Peter W. Flint, Ph. D. (1993) Notre Dame
University, is Professor of Biblical Studies
at Trinity Western University. He has published widely on the Scrolls, the Old Testament, and Second Temple Judaism – including *The Dead Sea Psalms Scrolls & the Book of
Psalms* (Brill, 1997) and *The Dead Sea Scrolls
Bible* (Harper, 1999) – and edited *The Psalms
Scrolls from Cave 4* (Oxford, 2000).

Patrick D. Miller is Charles T. Haley
Professor of Old Testament Theology at
Princeton Theological Seminary. He
has worked especially on the books of
Deuteronomy and Psalms and has written
books on Israelite religion and biblical
prayer.

THE BOOK OF PSALMS

# SUPPLEMENTS

## TO

# VETUS TESTAMENTUM

VOLUME XCIX

## FORMATION AND INTERPRETATION
## OF OLD TESTAMENT LITERATURE

### IV

EDITED BY

### CRAIG A. EVANS and PETER W. FLINT

# THE BOOK OF PSALMS

*Composition and Reception*

EDITED BY

PETER W. FLINT AND PATRICK D. MILLER, JR.

WITH THE ASSISTANCE OF

AARON BRUNELL

AND

RYAN ROBERTS

BRILL

LEIDEN · BOSTON

2005

This book is printed on acid-free paper.

**Library of Congress Cataloging-in-Publication Data**

The book of Psalms : composition and reception / edited by Peter W. Flint and Patric D.
   Miller, Jr. ; with the assistance of Aaron Brunell.
      p. cm. — (Supplements to Vetus Testamentum, ISSN 0083-5889 ; v. 99. Formation and
   interpretation of Old Testament literature ; 4)
   Includes bibliographical references and index.
   ISBN 90-04-13642-8 (hb : alk. paper)
      1. Bible. O.T. Psalms—Criticism, interpretation, etc. I. Flint, Peter W. II. Miller, Patrick
   D. III. Brunell, Aaron. IV. Supplements to Vetus Testamentum ; v. 99 V. Supplements to
   Vetus Testamentum. Formation and interpretation of Old Testament literature ; v. 4.

   BS410.V452 vol. 99
   [BS1430.52]
   221 s—dc22
   [223'.206]

                                                                        2003057084

ISSN   0083-5889
ISBN   90 04 13642 8

PRINTED IN THE NETHERLANDS

# CONTENTS

List of Contributors ................................................................. ix

Terms, Sigla and Abbreviations................................................. xi

PART ONE

GENERAL TOPICS

PATRICK D. MILLER AND PETER W. FLINT
Introduction and Overview of Psalms Scholarship in
this Volume.......................................................................... 1

KLAUS KOCH
Königspsalmen und ihr ritueller Hintergrund; Erwägungen
zu Ps 89,20-38 und Ps 20 und ihren Vorstufen ............................ 9

ROLF RENDTORFF
The Psalms of David: David in the Psalms ................................53

PART TWO

COMMENTARY ON OR INTERPRETATION OF SPECIFIC PSALMS

ADELE BERLIN
Psalms and the Literature of Exile: Psalms 137, 44, 69, and 78......65

DAVID NOEL FREEDMAN and DAVID MIANO
Non-Acrostic Alphabetic Psalms...............................................87

J. J. M. ROBERTS
Mowinckel's Enthronement Festival: A Review..........................97

BEAT WEBER
Zum sogennanten „Stimmungsumschwung" in Psalm 13............116

NANCY L. deCLAISSÉ-WALFORD
An Intertextual Reading of Psalms 22, 23, and 24......................139

DENNIS PARDEE
On Psalm 29: Structure and Meaning.......................................153

JOHN S. KSELMAN
Double Entendre in Psalm 59.................................................184

RICHARD J. CLIFFORD, S.J.
Psalm 90: Wisdom Meditation or Communal Lament?...............190

MICHAEL L. BARRÉ
The Shifting Focus of Psalm 101 ............................................ 206

SUNG-HUN LEE
Lament and the Joy of Salvation in the Lament Psalms .............. 224

CRAIG C. BROYLES
Psalms Concerning the Liturgies of Temple Entry ..................... 248

JAMES W. WATTS
Biblical Psalms Outside the Psalter ......................................... 288

PART THREE

THE PSALTER AS BOOK, INCLUDING SMALLER COLLECTIONS

HARRY P. NASUTI
The Interpretive Significance of Sequence and Selection in
the Book of Psalms .............................................................. 311

J. CLINTON MᶜCANN, JR.
The Shape of Book I of the Psalter and the Shape of
Human Happiness ............................................................... 340

MICHAEL GOULDER
The Social Setting of Book II of the Psalter ............................. 349

KLAUS D. SEYBOLD
Zur Geschichte des vierten Davidpsalters (Pss 138–145) ............ 368

GERALD H. WILSON
King, Messiah, and the Reign of God: Revisiting the Royal
Psalms and the Shape of the Psalter ....................................... 391

ERICH ZENGER
Theophanien des Königsgottes JHWH: Transformationen von
Psalm 29 in den Teilkompositionen Ps 28–30 und Ps 93–100 ...... 407

PART FOUR

TEXTUAL HISTORY AND RECEPTION IN JUDAISM AND CHRISTIANITY

ALBERT PIETERSMA
Septuagintal Exegesis and the Superscriptions of the
Greek Psalter ..................................................................... 443

MOSHE BERNSTEIN
A Jewish Reading of Psalms: Some Observations on the
Method of the Aramaic Targum .............................................. 476

ROBERT J. V. HIEBERT
  The Place of the Syriac Versions in the Textual History of
  the Psalter .........................................................................505

HARRY F. VAN ROOY
  The Psalms in Early Syriac Tradition.....................................537

CRAIG A. EVANS
  Praise and Prophecy in the Psalter and in the New Testament......551

PART FIVE

THEOLOGY OF THE PSALTER

WALTER BRUEGGEMANN
  The Psalms in Theological Use: On Incommensurability
  and Mutuality ....................................................................581

ERHARD S. GERSTENBERGER
  Theologies in the Book of Psalms............................................603

INDICES

1. Scripture Index ..................................................... 627
2. Apocrypha and Pseudepigrapha .......................................... 661
3. Dead Sea Scrolls................................................................ 662
4. Other Ancient Writings....................................................... 664
5. Modern Authors................................................................. 669

## LIST OF CONTRIBUTORS

*Michael L. Barré*
St. Mary's Seminary & University , Baltimore

*Adele Berlin*
University of Maryland

*Moshe J. Bernstein*
Yeshiva University, New York

*Craig C. Broyles*
Trinity Western University, British Columbia

*Walter Brueggemann*
Columbia Theological Seminary

*Richard J. Clifford, S. J.*
Weston Jesuit School of Theology, Cambridge, MA

*Nancy L. de Claisse-Walford*
McAfee School of Theology, Atlanta

*Craig A. Evans*
Acadia Divinity College, Nova Scotia

*Peter W. Flint*
Trinity Western University, British Columbia

*David Noel Freedman*
University of California, San Diego

*Erhard S. Gerstenberger*
Philipps Universität Marburg

*Michael Goulder*
University of Birmingham

*Robert J. V. Hiebert*
ACTS Seminary, Trinity Western University, British Columbia

*Klaus Koch*
Universität Hamburg

*John S. Kselman*
Weston Jesuit School of Theology, Cambridge, MA

*Sung-Hun Lee*
Sung-Kyul University, Korea

*J. Clinton McCann, Jr.*
Eden Theological Seminary, MO

*David Miano*
University of California, San Diego

*Patrick D. Miller*
Princeton Theological Seminary

*Harry P. Nasuti*
Fordham University, New York

*Dennis Pardee*
Oriental Institute, University of Chicago

*Albert Pietersma*
University of Toronto

*Rolf Rendtorff*
University of Heidelberg

*J. J. M. Roberts*
Princeton Theological Seminary

*Harry F. van Rooy*
Potchefstroom University, South Africa

*Klaus D. Seybold*
Universität Basel

*James W. Watts*
Syracuse University, NY

*Beat Weber*
Professor, Swiss Reformed Church

*Gerald H. Wilson*
Azusa Pacific University, CA

*Erich Zenger*
Westfälische Wilhelms Universität, University of Münster

# TERMS, SIGLA, AND ABBREVIATIONS

For most terms, sigla, and abbreviations of journals and other secondary sources, see P. H. Alexander et al. (eds.), *The SBL Handbook of Style for Ancient Near Rastern, Biblical, and Early Christian Studies* (Peabody, MA: Hendrickson, 1999). For Qumran sigla, see also J. A. Fitzmyer, *The Dead Sea Scrolls: Major Publications and Tools for Study* (rev. ed., SBLRBS 20; Atlanta: Scholars Press, 1990) 1–8.

## TERMS AND SIGLA

| | |
|---|---|
| (?) | Some doubt exists as to the identification of a verse or reading. |
| // | Two or more parallel texts (e.g. Ps 18//2 Sam 22) |
| + | Word(s) or a verse have been added. |
| > | Word(s) or a verse have been omitted. |
| * | What the scribe originally wrote (e.g. 4QDan$^{a*}$) |
| 2:4–5 | Dead Sea Scrolls: the second extant column of the manuscript, lines 4–5 |
| 10.4–5 | Dead Sea Scrolls: fragment 10, lines 4–5 |
| 10 ii.4–5 | Dead Sea Scrolls: fragment 10, column 2, lines 4-5 |
| §, §§ | Section(s), especially in Josephus and Philo |
| A$^1$ | Syriac translation of *Expositio in Psalmos* by Athanasius, Patriarch of Alexandria (c. 296–373). |
| A$^2$ | Abbreviated Syriac version of Athanasius' *Expositio* in Ms British Museum, Add. 12168, |
| abbr. | Abbreviation |
| *Adv. Haer.* | *Adversus Haereses (Against Heresies)* |
| ar | Aramaic |
| B | Barhebraeus' citations from the Peshitta |
| B$^y$ | Barhebraeus' excerpts from "the Greek" |
| *b.* | *Babylonian Talmud (Bavli)* |
| *b. Baba Bat.* | *Babylonian Talmud, Tractate Baba Batra* |
| *b. Ber.* | *Babylonian Talmud, Tractate Berakhot* |
| *b. Meg.* | *Babylonian Talmud, Tractate Megillah* |
| *b. Moʾed Qaṭ.* | *Babylonian Talmud, Tractate Moʾed Qaṭan* |
| *b. Pesaḥ.* | *Babylonian Talmud, Tractate Pesaḥim* |
| *b. Sanh.* | *Babylonian Talmud, Tractate Sanhedrin* |
| *b. Shab.* | *Babylonian Talmud, Tractate Shabbat* |
| *b. Roš Hašš.* | *Babylonian Talmud, Tractate Roš Haššanah* |
| *b. Suk.* | *Babylonian Talmud, Tractate Sukkah* |
| Beih. | Beihefte |

| | |
|---|---|
| BH | Biblical Hebrew |
| *bis* | Two times |
| *ca.* | *circa* |
| cf. | *confer*, compare |
| Chr. | Chrysostom |
| col(s). | Column(s) |
| corr. | *correctus, -a, um,* the corrected reading |
| Dead Sea Scrolls | (Scrolls from the Judean Desert) |
| CD | *Damascus Document* |
| 1QH[a] | *Hodayot* |
| 1QS[a] | *Rule of the Congregation* |
| 2Q23 | *Apocryphal Prophecy* |
| 4Q160 | *Vision of Samuel* |
| 4Q171 | 4QpPs[a] |
| 4Q174 | *Florilegium* or *4QMidrEsch*[a]? |
| 4Q177 | *Catena A* or *4QMidrEschat*[b]? |
| 4Q85 | 4QPs[c] |
| 4Q87 | 4QPs[e] |
| 4Q88 | 4QPs[f] |
| 4Q97 | 4QPs[p] |
| (*olim* 4Q237 | 4QPs[p]) |
| 4Q98g | 4QPs[x] |
| (*olim* 4Q236 | 4QPs[x]) |
| 4Q158–186 | *Miscellaneous Texts* |
| 4Q173 | 4QpPs[b] |
| 4Q380 | *Non-Canonical Psalms A* |
| 4Q381 | *Non-Canonical Psalms B* |
| 4Q394–399 | MMT (*Halakhic Letter*) |
| 4Q436 | *Barkhi Nafshi*[c] |
| 4Q500 | *papBenediction* |
| 4Q521 | *Messianic Apocalypse* |
| 11Q11 | *Apocryphal Psalms* |
| 11Q5 | 11QPs[a] |
| 11Q6 | 11QPs[b] |
| 11Q10 | 11QtgJob |
| 5/6Ḥev1b | 5/6ḤevPs |
| (*olim* 5/6Ḥev 40 | = 5/6ḤevPs) |
| (*olim* XḤev/Se 4 | = 5/6ḤevPs) |
| EA | El Amarna Tablets |
| ed(s). | Edition, editor(s), or edited |
| e.g. | *exempli gratia*, for example |
| eras. | *erasum*, erased |

| esp. | especially |
|---|---|
| ET | English translation |
| et al. | *et alii*, and others |
| frg(s). | Fragment(s) |
| 𝕲 or LXX | The Old Greek (as in the Göttingen editions) |
| 𝕲* | The (reconstructed) original reading of the Old Greek |
| θ′ | Theodotion's version of the Septuagint |
| Heb. | Hebrew |
| idem. | the same |
| i.e. | *id est*, that is |
| KE | Klagelied des Einzelnen |
| KTU | Die Keilaphabetischen Texte aus Ugarit |
| La | The Vetus Latina or Old Latin translation of the LXX |
| *Lev. Rab.* | Leviticus Rabbah |
| LXX | The Septuagint |
| *m.* | Mishnah |
| *m. Pesaḥ.* | *Mishna, Tractate Pesaḥim* |
| 𝕸 or MT | The Masoretic Text |
| 𝕸ed | An edition of the Masoretic Text (usually *BHS*) |
| 𝕸L or B19A | The Leningrad (St. Petersburg) Codex |
| 𝕸ms(s) | Masoretic manuscript(s) |
| 𝕸q | *qere* for the Masoretic Text |
| *Midr. Ps.* | Midrash Tehillim (Psalms) |
| MS(S) | Individual manuscript(s) |
| MT | Masoretic Text |
| n. | *nota*, note |
| no. | Number |
| n.p. | No publisher (cited) |
| n.s. | New series |
| NT | New Testament |
| OG | The Old Greek (original Septuagint) |
| P | Peshitta |
| *Pesiq. R.* | *Pesiqta Rabbati* |
| *Pesiq. Rab Kah.* | *Pesiqta de Rab Kahana* |
| *PG* | *Patrologia greaca* |
| Ps syr | Syric Psalm (e.g. Ps 155syr) |
| Ra | Rahlfs' edition of the Septuagint |
| recto | The front, inscribed side of a manuscript: the hair side of a leather scroll, or the side of a papyrus having horizontal ridges |
| repr. | Reprint(ed) |
| rev. | Revised |
| RIA | *Amherst Papyrus 63* |
| RS | Ras Shamra |

| | |
|---|---|
| *Sanh.* | *Sanhedrin* |
| SP | Samaritan Pentateuch |
| StU | Stimmungsumschwungs |
| *Tg.* | Targum |
| Th. or Theod. | Theodotian |
| Tht. | Theodoret |
| v(v). | Verse(s) |
| verso | The reverse side of a manuscript: the flesh side of a leather scroll, or the side of a papyrus having vertical ridges |
| Vgl. | Vergleiche (German, Compare) |
| Vorlage | Hebrew text used by the translator of the Greek or other Version |
| *y.* | *Jerusalem Talmud (Yerushalmi)* |
| *y. Meg.* | *Jerusalem Talmud, Tractate Megillah* |
| Z. | Zeile (German, Line) |
| z.B. | zum Beispiel (German, for example) |

## JOURNALS, BOOKS AND SERIES

| | |
|---|---|
| AASF | Annales Academiæ Scientiarum Fennicæ (Finland) |
| AASF.B | Annales Academiae scientiarum fennicæ, Series B |
| *AASOR* | *Annual of the American Schools of Oriental Research* |
| AB | Anchor Bible |
| *ABD* | *The Anchor Bible Dictionary* (6 vols., New York: Doubleday, 1992), ed. D. N. Freedman |
| *AfO* | *Archiv für Orientforschung* |
| *AfO* Beih | *Archiv für Orientforschung*, Beihefte |
| *AHw* | *Akkadisches Handworterbuch* (3 vols., Wiesbaden, 1965-1981), by W. von Soden |
| ALW | Archiv für Liturgiewissenschaft |
| AnBib | Analecta biblica |
| AOAT | Alter Orient und Altes Testament |
| ATA | Alttestamentliche Abhandlungen |
| ATD | Das Alte Testament Deutsch |
| AthANT | Abhandlungen zur Theologie des Alten und Neuen Testaments |
| AUSS | Andrews University Seminary Studies |
| *BA* | *Biblical Archaeologist* |
| *BASOR* | *Bulletin of the American Schools of Oriental Research* |
| BBB | Bonner biblische Beiträge |
| BDB | Brown, F., S. R. Driver, and C. A. Briggs. *A Hebrew and English Lexicon of the Old Testament* (Oxford, 1907) |
| *BHK* | *Biblia Hebraica* (R. Kittel) |

| | |
|---|---|
| *BHS* | *Biblia Hebraica Stuttgartensia* (Stuttgart, 1983), ed. K. Elliger and W. Rudolph |
| BHT | Beiträge zur historischen Theologie |
| BI | Biblical Illustrator |
| *Bib* | *Biblica* |
| *BibInt* | *Biblical Interpretation* |
| BiKi | Bibel und Kirche |
| *BiOr* | *Bibliotheca Orientalis* |
| BIOSCS | *Bulletin of the International Organization for Septuagint and Cognate Studies* |
| BIS | Biblical Interpretation Series |
| BJS | Brown Judaic Studies |
| *BK* | *Bibel und Kirche* |
| BK | Biblischer Kommentar |
| BKAT | Biblischer Kommentar: Altes Testament |
| *BN* | *Biblische Notizen* |
| BWA(N)T | Beiträge zur Wissenschaft vom Alten (und Neuen) Testament |
| *BZ* | *Biblische Zeitschrift* |
| BZAR | Beihefte zur Zeitschrift für Altorientalische und Biblische Rechtsgeschichte |
| BZAW | Beihefte zur *ZAW* |
| *CAD* | *The Assyrian Dictionary* of the Oriental Institute, University of Chicago (1956-) |
| CBNT | Coniectanea Biblica, New Testament Series |
| CBOT | Coniectanea Biblica, Old Testament Series |
| *CBQ* | *Catholic Biblical Quarterly* |
| CBQMon | Catholical Biblical Quarterly Monograph Series |
| CBQMS | Catholical Biblical Quarterly Monograph Series |
| *COS* | *The Context of Scripture* (3 vols., Leiden, 1997-), ed. W. W. Hallo |
| CRB | Cahiers de la Revue Biblique |
| CSCO | Corpus scriptorum christianorum orientaluim (Paris, 1903-), ed. B. Chabot et. al. |
| CthM.BW | Calwer theologische Monographien |
| *DCB* | *Dictionary of Christian Biography* (4 vols., London, 1877-1887), ed. W. Smith and H. Wace |
| *DDD* | *Dictionary of Deities and Demons in the Bible* (Leiden: Brill, 1995), ed. K. van der Toorn, B. Becking and P. W. van der Horst |
| DJD | Discoveries in the Judaean Desert |
| DJDJ | Discoveries in the Judaean Desert of Jordan |

| | |
|---|---|
| *DSD* | *Dead Sea Discoveries* |
| *Ebib* | *Études bibliques* |
| EdF | Erträge der Forschung |
| *EI* | *Eretz Israel* |
| *EstBib* | *Estudios bíblicos* |
| *ExpTim* | *Expository Times* |
| FAT | Forschungen zum Alten Testament |
| FB | Forschung zur Bibel |
| FIOTL | The Formation and Interpretation of Old Testament Literature |
| FMSt | Frühmittelalterliche Studien |
| FOTL | Forms of the Old Testament Literature |
| FRLANT | Forschungen zur Religion und Literatur des Alten und Neuen Testaments |
| FTS | Frankfurter Theologische Studien |
| FzB | Forschung zur Bibel |
| GCS | Griechischen christlichen Schriftsteller der ersten [drei] Jahrhunderte |
| GKC | *Gesenius' Hebrew Grammar* (2d. ed., Oxford, 1910), ed. E. Kautzsch, tr. A. E. Cowley, 1910 |
| *GM* | *Göttinger Miszellen* |
| *GNS* | *Good News Studies* |
| *HALAT* | *Hebräisches und aramäisches Lexikon zum Alten Testament*, ed. W. Baumgartner et al. |
| HAT | Handbuch zum Alten Testament |
| HBS | Herders Biblische Studien |
| HAR | Hebrew Annual Review |
| *HBC* | *Harper's Bible Commentary* |
| *HBT* | *Horizons in Biblical Theology* |
| HKAT | Handkommentar zum Alten Testament |
| HThKAT | Herders theologischer Kommentar zum Alten Testament |
| HTKAT (HthK) | Herders theologischer Kommentar zum Alten Testament |
| HNT | Handbuch zum Neuen Testament |
| *HTR* | *Harvard Theological Review* |
| *HUCA* | *Hebrew Union College Annual* |
| ICC | International Critical Commentary |
| *IDBSupp* | *Interpreter's Dictionary of the Bible, Supplement* (Nashville, 1976), ed. F. Crim et al. |
| *Int* | *Interpretation* |
| *ISBE* | *International Standard Bible Encyclopedia* (4 vols., Grand Rapids, 1979-1988), ed. G. W. Bromiley |
| *JAOS* | *Journal of the American Oriental Society* |

| | |
|---|---|
| *JBL* | *Journal of Biblical Literature* |
| JBTh | Jahrbuch für Biblische Theologie |
| *JNSL* | *Journal of Northwest Semitic Languages* |
| JNSLSup | *Journal of Northwest Semitic Languages*, Supplement Series |
| *JQR* | *Jewish Quarterly Review* |
| JQRMS | *Jewish Quarterly Review* Monograph Series |
| *JSJ* | *Journal for the Study of Judaism in the Persian, Hellenistic and Roman Period* |
| JSJSup | *Journal for the Study of Judaism in the Persian, Hellenistic and Roman Period*, Supplement Series |
| *JSNT* | *Journal for the Study of the New Testament* |
| JSNTSup | *Journal for the Study of the New Testament*, Supplement Series |
| *JSOT* | *Journal for the Study of the Old Testament* |
| JSOTSup | *Journal for the Study of the Old Testament*, Supplement Series |
| *JSP* | *Journal for the Study of the Pseudepigrapha* |
| JSPSup | *Journal for the Study of the Pseudepigrapha*, Supplement Series |
| *JSS* | *Journal of Semitic Studies* |
| JSSSup | *Journal of Semitic Studies*, Supplement Series |
| *JTS* | *Journal of Theological Studies* |
| KHC | Kurzer Hand-Commentar zum Alten Testament |
| LSJ | Liddell, H. G., R. Scott, and H. S. Jones, *A Greek-English Lexicon.* 9th ed. with revised supplement (Oxford, 1996) |
| MDOG | Mitteilungen der Deutschen Orient-Gesellschaft |
| *MGWJ* | *Monatschrift für Geschichte und Wissenschaft des Judentums* |
| MSU | Mitteilungen des Septuaginta-Unternehmens |
| MVAG | Mitteilungen der Vorderasiatisch-ägyptischen Gesellschaft. Vols. 1-44 (1896-1939) |
| *NAB* | *New American Bible* |
| NBL | Norsk Biografisk Leksikon |
| *NEB* | *New English Bible* |
| NEBAT | Die Neue Echter Bibel, Altes Testament |
| NEchBAT | Die Neue Echter Bibel, Altes Testament |
| *NETS* | *A New English Translation of the Septuagint* (Oxford, 2000-) |
| NIBC | New International Biblical Commentary |
| NICOT | New International Commentary on the Old Testament |
| *NJPS* | *New Jewish Publication Society Tanakh* |
| *NovT* | *Novum Testamentum* |
| NovTSup | *Novum Testamentum*, Supplement Series |
| *NRSV* | *The New Revised Standard Version* |
| *NTOA* | *Novum Testamentum et Orbis Antiquus* |

| | |
|---|---|
| *NTS* | *New Testament Studies* |
| NTTS | New Testament Tools and Studies |
| OBL | Orientalia et Biblica Lovaniensia |
| OBO | Orbis biblicus et orientalis |
| *Or* | *Orientalia (n.s.)* |
| OCD | *Oxford Classical Dictionary* (3d ed., Oxford, 1996), ed. S. Hornblower and A. Spawforth |
| ODCC | *The Oxford Dictionary of the Christian Church* (2d ed., Oxford, 1983), ed. F. L. Cross and E. A. Livingstone |
| *OLZ* | *Orientalistische Literaturzeitung* |
| OTL | Old Testament Library |
| OTS | Old Testament Studies |
| *OTS* | *Oudtestamentische Studiën* |
| *PEQ* | *Palestine Exploration Quarterly* |
| PFEG | Publications of the Finnish Exegetical Society |
| *PL* | *Patrologia latina*, ed. J. Migne |
| PTSDSS | The Princeton Theological Seminary Dead Sea Scrolls Project |
| QD | Quaestiones disputatae |
| *RB* | *Revue biblique* |
| RBib | Recherches Bibliques |
| *REB* | *Revised English Bible* |
| *REJ* | *Revue des études juives* |
| *RevQ* | *Revue de Qumran* |
| *RGG* | *Religion in Geschichte und Gegenwart* (7 vols., 3d. ed.; Tübingen, 1957-1965), ed. K. Galling |
| RILP | Roehampton Institute London Papers |
| RSB Richerche | Storico Bibliche |
| *RSV* | *Revised Standard Version* |
| SAA | State Archives of Assyria |
| SANT | Studien zum Alten und Neuen Testament |
| SB | Sources bibliques |
| SBLDS | Society of Biblical Literature Dissertation Series |
| SBLMS | Society of Biblical Literature Monograph Series |
| SBLRBS | Society of Biblical Literature Resources for Biblical Studies |
| SBLSCS | Society of Biblical Literature Septuagint and Cognate Studies |
| SBM | Stuttgarter biblische Monographien |
| SBS | Stuttgarter Bibelstudien |
| SBT | Studies in Biblical Theology |
| SC | Sources chrétiennes |
| *ScrHier* | *Scripta hierosolymitana* |

| | |
|---|---|
| SDSRL | Studies in the Dead Sea Scrolls and Related Literature |
| *SEL* | *Studi epigrafici e linguistici* |
| SESJ | Schriften der Finnischen Exegetischen Gesellschaft |
| SFEG | See PEFG |
| *SJT* | *Scottish Journal of Theology* |
| SNTS | Society for New Testament Studies |
| SNTSMS | Society for New Testament Studies Monograph Series |
| SNVAO | Skrifter utgitt av det Norske Videnskaps-Akademi i Oslo |
| SSEJC | Studies in Early Judaism and Christianity |
| SSN | Studia semitica neerlandica |
| *ST* | *Studia theologica* |
| STDJ | Studies on the Texts of the Desert of Judah |
| ThB | Theologische Bücherei |
| *TDNT* | *Theological Dictionary of the New Testament* (10 vols., Grand Rapids, 1964-1976), ed. G. Kittel and G. Friedrich |
| *TDOT* | *Theological Dictionary of the Old Testament* (Grand Rapids), ed. G. J. Botterweck and H. Ringgren |
| *THAT* | *Theologisches Handwörterbuch zum Alten Testament* (2 vols., Stuttgart, 1971-1976), ed. E. Jenni, with C. Westermann |
| *ThWAT* | *Theologisches Worterbuch zum Alten Testament* (Stuttgart, 1970-), ed. G. J. Botterweck and H. Ringgren |
| *ThZ* | *Theologische Zeitschrift* |
| *TLZ* | *Theologische Literaturzeitung* |
| *TRE* | *Theologische Realenzyklopadie* (Berlin: de Gruyter, 1977-), ed. G. Krause and G. Müller |
| *TUAT* | *Texte aus der Umwelt des Alten Testaments* (Gütersloh, 1984), ed. O. Kaiser |
| *TZ* | *Theologische Zeitschrift* |
| UB | Urban-Taschenbücher |
| UBL | Ugaritisch-biblische Literatur |
| UF | Ugarit-Forschungen |
| *Ug* | *Ugaritica* |
| *VT* | *Vetus Testamentum* |
| VTSup | *Vetus Testamentum*, Supplement Series |
| WBC | Word Biblical Commentary |
| WMANT | Wissenschaftliche Monographien zum Alten und Neuen Testament |
| WdO | Die Welt des Orients |
| WMANT | Wissenschaftliche Monographien zum Altern und Neuen Testament |
| WUNT | Wissenschaftliche Untersuchungen zum Neuen Testament |

WZKM          Wiener Zeitschrift für die Kunde des Morgenlandes
*YJS*           *Yale Judaica Series*
*ZAH*           *Zeitschrift für Althebräistik*
*ZAW*           *Zeitschrift für die alttestamentliche Wissenschaft*
ZBK           Zürcher Bibelkommentare
*ZNW*           *Zeitschrift für die neutestamentliche Wissenschaft*
*ZS*            *Zeitschrift für Semitistik und verwandte Gebiete*
*ZThK*          *Zeitschrift für theologie und Kirche*

# INTRODUCTION AND OVERVIEW OF PSALMS
## SCHOLARSHIP IN THIS VOLUME

The present volume was conceived and planned in the closing stages of the nineteen nineties, with the objective of producing a new collection of studies on the Psalter in the early years of a century's turning. The twenty-seven essays that comprise this volume — in addition to this introductory chapter — are a representative sampling of the extensive investigation of the Psalter in contemporary biblical scholarship. A wide range of contributors — from Europe, North America, Asia, and Africa — were selected. Essayists were invited with a view to representing the spectrum of opinion in the current interpretation of the Psalter, over a wide range of subjects. While this collection is in no sense exhaustive relative to either topics or individuals presently engaged in Psalms study, what is presented here should serve to identify the issues and concerns that belong generally to the study of the Psalms in the early years of a new millennium, as well as the emphases to be found in the present engagement of those issues by scholars in the field. The picture that comes forth gives some idea of the breadth of concern and research, while also lifting up some matters that are receiving particular attention.

Of special note is the lively interest in the Psalter as a collection or as a book comprised of various collections. The division of the Psalter into five great blocks is evidenced by the presence of the doxologies at strategic points in the book (Book I, Psalms 1–41; Book II, Psalms 42–72; Book III, Psalms 73–89; Book IV, Psalms 90–106; and Book V, Psalms 107–50). The interpretive significance of those divisions, as well as the many other groupings of the Psalter — some of them explicitly indicated by headings or otherwise, others more implicit but with linguistic and other markings — has been the object of vigorous study over the last quarter century. The result has been not only a focus upon the Psalter as a literary work, but a heightened reading of Psalms in relation to other psalms rather than simply reading them individually as an anthology. In this collection, one may see various manifestations of this development in Psalms study. Some of the treatments focus particularly upon the process of selection and redaction, such as Harry Nasuti's investigation of the interpretive significance of sequence and selection of the Psalms. His general discussion points to several particular examples and notes also that such literary and theological focus is not new to the interpretation of the Psalter but reaches back to very early Church Fathers. A more redactional examination of some of the groupings of the Psalter is evident in the essays by Erich Zenger, Klaus Koch, and Klaus Seybold. The work of these three European scholars, as well as that of others in the volume, indicates that attention to collections and groupings is productive but not necessarily apart from other entrees into the meaning of the psalms. So form critical inquiry continues to be a part of the process as Koch investigates the royal psalms and asks after their liturgical and literary roles, and Zenger's investigation of the place of the theophany of YHWH as king in the Psalms provides form critical analyses of the psalms but also looks at what happens when different types of psalms are combined with each other — in this case celebration of the kingship of YHWH, as in Psalm 29 —, or combined with more individual psalms reflective of a more private piety, as in the surrounding Psalms 28 and 30. Seybold's examination of the fourth Davidic Psalter (138–145) not only asks about the significance of the Davidic ascriptions for these psalms but also suggests that the group shares a common locus in the Jerusalem (second) temple and the experience of threat and imprisonment-asylum in the temple so that some sort of juridical process could determine guilt or innocence.

One of the persons who have most vigorously pursued the possible joining of psalmic sequence and ritual movement is Michael Goulder in a number of works. Representative of that continuing investigation is his essay on the social setting of Book II of the Psalter, arguing for a combination in the fall festival of the Korah Psalms (42–49), which probably came originally from Dan and celebrated God's protection and care of the people, with the David psalms (51–72), which celebrated the David-Solomon line in a group of psalms assembled as responses to the Succession Narrative of 2 Samuel–1 Kings.

Goulder's is a large proposal, incorporating historical claims as well. Others in these pages carry forward careful attention to the types and possible settings in life of the Psalms. Craig Broyles attends to the genre of temple entrance liturgy, exemplified for most readers of the Psalms in Psalms 15 and 24 but, in Broyles' analysis, to be found in different ways also in a number of other psalms more commonly regarded as individual laments. The question of a cultic Sitz im Leben comes to the fore in J. J. M. Roberts' vigorous defense of Mowinckel's theory of an autumn enthronement festival as the setting and interpretive context for understanding both the enthronement Psalms and a number of other Psalms. On the basis of a close reading of the classic lament, Psalm 13, Beat Weber takes up afresh one of the central outcomes of the form critical study of the Psalms, the famous turn in the individual lament from complaint and petition to assertions and expressions of confidence. He suggests that this turn rests less on some outside word, such as an oracle of salvation, than it does on the renewal of trust based on the *hesed* of the Lord, the saving presence of God over against the lamented absence of God. The expression of confidence by the sufferer serves to move God, on the basis of the renewed trust, to deliver while further strengthening the psalmist's conviction of God's gracious presence. Weber's identification of the centrality of the sufferer's claim on the Lord's *hesed* for the shift from complaint to confidence is carried forward in Sung-Hun Lee's essay on the Lament Psalms, and there generalized as the covenantal ground for the possibility of turning despair and sadness into confidence and joy. Richard Clifford chooses the familiar Psalm 90 in order to suggest that the common reading of this as a kind of sapiential meditation has failed to discern the presence of a communal lament, the shape of which he uncovers in his detailed study of the Psalm.

On the North American scene, three of the scholars who have devoted much attention to the arrangement of the Psalter into books and the significance of that for an interpretation of the Psalter as a whole are Gerald Wilson, J. Clinton McCann, and Nancy deClaissé-Walford. They carry forward that work in this volume as well, Wilson reviewing his thesis and then responding to issues that have been raised about it, such as the continuing place of David and royal psalms after the presumed shift from focus on the king in Books I–III to an emphasis in Book IV on the Lord's enthronement as a response to the failure of kingship. In the process, he takes up afresh the matter of what sort of messianic reading of the Psalms is appropriate in light of the analysis he has presented. McCann looks at the beatitudes in the Psalms, asking if there is something to the way in which they occur in Book I of the Psalter that is intentional and instructive about the shape of human happiness. DeClaissé-Walford focuses on Psalm 22 with a view to uncovering the "connectedness" among Psalms 22, 23, and 24, which together create a strong statement of trust in the Lord.

The headings or superscriptions of the Psalms, which have in the past been dismissed as later — and therefore unimportant — additions to the text, are the subject of close attention in a number of the essays in this volume. The ascription of many Psalms to David — whatever the precise meaning of that ascription — is central to Rolf Rendtorff's examination of the place of David in the Psalms. It also is the starting point for Seybold's study of the fourth Davidic Psalter, as well as the basis for Albert Pietersma's effort to uncover the levels of interpretation that take place in the Septuagint's translation of the Hebrew Psalms. This last essay is an indicator also of the important work going on in the textual history of the Psalter and the continuing discussion about the difference between translation and interpretation, textual history and reception history. His careful analysis of levels of interpretation in the Greek translation leads into the extensive work that is taking place in analyzing other versions of the Psalter and their place in its textual history. Research on the Syriac Psalter is reflected here in the essays of Robert Hiebert and Harry van Rooy, as well as into the interpretive history of the Psalms reflected on the one hand in the Jewish Targumim (see Moshe Bernstein's study of Jewish reading of the Psalms), and on the other in the New Testament and the appropriation of the Psalms by the early church as an interpretive key to the life, ministry, death, resurrection, and ascension of Jesus (see Craig Evans' study of the prophetic authority of the Psalms in the New Testament).

The poetry and style of the Psalms has been among the matters most intensively studied in recent years. That discussion is reflected here at several points. David Noel Freedman with David Miano continues his long-standing interest in the way in which the Psalms show acrostic patterns as a part of their poetic structure. In this instance, the authors suggest that there are important alphabetic patterns implicit in the psalms but these are not necessarily acrostic in form. They are, instead, identifiable by the totality of lines as multiples of 11 and are less obtrusive and more flexible than the alphabetic acrostics.

Dennis Pardee provides a detailed analysis of the poetic structure of Psalm 29 — the subject of a different kind of focus in Zenger's essay. Pardee examines the poetic structure and parallelism of the Psalm and brings to bear one of the relevant Ugaritic texts both with regard to its structure and its motifs. Like Zenger, he suggests that Psalm 96 is an expanded and revised form of Psalm 29.

In his classic study *Seven Types of Ambiguity*, William Empson long ago argued that all good poetry is ambiguous. That is no less true of the poetry of the Psalms, though this particular figure of thought has received less attention than some others in the poetic analysis of the Psalms. Building on the study of deliberate ambiguity in the Psalms by Paul Raabe (*JBL* 110 [1991] 213–27), John Kselman adds to our awareness of this poetic feature by proposing two instances in Psalm 59 and suggesting what their significance is for interpreting the Psalm as a whole.

While the ancient Near Eastern milieu of the Hebrew Psalms is not heavily to the fore in these essays, some of the authors draw upon textual evidence from the surrounding cultures to illumine their interpretation of the particular Psalms before them. That is evident, for example, not only in Pardee's examination of a Baal text from Ugarit, but also in Koch's comparison of the Aramaic Papyrus 63 with Psalm 20 and Michael Barre's citation of Neo-Assyrian royal grants to argue his case that the royal Psalm 101 had its original focus on the instruction of the king's courtiers on the occasion of the enthronement of the Judean king, a focus, he suggests that slowly disappears in the transmission of the Psalm.

The assumption that many of the Psalms were either composed during post-exilic times or were adapted to that context in the course of their transmission may be found in a number of the essays here and in Psalms scholarship in general. The possibility that some of the psalms were particularly associated with the fall or Jerusalem or the exile itself is explored with fruitful results in Adele Berlin's study of four psalms that seem to reflect that historical setting. Her aim is to show that each psalm approaches that situation differently and in so doing address the theoretical and practical problems of exile in several ways.

The reader of Scripture knows that not all Psalms are to be found in the Psalter. In fact, some of the Psalms themselves occur in other narrative contexts. James Watts calls attention not only to the large amount of psalmic material, largely hymnic, outside the Psalter but focuses his attention particularly on the way in which psalms set in narrative are to be interpreted very much in relation to their narrative setting. In the process he argues that the literary context does not reduce the liturgical application of the hymns or turn them into aesthetic and literary works alone. Rather, he argues, setting the hymn in the narrative is more likely an attempt to appropriate that literary context for use in liturgy. Inset hymns, therefore, may have a liturgical function as well as the more obvious role in scripturalization and canonization.

As a conclusion to the volume, two leading Old Testament theologians seek to address the question of the theology of the Psalter, a topic that is not altogether missing from some of the earlier essays. Walter Brueggemann, who has elsewhere provided a theological analysis of the canonical structure of the Psalter, turns in this instance to a more thematic approach but one that he argues is present also in the movement of the whole. It focuses upon the God who is addressed and praised in the Psalter but does so in terms of the relationship with the worshipping community. The key concepts that bring these together are incommensurability and mutuality, "the capacity of YHWH to be *assertive* or *interrupted* and Israel's capacity to be *receiving* or *interrupting*." The paradoxical coherence of these two features in the relationship between God and Israel is at the heart of the Psalter's theological claims.

In a quite different fashion, Erhard Gerstenberger argues for a view of the Psalter that is less coherent, seeing in the Psalter what he has elsewhere argued is true for the Old Testament or Hebrew Scriptures as a whole: a book of multilayered conceptions of God and thus varying theologies that are deeply determined by the social settings in which they arise — the family, the local clan, the state, and the kinship group —, a macro society that developed in the post-exilic community, what Gerstenberger calls the "exclusive congregation." The notion of oneness in conceptuality or the quest for unity is not to be abandoned, but that unity is hidden and is a goal for the community to pursue but not something that it can squeeze out of its varied writings.

In all the essays, the critical disciplines join with interpretive and theological concerns to uncover the continuing meaning and perduring effects of the Psalms on the communities of faith that hold them as Scripture and appropriate them as prayer, praise, and instruction. The whole is a kind of stratigraphic view of the contemporary study of the Psalms, one that both reflects the work of recent decades of Psalms scholarship and also provides some pointers for where the study of the Psalter may be headed.

\* \* \* \* \* \* \* \* \* \*

*The Book of Psalms: Composition and Reception* is fourth in the series "The Formation and Interpretation of Old Testament Literature" (FIOTL), the purpose of which is to examine and explore the prehistory, contents, and themes of the books of the Old Testament, as well as their reception and interpretation in later Jewish and Christian literature. The other three published volumes are: *Writing and Reading the Scroll of Isaiah: Studies in an Interpretive Tradition*, eds. Craig C. Broyles and Craig A. Evans (FIOTL 1.1-2 and VTSup 70.1-2, 1997); *The Book of Daniel: Composition and Reception*, eds. John J. Collins and Peter W. Flint (FIOTL 2.1-2 and VTSup 83.1-2, 2001); and *The Book of Leviticus: Composition and Reception*, eds. Rolf Rendtorff and Robert A. Kugler (FIOTL 3 and VTSup 93, 2003). Several more volumes are scheduled or in preparation.

The editors of the present collection, *The Book of Psalms: Composition and Reception*, extend thanks to several groups of people. First, to all the contributors for meeting various deadlines and working hard and harmoniously to render smooth and effective the editing of manuscripts which were sometimes very complex and difficult to process. Second, to several graduate assistants at Trinity Western University whose dedication, research, and computer skills have proved indispensable. Special thanks are due to Aaron Brunell — currently enrolled in the Ph.D. programme at the University of Michigan — for managing this project well and being closely involved with all aspects of the book from its inception until the final draft was being prepared. We are also grateful to Ryan Roberts for overseeing the final draft, and for the extensive task of preparing the abbreviation lists near the front of the book, and the extensive indices at the end. Thanks are also due to Professor André Lemaire and the VTSup Board for their support of the FIOTL volumes as part of the VTSup series. Finally, we express our appreciation to the team at Brill Academic Publishers, especially Desk Editor Mattie Kuiper and Senior Religion Editor Hans van der Meij, for their patience, guidance, and encouragement in the production of this book.

Patrick D. Miller                                                      31 August, 2004
*Princeton, New Jersey*

Peter W. Flint
*Langley, British Columbia*

# PART ONE

# GENERAL TOPICS

# KÖNIGSPSALMEN UND IHR RITUELLER HINTERGRUND; ERWÄGUNGEN ZU PS 89,20-38 UND PS 20 UND IHREN VORSTUFEN*

KLAUS KOCH

## WAS HEIßT KÖNIGSPSALMEN UND WAS WAR IHRE FUNKTION?

Über das Verhältnis von Poesie und Ritual wird in der Psalmenexegese seit rund 100 Jahren heftig gestritten, und es sieht nicht so aus, als ob es damit bald ein Ende hat. Den Apfel der Eris hat Hermann Gunkel auf den Tisch der Götter geworfen. Zwar hatte schon vor ihm Wellhausen mit seiner These vom Psalter als Gesangbuch des Zweiten Tempels breite Zustimmung gefunden und so schon dessen Poesie mit Ritual verbunden; da aber dessen Einzelheiten nicht interessierten, hatte die Einordnung keine Folgen für das grundsätzliche Verhältnis. Das wird anders, als es Gunkel gelingt, in seinem großen Psalmenkommentar von 1911 (und abschließend 1933 in seiner Einleitung in die Psalmen) die 150 Lieder auf Grund von Struktur und Inhalt bestimmten Gattungen der hebräischen Sprache zuzuweisen, die überwiegend ihren Sitz im Leben in unterschiedlichen Begehungen des israelitischen Kultus hatten, deren rituelle Funktion — z.B. für Gesänge vor dem Eingang zum Tempel an Jahresfesten oder beim kasualen Tempelbesuch eines Notleidenden — von ihm zu rekonstruieren versucht wurde. Doch seine Theorie war dadurch von vornherein dialektisch, daß er viele Psalmen zu „kultfreien" Nachahmungen einstmals kultischer Muster erklärte, da „ein außergottesdienstlicher Gebrauch ursprünglich kultischer Lieder von Jeremia bis in die Makkabäerzeit neben der Kultdichtung nachweisbar" sei, in seiner vorliegenden Endkomposition ist deshalb der Psalter als „ein Andachts- und Hausbuch für Laien" entstanden.[1] Die Mehrzahl deutschsprachiger Alttestamentler ist seither dieser Ansetzung der zwei Ebenen gefolgt, obwohl sich sonst für den Alten Orient wohl der Brauch von Büchern mit liturgischen Gesängen, nicht aber derartige Andachtsbücher

---

* Zuerst veröffentlicht in E. Zenger (Hrsg.), *Ritual und Poesie* (HBS 18; Freiburg: Herder, 2003) 211–49.

[1] H. Gunkel, *Einleitung* (1933) 447. 452.

nachweisen lassen.[2]

Für die Frage nach einer rituellen Verankerung ihrer Poesie scheinen die von Gunkel und andern als Königslieder ausgesonderten Gedichte im Psalter besonders geeignet, und das aus mehreren Gründen.

Einmal weisen die besonders markanten Beispiele dieser Liedgruppe wie Ps 2; 89; 132 die Merkmale einer *liturgischen Rahmengattung* auf, mit Gliedgattungen wie Hymnus oder Klagelied, die sonst selbstständig auftauchen, hier aber in sinnvoll erscheinende szenische Abfolgen eingebaut sind, die sich durchaus als kultisches Brauchtum auffassen lassen, wobei Ps 2; 20; 110 und 132 auf das Zionsheiligtum als „Schaubühne" zu verweisen scheinen.

Zum andern wird dreimal als Gliedgattung das Königsorakel verwendet (2,6-11; 89,4-5.20-38; 132,11-18) selbständig taucht es in Ps 110 auf; in allen Fällen fügt es sich nicht dem Muster der Gattung Profezeiung ein, wie es sich häufig in den prophetischen Büchern findet,[3] sondern entspricht weit eher dem der altorientalischen Königsorakel, die keiner schöngeistigen Dichtung Ausdruck geben wollten, sondern zur Legitimation von Herrschaft notwendig und deshalb meist rituell verankert waren.[4]

Beispiele wie 20; 21; 72 geben *Fürbitten eines Dritten für den König* wieder, wie sie sich für eine einzelne Person sonst nicht unter den Psalmen finden, wohl aber auf den Herrscher bezogen in der altorientalischen Nachbarschaft, dort aber gewöhnlich von einem höheren Kultfunktionär im Rahmen einer Begehung vorgetragen wurden[5] und gewiß nicht von irgendwelchen Privatleuten stammten.

Schließlich findet sich in 144 ein Klagegebet des Königs für seine eigene Rettung und das Heil seines Landes (hebr. noch Jes 38,9-20; Ps 155syr = 11QPs[a] 24:3-17). Die Gattung ist in den Umweltreligionen

---

[2] „Die babylonische, im ganzen (die) der israelitischen vorausgehende P(salmen)dichtung gehört zum Gottesdienst;" H. Gunkel, Art. „Psalmen," *RGG* (2. Aufl.) 4, 1611.

[3] K. Koch, *Formgeschichte* (1989) § 18.

[4] Zu Ps 89,20ff. ist H. U. Steymans, „Thron" (2002) den neuassyrischen Parallelen nachgegangen, zu ägyptischen für Ps 2,7ff. und 110 s. K. Koch, „König als Sohn Gottes" (2002).

[5] Vgl. die wohl im Rahmen der Krönung (oder Jubiläumsfeier?) Assurbanipals überlieferte Fürbitte bei M. Arneth, *Sonne der Gerechtigkeit* (2000) 58f. und dazu 64. Der Text auch mit weiteren Beispielen CoS I, 472-74.

beliebt und gehört dort zu einer entsprechenden Begehung.[6]

Welche Lieder aber gehören zu „Königspsalmen"? Darüber besteht heute eine weitgehende Übereinstimmung, die es nicht immer gegeben hatte. Zwar haben einige Psalmen, die sich mit dem von Gott eingesetzten König und seinem heilvollen Regieren befassen, besonders bei christlichen Auslegern seit alters ein hohes Interesse auf sich gezogen und sind bereits im Neuen Testament zu tragenden Pfeilern der Christologie geworden, wie Ps 2 wegen des Gottessohnprädikates für den Gesalbten oder Ps 110 mit dem Hinweis auf dessen Thronsitz zur Rechten Gottes. Da jedoch die Psalmen insgesamt um die Zeitenwende in Kreisen wie den Qumraniten und später bei frühen Rabbinen primär als eschatologische Weissagungen des Profeten Dawid gedeutet wurden,[7] nicht zuletzt wegen der häufigen Überschrift לְדָוִד, und die auf eine königliche Gestalt zentrierten Texte keineswegs innerhalb des Psalters in einem Verbund stehen, sind sie nicht als eigene Gruppe empfunden worden.

Das wurde erst anders, als zu Beginn des 20. Jahrh. Hermann Gunkel die Gattungskritik als maßgebliche Methode der Psalmenexegese einführte.[8] Er hat elf Königspsalmen als eigene Textsorte zwischen den von ihm entdeckten Gattungen eingeordnet, mußte aber, abweichend von der sonst von ihm befolgten formkritischen Methode bekennen: „Die Königspsalmen sind also nicht eine eigene, in sich geschlossene ‚Gattung'... sie bestehen aus einer ganzen Reihe von Gattungen."[9] In der Tat entspricht mindestens die Hälfte der ausgesonderten Texte dem Muster anderer Psalmengattungen; unter ihnen befinden sich z.B. ein Klagelied des Einzelnen Ps 144, ein Danklied des Einzelnen Ps 18 oder Fürbitten von seiten eines Dritten Ps 20; 21; 72.

Mehrfach gibt es unter ihnen, wie schon erwähnt, liturgisch wirkende Kombinationen mehrerer Gliedgattungen, so in Ps 2; 89; 132. Also ein bunter Blumenstrauß, zusammengebunden durch die Leitworte מָשִׁיחַ oder מֶלֶךְ, was aber nicht immer ausdrücklich geäußert

---

[6] Im Psalter fehlt sie sonst; es sei denn, man würde hier alle Psalmen mit der Rubrik לְדָוִד einordnen (s.u.), obwohl deren Text in der Regel nicht den Eindruck eines königlichen Sprechers erweckt und wenig Hinweise auf eine Ritualzugehörigkeit aufweist.

[7] Z.B. 11QPs[a] 27:11; *b.Sota* 48b; vgl. Apg 2,30f.

[8] Vor allem durch seinen HKAT-Kommentar, *Die Psalmen* (1911).

[9] H. Gunkel & J. Begrich, J. *Einleitung in die Psalmen* (1933) S.146f.

wird. Selbst wenn man sich dieser Rollen-zentrierten Auswahl anschließt, bleibt ungewiß, ob nicht weitere Stücke aus dem Psalter hierzu gezählt werden sollten, in denen das Ich eines frommen Individuums als maßgeblicher Sprecher oder Adressat der Gemeinde auftaucht. Schon Gunkel hat Ps 101 in die Gruppe eingereiht und die Neueren sind ihm darin ziemlich einhellig gefolgt; der anonyme Sänger weiß sich für die חֲסִידִים im Land verantwortlich und will die Frevler aus der Stadt Jahwäs ausrotten; so etwas kann ein König gelobt haben, aber ebensogut ein nachexilischer Hoherpriester oder Statthalter.[10] Ps 118 schildert eine Prozession, an deren Ende ein Einzelner begrüßt wird: „Gesegnet, der da kommt im Namen Jahwäs" (V. 26); haben erst die neutestamentlichen Evangelien dabei an eine messianische Gestalt gedacht oder schon der alte Text?[11] Ähnlich verhält es sich mit Ps 22, wo der schwer leidende Beter sich zwar wie ein Wurm und nicht ein Mensch vorkommt, dennoch nach seiner Errettung vor großer קָהָל aufzutreten in der Lage sein wird (V. 7.23.26), oder Ps 28, wo im Klagelied die abschließende Gewißheit der Erhörung die Heilshilfe für „seinen Gesalbten" betrifft. "What are 'royal' psalms?" fragt Mowinckel und antwortet zwar im Sinne Gunkels: "no particular psalm type but psalms in which the king takes a leading place,"[12] bezieht aber eine ganze Anzahl weiterer Psalmen ein. Auf den Umfang der Gruppe wird im Folgenden nicht eingegangen, sondern einer Minimalauswahl gefolgt; behandelt werden nicht einmal alle von den meisten Exegeten unter dieser Rubrik aussortierte Texte, sondern einige wenige, bei denen die Annahme eines rituellen Haftpunkts sich am ehesten nahelegt.

Zuvor soll jedoch Stellung und Funktion der von Gunkel ausgesonderten Beispiele (ohne 101) innerhalb bzw. außerhalb der Kleinpsalter erwogen werden, die der jetzigen Einteilung des Psalters in fünf Bücher als deren Bausteine vorangegangen waren, um Hinweise auf eine mögliche Überlieferungsgeschichte zu erhalten, die auf Nähe oder Ferne zu rituellen Begehungen schließen läßt.

### KLEINPSALTER UND EXEMTE KÖNIGSPSALMEN

Gunkel war es gelungen, durch die Verbindung der Analyse von Aufbaustrukturen, inhaltlicher Absicht und einer dazu gehörigen

---

[10] B. Duhm, *Psalmen* (1922) S. 364.

[11] A. Bentzen, *Messias* (1948) S.20.

[12] S. Mowinckel, *Psalms* (1962) III,2.

„Stimmung" die meisten Psalmen einem von vier oder fünf Haupt-
gattungen zuzuweisen, deren Grundmuster den Sitz im Leben jeweils
in einer kultischen Begehung hatte. Dabei bleiben die Einleitungsru-
briken (Überschriften) der Texte außer Betracht; denn Gunkel setzte
eine Ausformung der *langue* in Gattungen nur in der *oral tradition*
und dem vorliterarischen Sprachgebrauch voraus; die Rubriken hangen aber offensichtlich mit einer Verschriftung zusammen. Gunkel
nahm noch nicht zur Kenntnis, daß auch die Erzeugung von literarischen Texten sich an Gattungsmuster ausrichten muß, um Auftrag-
geber und Abnehmer zu finden, und das im Altertum gewiß mehr
noch als heutzutage. So übersieht er, daß Zuweisungen wie „Zu David
gehörend," „Zu Korach gehörend" u.ä. wie auch „Gattungs" kenn-
zeichnungen wie מִזְמוֹר, מַשְׂכִּיל, שִׁיר הַמַּעֲלוֹת Einzeltexte zu Ketten mit
eigenem Anliegen zusammenfügen, gegebenenfalls mit bestimmter
Stufenfolge der in der Überschrift angegebenen Merkmale.[13] Solche
*Kleinpsalter*, wie ich es zu benennen vorschlage, stellen eine wahrscheinlich eigene (literarische) Rahmengattung dar und sind als solche
in ihrem Aussagegefälle neben der Struktur der Einzelpsalmen zu
berücksichtigen, die vordem selbständig umgelaufen sein mögen,
dann aber von Redaktoren verklammert und dabei vielleicht überar-
beitet worden sind. Vor allem Hossfeld und Zenger haben sich
bekanntlich in letzter Zeit bemüht, diese weiterreichende Zusammenhänge aufzuklären.[14] In andern altorientalischen Literaturen lassen
sich ebenso religiöse Liedersammlungen nachweisen, die mehr sein
wollen als eine Anthologie von Einzeltexten, so etwa der demotisch-
aramäische Papyros Amherst 63, auf den unten einzugehen sein
wird.[15]

Wieweit gehörten Königspsalmen den älteren, David, Asaf oder
Korach zugewiesenen Kleinpsaltern bereits zu? Auffälligerweise he-

---

[13] Zu *genre terms* für Sammlungssegmente sowie zu gattungsverweisenden
und musikalischen Hinweisen auf die Entstehung eines Gesangs durch *demands
of public performance* im Unterschied zum *final shape* des Gesamtpsalters: G. H.
Wilson, *Shape* (1992) 131–38; vgl. K. Koch, „Redaktionsgeschichte" (1994).

[14] Zusammengefaßt in den beiden Kommentaren: F. Hossfeld & E. Zenger,
*Psalmen 1–50* (NEBAT, 1993) und *Psalmen 51–100* (HthKAT, 2000).

[15] Zu akkadischen Beispielen s. *RlA* 3,170; *TUAT* 2,775. Ein berühmtes ägyp-
tisches Beispiel bietet das „Buch der tausend Lieder" an Amon Pap. Leiden I 350,
dt. übersetzt von G. Roeder, *Ägyptische Götterwelt* (1959) S.276–301; in Aus-
zügen bei J. Assmann, *Ägyptische Hymnen und Gebete* (1999) Nr.132–42, und
*TUAT* 2,868–71.

ben sich gerade die besonders charakteristischen Belege aus dieser Gruppe durch fehlende oder singuläre Rubriken von denen der Kompositionen ab, vor denen oder nach denen sie jetzt eingestellt sind. Im Blick auf jene Vorstufen des Psalterbuches nehmen sie jeweils einen exemten Platz ein.

So steht Ps 2 ohne jede Überschrift vor den 39 Gesängen des 1. Davidpsalter, war also einmal wohl als vierzigster ein (nachträglich hinzugefügtes) Präludium zu einer לְדָוִד-Sammlung.[16]

Ps 72 folgt als einziger Salomo zugewiesener Psalm hinter dem 2.Davidpsalter,[17] womöglich als zwanzigster hinter 19 Davidpsalmen (ohne 71); er wird (hernach) zum Abschluß des zweiten Buchs im Psalter (vgl. die Doxologie V.18.19a), schließlich zu dem der beiden ersten Psalmbücher der masoretischen Sammlung (V.19b).

Ps 89 wird einem Korachpsalter (84–88*) angefügt, beschließt dann (vielleicht einen Asaf-Korach-Psalter und am Ende) die drei ersten Psalmenbücher. Auffälligerweise wird er einem Esrahiter Etan zugeschrieben, der nur noch 1Kön 5,11 als nichtisraelitischer Weiser erwähnt wird, eine Zuschreibung, die gewiß nicht erst ein nachexilischer Israelit vorgenommen hat, wenngleich das jetzt am Schluß angeschlossene Klagelied (V. 39-52) vermutlich exilisch oder nachexilisch sein wird. Die Ps 72,18f. ähnliche Doxologie (V. 53) ähnelt dem Abschluß sumerischer Hymnen-Kompositionen.[18]

Ps 110 trägt zwar mit לְדָוִד eine für Ursammlungen übliche Überschrift und folgt auf zwei ebenso überschriebene Gesänge Ps 108f., doch diese Kombination fehlt in den Qumranhandschriften, wo auf Ps 109 andere Stücke folgen.[19] Obwohl Ps 110 in den dort gefundenen Fragmenten nicht erhalten, scheint es nach Motiven und Vokabular ein vorexilisches Dokument zu sein;[20] dafür dürfte auch sprechen, daß einzig hier לְדָוִד nicht wie sonst (in späteren Zeiten) als Verfasserangabe verstanden werden kann, hebt der Sprecher doch an: „Jahwä hat zu meinem Herrn (David) gesprochen."

---

[16] Noch später ist Ps 1 hinzugekommen, Apg 13,33 D wird Ps 2 noch als erster Psalm zitiert. Vgl. G. H. Wilson, „Royal Psalms" (1986); Ders., „Shape" (1992) 132; E. Zenger, „Psalter als Wegweiser" (1993) S.29–47.

[17] F. Hossfeld & E. Zenger, *Psalmen 51–100* (HthKAT, 2000) 328.

[18] G. H. Wilson, „Shape" (1992) 130f.

[19] Ps 109 steht vor 118 in 11QPs^a+b; in 4QPs^e zwischen 105 und 115.

[20] K. Seybold, *Psalmen* (1996) S.437; K. Koch, „Der König als Sohn Gottes" (2002).

Ein Sonderfall stellt Ps 132 dar. Als שִׁיר הַמַּעֲלוֹת ist er zwar masoretisch den Wallfahrtsliedern 120–134 eingegliedert. In der großen Psalterhandschrift 11QPs[a] beschließt aber 132 deren Reihung; Ps 133 erscheint an viel späterer Stelle[21] in dieser Rolle. Indem 133 in der masoretischen Überlieferung zusammen mit 134 hinter 132 eingeordnet wird, wird die kultische Funktion anders bestimmt (in nachexilischer Korrektur?): nicht mehr David und „seine Priester" (132, 9.16), sondern der Hohepriester allein (Aaron 133,2f.) vermitteln Israel den Gottessegen. Dennoch läßt sich fragen, ob 132 von jeher zum Wallfahrtszyklus gehörte;[22] er ist erheblich länger als die vorangehenden, in denen nirgends auf einen König verwiesen wird. Betrachtet man ihn als nachträgliches Postludium, bleiben 12 Wallfahrtspsalmen übrig, und das war vielleicht eine beabsichtigte Zahl.

Ps 144 bildet im MT das vorletzte Glied eines Davidpsalters 138–145. In Qumran ist er jedoch nur in zwei Handschriften in der Folge 141–133–144 belegt (11QPs[a+b]), in einer davon ohne DavidÜberschrift.[23]

Einige Königspsalmen sind zwar in Kleinpsalter inkorporiert, so 18; 20 + 21[24] in die Mitte des 1. Davidpsalter, Ps 45 in eine Korachsammlung (vgl. Ps 144 MT); aber diese Lieder sind weniger markant in ihrer Königsideologie als die exemten. In ihnen kann zwar an ergangene Orakel erinnert werden (20,7; 21,5; vgl. 108,7f.), aber es wird keine direkte Gottesrede wiedergegeben wie Ps 2; 89,4f.20-38;110; 132,11-18). Auch wird in jenen der Herrscher nicht unmittelbar der Gottessfäre zugeordnet, sei es als Gottessohn (2,7; 89,27f.), sei es als Throngenosse und Mitregent (110).

Das Ergebnis der Übersicht ist im Blick auf die ersten drei Psalmbücher (nach masoretischer Ordnung) bemerkenswerter, da sich hier

---

[21] Zwischen 141 und 143; P. Flint, „Book of Psalms" (1998) 458; H. J. Fabry, „Psalter" (1998) 144.154.

[22] B. Duhm, *Psalmen* (1922) 447; J. M. Auwers, „Psaume 132" (1996).

[23] H. J. Fabry, „Psalter" (1998) 142.

[24] War im Zusammenhang des Davidpsalters auch in Ps 19(A) der Lauf des Bräutigams von einem Weltende zum andern (V.6f.) nicht mehr auf die Bahn der Sonne, sondern den Siegeszug des Königs bezogen und also als Königspsalm verstanden worden? Der Sänger stellt sich als Knecht Gottes vor und nennt YHWH seinen Fels wie 18,2.31.46. In jenem Sinn scheint Deuterojesaja (41,1-5; 45,1-3) die Stelle verstanden zu haben; s. K. Koch, „Die Stellung des Kyros im Geschichtsbild Deuterojesajas und ihre überlieferungsgeschichtliche Verankerung," *ZAW* 84 (1972) 352–56.

die Vorstufen älterer Kleinpsalter deutlich abgrenzen lassen, als hinsichtlich der Beispiele aus Buch 4 und 5, in denen die Umrisse früherer Sammlungen sowieso schwerer erkennbar bleiben. So liegt für Ps 2; 72; 89 auf der Hand, daß sie David- oder Korachpsalter exemt *zugeordnet*, aber überraschenderweise nicht *eingeordnet* worden sind. Redaktionelle Angleichungen an den neuen Kontext bleiben gering und beschränken sich wohl auf Anfangs- und Endabschnitte.[25] Selbst die im ersten Davidpsalter fest eingebundenen Psalmen 18 und 20 waren auch als Einzelgesänge im Umlauf, wie ihre Aufnahme in 2 Sam 22 und Pap.Amherst 63 (s.u.) beweisen. Die in den hinteren Teilen des Psalters aufgenommenen Beispiele 110; 132; 144 scheinen freischweifende Texte gewesen zu sein, die in den verschiedenen Überlieferungskreisen an unterschiedlichen Stellen eingefügt werden konnten.

Die mangelnde Einbindung der Königslieder in Psalmengruppen, die ein abweichendes Gepräge aufweisen, ließe sich dadurch erklären, daß es sich bei jenen durchweg um späte Dichtungen handelt. Schon B. Duhm hat für viele von ihnen eine makkabäerzeitliche Entstehungszeit vertreten und bis heute Nachfolger gefunden.[26] Dagegen sprechen jedoch die vielfältigen, bisweilen wörtlichen Parallelen in besonders exemten Texten zum altorientalischen, rituell verankerten Preis des Königs (mit Prädikaten wie Gottessohnschaft und kriegerischer Durchsetzung von Weltherrschaft) in vorpersischer Zeit. Von der zum Ausdruck gebrachten Königsideologie her legt sich nahe, zumindest einen Grundbestand dieser Lieder auf einen vorexilischen, in Jerusalem regierenden König zu beziehen und eine entsprechende Abfassungszeit anzunehmen;[27] vgl. die Nähe von Ps 2 und 110 zur

---

[25] Um den Übergang von Ps 88 zu Ps 89,1 vorzubereiten, wird die Überschrift des ersten durch die Nennung eines andern Esrahiter namens Heman erweitert, wohl im Zug einer allmählichen Israelitisierung der Esrahiter; vgl.88,1*G*; 2 Chr 2,6 (?); 6,16-29. Der Hinweis auf die Hinfälligkeit des Menschenlebens in 88,48f. ist vielleicht ein durch den Tenor von 88 veranlaßter Nachtrag. Weitere Querverbindungen vermuten F. Hossfeld & E. Zenger, *Psalmen 51–100* (HthKAT, 2000) 597.

[26] Z.B. H. Donner zu Ps 110 in: *Aufsätze zum Alten Testament* (BZAW 224; Berlin: de Gruyter, 1994) 213–23.

[27] Vgl. zu Ps 2 K. Seybold, *Psalmen* (1996) S.31; K. Koch, „Israel im Orient" (1999) 242–71. Zu Ps 18 K. Seybold, *Psalmen*, 83; F. Hossfeld & E. Zenger, *Psalmen 1–50* (NEBAT, 1993) 128. Zu Ps 20 K. Seybold, *Psalmen* (1996) 89; F. Hossfeld & E. Zenger, *Psalmen 1–50* (NEBAT, 1993) 128; zu Ps 21 K. Seybold,

ägyptischen,[28] von Ps 72 und 89 mehr zur neuassyrischen[29] Königs-
prädikation.

Wenn aber altes Textmaterial, warum sind dann die exemten Psalmen nicht in die frühen Kleinpsalter inkorporiert worden? Das läßt
sich kaum anders erklären als so, daß es neben jenen Kleinpsaltern als
Vorstufen des masoretischen Psalters lange Zeit, wenn nicht Jahrhunderte hindurch, mündliche oder schriftliche Überlieferung von eigenständigen, psalmenartigen Einzeltexten gegeben hat, die dem Anliegen der frühen Sammlungsverfasser wenig entsprochen oder sogar
widersprochen haben. Ausgeschlossen (oder ausgeschieden?) wurden
in bestimmten Überlieferungskreisen anscheinend Gesänge, die den
sakralen Charakter des (untergegangenen?) Königtums zu sehr herausgestrichen haben. In den 2.Davidspsalter werden noch zwei Lieder
mit kurzer Fürbitte für den König aufgenommen (61,7; 63,12), in den
2. Korachpsalter noch eines dieser Art (84,10), doch im Asafpsalter
73–83 und den kleineren Sammlungen des späteren 4. und
5. Psalmbuchs fehlen selbst Fürbitten für einen König. Darf man vermuten, daß zwischenzeitich große Gruppen von Psalmensängern
einem dynastischen Königtum völlig ablehnend gegenüberstanden,
aber David als Vorbild eines frommen Lebens von solcher Kritik aus-
genommen hatten? Irgendwann in nachexilischer Zeit werden jedoch
auch die Redaktoren von ehedem oppositionellen Kleinpsalter von
einer messianischen Begeisterung erfaßt, greifen das andernorts ge-
hütete Gut von Königsliedern auf und verwenden es zur Ein- oder
Ausleitung bisher „königsloser" Sammlungen.

Die „messianische" Interpretation von Teilsammlungen bzw. Teil-
büchern des Psalters durch Königsgesänge, die in dieser Art ange-

---

*Psalmen*, 92, F. Hossfeld & E. Zenger, *Psalmen 1–50*, 140f.; zu Ps 72 K. Seybold,
*Psalmen*, 277; F. Hossfeld & E. Zenger, *Psalmen 51–100* (HThKAT, 2000)
308ff.; zu Ps 110 K. Seybold, *Psalmen*, 437; K. Koch, „Der König als Sohn Gottes" (2002). Als Wallfahrtslied wird Ps 132 gemeinhin als nachexilisch eingestuft,
so wieder K. Seybold, *Psalmen* (1996) 497. In ihm wird aber die Lade als die
מְנוּחָה Gottes und Quelle des Heils für Israel in den Mittelpunkt gerückt. Was soll
sich ein Dichter nachexilischer Zeit dabei gedacht haben, wo es doch längst keine
Lade auf dem Zion mehr gab?

[28] K. Koch, „Israel im Orient" (1999); K. Koch, „Der König als Sohn Gottes"
(2002).

[29] M. Arneth, *Sonne der Gerechtigkeit* (2000); H. U. Steymans, „Ps 89,4-5,20-
38 zu Texten vom assyrischen Hof," in: E. Otto & E. Zenger (Hrsg.), *„Mein Sohn
bist du* (2002) 184–251.

gliedert worden und dadurch als Weissagungen auf einen künftigen nationalen Heilskönig begriffen worden sind — was nicht ihr ursprünglicher Sinn gewesen war —, wird heute von vielen Exegeten vertreten. Ch. Rösel hat dem ein eigenes Buch gewidmet[30] und Hossfeld/Zenger verweisen des öfteren darauf.[31] Demnach verheißen nun prophetisch Ps 2 die künftige Durchsetzung Jahwäs und seines Gesalbten gegen die aufrührerische Völkerwelt; Ps 72 dessen Ausbreitung von צֶדֶק über Land und Volk im Zusammenhang einer noch ausstehenden Weltherrschaft von Meer zu Meer, Ps 89 das Wiedererstehen einer ewigen Dawidsherrschaft, Ps 110 das Gericht eines auf Gottes eigenem Thron sitzenden Zionskönigs über die Völkerwelt (ähnlich 144). Dennoch bleibt der Begriff „messianisch" mißverständlich, weil zu schnell von neutestamentlichen Voraussetzungen her gefüllt. Vermutlich wird nämlich nicht der Person eines künftigen Heilskönigs Ewigkeit zugedacht, sondern seiner Dynastie in der Abfolge von Generationen. Zudem bleiben die in den Psalmen mit jenem verknüpften Hoffnungen weit hinter „messianischen" Weissagungen der prophetischen Literatur zurück; nichts verlautet davon, daß es dann überhaupt kein Böses im Land mehr geben wird, sondern Frieden sogar mit den Raubtieren (Jes 11,1-9), oder ein neuer Bund geschlossen wird mit der Wirkung einer bleibenden Internalisierung der Tora im Herzen jedes Kultgenossen (Jer 31,31-34).

Die besonders in der Sammlungen von Ps (1+) 2 bis 89 dominant werdende königsfreundliche Richtung hat die kritische Sicht nicht völlig verschwinden lassen. Das zeigt sich vielleicht auch im weiterenWachstum des Psalters. Nach dem Königspsalm 144 folgt wohl nicht von ungefähr 145 mit dem Eingang: „Ich will dich erheben, mein Gott, den König" und 146 mit der Mahnung, nicht den Herrschenden zu trauen (V.3f.). Auf Ps 89 folgt eine Reihe von YHWH-Königs-Psalmen (93–99); auch dahinter könnte sich eine Antithese verbergen.[32]

Trifft die Hypothese zu, daß das späte Auftauchen markanter Königslieder in Psalmensammlungen sich aus einer antiroyalistischen Tendenz früher Sammler einerseits wie der fortgesetzten Tradierung jener königsfreundlichen Texte bei andern Gruppen, deren mög-

---

[30] Ch. Rösel, *Die messianische Redaktion* (1999).

[31] Z.B. F. Hossfeld & E. Zenger, *Psalmen 1–50* (NEBAT, 1993) 51 zu Ps 2; *Psalmen 51–100* (HThKAT, 2000) 329 zu Ps 72.

[32] G. H. Wilson, „Shape" (1992) 139f.

licherweise schriftliche Hinterlassenschaft verloren gegangen ist, zu erklären wäre, dann war die Literatur- und die damit zusammenhängende Religionsgeschichte Israels in exilischer und frühnachexilischer Zeit viel differenzierter, als zumeist angenommen wird. Die Entstehungsstufen des kanonischen Psalters wird in der Regel stromlinienförmig vorgestellt, als ununterbrochene „Fortschreibung" eines ersten Kernbestands. Der Bildungsprozeß verlief wohl eher auf mehreren, auseinanderliegenden Gleisen mit sehr unterschiedlichen Tendenzen. Auch im Blick auf das Königsbild gab es keine kompakte „Königsideologie," sondern ein breites Raster von begeistertem Preis eines Gottessohns bis hin zur völligen Mißachtung einer monarchischen Verfassung.

Für eine eigenständige Vorgeschichte der exemten wie der in zwei Sammlungen früh inkorporierten Königspsalmen spricht der Befund, daß gerade von ihnen — mehr als von andern Psalmengruppen — Varianten außerhalb des Psalters nachweisbar sind. Das gilt schon für Ps 18, der in 2 Sam 22[33] in einen ganz anderen Kontext eingegliedert worden ist, also als selbstständiger Text betrachtet wurde.

Es gilt noch mehr für den mittleren Teil von Ps 89 und für Ps 20. Die Überlieferungsgeschichte dieser beiden Stücke soll eingehender untersucht und schließlich auf einen möglichen rituellen Hintergrund befragt werden. Beide Beispiele lassen erkennen, daß der Weg von einer möglichen rituellen Vorstufe bis zur vorliegenden poetischen Fassung ein sehr weiter gewesen sein kann.

### DAS KÖNIGSORAKEL IN PSALM 89, EINER QUMRANHANDSCHRIFT UND 2 SAM 7

Ps 89,20-38 gibt eine göttliche Verheißung an David wieder, die „damals" Jahwäs ḥasîdîm als חָזוֹן mitgeteilt worden war. Davon hebt sich das den Psalm beschließende Volksklagelied deutlich ab, wo der im Orakel verkündete herausgestrichene ewige Bestand von Bund und Thron (V. 29f.34f.) als ungültig geworden beklagt wird (V. 40).[34] Was V.20-38 geschrieben steht, ist wegen dieser Diskrepanz kaum

---

[33] Dazu jetzt F. Hartenstein, „Wolkendunkel und Himmelsfeste," in: B. Janowski & B. Ego, *Das biblische Weltbild und seine altorientalischen Kontexte* (FAT 32, 2001) (125ff.) 131–36.

[34] Es „wird Jhwh (vgl. V.40.50 im Gegensatz zu V.29.35.36) des Meineids bezichtigt. Der Gott Israels steht als Lügner da;" M. Emmendörfer, *Der ferne Gott* (FAT 21, 1998) 229; vgl. H. U. Steymans, „Bund" (1998) 129–33.

eine Fiktion des Psalmautors, sondern setzt tatsächlich ein älteres Orakel voraus. Dem entspricht, daß die Natanweissagung in 2 Sam 7 nur zu diesem Teil des Psalms direkte Parallelen zeigt, und zudem sich in Qumran ein Fragment gefunden hat, das allein dieses Stück des Psalms bietet, allerdings in erheblich verkürzter Form, und mit ihm ein eigenes Blatt begonnen hatte, wobei die Fortsetzung nach einer Wiedergabe des Anfangs von V.31 allerdings weggebrochen ist.[35] Zuerst als 4Q236 gezählt, wurde es 2000 in DJD 16 als 4QPs[x] abschließend veröffentlicht.[36] Das Fragment, "one of the most unusual Psalm manuscripts found at Qumran,"[37] stellt neben der berühmten Rolle 11QPs[a] die älteste dort gefundene Psalmenhandschrift dar, geschrieben in hasmonäischer Zeit, aber mit einer vom DJD-Autor *archaic* genannten Orthografie, es stammt also vermutlich aus dem 3.Jh.v.Chr., wenn es nicht noch älterer Herkunft ist.

Es handelt sich um einen für die alttestamentliche Literatur wohl einmaligen Fall, daß vier Texte in unterschiedlichen Literaturwerken womöglich auf denselben Grundtext zurückgehen. Für den Chroniktext gilt das allerdings nur bedingt, da dieser gewiß auf den Samueltext zurückgreift und ihn nur an wenigen Stellen auf Grund seines eigenen Anliegens umformuliert. Auch zwischen dem Qumranfragment und Ps 89 besteht wohl direkte Abhängigkeit, auf welcher Seite sie liegt, ist umstritten.[38] Die Beziehung zwischen Psalm und Natanweissagung wird zwar seit langem gesehen, doch so, daß meist von vornherein dem Samueltext die *pole-position* eingeräumt wird, wohl schon deshalb, weil er im Kanon voransteht, gegenwärtig vor allem deshalb, weil er dem Deuteronomistischen Geschichtswerk zugeschrieben wird und von da aus eine modische „deuteronomistizistische" Woge bei vielen Exegeten über alle andere alttestamentliche Literatur flutet,[39] die keine Beweise im Detail benötigt. Wer diesen

---

[35] Synopse bei U. Gleßmer, „Das Textwachstum von Ps 89 und ein Qumranfragment," *BN* 65 (1992) 55–73, bes. 64f.

[36] Ulrich et. al., *Psalms to Chronicles* (DJD 16, 2000) 163–67.

[37] DJD 16 (2000) 163.

[38] S. die Auseinandersetzung mit E. Lipinski, „Le poème royal du psaume LXXXIX 1.5,20-38" (CRB 6; Paris; Gabalda, 1967) bei J. B. Dumortier, „Un rituel d'inthronisation: le Ps LXXXIX 2-38," *VT* 22 (1972) 176–86.

[39] Vgl. schon B. Duhm, *Psalmen* (1922) 337–39 und H. Gunkel, *Psalmen* (1926) 392f. Ausführlich hat sich T. Veijola, *Verheißung* (1982) anhand eines statistischen Vergleichs einzelner Wörter um den Nachweis bemüht, daß, weil

imponierend geschlossen wirkenden literarkritischen Theoremen skep
tisch gegenübersteht, wird einen synchronen Vergleich der vier Fassungen in die historischen Verhältnisse als Einstieg für nötig halten.
Er folgt hier auf eine Synopse der Texte in deutscher Übersetzung.
Einige Erläuterungen zu ihrer Gestaltung. Die beiden linken Spalten
bieten den Qumran- und den Psalmtext; Fettdruck wird dann benutzt,
wenn masoretischer Text und Fragment übereinstimmen, wobei die
durch Textverderbnis entstandenen Lücken im zweiten Text, die
gemäß der Zeilenbreiten dem entsprechen, was der erste ausdrücklich
bietet, mit der DJD-Ausgabe nach MT ergänzt worden sind. Dagegen
erscheint im Normaldruck, wo die Texte divergieren. Die beiden
rechten Spalten geben den Samuel- und den Chroniktext wieder.
Fettdruck weist auf Übereinstimmung, Normaldruck auf Besonder-
heiten. Unterstrichen erscheinen Wörter, die mindestens in drei der
Fassungen auftauchen.

| 4Q236/Ps[x] | Ps 89 | 2 Sam 7 | 1 Chr 17 |
|---|---|---|---|
| | 4 Geschlossen habe ich einen Bund für meinen Erwählten, / geschworen dem David, meinem Knecht: | | |
| | 5 „Für immer werde | | |

---

2 Sam deuteronomistisch ist, Ps 89 nachdeuteronomistisch sein müsse, vor allem
deshalb, weil ein Bund Gottes mit dem König sonst unbekannt sei. Das Wortfeld
בְּרִית und חֶסֶד ist aber für den Davidsbund mit Gottessohnschaft und Weltherr-
schaftsversprechen charakteristisch anders als beim Sinaibund, zum ersten lassen
sich zudem neuassyrische Analogien aufweisen. Zur Kritik an neueren Deutun-
gen: H. U. Steymans, „Bund" (1998) und „Thron" (2002) 945–47. Veijola hat jedoch breite Zustimmung gefunden, jüngst bei M. Pietsch, „‚Dieses ist der Sproß
Davids....' Studien zur Rezeption der Natanweissagung" (masch. Dissertation,
Hamburg 2001). Eine rühmliche Ausnahme macht E. J. Waschke, „Das Verhältnis alttestamentlicher Überlieferungen im Schnittpunkt der Dynastie-zusage und
die Dynastiezusage im Spiegel alttestamentlicher Überlieferungen," *ZAW* 99
(1987) 157–79, der mit „zwei eigenständigen Entwicklungen ein und derselben
Tradition" rechnet (174), ähnlich schon H. J. Kraus, *Psalmen* (1978) 790. W. M.
Schniedewind, *Society and the Promise to David. The Reception History of 2
Samuel 7:1-17* (Oxford: University Press, 1999) 93–95 sieht in Ps 89, 20-38 einen
eigenständigen Text aus der Zeit Josias.

| | | | |
|---|---|---|---|
| | ich Bestand verleihen deinem Samen, /erbauen von Generation zu Generation deinen Thron." | | |
| 1 [Im Gesicht] sprichst du zu deinen Erwählten: | 20 Damals hast du im Gesicht / zu deinen Getreuen gesprochen: | 8 Und nun sprich so zu meinem Knecht David: / So hat Jahwä Zebaot gesprochen: | 7 Und nun sprich so zu meinem Knecht David: So hat Jahwä Zebaot gesprochen: |
| „Eingesetzt habe ich einen He[lfer über einen] He[lden], / 2 [erhöht einen Er]wählten aus dem Volk. | „Eingesetzt habe ich Hilfe über einem Helden, / erhöht einen Erwählten aus dem Volk. | „Ich habe dich weggenommen von der Herde, / hinter dem Kleinvieh weg, um נָגִיד zu sein über mein Volk, über Israel. | „Ich habe dich weggenommen von der Herde, / hinter dem Kleinvieh weg, um נָגִיד zu sein über mein Volk Israel. |
| Gefunden habe ich 3 [David, meinen Knecht], von meinem heiligen Öl 4 ihn [gesalbt], | 21 Gefunden habe ich David, meinen Knecht, / mit meinem heiligen Öl ihn gesalbt, | | |
| dem seine Hand euch Bestand gibt,/ 5 [und stärkt euch.] Gelegt habe ich auf das Meer die Hand 6 auf die Ströme [seine Rechte]. | 22 dem meine Hand Bestand gibt,/ ja, mein Arm stärkt ihn. Vgl. V.26 | 9 Ich war mit dir, wohin immer du gegangen bist / | 8 Ich war mit dir, wohin immer du gegangen bist / |
| [Nicht wird fortfahren] ein Feind und ein Übler (?), ihn zu bedrücken. | 23 Nicht wird ihn überfallen ein Feind, / ein Schändlicher ihn nicht bedrücken. 24 Zerstoßen | und rottete alle deine Feinde vor dir aus. | und rottete alle deine Feinde vor dir aus. |

| | | | |
|---|---|---|---|
| | werde ich <u>vor ihm</u> seine <u>Feinde</u>, / seine Hasser werde ich schlagen. | **Vgl. V. 10b** | **Vgl. V. 9b** |
| | 25 meine Treue und meine Huld sind mit ihm, / in meinem <u>Namen</u> wird sich sein Horn erheben. | **Und ich habe dir einen großen <u>Namen</u> verschafft / gleich dem Namen der Größten auf Erden.** **10 Und ich habe einen (Kult-)Ort gesetzt meinem Volk Israel / und es eingepflanzt und es wohnt unter ihm.** | **Und ich habe dir einen großen <u>Namen</u> verschafft / gleich dem Namen der Größten auf Erden.** **9 Und ich habe einen (Kult-)Ort gesetzt meinem Volk Israel / und es eingepflanzt und es wohnt unter ihm.** |
| | Vgl. V. 23 | **Und es/er wird sich nicht mehr ängstigen / und die <u>Schändlichen</u> werden <u>nicht</u> fortfahren, (es) zu** bedrücken, **wie am Anfang** 11 **und seit der Zeit, da ich Richter eingesetzt habe über mein Volk Israel.** | **Und es/er wird sich nicht mehr ängstigen / und die <u>Schändlichen</u> werden <u>nicht</u> fortfahren, (es) aufzureiben, wie am Anfang 10 und seit der Zeiten, da ich Richter eingesetzt habe über mein Volk Israel.** |
| Vgl. Z. 5 f. | **26 Gelegt habe ich auf das Meer** seine **Hand, / auf die Ströme seine Rechte.** | Und ich habe dir Ruhe verschafft vor **all deinen Feinden."** | Und ich habe gedemütigt **alle deine Feinde.** |
| **7 [Er wird mich anrufen: Mein <u>Vater</u> bist Du.]** / | **27 Er ist, der mich anrufen wird: Mein <u>Vater</u> bist du,** / meine Gottheit und Fels meiner Heilshilfe. | Vgl. V. 14 | Vgl. V. 13 |

| | | | |
|---|---|---|---|
| [Ich habe als Erstgeborenen ihn eingesetzt, / zum עֶלְיוֹן der Könige] der Erde | 28 Ja, **ich habe als Erstgeborenen ihn eingesetzt, / zum** עֶלְיוֹן **unter den Königen der Erde.** 29 Für immer werde ich ihm meine Huld bewahren, mein Bund ist verläßlich für ihn. | | |
| | | Und **kund**getan hat dir Jahwä, daß ein **Haus wird dir** verschaffen wird **Jahwä.** | Und ich tat dir (es) **kund**, und ein **Haus wird dir** bauen **Jahwä.** |
| | 30 Ich setze für alle Zeit seinen <u>Samen</u> ein, / | 12 **wenn voll** sein werden **deine Tage und du** bei **deinen Vätern** / liegen wirst, **dann werde ich aufrichten deinen <u>Samen</u> nach dir,** / der aus deinem Leib kommt. | 11 Geschehen wird, **wenn voll** geworden **deine Tage** / und du mit **deinen Vätern** (davon) gehst, **dann werde ich aufrichten deinen <u>Samen</u> nach dir,** der aus deinen Söhnen entsteht. |
| | seinen <u>Thron</u> wie die Tage des Himmels. | **Und ich werde beständig machen sein Königtum.** 13 **Er wird** meinem Namen **ein Haus bauen,** / und **ich werde fest** gründen den **<u>Thron</u>** seines Königtums **für immer.** | **Und ich werde beständig machen sein Königtum.** 12 **Er wird** mir **ein Haus bauen,** und **ich werde befestigen** seinen **<u>Thron</u> für immer.** |
| | Vgl. V. 27 | 14 **Ich werde ihm zum <u>Vater</u> werden,** / **und er wird mir zum** | 13 **Ich werde ihm zum <u>Vater</u> werden,** / **und er wird mir zum Sohn werden.** |

| | | Sohn werden. | |
|---|---|---|---|
| **Wenn verlassen ...** | 31 **Wenn verlassen** seine Söhne meine Weisung / und in meinen Rechtssetzungen nicht wandeln, 32 wenn sie meine Gesetze entweihen / und meine Gebote nicht wahren, | Wenn er schuldig wird, | |
| | 33 dann werde ich ahnden **mit dem Stab** ihre Vergehen / **und mit Schlägen** ihre Schuld. | werde ich ihn züchtigen **mit dem Stab** von Menschen / **und mit Schlägen** von Menschenkindern. | |
| | 34 Doch **meine Huld** lasse ich <u>nicht von ihm weichen</u>, / nicht trügerisch machen meine Treue. 35 Nicht werde ich entweihen meinen Bund, / die Äußerung meiner Lippen nicht ändern. | 15 Doch <u>**meine Huld**</u> wird <u>**nicht von ihm weichen,**</u> **wie ich sie weichen ließ** von Saul, den ich weichen ließ vor dir. | Und <u>**meine Huld**</u> lasse ich <u>**nicht von ihm weichen, wie ich sie weichen ließ** von</u> dem, der vor dir gewesen war. |
| | 36 Eines habe ich geschworen bei meiner Heiligkeit: / Fürwahr, Dawid täusche ich nicht! | | |
| | 37 Sein Same soll <u>für immer</u> bestehen, / sein **Thron** wie die Sonne vor mir. 38 Wie der Mond wird er immer **Bestand** haben, / und der Zeuge in den Wolken ist verläßlich | 16 und verläßlich wird sein Haus sein, / und sein Königtum <u>für immer</u> vor dir. Dein **Thron** wird **beständig** sein für immer. | 14 Und ich werde ihn auftreten lassen in meinem Haus und meinem Reich <u>für immer</u>. Sein **Thron** wird **beständig** sein <u>für immer</u>. |

Zunächst ein Vergleich von Qumran- und Psalmspalte, wobei nicht jedes Detail besprochen werden kann. Das Fragment weist offensichtlich einen strafferen Aufbau auf und läßt nichts von einer inhaltlichen Lücke erkennen. Der DJD-Band folgert daraus, daß es sich bei ihm um *"one of the sources of Ps 89 or ... a very early form of this psalm"* handelt. Ist der Überschuß im Psalm auf diese Weise zu erklären? Es handelt sich vornehmlich um zwei Themenkreise:

a) In 4Q fehlt die wiederholte Berufung auf בְּרִית, חֶסֶד, אֱמוּנָה, die im Psalm die eigentliche Begründung für den uneingeschränkten göttlichen Beistand liefern (89,25.29.34f.). Sie war im Vorgriff schon im Eingang des Psalms angeführt worden (V. 3-6) in der 3.Person. Allerdings könnte wenigstens eine einmalige Erwähnung von חֶסֶד, 89,34a entsprechend, im jetzt verlorenen Ende des Fragments gestanden haben, da sie sich dort auch parallel in 2 Sam 7,15 findet (s.u.). Die redundanten Einfügungen im Psalm finden im Kontext des Psalms weitere Parallelen (V. 2-4.6.40.50), hangen also mit dem speziellen Anliegen des Psalmisten zusammen und erweisen sich dadurch als Nachtrag.

b) Ebenso mangelt es im Fragment an der ersten Verheißung ewiger Dauer von Dynastie und Thron (V. 29f.). Nahezu wörtlich gleich, aber mit mythologischen Vergleichen verbunden, taucht sie 89,36-38 erneut auf, wo sie dann als eigener Gottesschwur eingeführt wird. Der Dynastie-Thron-Verheißung war schon im Psalmeingang V. 4f. als für sich stehendes Jahwäwort zitiert worden. In V. 30 wird sie dann in das Beistandsorakel wohl deshalb zusätzlich eingefügt, um in V.31-34 die (in der Überlieferung vorgegebene) Androhung beschränkter göttlicher Sanktionen für allfällige Vergehen der Nachkommen noch weiter zu relativieren.[40] In jedem Fall aber handelt es sich um Redundanzen, die nur der Psalmist gebraucht und seiner eigenen Absicht entsprungen sein werden.

Doch Qumran liefert nicht die einzige Parallele zu Psalm 89, wie die rechten Spalten der Übersicht ergeben mit dem Wortlaut der Natanweissagung von 2 Sam 7 und 1 Chr 17. Die Chronik legt offenkundig

---

[40] Zur Palindromie in V.29-38: H. U. Steymans, „Bund" (1998) 127.

den Samueltext zugrunde und formuliert ihn nur an einigen Stellen bewußt um. Die Spalte mit 2 Sam 7 ist etwa von gleicher Länge wie die Psalmenfassung, aber mit Unterschieden in der Ausgestaltung der Einzelabschnitte und bei belangreichen Formulierungen.[41] Das wichtigste sei aufgezählt:

a) 2 Sam gibt eine göttliche Verheißung durch den Profeten Natan als Anrede an den König in der *2. Person sing.* wieder, Ps 89 führt sie auf eine Vision von anonymen Getreuen (so MT)[42] zurück — eine eigenartige Bezeichnung —, unterrichtet werden dritte über den König in der *3. Person sing.* Orakel an Könige gibt es auch in der Umwelt Israels entweder mit unmittelbarer Anrede oder mit Verweis auf den Herrscher in

b) Der Psalm ist *streng poetisch*, fast durchweg mit Parallelismus membrorum, abgefaßt; der Natantext weist mehrmals *prosaische Einsprengsel* auf; in ihnen — und fast nur in ihnen — taucht deuteronomistische Terminologie auf, so beim Rückblick auf die Volksgeschichte (V. 10bβ.11.15) und bei der für den erzählenden Kontext bezeichnenden Koppelung von Gottes- und Königshaus (V. 12aαβ.13a); diese Sätze stammen wahrscheinlich von einem Redaktor der Samuelbücher.

c) *Rückblick auf die Vergangenheit* nimmt der Psalm nur mit

---

[41] Seit L. Rost, *Thronnachfolge* (1926), die Bedeutung von 2 Sam 7 und der darin erhaltenen Natanweissagung für die von ihm konstruierte Schrift über die Thronnachfolge Davids herausgestellt und als ursprünglichen Kern der Verheißung einzig V. 11b.16 gelten gelassen hat, reißen die literarkritischen Thesen zur Trennung von Schichten im Kapitel nicht mehr ab, ohne daß ein Konsens in Aussicht steht. W. Dietrich & T. Naumann, *Samuelbücher* (1995) bieten einen instruktiven Überblick; es ist bezeichnend, daß in ihrem Referat nirgends Ps 89 als belangreiche Variante auftaucht. Müßte aber nicht gegenüber der Literarkritik, die ein westlicher Stubengelehrter anhand eines einzigen antiken Textes zu rekonstruieren unternimmt — unter der naiven Voraussetzung, daß die Alten nicht anders gedacht haben als wir heute —, jeder Analyse, die sich auf mindestens zwei Textvarianten stützt, bei denen die Abhängigkeit der einen von der anderen nicht offenkundig ist, die größere historische Wahrscheinlichkeit zugebilligt werden?

[42] חֲסִידִים wird gewöhnlich auf Natan und andere Profeten bezogen (vgl. F. Hossfeld & E. Zenger, *Psalmen 51–100* [HthKAT,2000] 593), was aber eine sonst nicht belegte Ausdrucksweise ist. H. J. Kraus, *Psalmen* (1978) 790 vermutet eine Bezugnahme auf Orakel mehrerer Profeten, was zum gesonderten Neueinsatz in Ps 89,36; 2 Sam 7,11b (s.u.) passen würde. 4QPs^x liest בחריך und bezieht sich wahrscheinlich auf David und seine Nachkommen, vgl. die folgende Zeile: „eine Vision *betreffs* deiner Erwählten."

zwei Doppelzeilen am Eingang vor, die sich anscheinend auf eine einzige, kurz zurückliegende Gottesaktion beziehen, bei der der König „aus dem Volk erwählt," ihm eine — unerklärt bleibende — „Hilfe"[43] übereignet wurde, und das durch den Ritus der Salbung. 2 Sam 7 verweist hingegen — in Entfaltung der Aussage: „Gefunden habe ich David, meinen Knecht" — auf die Aufstiegsgeschichte Davids von ihren Anfängen an, übergeht jedoch die Salbung und sieht, was Ps 89, 23-26 als Verheißung für die Zukunft schildert, als bereits erfüllt an.[44] Der Psalm steht altorientalischen Parallelen näher; die Natanweissagung paßt den Text in den Erzählduktus der Samuelbücher ein.

d) Der Psalm begnügt sich mit der kurzen Notiz, daß der Gesalbte aus dem Volk erwählt ist, was ebenso Abstand wie Zugehörigkeit signalisieren kann. Natan schildert hingegen David als einen Nagid, der erhöht wurde, um für das Volk tätig zu sein, das selbst als Objekt des Gotteshandelns erscheint; es war von den Feinden seit langem bedrückt (V. 8-11a). Gerade deshalb hatte David über alle Maßen Erfolg, sind sämtliche Feinde ausgerottet, kann er ungestörte Ruhe genießen, kommt dem Ruhm seines Namens niemand auf Erden gleich. Das stellt vermutlich eine Bearbeitung der Vorlage nach dem

---

[43] 4QPs$^x$ liest das Partizip „Helfer" und versteht darunter wohl die Person des Königs, die über den „Held" das kollektiv gedachte Volk eingesetzt wird. Hier zeigt sich im Fragment gegenüber Ps 89 eine (sekundäre) Tendenz zur Demokratisierung, vgl. das „euch" Z. 4.f.

[44] Wie die „Tempora" der Verben in 2 Sam 7 zu übersetzen sind, ist seit langem umstritten, was sich bis in die gebräuchlich Bibelübersetzungen hinein auswirkt. Luther hat V. 9b noch präterital, V. 10 dann futurisch und V. 11b präsentisch wiedergegeben; die Revision von 1984 beginnt mit dem Übergang schon V. 9b, ebenso die Einheitsübersetzuung, die dann aber bereits V. 11a als Präsens faßt und V. 11b betont absetzt: „Nun verkündet der Herr." Nach dem Kontext des Kapitels ist gewiß וְאֶהְיֶה in V. 9a wie in V. 6 präterital gemeint, ebenso (kopulativ) die anschließenden w$^e$qāṭal-Formen V. 9-11a; denn Dawid hat seine Ruhe vor den äußeren Feinden nach V. 1 bereits gefunden (nur innerer Zwist steht noch bevor Kap. 9ff.) und das Volk hat den maqôm gefunden, wo es gedeihlich wohnen kann. Auch der Verweis auf eine Orakelmitteilung in V. 11b gibt besseren Sinn, wenn damit auf ein bereits früher ergangenes Wortverwiesen wird (s.u.). Dagegen haben die auf „nacktes" AK (impf) folgenden w$^e$qāṭal- Verben in V. 12.13b.14b. offensichtlich konstatierende und zugleich zukünftige Bedeutung.

Kontext der Samuelbücher dar; anders wäre nicht erklärlich, warum Ps 89 diese Bezüge übergeht. Nüchterner und jenen Erzählungen ferner erscheint hier die Stellung des Königs, aber auch betonter wieder auf eine Königsideologie nach altorientalischer Weise konzentriert: die Feinde, die es nach wie vor gibt, werden ihn nie bezwingen; statt Hinweis auf seinen Anfang unter dem Kleinvieh und auf spätere Siege wird das Ereignis der Salbung hervorgehoben, das den Mann so erfolgreich hat werden lassen, daß er künftig chaotische Völkerfluten bezwingen wird.[45] Nicht der Name des Königs, sondern der seines Gottes wird thematisiert (V. 25).

e) Ähnliches gilt für die Voraussage des Tempelbaus durch den Sohn, die sich nur bei Natan findet. Sie gehört innerhalb des Kapitels zur kunstvollen *Gegenüberstellung von Gotteshaus und Königshaus*, die בַּיִת zum Leitwort des Kapitels werden läßt (V. 1f.5-7.16.18f.25.27.29). Warum sollte der Psalmist den wichtigen Hinweis auf den Tempel ausgelassen haben, falls er ihn in seiner Vorlage gefunden hätte?

f) Zum erstgeborenen *Gottessohn* hat nach Ps 89 David die Salbung erhöht. Nach der Natanweissagung hingegen wird sein Sohn Salomo der Gottessohnschaft teilhaftig, weil erst er das Haus Gottes baut; dies ist sicherlich eine sekundäre Verschiebung, und der Psalm an dieser Stelle ursprünglicher. Doch auch von der Samuelkonzeption distanziert sich der Chronist; für ihn ist der zum Gottessohn erkorene Nachkomme Davids erst noch zu erwarten, nicht mit Samuel bereits erschienen. Keiner der bisherigen israelitischen Könige hat also schon eine so innige Beziehung zum einzigen Gott innegehabt, wie sie Natan verheißen hat. Verwundert es, daß ein chronistischer Leser des Deuteronomistischen Geschichts-werkes zu solcher Folgerung gelangen mußte?

g) Auffälligerweise verweisen Psalm wie Samuelbuch auf *zwei gesonderte Orakel*, die sie nunmehr zu einem Text zusammenbinden. Natan setzt 7,11b erneut an: „Jahwä hat dir kundgetan." Ebenso verweist Ps 89,36 auf ein zweites Gotteswort, diesmal sogar einen Schwur: „Eins habe ich bei meiner Heiligkeit geschworen."[46] Dieses Orakel war Ps 89,4f.

---

[45] Vgl. F. Hossfeld & E. Zenger, *Psalmen 51–100* (HthKAT, 2000) zu V.26.

[46] F. Hossfeld & E. Zenger, *Psalmen 51–100* (HthKAT, 2000) 582.585

bereits im Vorgriff und in einer ursprünglicher wirkenden Fassung zitiert, ist also offensichtlich einmal selbständig umgelaufen. Erst der Chronist verwischt (V. 10b) durch Auslassen des Subjekts (und PK statt AK) den Neueinsatz.

h) In 2 Sam ist das zweite Orakel erheblich länger als in der Psalmversion, bietet anders als diese die *Bestandszusage für Dynastie und Thron* nur in einem Abschnitt, aber so, daß von „Haus" und „Samen" viermal die Rede ist, während der Psalmist es nur zweimal tut und dabei die erste Erwähnung schon in sein erstes Orakel hineingenommen hat; das 4Q-Fragment hat davon wohl nur einmal und das sinngemäß in der zweiten Gottesäußerung berichtet, wenn man ein Äquivalent zu V. 37f.MT bei ihm voraussetzen darf. Von der Beständigkeit des Throns ist in beiden Spalten zweimal gesprochen; in 2 Sam wird sie jeweils auf das „Königtum" ausgedehnt (V. 13.16). Dem Chronisten geht so viel Verheißung für ein irdisches Königtum zu weit. So läßt er Natan V. 14 von Gottes Haus und Königtum reden, worin der Davidide eingebunden ist und von wo aus ihm allererst für sein Regieren Bestand zukommt.

i) Der Hinweis auf mögliche *Vergehen mit begrenzter Sanktion* bleibt in 2 Sam kurz und pauschal, während er in Ps 89 mit deuteronomistisch klingenden (?) Wendungen[47] erweitert ist. Im Fragment war er vorhanden, doch bleiben seine Länge und Einzelformulierungen unbekannt. Der Chronist hat den Absatz gestrichen, für ihn kann es anscheinend bei Gott keine Sonderbehandlung gekrönter Häupter geben. In diesem Fall hat gewiß der Psalmist erweitert.

Das Ergebnis des Vergleichs läßt m.E. erkennen, daß sich 2.Sam im Vergleich mit der Psalmversion in den meisten Fällen als eine jüngere Überlieferungsstufe erweist, jedoch nicht in allen (vgl. den letzten oben genannten Punkt). Wahrscheinlich ist also nicht eine von beiden Fassungen von der andern abhängig, sondern beide kanonisch gewordene Fassungen haben auf dieselbe Vorlage zurückgegriffen und sie erweitert.

---

erkennen den Neueinsatz, erklären ihn als redundant und für einen Zusatz.

[47] Vgl. F. Hossfeld & E. Zenger, *Psalmen 51–100*, 594. Die deuteronomistische Ableitung ist nicht unbestritten: H. U. Steymans, „Thron" (2002).

War diese Vorlage mit dem Qumran-Fragment identisch? Was dort steht, taucht tatsächlich beim Psalmisten wie bei Natan wieder auf. Was der Psalm über das Fragment hinaus aufweist, fehlt in der Regel in 2 Sam 7; was 2 Sam 7 über den Psalm hinaus an Aussagen bietet, fehlt auch in 4QPs^x. Allerdings weisen diese beiden kanonischen Stücke annähernd übereinstimmende Zuwächse über den Qumrantext hinaus auf. So die Verdopplung der Feindabwehrzusicherung (Ps 89,24.23; 2 Sam 7,9.11). Das erklärt sich am ehesten dadurch, daß die in 4Q erhaltene *ursprüngliche Fassung* schon unterschiedlich erweitert war, bevor sie durch redaktionelle Überarbeitung einerseits dem Psalmen-, andrerseits dem Samueltext einverleibt wurde.

Läßt sich hinter der im Fragment sichtbaren Textgestalt ein ritueller Sitz im Leben voraussetzen, sei es eine Krönung oder eine Jubiläumsfeier eines Königs? Oder gehörte schon diese einer schriftlichen Orakelsammlung für den König an, einer Art Florilegium, wie es z.B. für Assurbanipal[48] nachzuweisen ist und vielleicht zu Feiern der Inthronisation zusammengestellt (aber nicht rezitiert, sondern im Heiligtum deponiert?) wurde?[49] Die Verbindung von zwei Orakeln sowohl im Psalm wie im Samuelkapitel legt eher die letzte Lösung nahe. Eine direkte Verwendung in kultischen Zeremonien bleibt für die zwei Vorlagen möglich, wenn nicht sogar wahrscheinlich; sie läge dann aber eine überlieferungsgeschichtliche Stufe weiter zurück.

Ritueller Bezug legt sich besonders für das in beiden mittleren Spalten mit eigener Einführung angeschlossene zweite Orakel über den Bestand von Dynastie und Thron nahe. Wie angedeutet, findet es sich in einer kürzeren Form, ohne den Blick auf im Voraus eingeräumte mildernde Umstände bei möglichen Vergehen, bereits Ps 89 an früherer Stelle (V.4f.) als eigene Gottesrede, vom Psalmisten einleitend durch den Bundesgedanken erläutert: „Geschlossen habe ich den Bund für meinen Erwählten,/ geschworen dem David, meinem Knecht:"

---

[48] H. U. Steymans, „Bund" (1998) 136ff. Zu Liedern des Königs: A. Falkenstein & W. v. Soden, *Sumerische und akkadische Hymnen und Gebete* (Zurich & Stuttgart: Atemis, 1953) 292–94, „Wahrscheinlich … eine Zusammenstellung von aus verschiedenen Anlässen gesprochenen Gebeten, nach denen der König die Stimme seines Gottes zu hören glaubte," S.393. W. W. Hallo (Hg.), *The Context of Scripture* (= CoS 1997) 1,475f.

[49] „Für fast jeden Vers" des Psalm lassen sich neuassyrische Analogien anführen, nicht jedoch für Themen wie Salbung und bedingte Beistandszusage, die eher auf syrisches Erbe weisen; H. U. Steymans, „Thron" (2002).

Auf immer werde ich deinen Samen ausrüsten,
werde bauen von Geschlecht zu Geschlecht deinen Thron.[50]

In einer etwas anderen Formulierung findet sich dieser Gottesschwur zusammen mit der bedingten Beistandsversicherung bzw. Eingeschränkten Sanktionsandrohung auch Ps 132,11f.

### DIE ARAMÄISCHE ENTSPRECHUNG ZU PSALM 20.

Für den langen überlieferungsgeschichtlichen Weg, den manche Königspsalmen von ihrer Erstformulierung bis zur masoretischen Endfassung gefunden haben, ist ebenso der Vergleich der Fürbitte für den König nach Ps 20 mit dem in demotischer Schrift erhaltenen aramäischen Gebet des Papyros Amherst 63 Kol. XI (so die Zählung von Steiner) oder Kol.XII 11–19 (nach herkömmlicher Zählung)

---

[50] Die Bestandssicherung wird im Psalm wie in V. 29.35f. mit einem eigenen Bund begründet, den Jahwä mit dem Herrscher geschlossen hat, während der deuteronomistische Samuelverfasser (mit dem Chronisten) zwar auf den im Psalm wie auch sonst häufig mit בְּרִית verbundenen חֶסֶד verweist (V. 15), aber von einem mit dem Volksbund konkurrierenden Sonderbund Gottes mit dem König nichts weiß oder nichts wissen will (vermutlich ein Redaktor fügt ihn in 2 Sam 23,5 ein). Auch die übrigen Königspsalmen (außer 132,12?) meiden einen Hinweis auf einen Bund mit dem König. Es ist auch schwer einzusehen, wie ein solcher sich mit dessen Gottessohnschaft verträgt (vgl. Ps 89.27; 2,7), mit seinem eigenen Sohn schließt man gewöhnlich keinen besonderen Bund. Wegen seiner wichtigen politischen Implikation setzt der altorientalischem Politikverständnis entsprungene Bundesbegriff ein Abstandsgefühl voraus. Die Vorstellung eines *paritätischen* Bundes zweier politischer Parteien ist m.E. im Alten Orient nirgends sicher nachzuweisen. Die Rede vom Bund eines Gottes mit dem Herrscher scheint in neuassyrischer Zeit aufgekommen zu sein. So ist sie in Juda kaum erst der nachexilischen Erwartung eines Heilskönigs entsprungen, sondern scheint im letzten vorexilischen Jahrhundert in Jerusalem zum Bestandteil der Königsideologie geworden zu sein. War dann der Bundesschluß bei jedem neuen Herrscher als symbolischer Ritus notwendig gewesen? Das eigenartige Nebeneinander von zwei Bünden Gottes, einem mit Israel, der andere — mit abweichendem Inhalt — mit dem König, hatte vor einem halben Jahrhundert noch Diskussion hervorgerufen, vor allem ausgelöst durch L. Rost, „Davidsbund und Sinaibund," *TLZ* 72 (1947) 129–34; aufgenommen z.B. bei M. Sekine, „Davidsbund und Sinaibund bei Jeremia," *VT* 9 (1959) 47–57; A. H. J. Gunneweg, „Sinaibund und Davidbund," *VT* 10 (1960) 335–41 u.a. Gegenwärtig jedoch findet der Davidsbund so wenig Interesse, daß er im Artikel „Bund" der neu aufgelegten *RGG* 1 (1998) 1861–65 nicht einmal erwähnt wird; vgl. schon die kurze, beiläufige Bemerkung im entsprechenden Artikel der *TRE* 7 (1981) 339, 44–47. Anders G. E. Mendenhall & G.A.Herion, „Covenant", *ABD* 1 (1992) 1.1188–90.

aufschlußreich.[51]

Die enge Verwandtschaft mit dem biblischen Text ist erst seit zwei Jahrzehnten bekannt und seither kontrovers diskutiert worden: die ungewöhnliche Verwendung demotischer Schrift für einen aramäischen Text macht begreiflich, warum an vielen Stellen bis heute noch keine sichere Übersetzung möglich ist. Die Übersicht, die ich beifüge, spiegelt die divergenten Ergebnisse bisheriger Forschung, indem sie links die Übersetzung des Papyros durch R. C. Steiner von 1997,[52] in der Mitte diejenige von J. W. Wesselius 1991[53] abdruckt und rechts die Übersetzung des Psalms in Anlehnung an die Synopse von M.Rösel im Jahr 2000.[54] Steiner hat dankenswerterweise den gesamten Papyros übersetzt. Wohl zu Recht setzt er voraus, daß es sich — abgesehen von einer Assurbanipal-Sage am Ende — um eine nachträglich in einen polytheistischen Kontext einbezogene liturgische Komposition handelt, ob aber zu einer einzigen Begehung, bleibt fraglich.[55]

Die demotische Handschrift stammt wohl aus dem 4.Jh.v.Chr. und erweckt nicht den Eindruck eines Originaldokuments.[56] Die Übereinstimmung beider Texte geht so weit — siehe die in der Übersicht unterstrichenen Wörter —, daß sie nicht unabhängig voneinander entstanden sein können. Drei Erklärungen sind vertreten worden: (1) Der Psalm hangt vom Text des Papyros ab und ist entsprechend spät anzusetzen; (2) dieser ist umgekehrt von jenem abhängig, der Psalm also vermutlich älter als das 4.Jahrhundert; (3) beide Fassungen gehen auf eine verlorene ältere Vorlage zurück.[57]

Der Kontext des Liedes im Papyros selbst weist auf eine religiöse

---

[51] S. P. Vleeming & J. W. Wesselius, „An Aramaic Hymn," (1982) 501–509; Dies., *Studies in Papyrus Amherst 63* (1990); F. Nims & R. C. Steiner, „A Paganized Version," (1983) 261–74. I. Kottsieper, „Anmerkungen" (1988, 217–44; mit einer von den zwei in der Synopse abgedruckten Beispielen oft abweichenden Textabtrennung und Übersetzung).

[52] In: W. H. Hallo (Hg.), *The Context of Scripture* (CoS) 1 (1997) 309–327.

[53] *TUAT* 2,932f.

[54] M. Rösel, „Israels Psalmen in Ägypten? " (2000) 81–99.

[55] R. C. Steiner sieht darin das Ritual eines Neujahrsfestes nicht ohne eine dazu gehörige — für westliche Gelehrte offenbar schwer entbehrliche — Heilige Hochzeit. Vgl. Ders., „The Aramaic Text" (1991).

[56] *TUAT* 2,390. I. Kottsieper, „Papyrus Amherst 63," in: O. Loretz, *Die Königspsalmen* (1988) 55–75.

[57] F. Hossfeld & E. Zenger, *Psalmen 1–50* (NEBAT, 1993) 136.

Gemeinschaft, die aus Syrien oder Palästina in Ägypten eingewandert war. Stammt der Papyros aus der späten Perserzeit, dann aus einer Epoche, in der Ägypten sich gegen die Achaimeniden erhoben, Jahrzehnte lang selbständig gemacht und dadurch gegen Vorderasien abgegrenzt hatte. Das war gewiß keine Zeit engeren kulturellen und religiösen Kontakts mit Gesängen aus Juda-Jerusalem. Der ungewöhnliche Gebrauch der demotischen Schrift durch eine aramäisch sprechenden Gemeinschaft setzt voraus, daß diese schon geraume Zeit im Niltal sich angesiedelt und akkulturiert hatte. Die Entlehnung — welche Seite auch immer die empfangende war — geschah wahrscheinlich früher als im 4.Jahrhundert, sei es im 5.Jahrhundert, wofür gewisse Anklänge der aramäischen Fassung an die Religion der Judäer in Elefantine sprechen könnten, sei es bereits in der Zeit vor dem Untergang Judas 587/6 oder gar Nordisraels 722 v.Chr.[58]

Ein Wort vorweg zu den Gottesnamen, wo die Frage nach einer gegenseitigen Bezugnahme besonders interessant erscheint. Verwirrung herrscht gleich beim ersten Beispiel, wo auf ein ʾAlef ein Silbenzeichen folgt, das normalerweise *HR* bedeutet, dem an einigen Stellen, wo es im Lied erneut benutzt wird, ein *Waw* zu folgen scheint. Als Wiedergabe entscheidet sich Steiner (s. die CoS-Spalte) für den ägyptischen Gott Horus, obwohl dieser sonst nie mit anlautendem ʾAlef geschrieben wird. Kottsieper plädiert für die Wiedergabe El,[59] obwohl dieser Name an weiteren Stellen im Papyros anders (und eindeutiger) geschrieben wird. Der Ägyptologe Zauzich denkt dagegen an den hebräischen Gottesnamen Jah(u/o), indem er das ʾAlef (wie im Ägyptischen möglich) als anlautendes *Jod* liest und das Silbenzeichen als Schreibung für konsonantisches *He*;[60] dem haben sich wohl mit Recht Wesselius (s. TUAT-Spalte) und Rösel angeschlossen. Wahrscheinlich dürfte also sein, daß hier (wie vorher schon in Elefantine) der aus dem Alten Testament bekannte Name benutzt worden war. Dafür spricht ebenso das glücklicherweise eindeutige Adonaj als Wechselglied im Parallelismus, das auch sonst im Papyros zu belegen ist; als hebräische Bezeichnung liefert es ein Indiz dafür, daß der Grundtext hebräisch abgefaßt gewesen war. Offenbar gleichbedeutend kann das

---

[58] *TUAT* 2,930.

[59] I. Kottsieper, „Anmerkungen II–IV" (1997) 385–434, bes. 399–406; vgl. aber M. Rösel, „Israels Psalmen" (2000) 91f.

[60] Z. Zauzich, „Der Gott des demotisch-aramäischen Papyrus Amherst 63," *GM* 85 (1985) 89f.

aramäische Äquivalent Mar in Z.15.17 (und anderswo im Papyros) gebraucht werden, das in den ersten und letzten Kolumnen des Lieds im Vordergrund steht, während Adonaj wie der durch ʾ*ḥr* wiedergegebene Ausdruck nur in den Kolumnen XII.XIII (bzw.XI.XII) auftaucht, wo die Nähe zur alttestamentlichen Psalmensprache besonders sichtbar wird. Mit Adonaj wird nicht strikte Ausschließlichkeit, aber doch Unvergleichlichkeit im Götterhimmel verbunden, wie das an den in Frage stehenden Text angeschlossene nächste Lied in den Zeilen XII (XIII) 1-3 betont (s.die linken Spalten der Übersicht).

Ps 20 kennt den wahlweisen Austausch des Gottesnamens durch eine Herrentitulatur noch nicht, während er dem Papyros vertraut zu sein scheint, insofern scheint dessen Sprachgebrauch „jüdischer". Allerdings ist der Wechsel eines Gottesnamens außerisraelitisch mit der aramäischen „Herren"-bezeichnung Mar seit dem 9. Jahrh.v.Chr. und der phönikischen Entsprechung Adon schon seit dem 8.Jahrh. v.Chr. belegt.[61] Doch die erweiterte Form Adonaj wird sonst nur hebräisch verwendet. Sie taucht in wahlweisem Wechsel mit JHWH fast nur im Psalter auf (30,9; 38,16 usw.), das läßt für den Papyros auf eine Psalmvariante als Vorlage schließen.

In der Synopse folgt auf die Wiedergabe der Parallele zu Ps 20 noch der Anfang des nächsten Lieds, weil da die im vorangehenden Text fehlende Opferthematik (vgl. Ps 20,4) auftaucht.

## PAPYROS AMHERST 63

| CoS I 318 | TUAT II, 932f. | Psalm 20 |
|---|---|---|
| A Psalm from Bethel (XI.11-19) | Kol.XII | 1. Dem Musikmeister(?). Ein Psalm Dawids |
| May Horus <u>answer</u> us in <u>troubles</u>; may <u>Adonai</u> answer us in troubles. | 11. Möge <u>Yaho</u> uns in unseren <u>Bedrängnissen antworten,</u> <br> 12. möge Adonay uns in unseren Bedrängnissen antworten. | 2. <u>JHWH antworte</u> dir am Tag der <u>Bedrängnis</u>, der Name des Gottes Jakobs schütze dich! |
| O crescent (lit.bow) / | Er schmückt den Mond im | |

---

[61] M. Rösel, *Adonaj* (2000) 38f.44–49.

| | | |
|---|---|---|
| bowman in heaven, Sahar/ Shine forth; | Himmel | |
| send your emissary from the temple of Arash, and from Zephon may Horus help us. | 13. und sendet vom ganzen Resch und vom Zaphon, was auf Erde gesehen wird. | 3. Er sende deine Hilfe vom Heiligtum und stärke dich aus Zion. 4. Er gedenke deines ganzen Speisopfers, und dein Brandopfer lasse er fett werden. SELA. |
| May Horus grant us what is in our hearts; may Mar grant us what is in our hearts. All (our) plans may Horus fulfill. | 14. Möge Yaho uns unterstützen, möge Yaho uns gemäß unserem Herzen geben | 5. Er gebe dir, was dein Herz (begehrt), und alle deine Pläne erfülle er. |
| | 15. Möge der Herr uns gemäß unserem Herzen geben | 6. Wir wollen jubeln über deine Heilshilfe. Und im Namen unsres Gottes erheben wir das Banner. |
| May Horus fulfill - may Adonai not fall short in satisfying - every request of our hearts. | Möge Yaho alle Wünsche erfüllen, möge Yaho erfüllen möge Adonay nicht unerfüllt lassen, (16.) irgendeinen Wunsch den wir haben. | JHWH erfülle alle deine Wünsche. |
| | | 7. Nun habe ich erkannt, daß JHWH seinem Gesalbten geholfen hat. Er wird ihm antworten von seinem heiligen Himmel, durch die Kräfte der Heilshilfe seiner rechten Hand. |
| Some with the bow, some with the spear; but (lit., behold) as for us - Mar is god; Horus-Yaho, our bull, is with us. | Manche leben vom Bogen, manche leben vom Speer, aber (17.) wir - der Herr, unser Gott Yaho, wird uns erhalten. | 8. Jene (verlassen sich) auf Wagen und jene auf Rosse; wir aber denken an den Namen (JHWH) unsres Gottes. 9. Sie sind gestürzt und gefallen, wir aber stehen und |

| | | halten stand. |
|---|---|---|
| May the lord of Bethel <u>answer</u> us on the morrow. May Baal of Heaven Mar grant blessing / bless you; to your pious ones, your blessings | Morgen werden (auch) sie mit uns (18.) Bethel <u>antworten</u>. Möge Baal Schamayn, mein Herr, Deine Segen zugunsten deiner Getreuen sprechen. Ende. | 10. Hilf, JHWH! 'dem König! Er wird uns <u>antworten</u> am Tage unseres Rufens. |

| **Col. XII** | **Kol. XIII (2.Psalm)** | |
|---|---|---|
| Lambs of Adonai (XII, 1-3) | | |
| (H)ear me, my (go)[d], my king. Choice (lamb)s, sh(ee)p, | 1. Höre auf mich [...] schön [...] | |
| we sacrifice to you (alone) among the gods; our banquet is for you (alone) out of all the supreme beings /from the shepherds/chiefs of the people, | 2. werden wir opfern, zu Dir unter den Göttern rufen wir, zu Dir (rufen wir) mitten unter den Mächtigen des Volkes, | |
| Adonai, for you (alone) out of all the supreme beings /from the shepherds/chiefs of the (peo)ple. | 3. Adonay, zu Dir (rufen wir) mitten unter den Mächtigen des Volkes. | |
| | 4. Adonay, das Volk möge Dich loben. Wir werden die Ordnung Deines Jahres empfangen: | |
| | 5. Gib auserlesene Bewässerung und Frühregen! | |

Einige Bemerkungen zum Vergleich der einzelnen Abschnitte:[62]

---

[62] Vgl. O. Loretz, *Königspsalmen* (1988) 20–31.

a) Die erste Doppelzeile mit der generellen Anrufung um Gotteshilfe wird aramäisch als tautologischer, hebräisch als synonymer Parallelismus inhaltlich gleichlaufend formuliert; älter als das Wechselglied Adonaj im ersten Fall wird der „Gott Jakobs" im zweiten sein, wobei שֵׁם womöglich sekundär hinzugefügt wurde.[63]

b) Nur im Papyros folgt mit Z.12b ein möglicherweise mythologischer Hinweis, bei dem das zweite Kolon fehlt.[64]

c) Beide Fassungen verweisen Z.13//V.3 im synonymen Parallelismus auf die irdische Verankerung göttlicher Hilfe (hebr. עזר wie 89,20); aramäisch werden zwei Heiligtümer genannt, zuerst ein Berggipfel (reš), vielleicht der Karmel (1Kön 8,42),[65] und der Ṣapon, wie einst der heilige Nord-Berg der Ugariter geheißen hatte, was wohl später auch auf andre Heiligtümer übertragen wurde. Der Psalm führt nur Zion als „das Heiligtum" an, aber auch dieser Berg konnte Ṣapon heißen (Ps 48,3).[66]

d) Nur das hebräische Lied fügt dem eine Bitte um Opferannahme an V. 4, setzt also Anwesenheit und Kulthandlung des Angesprochenen am Tempel voraus.

e) Die Doppelzeile, die um Erfüllung der Planungen des Herzens ersucht, lautet Z.14//V.5 inhaltlich gleich. Während aber der Aramäer sie ähnlich in Z.15 wiederholt, wendet sich der Hebräer in V.6 zu einer kollektiven Selbst-

---

[63] S. Einheitsübersetzung. „Gott Jakobs" als für sich stehender Titel taucht fast nur in den Psalmen auf; H. J. Zobel, Art. „Jaʿaqob," *ThWAT* 3,752–77 (768f.). Im Papyros wird er auch bei einer Parallele zu Ps 75,10 durch Adonaj ersetzt; M. Rösel, „Psalmen" (2000) 94.

[64] Statt der für Z.12b in CoS und TUAT gebotenen Wiedergaben (s.die Synopse) ist wahrscheinlich zu übersetzen: „Er ist es, der am/im Himmel den Glanz bereitet" (*hû yaqaššeṭ bašamajn zahrā*), so nach I. Kottsieper, „Anmerkungen" (1988) 222f.227, wegen des voranstehenden *hû* jedoch kaum als Jussiv (so K.).

[65] Ra/esch, was hebräisch רוֹשׁ entspricht, könnte in der Vorgeschichte der Parallelisierung mit apon den zum nordsyrischen Dschebel el ʾaqra parallelen Namni/Nanni bedeutet haben. K. Koch, „Ṣapôn" (1993) 199–202. Zu Lokalisierungsvorschlägen: *TUAT* 2,931⁷ᵃ; R. C. Steiner, in: W. W. Hallo (Hg.), CoS 1,310 (ziemlich spekulativ); M. Rösel, „Israels Psalmen" (2000) 88.

[66] Baʿal Ṣapôn ist auch der Name einer Höhe beim ägyptischen Pelusium, die wohl als „Erstreckung" des syrischen Berges verehrt wurde (vgl. יַרְכְּתֵי Ps 48,3). K. Koch, „Ṣapôn" (1993) 171–223.

verpflichtung, nämlich zu jubeln und ein Banner (im Umkreis des Heiligtums? Vgl Num 1,52; 2,2) hochzuhalten. Danach wird nochmals um Wunscherfüllung gefleht, aramäisch Z.15b.16 zum dritten Mal, hebräisch wird die Wiederaufnahme durch V.6b auf ein einziges Kolon beschränkt.

f) Eigene Wege beschreitet der Psalm in V.7. Eine prosaisch wirkenden Zeile gibt die Kunde eines anonymen Ich[67] wieder, daß ihm Gott die Gewißheit der Erhörung des Gesalbten zuteil hat werden lassen; ein angeschlossener synonymer Parallelismus preist die himmlische Allmacht. Erst jetzt erfährt der Leser, daß die bisherige Fürbitte für das Du einer königlichen Figur gegolten hat.

g) Ausgerechnet die nach unsrer Ansicht für die JHWH-Religion besonders bezeichnende Aussage, daß dieser Gott sich ohne militärische Rüstung als stärker erweist als all irdischen Armeen, so V.8, findet den vollen Widerhall im Papyros Z.16b.17, doch so, daß er noch auf eine archaische Ausrüstung mit Bogen und Speer, der Psalm hingegen auf eine moderne mit Streitwagen und Rossen hinweist. Die Aussage widerspricht dem Selbstruhm altorientalischer Potentaten; stattdessen wird der Furcht vor fremden Bedrängern das Vertrauen in eine jederzeit mögliche direkte Gottesintervention entgegengesetzt.

h) Beide Fassungen nehmen am Ende mit Z.17f.// V.10 die Bitte des Anfangs um göttliche Antwort (הניו) wieder auf, der Papyros anscheinend mit der Erwartung der Hilfe Gottes „am Morgen,"[68] was der Psalm verallgemeinert: „am Tag unsres Anrufens," während der Papyros sie allein auf den König[69] bezieht. Der Aramäer erwartet sie von Betel statt Jaho und hofft statt auf dessen Heilshilfe auf den Segen eines Baal Schamajn. Schon Jer 48,13 galt Betel als ein Gott, auf den „das Haus Israel" sein Vertrauen setzte,

---

[67] K. Seybold, *Psalmen* (1996) vermutet als Sprecher den König.

[68] B. Janowski, *Rettungsgewißheit und Epiphanie des Heils* (1989).

[69] הַמֶּלֶךְ ist in V.10 gegen MT zu V.a zu ziehen, dann eher als Akkusativ (Zenger) und nicht als Vokativ (Seybold). Die frühmittelalterlichen Masoreten „entmessianisieren" den Schluß und beziehen gegen jedes Metrum den König auf Gott. Anders O. Loretz, *Königspsalmen* (1988) 28–31.

was sicher keinen zweiten Gott neben YHWH, sondern dessen nordiraelitische Anrufung und Verehrung meinte. Im 5.Jahrhundert v.Chr. nennen die Judäer in Elefantine/Syene neben Jaho einen (Herem-)Betel und einen „Namen (אֱשֶׁם) Betels" als ihren Gott; der letzte Name taucht auch im Papyros Amherst auf.[70]

Abgesehen von unserm Text erscheinen Betel und Mar im Papyros mehrfach nebeneinander in ähnlicher Funktion.[71] Wenn der antwortende Gott sowohl als Jaho wie als Betel angerufen werden kann, setzt das doch wohl eine Herkunft der Überlieferungsträger aus Palästina voraus.[72] Auch Baal Schamajn wird mehrfach an andern Stellen im Papyros erwähnt, wenngleich nicht im Zusammenhang mit Betel. Er bezeichnet einen seit Beginn des 1.Jahrt. v. Chr. in phönikischen und aramäischen Texten auftauchenden und bald zur Spitze des Pantheons aufrückenden „Himmelsmeister", dessen Hochschätzung mit der aus Mesopotamien kommenden Astralisierung der Religionen zusammenhängen dürfte.[73] Er war wahrscheinlich mit dem in neuassyrischer Zeit in Jerusalem zusammen mit dem „Heer des Himmels" verehrten Baal identisch, den bzw. dessen Parhedra die Josianische Reform nicht nur in Jerusalem, sondern gerade auch in Betel (2 Kön 23,15) bekämpft hat (mit nur zeitweiligem Erfolg?).[74] Der Psalm meidet den Namen, schreibt aber seinem Gott, der nach V.7 vom Himmel her seine Machttaten vollbringt, eine ähnliche Funktion zu wie andere dem Baal Schamajn.

*Ergebnis:* Die Vergleichung ergibt keine eindeutige Antwort auf die Frage, was als Original und was als Nachahmung zu bestimmen ist. Der Papyros weist mehr stilvolle Parallelismen auf als der Psalm, was ursprünglicher wirkt. Er nennt zwei Heiligtümer des Gottes, die am ehesten nach Nordisrael oder Phönikien weisen, darunter einen Ṣapôn,

---

[70] Kol. XV(XIV) 13-17; CoS I 321. W. Röllig, Art. „Bethel," *DDD* (1995) 331–34. E. R. Dalglish, Art. „Bethel," *ABD* 1 (1992) 706–710.

[71] CoS I 314.315.316.321.

[72] Juda und Samaria werden wohl Kol. XVII(XVI) 1-6 genannt; CoS I 321.

[73] H. Niehr, „Der höchste Gott," *BZAW* 190 (1990); dazu die z.T. berechtigte Kritik von K. Engelken, „BAʿAL ŠAMEM," *ZAW* 108 (1996) 233–48.391–407. K. Koch, „Ṣapon" (1994) 159–74.

[74] K. Koch, „Gefüge und Herkunft des Berichts über die Kultreformen des Königs Josia," in: J. Hausmann & H. J. Zobel (Hg.), *Alttestamentlicher Glaube und Biblische Theologie. FS H. D. Preuß* (1992) 80–92.

während der Psalm nur den judäischen Zion anführt, der allerdings auch als Ṣapôn gerühmt werden konnte. Vor allem aber weist der Papyros auf eine altertümlichere Bewaffnung und enthält wohl eine mythologische Reminiszenz, die im Psalm fehlt (Z.16 vs. V.8; Z.12b). Was der Psalm über den Papyros hinaus beschreibt (V.4.7.8), läßt sich als Nachtrag ausklammern, ohne daß das Aussagegefälle Brüche zeigen würde;[75] der Nachtrag ist wohl vor der Aufnahme des Gebets in den Davidspsalter erfolgt, da er zu diesem keinen eigenen Bezug aufweist.[76]

Andererseits weist auch der Papyros jüngere Züge auf. Er kennt und gebraucht schon eine Wahlmöglichkeit zwischen dem Gottesnamen und den Herrenprädikaten Adonaj und Mar; es ist schwer denkbar, daß der Psalmist diese ab der nachexilischen Zeit beliebt werdende Redeweise gegen seine Vorlage getilgt hätte, das von ihm als Wechselglied benutzte „Gott Jakobs" dürfte älter sein. Der hebräische Titel Adonaj läßt zwar vermuten, daß die aramäische Fassung auf eine hebräische zurückgreift; diese hat dann aber schon Adonaj geboten, hatte also den mit Ps 20 gemeinsamen Grundtext schon verändert. Demnach beruhen Papyros und Psalm auf *unterschiedlichen Weiterentwicklungen des gleichen hebräischen Klagelieds.*

Der wichtigste Unterschied besteht darin, daß der aramäische Text mit einem durchgängigen Wir-Subjekt ein *Volks-* (oder *Gemeinde-*) *Klagelied* vorträgt, während der Psalm ein *Königslied* darbietet, bei dem von Anfang bis Ende das Du eines anscheinend anwesend gedachten Gesalbten im Vordergrund steht, während das „Wir" seiner Gefolgschaft nur im zweiten Teil auftaucht, in V.7 durch die Aussage eines anonymen Ich über die eingetretene Erhörung unterbrochen. Stand am Anfang ein Königslied, das für eine nach Ägypten abgewanderten Gruppe keinen Bezug mehr hatte, oder ein Gemeindegesang, den dann der Psalmist „umfunktioniert" hätte?[77] Zu bedenken bleibt weiter, daß der Papyros eine generelle Not beklagt, der Psalm dagegen nach einer anscheinend konkreten Heilshilfe (יֵשַׁע) Ausschau

---

[75] I. Kottsieper, „Anmerkungen" (1988) 242; zu V.7 vgl. F. Hossfeld & E. Zenger, *Psalmen 1–50* (NEBAT, 1993) 135f.

[76] Dagegen schließt Ps 21 deutlich an den Grundtext von Ps 20 an mit dem Preis einer dem König gewährten Heilshilfe und Wunscherfüllung V.2f.

[77] So I. Kottsieper, „Anmerkungen" (1998) 243. Der Papyros weist allerdings an andrer Stelle vielleicht ein Orakel an einen König auf, in Kol VI 12–18 nach der Übersetzung in CoS 1,313.

hält und sie (teilweise) schon verwirklicht sieht, weshalb Zenger das
betreffende Nomen mit „Sieg" übersetzt (V.6.10, vgl. V.7); zu diesem
Zweck soll eine Opferhandlung wohlgefällig angenommen werden
(V.4), was der Papyros unerwähnt läßt.[78] Der Hinweis auf die
Planungen des Herzens, die durch Gottes Hilfe zum Erfolg gelangen
sollen, lassen eher an die Maßnahmen eines Regenten als die Wün-
sche von Privaten denken.[79] Auch die Feststellung, daß dem Gegner
seine militärische Aufrüstung nichts hilft, paßt zu einer hochpoli-
tischen und nicht zu einer privaten Auseinandersetzung. So neigt sich
doch wohl die Waagschale auf eine Herkunft aus dem Herrscherkult,
ohne daß sich eine letzte Sicherheit für die Zuweisung erreichen läßt.
Immerhin ist die nachträgliche Demokratisierung von ursprünglich
auf den Herrscher gemünzten Aussagen auf solche für Land und Volk
im Alten Orient weit häufiger nachzuweisen als der umgekehrte Vorgang.[80]

Woher stammt die Papyros-Version, was war ihr Sitz im Leben und
was ihr vermutliches Alter? Das zitierte Stück stammt einer *Sammlung von liturgischen Stücken*, die sich vorher zuerst an Mar bzw.
Betel klagend gewendet hatten und jeweils von einem Chor (so nach
Steiner) mit der Beteuerung der Gewißheit der Erhörung und einem
Amen beantwortet worden waren (IX (X)1-13 mit 13-17; IX(X) 17-20
mit 20-23); worauf einige nicht mehr ganz durchsichtige Klagen fol-
gten, dann das hier in Frage stehende Stück, ehe in der Fortsetzung
Adonaj um Annahme von Opfern und Lieder angegangen und mit
einem abschließenden Hymnus gepriesen wird (XII/XIII). Der Papyros, wohl in der Nähe von Theben gefunden, ist gewiß in Ägypten
niedergeschrieben worden; wenn nicht zu einem rituellen, so doch zu
liturgischen Zwecken für eine Gemeinde ohne Tempel.

Wohl die gesamte liturgische Komposition,[81] wenigstens aber das

---

[78] In Kol. XII (XIII) folgt jedoch ein Bittegebet an Adonaj, Opfer gnädig anzunehmen.

[79] K. Seybold, *Psalmen* (HAT 1/15; Tübingen: Mohr Siebeck, 1996) 90.

[80] Zu einem hethitische Beispiel: M. Greenberg, „Hittite Royal Prayers and
Biblical Petitionary Psalms," in: E. Zenger (Hg.), *Neue Wege* (1994) 15–27,
bes.25f. O. Loretz, *Königspsalmen* (1988) 34 möchte freilich aus dem Tat-
bestand, daß in V.7 ein Ich-Sprecher von einem Messias im Singular spricht, um-
rahmt von Wir-Stimmen in V.6.8f., ableiten, daß auch in Ps 20 der Gesalbte
kollektiv zu verstehen, die Vorstellung also demokratisiert sei. Der militärische
Kontext der Fürbitte spricht gegen eine solche Annahme.

[81] Eine von der Steinerschen sehr abweichende Übersetzung der Kol. XII

zitierte Lied dürfte auf hebräische Texte (dafür sprechen das Adonaj-Prädikat, aber auch das Amen in den vorangehenden Stücken) zurückgehen und wegen des häufigen, mit Jaho und Adonaj anscheinend gleichsinnigen Betel-Namens[82] aus Nordisrael stammen. (Auf Juda, Samaria und Jerusalem wird wohl noch XVI 1-6 [CoS 1,321] verwiesen, die Erinnerung an das Mutterland ist also noch bei den Verfassern des gesamten Papyros lebendig.)

War der oben vermutete ursprüngliche Bezug des Liedes auf den König schon im Heimatland nach 722 getilgt worden oder erst in der ägyptischen Diaspora? Hatte dort, wo es keine der „Natanweissagung" vergleichbare Dynastiezusage, aber auch keine Verheißung eines künftig erscheinenden Heilskönigs gegeben zu haben scheint, die Katastrofe von 722 jedes politische und religiöse Bedürfnis nach Monarchie verlöschen lassen (vgl. Richt 9,7-15)? (Immerhin gab es auch judäische Psalmensammlungen wie den Asafpsalter, die keinen König als Garant ihrer Gottesbeziehung zu kennen scheinen.)

Aus der aramäischen Parallele lassen sich zunächst drei Folgerungen ableiten:

(1)  Der jetzt in den ersten Davidpsalter inkorporierte Text muß einst „freischweifend" außerhalb dieser Sammlung in Umlauf gewesen sein, wie lange Zeit und in welchem Sitz im Leben auch immer (vgl. die isolierte Verwendung von Ps 18 aus der gleichen Sammlung und 2 Sam 22). Eine Vorstufe des Textes konnte deshalb auch früher (kaum später) in eine andere Liedsammlung wahrscheinlich nordisraelitischer Herkunft, wie sie hinter den Kol. IX–XII (X–XIII) des Papyros insgesamt zu vermuten ist (s.u.), eingegliedert gewesen sein.

(2)  Das Lied im Papyros Amherst ist in seinem hebräischen Grundbestand einmal die Vorlage für den Psalmisten gewesen. Zwar verweisen Loretz[83] (wie Kottsieper) seine Entle-

---

(XIII) zusammen mit dem psalmenartigen Gebet aus der vorangehenden Kolumne bringt J. W. Wesselius in *TUAT* 2,932–34 unter der Überschrift „Drei israelitische Hymnen" Der Anfang jener Kolumne erinnert an Ps 75,8-10; M. Rösel, „Israels Psalmen" (2000) 93f.

[82] Bethel wird mehrfach neben Mar in gleicher Funktion erwähnt, CoS I 314.135.316.321.

[83] O. Loretz, *Königspsalmen* (1988) 20.43.

hung in die nachexilische Epoche. Was sollte aber in dieser
Epoche einen auf den Zion ausgerichteten Judäer bewogen
haben, ausgerechnet das Gebet einer in Ägypten ansässigen
häretischen Sondergruppe sich anzueignen? Eher ist Psalm
20 zumindest in den zum Papyros parallelen Sätzen vorexilisch anzusetzen, da die Verschiedenheit im Anliegen wie
im Gebrauch der Gottesnamen und deren Verortung eine
längere Sondergeschichte wohl beider Texte voraussetzt.
Aber auch die Erweiterungen mit Opfer- und Messiashin-
weis (v.4f.7) lassen sich wohl eher aus den Verhältnissen der
Königszeit als denender Spätzeit ableiten.

(3) Der Maschiach meinte einst hier (V.7) wie in ähnlichen
Psalmen nicht einen künftigen Dawididen, sondern den
gegenwärtig auf dem Zion regierenden Herrscher.

War also der Text des ursprünglichen Gesangs von Juda nach Betel
gelangt — oder umgekehrt? Stammt der Königspsalm aus Nordisrael
— wie vielleicht auch das königliche Hochzeitslied Ps 45 (wegen
V.13) —,womöglich aus dem Reichsheiligtum Betel (Am 7,13)? Stellt
die Ausrichtung auf den Zion in Ps 20 eine nachträgliche Şapon
Uminterpretation[84] dar? Die Herkunft aus dem Norden ist wahrscheinlicher, wenngleich nicht eindeutig beweisbar.

Handelt es sich bei Ps 20 oder seiner Vorstufe um Gesang, der mit
einem *Ritus* gekoppelt war? Die Antwort hangt von der andern Frage
ab, wer zu solcher Fürbitte für den König befähigt und berechtigt war
und die Rolle des Ich in V.7 wahrgenommen hatte, welches die
geschehene Erhörung proklamieren konnte. In Assyrien ist gehört eine
entsprechende Gattung wohl zum Krönungsritual, belegt ist sie schon
für Tukulti-Ninurta I. und noch bei Assurbanipal,[85] in abgekürzter
Form findet sie sich im Ritual des babylonischen Neujahrsfests.[86] Sie
ist aber gewiß auch in Fällen außergewöhnlicher Not, insbesondere
kriegerischer Verwicklungen, den Göttern bei Begehungen an
kultischer Stätte vorgetragen worden. In Mesopotamien waren die
Sprecher gewiß keine Laien, sondern hohe Kultfunktionäre. Gleiches
wird man für Israel anzunehmen haben, da man Ps 20 (und ähnlich die

---

[84] M. Rösel, „Israels Psalmen" (2000) 97.

[85] CoS 1,472-474; M. Arneth, *Sonne der Gerechtigkeit* (2000) 58–69, bes. 64
n. 99.

[86] *TUAT* 2,217; vgl. RlA 165a.

Fürbitte für den König in Ps 72 oder seiner Vorstufe) vermutlich in vorexilische Zeit zu datieren hat, obwohl wir über den genauen Sitz im Leben keine Nachricht besitzen.

## WAS NÜTZT DEM VOLK EIN KÖNIG?

Die verschlungenen Wege der Überlieferungsgeschichte, wie sie oben nachzuzeichnen versucht wurde, laden zu einigen generellen Erwägungen ein, die über die Suche nach ritueller Verankerung dieser Lieder hinausführen. Warum hat Israel Königspsalmen weiterhin gesungen und gebetet, obwohl die Monarchie längst untergegangen war? Warum hat sich nicht das Programm einer Hierarchie durchgesetzt, obwohl Jahrhunderte lang Hohepriester die Ethnarchen gewesen sind? Oder gar eine Demokratie (nach Ex 19,3ff.)? Trifft das Ergebnis des redaktionsgeschichtlichen Hin und Her von zeitweiser Verwerfung solcher Texte durch bestimmte Überlieferungsträger und beharrlicher Pflege und Weitergabe durch andere sowie eine gewisse allgemeine Akzeptanz am Ende der althebräischen Psalmendichtung wirklich zu, war die Monarchie keineswegs für alle Störungen im Volk die eigentliche, gottgewollte Verfassung; dennoch stand am Ende eine verbreitete eschatologische Erwartung einer wiederkehrenden davidischen Dynastie, deren Majestät alles übertreffen sollte, was es zuvor an israelitischen, ja menschlichen Herrschaftssystemen überhaupt gegeben hatte. Die folgenden Überlegungen gelten also nicht mehr dem primären Stadium der Königspsalmen, die auf einen regierenden zeitgenössischen Herrscher bezogen (und dafür rituell u.U. verwendet worden waren), sondern dem redaktionsgeschichtlichen Endstadium des Psalters.

Die Konstanz der Überlieferung läßt sich zunächst psychologisch aus den Stimmungen einer unter Fremdherrschaft leidenden ethnischen Minderheit mit einem eigenbewußten kulturellen Gedächtnis begreifen. Das Volk sehnt sich nach Befreiung und vermag sie sich im Rückblick auf eine glorifizierte Vergangenheit nicht anders vorzustellen als durch einen die Masse mitreißenden und die Feinde endgültig besiegenden Helden, deshalb die Aufnahme von Psalmen wie 2; 18; 110; 144 in die Sammlungen. Einem König Israels wird dann jene universale Macht zuteil, welche fremde Großkönige derzeit ausüben. Das aber läßt sich von menschlicher Seite nicht organisieren. Im Gefolge der religiösen Überzeugungen der Väter wird erwartet, daß Gott durch eine plötzliche Intervention die Feinde niederwirft oder den König so siegreich kämpfen lehrt, daß er Israels Feinde ein

für alle Mal zerschmettert (2,9;18; 21,9-14; 89,23f.; 144). Auffälligerweise stellen vor allem jene Palmen den militärischen Befrei-
ungsschlag in den Mittelpunkt, die anscheinend als letztes Glied
einem Kleinpsalter oder Psalmbuch angefügt worden sind wie (ohne
Überschrift) Ps 2, der freischweifende (s.o.) Ps 110 oder der wohl der
jüngsten Sammlung zugehörige Ps 144. Vom kommenden Siegesfürst
(oder seiner Dynastie) wird erhofft, daß Gott seine Herrschaft לְעֹלָם
errichtet.

Es überrascht, daß weder in diesen noch in den übrigen Königsliedern auf die innenpolitischen Wirkungen der großen Wende näher
eingegangen wird. Bedenkt man, daß die Institution des Königtums
im vorhellenistischen Syrien-Palästina gewöhnlich sowohl territorial
wie ethnisch wie sakral definiert war, verwundert, daß — anders als in
den „messianischen" Abschnitten der Profetenbücher — von der
Wiederherstellung einer Integrität von Land und Volk nicht die Rede
ist. Nichts von einer Wiedervereinigung des verstreuten Israel, in
einem Land, das von Dan bis Beerscheba reichen soll; stattdessen
vage Andeutungen einer ungefährdeten Weltherrschaft. Kaum etwas
von einer Verbesserung der sozialen, rechtlichen und ökonomischen
Verhältnisse im Innern, höchstens allgemeine Aussagen über einen
sich ausbreitenden צֶדֶק (45,7; 72,1-7; 132,9) und künftigen großen
Segen (144,12ff.). Wichtiger die Residenz auf dem Zion, der zur
Quelle aller Umwandlungen im Land wird (2; 110; 18,7; 20,3).

In den andern, je einem Kleinpsalter wohl früher ein- oder angeg-
liederten Königsliedern fällt eine eigentümliche *Verschränkung im
Geschick des Heilskönigs und dem seines Volkes* auf, die in dieser Art
m.E. im Alten Orient ohne Parallele bleibt. Schon dem regierenden
Monarchen im alten Einzellied, dann aber dem im Zusammenhang
einer Sammlung in Zukunft erwarteten Heilskönig wird die Ehren-
bezeichnung eines auserwählten עֶבֶד, eines „Knechtes" (eigentlich:
eines bevollmächtigten Dieners) JHWHs zuteil (18,1; 89,4.20.40;
132,10; 144,10, auch 36,1; 78,70f.), als solcher ist er über das Volk
erhöht (89,20). Doch „Knechte" des Gottes sind ebenso die Glieder
der Kultgemeinde (89,51, weiter 79,2.20; 90,13.16 u.ö.), ja jeder
Psalmbeter (86,2.4.16; 116,16; 119,17 usw.). Die besondere Funktion
des Königs kommt also partiell auch dem Volk zu, aus dem und für
das er erhöht ist, dessen Horn und Schild (89,18.20; vgl. 84,10) und
damit Zentrum der Selbstbehauptung er ist.

Was für den König von Gott erbeten oder als erfahren vorausgesetzt
wird, fassen die Psalmisten mit dem Lexem יֵשַׁע zusammen

(18,3.51;20,6.7bis.10; 21,2.6); das mag sich im Einzelfall einst auf den militärischen Sieg beziehen, meint aber im Verbund einer Sammlung wohl jede Art spontaner göttlicher Intervention, womöglich als Theofanie (Ps 18;144), die als wunderhafte „Heilshilfe" erfahren wird. Sie betrifft nicht den König allein. Siegt er über Feinde, erfährt das arme Volk, daß Gott sie ihm zugewandt hat (18,28), jubelt über die יְשׁוּע, die der Regent erfahren hat (20,6). Gibt Gott Königen wie seinem Knecht Dawid תְּשׁוּעָה, breitet sich eine wunderbare Fruchtbarkeit im Land aus (144,10-15; vgl. 28,8). Um des Knechtes Dawid willen werden die Priester mit צֶדֶק und יֵשַׁע bekleidet, was sie dann gewiß segnend weitergeben (132,9f.16). Die Wurzel ישׁע ist zwar für viele Psalmbeter Inbegriff der Heilshilfe, die er von JHWH erwartet (13,6; 35,9 usw.),[87] doch nach den Königsliedern kommt dabei dem Herrscher eine unabdingbare Mittlerrolle zu, nicht zuletzt für die Armen (72,4.13; 89,27).

Der König dieser Lieder hat zwar als Sohn Jahwäs und als Gesalbter eine einzigartige Nähe zum göttlichen Wesen, die von keinem andern Menschen erreicht wird (vgl. 45,7). Dennoch wird er nicht als ein für sich stehendes Individuum begriffen, sondern als die repräsentative wie effektive „Auskörperung" der *Corporate Personality* Israel. Als sichtbares und wirksames Zeichen kollektiver Identität transzendiert er den Gegensatz von Herr und Knecht, von Herrscher und Untertan.

> There are plenty of cases in which the speaker ranges himself, as an individual person, alongside his "brethren" in "the great assembly" ... But on some occassions he represents all the others and speaks on their behalf and is in so far one with them. In most of these cases this person is the king.[88]

Die Überzeugung einer solchen Bruderschaft hat wiederholt in der Sprachgeschichte Israels zur Demokratisierung von Elementen der Königsideologie geführt. Die eben erwähnte Stellung des Knechtes JHWHs wird zuerst dem König, dann jedem Kultgenossen beigelegt. Das wichtige Prädikat einzigartiger göttlicher Erwählung (בחר) wird wahrscheinlich einst nur jenem, später dem Volksganzen zugesprochen.[89] Ps 89,28 schreibt dem König den Rang des Erstgeborenen Jahwäs wie des „Allerhöchsten" (עֶלְיוֹן) über die Könige der Erde zu,

---

[87] J. F. Sawyer, Art. „ישׁע," *ThWAT* 3, 1035ff., bes. 1055–58.

[88] S. Mowinckel, *Psalms* (1962) I 76; O. Loretz, *Königspsalmen* (1988) 7.

[89] K. Koch, „Zur Geschichte der Erwählungsvorstellung in Israel," *ZAW* 67 (1955) 205–26.

das erste wird Exod 4,22, das zweite (später) Dtn 26,19; 28,1 von Israel gerühmt.

Dennoch führt der eingefahrene Begriff Demokratisierung (besser wäre: Demotisierung) zu dem Mißverständnis, daß damit eine monarchische Verfassung für Israel als obsolet erklärt würde. So sehr solche Ausweitungen religiöser Prädikate von sozialen und politischen Wandlungen begleitet gewesen sein mögen, so sprechen doch analoge „Demokratisierungen" in der Geschichte der Nachbarkulturen gegen eine grundsätzliche Ablehnung des Königtums, für das in solchem Fall oft neue Titel aufkommen und die Sonderstellung sichern.[90]

In Israel hat es zwar mehr als irgendwo sonst Gegenströmungen gegeben, die zeitweise die sakrale Mittlerposition eines Monarchen abgelehnt (Richt 9; 1 Sam 8) oder zumindest entscheidend relativiert haben. Schon das Deuteronomium verlangt eine Teilung der Gewalten in Israel,[91] der Verfassungsentwurf des Ezechielbuchs schließt sich dem auf seine Weise an. Die Priesterschrift anerkennt einzig den Hohenpriester als Gesalbten.[92] Seit Haggai und Sacharja bis zur qumranischen Literatur hoffen andere auf einer Dyarchie von königlichen und priesterlichen Gesalbten. Doch solche Tendenzen zeigen keine direkten Beziehungen zu den angeführten Demokratisierungen. Zwar setzen einige Exegeten voraus, daß selbst der Titel „Gesalbter" in den Psalmensammlungen bereits nationalisiert worden sei; ausdrücklich wird eine solche Meinung in den dafür angeführten Texten jedoch nicht, jedenfalls nicht zweifelsfrei.[93] Gewiß gibt es neben den

---

[90] Vgl. die häufigen Schübe einer Demokratisierung bei Totenkult und Jenseitserwartung in Ägypten; K. Koch, *Geschichte der ägyptischen Religion* (Stuttgart: Kohlhammer, 1993) 671 s.v.

[91] N. Lohfink, „Die Sicherung der Wirksamkeit des Gotteswortes durch das Prinzip der Schriftlichkeit der Tora und durch das Prinzip der Gewaltenteilung nach den Ämtergesetzen des Buches Deuteronomium," in: H. Wolter S. J. (Hg.), *Testimonium Veritatis, FS W. Kempf* (Frankfurter Theologische Studien 7; Frankfurt a.M.: J. Knecht 1971) 143–55.

[92] K. Koch, „Die Eigenart der priesterschriftlichen Sinaigesetzgebung," *ZTK* 55 (1958) 36–50, bes.40f.

[93] O. Loretz, *Königspsalmen* (1988) 34–39 nennt als Belege einer kollektiven Verwendung Ps 28,8; 84,1o; 89,39.52; 105,15; 132,10.17. Keine dieser Stellen scheint mir für einen Beweis ausreichend. Für die Übertragung des Gedankens der Messianität vom Davididen auf das Volksganze wird gern Jes 55, 3-5 bemüht. Vgl. jedoch die eingehende Auseinandersetzung mit Westermanns Kommentar z.St. durch K. M. Heim, „King of Psalm 89" (1998) 309: „Isaiah 55.3 clearly includes the whole people in the promised covenant renewal, and may thus justific-

Königen andere wie Priester und Profeten, die als gesalbt aufgefaßt, aber dadurch stets vom Volk der Laien geschieden werden. Läßt sich, wenn z.B. Ps 89,51f. bei der Klage über die „Schmach deiner Knechte" (plur.) durch die Umtriebe der Feinde hinzugefügt wird, daß sie auch „deinen Gesalbten" (sing.) schmähen, wirklich auf eine absichtliche Identifikation beider Größen schließen? Sie taucht auch nicht in der nachfolgenden Rezeptionsgeschichte, etwa in der Qumranliteratur[94] oder den Targumen, irgendwo sicher auf. In der Endkomposition des masoretischen (und griechischen) Psalters hat sich doch wohl die Überzeugung von der Notwendigkeit eines königlichen Zentralindividuums für das Gottesvolk durchgesetzt.

Das hat zu eigentümlichen, sich von der altorientalischen Umwelt abhebende Verklammerung von Königsherrschaft einerseits und Volks- und Kultgemeinde andrerseits geführt, die weder der Idee einer absoluten menschlichen Monarchie noch der einer unvermittelten „Demokratie" vor Gott für alle Gläubigen Raum gelassen hat, wenngleich der Psalter in seiner Endgestalt keine in sich ausgeglichene Konzeption bietet. Die einzelnen Königspsalmen, erst recht ihr Kontext in den jeweiligen Teilsammlungen, setzen unterschiedliche Akzente, gerade auch im Blick auf das Verhältnis der messianischen zur Königsherrschaft Gottes. So verwundert es nicht, daß nach der Zeitenwende die christliche Gemeinde in solchen Liedern die Mittlerrolle des Gottessohns Jesus Christus geweissagt finden, daß das Judentum aber — nicht zuletzt wohl mit Berufung auf andere Psalmenaussagen — auf dem einen göttlichen Adonaj bestand, der allein als König verehrt werden will.

---

ably called ‚democratic,‘ but this by no means excludes the Davidic dynasty (although the inclusion of a Davidic king would not necessarily make the verse messianic)."

Er verweist zudem für die Identification des Jes 55,4 genannten Zeugen mit dem königlichen Gottesknecht der berühmten Lieder auf J. A. Motyer, *The Prophecy of Isaiah* (Leicester: Inter-Varsity Press, 1999) 153,13f. Ebenso K. Koch, *Die Profeten II* (2. Aufl., UB 281; Stuttgart: Kohlhammer, 1988) 146f.

[94] Vgl. C. A. Evans, Art. „Messiahs," in: L. H. Schiffman, & J. C. VanderKam (Hrsg.), *EncDSS* (2000) 537–42. G. J. Brooke, „Kingship and Messianism in the Dead Sea Scrolls," in: J. Day (Hrsg.), *King and Messiah* (1998) 434–55, meint den kollektiven Messias in 4Q174 (*Florilegium* = 4QMidrEsch[a]) 3:18f. zu finden; nach einem ausführlichen Bezug auf 2 Sam 7 und den „Sproß Davids" als Einzelfigur werde kurz auf den Gesalbten JHWHs in Ps 2 eingegangen, der das Volksganze meine, weil nachher im ziemlich zerstörten Text von „Erwählten Israels" im Plural gesprochen werde.

## LITERATURVERZEICHNIS

Ahlström, G. W. *Psalm 89. Eine Liturgie aus dem Ritual des leidenden Königs* (Lund: CWK Gleerups, 1959).

Arneth, M. *Sonne der Gerechtigkeit. Studien zur Solarisierung der Jahwe-Religion im Lichte von Ps 72* (BZAR 1; Wiesbaden: Harrassowitz, 2000).

Assmann, J. *Ägyptische Hymnen und Gebete* (2. Aufl., OBO Sonderband; Fribourg: Universitätsverlag; Göttingen: Vandenhoeck & Ruprecht, 1999).

Auwers, J. M. „Le Psaume 132 parmi les graduels," *RB* 103/4 (1996) 546–60.

Bentzen, A. *Messias, Mose redivius, Menschensohn* (AthANT 17; Zürich: Zwingli Verlag, 1948).

Day, J. (Hrsg.). *King and Messiah in Israel and the Ancient Near East. Proceedings of the Oxford Old Testament Seminar* (JSOTSup 270; Sheffield: Sheffield Academic Press) 1998.

Dietrich, W. D. & T. Naumann. *Die Samuelbücher* (EdF 287; Darmstadt: Wissenschaftliche Buchgesellschaft, 1995).

Duhm, B. *Die Psalmen* (KHC 14; Tübingen: Mohr Siebeck, 1922).

Emmendorfer, M. *Der ferne Gott* (FAT 21; Tübingen: Mohr Siebeck, 1998).

Fabry, H. J. „Der Psalter in Qumran," in: E. Zenger (Hrsg.), *Der Psalter in Judentum und Christentum* (HBS 18; Freiburg: Herder, 1998) 137–63.

Flint, P. „The Book of Psalms in the Light of the Dead Sea Scrolls," *VT* 48 (1998) 453–72.

Gunkel, H. *Die Psalmen* (4. Aufl., HKAT II/2; Göttingen: Vandenhoeck & Ruprecht, 1926).

Gunkel, H. & J. Begrich, J. *Einleitung in die Psalmen. Die Gattungen der religiösen Lyrik Israels* (HK–Ergänzungsband zur II. Abteilung; Göttingen: Vandenhoeck & Ruprecht, 1933).

Hallo, W. W. *The Context of Scripture*. Vol. 1: *Canonical Compositions from the Biblical World* (Leiden: Brill, 1997).

Hartenstein, F. „Wolkendunkel und Himmelsfeste," in: B. Janowski & B. Ego, *Das biblische Weltbild und seine altorientalischen Kontexte* (FAT 32; Tübingen: Mohr Siebeck, 2001) (125ff.) 125–79.

Heim, K. M. „The (God) Forsaken King of Psalm 89," in: J. Day (Hrsg.), *King and Messiah in Israel and the Ancient Near East. Proceedings of the Oxford Old Testament Seminar* (JSOTSup 270; Sheffield: Sheffield Academic Press, 1998) 296–322.

Hossfeld, F.-L. & E. Zenger. *Die Psalmen II: Psalmen 51–100* (2.Aufl., HThKAT; Freiburg: Herder, 2001).

—. *Die Psalmen I. Psalmen 1–50* (NEBAT; Würzburg: Echter, 1993).

Janowski, B. *Rettungsgewißheit und Epiphanie des Heils. Das Motiv der »Hilfe Gottes am Morgen« im Alten Orient und im Alten Testament* (WMANT 59; Neukirchen-Vluyn: Neukirchener, 1989).

Koch, K. *Was ist Formgeschichte?* (Neukirchen-Vluyn: Neukirchener, 1989).

—. „Gefüge und Herkunft des Berichts über die Kultreformen des Königs Josia," in: J. Hausmann & H. J. Zobel (Hg.), *Alttestamentlicher Glaube und Biblische Theologie. FS H. D. Preuß* (Stuttgart: Kohlhammer, 1992) 80–92.

—. „Hazzi, Ṣapôn, Kasion," in: B. Janowski, K. Koch & G. Wilhelm (Hrsg.), *Religionsgeschichtliche Beziehungen zwischen Kleinasien, Nordsyrien und dem Alten Testament* (OBO 129; Fribourg & Göttingen: Vandenhoeck & Ruprecht, 1993) 171–224.

—. „Ba'al Ṣapon, Ba'al Šamem and the Critique of Israel's Prophets," in: G. J. Brooke, A. H. W. Curtis & J. F. Healey (Hrsg.), *Ugarit and the Bible. Proceedings of the International Symposium on Ugarit and the Bible, Manchester, September 1992* (UBL 11; Münster: Ugarit-Verlag, 1994) 159–74.

—. „Der Psalter und seine Redaktionsgeschichte," in: K. Seybold & E. Zenger (Hrsg.), *Neue Wege der Psalmenforschung. FS W. Beyerlin* (HBS 1; Freiburg: Herder, 1994) 243–77.

—. „Israel im Orient," in: B. Janowski & M. Köchert (Hrsg.), *Religionsgeschichte Israels. Formale und materiale Aspekte* (Veröffentlichungen der Wissenschaftlichen Gesellschaft für Theologie 15; Gütersloh: Kaiser, 1999) 242–71.

—. „Der König als Sohn Gottes in Ägypten und Israel," in: E. Otto & E. Zenger (Hrsg.), *„Mein Sohn bist du" (Ps 2,7). Studien zu den Königspsalmen* (SBS 192; Stuttgart: Katholisches Bibelwerk, 2002) 1–32.

Kottsieper, I. „Anmerkungen zu Pap. Amherst 63 Teil II–V," *UF* 29 (1997) 385–434.

—. „Anmerkungen zu Pap. Amherst 63 Teil I: 12,11-19, Eine aramäische Version zu Ps 20," *ZAW* 100 (1988) 217–44.

Kraus, H. J. *Psalmen* (BKAT XV 1,2; Neukirchen-Vluyn: Neukirchener, 1989).

Loretz, O. *Die Königspsalmen. Mit einem Beitrag von I. Kottsieper zu Papyrus Amherst* (UBL 6; Münster: Ugarit-Verlag, 1988).

Mowinckel, S. *The Psalms in Israel's Worship I–II* (New York and Nashville: Abingdon, 1962).

Nims, F. & R. C. Steiner. „A Paganized Version of Ps 20:2-6 from the Aramaic Text in Demotic Script," *JAOS* 103 (1983) 261–74.

Roeder, G. *Ägyptische Götterwelt* (Zürich: Artemis 1959).

Rösel, Ch. *Die messianische Redaktion der Psalmen. Studien zur Entstehung und Theologie der Sammlung Psalm 2–89\** (CthM.BW 19; Stutgart: Calwer, 1999).

Rösel, M. *Adonaj–Warum Gott ‚Herr' genannt wird* (FAT 29; Tübingen: Mohr Siebeck, 2000).

—. „Israels Psalmen in Ägypten? Papyrus Amherst 63 und die Psalmen XX und LXXV," *VT* 50 (2000) 81–89.

Rost, L. *Die Überlieferung von der Thronnachfolge Davids* (BWANT 42; Kohlhammer, 1926).

—. *Das kleine Credo und andere Studien zum A. T.* (Heidelberg: Quelle & Meyer Verlag, 1965) 119–253.

Schiffman, L. H. & J. C. VanderKam (Hrsg.). *Encyclopedia of the Dead Sea Scrolls* (Oxford: Oxford University Press, 2000).

Seybold, K. *Die Psalmen* (HAT I/15; Tübingen: Mohr Siebeck, 1996).

Seybold, K. & E. Zenger (Hrsg.). *Neue Wege der Psalmenforschung. FS W. Beyerlin* (HBS 1; Freiburg: Herder, 1994).

Steiner, R. C. „The Aramaic Text in Demotic Script: The Liturgy of a New Year's Festival imported from Bethel to Syene by Exiles from Rash," *JAOS* 111 (1991) 362–63.

Steymans, H. U. „Der (un)glaubwürdige Bund von Ps 89," *ZAR* 4 (1998) 126–42.

—. „'Deinen Thron habe ich unter den großen Himmeln festgemacht.' Die formgeschichtliche Nähe von Ps 89,4-5,20-38 zu Texten vom assyrischen Hof," in: E. Otto & E. Zenger (Hrsg.), *„Mein Sohn bist du" (Ps 2,7). Studien zu den Königspsalmen* (SBS 192; Stuttgart: Katholisches Bibelwerk, 2002) 184–251.

Ulrich, E. et al. *Qumran Cave 4.XI: Psalms to Chronicles* (DJD 16; Oxford: Clarendon Press, 2000).

Veijola, T. *Die ewige Dynastie* (AASF 193; Helsinki: Academia Scientiarum Fennica, 1975).

—. *Verheißung in der Krise. Studien zur Literatur und Theologie der Exilszeit anhand des 89. Psalms* (AASF.B 220; Helsinki: Academia Scientiarum Fennica, 1982).

—. „Davidsverheißung und Staatsvertrag," in: Ders., *Gesammelte Studien zu den Davidsüberlieferungen des Alten Testaments* (SFEG 52; Helsinki: Finnish Exegetical Society, University of Helsinki = SESJ 52; Göttingen: Vandenhoeck & Ruprecht, 1990) 128–53.

Vleeming, S. P. & J. W. Wesselius. *Studies in Papyrus Amherst 63. Essays on the Aramaic texts in Aramaic-demotic Papyrus Amherst 63* (Amsterdam: Juda Palache Instituut) I 1985, II 1990.

—. „An Aramaic Hymn from the Fourth Century B.C.," *BiOr* 39 (1982) 501–509.

Wilson, G. H. „The Shape of the Book of Psalms," *Int* 46 (1992) 129–41.

—. „The Use of Royal Psalms of the 'Seams' of the Hebrew Psalter," *JSOT* 35 (1986) 85–94.

Zenger, E. „Der Psalter als Wegweiser und Wegbegleiter. Ps 1–2 als Proömium des Psalmenbuchs," in: A. Angenendt & H. Vorgrimler (Hrsg.), *Sie wandern von Kraft zu Kraft. Aufbrüche–Wege–Begegnungen. FS Bischof R. Lettmann* (Kevelaer: Butzon und Bercker, 1993) 29–47.

# THE PSALMS OF DAVID: DAVID IN THE PSALMS

ROLF RENDTORFF

## PSALMS WITH HEADINGS THAT MENTION DAVID

Almost half the psalms bear a headline including the name of David: in the Hebrew canon 73 of the 150 psalms, and in the Septuagint an additional 14, including the 151st psalm which is "out of count." The superscriptions vary remarkably, but what all have in common is the phrase לדוד. The exact meaning of this formulation is contested. It appears to be a rather formulary phrase that can be used by itself, as well as in different combinations with other words or phrases or even sentences. It appears thirty-five times in the formula מזמור לדוד (or לדוד מזמור), usually translated "a psalm of David." This formula can be extended to a sentence, for example, "when he fled from his son Absalom" (Ps 3:1[0]), or "when he was in the Wilderness of Judah" (63:1[0]). In these cases לדוד is obviously understood as naming David to be the author of the psalm. This is even more evident in cases like Ps 18:1(0), where לדוד is followed by "who spoke to Yhwh the words of this song."

In later tradition David is seen to be the author of the psalms in general. 2 Macc 2:13 mentions the "writings of David," and according to the large Qumran scroll (11QPs<sup>a</sup> col. 27) David "wrote" and "spoke" no less than 3,600 psalms (תהלים) and 450 "songs" (שירים). In the New Testament several times psalms are quoted as spoken by David "by the Holy Spirit" (Mark 12:36, cf. Acts 1:16) or "in the book of Psalms" (Luke 20:42, cf. Act 2,25, 4:25, Rom 4:6, 11:9). In rabbinic literature David as author of the "five books of Psalms" is compared to Moses as the author of the "five books of the Torah" (*Midr. Tehillim* to 1:2, cf. *b.Baba Batra* 14b, 15a; *b.Pesachim* 117a).

But what David is it who could be seen as the author of psalms[1] and even as "the sweet singer of the songs of Israel" (2 Sam 23:1)?[2] Is it

---

[1] "An essay on a subject like 'The David of the Psalms' is a sign of what is going on in biblical studies in our time." (J. L. Mays, "The David of the Psalms," *Interp* 40 [1986] 143–155, here 143)

[2] The *NRSV* understands this verse differently.

the great king who ruled Israel and half the surrounding world for decades? The one who did not hesitate to kill two thirds of the Moabite warriors when he had already defeated them (2 Sam 8:2)? To whom did he sing his psalms? To his wives? To Bathsheba? Or earlier to Abigail? Nothing is said about this. There is only one element in the narrative David tradition that shows a certain relation to singing psalms: David had been brought to the court of Saul to play the lyre before the king in order to chase away the evil spirit that had come upon Saul (1 Sam 16:14-23; 18:10; 19:9). But this was in his youth before he became king, and nowhere is anything mentioned about David playing his instrument in later times. One might mention 2 Sam 1:17, which says that David "sang" or "intoned" a lamentation or dirge over Saul and his son Jonathan. But it does not say he was the author of the song (nor in the following verse, which is "uncertain" [*JPS*]). Other traditions are even less clear: In Amos 6:5 the MT speaks of people "singing to the sound of the harp, like David inventing musical instruments;" but here again, according to commentators and translators, the meaning of the Hebrew text is "uncertain."

The "musical instruments of David" are also mentioned in Neh 12:36; 1 Chron 23:5; 2 Chron 29:26-27. This leads in another direction: according to the tradition of the Chroniclers (including Nehemiah, irrespective of the question of authorship) it was David who installed the institution of Temple singers and musicians (1 Chron 6:16; 16:4-7; etc.). The image of David in the chronistic literature is quite different from that in the Books of Samuel and Kings. According to our understanding of the historical setting of the Psalms, at least parts represent traditions more ancient than that of the Chronicler. Therefore this tradition cannot help us understand why David's name appears in the superscriptions of so many psalms. Even later is the view of the Qumran scroll 11QPs[a], which says that David wrote his songs to sing "before the altar" at the occasion of sacrifices and festivals.

## EXPANDED SUPERSCRIPTIONS THAT MENTION DAVID

A number of expanded superscriptions mention specific situations in the life of David when he had spoken or sung the respective psalm. All of these circumstances are reported in the Books of Samuel. The references make it clear that the psalms in their given shape are to be read in the larger framework of the Hebrew Scriptures. It is thus possible to understand these psalm titles as a kind of inner-biblical exegesis.[3] They provide insight into a way that David's personality was viewed by later generations of readers and writers of biblical texts.[4]

The first occurrence of such an expanded superscription is in Psalm 3, "A psalm of David when he fled from his son Absalom." This quotation refers to the events reported in 2 Samuel 15–17. Here David is seen neither as the mighty king nor as the sweet singer, but as a powerless fugitive whose future is quite uncertain. Following B. Childs, we can read some details in the psalm in the light of the narration in 2 Samuel. "How many are my foes! Many are rising against me." (Ps 3:2[1]) can be read as referring to 2 Sam 15:12: "The conspiracy gained strength, and the people supported Absalom in increasing numbers." The following verse "Many are saying of me: 'There is no help for him in God'" (Ps 3:3[2]) can be related to the many supporters of Absalom, and also to the cursing words of Shimei in 2 Sam 16:8. "I cry aloud to the LORD, and he answers me from his holy hill" (Ps 3:5[4]) recalls David passing the summit, "where God is worshiped" (2 Sam 15:32), perhaps suggesting that he had prayed there. The Psalm continues "I lie down and sleep; I wake again, for the LORD sustains me" (Ps 3:6[5]). This may be read in the light of 2 Samuel 17 which emphasizes how important it was for David to have the night — against the counsel of Ahitophel — to gain time to cross the Jordan. Finally, the call "Rise up, O LORD" (Ps 3:8[7]) is connected with the ark (Num 10:35) that David had brought to Jerusalem (2 Samuel 6). Psalm 3 is an individual lamentation. In the light of its superscription it may be read as a Midrash to an important chapter of David's history: a chapter of persecution and danger, but also of final divine help.

Psalm 7, the next to mention a situation in David's life, is also a lamentation. Its superscription says: "...which he sang to the LORD concerning Cush, the Benjaminite," referring to the Cushite who brought the news of Absalom's death to David (2 Sam 18:21-32).[5]

---

[3] Cf. B. S. Childs, "Psalm Titles and Midrashic Exegesis," *JSS* 16 (1971), 137–50; see also E. Slomovic, "Toward an Understanding of the Formation of Historical Titles in the Book of Psalms," *ZAW* 91 (1979) 350–80.

[4] For details, see in addition to Childs and Slomovic M. Kleer, „Der liebliche Sänger der Psalmen Israels": Untersuchungen zu David als Dichter und Beter der Psalmen (BBB 108; Bodenheim: Philo), 1996, esp. 78–85.

[5] This Cushite might have been a Benjaminite slave (cf. M. Millard, *Die Komposition des Psalters* [FAT 9; Tübingen: Mohr Siebeck 1994] 131).

This is the same context to which the superscription of Psalm 3 refers: David's flight from Absalom and finally Absalom's death. Here David is still in the position to intone a lamentation; but at the end the psalm turns to thanks and praise to God. Psalm 9 takes up this theme, thanking God about the defeat and even the death of the enemies. This psalm can be read in continuation with earlier psalms that mirror this specific phase in David's life. The headline of the psalm may be read: "about the death (עַל־מוּת), concerning the son" (9:1[0]).[6]

Psalms 3–9 are the first continuous group of psalms to bear a heading with the name of David. Reading this group as a kind of cluster composition,[7] Psalms 4–6 fit in with their speaking of the night (4:9[8]; 6:7[6]) and the morning (5:4[3]), recalling the night in 3:6(5), which reflect the importance of the night for the fleeing David (2 Samuel 17). While Psalms 3–7 are lamentations, Psalm 8 is a thanksgiving. It bridges the expression of thanks at the end of Psalm 7 with the thanksgiving Psalm 9, building together with these a strong, thankful conclusion to this group of psalms.

In this cluster of psalms David appears as a suffering and lamenting individual, far from the heights of kingship, dependent on the help and mercy of God. And indeed, in the narratives in the Books of Samuel and Kings David's misfortune and suffering is described much more broadly and in far greater detail than are his victories and his kingship. By setting this side of David's image in the foreground, these psalms make David a figure to be identified with by the individual reader as well as by the praying congregation — the more so because almost every psalm of lamentation ends with an expression of hope and confidence in the help of God, sometimes even with thanks for God's help already received.

The experience of God's help dominates the next psalm mentioned here: Psalm 18. According to the introduction, David spoke this song "... when the LORD delivered him from the hand of all his enemies, and from the hand of Saul" (Ps 18:1[0]). This psalm is different in several respects from those we have dealt with so far. First of all, it is not a lamentation but a thanksgiving. It praises God for his mighty deeds in delivering the psalmist from all kinds of crises. Furthermore, the introduction does not mention one specific situation in David's life, but rather speaks in general terms of his deliverance from "all his

---

[6] Millard, *Komposition des Psalters*, 133.

[7] Millard, *Komposition des Psalters*, 51.

enemies."[8] These enemies are, at least in the latter parts of the psalm, clearly the enemies of the ruling king, against whom he fought and over whom he triumphed, which made him "head of the nations" (v. 44[43]). Therefore Psalm 18 may partially be taken as a royal psalm (vv. 33-51[32-50]. The David of this psalm is not mainly one who suffers, but one who is victorious. But David is victorious only by the help of God. His whole life is looked at from this point of view. That makes Psalm 18 a kind of summary of what had been alluded to in the former psalms: the merciful guidance of God.[9] (I will return later to other aspects of Psalm 18.)

Finally, one more psalm in the first "book" of the Psalter (Psalms 1–41)[10] refers to a certain situation in David's life: "...when he feigned madness before Abimelech, so that he drove him out, and he went away" (Ps 34:1[0]). Again, this psalm is different from the aforementioned group: it is an acrostic wisdom psalm. But at the same time it is close to them by speaking of need and salvation by the LORD. The mentioning of David's simulation of madness clearly refers to 1 Sam 21:11-16(10-15).[11]

This leads to a much earlier period in David's life when he had not yet become king and had to flee from Saul. In Ps 34:5(4) the psalmist confesses that God "delivered me from all my fears;" the only explicit reference to David's fear in Samuel comes in this very episode in 1 Sam 21:13(12). The story of David in Gath continues with "David went away" (וילך, 1 Sam 22:1) —the same word by which the superscription of the psalm ends. The psalmist thanks God that he answered him (Ps 34:5[4]); later in the David Story it is told that God had answered David when he asked him by the ephod (1 Sam 23:2, 4, 11, 12; cf. in particular ויענהו in v. 4 with וענני in Ps 34:5[4]). Moreover, the "angel (מלאך) of the LORD," who protects and delivers those who fear the LORD (Ps 34:8[7]), can be related to the messenger (מלאך) who notified Saul of an invasion of the Philistines so that he had to give up his pursuit of David (1 Sam 23:27).

---

[8] That Saul is singled out separates him from the "enemies," and also alludes to the long story of David's persecution by Saul.

[9] See Mays, "David of the Psalms," 152.

[10] The question of the redactional history of the individual "books" of the Psalter is beyond the scope of this essay.

[11] The confusion of names (Ahimelech instead of Achish) could be explained differently; cf. Childs, "Psalm Titles," 144; Kleer, *Der liebliche Sänger*, 91.

## DAVID IN BOOK II OF THE PSALTER

The second "book" of the Psalter (Psalms 42–72) includes a compact group of lamentations in the "cluster" of Psalms 51–64.[12] In this group are assembled the majority of psalms with biographical references to the life of David: Psalms 51, 52, 54, 56, 57, 59, 60, 63. They refer to different periods in David's life. The first, Psalm 51, belongs to the few psalms that refer to events in a time when David really ruled as king, namely to David's sin with Bathsheba (2 Samuel 11–12); only Psalm 60 refers also to that time, in this case to David's wars with other nations (2 Samuel 8 or 10). The next five, Psalms 52, 54, 56, 57, 59, go back to the time already referred to in Psalm 34, when David had to flee and to hide before Saul (1 Samuel 19–24). Psalm 63 either refers to the same period, or to the time when David had to flee before Absalom as referred to in Psalms 3 and 7.[13]

Psalm 51 begins: "…when the Prophet Nathan came to him, after he had gone in to Bathsheba" (v. 2[0]). The reference to 2 Samuel 12 is obvious; this was one of the lowest in David's life, and Psalm 51 is one of the most explicit and deep confessions of guilt in the psalter. The confession "I have sinned" in v. 6(4) corresponds to 2 Sam 12:13; the reference to blood guiltiness (v. 16[14]) calls to mind Uriah's murdering; the "broken spirit" and "contrite heart" (v. 19[17]) parallel closely the repentance of David following Nathan's accusation. Again, it is not the victorious and happy David we encounter, but the great sinner and penitent.

Psalm 52 leads back to the earliest period in David's life, when he was fleeing and hiding before Saul. Then it happened that "Doeg the Edomite came to Saul and said to him, 'David has come to the house of Ahimelech'" (Ps 52:2[0]). This refers to 1 Samuel 22, in particular to v. 9. By this superscription Doeg the Edomite is portrayed as the prototype of a denouncing traitor. The psalm announces the destruction of the traitor (v. 7[5]); for the reader this fills a gap, because in the report of 1 Samuel nothing is revealed about Doeg's fate.

Psalm 54 refers to the same period: "…when the Ziphites went and told Saul, 'David is hiding among us'" (v. 2[0]). The reference to 1 Sam 23:14-28 is obvious, even if not all details are clear. The same

---

[12] Cf. Millard, *Komposition des Psalters*, 116–20.

[13] For details on the following psalms see also F. L. Hossfeld & E. Zenger, *Psalmen 51–100* (HTKAT; Freiburg: Herder 2000).

is true of Psalm 56, "…when the Philistines seized him in Gath" (v. 1[0]), referring to 1 Sam 21:11-16, as does Psalm 34 (see above). Again, the element of David's "fear" is mentioned (vv. 4, 5, 12[3, 4, 11]). That the Philistines had "seized" David might be an interpretation of "in their hands" (בידם 1 Sam 21:14[13]). In both psalms the tenor is the psalmist's trust in God's help, which according to Ps 56:14(13) he had already received. Psalm 57 "…when he fled from Saul, in the cave" (v. 1[0]) seems to refer rather to 1 Samuel 24 than to 1 Sam 22:1. Possibly there is an allusion from the shadow of God's "wings" (כנפיך Ps 57:2[1]) to the "corner" (כנף) of Saul's cloak, which David stealthily cut off (1 Sam 24:5[4]).

Psalm 59 goes even farther back to the very beginning of the conflict between David and Saul, when Saul "ordered his house to be watched in order to kill him" (v. 1[0]). This introduction corresponds exactly with what is reported in 1 Sam 19:11; corresponding to the same verse is Ps 59:4(3) "they lie in wait for my life." The psalmist's protestation "no sin of mine" (לא־חטאתי, v. 4[3]) corresponds with Jonathan's declaration before Saul that David "has not sinned against you" (לוא חטא לך 1 Sam 19:4). The psalmist's wish "Do not kill them" (Ps 59:12[11]) shows that David has no feelings of revenge, but leaves everything to God.

Finally, the introduction to Psalm 63 reads: "A Psalm of David, when he was in the Wilderness of Judah." This is rather vague and could refer to different periods in David's life. Most likely it is to be understood with regard to David's flight from Absalom (2 Samuel 15–17), where the wilderness is mentioned several times (15:23, 28, 16:2). The psalmist wants to behold (ראה) God's power and glory in the sanctuary (Ps 63:3[2]), as David hopes, that God will let him see again (הראה) the ark and its place in the sanctuary (2 Sam 15:25). That "the king shall rejoice in God" (Ps 63:12[11]) is now to be understood as spoken by the king himself. Again, the fleeing David hopes and trusts in God's final help.

Psalm 60 is difficult. Mentioned in its introduction are wars that David had fought against neighboring nations; other nations are mentioned in vv. 8-10(6-8). This seems to refer to 2 Sam 8:1-14, even though not all details are comparable. The main problem is that in those wars David was victorious, while the psalm is a lamentation after a bad defeat. A possible solution might be found in the word ללמד ("for instruction"), which in the superscription follows לדוד. Accordingly, this psalm may be understood as an instruction or direction to be issued in times of war.[14]

## DAVID AND THE TEXT (BODY) OF VARIOUS PSALMS

In the majority of the psalms with biographical introductions the name David appears only in the introduction itself and not in the following text; the only exception is Psalm 18. (In two more psalms David is mentioned in both the superscription and the text itself, but without biographical extensions in the superscription: Ps 122:1, 5 and 144:1, 10.) As noticed above, Psalm 18 is regarded as a combination of an individual thanksgiving and a royal psalm. At the very end of this long psalm the name David appears: "Great triumphs he gives to his king, and shows steadfast love to his anointed, to David and his descendants forever" (v. 51[50]). Here David is called God's משׁיח, his anointed. This title is used for David almost exclusively in psalms, including 2 Samuel 22 (the parallel to Psalm 18) and 2 Sam 23:1. (The only exception is 2 Sam 19:22[21].)

The title משׁיח appears first in Psalm 2: the "kings of the earth" revolt "against the LORD and his anointed" (v. 2). The "anointed" is the king of whom God says: "I have set my king on Zion, my holy hill" (v. 6). The name David is not actually mentioned, but it is obvious that it is he who had been enthroned by God on Zion. This is the dominating feature of Psalm 2. Another aspect appears when Psalm 1 and 2 are read in continuation: both are speaking about the opposition of the "righteous" and the "wicked." In Psalm 1 it is the righteous[15] who follows the Torah (v. 2: תורת יהוה), and their way[16] will be watched over by the LORD, while the way of the wicked will perish. If the reader moves on to Psalm 2, the theme of the "wicked" is spelled out in terms of nations and their rulers.[17] These are identified with those who walk the way of the sinners and the wicked in Psalm 1. In contrast to them, the king is depicted as the one who walks in the way of the righteous. This is exactly how in Psalm 18 the psalmist speaks

---

[14] Cf. Kleer, *Der liebliche Sänger*, 102–106; Hossfeld & E. Zenger, *Psalmen 51–100*, 160–61.

[15] In Hebrew vv. 1-3 are singular: "Happy the man" etc.

[16] In Hebrew v. 6 is plural.

[17] Cf. G. Sheppard, *Wisdom as a Hermeneutical Construct: A Study in the Sapientalization of the Old Testament*, BZAW 151 (1980) 136–44; P. D. Miller, "The Beginning of the Psalter," J. C. McCann (ed.), *The Shape and Shaping of the Psalter* (JSOTSup 159; Sheffield: Sheffield Academic Press, 1993) 83–92.

of himself: "I have kept the ways of the LORD, and have not wickedly departed from my God" (v. 22[21]); he also speaks explicitly about his own righteousness (vv. 21, 25[20, 24]). Here Psalm 18 presents an additional image of the anointed: he is not only the persecuted and suffering one, nor only the one whom God saves from his needs and give victory, but he is also the exemplary righteous one. This is reminiscent of 1 Kgs 2:1-4, 3, 14, which depicts David as the one who kept all the divine statutes and commandments. Finally, included in Psalm 18 are the entire people, who are called "humble" (עני, v. 28[27]). The king is also the representative of his suffering people, confirming to them that God will be the shield for all who take refuge in him (חסה, v. 31[30]). This is reminiscent of the last verse of Psalm 2: "Happy are all who take refuge in him" (Ps 2:12).

The so-called "royal psalms" mirror the different sides of the Davidic king. The theme of God's help for the king is the main topic in Psalm 20: "Now I know that the LORD will help his anointed; he will answer him from his holy heaven with mighty victories by his right hand" (v. 7[6]). The interrelation between the king ruling on earth and God being in heaven is expressed in several psalms. Psalm 21 also deals with God's help for the king, if even in a more drastic way by speaking of the king's power and splendor and the destruction of his enemies.

In other royal psalms the king's righteousness plays an important role. Psalm 101 as a whole deals with this topic; it may be described as a "loyalty vow"[18] of the king, who describes his devoted commitment to maintaining the law in his kingdom. In Psalm 72 God is called upon to give his justice (משפט) and his righteousness (צדקה) to the king, so that the latter can judge his people in righteousness in order to bring peace (שלום) and righteousness to the country (vv. 1-3). The king will help in particular the needy (אביון) and the poor (עני, vv. 12-14). Even nature will prosper (v. 16) because of the beneficial work of the king.

In Psalm 132 the main topic is the relation of the Davidic kingdom to mount Zion. At the beginning an important event in the life of David is recalled: when he brought the ark to mount Zion (vv. 1-5). This event is celebrated in a liturgical ceremony, in which the actual

---

[18] H. J. Kraus, *Psalms 60–150: A Commentary* (Minneapolis: Augsburg, 1989) [on Psalm 101].

king reminds God of the oath he had sworn to David (v. 11), and asks God: "For your servant David's sake do not turn away the face of your anointed one" (v. 10). Here the "anointed" is actually the praying king himself. At the end of the psalm David is called the משׁיח (v. 17), for whom God had prepared a "lamp," i.e. continuous succession on the throne (cf. 1 Kgs 11:36). This shows an interchange between David himself and the Davidic dynasty. In this psalm the theme of the king's righteousness emerges as well: in the quoted divine oath God has said he would always give David a successor on the throne from among his sons — if they keep God's covenant and his decrees (vv. 11-12). Here the righteousness of the king is connected with the Zion tradition.

In Psalm 110 the enthronement of the king on Zion as ruler over all nations is impressively depicted. Again, it is only God himself who gives the king the rule over his enemies and who will execute judgment among the nations (vv. 5-6). Here a specific Jerusalem tradition comes in, when the king is called "a priest forever according to the order of Melchizedek" (v. 4). This refers to Gen 14:18-20; but the historical and cultic background of this tradition is uncertain and contested.

Psalm 89 is of special importance. This psalm builds the end of the third "book" of the Psalter (Psalms 73–89), and at the same time marks a high point in the utterances on Davidic kingship in the Psalter. In its earlier portions the psalm speaks of the king in lofty terms, in particular about God's attitude towards him: God has made a covenant with David, his chosen one (בחיר, v. 4[3]), which he will never break (vv. 29, 35[28, 34]); he made him "the firstborn, the highest of the kings of the earth" (v. 28[27]), whose throne shall exist "as long as the heavens endure" (v. 30[29]), and whose "line (זרע) shall continue forever" like the sun and the moon (vv. 37-38[36-37]. Here Psalm 89 turns from David to his "line," his descendants, the Davidic dynasty. But then it breaks off: now God has rejected his anointed, renounced the covenant and defiled his crown in the dust (vv. 39-40[38-39]). This is followed by a lamentation without any expression of hope or thanks for God's help (vv. 47-52[46-51]). But even at this lowest point the fact that the king is "your anointed" (משׁיחך) it is called to God's memory.

## IMAGES OF DAVID IN THE PSALTER

Again: What kind of David is represented in the Psalter? The image of David in the psalms has very different features, but the main aspects appear in a concentrated way in the first three psalms. Psalm 2 speaks of the "anointed" (מָשִׁיחַ) king, whom God has set on Zion, his holy hill; whom he calls "my son, today I have begotten you" (v. 7), and whom he will make the ruler over all the nations. This is the first aspect: David, the "messianic" king, whom God has enthroned on Zion. Reading Psalm 2 in continuation with Psalm 1, David appears to be the exemplary righteous king who follows the divine Torah. In several psalms one of the most important elements of the king's image is that he will rule in righteousness. Psalm 3 shows a quite different side of David: he is the powerless fugitive, who in a lamentation asks for God's succor in his need, and who trusts in God's help.

Following the superscriptions with biographical elements (see Books II and III) the last-mentioned aspect dominates by far. The majority of psalms with this kind of superscription are lamentations. David is presented as suffering and lamenting — but at the same time as hoping and trusting in God's help. In these psalms David does not come in view as a king. Rather, David is presented as an example and a figure with whom the individual reader as well as the praying congregation can identify with in times of need and distress. In particular, David stands as an example because almost every lamentation psalm related to David's name ends with an expression of hope and confidence in God's help. David is not only the exemplary sufferer, but also the exemplary believer. And because this David expressed his sufferings and his belief through psalms, everybody can speak and sing these psalms and identify with David.

In the royal psalms the name of David is mentioned very rarely. Psalm 132 begins with an event in David's life (vv. 1-5), then turns to the praying king who speaks of himself as the "anointed" (v. 10), and finally returns to David, the "anointed" (v. 17). This transition from David to his successors and back again shows the focus to be not only on the "historical" David, but on that the name David represents the Davidic dynasty through the centuries. The same is true for Psalm 89: at the beginning God has "found" his "servant David" (v. 21[20]), but later the psalm moves to the actual king who recalls God's "steadfast love of old" which he had sworn to David (v. 50[49]), and it is the actual king who complains that the enemies "taunt the footsteps of your anointed" (v. 52[51]). Psalm 144:9-10 shows a similar use of David's name in a kind of identification with the actual king. The king will sing a new song to God, "the one who gives victory to kings, who rescues his servant David." Since the psalm speaks in the present tense, the rescued "David" can be no other one than the actual king himself.

This survey shows that only in a minority of psalms is the "historical" David portrayed as king. In a number of other psalms the name David represents the royal dynasty, and even later kings can be identified or identify themselves with this name. The same holds true for the title מָשִׁיחַ. In several of these psalms the righteousness of the king plays an important role. This is the case in particular in Psalms 18, 72, 101, and 132. This shows that even in those psalms in which the name David stands for the ruling king, it is not the image of the ruling and victorious one that is in the foreground, but that of the righteous one who serves and helps his people.

## SELECT BIBLIOGRAPHY

Childs, B. S. "Psalm Titles and Midrashic Exegesis," *JSS* 16 (1971), 137–50.

Hossfeld, F. L. & E. Zenger. *Psalmen 51–100* (HTKAT; Freiburg: Herder 2000).

Kleer, M. „*Der liebliche Sänger der Psalmen Israels": Untersuchungen zu David als Dichter und Beter der Psalmen* (BBB 108; Bodenheim: Philo), 1996.

Kraus, H.-J. *Psalms 1–59: A Commentary* (Minneapolis: Augsburg, 1988).

—. *Psalms 60–150: A Commentary* (Minneapolis: Augsburg, 1989).

Mays, J. L. "The David of the Psalms," *Interp* 40 (1986) 143–155.

Millard, M. *Die Komposition des Psalters* (FAT 9; Tübingen: Mohr Siebeck 1994).

Miller, P. D. "The Beginning of the Psalter," J. C. McCann (ed.), *The Shape and Shaping of the Psalter* (JSOTSup 159; Sheffield: Sheffield Academic Press, 1993) 83–92.

Sheppard, G. *Wisdom as a Hermeneutical Construct: A Study in the Sapientalization of the Old Testament*, BZAW 151 (1980) 136–44.

Slomovic, E. "Toward an Understanding of the Formation of Historical Titles in the Book of Psalms," *ZAW* 91 (1979) 350–80.

PART TWO


COMMENTARY ON
OR INTERPRETATION OF SPECIFIC PSALMS

# PSALMS AND THE LITERATURE OF EXILE:
## PSALMS 137, 44, 69, AND 78

ADELE BERLIN

The destruction of Jerusalem and the exile to Babylonia left its mark on much of biblical literature, including the book of Psalms. Indeed, the extent to which these events figure in the psalms is rarely appreciated. It is not only a question of dating psalms to the post-destruction period, the period increasingly favored by scholars for the dating of much of biblical literature, but of the importance of the theme of destruction and exile in many of the psalms. In this essay I will consider four psalms whose main theme relates to the fall of Jerusalem or to the exilic condition. Each presents a different "take" on the theme; each approaches the theme from a different perspective, with a different goal in mind. They all address the problem of exile in stereotypical language and style, and they share certain theological assumptions; yet each has its own thesis, its own particular concern about an aspect of the exilic experience.

The first psalm to be discussed, Psalm 137, has long been recognized as a lament for Jerusalem. I will focus on what it says about the phenomenon of lamenting Jerusalem, which is part of the larger question of worshipping God in exile. "Exile" does not necessarily mean living outside of the former Kingdom of Judah. People living in the Land of Israel after 538 BCE also felt that they were in exile as long as the Temple was not rebuilt and even afterwards, as long as they were under the rule of a foreign power. Exile is not only a geographic place, it is a religious state of mind.

The other psalms, 44, 69, and 78, have, in my view, been misunderstood wholly or in part, even by those who date them to the exilic or postexilic period — so I will endeavor to show how they relate to the literature of exile. Psalm 44 is an argument for why the exile should come to an end. Psalm 69 presents the perspective of a mourner for Zion. Psalm 78, not usually considered under the rubric of exile, presents its interpretation of history as a proof that the Temple will be rebuilt and the Davidic line will continue.

Other psalms besides the four I have singled out invoke the theme of destruction and exile or its permutations, including the hope for the restoration of Zion or the return of the exiles, or an acknowledgement of the restoration as a prelude to another request for God's favor. I would include in this group Psalms 74, 79, 85, 89, 102, 105, 106, and 126, but this list is not exhaustive, nor is it definitive. Other psalms might be included; and not everyone will agree that the psalms I have chosen should be on the list.[1]

The dating of psalms is notoriously difficult, and opinions on the date of the aforementioned psalms diverge widely. Dating entraps us in a hermeneutic circle whereby we interpret the meaning of the psalm and then date it to the period when that meaning would be most relevant. Moreover, dating the psalms also follows more general trends in dating biblical texts, the favored period having moved from the Maccabean period, to the monarchal period, to the Persian period, wherein today much of the Hebrew Bible is thought to have taken shape. To say that a psalm speaks of the destruction and exile is to date it no earlier than 586 BCE; I would place all of these psalms in the exilic or postexilic period.

## PSALM 137

This psalm locates its speakers "by the rivers (or canals) of Babylon" (v. 1), contrasting that location with Jerusalem, the place never to be forgotten (v. 5).[2] The psalm does not ask for the restoration of Zion but rather for revenge on Edom and Babylonia. More important in terms of the present essay, this psalm holds a key for understanding the concept of lamenting Jerusalem, and that will be the focus of my

---

[1] For instance, I have not included Psalms 60, 80, and 83, in which F. W. Dobbs-Allsopp, *Weep, O Daughter of Zion: A Study of the City-Lament Genre in the Hebrew Bible* (Rome: Editrice Pontificio Istituto Biblico, 1993) 154–55, sees evidence of city-lament influence because I find them too general to identify as exhibiting the Jerusalem lament theme. Peter R. Ackroyd, *Exile and Restoration* (Philadelphia: Westminster, 1968) 225–28, summarizes previous scholarly opinion that includes Psalms 40, 44, 51, 66, 69, 74, 79, 89, 102, 106, 136, and 148 as containing references to the exile. Ackroyd himself is confident only of Psalms 44, 74, 79, and 137. Ralph W. Klein, *Israel in Exile. A Theological Interpretation* (Philadelphia: Fortress, 1979) 18–22 discusses Psalms 44, 74, 79, and 102. Dalit Rom-Shiloni, *God in Times of Destruction and Exiles*, 28–40, finds that the following psalms were written as reactions to the destruction of Jerusalem, either shortly after the event or at a greater distance: Psalms 9–10, 42–43, 44, 74, 77, 79, 80, 89, 90, 94, 102, 103, 106, 123, 137.

[2] The question of whether the speakers are in Jerusalem or in Babylonia has vexed many commentators. My point is that, wherever the speakers are, the "there" — the "other" place — is Babylonia.

exposition. Several literary interpretations of the psalm have appeared in recent years and they inform my understanding of it.[3]

1 Among Babylon's waterways, there we dwelled, wailing our Zion memories.

2 Among the willows throughout it we hung up our lyres.

3 For there our captors demanded songs, our abductors joy: "Sing for us one of the Zion-songs."

4 How could we sing a YHWH-song on alien soil.

5 "If I forget you, Jerusalem, let my right hand hang limp.

6 Let my tongue stick to my palate if I do not remember you, if I do not elevate Jerusalem to/above my highest joy.

7 Remember, Lord, to the discredit of the Edomites, the day of Jerusalem; those who said: 'Strip it down, strip it down till its very foundation.'

8 Dear doomed Babylon, fortunate[4] is he who will pay you back what you deserve for what you did to us.

9 Fortunate is he who seizes and smashes your little children against The Rock."

*Verses 1-2.* The canals of Babylonia are emblematic of that country. These canals, and the willows that grow alongside them, formed a network throughout southern Mesopotamia. Verses 1 and 2 say that wherever in Babylonia the Judean exiles resided (and that may even include Judah under Babylonian rule) they could only utter sounds of sadness; they could not produce joyful music: The "otherness" of this location is marked twice by the word "there" (שָׁם) as well as by "alien soil" in v. 4. Scholars disagree on whether the speakers are located in Babylonia or in Judah, but in either case, the sense of alienation remains the same. The verb בכה means to utter a sad sound or cry. I have taken the liberty of translating "our Zion memories" because I think it better captures the sense of the phrase בְּזָכְרֵנוּ אֶת־צִיּוֹן. Zion-songs are sung and Zion memories are wailed. The exiles do not sim-

---

[3] Especially Shimon Bar-Efrat, "Love of Zion; a Literary Interpretation of Psalm 137," in Mordechai Cogan, Barry L. Eichler, Jeffrey H. Tigay (eds.), *Tehillah le-Moshe: Biblical and Judaic studies in honor of Moshe Greenberg* (Winona Lake, IN: Eisenbrauns, 1997) 3–11; George Savran, "How can we sing a song of the Lord?" The Strategy of Lament in Psalm 137," *ZAW* 112 (2000) 43–58; Yair Zakovitch, "על נהרות בבל: תהלים קלז — זיכרון בצל הטראומה" ["'By the Rivers of Babylon': Psalm 137 — Memory in the Shadow of Trauma"], in Z. Talshir et al. (eds.), *Homage to Shmuel. Studies in the World of the Bible* (Jerusalem: Ben Gurion University Press and Mosad Bialik, 2001) 184–93.

[4] The word אַשְׁרֵי is impossible to render properly in English. It means declared to be in a good or favored state.

ply cry when they think of Zion, but, here quite literally, they are crying a "song" to the memory of Zion — they utter a cry, the antithesis of a song, to memorialize Zion. This cry has no musical accompaniment; the lyres are hanging useless.

*Verses 3-4.* Among the deportees mentioned in Mesopotamian booty lists and depicted on reliefs were musicians with their instruments, who were required to perform for their captors.[5] The word תּוֹלָלֵינוּ is often rendered "tormentors," though A. Guillaume prefers "slave-drivers," or those who drive the prisoners.[6] This word may play on the sound of תָּלִינוּ, "we hung up," in v. 2.[7] The phrase דִּבְרֵי־שִׁיר means songs with words, or chants (cf. Judg 5:12, דַּבְּרִי־שִׁיר, "speak a song"). The captors request a Zion-song, presumably a Judean song but not necessarily a cultic song. "Sing for us one of your native songs," they demand. The use of "Zion" put into the mouths of the Babylonians is, however, strange, and already marks the Judean point of view, made explicit in the following verse, that a Zion-song is a "YHWH-song." Any reference to Zion has religious overtones; so by calling it a Zion-song, it becomes a cultic song. What the Babylonian captors may have intended as an accepted form of secular amusement is recast by the exiles as a religious affront. The term שִׂמְחָה ("joy") participates and reinforces this recasting. The musical entertainment (שִׂמְחָה) that the Babylonians hoped for has been explained as being a victory song that the vanquished must perform for the victors,[8] but by the time we get to verse 4, it is more obviously a reference to Temple worship. "Joy" has the cultic meaning of being in God's presence, worshipping in the Temple (see below). This kind of joy, this kind of Zion/Lord-song is impossible to perform in a foreign land, removed from the Temple.

*Verses 5-6.* This oath formula, a "pledge of allegiance to Jerusalem" as it is sometimes designated, is the beginning of the song that the speakers sing in place of the song that they can no longer sing. Their song continues until the end of the poem. Verses 5-6 set the memory

---

[5] See Bathja Bayer, "The Rivers of Babylon," *Ariel* 62 (1985) 43–52.

[6] "Meaning of *twll* in Psalm 137:3," *JBL* 75 (1956) 143–44. A different stream of interpretation is reflected in the Targum, which reads בזוזנא ("our plunderers").

[7] See Gary and Susan Rendsburg, "Physiological and Philological Notes to Psalm 137," *JQR* 83 (1993) 399; and Zakovitch, "By the Rivers of Babylon," 188.

[8] Harris Lenowitz, "The Mock-'Simha' of Psalm 137," in E. Follis (ed.), *Directions in Biblical Hebrew Poetry* (Sheffield: JSOT Press, 1987) 149–59.

of Jerusalem at the top of the list of "joys." If Jerusalem is not the chief joy, there can be no other joy, no other music or song. The hand that plays the lyre will atrophy and the tongue that sings will be immobilized.[9] The gist of these verses is that the joy of worshipping in the Temple is now to be replaced by the celebration of the memory of Jerusalem — that songs that memorialize Jerusalem will now replace the songs once sung in the Jerusalem Temple. Our psalm is just such a song to Jerusalem's memory; it is a Jerusalem lament, a song that replaces Zion-songs and that formalizes in song the wailing of Zion memories. It is a song about cultic singing in the absence of the Temple. It is a poetic explanation of the idea of the Jerusalem lament.

*Verses 7-9.* If the poet must remember Jerusalem, then God must remember Jerusalem's enemies. These verses contain thoughts of retaliation that typify complaints, especially at their close (compare Pss 5:11; 35:4-8; 69:23-28; 79:10; Lam 1:21-22; 3:64-66; 4:21-22). Moreover, they themselves are a kind of retaliation, for instead of the songs of joy that were demanded, the captors receive a song of doom, a curse. Modern readers have been repelled by the image of smashing little children against rocks, but, while not pleasant, the idea occurs elsewhere in the Bible (2 Kgs 8:12; Isa 13:16; Hos 14:1; Nah 3:10). The choice of words here is unusual, however, and contains a wordplay that is often missed. The last phrase is אֶל־הַסֶּלַע, literally "to the rock" (although many translations render "against the rocks" [*NRSV, NJPS*]). But the reference is not just to any rock or rocks. As Graham S. Ogden pointed out, "The Rock" is "synonymous with Edom itself" — that is, it is a title or epithet for Edom, set on cliffs.[10] Moreover, Ha-Sela' is the name of a fortress city in Edom (2 Kgs 14:7), so the reference is even more specific than Ogden suggested.[11] At work is a

---

[9] G. and S. Rendsburg, "Physiological and Philological Notes to Psalm 137," 388, suggest that a stroke in the left side of the brain is being described here.

[10] Graham S. Ogden, "Prophetic oracles against foreign nations and Psalms of communal lament: the relationship of Psalm 137 to Jeremiah 49:7-22 and Obadiah," *JSOT* 24 (1982) 91. According to Yair Zakovitch, Ps 137:7-9 is the source for 2 Chron 25:11-12: " ... another ten thousand the men of Judah captured alive and brought to the top of Sela. They threw them down from the top of Sela and everyone of them was burst open" ("Poetry Creates Historiography" in *"A Wise and Discerning Mind,"* in S. Olyan and R. Culley (eds.), *Essays in Honor of Burke O. Long* [Providence, RI: Brown Judaic Studies, 2000] 312).

[11] See G. Savran, "How Can We Sing," 56 with note 50; and Ulrich Kellermann, "Psalm 137," *ZAW* 90 (1978) 47. Some scholars have identified the city

wordplay invoking the city name, not unlike the wordplay on other foreign cities (e.g. Amos 6:13; Zeph 2:4).[12] The gist of verse 9 is that the rock-fortress protecting Edom will be the instrument for Edom's own punishment. The idea is similar to Ps 69:23, "may their table before them be a trap."

Form critics consider Psalm 137 a communal complaint (or lament), but it subverts the expectations for complaints. There is no immediate danger, and there is no request to save Israel, or to restore Israel to its land (except indirectly, as a result of the punishment of Edom and Babylonia). God is asked to remember Edom; the speakers remember Jerusalem. Ironically, by so doing they memorialize the very exile that they lament.

If memory is one major theme of the poem, singing is another. This psalm is about the type of song that can and cannot be sung after the destruction of Jerusalem. The type that cannot be sung is Zion-songs and/or YHWH songs. It is not immediately clear what these refer to. Based on v. 3, modern scholars have posited a category of psalms called Zion psalms, songs that praise Jerusalem's beauty and holiness (Psalms 46, 48, 50, 76, 84, 87, and 122). We do not know if this genre was recognized as such in ancient Israel, and we should be cautious about reading a modern generic label back into ancient times. Nevertheless, even without a specific genre called Zion-songs, we can understand Psalm 137 to be saying that songs praising the glory of Zion must cease, and that in their place one can sing only songs to the memory of Zion.

"Zion-song" and "YHWH-song" refer to the songs used in connection with praising God, most frequently in Temple worship. Gary A. Anderson's investigation into the religious phenomenology of joy and mourning provides the insight and the conceptual framework to understand our psalm. Song and praise for God are closely linked in Psalms and elsewhere. Singing (and other forms of music) is one of many public rituals of joy, along with appearing in God's presence and praising him. As Anderson puts it, verses 3-4

> make clear not only the relationship between songs and joy, but also the
> particular type of song that is implied by the term 'joy.' The captors do not

---

with Petra (which also means "Rock"), but that now seems unlikely. See "Sela," *ABD* 5.1073–74.

[12] Cf. Mordechai Cogan, *Obadiah* (Miqra Leyisrael, Tel Aviv: Am Oved, 1992) 22. [Hebrew]

want just any type of song ..., but a joyous song ..., a song that declares ... in the present tense the glory due Zion.[13]

Anderson notes that even while the Temple stood in Jerusalem, a
mourner or penitent was not permitted to engage in acts of public joy;
and any person cut off from God was considered a mourner. After the
destruction of Jerusalem, all Judeans were, in this sense, mourners, for
they were cut off from access to God and to Zion. They were therefore
forbidden, in a cultic sense, to sing praise to God or his chosen place,
and so could not acquiesce to their captors' request. What, then, could
they sing? What could take the place of Zion-songs? Psalm 137 transforms the Zion-song into the Jerusalem lament. Or, more correctly,
Psalm 137 shows the demise of the Zion-song and the birth of the Jerusalem lament. Jerusalem laments are the antithesis of Zion-songs;
they are songs for the lost Jerusalem.

I am not suggesting that Psalm 137 portrays the actual history of the
origin of Jerusalem laments. It offers, rather, a poetic conception of
the relationship between Zion-songs and Jerusalem laments, which is
part of the larger issue of the discontinuity of cultic practice after the
destruction of the Temple. The question of whether Israelite worship
of God can continue without the Temple is framed here in terms of the
language of prayer, not the cultic rituals of sacrifice. About sacrifice
there is really no question: without the Temple there can be no sacrifice. But what about prayer? What kinds of prayer are now appropriate and what kinds must be abandoned? The poet is exquisitely aware
that in the wake of the destruction the poetic discourse about Jerusalem (an important earlier form of praise to God) must change from
praise to lament. The idea of lamenting Jerusalem promoted in Psalm
137 became a theme in many exilic and postexilic pieces, and the related idea of being in exile became a hallmark of postexilic prayer.

## PSALM 44

This psalm does not mention Jerusalem and the events to which it
refers are expressed in such general terms that there has been little
consensus regarding its date, with some scholars placing it in the pre-
exilic period and others in postexilic times. In favor of its exilic dating
and its inclusion under the rubric of literature of exile is language

---

[13] Gary A. Anderson, *A Time to Mourn, A Time to Dance: The Expression of
Grief and Joy in Israelite Religion* (University Park, PA: Pennsylvania State University Press, 1991) 43.

about destruction and dispersal that calls to mind Lamentations and
other psalms that clearly lament Jerusalem: rejection by God and disgrace (v. 10), dispersal among the nations (v. 11), the butt and scorn
of the neighbors (vv. 14-15, 17), the place of jackals and deep darkness (v. 20), the call to God to rouse himself and not to hide his face
(vv. 24-27). The idea that the exile was a form of slavery into which
Judah was sold for no money, in v. 13, has an echo in Isa 52:3: "For
nothing were you sold, and for no money you will be redeemed."

Verses 18-22 have been a stumbling-block to modern commentators on the Psalms:

18  כָּל־זֹאת בָּאַתְנוּ וְלֹא שְׁכַחֲנוּךְ וְלֹא־שִׁקַּרְנוּ בִּבְרִיתֶךְ

19  לֹא־נָסוֹג אָחוֹר לִבֵּנוּ וַתֵּט אֲשֻׁרֵינוּ מִנִּי אָרְחֶךָ

20  כִּי דִכִּיתָנוּ בִּמְקוֹם תַּנִּים וַתְּכַס עָלֵינוּ בְצַלְמָוֶת

21  אִם־שָׁכַחְנוּ שֵׁם אֱלֹהֵינוּ וַנִּפְרֹשׂ כַּפֵּינוּ לְאֵל זָר

22  הֲלֹא אֱלֹהִים יַחֲקָר־זֹאת כִּי־הוּא יֹדֵעַ תַּעֲלֻמוֹת לֵב

The crux is v. 18 [17 in English], which many commentators take to
be a denial of Israel's guilt *prior to the exile*, although it is hard to see
how the syntax supports this view. Typical is the comment of J. J.
Stewart Perowne, who describes the psalm as

> A complaint that all these calamities have come upon them without any
> fault or demerit on the part of the nation. Such a complaint is doubly re-
> markable. First, because as an assertion of *national* innocence ... it is
> without parallel in the Old Testament, and next, because it wears the air of
> a reproach cast upon the righteousness of God.[14]

A look at English translations shows that there is disagreement on the
interpretation of v. 18, but individual commentators do not entertain
alternatives, apparently seeing none. I group the translations according
to the way they convey the temporal relationship between the clauses.
(In some cases this requires paraphrasing; italics are mine).

*KJV, NJPS, NRSV:* "All this has come upon us, yet we have not forgotten you."
*RSV, NAB:* "All this has come upon us *though* we have not forgotten you."
*NIV:* "All this happened to us, *though* we *had not* forgotten you."
*NEB:* "All this has befallen us, but we *do not* forget you."
*REB:* "*Though* all this has befallen us, we *do not* forget you."

The *KJV* and its companions are apparently ambivalent; they have
been understood (as Perowne does) to mean that the "have not for-

---

[14] J. J. S. Perowne, *The Book of Psalms* (Grand Rapids: Zondervan, 1976 [first
published 1878]) 1.364.

gotten" preceded what came upon the people, although I could just as easily read them the opposite way. The *RSV*, *NAB*, and especially *NIV* (Kraus's translation, as rendered in English, is similar to the *NIV*) clearly put the forgetting of God before the exile, making it sound like the speaker is denying all guilt, and thereby rejecting the Deuteronomic idea that exile is the result of sin. The *NEB* and *REB*, on the other hand, clearly make the exile prior to the forgetting of God.

I side with the *NEB* and *REB*, and take the "forgetting" clause to apply to the period during the exile, not before it.[15] It is not that the people have been exiled in spite of the fact that they had not forgotten God, but rather that *they have not forgotten and still do not forget God in spite of the fact that they have been exiled.* Notwithstanding their trouble and disgrace, the people have been true to the covenant and have not sought other gods, for if they had, God would know it (v. 22). The last point is a striking attestation to God's omniscience, even in Babylonia.

Verses 18-22 is not a denial that sin led to the exile, but a statement of the faithfulness of the people under circumstances adverse to the practice of their religion. Forgetting the name of God and spreading out the hands to a strange god (v. 21) are precisely the temptations faced by the exiled community in a foreign country, far from the "place where the name of the Lord resides," where pagan worship was readily accessible and where worship of the God of Israel was problematic, theologically speaking. Despite being in this pagan environment, the exiles continued to pray to God (v. 21), and to keep the covenant and obey its stipulations (vv. 18-19).

The phrasing is very Deuteronomic. Far from rejecting the Deuteronomic view that the sin of idolatry leads to the punishment of exile, Psalm 44 embraces it and builds on it. It declares that during the exile the people desisted from this sin; and that *therefore the exile should end, because the reason for it no longer exists.* Verses 18-19 echo Deut 28:9: "The Lord will establish you as his holy people ... if you keep the commandments of the Lord your God and walk in his ways."

---

[15] As does Amos Hakham, *Sefer Tehillim* (2 vols., Jerusalem: Mosad Harav Kook, 1970) 1.251. The syntax also supports this interpretation. Compare the two *qatal* (perfect) verbs that occur in a similar context in 2 Sam 12:18: בִּהְיוֹת הַיֶּלֶד חַי דִּבַּרְנוּ אֵלָיו וְלֹא־שָׁמַע בְּקוֹלֵנוּ, "While the child was alive, we spoke to him [David] but he did not (or: would not) listen." The second verb is clearly not pluperfect, and is likewise not pluperfect in Ps 44:18.

The psalmist pleads for the positive side of the Deuteronomic promise, without addressing the justification for the negative side (the
punishment of exile), except to say that that is how God wanted it
(cf. v. 4). The psalm prays for the end of the exile, using the same
theological reasoning that was used in Deuteronomic and prophetic
literature to predict it.

## PSALM 69

Psalm 69 initially presents itself as a typical individual complaint
that does not specify the danger its psalmist faces, although the mention of "My zeal for Your house" (v. 10) and the reference to the deliverance of Zion and the rebuilding of the towns of Judah (vv. 36-37),
suggests postexilic concerns. As the psalm now stands (some opine
that these verses are later additions to an earlier lament), those concerns are paramount. Hans-Joachim Kraus is not far off the mark
when he conjectures that "the petitioner of the psalm belonged to the
group that was enthusiastic about rebuilding the temple."[16] Kraus here
sees the psalmist as one of those in favor of rebuilding, beset by the
opponents mentioned by Haggai who urged against rebuilding. But we
can identify the psalmist even more precisely. In his comment to
vv. 10-12, Kraus adds: "Perhaps he is one of those 'rigid conserva-
tives' who still flagellate themselves 'for the sake of the house of
Yahweh' (Zech 7:3)."[17] What Kraus reluctantly admits but dismisses
as rigid conservatism describes more accurately who the speaker is
and of what his piety consists. Verses 10-12 portray a person consumed with zeal for the Temple, who weeps and fasts and wears sack-
cloth. He is one of the mourners for Zion mentioned in Isa 61:2-3 and
Zech 7:3-5. His public mourning is the reason he is mocked by his
friends and family and by society at large (from the city leaders to the
drunkards; and, one might add, by Kraus). He may be living in Jerusalem but he feels like he is in exile; he uses terms like "those you
have struck" (v. 27) and "captives" (v. 34) — terms evocative of exile — to refer to himself. He prays that the mockery end, and that the
mockers be punished; and when that occurs he will praise God. But
notice that he will praise God with song that will be more pleasing
than animal sacrifice (vv. 31-32). This is not a rejection of sacrifice,

---

[16] H.-J. Kraus, *Psalms 60–150: A Commentary* (Minneapolis: Augsburg, 1989)
61.

[17] Kraus, *Psalms 60–150*, 62.

but evidence that the Temple has not yet been rebuilt and that therefore animal sacrifice may not be performed.

Mourning for Zion was apparently well-entrenched, at least by a segment of the population (as Isa 61:3 suggests). The question in Zech 7:3-5 is whether this practice should continue when the Temple was rebuilt and about to be rededicated. Our psalmist seems to predate Zechariah and was one of the presumably small number of Mourners for Zion, perceived by some, if we are to believe the psalm, as eccentric in their piety. The speaker will not give up his persistent mourning until God "will deliver Zion and rebuild the cities of Judah" (v. 36) — which may go even beyond the rebuilding of the Temple to include the full restoration of Judah as it was before the destruction. That may have been the hope in the early days of the exile and return. In any case, the last verse is both a hope and a comfort, a way for the psalmist to gain the strength to continue his pious practice in the face of mockery.

PSALM 78: 59-70

Although well-studied over the years, the questions of how and when Israel adopted city laments that were current much earlier in Mesopotamia remain unanswered. Biblical city laments have been preserved only for the destruction of Jerusalem, and most scholars heretofore have assumed that city laments were unknown or unused in Israel prior to 586 BCE. An exception is F. W. Dobbs-Allsopp, who, while not denying the prior existence and probable influence of the Mesopotamian city-lament tradition, has proposed the existence of an Israelite city-lament tradition some two centuries before 586.[18] He bases his case primarily on the ironic use of the lament for cities found in the prophetic oracles against the nations. Secondly, he points to the use of similar language, themes, and imagery in the texts he identifies as influenced by an Israelite city-lament genre, including certain other prophetic passages and parts of a few psalms.[19]

I expressed reservations in the past about Dobbs-Allsopp's interpretation of this evidence in his monograph, and I remain unconvinced that he has proven his case.[20] I will not rehearse my argument

---

[18] First in *Weep, O Daughter of Zion*; and then clarified in "Darwinism, Genre Theory, and City Laments," *JAOS* 120 (2000) 625–30.

[19] See "Darwinism," 627 n. 17.

[20] See my review in *JAOS* 115 (1995) 319.

here, but some comment on his use of the material from psalms is relevant at this point, though admittedly the psalms passages are not central to Dobbs-Allsopp's argument. He cites Psalms 44, 60, 74, 79, 80, and 83 as instances of communal complaints containing formal elements that resemble Lamentations 5 and the Sumerian *balags*. There is no question that Psalms 44, 74, and 79 bear a resemblance to city laments, but since they are, according to most experts, post-586 psalms, they prove nothing about the earlier Israelite use of city laments. Psalms 60, 80, and 83 are more difficult to date, with little agreement among scholars; but at least some scholars date them to exilic or postexilic times. Since it is impossible to prove that these are pre-exilic psalms, they cannot be used with confidence to prove the pre-exilic existence of a city-lament theme or tradition, even if one agrees with the tenuous argument that they were influenced by city laments and that those city laments were Israelite and not Mesopotamian.[21]

In sum, the evidence that Dobbs-Allsopp cites from psalms does not lend support to his argument for a pre-586 Israelite tradition of city laments. However, his recognition of the Jerusalem lament theme in the psalms he discusses strengthens the argument that the theme of destruction and exile is present (in post-586 psalms) more often than is generally acknowledged.

Edward L. Greenstein, following Dobbs-Allsopp's lead, has found the remnant or echo of an ancient city lament for Shiloh in Ps 78:56-64.[22] If he is correct, this would be incontrovertible proof for

---

[21] There are other problems with the way Dobbs-Allsopp invokes formal elements and imagery to support his contention, but I will not address them here since the case can be made on dating alone. Along the same lines but even more peculiar is the dating by C. Bouzard, Jr of Psalms 74 and 79 to before 586, opining that it was not necessary for Jerusalem to have been destroyed in order to write a lament about its destruction, since the model for doing so already existed in Mesopotamian literature (*We Have Heard with Our Ears: Sources of the Communal Laments in the Psalms* [Atlanta: Scholars Press, 1997] 174–200). His aim is to show that the biblical communal laments have as their literary precursors the Mesopotamian *balags* and *er Shemmas*, but he takes his argument beyond the realm of reason here. Why would the loss of Jerusalem be commemorated in the cult before it occurred?

[22] "קינה על חורבן עיר ומקדש בספרות הישראלית הקדומה" [Lament over the destruction of city and temple in ancient Israelite literature]," in Z. Talshir et al. (eds.), *Homage to Shmuel. Studies in the World of the Bible* (Jerusalem: Ben

the early existence in Israel (presumably the 11th century BCE, when Shiloh was destroyed) of a tradition of lamenting destroyed cities or temples. But is this the best interpretation of the passage? Indeed, this passage sounds much like parts of Lamentations, as Greenstein diagrams in detail. Erhard Gerstenberger, also noticing the resemblance to Lamentations, wonders "if the name Shiloh as the sanctuary destroyed (v. 60) is correct. Could it be a pseudonym for Jerusalem?"[23] Gerstenberger's suggestion, however, is hard to maintain in light of the clear rejection of "the tent of Joseph" and the "tribe of Ephraim" in v. 67 and the choice of the tribe of Judah in v. 68. It is a serious misunderstanding of the poem, as I will show below.

The Shiloh sanctuary in v. 60 is not a pseudonym for anything; it stands for itself, as most scholars, including Greenstein, readily see. But, contra Greenstein, one need not see a fragment of an old lament for Shiloh in the adjacent verses. More than likely, a poet living long after Shiloh is describing that sanctuary's demise in the form and style common in his own day (that's why it sounds so much like Lamentations). The "ancient lament" is better explained as an anachronistic retrojection of the city-lament from to a time before that form was used in Israel, not a remnant of an authentic ancient lament for Shiloh. Once again, proof that laments for cities were used in Israel before 586 BCE is not forthcoming.[24] But Ps 78:56-64 does show that the Je-

---

Gurion University Press and Mosad Bialik, 2001) 88–97, esp. 95–97. Greenstein concludes, based on the similarities between Ps 78: 59-63 and Lamentations, that "the descriptions of the destruction at Shiloh ... are taken from a lament that was recited over that national catastrophe or are based on a work of that type" (p. 97, my translation). He references Shmuel Abramsky "חזיקה שבין שילה וירושלים" ["The Connection between Shiloh and Jerusalem"], in *SeferBen-Zion Luria. Studies in the Bible and the History of Israel Presented to Him on his Seventieth Birthday.* (Jerusalem: Kiryat Sefer, 1979) 342, as the only other scholar to identify the Psalm 78 passage as an ancient lament.

[23] *Psalms, Part 2 and Lamentations* (FOTL 15, Grand Rapids: Eerdmans, 2001) 118.

[24] Another attempt to find city-laments before 586 is Leslie J. Hoppe, "Vengeance and Forgiveness: The Two Faces of Psalm 79," in Lawrence Boadt and Mark S. Smith (eds.), *Imagery and Imagination in Biblical Literature. Essays in Honor of Aloysius Fitzgerald, F.S.C.* (CBQMon 32; Washington, DC: The Catholic Biblical Association of America, 2001) 1–22. Hoppe proposes that Psalm 79 existed in a pre-exilic form for use in ceremonies for rededicating the Temple, such as those in the times of Hezekiah and Josiah (cf. 2 Chronicles 29). The psalm was later updated in light of Deuteronomistic thought following the destruction of the

rusalem lament theme had caught on, and could be applied in the exilic and postexilic periods as a literary trope to other destructions as
well.

Psalm 78, a post-586 poem in my view,[25] draws heavily on Deuteronomistic sources (including Deuteronomy, 1 Samuel 4–6, 2 Samuel
7, 1 Kings 8, Jeremiah 7, and Lamentations). It also draws on traditions in Exodus and Numbers and on other biblical traditions), and is
structured on the Deuteronomistic principles of sin and punishment
and of the Davidic covenant. Although it has received its share of
treatment, it has not been adequately interpreted, especially in regard
to its use of Shiloh. The relevant verses are 59-70:

59 God heard and became angry, and he utterly rejected Israel.
60 He abandoned the Shiloh tabernacle (מִשְׁכָּן), the tent where he dwelled
    among people.
61 He gave his power into captivity, and his glory into the hand of the foe.
62 He consigned his people to the sword, and became angry at his inheri-
    tance.
63 Fire consumed its young men, and its maidens sang not.[26]
64 Its priests fell by the sword, and its widows wailed not.
65 The Lord awoke as if asleep, like a warrior dazed from wine.[27]
66 He drove away his foes, to eternal shame he put them.
67 He rejected the tent of Joseph, and the tribe of Ephraim he did not
    choose.

---

Jerusalem Temple. Hoppe's strongest argument is that Ps 79:6-7 appears also in
Jer 10:25, and he concludes that this part of the psalm must have been known in
Jeremiah's time. He also finds linguistic similarities with other pre-exilic pro-
phetic writings. Hoppe seems unaware of Dobbs-Allsopp's work but does cite
Bouzard.

[25] The proposed dates for this psalm range from the Solomonic period to the
postexilic period, with most scholars opting for the period between 722–586 BCE.
Philip D. Stern, "The Eighth Century Dating of Psalm 78 Re-argued," *HUCA* 66
(1995) 41–65, reviews the arguments up till 1995 for dating the psalm and concludes that it comes from the eighth century. Ernst Haag, "Zion und Schilo; Traditionsgeschichtliche Parallelen in Jeremia 7 und Psalm 78," in Josef Zmijewski
(ed.), *Die alttestamentliche Botschaft als Wegweisung. Festschrift für Heinz
Reinelt* (Stuttgart: Katholisches Bibelwerk, 1990) 85–115, dates the core of the
psalm to the time of Josiah, with revisions in the postexilic period. See pp.
110–112.

[26] Traditionally interpreted as referring to their wedding songs.

[27] The word מִתְרוֹנֵן is difficult and the entire image is problematic. For the image, see most recently Andrzej Mrozek, "The Motif of the Sleeping Divinity,"
*Biblica* 80 (1999) 415–19.

68 He chose the tribe of Judah, Mount Zion which he loves.

69 He built his Temple (מִקְדָּשׁוֹ) like an acropolis, like the earth that he founded for eternity.

70 He chose David his servant, he took him from the sheepfolds.

I read the poem as making a sharp distinction between the destiny of the Shiloh sanctuary and the destiny of the Jerusalem Temple. Jeremiah (7:12-14; 26:6, 9) used Shiloh as an example of what would happen to a legitimate sanctuary if the people sinned. He equated the sanctuary at Shiloh with the Temple in Jerusalem because he wanted to equate the fate of Shiloh with the fate of the Jerusalem Temple. The equation is explicit in the wording of 7:12: "my place that is in Shiloh, *where I caused my name to dwell* at first" — note the application to Shiloh of the Deuteronomic phrase designating the Temple. But our psalmist does not want to equate the Jerusalem Temple with the Shiloh sanctuary, because to do so in the post-destruction era would remove all hope of its restoration. The sanctuary at Shiloh, after all, was long gone, never to rise again. Instead, the psalmist reverses Jeremiah's use of Shiloh.[28] He says in v. 60 of the ancient sanctuary וַיִּטֹּשׁ מִשְׁכַּן שִׁלוֹ אֹהֶל שִׁכֵּן בָּאָדָם ("he abandoned the Shiloh tabernacle, a tent where he dwelled among people)." This is an allusion to 2 Sam 7:6, וָאֶהְיֶה מִתְהַלֵּךְ בְּאֹהֶל וּבְמִשְׁכָּן ("I would move around in a tent and in a tabernacle [or a tent-sanctuary])." This is the way God's presence was manifest before the building of the Temple. By invoking this phrase, the psalmist is implying that the Shiloh sanctuary (which was not actually a tent but a permanent structure that housed the portable Ark) is to be seen not only as prior to the Temple (as in Jeremiah) but also as an obsolete form of sanctuary that was appropriately replaced by the Temple. The psalm's characterization of the Jerusalem Temple and the Shiloh tabernacle is quite different from Jeremiah's.

The end of v. 60, "where he dwelled among people," is even more subtle, and is in direct contrast to Jeremiah's Deuteronomic phrase "where I caused my name to dwell at first." The God of Deuteronomic thought is transcendent; he does not dwell among the people but in

---

[28] I have found only one scholar who remarks about the relationship of reversal between the psalm and Jeremiah 7: E. Beaucamp, *Le Psautier. Ps 73–150* (Paris: Gabalda, 1979) 32. Accepting the consensus in his day that the psalm predates Jeremiah, he says: "Le prophète semble vouloir, en l'occurrence, contrer la thèse de notre psaume." He then goes on to say that the psalm's being prior to Jeremiah is "toute relative en somme, puisqu'à l'époque du prophète, l'influence en était encore sensible." Beaucamp does not elaborate further on his observation.

heaven. "Look from your holy abode, from heaven," says Deut 26:15. The location that God chose "to cause his name to dwell there," is not where he lives, but where sacrifices and prayer take place. That God lived in a sanctuary among people is a pre-Deuteronomic idea, found in Exod 25:8; 29:45-46: "I dwell among them/among the Israelites."[29] For a Deuteronomistic psalm like this one to ascribe to Shiloh the notion that it was the site where God "dwelled among people" is to locate Shiloh, theologically speaking, in a more primitive level of religious thought, in terms of its conception of God. Shiloh, says Psalm 78, is not the model to look to in order to understand the future of Jerusalem, for Shiloh was primitive, inferior, and obsolete; it was never intended to be permanent. The Temple in Jerusalem, on the other hand, (associated with the more sophisticated notion of "the place where God causes his name to dwell) was built like the earth itself — established in perpetuity (78:69).

Many commentators see in v. 61-66 a retelling of parts of 1 Samuel 4–6: the capture of the Ark by the Philistines (v. 61), the death of Eli's sons (v. 64), and a hint of the tumors that afflicted the Philistines (v. 66).[30] That may be, but sandwiching the Ark-Shiloh passage is the condemnation of the idolatry of the high places and the rejection of "the tent of Joseph" and "the tribe of Ephraim." God's abandonment of Shiloh follows from his anger at the idolatry of the *bamot* (vv. 58-60), and results in the rejection of the northern kingdom (v. 67). Jeremiah makes a similar link between the destruction of Shiloh and of the northern kingdom, "see what I did to it [Shiloh] because of the evil of my people Israel" (7:12). He does so in order to equate the evil-doing of the northern kingdom and the evil-doing of Judah in his own day, which in both instances leads to the destruction of God's holy place. Jeremiah does not specify the evil, but the psalm recounts it in detail, thereby heaping condemnation on the Northern Kingdom, which is sharply contrasted with Judah: God did not choose the Northern Kingdom, he chose Judah (vv. 67-68). Both the prophet and the psalmist telescope the destruction of Shiloh and of the Northern Kingdom, (perhaps this is a retrojected analogy from the destruc-

---

[29] See Jeffrey Tigay, *Deuteronomy* (Philadelphia: Jewish Publication Society, 1996) xiii; and Moshe Weinfeld, *Deuteronomy 1–11: A New Translation with Introduction and Commentary*, (AB 5; New York: Doubleday, 1991) 37–38.

[30] See, for example, Edward L. Greenstein, "Mixing Memory and Design: Reading Psalm 78," *Prooftexts* 10 (1990) 208.

tion of the Temple and of Judah), but they use the Shiloh-Northern Kingdom link to different ends.[31] Jeremiah wants to warn Judah that its destiny will be the same as that of Shiloh/the Northern Kingdom, while the psalmist wants to prove that the destinies of Shiloh/Israel and Jerusalem/Judah are diametrically opposed. Unlike the provisional tent-tabernacle at Shiloh, says the psalm, the Temple was constructed to be as permanent as the world itself.[32]

Is this simply an extreme form of the concept of the inviolability of Jerusalem in the pre-exilic era, when the thought of the Temple's destruction seemed inconceivable? I don't think so. As I read it, the psalm is better placed in the post-destruction era.[33] The psalm knows the Deuteronomistic traditions, and, it seems to me, knows and is responding to Jeremiah 7.[34] The psalm's silence about the events of 586 does not mean that it was written before they occurred. In fact, the

---

[31] Perhaps this was a popular tradition by the time of Jeremiah, but it is not reflected in 2 Kings 17, the account of the destruction of the northern kingdom, which also resonates in our psalm. On the connections between 2 Kings 17 and Psalm 78 see Stern, "The Eighth Century Dating," 61–62. Note that Stern posits that Psalm 78 was the source and 2 Kings 17 the borrower (from Psalm 78 or similar material). He must opt for this direction to maintain an 8$^{th}$ century date for the psalm.

[32] Samuel E. Loewenstamm, *The Evolution of the Exodus Tradition* (trans. Baruch J. Schwartz; Jerusalem: Magnes, 1992) 75, n. 12, comments on "he built" and compares v. 69 to the prologue of the Code of Hammurabi "which relates how Anu established for Marduk in the midst of Babylon an everlasting kingdom, the foundations of which are as strong as the heavens and the earth. The words *kemo ramim*, lit. 'like the heights,' in v. 69 are a reference to the heavens ..."

[33] The continuities between Psalm 78 and 79, mentioned by Hoppe, "Vengeance and Forgiveness," 16–17, reinforce the idea that both psalms date from the same period. I place them both after 586, although Hoppe prefers a pre-exilic date for both, with postexilic reworking for Psalm 79 (he does not discuss Psalm 78).

[34] This is all the more likely if, as many scholars have concluded, Jeremiah 7 is a Deuteronomistic composition, or a post-destruction Deuteronomistic reworking of an earlier sermon. We might then be seeing evidence of a difference of opinion within the so-called Deuteronomistic school. On the issue of the Deuteronomists, see Linda S. Schearing and Steven L. McKenzie (eds.), *Those Elusive Deuteronomists. The Phenomenon of Pan-Deuteronomism* (Sheffield: Sheffield Academic Press, 1999). Note especially the essay by Thomas C. Römer, "How Did Jeremiah Become a Convert to Deuteronomistic Ideology?" 189–99. On Deuteronomistic influence in Psalms, see the remarks in the same volume by Robert R. Wilson, "Who Was the Deuteronomist? (Who Was Not the Deutero-nomist?): Reflections on Pan-Deuteronomism," esp. 77.

best reading of the psalm takes those events as implied, as understood by the audience, and as the subtext against whose background the poet writes. The "historical review" is selective and is calculated to provide a negative answer to the question: Will history repeat itself? More specifically, will the history of Ephraim be repeated in the case of Judah? This is the "riddle," the wisdom lesson, that the psalm poses to the current generation, who were, like Israel of old, commanded to learn and teach about God's wondrous deeds (vv. 2-4). Those who forgot God's deeds and wonders (v. 11) are the people of Ephraim (v. 9), and they came to a bad end, for they repeated the errors of the ancestors and even went beyond them, adding idolatry to ingratitude and lack of trust.[35] Verse 9 is admittedly a crux, but it may be that we should read the entire psalm as simultaneously the story of the early days of Israel and the story of the destruction of the Northern Kingdom. That seems to be the case in vv. 54-66, as well as in part of the plague section.[36]

Judah, unlike Ephraim, stands as a beacon at the climax of the poem. The history of the ingratitude of premonarchal Israel applies equally to Ephraim and to Judah; but Judah is differentiated from Ephraim in that Judah is not specifically accused of any disobedience, especially idolatry. (As noted above, post-586 psalms about the destruction rarely dwell on Judah's sins.) The psalm, then, offers no explicit (Deuteronomic) reason that Judah should be punished as Ephraim was — as long as she remembers God's great deeds. Moreover, through this poem's instruction, Judah will come to understand that she is the beneficiary of the greatest of God's deeds, the Temple and the Davidic monarchy, permanent by their very nature. This, above all, Judah should never forget. The psalm, then, is not about history per se, nor is it a condemnation of past sins, an anti-northern polemic, an ode to Zion, a call to unite all Israel under the Davidic monarchy and the Jerusalem Temple,[37] or even just a lesson in mem-

---

[35] In addition to other studies of this psalm, see Frank A. Gosling, "Were the Ephraimites to Blame?" *VT* 49 (1999) 505–13.

[36] I take the enemy who was put to eternal disgrace (v. 66) to be Assyria. On the connection between the plagues and the Assyrian conquest of the north see Archie, C. C. Lee, "The Context and Function of the Plagues Tradition in Psalm 78," *JSOT* 48 (1990) 83–89.

[37] Richard J. Clifford, "In Zion and David a New Beginning: An Interpretation of Psalm 78," in B. Halpern and J. D. Levenson (eds.), *Traditions in Transforma-*

ory to motivate the people to maintain their side of the covenant.[38] It is a psalm of restoration — of comfort and hope in the belief that Judah, unlike Ephraim, will not be rejected forever. The psalm paints a picture of the past to give hope for the future. If Psalm 106 draws on earlier traditions to show that they will be repeated,[39] Psalm 78 draws on them to show that they will not.

To return briefly to vv. 56-64 — this is a version of the Jerusalem lament theme, perhaps borrowed from Lamentations or perhaps not. To the extent that this theme had become a conventional literary trope by the time of this psalm, it need not have been borrowed from any specific text. If, as I suggest, it is not an ancient lament but a lament fashioned by the psalmist for this poem, then the use of this conventional trope helps to emphasize the completeness of the destruction of Shiloh in a contemporary poetic way, by using a lament similar to those used for Jerusalem. At the same time, there may be an additional nod to Jeremiah 7:29:

גָּזִּי נִזְרֵךְ וְהַשְׁלִיכִי וּשְׂאִי עַל־שְׁפָיִם קִינָה כִּי מָאַס ה' וַיִּטֹשׁ אֶת־דּוֹר עֶבְרָתוֹ

Cut your hair and throw it away, and raise on the heights a lament, for the LORD has rejected and abandoned the generation that angered him.

Psalm 78:59-60 shares the vocabulary in the words עבר, מאס, נטש ("anger," "to reject," and "to abandon"). It may not be too much to see our psalmist taking Jeremiah's directive to lament but applying it to Shiloh instead of to Jerusalem — another way of deflecting onto Shiloh all of the negative attributes and experiences that the psalmist wants to distance from Jerusalem. It is not Jerusalem that needs lamenting, says the psalm, it is Shiloh — for it is Shiloh that God has rejected and abandoned because it angered him. Note that in this Shiloh lament there is no physical ruin and no exiled people, only suf-

---

*tion* (Winona Lake, IN: Eisenbrauns, 1981) 121–41.

[38] So Greenstein, "Mixing Memory," 201. Greenstein's analysis is very good but does not go far enough.

[39] Psalm 106 presents a history of Israel's sins that culminates in the sin of idolatrous practices that polluted Israel and its land and led to the destruction and exile. The catalogue of sins is meant to show how forbearing and forgiving God has been throughout the past and, by implication, how forgiving he will continue to be, since he maintains his covenant and is merciful. The past history of God and Israel is the model for the future; the exile of 586, says this psalm, is no different from earlier punishments, after which God took Israel back into his good graces.

fering and death, the cessation of individual and communal life (male and female, young and old, priests who engage in cultic praise and widows who are the public lamenters). The rhetorical effect of this mini-lament is to say that no trace remains of all the people of Shiloh and/or of the Northern Kingdom. Moreover, the phrase "its widows did not wail" implies that Shiloh's destruction was never commemorated in a lament (other than the lament the poet supplies here). Shiloh, in contrast to Jerusalem, had no survivors to lament its destruction, and without survivors there is no hope for restoration.

## CONCLUDING COMMENT

I have touched on a few ways in which the psalms address the theoretical and practical problems of exile. There is, of course, much more to be said on this topic, both within the Psalms and beyond, where the theme of exile and return is prominent.[40] In the literature of exile, the destruction of Jerusalem and the exile became the subject of lament and complaint par excellence, and the hope for the restoration became the symbol of the continuity of God's special protection of Israel in the future. The cases illustrated here show that more nuanced interpretations of the psalms in their historical and theological contexts will lead to more meaningful readings of the psalms and a better understanding of the times from which they emerged.[41]

## SELECT BIBLIOGRAPHY

Abramsky, Shmuel. "הזיקה שבין שילה וירושלים" ["The Connection between Shiloh and Jerusalem"], in *Sefer Ben-Zion Luria. Studies in the Bible and the History of Israel Presented to Him on His Seventieth Birthday* (Jerusalem: Kiryat Sefer, 1979) 335–55. [Hebrew]

Bar-Efrat, S. "Love of Zion; A Literary Interpretation of Psalm 137," in M.

---

[40] See, for example, M. Knibb, "The Exile in the Literature of the Intertestamental Period," *Heythrop Journal* 17 (1976) 253–72; D. Rom-Shiloni, "God in Times of Destruction and Exile," in J. Scott (ed.), *Exile. Old Testament, Jewish, and Christian Conceptions* (Leiden: Brill, 1997); Rodney A. Werline, *Penitential Prayer in Second Temple Judaism. The Development of a Religious Institution* (Atlanta: Scholars Press, 1998); Marc Wischnowsky, *Tochter Zion. Aufnahme und Überwindung der Stadtklage in den Prophetenschriften des Alten Testaments* (Neukirchen-Vluyn: Neukirchener, 2001).

[41] Work on this paper was completed while I was a Fellow at the Center for Advanced Judaic Studies, University of Pennsylvania. I thank the Center and its library staff for facilitating my research.

Cogan, B. L. Eichler, and J. H. Tigay (eds.), *Tehillah le-Moshe: Biblical and Judaic Studies in Honor of Moshe Greenberg* (Winona Lake, IN: Eisenbrauns, 1997) 3–11.

Bayer, B. "The Rivers of Babylon," *Ariel* 62 (1985) 43–52.

Beaucamp, E. *Le Psautier. Ps 73–150* (Paris. Gabalda. 1979).

Clifford, R. J. "In Zion and David a New Beginning: An Interpretation of Psalm 78," in B. Halpern and J. D. Levenson (eds.), *Traditions in Transformation* (Winona Lake, IN: Eisenbrauns, 1981) 121–41.

Dobbs-Allsopp, F. W. "Darwinism, Genre Theory, and City Laments," *JAOS* 120 (2000) 625–30.

—. *Weep, O Daughter of Zion: A Study of the City-Lament Genre in the Hebrew Bible* (Rome: Editrice Pontificio Istituto Biblico, 1993).

Füglister, N. "Psalm LXXVIII [78]: Der Rätsel Lösung?" in J. A. Emerton (ed.), *Congress Volume, Leuven, 1989* (VTSup 43; Leiden: Brill, 1991) 264–97.

Greenstein, E. "Mixing Memory and Design: Reading Psalm 78," *Prooftexts* 10 (1990) 197–218.

Greenstein, E. "קינה על חורבן עיר ומקדש בספרות הישראלית הקדומה" ["Lament over the destruction of city and temple in ancient Israelite literature"], in Z. Talshir et al. (eds.), *Homage to Shmuel. Studies in the World of the Bible* (Jerusalem: Ben Gurion University Press and Mosad Bialik, 2001) 88–97. [Hebrew]

Haag, E. "Zion und Schilo. Traditionsgeschichtliche Parallelen in Jeremia 7 und Psalm 78," in Josef Zmijewski (ed.), *Die alttestamentliche Botschaft als Wegweisung. Festschrift für Heinz Reinelt* (Stuttgart: Katholisches Bibelwerk. 1990) 85–115.

Hartberger, B. *"An den Wassern von Babylon ..."* (Frankfort am Main: Peter Hanstein, 1986).

Knibb, M. "The Exile in the Literature of the Intertestamental Period," *Heythrop Journal* 17 (1976) 253–72.

Lee, A. C. C. "The Context and Function of the Plagues Tradition in Psalm 78," *JSOT* 48 (1990) 83–89.

Loewenstamm, S. E. *The Evolution of the Exodus Tradition* (Jerusalem: Magnes, 1992).

Ogden, G. S. "Prophetic Oracles against Foreign Nations and Psalms of Communal Lament: The Relationship of Psalm 137 to Jeremiah 49:7-22 and Obadiah," *JSOT* 24 (1982) 89–97.

Rom-Shiloni, D. *God in Times of Destruction and Exile* (Dissertation, Hebrew University: Jerusalem, 2000). [Hebrew, with English summary]

—. "God in Times of Destruction and Exile," in J. Scott (ed.), *Exile. Old Testament, Jewish, and Christian Conceptions* (Leiden: Brill, 1997).

Savran, G. "How Can We Sing a Song of the Lord?" The Strategy of Lament in Psalm 137," *ZAW* 112 (2000) 43–58.

Schreiner, J. "Geschichte als Wegweisung; Psalm 78," in Josef Zmijewski (ed.), *Die alttestamentliche Botschaft als Wegweisung. Festschrift für Heinz Reinelt* (Stuttgart: Katholisches Biblewerk, 1990) 307–328.

Scott, J. M., (ed). *Exile. Old Testament, Jewish, and Christian Conceptions* (JSJSup 56; Leiden: Brill, 1997).

—. *Restoration. Old Testament, Jewish and Christian Perspectives* (JSJSup 72; Leiden: Brill, 2001).

Stern, P. D. "The Eighth Century Dating of Psalm 78 Re-argued," *HUCA* 66 (1995) 41–65.

Weber, B. "Psalm 78; Geschichte mit Geschichte deuten," *TZ* 56 (2000) 193–214.

Werline, R. A. *Penitential Prayer in Second Temple Judaism. The Development of a Religious Institution* (Atlanta: Scholars Press, 1998).

Wischnowsky, M. *Tochter Zion. Aufnahme und Überwindung der Stadtklage in den Prophetenschriften des Alten Testaments* (Wissenschaftliche Monographien zum Alten und Neuen Testament, 89; Neukirchen-Vluyn: Neukirchener, 2001).

Zakovitch, Y. "על נהרות בבל: תהלים קלז—זיכרון בצל הטראומה" ["'By the Rivers of Babylon': Psalm 137 — Memory in the Shadow of Trauma"], in Z. Talshir et al. (eds.), *Homage to Shmuel. Studies in the World of the Bible* (Jerusalem: Ben Gurion University Press and Mosad Bialik, 2001) 184–93.

—. "ויבחר את שבט יהודה... ויבחר בדוד עבדו תהילים עח. מקורות, מבנה, משמעות ומגמה" ["He chose the tribe of Judah ... He chose David his servant. Psalm 78. Sources, Structure, Meaning and Purpose"], in H. Baron and O. Lipshitz (eds.), *David King of Israel Alive and Enduring?* (Jerusalem: Simor, 1997) 117–202. [Hebrew]

# NON-ACROSTIC ALPHABETIC PSALMS

DAVID NOEL FREEDMAN AND DAVID MIANO

## STRUCTURE OF THE ALPHABETIC PSALMS

One of the sad consequences of the long transmission of the Hebrew text is the loss of the original stichometry of its songs and poems. That much of the Bible's poetry was copied as if it were prose has resulted in the obscuration of the original arrangement of poetic lines. This has given analysts much over which to ruminate. Of all the types of poems in the Hebrew Bible, the alphabetic acrostic has a structure that is easiest to determine.[1] Because the lines of these poems are organized and arranged by means of the normal sequence of the letters in the Hebrew alphabet, students can determine line and stanza length with a considerable degree of objectivity and accuracy. Although various methods of measuring quantity in line length are employed by scholars today, we find that no matter what system is used, there is variation in line and stanza length among the poems of this type. The basic pattern is a poem of 22 lines or bicolons with an average syllable count of 8 in each colon ($8 + 8 = 16$ syllables per bicolon) and 3 or 4 stresses per colon ($3 + 3 = 6$ stresses, or $4 + 4 = 8$ stresses, per bicolon), if we use the usual (Ley-Budde-Sievers) method of counting stresses.[2] However, the majority of the alphabetic acrostics in the Hebrew Bible deviates from this norm, exhibiting variations, adaptations, and elaborations of the basic structure. Some poems follow a 9-syllable / 3- or 4-stress design, while others follow a 10-syllable / 4-stress design. While some researchers prefer to emend the text so as to make these poems conform to the "ideal" paradigm, careful study has shown that such deviations are intentional and that the poets were not content to follow the simplest pattern so strictly.[3]

Alphabetic poems may be divided into the following classes:

---

[1] For an introduction to acrostics, see W. G. E. Watson, *Classical Hebrew Poetry: A Guide to Its Techniques* (Sheffield: JSOT Press, 1984) 190–200.

[2] D. N. Freedman, "Acrostics and Metrics in Hebrew Poetry," *HTR* 65 (1972) 367–92.

[3] See D. N. Freedman and J. C. Geoghegan, "Alphabetic Acrostic Psalms" in *Psalm 119: The Exaltation of Torah* (Winona Lake, IN: Eisenbrauns, 1999) 1–23.

1. *Standard Alphabetic*: 22 lines (bicolons) of approximately 16 syllables each (8 per colon); no examples from the Bible are perfect, but the following fit into this class while exhibiting some acceptable deviations: Proverbs 31 (contains one tricolon), Psalms 25 and 34 (omit the *waw* line and add a *pe* line at the end; the former also contains two tricolons) and Psalm 145 (contains one tricolon and averages 18 syllables per bicolon instead of 16).

2. *Half-line Alphabetic*: 22 lines (colons) of approximately 8 syllables each (1 colon per letter of the alphabet); for example, Psalms 111 and 112.

3. *Double-line Alphabetic*: 22 stanzas (tetracolons) of approximately 32 syllables each (8 per colon); no examples from the Bible correspond perfectly, but Psalm 37 fits into this class while exhibiting some acceptable deviations (it contains one bicolon and one hexacolon, which end up evening each other out).

4. *Qina Alphabetic*: 22 lines (bicolons) of approximately 13 syllables each (8 in the first colon, 5 in the second). Conceptually speaking, this derives from the standard form, except that the final stress in the second colon and its corresponding unstressed syllables are purposely omitted. The result is an unbalanced rhythm, for example, Lamentations 1–4.

Psalm 119, the greatest of all alphabetic acrostics, stands by itself, as it is made up of 22 stanzas, each consisting of eight standard bicolons.[4]

In the past, attention has been drawn to the fact that other poems of a non-acrostic nature conform to the structure of the alphabetic acrostic.[5] Some poems from this group include Lamentations 5, Psalms 33 and 94, and several examples from the Book of Proverbs (especially from chaps. 1–9, such as 2, 5, 8:1–11, 12–21, 22–31, 32–36 and 9:1–18). All of them build on the basic 22-line foundation, but the

---

[4] For an analysis of this poem, see D. N. Freedman, *Psalm 119: The Exaltation of Torah* (Winona Lake, IN: Eisenbrauns, 1999) 25–86.

[5] P. W. Skehan, "The Structure of the Song of Moses in Dt 32,1-43," *CBQ* 13 (1951) 153–63; "Strophic Patterns in the Book of Job," *CBQ* 23 (1961) 125–42; P. W. Skehan and A. A. Di Lella, *The Wisdom of Ben-Sira* (AB 39; New York: Doubleday, 1987) 74; Watson, 199; D. N. Freedman, "Acrostic Poems in the Hebrew Bible: Alphabetic and Otherwise," *CBQ* 48 (1986) 408–31; "Proverbs 2 and 31: A Study in Structural Complementarity," in M. Cogan et al. (eds.), *Tehillah le-Moshe: Biblical and Judaic Studies in Honor of Moshe Greenberg* (Winona Lake, IN: Eisenbrauns, 1997) 47–55.

initial letters in each line do not form the alphabet in sequence. The designation "non-alphabetic acrostic" has been used for these poems in the past;[6] however, we now prefer to call them "non-acrostic alphabetic." They are alphabetic in that they are structured according to the number of letters in the Hebrew alphabet, but they are not acrostic in that none of them, as far as we can tell, carries a set of letters that form a word or phrase or familiar sequence of letters.

## NON-ACROSTIC ALPHABETIC POEMS

In the present study, we wish to draw attention to a few more examples of the non-acrostic alphabetic poem from the Psalter. In regard to counting syllables, we will continue to employ the method used by David Noel Freedman over the years. While the Masoretes no doubt faithfully reproduced the traditional pronunciation of the biblical text in their day, their system of vocalization includes some postbiblical changes and non-biblical forms, which do not correctly reflect the actual morphology and phonology of the biblical period. Since our objective is to recover and reproduce the syllable count as it existed in classical times, we must make some modifications to the received text according to our knowledge of Biblical Hebrew in the historic period.

However, since we are only concerned with syllables and stresses at this point, we will make adjustments only when we feel the syllable count would be affected. Thus we treat masculine singular segholate formations as single syllables and do not count secondary vowels, especially the *hatefs* associated with laryngeals (including the so-called furtive *patah*). The "resolution" of original diphthongs will be reversed (for example, words like *mayim* will be restored to *maym*, *mawet* to *mawt*, and *bayit* to *bayt*). Contractions and mergings of syllables will also be rejected. When there is some uncertainty as to the original syllable count (as is often the case with 2nd masc. sing. and 3rd fem. sing. pronominal suffixes or with the question of whether a *shewa* is vocalized or not), we will provide two numbers separated by a slash, the lower syllable count followed by the higher. In the end we will end up with a syllable range rather than an exact figure. We can never pretend to recover fully the original vocalization, but we should try our best to come as close to the practice of the poet as possible.

---

[6] D. N. Freedman, "Acrostic Poems in the Hebrew Bible," *CBQ* 48 (1986) 408–31; "Proverbs 2 and 31," (1997) 47–55.

FIVE CASE STUDIES: PSALMS 103, 58, 20, 105, AND 100

Psalm 103 has the earmarks of a standard alphabetic poem. It has 22 lines, corresponding to the number of letters in the Hebrew alphabet. Its syllable and stress count also conforms to the pattern. The poem has three tricolons, an acceptable variation that is seen also in certain acrostic poems.

*Psalm 103*

Syllable Count:

| Line | A-colon | B-colon | C-colon | Total |
|------|---------|---------|---------|-------|
| 1 | 8 | 9 | | 17 |
| 2 | 8 | 9 | | 17 |
| 3 | 8/9 | 8/9 | | 16/18 |
| 4 | 7/8 | 10/11 | | 17/19 |
| 5 | 7 | 8/9 | | 15/16 |
| 6 | 7 | 9 | | 16 |
| 7 | 8 | 10 | | 18 |
| 8 | 7 | 6 | | 13 |
| 9 | 5 | 7 | | 12 |
| 10 | 10 | 13 | | 23 |
| 11 | 9 | 8 | | 17 |
| 12 | 8 | 10 | | 18 |
| 13 | 7 | 8 | | 15 |
| 14 | 7 | 8 | | 15 |
| 15 | 7 | 8 | | 15 |
| 16 | 10 | 10 | | 20 |
| 17 | 7 | 8 | 9 | 15 + 9 = 24 |
| 18 | 7 | 12 | | 19 |
| 19 | 9 | 9 | | 18 |
| 20 | 8 | 9 | 8 | 17 + 8 = 25 |
| 21 | 9 | 9 | | 18 |
| 22 | 8 | 8 | 8 | 16 + 8 = 24 |
| *Totals*: | 170/72 | 197/200 | 25 | 367/372 (+ 25 = 392/397) |
| *Averages*: | 7.73–7.82 | 8.95–9.09 | 8.3 | 16.68–16.91 |

We find that the syllable count for this psalm is not far from what we would expect. In the A-colon, the number of syllables averages very close to 8. The B-colon average is slightly higher at around 9. As a result, the average line length of close to 17 syllables (not counting the C-colons) is part way between an 8 syllable per colon standard and a 9 syllable per colon standard. The unbalanced syllable count may be intentional. This psalm is comparable to Psalm 145, which contains a tricolon and whose syllable count is between 395 and 416 syllables.[7] None of the deviations present exceeds the range of deviation that we find in the known alphabetic acrostic poems, so we may view it as a member of the non-acrostic alphabetic group.

The next two psalms we present — 58 and 20 — could well be classified as non-acrostic half-line alphabetic poems. They each consist of 22 colons (or, alternately, 11 lines of the standard bicolon length):

### Psalm 58

Syllable Count:

| Line | A-colon | B-colon | Total |
|------|---------|---------|-------|
| 1 | 9 | 10 | 19 |
| 2 | 8/9 | 11[8] | 19/20 |
| 3 | 7/8 | 9 | 16/17 |
| 4 | 10/11 | 9 | 19/20 |
| 5 | 11 | 8 | 19 |
| 6 | 11 | 10/11 | 21/22 |
| 7 | 13 | 10 | 23 |
| 8 | 8 | 6/7 | 14/15 |
| 9 | 11 | 11 | 22 |
| 10 | 9 | 10 | 19 |
| 11 | 11 | 10 | 21 |
| *Totals*: | 108/111 | 104/106 | 212/217 |
| *Averages*: | 9.82–10.09 | 9.45–9.64 | 19.27–19.73 |

### Psalm 20

Syllable Count:

| Line | A-colon | B-colon | Total |
|------|---------|---------|-------|
| 1 | 8/9 | 10 | 18/19 |
| 2 | 6/7 | 7/8 | 13/15 |
| 3 | 6/7 | 8/9 | 14/16 |
| 4 | 6/9 | 8/9 | 14/18 |
| 5 | 8/10 | 9 | 17/19 |
| 6 | 5 | 5/6 | 10/11 |
| 7 | 5/7[9] | 8 | 13/15 |
| 8 | 8 | 7/8 | 15/16 |

---

[7] Freedman, *Psalm 119*, 20.

[8] Reading באריץ with the B-colon. (If we saw this as a "Janus" construction, באריץ would sit *between* the two colons. The resulting scansion would be perfectly balanced [9 + 2 + 9 = 20].)

[9] Cf. note 7ª in *BHS*.

| 9 | 10 | 12/14[10] | 22/24 |
| 10 | 9 | 10 | 19 |
| 11 | 7 | 8 | 15 |
| *Totals*: 78/88 | | 92/99 | 170/187 |
| *Averages*: 7.09–8.00 | | 8.36–9.00 | 15.45–17.00 |

The standard total syllable count for a half-line alphabetic is 176, and Psalm 20 fits neatly into the expected norm. Its low count matches precisely the syllable counts for Psalms 111 and 112, whose structures are similar. The syllable count for Psalm 58 (212–217 syllables) is considerably higher than that of Psalm 20 (170–187 syllables), averaging closer to ten syllables per colon than the standard eight.[11] The 11-line structure and the balanced rhythm are indicators that it is to be regarded as a member of the alphabetic group, but is the longer line length within the acceptable limits of deviation? It appears to be another type of poem that adheres to the alphabetic line count, but has a norm of 10 syllables per line and a stress count of 4:4, rather than 3:3.[12]

We could well ask if the syllable and stress counts are necessarily significant and whether they ought to be used as components of the benchmark for alphabetic poems. It may be that they mean nothing, and the true criterion is simply the number of lines or stanzas in a poem. Most of the alphabetic acrostics have similar line lengths, but not all, and although we should expect that the non-acrostic alphabetics would approach an established norm, there may be more than one norm.

The third psalm considered here appears to conform to the pattern of the double-line alphabetic poem. It has the requisite 22 tetracolons (or alternately, 44 bicolons), plus one additional bicolon, which separates the two halves of the poem. The addition of an extra line is a device we find in acrostic alphabetic poems such as Psalms 25 and 34.

---

[10] Cf. note 8ª in *BHS*.

[11] It may be that in Psalm 58 a syllable was lost at the beginning of line 3 (v. 4; see note 8ª in *BHS*), and perhaps a word in line 10 (v. 11; see Greek). In the latter case, the word פשעים may have been lost as a result of haplography caused by the repetition of two letters (-פ, ם-) in the sequence (נקם [פַשְׁעָים] פַעֲמָיו). Restoration of these would bring the total syllable count closer to an expected 220 for a poem of eleven lines, with 10 syllables per line.

[12] An interesting and unusual feature of this poem is the chiasm of divine epithets in the middle colon (אֱלֹהִים and יְהוָה).

*Psalm 105*

Syllable Count:

| Line | A-colon | B-colon | Total |
|------|---------|---------|-------|
| 1 | 10 | 10 | 20 |
| 2 | 7 | 8 | 15 |
| 3 | 8 | 8/9 | 16/17 |
| 4 | 7 | 7 | 14 |
| 5 | 10 | 8 | 18 |
| 6 | 6/7 | 7 | 13/14 |
| 7 | 7 | 7 | 14 |
| 8 | 8 | 7 | 15 |
| 9 | 8 | 8 | 16 |
| 10 | 9/10 | 8 | 17/18 |
| 11[13] | 6/8 | 6 | 12/14 |
| 12 | 7/8 | 6/7 | 13/15 |
| 13 | 9 | 8 | 17 |
| 14 | 8 | 9 | 17 |
| 15 | 7/8 | 8/9 | 15/17 |
| 16 | 8 | 6/7 | 14/15 |
| 17 | 6/7 | 6 | 12/13 |
| 18 | 6 | 6/8 | 12/14 |
| 19 | 6 | 8/9 | 14/15 |
| 20 | 8 | 8 | 16 |
| 21 | 7 | 8 | 15 |
| 22 | 7 | 7 | 14 |
| 23 | 8 | 7 | 15 |
| 24 | 7 | 8 | 15 |
| 25 | 8/9 | 8 | 16/17 |
| 26 | 6 | 8/9 | 14/15 |
| 27 | 8/9 | 7 | 15/16 |
| 28 | 6 | 8 | 14 |
| 29 | 8 | 7 | 15 |
| 30 | 8 | 6/7 | 14/15 |
| 31 | 7 | 7 | 14 |
| 32 | 7 | 7 | 14 |
| 33 | 9 | 8 | 17 |
| 34 | 7 | 6 | 13 |
| 35 | 8 | 8 | 16 |
| 36 | 8 | 6 | 14 |

---

[13] We divide the line as follows: לֵאמֹר לְךָ אֶתֵּן אֶת־אֶרֶץ / כְּנָעַן חֶבֶל נַחֲלַתְכֶם ("Saying, 'To you I give the land / Canaan is the allotment of your inheritance'").

| 37 | 9/10 | 7/8 | 16/18 |
|----|------|-----|-------|
| 38 | 7 | 8 | 15 |
| 39 | 7 | 7/8 | 14/15 |
| 40 | 7/8 | 7 | 14/15 |
| 41 | 8 | 8 | 16 |
| 42 | 8 | 6 | 14 |
| 43 | 8 | 7/8 | 15/16 |
| 44 | 9 | 9 | 18 |
| 45 | 8 | 7 | 15 |

*Totals*:  341/352    331/343    672/695
*Averages*: 7.57–7.82    7.36–7.62    14.93–15.44

The syllable count for this psalm is slightly less than the standard eight, but the writer may have been deliberately steering a middle course between a 7-syllable colon and an 8-syllable colon. Regardless, the poem still falls into the general parameters for an alphabetic composition.

The final psalm we will consider is an alphabetic that not only contains lines that are half the standard length, but whose total line count is similarly half the standard. For this reason, it does not fall neatly into one of our four main categories. However, it is comparable to the acrostic in Nahum 1, which is, complete or not, also half the standard length.

*Psalm 100*

Syllable Count:

| Line | Total |
|------|-------|
| 1 | 9 |
| 2 | 8/9 |
| 3 | 8/9 |
| 4 | 9 |
| 5 | 9 |
| 6 | 7 |
| 7 | 8 |
| 8 | 8 |
| 9 | 8 |
| 10 | 9 |
| 11 | 9 |

*Total*:  92/94
*Average*: 8.36–8.55

The total syllable count is slightly higher than the expected 88 but is not far from the mark. The middle line of the poem has the shortest syllable count of them all, but it may be defective. The Greek witness of Codex Alexandrinus adds "and we" to the beginning of the colon, which represents Hebrew ואנחנו and makes for a smoother reading. The occurrence of the word אנחנו at the end of the preceding line is usually understood to play double duty to complete the sense of line 6. However, it could also have been the cause of a scribal oversight, as the repetition of five letters would easily induce parablepsis.[14] Moreover, the reading at Psalm 79:13, which is almost identical, carries the missing ואנחנו. This adds four syllables to the line and brings the total count for the poem up to 96/98. It falls three syllables short (at most) and one syllable short (at least) from an expected symmetrical 99. The phrase ואנחנו עמו is the centerpiece of the poem, both in meaning and in structure, as exactly 20 words both precede and follow it.[15]

CONCLUSION

The purpose of this study was to demonstrate that the alphabetic pattern is not confined to the acrostic poems of the Bible but carries over into other poems. They may be identified by the number of lines they contain, i.e., the total number of lines in a non-acrostic alphabetic poem should be a multiple of 11. In some cases, it may be one line short or one line too many. Syllable and stress counts most frequently average eight syllables/three stresses per line, but variants occur—eight syllables/four stresses per line, nine syllables/three or four stresses per line and ten syllables/four stresses per line. Although lack of precision will not allow us to make a definite conclusion in this matter, it is possible that the poets deliberately designed the poems to carry a total number of syllables equal to the total number of lines multiplied by 8, 9, or 10. We would therefore expect syllable counts of 88, 99, or 110 for half-line alphabetics, 176, 198, or 220 for standard alphabetics, and 352, 396, or 440 for double-line alphabetics. Another possibility is that some poems may be deliberately unbalanced, halfway between and 8 and 9 syllables per colon (that is, 17 syllables per bicolon) or between 9 and 10 syllables per colon (that is, 19 syllables per bicolon). Many more poems in the Bible are sure to fit into the alphabetic pattern. The non-acrostic alphabetic poem, al-

---

[14] Cf. D. M. Howard, Jr., *The Structure of Psalms 93–100* (Winona Lake, IN: Eisenbrauns, 1997) 95.

[15] Howard, *Structure of Psalms 93–100*, 96.

though certainly posterior to the acrostic type and based upon it, out-
numbers its precedent. Its popularity in comparison arose no doubt
because it was much simpler to construct. Blank verse in English by
Henry Howard, Earl of Surrey, in the 16ᵗʰ century and made popular
by John Milton in *Paradise Lost* (1667), caught on for much the same
reason. By freeing itself of its rhyming pattern, this new form of iam-
bic pentameter became more easily adapted to the various levels of
English speech and allowed more elbow room for composers. The
non-acrostic alphabetic poem in Hebrew likewise is less artificial and
obtrusive than the acrostic and grants greater flexibility in composition. In our minds, those loyal to the old acrostic form even in later
periods were, to borrow a phrase, "carried away by custom, but much
to their own vexation, hindrance, constraint to express many things
otherwise, and for the most part worse, than else they would have expressed them."[16]

## SELECT BIBLIOGRAPHY

Freedman, D. N. "Acrostic and Metrics in Hebrew Poetry," *HTR* 65 (1972)
    367–92.

—. "Acrostic Poems in the Hebrew Bible: Alphabetic and Otherwise," *CBQ* 48
    (1986) 408–31.

—. "Proverbs 2 and 31: A Study in Structural Complementarity," in M. Coogen et
    al (eds.), *Tehillah le-Moshe: Biblical and Judaic Studies in Honor of Moshe
    Greenberg* (Winona Lake, IN: Eisenbrauns, 1997) 47–55.

—. *Psalm 119: The Exaltation of Torah* (Winona Lake, IN: Eisenbrauns, 1999).

Freedman, D. N. and J. C. Geoghegan. "Alphabetic Acrostic Psalms" in *Psalm
    119: The Exaltation of Torah* (Winona Lake, IN: Eisenbrauns, 1999) 1–23.

Howard, D. M., Jr. *The Structure of Psalms 93–100* (Winona Lake, IN: Eisen-
    brauns, 1997).

Skehan, P. W. "The Structure of the Song of Moses in Dt 32, 1–43," *CBQ* 13
    (1951) 153–63.

—. "Strophic Patterns in the Book of Job," *CBQ* 23 (1961) 125–42.

Skehan, P. W. and A. A. Di Lella. *The Wisdom of Ben-Sira* (AB 39; New York:
    Doubleday, 1987).

Watson, W. G. E. *Classical Hebrew Poetry: A Guide to Its Techniques* (Sheffield:
    JSOT Press, 1984).

---

[16] John Milton, "The Verse" (Preface to *Paradise Lost*).

# MOWINCKEL'S ENTHRONEMENT FESTIVAL: A REVIEW

J. J. M. ROBERTS

## AN OUTLINE OF MOWINCKEL'S THEORY

Sigmund Mowinckel, the illustrious Norwegian student of the famous German form critic Hermann Gunkel, first put forward his theory of the enthronement festival in 1922.[1] In contrast to Gunkel, who still held to the primarily Protestant view of classical liberalism that true piety was individual piety and thus tended to be dismissive of communal expressions of piety, Mowinckel, influenced by the new interest in primitive religion and by the stirrings of the liturgical renewal movement, was far more open to the genuineness and importance of communal piety. Thus Mowinckel regarded the Psalms as primarily the product of the communal, mainly pre-exilic cult, not as late, post-exilic expressions of individual piety based on earlier, no longer preserved, cult Psalms.

He also argued that the form critical approach of Gunkel needed to be supplemented by what he called a cult functional approach, since Psalms of different types could be used at different points in the same ritual of worship. Beginning with the classical enthronement Psalms celebrating Yahweh's kingship — Psalms 47, 93, 95, 96, 97, 98, 99, 100 — and supplementing them with a number of other Psalms that are linked to these by shared motifs and vocabulary — Psalms 8, 15, 24, 29, 33, 46, 48, 50, 66A, 75, 76, 81, 82, 84, 87, 114, 118, 132, 149,

---

[1] Sigmund Mowinckel, *Psalmenstudien II: Das Thronbesteigungsfest Jahwäs und der Ursprung der Eschatologie* (Kristiania, Norway: J. Dybwad, 1922). Mowinckel republished all six volumes of his *Psalmenstudien* in two volumes (vol. 1 = Buch I–II; vol. 2 = Buch III–VI) in 1966 with corrections and annotations (Amsterdam: P. Schippers, 1966), and any references to his work in this paper will be to this later edition. In the foreword to this edition he cites his many later works on the Psalms in which he modified or revised many of the ideas he had expressed in his original work (the page is unnumbered, but follows vi). Among his later works, one should especially mention *The Psalms in Israel's Worship I–II* (New York and Nashville: Abingdon, 1962), a translation (by D. R. AP-Thomas) and revision of his Norwegian work *Offersang og Sangoffer* (Oslo: H. Aschehoug, 1951).

Exod 15:1-18 — Mowinckel reconstructed an annual cult festival involving the procession of the ark and a symbolic re-enactment of the enthronement of Yahweh as the cultic background to these Psalms. On the basis of parallels with the New Year's Festival in Babylon, late prophetic material associating the fall festival with Yahweh's kingship (e.g. Zech 14:16), and later Mishnaic traditions, Mowinckel reconstructed his festival as a seven-day autumn New Year's festival that later disintegrated into the three separate celebrations of New Year's Day, the Day of Atonement, and the Feast of Tabernacles. According to Mowinckel, the ritual re-enactment of Yahweh's enthronement took place on a particular day during this extended festival. In elaborating on the different ritual moments during the festival, Mowinckel also drew on many other Psalms that he associated with the festival in a more secondary fashion.

In order to sustain his reconstruction, it was important to Mowinckel to date the enthronement Psalms to the pre-exilic period when the royal cult was still an experienced fact of religious life. He rejected both the older historical interpretations of these Psalms and the eschatological interpretation favored by his teacher Gunkel as inadequate. Against the eschatological interpretation Mowinckel stressed two points:

1. These Psalms give no indication of awaiting a distant future.

2. They are lacking any feature of prophetic style.

In short, they are not prophetic oracles but statements of ritual experience. Moreover, the ritual formula מלך יהוה or יהוה מלך should be translated "Yahweh has become king," not "Yahweh reigns" or "Yahweh is king." The expression reflects a cultic re-enactment of Yahweh's taking of the throne.

## RESPONSES TO MOWINCKEL'S THEORY

Few scholarly publications have ever had either the immediate impact or the lasting influence on the field as Mowinckel's theory. In one of the earliest reviews of his work, Hans Schmidt accepted Mowinckel's theory of an enthronement festival as the background to the enthronement Psalms with great enthusiasm:[2]

---

[2] Hans Schmidt, "Rezension über: Sigmund Mowinckel, *Psalmenstudien II*: Thronbesteigungsfest Jahwäs und der Ursprung der Eschatologie," *TLZ* 4/5 (1924) 77–81. This review was reprinted along with a number of other important

> We stand here, as I believe, before a worthwhile discovery rich with con-
> sequences. It is as though scales fall from one's eyes, when one reads the
> aforementioned Psalms in the light of this new discovery.... In short, the
> significance of this book goes far beyond what an exegetical study di-
> rected to a relatively short section would at first lead one to expect.[3]

Schmidt's enthusiasm was echoed to one degree or another by many other adherents to Mowinckel's theory, but there were other scholars who were just as enthusiastic in their rejection of his theory. What no one in Psalms study could do, however, was ignore Mowinckel. His work required a response.

Gunkel, Mowinckel's teacher, reluctantly adjusted his views in response to his student's work. He grudgingly admitted that there was an enthronement festival for Yahweh in pre-exilic Israel, but, according to Gunkel, this was only introduced late in the monarchy under the influence of the Babylonian New Year's festival and the enthronement festivals associated with human Israelite kings. There were enthronement hymns composed for this festival of Yahweh's enthronement, and Deutero-Isaiah was influenced by them, but he transformed them into eschatological hymns. None of these cultic enthronement hymns are preserved in the Psalter; the enthronement hymns preserved there are all secondary eschatological hymns influenced by Deutero-Isaiah.[4] In short, Gunkel was unwilling to allow a genuinely cultic hymn into his spiritualized and eschatologized Psalter.

In contrast, Artur Weiser, while he rejected the notion of a separate enthronement festival of Yahweh,[5] argued that the enthronement of Yahweh was a single scene within the whole drama of the autumn festival of Covenant Renewal.[6] Although he regarded the celebration as more genuinely Israelite and less dependent on foreign models than he assumed Mowinckel thought, Weiser nonetheless accepted an early pre-exilic cultic celebration of Yahweh's accession to the throne. Note

---

essays in Peter H. A. Neumann (ed.), *Zur neueren Psalmenforschung* (Wege der Forschung 192; Darmstadt: Wissenschaftliche Buchgesellschaft, 1976) 55–61.

[3] *Zur neueren Psalmenforschung*, 55, 57.

[4] Hermann Gunkel and Joachim Begrich, *Einleitung in die Psalmen: Die Gattungen der religiösen Lyrik Israels* (Göttingen: Vändenhoeck & Ruprecht, 1933; 2nd ed. 1966) 100–116.

[5] Artur Weiser, *The Psalms: A Commentary* (OTL; Philadelphia: Westminster, 1962 [trans. from the 5th ed. of *Das Alte Testament Deutsch* 14/15 (Göttingen: Vandenhoeck & Ruprecht, 1959)]) 62.

[6] Weiser, *The Psalms*, 62–63, 378, 617.

his comment on Ps 47:8: "The psalm pictures the King-God as he ascends his heavenly throne and sits down in his holy majesty to signify
that he has entered upon his reign as King in the sight of the whole
world."[7] Weiser recognized that such a cultic act did not necessarily
imply that Yahweh had ceased to be king prior to that cultic act: "The
comparison of v. 8 with vv. 2 and 7 shows that the ceremony has in
mind the Yahweh who is already the King, whose kingship, however,
gains by his cultic enthronement a renewed actual significance for the
present and for the future."[8]

Hans Joachim Kraus was also compelled by Mowinckel's work to
recognize that the enthronement Psalms implied an enthronement of
Yahweh in some sort of cultic ceremony. After a lengthy discussion of
the expression יהוה מלך, he concluded that the expression meant,
"Yahweh has become king," and therefore justified the designation
"enthronement Psalms."[9] Because Mowinckel's treatment of
2 Samuel 6, 7 and 1 Kings 8, in the light of numerous Psalms, made it
clear that some sort of regular festival celebration took place in preexilic Jerusalem involving the procession of the ark into Jerusalem
and the installation of Yahweh in the temple,[10] Kraus, in order to
counter Mowinckel's theory, created a rival festival that he named the
royal Zion festival. This festival, which took place in the fall, celebrated Yahweh's choice of both Zion and David, but had nothing to
do with an enthronement of Yahweh.[11] Psalms 2, 24, 72, 78, 84, 87,
89, 122, 132 may be associated with this festival, but none of the classical enthronement Psalms were connected with it, despite the allusions to some of them in 1 Chronicles 16.[12] It was only with the exile,

---

[7] Weiser, *The Psalms*, 378.

[8] Weiser, *The Psalms*, 378, n. 1.

[9] Hans-Joachim Kraus, *Die Königsherrschaft Gottes im Alten Testament* (BHT
13; Tübingen: Mohr Siebeck, 1951) 3–9. Note especially his comment on p. 5:
"Und doch sind es vier gewichtige Gründe, die uns dazu veranlassen, an dem traditionellen Verständnis der Formel יהוה מלך = 'Jahwe ist König geworden!'
festzuhalten und damit die Existenz von 'Thronbesteigungspsalmen' unbedingt zu
bejahen."

[10] Heinz Kruse ("Psalm cxxxii and the Royal Zion Festival," *VT* 33 [1983]
279–97) has rejected the need for reconstructing any festival, but his comment
that the whole theory of the festival hinges on the interpretation of three verses of
Psalm 132 (p. 280) shows that he simply has not understood the discussion.

[11] Kraus, *Die Königsherrschaft Gottes*, 84–86.

[12] Kraus, *Die Königsherrschaft Gottes*, 46–85.

the loss of the Davidic kingdom, and the influence of the Babylonian culture that Second Isaiah began to speak of Yahweh coming again as king to his people. Under Second Isaiah's influence, in the post-exilic period the old royal Zion festival was transformed into a celebration of Yahweh's kingship, and it is in this transformed post-exilic festival that the enthronement Psalms have their *Sitz im Leben*.[13] Later, in his commentary on the Psalms, Kraus changed his mind and argued that the expression יהוה מלך in "Pss 93:1; 96:10; 97:1; 99:1 must be translated, 'Yahweh is king!'"[14] Only Ps 47:8 with its different word order מלך יהוה remained, according to Kraus' new view, as a proclamation of an actual enthronement. There could not be an enthronement of Yahweh in OT worship, according to Kraus, because: (1) there was no divine image to be carried and the ark itself was God's throne, (2) Israel rejected any mythicization of Yahweh, and (3) Yahweh's kingship was unchangeable and continuous.[15] Psalm 47, however, still implies an enthronement of Yahweh, and that bothers Kraus so much that he offers several different possibilities for explaining it, including his older view that it represents a product of the post-exilic cult influenced by Second Isaiah.[16] Since he has rejected any idea of Yahweh's enthronement in the other classical enthronement Psalms, Kraus is now free to date some of them in the pre-exilic period (Psalm 93 "in the early time of the kings;"[17] Psalm 99 "in the time of the kings").[18] As a result of this shift in his opinion, Kraus' older view of a post-exilic transformation of the old royal Zion festival into a celebration of Yahweh's kingship has lost much of its coherence.

J. J. Stamm, who summarized a quarter century of Psalms research in 1955, offers a good review of the other responses to Mowinckel's work.[19] According to Stamm,[20] Mowinckel's theory was accepted,

---

[13] Kraus, *Die Königsherrschaft Gottes*, 119–43.

[14] Hans-Joachim Kraus, *Psalms 1–59: A Commentary* (Minneapolis: Augsburg, 1988) 87.

[15] Kraus, *Psalms 1–59*, 87.

[16] Kraus, *Psalms 1–59*, 88–89.

[17] Hans-Joachim Kraus, *Psalms 60–150: A Commentary* (Minneapolis: Augsburg, 1989) 233.

[18] Kraus, *Psalms 60–150*, 269.

[19] Johann Jakob Stamm, "Ein Vierteljahrhundert Psalmenforschung," *Theologische Rundschau* 23 (1955) 1–68, esp. 47–50.

even if with some reservations, by Böhl,[21] Pedersen,[22] Bentzen,[23] Engnell,[24] Johnson,[25] and Widengren.[26] Stamm also mentions Humbert,[27] Leslie,[28] and von Rad[29] among those who accepted some form of Mowinckel's enthronement festival.[30] It was rejected, but with hardly any argument,[31] by Calès,[32] Herkenne,[33] Kissane,[34]

---

[20] Stamm, "Ein Vierteljahrhundert Psalmenforschung," 47.

[21] F. M. Th. Böhl, in F. M. Th. Böhl and A. van Veldhuisen (eds.), *De Psalmen I–II* (Tekst en Uitleg. Praktische Bijbelverklaring; Groningen-Batavia, 1946–1947); and in J. A. vor der Hake (ed.), *Psalmen* (Commentar op de Heilige Schrift; Amsterdam, 1956) 397–466. For a more detailed discussion of Böhl's changing views, see E. Lipinski, "Psaumes de la royauté de Yahwé," in Robert De Langhe (ed.), *Le Psautier: Ses origines. Ses problèmes littéraires. Son influence. Études présentées aux XIIe Journée Bibliques (29–31 août 1960)* (OBL 4; Louvain: Institut Orientaliste, 1962) 212–15.

[22] Johannes Pedersen, *Israel, its Life and Culture* III–IV (London: Oxford University Press, 1926).

[23] Aage Bentzen, *Forelaesninger over Indedning til de gesammelttestamentlige salmer* (Copenhagen: Gad, 1932) 183; *Introduction to the Old Testament* I–II (2nd ed.; Copenhagen: Gad, 1952) 1.146–67, 2.163–70.

[24] Ivan Engnell, *Studies in Divine Kingship in the Ancient Near East* (Uppsala: Almqvist & Wiksells, 1943) 71–96, 174–77.

[25] Aubrey R. Johnson, "The Role of the King in the Jerusalem Cultus," in S. H. Hooke (ed.), *The Labyrinth: Further Studies in the Relation between Myth and Ritual in the Ancient World* (London: SPCK, 1935) 71–111. See also Aubrey R. Johnson's later works, *Sacral Kingship in Ancient Israel* (Cardiff: University of Wales Press, 1955) 53–93; and *The Cultic Prophet and Israel's Psalmody* (Cardiff: University of Wales Press, 1979) 91.

[26] Geo Widengren, *Sakrales Königtum im Alten Testament und im Judentum* (Stuttgart: Kohlhammer, 1955) 62–79.

[27] Paul Humbert, "La relation de Genèse 1 et du Psaume 104 avec la liturgie du nouvel-an Israëlite" (Extrait de la Revue d'Histoire de de Philosophie Religieouses; Stasbourg, 1935).

[28] Elmer A. Leslie, *The Psalms: Translated and Interpreted in the Light of Hebrew Life and Worship* (New York and Nashville: Abingdon-Cokesbury, 1949) 55–89.

[29] Stamm cites a passage of Gerhard von Rad found in *Theologisches Wörterbuch zum Neuen Testament* I (Stuttgart: W. Kohlhammer, 1957) 567, but one can also find von Rad's views expressed in his *Old Testament Theology, I: The Theology of Israel's Historical Traditions* (New York: Harper, 1962) 362–64.

[30] Stamm, "Ein Vierteljahrhundert Psalmenforschung," 47, n. 1.

[31] Stamm, "Ein Vierteljahrhundert Psalmenforschung," 48.

Nötscher,[35] Podechard,[36] Schulz,[37] Tournay,[38] Barnes,[39] Eerdmans,[40] Eissfeldt,[41] de Groot,[42] Pfeiffer,[43] Sellin-Rost,[44] and Buttenweiser.[45] The only scholars to make a sustained argument against Mowinckel's reconstruction were Pap,[46] Snaith,[47] Aalen,[48] and Kraus,[49] and of

---

[32] Jean Calès, "La doctrine des Psaumes," *Nouvelle Revue Théologique* 67 (1953) 561–90; *Le livre des Psaumes* I–II (Paris: Beauchesne, 1936).

[33] Heinrich Herkenne, *Das Buch der Psalmen* (Die Heilige Schrift des Alten Testaments; Bonn: Peter Hanstein, 1936).

[34] Edward J. Kissane, *The Book of Psalms* I–II (Dublin: Browne and Nolan, 1953/54) 1.xxi.

[35] Friedrich Nötscher, *Die Psalmen* (Die Heilige Schrift in deutscher Übersetzung, Echter Bibel; Würzburg: Echter, 1947).

[36] Emanuel Podechard, *Le Psautier I, Psaumes 1–75* (Bibliothèque de la Faculté Catholique de Théologie de Lyon, vols. III and IV; Lyon: Facultés Catholiques, 1949).

[37] Alphons Schulz, "Kritisches zum Psalter," *Alttestamentliche Abhandlungen* 12/1 (Münster: Aschendorff, 1932); "Psalmen Fragen," *Alttestamentliche Abhandlungen* 14/1 (Münster: Aschendorff, 1940).

[38] Raymond J. Tournay, *Les Psaumes* (La Sainte Bible traduite en francais sous la direction de l'Ecole Biblique de Jérusalem; Paris: Cerf, 1950).

[39] W. Emery Barnes, *The Psalms: With Introduction and Notes*, I–II (London: Methuen, 1931).

[40] Bernardus Dirks Eerdmans, "Essays on Masoretic Psalms," *OTS* 1 (1942) 224–30.

[41] Otto Eissfeldt, *Einleitung in das Alte Testament* (Tübingen: Mohr Siebeck, 1934) 114–37, 497–505.

[42] Johannes de Groot, *In de Binnenkamer van het Oude Testament, uitleg van tien Psalmen* (Nijkerk: Callenbach, 1939).

[43] Robert Henry Pfeiffer, *Introduction to the Old Testament* (New York and London: Harper and Brothers, 1941 [2nd ed., 1948]) 619–44.

[44] Ernst Sellin, *Einleitung in das Alten Testament* (6th ed., Leipzig: Quelle & Meyer, 1933) 128–35; (7th ed., 1935) 126–34; (8th ed., edited by L. Rost, 1950) 147–55.

[45] Moses Buttenwieser, *The Psalms, Chronologically Treated With a New Translation* (Chicago: University of Chicago Press, 1938).

[46] László István Pap, *Das israelitsche Neujahrsfest* (Diss. theol. Utrecht; Kampen: Kok, 1933).

[47] Norman H. Snaith, *The Jewish New Year Festival* (London: SPCK, 1947).

[48] Sverre Aalen, *Die Begriffe "Licht" und "Finsternis" im Alten Testament, im Spätjudentum und im Rabbinismus* (SNVAO II Hist.-Filos. Kl. No. 1; Oslo: J. Dybwad 1951).

those, according to Stamm, the only one to make a persuasive case was Kraus.[50]

One may question whether Kraus has made a persuasive case, a point to which we will return, but Stamm's observation that most of those who rejected Mowinckel's theory failed to engage it seriously is certainly correct. This failure has also been noted by Peter Welten.[51] He characterized the history of research on the issue as divided into two phases, a productive phase associated with Gunkel, Mowinckel, and Schmidt, and a later phase of processing. According to Welten, "the first phase was marked by a certain delight in hypotheses, an intensive involvement with the newly discovered Ancient Near Eastern textual material, and a wide outlook incorporating the Near East and the Old and New Testaments."[52] In contrast, the second phase was marked by incomplete argumentation, an unhelpful reticence to engage the Near Eastern material, and an attitude he well characterizes as "a certain horror at the boldness of the fathers."[53]

THE ARGUMENTS AGAINST MOWINCKEL'S THEORY

The main arguments used against Mowinckel's reconstruction were the following:

1. The Old Testament does not mention a New Year's enthronement festival, so such a festival is an unattested, unproven, and unnecessary hypothetical reconstruction.

2. If one accepted Mowinckel's reconstruction, it would imply that Israel shared the cyclic, mythical outlook of other Ancient Near Eastern religions, that they saw Yahweh as a dying and rising God, and that they believed that there was a time when Yahweh was not yet ruler of the universe.

3. Syntactically, the Hebrew expressions מלך יהוה and יהוה מלך cannot mean "Yahweh has become king," but must mean "Yahweh reigns" or "It is Yahweh who is king."

---

[49] Hans-Joachim Kraus, *Die Königsherrschaft Gottes im Alten Testament* (Beiträge zur historischen Theologie 13; Tübingen: Mohr Siebeck, 1951).

[50] Stamm, "Ein Vierteljahrhundert Psalmenforschung," 48–52.

[51] "Königsherrschaft Jahwes und Thronbesteigung: Bemerkungen zu unerledigten Fragen," *VT* 32 (1982) 297–310.

[52] "Königsherrschaft Jahwes und Thronbesteigung," 297.

[53] The German original reads "ein gewisser Horror vor der Kühnheit der Väter" ("Königsherrschaft Jahwes und Thronbesteigung").

4. Mowinckel tries to explain too many Psalms of widely varied form and content against the background of this single cultic festival. With this last argument, which was also made against Weiser's covenant renewal festival, many of Mowinckel's defenders would agree. The theory cannot explain all the Psalms, and there must be some limit to what Psalms can be cited in evidence for the various movements and motifs in the course of the festival. Moreover, shared motifs are not sufficient evidence for the exclusive use of a particular Psalm in this particular cultic context.

The other arguments, however, are far less compelling. As Mowinckel stated clearly in *Psalmenstudien II* and has reiterated numerous times since, it is not a question "'of a new festival unattested in the sources' but of a little regarded or totally ignored aspect of the well known and well attested autumn and New Year's festival, the feast of tabernacles."[54] Moreover, the apologetic fear associated with the second objection is largely misplaced. It goes well beyond anything Mowinckel actually claimed, and our increased knowledge of the Babylonian New Year festival shows that, even with regard to this Near Eastern parallel, one cannot legitimately speak of a dying and rising God.[55] Welton has already noted this point, and his conclusion is worth quoting in detail:

> That means that, even if Israel's enthronement Psalms with great probability have their *Sitz im Leben* in the context of the autumn New Year festival, the question about Yahweh's being and becoming king can be asked quite free and unconnected from the question about the dying and rising God.[56]

A large number of scholars have written on the syntax of the Hebrew expressions יהוה מלך and מלך יהוה,[57] but even this grammatical dis-

---

[54] From the *Vorwort* to the 1966 re-edition of Mowinckel's *Psalmenstudien*.

[55] For the best recent treatment of the Mesopotamian material, see Mark E. Cohen, *The Cultic Calendars of the Ancient Near East* (Bethesda, MD: CDL Press, 1993) 400–453. One should also consult Alasdair Livingstone, *Court Poetry and Literary Miscellanea* (State Archives of Assyria III; Helsinki: Helsinki University Press, 1989) 82–91, nos. 34–35, and the literature cited there.

[56] Welton, "Köningsherrschaft Jahwes," 307.

[57] L. Koehler, "Jahwäh Mālāk," *VT* 3 (1953) 188–89; J. Ridderbos, "Jahwäh Malak," *VT* 4 (1953) 87–89; A. E. Combs, *The Creation Motif in the "Enthronement Psalms"* (Ph.D. Diss., Columbia University, 1987) 34–38, 81–82, 107–108, 219–21; D. Michel, "Studien zu den sogenannten Thronbesteigungs-psalmen," *VT* 6 (1956) 40–68; A. Gelston, "A Note on יהוה מלך," *VT* 16 (1966) 507–12; J. H.

cussion has with few exceptions been overly influenced by the apologetic desire to rescue Yahweh from any suspicion of being a cyclic, dying and rising God.[58] Those who reject Mowinckel's reconstruction, and even some who accept it, often refer to D. Michel's study as though he had demonstrated once and for all that neither expression should be translated ingressively with Mowinckel as "Yahweh has become king."[59] Brettler, however, though he rejects Mowinckel's theory, has clearly demonstrated, following Ulrichsen,[60] how methodologically flawed Michel's syntactical study was.[61] The debate over the proper translation of these expressions in the enthronement Psalms still remains unresolved.

In some ways, however, the debate is chasing after a red herring.[62] Those who reject Mowinckel's translation seem to assume that such a translation would imply that Yahweh's reign was neither eternal nor continuous, that such a festal shout would imply a cessation of Yahweh's rule for a brief period each year — but this would appear to be a rationalistic misunderstanding of cultic language.[63] The yearly cultic

---

Ulrichsen, "JHWH *mālāk*: einige sprachliche Beobachtungen," *VT* 27 (1977) 361–74; K. A. Kitchen, *Ancient Orient and Old Testament* (Downers Grove, IL: Inter Varsity Press, 1966) 102–106; H.-J. Kraus, *Worship in Israel: A Cultic History of the Old Testament* (Richmond, VA: John Knox, 1966) 203–208; *Psalmen* (5th ed., 2 vols; BKAT 15/1–2; Neukirchen-Vluyn: Neukirchener, 1978) 94–108, 817; E. Lipinski, *La royauté de Yahvé dans la poésie et le culte de l'ancien Israël* (2ed ed., Brussels: Academie voor Wetenschappen, Letteren en Schone Kunsten van Belgie, 1968) 336–91.

[58] See Welton, "Köningsherrschaft Jahwes," 302: "Even with D. Michel one cannot be entirely free of the impression that he is led in his formcritical as well as in his grammatical discussion by the prejudgment that the conclusion must be avoided that it is said of Yahweh, 'he has become king.'"

[59] See, for example, David M. Howard, Jr., *The Structure of Psalms 93–100* (BJS 5; Winona Lake, IN: Eisenbrauns, 1997) 36.

[60] J. H. Ulrichsen, "JHWH *mālāk*:," 361–74.

[61] Marc Zvi Brettler, *God is King: Understanding an Israelite Metaphor* (JSOTSup 76; Sheffield: JSOT Press, 1989) 142–44.

[62] Cf. Ben C. Ollenburger, *Zion, The City of the Great King: A Theological Symbol of the Jerusalem Cult* (JSOTSup 41; Sheffield: JSOT Press, 1987) 28.

[63] Note the very recent discussion of Marvin E. Tate, *Psalms 51–100* (WBC 20; Dallas: Word, 1990) 472. Tate is clearly not impressed by Howard's claim that Michel's argument against Mowinckel's translation, "Yahweh has become king," has settled the question. He points to very serious problems in Michel's treatment of 1 Kgs 1:11, 18: "The durative aspects of Adonijah's kingship could

celebration of Yahweh's primeval enthronement no more implies the yearly cessation of Yahweh's rule than the yearly cultic cry of the Easter vigil, "The Lord is risen, the Lord is risen indeed!" implies a yearly death and resurrection of Jesus. Both cries do suggest a cultic representation of the primeval or historical event, however. Brueggemann expresses this central point in Mowinckel's argument quite well:

> Mowinckel's argument (which I support and urge) is that the ontology need not be denied, but must be bracketed out if we are to understand the intent of the psalm, which focuses on the action in this moment. Such bracketing out of ontological matters is in fact what we do if we are serious about liturgy. Liturgy is not an appeal to any enduring ontology, but is an enactment of a fresh drama in this moment.
>
> Dramatically, experientially, realistically, this    liturgic formula, "the Lord reigns," is not a remembering, but is an enactment, a making so. If this moment of announcement is not a real enactment, then in fact there is no news, but only reiteration, the unveiling of what has always been.[64]

In short, Kraus and Michel's objections to translating יהוה מלך as "Yahweh has become king" are, at best, inconclusive. Kraus's objections to the assumed illegitimate mythicization of Yahweh in Israelite worship is unconvincing, and his view that the "unchanging and continuous" rule of Yahweh excludes a cultic celebration of Yahweh's accession to the throne is simply wrong. Moreover, one should note that Yahweh's choice of Zion and David, which Kraus sees as the

---

hardly be the major subject of Nathan (v. 11) and Bathsheba (v. 18). They are concerned with the fact that Adonijah has seized power and *become* king. The context of Ps 47:9[8] may favor the translation 'God has become king' rather than 'God is king.'"

But Tate also cites with approval Mowinckel's claim "that the argument for a shout of homage does not depend on the translation." Tate says, "Mowinckel ... is surely justified in arguing that the treatment of יהוה מלך as a cry of homage in the sense that 'Yahweh has become king,' or 'Yahweh reigns (anew)' does not destroy the idea that Yahweh always *is* king. Cultic terminology should not be pushed into such rationalistic modes of thinking. The dramatic nature of worship does not require an exact metaphysical delineation of words in liturgie." Tate adopts "Yahweh reigns" for his translation, but he understands it "in an acclamatory sense which celebrates the repeatedly new enthronement of Yahweh."

[64] Walter Brueggemann, *Israel's Praise: Doxology against Idolatry and Ideology* (Philadelphia: Fortress, 1988) 34. Cf. his later comments in *Theology of the Old Testament: Testimony, Dispute, Advocacy* (Minneapolis: Fortress, 1997) 655, esp. n. 18.

points celebrated in his pre-exilic royal Zion festival, presupposes the imperial kingship of Yahweh. Psalm 2, for instance, which Kraus still dates to the era of the Jerusalem monarchy in Judah,[65] presupposes that Yahweh is the real emperor, that the Davidic king is his human vice-regent, and that the rebellious nations are his legitimate vassals. It is worth noting that in the prologue to the Code of Hammurabi, the elevation of the god Marduk to kingship is linked to the elevation of his human king and his royal city to imperial prominence.[66] Moreover, Psalm 24, according to Kraus, celebrates Yahweh as king in a festal ritual of the monarchic period involving a procession of the ark into the sanctuary.[67]

If this is part of the royal Zion festival, then it certainly celebrated the kingship of Yahweh, not just the kingship of his Davidic agent. Kraus's objection that one could not ritually represent Yahweh's accession to his throne because of the lack of any cult object representing Yahweh is just silly. The ark is often seen as a cultic symbol representing the presence of Yahweh,[68] and the carrying of this object into the temple and the placing of it under the giant cherubim throne in the inner sanctuary,[69] where Yahweh was visualized as invisibly enthroned with his feet hanging down to rest on the ark as his footstool,[70] would be quite sufficient to symbolize Yahweh mounting his throne.

Despite the weaknesses and inconclusiveness of Michel's and Kraus's arguments against Mowinckel's thesis, however, their relatively wide-spread acceptance seems to have resulted in Mowinckel's work on the enthronement Psalms being increasingly ignored, particularly in Germany. Bernd Feininger's review of German Psalms scholarship during the years 1970–1980 makes hardly any mention of

---

[65] Kraus, *Psalms 1–59*, 126.

[66] See my discussion of this point in "God's Imperial Reign According to the Psalter," *Horizons in Biblical Theology* 23/2 (2001) 211–21, esp. 212–14 and the literature cited there.

[67] Kraus, *Psalms 1–59*, 312.

[68] Num 10:35; 14:44-45; 1 Sam 4:4-6; 2 Sam 11:11; 15:29; Ps 132:8.

[69] For the cherub throne, see 1 Kgs 6:23-28; for the placement of the ark under this throne, see 1 Kgs 8:6-7.

[70] For the ark as Yahweh's footstool, see 1 Chron 28:2; Pss 99:5; 132:7; Lam 2:1. For this visualization of Yahweh with his feet hanging down from the fifteen-foot high cherub throne, see Isa 6:1.

Mowinckel or his enthronement festival,[71] though one should note that Odil Hannes Steck still argues for an early pre-exilic festival of Yahweh's enthronement in which Yahweh's taking possession of Zion was re-enacted in the cult by a procession of the ark.[72] The recent tendency to concentrate on the literary shaping of the Psalter as a whole rather than on the meaning of individual Psalms has also directed attention away from the kind of issues raised by Mowinckel, since the process of final literary shaping is normally assigned to the post-exilic, second temple period. The new historical skepticism of the minimalists along with their penchant for the late dating of everything in the Old Testament has also had some impact on Psalm studies, where the very late dating of even royal Psalms is no longer as unfashionable as it once was.

As regards the enthronement Psalms, their late dating simply continues the tradition of Gunkel, Kraus, and others who saw an influence of Second Isaiah on them. Welton, who in other respects is quite critical of Kraus, accepts Kraus's original very late dating of the enthronement Psalms, and sees the enthronement festival reflected in them as a product of the post-exilic cult.[73] Such a late date raises a number of very serious questions, however. Mowinckel's critics attacked him because his enthronement festival is nowhere specifically mentioned in any of the lists of cultic festivals (Exod 23:14-17; 34:18-24; Leviticus 16; 23:4-44; Deut 16:1-17). His response to this critique was that Yahweh's enthronement was just one aspect of the fall festival in which New Year's, atonement, and the feast of booths were all part of the same extended festival. If one assumes an early monarchical festival that later disintegrated into several separate festivals, the lack of any specific mention of the enthronement festival in these lists is reasonable. If, however, one dates the creation of the enthronement festival to the post-exilic period, the lack of any mention of it in relatively late texts like Lev 23:4-44 is far more problematic.

Erhard S. Gerstenberger has recently argued for the late dating of these Psalms on the basis that the early Israelite monarchy had no models for imperialistic expectations and that there was no time dur-

---

[71] Bernd Feininger, "A Decade of German Psalm-Criticism," *JSOT* 20 (1981) 91–103.

[72] Odil Hannes Steck, *Friedensvorstellungen im alten Jerusalem* (Theologische Studient 111; Zürich: Theologischer Verlag, 1972) 15 n. 16.

[73] Welton, "Köningsherrschaft Jahwes," 297–310.

ing the reigns of David and Solomon for such an imperialistic ideology to develop.[74] He says,

> Only such states or national alliances could seriously claim world leader-
> ship which outranked possible competitors by a large margin. Israel has
> hardly had opportunities to cultivate such ambitions on account of her own
> royal history .... Not even the Davidic-Solomonic 'reign' was strong,
> large, and enduring enough to give rise to any true imperial notions.[75]

This argument, however, is baseless.

As far as imperial models go, Israel originated in the shadow of
Egypt, the greatest imperial power of the second millennium BCE. The
rulers of many former city states incorporated in the Israelite kingdom, including its capital Jerusalem, had carried on extensive diplomatic correspondence with the Egyptian imperial court. The northern
border of the state claimed for David and Solomon extended into the
region vigorously contested between Egypt and the other major imperial power of the late second millennium BCE, the Hittite empire. Damascus, which was subject to David (2 Sam 8:6), had fallen to the
Hittites after the climactic battle between Ramses II and the Hittite
emperor Muwattalis at Qadesh, a site that lay only a few miles north
of Lebo-Hamath (1 Kgs 8:65).[76] Moreover, the celebrated parity
treaty between Ramses II and Hattusilis III, which eventually followed that battle and required extensive diplomatic exchanges between the Hittite court and the Egyptian court, would hardly have escaped the attention of their vassals in Palestine, Syria, and the Lebanon. Unless one holds to the antiquated notion that the Israelites had
totally exterminated all the nobility of the former Canaanite city states
and all the scribal families that had served them, it is hard to believe
the Davidic court would have been ignorant of Egypt's former power
and of the imperialistic ideology associated with it — particularly
since Egypt's imperial pretensions continued well into the time of
David and Solomon, and Solomon is reported to have had diplomatic
relations with Egypt (1 Kgs 3:1).

---

[74] E. Gerstenberger, "'World Dominion' in Yahweh Kingship Psalms: Down
to the Roots of Globalizing Concepts and Strategies," in: *Horizons in Biblical
Theology* 23/2 (2001) 192–210.

[75] "'World Dominion,'" 208.

[76] How many miles depends on whether one locates Lebo-Hamath at Riblah or
at Lebweh. See the discussion in Tom F. Wei, "Hamath, Entrance of," in *The An-
chor Bible Dictionary* (New York: Doubleday, 1992) 3.37.

As to the strength, size, and endurance of the united monarchy, several comments are in order. According to the biblical material, David's conquests of all the surrounding states (2 Samuel 8) and Solomon's continued dominion over them, at least early in his reign (1 Kgs 5:1), means that during the period of their rule they outranked any possible competitors by a large margin. They had no real rival between the Euphrates and the Egyptian frontier. Each had a long reign of some 40 years (1 Kgs 2:11; 11:42), making a combined reign of approximately 80 years for the united monarchy, or 73 years if one subtracts the 7 years of David's early reign in Hebron. But the whole issue of how long the Davidic-Solomonic empire existed is irrelevant to the question of whether the Davidic court created an imperial ideology. Contrary to Gerstenberger's claim that an empire must endure a long time before it can create an imperial ideology, the examples from the Ancient Near East show that such ideologies were created relatively quickly during the reign of the king who first achieved imperial status. Sargon the Great, a pretender to the throne who founded the dynasty of Akkad, conquered the Sumerian south, and continued his conquests to the north and west, already had an imperial ideology in place during his lifetime, even though his control over the south was seriously threatened by revolt on at least one occasion. Hammurabi, though not the founder of his dynasty, was the first king of Babylon to achieve imperial status. He only overcame his major rivals in Larsa, Eshnunna, Ekallatum, and Mari late in his reign, but despite that fact, Hammurabi's imperial ideology was firmly in place prior to his death, as the prologue to his famous law code makes abundantly clear. Imperial ideologies are created in the glow of imperial success; their creators do not wait generations to see if the success lasts. Parenthetically, one should note that the ideology of the Third Reich boasted of a thousand year reign, though Hitler's state lasted only slightly more than ten years.

Finally, one should note that Gerstenberger has Israel adopting an imperialistic religious ideology precisely in a period of Israel's most abject weakness. As far as I can see, this is absolutely without parallel in the Ancient Near East.

One should also note that there is no convincing linguistic evidence for the late dating of the classical enthronement Psalms. Even Kraus backed away from a late dating of Psalms 93 and 99, and hedges con-

siderably on Psalms 45 and 95. Brettler[77] and Howard,[78] two of the
more recent scholars to study the enthronement Psalms, neither of
whom accept an enthronement festival, nonetheless agree in dating
these Psalms to the pre-exilic period. Howard, using dating criteria derived from Cross, Freedman, Andersen, and others, dates Psalm 93 "to
the earliest stages of Hebrew poetic writing, probably the 10th century;" for Psalm 94 he suggests a pre-exilic date is plausible; Psalm 95
he regards as "most likely preexilic" and possibly early monarchial;
Psalm 96 he treats as probably pre-exilic but post-9th century; Psalm
97 is probably pre-exilic; Psalm 98 "could conceivably have come
from either the premonarchic, the late preexilic, or the exilic period;"
Psalm 99 is monarchic; and "a preexilic date for Psalm 100 is a reasonable guess."[79] Brettler argues that of Psalms 96, 97, and 99, not
one exhibits "signs of post-exilic Hebrew diction," and points out that
"with one exception, all the psalms that according to [Hurvitz's][80]
linguistic criteria are clearly post-exilic are found in the fifth book of
the Psalter (107–150)." [81] He therefore assumes these psalms are pre-
exilic and "do not show the influence of Deutero-Isaiah."[82] Brettler
appears to hold the same view with regard to Psalm 47, though his
comments on it are less specific.[83]

Brettler argued against the cultic interpretation of these psalms because they call for the participation of foreigners in the Jerusalem
temple cult. Since there is very limited evidence for foreign participation in the Temple cult, according to him, "the lack of a contingent of
non-Israelites at the Temple presents a serious problem for our understanding of the pre-exilic Psalms 96, 97, and 99 as 'enthronement
psalms.'"[84] Instead of these psalms representing a cultic reality, Brettler sees them "as a (wishful) *projection* into the present of a period in
which God is sovereign, and his sovereignty is recognized by all, al-

---

[77] Mark Zvi Brettler, *God is King*.

[78] David M. Howard, Jr., *Structure of Psalms 93–100*.

[79] Howard, *Structure of Psalms 93–100*, 184–92.

[80] Avi Hurvitz, *The Transition Period in Biblical Hebrew: A Study in Post-Exilic Hebrew and Its Implications for the Dating of Psalms* (Jerusalem: Bialik Institute, 1972 [Hebrew]).

[81] Brettler, *God is King*, 148.

[82] Brettler, *God is King*, 148.

[83] Brettler, *God is King*, 156.

[84] Brettler, *God is King*, 149.

lowing Israel to live in peace and prosperity."[85] This writer finds Brettler's objection to the cultic interpretation very problematic and his rival interpretation quite flimsy. It is not at all clear that one should expect the historical books or the priestly works to have any great interest in mentioning the presence of foreign dignitaries at Israelite festivals, though if David, Solomon, and their successors ever ruled as suzerains over the surrounding states, as the historical books claim, then one must assume that their vassals brought tribute up to Jerusalem and that their presence in the royal capital was noted.[86] On the analogy with other Near Eastern states, one might also expect representatives of these vassals to be present on such occasions as the dedication of a new temple whether such presence is noted in the historical books or not. But quite apart from this issue, one must question whether the cultic interpretation of these psalms necessarily requires the actual physical presence of foreign vassals. No one, to my knowledge, has ever suggested that the appeal to the foreign gods to worship Yahweh (Pss 29:1; 47:7; 97:7) required that images of these deities be present in the cult. Nor does the appeal to heaven, earth, the sea, mountains, all that is in them, and all the trees of the forest (Ps 96:11-12) require the presence of all sea and mountain creatures in the temple for one to assume that this psalm was sung in a cultic ritual. A fictive audience is just as possible in a cultic ritual as it is in a prophetic oracle, and prophetic oracles are full of fictive audiences.

## CONCLUDING COMMENT

It should be clear from the preceding discussion that this writer still regards a modified version of Mowinckel's theory of an autumn enthronement festival as offering the most adequate interpretative context for understanding both the classical enthronement Psalms and a large number of other Psalms. In reaching this conclusion, I find myself in total agreement with all the points articulated by Patrick D. Miller in his treatment of this issue in 1985.[87] In my view, this festival developed as an important part of the pre-existing autumn agricultural festival early in the period of the united monarchy to celebrate Yah-

---

[85] Brettler, *God is King*, 150.

[86] See 2 Sam 8:1-13; 1 Kgs 5:1-8; 10:23-25; and Ps 68:19, 30.

[87] Patrick D. Miller, "Israelite Religion," in Douglas A. Knight and Gene M. Tucker (eds.), *The Hebrew Bible and Its Modern Interpreters* (Philadelphia: Fortress, 1985) 220–22.

weh's rise to imperial rank.[88] I think it was influenced by general
Near Eastern modes of thought, but was adopted in response to Israel's particular political development in a period of imperial
power—not just as an aping of insignificant Israel's more powerful
neighbors. I think the festival included a ritual re-enactment of Yahweh's accession to the throne symbolized by a procession of the ark
into the sanctuary, and the placing of the ark under Yahweh's cherub
throne in the inner sanctum of the temple. Finally, after all the linguistic and syntactical debate, I would argue that the ritual meaning of
the Hebrew expressions מלך יהוה and יהוה מלך is still best captured
by Mowinckel's translation, "Yahweh has become king!"

SELECT BIBLIOGRAPHY

Brettler, Marc Zvi. *God is King: Understanding an Israelite Metaphor* (JSOTSup
   76; Sheffield: JSOT Press, 1989).

Brueggemann, Walter. *Israel's Praise: Doxology against Idolatry and Ideology*
   (Philadelphia: Fortress, 1988).

Howard, David M. Jr. *The Structure of Psalms 93–100* (BJS 5; Winona Lake, IN:
   Eisenbrauns, 1997).

Michel, D. "Studien zu den sogenannten Thronbesteigungs-psalmen," *VT* 6
   (1956) 40–68.

Miller, Patrick D. "Israelite Religion," in Douglas A. Knight and Gene M. Tucker
   (eds.), *The Hebrew Bible and Its Modern Interpreters* (Philadelphia: Fortress,
   1985) 201–37.

Mowinckel, Sigmund. *Psalmenstudien II: Das Thronbesteigungs-fest Jahwäs und
   der Ursprung der Eschatologie* (Kristiania, Norway: J. Dybwad, 1922). Repr.
   in six vols. with corrections and annotations (Amsterdam: P. Schippers, 1966).

—. *The Psalms in Israel's Worship I–II* (New York and Nashville: Abingdon,
   1962).

Roberts, J. J. M. "The Religio-Political Setting of Psalm 47," *BASOR* 221 (1976)
   129–32.

—. "God's Imperial Reign According to the Psalter," *Horizons in Biblical Theology* 23/2 (2001) 211–21.

Schmidt, Hans. "Rezension über: Sigmund Mowinckel, *Psalmen-studien II*:
   Thronbesteigungsfest Jahwäs und der Ursprung der Eschatologie," *TLZ* 4/5
   (1924) 77–81.

---

[88] See my "God's Imperial Reign According to the Psalter," *Horizons in Biblical Theology* 23/2 (2001) 211–21; and my earlier works cited there, particularly
"The Religio-Political Setting of Psalm 47," *BASOR* 221 (1976) 129–32.

Stamm, Johann Jakob. "Ein Vierteljahrhundert Psalmenforschung," *Theologische Rundschau* 23 (1955) 1–68.

Ulrichsen, J. H. "JHWH *mālāk*: einige sprachliche Beobachtungen," *VT* 27 (1977) 361–74.

Welten, Peter. "Königsherrschaft Jahwes und Thronbesteigung: Bemerkungen zu unerledigten Fragen," *VT* 32 (1982) 297–310.

# ZUM SOGENANNTEN „STIMMUNGSUMSCHWUNG"
# IN PSALM 13

BEAT WEBER

## ZUM PROBLEM DES „STIMMUNGSUMSCHWUNGS" IN DEN PSALMEN

Zu den noch kaum gelüfteten Geheimnissen, welche die alttestamentlichen Psalmen in sich bergen, gehört das Phänomen des
sogenannten „Stimmungsumschwungs" (= StU).[1] Damit ist der Umstand gemeint, dass in vielen Psalmen, insbesondere solchen, die man
der Gattung „Klagelied des Einzelnen" (= KE) zurechnet, ein recht
abrupter Wechsel von Klagen und Bitten, die eine Situation der Not
spiegeln, zu Aussagen und Beteuerungen stattfindet, die durch Zuversicht, ja sogar Lobpreis(-Versprechen) gekennzeichnet sind. Dieser
„Stimmungsumschwung" ist umso frappierender, als kaum Indizien
vorzuliegen scheinen, aus denen ersichtlich würde, dass sich die Not
des Betenden bereits gewendet hat.[2]

Die Rätselhaftigkeit dieses Phänomens bedeutet nicht, dass man
dafür keine Erklärung gesucht und gefunden hätte. Am nachhaltigsten
hat die Psalmenforschung die von Joachim Begrich vorgelegte Deutung des StUs geprägt, die an dieser Stelle kurz skizziert werden soll.[3]

Nach Begrich ist ein „priesterliches Heilsorakel" für den „jähen
Umschwung der Stimmung, der im Klageliede des Einzelnen gegen das

---

[1] Die Bezeichnung des Sachverhalts ist unglücklich, da sie atmosphärische und
emotionale Momente in den Vordergrund schiebt. Da sie sich eingebürgert hat,
bleibe ich bei der Ausdrucksweise, setze sie aber in Anführungszeichen.

[2] In einzelnen Psalmen ist der Wechsel von Klage- und Bittaussagen zu Ver-
trauens- und Lobäusserungen sogar mehrfach zu beobachten, z.T. auch in um-
gekehrter Abfolge (vgl. u.a. Psalmen 3; 7; 22; 31; 35; 56; 70).

[3] J. Begrich, „Das priesterliche Heilsorakel," *ZAW* 53 (1934) 81–92 (= Ders.,
*Gesammelte Studien zum Alten Testament* [ThB 21; München: Kaiser, 1964]
217–31). Hinweise dazu finden sich auch bei H. Gunkel (und J. Begrich), *Einleitung in die Psalmen. Die Gattungen der religiösen Lyrik Israels* (HK– Ergänzungsband zur II. Abteilung; Göttingen: Vandenhoeck & Ruprecht, 1933)
243–51. H. Gunkel verweist darauf, dass schon Friedrich Küchler auf das Prie-
sterorakel als Erklärung des StUs hingewiesen habe.

Ende hin wahrzunehmen ist",[4] verantwortlich: „Wenn ein Einzelner, der im Heiligtum mit seinem Klageliede vor Jahwe getreten ist, seine Klagen und Bitten erschöpft hat, so tritt ein Priester auf, der, vielleicht aufgrund eines Opferbescheides, sich an den Beter mit einem Orakel Jahwes wendet und, auf sein Klagen und Bitten bezugnehmend, ihm die Erhörung und Hilfe seines Gottes zusichert. Getröstet durch das göttliche Orakel, spricht der Betende nunmehr die Gewissheit seiner Erhörung aus und schliesst mit den Worten des Gelübdes."[5] Der StU wird also von Begrich textextern, nämlich durch ein gottesdienstliches bzw. kultisches Geschehen, erklärt. Die vom Priester zugesprochene Heilszusicherung Gottes, die im Psalm selbst nicht aufbehalten wurde, erklärt den StU von der Klage und Bitte zur Erhörungsgewissheit und dem Lobgelübde. Zu dieser Folgerung gelangt Begrich aufgrund eines Textvergleichs dieser Psalmen mit Deuterojesaja, indem er in den Heilsworten von DtJes[6] das entsprechende Gegenstück, nämlich das priesterliche Heilsorakel, sieht, das in den Psalmen fehlt. Dabei kann er zeigen, dass die aus DtJes entnommenen Formen der Heilszusicherung durchaus den aus den Ps entnommenen Formen der Bitte (und Klage) entsprechen. Das Heilsorakel als unmittelbares JHWH-Wort beginnt gewöhnlich mit den Worten: „fürchte dich nicht!" (vgl. Jes 41,10.13.14; 43,1.5 u.ö.). Es folgt die Bezeichnung des Angeredeten sowie eine Versicherung der hilfreichen Nähe JHWHs.[7]

Dieses Erklärungsmodell des StUs ist in der Folge weithin auf Akzeptanz gestossen.[8] Allerdings fällt auf, dass die Gewissheit der Richtigkeit dieser Erklärung in neuerer Zeit zusehends abhanden gekommen ist, zumal ihre Schwäche wegen des Fehlens eines textlichen Anhalts in den Psalmen selber offenkundig ist. Zudem ist auch die

---

[4] Begrich, „Heilsorakel," 81.

[5] Begrich, „Heilsorakel," 82.

[6] Begrich, „Heilsorkel," 81, führt folgende Belege auf: Jes 41,8-13.14-16; 43,1-3a.5; (44,2-5); 48,17-19; 49,7.14-15; 51,7-8; 54,4-8, ferner Jer 30,10 = 46,27; 30,11 = 46,28, schliesslich Ps 35,3; Klgl 3,57.

[7] Vgl. Begrich, „Heilsorakel," 83.

[8] Vgl. u.a. C. Westermann, *Lob und Klage in den Psalmen* (6. Auflage; Göttingen: Vandenhoeck & Ruprecht, 1983 [1977]) 50–51; H.-J. Kraus, *Psalmen. 1.Teilband: Psalmen 1–59* (5. Auflage; BK XV/1; Neukirchen-Vluyn: Neukirchener, 1978) 51; P. C. Craigie, *Psalms 1–50* (WBC 19; Waco, TX: Word, 1983) 141; K. Seybold, *Die Psalmen. Eine Einführung* (UB 382; Stuttgart: Kohlhammer, 1986) 72. Im Blick auf Psalm 13 nimmt auch noch E. Zenger, *Die Nacht wird leuchten wie der Tag. Psalmenauslegungen* (Freiburg: Herder, 1997) 83–84 an, dass vor 6 bzw. 5b in der institutionellen Vorgeschichte dieses Psalms der göttliche Zuspruch aus dem Munde des leitenden Liturgen (Prophet, Priester) fällig gewesen sei.

Annahme Begrichs, dass die KE (ausschliesslich) am Heiligtum entstanden bzw. angestimmt wurden, keineswegs so sicher.[9]

So ist in neuerer und neuster Zeit die Forschungslage dadurch gekennzeichnet, dass das Verstehensmodell Begrichs angezweifelt und
nach neuen Erklärungen gesucht wird.[10] Nach Christoph O. Schroeder[11] sind bei den KE zumindest zwei unterschiedliche Formen göttlichen Eingreifens zu konstatieren: Bei einigen Psalmen (u.a. den
Psamen 6; 13; 71) bestehe die Krise in der Gottferne bzw. einem Sich-
Zurückziehen Gottes, die durch eine Wiederherstellung der göttlichen
Präsenz behoben werde. Dabei stützt er sich auf die beachtenswerte
Studie von Fredrik Lindström, nach der der Hintergrund des Leidens
in den KE nicht in der Sünde zu suchen ist; vielmehr interpretiere der
Betende seine Erfahrungen auf dem Hintergrund eines tempeltheologischen Verstehensmodelles, dem gemäss die (als unmotiviert er-
fahrene) Abwesenheit Gottes und damit seiner Heilssphäre die Ursache der Not ist. Als Folge davon gerät der Mensch in die Ein-
flusssphäre des Todes und von „Feinden", die übermenschlich-
dämonische Züge annehmen.[12] Bei einer andern Gruppe von Psalmen
(u.a. den Psalmen 7; 57; 64) steht nach Schroeder die Feindbedrängnis

---

[9] Vgl. u.a. E. Gerstenberger, *Der bittende Mensch. Bittritual und Klagelied des
Einzelnen im Alten Testament* (WMANT 51; Neukirchen-Vluyn: Neukirchener,
1980) 151–60.

[10] Vgl. dazu knapp zusammenfassend und mit Literaturangaben K. Ehlers,
„Wege aus der Vergessenheit. Zu einem neuen Sammelband zum Thema
‚Klage‘," *JBTh* 16 (2001) 383–96, 387; G. Etzelmüller, „Als ich den Herrn suchte,
antwortete er mir. Zu Patrick Millers Monographie über Form und Theologie des
biblischen Gebetes," *JBTh* 16 (2001) 397–406, 400–404. Frühe Kritiker der
„Heilsorakel"-Erklärung sind (im Blick auf Psalm 22) R. Kilian, „Ps 22 und das
priesterliche Heilsorakel," *BZ* 12 (1968) 172–85; O. Fuchs, *Die Klage als Gebet.
Eine theologische Besinnung am Beispiel des Psalms 22* (München: Kösel, 1982)
314–22, und, die Überlegungen von Fuchs weiterführend, A. R. Müller, „Stimmungsumschwung im Klagepsalm. Zu Ottmar Fuchs ‚Die Klage als Gebet‘,"
*ALW* 28 (1986) 416–26.

[11] C. O. Schroeder, *History, Justice, and the Agency of God. A Hermeneutical
and Exegetical Investigation on Isaiah and Psalms* (BIS 52; Leiden: Brill, 2001)
87–100, 203–206.

[12] Vgl. F. Lindström, *Suffering and Sin. Interpretations of Illness in the Indi-
vidual Complaint Psalms* (ConBOT 37; Stockholm: Almqvist & Wiksell, 1994).
In eine ähnliche Richtung zielen die Überlegungen von M. R. Hauge, *Between
Sheol and Temple. Motif Structure and Function in the I–Psalms* (JSOTSup 178;
Sheffield: Sheffield Academic Press, 1995).

im Vordergrund, die durch JHWHs Auftreten als Richter überwunden werde. Zumindest bei der zweiten Gruppe nimmt er an, dass das Handeln Gottes durch die Rezitation des Gebets in Kraft tritt.

Nach Gregor Etzelmüller transformiert sich bereits in vorexilischer Zeit die israelitische Religion mehr und mehr weg von der institutionellen Priester- oder Propheten-Befragung hin zur Erschliessung des Willens Gottes durch die Schrift. Die Psalmbeter sind in den „heiligen Schriften" beheimatet und können sich inmitten der Klagen an Gottes Zusagen erinnern, womit sich der StU erklären lässt. Er geschieht in der Interaktion von Gebet und Hören auf die Schrift.[13] Christoph Markschies vertritt die These, dass Vertrauensäusserungen das „Grundmotiv" der KE und Ausdruck der das Beten tragenden Gewissheit sind:

> Das Vertrauensmotiv ist nichts anderes als die allem Beten in den KE zugrunde liegende Forderung an YHWH, das Leben des Beters, der sein Vertrauen in Gottes Hand legt, in seinen Schutz zu nehmen. Die Bitte wird als Vertrauensäusserung formuliert, weil der Beter schon vor allem konkreten Bitten zuversichtlich hoffen kann, dass YHWH tatsächlich zu seinen Gunsten eintreten wird. Denn in eben dieser Zuversicht besteht ja sein Glaube, der ihn zu YHWH beten lässt.[14]

Die Grundstruktur des Vertrauens ist in den KE also nicht nur ab und mit dem StU gegeben, sondern auch schon in Klage und Bitte eingewoben. Auf Markschies Bezug nehmend schreibt Bernd Janowski:

> Die Klagepsalmen ... sind zwar in der Situation der Gottverlassenheit bzw. Gottesferne gesprochen, aber doch in der Hoffnung, dass Gott gerade *in* dieser Not nahe ist. Diese Spannung zwischen *erfahrener Gottverlassenheit* und *erhoffter Gottesnähe* ist für die Klagepsalmen insgesamt und für die Frage des „Stimmungsumschwungs" im besonderen konstitutiv.[15]

Jüngst hat auch Dorothea Erbele-Küster den Sachverhalt thematisiert und den StU literaturwissenschaftlich als „Leerstelle" im Übergang von Klage und Bitte zur Erhörungsgewissheit bezeichnet und davor gewarnt, diese (zu) schnell aufzufüllen und damit zu beseitigen.[16] Sie

---

[13] Vgl. Etzelmüller, „Als ich den Herrn suchte," 403–404.

[14] C. Markschies, „‚Ich aber vertraue auf dich, Herr!'—Vertrauensäusserungen als Grundmotiv in den Klageliedern des Einzelnen," *ZAW* 103 (1991) 386–98 [bes. 386–87].

[15] B. Janowski, „Das verborgene Angesicht Gottes. Psalm 13 als Muster eines Klagelieds des einzelnen," *JBTh* 21 (2001) 25–53 [bes. 45].

[16] D. Erbele-Küster, *Lesen als Akt des Betens. Eine Rezeptionsästhetik der Psalmen* (WMANT 87; Neukirchen-Vluyn: Neukirchener, 2001) 160. Vgl.

meint drei auslösende Momente für das Eintreten der Erhörungsgewissheit und damit den Gebetsprozess insgesamt erkennen zu können:
(a) die Erkenntnis des Schicksals der Feinde; (b) die Gotteserkenntnis;
(c) die Erlangung der Sprachfähigkeit.[17] Dabei sei die Veränderung
weniger als emotionaler Stimmungswandel denn als Erkenntnis-
prozess realisiert, der sich in konkreten Erfahrungen des Beters wider-
spiegele.[18] Das Nebeneinander der verwendeten hebräischen Tem-
pussysteme interpretiert sie als „Ineinander von geschehener Erhörung
und erwartungsvollem Ausblick. Die Leerstelle gibt der Fragmen-
tarität menschlicher Gewissheit Ausdruck. Der Beter ist erhört worden, und zugleich lebt er in Erwartung."[19]

Überblickt man die neuste Forschungssituation zum StU so lässt
sich deutlich erkennen, dass man weitgehend von textexternen Erk-
lärungsmustern im Zusammenhang mit institutionalisierten Geschehenszusammenhängen abgerückt ist und den StU textintern im
Zusammenhang mit dem Psalm selber und dem in ihm abgebildeten
Gebetsprozess zu verstehen sucht.[20] Hier ist anzuknüpfen. Eine umfassende Untersuchung hätte dem StU in sämtlichen relevanten
Psamen nachzugehen. Das kann hier nicht geleistet werden. Ich
beschränke mich nachfolgend im Sinne einer kleinen Einzelstudie auf
Psalm 13, der diesbezüglich drei „Vorzüge" aufweist: (a) er ist kurz;
(b) er gilt als klassisches Beispiel für das KE,[21] ist diesbezüglich also
nicht umstritten; (c) der StU kommt signifikant zum Ausdruck und
fällt mit der strophischen Gliederung zusammen.

Für dieses Unterfangen kann uns die sprechaktanalytische Erarbei-
tung von Psalm 13 durch Hubert Irsigler[22] wertvolle Dienste leisten.

---

ähnlich bereits Müller, „Stimmungsumschwung," 425.

[17] Vgl. Erbele-Küster, *Lesen*, 162–63.

[18] Vgl. Erbele-Küster, *Lesen*, 166, ferner auch F.-L. Hossfeld, „Von der Klage
zum Lob — die Dynamik des Gebets in den Psalmen," *BiKi* 56 (2001) 16–20
[bes. 18].

[19] Erbele-Küster, *Lesen*, 164.

[20] Vgl. Janowski, „Angesicht Gottes," 46, im Blick auf Ps 13,6 auch F.-L.
Hossfeld & E. Zenger, *Die Psalmen I. Psalm 1–50* (NEchB.AT; Würzburg:
Echter, 1993) 98: „Der ‚Stimmungsumschwung' ... gehört zur Dynamik des
Psalms als Gebetsgeschehen."

[21] Vgl. H. Gunkel, *Die Psalmen* (4. Auflage; HK II/2; Göttingen: Vandenhoeck & Ruprecht, 1926) 46; Westermann, *Lob und Klage*, 50ff., 139ff. u.ö.

[22] Vgl. H. Irsigler, „Psalm-Rede als Handlungs-, Wirk- und Aussageprozess.
Sprechaktanalyse und Psalmeninterpretation am Beispiel von Psalm 13," in: K.

Zudem hat jüngst Bernd Janowski, aufbauend auf Irsigler (und Markschies), diesen Psalm analysiert und dabei dem StU ein eigenes Kapitel gewidmet.[23] Diese beiden neueren Studien zu Psalm 13 bilden gleichsam die Ausgangslage für die folgenden Erörterungen.

## PSALM 13 UND DER „STIMMUNGSUMSCHWUNG"

### 1. Übersetzung

Obwohl an dieser Stelle keine umfassende Auslegung von Psalm 13[24] angestrebt wird, soll doch vorab eine Arbeitsübersetzung dieses Psalms dargeboten werden. Damit werden einige Übersetzungsentscheidungen vorweggenommen; diese werden weiter unten erörtert. Im Zentrum meiner Analyse steht insbesondere das Schlusstrikolon 6abc.[25]

**Überschrift**

1 Dem Musikverantwortlichen – ein Psalm – David zugehörig.

**Klagen**

I 2 a Wie lange noch, JHWH? Willst (wirst) du mich für immer vergessen?

b Wie lange willst (wirst) du dein Antlitz verbergen vor mir?

3 a Wie lange noch muss (soll, werde) ich Sorgen[26] in meiner Seele hegen?

b [Wie lange noch ist][27] Kummer in meinem Herzen tagelang?

c Wie lange noch darf (wird) sich mein Feind über mich erheben?

**Bitten**

II 4 a Schau bitte her! Antworte mir, JHWH;

---

Seybold & E. Zenger (Hrsg.), *Neue Wege der Psalmenforschung. FS W. Beyerlin* (HBS 1; Freiburg: Herder, 1994) 63–104.

[23] Janowski, „Angesicht Gottes," zum StU vgl. 43–50.

[24] Ich habe mich zu Psalm 13 bereits geäussert: B. Weber, *Werkbuch Psalmen I. Die Psalmen 1 bis 72* (Stuttgart: Kohlhammer, 2001) 87–89; B. Weber, „Lob und Klage in den Psalmen des Alten Testaments als Anfrage und Herausforderung an unsere Gebets- und Gottesdienstpraxis," *Jahrbuch für evangelikale Theologie* 13 (1999) 33–47, bes. 34–37. Die bisherigen Beobachtungen werden aber hiermit teilweise modifiziert.

[25] In runden Klammern sind mögliche Übersetzungsvarianten genannt, in eckigen Klammern Aussagen, die nicht im Text stehen, aber aufgrund des Vorliegens elliptischer Redeweise zu ergänzen sind.

[26] עצת, von עצה „Rat(schluss), Plan," auch „Sorge" (vgl. Sir 30,21); einige ändern — wohl unnötig — zu עצבות, von עצבת „Schmerz, Plage, Kummer" (vgl. HALAT, 819–20).

[27] Die Frage עד־אנה von 3a (vgl. 3c) bestimmt virtuell auch 3b. 3b kann man entweder – wie vorgeschlagen – als Nominalsatz bestimmen oder aber annehmen, dass der Teilvers (ebenfalls) vom finiten Verb aus 3a regiert wird („double duty").

b mein Gott, mache bitte hell meine Augen![28]

c Damit ich nicht [zu] dem Tod entschlafen muss (werde);[29]

5 a damit mein Feind nicht sagen kann (wird): „Ich habe ihn überwältigt!";

b [damit nicht] meine Bedränger jubeln dürfen (werden), wenn (dass) ich wanke.

[„S t i m m u n g s u m s c h w u n g"]

**Vertrauen + Lob/Dank**

III 6 a Ich aber, ich habe aufgrund[30] deiner Gnade vertraut.

b Es soll jubeln mein Herz aufgrund[31] deines Heilshandelns:

c „Ich will JHWH (be)singen, denn er hat [wohl] an mir getan."

## 2. Zu Gattung, Struktur, Kolometrie, Literarkritik und Datierung

Die Gattungsbestimmung von Psalm 13 als KE ist — wie gesagt — unbestritten, ebenfalls die Dreistrophigkeit, die mit den Gattungselementen „Klagen", „Bitten" und „Vertrauensbekenntnis / Dankversprechen" übereinstimmt. Am nächstliegenden scheint es — bis auf die Verstrennung von 4 und 5 —, die masoretische Lesart zu übernehmen. Obwohl Strophe II dieselbe Zahl von Verszeilen aufweist wie I, ist sie doch erheblich kürzer. Im Blick auf die Gesamtanlage des Psalms ist daher von einer „Trichterstruktur" auszugehen, die

---

[28] Mit J. P. Fokkelmann, *Major Poems of the Hebrew Bible at the Interface of Prosody and Structural Analysis. Volume II: 85 Psalms and Job 4–14* (SSN; Assen: Van Gorcum, 2000) 87–88, ist Strophe II nicht als zwei Bikola, sondern wohl als Bikolon (4ab) + Trikolon (4c5ab) zu lesen, auch wenn 4c mit zwei Hebungen dadurch relativ kurz ist. Für diese Kolometrie spricht: (a) der Aufteilung von יהוה אלהי auf zwei Zeilen ist der Vorzug zu geben; (b) die Versaufteilung in Bitten (Imperative) und Negativ-Begründungen (פֶּן-Sätze) entspricht stärker dem inhaltlichen Duktus; (c) die Parallelisierung der Satzglieder der beiden Vershälften 4ab ist nun ungleich deutlicher (phono-semantische abcc'a'b'-Struktur); (d) die drei Imperative entsprechen den drei פֶּן-Sätzen in gegenläufigem Sinn (ABCC'B'A'-Struktur); (e) die Analogie zwischen Strophe I und II ist dadurch verstärkt. Hossfeld & Zenger, *Die Psalmen I*, 97, lesen 4 als Trikolon sowie 5 und 6 je als Bikola. Zenger, *Nacht*, 73, dagegen liest 5 zwei- und 6 dreizeilig.

[29] Möglicherweise Breviloquenz für „(damit) ich (nicht) den Schlaf des Todes schlafen muss" (שְׁנַת הַמָּוֶת אִישָׁן), vgl. Janowski, „Angesicht Gottes," 26.

[30] E. Jenni, *Die hebräischen Präpositionen. Band 1: Die Präposition Beth* (Stuttgart: Kohlhammer, 1992) 104–105, hat darauf hingewiesen, dass die Präposition *Beth* an der vorliegenden Stelle im Sinne eines *Beth causae* verstanden werden muss; בטח ב ist also nicht — wie von den meisten Auslegern angenommen — mit „vertrauen auf" (terminativ) zu übersetzen, sondern mit „vertrauen durch / wegen / aufgrund".

[31] Auch hier ist von einem *Beth causae* auszugehen, vgl. Jenni, *Präpositionen 1*, 106.

eine Fokussierung auf die Schluss-Strophe hin mit sich führt.[32] Dabei ist eine literarkritische Ausscheidung von 3b[33] genauso unnötig wie eine Strophentrennung zwischen 5a und 5b unter Verbindung von 5b und 6a zu einem Bikolon.[34] Was die zeitliche Einordnung des Psalms angeht, so gibt die formularisch offene Diktion kaum Datierungshinweise. Meist wird der Psalm jedoch als vorexilisch eingestuft.[35]

---

[32] Ich gehe im Blick auf die drei Strophen von 19 (4+4 / 4+3+4) – 14 (3+3 / 2+3+3) – 10 (3+3+4) Hebungen aus.

[33] Dazu neigen Hossfeld & Zenger, *Die Psalmen I*, 96; Zenger, *Nacht*, 73. Die dort beigebrachten Argumente sind zu wenig gewichtig für einen Texteingriff bzw. lassen sich anders erklären (die Fragepartikel von 3a kann — mit oder ohne Verb — problemlos auch 3b regieren; die Varianz zwischen לבב 3b und לב 6b ist stilistisch, nicht literarkritisch zu interpretieren; die fehlende Hebung aufgrund der Elliptik und damit das Trikolon-Muster 4+3+4 ist nicht aussergewöhnlich; zwar ist die Feind-Zeile unparallelisiert, doch beim Wegfall von 3b ist wenig gewonnen, denn ein „antithetischer Parallelismus," wie Hossfeld & Zenger behaupten, stellt sich damit nicht ein).

[34] Vgl. dazu insbesondere O. H. Steck, „Beobachtungen zur Beziehung von Klage und Bitte in Psalm 13," *BN* 13 (1980) 57–62, bes. 61–62, ferner Zenger, *Nacht*, 73–74, 84–85, der damit zugleich drei gleichmässige Strophen zu je 4 Zeilen erreicht (durch Ausscheidung von 3b und dreizeilige Lesung von 4). Das Bikolon 5b6a wird dann etwa so wiedergegeben: „Meine Widersacher (mögen) jubeln, dass ich wanke, doch ich, ich vertraue auf deine Güte." Gegen die von Steck angeführten Gründe ist folgendes zu sagen: (a) die Varianz von Singular („mein Feind") und Plural („meine Bedränger / Widersacher") findet sich auch anderswo und kann hier nicht kolometrisch ausgewertet werden (vgl. dazu O. Keel, *Feinde und Gottesleugner. Studien zum Image der Widersacher in den Individualpsalmen* [SBM 7; Stuttgart: Katholisches Bibelwerk, 1969] 68–69; (b) elliptische Ausdrucksweise (= Nachwirkung von פן von 5a in 5b) ist typisch für die Psalmenpoesie (vgl. bereits עד־אנה in 3a für 3b), auch wenn die Nachwirkung der Partikel hier über das Feindzitat hinaus wie auch die Wortstellung in 5b einmalig sein mag; (c) ואני mit seinem adversativen Akzent („ich aber, ich jedoch") hat deutlich vers- oder sogar strophen-eröffnenden Charakter (vgl. ähnlich u.a. Pss 2,6; 5,8; 26,11; 30,7; 31,15.23, dagegen Ps 31,7); (d) die in allen drei Strophen angelegte Abfolge der Bezugsgrössen „Gott—Ich (selbst)—Mitmensch (Feind oder Mitfeiernder)" (dazu s.u.) würde durch eine Hinzunahme von 5b zu Strophe III ebenso gestört wie die kolometrische Gesamtanlage (s.o.). Vgl. auch Irsigler, „Psalm-Rede," 73.

[35] Vgl. u.a. Craigie, *Psalms 1–50*, 141; Hossfeld & Zenger, *Die Psalmen I*, 96 (aufgrund des Fehlens der in jüngeren Psalmen stärker auftretenden Vernichtungswünsche).

## 3. Zu den Klagen und Bitten (Verse 2–5)

Obwohl das Hauptgewicht dieser Untersuchung auf dem StU und Vers 6 (Strophe III) liegt, sind auch die ersten beiden Strophen und damit die „Klagen" (I) und „Bitten" (II) kurz ins Auge zu fassen. Es ist verschiedentlich darauf hingewiesen worden, dass Psalm 13 in seinen ersten beiden Teilen Momente aufgreift, die gemeinorientalisch sind. So hat etwa Hans-Joachim Kraus im Blick auf die mit עד־אנה eröffnende Fragereihe der Klage auf eine babylonische Parallele (Klagelied Nebukadnezars I) hingewiesen.[36] Dass im zeitlichen Verzug der Hilfe das wesentliche Problem liegt, wird allein schon durch die Fragestaffel (עד־אנה 4mal sowie 1mal virtuell) mit ihrem „einhämmernden" Charakter deutlich.[37] Die Klagereihe entfaltet sich in den drei „Sozialdimensionen" als Gott-Klage („anklagen", 2ab), als Ich-Klage („sich beklagen", 3ab)[38] und als Feind-Klage („verklagen", 3c). Damit wird deutlich, wie umfassend die Notlage für die Existenz des Betroffenen ist. Adressiert sind die drei Klage-Dimensionen alle an Gott (vgl. יהוה als invocatio, 2a).[39] Dieser Umstand sowie die Anfangsstellung der Gott-Klage lassen deutlich werden, dass das theologische Problem (anhaltende Gottesabwesenheit) die grundlegende Not des Betenden ausmacht. Ist diese behoben, so ist damit implizit der Kummer behoben wie auch die Feind-Bedrängnis abgewehrt. Mit andern Worten: Die Aspekte des Gottes-, des Selbst- und des Feind-Leidens sind Facetten ein- und derselben Not, die — mit Lindström — als (unerklärbare) Gottes-Absenz zu bestimmen ist.[40]

Odil Hannes Steck hat nun darauf hingewiesen, dass das Dreierschema: Gottesbezug — Selbstbezug — Feindbezug in der durch Imperative geprägten Bitt-Strophe (II) in gleicher Reihenfolge aufgenommen wird.[41] Dies gilt noch verstärkt bei der oben skizzierten, von derjenigen von Steck abweichenden kolometrischen Auffassung des Psalms. Die Abfolge: Gott – Ich – Feind(e) ist dieselbe, nur dass in I der „Ich"-Aussage zwei (3ab) und der „Feind"-Aussage eine Zeile (3c) zugeordnet wird, in II aber das Verhältnis gerade umgekehrt ist

---

[36] Vgl. Kraus, *Psalmen*, 241 (mit Abdruck des babylonischen Liedes).

[37] Vgl. ferner die Zeitdauerangaben נצח (2a) und יומם (3b).

[38] Verbunden mit einer Elendsschilderung.

[39] Mit andern Worten: Es findet weder ein Selbstgespräch statt noch werden Worte dem Feind entgegengeschleudert.

[40] Vgl. Lindström, *Suffering and Sin*, 97–101 (zu Psalm 13).

[41] Steck, „Beobachtungen," 57–62.

(4c bzw. 5ab). Die „Gott"-Klagen bzw. -Bitten finden sich je in einem Bikolon am Strophenanfang (2ab bzw. 4ab). Dabei sind einerseits die Bitten zu „sehen" und zu „(er)hören" (4a) auf die Klagen des „vergessens" und „verbergens" des Eingangsverses (2ab) zurückbezogen (nach dem Muster: abb'a'). Andererseits liegt eine deutliche Parallele zwischen der Klage, „dein Antlitz zu verbergen" (2b), und der Bitte, „meine Augen hell zu machen" (4b),[42] vor. Wie die Todesnähe aufzufassen ist, wird nicht gesagt. Vermutet wird oft eine schwere Krankheit, aber von 3ab her kommt mindestens so stark eine psycho-soziale Komponente ins Spiel, die an ein Schwinden von Lebensmut und -kraft denken lässt.[43]

Wie schon in der Klage-Eröffnung wird auch in der Bitt-Eröffnung Gott angerufen, nur dass jetzt neben dem Tetragrammaton noch der Vokativ „mein Gott" (אלהי) erscheint. Durch die Anführung des persönlichen Gottesverhältnisses bekommen die Bitten einen insistierenden Charakter, d.h. Gott soll damit (wie mit den nachher angeführten Eingreif-Motiven) verstärkt zum Heilshandeln bewogen werden. Wenn man den virtuellen Anfang von 5b mitzählt, knüpfen die drei פן-Aussagen des Trikolons 4c5ab nach dem spiegelsymmetrischen Muster abcc'b'a' an die drei Imperative von 4ab an. Sie wollen mit Hilfe negativ formulierter, konjunktivisch aufzufassender *yqtl*-Formulierungen, die *worst case*-Szenarien enthalten, Gott zum Eingreifen motivieren — weil ansonsten Rechtsbeugung und Chaos dominieren und Gott seiner Ehre berauben würden. Der Ich-Klage von 3ab entspricht die Verszeile 4c, also die Bitte um Abwehr der todesbedrohenden Lage des Betenden bzw. um Wiederherstellung seiner Lebenskraft. Die „Feind"-Klage schliesslich (3c) wird nun in zwei Zeilen mit Abwehr-Formulierungen Gott anheim befohlen (5ab).[44] Dabei wird festgestellt, dass die „Überhebung" (3c) zur „Überwältigung" (5a) führen würde. Nun hat Steck darauf hingewiesen, dass signifikanterweise dem „Feind" ein „Wie lange?"-Satz eingeräumt, der Feindaspekt aber nicht Gegenstand einer eigenen Bitte sei.[45] Daraus schliesst er, in Verbindung mit dem betont je am Anfang stehenden

---

[42] Vgl. zur Augen-Metapher für die Todesbedrohung (mit Belegstellen) Hossfeld & Zenger, *Die Psalmen I*, 98.

[43] Die Verbindung von 3ab und 4b auch wird durch die Alliteration der beiden Verben *yqtl* 1 sg אשית und אישן unterstützt.

[44] Vgl. beide Male איבי „mein Feind" (3c.5a).

[45] Steck, „Beobachtungen," 59–61.

Gottesaspekt — zu Recht —, dass nicht der Feind die eigentliche Ursache der Notlage sei. Diese ist Gott selbst in seiner anhaltenden Verborgenheit. Sie wird nicht erklärt und ist — wie die Klage deutlich macht — für den Betenden auch nicht erklärbar.[46] Dass der „Feind", das jede (Heils-)Ordnung erschütternde „Chaos" und der „Tod" Verbündete sind, zeigt sich am Trikolon 4c5ab.[47]

### 4. Zu „Stimmungsumschwung" und Vertrauensbekenntnis / Dankversprechen (Vers 6)

Mit dem Begriff „Stimmungsumschwung" verbindet sich v.a. das Moment des Neuen, der Umkehr des Bisherigen. Doch bei genauem Hinsehen ist die strophische Zäsur zwischen 5 und 6 sowohl durch Anknüpfung als auch durch Absetzung gekennzeichnet. Was die Anknüpfung betrifft, lässt sich sogar überlegen, ob sich die drei Sozialdimensionen „Gott–Ich–Feind" nicht über den StU hinweg in die Schlussstrophe III hinein — wenn auch unter Modifizierung der Reihenfolge — fortsetzen. So betont die Verszeile 6a deutlich den „Ich"-Aspekt, und im Schlusskolon 6c tritt ebenso deutlich der „Gott"-Bezug hervor, nur dass hier JHWH nicht mehr angerufen (Vokative 2a und 4ab), sondern besungen wird, womit ein Moment der Verkündigung vor der Gemeinde hinzutritt.[48] Nur virtuell präsent ist allerdings der „Feind"-Aspekt, zumal er ja mit Gottes Eingreifen seinen bedrohlichen Status verliert. Doch darf man ihn vielleicht hinter 6b durchscheinen sehen, da durch die Aufnahme des Verbes גיל („jubeln") aus 5b dieser Aspekt gleichsam „aufgerufen" und kontrastiv neuakzentuiert wird: Es soll hier — in Abgrenzung zum „Feind"-Verhalten — gerade nicht über den Feind, sondern aufgrund von Gottes Heilshandeln gejubelt werden. Zudem kann ja auch im Heilshandeln die Befreiung von Feindesnot mitgemeint sein. Mit dieser Vermutung, dass sich Gott-, Selbst- und Feindbezug auch in die

---

[46] Vgl. Lindström, *Suffering and Sin*, 98–99. Lindström ist auch darin beizupflichten, dass eine Verbindung zwischen dem Leiden und einer Sündenproblematik im Psalm nicht hergestellt wird und es damit auch nicht legitim ist, eine solche anzunehmen. Vielmehr spricht die Behaftung Gottes gerade gegen eine Verlagerung der Ursache auf den Betenden.

[47] Vgl. Lindström, *Suffering and Sin*, 100. Damit ist Lindström auch Recht zu geben, wenn er sagt, dass die „Feinde" in den KE im Dienst der Todesmächte und damit einer widergöttlichen Gegenmacht stehen bzw. deren Ausdruck sind.

[48] Dies wird auch durch die Verschiebung von der „Du / Gott"- zur „Er / Gott"-Rede deutlich. Vgl. auch Irsigler, „Psalm-Rede," 74, 81.

Schlussstrophe hinein fortsetzen, ist die Kontinuität über den StU
bzw. die „Leerstelle" hinweg betont: Die drei Aspekte werden weitergeführt, auch wenn sie in der fokussierten Schlussstrophe anders zum
Klingen kommen.

Konnektivität und Adversativität ist auch mit dem sogenannten
„waw-adversativum" vor dem betonten Personalpronomen (יַאֲנִי „aber
ich...“), das hier als Satz-, Vers- und Stropheneröffner fungiert, gegeben.[49] Nun erscheint das Verb innerhalb der Verszeile 6a in auffäl-
liger Schlussstellung. Wir haben — um mit Walter Gross zu sprechen — ein „doppelt besetztes Vorfeld" insofern, als zwei pronomi-
nale bzw. nominale Wortbildungen dem Verb vorangestellt sind.[50]
Das hier sprechende „Ich" ist *verbunden* mit den vorherigen Ich-
Aussagen, insbesondere dem unmittelbar vorangehenden Zeilen-
schluss von 5b, der (abgewehrten) Aussage: „...wenn (dass) ich
wanke" (כִּי אֶמּוֹט).[51] Doch וַאֲנִי knüpft nicht nur an 5b an, sondern es
findet auch eine deutliche *Absetzung* (und damit verbunden eine Fokussierung) im Vergleich zum Vorhergehenden statt. Damit stimmt
überein, dass eine mit וַאֲנִי eröffnete Aussage auch anderswo in den
KE als Sprach- und Gattungselement auftaucht,[52] eine Zäsur markiert
und ein „Bekenntnis der Zuversicht" oder eine „Gewissheit der
Erhörung" initiiert.[53] Nachdem die Notlage beklagt und die Hilfe
JHWHs erbeten worden ist, ist hier erstmals von einer positiv bestimmten Handlung die Rede, die der Betende betont *selbst* initiiert
und vollzieht.[54] Dies in auffälligem Kontrast zu den vorangegangenen

---

[49] Grundsätzlich ist das „waw" als Verbindungspartikel aufzufassen und die
adversative Verwendung als eine Bedeutungsnuancierung davon. Vgl. dazu R. C.
Steiner, „Does the Biblical Hebrew Conjunction -ו Have Many Meanings, One
Meaning, or No Meaning at All?," *JBL* 119 (2000) 249–67, bes. 265–67.

[50] Vgl. W. Gross, *Doppelt besetztes Vorfeld. Syntaktische, pragmatische und
übersetzungstechnische Studien zum althebräischen Verbalsatz* (BZAW 305;
Berlin: de Gruyter, 2001). Zu Ps 13,6ab vgl. 99.

[51] Das „Wanken" steht in Verbindung mit dem Chaos, womit die Gefährdung
des Einzelnen mit einer solchen von Gottes Weltordnung verbunden ist.

[52] Vgl. v.a. Pss 31,7.15; 52,10; 55,24; 71,14; 73,23.

[53] Vgl. etwa Westermann, *Lob und Klage*, 52–56; Markschies, „Ich aber vertraue auf dich, Herr!," 390–98.

[54] In gewisser Weise kann das zwar auch von den Klagen und den Bitten
gesagt werden, doch steht vor diesen das Vorzeichen der Not, das hier erstmals
unerwähnt bleibt. Irsigler, „Psalm-Rede," 79–80, spricht im Blick auf 6a von
„Aufschwung" und dass der Sprechakt von 6a einen „initiativen Sinn" gewinne.

פ-Sätzen, in denen zwar auch von „Ich"-Handlungen die Rede ist, die jedoch als *erzwungen* befürchtet bzw. dem Eingreifen JHWHs anheim gestellt werden. So erscheint auffälligerweise mit dem Verb בטח „vertrauen" (6a) der Gegenbegriff zu מוט „wanken" (5b).[55] Durch die betonte Subjektsvoranstellung ist hier — wie andernorts[56] — die Vertrauen ausdrückende Handlung des Betenden noch verstärkt. Wird in 4ab (als Kehrseite der Not-Klage) um Gottes Handeln gebeten, so setzt nun der Betende eine eigene Aktivität: die des Vertrauens.

Aufgrund der Wortfolge in 6a ist nun בחסדך (ebenfalls) hervorgehoben, womit jedoch nicht das Ziel, sondern die Ermöglichung und Begründung des Vertrauens genannt wird (vgl. Übersetzung).[57] Es ist die göttliche „Gnade" bzw. „Güte", die Vertrauen gestiftet hat und damit gleichsam den StU ermöglicht.[58] Wird also in der Klage die Ursache der persönlichen Not und der Feindbedrängnis als Vergessen vonseiten Gottes benannt, so liegt die Ursache für das Vertrauen des Beters wiederum — und das ist theologisch bedeutsam — bei Gott selber: „Aufgrund seiner Gnade" (בחסדך) konnte bzw. kann der Betende Vertrauen investieren und ausdrücken. Mit חסד ist ein besonderes, über das Selbstverständliche hinausgehendes, geschenkweises und vielleicht auch spontanes Verhalten JHWHs gegenüber dem Betenden gemeint, das mit unseren Begriffen „Gnade", „Güte" nur annähernd erfasst wird.[59]

Der חסד ist heilvolle Gottes-Präsenz und damit gerade das Gegenteil der eingangs beklagten Gottes-Absenz. Wie und wann „Gottes Gnade" dem diesen Psalm (Nach-)Betenden so plötzlich zukommt, sind Fragen, die der Text scheinbar nicht explizit. Es ist möglich, dass in der Tatsache des Betens selbst bzw. des Anrufens JHWHs als „mein Gott" (4b, vgl. 2b) ein grundlegendes Vertrauensmotiv, das

---

[55] Vgl. auch Pss 21,8; 125,1, ähnlich im Blick auf das synonyme מעד Ps 26,1; dazu Janowski, „Angesicht Gottes," 38–39, 42.

[56] Vgl. Pss 26,1; 27,3; 31,7.15; 52,10; 55,24; 56,4.

[57] Dazu Gross, *Vorfeld*, 310–17.

[58] Als Variante dazu ist das *qtl* als Koïnzidenz im Sinne einer Sprechhandlung als Vertrauensvollzug interpretierbar.

[59] Vgl. H. J. Stoebe, „חֶסֶד *ḥésed* Güte," *THAT* I (3. Auflage; 1978) 600–21; E. Kellenberger, *ḥäsäd wäʾämät als Ausdruck einer Glaubenserfahrung. Gottes Offen-Werden und Bleiben als Voraussetzung des Lebens* (AThANT 69; Zürich: Theologischer Verlag, 1982) u.a. 37–41, 135–36; Lindström, *Suffering and Sin*, 101, 437–39.

wiederum auf Gottes Gnade fusst, durchscheint.[60] Der Gottes-Name markiert die Präsenz des Angerufenen und hat in sich die Potenz, die notvolle in eine heilvolle Situation zu wandeln.[61] Im Blick auf die im *qtl* gemachte Aussage von 6a lässt sich annehmen, dass der mit Gott Sprechende auf frühere „Gnadenerfahrungen" zurückgreift und diese in einer Vertrauensäusserung aktualisiert bzw. neu realisiert. Das „Bekenntnis der Zuversicht" hat wohl die doppelte Zielsetzung, Gott aufgrund der (neuen) Vertrauenssetzung zum rettenden Handeln zu bewegen und durch das deklarierende Aussprechen das eigene Vertrauen zu JHWH angesichts der in der Klage angesprochenen „Beziehungsstörung" neu zu stärken. Man kann mit Irsigler diese Sprechhandlung als „implizit performatives Beteuern und Versichern des eigenen Vertrauens" oder aber — im Koïnzidenzfall — als „direkter und explizit performativer Sprechakt" verstehen.[62] Während die Klage einen sowohl von Gott wie auch von der Glaubensgemeinschaft isolierenden Aspekt enthält, ist mit dieser Vertrauensaussage auch eine Reintegration in die Glaubens- und Gottesdienstgemeinde verbunden — ein Umstand, der dann in 6c explizit wird.

Im Kolon 6b, das mit dem vorangehenden 6a im Blick auf die Satzglieder teilchiastisch verbunden ist (abcc'a'b'),[63] wechselt die Aussage von einer perfektiven zu einer jussivischen. Damit verändert sich die Rederichtung von einer retrospektiven zu einer prospektiven. Das Personalpronomen wird nun durch לבי „mein Herz" substituiert. Damit wird die Willenskundgabe kontrastierend zurückgebunden an die Elendsschilderung von 3b, zumal dort die Langvariante für „mein Herz" (לבב[י]) nicht nur ebenfalls auftaucht, sondern auch die jeweils kontiguierten יגון und יגל lautspielartig miteinander verbunden sind: Hat vorhin „Kummer" das Herz gefüllt, so wird es jetzt geheissen zu jubeln. Mit Hilfe des Verbes גיל findet — wie schon erwähnt —

---

[60] So Irsigler, „Psalm-Rede," 79, und im Anschluss an Markschies („Ich aber vertraue auf dich, Herr!") v.a. Janowski, „Angesicht Gottes," 50–53. Es ist allerdings eine gewisse Zurückhaltung angebracht, wenn Markschies („Ich aber vertraue auf dich, Herr!") und in seinem Gefolge und in Anwendung auf Psalm 13 Janowski („Angesicht Gottes," 50–51) dem „Vertrauensmotiv" und damit dem Betenden diese Veränderungspotenz zutrauen. Die andere Gefahr besteht darin, dass man die Krise und damit die Erfahrung der Gottverlassenheit herunterspielt und marginalisiert.

[61] Vgl. Lindström, *Suffering and Sin*, 97.

[62] Vgl. Irsigler, „Psalm-Rede," 79.

[63] Vgl. Gross, *Vorfeld*, 99.

eine zweite kontrastive Rückkoppelung zur Feind-Problematik von 5b
statt: Es geht um die Frage, wer zuletzt und aufgrund der wahren Ur-
sachen jubelt. Die Präpositionalfügung בישׁועתך „aufgrund deines
Heilshandelns" ist analog zu בחסדך zu verstehen, nur dass damit die
„Gnade" stärker konkretisiert ist. Worauf dieses „Heilshandeln" Gottes, das zum Ausgangspunkt des Lobpreises wird, Bezug nimmt,
bleibt ungesagt. Es können persönliche Rettungserfahrungen früherer
Zeiten angesprochen werden. Wahrscheinlicher ist proleptisch die
vorhin vermisste und nun wiederhergestellte Heilsgegenwart Gottes
gemeint.

Denkbar ist auch eine Bezugnahme auf die Heilsgeschichte Israels
als Quellgrund, aus dem Vertrauen, Hoffnung und dann Jubel möglich
wird.[64] Die Vertrauensäusserungen von 6a, aber auch „dein Heilshandeln" werden zur Antriebsfeder für das Lobversprechen von 6b,
das mit dem Jussiv gewissermassen jetzt schon ausgelöst wird. Das
ein künftiges Dankbekenntnis (תודה) anvisierende Gelübde dürfte abgesehen von der Selbstverpflichtung im Gebet eine ähnliche Funktion
haben wie die 4c5ab negativ genannten Motive: die Verstärkung der
Bitte insofern, als Gott zur Erhörung „gedrängt" werden soll.[65]

6c führt 6b in dem Sinn weiter, als אשׁירה ליהוה einerseits יגל לבי
und כי גמל עלי andererseits בישׁועתך konkretisierend aufnimmt.[66]
Dabei geht 6c über 6b auch insofern hinaus, als das Lob des Herzens
nun durch den Mund geht und damit hörbar wird. 6c besteht aus zwei
Satzaussagen, zunächst einer Kohortativ-Formulierung, einem „Lobgelübde", mit dem der Psalmist ein zukünftiges Danklied ankündet.
Dieser Entschluss wird anschliessend mit einer *qtl*-Aussage begründet
(כי). Irsigler hält 6c für ein „(Lob-)Redezitat", dessen Zielebene allerdings nur „vorwegnehmend" erreicht werde,[67] und sagt:

> Aus dem indirekten Lobversprechen von 6b wird satzsemantisch in 6c ein
> direktes, das jedoch kontextuell in 6c-d das Lob für Jahwe direkt vollzieht

---

[64] Dafür könnte die Anlehnung von 6c an Ex 15:1, 21 angeführt werden.

[65] Vgl. H. Tita, *Gelübde als Bekenntnis. Eine Studie zu den Gelübden im Alten
Testament* (OBO 181; Freiburg: Universitätsverlag; Göttingen: Vandenhoeck &
Ruprecht, 2001) 44, 226–27.

[66] Vgl. Irsigler, „Psalm-Rede," 81.

[67] Vgl. Irsigler, „Psalm-Rede," 81–83. Janowski („Angesicht Gottes," 51)
spricht im Blick auf 6c ähnlich von einem „Lobzitat" als „deklarativem Sprechakt," ähnlich Hossfeld & Zenger (*Die Psalmen I*, 99), die von einem „Zitat des
Dankklieds" reden.

und in der Retrospektive darauf, dass Jahwe ‚gehandelt' hat, indirekt ebenso Dank verwirklicht.[68]

Dem wird man beipflichten können, wenn man Kontext und Intertext einbezieht: Die Selbstaufforderung, die schon in 6b gefasst wurde, wird nun gleichsam proleptisch vollzogen. Dass hier eine Zitat-artige Einspielung vorliegt und damit die Ankündigung und Durchführung sowohl des Gott zusingenden Lobpreises als auch des Bezeugens vor der Gemeinde gleichsam zusammenfallen, ist auch deshalb anzunehmen, weil 6c den Anfang des „Schilfmeerlieds" (Ex 15,1) intoniert (אָשִׁירָה לַיהוה כִּי). Der Psalmist bringt damit den Siegeshymnus seines Volkes zum Klingen, modifiziert ihn aber nach der Begründungspartikel כִּ zu einem Danklied des Einzelnen (תודה): גמל עלי „er hat [wohl] an mir getan".[69]

Mit diesen Worten wird die Wiederherstellung des Heils bekannt, und damit schliesst der Psalm — nicht ohne am Schluss nochmals einen Gegenakzent zwischen dem Verhalten des Feindes und demjenigen seines Gottes zu evozieren: Hat der Feind sich „über mich" (עלי, Vers- und Strophenschluss) erhoben, so hat nun JHWH „über" bzw. „an mir" (עלי, Vers-, Strophen- und Psalmschluss) wohl getan.[70] Es wird also eine glaubende Vorwegnahme von Gottes Heilseingreifen gefeiert.

Psalm 13 enthält also ein Gebet, das den Weg von der Anrufung JHWHs inmitten der Not bis zur Besingung JHWHs und der Bezeugung seines Heilshandelns und damit der Beendigung der Not abschreitet. Der Psalm setzt ein bei der Klage über die Gott-Verlassenheit des Betenden und führt über das Flehen um rettendes Eingreifen hin zum Lobpreis seines Rettungshandelns. Letzteres liegt noch in der Zukunft, aber zugleich auch schon in der Vergangenheit — deshalb kann das Lob proleptisch schon erklingen, weil es aus der Retrospektive genährt wird.

### FAZIT UND WEITERFÜHRENDE ÜBERLEGUNGEN

(1) Psalm 13 ist ein Individualgebet, das exemplarischen bzw. paradigmatischen Charakter hat. Es ist nicht (direkter) Ausfluss einer individuellen biographischen Erfahrung, sondern umgekehrt ein Ge-

---

[68] Irsigler, „Psalm-Rede," 81.

[69] Vgl. Pss 116,7; 142,8.

[70] Das *qtl* von 6c könnte wohl sachgemäss auch im Sinne eines Futur II übersetzt werden: „denn er wird [wohl] an mir getan haben".

betsformular, das von seinen einzelnen Nachbetern je neu biographisch zu füllen ist.

(2) Die dem Gebet zugrunde liegende Not besteht in erster Linie in der Erfahrung der Abwesenheit Gottes im Lebensbereich des (Nach-) Betenden. Dabei wird insbesondere das zeitliche Andauern und die Gefahr der Endgültigkeit dieser Situation als notvoll erfahren und eingeklagt. Diese Not ist eng verzahnt mit einer starken, als Todesnähe erfahrenen psycho-physischen Beeinträchtigung des sprechenden Ichs und mit massiver Feind-Bedrängnis, die Ordnungs-umstürzend wirkt bzw. zu wirken droht („Chaos") und damit überindividuelle Züge einer Gegenmacht JHWHs annimmt. Die Notlage ist — soweit ersichtlich — nicht auf wie auch immer geartete Vergehen zurückzuführen. Sie ist im Gegenteil von Gott veranlasst und im Grunde genommen unverständlich. Im Blick auf Psalm 13 scheint das tempeltheologische Erklärungsparadigma (Lindström) plausibel, demgemäss die Individualerfahrungen von Not und Heil mit kollektiven, d.h. gottesdienstlichen bzw. kultischen Vorstellungen und Erfahrungen von Gottes-Nähe bzw. Gottes-Ferne interpretiert werden.[71] Dabei sind mit der Abwesenheit Gottes das Abgleiten in den Einflussbereich von Todes- und Feindmächten sowie psycho-physische und soziale Beeinträchtigungen verbunden.

(3) Entsprechend wird die Wende von der Not zum Heil von der Neu-Zuwendung und dem hilfreichen Eingreifen Gottes erwartet, d.h. mit der Gegenwart JHWHs in Verbindung gebracht. Als Weg bzw. „Mittel" zur Behebung der angesprochenen Notlage des Einzelnen dient ein Gebet zu JHWH, wie es uns mit Psalm 13 erhalten ist. Hier wird Gott angerufen, ihm die Not geklagt und um sein Eingreifen gebittet, damit nicht noch unheilvollere Folgen für den Betenden eintreten mögen.

(4) Die als StU bezeichnete Wende von den Klagen und Bitten zum Vertrauensbekenntnis und Lob (Gelübde und proleptischer Vollzug) ist gegenüber der traditionellen Auffassung zu modifizieren. Zum einen ist der Umschwung nicht so jäh bzw. unvermittelt wie allgemein

---

[71] Damit ist noch nicht geklärt, ob bzw. inwieweit die Erfahrungen der Not selber, die Bearbeitung der Not mit Hilfe des Klagepsalms und die Behebung der Not mit einer eigentlichen, d.h. örtlichen Anwesenheit des (Nach-)Betenden am Kultort zu verbinden sind. Am Sichersten ist damit im Nachgang zum Betens des Psalms (vgl. Vers 6), d.h. im Erhörungsfall zu rechnen, der in der Regel jeweils zur Darbringung eines Dank(opfer)bekenntnisses (תודה) führt.

angenommen, zum andern ist mit dem Umschwung nur der eine von
zwei Aspekten, nämlich der des Einschnitts, der Absetzung, nicht aber
der ebenfalls vorhandene Aspekt der Anknüpfung und damit der
Kontinuität, angesprochen. Damit soll die mit dem Begriff des StUs
bezeichnete Wende nicht marginalisiert werden, vielmehr soll die
Spannung, die mit dem StU und den im Gebet integrierten Befindlich-
keiten der Not (Klagen und Bitten) einerseits sowie der zum Heil ge-
wendeten Not (Vertrauen und Lob / Dank) andererseits verbunden ist,
sorgfältig wahrgenommen und bedacht werden. Die sich in Psalm 13
anzeigenden Unheils- bzw. Heilssphären von Abwesenheit und Anwesenheit Gottes im Erfahrungsbereich des Betenden stehen also in
einer dialektischen Spannung von „noch nicht" und „schon", die genauer zu beschreiben ist.

(5) Unter den die Psalmteile vor und nach dem StU verbindenden
Momenten ist neben der Identität des Betenden und der die Schluss-
Strophe eröffnenden Konjunktion[72] zunächst das anzuführen, was ich
die „Strategie der Motivierung Gottes" nennen möchte. Dazu gehört,
dass zu JHWH gebetet wird, auch wenn er sich verbirgt und den Betenden verlassen zu haben scheint; implizit wird also „trotz allem" mit
der Möglichkeit der Erhörung gerechnet. Die eingeklagte Abwesenheit Gottes ist nicht total und absolut. Es wird ersichtlich, dass der
Betende jenseits der momentanen Not der Gottes-Ferne JHWH als
Gott kennt, der ihm früher heilvoll gegenwärtig war. Zu dieser
„Strategie" gehört ferner eine Überzeugungs-Rhetorik des Betenden
im Blick auf Gott, mit der die für den Betenden wie für Gott geltende
„Unhaltbarkeit" der Situation benannt und dieser zum Heilshandeln
motiviert werden soll. Diese drückt sich in der Frage-Staffel der Klage
und in den „damit nicht …"-Sätzen im Bitt-Teil aus. Das bittende
Moment setzt sich über den StU hinweg in die Schluss-Strophe hinein
insofern fort, als auch die Vertrauens-Bekundung und das Lob-Gelüb-
de einen Aspekt nicht nur der Selbst-, sondern auch der Gottes-Mo-
tivierung enthalten. Hinter den genannten Aspekten wird ein alle Teile
des Gebetspsalms verbindendes Grundvertrauen ansichtig, das vor
dem StU am deutlichsten in den Gottes-Anrufungen (2a, 4ab), insbesondere in der auf das persönliche Verhältnis rekurrierenden Anrede
„mein Gott" (4b), erkennbar wird (Markschies; Irsigler; Janowski).
Mit den Gottes-Anrufungen ist Namens-theologisch auch eine Präsenz

---

[72] Vgl. auch die mögliche Weiterführung der drei Sozialdimensionen „Gott –
Ich – Feind" in die Schluss-Strophe hinein.

des Angerufenen und damit eine Realitätsveränderung hin zum Heil,
die sich auch auf frühere „Gnaden"-Erfahrungen abstüen kann — wie
6a explizit sagt —, evoziert (Lindström).

(6) Die neuen, d.h. im Vergleich zu den beiden vorangegangenen
Strophen (Klagen, Bitten) kontrastiven Elemente der Schluss-Strophe
wurden bisher meist gut gesehen und entsprechend herausgestrichen.
Mit dem die Schluss-Strophe eröffnenden „Ich aber…" wird sowohl
durch die adversativ nuancierte Konjunktion wie auch durch das betont vorangestellte, eine Ich-Handlung einführende Personalpronomen
ein neuer Akzent gesetzt. Von der in all den vorangehenden Versen
ansichtig gewordenen Notsituation ist in 6 nichts mehr spürbar (allenfalls implizit durch den durchschimmernden Toda-Horizont).[73] Der
atmosphärische Einschnitt geht einher mit neuer Begrifflichkeit, die
Vertrauen, Heil und Lobpreis als Zeichen einer heilvollen Gottes-
präsenz zum Ausdruck bringt. Das gegenüber den vorangehenden
Versen Neue wird im Schlussvers auch durch eine Reihe von kontrastiven Rückbezügen ersichtlich: So steht das vom Betenden bezeugte
(Wohl-)Tun im Gegensatz sowohl zu den Klagen am Psalmanfang als
auch zum Verhalten des Feindes gegenüber dem Beter. Das auch in
den suffigierten Nominalbegriffen von 6ab zum Ausdruck kommende
Heilshandeln Gottes steht im Kontrast zu dessen bisherigem Nicht-
Handeln. Zudem ist auch der Gegensatz im Blick auf das betende
Subjekt auffällig: Wie schon das eröffnende „Ich aber…" zeigt, ist
die in Strophe I und II doch eher unterschwellig präsente Vertrauensäusserung in Strophe III explizit gemacht, ja erst eigentlich initiiert.
Hier kommt — gerade auf dem Hintergrund der befürchteten Handlungen des Feindes, der das betende Ich zu überwältigen
trachtet — eine neue Entschiedenheit, eine Form von „Ich-Stärke"
zum Vorschein, die trotz und wider die vorfindliche Situation und die
Todesmächte bewusst auf Gott und dessen Gnade setzt. So steht das
„Vertrauen" gegen das „Wanken" (5b, 6a), das jubelnde „Herz" dem
kummervollen „Herz" gegenüber (3b, 6b), und das „Jubeln" der Bedränger über den wankenden Beter wird durchkreuzt durch das
„Jubeln" desselben zu Gott aufgrund seines Heilshandelns (5b, 6a).
Die Klage an Gott wird vom Lobpreis zu und über ihn abgelöst. Dabei
ist zu beachten, dass Vertrauen und Lob nicht zu „Gnade" und „Heilshandeln" Gottes hinführen, sondern umgekehrt von diesen herkom-
men. Damit liegt — ohne die neue Vertrauenssetzung des Betenden

---

[73] Aufgrund von 6 allein wüsste man nicht, dass man ein KE vor sich hat.

beiseite schieben zu wollen — die Letztbegründung für die neuerliche
Wende zum Heil und damit für den StU im Sein und Handeln Gottes
selber.

(7) Nun sind über den StU hinweg Anknüpfung und Absetzung
*zugleich* gegeben. Klage und Bitte sind mit Vertrauensäusserung und
Lob im selben Psalm vereint. Dieses „Zugleich" macht die Spannung
gerade aus. Aufgrund der oben skizzierten Momente von Anküpfung
und Absetzung wird man gegenüber Verstehensmodellen, die mit dem
StU eine einfache „Ablösung" von der Klage und Bitte zu Vertrauensäusserung und Lob(gelübde) verbinden, skeptisch sein. Zwar ist die
Reihenfolge der Strophen und damit die Abfolge der darin explizier-
ten Gebetsäusserungen samt der Fokussierung auf Strophe III hin we-
sentlich und konstitutiv für das Verständnis des Psalms. Sie ist aber
aufgrund der Zugehörigkeit des Psalms zur verspoetischen Textsorte,
die Räumlichkeit (Stereometrie) impliziert,[74] nicht (nur) im Sinne
einer strikt linearen Abfolge auszuwerten. Es ist vielmehr auch von
einem „Zugleich", also einer Simultanität der einzelnen Gebetsäusserungen auszugehen.[75] So ist ein „Gebetsprozess" (Janowski) nicht
einfach in Abrede zu stellen, aber auch nicht überzubetonen. Die Deutung des StUs im Sinne einer zeitlichen bzw. biographischen Zäsur ist
eine Art der Auffüllung der „Leerstelle", die Wahrheitsmomente enthalten mag, aber im Text selber keinen Anhalt hat. Im Gebetstext,
wie er mit Psalm 13 vorliegt, sind alle Teile — damit auch Klagen und
Bitten, die nicht „abgestossen" wurden — in ein poetisches Ganzes
eingebunden. Die Beobachtungen hinsichtlich des „Zugleichs" von
Klage und Lob und damit von erfahrener und behobener Not verschär-
fen sich noch, wenn man die zwischen Retrospektive und Prolepse
pendelnden Zeithorizonte in 6 beachtet: Einstiges Heilshandeln, die
vertrauensvolle Aktualisierung früherer Heilserfahrungen in der
Gegenwart und die VorabBezeugung, dass Gott wieder neu heilvoll
am Betenden gewirkt hat bzw. gewirkt haben wird, greifen gleichsam
ineinander. V.a. wird das zukünftige Heil, das bejubelt und vor Gott
wie der Gemeinde bekannt werden soll bzw. wird, bereits in die

---

[74] Vgl. zur theoretischen Grundlegung B. Weber, *Psalm 77 und sein Umfeld.*
*Eine poetologische Studie* (BBB 103; Weinheim: Beltz Athenäum, 1995) v.a.
7–11, 29–32.

[75] In diese Richtung deuten auch Hinweise von KE, die mehrere Durchläufe
von Klagen / Bitten und Vertrauensäusserungen aufweisen (vgl. z.B. die Psalmen
3; 22).

Gegenwart hineingeholt. Damit wird die in der Gottes-Ferne
gründende Notsituation durch den im Vertrauen auf Gottes „Gnade"
realisierten Lobpreis überblendet, der die Gottes-Nähe schon hereinbrechen lässt. Offensichtlich führt das bewusste Aussprechen des
Vertrauens und des Lob(versprechen)s vor Gott aufseiten des Betenden zu einer veränderten Wahrnehmung und Einschätzung der
Wirklichkeit. Es stellt sich im (Nach-)Beten des Psalms — trotz
scheinbar noch ausstehender Heilswende — nicht nur Erhörungsgewissheit ein, sondern die Heilswende und die darauf erfolgende Toda
vor Gott und der versammelten Gemeinde wird antizipiert. Die ver-
trauende und lobpreisende Vorwegnahme der erwarteten Gottes- und
Heilsgegenwart ist der letzte Schritt, den dieses Gebet geht und — vor
der Erhörung durch Gott — gehen kann. Die Überlieferung, Aufbe-
wahrung und Kanonisierung von Psalm 13 ist ein Hinweis darauf,
dass diese Psalmworte bei vielen (Nach)Betenden „wirksam" waren
und von Gott durch sein Eingreifen zum Heil beantwortet wurden.

(8) Das Ergebnis der Untersuchung beschränkt sich auf Psalm 13.
Es ist im Hinblick auf andere KE und deren StU, evtl. auch auf Toda-
Psalmen zu prüfen, zu modifizieren und zu variieren. Im Blick auf die
Praxis des Psalm-Lesens bzw. -Betens ist auch die Möglichkeit eines
wiederholten Lesens und Betens durch den jeweiligen Verwender des
Psalms (Relecture) und damit einer performatorischen Zyklizität zu
bedenken. Dadurch könnte sich eine Vertiefung der Gebetsäusserun-
gen und eine Art von „Vertrauens-Akkumulierung" eingestellt haben.
Im Blick auf unser Thema des StUs ist schliesslich auch darüber
nachzudenken, ob sich durch die Einbettung von Psalm 13 in seinen
jetzigen Kontext (insbesondere die Kleingruppe Psalmen 11–14) neue
Aspekte ergeben.

(9) Die angeführten Erwägungen und tastenden Erklärungsversuche
zum StU in Psalm 13 können und sollen die damit verbundene Leerstelle nicht auffüllen. Psalmen als poetische Texte mit ihrem Ambi-
guitäts-Charakter sind auf Offenheit hin angelegt. Die hier sprachlich
zum Ausdruck kommende, von Gott erflehte und göttlich gewirkte
Wende vom Unheil zum Heil ist im Letzten nicht erklärbar. Ob sie
kommt und wie sie kommt, bleibt Gott vorbehalten. So bleibt in den
mit dem StU verbundenen Geschehenszusammenhängen eine Nähe
zum Geheimnis, zum Wunder, denn Gottes „Gnade" (חסד) ist nicht
verrechenbar und im Letzten auch nicht einsichtig. Damit tritt zur po-
etologischen eine theologische Begründung der gerade auch im StU
angelegten Offenheit dieses Psalms.

## VERWENDETE LITERATUR

Begrich, J. „Das priesterliche Heilsorakel", *ZAW* 53 (1934) 81–92 (= Ders., *Gesammelte Studien zum Alten Testament* [ThB 21; München: Kaiser, 1964] 217–31).

Craigie, P. C. *Psalms 1–50* (WBC 19; Waco, TX: Word, 1983).

Ehlers, K. „Wege aus der Vergessenheit. Zu einem neuen Sammelband zum Thema ‚Klage', "*JBTh* 16 (2001) 383–96.

Erbele-Küster, D. *Lesen als Akt des Betens. Eine Rezeptionsästhetik der Psalmen* (WMANT 87; Neukirchen-Vluyn: Neukirchener, 2001).

Etzelmüller, G. „Als ich den Herrn suchte, antwortete er mir. Zu Patrick Millers Monographie über Form und Theologie des biblischen Gebetes", *JBTh* 16 (2001) 397–406.

Fokkelmann, J. P. *Major Poems of the Hebrew Bible at the Interface of Prosody and Structural Analysis. Volume II: 85 Psalms and Job 4–14* (SNN; Assen: Van Gorcum, 2000).

Fuchs, O. *Die Klage als Gebet. Eine theologische Besinnung am Beispiel des Psalms 22* (München: Kösel, 1982).

Gerstenberger, E. *Der bittende Mensch. Bittritual und Klagelied des Einzelnen im Alten Testament* (WMANT 51; Neukirchen-Vluyn: Neukirchener, 1980).

Gross, W. *Doppelt besetztes Vorfeld. Syntaktische, pragmatische und übersetzungstechnische Studien zum althebräischen Verbalsatz* (BZAW 305; Berlin: de Gruyter, 2001).

Gunkel, H. *Die Psalmen* (4. Auflage; HKAT II/2; Göttingen: Vandenhoeck & Ruprecht, 1926).

—. (& Begrich, J.). *Einleitung in die Psalmen. Die Gattungen der religiösen Lyrik Israels* (HK–Ergänzungsband zur II. Abteilung; Göttingen: Vandenhoeck & Ruprecht, 1933).

Hauge, M. R. *Between Sheol and Temple. Motif Structure and Function in the I-Psalms* (JSOTSup 178; Sheffield: Sheffield Academic Press, 1995).

Hossfeld, F.-L. & E. Zenger. *Die Psalmen I. Psalm 1–50* (NEchB.AT; Würzburg: Echter, 1993).

Irsigler, H. „Psalm-Rede als Handlungs-, Wirk- und Aussageprozess. Sprechaktanalyse und Psalmeninterpretation am Beispiel von Psalm 13", in: K. Seybold & E. Zenger (Hrsg.), *Neue Wege der Psalmenforschung. FS W. Beyerlin* (HBS 1; Freiburg: Herder, 1994) 63–104.

Janowski, B. „Das verborgene Angesicht Gottes. Psalm 13 als Muster eines Klagelieds des einzelnen", *JBTh* 21 (2001) 25–53.

Jenni, E. *Die hebräischen Präpositionen. Band 1: Die Präposition Beth* (Stuttgart: Kohlhammer, 1992).

Keel, O. *Feinde und Gottesleugner. Studien zum Image der Widersacher in den Individualpsalmen* (SBM 7; Stuttgart: Katholisches Bibelwerk, 1969).

Kellenberger, E. *ḥäsäd wäᵃʾmät als Ausdruck einer Glaubenserfahrung. Gottes Offen-Werden und Bleiben als Voraussetzung des Lebens* (AThANT 69; Zürich: Theologischer Verlag, 1982).

Kilian, R. „Ps 22 und das priesterliche Heilsorakel", *BZ* 12 (1968) 172–85.

Kraus, H.-J. *Psalmen. 1. Teilband: Psalmen 1–59* (5. Auflage; BK XV/1; Neu-kirchen-Vluyn: Neukirchener, 1978).

Lindström, F. *Suffering and Sin. Interpretations of Illness in the Individual Complaint Psalms* (CBOT 37; Stockholm: Almqvist & Wiksell, 1994).

Markschies, C. „„Ich aber vertraue auf dich, Herr!'—Vertrauensäusserungen als Grundmotiv in den Klageliedern des Einzelnen", *ZAW* 103 (1991) 386–98.

Müller, A. R. „Stimmungsumschwung im Klagepsalm. Zu Ottmar Fuchs, ,Die Klage als Gebet', "*ALW* 28 (1986) 416–26.

Schroeder, C. O. *History, Justice, and the Agency of God. A Hermeneutical and Exegetical Investigation on Isaiah and Psalms* (Biblical Interpretation Series 52; Leiden: Brill, 2001).

Seybold, K. *Die Psalmen. Eine Einführung* (UB 382; Stuttgart: Kohlhammer, 1986).

Steck, O. H. „Beobachtungen zur Beziehung von Klage und Bitte in Psalm 13", *BN* 13 (1980) 57–62.

Steiner, R. C. „Does the Biblical Hebrew Conjunction -ו Have Many Meanings, One Meaning, or No Meaning at All?", *JBL* 119 (2000) 249–67.

Stoebe, H. J. „חֶסֶד *ḥésed* Güte", *THAT* I (3. Auflage; 1978) 600–21.

Tita, H. *Gelübde als Bekenntnis. Eine Studie zu den Gelübden im Alten Testament* (OBO 181; Freiburg: Universitätsverlag; Göttingen: Vandenhoeck & Ruprecht, 2001).

Weber, B. *Psalm 77 und sein Umfeld. Eine poetologische Studie* (BBB 103; Weinheim: Beltz Athenäum, 1995).

—. „Lob und Klage in den Psalmen des Alten Testaments als Anfrage und Herausforderung an unsere Gebets- und Gottesdienstpraxis", *Jahrbuch für evangelikale Theologie* 13 (1999) 33–47.

—. *Werkbuch Psalmen I. Die Psalmen 1 bis 72* (Stuttgart: Kohlhammer, 2001).

Westermann, C. *Lob und Klage in den Psalmen* (6. Auflage; Göttingen: Vanden-hoeck & Ruprecht, 1983 [1977]).

Zenger, E. *Die Nacht wird leuchten wie der Tag. Psalmenauslegungen* (Freiburg: Herder, 1997).

# AN INTERTEXTUAL READING OF PSALMS 22, 23, AND 24

## NANCY L. deCLAISSÉ-WALFORD

אֵלִי אֵלִי לָמָה עֲזַבְתָּנִי, "My God, my God, why have you forsaken me?" Thus begins one of the most heartfelt laments in the Hebrew Psalter. It is a lament made more poignant, perhaps, because of its connection with the passion narratives of Jesus of Nazareth. According the writers of the Gospels of Matthew and Mark, Jesus spoke the opening words of Psalm 22 in his dying moment as he hung on the crucifixion cross.[1] In addition, Psalm 22 is the traditional psalm read at the feast of Purim, words placed on the lips of Esther as she risks her life to save her people.

But Psalm 22 is poignant in itself, without any connection to the heroic efforts of Esther or to the passion narratives of the Christian scriptures. J. Clinton McCann, Jr., observes, in fact, that "Psalm 22 is not unique because it is used in the New Testament (and, we might add, used at Purim); rather it is used in the New Testament (and at Purim) because it is unique."[2] The words of this psalm are gutsy, graphic, and grief-filled. They give the reader pause; they make the reader stop and consider. So let us pause for a moment and consider the words of Psalm 22.

We will begin by observing that Psalm 22 is a usual psalm and yet an unusual psalm. In what ways is it usual?

1. It is a lament.
2. It is ascribed to David.

In Book I of the Psalter, where Psalm 22 is located, twenty-seven of the forty-one psalms are laments. And all of the psalms in found here, except for Psalms 1 and 2, are "psalms of David."[3] The superscription

---

[1] Angela M. Hubbard, in "Psalm 2 and the Paschal Mystery," *The Bible Today* 36 (1998) 111, states: "The passion story is probably the oldest continuous narrative about Jesus and Psalm 22 is tightly woven into that narrative."

[2] J. Clinton McCann, Jr., "The Book of Psalms," in Leander E. Keck (ed.), *The New Interpreter's Bible* (Nashville: Abingdon, 1996) 4.762.

[3] Psalm 10 is strongly linked to Psalm 9. See H.-J. Kraus, *Psalms 1–59: A Commentary* (Minneapolis: Augsburg, 1988) 188–89; and William L. Holladay, *The Psalms through Three Thousand Years: Prayerbook of a Cloud of Witnesses* (Minneapolis: Fortress, 1993) 77. Psalm 33 has solid linguistic links to Psalm 32.

of Psalm 22 reads, for the leader: אַיֶּלֶת הַשַּׁחַר—translated variously as "upon the deer of the dawn," "upon the doe of the morning," or "according to the hind of the dawn." It is usual; it is a lament; it is "of David."

But Psalm 22 is also unusual. It is located in a portion of Book I of the Psalter that is different from the rest of the Book. Beginning with Psalm 18, the psalms in Book I change for a short while from the persistent lamenting of Psalms 3–17,[4] to psalms of different types. Psalm 18, which is categorized as a royal psalm, praises the kind and good deliverance which God brings to the king:

| PSALMS 18–24 |
| --- |
| 13 of the first 17 psalms in Book I are laments: |
| Psalm 18 — Royal Psalm |
| Psalm 19 — Creation Psalm |
| Psalm 20 — Royal Psalm |
| Psalm 21 — Royal Psalm |
| *Psalm 22 — Lament Psalm* |
| Psalm 23 — Trust Psalm |
| Psalm 24 — Entrance Liturgy |
| 10 of the 17 remaining psalms are laments. |

> The LORD is my rock, my fortress and my deliverer,
> My God, my rock, in whom I take refuge;
> My shield and the horn of my salvation, my stronghold.
> I call upon the LORD, who is worthy to be praised,
> And I am saved from my enemies. (vv. 1-3)[5]

Next comes Psalm 19, a creation psalm, which celebrates God's sovereignty over the created world:

> The heavens are telling of the glory of God;
> And their expanse is declaring the work of God's hands. (v. 1)

Psalms 20 and 21, are — like Psalm 18 — royal psalms of thanks and praise:

> Now I know that the LORD saves the LORD's anointed ...
> For the king trusts in the LORD and through the steadfast love of the Most High;
>     the king will not be shaken. (20:6; 21:7)

Thus we find four psalms of thanksgiving and praise (Psalms 18–21) clustered at the end of an extended collection of laments — a break for the reader from the words of Psalms 3–17. Quite dramatically, though, the reader is returned to the realm of lament in Psalm 22:

> My God, My God, why have you forsaken me? ...
> Oh my God, I cry by day, but you do not answer

---

See Gerald H. Wilson's treatment in *The Editing of the Hebrew Psalter* (SBLDS 76; Chico, CA: Scholars Press, 1985) 174–75.

[4] In Psalms 3–17, only Psalms 8 and 15 are not laments.

[5] We will use English verse designations throughout the article.

> And by night, but find no rest ...
> I am a worm and not human;
> Scorned by others, and despised by the people....
> Many bulls encircle me,
> Strong bulls of Bashan surround me; ...
> I am poured out like water,
> And all my bones are out of joint ...
> My mouth is dried up like a potsherd,
> And my tongue sticks to my jaws ...
> Dogs are around me;
> A company of evildoers encircle me. (vv. 1, 2, 6, 12, 14-16)

Immediately following is Psalm 23, which is classified as a psalm of trust in the LORD:

> The LORD is my shepherd, I shall not want.
> The LORD makes me lie down in green pastures;
> The LORD leads me beside still waters ...
> Even though I walk through the darkest valley,
> I fear no evil ...
> And I shall dwell in the house of the LORD
> For length of days. (vv. 1-2, 4, 6)

And the next psalm, Psalm 24, is an entrance liturgy:

> Lift up your heads, O gates,
> And be lifted up, O ancient doors,
> That the king of glory may come in.
> Who is the king of glory?
> The LORD, strong and mighty ...
> Lift up your heads, O gates!
> And be lifted up, O ancient doors!
> That the king of glory may come in. (vv. 7-9)

With Psalm 25, the reader is returned to the characteristic lamenting of Book I. And of the seventeen psalms remaining in the Book, ten are laments.[6] The pause in the lamenting of Book I which begins with Psalm 18 and ends with Psalm 24 is intriguing. And the placement of Psalm 22 in the midst of that pause is perhaps most intriguing of all. Those concerned with the shape and shaping of the Hebrew Psalter are well-justified in asking the question, "Why is this psalm in this particular place and in this particular relationship with the psalms surrounding it?" Can we find a satisfying explanation?

We will begin our study at the beginning. Book I of the Psalter appears to be an ancient collection of psalms of David which was placed

---

[6] Psalms 25–28, 31, 35–36, and 38–40.

as a unit at the beginning of the Psalter, with Psalms 1 and 2 as introductory material to both Book I and to the entire Psalter.[7]

The first question to be asked is whether we are permitted to read
the psalms in Book I as a unit that is ancient and traditional. All of our
textual evidence — the Septuagint, the Dead Sea Scrolls (especially
the Cave 4 Psalms scrolls and the Naḥal Ḥever manuscripts),[8] and the
Midrash on the Psalter — indicates a
traditional connectedness between the
psalms of Book I. If we search for evidence for the connectedness of Psalms
22, 23, or 24, the only concrete data
come from the Naḥal Ḥever Psalms
scroll (5/6 ḤevPs). The surviving fragments preserve portions of Psalms 22,
23, and 24, grouped together in succession in the midst of Psalms 7–14, 18, and
then 25, 29, and 31.[9]

| NAḤAL ḤEVER (5/6 ḤevPs) | |
|---|---|
| Psalms 7 | 18 |
| 8 | 22:4-9, 15-21 |
| 9 | 23:2-6 |
| 10 | 24:1-2 |
| 11 | 25 |
| 12 | 29 |
| 13 | 31 |
| 14 | |

None of the extant scrolls from Qumran has Psalms 22, 23, and 24,
with the sole exception of 4QPs[f] (4Q88), which contains Psalms
22:15-17, followed by portions of Psalms 107, 108, and 109. We may
conclude that the ancient evidence permits us — perhaps it would be
better to say does not forbid us — to read Book I of the Psalter as a
unit and to read Psalms 22, 23, and 24 as a connected sequence.

J. Clinton McCann has already observed a number of links between
the first five verses of Psalm 22 and Psalms 20 and 21—two of the
psalms that begin the pause in lamenting in Book I.[10] He cites a number of words that the three psalms have in common, such as ישׁע
("help") in Pss 20:5-6, 9; 21:1, 5; and 22:1; ענה ("answer") in 20:1, 6,
9; and 22:2; and בטח ("trust") in 21:7 and 22:4-5. McCann writes:

> In Psalms 20–21 [which, let us recall, are classified as royal psalms], there
> is the certainty that the sovereign God will answer and help the king, who

---

[7] See Nancy L. deClaissé-Walford, *Reading from the Beginning: The Shaping
of the Hebrew Psalter* (Macon, GA: Mercer University Press, 1997) 37–48; Patrick D. Miller, "The Beginning of the Psalter," in J. Clinton McCann (ed.), *The
Shape and Shaping of the Psalter* (JSOTSup 159; Sheffield: JSOT Press, 1993)
84–88; and McCann, "The Book of Psalms," 664–65.

[8] Peter W. Flint, *The Dead Sea Psalms Scrolls and the Book of Psalms* (STDJ
17; Leiden: Brill, 1997) 257–63.

[9] Flint, *Dead Sea Psalms Scrolls*, 257–63

[10] McCann, "The Book of Psalms," 754–59.

lives by his trust in God. Thus the canonical sequence emphasizes the sharp contrast between Psalms 20 and 21 and Psalm 22:1-5:

> My God, my God, why have you forsaken me?
> Oh my God, I cry by day, but you do not answer;
> And by night, but find no rest.

For in the first five verses of Psalm 22, there is no help and no answer for the psalmist.[11]

This writer is fully in agreement with David M. Howard, who cautions in an essay in *The Shape and Shaping of the Psalter* that if research into the connections between adjacent psalms continues to be carried out, soon "every pair of adjacent psalms will be shown to have some significant—or logical—links between them" (a case of "be careful what you go looking for, because you will probably find it").[12] Nevertheless, this reader sees a strong connectedness between Psalms 22, 23, and 24.

Psalm 22 is classified as an individual lament. And if we accept McCann's tying together of Psalms 20, 21, and 22, then we can hear in the words of Psalm 22 the laments of a king of ancient Israel. Laments consist of a number of elements.[13] Psalm 22 expresses those elements in the following ways:

1. In the *Invocation*, the psalmist cries out to God to hear and listen: "My God, my God" and "O my God" (vv. 1, 2).

2. In the *Complaint* (or the *Lament*), the psalmist tells God what is

---

[11] McCann, "The Book of Psalms," 762.

[12] David M. Howard, "Editorial Activity in the Psalter," in McCann (ed.), *The Shape and Shaping of the Psalter*, 68.

[13] William H. Bellinger, Jr., *Psalms: Reading and Studying the Book of Praises* (Peabody MA: Hendrickson Publishers, 1990) 45–46, cites four elements in a lament psalm: invocation, complaint, petition, and expression of confidence. This four-fold division is a simplification of Bellinger's previous six-element analysis, found in his *Psalmody and Prophecy* (JSOTSup 27; Sheffield: JSOT Press, 1984) 22–24. James Limburg, in *Psalms* (Westminster Bible Companion; Louisville KY: Westminster John Knox Press, 2000) 8, cites three elements in a lament psalm: complaint, affirmation of trust, and call for help or request. McCann, in "The Book of Psalms," 644–45, outlines five elements: opening address, description of trouble or distress, plea or petition to God, profession of trust or confidence in God, and promise or vow to praise God or to offer a sacrifice. I have adopted a five-fold format for the lament, but with somewhat different category titles than McCann uses: invocation, complaint, petition, expression of trust, and expression of praise. This is modified from my own previous four-fold division; see deClaissé-Walford, *Reading from the Beginning*, 50.

wrong. "I am a worm and not a human being." "Dogs have surrounded me; a band of evildoers have encompassed me" (vv. 6, 16).

3. In the *Petition*, the psalmist tells God what the psalmist wants God to do. "Deliver my being from the sword and my only life from the power of the dog." "Save me from the lion's mouth" (vv. 20, 21).

4. In the *Expression of Trust*, the psalmist tells God why he or she knows that God can do what the psalmist asks. "Yet you are the one who brought me forth from the womb; you made me trust when upon my mother's breasts. Upon you I was cast from birth; you have been my God from my mother's womb" (vv. 9, 10).

5. And in the *Expression of Praise and Adoration*, the psalmist celebrates the goodness and sovereignty of the LORD. "All of the ends of the earth will remember and turn to the LORD—and all of the families of the nations will worship before you. For the kingdom is the LORD's and the LORD rules over the nations" (vv. 27, 28).

| 1. Invocation | — vv. 1-2 |
| 2. Complaint/Lament | — vv. 1-2, 6-8, 12-18 |
| 3. Petition | — vv. 11, 19-21 |
| 4. Expression of Trust | — vv. 3-5, 9-10 |
| 5. Expression of Praise | — vv. 22-31 |

Psalm 22 contains all of the elements of a lament; and the lament's resolution, in the form of expressions or praise and adoration, is lavished upon the reader at the end of the psalm, in verses 22-31. But Psalm 22 is powerful, and this writer exited the psalm with puzzled feelings of depression and despair.

We might wonder if the despair and depression would not be so deep if we had a specific instance in the life of the psalmist David to which to tie the Psalm, to give it a story-world to inhabit — as we have in Psalms 3, 18, 56, and ten others in the Psalter.[14] These psalms give the reader a context within which to understand the words of the psalm, one that provides the reader with "hooks" on which to hang the words of the lament, the feelings of despair, and the heartfelt petitions to God. The superscription of Psalm 56, for instance, reads "of David: a Miktam, when the Philistines seized him in Gath." And that gives the reader an initial context for understanding the words of the Psalm:

Be gracious to me, O God, for people trample on me;
all day long foes oppress me;

---

[14] Thirteen psalms in the Hebrew Psalter locate themselves, in their superscriptions, in specific events in the life of David: 3, 7, 18, 34, 51, 52, 54, 56, 57, 59, 60, 63, and 142.

my enemies trample on me all day long,
for many fight against me. (vv. 1, 2a)

Psalm 51's superscription reads "to the leader: a psalm of David, when the prophet Nathan came to him, after he had gone in to Bathsheba," a setting for the words:

Have mercy on me, O God,
according to your steadfast love;
according to your abundant mercy
blot out my transgressions.
Wash me thoroughly from my iniquity,
and cleanse me from my sin. (vv. 1, 2)

But Psalm 22 does not give the reader such a context. Its superscription reads simply, "to the leader: upon אַיֶּלֶת הַשַּׁחַר (the deer of the dawn), a psalm of David." And then:

My God, my God, why have you forsaken me?
Why are you so far from helping me,
from the words of my groaning?
O my God, I cry by day, but you do not answer;
and by night, but find no rest. (vv. 1, 2)

No hooks, no initial context for the reading of these difficult words.

The rest of the psalm has no more concrete contextual clues. Its form, though, may give us some clues. Ellen Davis, in a 1992 article in *JSOT,* describes the psalm as extravagant — extravagant in both its expressions of lament and in its expressions of praise.[15]

The lament (or complaint) of Psalm 22 occurs in three sections. The first two sections of laments, verses 1-2 and 6-8, are followed by expressions of trust in God. In verse 3, we read:

Yet you are holy,
enthroned on the praises of Israel.
In you our ancestors trusted;
they trusted and you delivered them.

And in verse 9, we read:

Yet it was you who took me from the womb;
you kept me safe on my mother's breast.
On you I was cast from my birth,
and since my mother bore me you have been my God.

The two laments conclude in verse 11 with the petition אַל־תִּרְחַק מִמֶּנִּי

---

[15] Ellen F. Davis, "Exploding the Limits: Form and Function in Psalm 22," *JSOT* 53 (1992) 93–105.

"(do not be far away from me), for trouble is near and there is no one
to help."

The third lament, found in verses 12-18, is longer and more vivid
than the previous two, using
strong metaphorical images to
depict the psalmist's despair:

| STRUCTURE OF PSALM 22 |
| --- |
| Lament (vv. 1-2) |
| Trust (vv. 3-5) |
| Lament (vv. 6-8) |
| Trust (vv. 9-10) |
| Petition (v. 11) |
| Lament (vv. 12-18) |
| Petition (vv. 19-21) |
| Praise (vv. 22-31) |

> many bulls surround me ...
> my heart is like wax ...
> my mouth is dried up like a
> potsherd ...
> dogs are all around me ...
> I can count all my bones.

This lament is not followed by an
expression of confidence and trust in God, but only by a terse petition,
found in verses 19-21, which begins with the same word as the petition that follows the previous two laments:

> But you, O LORD, אַל־תִּרְחָק (do not be far away)!
> O my help, come quickly to my aid!
> Deliver my being from the sword,
> my life from the power of the dog!

Ellen Davis characterizes the conclusion of Psalm 22, verses 22-31, as
"a flood of praise." Indeed, the words of the psalmist in these verses
are joyous and full of praise:

> I will tell of your name to my brothers and sisters;
> in the midst of the congregation I will praise you:
> You who fear the LORD, praise him!
> All you offspring of Jacob, glorify him;
> stand in awe of him, all you offspring of Israel! ...
> Posterity will serve him;
> future generations will be told about the LORD,
> and proclaim his deliverance to a people yet unborn,
> saying that he has done it.

An extravagance of lament; and an extravagance of praise. A self-
contained unit of lamenting. But, as stated earlier, this writer exited
the psalm with feelings of depression and despair. The strong bulls
and the dogs still surround us; our mouth is like a potsherd; our enemies are still staring and gloating.

Does the extravagance of lament in Psalm 22 need further words of
trust in order to move it to resolution? Might we be permitted to read
Psalm 23's words of trust as an answer to the extravagant lamenting

found in Psalm 22? Words of trust are, after all, missing after Psalm 22's third lament, found in verses 12-18.

Might we further be permitted to read Psalm 24 as the final words of "extravagant" praise in this sequence of psalms? The evidence from the Septuagint and from the Dead Sea documents indicates that Psalms 23 and 24 seem to be fixed firmly in their positions following Psalm 22.

The three psalms together form an interesting structure. The extravagant lament found in 22:12-18 forms the center of the structure. Petitions lie on either side — verse 11 and verses 19-21. The edges of this structure are formed in the following ways. At the beginning of Psalm 22, we find a lament in verses 1-2, an expression of confidence in verses 3-5, another lament in verses 6-8, and another expression of trust in verses 9-10. At the end of the Psalm 22, we find an expression of praise in 22-31, an expression of trust in Psalm 23, and another expression of praise in Psalm 24.[16] A lament and petitions in the middle of the structure, introduced by laments and expressions of trust and concluded with praise and an expression of trust.

> STRUCTURE OF PSALMS
> 22, 23, AND 24
>
> Lament (22:1-2)
>   Trust (22:3-5)
>     Lament (22:6-8)
>       Trust (22:9-10)
>         Petition (22:11)
>           *Lament (22:12-18)*
>         Petition (22:19-21)
>       Praise (22:22-31)
>     Trust (Ps 23)
>   Praise (Ps 24)

The vocabulary of the three psalms also reveals some interesting connections. The *Midrash Tehillim* associates Psalm 22 with David's early life as a shepherd. According to the *Midrash*, David spoke the words of Psalm 22:21, "Save me from the lion's mouth; from the horns of the wild oxen you have answered me," at a time when he was shepherding and being threatened by these two animals. God rescued David after the wild oxen had lifted him in its horns by sending first a lion to compel the ox to kneel in homage before the king of beasts and then a wild gazelle to distract the threatening lion while David escaped.[17] The superscription of Psalm 22, עַל־אַיֶּלֶת הַשַּׁחַר, is usually

---

[16] And, in fact, we might argue that the laments of Psalms 25–28 would complete the chiastic structure of this group of psalms.

[17] See William G. Braude, *The Midrash on Psalms*, vol. 1 (New Haven CT: Yale University Press, 1959) 322.

translated "according to the deer of the dawn," but might better be rendered "concerning the deer of the dawn," in reference to the deer-like creature that saved David from the lion and the wild ox.

Psalm 23 expresses confidence in the LORD as רֹעֶה — as shepherd — to the psalmist, a shepherd who supplies everything the psalmist needs: green pastures, still waters, right paths, protection, abundant sustenance, and a secure dwelling. The imagery in Psalm 23 certainly stands in sharp contrast to the imagery of the lament portions of Psalm 22. In Psalm 22, the psalmist cries out to God and accuses God of being far away and of not answering the psalmist's cry for help; of being silent when those around mock and shake their heads; of paying no heed when bulls and lions and dogs and evildoers surround; and of ignoring the fact that the psalmist's body is shriveled and emaciated.

Indeed, God lays the psalmist in עֲפַר מָוֶת ("the dust of death"), כִּי ("because") עֲדַת מְרֵעִים ("a band of evildoers") surround the psalmist. In verses 11 and 19, the psalmist cries out: וְאַתָּה יְהוָה אַל־תִּרְחָק מִמֶּנִּי ("but you, O LORD, do not be far from me"), כִּי ("because") צָרָה קְרוֹבָה ("trouble is nearby").

| PSALM 22 | PSALM 23 |
|---|---|
| עֲפַר מָוֶת | גֵּיא צַלְמָוֶת |
| "the dust of death" (v. 15) | "the valley of deep darkness" (v. 4) |
| כִּי | רָע |
| "because" (v. 16) | "evil" (v. 4) |
| עֲדַת מְרֵעִים | כִּי |
| "a band of evildoers" (v. 16) | "because" (v. 4) |
| וְאַתָּה יְהוָה אַל־תִּרְחָק מִמֶּנִּי | אַתָּה עִמָּדִי |
| "but you O LORD, do not be far from me" (v. 11, 19) | "you are with me" (v. 4) |
| צָרָה קְרוֹבָה | נֶגֶד צֹרְרָי |
| "trouble is nearby" (v. 11) | "in front of my troublers" (v. 5) |

In Psalm 23, in contrast, even while walking through גֵּיא צַלְמָוֶת ("the valley of deep darkness" or "the valley of the shadow of death"),[18] the psalmist will not fear רָע ("evil)", כִּי ("because") אַתָּה עִמָּדִי ("you are with me"). And in fact, YHWH "prepares a table" for the psalmist נֶגֶד צֹרְרָי ("in front of my troublers").

The verbal connections between Psalm 22 and 23 are striking. And

---

[18] In Job 10:22, the word צַלְמָוֶת describes the realm of the dead (McCann, "The Book of Psalms," 768).

the contextual connections between the laments of Psalm 22 and the expression of trust in Psalm 23 are compelling. In Psalm 22 the psalmist feels surrounded, threatened, and bereft of the presence of God. In Psalm 23, the psalmist is still surrounded and threatened, but God is present, and for the psalmist, that fact makes all the difference. The words of the first five verses of Psalm 23 seem to fit well with the third lament of Psalm 22 (vv. 12-18) and its petition (vv. 19-21) — the very lament and petition in Psalm 22 which have no expression of trust attached to them.

In the middle of verse 21 of Psalm 22, the psalmist's petition to God ceases, and we find the words, "from the horns of the wild oxen you have answered me ... I will tell of your name to my kindred." Here we find the turning point of Psalm 22's third lament. The psalmist's despair is answered with words of hope: "from the

| STRUCTURE OF PSALM 22 |
|---|
| Lament (vv. 1-2) |
| Trust (vv. 3-5) |
| Lament (vv. 6-8) |
| Trust (vv. 9-10) |
| Petition (v. 11) |
| Lament (vv. 12-18) |
| *No words of trust* |
| Petition (vv. 19-21) |
| Praise (vv. 22-31) |

horns of the wild oxen you have answered me." McCann comments on verse 21: "The answer comes not beyond suffering, but precisely in the midst of and even from the suffering! God is somehow present—in the depths and even amid death."[19] McCann's analysis is also appropriate for the expression of confidence we find in Psalm 23. God is present in the midst of the "valley of deep darkness," and, in fact, the shriveled and emaciated psalmist can sit down and eat at the table God has prepared "in the presence of" the psalmist's "troublers."

Psalm 23 ends with words of praise in which the psalmist confidently states: "I shall dwell in the house of the LORD for length of days" (v. 6). And in Psalm 22's extended words of praise in verses 22-31, the psalmist says: "I will tell of your name to my kindred. In the midst of the congregation I will praise you" (v. 31). That brings the reader to Psalm 24.

Psalm 24 is classified by form critics as an entrance liturgy.[20] It was most likely sung in ancient Israel as worshipers entered the sanctuary or the temple in Jerusalem during the three pilgrimage festivals of an-

---

[19] McCann, "The Book of Psalms," 764.

[20] See for example, Bellinger, *Psalms*, 89; and McCann, "The Book of Psalms," 772.

cient Israel: the Feasts of Unleavened Bread, First Fruits, and Tabernacles.[21] In the postexilic period, Psalm 24 was read as a celebration
of creation in a group of psalms called the *Tamid*, which were read
during the daily service at the temple.[22] In modern synagogue worship, the Psalm is recited on the Sabbath as the Torah scroll is being
returned to the ark; in the wider Christian tradition, Psalm 24 is traditionally read on Ascension Sunday; and in the Reformed tradition,
verses 7-10 of the Psalm are recited when the elements of the Eucharist are brought to the table.[23]

In the form preserved in the Hebrew Psalter, Psalm 24 is a celebration of the kingship of the LORD and of the LORD's sovereignty over
all creation. It opens with the words:

> The earth is the LORD's and all that is in it,
> the world, and those who live in it;
> for God has founded it on the seas,
> and established it on the rivers. (vv. 1-2)

God, the creator, ordered the world out of the chaos of the waters, the
יַמִּים and the נְהָרֹת, and thus the world and all those who live it in belong to God.

The Psalm continues in verses 3-6 to outline, in a question and answer format, the required demeanor of those who would enter the holy
place.

> Who shall ascend the hill of the LORD?
> And who shall stand in God's holy place? (v. 3)

Only those with "clean hands and pure hearts, who do not lift up their
beings to what is false, and do not swear deceitfully" (v. 4), only
those, declares the psalmist, will receive blessing and צְדָקָה ("justice")
from the LORD (v. 5).

The God of Israel is a God of order (in creation) and a God of justice. Walter Brueggemann writes: "Israel's very existence as a historical community is dependent upon and derived from the LORD's ini-

---

[21] Nahum Sarna, *On the Book of Psalms* (New York: Schocken, 1993) 103.

[22] Mishnah, *Tractate Tamid*, 7.4. The psalms read were: Sunday–Psalm 24;
Monday–Psalm 48; Tuesday–Psalm 82; Wednesday–Psalm 94; Thursday–Psalm
81; Friday–Psalm 93; Saturday–Psalm 92. The superscription to Psalm 24(23) in
the Septuagint reads ψαλμὸς τῷ Δαυιδ τῆς μιᾶς σαββάτων ("a psalm of David,
the one for the Sabbath").

[23] Robert Davidson, *The Vitality of Worship* (Grand Rapids: Eerdmans, 1998)
88–89.

tial, even primordial, preoccupation with justice."[24] Thus the psalmist who is surrounded by dogs (22:16) and mocked and scorned by others (22:6, 7) can state with confidence that "even though I walk through the valley of deep darkness, I will fear no evil" (23:4) and that, indeed, "the earth is the LORD's and all that is in it" (24:1). Why? We find our answer in Psalm 22; there the psalmist reminds God:

> It was you who took me from the womb;
> you kept me safe on my mother's breast.
> On you I was cast from my birth,
> and since my mother bore me you have been my God. (9, 10)

God is sovereign, and even in the midst of bulls and dogs and lions and evildoers, in the midst of mocking and sneering, in the midst of joint-breaking, heart-melting emaciation, God prepares a table and feeds and cares for "those who have clean hands and pure hearts, who do not lift up their beings to what is false, and do not swear deceitfully" (24:4).

The lamenting king in Psalm 22, who is surrounded by bulls and dogs and evildoers, expresses confidence in Psalm 23 in the LORD as the "shepherd-king" who provides for the psalmist's needs — green pastures, still waters, right paths, protection, a secure dwelling place. And in Psalm 24, the king leads the congregation in a celebration of the LORD's sovereignty, justice, kingship, and glory:

> Lift up your heads, O gates!
> and be lifted up, O ancient doors!
> that the king of glory may come in. . . .
> Who is this King of glory?
> The LORD of hosts,
> he is the king of glory. (vv. 9,10)

Why are these psalms in this particular place in the Hebrew Psalter and in this particular relationship with one another? The community of Israelites who shaped the collection of psalms of David which are preserved for us in Book I of the Psalter saw a connectedness between Psalms 22, 23, and 24 — a connectedness that does not diminish the individual poetic and theological character of any one of them, but when read together, creates a powerful statement of trust in the LORD God of the Israelites.

---

[24] Walter Brueggemann, *The Psalms and the Life of Faith* (Minneapolis: Fortress, 1995) 61.

SELECT BIBLIOGRAPHY

Braude, William G. *The Midrash on Psalms*, vol. 1 (New Haven CT: Yale University Press, 1959).

Brueggemann, Walter. *The Psalms and the Life of Faith* (Minneapolis: Fortress, 1995).

Davis, Ellen F. "Exploding the Limits: Form and Function in Psalm 22," *JSOT* 53 (1992) 93–105.

deClaissé-Walford, Nancy L. *Reading from the Beginning: The Shaping of the Hebrew Psalter* (Macon, GA: Mercer University Press, 1997).

Flint, Peter W. *The Dead Sea Psalms Scrolls and the Book of Psalms* (STDJ 17; Leiden: Brill, 1997).

Holladay, William L. *The Psalms through Three Thousand Years: Prayerbook of a Cloud of Witnesses* (Minneapolis: Fortress, 1993).

Kraus, H.-J. *Psalms 1–59: A Commentary* (Minneapolis: Augsburg, 1988).

McCann, J. Clinton, Jr. "The Book of Psalms," in Leander E. Keck (ed.), *The New Interpreter's Bible* (Nashville: Abingdon, 1996) 4.639–1280.

—. *The Shape and Shaping of the Psalter* (JSOTSup 159; Sheffield: JSOT Press, 1993).

Miller, Patrick D. "The Beginning of the Psalter," in McCann (ed.), *The Shape and Shaping of the Psalter*, 84–88.

Sarna, Nahum. *On the Book of Psalms* (New York: Schocken, 1993).

# ON PSALM 29: STRUCTURE AND MEANING[*]

D. PARDEE

## INTRODUCTION

The object of the present essay is one of the most studied of the Psalms and I have no intention of doing a thorough bibliographical overview. Some years ago, in a review of one of the major studies of Psalm 29 in recent decades,[1] decades, I offered a translation of the psalm arranged in poetic verses prefaced by the remark that "some day I would like to make a case for the structure of the core of the poem being made up of tricola."[2] This is what I intend to do below in the section devoted particularly to structure. Because of the importance of the Ugaritic parallels that have been cited ever since H. L. Ginsberg's proposal to see in Psalm 29 "A Phoenician Hymn in the Psalter,"[3] I will discuss the relationship of structure and meaning both in terms of the poem's own internal structure and in terms of similarity with the meaning and structure of one of the more representative of the relevant Ugaritic texts.

The comments that follow are with reference to the table on the next two pages ("Semantic Parallelism in Psalm 29").

[*] I wish to thank the members of the various Hebrew and Ugaritic classes in which over the years the interpretations of the texts discussed here have evolved. Though too many have contributed to be named here, my gratitude to them all is no less great.

[1] Carola Kloos, *Yhwh's Combat with the Sea. A Canaanite Tradition in the Religion of Ancient Israel* (Amsterdam: Oorschot, 1986).

[2] D. Pardee, Review of C. Kloos, *Yhwh's Combat with the Sea*, in *AfO* 35 (1988) 229–32, quotation from p. 231.

[3] *Atti XIX Congresso intrenazionale degli Orientalisti* (Rome: Tipografia del Senato, 1938) 472–76 (the congress at which the paper was read took place in 1935, only six years after the discovery of Ugaritic).

SEMANTIC PARALLELISM IN PSALM 29

| | Text (verse)[4] | Translation (verse) | Semantic parallelism (text)[5] | Macro-parallelism | Semantic parallelism |
|---|---|---|---|---|---|
| 1) | הָבוּ לַיהוָה בְּנֵי אֵלִים | Ascribe to YHWH, O sons of the gods, | a b c$^2$ (x + b') | A | 1 I$^1$ 2 I$^1$ 3 I$^1$ 4$^1$ 3 II$^1$ |
| | הָבוּ לַיהוָה כָּבוֹד וָעֹז | Ascribe to YHWH glory and strength, | a b d$^2$ (y + y') | A' | 1 I$^2$ 2 I$^2$ 3 I$^2$ 5 I$^1$ 5 II$^1$ |
| 2) | הָבוּ לַיהוָה כְּבוֹד שְׁמוֹ | Ascribe to YHWH the glory (due) his name, | a b d'$^2$ (y + z) | A'' | 1 I$^3$ 2 I$^3$ 3 I$^3$ 5 I$^2$ 6$^1$ |
| | הִשְׁתַּחֲווּ לַיהוָה בְּהַדְרַת־קֹדֶשׁ | Bow down to YHWH in the splendor of the sanctuary. | a' b e$^2$ (y'' + m) | B | 7$^1$ 2 I$^4$ 3 I$^4$ 2 II$^1$ 5 III$^1$ 8 I$^1$ |
| 3) | קוֹל יְהוָה עַל־הַמָּיִם | The voice of YHWH, over the waters, | a b c | A | 9$^1$ 3 I$^5$ 2 III$^1$ 10$^1$ 11 I$^1$ |
| | אֵל־הַכָּבוֹד הִרְעִים | The god of glory does thunder, | b'$^2$(b' + x) d | B | 3 II$^2$ 10$^2$ 5 I$^3$ 12$^1$ |
| | יְהוָה עַל־מַיִם רַבִּים | YHWH (does thunder) over the many waters. | b c$^2$ (c + y) | A' | 3 I$^6$ 2 III$^2$ 11 I$^2$ 5 IV$^1$ |
| 4) | קוֹל־יְהוָה בַּכֹּחַ | With might does the voice of YHWH, | a b c | A | 9$^2$ 3 I$^7$ 2 II$^2$ 10$^3$ 5 V$^1$ |
| | קוֹל יְהוָה בֶּהָדָר | With splendor does the voice of YHWH, | a b c' | A' | 9$^3$ 3 I$^8$ 2 II$^3$ 10$^4$ 5 III$^2$ |
| 5) | קוֹל יְהוָה שֹׁבֵר אֲרָזִים | Does the voice of YHWH break cedars. | a b d e | B | 9$^4$ 3 I$^9$ 13 I$^1$ 14 I$^1$ |
| 6) | וַיְשַׁבֵּר יְהוָה אֶת־אַרְזֵי הַלְּבָנוֹן | YHWH has broken the cedars of Lebanon | a b c$^2$ (x + y) | A | 15$^1$ 13 I$^2$ 3 I$^{10}$ 16 I$^1$ 14 I$^2$ 10$^4$ 17 I$^1$ |
| | וַיַּרְקִידֵם כְּמוֹ־עֵגֶל לְבָנוֹן | And has caused Lebanon to dance like a calf, | d e c' (y) | B | 15$^2$ 18 I$^1$ 19 I$^1$ 2 IV$^1$ 20 I$^1$ 17 I$^2$ |
| | וְשִׂרְיֹן כְּמוֹ בֶן־רְאֵמִים | Even Siryon like a young bovid. | c'' (y') e'$^2$ (z + e') | B' | 17 II$^1$ 2 IV$^2$ 4$^2$ 20 II$^1$ |
| 7) | קוֹל־יְהוָה חֹצֵב לַהֲבוֹת אֵשׁ | The voice of YHWH splits off flames of fire, | a b c d$^2$ | A | 9$^5$ 3 I$^{11}$ 13 II$^1$ 21 I$^1$ 21 I$^2$ |
| 8) | קוֹל יְהוָה יָחִיל מִדְבָּר | The voice of YHWH causes the steppe to writhe, | a b e f | B | 9$^6$ 3 I$^{12}$ 18 II$^1$ 22$^1$ |
| | יָחִיל יְהוָה מִדְבַּר קָדֵשׁ | YHWH causes the steppe of Qadeš to writhe. | e b f$^2$ (f + x) | B' | 18 II$^2$ 3 I$^{13}$ 22$^2$ 17 III$^1$ |

| |  |  | | |
|---|---|---|---|---|
| 9) | קוֹל יְהוָה יְחוֹלֵל אַיָּלוֹת / וַיֶּחֱשֹׂף יְעָרוֹת / וּבְהֵיכָלוֹ כֻּלּוֹ אֹמֵר כָּבוֹד | The voice of YHWH makes the hinds writhe / And has stripped bare the forests; / And (as a result) in the temple all says 'Glory'. | a b c d / e f / g h i j | A $9^7$ 3 $I^{14}$ 18 $II^3$ 20 $III^1$ / A' $15^3$ $23^1$ 14 $II^1$ / B $15^4$ 2 $II^4$ 8 $II^1$ $24^1$ $25^1$ 5 $I^4$ |
| 10) | יְהוָה לַמַּבּוּל יָשָׁב / וַיֵּשֶׁב יְהוָה מֶלֶךְ לְעוֹלָם | YHWH at the flood did sit, / Yea, he sat as king of all time. | a b c / c a d e | A 3 $I^{15}$ 2 $I^3$ $10^6$ 11 $II^1$ $26^1$ / A' $15^5$ $26^2$ 3 $I^{16}$ $27^1$ 2 $I^4$ $28^1$ |
| 11) | יְהוָה עֹז לְעַמּוֹ יִתֵּן / יְהוָה יְבָרֵךְ אֶת־עַמּוֹ בַשָּׁלוֹם | YHWH constantly gives strength to his people, / YHWH constantly blesses his people with well-being. | a b c d / a e c f | A 3 $I^{17}$ 5 $II^2$ 2 $I^5$ $29^1$ 1 $II^1$ / A' 3 $I^{18}$ $30^1$ $16^2$ $29^2$ 2 $II^5$ $10^7$ 5 $VI^1$ |

---

[4] Only major constituent elements are indicated here, in the traditional manner; letters in parentheses break a two-word formula down into its component parts. For example, in v. 1 "x + b" describes the phrase בְּנֵי אֵלִים as made up of a new semantic entity of which the second word belongs to the same semantic group as YHWH.

[5] Here all words are tabulated, including particles, and designated according to the semantic group to which each belongs (the groups are listed on the following page): the Arabic numeral designates the group, the Roman numeral the member of the group (if the group contains more than one member), the raised Arabic numeral the n-occurrence of a given word (1 ...). For this method of charting semantic parallelism through a poem, see D. Pardee, "The Semantic Parallelism of Psalm 89," in W. B. Barrick and J. R. Spencer (eds.), *In the Shelter of Elyon: Essays on Ancient Palestinian Life and Literature in Honor of G. W. Ahlström* (JSOTSup 31; Sheffield: Journal for the Study of the Old Testament, 1984) 121–37; idem, *Ugaritic and Hebrew Poetic Parallelism: A Trial Cut (nt I and Proverbs 2)* (VTSup 39; Leiden: Brill, 1988) 9–12, 77–81.

Here now is a list of the semantic groups that emerge from the right-most
column in the table:

1. Giving

    I. יהב (vv. 1bis, 2) [כָּבוֹד + יהב ≈ אמר + כָּבוֹד (#25 + #5 I)]

    II. נתן (v. 11) [עֹז + נתן ≈ ברך (#30)]

2. Prepositions

    I. לְ (vv. 1bis, 2bis, 10bis, 11)

    II. בְּ (vv. 2, 4bis, 9, 11)

    III. עַל (v. 3bis)

    IV. כ: כְּמוֹ (v. 6bis)

3. Divinity

    I. יהוה (vv. 1bis, 2bis, 3bis, 4bis, 5bis, 7, 8bis, 9, 10bis, 11bis)

    II. God(s) (v. 1 אֵלִים, vs. 3 אֵל)

4. Son: בֵּן (vv. 1, 6)

5. Glory

    I. כָּבוֹד, "glory" (vv. 1, 2, 3, 9)

    II. עֹז, "strength" (vv. 1, 11)

    III. הדר: הֲדָרָה, "splendor" (v. 2), הָדָר (v. 4)

    IV. רַב, "numerous, great" (v. 3)

    V. כֹּח, "might" (v. 4)

    VI. שָׁלוֹם, "well-being" (v. 11)

6. Name: שֵׁם (v. 2)

7. Prosternation: חוה, "bow down" (v. 2) [functionally ≈ כָּבוֹד + יהב (וְעֹז)
(#1 I + #5 II)]

8. Divine dwelling

    I. קֹדֶשׁ, "sanctuary" (v. 2) [cf. קָדֵשׁ, v. 8 (#17 III)]

    II. הֵיכָל, "temple" (v. 9)

9. Voice: קוֹל (vv. 3, 4bis, 5, 7, 8, 9)

10. Definite article (vv. 3bis, 4bis, 5, 10, 11)[5]

11. Water

    I. מַיִם, "water" (v. 3bis)

    II. מַבּוּל, "flood" (v. 10)

12. Thundering: רעם (v. 3) [= קוֹל + נתן (#1 II + 9)]

13. Breaking asunder:

    I. שׁבר, "to break" (v. 5bis)

    II. חצב, "to split" (v. 7)

14. Trees

    I. אֶרֶז, "cedar" (v. 5bis)

---

[5] Because the definite article is attested consonantally, I include all tokens of
the particle, including those that appear only in the Masoretic vocalization; it is
evident that these may not have been part of the older tradition.

II. יַעַר, "forest" (v. 9)

15. Conjunction: וַ (vv. 5, 6bis, 9bis, 10)

16. Definite Direct Object Marker: אֵת (vv. 5, 11)

17. Place Names

    I. לְבָנוֹן (vv. 5, 6)

    II. שִׂרְיֹן (v. 6)

    III. קָדֵשׁ (v. 8) [√קדשׁ = #8 I]

18. Turning

    I. רקד, "to dance" (v. 6)

    II. ח(ו)ל, "to whirl" (vv. 8bis, 9)

19. Enclitic ם (v. 6)[6]

20. Animals

    I. עֵגֶל, "calf" (v. 6)

    II. רְאֵם, "wild bull" (v. 6)

    III. אַיָּלָה, "female deer" (v. 9)

21. Fire

    I. לֶהָבָה, "flame" (v. 7)

    II. אֵשׁ, "fire" (vs. 7)

22. The steppe: מִדְבָּר (v. 8bis)

23. Stripping: חשׂף (v. 9)

24. Entirety: כֹל (v. 9)

25. Saying: אמר (v. 9) [כָּבוֹד + אמר ≈ יהב + כָּבוֹד (#1 I + #5 I)]

26. Sitting ישׁב (v. 10bis)

27. King: מֶלֶךְ (v. 10)

28. Long stretch of time: עוֹלָם (v. 10)

29. People: עַם (v. 11bis) [functional antonym of בְּנֵי אֵלִים (v. 1)]

30. Blessing: ברך (v. 11) [as *benefacere* ≈ נתן + עֹז here; as *bendicere* ≈ כָּבוֹד + אמר / יהב (see #25)]

## POETIC UNITS

Though I would be the first to admit that the division of an ancient Semitic poem into poetic units contains an element of artificiality, the exercise nonetheless continues to appear to me to be useful and fruitful. In the present case, the poem can be divided into meaningful rhetorical units that correspond to meaningful poetic units and such an analysis goes a long way towards refuting attempts to reorder the elements of the poem or to excise elements from it.[7]

---

[6] Ginsberg pointed out this feature in his 1935 paper (reference note 3).

[7] For reordering, see (e.g.) S. Mittmann, "Komposition und Redaktion von Psalm xxix," *VT* 28 (1978) 172–94, followed by P. Auffret, "Notes conjointes sur la structure littéraire des psaumes 114 et 29," *EstBib* 37 (1978) 103–13, esp.

Part and parcel of the attempt to provide a structural analysis of the psalm as it has come down to us is the belief that this poem is not an old Phoenician poem that has been adapted to Hebrew but that it was an original composition in Hebrew.[8] The idea is that a poem originally conceived in Hebrew as a piece of anti-Baal propaganda is less likely to have undergone radical editorial restructuring than would have been the case of a work that began its life as derivational from a work in another language from another religion and culture. The function of "so transparent a presentation of Yahweh in Baalistic imagery" was to provide "a repudiation of the need to offer a cult to Baal."[9]

As for the verse structure, it is widely recognized that: (1) verses 10 and 11 constitute two bicola that are closely linked together; (2) verses 1 and 2 are similarly linked, though there is less agreement on the precise structure of these four cola. There is, on the other hand, no consensus on the structure of verses 3-9: do they consist of all bicola (which could, on the pattern of vv. 1-2 and 10-11, be paired off to form four-unit verses)[10] or a mixture of bicola and tricola?[11] Those

---

108–11. For attempts to excise, see (e.g.) O. Loretz, *Psalm 29. Kanaanäische El- und Baaltraditionen in jüdischer Sicht* (UBL 2; Münster: Ugarit-Verlag, 1984) 23 and *passim*.

[8] This conclusion was reached by Kloos and I have already expressed my agreement with it (references in notes 1 and 2). The rejection of the hypothesis that Psalm 29 is the Hebrew adaptation of a Phoenician or Canaanite poem seems to have begun in the early 70s of the last century: B. Margulis, "The Canaanite Origin of Psalm xxix Reconsidered," *Bib* 51 (1970) 332–48; P. C. Craigie, "Psalm xxix in the Hebrew Poetic Tradition," *VT* 22 (1972) 143–51. J.-L. Cunchillos rejected both the Phoenician/Canaanite origin of the poem and the fourth-century date for the text which had been proposed (*Estudio del Salmo 29* [Institución San Jerónimo 6; Valencia, Spain: Libreria Diocesana, 1976] 169–96). See also M. Girard, *Les Psaumes. Analyse structurelle et interprétation, 1–50* (Recherches, Nouvelle Série 2; Montréal: Bellarmin; Paris: Cerf, 1984) 240–41, who rejects the Phoenician / Canaanite origin but does not take up the question of dating.

[9] Pardee, Review of C. Kloos, *Yhwh's Combat with the Sea*, 229.

[10] Thus Mittmann presents the poem as consisting of four four-unit verses, which he achieves by reordering some units and omitting v. 11 (*VT* 28 [1978] 191; followed by Auffret, "Notes conjointes," 108). B. Duhm created the same effect by reading v. 4 as a single colon joined to v. 3 and by inserting a colon into v. 9 (*Die Psalmen erklärt* [Kurzer Hand-Kommentar zum Alten Testament 14; Tübingen: Mohr Siebeck, 1922] 118–20: "Es fürchten ihn alle Enden der Erde" is given as the third colon of vs. 9).

who do not consider, as do I, "the bicolon or tricolon to be the building-block of poetic structure"[12] will propose longer poetic units.[13] What appears in my view to have been the deciding factor in these various divisions is the perceived need to maintain the repetitive parallelism of שׁבר, יהוה, and אֶרֶז within the confines of a single verse, as did the Masoretes in delimiting what we know as verse 5 as a unit. If one be willing to admit, however, as I have attempted to show in my various studies of the distributions of parallelisms of all types through a poem, that "regular" parallelism (i.e. that which occurs between the segments of a given verse) was only one of several distributions; that "near" parallelism (i.e. that which occurs between adjacent verses) is a standard distribution, sometimes attaining equal or even superior status as compared with "regular" distribution,[14] then the way is open to recognizing a verse division at the half-way point of verse 5. Why do so? The principal reason is because taking בַּכֹּחַ and בֶּהָדָר in v. 4 as adverbials is preferable to the analysis as examples of the rare בְּ essentiae (see comment below). Against the division into a series of bicola must stand v. 3 in its present form: unless one be willing to emend, that verse clearly constitutes a tricolon and the scansion of the rest of the poem must proceed therefrom to the extent that such a division is plausible. Unless one be willing to add a line somewhere, it is impossible to divide the poem as having a chiastic macro-structure on the pattern 4 3 2 ... 2 3 4. A quadricolonic pattern throughout has actually been proposed, though this is only possible by means of emendation of one kind or another.[15] Because re-ordering the units that have come down to us is a completely arbitrary procedure that has no basis in the versions and no real basis in the theory of oral or written tradition,[16] because more

---

[11] E.g. Cunchillos, *Salmo 29*, 156; Loretz, *Psalm 29*, 23.

[12] D. Pardee, *Ugaritic and Hebrew Poetic Parallelism: A Trial Cut / ʾNt I and Proverbs 2* (VTSup 39; Leiden: Brill, 1988) xvi.

[13] E.g. Girard, *Les Psaumes*, 234, divides the poem into cola as follows: 4 + 5 + 2 2 1 2 2 + 5, where the first and last units form an inclusio and the five central units a chiasmus, whereas the second unit stands alone.

[14] See in particular "Acrostics and Parallelism: The Parallelistic Structure of Psalm 111," *Maarav* 8 (*Studies in Memory of Stanley Gevirtz*, 1992) 117–38.

[15] For references, see note 11.

[16] In oral tradition, any one organization is as valid as another; in textual transmission, the radical reshuffling of units such as those envisaged by Mittmann

radical emendations are even less plausible, the version attested by the MT and all the versions must, in spite of its problematic features, be considered the only one worthy of consideration in our day.

Though the different vocabulary in v. 2b as compared with v. 1 makes the analysis of these verses as constituting a "strophe,"[17] rather than a single verse, at first sight appealing, the analysis as an expanded "staircase" is in the long run much more satisfying. E. L. Greenstein has successfully defended the "staircase" pattern as a distinct variant of the "expanded colon," defined as consisting of a basic A A' B macro-structure wherein A and A' differ by their syntactic structure, that is, A' usually contains a major syntactic unit omitted from A. One often encounters the structure made up of verb + vocative // verb + object, which is that of verse 1 here. The third segment of such a tricolonic structure is syntactically patterned on the second but semantically distinct.[18] With this definition in mind, the examination of verses 1-2a shows that its structure is A A' A', not A A' B. The conclusion appears obvious that the third segment of Ps 29:1-2 is simply an expansion on the second in Greenstein's classic "staircase" and that it is v. 2b that constitutes the B element of that structure.[19]

Because of its apparently aberrant structure, v. 3 has been taken as the key to unlocking the structure of the poem, whether by emendation or, as I prefer, by retaining the only version that has come down to us and observing what it has to say. It is this verse that is redistributed through the poem in the re-ordering proposed by Mittmann, whereas Loretz elides the second segment. Again, however, unless one be willing to admit editorial re-ordering in the

---

could only be classified as purposely editorial — simple scribal confusion of the classic types could only with difficulty have produced such a result. There is, however, no textual evidence for the version envisaged by Mittmann, and there is no reason to suspect that an editor would have produced the "defective" version that has come down to us (here the old textual dictum *lectio difficilior preferenda est* appears to have validity).

[17] Cunchillos, *Salmo 29*, 157.

[18] E. L. Greenstein, "One More Step on the Staircase," *UF* 9 (1977) 77–86.

[19] Though Girard, *Les Psaumes*, 239, refers to vv. 1-2a as an example of "parallélisme en cage d'escalier," the facts that this analysis leaves v. 2b standing alone and that vv. 1-2 constitute so beautiful an example of Greenstein's "staircase" if only one be willing to admit that the one more step may be added to the staircase make the Greenstein-inspired structure infinitely preferable.

direction of a *lectio difficilior*, one is constrained to interpret the text as it has been transmitted to us. When one faces that requirement and when one looks at what the verse says, one must conclude that the poet has subtly inserted the El-concept here, as in v. 1, in the form of a common noun rather than as the divine name *per se*.[20]

I have already observed above that taking the prepositional phrases בֶּהָדָר // בַּכֹּחַ as adverbials rather than as predicates (i.e. identifying the preposition as בְּ *essentiae*, that is, as introducing a nominal predicate rather than an adverbial phrase)[21] is preferable because of the rarity of the use of בְּ *essentiae*. But the facts that בְּ *essentiae* exists as a grammatical phenomenon in Biblical Hebrew and that this poem shows at least one archaic feature (the enclitic מ in v. 6) mean that other reasons must be provided for preferring the analysis as adverbials; it must be shown that seeing these cola as two elements of a tricolon is at least as poetically satisfying as the other analysis, if not more so. One argument is provided by the structure of v. 3, an indubitable tricolon unless one be willing to emend (see discussion above). Another is provided by the plausible analysis of the tricolon of vv. 4–5a as a variation on the "staircase," i.e. as showing simple semantic parallelism of same syntactic constituents in the first two cola (as opposed to the different syntactic constituents of the "staircase") but with replacement of a syntactic unit in the third (S M // S M // S V O).[22] Another variant feature is identifiable in the

---

[20] Many since the discovery of Ugaritic have parsed אֵלִים in v. 1 as consisting of אֵל + י + enclitic מ; the use of the genitive construction following a divine name in Ugaritic as well as in the Hebrew inscriptions from Kuntillet ʿAjrud (יהוה שמרן and יהוה תמן) makes such an analysis of אֵל־הַכָּבוֹד plausible. These analyses would give "sons of El" and "El of glory = glorious El." In a poem to the glory of YHWH, it appears more likely to me that the use of the two terms is meant as an allusion to the admitted identity of YHWH and El rather than the mention of El as a distinct divinity.

[21] A classic quasi-literal translation is found in T. K. Cheyne, *The Book of Psalms or the Praises of Israel. A New Translation, with Commentary* (New York: Whittaker, 1892) 79: "The voice of Jehovah is with power!" See also M. Dahood, *Psalms I: 1–50* (AB 16; New York: Doubleday, 1965) 174, 177: "is strength itself;" G. B. Gray, *The Biblical Doctrine of the Reign of God* (Edinburgh: Clark, 1979) 40: "is the essence of strength;" Loretz, *Psalm 29*, 23, 37 (translates without providing a lexical marker of predication in the German — the exclamation mark placed after the second colon is apparently meant to have this function — but refers to the verse as a bicolon).

[22] S = subject, M = modifier phrase, V = verb, O = direct object.

repetitive parallelism characteristic of this poem, visible here in the phrase קוֹל יְהוָה which begins each line, for a "standard staircase" shows semantic parallelism in the third colon, not repetitive parallelism. The willingness of this poet to modify standard structures is proven by what he did in vv. 1-2 and the varying patterns of the following verses underscore his originality. Indeed, if the analysis of the core of this poem as consisting of tricola be accepted, the structural variety visible as one progresses from one poetic verse to the next is remarkable.

Verse 9 presents another sort of challenge to the hypothesis that the basic structure of vv. 3-9 is tricolonic in structure, indeed two, one at the lexical level, the other at that of the verse. First, according to the consonantal text of the Masoretic version, the nouns of the object phrases belong to different categories of the natural world, animals and trees, and there has for that reason been a tendency to emend one or the other of the words to constitute a closer parallelistic pair, אַיָּלוֹת to אֵלוֹת ("terebinths"), or יְעָרִים to יְעָלִים ("wild goats"). In my preliminary translation, I chose the former option,[23] but I now ask myself if it is not better, in this last verse of this center section, to see a purposeful summing up of the natural world, of which both vegetal and animal categories have already been mentioned (see semantic groups ##14 and 20). Both the temple and the palace described in 2 Kings 6–7 as constructed under Solomon were decorated with vegetal and animal motifs; this poem and the summary in this verse may be seen as a verbal version of a similar ideology.[24]

The other aspect of v. 9 that resists classification as a tricolon is the semantic and grammatical parallelism. Though the first two cola show tight grammatical parallelism, the semantic parallelism is weak ("causing to writhe" // "stripping off" and "female deer // trees"); the third colon shows neither semantic nor grammatical parallelism with the preceding two. The differences between the first two cola may plausibly be ascribed to the poet's desire to provide the summary that I have just proposed to be the function of putting animal and vegetal

---

[23] Review of C. Kloos, *Yhwh's Combat with the Sea*, 231.

[24] I now believe, therefore, that the "dissonance" of the semantic parallelism here may be part of the message of the poem rather than a simple vocalization error in the Masoretic tradition, as so many have thought, including Girard, *Les Psaumes*, 234, who elsewhere avoids emending the Masoretic version of the poem.

elements in parallel. The function of the third colon, on the other hand, is best explained by a feature common to Ugaritic narrative poetry: there junctures marked by verbs of speech may take the form of either a bicolon or a monocolon.[25] The distant parallelism of v. 9c, with הֵיכָל recalling קֹדֶשׁ in v. 2, with the explicit naming of "all," and with כָּבוֹד + אמר recalling the entire כָּבוֹד chain (group #5) and, in particular, כָּבוֹד + יהב in v. 1, identifies this colon both as a summary line and, by the presence of a verb of speech, as the lyric version of the narrative use of such verbs to mark a transition. At one level, therefore, v. 9 is best defined as a bicolon followed by a monocolon.[26] But, within the larger poem, its relationship to the preceding tricola is analogical to the relationship of vv. 10-11 to vv. 1-2: just as vv. 10-11 are readily identified as two closely linked bicola that mirror the tightly structured quadricolon of vv. 1-2, so v. 9 fits into the central structure of the poem by consisting of three cola. It is distinct from the other tricola in that the first two cola here show a form of parallelism (grammatical) and exemplify the categories of nature while the third expresses that concept in even broader terms that include verbal praise but without strongly marked semantic or grammatical parallelism. The absence of any real "regular" semantic parallelism is paralleled in Ugaritic poetry,[27] and here, as there, its place in the poem is assured by the tighter semantic (and other) structures that surround it. The function of the entire verse as a summary is seen clearly in the chart of semantic parallels for the text as a whole, where every lexical item but two is paralleled above and the first of these two exceptions is a lexical expression of summary (כֹּל, #24) while the second (אמר, #25), when joined with its object (כָּבוֹד), constitutes a functional semantic and grammatical parallel with כָּבוֹד + יהב (as noted above at #25).[28]

---

[25] See as examples here below in the Ugaritic text cited, lines 14-15 and 37-38. A variation is found in lines 23-25, where a reference to a previous speech and a quotation from it are placed in adjacent cola.

[26] This is how I set it out in my preliminary translation (Review of C. Kloos, *Yhwh's Combat with the Sea*, 231).

[27] Pardee, *Trial Cut*, 9, 23 (on §X of the text under examination).

[28] Girard, *Les Psaumes*, 234–41 takes this functional equivalence as an indication that v. 9c belongs structurally with vv. 10-11 (cf. already Auffret, "Notes conjointes," 108–113). I believe strongly that this is a misinterpretation of the function of 9c, that it is better explained as transitional, as a part of the summary that is the function of v. 9 as a whole, and that this analysis is supported by the presence of כָּבוֹד in v. 3 (in this respect, כָּבוֹד in v. 9 forms an *inclusio* with

## THE MEANING OF THE POEM AS EXPRESSED BY
## REPETITIVE AND SEMANTIC PARALLELISM

As admitted above, the division of the central section into discrete
verses contains an element of artificiality and is to a certain extent an
exercise in modern esthetics, in this case a search for symmetry. What
is more important for the meaning of the poem, however, is the
distribution of repetitive and semantic parallels through the poem. J.-
L. Cunchillos has charted the former, by the conventional letters of
the alphabet within a verse and by arrows joining repetitions situated
at a greater distance from each other.[29] But the message of the poem
comes out even more clearly when one notes the combination of
repetitive and semantic parallels in all possible distributions. The
central message must be judged to be the reciprocal "giving" and
possessing of the various qualities designated by the terms in group 5
that function in internal or regular parallelism within a verse and then
again in various distributions throughout the poem. The sons of the
Gods are called upon to "ascribe" (= "give") "glory and power" to
YHWH in v. 1; to bow down in the splendor of the sanctuary in v. 2;
YHWH thunders as "god of glory" in v. 3; he breaks cedars with
"might" and "splendor" in v. 4;[30] at the end of the recital of his
powers as storm god, everything and everyone pronounces the word
"glory;" YHWH enthroned imparts "strength" and "well-being" to his
people.[31] That all of the storm imagery is expressed in terms of
YHWH's possessing his own dwelling is made clear by the distant
parallelism of "sanctuary" (v. 2) and "temple" (v. 9)[32] and the point is

---

v. 3, not with vv. 1-2; it is the phrase עֹז + נתן in v. 11 that explicitly forms the
*inclusio* with יהב + כָּבוֹד + עֹז in vv. 1-2, hence providing the basic message of the
poem — see below.

[29] *Estudio del Salmo 29*, 156.

[30] Girard, *Les Psaumes*, 234, 235, correctly analyses הַדְרַת in v. 2 as a variant
form of הָדָר in v. 4, but does not make this "mini-structure" (see note bottom of
p. 234 with its reference to "un rôle mini-structurel" played by the two words) an
integral part of the larger structure provided by כָּבוֹד and עֹז (in his coded
translation, "*splendeur*" is each time in italics, whereas "**GLOIRE**," "**FORCE**,"
and "**VIGUEUR**" are in bold caps).

[31] Girard, *Les Psaumes*, 236, has very correctly pointed out the inclusional
function of vv. 1-2 and 10-11 and the reversal of the actors' roles: in vv. 1-2 glory
and strength are ascribed to YHWH; in v. 11, YHWH gives strength and well-
being to his people.

[32] This important point has been made by Girard, *Les Psaumes*, 235–36, who

driven home in the conclusion to the poem where the principal motif is YHWH's kingship (the phrase "sits as king" implies a "palace;" a deity's house is, of course, his palace / temple — see the Ugaritic text cited below), the proof positive of his ability to provide commensurate benefits for his people.

Of particular interest in this presentation of YHWH's powers as storm deity is the mixing of the storm motif with that of the defeat of the watery powers of chaos. As noted below in comparing the motifs present in Psalm 29 and the Ugaritic text cited as parallel, the defeat of the watery powers is not present in the Ugaritic text but, according to the standard organization of the tablets of the Baal Cycle, it was the object of a long narrative earlier in the cycle. What Psalm 29 has done, then, is to join these two facets of the much longer Baal myth in a very succinct fashion, the previous defeat of the waters of chaos being evoked in v. 3 by the fact that YHWH can thunder over them at will.[33] It may be added that, if the description of YHWH as מֶלֶךְ לְעוֹלָם (v. 10) has a connotation of ruling over the dead as well as over the living,[34] the last two verses of the poem join to the theme of defeating the waters of chaos (allusively, as we shall see, by the use of the term מַבּוּל) that of doing battle with the forces of death (Baal's battle with Mot comes after the text cited below, nearer the end of the

---

correctly remarks that "… le sanctuaire est toujours le micro-symbole, la synthèse et le centre du cosmos.…"

[33] Those who have commented on the psalm since the discovery of Ugaritic have tended to identify the "many waters" with the Mediterranean Sea (Ginsberg, "שם קדמון למדבר סוריה," *Yediot* 6 [1938–1939] 96–97; idem, "A Strand in the Cord of Hebraic Hymnody," *EI* 9 [1969] 45–50, esp. 45 n. 2; Cunchillos, *Salmo 29*, 164 [cf. pp. 73–76, where a broader connotation is accepted]; Loretz, *Psalm 29*, 34–36, 89. Though at one level this is certainly correct even for the Ugaritic mythological texts (cf., for example, M. Yon, "Šḥr mt, la chaleur de Mot," *UF* 21 [1989] 461–66), at another level the very use of the term מַיִם רַבִּים ("many waters," not, primarily at least, "great waters") must be taken as connoting the various forms taken by the water chaos. As known from the Ugaritic texts, these are "the (salt) sea" (*Yammu*) and "the river" (*Naharu*), which apparently stand for all the watery forces that were once threatening or still potentially are.

[34] D. Pardee, *Les textes para-mythologiques de la 24ᵉ campagne* (Ras Shamra Ougarit 5; Paris: Editions Recherche sur les Civilisations, 1988) 89–90, commentary on RS 24.252:1. Texts from Ras Shamra are here cited by excavation number; for a key to the various editions and collections, see P. Bordreuil and D. Pardee, *La trouvaille épigraphique de l'Ougarit. 1 Concordance* (Ras Shamra —Ougarit 5/1; Paris: Éditions Recherche sur les Civilisations, 1989).

Baal cycle as we know it). If this last point be granted, the overall structure of Psalm 29 replicates that of the Baal myth: YHWH defeats the waters of chaos, he gives forth his thunder and lightning from his heavenly dwelling, he exercises power even over the realm of death. Missing is any allusion to the episode of Baal's temporary defeat by Mot, which entailed Baal's descent into the nether world and his forced seclusion there for a time. At least in this presentation of YHWH's powers, his having taken on the characteristics of both El and Baal permitted him to avoid this episode of Baal's divine cycle, for, El, of course, never entered the underworld. On the other hand, a story such as that of Elisha and the priests of Baal (1 Kings 17–18) shows that the annual and irregularly more severe droughts must have placed strains on the concept of YHWH as the ever-active rainmaker. Also missing in Psalm 29 is any allusion to the fact that Baal does not destroy Mot ("death") in their battle as described near the end of the Baal Cycle. Indeed, an important feature of Ugaritic theology, one that implicitly recognizes the reality of life and death, is that Baal's fertilizing powers and Mot's insatiable appetite must be accepted as coexisting.[35] If there is anything to the proposal that מֶלֶךְ לְעוֹלָם in Ps 29:10 expresses a concept similar to that of *mlk ʿlm* in RS 24.252:1 (reference note 37), the psalm is claiming for YHWH a power over the realm of the dead that is certainly superior to anything claimed for Baal in the Ugaritic texts but one that also recognizes the reality of death.

## SOME MAJOR ISSUES OF INTERPRETATION

Based on the single occurrence of *hdrt* in Ugaritic (RS 2.[003]+ iii 51), where the context and parallel passages containing *ḏhrt* and *ḏrt* show the meaning to be "appearance, vision," some have interpreted הַדְרַת־קֹדֶשׁ as "when he appears in holiness"[36] or "at His theophany."[37] Whether or not the Ugaritic word be a "ghost word," as

---

[35] See, for example, my translation in W. W. Hallo and K. L. Younger (eds.), *The Context of Scripture*. Vol. I: *Canonical Compositions from the Biblical World* (Leiden: Brill, 1997) 272–73.

[36] F. M. Cross, "Notes on a Canaanite Psalm in the Old Testament," *BASOR* 117 (1950) 19–21, quotation from p. 21; cf. idem, *Canaanite Myth and Hebrew Epic. Essays in the History of the Religion of Israel* (Cambridge, MA: Harvard University Press, 1973) 152 (n. 28), 154–55.

[37] Gray, *Biblical Doctrine*, 40.

appears probable since the Ugaritic root was in all likelihood ḎHR,[38] the parallelistic structure of this poem shows that the Hebrew word is a form of the Hebrew root הדר that denotes "splendor, glory, wealth, etc."[39]

A significant number of scholars have taken קוֹל as an interjection, translatable in English as "Hark!" or the like.[40] As this goes against the Ugaritic and Hebrew tradition of describing thunder meta-phorically as the "voice" of the weather deity, I find the notion misplaced, particularly when this is the one aspect of the Baal myth which is attested as already current in Late Bronze Canaan. I refer, of course, to the attestation in Amarna Akkadian of the formula {ša id-din ri-ig-ma-šu i-na sa-me ki-ma ᵈIM}, "who gives forth his voice in the heavens like Haddu."[41]

The meaning and function of חֹצֵב לַהֲבוֹת אֵשׁ in v. 7 has elicited the most diverse reactions, including that of emendation.[42] It is clear from biblical usage of the verb חצב that it is transitive and that it expresses various acts of hewing, from hollowing out a pit to producing an object such as a pillar or a piece of ashlar building stone to chopping

---

[38] J. Tropper, "Ugaritic Dreams. Notes on Ugaritic ḏ(h)rt and hdrt," in N. Wyatt, W. G. E. Watson, and J. B. Lloyd (eds.), *Ugarit, Religion and Culture. Proceedings of the International Colloquium on Ugarit, Religion and Culture, Edinburgh, July 1994. Essays Presented in Honour of Professor John C. L. Gibson*, UBL 12 (1996) 305–313. That Ugaritic {hdrt} is probably a scribal error had already been observed by M. Dietrich and O. Loretz, "Zur ugaritischen Lexikographie (II)," *OLZ* 62 (1967) 533–51, esp. col. 538; cf. eidem, "Das ug. Nomen ḏ(h)rt 'Traum, nächtliches Gesicht' (?)," *SEL* 1 (1984) 85–88, esp. 87.

[39] As correctly observed by Girard, but only for the "mini-structure" of vv. 2-4 (see above, note 31).

[40] Bibliography in E. L. Greenstein, "YHWH's Lightning in Psalm 29:7," *Maarav* 8 (1992) 49–57, esp. 56 n. 40.

[41] EA 147:13-14. Girard, *Les Psaumes*, 238 correctly sees in קוֹל "la voix puissante et tonitruante" of YHWH, but attempts to find corresponding human cultic cries embedded in the poem, particularly כָּבוֹד וָעֹז and כְּבוֹד שְׁמוֹ (p. 235). As Girard very clearly sets forth, the "voice" of YHWH is the central element in the depiction of his powers as weather deity, and its semantic and morpho-syntactic function as a common noun is not changed by that fact, i.e. it plays, in this poem, its proper syntactic function in each phrase in which it appears regardless of whether ancient Israelites ever in their cult shouted קוֹל יְהוָה as a complete utterance. The same is true, however, of כָּבוֹד וָעֹז and of כְּבוֹד שְׁמוֹ. In this poem, the only utterance presented as such is כָּבוֹד in v. 9.

[42] Greenstein, "YHWH's Lightning," 56, reading חִצָּיו ("his arrows").

up one's adversaries. The last meaning is the only one attested in the occurrences of the root ḤṢB in Ugaritic (RS 2.[014]⁺ ii 6, 20, 24, 30). Unless a distinct etymology be found for the verb in Ps 29:7 (Hebrew /ḥ/ may derive from either proto-Semitic /ḥ/ or /ḫ/, Hebrew /ṣ/ from /ṣ/, /ḍ/, or /ẓ/), it appears best to interpret v. 7 as expressing the chipping off of lightning bolts by striking some heavenly substance that would be analogous to earthly flint. Just as by striking a piece of stone with a sharp implement a piece is detached from it, so by striking a piece of flint a spark is detached. In the view of lightning expressed in Ps 29:7, it would be produced by the weather deity's voice (thunder) chipping lightning bolts (from an unnamed substance). It becomes clear from examining the biblical attestations that the direct object of the verb can be either the material upon which the actor works (as in the occupational title חֹצֵב אֶבֶן) or the finished product. Examples of the latter are: the יֶקֶב ("wine-vat") in Isa 5:2, the קֶבֶר ("tomb) in Isa 22:16, or וּנְחֹשֶׁת ("copper") said to be "hewn" from the mountains in Deut 8:9. The Ugaritic metaphor also involves a concept of producing a division or separation, but there it is that of producing a rift or a rent within a homogeneous entity. The word is *bdqt* (see below, lines 19 and 28 of the Ugaritic text cited). In biblical Hebrew, the root is expressed as a noun, בֶּדֶק, designating a fissure in a building that requires repair while in Mari Akkadian *bitqu* expresses a hole that has opened up in a weir or a dam, which allows more water through than is desired.[43] The Ugaritic view of lightning was apparently, therefore, that it rent the clouds to allow the rain to pass.[44]

From the consistent perspective of this poem, where Baal's functions in the Canaanite cosmology are attributed to YHWH and where the geographic center of the weather deity's activity is explicitly placed in the Lebanon and anti-Lebanon mountain chains,[45]

---

[43] B. Lafont, "Nuit dramatique à Mari," in J.-M. Durand (ed.), *Florilegium marianum. Recueil d'études en l'honneur de Michel Fleury* (Mémoires de N.A.B.U. 1; Paris: SEPOA, 1991) 93–105. The word *bitqu* appears in lines 26 and 28 of the text on which the article is based (transcription p. 94, hand-copy p. 95) and is translated "brèche" by the author. It is not, in this case at least, a purposeful "sluice" (the standard translation of *bitqu*) but a "tear" in the fabric of the dam.

[44] I follow previous commentators in taking *bdqt* in the Ugaritic text cited below as denoting a "rift" and do not follow the lead of Akkadian *butuqtu*, which can mean "flood" as well as "sluice." On the separateness of the "rift" in the structure of that text, see below, note 60.

[45] The contrast with Psalm 89, where in v. 13 reference is made to north and

the מִדְבַּר קָדֵשׁ, if correctly vocalized in the Masoretic tradition, can only refer to an area in the vicinity of Qadesh, either the Syrian desert, as Ginsberg thought,[46] to which the Homs Gap provides one of the principal accesses when one is arriving from the coast, or the Beqa Valley, which stretches south from Qadesh on the Orontes, between the Lebanon and the anti-Lebanon chains, and which included relatively wild areas in the Late Bronze Age, particularly on the east and west fringes that reached up towards the mountains on either side.[47] For that matter, if this מִדְבָּר was situated on the north-south axis, it may have included part of the Orontes Valley north of Qadesh. When attempting to determine the area designated by the phrase, it is important to remember that Ugaritic/Hebrew *mdbr* does not mean "desert," at least in the commonly accepted English use of the term, but "uninhabited territory (that is usually fit for pasturing sheep and goats)."

This general interpretation of Ps 29:8 is supported, as many have observed, in part by the occurrence in Ugaritic of the phrase *mdbr qdš* (RS 2.002:65) — though only in part, for that phrase is neither placed in a context having to do with Baal's activities as weather god, nor can it be said with any certainty that it refers to Qadesh on the Orontes; indeed *qdš* in the phrase is often taken as the adjective "holy."[48] In this text, as well, perhaps, as in RS 24.258:23-24,[49] the *mdbr qdš* is considered an area appropriate for hunting (ṢD) and, in RS 2.002, it is placed in explicit contrast with *šd* ("field, arable land"), and with *mdrᶜ* ("sown land"). Because no one has ever been able to explain why this "uncultivatable land" would have been qualified as "holy," however, it is perhaps best to take the cue from Ps 29:8 and

---

south (צָפוֹן וְיָמִין) and to two mountains (תָּבוֹר וְחֶרְמוֹן), is stark.

[46] See below, note 52.

[47] L. Marfoe, "The Integrative Transformation: Patterns of Socio-political Organization in Southern Syria," *BASOR* 234 (1979) 1–42.

[48] Cf. Pardee, *Context*, 282 n. 65, 304 n. 18. A striking example is found in Gray, *Biblical Doctrine*, 41, who translates "awful desert," with no discussion of how to get there from the Masoretic vocalization of the second word as קָדֵשׁ. The facility with which many have taken קָדֵשׁ as a simple adjective meaning "holy" when no such word is attested in Biblical Hebrew (קָדֵשׁ and קְדֵשָׁה are only attested as substantives with the function of a *nomen professionalis*) can only, in retrospect, be described as astounding.

[49] Cf. Gray, *Biblical Doctrine*, 41; Pardee, *Les textes para-mythologiques*, 15, 19, 23, 65–66.

conclude that, for reasons that remain unclear, *midbar qādēš* (to use the Hebrew vocalization),[50] designated a sparsely populated area in the vicinity of Qadesh on the Orontes that was widely known as "the steppe-land of Qadesh." This would be consonant with other specific geographical allusions in the Ugaritic mythological texts, for example, *aḫ smk*, plausibly a reference to the Hule Valley.[51] Though it may not be improper to see in the use of the Canaanite formula in the poem an indirect allusion to the events of Israel's salvific history that took place at Qadesh-Barnea, it is literarily unlikely that, in this central section, where the benefits of YHWH's reign for "his people" have not yet become the theme, a specific reference would have been made to this southern Qadesh.[52]

The meaning and function of the term מַבּוּל in v. 10 has elicited virtually opposite interpretations. Because of the other clear references to Baal-like activities and hence to the Ugaritic texts, Cunchillos argues for interpreting the term as having nothing to do with the Mesopotamian concept of a river-flood but as having to do with rainfall; he ends up by identifying the term with the source of

---

[50] In the Akkadian of Ugarit, Qadesh was written {kín-za} (e.g. *Ugaritica* V [1968], texts 38, 39); but, in Ugaritic, the expected consonants {qdš} appear (RS 94.2391:16').

[51] Bibliography in G. del Olmo Lete and J. Sanmartín, *Diccionario de la Lengua Ugaritica* I (Sabadell, Spain: AUSA, 1996) 17.

[52] Ginsberg, in his pioneering article on the Canaanite interpretation of Psalm 29, already considered the idea that the reference in the psalm could no longer be taken as referring to Qadesh-Barnea and that both this reference and the *mdbr qdš* of RS 2.002 might be to the region of Qadesh on the Orontes ("A Phoenician Hymn," 89); later he identified the *midbar* with the Syrian desert to the east of the anti-Lebanon range ("שם קדמון למדבר סוריה," 96–97; A Strand," 45 n. 2). Such an interpretation, based on the order of mention in the psalm ("many waters" = Mediterranean, Lebanon, Siryon, מִדְבַּר קָדֵשׁ), cannot be ruled out, but the Ugaritic reference(s) to hunting there would make of the Beqa a more appropriate candidate. Cunchillos, *Salmo 29*, 100–102, 164–65 rejects any reference to Qadesh-Barnea but maintains the translation "estepa santa" (p. 100). Loretz, *Psalm 29*, 87–92, accepts unreservedly that the psalm refers to Qadesh on the Orontes, but doubts the same interpretation for the Ugaritic text, basing his doubt on the absence of direct connection between the Ugaritic and Hebrew texts. One cannot fault his methodology on this point, but in the absence of contrary evidence, one may leave open the possibility of a perennial Canaanite tradition identifying the *midbar qādēš* as an area defined by the most famous of the Late Bronze Age towns bearing the name of Qadesh.

rainfall, viz., "el Océano celeste."[53] Loretz, on the other hand, takes as the most meaningful datum the fact that the Hebrew term refers only to the biblical Flood and concludes that it is out of place in this poem in honor of YHWH as weather deity. On this basis, he removes the term by emendation, replacing it by כִּסְאוֹ ("his throne").[54] Observing the structure of the poem, it may be argued, allows one to escape this dialectic of exclusivity: because vv. 10-11 stand structurally distinct from vv. 3-9 and because v. 11 explicitly mentions YHWH's people, it may be argued that מַבּוּל in v. 10 should be interpreted in a strictly Israelite sense, as indeed referring to the Israelite Flood tradition. But, it may further be argued, because the burden of the poem as a whole is to present YHWH as the Israelite Baal, the use of the Hebrew word for "flood" may be seen as expressive of YHWH's power over water in general, i.e. as the one capable of defeating destructive waters and of providing rainwater, source of all vegetal and animal fertility.

The precise nuance of יְהוָה לַמַּבּוּל יָשָׁב has been the source of much discussion in recent decades and the range of translations of the verb-preposition combination has been broad, such as "'from' in a temporal sense," that is, since (the flood),[55] or "sit upon (the flood)" (the standard literal translation). The latter is inspired by the Ugaritic idiom YṮB *l*, "sit on/upon," for example, "a throne." The former, that is, as marking a temporal point of departure, is based on what I consider to be a faulty analogy with Ugaritic: because Ugaritic *l* may be translated by "from," the corresponding Hebrew word may be so translated anywhere, irrespective of context. Because Ugaritic YṮB *l* is not attested as meaning "to be seated since," I find it dubious that that idiom would ever have occurred in Hebrew. In the Ugaritic text cited here below, one finds another idiom: YṮB + *l* + "house," where it is unlikely that the meaning is "sit upon" (l. 42).[56] One may

---

[53] *Salmo 29*, 111–21. For this author, the meaning of "inundation" would be specific to the P source and would reflect a secondary development of the term. The interpretation of מַבּוּל as referring to the waters of the heavens, which goes back at least to J. Begrich ("*Mabbūl*. Eine exegetisch-lexikalische Studie," ZS 6 [1928] 135–53), was also adopted by Kloos and criticized in my review of her book, pp. 230–31 [see note 2 above].

[54] *Psalm 29*, 24, 49–51, 91–96.

[55] Dahood, *Psalms* I, 180.

[56] The orthography would allow for the interpretation "return to," but since no notice has been given of Baal departing his house, that option, though preferred by some scholars, is not the obvious choice.

conclude that the phrase was less specific than the simple designation of that upon which one sits. If that observation may be extrapolated to the corresponding Hebrew idiom, always a dangerous procedure but rendered at least plausible by the presence in this text of enclitic מ, another feature far more characteristic of Ugaritic idiom than of Hebrew, then one is not required to translate "sit upon the flood." Though I, like many of my predecessors, have adopted that translation, I have never known just what it was supposed to mean. If the nuance of the Ugaritic text is "because Baal has taken his kingly throne with respect to his palace," that is, the emphasis is not on location but on interlocking functions (the deity's "chair" is a "throne" because it is in a "palace," the "house" is a "palace" because a deity "sits" enthroned there), the same may be true of the Hebrew idiom: the phrase does not mean that YHWH sat upon the Flood, treating it like a chair, but that he sat upon his kingly throne with respect to the Flood, i.e. acted as sovereign towards it. This interpretation would fit the biblical view of the Flood, which was brought about by YHWH and which made use of both the heavenly reservoir and of the subterranean fresh water, the תְּהוֹם, neither of which was a malefic figure according to Ugaritic mythology. It appears possible, then, to take the mention of מַבּוּל as tweaking the Canaanite ear, as it were, by referring to an episode of cosmic proportions and having to do with watery forces, but in Israelite terms according to which certain watery forces are harnessed by the divinity for the purpose of subduing evil. If this be the case, the allusion is to a Flood story that is more closely related to the Mesopotamian flood stories than to the North-Syrian myth of Baal defeating Sea. The implications for dating Psalm 29 are difficult to draw for lack of data: the time is necessarily one when the "Canaanite" Baal mythology was still well known but when the Israelite flood story had become part of the received view of YHWH.

## ONE UGARITIC VIEW OF BAAL'S RAIN-MAKING POWERS

Loretz has cited a comprehensive group of Ugaritic texts wherein parallels with Psalm 29 have been identified.[57] For this much briefer coverage of the issues, however, it may suffice to cite only the text RS 2.[008]+ vii 14-52, in which a series of terms and motifs are found which largely parallel those in the psalm. It should be observed immediately, however, that the Ugaritic poem is part of a long

---

[57] *Psalm 29*, 111–26.

RS 2.[008] + VII 14-52

| Text | Vocalization | Translation |
| --- | --- | --- |
| 14) w yʕn . dlı ʾyn (15) bʕl [.] | wa yaʕni ʾalʾiyánu baʕlu | Mighty *Baʕlu* speaks up: |
| à štm . ktr bn (16) ym . ktr . bnm . ʕdt | ʾašitama kôṯara bina yômi kôṯara binama ʕidati | "I believe I'll charge *Kôṯaru* this very day, Yea, *Kôṯaru*, this very moment, |
| 17) ypth . hln . b bhtm | yiptaḥa ḥallâna bi bahatima | With opening a window in (my) house, |
| 18) úrbt . b qrb . hkl(19) m . w [l] pth . bdqt . ʕrpt | ʾurbata bi qirbi hêkalima wa ʾiptaḥa buduqta ʕurapâti | A latticed window in (my) palace; But I'll open up the rift of the clouds." [59] |
| 20) ʕ hwt . ktr . w hss | ʕalê huwâti kôṯari wa ḥasîsi | On account of *Kôṯaru-wa-Ḫasîsu*'s (previous) speech,[60] |
| 21) sḥq . ktr . w hss | ṣaḥiqu kôṯaru wa ḥasîsu | *Kôṯaru-wa-Ḫasîsu* begins laughing, |
| 22) yšu [.] gh [.] w ysh | yiššaʾu gâhu wa yaṣîḥu | Lifting up his voice and crying out: |
| 23) l rgmt . lk . l dlı ʾ(24) yn . bʕl . ttbn . bʕl (25) l hwty | lâ ragamtu lêka lê ʾalʾiyâni baʕli tatûbuna baʕli lê huwâtiya | "Did I not say to you, O Mighty *Baʕlu*: 'You'll come around, O *Baʕlu*, to my word'." |
| ypth . h(26)ln . b bhtm . úrbt (27) b qrb . hk[lm . yp]th (28) bʕl . bdqt [. ʕrp]t | yiptaḥ ḥallâna bi bahatima ʾurbata bi qirbi hêkalima yiptaḥ baʕlu buduqta ʕurapâti | He opens a window in the house, A latticed window in the palace; *Baʕlu* opens up the rift of the clouds. |
| 29) qlh . qdš [.] b[ʕ . y]tn | qâlahu qaduša baʕlu yattinu | His holy voice *Baʕlu* gives forth repeatedly, |
| 30) ytny . bʕl . ṣ[dt . š] pth | yaṯniyu baʕlu šiʕata šiptêhu | Repeatedly pronounces, does *Baʕlu*, the outpouring of his lips. |

| Transliteration | Normalization | Translation |
|---|---|---|
| 31) qlh . q[dš . tr]r . ảrṣ<br>32) [ṣảt . špth .] ġrm [.] tʾḫšn | qāluhu qaduši tarrira ảrṣa<br>šiʾata šaptêhu ġurūma taḫīšūna | His holy voice causes the earth to tremble,<br>At the outpouring of his lips, the mountains take fright.[61] |
| 33) rq [          ] (34) qdmym .<br>bmt . ả[ rṣ] (35) tṭṭn . | bamātu ảrṣi tiṭṭutna | the high places of the earth totter. |
| ỉb . bʿl . tỉḫd (36)   yʿrm .<br>šnủ . hd . gpt (37) ġr . | ỉêbū baʿli taʾḫudū yaʿrima<br>šāniʾū haddi gipāti ġūri | Baʿlu's enemies grasp the trees,<br>Haddu's adversaries (grasp) the slopes of the mountain. |
| w yʿn . ảlỉyn (38) bʿl . | wa yaʿni ʾalʾiyānu baʿlu | Mighty Baʿlu speaks up: |
| ỉb . hdm ʾ . lm . tḫš<br>39) lm . tḫš . ntq . dmrn | ỉêbi haddima lêma taḫīšū<br>lêma taḫīšū nātiqi dimarāni | "O enemies of Baʿlu, why have you taken fright?<br>Why have you taken fright, you who arm yourselves against Dimarānu? |
| 40) ʿn . bʿl . qdm . ydh<br>41) ktġd . ảrz . b ymnh | ʿana baʿlu qudāma yadihu<br>kittuġaddu ʾarzi bi yaminihu | Does not Baʿlu sight where his hand (will strike),<br>(when) the kittuġaddu of cedar (is) in his right hand? |
| 42) bkm . ytb . bʿl . l bhth<br>43) ủ mlk . ủ bl mlk<br>44) ảrṣ . drkt . yštkn | bikama yatābi baʿli lê bahatihu<br>ʾô malku ʾô balû malki<br>ʾarṣa darkata yištakīnu | With Baʿlu enthroned at his house,<br>What person, king or commoner,<br>can set up his own dominion in the earth? |
| 45) dll . ảl . ʾlảk .<br>l bn (46) ỉlm . mt .<br>ʿdd [.] l ydd (47) ỉl . ġzr . | dalila ʾal ʾilʾak<br>lê bini ʾilima môti<br>ʿadida lê yadidi ʾili ġazri | So why don't I send a courier<br>to Môtu, son of ʾIlu,<br>a messenger to the beloved lad of ʾIlu? |
| yqrả . mt   (48) b npšh .<br>ystrn ydd (49) b gngnh . | yiqraʾa môtu bi napšihu<br>yistarran yadidu bi ganganihu | Let Môtu cry out (all he wants) from his throat,<br>Let the beloved one repeat from his very innards: |

| | | |
|---|---|---|
| *āḫdy . d ymn*(50) *lk . ʿl . ilm .* | *ʾaḫhadāya dū yamluku ʿalê ʾilima* | 'I alone am the one who rules over the gods, |
| *dʿ ymriʾ* (51) *ilm . w . nšm .* | *dū yamarriʾu ʾilima wa našima* | who fattens gods and men, |
| *d yšb*(52)[ʿ] . *hmlt . arṣ* | *dū yašabbiʿu hamullata ʾarṣi* | who sates the hordes of the earth.' |

---

[59] For the restoration of a 1st person form, inspired by the explicit statement in lines 27–28 that it is Baal himself who opens the rift in the clouds, see Miller Prosser, "Reconsidering the Reconstruction of KTU 1.4 vii 19," *UF* 33 (2001) 467–78.

[60] Baal had previously said that he did not want a window in his house and Kôthar-wa-Ḫasis had said that he, Baal, would come around to his "word" (see vi 15 and the reference thereunto here below, lines 24–25). I have changed my view of the verse divisions here (as compared with *Context* [1997] 262, where this colon was taken with the preceding as forming a bicolon) because Kôthar-wa-Ḫasis said nothing in their previous speech about a rift in the clouds: that concept appears for the first time here in Baal's speech. This observation and the clear distinction in lines 25-28 (and in line 19, as restored) between the roles of Kôthar-wa-Ḫasis and Baal casts doubt on the identification of *bdqt* ʿ*rpt* as a metaphor for the window (M. C. A. Korpel, *A Rift in the Clouds. Ugaritic and Hebrew Descriptions of the Divine* (UBL 8; Münster: Ugarit-Verlag, 1990) 375, 381-82.

[61] The last word in line 32 is {*dḥs ʾn*}, which is either to be emended to {*tḥšn*} or to be retained and translated as a factitive "I will lay fright on RTQ[...]" (no satisfactory explanation of this last word has been proposed and the broken context makes any solution uncertain).

narrative cycle, that it is not lyrical in nature as is Psalm 29 and, for this reason, the motifs are presented differently. The following motifs are common to the two texts:

|              | Psalm 29                           | RS 2.[008]                                      |
|--------------|------------------------------------|-------------------------------------------------|
| Dwelling     | הֵיכָל, קֹדֶשׁ (vv. 2, 9)           | *bhtm, hklm* (ll. 17-19 etc.)                   |
| Thunder      | הָרְעִים, קוֹל (v. 3, etc.)          | *ql* + YTN, *ṣit špt* + ṮNY, *ql qdš* (ll. 29-30) |
| Lightning    | חצב + לַהֲבוֹת אֵשׁ (v. 7)          | *bdqt ʿrpt* + PTḤ (ll. 19, 27-28)               |
| Trees        | יְעָרוֹת, אֶרֶז (vv. 5, 9)           | *ʾrz, yʿrm* (ll. 35-36, 41)                      |
| Mountains    | שִׂרְיֹן, לְבָנוֹן (vv. 5-6)         | *bmt árṣ, gpt ġr* (ll. 35-37)                    |
| Trembling    | ח(ו)ל, רקד (vv. 6, 8-9)            | TRR, NṬṬ (ll. 31, 34-35)                         |
| Kingship     | מֶלֶךְ, ישׁב ל (v. 10)               | YṮB *l, mlk, drkt* (ll. 42-43)                   |
| Blessings    | ברך בַּשָּׁלוֹם, עֹז + נתן (v. 11)   | MRʾ, ŠBʿ (ll. 50-52)                             |
| …for Clients | עַמּוֹ (v. 11)                       | *ilm w nšm, hmlt á rṣ* (ll. 51-52)              |

The primary motif present in Psalm 29 but absent in the Ugaritic passage is that of the many waters; as the structure of the *Baʿlu* cycle is usually understood, this motif was present in tablet 2, col. iv, where *Baʿlu* defeated *Yammu/Naharu* in single combat. Also absent in the Hebrew lyric poem is the architectural detail of the window (this motif appears in the biblical Flood story: Gen 6:11), clearly important for the Ugaritic narrative, though its precise signification is obscured by lacunae in the text.[60] An important difference is that the Hebrew lyric poem describes YHWH's powers as causing the natural world to tremble, but the Ugaritic poem includes a reference to Baal's enemies.

What stands out from this charting of the motifs is not only the number and importance of the parallels, but the fact that several appear in the same order, almost all in roughly similar order. This fact may be taken as reflecting an institutional paradigm for the weather divinity's activity: his authority is established in his dwelling, from that dwelling he gives his orders (explicitly in the Ugaritic text, implicitly in the psalm), the divine orders take the form of thunder and lightning, these cause the earth and all its inhabitants to tremble and fear; all these divine manifestations confirm that the deity is indeed king of the universe and that from him flow the blessings necessary for the well-being of the denizens of the universe, whether divine or human (at the end of the passage quoted above, Baal accuses Mot of claiming falsely to be at the origin of these benefits).

---

[60] Cf. Pardee, *Context*, 261 n. 173.

## CONCLUSIONS REGARDING THE STRUCTURE
## AND MEANING OF PSALM 29

The internal structure of Psalm 29 as well as external comparisons with Ugaritic, the only pre-biblical West-Semitic literature attested to date, show this psalm to be a tightly constructed paean to YHWH, who is depicted in terms known from the Ugaritic texts as applicable to the weather deity Baal. None of the multitudinous emendations that have been practiced on this text in the interest of creating a text more appealing to the modern mind has any foundation in the textual tradition nor, consequently, any real validity — with the possible exception of the excision of the so-called "prose particles"[61] — and the text is perfectly understandable without them. A common thread running through the text is provided by the terms that are parallel with כָּבוֹד and that proceed from the "glory" of YHWH in v. 1 through to the "well-being" of his people in v. 11.

For lack of data, it is difficult to determine at what stage in Israelite history such a work may most plausibly be fixed: the requirements are both that belief in the Baal figure in a form similar to that known from the Ugaritic texts be still alive and that that belief be appealing to Hebrew-speaking "Israelites" — if the mythological presuppositions were no longer alive or if they no longer held allure, the poem would have been a purely scholarly exercise. Proposed dates have ranged from the 12th century[62] to well after the exile.[63] The text does show one feature that is, on the basis of present evidence, archaic (the enclitic מ in v. 6), but such archaisms have been explained by some as late manifestations of the Israelite culture on Judaeans. Viewed from a

---

[61] If it could be proven that the text is early, it is plausible that the presence of the definite direct object marker אֵת and the definite article, both of relatively recent date were later accretions (cf. D. N. Freedman, "Prose Particles in the Poetry of the Primary History," in A. Kort, S. Morschauser [eds.], *Biblical and Related Studies Presented to Samuel Iwry* [Winona Lake, IN: Eisenbrauns, 1985] 49–62).

[62] D. N. Freedman, "'Who is Like Thee Among the Gods?' The Religion of Early Israel," in P. D. Miller, Jr., P. D. Hanson, and S. D. McBride (eds.), *Ancient Israelite Religion. Essays in Honor of Frank Moore Cross* (Philadelphia: Fortress, 1987) 315–35, esp. 317: "perhaps twelfth century." The poem is also identified here as "an old Canaanite hymn appropriated and adapted for Israelite usage...."

[63] R. Tournay, "En marge d'une traduction des Psaumes," *RB* 63 (1956) 161–81, esp. 180.

purely biblical perspective, this poem should respond to the issues raised in the Book of Hosea, where the conflict between Baal and YHWH is depicted as a living issue. This may provide an indication that the poem was pre-exilic; the two mountain names (vv. 5-6) certainly give to the poem a northern flavor and such is probably the case as well of מִדְבַּר קָדֵשׁ (v. 8), as we have seen.[64] But whether the context be identical to that of the Book of Hosea (northern kingdom before its demise in 722 BCE), a similar one in Israel or Judah, the result of Israelite influence on Judaean thinking, or a later product of literary artifice is beyond our ability to determine.

Even this more superficial analysis, without the full semantic breakdown for the entire text, shows very important differences as compared with Psalm 29.[65] First, the verse structure is almost entirely bicolonic, and clearly so, with few ambiguities[66]—the exercise of laying out the poetic verses here is hence less artificial than in the case of Psalm 29, for the poet appears to have been thinking in bicola. Second, though repetitive parallelism was a part of this poet's repertory, he did not use it as extensively as did the poet of Psalm 29. Third, this poet relied less on semantic parallelism and more on grammatical parallelism within verses; if one minded only the grammatical parallelism, the incidence of primed numbers would be much higher (e.g. in v. 2, "singing," "blessing," and "telling good news" are not synonyms, though one could group them into a broad

---

[64] G. A. Rendsburg's linguistic arguments for a northern origin of the poem (*Linguistic Evidence for the Northern Origin of Selected Psalms* [SBLMS 43, 1990]) cannot be taken at face value (see my review in *JAOS* 112 [1992] 702–704), but the indubitable presence of enclitic מ in v. 6 may constitute a nod to a language where the particle was used with some frequency—the only one presently known is Ugaritic.

[65] I do not follow the lead of Ginsberg ("A Strand in the Cord," 47–50), who saw Psalms 29 and 96 as representing two stages of use of an old Canaanite poem, these two followed by two others, visible in Psalms 98 and 147. The point has already been made above that Psalm 29 is more plausibly of Israelite origin, laying claim in "Canaanite" diction to Baal's powers for YHWH. Psalm 98 and 147 may well represent a continuation of the hymnic tradition as compared with Psalm 96 but, as they show no direct influence from Psalm 29, they are not considered here.

[66] The only exceptions are in vv. 10 and 11: in 10 because the present verse is tricolonic and the only question is whether the third colon is secondary, in 11 because the a b a' b' structure in the first colon could be divided into two cola.

category of "voice production" if one wished; nevertheless, they all appear in an identical verbal form, the m.pl. imperative).

In the specific matter of the overlapping material in the two psalms, the phrase מִשְׁפְּחוֹת עַמִּים appears to be a demythologization of בְּנֵי אֵלִים in Ps 29:1 and hence to be based on knowledge of the poetic tradition behind Psalm 29. If such be the case, then Ps 96:7-9 are rather clearly an expansion of Ps 29:1-2, transforming the "staircase" quadricolon into three bicola, with the third and fourth cola of the quadricolon each expanded into a bicolon by means of a new colon that is characterized primarily, as elsewhere in this poem, by grammatical parallelism.

Indeed, a case could be made for Psalm 96 consisting of an expanded and revised version of Psalm 29. Verses 1-6 of Psalm 96 would be an expansion on the theme of ascribing glory to YHWH, culminating in a paroxysm of synonymous parallelism in v. 6, where two of the words characteristic of Psalm 29 (הָדָר and עֹז) each appears in parallel with a new term. The kernel of the new poem consists of the expansion of Ps 29:1-2 described in the preceding paragraph. The big revision would have been in vv. 10-13, where the motif of kingship is mentioned immediately and the Baal imagery disappears entirely — to the point that the sea is here depicted as "thundering" in praise of YHWH (רעם in v. 11). The image of YHWH thundering over the mighty waters (רעם in Ps 29:3) is thus turned on its head, hardly a coincidence. The categories of nature mentioned in Ps 29:5-9 are not here depicted as cowering at the ambiguous power of the thunderstorm but as happily offering up praise to YHWH. Finally, the vision throughout this poem is not one of blessing reserved for the people of YHWH, as in the conclusion to Psalm 29, but of YHWH dealing with all the peoples of the earth: the poem begins and ends with עַמִּים and, as we have seen, it is part of the phrase inserted in place of בְּנֵי אֵלִים. The peoples of the earth are not offered unqualified access to YHWH's bounties, but the final promise is that they will be judged/ruled — a decision will be reached in their case by him who exercises rule (שׁפט) — according to the rule of right as upheld faithfully by YHWH.[67] Thus the extended parallelism of מלך and שׁפט

---

[67] Ginsberg, in his comparison of Psalms 29 and 96 did not view Psalm 96 as from beginning to end a revision of Psalm 29; rather, he treated it as a quotation of only the first two verses of Psalm 29 with insertions; he did, however, mention the possibility of the kingship motif in Psalm 96 reflecting Ps 29:10. In Loretz's

in vv. 10-13 expresses YHWH's absolute rule over the cosmos, the willing participation in this economy by the elements of nature, and at least the possible integration into it of all the peoples of the earth. If the socio-religious context of Psalm 29 reminds one of Hosea, that of Psalm 96 is much closer to certain passages of Isaiah, in particular Isaiah 2.[68]

SELECT BIBLIOGRAPHY

Auffret, P. "Notes conjointes sur la structure littéraire des psaumes 114 et 29," *EstBib* 37 (1978) 103–113.

Begrich, J. "*Mabbūl*. Eine exegetisch-lexikalische Studie," *ZS* 6 (1928) 135–53.

Cross, F. M. "Notes on a Canaanite Psalm in the Old Testament," *BASOR* 117 (1950) 19–21.

Cunchillos, J.-L. *Estudio del Salmo 29* (Institución San Jerónimo 6; Valencia, Spain: Libreria Diocesana, 1976).

Freedman, D. N. "'Who is Like Thee Among the Gods?' The Religion of Early Israel," in P. D. Miller, Jr., P. D. Hanson, and S. D. McBride (eds.), *Ancient Israelite Religion. Essays in Honor of Frank Moore Cross* (Philadelphia: Fortress, 1987) 315–35.

Ginsberg, H. L. "A Phoenician Hymn in the Psalter," *Atti XIX Congresso intrenazionale degli Orientalisti* (Rome: Tipografia del Senato, 1938) 472–76.

—. "שם קדמון למדבר סוריה," *Yediot* 6 (1938–1939) 96–97.

—. "A Strand in the Cord of Hebraic Hymnody," *EI* 9 [1969] 45–50.

Girard, M. *Les Psaumes. Analyse structurelle et interprétation, 1–50* (Recherches, Nouvelle Série 2; Montréal: Bellarmin; Paris: Cerf, 1984).

Greenstein, E. L. "One More Step on the Staircase," *UF* 9 (1977) 77–86.

—. "YHWH's Lightning in Psalm 29:7," *Maarav* 8 (1992) 49–57.

Kloos, C. *Yhwh's Combat with the Sea. A Canaanite Tradition in the Religion of Ancient Israel* (Amsterdam: Oorschot, 1986).

Loretz, O. *Psalm 29. Kanaanäische El- und Baaltraditionen in jüdischer Sicht* (UBL 2; Münster: Ugarit-Verlag, 1984).

---

comparison of the two poems (*Psalm* 29, 127–33), Ps 96:7-10 is described as a post-exilic commentary on Ps 29:1-2 by means of glosses and quotations (from other psalms). No place is left for oral tradition nor for Psalm 96 being the product of an authentic poet who preferred to compose in bicola. Nor is any attempt made to see Psalm 96 as covering similar ground, as compared with Psalm 29, from beginning to end but with a different view of YHWH's relationship with nature and with mankind.

[68] As Cunchillos remarks, "El carácter universalista del Ps 96 ... ha sido puesto relieve por todos los comentaristas" (*Salmo 29*, 44).

Korpel, M. C. A. *A Rift in the Clouds. Ugaritic and Hebrew Descriptions of the Divine* (UBL 8; Münster: Ugarit-Verlag, 1990).

Mittmann, S. "Komposition und Redaktion von Psalm xxix," *VT* 28 (1978) 172–94.

Tournay, R. "En marge d'une traduction des Psaumes," *RB* 63 (1956) 161–81.

## APPENDIX: PSALM 96

| | Text | Translation | Semantic parallelism |
|---|---|---|---|
| 1) | שִׁירוּ לַיהוָה שִׁיר חָדָשׁ<br>שִׁירוּ לַיהוָה כָּל־הָאָרֶץ | Sing to YHWH a new song,<br>Sing to YHWH, all the earth; | a b c² (a + x)<br>a b d² |
| 2) | שִׁירוּ לַיהוָה בָּרְכוּ שְׁמוֹ<br>בַּשְּׂרוּ מִיּוֹם־לְיוֹם יְשׁוּעָתוֹ | Sing to YHWH, bless his name,<br>Proclaim day by day the good news of victory. | a b c d<br>e f² (x + x) g |
| 3) | סַפְּרוּ בַגּוֹיִם כְּבוֹדוֹ<br>בְּכָל־הָעַמִּים נִפְלְאוֹתָיו | Recount among the nations his glory,<br>Among the peoples his wondrous acts. | a b c<br>b'² c' |
| 4) | כִּי גָדוֹל יְהוָה וּמְהֻלָּל מְאֹד<br>נוֹרָא הוּא עַל־כָּל־אֱלֹהִים | For great is YHWH and greatly to be praised,<br>Fearful is he above all the (other) gods. | a b c²<br>e² b'² (x + b') |
| 5) | כִּי כָּל־אֱלֹהֵי הָעַמִּים אֱלִילִים<br>וַיהוָה שָׁמַיִם עָשָׂה | For all the gods of the peoples are but shams,<br>Whereas YHWH made the earth. | a³ (x + a + y) a'<br>a" c d |
| 6) | הוֹד־וְהָדָר לְפָנָיו<br>עֹז וְתִפְאֶרֶת בְּמִקְדָּשׁוֹ | Majesty and splendor (are) before him,<br>Strength and beauty (are) in his sanctuary. | a a' b<br>a" a"' c |
| 7) | הָבוּ לַיהוָה מִשְׁפְּחוֹת עַמִּים<br>הָבוּ לַיהוָה כָּבוֹד וָעֹז | Ascribe to YHWH, O tribes of the peoples,<br>Ascribe to YHWH glory and power. | a b c² (x + y)<br>a b d² (z + z) |
| 8) | הָבוּ לַיהוָה כְּבוֹד שְׁמוֹ<br>שְׂאוּ־מִנְחָה וּבֹאוּ לְחַצְרוֹתָיו | Ascribe to YHWH the glory (due) his name,<br>Bring an offering and enter his courts. | a b c²<br>d e f g |

9) הִשְׁתַּחֲווּ לַיהוָה בְּהַדְרַת־קֹדֶשׁ
   חִילוּ מִפָּנָיו כָּל־הָאָרֶץ׃

Bow down to YHWH in the splendor of the sanctuary,
Dance at his presence, all you inhabitants of the earth.

a b c²
d e f²

10) אִמְרוּ בַגּוֹיִם יְהוָה מָלָךְ
    אַף־תִּכּוֹן תֵּבֵל בַּל־תִּמּוֹט
    יָדִין עַמִּים בְּמֵישָׁרִים׃

Say among the nations: "YHWH is king;"
Hence the world is solid, it shall not totter;
He shall judge the peoples with righteousness.

a b c d
e f g
h i j

11) יִשְׂמְחוּ הַשָּׁמַיִם וְתָגֵל הָאָרֶץ
    יִרְעַם הַיָּם וּמְלֹאוֹ׃

Rejoice O heavens, let the earth be glad,
Let the sea and all that fills it make thunderous noise.

a b a' b'
c b" d

12) יַעֲלֹז שָׂדַי וְכָל־אֲשֶׁר־בּוֹ
    אָז יְרַנְּנוּ כָּל־עֲצֵי־יָעַר׃

Let the fields rejoice and all that pertains to them,
Then let all the trees of the forest shout aloud

a b c²
a' b'³ (x + b' + b")

13) לִפְנֵי יְהוָה כִּי בָא
    כִּי בָא לִשְׁפֹּט הָאָרֶץ

Before YHWH, for he comes,
For he comes to rule the earth.

a b c
c d e

    יִשְׁפֹּט־תֵּבֵל בְּצֶדֶק
    וְעַמִּים בֶּאֱמוּנָתוֹ׃

He will rule the world with right,
Even the peoples with his faithfulness.

a b c
d c'

# DOUBLE ENTENDRE IN PSALM 59

JOHN S. KSELMAN, S. S.

In a recent article, Paul Raabe examined a number of cases of *double entendre*, or what he calls "deliberate ambiguity," in the Book of Psalms.[1] Two of his instances come from Psalm 59.[2] What is proposed here is that there is at least one more example of such double-meaning speech, intended by the poet, in the refrain in Pss 59:7 and 59:15.[3]

Psalm 59 contains two refrains, the first of which is found in vv. 7 and 15, and the second in vv. 10-11 and 18.[4] It is the first of these refrains (vv. 7 and 15) that is under consideration here. The text and standard translation of v. 7 are as follows:

| | |
|---|---|
| יָשׁוּבוּ לָעֶרֶב | In the evening they return; |
| [5]יֶהֱמוּ כַכָּלֶב | they howl like dogs; |
| וִיסוֹבְבוּ עִיר | they prowl about the city. |

---

[1] P. R. Raabe, "Deliberate Ambiguity in the Psalter," *JBL* 110 (1991) 213–27.

[2] Raabe, "Ambiguity," 217–18 (on Ps 59:16); 224 (on Ps 59:14). On Ps 59:16, see now J. Tropper, "'Sie knurrten wie Hunde.' Psalm 59,16, Kilamuwa:10 und die Semantik der Wurzel *lun*," *ZAW* 106 (1994) 87–95; on pp. 87–91, Tropper advances strong arguments against deriving יְלִינוּ from לוּן, "complain, murmur."

[3] There are other poetic devices in Psalm 59 besides deliberate ambiguity. An *inclusio* is formed by תְּשַׂגְּבֵנִי in v. 2 and מִשְׂגַּבִּי ... מִשְׂגָּב in vv. 17-18. There are also three instances of talionic reversal: in vv. 2 and 12, the psalmist prays that "those who rise against me" (מִמִּתְקוֹמְמַי) God will "bring down" (וְהוֹרִידֵמוֹ); the hostile "mighty" (עַזִּים) of v. 4 are confronted by God's "might" in vv. 10 (עֻזּוֹ) and 17-18 (עֻזֶּךָ ... עֻזִּי); the roaming around for food by predatory enemies (K יְנוּעוּן; Q יְנִיעוּן, v. 16) leads the psalmist to pray "Make them totter" (הֲנִיעֵמוֹ). Finally, there is a probable instance of hysteron-proteron in v. 5: "they charge (יְרוּצוּן), they form themselves in battle array" (וְיִכּוֹנָנוּ; on this assimilated *hitpolel* with this meaning, see D. J. A. Clines, *Dictionary of Classical Hebrew* 4 [Sheffield: Sheffield Academic Press, 1998] 376).

[4] The presence of more than one refrain in a psalm is not unparalleled; Psalm 42–43 has three refrains (42:4d and 11d; 42:6, 12 and 43:5; 42:10 and 43:2), none of which is exactly repeated.

[5] The simile כַּכָּלֶב is taken as a collective: "As often with animal names, Hebrew uses the singular collective preceded by the definite article" (W. H. C. Propp, *Exodus 1–18* [AB 2; New York: Doubleday, 1999] 591).

This line is repeated in v. 15, the only difference being the conjunction (וִישׁוּבוּ).

Commentators and translators understand the simile כְּכֶלֶב ("like dogs") as referring to enemies, either national enemies or (if Psalm 59 is a royal psalm) enemies of the king.[6] The simile likens the enemies to an urban phenomenon, scavenging dogs roaming about a city in search of food (cf. 1 Kgs 14:11; 16:4; 21:24).

## THE DOUBLE ENTENDRE IN THIS PSALM

The *double entendre* proposed here requires no change in the text, but rather a reunderstanding. First, the verb שׁוּב (וִישׁוּבוּ) is taken in its political sense, as "turn away," i.e. be disloyal.[7] This political sense of שׁוּב is reinforced by the immediately preceding כָּל־בֹּגְדֵי אָוֶן ("all malicious traitors") in v. 6.[8] Similarly in Jer 3:6-8, "faithless Israel" (מְשֻׁבָה יִשְׂרָאֵל) is twice paired with "her traitorous sister Judah" (בֹּגְדָה יְהוּדָה אֲחוֹתָהּ / בָּגוֹדָה אֲחוֹתָהּ יְהוּדָה); and again in 3:11, note מְשֻׁבָה יִשְׂרָאֵל מִבֹּגֵדָה יְהוּדָה.

In the second colon, while the verb הָמָה (יֶהֱמוּ) can mean "howl,

---

[6] J. Botterweck, *TDOT* 7.156: "In the Psalms, the כְּלָבִים represent the enemies who oppress the individual worshipper. They, the band of the wicked (sometimes with demonic overtones) surround the faithful psalmist ... like a pack of growling dogs on the prowl ... they greedily beset the psalmist ...." Among the many who consider Psalm 59 a royal psalm are S. Mowinckel, *The Psalms in Israel's Worship* (New York and Nashville: Abingdon, 1962) 1.226; J. H. Eaton, *Kingship and the Psalms* (SBT 32; London: SCM, 1976) 47; M. E. Tate, *Psalms 51–100* (WBC 20; Dallas: Word, 1990) 95; G. Ravasi, *Il libro dei Salmi 2* (Bologna: Dehoniane, 1986) 190; M. Dahood, *Psalms II* (AB 17; Garden City, NY: Doubleday, 1968) 66–67. As will be seen below, I depart from Dahood's understanding of "the nations" (הַגּוֹיִם, vv. 6 and 9) as foreign enemies and the "dogs" as domestic foes. I will argue that both nations and dogs refer to rebellious vassal states.

[7] W. L. Holladay, *The Root Šûbh in the Old Testament* (Leiden: Brill, 1958) 80: שׁוּב as "withdraw (from God), become apostate"; "turn back (from good, the covenant, etc., to evil), become apostate"; and see pp. 134, 137, 151–52. Dahood (*Psalms II*, 69) derives יָשׁוּבוּ from שׁוּב II, a biform of יָשַׁב, meaning "reside, sit." This analysis does not affect the point being made here. If Dahood is correct, then יָשׁוּבוּ from שׁוּב II ("they reside") is reread in the *double entendre* as derived from שׁוּב I ("turn" politically).

[8] On בגד as meaning "faithless (to a relationship)," see Pss 25:3; 78:57; Hos 5:7; Mal 2:11; S. Erlandsson, *TDOT* 1.470–73. Acording to C. A. and E. G. Briggs (*The Book of Psalms* 2 [ICC; Edinburgh: T & T Clark, 1907] 156), בגד means treachery to covenant relationships.

bay" of dogs, it can also be used of the roar of attacking enemies (Pss 46:7; 83:3; Isa 17:12). And on the simile כְּכֶלֶב in this colon, two observations can be made. First, the description of enemies as savage predators is a common motif in biblical poetry (Pss 7:2-3; 10:9; 7:12; 22:13-14, 22, etc.). Second, we turn to an extrabiblical source, the Amarna letters, especially important because of their Northwest Semitic context.[9] In these cuneiform texts, there are two ways in which "dog" (*kalbu*, or the sumerogram UR.KU) is used. It can be part of a self-abasement formula in a subject's self-presentation to the king, as in EA 60:7 ("... and I am a servant and a dog of his house").[10] Far more frequent (more than 20 times) is the use of "dog" for an enemy, specifically a traitorous and rebellious vassal. A good example occurs in EA 67, where an unnamed individual is reported to the Pharaoh as disloyal (67:15-18): "He made a treaty with the ruler of Gubla and the ruler of ... and all the fortress commanders of your land became friendly with him, my lord. Now he is like a runaway dog, and he has seized Sumur, the city of the Sun, my lord ..."[11]

In the third colon, the verb וִיסוֹבְבוּ is understood to mean "roam" or the like: "they roam around the city."[12] The verb סבב has this intran-

---

[9] W. L. Moran, *The Amarna Letters* (Baltimore and London: Johns Hopkins University Press, 1992). I must credit M. L. Barré for help with these materials.

[10] Other occurrences of this self-abasement formula include EA 61:3; 201:15; 202:13; 247:15. This is the usage found in the Hebrew Bible (2 Sam 9:8; 2 Kgs 8:13; cf. 1 Sam 24:15) and in three sixth-century ostraca from Lachish (2.4; 5.4; 6.3): "Who is your servant (but) a dog ...." See P. K. McCarter, *I Samuel* (AB 8; Garden City, NY: Doubleday, 1980) 384–85; idem, *II Samuel* (AB 9; Garden City, NY: Doubleday, 1984) 261; G. W. Coats, "Self-Abasement and Insult Formulas," *JBL* 89 (1970) 14–26.

[11] Moran, *Amarna Letters*, 137. For "friendship" as a treaty term, see n. 59 of Moran's introduction, and the literature cited there; see also J. S. Croatto, "ṬŌBÂ como 'amistad de Alianza)' en el Antiguo Testamento," *AION* 18 (1968) 385–89; I. Johag, "*ṭwb* — Terminus Technicus in Vertrags- und Bündnis-formularen des alten Orients und des Alten Testaments," in H.-J. Fabry (ed.), *Bausteine biblischer Theologie*, Festschrift G. J. Botterweck (BBB 50; Cologne and Bonn: Peter Hanstein, 1977) 3–23; J. M. Galán, "What is he, the dog?" *UF* 25 (1993) 573–80. In a private communication, Barré notes: "My guess is that [*kalbu halqu*, runaway dog] probably can refer to those people in this era who simply abandoned their cities and city-rulers and ran off with the Apiru."

[12] The absence of a preposition with עִיר is unobjectionable in the terse language of poetry; see P. R. Raabe, *Psalm Structures: A Study of Psalms with Refrains* (JSOTSup 104: Sheffield: JSOT, 1990) 135. The absence of the preposition

sitive meaning in several biblical texts (Isa 23:16; Ps 48:13; Cant 3:2, 3; 5:7). But more commonly the verb is transitive, meaning "encircle, surround, besiege." In the account of the Israelite attack on Jericho in Joshua 6, עִיר is the direct object of the verb סבב (*qal*) six times (6:3, 4, 7, 14, 15 [twice]).[13] Similar usage (סבב [*qal*] + עִיר [direct object]) occurs in 2 Kgs 6:15 and Qoh 9:14.

## EVIDENCE CONFIRMING THIS INTERPRETATION

To summarize the discussion thus far: the proposal is that the obvious first sense of vv. 7 and 15 (the nations are like scavenging dogs, roaming the city by night in search of food) is complemented by a *double entendre*, in which vv. 7 and 15 refer to rebels who treacherously attack the city of their suzerain:

> By night they prove faithless;
> they roar like dogs,
> they surround the city.

Under cover of darkness, the time for wrongdoing and treachery (Job 24:13-17; Prov 4:19; Luke 22:53; John 13:30), traitorous allies or vassals besiege the city.[14]

There are several pieces of confirmatory evidence in Psalm 59 that support this interpretation. First, v. 8 speaks of the baying of the dogs, "with swords on their lips."[15] The "swords" that are issuing from the mouths of the psalmist's enemies may be not simply a metaphor for malicious, damaging speech, but more specifically disloyal, seditious speech, involving plots against the king and rebellion by vassal or treaty partner. Such subversive and seditious speech is a constant concern of ancient Near Eastern monarchs.[16] And the background of the appeal to God to "see" (v. 5) and the boast of the rebels, "Who hears?" (v. 8) may be found in the ancient Near Eastern version of a

---

also permits the intentional ambiguity, where עִיר is taken as the direct object of the verb.

[13] But note וַיַּסֵּב אֲרוֹן־יְהוָה אֶת־הָעִיר in Josh 6:11: "He caused the ark of Yhwh to go around the city."

[14] Note the reference to stealth and warfare in v. 4: "They lie in wait for my life; the mighty war against me."

[15] Other instances of this metaphor of the mouth (or words) as weapons are found in Pss 52:3; 55:22; 57:5; 64:4-5; Job 5:15; and see Rev 1:16; 19:15.

[16] M. Weinfeld, "The Loyalty Oath in the Ancient Near East," *UF* 8 (1976) 379–414.

secret service, spoken of as "the eyes and ears of the king," whose responsibility it was to search out such dangerous speech.[17] When the evildoers ask "Who hears?," they are expressing their confidence that their treachery has not become known to the king's agents, his "eyes and ears." Given this context, the "sins and transgressions" and "guilt" spoken of in vv. 4 and 13 may be more precisely defined as treaty violations.[18] In v. 5 the king denies that he has broken the treaty ("for no misdeed [covenant breach] on my part, they charge ..."); and in vv. 8 and 13 he accuses his enemies of subversive and threatening speech ("There are swords on their lips ... the sins of their mouths, the words of their lips ... their cursing and lies"). According to Milgrom, the last of these terms (כַּחַשׁ, "lie") means false denial, "especially in oath-taking."[19]

The verb לכד (nipʿal) in v. 13 is appropriate to the *double entendre* of the refrain, since it can refer both to snaring and trapping animals (the "dogs" of vv. 7 and 15) and human beings (Jer 5:26; Ps 35:8; Prov 5:22; Job 5:13) and to taking a city in war (Deut 2:35; Josh 1:8, 12; 10:1; Judg 1:8, 12, etc.).[20] Even Yhwh's mocking laughter (v. 9) at the pretensions of the rebels calls to mind the similar scene in Ps 2:4, where the divine Suzerain laughs at the planned revolt of the vassals in vv. 1-3 and establishes the Israelite king's rule "to the ends of the earth" (Pss 2:8; 59:14).

Finally, in the context of treaties of the suzerain-vassal type, a context that I have argued is present in the political reading of vv. 7 and 15, it is appropriate for the king to call upon the divine Suzerain to annihilate his (and the king's) enemies (Ps 2:2), thereby demonstrating his royal dominion. This recognition of God's supremacy by the defeat of his enemies occurs twice in Psalm 59:

> v. 6: You alone, O Yhwh, are the God of hosts, the God of Israel;
> awake to punish all the nations.

---

[17] A. L. Oppenheim, "The Eyes of the Lord," *JAOS* 88 (1968) 173–80.

[18] H. Tadmor, "Treaty and Oath in the Ancient Near East," in G. M. Tucker and D. A Knight (eds.), *Humanizing America's Iconic Book: Society of Biblical Literature Centennial Addresses 1980* (Biblical Scholarship in North America 6; Chico, CA: Scholars Press, 1982) 145.

[19] J. Milgrom, *Leviticus 1–16* (AB 3; New York: Doubleday, 1991) 335; see also H. C. Brichto, *the Problem of "Curse" in the Hebrew Bible* (Philadelphia: Society of Biblical Literature, 1963) 57–59.

[20] On being caught in/by one's words, see the striking parallel in Prov 6:2.

v. 14: Destroy them in your rage, destroy them until they are no more;
let them recognize that God rules in/from Jacob to the ends of the earth.[21]

These two statements of God's supremacy immediately precede the refrains in vv. 7 and 15. If this proposal of intentional ambiguity, of a *double entendre* with a political sense, has merit, then this proposal provides further evidence that the psalm is royal, and that the speaker is the king.

## SELECT BIBLIOGRAPHY

Briggs, C. A. and E. G. *The Book of Psalms* 2 (ICC; Edinburgh: T & T Clark, 1907).

Clines, D. J. A. *A Dictionary of Classical Hebrew* 4 (Sheffield: Sheffield Academic Press, 1998).

Dahood, M. *Psalms II* (AB 17; Garden City, NY: Doubleday, 1968).

Eaton J. H. *Kingship and the Psalms* (SBT 32; London: SCM, 1976).

Galán, J. M. "What is he, the dog?," *UF* 25 (1993) 573–80.

Holladay, W. L. *The Root Šubh in the Old Testament* (Leiden: Brill, 1958).

Mowinckel, S. *The Psalms in Israel's Worship* (New York and Nashville: Abingdon, 1962).

Moran, W. L. *The Amarna Letters* (Baltimore and London: Johns Hopkins University Press, 1992).

Oppenheim, A. L. "The Eyes of the Lord," *JAOS* 88 (1968) 173–80.

Raabe, P. R. *Psalm Structures: A Study of Psalms with Refrains* (JSOTSup 104; Sheffield: JSOT, 1990).

—. "Deliberate Ambiguity in the Psalter," *JBL* 110 (1991) 213–27.

Ravasi, G. *Il libro dei Salmi 2* (Bologna: Dehoniane, 1986).

Tadmor, H. "Treaty and Oath in the Ancient Near East," in G. M. Tucker and D. A. Knight (eds.), *Humanizing America's Iconic Book: Society of Biblical Literature Centennial Addresses 1980* (Biblical Scholarship in North America 6; Chico, CA: Scholars Press, 1982) 127–52.

Tate, M. E. *Psalms 51–100* (WBC 20; Dallas: Word, 1990).

Tropper, J. "'Sie knurrten wie Hunde.' Psalm 59,16, Kilamuwa:10 und die Semantik der Wurzel *lun*," *ZAW* 106 (1994) 87–95.

Weinfeld, M. "The Loyalty Oath in the Ancient Near East," *UF* 8 (1976) 379–414.

---

[21] Note the chiastic order of the two passages: God's rule : the punishment of the nations : : the punishment of the nations : God's rule. Note also that both passages are followed by סֶלָה.

# PSALM 90:

## WISDOM MEDITATION OR COMMUNAL LAMENT?

RICHARD J. CLIFFORD, S. J.

Readers through the ages have found in Psalm 90 a rich and diverse trove of sentiments. The author of 2 Pet 3:8 discovered in its portrayal of God's nature an explanation for the apparent delay of the coming of the Lord: "with the Lord one day is like a thousand years, and a thousand years are like one day." Francis Bacon in the seventeenth century regarded Ps 90:11-12 as an invitation to remember our mortality and gain wisdom, "Teach us, O Lord, to number well our days ... for that which guides man best in all his ways, is meditation of mortality." Isaac Watts in the early eighteenth century emphasized the contrast between the eternal God and ephemeral human beings: "Time, like an ever-flowing stream, bears us all away." The psalm is no less fascinating to modern readers as the continuing stream of scholarly studies makes clear.

In an important study that appeared in 1994, Thomas Krüger of the University of Zurich described the scholarly consensus regarding the interpretation of Psalm 90: it laments the transience of human beings, a transience that is attributed to God's anger at human sin. The major disagreement among commentators is whether guilt and transience are to be accepted as part of the human condition or are to be protested against.[1] Since Krüger's assessment, studies and commentaries have added nuance, but have not significantly departed from the consensus. Klaus Seybold regards Psalm 90 as a late and much redacted prayer on the "wisdom-philosophical" theme of time (God's and ours), which is provoked by a severe crisis or by an "experience of loss of time or life."[2] Johannes Schnocks disregards genre considerations as unhelpful for analyzing what is essentially a wisdom meditation on time and eternity.[3] To James Luther Mays, the psalm is "the theological ac-

---

[1] "Psalm 90 und die 'Vergänglichkeit des Menschen,'" *Bib* 75 (1994) 191–219. Professors John Kselman, S. S, and Michael Barré, S. S., have read earlier versions of the manuscript and offered helpful suggestions.

[2] *Die Psalmen* (HAT I/15; Tübingen: Mohr Siebeck, 1996) 356–57.

[3] "Ehe die Berge geboren wurden, bist du": Die Gegenwart Gottes im 90.

count of the human predicament ... the wrath of God at human sinfulness."[4] Christine Forster's study of the theme of human transience in wisdom Psalms (chiefly Psalms 39, 49, and 90) views the psalm as an attempt to incorporate wisdom reflection into prayer so that pray-ers will be better able to cope with their limited span of life.[5] Erich Zenger also sees the poem as a wisdom-inspired reflection on human transience that aims at attaining wisdom about life. Though conceding the artistic unity of the present poem, Zenger (also Seybold and others) follows Hermann Gunkel in viewing vv. 1-12 as the core that was later expanded.[6]

The present essay challenges the consensus. It argues that the poem is not a wisdom meditation on mortality and the brevity of human life, but a communal lament that asks God to bring an end to a lengthy period marked by divine wrath. The theme of brevity of life is only a piece in the argument that a whole generation of Israelites will die without knowing the gracious God of their ancestors! Krüger and Forster correctly judge that vv. 7-10 are distinct from vv. 1b-6 and describe a specific period of wrath. Verses 11-12 ask to know the duration of the divine punishment rather than of human life.[7] Among the weaknesses of the "wisdom-meditation on mortality" interpretation is its vague definition of "wisdom" and its inability to explain the psalm without postulating a two-stage composition.

Why has the consensus ("wisdom-meditation on the brevity of life") stood for so long? I suggest that factors extrinsic to the psalm have played an inordinate role. One can name three such factors: (1) the

---

Psalm," *BK* 54 (1990) 163–69.

[4] *Psalms* (Interpretation; Louisville, KY: John Knox, 1994) 292. Robert Davidson notes that the psalm "addresses no specific crisis in the life of the community. Indeed, it deals with a basic human problem, the universal need for wisdom (v. 12)" in *The Vitality of Worship: A Commentary on the Book of Psalms* (Grand Rapids: Eerdmans, 1998) 299–300.

[5] *Begrenztes Leben als Herausforderung: Das Vergänglichkeitsmotiv in weisheitlichen Psalmen* (Zurich: Pan, 2000). Forster deals with Psalm 90 on pp. 137–200. She departs from the consensus in accepting Krüger's view that vv. 7-10 refer to a specific past event rather than to the general transience of the human race.

[6] Frank Hossfeld and Erich Zenger, *Psalm 51–100* (HTKAT; Fribourg: Herder, 1998).

[7] The interpretation of vv. 11-12 is taken from my "What is the Psalmist Asking for in Psalms 39:5 and 90:12?" *JBL* 119 (2000) 59–66.

genre of *consolatio*, well known since classical antiquity, invites a similar interpretation of Psalm 90; (2) interpreters blend two topoi that are ordinarily distinct, human transience and the effects of divine wrath[8]; and (3) the Western philosophical problem of time and eternity inclines interpreters to view the poem as a philosophical reflection.

One of the above factors merits a brief excursus. The genre of *consolatio* developed in Greco-Roman antiquity and continued into the Middle Ages and beyond. Among its sub-genres were philosophical treatises on death, letters to those suffering bereavement, exile, or other loss, and funeral speeches. Writers drew on a relatively narrow range of arguments: all are born mortal, death brings release from the miseries of life, time heals all griefs, future ills should be anticipated, the deceased was only "lent" to us for a time. Examples of *consolationes* are Cicero's *Consolatio* (now lost), Sulpicius Rufus' letter to Cicero on the death of his daughter Tullia, and Seneca's *Ad Marciam*. Christian writers such as Ambrose, Jerome, and the Cappadocian Fathers employed the genre in continuity with the classical tradition.[9] Familiarity with the genre has disposed ancient and even modern readers of Psalm 90 to read it as a *consolatio* in the face of the fragility and brevity of life.

Given the subtlety of the argument that Psalm 90 makes to God and the fact this argument has been missed by most commentators, it seems best to begin with another, similar, psalm where the same argument is made in a more accessible way. Hence this essay begins with Psalm 39. It too makes the request "to know the measure of my days" (Ps 39:5 = Ps 90:12) and makes it part of its plea. Psalm 39 can therefore serve as a convenient entry into the problematic Psalm 90.

## PSALM 39

The narrative logic of Psalm 39 is relatively simple. In vv. 2-4a, the psalmist resolves to remain silent in the face of enemies eager to use any utterance in a malicious manner. Turning to the one person to

---

[8] In the first topos, sufferers *tell God* of their misery, whereas in the second, they *ask God to tell them* its duration.

[9] J. H. D. Scourfield, *Consoling Heliodorus: A Commentary on Jerome, Letter 60* (Oxford Classical Monographs; Oxford: Clarendon Press, 1993) especially pp. 22–24. A synopsis can be found in Scourfield's article, "Consolation," in *OCD*, 378.

whom it is permissible to talk, that is, God, the psalmist asks how long the present suffering will go on (v. 5, for this interpretation see below). The psalmist argues that human life is too short to be spent entirely in suffering (vv. 6-7). Verses 8-12 take the argument a step further: since my affliction is entirely from you, only you can take it away. Verses 13-14 are a final plea.

Ps 39:5 is particularly relevant for this essay, and the argument of which it is a part. Virtually all commentators and translators are in agreement that v. 5 asks for an understanding of the brevity of human life so as to accept the present distress with equanimity and to cease worrying about what cannot be changed. The translation of the *NRSV* reflects the consensus: "LORD, let me know my end, and what is the measure of my days; let me know how fleeting my life is." Similarly, *NAB*: "LORD, let me know my end, the number of my days, / that I may learn how frail I am."

The above interpretation and translation, though well-nigh universal, runs into major logical and lexical difficulties. The logical problems: (1) why would the psalmist, well aware of the transience of life (vv. 6-7, 12c), ask for further awareness?; (2) how would knowing one's life span make it easier to bear suffering? The lexical difficulties are equally serious. Hebrew קֵץ in v 5a simply means the end of a defined time; it does not imply shortness of time. Though the phrase מִדַּת יָמַי, "measure of my days," is unique in the Bible, the semantically similar phrase מִסְפַּר יְמֵי / יָמֶיךָ,[10] means a set time in Exod 23:26; Qoh 2:3; 5:17; and 6:12. The related idiom סָפַר יָמִים, "to count the days," occurs in Lev 15:13, 28; 23:16; and Ezek 44:26 in the sense of counting off or noting a determined time period. Therefore, מִדַּת יָמַי means the number or quantity of my days. The *NRSV* rendering of the adjective חָדֵל as "fleeting" (cf. *NAB* "frail" and *REB* "short") in v. 5 is an *ad hoc* rendering[11] and unlikely. The other occurrences of the adjective are Ezek 3:27 (negating the previous verb, "one refusing [to hear]") and Isa 53:3 ("abandoned" or the like). To judge from the

---

[10] The verbs מָנָה and סָפַר in the *nip'al* conjugation are synonyms in 1 Kgs 3:8; 8:5; and 2 Chron 5:6.

[11] Franz Delitzsch correctly observes that חָדֵל means "that which leaves off and ceases," but wrongly allows also the meaning "transitory" or "frail." To cease doing something is not the same as to be fleeting or frail. See C. F. Keil and F. Delitzsch, *Psalms* (Commentary on the Old Testament; Grand Rapids: Eerdmans, 1991, repr. of 1871 edition) 5/2.29.

cognate verb חָדַל, "to cease, come to an end; leave off (doing)," the adjective חָדֵל means something like "ceasing; ending; final." The proper translation of the adjective in Ps 39:5 is "how I cease"; "cease" in this case is like Ezek 3:27, negating a previous verb (understood) of suffering. Even apart from the lexical problems, however, the traditional translation of the third colon (v. 5c), "let me know how fleeting/frail I am," does not make a logical transition to vv. 6-7, where the psalmist is well aware of the transience of his life, "Look, you have made my days just handbreadths long."

The lexical and logical problems noted above are resolved if one takes v. 5 as a request to know the end of the psalmist's *affliction* rather than of the psalmist's *life*. The psalmist expresses the very human desire to know exactly how long the divine wrath will go on. Such a desire is well attested in the ancient Near East. "That there were predetermined limits to the periods of divine wrath which the gods might reveal through omens or oracles was widespread in the ancient Near East" has been amply demonstrated by J. J. M. Roberts.[12] He shows convincingly that Ps 74:9 ("We do not see our signs, there is no longer any prophet, and there is no one among us who knows how long") refers to an expected oracular or prophetic statement on the duration of the affliction. The frequent prayer in the Psalms, "How long, O Lord?" thus is a genuine question.

Biblical examples of set periods of punishment are the seventy years of the exile in Jer 25:11-12 and 29:10, and the three punishments Gad lays before David in 2 Sam 24:13: "Shall three years of famine come to you on your land? Or will you flee three months before your foes while they pursue you? Or shall there be three days' pestilence in your land? Now consider, and decide what answer I shall return to the one who sent me." The length of time one must suffer is important.

Roberts gives examples from Mesopotamia of set periods of divine wrath toward human beings. One is Marduk's famous decision to leave Babylon for seventy years.[13] Another is an omen text on the Elamite captivity of Bel:

---

[12] "Of Signs, Prophets, and Time Limits: A Note on Psalm 74:9," *CBQ* 39 (1977) 474–81, here p. 478. References to Mesopotamian texts in notes 13–17 are from Roberts' article.

[13] R. Borger, *Die Inschriften Asarhaddons Königs von Assyrien* (AfO Beiheft 9; Graz: E. Weidner, 1956) 14–15, episodes 6-10.

... the Umman-manda will arise and rule the land. The gods will depart from the daises, and Bel will go to Elam. It is said that after thirty years vengeance will be exercised, and the gods will return to their place.[14]

In another text Nabonidus declares:

For twenty-one years [Marduk] established his seat in Ashur, but when the days were fulfilled and the set time (*adannu*) arrived, his anger abated, and the heart of the king of the gods, the lord of lords, remembered Esagil and Babylon, the seat of his lordship.[15]

The phrase "when the days were fulfilled" implies a pre-determined number of days after which ("set time") divine anger came to an end.

Two Mesopotamian texts are especially relevant to Psalm 39, for they show time limits of *individual* suffering. In *Ludlul bel nemeqi*, the sufferer complains, "Nor has the diviner put a time limit (*adanna*) on my illness."[16] In a text from Ras Shamra, a sufferer complains: "The experts have carefully pondered my tablets, but they have not set a limit (*ada[n]*) to my illness."[17] Michael Barré has found that most of the omens in the Akkadian medical omen series end with a prognosis stating the patient's prospects for recovery. Many indicate how long it will be before the patient gets well, for example, "within seven days," "within ten days," "quickly, soon," and "within three days."[18] These urgent pleas show how strong was the desire of sufferers to know exactly when their ailments would end.

Ps 39:5 similarly attempts to learn how long the affliction will last. Such an interpretation is the only one that avoids the logical and lexical problems noted above. The following translation (paraphrasing slightly for the sake of clarity) brings out the meaning.

Let me know my term [= the term of my affliction],
what the number of my days is [= the allotted length of my affliction].
May I know how I am ceasing [from my affliction]! (Ps 39:5)

---

[14] G. Smith, *Cuneiform Inscriptions of Western Asia* (London: British Museum, 1861-64) 3/61, no. 2:21'–22'.

[15] H. Winckler, "Einige Bermerkungen zur Nabunid-Stele," *MVAG* 1/1 (1896) 73–83 (copy), 1.23-24.

[16] W. G. Lambert, *Babylonian Wisdom Literature* (Oxford: Clarendon Press, 1970), 44–45.111.

[17] *Ugaritica V* (ed. J. Nougayrol *et al.*; Mission de Ras Shamra 16; Paris: Imprimerie Nationale, 1968) 267.7-8. See also B. R. Foster, *Before the Muses: An Anthology of Akkadian Literature* (Bethesda, MD: CDL Press, 1993) 326–27.

[18] "New Light on the Interpretation of Hosea VI 2," *VT* 28 (1978) 139.

No less important is how the above sentiments fit within the rhetorical strategy of the psalm. In vv. 2-3, the psalmist resolves to accept silently the divine chastisement for sin (cf. vv. 10-11) in accord with the age-old view that suffering is a result of one's sins (even if one is not conscious of having done anything wrong). Presumably, enemies will interpret cries of complaints as blasphemy (as Job's friends did). Though forced to be silent before human beings, the psalmist need not be silent before God. Verse 5 is the first word directed to God and it is a plea — tell me how long I must bear the pain. Verses 6-7 give the basis for the plea: human life is "just handbreadths long," lasting no longer than a breath (הֶבֶל in the sense of Job 7:16). Human life is momentary when assessed in relation to God, "my duration is as nothing *in your sight*" (Ps 39:6b). The divine-human comparison will be elaborated in Psalm 90. Sometimes by implication, sometimes by direct statement, Ps 39:5-7 argues that human life is already so short it is unworthy of God to make it pass entirely under divine wrath.

Ps 39:8 gains specific meaning when understood in the context suggested above. Its meaning is muted in renderings such as the *NRSV*, "Now, Lord, what do I wait for? / My hope is in you," or the *NAB*, "And now, Lord, what future do I have? / You are my only hope." Verse 8 actually resumes v. 5, and should be rendered: "And now, what (term of the fixed period of suffering) must I wait for? / My hope (objective sense = *what* is hoped for, the termination of suffering) lies with you!" Verse 9 asks for the same thing in different words — deliverance from the sufferings associated with transgressions. The remaining verses (vv. 10-14) plead that the suffering be brought to an end.

This examination of Psalm 39, it is hoped, has demonstrated that the request to know "my end" does not mean to know my life span but to know the end of my affliction, and the request to know "the number of my days" does not mean the days allotted to me but the period of wrath allotted to me. It also shows how the theme of brevity of human life in vv. 6-7 contributes to the argument of the poem. Human life is so short that it is unworthy of God to prolong the period of suffering. We are now in a position to see how the same arguments proceed in Psalm 90, a communal lament.

## PSALM 90

Before looking at the use of the themes in Psalm 90, I should say a few words about its genre and rhetorical strategy. All commentators recognize the unusual nature of the psalm, though most acknowledge it has elements of a communal lament, for in the poem "we" complain about God's wrath, asking that God give up the wrath and regard "us" again with favor. At first glance, Psalm 90 seems to lack one feature of communal laments — the narrative of a glorious past event that stands in contrast to the miserable present (see Pss 44:2-9, 74:12-17; 77:12-21; 80:9-12; 83:10-13; 89:2-38; and Isa 63:7-14). The singer in such laments asks God to renew now the past event. The "glorious past" in Psalm 90 is the time in the past when God was actually "our refuge" (vv. 1b-2). The psalm prays for the return of divine favor when God blessed Israel and brought its projects to a happy conclusion (vv. 13-17).

Before going further, it is well to remind ourselves that ancient prayers took for granted that the world was made by the gods for the gods, and that human beings were merely slaves or servants maintaining it. Prayers had to make clear that granting the petition would actually benefit the god. Ancient petitions were thus "rhetorical" in that they were carefully framed to persuade the god to act for the client. Petitioners asked for health, for example, on the grounds that healthy servants could properly serve the god and perform required rituals; they asked for prosperity on the grounds that prosperous clients made the divine patron appear generous, powerful, and compassionate in the eyes of others; they promised thanksgivings if a prayer was granted. Psalm 90, no less than other laments, has a rhetorical strategy.

What is the strategy of Psalm 90? First, like other communal laments, it seeks a renewal of a favorable past time, in this case the time when God looked with favor upon the people, protecting them, bestowing abundance, and prospering their efforts. What argument does the psalmist use to invite God again to regard the people with favor? The divine "self interest" to which the psalmist appeals is God's care for his name. The psalmist implicitly asks: will you let the title under which we have invoked you, "a refuge for us in every generation" (v. 1b), be invalidated? Though the argument is made indirectly out of reverence, it is unmistakable: you are known as our God in *every generation* (vv. 1b-2); you live forever and have decreed that we live only briefly (vv. 3-6); your wrath has long been upon us and *this generation* (measured by "seventy ... eighty years") is passing away without ever knowing you as our "refuge" and favoring God (vv. 7-10). For God not to allow his people to languish will suggest to people that he is without the power to live up to his name.

Demonstrating this interpretation requires analysis of the psalm structure. Verse 17 reprises vv. 1-2, for (apart from the tetragrammaton in v. 13) only these verses have divine names (אֲדֹנָי and אֵל in vv. 1-2, אֲדֹנָי and אֱלֹהִים in v. 17). נֹעַם אֲדֹנָי in v. 17 reverses אֲדֹנָי מָעוֹן of v. 1, suggesting perhaps that v. 17 expects the actualization of the divine title mentioned in v. 1. Coherence is provided by vocabulary cross-references between vv. 3-10 and 13-16 and within the two sections: שׁוּב in vv. 3 and 13; עֶבֶד in vv. 13 and 16; בֹּקֶר in vv. 6 and 14; יוֹם in vv. 9-10 and 14-15; שָׁנָה in vv. 9-10 and 15; and בָּנִים in vv. 3 and 16. Thematically, vv. 1b-6 deal with the contrast between time without limit in God and time with limit in human beings, and vv. 7-10 deal with the theme of living under divine wrath.

Verse 1 forms a chiasm, which is marked below by different type faces.

> Lord, a refuge have <u>you</u> been for us IN EVERY GENERATION
>> before the mountains were brought forth
>> and you brought forth the earth and world,
> FROM EVERLASTING TO EVERLASTING, <u>you</u> are <u>God</u>.

The chiastic pairing of "Lord, a refuge have you been for us [= Israel]"[19] and "you are God" makes the important point that the phrase "you are God" is not an apostrophe to God in a generic sense, but to Yahweh, Lord of Israel. The poem collapses into one act what is narrated in Genesis and Exodus as two distinct events—the creation of the world and the formation of Israel. Israel is here created in the creation of the world; Israel is "the people." As the people are created, they are also created mortal. As H.-P. Müller has correctly observed, the verb in v. 3a, תָּשֵׁב, "you return (man to dust)," has a preterite meaning and refers to the primordial decision to make human beings mortal.[20]

---

[19] For the argument that הָיִיתָ in v. 1 refers to the past, i.e. God *has been* a refuge for the people, see Krüger, "Psalm 90 und die 'Vergänglichkeit des Menschen,'" 196–97.

[20] H.-P. Müller, "Der 90. Psalm: Ein Paradigma exegetischer Aufgaben," *ZTK* 81 (1984) 271: "du hast in der Urzeit der Schöpfung bestimmt, das der Mensch sterben muss." The divine decree of mortality at creation was an important theme in Mesopotamian as well as biblical literature. In *Gilgamesh* X.vi, Utnapishtim explains to Gilgamesh, "

After [the gods] had pronounced the blessing on me,
The Anunnaku, the great gods, were assembled,

Verses 3-5 are not a protest against mortality. There are no protests in the Bible against mortality as such, only against premature or shameful death. Outside the Bible, Gilgamesh, to be sure, tried to conquer death and obtain immortality, but his motives came from his unique situation — his love for Enkidu and his heroic and untamed spirit. The epic ends with the king returning to the walls of Uruk with the realization that whatever immortality he may attain will be through his royal achievements. Psalm 90 is only being traditional, therefore, in calmly stating that for a human being, especially in comparison with God's eternity, life is over in a day (vv. 4-6). The same sentiments are expressed in Job 7:7-8; 14:2; Pss 102:3-11; 103:15-16; Isa 40:7-8. The comparison is further elaborated through the contrast of "thousand" and "one" (as in Deut 32:30; Josh 23:10; Qoh 7:28; Isa 30:17) and "year" and "day."

Brevity of life is a stage in an argument used to persuade God to change from wrath[21] to favor. To grasp its import, one must recognize that the topos of mortality/brevity of life (vv. 1-6) is distinct from the topos of divine wrath. The two topoi do not say the same thing and are not logically linked. The singers of Psalms 6, 38, 74, 77, 85, and 88 are under divine wrath yet say nothing about mortality and brevity of life. Psalms 39, 102:3-11 and 103:15-16, on the other hand, deal with both topoi. Though Psalm 90 also contains both topoi, it makes a separate use of them: mortality and brevity of life in vv. 3-6, and divine wrath in vv. 7-12. Inclusions mark off vv. 7-12 as distinct from vv. 3-6: כָּלִינוּ in vv. 7a and 9b; עֶבְרָה in vv. 9 and 11; and אַפֶּךָ in vv. 7 and 11. The past tenses of vv. 7-10 also mark them as different from vv. 1b-6; they describe a specific event rather than a general

---

And Mammitum, creatress of destiny,
Decreed destinies with them.
They established life and death.
Death they fixed to have no ending."

*Atrahasis* III:6 tells of the mortality imposed by the gods to limit human population in the post-flood order, "[You], birth-goddess, creatress of destinies, / [Assign death] to the peoples." See R. Clifford, *Creation Accounts in the Ancient Near East and in the Bible* (CBQMS 26; Washington, DC: Catholic Biblical Association, 1994) 146–47.

[21] Wrath in these psalms is something like an objective state characterized by the withdrawal of divine blessings. An individual or a community lives without the customary fertility, protection, prosperity, and "happiness" that enable them to live rather than merely exist.

condition as T. Krüger correctly points out.[22]

The topic changes in vv. 7-12 to divine wrath, for words for wrath occur five times and the verbs "consume" (כָּלָה, twice) and "confuse" (בָּהַל) describe its effects. It is easy to miss the specific reference of vv. 7-12 and understand its statements as applying to life generally rather than life under wrath. Verse 10c, וְרָהְבָּם עָמָל וָאָוֶן, "and the best of them (?) are toil and trouble," describes a particular period rather than life as such.[23] Though the exact sense of רָהְבָּם is unclear, "trouble and toil" are quite clear. They describe life at a particular period rather than human life generally. Though v. 10d, וְנָעֻפָה כִּי־גָז חִישׁ, "they (the years) are quickly cut off and we fly away," has some uncertainties,[24] it too describes the period of wrath. In Hos 9:11, Job 20:8, and Prov 23:5, the verb עוּף has the nuance of "disappear never to reappear," which is exactly the argument made in Psalm 90: let us see your gracious side, for we are passing away never to return. The next three lines say essentially that *all* our days are spent in this period of wrath; someone living to a very old age will never know what divine favor means. The numbers "seventy ... eighty" suggest perhaps that the community has been afflicted for a very long time. It is conceivably a reference to the exile, for "seventy years" is a round number for the exile in Jer 25:10-11 and 29:10.

To summarize the argument up to this point: vv. 1b-2 say that the Lord has been our God in every generation; vv. 3-6 say that mortals have a limited life span; and vv. 7-12 say that an entire generation is passing away without seeing the Lord as their God. The complaint is that the Lord has not lived up to the title under which he is invoked, viz., being our God in every generation.

I must now deal with the difficult verses 11-12. These are almost universally interpreted like Ps 39:5 — a prayer to realize the transitory nature of human life so the afflicted person can find the wisdom to

---

[22] "Psalm 90 und die 'Vergänglichkeit' des Menschen," 192, 201–203.

[23] עָמָל, "toil," in v. 10 suggests to Zenger and Forster a link to Qoheleth's use of עָמָל as in Qoh 1:3, "What profit is there for a man for all his labor (עֲמָלוֹ) at which he has labored (יַעֲמֹל) under the sun." The usages in Psalm 90 and Qoheleth are completely different, however. Qoheleth counsels acceptance of unremitting toil as an inescapable part of life, whereas Psalm 90 regards it as an aberration and prays that God will take it away.

[24] גָז is 3rd person masc. sing., though its antecedent is fem. pl. (שָׁנוֹת, "years"); חִישׁ is a verb in an adverbial sense. Death as "flying away" occurs also in Job 20:8.

face suffering. Verse 11 is taken as a rhetorical question expressing the human inability to appreciate the devastation of divine wrath (e.g. *NAB*, "Who comprehends your terrible anger?"). Verse 12 is regarded as a plea to accept one's mortality and fragility. H.-M. Wahl, in the most through recent study of v. 12, paraphrases the verse: "Teach us to realize that humanity is subject to mortality, to finitude!" He describes the poetic logic:

> The realization — awareness of finitude — makes it possible to share in divine wisdom, which brings those who are touched by it from dissolution to life. This understanding of life through death-as-referring-to-God can be viewed as a *hermeneutic of death*; one finds it only in Ps 90:12.[25]

J. L. Mays goes in a similar direction though employing less philosophical language: "The question [in v. 11] is rhetorical; it has a critical and instructional function.... The psalmist has the congregation pray for the wisdom of heart/mind that comes from considering the finitude of human existence, its frustration and brevity."[26]

The major translations reflect this interpretation. The reading of the *NRSV* is typical:

[11]Who considers[27] the power of your anger?
Your wrath is great as the fear that is due you.[28]

---

[25] "Psalm 90,12: Text, Tradition und Interpretation," *ZAW* 106 (1994) 116-123. The two quotations are on pp. 122 and 123. Wahl's italics, my translation.

[26] *Psalms* (Interpretation: Louisville: John Knox, 1994) 293. According to H.-J. Kraus (*Psalms 60–150* [Minneapolis: Augsburg, 1989] 217):

> ... the psalmist in agitation asks who could possibly be able to perceive the whole sweep of the effects of the wrath of God. At this point, the trend of the statements in vv. 3ff. is revealed. With the perceptions of חָכְמָה the singer wants to lead the lamenting community to a more profound view of its misery. He imports the general reflections of wisdom teaching into his prayer song in order to illustrate the weight of divine wrath. The psalmist therefore takes the view that one can appear before God only with a wise heart.

Seybold takes the theme of vv. 10-12 to be the determined nature of human life. Verse 12 asks for the intelligence to count the days and to adopt an attitude of *carpe diem* toward the time still remaining to us, in *Die Psalmen*, 359.

[27] *NRSV*, "Who considers?" (מִי־יוֹדֵעַ, lit. "Who knows?), attempts to finesse the problem that the psalmist already knows the divine wrath in vv. 7-10. The rendering, "Who considers?" suggests no one fully comprehends the divine suffering. The translation ignores the plain sense of the idiom "Who knows?" See note 29.

[28] I translate the MT literally, but the verse is corrupt. A common emendation, וּמִי רָאֵה תֹּךְ, "Who sees the oppression (of your wrath)?," makes a satisfactory

¹²So teach us to count our days
    that we may gain a wise heart. (Ps 90:11-12)

The usual explanation here (as in Ps 39:5) leaves several questions unanswered. If the question "Who knows?" (מִי־יוֹדֵעַ) in v. 11 means "nobody knows," as it seems to,[29] why would the psalmist, who has just described in vv. 7-10 the effects of wrath, assert no one knows its force? Why should v. 12 ask that the community be taught "to count our days" in the sense of becoming aware of the transience of life when vv. 1-5 have already spoken at length on the topic? A. B. Ehrlich correctly noted long ago: "It is utterly inconceivable how one can bring oneself to follow the traditional explanation here. 'Who knows the strength of your anger?' could never be asked by the poet who, according to vv. 7 and 9, has known so well the powerful anger of his God."[30]

As with Psalm 39, the best solution to these problems is to suppose that the poet is asking to know the term not of human life but of the divine anger causing the community's tribulations. This interpretation finds support from the vocabulary of vv. 11-13: עֹז אַפֶּךָ, "the force of your anger," לִמְנוֹת יָמֵינוּ, "to count our days," and כֵּן, "correctly, accurately." In v. 11a, עֹז cannot mean simply "force," for the community already knows the force of divine anger (vv. 7-10). עֹז must refer to an aspect of divine anger not yet experienced by the community, which can only be the full extent, the duration, of the anger. Only then can the question be genuine: "Who knows the *full extent* (= duration) of your anger?" The implied answer is "no one!"

The phrase "to count our days aright" (לִמְנוֹת יָמֵינוּ כֵּן) cannot mean "let us know the brevity of human life." As noted under Psalm 39, "to count our days" means numbering or counting days, months, and years. The Hebrew כֵּן can be either of two words, "thus, so" (so *NRSV*

---

parallel semantically but is far from certain. For variations of the emendation, see Gunkel, *Die Psalmen* (6th ed., Göttingen: Vandenhoeck & Ruprecht, 1968) 401.

[29] The expression bears this meaning in 2 Sam 12:22; Prov 24:22; Qoh 3:21; 6:12; Joel 2:14; Jon 3:9. For discussion of the phrase, see J. L. Crenshaw, "The Expression *mî yôdîa* in the Hebrew Bible," *VT* 36 (1986) 274–88, reprinted in his *Urgent Advice and Probing Questions* (Macon, GA: Mercer University Press, 1995) 179–91. I differ from Crenshaw in seeing this instance of "Who knows?" as expressing the community's ignorance of the duration of divine wrath.

[30] In *Die Psalmen* (Berlin: M. Papillar, 1905) 219. Ehrlich's own solution — "who knows how to deal with your anger? — suffers from the same defects as *NRSV*, "Who considers the power of your anger?"

and *REB*) or "right, accurate; right, righteous" (so *NAB* and *NJPS*). The second meaning is apt here; the usage is similar "to speak accurately" (כֵּן) in Judg 12:6 and "to know accurately" (כֵּן) in 1 Sam 23:17. Ps 90:12 thus refers to an accurate knowledge of the time period of the divine wrath.

The idiom "to count the days" (סָפַר יָמִים), though treated briefly before, deserves more attention here. The idiom "to count days/months" is found in Ugaritic and Akkadian. The relevant Ugaritic example is found in the Aqhat Epic: *ytb.dnil.[ls]pr.yrḫn yrḫ.[ ]tlt.rb[ʿ]* (*KTU* 1.17.2.43), "Daniel sits to count her months, a month, ... a third, a four[th] ...." King Daniel is simply counting or noting a pre-determined period of time, the months of his wife's pregnancy. The meaning is that he will simply check the years and month as they pass.[31] The corresponding verb in Akkadian is *manû*, "to count," which is the same etymological root as in Ps 90:12. It occurs in *Atrahasis* (I.279) in the same idiom that appears in the Ugaritic text just cited, namely, "to count months" (in the sense of waiting for a certain number of months to come to an end): [278]*[wa-aš-ba]-at* ᵈ*nin-tu* [279]*[i-ma]-an-nu ar-ḫi*, "And Nintu [sat] counting the months."[32] The goddess is ticking off the months of human pregnancy. In both the Akkadian and Ugaritic examples the meaning is to count off or take note of a set period of time. The extra-biblical evidence thus suggests that "to number our days" in Ps 90:12 means simply to know accurately a pre-determined time period rather than to be aware of mortality.

In the light of the foregoing evidence, Ps 90:11-12 should be rendered as follows:

[11]Who knows the full force of your anger,
    the (?) of your wrath?
[12]Let (us) know how to compute accurately our days (of affliction);
    let us bring wisdom into our minds.

---

[31] A second Ugaritic example is interesting but not directly parallel: *ašprk.ʿm.bʿl šnt.ʿ m.bʿl.tspr.yrḫm* (*KTU* 1.17.6.29), "I will cause you to count years with Baal, you will count months with the son of El." The goddess Anat promises the youth Aqhat that he will spend his life with the gods, that is, "count years" and "count months" with them.

[32] A second Akkadian example from *Atrahasis* is noteworthy but not directly parallel: (I.34 and 36) [*šanātim im*]-*nu-ù ša šu-up-ši-ik-ki*, "[they] counted [the years] of the toil." The junior gods are recalling the number of the years of their past servitude.

"Wisdom" (חָכְמָה) in v. 12b is not philosophical or theological insight as Wahl and others propose, but, as elsewhere in the Bible, practical knowledge enabling one to act rightly in a situation.

The test of an interpretation is the sense it makes of the entire poem. Verses 13-17 follow logically from the interpretation given here of vv. 1b-12. There is no need to postulate two stages of the composition. Verse 13a is a genuine question, asking "how long" this terrible period will go on. The word שׁוּבָה, "turn," in v. 13a has the same sense as in Ps 85:5, "Turn, O God of our salvation, // and break off your wrath toward us." Ps 90:13b asks the same favor positively: have mercy on us! The remaining verses make the same request in different ways. To be filled with God's חֶסֶד, "steadfast love," is to be in right relationship to him, which causes "rejoicing" that will last all our days (v. 14; cf. "all our days" in v. 9). Verse 15 hints, perhaps, at how long the anguish has been going on, for the psalmist asks that the period of favor be equivalent to the period of wrath. The wrath must have lasted a very long time!

Verse 16 asks that "your deed (pōʿal)" appear to "your servants." The pōʿal is common for a divine deed that in prayer is to be remembered (as in Pss 44:2; 77:13; 143:5) or praised (as in Deut 32:4; Pss 64:10; 93:5; 111:3). As mentioned, the divine deed here is the peace that once prevailed between God and people. The context of v. 16b makes understandable the seemingly odd request for glory — the divine presence — for the children. The wrath is affecting the upcoming generation.[33]

It has already been pointed out that נֹעַם אֲדֹנָי in v. 17a reverses אֲדֹנָי מָעוֹן of v. 1, an indirect way of asking that divine "refuge" now show itself by granting divine "favor." The plea that our work be established makes sense if God has withdrawn and ceased to bless the people's enterprises. Deuteronomy several times associates the fruitfulness of the work of one's hands with divine blessing as in 2:7; 14:29; 24:19; 28:12 ("to bless all the work of our hands"). Without a blessing, one's work does not endure. "Unless the Lord builds the house, those who build it labor in vain" (Ps 127:1).

Though the interpretation offered here may appear more conventional than the philosophical and reflective readings of others, it is no

---

[33] The mention of the children may be another indication of an exilic date. That a major problem of the exile was the suffering borne by the innocent younger generation is shown by Jeremiah 31 and Ezekiel 18.

less moving or relevant. An anguished community pleads that it may live before God. It refuses to believe that God would not live up to his name as the refuge of his people. Reflecting on God's history with this people, it insists that God live up to promises made to their ancestors and bless these creatures of a moment with prosperity. Though limited and vulnerable, the people place all their hope in their compassionate and powerful Patron. The poem can thus serve as a prayer for God's community in every period of crisis and loss.

## SELECT BIBLIOGRAPHY

Booij, T. "Psalm 90, 5-6: Junction of Two Traditional Motifs," *Bib* 68 (1987) 393–96.

Clifford, R. "What is the Psalmist Asking for in Psalms 39:5 and 90:12?" *JBL* 119 (2000) 59–66.

Forster, C. *Begrenztes Leben als Herausforderung: Das Vergänglichkeitsmotiv in weisheitlichen Psalmen* (Zurich: Pan, 2000) 137–200.

Greinacher, N. "Psalm 90," in *Die Freude an Gott—unsere Kraft* (O. B. Knoch volume; Stuttgart: Katholisches Bibelwerk, 1991) 366–77.

Harrelson, W. A. "A Meditation on the Wrath of God: Psalm 90," in A. L. Merrill and T. W. Overholt (eds.), *Scripture in History and Theology* (C. Rylaarsdam volume; Pittsburgh: Pickwick, 1977) 181–91.

Krüger, T. "Psalm 90 und die 'Vergänglichkeit des Menschen,'" *Bib* 75 (1994) 191–219.

Müller, H.-P. "Der 90. Psalm: Ein Paradigma exegetischer Aufgaben," *ZTK* 81 (1984) 265–85.

—. "Sprachliche Beobachtungen zu Ps. XC 5f.," *VT* 50 (2000) 394–400.

Rad, G. von. "Der 90. Psalm," *Gottes Wirken in Israel* (Neukirchen: Neukirchener, 1974) 268–79.

Schmidt, W. H. "'Der Du die Menschen lässest sterben': Exegetische Anmerkungen zu Ps 90," in F. Crüsemann et al. (eds.), *Was ist der Mensch ...? Beiträge zur Anthropologie des Alten Testaments* (H. W. Wolff volume; Munich: Kaiser, 1992) 115–30.

Schnocks, J. "'Ehe die Berge geboren wurden, bist du': Die Gegenwart Gottes im 90. Psalm," *BK* 54 (1990) 163–69.

Schreiner, S. "Erwägungen zur Struktur des 90. Psalm," *Bib* 59 (1978) 80–90.

Soden, W. von. "Zum Psalm 90,3," *UF* 15 (1983) 307–308.

Tsevat, M. "Psalm XC," *VT* 35 (1985) 115–17.

Wahl, H.-M. "Psalm 90,12: Text, Tradition, und Interpretation," *ZAW* 106 (1994) 116–23.

Whitley, C. "The Text of Psalm 90,5," *Bib* 63 (1982) 555–57.

# THE SHIFTING FOCUS OF PSALM 101

MICHAEL L. BARRÉ

The history of the interpretation of Psalm 101, generally classified as a royal psalm, reveals a good deal of controversy as to its original focus.[1] I shall present here evidence as to what that focus was and show that this focus has shifted through a series of changes to the text, some possibly deliberate and some possibly due to scribal error. This process has not been carried through rigorously, with the result that the latest form of the text (the MT) is not altogether homogeneous. Essentially, I shall argue in favor of the frequently proposed view that the poem was composed for the occasion of the enthronement of a Judahite king.[2] Specifically, its original focus was the instruction of the king's courtiers (especially his advisers) in conduct becoming to such personnel. Over time the theme of instruction has been downplayed to the point that it has all but disappeared, resulting in a text whose main concern is now the glorification of the Davidic king as the royal paragon of righteousness and virtue.

## BASIC STRUCTURE

Ideally, every treatment of an ancient Hebrew poem should include a discussion of its structure. Therefore I shall begin with an overview of the structure of Psalm 101, especially since certain aspects of this bear significantly on matters of interpretation.[3]

One persistent question in the study of this psalm is where to mark off its second major division. It comes down to whether to include v. 2b[4] as part of the first or the second stanza. Although a number of

---

[1] For the background, see Hans-Joachim Kraus, *Psalms 60–150: A Commentary* (Minneapolis; Augsburg, 1989) 277–78; Gianfranco Ravasi, *Il Libro dei Salmi: Volume III (101–150)* (3 vols., Bologna: Edizioni Dehoniane, 1985) 15–18.

[2] See, for example, Sigmund Mowinckel, *The Psalms in Israel's Worship* (2 vols., Nashville: Abingdon, 1962) 1.65–66; Claus Westermann, *The Living Psalms* (Grand Rapids; Eerdmans, 1989) 57.

[3] For the structure of Psalm 101, see John S. Kselman, "Psalm 101: Royal Confession and Divine Oracle," *JSOT* 33 (1985) 45–62, esp. 46–50.

[4] I.e. אֶתְהַלֵּךְ בְּתָם־לְבָבִי בְּקֶרֶב בֵּיתִי.

modern translations and commentators opt for placing this bicolon at the beginning of the second division,[5] rhetorical devices in vv. 3-7 show that these verses constitute a major unit of the poem and consequently that the second major unit must begin with v. 3, not v. 2b. John S. Kselman has pointed out a chiastic structure spanning these verses and composed of four elements.[6] In their most basic form they are as follows:

| 3a | לְנֶגֶד עֵינָי | a | 6a | עֵינָי | d´ |
| 3a | דְּבַר | b | 7a | עֹשֵׂה | c´ |
| 3b | עֹשֵׂה | c | 7b | דבר | b´ |
| 5b | עֵינָיִם | d | 7b | לנגד עיני | a´ |

This four-part chiasmus gives the strongest possible indication that vv. 3-7 comprise one of the major units of the poem (Part II).[7] Hence the view that v. 2b begins a major division of the poem is highly unlikely. The chiasmus and the two inclusions created by עֵינִ(ם) also point to a subdivision within vv. 3-7, namely, into vv. 3-5 (IIA) and 6-7 (IIB). Finally, these literary devices also indicate that the last major division of the psalm begins after v. 7 — that is, v. 8 (Part III).

## THE ORIGINAL FOCUS OF PSALM 101

### Evidence from Part I

Although a number of interpreters believe that Psalm 101 (in its original form) was a Judahite coronation hymn, others classify it as a lament. The two genres are mutually exclusive. It is hardly possible to imagine that an occasion of national celebration such as the coronation of a king could have allowed for lamentation.

Verse 2 is widely regarded as the most controversial line in the psalm, particularly the end of the first bicolon, מָתַי תָּבוֹא אֵלָי, "When will you come to me?" As we shall see, it is this verse — in its original reading — that clearly indicates the original focus of Psalm 101. Now it is well known that the interrogative term מָתַי, "when," like לָמָּה, "why," is an element commonly found in lament psalms. This is no doubt why Psalm 101 is categorized by some as a lament. How-

---

[5] E.g. *RSV, NIV.*

[6] Kselman, "Psalm 101," 47

[7] Konrad Schaefer (*Psalms* [Berit Olam; Collegeville, MN: Liturgical Press, 2001] 248) has proposed an ABCDEF // ABDCFE pattern spanning vv. 2a-5a, 6b-8a. This structure is a matching pattern that *almost* works, but ignores v. 1 altogether, and hence is far from convincing.

ever, such a classification is hardly possible for Psalm 101. Nine psalm passages contain מָתַי as the beginning of a question addressed to God.[8] It is true that all of these occur in a lament context.[9] But all of the psalms in which these occur also contain the more *constitutive* elements of the lament, namely the petition to God for help or deliverance and the recitation of various sufferings about which the psalmist is complaining. With the absence of the latter two elements one cannot classify a Biblical Hebrew poem as a lament. Hence Psalm 101 cannot be so classified, despite the presence of מָתַי, since it contains no hint of either element. This fact pointedly raises the question of whether the standard interpretation of v. 2aβ is correct.

Many modern translations take אַשְׂכִּילָה in v. 2 as a transitive verb with בְּדֶרֶךְ as its object: "I will give heed to" (*RSV*), "I will study" (*NRSV, JPS*). But the *hipʿil* form functions in some instances as a causative of the *qal* stem: "to cause (someone) to be wise > instruct." A clear example of this usage is found in Ps 32:8a, where precisely this nuance of the 1st sing. form appears, again followed by בְּדֶרֶךְ:

אַשְׂכִּילְךָ וְאוֹרְךָ בְּדֶרֶךְ־זוּ תֵלֵךְ
*I will instruct you* and teach you
    (about) the path you should walk.

In light of this one may translate Ps 101:2aα: "I will instruct in/about the way of blamelessness …"

One problem with this interpretation of the verb is the lack of an object. Ps 32:8a has "I will instruct you," but there is no personal object in Ps 101:2a. Rather, the object of this verb is the second colon itself. In an earlier, "defective" orthography this would have read מתי תבא אלי. I would vocalize as follows: מְתֵי תָּבֹא אֵלָי; thus the original meaning of v. 2a was:

I will instruct in the way of blamelessness
    the men you bring to/before me.

On this reading the second colon would be an example of a somewhat rare construction in Biblical Hebrew in which a noun in the construct state is the virtual *nomen regens* of a finite verb clause.[10]

---

[8] Pss 6:5; 42:3; 74:10; 80:5; 90:13; 94:3, 8; 119:82, 84

[9] Even though Psalm 119 is not a lament, its *kap* section (vv. 81-88) is a mini-lament that concludes the first half of the psalm. See Will Soll, *Psalm 119: Matrix, Form, and Setting* (CBQMS 23; Washington, DC: Catholic Biblical Association, 1991) 100–101.

[10] For this construction in Biblical Hebrew, see GKC §130d (p. 422); Bruce K.

The translation given here, however, raises several questions. Who are these "men" whom God "brings to/before" the king? And why does the poet say that "Yahweh" brings them?

As to the first question, I argue that in this bicolon the newly crowned king expresses his intention to instruct in the ways of righteousness those men admitted into his presence as the final step in the process of their induction as courtiers (especially advisers) into the royal court. Two Old Testament passages allude to this process.

Genesis 41 tells the story of Pharaoh's attempt to find an interpreter of his perplexing dream. He hears that a certain imprisoned Hebrew, Joseph, has the gift of interpreting dreams and so he sends for him. After being whisked out of prison and hastily cleaned up, he "came in before Pharaoh"[11] (v. 14: וַיָּבֹא אֶל־פַּרְעֹה). Pharaoh listens to Joseph's interpretation, is impressed, and comments on his wisdom.[12] He makes him second in command in the land. Afterwards the text notes (v. 46) that by such an appointment Joseph had "entered the service of Pharaoh" — lit., "stood before Pharaoh" (בְּעָמְדוֹ לִפְנֵי פַרְעֹה).

A second significant passage is Daniel 1, which speaks of the preparation of certain young men for service in Nebuchadnezzar's court. After a three-year period of training, the chief eunuch "brought them in before Nebuchadnezzar" (וַיְבִיאֵם ... לִפְנֵי נְבֻכַדְנֶצַּר, v. 18). Here the king speaks with the new trainees for a time and then the text states, וַיַּעַמְדוּ לִפְנֵי הַמֶּלֶךְ, "and so they stood before the king" (v. 19). Immediately after this the narrator adds that the king had found these men to excel in "wisdom and understanding" (חָכְמַת בִּינָה).[13] Like Genesis 41, the scenario described here speaks of certain potential courtiers being "brought in before" the king, who then speaks with them to discern the level of their wisdom, apparently the final step before officially accepting them as courtiers and admitting them to the royal service — lit., being allowed to "stand before the king."

---

Waltke and Michael O'Connor, *An Introduction to Biblical Hebrew Syntax* (Winona Lake, IN: Eisenbrauns: 1990) §9.6d (p. 156). Note קִרְיַת חָנָה דָוִד, "the city where David camped" (Isa 29:1). This grammatical construction also occurs in Akkadian (see Arthur Ungnad and Lubor Matouš, *Grammatik des Akkadischen* [5th ed., Munich: C. H. Beck, 1969] §114b [p. 128]: *awāt iqbû*, "the word he spoke").

[11] Thus *RSV*.

[12] Verse 39: ‏אין נבון וחכם כמוך.

[13] Cf. Pharaoh's comment about Joseph in Gen 41:39.

In a similar way, I understand Ps 101:2a as the keynote statement in this coronation hymn declaring the king's intention to instruct would-be courtiers in the ways of righteous conduct, which can also be described as the ways of wisdom.[14] It was most important that in exercising rulership the king not be led astray by the advice of corrupt counselors. Rather, he must take care to surround himself with righteous advisers so that his rule would be righteous. Should he fail to give this instruction, he would run the risk of being influenced by corrupt counselors and thus fail to fulfill his kingly responsibilities.[15]

As to the second question, although the OT mentions the importance of kings having good counselors and the pitfalls of evil ones,[16] the statement that Yahweh brings counselor candidates before the king is unique in this literature. A close parallel, however, may be found in the concluding section of a neo-Assyrian hymn composed for the coronation of Ashurbanipal.

This section of the hymn has three main parts. The most important line for our purposes is the last one in the first part, in which five major gods are listed as presenting certain "gifts" to the new king: Anu, Enlil, Ninurta, Nergal, and Nusku. Each one bestows an aspect of kingship that is appropriate to that particular god. Nusku was regarded as the counselor par excellence among the gods.[17] Thus his gift to the king has to do with good counsel. The relevant line reads: *umta<sup>ɔ</sup>ɔirma Nusku mālikī maḫaršu ulziz.* This could be translated, "Nusku sent and placed advisers before him"[18] or possibly, "Nusku instructed

---

[14] I believe that the strong "wisdom" tone that Helen A. Kenik detects in this psalm ("Code of Conduct for a King: Psalm 101," *JBL* 95 [1976] 391–403) does not derive originally from the topos of the king as sage par excellence so much as from the traditional insistence upon the wisdom — i.e. moral probity — of his royal counselors.

[15] This is precisely what happens to Ahaziah according to 2 Chron 22:3-4: "He also *walked in the ways* of the house of Ahab, for his mother (Athaliah) was his *counselor in doing evil* .... After the death of his father they (the house of Ahab) were his *counselors, to his undoing*" (*RSV*).

[16] On this theme, see 2 Chron 22:3-4; Prov 16:12; 25:4-5; and 29:12.

[17] He bears epithets in Akkadian literature such as *šurbû mālik ilī rabûti*, "the supreme counselor of the great gods," *CAD* M/1, 164 (the text is *Maqlu* I 144). For other epithets of Nusku relating to his role as counselor among the gods, see Knut L. Tallqvist, *Akkadische Götterepitheta* (Studia Orientalia edidit Societas Orientalis Fennica, 7; Helsinki: Finnish Oriental Society, 1938) 433–34.

[18] For the Akkadian text and translation, see Alasdair Livingston, *Court Poetry*

(him) by causing advisers to stand before him."[19] The reference to a god causing advisers to enter the service of the king may be unique to Ashurbanipal's coronation hymn.[20] In any case, the concept is quite close to Psalm 101:2aβ as I read it.[21] The main connection is the idea of a deity causing advisers to stand before the king, which is similar to that of Yahweh "bring[ing]" (תָּבֹא) potential advisers before the psalmist-king.[22]

---

*and Literary Miscellanea* (SAA 3; Helsinki: Helsinki University Press, 1989) 27.

[19] One must compare this to a variant of this line that appears in a closely related Babylonian mythological text dealing with the creation of the king, VS 24.92 (see Werner R. Mayer, "Ein Mythos von der Erschaffung des Menschen und des Königs," *Or* 56 [1987] 55–68; Eva Cancik-Kirschbaum, "Konzeption und Legitimation von Herrschaft in neuassyrischer Zeit: Mythos und Ritual in VS 24.92," *WdO* 26 [1995] 5–20). This text also mentions Anu bestowing his crown upon the newly created king, Enlil his throne, Nergal his weapon, etc., as in the coronation hymn. But the text of the Nusku line is somewhat different: *umaʾʾir Nusku umallikma izz[iz maḫaršu]*, which I would translate, "Nusku instructed (him), acted as counselor (to him), and stoo[d before him (as adviser)]." Cancik-Kirschbaum notes that (*w/m)âru* in the D stem is in some texts a semantic equivalent of *malāku*, "to counsel" (ibid., 17) and thus translates the first word — which is immediately followed by this verb — as "Anweisung gab" (ibid., 7). Hence it is possible that the verb (*w/m)âru* in the D stem has this meaning in the Ashurbanipal hymn as well.

[20] His father, Esarhaddon, in an apparent allusion to his own coronation, mentions the same gifts of Anu, Enlil, Ninurta, and Nergal in the same sequence as in the Ashurbanipal coronation hymn but there is no mention of Nusku and his gift. See Riekele Borger, *Die Inschriften Asarhaddons Königs von Assyrien* (AfO Beiheft 9: Osnabrück: Biblio-Verlag, 1967) 81 rev. 1.

[21] Note the mention of other "gifts" of Yahweh to the new king in Part I— מִשְׁפָּט and חֶסֶד (on these two nouns as divine gifts to the king; see Kraus, *Psalms 60–150,* 280).

[22] There are a number of parallels between the tripartite conclusion of the Ashurbanipal coronation hymn and tripartite Psalm 101 that suggest the latter may have been influenced by the first two sections of the former. (1) The first major section in the conclusion to the Ashurbanipal hymn (lines 5–8) contains a series of gifts various gods bestow on the new king. But in contradistinction to the others, the gift of *Nusku*, the last god mentioned, is not a single word but the statement that the god sent counselors and had them *stand before* the king (or perhaps had instructed the king by having them stand before him). The first bicolon of Psalm 101 (v. 1b) also lists several divine gifts to the king, חֶסֶד וּמִשְׁפָּט (see previous note). The penultimate bicolon of Part I (v. 2a) speaks of the king instructing certain persons whom *Yahweh* had *brought before* him as advisers. (2) The second section of the Assyrian hymn (lines 9–14) lists a series of three kinds

Further, I believe that the first part of next bicolon, v. 2b, is not the original reading. Theoretically, this bicolon would fit satisfactorily with the interpretation of v. 2a I have proposed. In this case it would stress the fact that by taking care to instruct potential advisers in right-eousness the king is acting as a just monarch should, i.e., walking in the דֶּרֶךְ תָּמִים, which is perhaps best translated "the way of blameless-ness/irreproachableness." But as I have indicated above, this was not the original thrust of these verses.

I propose that v. 2bα originally read: להתהלך בתם לבב With this reading v. 2 as a whole can be translated as a tetracolon:

> I will instruct in the way of blamelessness
> > the men you bring before me,
> That they may walk with wholehearted (fidelity)[23]
> > within my palace.

When so read, the predicate of v. 2b is not a finite verb but an infini-tive, with no explicit subject. As such it is ambivalent: in theory the subject could be the psalmist or those he intends to instruct. I suggest that this ambivalence was "clarified" by a scribe who understood the psalmist to be the subject. The best evidence of this can be found in a comparison of Ps 56:14 with 116:9. The former reads:

> For you have delivered my life from death,
> > yea, my feet from stumbling,
> *To walk* (לְהִתְהַלֵּךְ) in the presence of Yahweh
> > in the land of life/the living.[24]

It is hardly doubtful that the author of Psalm 116 has used this con-cluding verse of Psalm 56 with a few modifications to end the first half of his psalm (vv. 8-9). One of these was to replace the infinitive construction with a finite verb:[25]

> For you have delivered my life from death,
> > my eyes from tears,
> > my feet from stumbling;

---

of persons disloyal to the king. Like Part II of Psalm 101, the series begins and ends with "the one who *speaks* (improper things) ..." (*ša ... idbubu, ša ... itammû*).

[23] On the precise meaning of the phrase בתם לבב, see below, n. 32.

[24] On this translation of the expression, see Michael L. Barré, "ʾrṣ (h)ḥyym— 'The Land of the Living?'" *JSOT* 41 (1988) 37–59, esp. 46–50.

[25] Note that the Syriac translates the infinitive להכרית in v. 8b with a 1st per-son form, viz., ܘܐܘܒܕ , "and I do away with, slay."

*I shall walk* (אֶתְהַלֵּךְ) in the presence of Yahweh
   in the "lands" of life/the living.

It us possible, then, that אתהלך in Ps 101:2bα represents a scribal clarification of an original להתהלך, and its reference to courtiers. There is no extant versional evidence in support of the reading להתהלך בתם לבב in Ps 101:2bα, but there are a number of indirect indications in favor of it.

First and most important, clues to the originality of this reading may be found within the poem itself:

- The first is v. 6bα: הֹלֵךְ בְּדֶרֶךְ תָּמִים, "the one who walks in the way of blamelessness." This is the only other occurrence of the root הלך in the psalm.[26] If the king is the speaker here,[27] it can only refer to one of the king's courtiers, as it is followed by הוּא יְשָׁרְתֵנִי[28] — "he shall minister to me." Since the language of v. 6bα refers to the actions of a courtier/adviser, it is reasonable to think that the same phraseology in v. 2b also refers to actions by such personnel.

- The second clue is the phrase בְּקֶרֶב בֵּיתִי, "within my house," in v. 2bβ. There are only two examples in the MT of the expression בְּקֶרֶב בַּיִת where בַּיִת refers to a building — Ps 101:2b and 7a. Note that in the latter case בְּקֶרֶב בֵּיתִי occurs in a sentence in which the subject is someone *other than the king*, someone who may not dwell (יֵשֵׁב) "within my house." The reference to this person as to whether he may or may not "dwell" in the king's house presumes court personnel. Again, the use of the same phrase in v. 2bβ suggests that there, too, it refers to courtiers.[29]

- A third clue from the psalm in support of the reading proposed above is structural in nature and suggestive rather than proba-

---

[26] It is true that in v. 6bα the verb הלך is associated with the prepositional phrase בתם לבב rather than with בדרך תמים as in v. 2bα. But since in v. 2 the king expresses his intention to instruct his would-be courtiers in the "*way of* blamelessness" the implication is that *they should walk* in this way.

[27] Kselman's thesis is that it is God, not the king, who is speaking in vv. 6-7 ("Psalm 101," 45).

[28] The verb שרת can refer either to the service of a human superior (e.g. Gen 39:4; 40:4; Exod 24:13; 33:11; Num 11:28) or, in a cultic context, to that performed for a deity (e.g. Exod 28:35; Num 1:50; Deut 17:12; 1 Sam 2:11; 1 Kgs 8:11; 1 Chron 6:17).

[29] Note the juxtaposition of הלך בדרך and ישב בבית in Deut 6:8, which suggests that vv. 6b and 7a are more closely connected than first appears.

tive. Only two infinitives occur in Psalm 101, three if one accepts the emendation of v. 2bα. If one reads להתהלך, there is a balanced distribution of infinitives throughout the psalm.[30]

Second, further evidence that the language of v. 2b finds its *Sitz im Leben* in the world of courtiers and royal advisers comes from another neo-Assyrian document relating to Ashurbanipal. Among the surviving inscriptions of this king is a particular form of royal grant containing certain phrases that do not appear in other grants issued by him, or apparently by any other king. According to a recent edition of all the neo-Assyrian royal grants published to date eight exemplars of this grant form, or fragments thereof, have survived.[31] The second section of the document contains a number of expressions that describe the dutiful courtier, several of which are echoed in Ps 101:2.

[11]Baltaya, the chief of the fodder supplies of Ashurbanipal ...

[15]who ... was devoted to the king his lord,

[16]who was wholehearted(ly loyal)[32] to his lord,

---

[30] The distribution of these terms is as follows:

| Location in Poem | Verse | 1st or 2d Colon | Infinitive | |
|---|---|---|---|---|
| End of Part I | 2b | 1st word in 1st | x x | להתהלך |
| Start of Part IIB | 6a | 1st word in 2d | x | לשבת |
| End of Part III | 8b | 1st word in 1st | x x | להכרית |

Note the similar distribution of the term לבב. It is clear that the author has consciously arranged the three occurrences of this term from the striking fact that it occurs as the 15th, 30th, and 45th word in the psalm:

| Location in Poem | Verse | Colon | Position |
|---|---|---|---|
| End of Part I | 2a | first | last |
| Middle of Part IIA | 4a | first | first |
| End of Part IIA | 5b | first | last |

[31] Laura Kataja and Robert Whiting, *Grants, Decrees and Gifts of the Neo-Assyrian Period* (SAA 12; Helsinki: Helsinki University Press, 1995) 24–28, 31–35 (##25–26, 29–34)

[32] The term used here, *gummuru*, is an intensive form of the adjective *gamru*, "complete, total." Line 16 (*libbašu gummuru ana bēlišu*) is virtually equivalent to לבבם שלם אליו, "whose heart was whole toward him," in 2 Chron 16:9. As to the translation "wholehearted(ly)," note that Jacob M. Myers gives this translation for בלבב שלם in 2 Chron 25:2 (*II Chronicles* [AB 13; 2d ed.; Garden City, NY: Doubleday, 1974] 140). *Libbašu gummuru* is also equivalent to ת(ו)ם־לבב. In a discussion of the Biblical Hebrew root תמם, Klaus Koch notes the virtual synonymity of the Semitic roots *t-m-m*, *k-l-l/k-l-y*, *š-l-m*, and *g-m-r* (*THAT*, cols. 1045–51, esp. 1045). In light of this datum, there can be little doubt that the phrases (ב)לבב שלם (ב)לב, בת(ו)ם לב(ב), / לב תמים בכל, and Akkadian *libbu gummuru/ina gum-*

[17](who) stood before me (= served me as a courtier) faithfully,
[18]walked (= behaved) irreproachably,[33]
[19](who) grew (up?) in good repute within my palace,
[20](who) guarded my royal person.[34]

I give below the neo-Assyrian of lines 17-19, which are important for the point I wish to make:

---

*murti libbi* are virtually synonymous. Given that all these roots have "whole(ness)" as the common denominator, the meaning of the phrases given above is more properly "*whole*hearted(ness)" rather than "perfect(ion), blameless(ness)" or the like. Hence in the context of the relationship to God they denote wholehearted (as opposed to "halfhearted") service. Note the editorial comment in 2 Chron 25:2: "He (Amaziah) did what was right in the eyes of the Lord, but not wholeheartedly (רק לא בלבב שלם)." See also Moshe Weinfeld, *Deuteronomy and the Deuteronomic School* (Oxford: Clarendon Press, 1972) 335.

[33] The exact meaning of this line, *itallaku šalmeš*, is controverted. Specifically, the issue is how to render *šalmeš* in this context. J. N. Postgate (*Neo-Assyrian Royal Grants and Decrees* [Studia Pohl: Series Maior 1; Rome: Pontifical Biblical Institute, 1969] 36), followed by Kataja and Whiting (*Grants, Decrees and Gifts*, 25, 27, 32), translates it "in safety." The expression can have this meaning in certain contexts (see *CAD* Š/1, 255b). But prescinding from this line, lines 15-20 all express the courtier's loyal service to Ashurbanipal. One would expect this line, occurring in the midst of such a context, to do the same. The *Chicago Assyrian Dictionary* marks an improvement over Postgate's translation with "properly" (ibid.). But Yochanan Muffs is certainly correct in his comment: "Just as *ina kīnāti* describes the faithfulness of the [courtier's] service, so *šalmeš* must somehow describe the loyalty, more specifically, the fullness and exactitude with which the courtier performed his duties" (*Studies in the Aramaic Legal Papyri from Elephantine* [Studia et Documenta ad Iura Orientis Antiqui Pertinentia 8; Leiden: Brill, 1969] 203).

Perhaps the most accurate translation in this context is "irreproachably" or "blamelessly." As early as 1915 Maximilian Streck had suggested this meaning for *šalmeš* in our text (*Assurbanipal und die letzten assyrischen Könige bis zum Untergange des Niniveh's* [3 vols., Vorderasiatische Bibliothek; Leipzig: J. C. Hinrichs, 1916] 1.CLIV: "unbescholten"). The word *šalmeš/šalmiš* is an adverb formed from the G-stem verbal adjective (*šalmu*) of the verb *šalāmu*, one of whose meanings according to Wolfram von Soden is "sein einwandfrei" (*AHw*, 1144).

[34] Translation mine. For the text, see Postgate, *Neo-Assyrian Royal Grants and Decrees*, 36, and more recently Kataja and Whiting, *Grants, Decrees and Gifts*, 27. Disappointingly, although Kataja and Whiting's edition of these texts appeared over 25 years after Postgate's, they provide no new translation but simply reproduce that of Postgate, errors and all (e.g. Postgate neglected to translate line 16 and Kataja and Whiting follow suit).

<sup>17</sup>*ina maḫriya ina kīnāti izzizuma*
<sup>18</sup>*itallaku šalmeš*
<sup>19</sup>*qereb ekalliya ina šumi damqi irbû(ma)*

If one takes line 18 with the first two words of the subsequent line, it is possible to read "(who) walked irreproachably within my palace ...." Yochanan Muffs, followed by Moshe Weinfeld, has argued that the passage is to be translated in this way,[35] but this is incorrect. As the line-division clearly indicates, in the neo-Assyrian text *qereb ekalliya* goes with the following verb, *irbû* or *irbûma*.[36] But it is quite possible that this widely disseminated legal document from Ashurbanipal, or at least some of its phraseology, was known in an Aramaic translation. The "sense-line" division of the neo-Assyrian text, so well entrenched in Akkadian writing practice, would not have been reproduced in the written Aramaic translation with its typical "run-on" style. This is obvious, for example, from the Tell Fekherye bilingual inscription.[37] Finally, lines 17-19a of the grant have the appearance of a chiastic arrangement,[38] which would be another reason for someone working from a translation to take "within my palace" with the preceding line.

In summary, there are a number of pieces of evidence in Psalm 101 and in extrabiblical literature supporting the position that v. 2b originally did not refer to the king but to his advisers. Hence it is possible that v. 2 originally voiced the king's intention to instruct his potential courtiers in the ways of righteous conduct, so that *they* might walk in wholehearted loyalty to God and king.[39]

---

[35] Muffs, *Studies in the Aramaic Legal Papyri from Elephantine,* 203; Weinfeld, *Deuteronomy and the Deuteronomic School,* 76 n. 2.

[36] Since no variant of this Ashurbanipal grant preserves the end of this verb, either reading is possible. See Postgate, *Neo-Assyrian Royal Grants and Decrees,* 35.

[37] See Ali Abou-Assaf et al., *La statue de Tell Fekherye et son inscription bilingue assyro-araméenne* (Etudes Assyriologiques; Paris: Editions Recherche sur les civilisations, 1982) 13–14, 23–24.

[38] The chiasmus is: A: *ina maḫriya* (adverbial phrase of place) B: *ina kīnāti* (adverbial phrase of manner) C: *izzizuma* (verb) C´: *italluku* (verb) B´: *šalmeš* (adverb of manner) A´: *qereb ekalliya* (adverbial phrase of place).

[39] Of course, precisely because the infinitive להתהלך has no stated subject this reading has the advantage of *ambivalence*. Although I believe that the author of the psalm intended the courtiers to be the subject, such a construction leaves open the possibility of a reference to the king. The theme of the righteous king is pre-

*Evidence from Part II*

In Part II of Psalm 101 the king instructs his (potential) courtiers about unacceptable types of court personnel — precisely what he had announced in v. 2aα. I maintain that in the original version of the psalm all the references to evil in this section were references to *evil persons* rather than *abstract evils*,[40] and more specifically to morally objectionable types of courtiers whose behavior makes them unsuitable to serve in his household. In Part III the king's aversion for the wicked is extended beyond the royal household to "*all* evildoers" and beyond the palace to the holy city (v. 8b).

Even according to the MT some verses in Part II must refer to persons. First, the MT points certain words in this section as participles: מְלָוְשְׁנִי (v. 5a), הֹלֵךְ (v. 6b), עֹשֵׂה (v. 7a), and דֹּבֵר (v. 7b). Second, v. 5a uses two adjectives that refer to certain types of individuals:

___

sumed in the original version of the psalm. True, I do not believe it is the predominant focus, but a king who properly instructs his advisers lest they corrupt his administration of justice is by that very fact righteous. Thus later tradition simply took this theme, already present in the psalm, and made it predominant.

[40] On this point see also Kselman, "Psalm 101," 49. The closest parallel in the Psalter to the language of Parts II–III of Psalm 101 is Ps 5:5-7, which contains a number of the same or similar terms. In Ps 5:5-7 the issue is not those who may dwell in the king's house but those who may dwell in Yahweh's house. But one must keep in mind that much of the language of service to God in the temple was patterned on that of service to the *king*. In this passage all the references are to evil *persons*, not abstract evil:

> [5] For you are not a god who delights in the wicked (רשע; Ps 101:8a),
>     no evil person (רע; Ps 101:4b) can dwell with you;
> [6] The boastful may not stand
>     before your eyes (לנגד עיניך; Ps 101:3a, 7b);
> You hate (שנאת; Ps 101:3b) all evildoers (כל־פעלי און; Ps 101:8b),
>     [7] you destroy those who speak lies (דברי כזב; Ps 101:7b).
> The man of bloodshed and treachery
>     Yahweh abhors.

Note that all of these refer to *personal* manifestations of evil except the first, which the MT vocalizes as רֶשַׁע, "wickedness" (so also the Versions). But given the fact that all the others are personal, it is likely that this word is rather to be pointed רָשָׁע, "wicked (person)." Even if one retains the MT's reading the reference is still more likely to a wicked person rather than to the abstract, since an abstract term can be used to denote the concrete (W. G. E. Watson, *Classical Hebrew Poetry: A Guide to its Techniques* [JSOTSup 26; Sheffield: JSOT Press, 1984] 314–16). This parallel passage provides support for the contention that Ps 101:3-7 is concerned with evil individuals, not evil in the abstract.

גְּבַהּ־עֵינַיִם וּרְחַב לֵבָב, lit., "the one who is high of eyes and broad of heart"—i.e., the haughty and the arrogant. Third, it is likely that even the MT understood לֵבָב עִקֵּשׁ ("a perverse heart/mind") in v. 4a not as the physical organ or even the mental faculty but as metonymy[41] for "a person of a perverse mind."[42]

Other words in Part II are likely to be understood in a personal sense. Two further terms are to be parsed as participles.[43] In v. 3a the MT vocalizes דבר as the construct of דְּבָר, "thing." There are a number of reasons why a copyist may have understood this as a noun rather than a participle. There is one other example of the phrase דְּבַר־בְּלִיַּעַל in the MT, Ps 41:9. The phrase שִׁית לְנֶגֶד, "to set before X," also appears elsewhere only once, in Ps 90:8: שַׁתָּ עֲוֹנֹתֵינוּ לְנֶגְדֶּךָ, "You have placed our iniquities before you." Here, as in Ps 101:3a (MT), what is placed before some one is also some kind of iniquity. In response one should note that in Ps 41:9 the context is clearly one of terminal illness, so that דבר should probably be vocalized as דֶּבֶר — thus דֶּבֶר־בְּלִיַּעַל, "a noxious plague." As for שִׁית לְנֶגֶד, it is true that no other example of the idiom can be found in the MT, but compare the similar שׁוּה לְנֶגֶד in Ps 16:8a: שִׁוִּיתִי יְהוָה לְנֶגְדִּי תָמִיד, "I have placed Yahweh before me always." The strongest evidence that דבר here is a participle is the chiastic connection with the end of Part II in v. 7b. The two bicola are identical in meaning and chiastic in structure: compare דבר שרקים[44] // לא אשית לנגד עיני // דֹּבֵר בליעל (v. 3a), and דבר שרקים // לא יכון לנגד עיני (v. 7b). The phrases דבר בליעל and דבר שרקים are virtually synonymous, referring to persons who utter various kinds of objectionable speech.

עשׂה in v. 3b is also to be pointed as a participle. The MT points this

---

[41] Cf. Prov 6:16-19. This passage contains a list of seven "abominations" to Yahweh. Even though the first five are body parts ("eyes, ... tongue, ... heart, ... hands, ... feet") it is clear that these stand for certain types of unrighteous *persons* by metonymy. This is evident from the last two items in the series, which unambiguously refer to people: "a false witness" and "one who sows discord among brothers." See also Kselman, "Psalm 101," 49.

[42] The *RSV* is definitely wrong in turning this into an abstract, "perverseness of heart." The Hebrew cannot bear such a sense.

[43] See Kselman, "Psalm 101," 51–52.

[44] I opt for this scansion of the bicolon, which contradicts the standard view. Up to this point in the psalm all bicola have the pattern *long // short* — i.e. the second colon has fewer words than the first. Reversing this is one way to indicate the conclusion of a major section of the poem.

as an infinitive, עֲשֹׂה, as if the phrase were to be translated "the doing of סְטִים." But again the matching term in the chiasmus is a participle: עֹשֵׂה in v. 7a. The Versions also read a participle.[45] The translation should be "one who commits iniquities,"[46] again referring to the immoral behavior of an individual other than the king.

In v. 4b רע in the sentence רע לֹא אֵדָע could theoretically refer either to an "evil thing" or an "evil person." Both possibilities work satisfactorily as objects of the verb יָדַע: "I do not acknowledge one who is evil" or "I do not know (= have experience of?) evil." But if the latter is correct, רע would stand out as the only abstract term in a series of personal terms in Part II. Hence it is probable that this term also has a personal reference.[47]

It is axiomatic in OT wisdom literature that the righteous must avoid the company of the wicked, lest they be corrupted by their influence.[48] This was *a fortiori* true of the king. "Take away the wicked *from the presence of* the king, and his throne will be established in righteousness."[49] This explains why in the psalm the king insists that he wants no immoral persons "before [his] eyes" or to "live within [his] house." Since the access of ordinary citizens to the king was limited, most if not all of those alluded to in Part II who are living within his view or in his house could hardly be persons other than members of the royal household.

Several expressions in Part II almost certainly refer to (potential) courtiers:

- The clearest example is v. 6b, where it is said of the one who walks "in the way of blamelessness," so that "*he* may minister to me (הוּא יְשָׁרְתֵנִי)." If the speaker is the king, this can only refer to

---

[45] LXX: ποιοῦντας; Vulgate [iuxta Hebr.]: *facientem*; Syriac: ܥܒ̈ܕܝ.

[46] The *hapax legomenon* סֵטִים is most likely to be derived from the root סטי = שׁטי or a by-form, סוט = שׁוט, "to go astray" (see *HALAT*, 709). The term is probably related to Akkadian šēṭu/šeṭṭu and šettu (< *šeṭṭu), a comparatively rare term for "sin" from šēṭu, "to miss the mark" (see *CAD*, Š/2, 339–40; *AHw*, 1221). Such a translation accords well with the LXX's παραβάσεις ("trangressions)" and the Syriac's ܪܘܫܥܐ ("wickedness"). The *Psalms Targum* (hereafter Tg. Pss.) relates סֵטִים to this root with its paraphrase, עבדי בישין ושטין מן פיקודיא, "those who do wicked things and *stray* from the commandments." Note that a few later Hebrew manuscripts read שׂטים.

[47] So also Kselman, "Psalm 101," 49.

[48] See, for example, Pss 1:1; 26:4-5; Prov 4:14; 24:1.

[49] Prov 25:5 (*RSV*).

someone admitted to the circle of royal attendants.

- In two cases the predicate contains the verb ישב, "to dwell" (vv. 6a, 7a). The first is followed by עמדי, "with me," and the second by בקרב ביתי, "within my house." Verses 6a and 6b are the only two positive statements in Part II. As for v. 6a, it is hardly possible to think that the king intends to admit the righteous en masse to live with him in his palace.[50] These sentences must refer to potential courtiers.

- לנגד עיני, "before my eyes," occurs only twice, at the beginning and end of Part II. The fact that in Psalm 101 it occurs twice in proximity to בקרב ביתי, "within my house" (vv. 2b-3a, 7ab)[51] supports the view that it refers to someone in proximity to the king, that is, a member of the royal household.

- Another expression clearly refers to the royal household if the reading of the Versions is correct. The LXX and the Syriac read v. 5bβ as אתו לא אוכל, "with him I will/do not dine" (rather than the MT's אתו לא אוכל, "I cannot endure[52] him"). People who dine at the king's table would most likely be courtiers, as presumably in Prov 23:1.[53]

SHIFTING THE FOCUS OF PSALM 101

In the foregoing section I have argued that Psalm 101 was the coronation hymn of a Judahite king whose primary focus was the instruction of his courtiers in the ways of righteousness, and that this instruction is given in Part II. It is clear, however, that the MT reflects a process that changed the focus from the king's instruction to the king's own righteousness.

---

[50] The phrase נאמני ארץ in v. 6a is usually translated "*the* faithful in the land" (*RSV*), which strictly speaking is not accurate. Such a translation would imply that the king wished *all* faithful persons in Judah to move into his palace! Rather the term should be taken in a restrictive sense: "faithful/trustworthy persons in the land." The bicolon could be paraphrased: "I am on the lookout for trustworthy persons in the land // that they may join my household" — i.e. he is looking for good candidates as courtiers and advisers.

[51] Note the equivalent expressions *ina maḫriya* and *qereb ekalliya* in the Ashurbanipal grant cited above (lines 17, 19), both modifying verbs whose subject is the dutiful courtier.

[52] For this meaning of יכל see Isa 1:13.

[53] Even if one opts for the MT's reading here the reference still *could* be to a courtier, but less clearly so.

The shift of focus was effected primarily through the various changes to the text discussed above. Most significant were changes to the original text of v. 2 that set forth the theme of the psalm. The first was the revocalization of the phrase מתי תבא אלי as a pious wish, "When will you come to me?" Once this had happened, its governing verb אשׂכילה would have to bear a meaning such as "I will give heed to (the way of blamelessness)" or perhaps "I shall act wisely = behave virtuously."[54] The MT no doubt intends it to be read this way. The second change was that of להתהלך to אתהלך (and לבב to לבבי). With these two alterations, the focus of the psalm is radically shifted.

Further changes were made to various terms in Part II. So, for example, when one reads the colon דבר־בליעל in v. 3a as "(any) base thing" rather than the original sense of "the one who speaks base things" the point of the bicolon now becomes that the king is so righteous he refuses even to look upon evil. Similarly in v. 3b עשׂה סטים no longer states the king's hatred of "one who commits transgressions" but of the very concept of "committing transgressions" — i.e. by the king. In v. 4aβ, רע לא אדע no longer means "I do not acknowledge one who is evil" but rather "I do not know (have experience of?) evil."

At some stage in the transmission of Psalm 101 it was given a superscription like the majority of psalms. In the case of this psalm the superscription served to associate the anonymous king who speaks in the poem with David. It is evident from the works of the Deuteronomistic Historian and the Chronicler that that the portrait of David became more and more idealized in post-exilic Judahite tradition. Thus the attribution of Psalm 101 to David was another step in transforming it into a portrait of the pious king. Later Tg. Pss. makes the connection with David even more explicit by mentioning him within the body of the psalm, viz., by introducing v. 2b with אמר דוד, "David said."

The Versions contribute in other ways to the shift of focus. In the LXX all the verbs from v. 2b to the end of the poem are in a past tense, aorist or imperfect. The Syriac is similar with its predominance of *qtl* verb forms. This reinforces the interpretation of the psalm as a "confession of innocence" on the part of the king. The poem thus becomes a catalog of sins he *has not* committed, which is another way of emphasizing his total righteousness. For its part Tg. Pss. enhances the picture of the king in the psalm as a wisdom figure. It paraphrases

---

[54] As in Ps 36:4.

בקרב ביתי, "within my house," in v. 2b with בגו בית אולפני, "within my house *of instruction*."

## CONCLUSION

The thesis argued in this article is that the issue of the focus of Psalm 101 as well as its form-critical classification cannot be answered from present textual evidence alone. One of the reasons for this is that the MT, the final version of the text, reflects a focus different from the original one, a focus based on departures from the original text of the psalm in several places. It departs from the original consonantal text of the psalm in the case of one colon, v. 2bα: אתהלך (originally להתהלך) and לבבי (originally לבב). And it departs from the original vocalization of several nominal in Parts I and II. These changes to the text predate textual evidence currently available, and yet indirect evidence for them can be found within the psalm itself as well as in two neo-Assyrian texts from the reign of Ashurbanipal (668-627 BCE). The fact that the keynote v. 2 shows neo-Assyrian influence argues that this psalm dates from a period of neo-Assyrian political influence or domination in Judah, specifically during the reign of Ashurbanipal in the seventh century BCE. Hence I tentatively suggest that Psalm 101 was the coronation hymn of a Judahite king in the mid-seventh century.[55]

## SELECT BIBLIOGRAPHY

Cancik-Kirschbaum, E. "Konzeption und Legitimation von Herrschaft in neuassyrischer Zeit: Mythos und Ritual in VS 24.92," *WdO* 26 [1995] 5–20).

Kataja. L. and R. Whiting. *Grants, Decrees and Gifts of the Neo- Assyrian Period* (SAA 12; Helsinki: Helsinki University Press, 1995).

Kenik, H. A. "Code of Conduct for a King: Psalm 101," *JBL* 95 (1976) 391–403.

Kraus, H.-J. *Psalms 60–150: A Commentary* (Minneapolis; Augsburg, 1989).

Kselman, J. S. "Psalm 101: Royal Confession and Divine Oracle," *JSOT* 33 (1985) 45–62.

Livingston, A. *Court Poetry and Literary Miscellanea* (SAA 3; Helsinki: Helsinki University Press, 1989).

---

[55] The most likely candidate would be Amon (642-640), whose reign began during a period of Assyrian influence. It would be particularly ironic if Psalm 101 was this king's coronation hymn. For it would mean that after having instructed his courtiers to walk blamelessly "within my house" they ended up conspiring against him and assassinating him "in his house" (2 Kgs 21:23; 2 Chron 33:24).

Mowinckel, S. *The Psalms in Israel's Worship* (2 vols., Nashville: Abingdon, 1962).

Postgate, J. N. *Neo-Assyrian Royal Grants and Decrees* (Studia Pohl: Series Maior 1; Rome: Pontifical Biblical Institute, 1969).

Westermann, C. *The Living Psalms* (Grand Rapids; Eerdmans, 1989).

# LAMENT AND THE JOY OF SALVATION
# IN THE LAMENT PSALMS

SUNG–HUN LEE

Commentators on the lament psalms are usually impressed by their remarkably sombre tone. Yet readers of Individual Lament Psalms would also be struck by the fact that — along with an extended pre-occupation with great present distress in the midst of suffering and affliction — there appears, interspersed, the expression of assurance in God's salvation. It would be even more surprising that the Individual Lament psalms, in most cases, end jubilantly in abrupt praise of God. This sudden transition is clearly seen in Psalm 57:

*The Petitioner's Petition:*

1. Be merciful to me, O God, be merciful to me for in you my soul takes refuge; in the shadow of your wings I will take refuge.
2. I cry to God Most High, to God who fulfils his purpose for me.
3. He will send from heaven and save me; he will put to shame those who trample on me. Selah.
4. I lie down among lions that greedily devour human prey; their teeth are spears and arrows, their tongues sharp swords.
5. Be exalted, O God, above the heavens, let your glory be over all the earth.
6. They set a net for my steps; my soul was bowed down. They dug a pit in my path, but they have fallen into it themselves.

[Transition]

*The Petitioner's Expression of Confidence (or Praise):*

7. My heart is steadfast, O God, my heart is steadfast. I will sing and make melody.
8. Awake, my soul! Awake, O harp and lyre! I will awake the dawn.
9. I will give thanks to you, O Lord, among the peoples; I will sing praises to you among the nations.
10. For your חֶסֶד is as high as the heavens; your faithfulness extends to the clouds.
11. Be exalted, O God, above the heavens, let your glory be over all the earth. (*NIV*)

Though this abrupt shift in mood in the lament psalms has long been discussed by scholars, no satisfactory explanation has yet been suggested.[1] The present essay proposes an answer for the transition from lament to praise in the lament psalms, in the light of several previous attempts to do so.

## PAST INTERPRETATIONS OF THE TRANSITION

### 1. The Psychological Interpretation

Earlier interpretations for the shift on the basis of unconscious inner psychological conflicts cannot alone constitute the ultimate solution, since they offer only a partial understanding of the shift aside from theological motives. Because the origins of the transition from lament to praise require some consideration of the psychological processes implicit in the moods and emotions of the text, in this approach the petitioner's confidence is based on his awareness of the granting of God's חֶסֶד within the covenant relationship. This does not rule out the psychological explanation, but is concerned to root the motivation for such a shift in the character of God and his חֶסֶד.

### 2. The Cultic Interpretation

An inferred priestly oracle of salvation based on the cultic interpretation has also been suggested as a cause of the transition in the lament psalms; J. Bergrich has reconstructed a formula or *Gattung*, based on an oracle in Second Isaiah. This suggestion proves inadequate, however, firstly because the form postulated is absent in the lament psalms. Secondly, where in other OT texts the oracle fits its suggested context as an oracle of salvation, being associated with a lament, its form does not fit the suggested *Gattung*.

Conversely, in cases where the oracle form does fit, it is not associated with a lament element, and thus cannot be transposed

---

[1] F. Küchler, "Das Priesterliche Orakel in Israel und Juda," in W. W. Grafen von Baudissin (ed.), *Abhandlungen zur semitische Religionskunde und Sprachwissenschaft* (BZAW 33; Berlin: de Gruyter, 1918) 285–301; H. Gunkel & J. Begrich, *Einleitung in die Psalmen* (HAT suppl.; Göttingen: Vandenhoeck & Ruprecht, 1933); H. Gunkel, *The Psalms* (London: SCM, 1962); S. Mowinckel, *The Psalms in Israel's Worship II* (Oxford: Blackwell, 1962); C. Westermann, *Praise and Lament in the Psalms* (Edinburgh: T. &T. Clark, 1981) 65, 79; J. Muilenburg, *The Way of Israel* (New York: Harper & Row, 1961) 124ff; idem, *The Psalms* (London: SCM, 1962); H.-J. Kraus, *Psalms 1–59*, (Minneapolis: Augsburg, 1988); T. W. Cartledge, "Conditional Vows in the Psalms of Lament: A New Approach to an Old Problem," in K. G. Hoglund et al., *The Listening Heart: Essays in Wisdom and the Psalms in Honour of Roland E. Murphy* (Sheffield: JSOT Press,1987) 77–94

easily to the context of the lament psalms. Indeed, the suggested *Gattung* for the oracle seems to fit only Second Isaiah, from which it has been extrapolated. Nevertheless, there is still room for the idea of a prophetic oracle of salvation in some lament psalms, which works very plausibly as a suggestion for the transition. The direct reference to an oracle is, however, absent in some lament psalms. In such cases, the identification of confidence in the granting of God's *hesed* offers an explanation for the transition that is more clearly theological than explicitly cultic. These two approaches need not be seen as mutually exclusive.

An obvious feature of Individual Lament Psalms is that they are prayers written in the first person singular, in the persona of one who complains of dire troubles, and are addressed to a deity apparently capable of rescuing individuals from the trouble. This suggests that the cause of the shift could be understood in relation to the "covenant" between God and his people, since this is a key concept in OT thought, elucidating the nature of the relationship between humans and the divine.[2]

Moreover, the biblical term חֶסֶד is often found in close connection with the concept of covenant, as an "agent" or expression of God's willingness to deliver his people from harmful situations; the term may thus be examined for the light it sheds on the covenant as a likely cause of the shift from lament to praise in the lament psalms. Towards this end, the attributes of חֶסֶד will now be discussed in terms of textual usage.

## THE MEANING OF *ḤESED*

No Hebrew word in the Old Testament arouses more debate than חֶסֶד, which appears 245 times. It has proved virtually impossible to define the term by a single word in translation, since חֶסֶד denotes various connotations in each text, with particular nuances in meaning depending on the context. Different renderings of the word in the various translations of the OT testify to the difficulty of interpretation. For example, the Peshitta (Syriac) Psalter renders the term חֶסֶד

---

[2] W. Eichrodt states: "The concept in which Israelite thought gave definitive expression to the binding of the people to God and by means of which they established firmly from the start the particularity of their knowledge of him was the covenant" (*Theology of the Old Testament* [Philadelphia: Westminster, 1961 {first published in German, 1935}] 36).

with ܪܚܡ,[3] ܐܬܪܚܡ,[4] or ܚܘܒܠܐ,[5] and R. P. Smith[6] in his Syriac dictionary translates ܪܚܡ to "love," "delight," "have mercy upon," or else "show pity," whether explicitly or implicitly, to another. Yet if one looks at Smith's English equivalents of the Syriac for חֶסֶד, "active goodness," "kindness," "grace" traslates ܚܘܒܠܐ,[7] — from the root ܚܒܠ (pa'el) a different root from ܪܚܡ — which highlights the difficulties in capturing the concise meaning of חֶסֶד in another language. The LXX generally renders חֶסֶד as ἔλεος ("mercy"),[8] but also (rarely) as ἐλεήμων ("the one who has mercy, or pity"), or πολυέλεος ("richly merciful").

The difficulty of translating חֶסֶד is further evident in the various approaches adopted over the last century in order to define its meaning. Etymological methods[9] have struggled, despite the investigation of various linguistic origins, to find a satisfactory rendering of the noun,[10] and the question of the "correct" translation of חֶסֶד remains a moot point.

Major differences over the meaning are partly due to the bilateral attributes of the term in its "conditional" and "unconditional" aspects. The English translation "mercy," for instance, seems more focused on the unconditional view of חֶסֶד, while L. Köehler's translation "bond" appears more focused on the conditional view. Since חֶסֶד is treated in this study in its bilateral aspects, it will not be rendered by a single word; no single English term suffices to convey its meaning.

*1. Conditional Aspect*

*(a) Attributes of חֶסֶד in the Reciprocal View*

The term חֶסֶד in its conditional aspect, stressed most noticeably by

---

[3] E.g. Pss 33:5; 42:8; 51:1.

[4] E.g. Pss 36:5 36:7; 40:10; 44:26.

[5] E.g. Pss 5:7; 6:4; 13:5; 18:50; 33:22; 40:9; 57:3.

[6] R. P. Smith, *A Compendious Syriac Dictionary* (Eugene, OR: Wipf & Stock, 1999 [founded upon J. P. Smith, *Thesaurus Syriacus* [Oxford, Clarendon Press, 1903]) 537.

[7] Smith, *A Compendious Syriac Dictionary*, 171.

[8] E.g. Ps 41:9 [42:9].

[9] Cf. N. H. Snaith, *The Distinctive ideas of the Old Testament* (London: Epworth, 1945) 95–98; H.-J. Zobel, "חֶסֶד," *TDOT* 5.45.

[10] H. W. Robinson, *Inspiration and Revelation in the Old Testament* (Oxford: Clarendon, 1946) 58; W. R. Smith, *The Prophets of Israel* (London: Black, 1919) 408.

N. Glueck,[11] is associated with mutuality, reciprocity, mutual
assistance, and service rendered in return for help given.[12] According
to this aspect, something is directly and reciprocally required of the
receiver of חֶסֶד within a mutual relationship of rights and duties, or
conduct, both within the context of human-divine and human-human
relation-ships.

Such reciprocal attributes are also applicable to the relationship
between God and man, in which those who ask for his חֶסֶד are required to behave correspondingly.[13] For example, Abraham's servant
refers to God as the God of Abraham, before he expects and asks for
חֶסֶד from Yahweh on Abraham's behalf: "... show חֶסֶד to my master
Abraham" (Gen 24:12). Abraham's servant thus expects and asks for
God's חֶסֶד because of the special relationship between God and Abraham, as summarized in the phrase יהוה אֱלֹהֵי אֲדֹנִי אַבְרָהָם ("O Lord,
God of my master Abraham" [Gen. 24:12, 27, 42, 48]).[14] Mic 6:8
presents another example of חֶסֶד in the context of mutually reciprocal
conduct of men among men, and vis-à-vis God[15]: "He has told you, O
mortal, what is good; and what does the Lord require of you ... to
love חֶסֶד, ...?"

This verse also shows what conduct God demands: עֲשׂוֹת מִשְׁפָּט ("to
do justice"), וְאַהֲבַת חֶסֶד ("to love חֶסֶד"), וְהַצְנֵעַ לֶכֶת עִם־אֱלֹהֶיךָ ("and
to walk humbly with your God"). In this light, חֶסֶד, is understood in
the context of a relationship of "mutual reciprocity," and as expressing this relationship.[16] These references also show that the granting
of חֶסֶד is considered a reciprocal act towards the other party, since
one side's granting it is contingent on the other side's behaviour, and
thus חֶסֶד is conditionally reserved for those who deserve it.[17] As seen
above, those who receive חֶסֶד are required to show a proper attitude

---

[11] N. Glueck, *"Hesed"* in the *Bible* (Cincinnati: Hebrew Union College Press,
1967) 35–55. Cf. Gen 19:19; 20:13; Ruth 2:20; Josh 2:12, 14; 1 Sam 15:6; 20:14,
15; 2 Sam 3:8; I Kings 20:31; 2 Chron 24:22.

[12] Glueck, *'Hesed' in the Bible*, 54–55.

[13] Some two-thirds (187/282) of the total number of occurrences of חֶסֶד have
God as the agent; cf. G. R. Clark, *The Word "Hesed" in the Hebrew Bible*
(JSOTSup 157; Sheffield: JSOT Press, 1993) 49, 53.

[14] Cf. Ps 105:6, 42; Deut 9:27; Isa 41:8.

[15] Glueck, *"Hesed"* in the *Bible*, 61.

[16] Glueck, *"Hesed"* in the *Bible*, 71.

[17] Glueck, *"Hesed"* in the *Bible*, 102.

— for example, by loving God, confessing sins, and hearing and obeying God's commandments as servants.

### (b) Meaning of חֶסֶד in the Obligatory Sense

In the conditional aspect, the usage of חֶסֶד places great import on the "loyalty," "duty," and "faithfulness" which both parties to the covenant should observe towards each other. For example, when David seeks Jonathan's help in discovering what Saul's attitude towards him may be, he does so secure in Jonathan's obligations under the covenant: "Therefore deal kindly (חֶסֶד) with your servant, for you have brought your servant into a sacred covenant (בְּרִית) with you" (1 Sam 20:8). While Jonathan, if he performs his obligations under their own covenant, will finally be doing a חֶסֶד, it is obvious that David is really calling upon him to do more, i.e. to "act loyally" or "show loyalty." It is thus obligatory for David to show חֶסֶד to Mephibosheth, the survivor of Saul's house, in turn, since Jonathan's past חֶסֶד was done to David within the same covenant (2 Samuel 9) This obligatory sense of חֶסֶד is also applicable to the relationship between God and the people of Israel. In Exod 20:5b-6,[18] for example, where only the duties of the people are mentioned, God's חֶסֶד is promised categorically to those who, in return, love him and keep the commandments.

Such an understanding based on the strictly conditional sense of חֶסֶד, distinguishes it from "mercy" or "goodness," which — according to N. Glueck — only carry a secondary meaning. For him, חֶסֶד also cannot be equated with "grace," although it is based on grace

Some scholars understand חֶסֶד differently by weakening the significance of the strictly conditional aspects. H. W. Robinson[19] posits a "supreme moral value" which prompts a man to assist his neighbour even though no strictly legal obligation enforces this; however, he also perceives חֶסֶד to include "loyalty" and "moral obligation." He concludes that חֶסֶד denotes a nonenforceable obligation engendered by social bonds, rather than by strict compulsion.[20] L. J. Kuyper[21] also

---

[18] E.g. Deut. 7:9, 12; 1 Kgs 8:23; 2 Chron 6:14; Neh 1:5; 9:32; Dan 9:4

[19] H. W. Robinson, *Inspiration and Revelation in the Old Testament* (Oxford: Clarendon Press, 1946) 57, 84-85.

[20] Robinson, *Inspiration and Revelation*, 84.

[21] L. J. Kuyper, "Grace and Truth." *Reformed Review* 16 (1962) 1–16; "Grace and Truth," *Int* 18 (1964) 3–19.

softens the reading of strict obligation, by regarding חֶסֶד as a
"generous act" by which the superior protects the welfare of the
inferior.

L. Koehler,[22] W. F. Lofthouse,[23] and J. B. Bauer[24] also emphasise
the strict conditional aspects of חֶסֶד, but highlight the obligatory view
by replacing typical renderings such as "mercy," "goodness," and
"faithfulness" with "communal responsibility" (*Gemeinschaftspflicht*,
*Verbundenheit*, and *Solidarität*).

## 2. Unconditional Aspect

### (a) Meaning of חֶסֶד within the One-Sided Action

In the unconditional view, חֶסֶד may be understood as an essentially
one-sided action, similar to a promise, since חֶסֶד would be granted
mainly by God to His people, ultimately without condition:[25] "In
overflowing wrath for a moment I hid my face from you, but with חֶסֶד
I will have compassion on you, says the Lord, your Redeemer" (Isa
54:8). For a brief time (רֶגַע [vv. 7, 8]) Yahweh had turned away from
Israel, (עָזַב [v. 7]; סָתַר [v. 8]). Now Yahweh's temporary abandonment of Zion is followed by a disputation announcement of salvation,
promising a bright future, in two parts, each beginning with the
preposition *bet*: וּבְרַחֲמִים גְּדֹלִים אֲקַבְּצֵךְ ("with great compassion I will
gather you," 7b); and וּבְחֶסֶד עוֹלָם רִחַמְתִּיךְ ("with חֶסֶד I will have
compassion on you," 8bα). Thus the promised חֶסֶד, significantly
paralleled here with the covenant, will not be removed without the
attached stated condition.[26] This amounts to a unilateral action on
God's part, despite the sinful behaviour of the other party.

This one-sided unconditional aspect of חֶסֶד has also influenced
modern understandings of the term. K. D. Sakenfeld's survey of חסד,
for example, is mostly similar to that of Glueck in focusing on its
contextual side. Sakenfeld is aware of both the conditional and

---

[22] L. Köehler & W. Baumgartner, *Hebrew and Aramaic Lexicon of the Old Testament* (2 vols., Leiden: Brill, 1994).

[23] Cf. W. F. Lofthouse, "*Hen* and *Hesed* in the Old Testament," *ZAW* 51 (1953) 29–35.

[24] Cf. J. B. Bauer, "Love," in Bauer (ed.), *Encyclopaedia of Biblical Theology* (3rd ed., London and Sydney: Sheed and Ward, 1963) 2.526.

[25] Cf. Hos 2:19; Isa 54:8; Ps 89:28, 33; Jer 3:12; 2 Sam 7:15.

[26] R. F. Melugin, *The Formation of Isaiah 40–55* (BZAW 141; Berlin: de Gruyter, 1976) 171.

unconditional perspectives, but judges the former to dominate:

> "*Hesed* involves the sovereign God's free willingness to hear and rescue the one who trusts in him, who is in dire straits, who has no other help but God."[27]

She concludes that the action of חֶסֶד is fundamentally one-sided, in that a superior party has a special responsibility towards an inferior party,[28] giving rise to an essentially unilateral interpretation of God's actions in favour of his people, despite humans' sinful tendencies.

David is only a commander when Hushai performs חֶסֶד for him (2 Sam 16:17). Based on these observations, Sakenfeld, argues that in granting חֶסֶד, one party such as God (the superior party), would be able to fulfill the needs of another party, in this case man (the inferior party). This means that חֶסֶד is done in special situations, with specific circumstances being reflected in appropriate usage of the word.

### (b) Meaning of חֶסֶד within the Concept of Grace

Advocates of a more softened interpretation often equate חֶסֶד with mercy or grace, and try to demonstrate a closer relationship between חֶסֶד and these concepts. Examples of unconditional usage are used to support this view, which criticizes strictly conditional renderings such as "rights" or "duties."[29] One example is God's promise to David: "I will be a father to him, and he shall be a son to me. I will not take my חֶסֶד, from him, ..." (1 Chron 17:13). God's חֶסֶד and eternal kingship (cf. v. 16) are clearly promised to David and his dynasty in contrast to the house of Saul, despite the apparent presupposition of David's sin. In this passage חֶסֶד may be regarded as God's one-sided favour to David and his descendants, which will remain in perpetuity.[30] God acts favourably towards David despite his sinful behaviour, not based on the doctrine of reward, but on that of חֶסֶד, which contains a special responsibility on God's side.

The unconditional aspect of חֶסֶד thus moves, as W. F. Lofthouse

---

[27] K. D. Sakenfeld, *The Meaning of Hesed in the Hebrew Bible* (Missoula, MT: Scholar's Press, 1978) 147–48.

[28] Sakenfeld, *Meaning of Hesed*, 233–39.

[29] Sakenfeld, for example, observes that Glueck creates a false dichotomy between obligatory action and action that is freely done (*Meaning of Hesed*, 3).

[30] P. K. McCarter, Jr., *II Samuel: A New Translation with Introduction, Notes and Commentary* (AB 9; New York: Doubleday, 1984) 208. Cf Sakenfeld, *Meaning of Hesed*, 105, 144.

maintains,[31] beyond a conditional obligation of loyalty, since חֶסֶד has been shown indefinitely by God — even though the covenant can be broken by one of the parties, man. God's חֶסֶד is ultimately identical with his steadfast determination to be true to his side of the covenant obligation, even if individuals or the people of Israel should fail on their part to show the corresponding proper attitude to God's חֶסֶד.[32]

In this light חֶסֶד seems to share features with הֵן and רַחֲמִים, though they cannot be identical. Beginning with an analysis of הֵן and רַחֲמִים, H. J. Stoebe[33] points out that apparent synonyms within a language are often not identical in meaning. For example, הֵן is normally oriented toward the object of action (i.e. the recipient), whereas רַחֲמִים (as well as חֶסֶד) is oriented toward the subject (i.e. the giver). Moreover, since חֶסֶד is invariably the preceding word when paired in singular form with רַחֲמִים in poetry, Stoebe identifies חֶסֶד as the dominant concept denoting the abstract quality of "good-hearted sentiment" or "kindness."

In contrast, רַחֲמִים represents the concrete working out of this quality. He concludes that God looks upon man with a goodness and generosity that is ultimately free from any imposed condition.

Understanding חֶסֶד as approximating the concept of grace thus seems fairly justified, but care must be taken when applying later concepts, as T. F. Torrance recognizes:

> There is no one word for grace in the Old Testament as there is in the New, nor are the precise lineaments of the New Testament thought manifest, but the substance of the doctrine is there.[34]

---

[31] W. F. Lofthouse, "*Hen* and *Hesed* in the Old Testament," *ZAW* 51 (1953) 29–35.

[32] N. H. Snaith, *The Distinctive Ideas of the Old Testament* (London: Epworth, 1945) 111.

[33] H. J. Stoebe, on account of the overlegalistic and formalised nature of this view, criticises any directly obligatory sense of חֶסֶד. Clark, too, suggests that such a relationship might be expressed in the phrase "One good turn demands another" (*The Word "Hesed,"* 15–17). See Stoebe, "חֶסֶד-Güte," in E. Jenni & C. Westermann (eds.), *Theologisches Handwörterbuch zum Alten Testament* (Munich: Kaiser, 1971) 1.600–21; idem, "Die Bedeutung des Wortes HÄSÄD im Alten Testament," *VT* 2 (1952) 247–48.

[34] T. F. Torrance, "The Doctrine of grace in the Old Testament," *SJT* 1 (1948) 55. Cf. J. A. Montgomery, "Hebrew HESED and Greek CHARIS," *HTR* 32 (1939) 97–102.

## חֶסֶד IN THE INDIVIDUAL LAMENT ("IL") PSALMS

The term חֶסֶד displays diverse nuances in both its conditional and unconditional aspects, and can support a wide range of translations. In addition, חֶסֶד may also share common meanings with other terms in the lament psalms.

### 1. חֶסֶד in Its Aspect of Deliverance

חֶסֶד in the lament psalms may be related to other terms such as יְשׁוּעָה ("salvation"), צְדָקָה ("righteousness") אֱמֶת ("truth"), or רַחַם ("mercy"), since these share a common semantic field in some passages.[35] For example, the relationship between חֶסֶד and the verb יָשַׁע seems distinctive in the Individual Lament Psalms, since חֶסֶד is regularly manifested in Yahweh's acts such as rescue from dire straits.[36] This need not necessarily be taken as synonymous with deliverance (יָשַׁע),[37] nor rendered as power, might, or fortitude.[38] חֶסֶד

---

[35] Clark, *The Word "Hesed,"* 109–61. Note also the following: "Hebrew may be called primarily a language of the senses. The words originally expressed concrete or material things and movements or actions which struck the senses or started the emotions" (G. A. Smith, *The Hebrew Genius as Exhibited in the Old Testament* [Oxford: Clarendon Press, 1927] 10). In similar vein, S. A. Cook remarks: "To 'remember' [with the Hebrew] implies action: and words for love, hate, anger, cover or desire, cover the practical results of those feelings. ... Hebrew has no empty or abstract terms" (*The Old Testament: A Reinterpretation* [Cambridge: Heffer; New York: Macmillan, 1936] 106).

[36] This approach also supported by H.-J. Zobel, who regards יְשׁוּעָה as related to חֶסֶד within the framework of his linguistic approach. Zobel attempts to connect the terms as nouns used in parallel with חֶסֶד, or forming part of its semantic field: יְשׁוּעָה, מִשְׁפָּט, צְדָקָה, רַחֲמִים, אֱמֶת, and אֱמוּנָה. In his analysis of the different contexts of חֶסֶד, with reference to syntax, semantics, history, literature and theology, Zobel ("חֶסֶד," 44–56) makes passing reference to other words used in conjunction. חֶסֶד also seems to express divine attributes while denoting active character, in most cases with the object suffix of the first person singular (cf. Pss 3:8; 6:5; 7:2; 22:22; 31:17; 54:3; 59:3; 69:2; 71:2; 109:26). For more details on the usage of those terms in the psalms, see: A. Aejmelaeus and L. Schmidt, *The Traditional Prayer in the Psalms/Literarische Studien Zur Josephsgeschichte* (BZAW 167; Berlin: de Gruyter, 1986) 16–21, 62–67; W. Beyerlin, *Die Rettung der Bedrängten in den Feindpsalmen der Einzelnen auf institutionelle Zusammenhänge untersucht* (FRLANT 99; Gottingen: Vandenhoeck & Ruprecht, 1970) 134.

[37] The words "deliverance" and "salvation" are be used interchangeably, as synonyms.

[38] C. F. Whitley, "The Semantic Range of Hesed," *Bib* 62 (1981) 518–26.

and יְשׁוּעָה are closely associated with each other, since, they frequently appear in parallel:[39]

וִיבֹאֻנִי [40]חֲסָדֶךָ יְהוָה          Let your חֶסֶד come to me, O Lord,

//

תְּשׁוּעָתְךָ כְּאִמְרָתֶךָ          Your salvation according to your promise (Ps 119:41).

חֶסֶד and יְשׁוּעָה also occur contiguously in Ps 98:2-3, in which the house of Israel experiences Yahweh's חֶסֶד while his יְשׁוּעָה is made known to the nations of the earth:

[2]הוֹדִיעַ יְהוָה יְשׁוּעָתוֹ לְעֵינֵי הַגּוֹיִם גִּלָּה צִדְקָתוֹ [3]זָכַר חַסְדּוֹ וֶאֱמוּנָתוֹ לְבֵית יִשְׂרָאֵל

The LORD has made known his victory; he has revealed his vindication in the sight of the nations. He has remembered his חֶסֶד and faithfulness to the house of Israel. (Ps 98:2-3)

Yahweh's חֶסֶד is obviously here a manifestation of his יְשׁוּעָה. Regarding their relationship, Glueck thus sees God's יְשׁוּעָה and צְדָקָה expressed in acts by which Yahweh shows his חֶסֶד and אֱמוּנָה in history.[41] J. L. Mays accordingly comments: "Yahweh's salvation of Israel was at once the exercise of his חֶסֶד and אֱמוּנָה toward Israel and the revelation of his righteousness to the nations as king."[42] A similar association between the words is contextually evident in Psalms 106 and 118:

הוֹדוּ לַיהוָה כִּי־טוֹב כִּי לְעוֹלָם חַסְדּוֹ

O give thanks to the Lord, for He is good; for his endures forever. (Pss 106:1; 118:1, 29)

Both of these Psalms keep Yahweh's חֶסֶד clearly in mind, and bring it

---

[39] Cf. R. G. Bratcher & W. D. Reyburn, *A Translator's Handbook on the Book of Psalms* (New York: United Bible Societies, 1991).

[40] A. A. Anderson, followed by W. S. Plumer (*Psalms* [Edinburgh: T. & A. Constable, 1978] 1039), believes the plural form is used either for the sake of emphasis, or denotes Yahweh's numerous gracious deeds whereby the Covenant relationship is maintained. A. Deissler observes (*Psalm 119 [118] und seine Theologie: ein Beitrag zur Erforschung der anthologischen Stilgattung im Alten Testament* [München: Karl Zink, 1955] 140) that only in the psalms would a plural of חֶסֶד, occur and that Codex Sinaiticus of the Septuagint, which has a plural, is not a reliable guide, since it wrongly renders v. 64. The MT vocalizes חסדך as plural, probably influenced by רַחֲמֶיךָ in v. 77. M. Dahood also regards it as the singular form, referring to the parallelism with תְּשׁוּעָתְךָ later in the verse (*The Psalms III: 101–150* [AB 17A; Minneapolis: Fortress, 1970]).

[41] Glueck, *"Hesed" in the Bible*, 73.

[42] J. L. Mays, *The Lord Reigns: A Theological Handbook to the Psalms* (Louisville, KY: Westminster John Knox, 1994) 15.

vividly into focus, whilst recalling many of Yahweh's mighty deeds on behalf of his people, including instances of his יְשׁוּעָה.

זָכְרֵנִי יְהוָה בִּרְצוֹן עַמֶּךָ פָּקְדֵנִי בִּישׁוּעָתֶךָ

Remember me, O Lord, when you show favour to your people; help me when you deliver them. (Ps 106:4)

עָזִּי וְזִמְרָת יָהּ וַיְהִי־לִי לִישׁוּעָה

The Lord is my strength and my might; he has become my salvation. (Ps 118:14)

קוֹל רִנָּה וִישׁוּעָה בְּאָהֳלֵי צַדִּיקִים

There are glad songs of victory in the tents of the righteous. (Ps 118:15a)

אוֹדְךָ כִּי עֲנִיתָנִי וַתְּהִי־לִי לִישׁוּעָה

I will give you thanks, for you answered me; you have become my salvation. (Ps 118:21)

D. Sylva offers the reasonable hypothesis that "God's חֶסֶד is expressed by delivering people from problems with shelter, sustenance, persons, sickness, nature and business, and by blessing them in these areas."[43]

## 2. חֶסֶד as a Motivation for God's Deliverance

In the lament psalms God's חֶסֶד may also be given the nuance of providing the motivation or grounds for his saving action,[44] since his חֶסֶד is often manifested in help and salvation[45] for those who call to him in times of suffering.[46]

For example, in Psalm 86, the petitioner's desperate situation is conveyed by using terms typical of the lament psalms in the passages where God is asked for help.[47] The opening of the prayer contains an imperative petition for hearing, and the verb "to answer" with the first person object suffix:

הַטֵּה־יְהוָה אָזְנְךָ עֲנֵנִי כִּי־עָנִי וְאֶבְיוֹן אָנִי

Incline your ear, O Lord, and answer me, for I am poor and needy. (Ps 86:1)

The petitioner's suffering is here described as some sort of affliction

---

[43] D. Sylva, *Psalms and the Transformation of Stress: Poetic-Communal Interpretation and the Family* (Louvain: Peters, 1994) 154.

[44] חֶסֶד has been characterised as the "motivation for divine intervention" (Gunkel & Begrich, *Einleitung in die Psalmen*, 232).

[45] H. Ringgren, *The Faith of the Psalmists* (Minneapolis: Fortress, 1963) 22.

[46] Sylva, *Psalms and the Transformation of Stress*, 156.

[47] So Gunkel, Anderson, Weiser, Schmidt, Oesterley, Deissler.

or distress caused by an external agent, the enemies:

אֱלֹהִים זֵדִים קָמוּ־עָלַי וַעֲדַת עָרִיצִים בִּקְשׁוּ נַפְשִׁי וְלֹא שָׂמוּךָ לְנֶגְדָּם

O God, the insolent rise up against me; a band of ruffians seeks my life,
and they do not set you before them. (Ps 86:14)

Also typical of prayer seeking deliverance is the imperative verb
followed by the object: הוֹשַׁע עַבְדְּךָ ("save your servant" [v. 2]),
אֶקְרָאֶךָ ("I call on you" [v. 7]). The realization of God's salvation is
expressed in the particle כִּי, based on Yahweh's great חֶסֶד:[48]

כִּי־חַסְדְּךָ גָּדוֹל עָלָי וְהִצַּלְתָּ נַפְשִׁי מִשְּׁאוֹל תַּחְתִּיָּה

Because your ds,x, is great towards me, you have delivered my soul from
the depths of Sheol. (Ps 86:13)

חֶסֶד as a motivation for deliverance may also be discerned in Psalm
107 (especially vv. 8, 15, 21, 31), since the theme of this psalm is
God's חֶסֶד given to his people as expressed in their deliverance from
all types of difficulties.[49]

| יוֹדוּ לַיהוָה חַסְדּוֹ | Let them thank the Lord for his חֶסֶד, |
| // | |
| וְנִפְלְאוֹתָיו לִבְנֵי אָדָם | for his wonderful works to humankind (Ps 107:8) |

In the psalmist's expressed joy in God's salvation, חֶסֶד is paralleled
with נִפְלָאוֹת, a word associated with God's salvation;[50] חֶסֶד may thus
be understood as the motivation for his acts of deliverance. In this
light, Yahweh's חֶסֶד, by extension, is the motivation to deliver (גאל
[v. 2]) his people from their trouble (יַד־צָר [v. 2]), for example, when

---

[48] Cf. A. Aejmelaeus, "Function and Interpretation of כִּי in Biblical Hebrew."
*JBL* 105 (1986) 202–209; W. T. Classen, "Speaker-Oriented Function of *kî* in
Biblical Hebrew," *JNSL* 1 (1983) 29–46.

[49] J. H. Eaton, *The Psalms* (Torch Bible Commentary; London: SCM, 1967)
256; E. M. Blaiklock, *Commentary on the Psalms I* (Philadelphia: Holman, 1977)
73.

[50] This psalm is often interpreted in two ways: with reference to the Exodus (E.
Kissane, *The Book of Psalms* [Dublin: Browne and Nolan, 1952] 174–80; A. F.
Kirkpatrick, *The Book of Psalms* [The Cambridge Bible for Schools and Colleges;
Cambridge: University Press, 1906] 637–38; or to Exile traditions; cf. vv. 2-3 and
the desert imagery of vv. 4-9 and 33-39 (e.g. A. Weiser, *The Psalms* [London:
SCM, 1962] 686). Commentators have produced little hard evidence to buttress
this hypothesis. M. Dahood (*Psalms III: 101–150*, 81) sees references in this
psalm to both the Exodus and the Exile. Others, however, assume source and
redaction stratification of the psalm, considering vv. 2-3 as an insertion, but this is
an unlikely proposition (cf. W. Beyerlin, *Werden und Wesen des 107. Psalms*
[BZAW 153; Berlin: de Gruyter, 1979] 73-74, 78).

wandering in the desert wastes (בַּמִּדְבָּר בִּישִׁימוֹן [vv. 4-7]), in bondage
(מוֹסֵרָה [vv. 14-15]), and in distress (מְצוּקָה [v. 19]). The following
references also clearly show how Yahweh's חֶסֶד may reasonably be
understood as the grounds of his deliverance, although varying prepositions create different shades of meaning:

(1)        (Plea for deliverance) שׁוּבָה יְהוָה חַלְּצָה נַפְשִׁי הוֹשִׁיעֵנִי

           (Grounds for deliverance) לְמַעַן חַסְדֶּךָ

Turn O LORD, save my life; deliver me *for the sake of*[51] *your* חֶסֶד. (Ps 6:5 [4])

(2)        (Plea for deliverance) הָאִירָה פָנֶיךָ עַל־עַבְדֶּךָ הוֹשִׁיעֵנִי

           (Grounds for deliverance) בְחַסְדֶּךָ

Let your face shine upon your servant; save me *in your* חֶסֶד (Ps 31:17 [16])

(3)        בְּרָב־חַסְדֶּךָ

           (Grounds for an answer) עֲנֵנִי בֶּאֱמֶת יִשְׁעֶךָ

*in the abundance of your* חֶסֶד, answer me with your faithful help. (Ps 69:14 [13]b)

(4)        עֲנֵנִי יְהוָה

           (Grounds for an answer) כִּי־טוֹב חַסְדֶּךָ

Answer me, O LORD, *for your* חֶסֶד *is good."* (Ps 69:17 [16]a)

(5)        (Plea for deliverance) וְאַתָּה יְהוָה אֲדֹנָי עֲשֵׂה־אִתִּי לְמַעַן שְׁמֶךָ

           (Grounds for the plea for help) כִּי־טוֹב חַסְדְּךָ הַצִּילֵנִי

But you, O LORD my Lord, act on my behalf for your name's sake; *because
your* חֶסֶד, *is good*, deliver me. (Ps 109:21)

(6)        עָזְרֵנִי יְהוָה אֱלֹהָי הוֹשִׁיעֵנִי

           (Grounds for the plea for deliverance) כְחַסְדֶּךָ

Help me, O LORD my God! Save me *according to your* חֶסֶד (Ps 109:26)

## 3. The Instrumental Sense of חֶסֶד in Relation to Deliverance

Since חֶסֶד is closely associated with יְשׁוּעָה ("deliverance") and
corresponding terms, in the Individual Lament Psalms it sometimes
occurs instrumentally, in phrases such as "sending your חֶסֶד."

A case in point is Ps 61:8[7], where God's חֶסֶד is personified as an
agent or guardian which he might send to preserve the petitioner:
יֵשֵׁב עוֹלָם לִפְנֵי אֱלֹהִים חֶסֶד וֶאֱמֶת מַן יִנְצְרֻהוּ ("May he be enthroned for
ever before God; appoint חֶסֶד and faithfulness to watch over him").

In some cases the petitioner, in desperate need of God's חֶסֶד,
directly calls upon it to intervene and save him from his enemies,

---

[51] "For the sake of" is better expressed by "on account of" or "because." God's
חֶסֶד, is the ground, or basis, for the psalmist's prayer.

since Yahweh would manifest his חֶסֶד by delivering him. In Psalm 17, for example, he expresses his desire for God's חֶסֶד with different verbs referring to deliverance, of equivalent imperative form, such as "hear," "answer," and "deliver," with the first person object suffix:

שִׁמְעָה יְהוָה צֶדֶק הַקְשִׁיבָה רִנָּתִי הַאֲזִינָה תְפִלָּתִי

Hear a just cause, O LORD, attend to my cry; give ear to my prayer ... (17:1)

מִלְּפָנֶיךָ מִשְׁפָּטִי יֵצֵא עֵינֶיךָ תֶּחֱזֶינָה מֵישָׁרִים

From you let my vindication come; Let your eyes see the right (v. 2)

אֲנִי־קְרָאתִיךָ כִי־תַעֲנֵנִי אֵל הַט־אָזְנְךָ לִי שְׁמַע אִמְרָתִי

I will call upon you, for you will Answer me, O God, Incline your ear to me, hear my words (v. 6)

שָׁמְרֵנִי כְּאִישׁוֹן בַּת־עָיִן בְּצֵל כְּנָפֶיךָ תַּסְתִּירֵנִי

Guard me as the apple of the eye; hide me in the shadow of your wings (v. 8)

In the same psalm, the petitioner also asks God to destroy his enemies using the imperative, with the instrumental power of God's חֶסֶד implied:

קוּמָה יְהוָה קַדְּמָה פָנָיו הַכְרִיעֵהוּ פַּלְּטָה נַפְשִׁי מֵרָשָׁע חַרְבֶּךָ

Rise up, O LORD, confront them, overthrow them! By your sword deliver my life from the wicked, (v. 13)

מִמְתִים יָדְךָ יְהוָה מִמְתִים מֵחֶלֶד חֶלְקָם בַּחַיִּים

May their bellies be filled with what you have stored up for them (v. 14a)

The petitioner also seems to gain hope through reflection on past recorded instances of God's deliverance,[52] since the experience of the individual could be associated with public experiences.[53] The petitioner longs for deliverance from God who has shown his deliverance in the past, in biblical history — for example, in Exodus as described in the Song of the Sea in the Book of Exodus.[54]

This helps the petitioner to look forward with expectation. In view of past deliverance, he can now ask for God's חֶסֶד *from which* his

---

[52] W. H. Bellinger, *Psalms: Reading and Studying the Book of Psalms* (Peabody, MA: Hendrickson, 1990) 55.

[53] H. H. Rowley suggests the biblical concept of an organic whole between the individual and community, where the parts are knit together, without losing their individuality. This concept would make it possible to relate communal experience to that of the individual (*Individual and Community: The Faith of Israel* [London: SCM, 1955] 99–123; idem, "Individual and Community in the Old Testament," *TToday* 12 [1955-56] 491–510). See also P. C. Craigie and P. Campbell, *The Book of Deuteronomy* (NICOT; London: Hodder and Stoughton, 1976) 380–81.

[54] Cf. P. C. Craigie, *Psalms 1–50* (WBC 19; Waco, TX: Word, 1983).

salvation will be achieved, instrumentally:

הַפְלֵה חֲסָדֶיךָ מוֹשִׁיעַ חוֹסִים מִמִּתְקוֹמְמִים בִּימִינֶךָ

Wondrously show your חֶסֶד, O Saviour of those who seek refuge from their adversaries at your right hand" (v. 7)

The association of חֶסֶד with the idea of deliverance is particularly and concisely expressed in Psalm 85:

הַרְאֵנוּ יְהוָה חַסְדֶּךָ וְיֶשְׁעֲךָ תִּתֶּן־לָנוּ

Show us your חֶסֶד, O LORD, and grant us your salvation (Ps 85:8 [7])[55]

To sum up, major debates concerning the translation of the Hebrew term חֶסֶד have largely originated from its bilateral character, owing to its conditional and unconditional aspects. In its conditional aspect חֶסֶד may be considered a reciprocal act towards the other party in a relationship, since one side's חֶסֶד is contingent upon the behaviour of the other. In this view חֶסֶד would, in the case of the God-man relationship, be reserved for those who deserve it, fulfilling the requirements of their relationship to Yahweh. It also implies a mode of behaviour conforming to a relationship of appropriate mutual rights and duties, and of appropriate reciprocal conduct between humans, between Israel and Yahweh, and between humans and the divine.

In its unconditional aspect, חֶסֶד may be understood as a funda-mentally one-sided action. God, in the unconditional view, makes a unilaterally continuous commitment to providing his חֶסֶד to the other party, whether to Israel or to individuals. Because of this aspect חֶסֶד has acquired softer interpretations by being equated, for example, with the terms "mercy" or "grace."

## PSALM 130

A confident expression of assurance in God's salvation is evident in the Psalm 130. As is commonly the case with Individual Lament Psalms, this psalm may not refer to any one individual experience. We know that it expresses fully the petitioner's state of grievous anguish or abysmal agony as he becomes conscious of being separated from God, and entering a condition "like death"[56] (cf. מִמַּעֲמַקִּים, "out of the depths" [v. 1]). However, identifying here a specific event such as a near-death experience could seems tenuous or speculative. W. H.

---

[55] A. A. Anderson translates as "cause us to see and to experience your חֶסֶד" (*The Book of Psalms* [Century Bible, 2 vols.; London: Oliphants, 1972) 611.

[56] O. Keel, *The Symbolism of the Biblical World: Ancient Near Eastern Iconography and the Book of Psalms* (London: SPCK, 1978) 64, 186.

Schmidt argues:

> There is no mention of the nearness of death apart from terms indicating depth; in particular the required plea for a change in situation is missing, be it the plea for recovery or for rescue from the enemy.[57]

## 1. A Crisis of God's חֶסֶד

| | |
|---|---|
| Out of the depths I cry to you, O LORD. <br> ²Lord, hear my voice ! <br> Let your ears be attentive <br> To the voice of my supplications! <br> ³If you, O Lord, should mark iniquities, <br> Lord, who could stand? <br> ⁴But there is forgiveness with you, <br> so that you may be revered. | מִמַּעֲמַקִּים קְרָאתִיךָ יְהוָה <br> ²אֲדֹנָי שִׁמְעָה בְקוֹלִי <br> תִּהְיֶינָה אָזְנֶיךָ קַשֻּׁבוֹת <br> לְקוֹל תַּחֲנוּנָי <br> ³אִם־עֲוֹנוֹת תִּשְׁמָר־יָהּ <br> אֲדֹנָי מִי יַעֲמֹד <br> ⁴כִּי־עִמְּךָ הַסְּלִיחָה <br> לְמַעַן תִּוָּרֵא⁵⁸ |

His awareness of the common weakness of human nature leads the psalmist to conclude that there is no hope for human beings in themselves alone: אִם־עֲוֹנוֹת תִּשְׁמָר־יָהּ אֲדֹנָי מִי יַעֲמֹד (v. 3).[59] Nor is there any other way but through God in which man can obtain hope for himself, since man is infinitely small and ephemeral in comparison to Yahweh.[60] The petitioner thus speaks of the help that lies for him in Yahweh. This emphasis on humans being dependent on God is aptly summed up by J. L. Mays:

> In the long view, ultimately speaking, there is no technical or scientific solution to the reality of human finitude and sinfulness. To be human is to desire life and rightness and, because we cannot autonomously secure either, to be essentially needy. Could we use these prayers to learn that, admit that, learn from them to nurture a consciousness structured by an honest sense of our finitude and fallibility?[61]

---

[57] W. H. Schmidt, "Gott und Mensch in Ps.130 (Formgeschichtliche Erwägungen)," *TZ* 22 (1966) 243 (my translation).

[58] LXX ἕνεκεν τοῦ νόμου σου ("Thanks to your law"); Vulg. *et propter legem* ("and because of your law"); Peshitta ܫܘܒܩܢܐ ܐܝܬ ܡܢ ܠܘܬܟ ("because forgiveness is from you"); Targ. ארום גבך שביקותא מן בגלל דתחמי ("there is forgiveness with you because you may be seen"). Duhm reads תורא as טוּבֶךָ.

[59] Cf. Pss 25:11; 31:10; 32:5; 38:4; 38:18; 39:11; 40:12; 49:5; 51:2; 51:5; 51:9; 65:3; 90:8; 143:2.

[60] Cf. Pss 8:5; 49:7, 12; 90:4-8.

[61] J. L. Mays, "A Question of Identity: The Threefold Hermeneutic of Psalmody," *Asbury Theological Journal* 46 (1991) 94.

In the depths of his awareness of guilt, the petitioner discerns the total extent of his dependence on God, and cries out to God from his position of distress, since it is God alone who can offer him forgiveness:[62] כִּי־עִמְּךָ הַסְּלִיחָה (v. 4). Compare Ps 86:5: כִּי־אַתָּה אֲדֹנָי טוֹב וְסַלָּח ("For you, O Lord, are good and forgiving"); and Ps 25:11: לְמַעַן־שִׁמְךָ יְהוָה וְסָלַחְתָּ לַעֲוֹנִי כִּי רַב־הוּא ("For your name's sake, O Lord, pardon my guilt, for it is great").[63] This sense of dependence leads the petitioner to "fear" God, showing his proper attitude him: לְמַעַן תִּוָּרֵא (v. 4). On this basis the petitioner can call upon God to act and deliver as God should, and the fact that he expects it to happen is seen in the direct imperative form of his entreaty: שִׁמְעָה ("hear"! [v. 2]).

## 2. Confidence in the Granting of God's חֶסֶד

| | |
|---|---|
| [5]I wait[64] for the LORD, my soul waits. | [5]קִוִּיתִי יְהוָה קִוְּתָה נַפְשִׁי |
| and in his word I hope. | וְלִדְבָרוֹ הוֹחָלְתִּי |
| [6]My soul (waits for) the LORD | [6]נַפְשִׁי לַאדֹנָי |
| more than those who watch for the morning, | מִשֹּׁמְרִים לַבֹּקֶר |
| more than those who watch for the morning. | [65]שֹׁמְרִים לַבֹּקֶר |

In Psalm 130 the petitioner's understanding of the "correct attitude" towards God is also manifested in the verbs קוה ("to wait") and יחל ("to hope"). Since קוה and יחל can both mean "to trust" in God in addition to signifying expectation and longing, they seem to show no distinctive difference in meaning. Attempts have been made, however, to distinguish them in terms of slightly different theological usages.[66] One Lexicon, for example, differentiates these verbs by giving יחל the extra nuance "to wait" as well as the sense "to hope" which both

---

[62] H. McKeating, "Divine Forgiveness in the Psalms," *SJT* 18 (1965) 69–83.

[63] Cf. Pss 25:11; 86:5; 103:3.

[64] Literally, "I waited." This seems to be the perfect tense of experience. Peshitta ܒܗܘܢ ܣܒܪܬ ("I trust in the Lord"). Cf. LXX, *AV*, *RV*: "I wait."

[65] LXX: ἀπὸ φυλακῆς πρωΐας μέχρι νυκτός ("from the morning watch until night"). Vulg. *a custodia matutina usque ad noctem* ("from the morning watch until night"). Syr. ܡܢ ܡܛܪܬܐ ܕܨܦܪܐ ܘܥܕܡܐ ܠܡܛܪܬܐ ܕܨܦܪܐ ("the Lord from the dawn watch until the dawn watch").

[66] According to C. Westermann, יחל was considered both a non-theological and theological concept, while קוה was reserved mainly for theological usage (cf. G. Waschke, "קוה," *TDOT* (Grand Rapids: Eerdmans, 1989) 6.1225–34. While both terms are considered as being in the same category, קוה ("waiting") is distinguished from חכה and שבר, which are mainly understood as "hoping."

words share.[67] Nevertheless, קוה and יחל seem to have developed at least some equivalent meaning,[68] since they are often used as equivalent terms in the MT where they appear in parallel:[69]

| I wait for the LORD, my soul waits, | קִוִּיתִי יְהוָה    קִוְּתָה נַפְשִׁי |
| and in his word I hope. ( Ps 130: 5) | // וְלִדְבָרוֹ    הוֹחָלְתִּי |

The similarity in meaning is also apparent in their co-usage, as in the following instances: וְעַתָּה מַה־קִּוִּיתִי // אֲדֹנָי תּוֹחַלְתִּי לְךָ הִיא ("And now, O Lord, what do I <u>wait for</u>? My <u>hope</u> is in you" [Ps 39: 8{7}); תּוֹחֶלֶת צַדִּיקִים שִׂמְחָה // וְתִקְוַת רְשָׁעִים תֹּאבֵד ("The <u>hope</u> of the righteous ends in gladness, but the <u>expectation</u> of the wicked comes to nothing" [Prov 10:28]); בְּמוֹת אָדָם רָשָׁע תֹּאבַד תִּקְוָה // וְתוֹחֶלֶת אוֹנִים אָבָדָה ("When the wicked die, their hope perishes, and the expectation of the godless comes to nothing" [Prov 11:7]).

In the Septuagint, both terms are rendered as ἐλπίζειν ("to hope"):

יחל and ἐλπίζω (Ps 38:16)[70]

כִּי־לְךָ יְהוָה הוֹחָלְתִּי אַתָּה תַעֲנֶה אֲדֹנָי אֱלֹהָי

But it is for you, O LORD, that I <u>wait</u>; it is you, O Lord my God, who will answer.

ὅτι ἐπὶ σοί, κύριε, <u>ἤλπισα</u>· σὺ εἰσακούσῃ, κύριε ὁ θεός μου.

קוה and ἐλπίζω (Isa 25:9b)[71]

הִנֵּה אֱלֹהֵינוּ זֶה קִוִּינוּ לוֹ וְיוֹשִׁיעֵנוּ

Behold, this is our God; we have <u>waited for</u> him, so that he may save us.

Ἰδοὺ ὁ θεὸς ἡμῶν, ἐφ' ᾧ ἠλπίζομεν καὶ ἠγαλλιώμεθα.

Since both קוה and יחל have a grounding in Yahweh and are directed toward him, they indicate that, for the petitioner, the future and deliverance come solely from the hand of God, and do not lie in

---

[67] Cf. W. L. Holladay, *A Concise Hebrew and Aramaic Lexicon of the Old Testament* (Grand Rapids: Eerdmans, 1971).

[68] R. Bultmann, "ἐλπίς," *TDNT* (Grand Rapids: Eerdmans, 1966) 2.523.

[69] Cf. M. I. Gruber, "The meaning of Biblical Parallelism: A Biblical Perspective," *Prooftexts* 13 (1993) 289–93; W. G. E. Watson, *Classical Hebrew Poetry* (JSOTSup 26; Sheffield: JSOT Press, 1984) 118.

[70] Cf. also Pss 33:18, 22; 42:5, 11; 43:5; 69:3; 71:14; 119:43, 49, 74, 81, 114, 147; 131:3; 147:11, etc.

[71] Cf. also Job 4:6; 5:16; 6:8; 6:19; 7:6; 8:13; 11:18; 11:20; 14:7; 17:15; 19:10; 27:8; Prov. 10:28; 11:7; 11:23; 19:18; 23:18; 24:14; 26:12; 29:20

man's path and at his disposal: גַּם כָּל־קֹוֶיךָ לֹא יֵבֹשׁוּ יֵבֹשׁוּ הַבּוֹגְדִים רֵיקָם
("No one whose hope is in you is put to shame; but shame come to all
who break faith without cause" *[REB]*). The petitioner has abandoned
his search for human help and has completely entrusted himself to his
God from whom the salvation would come forth: מִי יִתֵּן מִצִּיּוֹן יְשֻׁעֹות
יִשְׂרָאֵל בְּשׁוּב אֱלֹהִים שְׁבוּת עַמּוֹ יָגֵל יַעֲקֹב יִשְׂמַח יִשְׂרָאֵל ("O that deliverance for Israel would come from Zion! When God restores the for-
tunes of His people" [Ps 53:6{7}]); אַךְ אֶל־אֱלֹהִים דּוּמִיָּה נַפְשִׁי מִמֶּנּוּ
יְשׁוּעָתִי ("For God alone my soul [waits] in silence; from him comes
my salvation" [Ps. 62:2{1}]).[72] The petitioner no longer sees anything
but God to whom he has turned his whole inner being, for it is only
God who can deliver him. He can thus preserve hope even in a
calamity which cannot be overcome by any human. God will save him
from his sins, preventing him from becoming the object of scorn and
blasphemy among fools: וְעַתָּה מַה־קִּוִּיתִי אֲדֹנָי תֹּוחַלְתִּי לְךָ הִיא מִכָּל־
פְּשָׁעַי הַצִּילֵנִי ("And now, O Lord, what do I <u>wait</u> for? My <u>hope</u> is in
you. Deliver me from all my transgressions ..." [Ps 39:7-8a{8-9a}]).
The guarantee for the future lies in the hands of the God who has
continually proven himself to be man's help and deliverance, and with
whom the petitioner knows himself to be united. It is only in God that
he is able to find comfort and support when every form of human
support has proved unreliable. The petitioner has thus made a bold
decision of faith, and has entrusted all his hopes and sorrows to God.

Since קוה and יחל connote incessant, looking forward to Yahweh,
both can also be linked to בטח ("trust"). קוה is close in meaning and
derivatives to בטח,[73] and all three terms share the notion of expectant
looking to the future, which implies not seeing and yet hoping. This
means that "to wait is to be faithful, to be confident and trusting."[74]
קוה and בטח may be placed in the same semantic category,[75] and the

---

[72] Pss 18:2; Ps 49:15; 50:23; 56:4; 62:1, 7; 69:13, 29; 70:4; 74:12; 98:3 (cf. Pss
3:7; 6:4; 7:1, 10; 12:1; 16:6; 17:3, 7; 18:3, 27; 20:6, 9; 21:21; 28:9; 31:2, 16; 34:6,
18; 36:6; 37:40; 44:3, 7; 54:1; 55:16; 59:2; 60:5; 69:1, 35; 71:2, 3; 72:4, 13; 76:9;
80:3, 7, 19; 86:2, 16; 98:1; 106:8, 10, 47; 107:13, 19; 108:6; 109:26, 31; 116:6;
118:25; 119:17, 94, 146; 138:7; 145:19).

[73] H.-J. Kraus, *Theology of the Psalms* (Minneapolis: Augsburg, 1979]) 71.

[74] R. J. Petty, "Psalm 130, A Song of Sorrow," in J. C. Knight & L. A. Sinclair
(eds.), *The Psalms and Other Studies on the Old Testament Presented to J. I. Hunt*
(Nashotah, WI: Nashotah House, 1990) 48.

[75] A. Weiser, "The Old Testament Concept," *TDNT* 6.182–96; Kraus, *Theology of the Psalms*, 158.

close relationship between them is evident in other texts such as the Septuagint, where both are rendered as ἐλπίζειν ("to hope"):

בטח and ἐλπίζω (Ps 115:9-10)[76]

יִשְׂרָאֵל בְּטַח בַּיהוָה עֶזְרָם וּמָגִנָּם הוּא

O Israel (the house of Israel LXX), trust in the LORD! He is their help and their shield.

οἶκος Ισραηλ ἤλπισεν ἐπὶ κύριον· βοηθὸς αὐτῶν καὶ ὑπερασπιστὴς αὐτῶν ἐστιν.

בֵּית אַהֲרֹן בִּטְחוּ בַיהוָה עֶזְרָם וּמָגִנָּם הוּא

O house of Aaron, trust in the LORD! He is their help and their shield.

οἶκος Ααρων ἤλπισεν ἐπὶ κύριον· βοηθὸς αὐτῶν καὶ ὑπερασπιστὴς αὐτῶν ἐστιν.

קוה and ἐλπίζω (Isa 26:8)

אַף אֹרַח מִשְׁפָּטֶיךָ יְהוָה קִוִּינוּךָ לְשִׁמְךָ וּלְזִכְרְךָ תַּאֲוַת־נָפֶשׁ

In the path of your judgments, O LORD, we wait for you; your name and your renown are the soul's desire.

ἡ γὰρ ὁδὸς κυρίου κρίσις· ἠλπίσαμεν ἐπὶ τῷ ὀνόματί σου καὶ ἐπὶ τῇ μνείᾳ.

This shows that the Septuagint translators found statements of hope where the emphasis was trust in God, considering hope as implicit in an attitude of trust and expectation.[77]

Since the petitioner's proper attitude or relationship with God is evident in his use of קוה and יחל, the theological concept of God granting his חֶסֶד to the petitioner within the covenant relationship once more comes to the fore, leading the petitioner to express his confidence in God's חֶסֶד: [18]הִנֵּה עֵין יְהוָה אֶל־יְרֵאָיו לַמְיַחֲלִים לְחַסְדּוֹ [19]לְהַצִּיל מִמָּוֶת נַפְשָׁם ... ("Truly the eye of the Lord is on those who fear him, on those who hope in his חֶסֶד, to deliver their soul from death ..." [Ps 33:18-19a]); יְהִי־חַסְדְּךָ יְהוָה עָלֵינוּ כַּאֲשֶׁר יִחַלְנוּ לָךְ ("Let your חֶסֶד, O LORD, be upon us, even as we hope in you" [Ps 33:22]). God will show his deliverance through his חֶסֶד in the covenant relationship: רוֹצֶה יְהוָה אֶת־יְרֵאָיו אֶת־הַמְיַחֲלִים לְחַסְדּוֹ ("but the LORD takes pleasure in those who fear him, in those who hope in his חֶסֶד [Ps 147:11]).

The fullness of the petitioner's confidence in God's חֶסֶד becomes his motivation to introduce a new tone in v. 7 of Psalm 130, beginning

---

[76] Cf. Pss 4:5; 13:5; 22:4, 5, 10; 26:1; 27:3; 28:7; 31:6, 14; 32:10; 33:21.

[77] W. Zimmerli, *Man and His Hope in the Old Testament* (London: SCM, 1971); R. K. Harrison, "Hope," *ISBE*, 752.

with כִּי,[78] and ascending to the hopeful expectation of redemption by God's חֶסֶד.[79] Such confidence prompts the petitioner to warn Israel to have hope (יחל) in God, who will redeem Israel from all her iniquities:

| | |
|---|---|
| [7]Let Israel hope in the LORD: | [81]יַחֵל יִשְׂרָאֵל אֶל־יְהוָה[7] |
| for with the LORD there is חֶסֶד, | כִּי־עִם־יְהוָה הַחֶסֶד |
| and with him is great power to redeem. | וְהַרְבֵּה עִמּוֹ פְדוּת |
| [8]It is he who will redeem Israel | [8]וְהוּא יִפְדֶּה אֶת־יִשְׂרָאֵל |
| from all its iniquities.[80] | מִכֹּל עֲוֹנֹתָיו |

The petitioner's proper attitude motivated by the realization that God will bestow his חֶסֶד within the covenant relationship cannot, however, be the ultimate condition for this granting by God, since the petitioner's attitude is not on absolute and self-contained norms. As he addresses God, the petitioner comes to realize there is no humanly possible remedy for the situation in which he finds himself, and so he acknowledges that his nature is sinful (עֲוֹנוֹת):[82] אִם־עֲוֹנוֹת תִּשְׁמָר־יָהּ אֲדֹנָי מִי יַעֲמֹד ("If you, O Lord, should mark iniquities, Lord, who could stand? [Ps 130:3;]); אֶת־עַבְדֶּךָ וְאַל־תָּבוֹא בְמִשְׁפָּט כִּי לֹא־יִצְדַּק לְפָנֶיךָ כָל־חָי ("Do not enter into judgment with your servant, for no one living is righteous before you" [Ps 143:2]).

This leads him to become solely dependent upon God, acknowledging that is effective forgiveness is only in God[83]: כִּי־עִמְּךָ הַסְּלִיחָה לְמַעַן תִּוָּרֵא ("But there is forgiveness with you, so that you may be revered" [Ps 130:4]). The petitioner is thus aware to whom he must

---

[78] So *NEB*, Briggs, Kissane, Anderson, Delitzsch, Barnes, Kirkpatrick, Sabourin, Gunkel, Dahood, Weiser. In general, the particle כִּי is used as "if," "lest," "indeed," and "because"; cf. C. Westermann, *Praise and Lament in the Psalms* (Edinburgh: T.&T. Clark, 1981) 80; A. Schoors, "The Particle כִּי," *OTS* 21 (1981) 240–76; B. K. Waltke & M. O'Connor, *An Introduction to Biblical Hebrew Syntax* (Winona Lake, IN: Eisenbrauns, 1990) 32, 322, 365, 510–11, 526, 636–37, 638–40, 640–46, 656–57, 663–67, 670–71, 675–76; Gunkel & Begrich, *Einleitung in die Psalmen*, 562–63.

[79] Petty, "Psalm 130," 45–53.

[80] Some translate as "punishment," suggesting that the term refers not only to sin, but to sufferings that are the result of sin. See H. McKeating, "Divine Forgiveness in the Psalms," *SJT* 18 (1965) 69–83.

[81] The LXX places this clause in the last colon of verse 6.

[82] For a discussion of עָוֹן, see G. Quell, G. Staehlin, and W. Grundmann, "ἁμαρτάνω," *TDNT* 1.267–93.

[83] Cf. Pss 32:5; 51:6, 9; 65:3; 78:38; 79:8; 85:2; 103:3.

pray, and what he can hope for in his present affliction; and so he addresses his prayer directly to God, who delivers salvation, and provides for and protects the weak against their oppressors in the day of trouble. Despite the petitioner's sinful nature, he is confident of God's חֶסֶד, since he knows to approach God with the correct attitude, using terms such as יחל, קוה and בטח, which indicate his total dependence on God.

This element of reciprocity, of the petitioner's expression of a correct attitude in exchange for a restored relationship with God and his resumed חֶסֶד, corresponds to the conditional aspect of חֶסֶד. God's repeated forgiveness of man, and willingness to restore an operating relationship with man despite his sinful nature, however, must rely on something other than a system of absolute norms of human behaviour. It could require a unilateral, ongoing commitment, on God's part, to providing his חֶסֶד, enshrined in his own immutable covenant with his people. God's unwavering commitment to his people is ultimately focused on the unconditional attributes of חֶסֶד, again within the covenant relationship. This leads to the conclusion that the petitioner's confidence in God's חֶסֶד is ultimately based on the unconditional aspect of his חֶסֶד in the covenant relationship.

## BIBLIOGRAPHY

Aejmelaeus, A. "Function and Interpretation of כי in Biblical Hebrew," *JBL* 105 (1986) 193–209.

Aejmelaeus, A. and L. Schmidt. *The Traditional Prayer in the Psalms: Literarische Studien Zur Josephsgeschichte* (BZAW 167; Berlin: de Gruyter, 1986).

Beyerlin, W. *Die Rettung der Bedrängten in den Feindpsalmen der Einzelnen auf institutionelle Zusammenhänge untersucht* (FLANT 99; Gottingen: Vandenhoeck & Ruprecht, 1970).

—. *Werden und Wesen des 107. Psalms* (BZAW 153; Berlin: de Gruyter, 1979).

Bultmann, R. "ἐλπίς," *TDNT* 2.517–34.

Clark, G. R. *The Word "Hesed" in the Hebrew Bible* (JSOTSup 157; Sheffield: JSOT Press, 1993).

Classen, W. T. "Speaker-Oriented Function of kî in Biblical Hebrew," *JNSL* 1 (1983) 29–46.

Gerstenberger, E. S. *Der bittende Mensch: Bittritual und Klagelied des Einzelnen im Alten Testament* (WMANT 51; Neukirchen Vluyn: Neukirchener, 1980).

Gruber, M. I. "The Meaning of Biblical Parallelism: A Biblical Perspective," *Prooftexts* 13 (1993) 289–93.

Keel, O. *The Symbolism of the Biblical World: Ancient Near Eastern Iconography and the Book of Psalms* (London: SPCK, 1978).

Lofthouse, W. F., "Ḥen and Ḥesed in the Old Testament," *ZAW* 51 (1953) 29–35.

Masing, U. "Der Begriff *Hesed* im Alttestamentlichen Sprachgebrauch," in *Haristeria Iohanni Kōpp: Octogenario Oblata* [*Papers of the Estonian Theological Society in Exile* 7 (1954)] 27–63.

Mays, J. L. "A Question of Identity: The Threefold Hermeneutic of Psalmody," *Asbury Theological Journal* 46 (1991) 87–94.

—. *The Lord Reigns: A Theological Handbook to the Psalms* (Louisville: Westminster John Knox, 1994).

McKeating, H. "Divine Forgiveness in the Psalms," *SJT* 18 (1965) 69–83.

Melugin, R. F. *The Formation of Isaiah 40–55* (BZAW 141; Berlin: de Gruyter, 1976).

Miller, P. D., Jr. "In Praise and Thanksgiving," *Theology Today* 45 (1988-89), 181–88.

Petty, R. J. "Psalms 130, A Song of Sorrow," in J. C. Knight and L. A. Sinclair (eds.), *The Psalms and Other Studies on the Old Testament Presented to J. I. Hunt* (Nashotah, WI: Nashotah House Seminary, 1990).

Sakenfeld, K. D. *The Meaning of Hesed in the Hebrew Bible* (Missoula, MT: Scholar's Press, 1978).

—. *Faithfulness in Action: Loyalty in Biblical Perspective* (Philadelphia: Fortress, 1985).

Schmidt, H. "Gott und Mensch in Ps.130 (Formgeschichtliche Erwägungen)," *TZ* 22 (1966) 241–53.

Stoebe, H. J. "Die Bedeutung des Wortes HÄSÄD im Alten Testament," *VT* 2 (1952) 244–54.

Sylva, D. *Psalms and the Transformation of Stress: Poetic-Communal Interpretation and the Family* (Louvain, Peters, 1994).

Torrance, T. F. "The Doctrine of Grace in the Old Testament," *SJT* 1 (1948) 55–65.

Whitley, C. F. "The Semantic Range of Hesed," *Bib* 62 (1981) 518–26.

# PSALMS CONCERNING THE LITURGIES OF TEMPLE ENTRY

CRAIG C. BROYLES

## I. TEMPLE ENTRY LITURGIES: PSALMS 15 AND 24[1]

Psalms 15 and 24 (especially vv. 3-6) have long been recognized as liturgies for worshipers entering the temple. They, along with Isaiah 33:14b-16, follow a set pattern: (a) a double question of who may visit Yahweh's holy hill, (b) a reply consisting of the qualifications for worshipers, and (c) a promise. In the chart below underlined words denote parallel terminology. [2]

|  | *Psalm 15* | *Psalm 24:3-6* | *Isaiah 33:14b-16* |
|---|---|---|---|
| *Questions* | 2-fold מִי (v. 1) | 2-fold מִי | 2-fold מִי |
|  | שׁכן // גור (impf) | קום // עלה (impf) | גור // גור (impf) |
|  | הר קדשׁך // אהל | הר־יהוה // מקום קדשׁו | burning |
| *Qualifications* | Pos: 3 ptc: הלך, פעל, דבר (qal, v. 2) | Pos: 2 adj + bodily part (in construct) | Pos: 2 ptc: דבר, הלך (qal) |
|  | • integrity, *righteousness*, truth • with his heart | • innocent, pure | • *righteous* acts, equity |
|  | Neg: 3 לא + pf + ל/על (v. 3) • slander with tongue, do *evil* (רעה), reproach against neighbor | Neg: 2 לא + pf + ל • lift soul to emptiness • *swear* to deceit | Neg: 4 ptc of refusing participation • extortion, *bribes*, bloodshed, *evil* (רע) |
|  | Neg: *nip* ptc + rejected one, & Pos impf + Yhwh-fearers (v. 4a) |  |  |

---

[1] The ideas in this article have undergone their own pilgrimage. They were first presented at the annual meeting of the Society of Biblical Literature in 1992, and developed further in my *Psalms* (NIBC 11; Peabody, MA: Hendrickson, 1999).

[2] Abbreviations in this chart: Adj = adjective, Impf = imperfect, Neg = negative, Nip = Nip'al, Pf = perfect, Pos = positive, Ptc = participle. For a more detailed analysis of the poetics of Psalm 15 and the "different ways of reading or speaking the psalm *that are there in the text*," see Patrick D. Miller, Jr., "Poetic Ambiguity and Balance in Psalm XV," *VT* 29 (1979) 416–24.

| | | | |
|---|---|---|---|
| | He *swears* (Nip) & does not change (impf, v. 4b) | | |
| | Neg: 2 לֹא + pf (v. 5a) • giving with interest • taking *bribe* | | |
| *Promise* • Recipient | Ptc: doer of these things (v. 5b) | Ptc: seekers of Yhwh's face | Personal pronoun + 3 pron. suffixes |
| • Action | Impf • stability | Impf • receiving blessing & *righteousness* from saving God | Impf Nominal clause 2 *Nip* ptc • security and provision |
| *Bodily Parts* (3) | *heart* (לבב) tongue *eyes* | *hands* (כף) *heart* (לבב) soul | *hands* (כף) ears *eyes* |

*Questions.* The interrogative מִי is searching not for a particular individual but for a character description — in other words, "what kind of person?" The verbs indicate the notion of a pilgrimage journey (on גור cf. 61:5, and on שׁכן cf. 65:5). In Psalm 24 the verb עלה is particularly suited to the context of the ark's processional ascent up Yahweh's "hill" (cf. 2 Sam 6:2, 12, 15). The particular attribute of Yahweh associated with his locale (whether אהל,[3] הר, or מקום) is his holiness.

*Qualifications.* In Psalm 15 this question is posed to Yahweh himself, implying it seeks an oracle of instruction or "torah." The answer should thus be regarded as an oracle delivered by a priest or temple prophet. (Although v. 4 does refer to Yahweh in the third person, it is part of a phrase that identifies a certain class of persons, namely "Yahweh-fearers.") This "torah" lists ten qualifications. Three positive character descriptions (v. 2) are matched by three negative actions related primarily to speech (v. 3). The positive descriptions focus on integrity, and the negative statements on not abusing people verbally. There follow two qualifications (each with a *Nip'al* verb and

---

[3] אהל need not imply pre-temple origins for this expression. See, for example, 27:4-6, where it is collocated with היכל, and 61:5, 7, where it is collocated with a reference to the "king." Its use here suits the notion of sojourning and echoes the ancient custom of the traveler who comes under the protection of the host, whose "tent" he has entered. In 61:5 "Let me sojourn in your tent" is paralleled by "Let me take refuge in the hiding place of your wings." Cf. also Psalm 23.

an imperfect verb, v. 4) referring to the company one keeps and to keeping oaths. The final two are negative statements (v. 5a) referring to money and not abusing one's resources and position. Four of the ten qualifications concern speech: (1) "who speaks truth with his heart," (2) "he does not slander with his tongue," (3) "a reproach he does not take against his neighbor," and (4) "he swears to his friend and does not change" (reading לְהָרֵעַ with LXX).

The number ten invites comparison with the "Ten Words." Although four of these "words" concern relationship with God, all ten qualifications in Psalm 15 concern human relationships. The only "word" with which these ten qualifications clearly overlap is the ninth, which concerns "false testimony against your neighbor" (Exod 20:16; Deut 5:20). The temple entry torah of Psalm 15 thus lays special emphasis on one's speech in social relationships as the "litmus test" to indicate one's true "color." The qualifications are ethical, not sacral, in nature (contrast Deut 26:13-14). Nothing is said about festival attendance, proper sacrifices, prayers, etc. They focus on social or civil, not criminal, behavior. Entrants may not casually assume they pass the requirements simply because they are not part of society's criminal element; these verses reflect sins that any citizen might commit. They do not point to singular, heinous crimes but to matters of daily conversation. Third, these qualifications point to inner attitudes, not merely to what is observable and legally enforceable (only usury and bribery would qualify). They transcend what comes under the jurisdiction of the legal system and go to matters of the heart. Thus, self-examination under the scrutiny of conscience was required.

According to the contrast in v. 4a, one demonstrates loyalty to Yahweh by the company one keeps: "Yahweh-fearers" are honored but "a rejected one" is "despised." It will become evident in other psalms connected with temple entry that Yahweh's worshipers must endorse any judgment pronounced on the wicked.

In Psalm 24 the qualifications contain two positive descriptions of character, the first related to behavior ("clean hands") and the second to thoughts and motives ("pure heart"). These are matched by two negative descriptions related to speech: "who does not lift up my/his soul to what is empty and does not swear to deceit." If "my soul" in the Leningrad Codex is correct (לֹא־נָשָׂא לַשָּׁוְא נַפְשִׁי) and the third of the Ten Words serves as a parallel (לֹא תִשָּׂא אֶת־שֵׁם־יְהוָה אֱלֹהֶיךָ לַשָּׁוְא, Exod 20:7; Deut 5:11; cf. Ps 139:20, where נָשׂא לַשְּׁוא parallels "speaking," אמר), then this phrase certainly matches its own poetic parallel, which prohibits swearing to deceit (also cf. Amos 6:8; Jer 51:14). If "his soul" (נַפְשׁוֹ in many Hebrew manuscripts and most ancient versions) is correct, the closest parallels to the phrase, נשׂא נפשׁ לאל/ל, appear in the very next psalm, 25:1, and also in 86:4 and 143:8. In these contexts "lifting one's soul to Yahweh" occurs in the act of reciting the psalm. Thus, with either alternative this phrase in Psalm 24 refers to a speech act. These qualifications for entering the temple are obviously not meant to be an exhaustive checklist, but they are a teaching that makes clear what is essential by a contrast: one is to be "innocent" and "pure" and not characterized by "vanity" or "deceit."

*Promise*. In Psalm 15 "the doer of these things" is promised stability, not by virtue of one's behavior alone but because this person is one who may "reside on your holy hill" (v. 1). This image of stability derives from the sacred mountain, which symbolizes steadiness and order in the traditions of the ANE. This background is made explicit in Psalm 24. Stability is not an explicit promise in Psalm 24, but it is implied by the opening question, "Who may stand …?"

From Psalm 15 itself one might infer that behavior alone establishes one as a "doer of righteousness" and therefore admissible to holy ground. But Psalm 24 makes clear that entrants are also promised to receive "blessing … and righteousness from his saving God" (v. 5). Righteousness is both prerequisite and gift. While in the promise of Psalm 15 an entrant is identified as a "doer of these things," in Psalm 24 they are "seekers of the face of the God of Jacob" (v. 6; see *BHS*). For purposes of clear pedagogy these entry torahs present only two alternatives: (a) those who "fear Yahweh," seek him, and aspire to the character profile contained therein, and (b) those who "slander … the neighbor" and "swear to deceit." The issue is not moral perfection but the character profile one chooses to "honor" and the profile one chooses to "despise." Properly understood within their OT usage, תמים does not denote moral "blamelessness" but "wholeness, integrity"; צדק must be understood not in the context of moral codes but relationships; and אמת does not point to abstract, absolute "truth" but to being "true" to a relationship (i.e. fidelity).

*The context of the entry formula in Psalm 24.* While the entirety of Psalm 15 is comprised of the threefold pattern of the temple entry torah, Psalm 24 provides a wider context in which such a dialogue can

take place, namely that of a corporate procession into the temple. In
the opening two verses Yahweh lays claim to the world on the basis of
his founding it upon the "seas" and "rivers" (יָם and נָהָר). In the
psalm's closing sections (vv. 7-10) he is celebrated under a new name
("new" because it is apparently unknown to the respondents in vv. 8a,
10a), "the king of glory." The meaning and significance of these
claims becomes clearer once we recognize the cultural context of the
ANE and of Canaan in particular. Here divine kingship was achieved
by the deity's victory over the chaotic seas and Prince Yam-Judge
Nahar in particular.[4] The opening verses are thus no mere doctrinal
confession but a victory shout that "to Yahweh" — not to any other
claimant, especially Baal — "belongs the earth" (following the
Hebrew word order).

Verses 7-10 clearly contain a dialogue: those in the procession
commanding the gates to open (vv. 7, 8b, 9, 10b) and the gatekeepers
(vv. 8a, 10a). The picture of gates having to open so Yahweh may
enter requires some physical symbol of his presence. The most likely
candidate is the cherubim-ark. The name of God used as a "password"
through the gates, "Yahweh of hosts," is in fact the name invoked
over the ark (see especially 1 Sam 4:4; 2 Sam 6:2). The depiction of
Yahweh as "a warrior of war" also suits both the cherubim-ark
symbol (see especially Num 10:35; Josh 6:4-13) and the name
"Yahweh of (military) hosts."

Now what is the connection between Yahweh's victory procession
into his temple-palace and the entry torah? The most obvious is that
the liturgy of Psalm 24 stands at the point of entry into sacred
precincts. Moreover, as Yahweh has "established" world order over
the forces of chaos, so his worshipers must reflect similar order within
the social world. While vv. 3-6 describe Yahweh's worshipers, they
are also presented as a reflection of Yahweh himself. A deity may be
known by the kind of worshipers he/she desires. This conqueror over
chaos is the kind who would be king over a society based on truth.
Because Yahweh's temple or royal palace symbolized the
achievement of world order, only those who conform to Yahweh's
right order may enter his royal palace. This combination of ritual entry
into Yahweh's "holy place," the qualifications for worshipers, the
celebration of Yahweh's cosmic victory, and the title, "God of Jacob"

---

[4] See esp. the *Baal Epic*, 2.iv.2–32, in J. C. L. Gibson, *Canaanite Myths and
Legends* (Edinburgh: T. & T. Clark, 1977) 43–45.

(which is at home in Zion psalms, royal psalms, and festival psalms) shows how this single psalm ties together the religious, ethical, cosmic, and political dimensions of Israel's faith.

## II. PSALMS 5, 26, 28, 36, AND 52:
### THEIR MUTUAL AFFINITIES TO PSALMS 15 AND 24

Psalms 5, 26, 28, 36, and 52 share several affinities with each other and with Psalms 15 and 24. Although each may not be unique to these psalms, this particular constellation of features does point to a special grouping.

- *No lament.* None of these psalms contains a typical lament. There is no "I" lament concerning the speaker's affliction, nor is there a "you" or "God" lament offering complaint.
- *Character description of the wicked.* While there are references to the wicked, and even sometimes to "my enemies," there is no formal "they" or "foe" lament decrying what opponents do to the speaker and his group. There is no explicit mention of threat directed to the speaker and no lament on behalf of victims. The wicked are described simply in terms of their character, especially their deceitful speech, with the use of common terminology.[5]
- *Temple setting.* Unlike most laments of the individual, each psalm makes explicit reference to the temple and implies the speaker is present there.
- *Speaker = liturgist.* All of these psalms contain hints that the speaking "I" is not a lone individual in a special emergency, but one who speaks on behalf of the general group of worshipers in the regular liturgy.
- *Affinities to temple entry liturgy.* These psalms contain affinities to Psalms 15 and 24, including indications of judgment where there is a parting of the ways: the "righteous" who may enter the temple and the "wicked" who may not and who will thus suffer the consequences.

In addition, several psalms appear to contain prophetic oracles (see the discussion below on 15:2-5; 28:5; 36:2-5; 52:3-7).

---

[5] In these profiles the prevailing image is that of the רשע, not the איב. See further O. Keel, *Feinde und Gottesleugner* (SBM 7; Stuttgart: Katholisches Bibelwerk, 1969).

## PSALM 5

*Previous Interpretations.* Most commentators have read this psalm as a lament of the individual. Some, including Kraus, have specified it further as "a psalm of the falsely accused," where the speaker seeks acquittal at Yahweh's sacral court.[6] This interpretation looks plausible because the chief fault of the wicked lies in their speech: they are "lying speakers" and are characterized as people of "deceit" (v. 7). Moreover, "Nothing in their mouth can be substantiated; their inward part is destruction" (v. 10a).

*Features shared by Psalms 5, 26, 28, 36, and 52*

*1. The Absence of Lament and 2. The Profile of the Wicked*

The only verse that might be formally called a lament is v. 10, which concerns the opponents. But the speaker is not singled out for attack, nor is there any reference to victims. A literal translation of v. 10b reveals that their words are deceitful and destructive for reasons other than false accusation: "their throat is an open grave; their tongues they make smooth (יַחֲלִיקוּן)" — an OT idiom for flattery (cf. 12:3-4; 36:3). Here is painted the graphic picture of someone being enticed by their flattering speech and slipping on their smooth tongue into their grave-like throat. They are likened to a slippery chasm to Sheol. In light of this image, their words are enticing and tempting,

---

[6] See Hans-Joachim Kraus's *Psalms 1–59: A Commentary* (Minneapolis: Augsburg, 1988) 153–58, and notably Walter Beyerlin, *Die Rettung der Bedrängten in den Feindpsalmen der Einzelnen auf institutionelle Zusammenhänge untersucht* (FRLANT 99; Göttingen: Vandenhoeck & Ruprecht, 1970) 90–95. While this theory may account for some verses in some psalms (esp. Psalms 7 and 17), it has its limitations. First, although texts such as Deut 17:8-13 and 1 Kgs 8:31-32 may imply there were "psalms of the accused," the ones we have in the Psalter are decidedly "psalms of the *falsely* accused." The speaker's innocence and his accusers' guilt are presumed. While 1 Kgs 8:31–32 refers to an oath, the only psalmic verses that come close to this description are 7:3-5. But the rest of the psalm is hardly an objective formulary for ritual interrogation — it clearly presupposes the innocence of the speaker and in effect grants him acquittal. Second, the proposed setting of a ritual of divine judgment for the accused hardly accounts for the content and development of Psalms 5, 26, 28, 36, and 52. Third, is it reasonable to think that texts written for accused criminals became meditative poetry foundational to Israel's worship and piety? It seems strange that these texts would have migrated from the experiences of an unfortunate few to the experiences of all God's people, and from the juridical sphere to the religious.

not accusatory. Kraus mentions "dangerous flattery that brings people down to ruin" and refers to Prov 2:16; 7:5; 28:23 for support.[7] But the first two passages speak of the "seductive words" of the adulteress, which are dangerous because the naive may be tempted, not because these words accuse anyone. And Prov 28:23 contrasts flattery with rebuke, which is a form of accusation. Kraus then characterizes these wicked in Psalm 5 as "slanderers," but this is precisely how the psalmist does not characterize them. Kraus's "false accusation" interpretation strains the text at another point. In his view vv. 2-4 show us that "we should have to imagine that early in the morning the petitioner brought an offering that accompanied his prayers and pleas for a divine verdict." The psalmist then "is on the lookout" and "waits," expecting that a "דבר of Yahweh ... sent through the mouth of the priest, will be transmitted to him."[8] Kraus must, therefore, see a hiatus between this and the following section. He strangely interprets vv. 5-8 as the assurance of being heard:

> The assurance of being heard is now won by the petitioner from the fact that the wicked are not allowed to appear before Yahweh, whereas he himself, the petitioner, has access to the sanctuary.[9]

But the כי introducing vv. 5-8 implies that it is connected — without interruption — to vv. 2-4.

Although vv. 5-7 describe the "workers of iniquity," they cannot be considered a lament. As phrased, they are a confession about God ("you are not a God who ..."). He is the principal subject of the verbs. The wicked are given mention simply as a foil to describe God in terms of the kind of company he cannot tolerate. God's character is presented as the antithesis of the wicked. In vv. 10-11 the reason why God should "banish" these "smooth-talkers" is, "for they have rebelled against you" (v. 11). The wicked are presented primarily as opponents of God.

The wicked also serve as a foil for the speaker. In contrast to the "boastful" who would dare "take their *stand* before your eyes" (v. 6), the speaker (וַאֲנִי) would enter this presence "in the abundance of your loyalty" (חסד) and "*bow down* ... in fear of you" (v. 8). Reference is indeed made to "my lurkers" (or "my watchers," שׁוֹרְרָי, v. 9).[10] While

---

[7] Kraus, *Psalms 1–59*, 156.

[8] Ibid., 154.

[9] Ibid., 155.

[10] שׁוֹרְרָי is probably a *Polel* participle derived from שׁור. The verb's negative

the psalm clearly identifies them as *my* enemies, they are not necessarily *personal* enemies. The next verse, as explained above, merely describes their tempting and consequent destructive behavior, not their personal attacks. They are smooth-talkers lurking with enticing words to lure one away from following Yahweh's "way" (v. 9) and into "an open grave." This reference to "my lurkers" surfaces in a petition that seeks simply to avoid their tempting influence ("Lead me in your righteousness because of my lurkers; make straight your way before me"). The petition for their indictment and banishment is grounded in their rebellion against Yahweh, not their attacks on the speaker (v. 11). When protection is petitioned, it is done on behalf of "all who take refuge in you" (v. 12), not the speaker alone.

In light of the above, the wicked do pose a threat, not by overt, personal attack but by tempting the righteous. And the psalm nowhere contains a lament concerning how they victimize others. They are given mention as those who contrast with God, and thus "cannot take their stand before your eyes," and as those who contrast with the speaker in terms of the posture they assume before that presence. Thus, the psalm hinges on this issue: given God's character, who is permitted to "enter (בוא) your house" (v. 8)?

### 3. Temple Setting

As already noted above, the speaker locates himself at the temple: "I enter your house; I bow down toward your holy temple" (אָבוֹא בֵיתֶךָ אֶשְׁתַּחֲוֶה אֶל־הֵיכַל־קָדְשְׁךָ, v. 8). Rendering the Hebrew imperfect verbs in the present and thus understanding these ritual actions as attending the singing of the psalm, not vowing future action, is confirmed by other allusions within the psalm. The speaker contrasts himself with those who do "evil," which "may not sojourn with you" (לֹא יְגֻרְךָ רָע, v. 5), that is, at Yahweh's sacred dwelling (cf. Yahweh, "who may sojourn [יָגוּר] ... on your holy [קָדְשֶׁךָ] hill?," 15:1). They characteristically "cannot take their stand before your eyes" (עֵינֶיךָ לֹא־יִתְיַצְּבוּ ... לְנֶגֶד, v. 6). And, as argued below, the closing description of "all those who take refuge in you" (v. 12) and the elliptical petition,

---

connotation, "to watch stealthily, lie in ambush," is evidenced in Jer 5:26; Hos 13:7 (see BDB, 1003–1004). Because the phrase, לְמַעַן שׁוֹרְרָי, appears to disturb the verse's metrical balance (otherwise 3 + 3), it would be tempting simply to regard this solitary reference to personal enemies as a later gloss. But the psalm does not display a clear, regular metrical pattern.

"and may you spread (your wings?) over them" (וְתָסֵךְ עָלֵימוֹ), make best sense in light of temple symbolism.[11]

## 4. Representative Speaker

Although vv. 2-4, 8-9 speak in the language of "I," vv. 5-7, 10-13 are devoted to general groups, "doers of iniquity" and "the righteous." Strictly speaking, this is not a psalm of the individual merely. The speaker may, in fact, be a representative on behalf of "the righteous."[12]

## 5. Parallels with Psalms 15, 24, and Other Psalms of Temple Entry

This psalm's connection to the liturgy of temple entry is supported by the following parallels with Psalms 15 and 24.

| | |
|---|---|
| (5:8) הֵיכַל־קׇדְשֶׁךָ<br>your *holy* temple | (15:1) בְּאׇהֳלֶךָ // בְּהַר קׇדְשֶׁךָ<br>on your *holy* hill // in your tabernacle |
| | (24:3) בְּהַר־יְהוָה // בִּמְקוֹם קׇדְשׁוֹ<br>in your *holy* place // on Yahweh's hill |
| (5:5) לֹא יְגֻרְךָ רָע<br>Evil may not *sojourn* with you | (15:1) מִי־יָגוּר בְּאׇהֳלֶךָ<br>Who may *sojourn* in your tabernacle? |
| (5:6) לֹא־יִתְיַצְּבוּ הוֹלְלִים לְנֶגֶד עֵינֶיךָ<br>The arrogant may not *stand* before<br>your eyes | (24:3) וּמִי־יָקוּם בִּמְקוֹם קׇדְשׁוֹ<br>And who may *stand* in your holy place? |
| (5:6) פֹּעֲלֵי אָוֶן<br>*doer*s of trouble | (15:2) פֹּעֵל צֶדֶק<br>a *doer* of righteousness |
| (5:7) תְּאַבֵּד דֹּבְרֵי כָזָב<br>You destroy *speaker*s (Qal ptc)[13]<br>of a lie | (15:2) וְדֹבֵר אֱמֶת בִּלְבָבוֹ<br>and a *speaker* (Qal ptc) of truth<br>in his heart |

---

[11] It is possible the elliptical phrase, בֹּקֶר אֶעֱרׇךְ־לְךָ, "at morning I will arrange/set out to you," indicates ritual sacrifice (Lev 1:8-9, 12; 1 Kgs 18:33).

[12] Because the subjects of the psalm appear in such distinct sections ("I" in 2-4 and 8-9, God vs. the wicked in 5-7 and 10-11, and the "righteous" in 12-13), it is possible that different speakers performed this liturgy. The "I" sections may be in the mouth of a liturgist speaking on behalf of pilgrims. The sections referring to corporate groups, the wicked and the righteous, may be in the mouth of a priest. This scenario, though it cannot be proven, certainly suits the alternation of topics treated in the psalm, as described above.

[13] Although דבר as a verb usually appears in the *Pi'el* stem, here in Pss 5:7; 15:2 and also 28:3 (see below) it appears as a *Qal* participle.

| | |
|---|---|
| (5:7) אישׁ־דמים וּמִרְמָה<br>a man of blood and *deceit* | (24:4) ולא נשבע לְמִרְמָה<br>and he does not swear to *deceit* |
| | (36:4) דברי־פיו אָון וּמִרְמָה<br>the words of his mouth are trouble and *deceit* |
| | (52:6) לָשׁוֹן מִרְמָה<br>a tongue of *deceit* |
| (5:13) כי־אתה תברך צַדִּיק יהוה<br>For you *bless* the *righteous*, Yahweh | (24:5) ישׂא בְרָכָה מאת יהוה וּצְדָקָה<br>מאלהי ישׁעו<br>He will receive *blessing* from Yahweh, and *righteousness* from his saving God. |
| | (15:2) פעל צֶדֶק<br>a doer of *righteousness* |

If we regard Psalms 15 and 24 as typical entrance liturgies and so combine them to gain a fuller picture of their typical expressions, we can see a clear correspondence with the confession of Ps 5:5-7.

| *Psalms 15 and 24* | *Psalm 5* |
|---|---|
| Setting: "your holy hill/tabernacle" and "his holy place" (15:1; 24:3) | "your holy temple" (v. 8) |
| "Who may sojourn (גּוּר) in your tent?" (15:1) | "Evil may not sojourn (גּוּר) with you" (v. 5). |
| "And who may stand in your holy place?" (24:3) | "Boasters may not take their stand before your sight" (v. 6). |
| "a doer (פעל) of righteousness" (15:2) | "doers (פעל) of iniquity" (v. 6) |
| "he who speaks (דּבֶר) the truth with his heart" (15:2) | "You destroy those who speak (דּבֶר) a lie" (v. 7). |
| "He does not swear deceitfully (מרמה)" (24:4). | "a man of blood and deceit (מרמה)" (v. 7) |
| "A doer of righteousness" (15:2) "will receive blessing from Yahweh" (24:5). | "You bless the righteous, Yahweh" (v. 13). |

The descriptions of the wicked, who may not sojourn with Yahweh, in Psalm 5 mirror in reverse the descriptions of the righteous, who may sojourn in his tent, in Psalms 15 and 24. Thus, Psalm 5 probably belongs to the same "rite of passage" as Psalms 15 and 24. They are the voice of the priests, and Psalm 5 contains the confessional response of pilgrims. As the description of the "doer of righteous" in Psalms 15 and 24 does not refer to a particular person or group but portrays a character profile, so the description of the "doers of iniquity" in Psalm 5 is also probably a character profile. Thus, their mention in Psalm 5 probably does not stem from the actual circumstances of the speaker but from the entry liturgy itself. Psalm 5 was probably not a special psalm designed for individuals who fell into the particular circumstances of false accusation; rather it was a regular liturgy for all entrants into Yahweh's presence. Thus, reference is made to their speech, not because of false accusation, but because this was the key "litmus test" for temple entry.

## 6. Thematic Coherence and Exposition as a Psalm of Temple Entry

In the language common to the individual laments, the opening section begins with petitions for Yahweh to hear (vv. 2-4). While the title, "my God," is typical of individual prayers, the title, "my king" (v. 3), is not. Elsewhere in the Psalms it appears in 44:5 (a corporate lament), 68:25 (a corporate hymn), and 74:12 (a corporate lament). Ps 84:4 (a psalm of pilgrimage to Yahweh's house on Zion) uses the same word pair, "my king and my God." Although the "I" form predominates in this psalm, the psalm sets the speaker in a representative role: his petition that God "hear *my* prayer" is followed immediately by one that he "behold *our* shield" (vv. 9-10).[14] In Psalm 5 addressing God as "my king" is consistent with the later confession that the speaker is entering Yahweh's "temple" or "palace" (הֵיכָל, v. 8). It also makes sense if we are correct in reading Psalm 5 as a response to an entry liturgy such as Psalm 24, which repeatedly acclaims Yahweh with the title, "king of glory" (vv. 7-10).

Verses 5-7 describe the divine addressee of these petitions for a hearing. Yahweh is characterized, even praised, by his mirror opposite, the kind of company denied an audience with him. Emphasis is given to face-to-face encounter ("sojourn *with you*," "in front of your eyes") and to Yahweh's emotional reaction ("does not delight in," "you hate," "you abhor"). The characteristics contrary to Yahweh are wickedness (רֶשַׁע, רָע, אָוֶן), boasting (הוֹלְלִים), deceit (מִרְמָה, כָּזָב), and violence (אִישׁ־דָּמִים). By implication Yahweh does delight in

---

[14] Psalm 84:12, "those who walk with integrity," also echoes the qualifications for temple entry (15:2; 26:1, 11).

righteousness, truth, and harmony (cf. 15:2-3).

The speaker then contrasts his entry (בוֹא, v. 8) into Yahweh's house with those denied access by referring to his attitude ("in fear of you") and basis of entry ("in the abundance of your loyalty" vs. "boasting") and to his posture ("bowing down" vs. "taking one's stand"). In this light, it is likely that the petitions, "Lead me in(to) your right-eousness" and "make straight your way before me," are not general petitions for guidance but for direct admittance into Yahweh's royal court (v. 9). Yahweh's "righteousness" is here used in the same sense as found in 24:5 ("he will receive ... righteousness from his saving God"). It is not presented as a threat to the worshiper's entry into Yahweh's "holy palace" (הֵיכַל־קָדְשֶׁךָ), as though it indicated retributive righteousness, rather it ensures his entry, thus indicating a kind of saving righteousness.

At first glance, the indictment of the wicked (v. 10) and the petition for a verdict and punishment (v. 11) seem to make little sense as a response to the entry liturgies of Psalms 15 and 24. But we must recall that the qualification for entry, "despised in his eyes is a rejected one, but fearers of Yahweh he honors" (15:4), entails an endorsement of Yahweh's rejection of and judgment on those who are denied entry into Yahweh's courts. As the speaker enters Yahweh's house "in the abundance of your loyalty" (בְּרֹב חַסְדְּךָ, v. 8), so the wicked are to be "banished" (הַדִּיחֵמוֹ) "in the abundance of their transgressions" (בְּרֹב פִּשְׁעֵיהֶם, v. 11), presumably from the same house.

As vv. 5-7, 10-11, have concerned the wicked in general, and not the speaker's personal enemies, so the closing section (vv. 12-13) concerns "*all* who take refuge in you." Although not apparent initially, by alluding to temple symbolism it petitions and confesses that they should have access to and enjoy the benefits of entering the temple, namely refuge, blessing, and joyful praise. In the petition, וְתָסֵךְ עָלֵימוֹ, the verb סכך is elsewhere frequently used in connection with the cherubim, whose wings "cover" the ark of the covenant (Exod 25:20; 37:9; 1 Kgs 8:7; 1 Chr 28:18; cf. Ezek 28:14, 16). Psalm 91:4 illustrates how the symbol of the protective cherubim became a metaphor for Yahweh himself: his feathers "cover" (סכך) the one who "takes refuge" (חסה) under his wings. Also like 91:4, Ps 5:13 shifts to a military metaphor for God: "as with a shield (both passages use צִנָּה) you surround him with favor." The symbol of the cherubim-chariot is in part a military image where "Yahweh of (the military) hosts" presides as warrior. In the Psalms "refuge" (חסה) is frequently taken specifically under Yahweh's "wings" (17:7-8; 36:8; 57:2; 61:5) located at his house (36:9; 61:5). (Cf. also 63:8, where "singing for joy," רנן, which also appears in 5:12, occurs under Yahweh's "wings.")

## PSALM 26

*Previous Interpretations.* Psalm 26, like Psalm 5, is generally regarded as an individual lament. Kraus and Beyerlin classify it more specifically among the "psalms of the falsely accused."[15]

*Features shared by Psalms 5, 26, 28, 36, and 52*

*1. The Absence of Lament and 2. The Profile of the Wicked*

What is the speaker's relation to the opponents? The psalm makes no reference to the wicked posing a personal threat directed to the speaker. They are mentioned twice. First, the worshiper confesses his rejection of evil company (vv. 4-5), and more specifically of "sitting" (ישב as an inclusio, vv. 4a, 5b) with them and "entering" (בוא) "an assembly (קהל) of evildoers." This serves as a contrast to the "assemblies" (מקהלים, v. 12) in which Yahweh is worshiped. Second, the worshiper petitions, "Do not take my soul away with sinners" (v. 9).

In verses preceding and following it becomes apparent that the place from which he does not want to be removed is Yahweh's "house" (v. 8, "assemblies" in v. 12). As phrased, the petition is not against the wicked, as though they have wronged the petitioner. Their judgment appears to be a given. Rather, the petition seeks the petitioner's welfare that he be spared their imminent judgment. The subsequent petitions are also for his sake: "redeem me and be gracious to me" (v. 11b).

While it is possible that the "evil scheme" and "bribes" mentioned in v. 10 could be used against the worshiper himself, this is unlikely because of how the preceding petition is phrased. "Do not take my soul away with sinners" reflects a concern that the worshiper might be misperceived as being in company with the wicked. This would certainly be an odd phrasing if they were obviously contrary parties as accusers versus the accused. (Further on the mention of "bribes," see below.) In light of these observations, the wicked are presented as a

---

[15] Kraus, *Psalms 1–59*, 325–29; and Beyerlin, *Die Rettung der Bedrängten*, 117–22.

foil to evidence the speaker's loyalty to Yahweh's house, saying in effect, "in contrast to entering their assemblies I choose to enter Yahweh's."

### 3. Temple Setting

Not only are there explicit references to Yahweh's "house"[16] and "assemblies" (8, 12), there are also clear references to rites performed by the speaker at the temple. The "altar" (v. 6) lies at "the entrance" (פתח) to the sanctuary (Lev 1:5).[17] The symbolic rite of "washing hands in innocence" (Ps 26:6) also probably occurred at its entry. According to O. Keel, a "model of a temple from Gezer shows two fonts of holy water, one at either side of the entrance."[18] Once these entry rites have been performed, the speaker can then "make heard a voice of thanksgiving" and "recount all your wonders" (v. 7). In addition, as noted above, the psalm contains an implicit contrast between Yahweh's "assemblies" (v. 12) and "an assembly of evil-oers" (v. 5), specifically mentioned the act of "entering" (בוא). This contrast suggests the evildoers' assembly is cultic in nature.

### 4. Representative Speaker

Nothing in the psalm itself suggests that the speaker is in immediate crisis. While it is possible the psalm may have been intended for use by a lone individual, we should note that the wicked are described generically and as a cultic group. It is therefore possible that the opposing "I" may speak on behalf of individuals in a congregation.

---

[16] It is interesting that one of the terms denoting Yahweh's sanctuary alludes to the ancient tradition of the "tabernacle" (משכן), as does Ps 15:1, which refers to Yahweh's "tent" (אהל, also probably 52:7).

[17] Paul G. Mosca argues that this act of "processing about the altar" (v. 6) was the sole prerogative of priests ("Psalm 26: Poetic Structure and the Form-Critical Task," *CBQ* 47 [1985] 230–36); cf. 2 Kgs 12:10. Even so, this rite would still be performed on behalf of the congregation, not for the priest alone. The altar was in clear view of "all the assembly of Israel" (1 Kgs 8:22). On the other hand, the Chronicler's relocation of Joash's money chest, from "beside the altar on the right as one enters the house of Yahweh" (2 Kgs 12:10) to "outside at the gate of the house of Yahweh" (2 Chr 24:8), implies that while postexilic practice denied the laity access to the inner court of the altar, pre-exilic practice admitted them. See Raymond B. Dillard, *2 Chronicles* (WBC 15; Dallas: Word, 1998) 191; H. G. M. Williamson, *1 and 2 Chronicles* (NCB; Grand Rapids: Eerdmans, 1982) 321.

[18] *The Symbolism of the Biblical World: Ancient Near Eastern Iconography and the Book of Psalms* (London: SPCK, 1978) 123, 127, 395.

## 5. Parallels with Psalms 15, 24, and Other Psalms of Temple Entry

| Psalm 26 | Psalm 15 / 24 |
|---|---|
| (26:1) כי־אני בתמי הלכתי<br>For I in my *integrity* have *walked*<br>(26:11) ואני בתמי אלך<br>But I in my *integrity walk* | (15:2) הולך תמים<br>who *walks* with *integrity* |
| (26:2, Qere) צרפה כליותי ולבי<br>Test my kidneys and my *heart*<br>(26:3) והתהלכתי באמתך<br>And I walk in your *truth* | (15:2) ודבר אמת בלבבו<br>and speaks *truth* in his *heart*<br>(24:4) ובר־לבב<br>and pure of *heart* |
| (26:4) לא־ישבתי עם־מתי־שוא ועם<br>נעלמים לא אבוא<br>I have not sat with men of *vanity*,<br>and with the secretive I do not enter. | (24:4, emended[19]) לא־נשא לשוא נפשו<br>He has not lifted to *vanity* his soul |
| (26:6) ארחץ בנקיון כפי ואסבבה<br>את־מזבחך יהוה<br>I wash in *innocence* my *hands*,<br>and I go about your altar, Yahweh.[20] | (24:4) נקי כפים<br>*innocent* of hands |
| (26:8) יהוה אהבתי מעון ביתך ומקום<br>משכן כבודך<br>ahweh, I love the dwelling of your house, and<br>the *place* of the *tent* of your *glory*. | (24:7-10) מלך הכבוד<br>the king of *glory*<br>(24:3) ומי־יקום במקום קדשו<br>And who may stand in his holy *place*?<br>(15:1) מי־ישכן בהר קדשך<br>Who may *tent* on your holy hill? |
| (26:10) אשר־בידיהם זמה וימינם מלאה שחד<br><br>in whose hands are a scheme,<br>and whose right hand is full of *bribes*. | (15:5) כספו לא־נתן בנשך ושחד על־נקי<br>לא לקח<br>His money he does not give with<br>interest, a *bribe* against the innocent<br>he does not take. |
| ...tability of the worshiper:<br>(26:12) רגלי עמדה במישור במקהלים<br>אברך יהוה:<br>My feet stand in a level place,<br>and in the assemblies I bless Yahweh. | (15:5) עשה־אלה לא ימוט לעולם<br>The doer of these things will never<br>totter. |

---

[19] Each text marked "emended" generally follows the text-critical apparatus in *BHS*. In most every case the change has no bearing on the adduced parallel.

[20] In the Psalms the terms נקיון/נקי and כף ("innocent" and "hand") occur only at these two references and in 73:13 (on which see below).

Psalm 26 appears to endorse what Psalms 15 and 24 prescribe as qualifications for temple entry. In this light we begin to grasp the importance of "walking in integrity," of "truth" and the "heart," of avoiding "vanity," of "innocent hands," and of the "place of the tent of your glory." We may also understand why "bribes" are specially mentioned here (in the Psalms שֹׁחַד appears only in these two passages). These parallels may also explain why attention is given to the motif of stability at the psalm's close.

| | |
|---|---|
| (26:5) שָׂנֵאתִי קְהַל מְרֵעִים וְעִם־רְשָׁעִים לֹא אֵשֵׁב | (5:6) שָׂנֵאתָ כָּל־פֹּעֲלֵי אָוֶן |
| I *hate* the assembly of the evil, and with the wicked I do not sit. | You *hate* all doers of trouble. |
| (26:9) אַנְשֵׁי דָמִים | (5:7) אִישׁ־דָּמִים |
| *men of blood* | a *man of blood* |
| (26:8) יהוה אהבתי מעון בֵּיתֶךָ וּמְקוֹם מִשְׁכַּן כְּבוֹדֶךָ: | (5:8) ואני ברב חסדך אבוא בֵיתֶךָ אשתחוה אל־הֵיכַל־קָדְשְׁךָ ביראתך: |
| Yahweh, I love the dwelling of *your house*, and the place of the *tent of your glory*. | But I in the abundance of your loyalty enter *your house*; I bow down toward *your holy temple* in your fear. |

Judgment that distinguishes the fates of the speaker and the wicked:

"Judge me" (26:1)

"Don't take me away with sinners" (26:9)

"Declare them guilty" (5:11)

"Lead me into your righteousness" (5:9)

"Banish them" (5:11)

The parallels with Psalm 5 are also striking: the importance of "hating" evil and of confessing one's affinity to Yahweh's house, the image of bloodthirsty men, and a judgment that distinguishes the fates of the speaker and the wicked. Thus, the concern for the wicked stems not from the supposed circumstances of the psalmist but from the entry liturgy itself. It was composed not for lone individuals who happen to have been accused falsely but for any pilgrim as a response to the entry instruction ("torah") found in Psalms 15 and 24.[21]

---

[21] E. Vogt has also argued that this psalm is not a lament but a "pilgrim prayer" connected with the liturgies of Psalms 15 and 24 ("Psalm 26, ein Pilgergebet," *Bib* 43 (1962) 328–37. Peter Craigie follows his interpretation (*Psalms 1–50* [WBC 19; Waco, TX: Word, 1983] 224).

·

## 6. Thematic Coherence and Exposition as a Psalm of Temple Entry

Psalm 26 opens with petitions that Yahweh recognize the worshiper's integrity and trust. He declares his loyalty to Yahweh's congregation by disclaiming associations with the evildoers' assembly and by affirming his love for Yahweh's house. He then petitions Yahweh to exempt him from their impending judgment. In closing he vows praise to God, thus implying other psalms followed in the larger liturgy. Key terms help to interlock the psalm's sections. The claim of "walking in integrity" (vv. 1, 11) underlies the two petition sections related to judgment (vv. 1-3 and 9-11). And references to "assemblies" and to Yahweh's "praise" tie together the confession of trust (vv. 4-8) and the vow of praise (v. 12).

Although the opening petition, "judge me" (שָׁפְטֵנִי) also appears in a psalm reflecting false accusation (7:9; cf. 35:24), it also makes good sense as a request to establish that the speaker does "walk with integrity" and "in truth" (see the parallels with Psalms 15 and 24 above), thus meeting the qualifications to "stand in his holy place" (24:3; cf. 15:1). The scope of Yahweh's examination goes to "my kidneys (כִלְיוֹתַי) and my heart" (v. 2), not merely to his conduct and words. Indeed, the qualifications for temple entry go to matters of the "heart" (15:2; 24:4). As noted above, Yahweh's judgment of sinners is presupposed in v. 9, so now the speaker petitions he be judged and found to be distinguished from them.

The speaker affirms the divine attribute that defines his goal ("your loyalty is before my eyes") and process ("I walk in your fidelity," v. 3). The following verses unpack these general claims in specific terms of ritual actions (vv. 4-8). The petition, "Do not take my soul away with sinners," reflects the fear of the "holy," noted in Pss 15:1 and 24:3.

Supporting the psalm's petitions (vv. 1-2, 9) is a contrast of behaviors. Those described in verses 4-8 are primarily religious, and those mentioned in verses 9-10 are social, focusing especially on the treatment of innocent people. As the entry liturgy of Psalm 15 prescribes that entrants "despise" vile company and "honor" fearers of Yahweh (v. 4), so in this psalm the worshiper must confess that he "hates the assembly of evildoers" (v. 5) and that he "loves the habitation of your house" (v. 8). The character profiles of the righteous and the wicked are constructed as mirror opposites: contrasting the worshiper's "hands" washed "in innocence" (v. 6, note also the "innocent hands" of 24:4) are those of sinners which are full of "evil schemes" and "bribes" (so 15:5).

The psalm closes with echoes from its beginning. He vows, "I, in my integrity, (will) walk" (Heb. imperfect, v. 11; the identical phrase though with the Heb. perfect in v. 1). As "I do not slip" because "in Yahweh I have trusted" (v. 1), so now "my foot stands on level ground" because "I bless Yahweh" (v. 12). This affirmation of stability matches the promise closing Psalm 15: "The doer of these things will never totter."

## PSALM 28

*Previous Interpretations.* The opening verse may be suggestive of sickness,[22] but this hypothesis does not account for the contents of the psalm, whose central section (vv. 3-5) concerns the destiny of the wicked. And the closing reference to the "salvation" of God's "anointed" and his "people" would seem out of place in a psalm focused on an individual's restoration. Kraus, unlike Beyerlin in this case, interprets this psalm as another one reflecting "a person who is falsely persecuted."[23]

*Features shared by Psalms 5, 26, 28, 36, and 52*

*1. The Absence of Lament and 2. The Profile of the Wicked*

The psalm lacks any complaint against God or any lament of personal anguish (an "I"-lament). There are statements describing the wicked, but they threaten society in general, not the speaker in particular: "those who speak peace with their neighbors but have evil in their hearts" (v. 3). The other indictment against them lies not in their abuse of the psalmist or even of the righteous in general but their disregard of "Yahweh's works" (v. 5). The petition, "Do not drag me away with the wicked" (v. 3), seeks to guard against the misperception that the speaker be seen as party with them. Thus, the supposition that they are personal accusers does not fit. The metaphor of protection, "my strength and my shield" (v. 7), may imply the wicked pose a threat to the speaker, but we should note that the next metaphor, "a stronghold of deliverances" is applied to the "anointed" and the "people" (reading לְעַמּוֹ with *BHS*) in general (v. 8). Thus, the

---

[22] See, e.g. Sigmund Mowinckel, *The Psalms in Israel's Worship* (2 vols., Oxford: Blackwell, 1962) 1.74; Mitchell Dahood, *Psalms I* (AB 16; Garden City, NY: Doubleday, 1966) 172.

[23] Kraus, *Psalms 1–59*, 340; Beyerlin, *Die Rettung der Bedrängten*, 11.

opponents are a societal threat, not an individual one. Moreover, these affirmations appear only after the speaker feels assured of being heard.

The petition of v. 3, like that in 26:9, reckons that judgment on the wicked is a given. What is at issue is their sentencing. Verse 4 thus petitions that their punishment should be commensurate with their crime.

### 3. Temple Setting and 4. Representative Speaker

The mention of "raising hands to your holy inner sanctuary" (i.e. not simply the outer building or היכל but its innermost room, the דביר, v. 2) places the speaker in close proximity to the sanctuary. This would be an odd word choice if hands were raised towards the temple from a remote location.

The psalm contains several shifts that are best explained by a liturgical setting. First, the shift from addressing Yahweh directly (vv. 1-4, 9) to referring to him in the third person (vv. 5-8) may imply that the psalm consists not merely of prayer but also of testimony to a congregation. Second, the shift from "Hear the voice of my supplications" (v. 2) to "he has heard the voice of my supplications" (v. 6) might best be explained by an intervening oracle of salvation. In fact, verse 5 may have served this very purpose. We should note that its meter is distinct and that the prophetic indictment in Isa 5:12 is very similar: "Yahweh's work (פעל) they do not behold and the work of his hands (מעשה ידיו) they do not see." And the word pair, to "tear down" and "build," is a favorite of the prophet Jeremiah (1:10; 24:6; 31:28; 42:10; 45:4). Third, the last two verses — without transition — shift to corporate interests. In v. 7 the speaker confesses Yahweh as "my strength and my shield," but in the next verse as the "strength" and "stronghold of deliverances" for his people and king.

The closing verse is an intercession for the people. In light of these observations, it is possible Psalm 26 was intoned by a variety of voices: a liturgist representing the individual members of the congregation offers the opening petitions (vv. 1-4), a prophet pro-nounces an oracle (v. 5), the liturgist sings the assurance of being heard and praises (vv. 6-7), and a priest offers corporate praises and a closing intercession (vv. 8-9).

## 5. *Parallels with Psalms 15, 24, and Other Psalms of Temple Entry.*

פַּעֲלֵי אָוֶן (28:3)
*doers* of iniquity
תֶּן־לָהֶם כְּפָעֳלָם וּכְרֹעַ מַעַלְלֵיהֶם (28:4)
כְּמַעֲשֵׂה יְדֵיהֶם תֵּן לָהֶם הָשֵׁב גְּמוּלָם לָהֶם:
Give to them according to their *action*,
according to the evil of their deeds.
according to the *work* of their hands give
to them, return their reward to them.

וּפֹעַל צֶדֶק ... עֹשֵׂה־אֵלֶּה (15:2, 5)
and a *doer* of righteousness ... he who
*does* these things

דִּבְרֵי שָׁלוֹם עִם־רֵעֵיהֶם וְרָעָה (28:3)
בִּלְבָבָם
those who *speak* peace with
*their neighbor*, but *evil* is in their *hearts*

וְדֹבֵר אֱמֶת בִּלְבָבוֹ (15:2)
and *speaks* truth *in his heart*
לֹא־עָשָׂה לְרֵעֵהוּ רָעָה (15:3)
He does no *evil* to *his neighbor*

בְּנָשְׂאִי יָדַי אֶל־דְּבִיר קָדְשֶׁךָ (28:2)
as I lift my hands toward *your holy* inner
sanctuary

מִי־יִשְׁכֹּן בְּהַר קָדְשֶׁךָ (15:1)
Who may tent on *your holy* hill?

דברי שלום עם־רעיהם ורעה (28:3b)
בלבבם
those who speak peace with their neighbor,
but evil is in their *hearts*
כמעשׂה יְדֵיהֶם תֶּן לָהֶם (28:4b)
... according to the work of their *hands* give
to them.

נְקִי כַפַּיִם וּבַר־לֵבָב (24:4)
innocent of *hands* and pure of *heart*

בנשׂאי ידי אל־דביר קָדְשֶׁךָ (28:2)
as I lift my hands toward *your holy inner
sanctuary*

אַל־תִּמְשְׁכֵנִי עִם־רְשָׁעִים וְעִם־פֹּעֲלֵי (28:3a)
אָוֶן
*Don't drag* me *away* with the *wicked* and
with *workers of iniquity*.

יְהוָה אָהַבְתִּי מְעוֹן בֵּיתֶךָ וּמְקוֹם (26:8)
מִשְׁכַּן כְּבוֹדֶךָ
Yahweh, I love *the dwelling of your
house*, and *the place of the tent of your
glory*.
אַל־תֶּאֱסֹף עִם־חַטָּאִים נַפְשִׁי (26:9)
וְעִם־אַנְשֵׁי דָמִים חַיָּי:
*Don't gather* my soul *with sinners* and
my life *with men of blood*.

שְׁמַע קוֹל תַּחֲנוּנַי בְּשַׁוְּעִי אֵלֶיךָ (28:2a)
*Hear* the *voice* of my supplications when I
*cry for help* to you.

הַקְשִׁיבָה לְקוֹל שַׁוְעִי (5:3a)
Heed the *voice* of my *cry for help*.
יְהוָה בֹּקֶר תִּשְׁמַע קוֹלִי (5:4a)
Yahweh, in the morning you *hear* my
*voice*.

The description of the "doers of iniquity" provides a clear contrast to
that of the "doer of righteousness" in 15:2-3, in terms of their speech

and treatment of the "neighbor" and what lies in their "heart," whether "evil" or "truth." Both psalms appear to have been performed directly before the "holy" place. Psalm 28 in its assessment of one's character refers to the same bodily parts as the other entry torah in Psalm 24: "hearts" and "hands." Seen in the light of these liturgies, the key issue may be, "Who may sojourn on your holy hill?" Since evildoers cannot, both Psalms 26 and 28 — immediately following an affirmation of affinity to his sanctuary — petition God not to remove the speaker with sinners. Thus, the reason the psalm shows such interest in the wicked is not because of the supposed circumstances of the psalmist but because of the key issue of the entry liturgies. Reading Psalm 28 in this context also explains how the negative petitions result in positive benefits for the speaker and why attention is turned from the speaking "I" to God's people. The speaking "I" was probably not a lone individual but a liturgist praying on behalf of fellow worshipers.

*6. Thematic Coherence and Exposition as a Psalm of Temple Entry*

Like Psalm 26, the speaker in this psalm seeks to be exempt from the impending judgment of the wicked but also includes praise for being granted the protection and privileges of the temple. In the context of temple entry, the psalm may have developed as follows. It opens before the Holy of Holies with petitions that the worshiper be spared the impending judgment on the wicked, which judgment he endorses by asking they be punished in like measure to their crime (vv. 1-4). A temple prophet responds by announcing Yahweh will bring them down because they disregard his works (v. 5). In return, the worshiper blesses Yahweh for hearing these petitions and vows to sing further praise (vv. 6-7). In closing, it is perhaps a priest who widens the horizons to Yahweh's people, and praises him for his salvation and petitions it continue forever (vv. 8-9). Repeated phrases link the psalm's parts. The petitioned "voice of my supplications" (v. 2) is heard in verse 6. From "my hands" uplifted toward the sanctuary (v. 2) attention shifts to "the work of their hands" (v. 4) and then to "the work of his (i.e. Yahweh's) hands" (v. 5). As the speaker "blesses" Yahweh (v. 6), he in turn is invoked to "bless" his "inheritance" (v. 9). As Yahweh is "my strength" (עֹז, v. 7), so he is "the strength (עֹז) of his people and a stronghold (מָעוֹז) of deliverances for his anointed" (v. 8).

Faced with the issue of entering or not entering the temple, we can now make sense of the opening petitions (vv. 1-4). The issue of life and death may be explained not with reference to the supposed circumstances of a particular psalmist (e.g. sickness or false accusers) but with reference to the imagery of the temple itself. As evident from Psalm 36 (discussed below), to have access to it is to have access to "light" and "life" itself; to be regarded as "wicked" and thus to be denied is to become like the "fallen" who are "not able to rise" (36:9-10, 13). As in the temple entry torah found in Psalms 15 and 24, the decisive distinction between the righteous and the wicked is what one says to one's "neighbor" and what resides in one's "heart" (28:3 and 15:2-3). Since the liturgy of entrance, though addressed to worshipers as individuals (15:1-5; 24:3-5), is performed within a congregation (Psalm 24, especially v. 6), the shift in verses 8-9 to corporate concerns comes as no surprise.

### PSALM 36

*Previous Interpretations.* Psalm 36 does not fit the standard form-critical genres. Initially the two sections vv. 2-5 and 6-10 appear to have little in common, and the abrupt change of subject matter between them may suggest they were artificially spliced together. What connection is there between describing the character of the wicked and praising Yahweh's loyalty and righteousness, along with the riches of his house?

Kraus describes Psalm 36 as "didactic poetry," and he determines the setting of this psalm solely from v. 12: the petitioner "is persecuted by insolent enemies" and thus looks for "asylum."[24] Peter Craigie describes Psalm 36 as "a literary and devotional composition" that "stands in the wisdom tradition."[25]

*Features shared by Psalms 5, 26, 28, 36, and 52*

*1. The Absence of Lament and 2. The Profile of the Wicked*

Using the standard form-critical categories, vv. 2-5 could be labeled a lament against foes. But, once again, the wicked are described simply in their own right. There is no mention of attacks or threats directed against the speaker or any other victims. Moreover, we should probably understand these verses as "an oracle," not as an individual's lament. This word opening v. 2, נְאֻם, probably belongs

---

[24] Kraus, *Psalms 1–59*, 397, 398, 399.

[25] Craigie, *Psalms 1–50*, 291.

with the psalm's superscription in v. 1, thus designating vv. 2-5 as divine speech.[26] The characteristics of the wicked that are in focus concern their godless "heart," their deceptive speech, and their evil plans. Threat is implied in the jussives of v. 12, but it appears merely as a possibility, not a present reality.

### 3. Temple Setting

Explicit reference is made to Yahweh's "house" and implicit reference to its ritual feasts (יִרְוְיֻן מִדֶּשֶׁן בֵּיתֶךָ, cf. 63:3-6). The symbolism of the cherubim-ark may also be implied because it can explain several associations within our psalm's hymnic section (vv. 6-10). Psalm 89:15-16 celebrates the same two pairs of divine attributes that are center stage in our psalm, namely חסד and אמת/אמונה, and צדק[ה] and משפט (36:6-7). Psalm 89 appears to do so in the context of a procession of the cherubim-ark.[27] Both psalms also celebrate Yahweh's "light" (36:10; 89:15). The reference in our psalm to refuge being taken "in the shadow of your wings" (v. 8) may also point to the cherubim symbol. The symbolism of the cherubim-chariot can also explain the juxtaposition of the word pair, "heavens-clouds" (שׁמים-שׁחקים), and Yahweh's "house." Psalms 18:7, 10-12 and 68:34-36 associate Yahweh's "riding" (רכב) a "cherub" in the "heavens-clouds" (שׁחקים-שׁמים) and his sanctuary/temple. The earthly temple symbolized both Yahweh's dwelling in the midst of his people and his palace in the skies/heavens.[28] The images of a "stream" (cf. 46:5) and a "spring" (מקור, 68:27; cf. 87:7) are also associated with the Zion temple elsewhere.

### 4. Representative Speaker

The first and only mention of an individual speaker does not occur until v. 12, and its parallel petition in the preceding verse suggests this speaker simply represents the group of "those who know you" and "the upright of heart."

---

[26] The construct phrase, נאם־פשׁע, is without parallel in the OT. Elsewhere נאם is always followed by a term for God or some human speaker. In addition, we should probably read with a few Mss, the Syriac, and the LXX לִבּוֹ, "his heart," instead of לִבִּי, "my heart." See further Craigie, *Psalms 1–50*, 290. Verse 2a should thus read, "An oracle. Transgression belongs to the wicked; (it is) in the midst of his heart."

[27] See further Broyles, *Psalms*, 356.

[28] See further Broyles, *Psalms*, 80, 104–105, 281–84.

*5. Parallels with Psalms 15, 24, and Other Psalms of Temple Entry.*

These parallels are most evident in the verses describing the wicked:

| | |
|---|---|
| לִבּוֹ (36:2, emended, 11) | בִּלְבָבוֹ (15:2) |
| (his) *heart* | in his *heart* |
| עֵינָיו (36:2, 3) | עֵינָיו (15:4) |
| his *eyes* | his *eyes* |
| פִּיו (36:4) | לְשֹׁנוֹ (15:3) |
| his *mouth* | his *tongue* |
| אֵין־פַּחַד אֱלֹהִים לְנֶגֶד עֵינָיו (36:2) | וְאֶת־יִרְאֵי יְהוָה יְכַבֵּד (15:4) |
| There is no *fear of God* before his eyes. | But *fearers of Yahweh* he honors. |
| רַע לֹא יִמְאָס (36:5) | נִבְזֶה בְּעֵינָיו נִמְאָס (15:4) |
| evil he does not *reject* | Despised in his eyes is a *rejected* one |
| דִּבְרֵי־פִיו אָוֶן וּמִרְמָה (36:4) | וְלֹא נִשְׁבַּע לְמִרְמָה (24:4) |
| the words of his mouth are trouble and *deceit* | and he does not swear to *deceit* |
| מְשֹׁךְ חַסְדְּךָ לְיֹדְעֶיךָ וְצִדְקָתְךָ לְיִשְׁרֵי־לֵב: (36:11) | בַּר־לֵבָב (24:4) |
| Prolong your loyalty to those who know you, | *pure of heart* |
| and your *righteousness* to the *upright of heart*. | יִשָּׂא בְרָכָה מֵאֵת יְהוָה וּצְדָקָה (24:5) |
| | מֵאֱלֹהֵי יִשְׁעוֹ: |
| | He will receive blessing from |
| | Yahweh, and *righteousness* from |
| | his saving God. |
| פֶּשַׁע לְרָשָׁע בְּקֶרֶב לִבּוֹ (36:2, emended) | קִרְבָּם הַוּוֹת (5:10) |
| *Transgression* belongs to the wicked; | their *inner part* is destruction |
| it is in the *midst* of his heart. | בְּרֹב פִּשְׁעֵיהֶם (5:11) |
| | in the multitude of their *transgressions* |
| כִּי־הֶחֱלִיק אֵלָיו בְּעֵינָיו (36:3) | לְשׁוֹנָם יַחֲלִיקוּן (5:10) |
| for he *flatters* himself in his eyes | with their tongues they *flatter* |
| דִּבְרֵי־פִיו אָוֶן וּמִרְמָה (36:4) | תְּאַבֵּד דֹּבְרֵי כָזָב (5:7) |
| *the words of his mouth are trouble and deceit* | You destroy *speakers of a lie* |
| בְּצֵל כְּנָפֶיךָ יֶחֱסָיוּן (36:8) | וְיִשְׂמְחוּ כָל־חוֹסֵי בָךְ (5:12) |
| in the shadow of your wings they *seek refuge* | and let all who *seek refuge* in you |
| | rejoice |
| | שַׁתִּי בַּאדֹנָי יְהוִה מַחְסִי (73:28) |
| | I have set in Lord Yahweh my *refuge*. |

(36:5) יִתְיַצֵּב עַל־דֶּרֶךְ לֹא־טוֹב

they *stand* upon a way that is not good

(36:13) שָׁם נָפְלוּ פֹּעֲלֵי אָוֶן דֹּחוּ וְלֹא־יָכְלוּ קוּם:

There *doers of trouble* have *fallen*;
they are thrust down and unable to *stand*.

לֹא־יִתְיַצְּבוּ הוֹלְלִים לְנֶגֶד עֵינֶיךָ

(5:6) שָׂנֵאתָ כָּל־פֹּעֲלֵי אָוֶן:

The arrogant may not *stand*
before your eyes; You hate
all *doers of trouble*.

(5:11) הַאֲשִׁימֵם אֱלֹהִים יִפְּלוּ מִמֹּעֲצוֹתֵיהֶם

Declare them guilty, O God,
let them *fall* by their schemes.

(Evil person uprooted, 52:7)

(24:3) וּמִי־יָקוּם בִּמְקוֹם קָדְשׁוֹ

And who may *stand* in his holy place?

(15:2) פֹּעֵל צֶדֶק

a *doer* of righteousness

Petition to avoid wicked influence (36:12) | Petition to avoid wicked influence (26:9; 28:3)

Psalms 15 and 36 draw their character profiles with the same three bodily parts: the "heart," the "eyes," and the "mouth" or "tongue." The wicked person dismisses the fear of God, and "does not reject" what should be "rejected." As in Psalm 24, attention is given to wicked speech which is characterized as "deceit." In both psalms, Yahweh's "righteousness" is to be bestowed to those of right "heart." Both Psalms 5 and 36 are clear how deeply evil has penetrated the wicked, how they flatter and deceive. They are also clear on their ultimately unstable destiny. Psalms 26, 28, and 36 all contain a petition to avoid the influence of the wicked.

## 6. Thematic Coherence and Exposition as a Psalm of Temple Entry

The context of the temple entry liturgies helps us to overcome the impasse of explaining the content and development of Psalm 36. The opening description of the wicked (vv. 2-5) is not an individual's lament over present circumstances but an oracle from Yahweh profiling those who are not permitted to enjoy the benefits of his house, which are hymned in vv. 8-10. This is similar to the temple entry liturgy of Psalm 15, where verses 2-5 should be regarded as an oracle describing "the doer of righteousness." As the description of the righteous answers the question, "LORD, who may dwell in your sanctuary?" in Psalm 15, so the description of the wicked in Psalm 36 informs God's people who may not "feast on the abundance of your house" (v. 9). In addition, as Psalm 5 uses the wicked as a foil to contrast Yahweh's character with theirs (vv. 5-7), so our psalm does the same. Displacing the "fear of God before his eyes, he flatters himself in his eyes." But to carry out this action, self-deception is necessary: "he hates to find his iniquity" (reading שָׂנֵא). Because transgression has penetrated his *heart* and self-flattery has displaced God in his *eyes*, now "the words of his *mouth* are injustice and deceit." He is both deceived and deceiving. Illustrating the comprehensive nature of his evil are polar bodily postures: "*on his bed* he plots injustice" and "*he takes his stand on a road* that is not good." He rejects what is good (הֵיטִיב and טוֹב) and deliberately chooses what is bad (רָע). Evil thus proceeds from one's thinking to one's speech and to one's actions.

A liturgist or choir then responds with hymnic praise (vv. 6-10) of Yahweh's attributes, using two common word pairs — "loyalty" and "faithfulness" and "righteousness" and "justice" — in their vast cosmic dimensions — to the "heavens-clouds" and comparable to "the mountains of El" and the "great deep." He "saves" all creatures (אָדָם־וּבְהֵמָה) and offers "refuge" to all humans (בְּנֵי אָדָם). At his "house" he provides a rich, life-giving banquet and "light."

The unity of these two sections is confirmed by the closing petitions (vv. 11-12). The first responds to the hymn and requests the continuance of Yahweh's "loyalty" and "righteousness" — the first member within the two word pairs hymned above ("loyalty-faithfulness," "righteousness-justice") — to his people, who are described first by their relationship to him ("those who know you") and then by their moral stature ("the upright in heart"). The second petition responds to the opening oracle and expresses the wish that the "wicked" not "make" the representative speaker "homeless" (נוד *Hipʿil*). Like the oracle, it also plays on the image of bodily parts: here their "foot" and "hand." As the temple entry torah of Psalm 15 closes with a promise of stability for temple entrants ("A doer of these things will never totter"), so our psalm closes with a confession about the instability of "doers of iniquity" (v. 13). Their judgment is consistent with their presumption: those who would "take their stand" (יִתְיַצֵּב, v. 5) now "have fallen ... and are unable to rise" (v. 13). Thus, the closing petition, "may the foot of the proud not come against me" (v. 12), is seen to have its effect.

While no single line of the psalm is a theodicy, as a whole it makes a clear statement in this regard. In the opening oracle Yahweh discloses that evil belongs to wicked people — they own it within themselves ("Transgression belongs to the wicked; it is in the midst of his heart," פֶּשַׁע לָרָשָׁע בְּקֶרֶב לִבּוֹ, v. 2). By contrast, the following hymn testifies that Yahweh's character is thoroughly just, saving, and life-giving.[29] Concluding petitions request that Yahweh exhibit these characteristics to those who know him and that the wicked not deter them. The whole psalm thus presents us with a lens on how evil and good in this world are to be interpreted and how individuals may obtain the good. Evil is clearly to be attributed to evil people. But despite the presence of this force in the world, the actions to be attributed to God remain thoroughly fair, salvific, and life-promoting. Moreover, those who are on God's side cannot take this state of affairs for granted, for they bear the responsibility to petition God to secure his goodness for themselves.

Yahweh is depicted as magnanimous in the extreme, willing to help all his creatures. He is a rich host par excellence and the source of life. But those who find fascination in themselves, instead of him, will find themselves excluded from his gifts.

## PSALM 52

*Previous Interpretations.* Psalm 52 is difficult to analyze according to the traditional form-critical motifs and difficult to locate with respect to a setting. Kraus posits that "the person addressed (vv. 1 ff.) is a rich (v. 7), cunning man of power (vv. 2, 4)" and "an influential accuser" of "a pious man."[30]

*Features shared by Psalms 5, 26, 28, 36, and 52*

*1. The Absence of Lament and 2. The Profile of the Wicked*

Because the opponents are the grammatical subject in vv. 3-6, this section might be labeled a lament against an enemy. His "tongue" practices "deceit" and "destruction," but no mention is made of victims[31] or direct threat to the speaker. If the suggestion found in

---

[29] The revelation that evil belongs to wicked people is in Yahweh's mouth, but the claims about Yahweh's own character are in the mouth of liturgist, perhaps to provide the force of independent testimony. This may explain the shift in liturgical motifs from oracle to hymnic praise.

[30] Kraus, *Psalms 1–59*, 510.

[31] In the taunt of the righteous against the wicked person (v. 9), the phrase, "he

*BHS* is correct,[32] the only possible explicit connection with another party appears in the opening verse: "Why do you boast in evil, O hero, *against the devout* all the day?" But this action is not one of threat, and it is later countered in the taunt of the righteous (v. 9). The psalm also lacks any formal petition. In fact, it expresses certainty that God will, in fact, bring judgment on the wicked person (v. 7). It does close with a vow of praise, but this response is predicated on this confession of impending judgment, not on a petition for deliverance.

The opening characterization of the wicked person (vv. 3-6) centers on his "tongue" (vv. 4, 6), which even serves as a synecdoche for the whole person. It is guilty of "boasting" in "evil" (רָעָה ,רָע) and practicing "deceit" (מִרְמָה ,שֶׁקֶר, רְמִיָּה). It acts like a "sharpened razor" and plots "destruction," and its words "devour." The taunt of the righteous against the wicked (v. 9) focuses simply on his choice to trust in "wealth" instead of God.

## 3. Temple Setting and 4. Representative Speaker

There is nothing in this psalm that clearly locates its performance at the temple, though there are allusions to it. The speaker confesses to being "like a leafy olive tree in *the house of God*" (v. 10; cf. 92:13-15). By contrast, the wicked person will be "torn away" and "uprooted" from a "tent" (אֹהֶל, v. 7). These contrasting parallels (note also the agricultural metaphors) may imply this tent is Yahweh's (cf. "who may sojourn in your tent [אֹהֶל]?", 15:1).

The psalm contains several unexpected shifts that are probably best explained by a liturgical setting. There are two shifts in addressee: the wicked are addressed directly in vv. 3-7 and then referred to in the third person in vv. 8-9, and God is referred to in the third person throughout except in the closing verse, where he is abruptly addressed. The former may reflect a development from direct address of the wicked (perhaps simply as a dramatic form — they need not be physically present) to a testimony about the wicked recited to a congregation. The closing verse then turns to address God in direct

---

prevailed in his destruction" (בְּהַוָּתוֹ יָעֹז), makes little sense. *BHS* suggests we read, "in his wealth" (בְּהוֹנוֹ), with appeal to the Syriac and Targum. This makes sense especially in light of the parallel phrase, "and he trusted in the abundance of his riches."

[32] It is difficult to make sense of the MT's חֶסֶד אֵל. *BHS*, with appeal to the Syriac, suggests reading אֶל־חָסִיד. If this is correct, the counter-taunt from the righteous (vv. 8-9) becomes more understandable.

praise. Another shift occurs between the group and the individual: from the righteous ones (vv. 8-9) to the speaking "I" (vv. 10-11), who may have been a representative of the righteous group.[33]

### 5. Parallels with Psalms 15, 24, and Other Psalms of Temple Entry

| | |
|---|---|
| (52:4) הַוּוֹת תַּחְשֹׁב לְשׁוֹנֶךָ<br>*Destruction* you *plot* with your *tongue*. | (36:4) דִּבְרֵי־פִיו אָוֶן וּמִרְמָה<br>the *words* of his mouth are trouble and *deceit* |
| (52:5) אָהַבְתָּ רַע מִטּוֹב שֶׁקֶר מִדַּבֵּר צֶדֶק<br>You love *evil* more than *good*, deception more than a *word* of righteousness (emended). | (36:5) אָוֶן יַחְשֹׁב עַל־מִשְׁכָּבוֹ<br>יִתְיַצֵּב עַל־דֶּרֶךְ לֹא־טוֹב רַע לֹא יִמְאָס<br>Trouble he *plots* upon his bed;<br>they stand upon a way that is not *good*;<br>*evil* he does not reject. |
| | (24:4) וְלֹא נִשְׁבַּע לְמִרְמָה<br>And he does not swear to *deceit*. |
| (52:6) לְשׁוֹן מִרְמָה<br>a *tongue* of *deceit* | |
| | (5:10, emended) כִּי אֵין בְּפִיהֶם נְכוֹנָה<br>קִרְבָּם הַוּוֹת קֶבֶר־פָּתוּחַ גְּרוֹנָם לְשׁוֹנָם יַחֲלִיקוּן:<br>For nothing in their mouth is established, their inner part is *destruction*; their throat is an open grace, with their *tongue* they flatter. |
| | (5:7, emended) תְּאַבֵּד דֹּבְרֵי כָזָב<br>אִישׁ־דָּמִים וּמִרְמָה תְּתַעֵב יְהוָה:<br>You destroy <u>*speakers of a lie*</u>;<br>a man of blood and *deceit* you treat as an abomination, Yahweh. |
| Evil person torn down & uprooted (52:7) | Evildoers thrust down & fallen (36:13) |
| | Worker of righteousness never totters (15:5) |
| Nourished in God's house: a flourishing olive tree (52:10) | Nourished in God's house: a rich banquet (36:9-10) |

---

[33] The closing verse is a vow of praise and thus points to future action, but it contains one unique twist. He vows not only the traditional "giving of thanks" (ידה *Hiphil*) but also to "wait for your name" (קוה in the imperfect used only here in the Psalms) "in front of your faithful ones." What he awaits specifically may be the judgment pronounced in v. 7.

| | |
|---|---|
| עֹשֵׂה רמיה (52:4)<br>*doer* of deceit | פֹּעַל צדק (15:2)<br>*worker* of righteousness<br>עֹשֵׂה־אלה (15:5)<br>*doer* of these things |
| מה־תתהלל ברעה (52:3)<br>Why do you boast in *evil*? | לא־עשׂה לרעהו רעה (15:3)<br>He does not do *evil* to his neighbor. |
| ויסחך מאהל (52:7)<br>And he will tear you away from (the) *tent*. | יהוה מי־יגור באהלך (15:1)<br>Yahweh, who can sojourn in your *tent*? |
| הנה הגבר לא ישׂים (52:9, emended)<br>אלהים מעוזו ויבטח ברב עשׁרו יעז בהונו:<br>Behold the man who did not make God his *stronghold* and *trusted* in the abundance of his riches and prevailed in his wealth.<br>בטחתי בחסד־אלהים עולם ועד (52:10)<br>I *trust* in God's loyalty forever and ever. | יהוה עֻזִּי ומגני בו (28:7a, 8, emended)<br>בטח לבי ...יהוה עז־לעמו ומעוז ישׁועות משׁיחו הוא:<br>Yahweh is my strength and my shield; in him my heart *trusts* ... Yahweh is the strength of his people and a *stronghold* of victories for his anointed.<br>וביהוה בטחתי (26:1)<br>And in Yahweh I *trust*. |

As noted in the psalms discussed above, the description of the evil person (vv. 3-6) concerns his character with no lament on behalf of victims. As in Ps 36:2-5, it is presented in the form of a prophetic oracle (see below) and focuses on his deceitful speech (as also in Psalm 5) and preference of evil over good. And both psalms refer to the instability of evildoers and to the nourishment Yahweh's worshipers receive in God's house. The speech of the "doer of deceit" in Psalm 52 contrasts with the truthful speech of the "worker of righteousness" in the oracular torah of 15:2-4 (cf. also 24:4). Their respective fates are also antithetical. The issue of "trusting" in God as one's "stronghold" is pivotal in both Psalms 52 and 28.

## 6. Thematic Coherence and Exposition as a Psalm of Temple Entry

These observed parallels may explain why the psalm lacks lament and petition. The opening description of the evil person is not a report on a particular person at a particular historical moment, nor was the psalm occasioned by a specific crisis. Rather, the psalm belongs to these liturgies of temple entrance, where there occurs the separation of the ways: the righteous who may enter and so become "like a leafy olive tree in the house of God" (v. 10), and the wicked who may not and so are "torn away from a tent" (probably Yahweh's, v. 7). The intent of the psalm is thus not to respond to a specific event but to teach would-be entrants of Yahweh's temple.

As noted above, the opening verses (vv. 3-6) do not lament; they simply describe the deceitful speech of a wicked person (similar to the "oracle" in 36:2-5). The subsequent pronouncement of impending judgment ("God will tear you down ...," v. 7) implies these verses function as an indictment. Verses 3-7 are similar to some prophetic judgment oracles (note esp. those that contain the rhetorical מָה: Ps 50:16-21; Isa 22:16-19; Hab 2:18-19).[34] Thus, a temple prophet indicts the evil person (actually or dramatically present) with a description of his character that focuses on his speech, which is boastful, deceptive and destructive. The vocative גִּבּוֹר contains an obvious tone of sarcasm. The prophetic voice then announces the punishment.

Next either the same speaker or another liturgist describes how "righteous ones" will respond to and endorse this judgment (cf. 15:4): they mock the evil person's misplaced trust and rejoice in God's judgment of reversing his fortunes. In the closing verses a liturgist speaks on behalf of the congregation, turning their attention to their vertical relationship to God. Here the welfare, character, and action of the worshiper are presented as an antitype to that of the evil person. The use of agricultural images links their respective fates: while the evil one will be "uprooted from the land of the living," the speaker is "like a leafy olive tree in the house of God." Another contrast lies in the object of one's trust: the evil person "trusted in the abundance of his riches," but the speaker "has trusted in God's loyalty" (חֶסֶד, v. 10). The object of trust is the issue that determines the fate of each. In fact, it is God's חֶסֶד that defines his adherents, the חֲסִידִים, in the opening and closing verses. A third contrast lies in the object of one's praising. The evil person "boasts" (הלל Hithpaᶜel 1, v. 3) in evil; the speaker "gives thanks" (ידה Hipᶜil) to God. Here we see that the descriptions of the righteous and the wicked are shaped by one another in the context of liturgy, not simply from actual, particular social groups in ancient Israel.

In the closing verse the speaker's vow to "wait for God's name" before the congregation may refer to their waiting for his self-revealing judgment promised in verse 7. The psalm clearly encourages the community of the righteous to commit the punishment of the

---

[34] See further Marvin E. Tate, *Psalms 51–100* (WBC 20; Dallas: Word, 1990), 35.

ungodly to God and not to take it into their own hands.

The psalm reflects a chronological sequence. First, a temple prophet indicts an evil person on the basis of his present speech (vv. 3-6) and then announces God's impending judgment (v. 7). Afterwards, verses 8-9 anticipate a lesson the righteous will draw from the fate of the wicked person, this time focusing on the object of his trust (vv. 8-9). Now, for the first time, we hear the voice of an individual (וַאֲנִי), a liturgist most likely, who testifies of his present and future trust for all time (עוֹלָם וָעֶד ... בָּטַחְתִּי Hebrew perfect) and of his blessing in God's house (v. 10). He closes promising future praise and present waiting before the devout, presumably for the impending judgment (v. 11). Thus, this psalm, in effect, calls the audience to trust in God's devotion and justice in the midst of contrary circumstances.

## PSALM 73

Psalm 73 is not a liturgy for temple entry. It may, however, function as a public testimony concerning what is disclosed during the liturgies of temple entry. In brief, the psalm puts its opening proverb to the critical test of life experience: "Surely God is good to Israel, to the pure of heart." The speaker's observations (אֶרְאֶה, v. 3), however, lead to the opposite conclusion: the wicked, who are cavalier about God (v. 11), enjoy שָׁלוֹם (v. 3) and the speaker, who has endeavored to "cleanse" his "heart," suffers punishment (vv. 13-14). Our analysis on the liturgies of temple entry may shed light on the psalm's interpretive crux, namely v. 17, which has always troubled commentators: "When I pondered to understand this, it was trouble in my sight, until I came to the sanctuary of God, then I considered their end" (vv. 16-17). The speaker's own searching was futile until understanding came from this external source. The pivot for the speaker occurs at the moment he enters the temple, but to what experience does he refer?

### 1. Parallels with Psalms 15, 24, and Other Psalms of Temple Entry

| | |
|---|---|
| (73:1) אַךְ טוֹב לְיִשְׂרָאֵל אֱלֹהִים לְבָרֵי לֵבָב | (24:4) נְקִי כַפַּיִם וּבַר־לֵבָב |
| Surely God is good to Israel, to those *pure of heart* | *innocent* of hands and *pure of heart* |
| (73:13) אַךְ־רִיק זִכִּיתִי לְבָבִי וָאֶרְחַץ בְּנִקָּיוֹן כַּפָּי | (26:6) אֶרְחַץ בְּנִקָּיוֹן כַּפַּי וַאֲסֹבְבָה אֶת־מִזְבַּחֲךָ יהוה |
| Surely in vain have I kept my *heart* pure, and *washed in innocence my hands.* | I *wash in innocence my hands,* and I go about your altar, Yahweh. |

(73:15) אם־אמרתי אספרה כמו הנה דור
בניך בגדתי

If I had said, "I will recount thus,"
Behold, I would have betrayed the
*generation* of your children.

(73:3) כי־קנאתי בהוללים שלום רשעים
אראה:

For I envied the *arrogant*, as I saw the
prosperity of the wicked.

(73:6) לכן ענקתמו גאוה
Therefore *pride* is their necklace.

(73:8-9) ימיקו וידברו ברע עשק ממרום
ידברו: שתו בשמים פיהם ולשונם תהלך
בארץ:

They mock and *speak* with *evil*; they
*speak* oppressively from on high. They put
in the heavens their *mouth*, and their
*tongue* struts through the land.

זה דור (24:6, *Qere* and emended)
דרשיו מבקשי פני אלהי יעקב

This is the *generation* of those who
seek him, those who seek the face of
the God Jacob.

(5:6) לא־יתיצבו הוללים לנגד עיניך
The *arrogant* may not stand before
your eyes
(*Hith* in 52:3.)

(36:12) אל־תבואני רגל גאוה
Let not the foot of *pride* come against
me.

(5:5) לא יגרך רע
*Evil* does not sojourn with you.
(5:7) דברי כזב
*speaker*s of a lie
(5:10, emended) אין בפימו נכונה ...
לשונם יחליקון
There is nothing trustworthy in their
*mouth*; ... with their *tongue* they
flatter.

(28:3) דברי שלום עם־רעיהם ורעה
בלבבם
those who *speak* peace with their
neighbor, but *evil* is in their hearts

(36:4) דברי־פיו און ומרמה
the *words* of his *mouth* are trouble and
deceit
(36:5) רע לא ימאס
*Evil* he does not reject.

(52:4) הוות תחשב לשונך
Your *tongue* plots destruction.
(52:5) אהבת רע מטוב שקר מדבר צדק
You love *evil* more than good,
deception more than a *word* of
righteousness (emended).
(52:6) לשון מרמה
O deceitful *tongue*

(73:12) הנה־אלה רשעים ושלוי עולם השגו־חיל:

Behold, these are the wicked, and ever at ease they increase *wealth*.

(73:18) אך בחלקות תשית למו הפלתם למשואות:

Surely in *slippery places* you set them; you cause them to *fall* to ruins.

(73:2) ואני כמעט נטיו רגלי כאין שפכו אשרי

But as for me, my *feet nearly slipped*, my *steps nearly faltered*.

(73:20, emended) כחלום מהקיץ אדני בהעיר צלמם תבזה:

Like a dream after awaking, O Lord, when you awake their image you will *despise*.

(73:27) כי־הנה רחקיך יאבדו הצמתה כל־זונה ממך:

For those far from you will *perish*; you will *ruin* all those unfaithful to you.

(15:2) ודבר אמת בלבבו

and a *speaker* of truth in his heart

(15:3) לא־רגל על־לשנו

He does not slander with his *tongue*.

(52:9, emended) ויבטח ברב עשרו יעז בהונו

And he trusted in the abundance of his *riches*; he prevailed with his *wealth*.

(36:13) שם נפלו פעלי און דחו ולא־יכלו קום:

There doers of trouble have *fallen*; they are thrust down and unable to stand.

(5:11) האשימם אלהים יפלו ממעצותיהם

Declare them guilty, O God, let them *fall* by their schemes.

(5:6) לא־יתיצבו הוללים לנגד עיניך

The arrogant may *not stand* before your eyes

(Evil person left with no foothold) (52:7)

(24:3) ומי־יקום במקום קדשו

And who may *stand* in your holy place?

(26:1) וביהוה בטחתי לא אמעד

and in Yahweh have I trusted and not *tottered*

(5:5) לא אל־חפץ רשע אתה

You are *not* a God who *delights* in wickedness.

(5:6) שנאת כל־פעלי און

You *hate* all workers of iniquity.

(5:7) תאבד דברי כזב

You *destroy* all speakers of a lie.

| | |
|---|---|
| (5:9) יהוה נַחֵנִי בצדקתך<br>Yahweh, *lead me* in your righteousness. | (73:24) בעצתך תַנְחֵנִי ואחר כבוד תקחני:<br>In your council you *lead me*, and afterwards with *glory* you receive me. |
| (24:7-10) מלך הכבוד<br>the king of *glory* | |
| (26:8) יהוה אהבתי מעון ביתך ומקום<br>משכן כבודך:<br>Yahweh, I love the dwelling of your house, and the place of the tent of your *glory*. | |
| (5:12) וישמחו כל־חוסי בך<br>and let all who seek *refuge* in you rejoice | (73:28) שתי באדני יהוה מַחְסִי<br>I have set in Lord Yahweh my *refuge* |
| (36:8) בצל כנפיך יחסיון<br>in the shadow of your wings they seek *refuge* | |
| (26:7) ולספר כל־נפלאותיך<br>to recount all your *wonders.* | (73:28) לספר כל־מלאכותיך<br>to recount all your *works.* |

The numerous echoes of the psalms of temple entry helps us to understand the importance of a "pure heart" and "innocent hands"; the designation of Yahweh's group of worshipers as a "generation"; the description of the wicked as "arrogant," with special attention to their evil speech and even "wealth"; the image of their instability and imminent "fall"; Yahweh's hatred toward them and promise to destroy them; Yahweh's "guiding" his pilgrims to his "glory"; the symbolism of Yahweh as "refuge"; and the promised "telling" of Yahweh's deeds. We should also note that the description of the wicked (vv. 3-12), like others discussed above, focuses on the character of the wicked themselves, not on their abuse of victims.

## 2. *Psalm 73 in Light of the Psalms of Temple Entry*

So how did the speaker's "entering (בוא)" into "the sanctuary of God" (v. 17) resolve the apparent contradiction of the prosperity of the wicked and the afflictions of the pure of heart? In the liturgies concerning temple entry the worshiper hears and perhaps sees dramatized the separation of "the two ways": the wicked are excluded from the temple and its rock of stability. God, thus, puts them on "slippery places" and "casts them down" (vv. 18-20). The "pure of heart," Yahweh's "refugees" (cf. v. 28), however, are admitted to the temple and so received into God's very presence. They, in turn, "proclaim" his "works," presumably in further psalms.

Implicit in this psalm is a contrast between what the speaker "sees" (ראה, v. 3) from his own observation and "understands" (בין, v. 17) from his entry into the temple. Verses 18-20 do not record what is immediately evident in human experience; they report what was revealed during temple entry concerning their ultimate "end" (v. 17).

Another line of the psalm that has raised considerable debate among commentators is, "With your counsel you guide (נחה) me, and afterward you receive (לקח) me with glory" (v. 24). This is often interpreted as a veiled reference to some kind of afterlife, especially on the basis of its use of לקח ("Enoch waked with God, and he was not for God *took* him," Gen 5:24; and "Surely God will ransom my soul from the hand of Sheol, for he will *take* me," Ps 49:16). But in the context of "entering the sanctuary of God" (Ps 73:17), this verse may refer to the processes of pilgrimage and admission into the temple. A motif of the psalms of pilgrimage and temple entry is the assurance that Yahweh "guides" his pilgrims (נחה, 5:9; 23:3; 43:3; 61:3; cf. 27:11; 31:4; 32:8; 139:24). This verse, thus, most likely refers to the pilgrim's reception into "the place where your glory dwells" (26:8) and into the presence of "the king of glory" (24:7-10). In other words, "after" you have "guided" me along the pilgrim path, you "take" me into the "glory" of your temple.

Psalm 73, therefore, functions as a testimony about the realization that only those "refugees" who enter God's dwelling enjoy true security and what is good, and that the wicked, far from God's temple presence, will indeed fall to their ruin. The speaker, although he had nearly slipped with the wicked, discovers that those who enter the temple have God as the "rock" of their failed heart and his nearness as their "good." This psalm testifies that these liturgies of temple entry shed revelatory light into his people's limited understanding and embittered confusion.

### III. CONCLUSIONS AND IMPLICATIONS

*Psalms 5, 26, 28, 36, and 52 as part of regular liturgy, not as emergency laments.* These psalms should not be categorized as laments for individuals to use in special emergencies; they belong to the regular liturgies that all worshipers would invoke, probably during pilgrimage festivals. In the analogy of the Anglican *The Book of Alternative Services*,[35] texts such as these psalms should be located among the regular liturgies of "Morning Prayer," "The Holy Eucharist," and "Good Friday," not among the "Occasional Prayers" at the back of the book (e.g. "For the Unemployed," "For Those in Mental Distress").

*The speaking "I" as a liturgist.* Not only are these psalms not "laments," they are also not "*individual* laments." The speaker is not a lone individual in particular circumstances of need; he speaks on behalf of the assembled worshipers. This liturgist acts as spokesperson for pilgrims in response to the entry "torahs" of Psalms 15 and 24.

*Encounter with the holy God.* Because more psalms should be connected with temple entry than previously thought, this brings center stage the momentous moment of meeting with God, who above all is holy. Belief in omnipresence can entail taking that presence for granted, but these psalms stand as profound reminders that seeking an audience with God is a holy encounter.

*Studying psalms by form-critical genres is helpful, but liturgical services may combine various genres.* This study has some methodological implications. Although Psalms 15 and 24 and Psalms 5, 26, 28, 36, and 52 belong to different literary forms or genres, they still belong to the same liturgical complex and should thus be studied together. In addition, we should note that most of these psalms close with the anticipation that other psalms, especially thanksgivings and hymns, will immediately follow (see esp. 26:12, but also 5:12; 28:7; 52:9; 73:28). Thus, while it is appropriate to examine psalms within their own generic categories, we must also endeavor to study them within the liturgical complex in which they were performed.

*Psalmic references from the temple, not from circumstances.* We have seen that the language of these psalms derives primarily from the symbolism and metaphors of temple liturgy, not from personal or social circumstances. Even though most scholars do not believe David was the historical author of the לדוד psalms, many commentators continue to interpret psalms as if they were a direct reflection of a "psalmist's" personal experience and circumstances. While psalms are certainly informed by experience — both personal and social — they reflect typical experiences of God's people, not an author's particular experience.

---

[35] *The Book of Alternative Services of the Anglican Church of Canada* (Toronto: Anglican Book Centre, 1985).

*The Righteous and the Wicked/Enemies.* As the description of the "righteous" in Psalms 15 and 24 does not identify a particular person, so the descriptions of the "wicked" in Psalms 5, 26, 28, 36, and 52 do not report on particular persons or social groups. Rather they are character profiles derived from the temple instruction. They need not point to personal enemies who aim attacks at the speaker of the psalm, but may simply be a typical portrayal of those who oppose Yahweh's adherents. In other words, these profiles are not comparable to a "letter of reference" reporting biographical facts about an actual individual. Respect for their literary form shows they are an oracular "torah" teaching God's will about the kind of person he desires and the kind of person he rejects. They are not descriptive reports; they are prescriptive models. They are not biographical accounts but stylized images or portraits. As a rule, the Hebrew Bible does not speak in abstract or purely spiritual terms but in terms that are concrete and tangible. "Righteousness" and "wickedness" were presented as concepts embodied as "the righteous one" and "the wicked one." The wicked are given mention not because they single the speaker out for attack but because loyalty to Yahweh is to be exhibited in part by one's disassociation from those whose character is contrary to Yahweh's. Their mention serves as an illustrative contrast.

*Liturgy as education.* For the sake of pedagogical clarity, the temple liturgies present the congregation with two alternatives — the two "ways." Each worshiper is presented with a clear choice: with what kind of company does one identify? Either one identifies with "the righteous" and is thus regarded as "righteous" or one identifies with "the wicked" and is thus regarded as "wicked." In this light, we should understand that claims to being "righteous" in the Psalms are not claims of moral blamelessness but claims of identifying with and aspiring to the righteous profile, as distinct from the wicked profile. We also see how liturgy educates: liturgy is putting words in a worshiper's mouth. Mere instruction can be cerebral, but hearing oneself make certain claims (or at least standing to be counted among those who endorse such claims) should lead to heart searching and changes in attitude and behavior. In addition, we see how these liturgies serve as models for interpreting life experience. In these liturgies especially, we see that opposition to the people of God is more the norm than the exception.

*God's values: treatment of the neighbor.* In these psalms we see an integral connection between worship and daily social life, especially treatment of the neighbor. They warn against both ritualism and privatized piety. There must be a concrete social reality behind one's claims to spirituality. Worshipers' character must be appropriate to the character of the God they claim to worship. The ritual for Temple entry goes to both matters of the heart (private) and matters of concrete social life (public). The qualifications are neither merely personal, nor merely behavioral. The litmus test God employs to determine the true color of his worshipers is dipped into their daily, public lives, not the private corners of "spirituality" or of their "personal" relationship with God. How they treat their neighbors Yahweh considers symptomatic of the inner life.

In view of these psalms, social justice was not an innovation of the Prophets. In answer to: "With what shall I meet Yahweh?", Micah says, "He has told you, O human, what is good and what Yahweh requires from you, except to do justice and to love loyalty and to walk humbly with your God" (6:8). This naturally begs the question, "when did God tell his worshipers what he requires when they meet?" The answer proposed here is during the temple entry liturgies.

## SELECT BIBLIOGRAPHY

Beyerlin, W. *Die Rettung der Bedrängten in den Feindpsalmen der Einzelnen auf institutionelle Zusammen-hänge untersucht* (FRLANT 99; Göttingen: Vandenhoeck & Ruprecht, 1970).

Broyles, C. *Psalms* (NIBC 11; Peabody, MA: Hendrickson, 1999).

Craigie, P. *Psalms 1–50* (WBC 19; Waco, TX: Word, 1983).

Dahood, M. *Psalms I* (AB 16; Garden City, NY: Doubleday, 1966).

Gibson, J. C. L. *Canaanite Myths and Legends* (Edinburgh: T. & T. Clark, 1977).

Keel, O. *Feinde und Gottesleugner* (SBM 7; Stuttgart: Katholisches Bibelwerk, 1969).

Keel, O. *The Symbolism of the Biblical World: Ancient Near Eastern Iconography and the Book of Psalms* (London: SPCK, 1978).

Kraus, H.-J. *Psalms 1–59: A Commentary* (Minneapolis: Augsburg, 1988).

Miller, Patrick D. Jr. "Poetic Ambiguity and Balance in Psalm XV," *VT* 29 (1979) 416–24.

Mosca, P. G. "Psalm 26: Poetic Structure and the Form-Critical Task," *CBQ* 47 (1985) 230–36.

Mowinckel, S. *The Psalms in Israel's Worship* (2 vols., Oxford: Blackwell, 1962).

Tate, M. E. *Psalms 51–100* (WBC 20; Dallas: Word, 1990).

Vogt, E. "Psalm 26, ein Pilgergebet," *Bib* 43 (1962) 328–37.

# BIBLICAL PSALMS OUTSIDE THE PSALTER

## JAMES W. WATTS

### THE COMPARATIVE STUDY OF INSET HYMNS

Psalms appear irregularly in the narrative and prophetic literature of the Hebrew Bible, at Exod 15:1-21, Deut 32:1-43, Jdg 5, 1 Sam 2:1-20, 2 Samuel 22, Isa 38:9-20, Jon 2:3-10, Habakkuk 3, Dan 2:20-23, 1 Chron 16:8-36; in the Apocrypha/Deuterocanon at Daniel 3, Jdg 16:1-17, Tobit 13; and in the New Testament at Lk 1:46-55, 67-79. More often, fragments of hymns and other poems are quoted as natural parts of story-lines (e.g. 2 Sam 1:17-27; 3:33-34) or are employed as elements in prophetic compositions (e.g. Am 4:13; 5:8; 9:5-6). Complete poetic compositions appear less frequently but more prominently. Many of these inset poems are, in form and content, "psalms" since they would fit perfectly well within the Book of Psalms. But instead of being placed in the Psalter,[1] these compositions have been inserted into narrative and prophetic books for literary and religious purposes. The comparative study of these psalms inserted whole into non-hymnic contexts is the subject of this review of research.

Most of these individual psalms have been studied extensively as to their internal structure, time of origin, and original message. Before 1990, however, very little attention had been given to comparing the roles they play in their literary contexts. That situation has now changed. As I was submitting my dissertation on the subject (1990),[2] Hans-Peter Mathys was completing his *Habilitationsschrift* (1989/90) covering the same range of texts and some others.[3] Three years later, Steven Weitzman added his dissertation (1993)[4] to the literature on

---

[1] Or in addition to appearing there, in the cases of 2 Samuel 22 = Psalm 18 and 1 Chron 16:8-36 = Pss 105:1-15, 96:1-13a, 106:1, 47-48.

[2] Published as James W. Watts, *Psalm and Story: Inset Hymns in Hebrew Narrative* (JSOTSup 139; Sheffield: JSOT Press, 1992).

[3] Published as Hans-Peter Mathys, *Dichter und Beter: Theologen aus spätalttestamentlichen Zeit* (OBO 132; Freiburg: Universitätsverlag, 1994).

[4] Published as Steven Weitzman, *Song and Story in Biblical Narrative: The History of a Literary Convention in Ancient Israel* (Bloomington, IN: Indiana

biblical songs outside the Psalter, while in the same year Johannes C. de Moor and Wilfred G. E. Watson published a collection of essays addressing the appearance of poetry in a variety of ancient Near Eastern prose literatures.[5] In 1994, Susan E. Gillingham published an introductory survey of "the poems and psalms of the Hebrew Bible" that included cultic poetry outside the Psalter.[6] In more narrowly focused studies, John Kleinig and Kurt Noll produced monographs on the role of hymnody in Chronicles and Samuel respectively.[7] This wave of research confirms Lyle Eslinger's observation that a new sub-field of biblical research has developed on the topic of inset psalms in their literary contexts.[8]

Examination of these various studies shows considerable overlap and agreement about the functions performed by inset psalms within their literary contexts, but also strong differences over certain aspects of the phenomenon and the methods used for its study. In what follows, I will first survey the common findings of the last decade's research before describing and evaluating disagreements over how to understand the literary and religious functions of inset psalmody.

## THE ROLES OF INSET HYMNS

The three monographs by Mathys, Weitzman, and myself agreed that almost all inset hymns are either late additions to pre-existing stories or are original parts of stories composed late in the Bible's compositional history. They reshape the surrounding literary structures in order to strengthen a theological focus on the acts of God, and/or provide models of proper worship through prayer and hymnody for readers to imitate. The appearance of inset hymns thus provides insight into the efforts of Jewish scribes in the Second Temple period to shape biblical literature for its use as scripture.

---

University Press, 1997).

[5] Johannes C. de Moor and Wilfred G. E. Watson (eds.), *Verse in Ancient Near Eastern Prose* (AOAT 42, Neukirchen-Vluyn: Neukirchener, 1993).

[6] S. E. Gillingham, *The Poems and Psalms of the Hebrew Bible* (Oxford: Oxford University Press, 1994) 136–69.

[7] John W. Kleinig, *The Lord's Song: The Basis, Function and Significance of Choral Music in Chronicles* (JSOTSup 156; Sheffield: Sheffield Academic Press, 1993); K. L. Noll, *The Faces of David* (JSOTSup 242; Sheffield: Sheffield Academic Press, 1997).

[8] Lyle Eslinger, review of *Faces of David* by K. L. Noll, in the *Review of Biblical Literature* (http://www.bookreviews.org/Reviews/1850756597.html).

The only clear example of an inset hymn in earlier biblical literature is Judges 5, which seems to have been placed after the battle narrative in Judges 4 prior to or during the composition of the book of Judges.[9] The evidence for the late insertion of the other psalms ranges from thematic gaps and plot disruptions to text-critical disturbances, but also includes in one case the existence of a version of the story without the hymn (Isaiah 38; cf. 2 Kings 20). All these point to the psalms being later additions to Exodus, Deuteronomy, Samuel, Isaiah, Daniel 2 and the Septuagint version of Daniel 3.[10] Many commentators have also considered the psalms in Jonah and 1 Chronicles to be secondary, but here attributing the hymns to the authors of the narratives makes better sense of their literary roles.[11] Yet the use of hymns in both books relies on and modifies the literary conventions of inset hymnody in the books of Samuel and Isaiah, while those at the end of Samuel imitate the end of Deuteronomy. Samuel, Jonah and 1 Chronicles thus represent the earliest examples we have of the tendency in Second Temple period literature (also Judith, Tobit, Luke, etc.) to place hymns and prayers in characters' mouths in imitation of biblical examples, which were themselves inserted into earlier literature.[12]

---

[9] Watts, *Psalm and Story*, 92–98; Weitzman, *Song and Story*, 57. Mathys suggested that Judges 5 is, like other inset hymns, also a late addition to its context (*Dichter und Beter*, 176).

[10] Watts, *Psalm and Story*, 32–37, 55–60, 74–79, 92–95, 110–14, 126–29, 149–52; Mathys, *Dichter und Beter*, 146, 156–57, 168, 173, 176, 179–80; Weitzman, *Song and Story*, 100–123; all building on the extensive bibliographies devoted to each of these hymns separately. On the text-criticism of 1 Samuel 1–2, see especially Emanuel Tov, "Different Editions of the Song of Hannah and of Its Narrative Framework," in M. Cogan, B. L. Eichler, and J. H. Tigay (eds.), *Tehillah le-Moshe: Biblical and Judaic Studies in Honor of Moshe Greenberg* (Winona Lake, IN: Eisenbrauns, 1997) 149–70.

[11] Watts, *Psalm and Story*, 141–43, 162–64. Mathys and Weitzman also credited 1 Chronicles 16 to the Chronicler, but Mathys evaluated Jonah 2 as an insertion (*Dichter und Beter*, 203, 215, 225), while Weitzman remained undecided as to its originality in context (*Song and Story*, 109–113).

[12] Watts, *Psalm and Story*, 175–81; and especially Weitzman, *Song and Story*, 59–123. For the contrary suggestion that the Deuteronomists of the late monarchic period were already responsible for the insertion of old hymns, see Johannes C. de Moor, "Poetic Fragments in Deuteronomy and the Deuteronomistic History," in F. García Martínez et al. (eds.), *Studies in Deuteronomy in Honour of C. J. Labuschagne* (VTSup 53; Leiden: Brill, 1994) 183–96.

The psalms emphasize God's role in the events recounted by the surrounding stories. This effect appears especially prominent when the stories, such as those of 2 Samuel, do not emphasize theological concerns. The realistic plots and characterizations of the stories about David and his family in 2 Samuel have been justly celebrated as great prose writing, but they produce in readers complex moral and religious evaluations of Israel's most celebrated king. On the other hand, David's thanksgiving psalm near the conclusion of the book (2 Samuel 22) depicts his religious devotion unambiguously. Together with Hannah's psalm in 1 Samuel 2, it brackets the books of Samuel with an explicit thematic summary in theo-political terms: God's absolute support for David.[13] In Exodus, God plays a more prominent role in the plot, yet the Song of the Sea (Exodus 15) goes further, placing exclusive emphasis on the divine warrior's victory over Egypt.[14] Deuteronomy 32 and Judges 5 also shape their contexts with similar theological agendas.

Because they are placed in the mouths of characters, inset psalms always characterize their speakers, such as David and Moses in the above examples. In some texts, characterization of the speaker seems to be a hymn's primary contribution to its context. The psalms shape readers' and hearers' evaluations of that individual and also model for them proper piety both in religious practice and in composing new literature.[15] Thus not only King David, but also King Hezekiah is given

---

[13] Watts, *Psalm and Story*, 107–109; Mathys, *Dichter und Beter*, 146. Also Randall C. Bailey, "The Redemption of YHWH: A Literary Critical Function of the Songs of Hannah and David," *BibInt* 3/2 (1995) 213–31; J. Vermeylen, *La loi du plus fort: Histoire de la rédaction des récits davidiques de 1 Samuel 8 à 1 Rois 2* (Leuven: University Press, 2000) 413–17. Walter Brueggemann analyzed the stories at the very beginning and end of Samuel to show that they, together with the psalms, create a thematic bracket around the book ("1 Samuel 1: A Sense of a Beginning," *ZAW* 102 [1990] 33–48).

[14] Watts, *Psalm and Story*, 51–55; Weitzman, *Song and Story*, 26–28.

[15] Watts, *Psalm and Story*, 189, 191–92; Mathys, *Dichter und Beter*, 225–27, 318, 321; Weitzman, *Song and Story*, 59, 63–70, 93–123. Noll took this point even further by arguing that the songs of 2 Sam 1:19-27, 22:1-51, and 23:1-7 contribute in crucial ways to David's characterization in the Deuteronomistic History as a whole: "There is a sense in which 2 Samuel 22 serves as the 'glue' which weds the complex portrait of David found in Samuel and early in Kings to the more simplistic image of David which is perpetuated through most of the remaining story" (*Faces of David,* 120).

a proper psalm in order to sing thanks for God's support (Isaiah 38), just as Daniel and his three friends do (Daniel 2 + Additions to Daniel 3). Jonah's psalm is particularly revealing: like Isaiah 38 and the Daniel psalms, it appears after deliverance has been promised but is not yet complete (Jonah sings thanks after being saved from drowning while he is still in the fish). These psalms thus model, not just a thankful attitude, but also trust in God's promised salvation. Yet the book of Jonah presents a stark discrepancy between the prophet's pious words in the psalm, as well as to the sailors (1:9) and even to God (4:2, quoting Exod 34:6-7), on the one hand, and his rebellious attitude that rejects God's mercy for Nineveh, on the other. The book thus seems already to expect reader recognition of the literary convention that inset hymnody characterizes the speaker's piety, setting up a false expectation that it undermines with its surprise ending.[16]

The use of inset hymnody reveals a sharp gender distinction in these models of piety. Men sing individualized thanksgiving psalms (e.g. David, Hezekiah, Jonah, Daniel and his three friends, and Tobit) while women sing nationalistic victory hymns (Deborah, Hannah, Judith, and Mary).[17] Though the precise form-critical classification of many of these hymns has been subject to considerable debate, the distinction between thanks for individual benefits and praise for national victories is clear enough. Thus David, though celebrating a career of military

---

[16] Watts, *Psalm and Story*, 135–40, 143–44; similarly Weitzman: "As I see it, however, such behavior—which really represents an attempt to parody the songs in biblical narrative—was only possible in a literary culture that expected biblical heroes to sing to God after he delivered them from danger" (*Song and Story*, 112). Mathys, on the other hand, found the tension between song and narrative too strong for both to have been written by the same author (*Dichter und Beter*, 225). For the minority view that the psalm's characterization of Jonah is completely consistent with that of the prose, see K. A. D. Smelik, "The Literary Function of Poetical Passages in Biblical Narrative," in J. Dyk (ed.), *Give Ear to My Words: Psalms and Other Poetry In and Around the Hebrew Bible* (Amsterdam: Societas Hebraica, 1996) 147–51.

[17] Watts, *Psalm and Story*, 29–30, 176, 180, 181. This women's tradition of hymnody was described at length by E. B. Poethig, "The Victory Song Tradition of the Women of Israel" (Ph.D. Diss., Union Theological Seminary, New York, 1985). The difference in gendered points of view in Judges 4–5 was also explored by Mieke Bal, *Murder and Difference: Gender, Genre, and Scholarship on Sisera's Death* (Bloomington, IN: Indiana University Press, 1988), and Athalya Brenner, "A Triangle and a Rhombus in Narrative Structure: A Proposed Integrative Reading of Judges IV and V," *VT* 40 (1990) 129–38.

victories, emphasizes God's support for himself personally, whereas Hannah, when celebrating the birth of her son, nevertheless emphasizes God's aid for Israel's victories. The chief exception to this rule would seem to be Exodus 15, where Moses and the Israelite men sing a victory song praising God's victory at the sea. Yet the women also sing, perhaps an antiphonal response to the whole song, and comparison with other stories of victory songs makes clear that it is the women who are playing their conventional role here. The men, however, are displaced from their conventional warrior role by God's single-handed victory over the Egyptians, and so join the women in the praise choir.[18]

Short fragments of hymns and songs may serve to motivate plot developments in biblical narratives: for example, a couplet from a victory hymn prompts Saul's jealousy of David (1 Sam 18:6-9; also 21:12 [11], 29:5), and David sings a dirge for Abner (2 Sam 3:33-34) to demonstrate publicly his innocence for Abner's murder. Balaam's Oracles (Numbers 23–24) are the only longer poems to play such plot roles. The other songs and hymns quoted in full within narrative contexts do not further the plot, that is, no subsequent action occurs as a consequence of their being sung. The levitical medley in 1 Chronicles 16 does illustrate the plot of its context, which concerns the ranks and duties of levitical musicians in the Temple. For the most part, however, inset hymns serve instead to structure blocks of material with the themes of God's deliverance and the singer's piety. While Deborah's Song simply concludes and amplifies the battle account in the previous chapter (Judges 4–5), psalms appear at the end of larger sections of text in Exodus (the Song of the Sea after the plagues and exodus story of chaps. 1–14), Deuteronomy (the Song of Moses and "Blessing" of Moses climax the book), and Samuel (bracketed by Hannah's Psalm near the beginning and David's Thanksgiving and "Last Words" near the end).[19] Thus inset psalms often serve to make

---

[18] Watts, *Psalm and Story*, 51–54; Weitzman, *Song and Story*, 28–29. Another exception may be found in Habakkuk 3. However, the oracular context and liturgical setting gives the issue of characterization in this psalm a different impact (see below).

[19] Watts, *Psalm and Story*, 186–89 and *passim*; Mathys, *Dichter und Beter*, 156–57, 179. Weitzman's strict distinction between the roles played by Exodus 15, Judges 5 and Deuteronomy 32 and those of other inset hymns is discussed below (under "Poetry, Parallels, and Literary Conventions").

explicit the themes and boundaries of textual units. As we have already seen, other hymns highlight their speaker's piety by appearing when deliverance has been promised but has not yet been fully manifested (Isaiah 38, Jonah 2, Daniel, Additions to Daniel). These psalms provide thematic emphasis primarily by characterizing their speakers.

The use of inset hymns to emphasize theological themes, to structure books, and to model characters' piety all suggest various efforts to shape older texts for their role as scripture, a process Weitzman called "scripturalization."[20] Gerald Sheppard pioneered the study of how editors employed inset hymns in the "canon-conscious" shaping of Samuel, arguing that the editing and arrangement of 2 Samuel 21–24 "is integral to the final, constitutive formation of biblical books."[21] The comparative studies by Matthys, Weitzman and myself suggested that similar motives lie behind the appearance of most other inset hymns as well, if one includes under "canonical" the concerns not only for the structure and boundaries of biblical books, but also for their use in modeling devotional and liturgical practices. Weitzman in particular has elaborated on the use of inset songs to emphasize study and prayer as proper Jewish piety.[22] Not only did it elevate the text's status as scripture, such modeling marked the contents of many biblical books profoundly: "The scripturalization of biblical narrative actually propelled its compositional development."[23]

This consensus about the function of inset hymnody grew out of studies motivated by different methodological concerns. While Mathys emphasized theological issues, Weitzman and I were concerned first of all with literary history and conventions. These two different approaches overlap a great deal, but they also point to two constellations of issues over which there remains considerable disagreement and which go to the heart of how to interpret the phenomenon of inset hymnody in its ancient literary and cultural contexts. In what follows, I will first discuss the problems involved in the literary history of inset hymns, then turn to contested issues surrounding their thematic and religious roles in context.

---

[20] Watts, *Psalm and Story*, 60–61, 116–17, 191; Mathys, *Dichter und Beter*, 125, 164, 180, 317; Weitzman, *Song and Story*, 12–13, 93–123.

[21] Gerald T. Sheppard, *Wisdom as a Hermeneutical Construct* (BZAW 151; Berlin: De Gruyter, 1980) 155; see also pp. 145–59.

[22] Weitzman, *Song and Story*, 59–92, 93–123.

[23] Weitzman, *Song and Story*, 129.

POETRY, PARALLELS, AND LITERARY CONVENTIONS

The works by Weitzman, Noll and myself have focused on the literary roles played by inset songs in their contexts, but have differed over how these should be analyzed. I focused on the interplay between literary analyses of the hymns' contextual roles and historical observations about their lack of originality to their contexts. So after synchronic analysis of each psalm's effects on the story's plot, themes and characterization, I factored these conclusions into long-standing arguments about its literary history.[24]

Others have focused primarily on one or another of these elements. Mathys emphasized thematic analysis (see SCRIPTURE, WISDOM, AND PERFORMANCE below). Noll evaluated the songs' contribution to characterizing their speakers. He used a theoretical distinction to argue that the discrepancy between 2 Samuel 22's glorification of David and the context's diminution of his accomplishments was produced by tension between the biased narrator and the implied author.[25] He concluded that the songs in Samuel serve to emphasize this discrepancy and therefore strengthen the literature's aesthetic cast, just the opposite of the scripturalizing tendency noted by Mathys, Weitzman, and myself. Noll argued, "The narratives were strung together to function aesthetically, not canonically ... the Former Prophets give every appearance that their authors were not interested in creating the kind of literary authority that the Bible eventually became for several religious communities."[26] Noll's conclusions developed out of frequently noticed tensions within the books of Samuel, but they look implausible from a comparative perspective on inset hymnody in biblical (and other) literature. The appearance of similar literary patterns in various other Second Temple period works suggest looking, not to unreliable narrators, but to scripturalizing editors and authors to account for

---

[24] Watts, *Psalm and Story*, 17–18 ("Shape of the Study") and 198–205 ("Methodological Conclusions"). This neat methodological distinction often faded in the face of textual details: "When the full complexity of the biblical text was taken into account in evaluating the compositional history of psalms in narrative contexts, the methodological dichotomy between synchronic and diachronic explanations frequently broke down. That is, the same psalm could be labeled both 'original' and 'secondary,' depending on the size of the contextual frame of reference" (p. 201).

[25] Noll, *Faces of David*, 28–30, 120.

[26] Noll, *Faces of David*, 37.

them.[27] Tension between narrative and hymnic characterizations of
the singers seem to be typical rather than unusual, even when the
same author wrote both, as in Jonah and Judith.[28]

I also argued that the inclusion of hymns into biblical narratives was
not usually done *ad hoc* but was informed by literary conventions. I
identified two different structural conventions: insertion of hymns as a
concluding climax or bracketing structure (Exodus 15, Deuteronomy
32, Judges 5, 2 Samuel 22, 1 Chronicles 16, Judith, Tobit), or insertion prior to deliverance to model faithful piety (Isaiah 38, Jonah 2,
Daniel 2, Add Dan). In addition, Deuteronomy 32 and 1 Chronicles 16
seemed to me to serve distinctive thematic purposes within those
books.[29] Weitzman made the exploration of such literary conventions
the focus of his work, and also found two kinds of conventions at
work in biblical literature. The first adapts several patterns from other
Ancient Near Eastern literature, such as the victory hymn after a battle
account and the topos of a sage's last words, to shape the use of Exodus 15, Judges 5, and Deuteronomy 32. The second enhances the piety
of biblical heroes by placing appropriate songs of praise in their
mouths, thereby enhancing the text's usefulness as scripture.[30] Unfortunately, Weitzman ignored my description of the two conventions,
thus missing an opportunity for constructive debate over how to characterize these larger patterns of inset hymnody as well as failing to
note our similar conclusions about many individual texts. His summary and critique of my work focused almost exclusively on the
methodological issues surrounding the distinction between prose and
poetry on the one hand, and the use of ancient Near Eastern literary
parallels on the other. It is therefore to these issues that I now turn
before addressing the debate over how to characterize the two traditions of inset hymnody.

---

[27] I do not rule out of hand the possibility of unreliable narrators in ancient lit-
erature, but think that the case for one in Samuel is very tenuous. For my applica-
tion of the concept, see James W. Watts, "The Unreliable Narrator of Job," in S.
L. Cook, C. L. Patton and J. W. Watts (eds.), *The Whirlwind: Essays on Job,
Hermeneutics and Theology in Memory of Jane Morse* (JSOTSup 336; London:
Sheffield Academic Press, 2001) 168–80.

[28] Linda Day described the ambiguous characterization of Judith, who claims
more credit in her psalm than the story grants her ("Faith, Character and Perspective in Judith," *JSOT* 95 [2001] 71–93). On Jonah, see above.

[29] Watts, *Psalm and Story*, 191–93.

[30] Weitzman, *Song and Story*, 124–31.

First, the prose-poetry distinction: inset hymns are frequently described as poems quoted in a prose narrative, but this raises the contentious question of how exactly to distinguish prose from poetry. The long history of wrestling with the definition and quality of Hebrew poetry was analyzed by James Kugel, who concluded that interpreters have mostly imposed later definitions of poetry onto biblical materials: "the concepts of poetry and prose correspond to no precise distinction in the Bible."[31] That conclusion has been contested by many scholars who have continued to put forward varying criteria for distinguishing poetry from prose.[32] Weitzman, a student of Kugel, carried this debate into his evaluation of inset hymnody by accusing many interpreters, including myself, of imposing our own notions of poetry onto the biblical texts.[33] He therefore wrote about "songs" rather than "poems" or "psalms" in an attempt to stay closer to the Hebrew terminology used in the literature itself.

Such methodological caution is to be applauded, but in his summaries of other scholars' work, Weitzman made no effort to distinguish *a priori* bias from inductive conclusions about the differences between kinds of Hebrew texts. My observations about the distinctiveness of inset poems were made at the end of my book on the basis of detailed examinations of nine different narratives that included psalms. Thus my conclusion that "prose narrative usually eschews direct commentary .... Poetry, by contrast, does not narrate sequentially, but offers vivid descriptions of feelings and emphatic statements of ideas instead" described an inductive observation about Hebrew literature, as was made clear by contrasting it with the epic literatures of the ancient Near East.[34] It is precisely the contrast between biblical use of poetry and prose and the epic poetry of other ancient cultures that makes this

---

[31] James L. Kugel, *The Idea of Biblical Poetry: Parallelism and its History* (New Haven, CT: Yale University Press, 1981) 302.

[32] See, for example, W. G. E. Watson, *Classical Hebrew Poetry: A Guide to Its Techniques* (JSOTSup 26: Sheffield: JSOT Press, 1984) 46–54; W. van der Meer and J. C. de Moor (eds.), *The Structural Analysis of Biblical and Canaanite Poetry,* JSOTSup 74; Sheffield: JSOT Press, 1988; W. T. Woldemar Cloete, "Distinguishing Prose and Verse," in De Moor and Watson (eds.), *Verse in Ancient Near Eastern Prose*, 31–40; Gillingham, *Poems and Psalms of the Hebrew Bible*, 18–43; Jichan Kim, *The Structure of the Sampson Cycle* (Kampen: Kok Pharos, 1993) 116–34.

[33] Weitzman, *Song and Story*, 1–3, 143–45.

[34] Watts, *Psalm and Story*, 194.

an interesting conclusion. Indeed, the comparison suggests that the real mystery involves, not the appearance of poetry in prose, but rather the exclusive use of prose rather than epic to narrate biblical stories.

This whole debate is irrelevant, however, for the study of inset hymnody. Distinguishing these texts from the surrounding stories does not depend on the prose-poetry distinction at all, for the simple reason that they are clearly marked with introductory formulas or labels to differentiate them from their contexts. The most common markers are nominal or verbal forms of שׁיר ("sing, song," Exod 15:1; Deut 31:19, 21, 22, 30; 32:44-45; Judg 5:1; 2 Sam 22:1; cf. also Num 21:17; Greek ὑμνέω/ὕμνος in Add Dan 1; Jdt 15:13). The Levitical personnel who voice the hymn in 1 Chronicles 16 are explicitly labeled משׁררים ("singers," 1 Chron 15:16, 19, 27) and David's compositions are labeled קינה ("lament/dirge") in 2 Sam 1:17, 3:33. Some labels might refer to either poetry or prose: Hannah and Jonah התפלל ("pray") their psalms (1 Sam 2:1; Jon 2:2) and Hezekiah's psalm is termed a מכתב ("writing, letter," Isa 38:9). The hymns sometimes contain internal markers of song, such as אשׁירה ("I will sing," Exod 15:1; Judg 5:3) or שׁירו ("Sing!" Exod 15:21; 1 Chron 16:9).[35] Thus biblical texts explicitly distinguish inset hymns and some other genres of poetry from their contexts.

The psalm in Habakkuk 3 shows how far ancient authors or editors could go to mark an inset hymn explicitly. Placed after prophetic oracles that share with it the usual characteristics of Hebrew poetry, this piece exhibits more explicit markers of its hymnic status than any other text in the Hebrew Bible. The technical jargon contained in both the superscription and colophon (Hab 3:1, 19) — together with the repeated liturgical interjection *Selah* (vv. 3, 9, 15) — make its psalmic nature impossible to miss, even if readers do not recognize its similarity to other hymns of victory (Exodus 15, Deuteronomy 33, Judges 5, Ps 77:16-20), most of which appear outside the Psalter. The author or editor of Habakkuk 3 wanted his readers to recognize very clearly that this was a psalm.[36]

---

[35] For full discussion, see James W. Watts, "'This Song': Conspicuous Poetry in Hebrew Prose," in de Moor and Watson (eds.), *Verse in Ancient Near Eastern Prose*, 345–48 (reproduced at http://web.syr.edu/~jwwatts/ThisSong.htm).

[36] For full discussion, see my "Psalmody in Prophecy: Habakkuk 3 in Context," in J. W. Watts and P. R. House (eds.), *Forming Prophetic Literature: Es-*

Now that is not to say that ancient Hebrew literature deploys consistent terminology for genre categories; it does not. The appearance of anthologies of similar compositions, such as in the Psalter and Song of Songs, when other kinds of poems (such as secular dirges and patriarchal or prophetic "blessings") appear only in narrative contexts, shows that the ancient editors worked with an awareness of a wider array of genres than this limited set of Hebrew terms suggests. Such collections warrant our application of genre labels such as "psalm" or "hymn" and even "poem" which have no equivalent in biblical Hebrew, so long as the definition of those terms arises inductively from the ancient texts rather than just from modern analogues. Then inductive observations about differences between such inset genres and their contexts, such as the absence of emotive responses in the narratives or the absence of narration in the songs, simply follow from the explicit distinctions made by the texts themselves. Comparative analysis of these texts does not depend on resolving the prose-poetry debate first.

The second issue involves the use of ancient Near Eastern parallels for understanding the phenomenon of biblical inset psalmody. In an appendix, I surveyed patterns of inset hymnody in various ancient narrative literatures.[37] Inset poetry and songs, a rare phenomenon in

---

*says on Isaiah and the Twelve in Honor of John D. W. Watts* (JSOTSup 235; Sheffield: Sheffield Academic Press, 1996) 209–223. (This article is reproduced at http://web.syr.edu/~jwwatts/Hab3.htm)

[37] Watts, *Psalm and Story*, 206–220. Weitzman chose to focus his strongest critique of my work, not on the body of my book whose contents most paralleled his own, but rather on this appendix because of its "rather imprecise use of comparative evidence" (*Song and Story*, 9). Weitzman confused my cataloguing of ancient literary practices, which demonstrated precisely the diversity that he ridiculed, with an argument for literary dependence, which I explicitly denied: "The similarities of these texts to Hebrew psalms in narrative contexts are in no case close enough for there to be any question of direct literary dependence." Nevertheless, the links between the Hebrew psalms and hymns embedded in other ancient Near Eastern texts, especially the Piye Stela from ca. 734 BCE, do suggest that the Hebrew usage developed out of a literary culture containing elements of both Mesopotamian and Egyptian provenance (Watts, *Psalm and Story*, 219). My point was simply that inset poetry and songs, a rare phenomenon in modern narrative, is relatively common in ancient literatures and so their appearance in biblical texts should cause no great surprise. I also pointed out that Egyptian literature provides closer parallels than do the Mesopotamian epic and historiographical traditions that have been cited more commonly in this regard. Weitzman under-

modern narratives, are relatively common in ancient stories. Their appearance in biblical texts, then, should cause no great surprise. The
closest parallel to biblical usage is found in the Egyptian Piye Stela,
an 8th century BCE royal inscription. The stela's restrained prose account of Piye's conquests incorporates two victory hymns sung by
enthusiastic crowds, the longer one at the very end of the inscription.[38] The placement of the Song of Deborah in Judges 5 after the
battle account in Judges 4 seems to reflect the same literary convention as the Piye Stela, and from roughly the same time period.[39]
Weitzman deepened the analysis of this parallel considerably, noting
that both the concluding song of the Piye stela and the Song of the Sea
in Exodus 15 aim "not only to celebrate the victory of the divine warrior over his foes but also to acclaim him as an eternal, invincible
ruler."[40]

He demonstrated that the stela's victory hymns are the culmination
of a five-century-old trend in Egyptian battle accounts to shape readers' evaluation of the king's actions. The songs model the desired
reader response. Weitzman thus explained the role of the Song of the
Sea on the basis of a literary convention produced by the political
concerns of Egyptian royal inscriptions. It was employed in Exodus
out of a similar concern to actualize for readers Israel's jubilant response to God's salvation.[41]

Weitzman argued, however, that the remainder of the Bible's inset
hymns have no relationship to this Egyptian convention. He tried to
explain the role of the Song of Moses in Deuteronomy 31–32 on the

---

mined his own methodological critique by accepting and elaborating on the closest parallel I discovered, the Piye Stela, to understand Exodus 14–15 and Judges
4–5. He concluded, "In my view, ... Exodus 15 and the Piye Stela preserve independent manifestations of a literary practice shared by Egyptian and Israelite
scribes" (*Song and Story*, 21) — precisely my point.

[38] Watts, *Psalm and Story,* 213–14, 219. For the texts, see N.-C. Grimal, *La
Stèle Triomphale de Pi('ankh)y au Musée du Caire* (Cairo: IFAO, 1978). For an
English translation, see Miriam Lichtheim, *Ancient Egyptian Literature: A Book
of Readings* (Berkeley: University of California Press, 1973, 1976, 1980)
3.66–84.

[39] Watts, *Psalm and Story,* 96–97, 196; Weitzman, *Song and Story*, 31–36.

[40] Weitzman, *Song and Story,* 19.

[41] Weitzman, *Song and Story,* 17–30. On actualization in Exodus 15 and elsewhere, see J. W. Groves, *Actualization and Interpretation in the Old Testament*
(SBLDS 86; Atlanta: Scholars Press, 1987); and Watts, *Psalm and Story,* 60–62.

basis of strained parallel with the Aramaic wisdom text, *Ahiqar*.[42] However, *Ahiqar* is a fragmentary text known only from late sources, and it contains no hymn or song. So despite the fact that Moses and *Ahiqar* both deliver warning speeches to rebellious sons or followers, the parallel explains nothing about the choice of a hymnic genre in Deuteronomy 32. Nevertheless, Weitzman's conclusion that different songs were incorporated on the basis of different literary conventions can be accepted readily enough, even if the specific conventions are more debatable.[43]

Much less plausible, however, was his sharp distinction between the songs whose placement is influenced by ancient Near Eastern conventions (Exodus 15, Deuteronomy 32, Judges 5) and those whose position reflects the emerging "canon-conscious culture" of Second Temple Judaism (e.g. 1 Samuel 2, 2 Samuel 22).[44] Like other investigators of the Samuel psalms, Weitzman noted that they imitate the earlier group of texts to "scripturalize" the literature of Samuel, in the process not only characterizing their speakers' piety but also providing a thematic bracket around the book.[45] But Weitzman's sharp distinction between the "two distinct literary cultures" led him to underestimate the large-scale structural roles also played by Exodus 15 and Deuteronomy 32.[46] Writers can and do draw on multiple genre conventions simultaneously: the Song of the Sea can both conclude the battle account that immediately precedes and climaxes the exodus story of the first third of the book, and various features of Exodus 1–15 suggest that it does just that.[47] Mathys also distinguished these

---

[42] Weitzman, *Song and Story*, 37–55.

[43] Weitzman, *Song and Story*, 55–58; similarly, Watts, *Psalm and Story,* 186–92.

[44] "The act of inserting songs within biblical narrative changed over the course of Israelite literary history, evolving from an assortment of disparate Near Eastern scribal practices into a fully formed literary convention unique to the Bible and the later religious literatures which sought to emulate it" (Weitzman, *Song and Story*, 58).

[45] Weitzman, *Song and Story*, 120, 124–31.

[46] Watts, *Psalm and Story*, 48–51, 55, 60–62, 71–72, 74, 79–80, 186–87.

[47] Watts, *Psalm and Story*, 49. Elaborating on this observation, Mark Smith and William Propp have argued that Exodus 15 serves as a pivot at the center of the whole book that "both concludes the first half of Exodus and opens the second half" (William H. C. Propp, *Exodus 1–18* [AB 2; New York: Doubleday, 1999] 38; building on Mark S. Smith, *The Pilgrimage Pattern in Exodus* [JSOTSup 239.

two groups of inset hymns, but only as to the degree of canon-consciousness that their positions reflect.[48] Some psalms serve to structure books (Deuteronomy) or large sections of books (Exodus 1–14) in a scripturalizing, if not a fully canon-conscious, way. (Only the role of Judges 5 role seems to be limited to its immediate context.) Weitzman admitted at the end of his book that several literary conventions for the use of inset hymnody can be at work at the same time — "The culture of canon-consciousness is defined in part by its need to emulate the culture which preceded it, and the earlier culture never completely gave way to its successor" — but he cited only Tobit.[49]

The fact is that some late Second Temple literature is, in its mix of hymnody and narrative, actually more like older Near Eastern epic and historiography than is the preponderance of earlier biblical narrative. For example, the rule that only characters voice hymns is broken by the narrators of Chronicles, Ezra and 1 Maccabees who themselves seem to join in the liturgical refrain "for his kindness is forever."[50] 1 Maccabees goes even further, placing hymns and praise songs in the narrator's voice in a way very reminiscent of epic style.[51] A broad survey of the use of inset songs in ancient literatures reveals the emergence of parallels at various stages in Israel's literary culture and helps guard against jumping to conclusions about unique developments.

What is clear enough is that biblical examples of inset hymnody were increasingly emulated as the Second Temple period progressed.[52] The constellation of 2 Samuel 22 and 23 within a four-chapter "appendix" to Samuel was clearly designed to emulate the role of Deuteronomy 32 and 33 in the ending of Samuel. 1 Chronicles 16 in turn probably adapts the tradition of David's hymns from Samuel to address its very different concerns for liturgical hymnody.[53]

---

Sheffield: Sheffield Academic Press, 1997] 30–39).

[48] Mathys, *Dichter und Beter*, 126, 180.

[49] Weitzman, *Song and Story*, 130.

[50] 1 Chron 16:41; 2 Chron 5:13; 7:3, 6; Ezra 3:11; 1 Macc 4:24; Watts, *Psalm and Story*, 157–58, 196–97.

[51] Watts, *Psalm and Story*, 178, 196. See G. O. Neuhaus, *Studien zu den poetischen Stücken im 1.Makkabäerbuch* (FzB 12; Würzburg: Echter, 1974).

[52] Watts, *Psalm and Story*, 181, 185.

[53] O. Plöger, "Reden und Gebete im deuteronomistischen und chronistischen

The tradition of victory hymns welding together Egyptian literary conventions with Israel's cultural tradition of women war singers emerges not just in battle contexts such as Exodus 14–15, Judges 4–5, and Judith, but also in Hannah's and Mary's songs (1 Samuel 2, Luke 1), the former clearly a model for the latter. Translations and retellings of biblical stories increasingly supplied additional psalms for characters to sing, and the multiplication of historical superscriptions in various versions of the Psalter pointed out the potential for additional insertions.[54] The four poems and poem-fragments of Luke 1–2, one of several stylistic imitations of the Greek Septuagint in Luke's prologue, show that, by the end of the period, inset psalmody had become an expected feature of "biblical" style. Weitzman described this development in detail, noting that "the scripturalization of biblical literature led early Jews to emulate its genres and stylistic characteristics in their own literary and liturgical compositions," which in turn effected the shape of the biblical literature itself, as we have seen.[55] There remains, however, some disagreement about the nature and purpose of this activity, so it is to this issue that I now turn.

## SCRIPTURE, WISDOM, AND PERFORMANCE

The historical development of the convention of inset hymnody has been characterized in different ways. I described it as an emerging trend in Jewish literature, especially of the Second Temple period, rooted in Egyptian conventions and perhaps reflecting the use of inset songs and poetry in a broader range of ancient Near Eastern narrative literatures.[56] Weitzman described the increasing use of inset songs for the purpose of scripturalization in much greater detail, but characterized the phenomenon of inset hymnody itself as "a literary constant" in Israel that reflected two distinct cultures and many different genre conventions.[57] Mathys, however, characterized the phenomenon as a

---

Geschichtswerk," in W. Schneemelcher (ed.), *Festschrift Günther Dehn* (Neukirchen-Vluyn: Kreis Moors, 1957) 39–41, 46; Watts, *Psalm and Story*, 165–67.

[54] Watts, *Psalm and Story*, 175–85.

[55] Weitzman, *Song and Story*, 128; see 59–123. See also Yair Zakovitch, "Poetry Creates Historiography," in S. M. Olyan and R. C. Culley (eds.), *"A Wise and Discerning Mind": Essays in Honor of Burke O. Long* (BJS 325; Providence, RI: Brown Judaic Studies, 2000) 311–20.

[56] Watts, *Psalm and Story*, 186–97, 218–20.

[57] Weitzman, *Song and Story*, 12 and *passim*.

uniquely "late post-exilic" development reflecting Jewish theological trends.[58]

Mathys looked for the theological and canonical significance of the songs from the start. He argued that the late addition of prayers, doxologies and psalms to biblical texts reflects a systematizing tendency in Second Temple Judaism. The inserted texts convert the specific stories around them into paradigms suitable for teaching.[59] Thus Mathys focused primarily on the inserts' thematic contributions to their contexts. (Kleinig's investigation of choral music in Chronicles also explored the thematic contribution made by inset hymns, as well as references to songs and singers, but with implications less for systematizing theology than for Second Temple liturgical practice and for the theological significance of song itself.[60])

Mathys's thematic emphasis depended explicitly on understanding later Second Temple psalmody in general and inset psalmody in particular as a product of Wisdom traditions. He contrasted the scribal, editorial, and didactic nature of inset hymnody with oral cultic poetry designed to address a variety of situations in an open-ended manner. Sigmund Mowinckel first elaborated this thesis of a "learned psalmography" dedicated to the composition of prayers and psalms as acts of piety. Scribes inserted appropriate psalms into narratives to provide models of the practice.[61] (Traditions of didactic hymnody also developed in other ancient cultures, such as New Kingdom Egypt.[62])

---

[58] Mathys, *Dichter und Beter*, 312.

[59] Mathys, *Dichter und Beter*, 1, 179–80, 317. He concluded: "Interpretation, Verallgemeinerung, Zusammenfassung, Kanonisierung — dafür eignen sich Gebete, Psalmen und Doxologien in besonders ausgezeichneter Weise" (p. 318).

[60] Kleinig, *The Lord's Song*, 14 and *passim*.

[61] Sigmund Mowinckel, "Psalms and Wisdom," in M. Noth and D. W. Thomas (eds.), *Wisdom in Israel and in the Ancient Near East* (Festschrift H. H. Rowley; VTSup 3; Leiden: Brill, 1955) 205–224, esp. 211, 222; *idem, The Psalms in Israel's Worship* (2 vols., Oxford: Blackwell, 1962) 2.115.

[62] Jan Assman observed that the earliest Egyptian hymns come from the Middle Kingdom and are found in three contexts: in the cult, in grave inscriptions, and in literature (e.g. the tale of Sinuhe). Royal hymns are at home in literature and also in the cult, but not in grave inscriptions, whereas divine hymns appear in grave inscriptions and no doubt arise from the cult, but do not appear in literature. But in the New Kingdom, divine hymns become a literary genre as well: "Das heisst: ihrer Hauptabsicht besteht darin, ein Wissen von Gott in den literarischen Diskurs einzubringen, der das fundierende Wissen und Weltbild vermittelt. Liter-

Mathys combined this thesis with Sheppard's observations about the use of psalms for canonical shaping, arguing that Jewish scribes composed and inserted didactic psalms to shape the literature theologically.[63] He pointed out that much of the Hebrew Bible recounts contingent history, and canonization presses the question of the significance of this history. Inset psalms answer by making the history of God's salvation of Israel less contingent and more paradigmatic, and by modeling Israel's appropriate response as thanksgiving.[64]

Mathys therefore emphasized that inset hymns were not composed for use in Temple liturgies, but were instead *kunst-psalmen*, products of a literary aesthetic that prized the composition of hymns and prayers as itself an act of piety.[65] He argued that Deuteronomy 32, 1 Samuel 2, 2 Samuel 22, Jonah 2, and 1 Chronicles 16 were all composed for insertion in these literary contexts, though incorporating traditional materials.[66] Their purpose is didactic, rather than cultic.[67] Susan Gillingham pushed the distinction even further, concluding that inset hymns reflect a scribal wisdom tradition, but that their placement in other literary contexts restricted their religious significance:

> A cultic poem (used in an entirely different context), when appropriated into a particular piece of literature, actually loses something of its more repeatable and more typical performative nature .... This more specific and particular adaptation contrasts with the liturgical poetry proper in the Psalter, where there is an open-ended orientation because of the re-usable nature of the psalms for all types of cultic occasions.[68]

---

arisch heisst in Ägypten zunächst und vor allem: edukativ" ("Verkünden und Verklären – Grundformen hymnischer Rede im alten Ägypten," in W. Burkert and F. Stolz (eds.), *Hymnen der Alten Welt im Kulturvergleich* [OBO 131; Freiburg: Universitätsverlag, 1994] 33–57 [41]).

[63] In the psalms outside the Psalter "entdeckt man zwar unterschiedliche, aber immer höchst kunstvolle, oft rabbinisch anmutende Theologie und stösst zugleich — so deutlich wie kaum noch im Alten Testament — auf Anfänge der Kanonisierung" (Mathys, *Dichter und Beter*, 125).

[64] Mathys, *Dichter und Beter*, 317–18.

[65] He also found the same tendencies at work in the Psalter, in Psalms 19, 33, 111/112, 117, 119, 130, 135, 144, 146 (*Dichter und Beter*, 231–316)

[66] Mathys, *Dichter und Beter*, 146, 168, 203, 219.

[67] Thus on Samuel, he concluded: "Die Kanonisierung beginnt hier mit Psalmen und Weisheit!" (*Dichter und Beter*, 164). And "Dtn 32 ist ein systematischer, lehrhafter Text in bunter Verkleidung" (p. 168).

[68] Gillingham, *Poems and Psalms of the Hebrew Bible*, 158, 169; see also pp.

Thus the insertion of the Song of the Sea into Exodus 15 "has limited its performative value to this context alone."[69] This distinction between cultic and literary hymnody derives from the old form-critical observation that hymnody developed through oral composition, but that some psalms can only have originated in writing (the most obvious cases are alphabetical acrostics). It also grows from the patent observation that those who inserted psalms showed considerable aesthetic sensitivity to traditional Jewish literature and hymnody.[70] This judgment about the different origins of particular compositions becomes misleading, however, when it is reified into an absolute distinction between the scribal and liturgical spheres. Not only is such separation highly unlikely in Second Temple Jewish society, but there is literary evidence of increasing interaction and influence between wisdom and priestly circles as the period progressed, even in regards to inset hymnody. On the basis of liturgical compositions from Qumran, Weitzman has shown that Philo's and Pseudo-Philo's rewriting of the Songs of Moses and Deborah reflected the liturgical practices of their own day. For these writers, "there was no clear line between the biblical past and the liturgical present."[71] Those who wrote and inserted hymns were expressing liturgical as well as aesthetic sensibilities.

Thus Mathys's observations about how inset hymns model pious thanksgiving are in some tension with his and Gillingham's insistence that they do not reflect liturgical practices. The root of the problem lies in an overly strict distinction between oral and literate cultures. Though particular pieces of literature can often be credited to oral or written composition, the activities of ancient people cannot be so neatly segregated. Even reading does not belong purely to the realm of literate culture, for ancient reading was almost always reading aloud and usually to an audience. Thus reading involved performance, and performance might invite audience participation. Here scribal and

---

159–60.

[69] Gillingham, *Poems and Psalms of the Hebrew Bible*, 145.

[70] See Weitzman, *Song and Story*, 65–70.

[71] Weitzman, *Song and Story*, 83; see 76–77, 80–83. On the basis of hymnic fragments in the Book of the Twelve, Erhard S. Gerstenberger has argued that liturgical influences shaped the depiction of prophets in the Second Temple biblical literature ("Psalms in the Book of the Twelve: How Misplaced are They?" *SBL 2000 Seminar Papers* [Atlanta: Society of Biblical Literature, 2000] 254–62).

cultic activities can easily merge into *liturgy*, where oral recitation, ritual action and reading coalesce. The growing authority of Torah in Second Temple Judaism was evidenced first of all by its public reading.[72] The oral reading and aural reception of the authoritative text marked Torah's status in Temple and synagogue. It was the fact that Torah was *haMiqra* "the reading" that made it also "scripture" and "canon."

Such liturgical use of biblical literature eventually found its logical conclusion in the liturgical *singing* of many if not all biblical readings, as evidenced in late antiquity by the liturgies of both synagogue and church. How far back in time such cantorial traditions go cannot be determined. There is, however, evidence that inset hymns were used liturgically in the late Second Temple period.[73] Taken together, these observations suggest that, far from losing their liturgical application when inserted into other literary contexts as Gillingham suggested, hymns preserved their liturgical orientation and carried it into their new literary contexts. That is, rather than seeing the insertion of hymnody into other literatures as reducing the hymns' liturgical application, it was more likely an attempt, obviously successful, to appropriate the surrounding literature for use in liturgy.

Several inset psalms in the Hebrew Bible seem to serve precisely such a function. The Song of the Sea concludes not just the story of the Reed Sea but the entire exodus account (Exodus 1–14) with a celebration of God's victory that takes the anachronistic perspective of later generations (that is, the readers and hearers), rather than the people with Moses at the sea. In the song, the exodus generation and the readers are merged into the one people of God, thereby appropriating the exodus story as the readers' story as well. Deuteronomy 31 depicts the Song of Moses as a summary of Moses' threats and warnings for the people to memorize, in contrast to the law which priests read aloud every seven years. The song thus emphasizes and actual-

---

[72] See James W. Watts, *Reading Law: The Rhetorical Shaping of the Pentateuch* (The Biblical Seminar 59; Sheffield: Sheffield Academic Press, 1999) 15–31.

[73] For rabbinic and Qumran evidence, see the discussion cited by Weitzman, *Song and Story*, 74 and 175 n. 69. One should also add the evidence of the Septuagint "Odes," which excerpt inset hymns from their contexts and append them to the Psalter for liturgical use, though again this development cannot be securely dated.

izes the authority of the book.[74] Perhaps the most emphatic evidence of the use of a psalm to "liturgize" its context comes from the book of Habakkuk. Here the prophet's questions and complaints are answered by a theophany which takes the form of, not a private revelation to the prophet, but a very clearly marked psalm, that is, a public liturgy available to all Temple worshipers.[75]

In these cases and, I think, the rest of the texts discussed above, an inset hymn shapes the literature for liturgical appropriation. So along-side the role of inset psalmody in scripturalization and canonization, we should emphasize even more its *liturgizing* role in shaping the Hebrew Bible.

## SELECT BIBLIOGRAPHY

Burkert, W. and F. Stolz, eds. *Hymnen der Alten Welt im Kulturvergleich* (OBO 131; Freiburg: Universitätsverlag, 1994).

Gillingham, S. E. *The Poems and Psalms of the Hebrew Bible* (Oxford: Oxford University Press, 1994).

Kleinig, J. W. *The Lord's Song: The Basis, Function and Significance of Choral Music in Chronicles* (JSOTSup 156; Sheffield: Sheffield Academic Press, 1993).

Mathys, H.-P. *Dichter und Beter: Theologen aus spätalttestamentlichen Zeit* (OBO 132; Freiburg: Universitätsverlag, 1994).

Moor, J. C. de and W. G. E. Watson (eds.). *Verse in Ancient Near Eastern Prose* (AOAT 42; Neukirchen-Vluyn: Neukirchener, 1993).

Noll, K. L. *The Faces of David* (JSOTSup 242; Sheffield: Sheffield Academic Press, 1997).

Watts, J. W. *Psalm and Story: Inset Hymns in Hebrew Narrative* (JSOTSup 139; Sheffield: JSOT Press, 1992).

—. "Psalmody in Prophecy: Habakkuk 3 in Context," in J. W. Watts and P. R. House (eds.), *Forming Prophetic Literature: Essays on Isaiah and the Twelve in Honor of John D. W. Watts* (JSOTSup 235; Sheffield: Sheffield Academic Press, 1996) 209–223. (Reproduced at http://web.syr.edu/~jwwatts/Hab3.htm)

—. "'This Song': Conspicuous Poetry in Hebrew Prose," in J. C. de Moor and W. G. E. Watson (eds.), *Verse in Ancient Near Eastern Prose* (AOAT 42; Neukirchen-Vluyn: Neukirchener Verlag, 1993) 345–58. (Also accessed at http://web.syr.edu/~jwwatts/ThisSong.htm)

Weitzman, S. *Song and Story in Biblical Narrative: The History of a Literary*

---

[74] Watts, *Psalm and Story*, 48–51, 60–62, 79–81, 191.

[75] Watts, "Psalmody in Prophecy," 222.

*Convention in Ancient Israel* (Bloomington, IN: Indiana University Press, 1997).

—. "Allusion, Artifice and Exile in the Hymn of Tobit," *JBL* 115 (1996) 49–61.

PART THREE


THE PSALTER AS BOOK,
INCLUDING SMALLER COLLECTIONS

# THE INTERPRETIVE SIGNIFICANCE OF SEQUENCE
# AND SELECTION IN THE BOOK OF PSALMS

HARRY P. NASUTI

The last twenty years have seen an important shift in the scholarly approach to the Psalms. Whereas most of the twentieth century was devoted to refining and developing the form-critical insights of Hermann Gunkel and Sigmund Mowinckel, recent attention has focused on the literary shape and theological orientation of the book of Psalms as a whole. Research has obviously continued on the literary and theological interpretation of the individual psalms, but considerable creative energy has been devoted to the place of these psalms—and the collections and genres to which they belong — in the larger whole.

Clearly, much very fruitful work has been done in this area in a remarkably short period of time. Nevertheless, one should also take note of a number of cautionary voices that are less convinced of either the possibility of isolating a single theological perspective for the book or the wisdom of focusing exclusively on the book nature of these texts.[1] One should perhaps also not ignore the larger question of whether the attempt to isolate the meaning of the Psalter's shape is in the end a redaction-critical or a canonical enterprise.[2]

This essay hopes to make a modest contribution to the present debate by examining two interpretive strategies that have played a sig-

---

[1] So, for example, E. S. Gerstenberger, "Der Psalter als Buch und als Sammlung," in K. Seybold and E. Zenger (eds.), *Neue Wege der Psalmenforschung* (Herders Biblische Studien 1: Freiburg: Herder, 1994) 3–13; and N. Whybray, *Reading the Psalms as a Book* (JSOTSup 222: Sheffield: Sheffield Academic Press, 1996).

[2] On this question, see M. Millard, "Von der Psalmenexegese zur Psalterexegese: Anmerkungen zum Neuansatz von Frank-Lothar Hossfeld und Erich Zenger," as well as the following responses by R. Rendtorff ("Anfragen an Frank-Lothar Hossfeld und Erich Zenger: Aufgrund der Lektüre des Beitrages von Matthias Millard"), F.-L. Hossfeld and E. Zenger ("Neue und Alte Wege der Psalmenexegese: Antworten auf die Fragen von M. Millard und R. Rendtorff"), and M. Millard ("Respons"), in *BI* 4 (1996) 311–45. Cf. also my *Defining the Sacred Songs: Genre, Tradition and the Post-Critical Interpretation of the Psalms* (JSOTSup 218; Sheffield: Sheffield Academic Press, 1999) 163–208.

nificant role in recent attempts to understand individual psalms as part of a larger entity. The first of these two strategies is that of sequence. Most form-critical scholars were not particularly interested in the order of the psalms, beyond attributing this order to historical factors in the development of the Psalter. However, for scholars interested in the shape of the book of Psalms, the sequence of the individual psalms is of crucial importance for the meaning of the larger whole. To take only one of the most commonly argued examples, such scholars have often seen the fact that the Psalter begins with Psalm 1 and ends with Psalms 146–150 as indicative of a significant and irreversible order in that book.

Despite the importance of sequence for such scholars, few have tried to argue that the movement from one psalm to the next has interpretive significance over the course of all the psalms in the book. It may simply be that such an argument is premature at this time and that it will be made at some point in the future. On the other hand, it may be that the book of Psalms is resistant to any analysis in which all the pieces neatly fit.[3] Such resistance may stem either from the inherently unwieldy (and non-sequential) nature of these texts or from constraints connected with the book's historical development.

Given the difficulty of accounting for the place of every psalm in the larger whole, scholars have generally coupled their interest in sequence with a second interpretive move, that of arguing that certain selected psalms are of particular significance. Some selections are based on the position of particular psalms at certain points in the book, such as the beginning and end of either the Psalter as a whole or the five individual "books" within the Psalter. Other selections are based on what is seen to be the significance of particular psalms or groups of psalms over against others. In such a vein, a number of scholars have argued for the significance of the lament psalms in the first half of the Psalter or of particular royal or torah psalms.

What needs to be seen in most of these cases is the interplay between the selection of certain psalms as significant and the overall point of the sequence of which they are seen to be a part. Thus, for example, highlighting the lament psalms in the first half of the Psalter and the psalms of praise at its end makes possible the argument that the book of Psalms moves "from lament to praise." Similarly, high-

---

[3] So Whybray, *Reading*. Cf. also B. S. Childs, *Introduction to the Old Testament as Scripture* (Philadelphia: Fortress, 1979) 522.

lighting the torah psalm at the beginning of the Psalter and the praise psalms at its end makes possible the argument for an "obedience to praise" sequence. For the scholars that make these arguments, it is the sequence of these selected psalms and psalm types that constitutes the theological point of the book of Psalms.

This essay will examine the ways that sequential arguments have been made for the Psalter, in both recent scholarship and throughout the Psalms' history of interpretation. It will also briefly consider the role of sequence in the interpretation of selected psalms that have been understood as groups. Finally, this essay will consider some possible reasons for the pervasiveness of the sequential understanding of the Psalms.

## SEQUENCE AND THE PSALMS: INITIAL CONSIDERATIONS

At its most basic level, a sequence may be seen as a series of connected elements whose order is significant for meaning. The key to understanding a particular sequence is being able to discern the nature of the connection between the elements. Over against other possible ways of arranging elements, a sequential arrangement is one distinguished by linear movement in a given direction. The order of the elements can not be reversed without affecting the meaning of the whole.

Perhaps the most easily recognizable sequence found in the Bible is that of narrative, which implies a temporal progression of events centered on a particular character or related set of characters. The temporal nature of narrative provides a basic structure for this sequence of events, although the order in which the reader is given access to information about these events is sometimes different than the temporal sequence itself. The difference between the temporal sequence and the order in which the reader learns about that sequence is, of course, of primary interpretive significance.

Obviously, the Psalter does not constitute a narrative sequence in the same way that such books as Genesis or Kings do. The Psalter does, however, contain narrative elements and historical allusions that have an impact on how one understands the sequence of the individual psalms. Especially prominent in this respect are references to events in the personal life of the first person speaker of the psalms (usually, though not always, identified with David in the tradition) and the historical life of Israel. As a first step, it will be useful to look at the implications for sequence of each of these possibilities.

THE FIGURE OF DAVID AND THE SEQUENCE OF THE PSALMS

One of the gains of the recent canonical approach to the Psalter has been its retrieval of the hermeneutical significance of the figure of David.[4] Many scholars now see the Davidic superscriptions as providing both a context for the interpretation of the individual psalms and an insight into the inner life of one of the main characters of 1 and 2 Samuel. Such scholars also have viewed this Davidic connection as helping to make the psalms available as the prayers of future generations.

Despite this recent interest in the David of the psalms, the significance of the Davidic superscriptions for how one understands sequence in the Psalter has received considerably less attention. In this respect, one may note the evidence of two types of superscriptions: those that simply ascribe a psalm "to" David and those that provide a more elaborate account of the historical circumstances under which David either composed or utilized a particular psalm. Also significant for the question of sequence is the Davidic postscript in Ps 72:20.

Given David's status as an historical figure with a well-known story, it would not be unreasonable to expect the psalms to be arranged in a chronological sequence according to the events of David's life. Along these lines, it has been suggested that the reference to the "conclusion" of David's prayers in Ps 72:20 also implies the end of that life.[5] In support of this is the fact that Ps 71:9 refers to the psalmist's old age and that Psalm 72 could be seen as David's prayer "for" Solomon, his son and successor. Such elements imply that one should understand the sequence of the first two Davidic collections (Psalms 3–41, 51–72) as basically chronological and biographical.

Despite the attractiveness of such an understanding of Psalms 71–72, it is doubtful that one can move from this to a similar understanding of the sequence of the entire Psalter or even of the first two Davidic collections, at least in their present form. Counting decisively against such a viewpoint is the evidence of the superscriptions, especially those that contain historical allusions to David's life.[6] Even a

---

[4] For a summary of recent scholarship on this issue, see my *Sacred Songs*, 128–62.

[5] So, for example, F.-L. Hossfeld, "Die unterschiedlichen Profile der beiden Davidsammlungen Ps 3–41 und Ps 51–72," in E. Zenger (ed.), *Der Psalter in Judentum und Christentum* (HBS 18; Freiburg: Herder, 1998) 59–74, esp. 66–68.

[6] The presence of even the simpler Davidic superscriptions later in the Psalter

quick overview of these psalms shows the difficulty of understanding the present shape of the Psalter in terms of the chronological sequence of David's life.

Thus, for example, the first of these psalms, Psalm 3, is situated during David's flight from his son, Absalom, an event recounted in 2 Samuel 15. On the other hand, the last of these psalms in the first two Davidic collections, Psalm 63, is situated during David's time "in the wilderness of Judah," apparently a reference to the period described in 1 Samuel 22–30. Even psalms right next to each other in the same Davidic collection show no interest in chronological sequence. Thus, Psalm 51 is situated after the confrontation with Nathan described in 2 Samuel 12, whereas Psalm 52 is situated at the time of David's flight from Saul in 1 Samuel 21.

Such evidence might well mean that those responsible for the historical superscriptions were faced with a psalms collection whose order was already largely fixed. It also, however, clearly indicates that either those same individuals did not consider sequence to be significant or they did not see the sequence of the psalms as chronological, at least with regard to the biographical details of David's life. One also notes that the last psalm in the Psalter with such a superscription, Psalm 142, is situated during David's early period in the wilderness, as described in 1 Samuel 26. Thus for the final shape of the Psalter, there is little to indicate any redactional interest in arranging the psalms according to the chronological sequence of David's life.[7]

This lack of chronological interest has long been apparent to interpreters of the Psalms, even before the modern era. This is clearly seen in the comments on the historical superscription of Psalm 3 found in *Midrash Tehillim*. There it is noted that the "exact order" of David's psalms (and apparently all of Scripture) is not known, except to God.[8] Indeed, the attempts of two rabbis to arrange the psalms in their

---

also counts against such a view.

[7] One should note the historical arguments of M. Goulder who contends that Psalms 51–72 are actually in chronological order corresponding to the historical events of David's life from the Bathsheba episode to the accession of Solomon. To argue this way, Goulder is, of course, forced to discount the canonical shape of the text, which includes the present historical superscriptions. See his *The Prayers of David Psalms 51–72: Studies in the Psalter II* (JSOTSup 102; Sheffield: Sheffield Academic Press, 1990).

[8] *Midrash Tehillim* 3.2; translations from W. G. Braude, *The Midrash on Psalms* (New Haven: Yale University, 1959).

"proper order" are thwarted, one by a command from a heavenly voice and the other by the rabbi's master. Whereas the heavenly voice warns against rousing "that which slumbers" (apparently David), the master cites Ps 111:7-8 to affirm the eternal validity, as well as the truth and righteousness, of the present order.[9]

In the Christian tradition, one may take note of Gregory of Nyssa's *Commentary on the Inscriptions of the Psalms*, which deals directly with this issue. Gregory freely acknowledges that "for anyone who may wish to examine the psalter, its order seems to differ from the course of historical events."[10] He continues, "Should a person consider the time in which David lived and the sequence of his deeds, he would not find the distribution of the psalms to agree with historical events." As will be seen below, this lack of chronological sequence in no way compromises what Gregory sees as the "well-thought-out order of the psalms."[11]

One should note that both *Midrash Tehillim* and Gregory are concerned to affirm the importance of sequence in the Psalter even as they recognize the difficulties of seeing this sequence in terms of the biographical narrative of David's life.[12] Indeed, these sources seem to see the Psalter's refusal to follow the expected biographical order as indicative of the existence of another type of sequence. It is, of course, the question of what constitutes the nature of that sequence that needs to be examined further.

## ISRAEL'S HISTORY AND THE SEQUENCE OF THE PSALMS

As noted above, recent scholars have increasingly retrieved the traditional significance of David both for the Psalter as a whole and for the individual psalms, especially those with historical superscriptions. There is, however, another way that David has functioned for modern

---

[9] Both Rashi and David Qimḥi (in their comments on Ps 72:20) also take note of the lack of chronological order in the Psalter.

[10] Book 2, Chap. 11. Translations in the text are from Saint Gregory of Nyssa, *Commentary on the Inscriptions of the Psalms* (transl. C. McCambley, OCSO; Brookline, MA: Hellenic College, n.d.).

[11] Gregory, *Inscriptions*, preface. One may compare this to the view of Diodore of Tarsus who sees their original order as having been disturbed because of the exile.

[12] So also Qimḥi, who connects the lack of chronological order to a desire to end the book with psalms of praise and future redemption from exile.

scholars, one that was less likely for earlier interpreters who tended to see David as in some way responsible for all the psalms. Because modern scholars do not share such a view, they have not restricted themselves to locating the psalms within the life of David. Instead, they have been able to view the psalms against a larger narrative, that of the history of Israel, of which David is only a part. It is the relationship between this historical narrative and the sequence of the psalms that makes this interpretive move of interest for the present analysis.

Particularly instructive along these lines is the work of Gerald Wilson, whose groundbreaking work on the shape of the Psalter has been particularly influential for later scholarship on the subject. As will be seen below, Wilson has taken note of a number of sequential aspects of the Psalms, such as the movement from lament to praise and from individual to communal concerns. It is, however, his more "historical" interpretation that will be examined in this section.

For Wilson, the royal psalms at the seams of the first three divisions of the Psalter have a particular importance for establishing the central question of that work. In Psalms 2, 72, and 89, Wilson sees allusions to the "institution, transmission, and failure" of the Davidic covenant.[13] It is the failure of this covenant that constitutes the theological crisis that lies at the heart of the Psalter. Wilson sees the answer to this crisis in the Mosaic Psalm 90 and the ensuing emphasis on God as the one true King that one finds in Book IV and the rest of the Psalter.

Wilson's argument has been much discussed in recent years, and that discussion need not be repeated here. What has perhaps not been adequately examined, however, is the sequential nature of Wilson's argument. By highlighting Psalms 2, 72, and 89, Wilson has set up an historical sequence that includes the origins of the Davidic covenant, its passing on to Solomon (Psalm 72), and its demise at the time of the exile (Ps 89:39-52). By taking note of this sequence, the reader is led to reflect on the larger narrative of Israel's history and the role of the Davidic covenant within that history.

It is significant that at this point Psalm 90 directs the reader's atten-

---

[13] See, for example, his "Shaping the Psalter: A Consideration of Editorial Linkage in the Book of Psalms," in J. C. McCann, Jr., (ed.), *The Shape and Shaping of the Psalter* (JSOTSup 159; Sheffield: Sheffield Academic Press, 1993) 72–82, esp. 78. See also his "The Use of Royal Psalms at the 'Seams' of the Hebrew Psalter," *JSOT* 35 (1986) 85–94; and "The Shape of the Book of Psalms," *Int* 46 (1992) 129–42.

tion to Moses, an allusion that clearly is counter to the historical progression that Wilson has described in Psalms 2, 72, and 89. As such,
the sequence no longer continues its straightforward account of Israel's history but instead reverts to an earlier stage of that history. In
more standard forms of narrative, such a manipulation of the temporal
sequence usually has interpretive significance for the reader. In Wilson's view, such is clearly also the case here, especially since this
temporal shift is coupled with an emphasis on an alternative theological tradition (the Mosaic over against the Davidic).

There is, however, a way in which Wilson's analysis of what happens at Psalm 90 goes beyond the usual manipulation of the temporal
sequence that one finds in standard narrative. Indeed, one may argue
that for Wilson the entire nature of the sequence changes at Psalm 90.
Up until this point, the reader who has followed the psalms in order to
Psalm 89 is looking back on what has happened in the past. At the end
of Psalm 89, the reader arrives at what seems to be his/her own point
of standing. There is no Davidic king on the throne, and the status of
the Davidic covenant is in serious doubt. For Wilson, the rest of the
Psalter is meant to encourage the reader to turn away from the mis-
takes of the past and embrace a different future.[14]

That is to say, the rest of the Psalter is not only the object of historical reflection but also a preferred theological stance that the reader is
meant to adopt. Unlike the earlier royal psalms, the psalms after
Psalm 90 express the proper sentiments of trust in and praise of God
as the one true King. For Wilson, the reader is clearly meant to adopt
these attitudes as his/her own.[15]

Two other aspects of Wilson's argument have implications for the
issue of sequence. First, the argument depends on a prior selection of
which psalms are to be a part of that sequence — namely, the royal
psalms that begin the first book and conclude the second and third
books of the Psalter. Secondly, the argument presumes the reader's

---

[14] Thus Wilson argues that in the psalms of Book IV Israel is "called ... to surrender — complete and absolute surrender to the eternal king whom they experience anew as creator and sustainer worthy of praise even in the midst of exile. ...
Israel is forced not only to acknowledge [Yahweh's] holiness but must also confront the reality of its own guilt" ("Shape," 140).

[15] As will be noted below, one finds a similar move in Wilson's more general
insights about the Psalter's move from lament to praise and individual to community.

familiarity with (and participation in) the narrative of Israel's history for an understanding of the proposed theological issues and a recognition of the disruption of the sequence at Psalm 90.

The importance of these aspects may be seen when one looks at other scholars who are indebted to Wilson's argument but who include other psalms in their sequence. Thus, for example, J. Clinton McCann has attempted to move beyond Wilson by considering "the psalms that begin Books I–III instead of concentrating principally upon the psalms that conclude these books."[16] McCann supports Wilson's view that "the editorial purpose of the Psalter was to address the problem posed by exile and dispersion, namely the apparent failure of the traditional Davidic/Zion covenant theology." However, his alternative selection of significant psalms leads him to the conclusion that while "an answer *does* come in Books IV and V, as Wilson suggests, ... Books I–III already begin to provide answers."[17]

Other scholars also see evidence of exilic concerns in Books I–III. Thus, for example, Frank-Lothar Hossfeld and Erich Zenger have argued for a view of the Psalter's development that includes exilic (and post-exilic) redaction of both the individual psalms and the psalms groupings in those books.[18] In such a view, the second David collection (Psalms 51–72) has been clearly shaped to address exilic concerns.[19] Indeed, even the predominantly pre-exilic first Davidic collection has undergone an exilic redaction in order to address the issues of the exile.

Obviously, these scholars raise a number of interesting possibilities for understanding both the historical development and the theological message of the Psalter. For the purposes of the present essay, however, it is the implication for how one understands the sequence that needs to be noted. By seeing a theological wrestling with the exile even in the earlier stages of the book, such scholars have significantly

---

[16] McCann, "Books I–III and the Editorial Purpose of the Hebrew Psalter," in his *Shape and Shaping*, 93–107, esp. 95. For a similar approach, see also N. L. deClaissé-Walford, *Reading from the Beginning: The Shaping of the Hebrew Psalter* (Macon, GA: Mercer University Press, 1997).

[17] McCann, "Editorial Purpose," 104.

[18] For a short summary of their view of the development of the Psalter, cf. F.-L. Hossfeld and E. Zenger, *Die Psalmen I: Psalm 1–50* (Würzburg; Echter, 1993) 14–15.

[19] Cf. Hossfeld, "Profile."

altered at least one aspect of Wilson's sequential argument. For them, the Psalter is not structured to evoke and then answer a particular historical problem as much as it assumes that problem from the start and addresses it throughout. Even if the answer to that problem is more directly present at later stages of the Psalter, it is "anticipated" or "foreshadowed" in a significant way at earlier stages of that work.[20]

One may clearly see the difference between these perspectives by raising the question of the reader's point of standing. For Wilson, the reader is one who both looks back on the historical sequence set forth in Psalms 2, 72, and 89 and is meant to adopt the theological stance of Psalm 90 and the following psalms. For scholars such as McCann, Hossfeld, and Zenger, the first part of the Psalter has received an exilic redaction that enables it to share in the preferred theological stance that the reader should assume. That is to say, the reader's point of standing is for the latter authors at least to a certain extent coterminous with all the psalms, since the first part of the Psalter is not completely "past" from the perspective of the reader.

The difference such a point of standing makes is perhaps especially clear when one considers the controversial question of the messianic interpretation of the royal psalms of the first part of the Psalter. If the reader's point of standing is between Psalms 89 and 90, Psalm 2 is most easily seen as something past, an object of historical reflection. If, on the other hand, the reader's point of standing is coterminous with all the psalms from the very start, Psalm 2 is free to function in a future messianic sense.[21]

---

[20] For redaction-critical scholars, the historical development of the Psalter is of interpretive significance. Because the redactional elements are seen as reflecting the intentionality of the final redactors, they are also seen as providing the key to the final shape of the Psalter. In a certain sense, the chronological sequence that is of interpretive significance for such scholars is one that exists "behind" the present text: the chronological sequence from the text that these redactors received to the text that they handed on. Such an understanding of the chronological development of the Psalter is, of course, very different from the type of chronological sequence that someone like Wilson has argued for "in" the text of the Psalter itself.

[21] A related issue is the similarly debated question of whether Psalm 2 is part of the introduction to the entire Psalter. On these issues, cf. the work of E. Zenger, summarized in "Der Psalter als Buch: Beobachtungen zu seiner Entstehung, Komposition, und Funktion," in Zenger (ed.), *Psalter*, 1–57, esp. 36–38; and S. Gillingham, "From Liturgy to Prophecy: The Use of Psalmody in Second Temple

One may conclude this section by noting that the question of point of standing is one that has been of some importance throughout the history of the Psalms' interpretation. The question is particularly raised by the fact that both Jewish and Christian traditions entertain the possibility that David was a prophet. As a result, one of the reader's tasks has always been to decide whether to understand a particular psalm with reference to David's own life or to later events in the reader's past, present, or future. That is to say, the reader must determine whether his/her point of standing is subsequent, contemporaneous, or even prior to that which is described in the psalm.[22] It is, of course, well worth noting that these traditions are often quite content to entertain multiple points of standing, depending on what function a psalm is being asked to perform at any given time.[23]

## SEQUENCE AND THE "LIFE OF FAITH" IN MODERN SCHOLARSHIP

The previous section examined the way that arguments for sequence in the Psalter also involve a situating of the reader in that sequence. This identification of what I have called the reader's point of standing was seen, on the one hand, to have a temporal dimension. In some cases, the reader is expected to reflect on events in Israel's history that have already taken place. In other cases, that reader is expected to reflect on the present situation or to look ahead to future events.

In addition to this temporal dimension, the reader's point of standing was also seen to have what might be called an existential aspect, as the reader is called upon to assume a particular theological stance. It is with this existential point of standing in mind that one may take note of other less overtly "historical" characterizations of sequence in the Psalter. Such attempts have been particularly interested in three elements of that book.

First, several scholars have taken note of the fact that the Psalter begins with a torah psalm and ends with a number of psalms of praise. Secondly, scholars have noted the fact that the first part of the Psalter

---

Judaism," *CBQ* 64 (2002) 470–89, esp. 476–79. I have also discussed the canonical implications of these issues in my *Sacred Songs*, 201–205.

[22] That is, with that to which the psalm is referring. The reader is, of course, subsequent to David's speaking of the psalm in any case.

[23] This is, for example, one implication of the well-known comment in *Midrash Tehillim* 18.1 that "all that David said in his Book of Psalms applies to himself, to all Israel, and to all the ages." Cf. my *Sacred Songs*, 149–54.

contains a sizable concentration of lament psalms, while the latter part contains a similar concentration of psalms of praise. Finally, scholars have noted a shift over the course of the Psalter from individual to communal psalms.

A number of comments are appropriate here. First of all, some of these analyses clearly depend on modern form-critical definitions of individual psalms, definitions that might not necessarily have been shared by those responsible for the shaping of the Psalter. While this does not necessarily mean that such analyses are mistaken, it does prompt a certain amount of caution about claims concerning the "intentionality" of the Psalter's shaping.[24]

Second, even given these modern genre definitions, the distribution of psalm "types" is more a matter of dominant tendencies than of exclusive groupings of certain types in different parts of the Psalter. That is to say, one can certainly find laments in the latter part of the Psalter and psalms of praise and thanksgiving in the earlier parts.

Third, the simple "fact" of this distribution of psalm "types" does not necessarily imply sequence. One could simply explain this distribution in terms of how the Psalter developed historically and not impute any interpretive significance to it. Most scholars who take note of these features do, however, argue that the order in which they occur is significant. Thus, for example, Wilson argues that the shift from lament to praise and from the individual to the community "influences profoundly the theology of the Psalter."[25] Similarly, Walter Brueggemann probes "the question of theological intentionality by asking how one gets from one end of the Psalter to the other."[26]

The reason that these scholars see a meaningful sequence here is readily apparent in their identification of the movement of the Psalter with the theological dynamics of the "life of faith." That is to say, such scholars see in the sequence of the Psalter a paradigm for the proper spiritual development of its readers. The exact nature of this spiritual paradigm differs from one scholar to another, depending on which psalms such scholars select as being of primary importance. For the most part, however, such scholars agree on the existential na-

---

[24] On this point, see my *Sacred Songs*, 197–99.

[25] Wilson, "Shape," 139.

[26] W. Brueggemann, "Bounded by Obedience and Praise: The Psalms as Canon," *JSOT* 50 (1991) 63–92, esp. 64.

ture of the sequence involved.[27]

One should not minimize the significance of this way of under-standing the sequence of the Psalter in terms of the "life of faith" of its "reader." Once again, these scholars see the sequence of the Psalter as goal-oriented in that the final part of the Psalter defines the preferred theological stance that its reader is meant to adopt. The articulation of this theological stance is the overall message of the Psalter and the adoption of this stance is the ultimate goal of meditating on that book.

Such a sequential approach raises a number of issues, even if one assumes a plausible description of the dynamics of the book. One may begin with the question of the reader's point of standing. When the reader is defined over against the history of Israel, that reader's point of standing is, to a certain extent, clear in that certain psalms can be situated in the reader's past, present, or future.[28] When, however, point of standing is defined over against the dynamics of the reader's spiritual life, that point of standing becomes much less clear. After all, one cannot simply assume every reader is at the same point in his/her spiritual development. Different readers of the same sequence may have different points of standing, as may the same reader at different times of his/her life.

The question of point of standing takes on particular significance when one raises the issue of the theological status of the earlier psalms in the sequence. On the basis of these sequential arguments, one could well argue that the earlier psalms have a status inferior to the later psalms, at least to the extent that their theological viewpoint is pre-liminary. So, for example, Brueggemann characterizes Psalm 1 as "a beginning point beyond which the faithful characteristically move."[29]

This is, of course, not a problem if one is meditating on an entire book whose message necessitates moving beyond an earlier theologi-cal point of view. If, on the other hand, one is using the psalms as they

---

[27] See, for example, Brueggemann's explicit statement that "the shape of the Psalter correlates with the shape of Israel's life with God" ("Obedience," 88).

[28] Though, as noted above, the question of the prophetic nature of the text is a complicating factor in this regard.

[29] Brueggemann, "Obedience," 70. For Brueggemann, the obedience of the be-ginning of the Psalter is both the condition for what follows and in a dialectical relationship with it. In the latter relationship, obedience is to be transcended in favor of the "joyous communion" of the Psalter's conclusion. Both of these moves presume a sequential reading of the Psalter.

have often (indeed most often) been used throughout their history — as prayer — such a view raises a number of questions. After all, most people do not normally pray the psalms of the first part of the Psalter with a view that they are of lesser theological value. Nor do they normally cease to pray these psalms because they feel that they have moved beyond them in some way. With such a dilemma in mind, it is useful to compare this modern sequential understanding of the Psalter with earlier approaches that view that book's sequence from the perspective of the "reader."

## SEQUENCE AND THE "LIFE OF FAITH":
### INSIGHTS FROM THE INTERPRETIVE TRADITION

One may begin by returning to a figure who has already been seen to take the sequence of the Psalter very seriously: Gregory of Nyssa. As noted above, Gregory sees the superscriptions as ruling out an understanding of sequence in terms of the chronology of David's life. Despite this, Gregory explicitly affirms the "well thought-out order of the psalms."[30] To understand this order, one must understand the purpose that lies behind the Psalter, which for Gregory is the fostering of a life in accord with virtue. In this, Gregory sees the purpose of the Spirit who is the "guide and teacher of our souls."[31]

For Gregory, "anything undertaken with a purpose has a certain, natural, necessary order which brings about the end one strives after." Gregory compares God's work in the book of Psalms to that of a sculptor who works to "conform stone to some kind of image." Just as the sculptor uses tools of increasing subtlety as he moves from a block of stone to a polished image, God uses different types of psalms to conform the believer ever more closely to the divine likeness. Along these lines, Gregory sees the Psalms as leading believers "by successive steps to the supreme height of blessedness."[32]

In light of recent scholarship, it is suggestive that Gregory identifies these successive steps with the five books of the Psalter that are distinguished by their concluding doxologies. As he explains these steps, Gregory pays particular attention to the first psalm in each book, though he also sees the final psalm of the Psalter as significant. Thus,

---

[30] Gregory, *Inscriptions*, preface.

[31] Gregory, *Inscriptions,* book 2, chap. 11.

[32] Gregory, *Inscriptions*, preface.

the Psalter begins with a "turning away from evil" and moves towards "the loftiest peak and degree of contemplation," as seen in the fifth book.[33] The last psalm sums up the "praise of God fulfilled in all the saints," a "union of our nature with that of the angels."[34]

In this movement from more basic spiritual necessities to a higher spirituality, one will not fail to see certain similarities to the way that modern scholars view the movement of the Psalter. Given these similarities, it is important to note the differences between how they understand this movement. First of all, while Gregory does see the earlier psalms as being on a lower level, he does not see them as inadequate in the same ways that modern scholars sometimes seem to suggest.[35] They are rather a necessary stage of a believer's spiritual development.[36]

Given this sequential view, it is significant that Gregory also claims that the earlier psalms contain within them an anticipation of the higher spirituality found later in the Psalter. He finds this especially in the presence of the *diapsalma* in these psalms, which he sees as leading to a "more sublime understanding of the good."[37] Through the insertion of this term in the middle of these psalms, the latter "have a role to teach loftier ideas." These ideas, imparted by the Spirit, are found following the *diapsalma*, and anticipate what one finds in the last section of the Psalter, which has no need for the *diapsalma*.[38]

Of particular interest for the present essay is the way that Gregory relates his sequential view of the Psalter to his understanding of the

---

[33] Gregory, *Inscriptions*, book 1, chap. 1.8.

[34] Gregory, *Inscriptions*, book 1, chap. 9. This union is symbolized by the union of the cymbals in the psalm.

[35] So, for example, Wilson sees the individual laments of the first part of the Psalter as connected with "human weakness" and "moments of doubt" that are "swallowed up in the community's collective vision" found in the second part of the Psalter ("Shape," 139). One may also note Brueggemann's view that Psalm 1 sets up a neatly ordered view of life that is at considerable tension with what one finds in the rest of the Psalter ("Obedience," 66).

[36] This is, of course, more similar to Brueggemann's argument that "only the obedient can praise" than to his view that Psalm 1 presents a view of life that is at odds with reality.

[37] Gregory, *Inscriptions*, book 2, chap. 10.

[38] Such anticipation complicates the sequence that Gregory sees in the Psalms in a way reminiscent of the way the anticipatory elements of such modern scholars as McCann complicate the sequence of the Psalter.

historical situations specified by the superscriptions. Along these lines, Gregory devotes several chapters to the cluster of psalms with detailed historical superscriptions found in the second book of the Psalter. As noted above, Gregory is quite aware that these psalms are not in chronological order with regard to their "temporal, carnal deeds."[39] The "intention" of these psalms' sequence, rather, is more concerned with "our ascent to better things."

Gregory's concern for the reader's spiritual ascent does not mean, however, that he ignores the historical settings specified in these psalms' superscriptions. Indeed, Gregory spends considerable time retelling the stories found in these settings and reflecting on the point of the respective psalms specifically in light of those settings. The sequence from one psalm to the next is from one spiritual lesson learned by the reader to another. In this respect, the David of the psalm is a model for the believer who becomes like him by adopting the attitude of the psalm.

To underscore the need for such an imitation of David, Gregory draws parallels between the believer's circumstances and David's historical situation, often through allegorical means. This allows him to portray the believer as the first person voice of the psalm. Thus, for example, in commenting upon Psalm 54 (MT), Gregory compares David's enemies to the forces of sin that assail believers. Like David, these believers "entrust the power of God's judgment for our good in his saving name exclaiming, 'God, by your name save me, and by your power judge me.'"[40]

In concluding this consideration of Gregory, one may note perhaps the most important difference between him and more modern scholars, namely, his view of how the movement in the Psalter is actualized in the reader's life. Modern scholars tend to emphasize the need for the believer to meditate on the Psalter so as to attain the desired life of praise. For Gregory, on the other hand, the spiritual development that takes place is one that God brings about in the believer, as may be seen in his argument that God is similar to a sculptor who chisels a block of stone into a finished image. To be sure, Gregory also sees the need for human effort in the attainment of virtue.[41] Nevertheless, God

---

[39] Gregory, *Inscriptions*, book 2, chap. 13.

[40] Gregory, *Inscriptions*, book 2, chap. 13.

[41] So in book 1, chap. 3 Gregory argues that virtue comes about for those who apply themselves to it.

is an active agent who by grace helps to make the virtues described in the Psalms present in the believer.[42]

Gregory is somewhat unusual in the extended and detailed attention he gives to the superscriptions. He is, on the other hand, far from unique in his attempt to find a theological understanding of the book of Psalms as a whole or to see a significance in the sequence of the individual psalms. As with modern scholars, however, other figures in the psalms' interpretive history have not always selected the same psalms as significant for their chosen sequence. Nor have they been particularly concerned to include all of the psalms in their sequential analyses.

As an example of an alternative selection and sequence, one may take note of another Christian tradition, which focused on what was felt to be a significant numerical sequence. In this tradition, Augustine and a number of medieval interpreters focused on the sequence of Psalms 50, 100, and 150 (according to the Greek/Latin numbering).[43] Such interpreters had many reasons for highlighting these particular psalms, among them the significance of the number fifty elsewhere in the Bible and especially its connection with the Jubilee year.

For these interpreters, the combination of the Jubilee reference with the Greek/Latin numbering of the most prominent penitential psalm (MT Psalm 51) brought to the fore the important themes of repentance and forgiveness. Even more significantly, however, such interpreters saw this psalm's emphasis on turning away from sin as the first step in a spiritual ascent. Thus, Augustine sees a progression from repentance to God's judgment and mercy (in MT Psalm 101) and finally to the praise of God in God's saints (Psalm 150).[44]

It is obvious that this sequential view shares many elements with modern views of the shape of the Psalter. Especially similar is the idea

---

[42] One sees a similar emphasis on God's active role in the psalms in such authors as Athanasius and John Cassian. Cf. my *Sacred Songs*, 107–16.

[43] H. Meyer, "Die allegorische Deutung der Zahlenkomposition des Psalters," *FMSt* 6 (1972) 211–31, esp. 217–20. One may also note that Augustine specifically argues against the fivefold division of the Psalter in his comments on Psalm 150.

[44] In this, Augustine is followed by many subsequent interpreters; cf. Meyer, "Deutung," 220. Meyer also notes a number of variations in this threefold tropological arrangement, with some arguing for a progression from faith to hope to love or from *ante lege* to *sub lege* to *sub gratia*. A common theme is that the praise of Psalm 150 is seen as signifying eternal life.

that the concluding praise of the Psalter has interpretive significance as the goal of the reader's spiritual development. Also similar is the selection of particular psalms as having special significance for the sequence. Since, however, the psalms selected are different, the movement of the sequence is different. Instead of a movement from lament to praise or obedience to praise, these interpreters see a movement from repentance to praise. For Christian interpreters, the difference between these movements has not been insignificant.

One should, of course, not fail to see the implications of these views for the important issue of the reader's point of standing. As was the case with modern reader-oriented views, these ancient interpretations of the Psalter's sequence do not allow for a fixed point of standing. Instead, the reader's point of standing in the sequence depends on where that reader is in his/her spiritual development. Moreover, as in the modern examples, this flexible point of standing raises the question of the theological status of the psalms that precede the point where the reader is at present. This essay will revisit these issues in its conclusions.

### SEQUENCE AND SELECTION IN THE SMALLER PSALMS GROUPS

To this point, the present essay has considered several ancient and modern attempts to distinguish a sequence in the Psalter by the selection of particular psalms that were seen to be of special significance. This section will examine another way in which sequence and selection intersect in the interpretation of the Psalter, namely, in the sequential interpretation of psalms that have been seen as self-contained smaller groups. Obviously, a comprehensive overview of these groups cannot be attempted here; nevertheless, even the following examples may help to illustrate the issues involved.

### The Psalms of Ascents

One may begin by looking at the Psalms of Ascents, Psalms 120–134. These psalms follow each other in the Psalter, share a common (or similar) superscription, and are usually seen to share other literary features and theological themes. As a result, both ancient and modern interpreters almost always treat these psalms as a group and look for a connection between them. Often, though not always, these interpreters see this connection as a sequential one.[45]

---

[45] For a non-linear view of these psalms, see H. Viviers, "The Coherence of the

This was, of course, a natural interpretive move, given that the idea of "ascending" implies movement from one place to another, most naturally, from a lower to a higher place. Along such lines, the question that interpreters felt they needed to answer was that of what type of ascending is present in these psalms. This question is, to a certain degree, complicated by the plural nature of these ascents.

Both ancient and modern interpreters have often seen the ascents of these psalms in historical terms, as a going up to the land of Israel (or Jerusalem) from outside that land. In this regard, a connection with the return from exile in Babylon is especially prominent.[46] On the other hand, many interpreters see a reference to the exiles of their own or future times. Thus, for example, *Midrash Tehillim* speaks of the time in the future "when the children of Israel get free of their troubles and go up out of exile."[47] Less specific, but still "historical," is the interpretation of the ascents in the context of pilgrimage to Jerusalem, an interpretation especially prominent among modern authors.[48]

After the previous section, it will come as no surprise that a number of interpreters have understood these psalms' ascents in terms of the reader's spiritual development. Thus, for example, Augustine sees the ascent in these psalms as a progression towards the understanding of things spiritual and a pilgrimage to the heavenly Jerusalem.[49] Cassiodorus develops the latter image further, noting how the fifteen psalms have led all the way to the heavenly Jerusalem, in a journey that begins with the renunciation of the world and ends with perfect love.[50]

---

*maᶜᵃlôt* Psalms (Pss 120–134)," *ZAW* 106 (1994) 275–89.

[46] Examples of this view may be found in such traditional interpreters as Theodoret, and the Syriac translation. Cf. C. C. Keet, *A Study of the Psalms of Ascents* (London: Mitre Press, 1969) 9–11. For a similar modern view, cf. M. D. Goulder, *The Psalms of the Return (Book V, Psalms 107–150): Studies in the Psalter, IV* (JSOTSup 258; Sheffield: Sheffield Academic Press, 1998).

[47] So *Midrash Tehillim* 120.1 (Braude's translation). References to later historical events can be found throughout this work's commentary on these psalms. Later interpreters such as Rashi, Ibn Ezra, and Qimhi specifically connect the references in v. 5 to Israel's future exile.

[48] Cf., for example, K. Seybold, *Die Wallfahrtspsalmen: Studien zur Entstehungsgeschichte von Psalm 120–134* (Neukirchen-Vluyn: Neukirchener, 1978); and L. D. Crow, *The Songs of Ascents (Psalms 120–134): Their Place in Israelite History and Religion* (SBLDS 148; Atlanta: Scholars Press, 1996).

[49] See his comments on Psalms 120 and 122 (MT) in the *Enarrationes*.

[50] So Cassiodorus, *Explanation of the Psalms* (vol. 3; transl. P. G. Walsh; New

Along somewhat different lines, a later interpreter, Michael Ayguan, groups these psalms into three sets of five and sees these sets as describing the purgative, illuminative, and unitive stages of the spiritual life, respectively.[51]

Such interpreters see the reader of these psalms as someone whose point of standing may certainly differ from that of other readers who are at different stages of their spiritual development. What all of these readers share is the fact that they are "on the way" from one spiritual state to another, pilgrims who have not reached the end of their journey. As such, this interpretation is similar to those historical interpretations that see these psalms in relation to Israel's future "goings up" from exile. Both of these approaches look forward to a future that is desired but not yet attained. In both their flexible point of standing and their future orientation, such views of this psalms group are similar to the sequential views of the Psalter as a whole that were seen earlier in this essay

### Hallel, Tamid, and Other Groups of Selected Psalms

Whereas a common superscription has obviously helped to distinguish the psalms of ascents as a group, such a marker is not always present in the case of other psalms that the interpretive tradition has treated in a collective way. Some of these latter groups are found as consecutive texts in the Psalter, while others simply consist of psalms that have been selected on the basis of liturgical usage or some other theological criteria.

One of the earliest of these is the group of psalms known as the Egyptian Hallel, Psalms 113–118.[52] In the Jewish tradition, these texts are used as a group on a variety of liturgical occasions and omitted on others where praise is not felt to be appropriate. Of particular interest for this essay is the fact that the tradition is concerned about both the group status and the order of these psalms. While some of this con-

---

York: Paulist, 1991) 340–41.

[51] For Ayguan, these different stages are for "the beginners, the progressors, and the perfect" and correspond to the psalms' emphasis on trouble, confidence, and communion. Cf. the reference in J. M. Neale and R. F. Littledale, *Commentary on the Psalms* (vol. 4; London: Joseph Masters, 1874) 164.

[52] This group is known simply as the Hallel in the Mishnah (so *m. Pesaḥ.* 5.7, 9.3; Hallelujah in *m. Pesaḥ.* 10.5). It is called the Egyptian Hallel (as in *b. Ber.* 56a), apparently to distinguish it from the little Hallel (Psalms 146–150) and the so-called great Hallel (the extent of which is debated in *b. Pesaḥ.* 118a).

cern may simply be attributed to a normal interest in ritual precision, there is also some indication that the group has received a more specifically sequential interpretation. Thus, for example, *b. Pesaḥ*. 118a sees a progression from events of the past in Psalm 114 to events of the future in Psalms 115–116.[53] It is, of course, significant for the reader's point of standing that this sequence is seen to contain both historical and eschatological elements. Indeed, these psalms' liturgical usage in the Passover Seder underlines the position of the reader being in the midst of a sequence whose completion has not yet occurred.[54]

Of similar antiquity is the group of psalms associated with the daily Tamid sacrifice in the temple (Psalms 24, 48, 82, 94, 81, 93, 92).[55] This group of psalms differs from the Hallel psalms in two respects. First, these psalms were not recited as a group on a single occasion but were instead recited one a day over the course of a week. Second, the order of these psalms' recital over the course of the week did not follow the canonical order of these psalms in the Psalter. Despite this, the tradition clearly tended to see these psalms as a distinct group.

The question is whether this group was understood in sequential terms. Pointing in such a direction is the rabbinic connection between the Tamid psalms and the seven days of creation in Genesis.[56] In light of what has already been observed above about other psalms sequences, it is suggestive that in this discussion Psalm 92 is given eschatological significance as the song for the "day which will be all Sabbath."[57] Again, this means the reader's point of standing in this sequence is one in which he/she both looks back and looks ahead.[58]

---

[53] Thus in Psalm 114 the rabbis see the exodus from Egypt (v. 1), the dividing of the sea (v. 3), and the giving of the Torah (v. 4), while in Ps 116:9 and in Ps 115:1 they see the resurrection of the dead and the pangs of the Messiah. R. R. Donin notes concerning the interpretive tradition that "because of this chronological continuity in the Hallel, it may only be said in the prescribed order" (*To Pray as a Jew* [New York: Basic, 1980] 270).

[54] Donin sees the shift in chronological reference as one reason why the Hallel psalms are split in the Passover service (*Pray*, 267–68).

[55] See *m. Tamid* 7.4.

[56] See *b. Roš Haš.* 31a. One should note, however, the somewhat different treatment in *Midrash Tehillim*.

[57] Cf. also *m. Tamid* 7:4, where this day of "all Sabbath" is specifically associated with the time that is to come and life everlasting."

[58] More recently, Peter Trudinger has suggested that the Tamid psalms have their own internal coherence as "narrative." He specifically argues that the "se-

One finds similar groupings of psalms in the Christian tradition. A particularly important selection of psalms, at least in western Christianity, is the group of seven penitential psalms (Psalms 6, 32, 38, 51, 102, 130, and 143). The exact origins of this grouping are unknown, as are the reasons for the selection of these particular psalms. Nevertheless, the interpretive tradition has tended to give this group a sequential interpretation from the very start.

Thus, for example, Cassiodorus, the first interpreter to number these psalms explicitly, sees them as a "course of blessed tears" and a "path of salvation."[59] Later interpreters speak in more detail of a "ladder of penitence" and specifically match each psalm to a stage in the progression from fear of punishment to the exultation of spiritual joy.[60] As has often been the case, the sequence is one that involves the spiritual development of the reader, whose exact point of standing will depend on that reader's present state of spiritual progress. It is also a sequence whose end has not yet been achieved.

These examples do not, by any means, exhaust the psalms groupings that may be found in either the Jewish or the Christian interpretive tradition. They are, however, sufficient to underline the existence of the same interplay between selection and sequence that was seen in the previous consideration of the Psalter as a whole. The selection of certain psalms as either a self-contained group or the organizing psalms of a larger whole almost always leads to a sequential interpretation of those psalms.

---

quential links between consecutive psalms" constitute a "plot" involving two developing characters, namely, God and the righteous. Trudinger further notes the similarity of this plot to Brueggemann's orientation-disorientation-new orientation sequence. While more research is needed here, the possibility that these psalms constitute a meaningful sequence of some kind is suggestive.

Trudinger's work on the Tamid psalms is currently found in his unpublished Emory University dissertation, parts of which were presented in his papers at the 2001 CBA and SBL national conventions. I am most grateful to him both for these stimulating papers and for making available to me part of chapter four from his dissertation.

[59] Cassiodorus, *Explanation*, 3.412.

[60] See, for example, the discussion of medieval interpreters in R. R. Rains, *Le sept psaumes allégorisés of Christine de Pisan* (Washington: Catholic University of America Press, n.d.) 33–34. That this view continued after the medieval period in a variety of Christian traditions may be seen from the detailed exposition of these psalms as a "ladder of repentance" by the seventeenth century Lutheran commentator, Reinhard Bakius.

## CONCLUSIONS

The present essay is clearly not comprehensive in its treatment of either the Psalter as a whole or its various psalms groupings.[61] However, even such a limited treatment as this has perhaps shown the importance of sequence in both traditional and modern psalms interpretation. The larger question that this overview raises is, of course, that of why sequence has been seen to be so significant for the Psalter. After all, it is perfectly possible to see the Psalter as either an antho logy of liturgical texts that does not have—or need—any particular order. It is also quite possible to see the order of the Psalter as resulting from that book's historical development, but not having interpretive significance. Why, then, has sequence so often played such an important role in the interpretive history of the Psalms?

One possible explanation is that the sequential understanding of the Psalter and its smaller psalms groups simply flows naturally from what one finds in the individual psalms. Many, indeed most, psalms describe movement from one state to another. Sometimes this is spatial movement from one place to another, such as in a pilgrimage. Sometimes it is chronological movement, from a troubled past to a more settled present or from a troubled present to a hoped for future. Sometimes the movement is even predominantly psychological or spiritual, taking place not so much in the world at large as within the psalmist's own self or in the relationship between the psalmist and God. These movements within the individual psalms to a large extent match the diverse ways in which ancient and modern interpreters have understood sequence in the Psalter and its smaller psalms groups.

Another possible explanation for the sequential interpretation of the Psalter has to do with its connections to the larger historical narrative of a people of which the reader feels him/herself to be a part. Clearly, the historical allusions found in the Psalter contribute to such a self-understanding, even though these allusions do not themselves allow for a consistent chronological reading of this text.[62] Also contributing to this interpretation is the liturgical use of the psalms in the context of such historically based feasts as Passover or Easter.

---

[61] For a more comprehensive overview (and a very detailed bibliography), see J.-M. Auwers, *La composition littéraire du Psautier: Un état de la question* (CRB 46; Paris, Gabalda, 2000).

[62] On the role of historical allusions in the Psalms, cf. my "Historical Narrative and Identity in the Psalms," *HBT* 23 (2001) 131–52.

It is important that those who participate in these liturgical events understand themselves as members of a people whose historical narrative is not yet complete. As such, these events tend not only to look back to an historical past but also to look forward to a future fulfillment.[63] In such a context, the psalms often serve both to actualize the past and to anticipate the future. As in the case of the individual psalms, there is a dynamic quality to such usage that readily lends itself to a sequential interpretation of the Psalter as a whole.

A third possible explanation for the persistence of sequence in the interpretation of the Psalter has to do with the role of its readers. As has often been pointed out, the emotions and situations that one finds in the psalms clearly echo those found in these readers' lives. Because of the broken nature of human existence, these lives conform to certain patterns marked by sin and suffering. However, because of the salvific purposes of the biblical God, these lives also share a common goal, a goal that has not yet been realized.

In other words, it may be that readers are inclined to interpret the Psalter sequentially because of the sequential nature of their own lives. Such an explanation fits well with the "turn to the reader" that marks many of the sequential interpretations described in this essay. The fact that these lives are still in process also helps to explain certain aspects of these sequential interpretations, especially those that have to do with the reader's point of standing.

Because the "life settings" of different readers are not the same, even readers who discern the same sequence in the Psalter may find themselves at different points of standing within that sequence. Indeed, the same reader will almost certainly have a different point of standing at different times of his/her own life. Since the path to holiness is seldom a smooth and steady ascent, that reader rarely leaves behind certain psalms once and for all.[64]

---

[63] Along these lines, one should note E. Zenger's understanding of the fifth book of the Psalter as a "'spiritual pilgrimage' to Zion" and a "meditative actualization of the canonical history of the origin of Israel (Ps. 113–118: the Exodus; Ps. 119: Sinai; Pss. 120–136: entry into the Promised Land with Zion/Jerusalem as the heart of the land)." For Zenger, there is also future hope in the messianic promises of Psalms 110 and 144 ("The Composition and Theology of the Fifth Book of Psalms. Psalms 107–145," *JSOT* 80 [1998] 77–102, esp. 100–101). Cf. also M. Millard, *Die Komposition des Psalters: Ein formgeschichtlicher Ansatz* (Tübingen: Mohr Siebeck, 1994) 228–29.

[64] In such a way, one may recall Augustine's emphasis on the penitential

One of the advantages of the sequential understanding of the psalms is that it works against an exclusively expressive use of these texts as a way of describing where one is at a particular time.[65] In reflecting upon (or praying) a sequence, one is required to remember where one has been (and may be again) and is enabled to anticipate where one is going. In that anticipation, the psalms even provide a foretaste of the goal and help to transform those who use them. In other words, a sequential understanding of the psalms means that one must be aware of and open to psalms beyond those that express one's current point of standing.

This interplay between the reader's point of standing and the larger sequence is reminiscent of a tension that one sees in the history of the Psalms' use. It is the tension between the use of particular psalms that are appropriate to personal or liturgical settings and the need to read or pray the entire Psalter. One sees this tension, for example, in Athanasius' *Letter to Marcellinus*, where this Church Father both specifies particular psalms for certain occasions and insists upon the praying of the entire book.[66]

One also sees this tension in the difference between the ancient cathedral and monastic offices.[67] The former specifies the use of certain psalms as appropriate to particular times or liturgical occasions, while the latter urges the continuous reading of the Psalter over a specific period of time. A similar tension between occasional and comprehen-

---

psalms at his deathbed, despite the fact that the most prominent penitential psalm occurs first in the Augustinian psalms sequence described above.

[65] On the difference between the expressive and transformative functions of the Psalms, cf. my *Sacred Songs*, 82–127.

[66] Athanasius specifically notes the need to read the entire Psalter in his *Letter to Marcellinus*, chap. 30.

[67] On the relationship between these offices and the psalms' early use for both prayer and meditation, see J. W. McKinnon, "The Book of Psalms, Monasticism, and the Western Liturgy," in N. Van Deusen (ed.), *The Place of the Psalms in the Intellectual Culture of the Middle Ages* (Albany, NY: State University of New York Press, 1999) 43–58. Cf. also A. Gerhards, "Die Psalmen in der römischen Liturgie. Eine Bestandaufnahme des Psalmengebrauchs in Stundengebet und Messfeier," in Zenger, (ed.), *Psalter*, 355–79; P. Bradshaw, "From Word to Action: The Changing Role of Psalmody in Early Christianity," in M. R. Dudley (ed.), *Like a Two-Edged Sword: The Word of God in Liturgy and History* (Norwich: Canterbury Press, 1995) 21–37; and R. Taft, S. J., *The Liturgy of the Hours in East and West: The Origins of the Divine Office and Its Meaning for Today* (Collegeville, PA: Liturgical Press, 1986).

sive usage is to be seen in the Jewish tradition, where the liturgical usage of certain psalms at particular times again exists alongside certain circles' practice of a continuous reading of the entire Psalter.

It is not too far-fetched to see an echo of the same tension in modern scholarship on the Psalms, which has moved from its traditional concern for individual psalms in their life settings to its more recent emphasis on the Psalter as a book.[68] The present author would obviously want to argue that both approaches are appropriate and that the tension between them is (or at least can be) a creative one. Along these lines, one does well to recall the view of Brevard Childs that the final form of the Psalter incorporated within itself a "variety of different hermeneutical moves."[69]

The history of the psalms' use is marked by a rich interplay between their settings in individual lives, communal history, and canonical text. What the present essay has tried to suggest is that the interpretive strategies of sequence and selection have played a significant role in all of these settings. As such, these strategies may function as a means to bring all these different approaches into a productive conversation with each other.

## SELECT BIBLIOGRAPHY

Auwers, J.-M. *La composition littéraire du Psautier: Un état de la question* (CRB 46; Paris, Gabalda, 2000).

---

[68] Along these lines, one may recall E. Gerstenberger's argument that the view of Psalter as a book for continuous reading and meditation is "monastic" in origin ("Psalter," 10). Even if Gerstenberger were correct, it would not necessarily invalidate such an approach to the Psalter.

[69] B. S. Childs, *Introduction*, 522. Childs continues: "Although the psalms were often greatly refashioned for use by the later generations, no one doctrinaire position received a normative role. The material was far too rich and its established use far too diverse ever to allow a single function to subordinate all others. The psalms were collected to be used for liturgy and for study, both by a corporate body and by individuals, to remind of the great redemptive acts of the past as well as to anticipate the hopes of the future." The present essay is obviously supportive of many of Childs' points here.

Bradshaw, P. "From Word to Action: The Changing Role of Psalmody in Early Christianity," in M. R. Dudley (ed.), *Like a Two-Edged Sword: The Word of God in Liturgy and History* (Norwich: Canterbury Press, 1995) 21–37.

Braude, W. G. *The Midrash on Psalms* (YJS 13; New Haven, Yale University Press, 1959).

Brueggemann, W. "Bounded by Obedience and Praise: The Psalms as Canon," *JSOT* 50 (1991) 63–92.

Cassiodorus. *Explanation of the Psalms* (vol. 3; trans. P. G. Walsh; New York: Paulist, 1991).

Childs, B. S. *Introduction to the Old Testament as Scripture* (Philadelphia: Fortress, 1979).

Crow, L. D. *The Songs of Ascents (Psalms 120–134): Their Place in Israelite History and Religion* (SBLDS 148; Atlanta: Scholars Press, 1996).

deClaissé-Walford, N. L. *Reading from the Beginning: The Shaping of the Hebrew Psalter* (Macon, GA: Mercer University Press, 1997).

Donin, R. R. *To Pray as a Jew* (New York: Basic, 1980).

Gerhards, A. "Die Psalmen in der römischen Liturgie. Eine Bestandaufnahme des Psalmengebrauchs in Stundengebet und Messfeier," in E. Zenger (ed.), *Der Psalter in Judentum und Christentum* (Herders Biblische Studien 18: Freiburg: Herder, 1998) 355–79.

Gerstenberger, E. S. "Der Psalter als Buch und als Sammlung," in K. Seybold and E. Zenger (eds.), *Neue Wege der Psalmenforschung* (Herders Biblische Studien 1: Freiburg: Herder, 1994) 3–13.

Gillingham, S. "From Liturgy to Prophecy: The Use of Psalmody in Second Temple Judaism," *CBQ* 64 (2002) 470–89.

Goulder, M. *The Prayers of David Psalms 51–72: Studies in the Psalter II* (JSOTSup 102: Sheffield: Sheffield Academic Press, 1990).

—. *The Psalms of the Return (Book V, Psalms 107–150): Studies in the Psalter, IV* (JSOTSup 258; Sheffield: Sheffield Academic Press, 1998).

Gregory of Nyssa, *Commentary on the Inscriptions of the Psalms* (transl. C. McCambley, OCSO; Brookline, MA: Hellenic College, n.d.).

Hossfeld, F.-L. "Die unterschiedlichen Profile der beiden Davidsammlungen Ps 3–41 und Ps 51–72," in E. Zenger (ed.), *Der Psalter in Judentum und Christentum* (Herders Biblische Studien 18: Freiburg: Herder, 1998) 59–74.

Hossfeld, F.-L. and E. Zenger. "Neue und Alte Wege der Psalmenexegese: Antworten auf die Fragen von M. Millard und R. Rendtorff," *BI* 4 (1996) 332–43.

Hossfeld, F.-L. and E. Zenger. *Die Psalmen I: Psalm 1–50* (Würzburg: Echter, 1993).

Keet, C. C. *A Study of the Psalms of Ascents* (London: Mitre Press, 1969).

McCann, J. C., Jr. "Books I–III and the Editorial Purpose of the Hebrew Psalter," in J. C. McCann, Jr. (ed.), *The Shape and Shaping of the Psalter* (JSOTSup 159; Sheffield Academic Press, 1993) 93–107.

McKinnon, J. W. "The Book of Psalms, Monasticism, and the Western Liturgy," in N. Van Deusen (ed.), *The Place of the Psalms in the Intellectual Culture of the Middle Ages* (Albany, NY: State University of New York Press, 1999) 43–58.

Meyer, H. "Die allegorische Deutung der Zahlenkomposition des Psalters," *FMSt* 6 (1972) 211–31.

Millard, M. *Die Komposition des Psalters: Ein formgeschichtlicher Ansatz* (Tübingen: Mohr Siebeck, 1994).

—. "Von der Psalmenexegese zur Psalterexegese: Anmerkungen zum Neuansatz von Frank-Lothar Hossfeld und Erich Zenger," *BI* 4 (1996) 311–28.

—. "Respons," *BI* 4 (1996) 344–45.

Nasuti, H. P. *Defining the Sacred Songs: Genre, Tradition and the Post-Critical Interpretation of the Psalms* (JSOTSup 218; Sheffield: Sheffield Academic Press, 1999).

—. "Historical Narrative and Identity in the Psalms," *HBT* 23 (2001) 131–52.

Neale, J. M. and R. F. Littledale. *Commentary on the Psalms* (vol. 4; London: Joseph Masters, 1874).

Rains, R. R. *Le sept psaumes allégorisés of Christine de Pisan* (Washington: Catholic University of America Press, n.d.)

Rendtorff, R. "Anfragen an Frank-Lothar Hossfeld und Erich Zenger: Aufgrund der Lektüre des Beitrages von Matthias Millard," *BI* 4 (1996) 329–31.

Seybold, K. *Die Wallfahrtspsalmen: Studien zur Entstehungsgeschichte von Psalm 120–134* (Neukirchen-Vluyn: Neukirchener, 1978).

Taft, R., S.J. *The Liturgy of the Hours in East and West: The Origins of the Divine Office and Its Meaning for Today* (Collegeville, MN: Liturgical Press, 1986).

Viviers, H. "The Coherence of the *ma*ᶜᵃ*lôt* Psalms (Pss 120–134)," *ZAW* 106 (1994) 275–89.

Whybray, N. *Reading the Psalms as a Book* (JSOTSup, 222; Sheffield: Sheffield Academic Press, 1996).

Wilson, G. H. "The Shape of the Book of Psalms," *Int* 46 (1992) 129–42.

—. "Shaping the Psalter: A Consideration of Editorial Linkage in the Book of Psalms," in J. C. McCann, Jr. (ed.), *The Shape and Shaping of the Psalter* (JSOTSup 159; Sheffield: Sheffield Academic Press, 1993) 72–82.

—. "The Use of Royal Psalms at the 'Seams' of the Hebrew Psalter," *JSOT* 35 (1986) 85–94.

Zenger, E. "The Composition and Theology of the Fifth Book of Psalms. Psalms

107–145," *JSOT* 80 (1998) 77–102.

—. "Der Psalter als Buch: Beobachtungen zu seiner Entstehung, Komposition, und Funktion," in E. Zenger (ed.), *Der Psalter in Judentum und Christentum* (Herders Biblische Studien 18; Freiburg: Herder, 1998) 1–57.

# THE SHAPE OF BOOK I OF THE PSALTER
# AND THE SHAPE OF HUMAN HAPPINESS

J. CLINTON McCANN, JR.

One of the few things that Psalms scholars of all backgrounds and methodological persuasions seem to agree upon is that Psalm 1 was placed intentionally at the beginning of the collection as a preface or introduction.[1] Of course, the next question is "Why?" or "What is the intended effect of Psalm 1?" And at this point, the consensus collapses. We need not review all the options. Suffice it to say that for the purposes of this essay, I assume that James L. Mays' conclusion is a sound one; and I shall take his conclusion as a starting point for the following investigation. Mays states concerning Psalm 1, and more specifically concerning the beatitude that begins Psalm 1:

> This opening beatitude ... serves as an introduction to the book. Its location as the first psalm is not accidental; the psalm is there to invite us to read and use the entire book as a guide to a blessed life.[2]

In other words, in some sense at least, all the rest of the Psalms are about what constitutes blessedness or happiness. This being the case, it makes sense that subsequent beatitudes would play a crucial role in the book of Psalms. Thus, it also makes good sense to investigate whether those subsequent beatitudes serve any discernable role either in the shaping of the Psalter, or parts thereof, or in communicating what may be the, or at least, a fundamental message of the book.

Such is the primary purpose of this essay. There are seven more beatitudes in Book I and seventeen more in Books II–V: that is, a total of 25, just over three times more than in the book of Proverbs (see Table 1). I shall begin with and focus primarily on Book I but shall extend the investigation briefly to Books II–V. I shall conclude with a consideration of how the Psalter's message about the shape of human

---

[1] For a recent review of contemporary Psalms study, see David M. Howard, Jr., "Recent Trends in Psalms Study," in D. W. Baker and B. T. Arnold (eds.), *The Face of Old Testament Studies: A Survey of Contemporary Approaches* (Grand Rapids: Baker, 1999) 329–68.

[2] James L. Mays, *Psalms* (Interpretation: A Bible Commentary for Teaching and Preaching; Louisville: John Knox, 1994) 40.

---

### TABLE 1: BEATITUDES IN THE BOOK OF PSALMS

#### BOOK I

| | |
|---|---|
| 1:1(-2) | Happy are those who[se] ... delight is in the *torah* of the LORD, and on God's *torah* they meditate day and night. |
| 2:12 | Happy are those who take refuge in God. |
| 32:1 | Happy are those whose rebellion is forgiven, whose sin is covered. |
| 32:2 | Happy are those to whom the LORD does not impute iniquity ... |
| 33:12 | Happy is the nation whose God is the LORD, the people whom God chose for a heritage. |
| 34:9 | ... happy are those who take refuge in God. |
| 40:5 | Happy are those who make the LORD their trust, ... |
| 41:2 | Happy are those who consider the poor; ... |

#### BOOK II

| | |
|---|---|
| 65:5 | Happy are those whom you choose and bring near ... |

#### BOOK III

| | |
|---|---|
| 84:5 | Happy are those who live in your house, ... |
| 84:6 | Happy are those whose strength is in you, ... |
| 84:13 | ... happy are those who trust in you. |
| 89:16 | Happy are those who know the shout; they walk in the light of your face. |

#### BOOK IV

| | |
|---|---|
| 94:12 | Happy are those whom you discipline, O LORD, and whom you teach from your *torah*. |
| 106:3 | Happy are those who keep justice, who do righteousness all the time. |

#### BOOK V

| | |
|---|---|
| 112:1 | Happy are those who fear the LORD, who delight greatly in God's commandments. |
| 119:1 | Happy are those whose way is integrity, who walk in the *torah* of the LORD. |
| 119:2 | Happy are those who keep God's decrees; they seek God with all their heart. |
| 127:5 | Happy is the one who has a quiver full of them [i.e. arrows=children]. |
| 128:1 | Happy are all those who fear the LORD, who walk in God's ways. |
| 137:8 | Happy shall they be who pay you back what you have done to us. |
| 137:9 | Happy shall they be who seize and shatter your little ones upon a rock. |
| 144:15a | Happy is the people to whom this [happens]; ... |
| 144:15b | ... happy is the people whose God is the LORD. |
| 146:5 | Happy are those whose help is the God of Jacob, whose hope is the LORD their God. |

---

happiness has been appropriated by and may continue to address the communities of faith which treasure the Psalms as Scripture, and how this message may also address a culture which claims to be decisively shaped by the Judeo-Christian tradition, whose the liturgical and devotional classic is the book of Psalms.

My initial observation concerns the distribution of the eight beatitudes in Book I and the seven psalms in which they are contained. As Table 1 suggests, beatitudes occur in the first two psalms of Book I (Psalms 1–2) and the last two psalms in Book I (Psalms 40–41). The other four beatitudes occur in three consecutive psalms in the midst of the book (Psalms 32–34). Granted, this distribution does not seem overly impressive; and some may conclude that it is simply coincidental. Clearly, for instance, the word "happy" does not occur at regular intervals in Book I so as to order the book into neat divisions. Indeed, I am willing to concede that the occurrences of beatitudes in the consecutive Psalms 32–34, while interesting, may be coincidental to the *shaping* of Book I — although not ultimately unimportant for its *message* about the shape of human happiness. The occurrences of the beatitudes in Psalms 1–2, 40–41 are another matter, however. This pattern seems to be more than coincidental; indeed, it seems highly significant. In any case, the *effect* of this pattern is to provide a frame for Book I that is especially noticeable, all the more so since the first and last psalms of the book *begin* with the beatitude. This framing device reinforces Mays' conclusion that the entire book, or at least Book I, is to be read as a guide to a "happy" life. In other words, not only are Psalms 1 and 41 about happiness, but so are all the psalms in between.

We shall return to Psalm 41; but to begin with, attention must be directed to the beatitudes in Psalms 1 and 2 and their effect. While the beatitudes in Pss 1:1 and 41:2 frame Book I, the beatitudes in Pss 1:1 and 2:12 frame what I take to be a paired introduction to the Psalter. Granted, there is not a scholarly consensus that Psalms 1–2 form a paired introduction; but almost certainly they do. They are only two of the four psalms in Book I without a superscription; and in the cases of the other two — Psalms 10 and 33 — these psalms have clear connections with the preceding psalm. So, too, do Psalms 1 and 2 have clear connections, including the verbal links represented by repetition of the verbs הגה in 1:2 and 2:1 (*NRSV* "meditate" and "plot") and אבד (*NRSV* "perish") in 1:6 and 2:12, the last verse of each psalm. Furthermore, Psalm 2 portrays in corporate terms the very thing that Psalm 1 presents in terms of individuals — that is, the sharp, life-or-death contrast between those who orient their lives to God and those who oppose God's sovereign claim. The clinching clue that Psalms 1–2 belong together is the appearance of "Happy" in 1:1 and 2:12 — a framework which suggests that these two psalms begin to paint the portrait of the happy life that will be given further depth and dimension in Psalms 3–41 and the rest of the Psalter.

In short, the beatitudes in Psalms 1 and 2 do play a role in the *shaping* of Book I; and they lay the foundation for the further construction of the Psalter's *message* about the shape of human happiness. Fundamental to this foundation is the contrast in Psalms 1 and 2 between the happy lives of those who are called "righteous" and the certain deaths of those who are called "wicked." These contrasting outcomes are the result of God's sovereign claim, for God "knows the way of the righteous" (1:6, *RSV*) and God's claim demands that even the "kings" and "rulers of the earth" be told, "Serve the LORD" (2:11). *And yet*, it is clear that the wicked do exist (Psalm 1) and so do kings and rulers who assert their own claims over against the LORD's sovereignty (Psalm 2). This apparent anomaly in itself necessitates a very particular understanding of the way God exercises sovereignty, and this understanding has profound implications for understanding the Psalter's message about the shape of human happiness and the proper content of associated words like "prosper" (1:3, *NRSV*), "righteous," and "wicked."

The sharp contrast laid out in Psalms 1–2 is immediately obvious in Psalm 3 and, indeed, throughout the prayers for help that constitute the large majority of psalms in Book I. The problem is that the righteous do not "prosper" in any generally recognizable sense of the term. In fact, they appear constantly on the brink of death while the wicked seem to be doing just fine. The wicked are proud and powerful while the righteous are pursued and persecuted. The wicked are outwardly prosperous and affluent while the righteous are poor and afflicted. The wicked, apparently healthy and at ease, terrorize the righteous who regularly appear to be plagued by illness and disease (see Ps 10:1-11). In short, the conditions of life for the righteous do not consist of anything that anyone, then or now, would readily associate with happiness — pain, poverty, persecution, and poor health! To introduce the Psalter under the rubric of "Happy are those ...," then to follow that introduction with an impressive series of poignant prayers for help, and then to provide a closing frame for Book I that also features the concept of happiness — all this serves to suggest that the shape of human happiness according to the Psalms has nothing to do with the normal definition of happiness or blessedness (one that is even found elsewhere in the Bible) in terms of material prosperity as well as physical security and well-being. Rather, according to the shape of the Psalter, happiness has to do with the fundamental orientation of the self to God, constantly delighting in God's "instruction" (Ps 1:2, *NRSV* "law"); and with finding "refuge in" God (Ps 2:12).

The paired introduction to the Psalter thus anticipates what will be a key concept throughout the book — "refuge" (חסה) — especially in

Book I where it occurs fourteen times.[3] Not surprisingly Psalm 34 asserts both "happy are those who take refuge in" God (34:9) and "many are the affliction of the righteous" (34:20). To "take refuge in" God means fundamentally to entrust self, life, and future to God. Again, not surprisingly, the beatitude in 40:5 explicitly portrays happiness in terms of trust: "Happy are those who make the LORD their trust."

While the beatitudes themselves in Pss 32:1-2 and 33:12 do not contain either "refuge" or "trust," both Psalms 32 and 33 conclude by portraying the "righteous" (32:11; 33:1) as those who "trust in the LORD" (32:10) or "trust in" God's "holy name" (33:21). The shape of human happiness in the Psalms is essentially this — trust. The beatitudes in Psalms 32 and 33 add an important dimension to the character of the relationship of trust that constitutes happiness. That is, it is established by God's initiative (Ps 33:12), and it is sustained by God's forgiveness (Ps 32:1-2). Righteousness in the Psalms is never self-righteousness. Again, righteousness, or prosperity, or happiness is essentially a matter of trust, of fundamental dependence upon God for life and direction and future. Each of the first seven beatitudes in the Psalter defines happiness in terms of such relatedness to God.

The apparent exception is Ps 41:2, the beatitude that opens the final psalm of Book I, and that, as suggested above, participates with Ps 1:1 in framing Book I with the concept of happiness. It defines happiness not in terms of orientation toward God, trusting God, or finding refuge in God, but rather in terms of orientation to the needs of other people. But the relationship between the beatitude in Ps 41:2 and the previous seven is not contradictory but rather complementary. While Psalm 1, for instance, portrays happiness in terms of openness to God's instruction, Psalm 41 portrays happiness in terms of openness to the needs of others.[4] In effect, then, the framework of Book I portrays the happy ones as those who love both God and neighbor.

---

[3] See Jerome F. D. Creach, *Yahweh as Refuge and the Editing of the Hebrew Psalter* (JSOTSup 217; Sheffield: Sheffield Academic Press, 1996). Creach suggests that Ps 2:12d is a late addition to Psalm 2 and that the concept of "refuge" both played a role in the shaping of the Psalter and is vitally important to a theological interpretation of the Psalms. See his conclusions on pp. 122–26.

[4] See W. Dennis Tucker, "Toward the Democratization of the Royal Ideal," a paper delivered Nov. 18, 2001 at the SBL Annual Meeting, Denver, CO. Tucker cites the coherence between Psalm 41 and Psalms 72 and 89, the psalms that conclude Books II and III; and suggests that this coherence makes especially good sense if the role of the monarchy has become the vocation of the whole people.

Ultimately, however, to say, "Happy are those who consider the poor," *is* to define happiness in terms of relatedness to God. To begin to explain the logic of this statement, I point out another verbal connection between Psalms 1 and 41. The root translated "delight" (חפץ) in Ps 1:2 is translated "pleased with" in 41:12: "By this I know that you are pleased with me; because my enemy has not triumphed over me" (*NRSV*). Thus, Book I opens with a portrayal of those who delight in God, and it concludes with an affirmation of God's delighting in the psalmist. The effect is to communicate the mutuality of the relationship between God and humanity. From the human side, the essence of the relationship is trusting or taking refuge in God, which as suggested above, is directly the subject of the beatitudes in Pss 2:12; 34:9; and 40:5 and indirectly in Pss 32:1-2 and 33:12. From the divine side, the relationship is grounded in the way God is — that is, fundamentally "gracious" (see Ps 41:4, 10, the petitions that frame the actual complaint) and steadfastly loving (see Pss 32:10; 33:5, 18, 22; 40:11). In particular, God's essential character is manifest in God's commitment to those described by several Hebrew words variously translated as "weak," "needy," "poor," "afflicted," "humble," "meek," and "oppressed." It is this conviction about God that underlies the appeal for help. It is also this conviction that underlies the opening beatitude of Psalm 41. To say "Happy are those who consider the poor" is to say, in effect, "Happy are those who are like God." Thus, even this final beatitude of Book I ultimately portrays human happiness in terms of essential relatedness to God.

While we have focused on the way the Psalms portray the psalmist, especially in terms of human happiness, we have also touched upon the portrayal of God. Strikingly, not only does human happiness take the shape of suffering servanthood; but also, God *suffers* too, as evidenced both by the opposition God experiences from the wicked, the kings and rulers of the earth, and the peoples and nations, *and* by God's commitment to be related to the poor and afflicted. Or, to put the same thing a bit differently, the theological perspective of the Book of Psalms is eschatological — that is, God's sovereignty is proclaimed amid persistent opposition that seems to deny it.

We shall return below to the appropriation by the Judeo-Christian tradition of these perspectives on human happiness and divine character, but first we turn briefly to the beatitudes in Books II–V. As Table 1 suggests, there are simply too few occurrences in Books II–IV for them to have played any significant role in the shaping of these

books, although it is interesting that the concluding psalms of both
Books III and IV contain a beatitude (Pss 89:16; 106:3). There are
more occurrences in Book V, but there appears to be no particular
pattern. Rather, the significance of the seventeen beatitudes in Books
II–V is that they recall and reinforce Book I's portrayal of the shape
of human happiness and of the character of God. Human happiness,
we are reminded, remains a matter of God's initiative and forgiveness
(see Pss 65:5; 84:5; 144:15; cf. Pss 32:1-2, 33:12); it remains a matter
of trusting God (Ps 84:13; cf. Ps 40:5), or synonymously, fearing God
(Pss 112:1; 128:1); it remains a matter of being open to God's instruction and being directed by God (Pss 94:12; 112:1; 119:1-2;
128:1; cf. 1:1-2); it remains a matter of being like God (Ps 106:3,
"Happy are those who observe justice / who do righteousness at all
times;" cf. 41:2). Perhaps coincidentally — but very appropriately and
certainly not surprisingly — Psalm 146, which initiates the final discrete collection in the Psalter (Psalms 146–150, all bounded by הלל),
contains both the explicit proclamation of God's reign (146:10) and a
beatitude that effectively summarizes all the others (146:5). Not surprisingly either, the beatitude follows upon the admonition, "Do not
put your *trust* in princes, / in mortals in whom there is no help"
(146:3; emphasis added). The beatitude reads: "Happy are those
whose help is the God of Jacob, whose hope is in the LORD their
God." Again, human happiness is essentially trust, utter dependence
upon God for life and future.

Given the shape of Book I of the Psalter and its portrayal of the
shape of human happiness, it is to be expected that the Psalms served
not only as an important liturgical resource for Israel and the church
but also as an important theological resource. The portrait of the righteous as suffering servants would have been particularly meaningful as
Israel struggled during the exilic and postexilic eras to understand its
past or present suffering, as well as its destiny. How much prophetic
interpretations of Israel's past and future, like that in Isaiah 40–55,
depended on the Psalms, we simply do not know.[5] What we do know
is that a later Jewish movement prominently used several of the
prayers for help from Book I of the Psalter to depict as a suffering

---

[5] See Creach, *Yahweh as Refuge*, 124, where he points out that "refuge" is also
an important concept in portions of the book of Isaiah, including chapters 40–55.
See also his "The Shape of Book IV of the Psalter and the Shape of Second
Isaiah," *JSOT* 80 (1998) 63–76.

servant the one whom it proclaimed as the Messiah — see especially Psalms 22 and 31, but also Psalm 41 (see v. 10), the concluding psalm of Book I that was discussed above. In view of this use of the Psalms by early Christian writers, it is interesting that what has become known perhaps as Jesus' teaching *par excellence* consists in part of a series of beatitudes which pronounce as "Happy" precisely those persons featured as "the righteous" in Book I of the Psalter—the poor, the meek, those who mourn, the seekers of righteousness, the persecuted. At least two of Jesus' beatitudes allude rather clearly to Psalms in Book I — compare Matt 5:5 concerning "the meek" with Ps 37:11, and compare Matt 5:8 concerning the pure in heart with Ps 24:4-6. The shape of human happiness in Jesus' Beatitudes matches precisely the shape of human happiness in the Psalms. In both cases, the portrayal adds up finally to love of God and love of neighbor (see Matt 22:34-39 and above on Psalms 1 and 41); and in both cases, the portrayal is predicated upon the proclamation of God's strange sovereignty — a divine power persistently opposed, in Jesus' case, all the way to a cross. The Christian church saw in Jesus the very incarnation of God, a claim that perhaps is not so surprising, given the portrayal of God in the Psalms as one intimately involved in the afflictions of God's people — in effect, a suffering servant.

What is perhaps more surprising is that the Christian church has seldom discerned the shape of human happiness as it is portrayed in the Psalms and by Jesus, and that this message has almost entirely escaped the consciousness of a Western culture that frequently claims to be shaped by the Judeo-Christian tradition. To be sure, we hear a lot about happiness; and one of the canonical documents of our culture even features the "pursuit of happiness" as what it calls an "inalienable right." Tellingly, however, this document is entitled "The Declaration of *Independence*." Thus, at least in a subtle way, it directs the pursuit of happiness on a course that is fundamentally opposed to that of the Psalms, which might accurately be described as "A Declaration of *Dependence*" — dependence first upon God and then upon other human beings. Right after the beatitude in Ps 2:12, the enemies of the psalmist assert, "There is no help for you in God" (Ps 3:3), or to cite the contemporary equivalent, "God helps those who help themselves." Psalm 3 concludes as the psalmist professes precisely the opposite: "Help belongs to God" (3:9; my translation). Quite simply, North American "self-made" women and men are not very inclined to believe this. And quite expectedly, if independence is a basic virtue and a fundamental goal, the pursuit of happiness in our cultural context produces, for the most part, a society of isolated and alienated selves, most of whom cannot even begin to comprehend what Psalm 1 might mean by delighting in or being open to God's instruction and most of whom would never, as in Psalm 41, associate the shape of human happiness with consideration of the poor. In short, the word of the Psalms is a counter-word to our prevailing religious and cultural script: Happy are those who delight in God's instruction; happy are those who consider the poor.

## SELECT BIBLIOGRAPHY

Creach, J. F. D. "The Shape of Book Four of the Psalter and the Shape of Second Isaiah," *JSOT* 80 (1998) 63–76.

—. *Yahweh as Refuge and the Editing of the Hebrew Psalter* (JSOTSup 217; Sheffield: Sheffield Academic Press, 1996).

Howard, D. M., Jr. "Recent Trends in Psalms Study," in D. W. Baker and B. T. Arnold (eds.), *The Face of Old Testament Studies: A Survey of Contemporary Approaches* (Grand Rapids: Baker, 1999) 329–68.

Mays, J. L. *Psalms* (Interpretation: A Bible Commentary for Teaching and Preaching; Louisville: John Knox, 1994).

Tucker, W. D. "Toward the Democratization of the Royal Ideal," Paper delivered Nov. 18, 2001 at the SBL Annual Meeting, Denver, CO.

# THE SOCIAL SETTING OF BOOK II OF THE PSALTER

## MICHAEL GOULDER

Book II of the Psalter is particularly provoking. It is in some sense a real unity because, alone of the Books,[1] it shows a strong preference throughout for אלהים over יהוה. But it is riven in two by its earliest commentators' ascriptions: 42–49 are psalms "of the Sons of Korah,"[2] while 51–72 are said to be "for David"[3] or "for Solomon" (72), and 72 is followed by the note, "The Prayers of David the son of Jesse are ended." Besides this, someone has taken one of the Asaph psalms, and inserted it between these two collections as Psalm 50. There are also some obscure indications of a relation to the shrine of Dan. The Korah psalmist speaks of remembering God from the land of Jordan, from the Hermons (42:7), and in the uttermost part of the north (48:3), and Psalm 68, which is clearly loyal to Zion, warns the high mountains of Bashan — again the Hermon range — not to look with envy at God's mountain (68:16-17). At the same time 48:3, 12-13 also speak unambiguously of Zion and Judah.

I propose a solution to these apparent contradictions in three steps. First, I will argue that the Korah psalms in the Book presuppose a series of public rituals, each of which might be expected to occupy most of a day. This will suggest that the social setting of Psalms 42–49 is of a national festival lasting a number of days, perhaps with Tabernacles as "the Feast" (1 Kgs 8:2). Second, I will make inferences from the David psalms, both their general ascription to David and their particular structure; they, too, are an ordered collection of public psalms, not personal laments and thanksgivings. Finally, I will draw the argument together, as implying given places and times.

## THE KORAH COLLECTION

The psalmist of 42 is on the move. He asks, "Why go I mourning because of the oppression of the enemy?" (42:10, 43:2), and the en-

---

[1] Book III also shows the same preference overall, but not in the last few of its psalms, 84–89.

[2] More exactly, Psalms 42, 44–49; but 43 is in some way a second part of 42.

[3] Psalms 66, 67 and 71 lack David's name; several terms are used for *psalm*.

emy here is "an ungodly nation" (43:1); they crush his bones, so to speak, with their malign taunts, "Where is thy God?" (42:4, 11).[4] He is apparently on pilgrimage. His soul is cast down within him, and he says, "Therefore will I remember thee (אזכרך) from the land of Jordan, from the Hermons, from the little hill" (42:7). Jerusalem is not in the Jordan valley, nor is it near the Hermon range (nor on a little hill); but these details all apply to Dan.[5] Dan stands at one of the four sources of the Jordan, on a spur (a little hill) off Mt. Hermon; and the kings of (northern) Israel used to lead pilgrimages to Dan each year for the great festival(s).[6] The site is also referred to in 42:8, "Deep calleth unto deep at the noise of thy cataracts":[7] it is only in the north of Israel, in the region of Dan, that there are waterfalls. In his depression he remembers happier times, "How I went with the throng and walked in procession with them to the house of God, With the voice of joy and praise, A multitude keeping holy day" (42:5). We may also think that the language of 42:2-3 is not just metaphorical. "As the hart panteth for the water brooks, So panteth my soul after thee, O God. My soul thirsteth for God, even for the living God: when shall I come and see the face of God?" One "saw the face of God" in early times at the pilgrimage-feasts (Exod 23:15; 34:20); and anyone who has been on a modern pilgrimage will know that the panting and thirsting are

---

[4] H.-J.Kraus (*Psalmen I–II* [BKAT; Neukirchen-Vluyn: Neukirchener, 1978]) draws a pathetic picture of a faithful Israelite fatally ill, walking about in dust-covered penitent's clothes by Mt. Hermon, pursued by the sarcastic cries of the heathen. But there are many indications ("my God," etc.) that this is no ordinary Israelite; in other psalms the taunt, "Where is thy God?" is addressed to Israel (79:10; 115:2); Israelites did not treat the sick Naaman like this. Cf. my *The Psalms of the Sons of Korah* (JSOTSup 29; Sheffield: JSOT Press, 1982) 23–25. References to Kraus and other commentators are to their commentaries as detailed in the bibliography. As such works are arranged in order, I have limited page numbers to other works.

[5] The specific details of the site (the Jordan, Hermon, the "little hill") suggest that the place is significant; as if a modern Catholic were to say, "I will pray for you in the Pyrenees, by the Pau river, at the grotto," meaning at Lourdes.

[6] Kraus (and most commentators) assume that the speaker is sad to be near Hermon, and wishes he were with the festal crowds in Jerusalem. But the text says, "My soul is cast down ... *Therefore* will I remember thee from [Hermon]" (42:7), and *RV* has wrongly imported the "Yet" in v. 9.

[7] H. Gunkel (*Die Psalmen* [Gottinger HKAT, 4th ed.; Göttingen: Vandenhoeck & Ruprecht, 1929]) takes the waves and cataracts as symbols of death, with their "grauenvolle Gesang": but the psalm speaks of "*thy* cataracts ... *thy* waves."

not just spiritual.

Psalm 43 reads like a continuation of 42, but the two are distinct. Psalm 42 seems to be an evening psalm, "in the night his song shall be with me" (42:9); while 43 is to be chanted at dawn, "O send out thy light and thy truth that they may lead me" (43:3). Psalm 43 does not provide for a full day's ritual, but only for a procession to the high place for the morning sacrifice: "Let [thy light and truth] bring me unto thy holy hill, and to thy tabernacles. Then will I go unto the altar of God" (43:3-4). The repeated refrain, "Why art thou cast down, O my soul ...?" suggests that the pilgrimage is taking place in a time of national trial. Perhaps the speaker is leading a party the hundred miles from Samaria to Dan, and 42 is the evening psalm on arrival. Psalm 43 will then be the psalm of sacrifice the next morning: all Israelite shrines were on "holy hills," high places, including Dan and Jerusalem. There would then be need of some time to complete arrangements before the Feast.[8]

Psalm 44 is a full-scale national lament, and it lasts all day: "In God have we made our boast all the day long" (44:9); "All the day long is my dishonour before me" (44:16). The situation presupposed is dire: God has cast Israel off, made them turn their backs on their enemies, appointed them like sheep for slaughter, sold them for nothing, made them a byword to their neighbours,[9] smitten them into a place for jackals (44:10-20). The army has been defeated and massacred, fine towns burned and left uninhabited to the wild animals.

In face of this the people gives itself to a day of lamentation. This is carefully structured to arouse God to action: "Awake, why sleepest thou, O Lord?" (44:24). First there are recitations of his saving acts of old, "We have heard with our ears, O God, our fathers have told us, What work thou didst in their days" (44:2).[10] These especially

---

[8] For a fuller exposition of Psalms 42–43, see my *Korah*, 23–37.

[9] F. Delitzsch (*Biblical Commentary on the Psalms* (4th ed., London: Hodder & Stougton, 1887-88) notes how much of the thought and expression of 44 echoes that of 42–43: God's people being cast off, the taunts of their neighbours, the oppression of the enemy, the speaker's soul bowed/cast down, the appeal to God's lovingkindness to command victory.

[10] Kraus takes this to refer to family and clan traditions, but A.Weiser (*The Psalms* [5th ed., ATD; London SCM Press, 1962]) thinks of a public recital of the *Heilsgeschichte* at the festival. The latter seems to be implied by 44:9; also Deut 31:9-11 requires the elders to recite the Law at Sukkot before all Israel "in their ears" (באזניהם), as at 44:2. See further my *Korah*, 85–98.

stressed his giving of the land (44:3-4). The people has then responded to these recitals with massive cries of "Hallelujah!": "In God have we made our boast (הללנו) all the day long" (44:9). The point of these moves, however, is to form a contrast with Israel's present plight (44:10-20), and when this is spoken of, the people fall on their faces in the dirt: "For our soul is bowed down to the dust, Our belly cleaveth unto the earth." Surely such a day's ritual must move the unpredictable heart of the deity: "Rise up for our help" (44:27). We have done nothing wrong: "Our heart is not turned back" (44:19).

Such a view of Psalm 44 is not too controversial. Many commentators have suggested a setting at a special fast-day following a defeat; or it could be an annual day of fast before the Festival, such as was later developed into Yom Kippur: All years contained some bad experiences, and 44 could have been written for a very bad year.[11]

Psalm 45 also implies a full day's ritual, but of a happier kind.[12] It is the consecration, or perhaps reconsecration, of the king. First there is a procession. The king wears his sword, his bow and ("very sharp") arrows; he is to put on his "glory and majesty," his helmet and breastplate, and to "ride on in behalf of righteousness." The ride symbolizes the defeat of his enemies, who fall with his arrows in their heart. Then he returns to the palace where he is enthroned as a divine ruler: "Thy throne, O divine one (אלהים), is for ever" (45:7). He is presented with "the sceptre of equity," with which he is to apply God's laws to his people. He is anointed with considerable amounts of scented oils, the oil of gladness mingled with myrrh, aloes, and cassia. An orchestra inside the royal house plays the while: "Out of ivory palaces stringed instruments make thee glad" (45:9).

The king has a harem, "his precious ones," to whom are now to be added "kings' daughters," that is, a foreign princess as the new queen

---

[11] While an occasional fast would be possible, a national day of affliction would need the gathering of the people, which would not be practicable more often than at the three festivals. The fasts of Joel 1–2 follow failed harvests, and are dated most naturally in the autumn.

[12] The order of the Korah psalms might be either accidental (as is usually supposed), like the hymns in a hymn-book, or deliberate, as the gospels and epistles follow an annual cycle in a Prayer Book. The association of Psalms 42–43 with the pilgrimage, and of Psalm 44 with a pre-festal lament, suggests an ordered sequence. It may also be thought that the king must preside over the whole festival: if the Korah psalms were written to accompany it, his reconsecration should come first.

("forget also thine own people," 45:11). She is probably "the daughter of Tyre" (45:13).[13] Kings of (northern) Israel could marry foreign princesses like Jezebel, while kings of Judah usually married the daughters of Jewish aristocrats. She is dressed in cloth of gold ("of Ophir"), and makes her obeisance to her lord, after which she receives gifts from the Israelite nobles, "the rich among the people" who "smooth her face." She then goes into the women's house to change into her night-attire, and is carried over in a palanquin "upon broidered work" to the king's palace, escorted by her bridesmaids for her wedding-night. The royal party is followed by wild cheering, "gladness and rejoicing" (45:16): Israel will not lack a king, and there will be stability and peace.

Psalm 46 probably also implies a day's ritual.[14] It celebrates God's preservation of his holy city against the onslaughts of two kinds of enemies: the waters below that "roar and are troubled," and make the mountains shake with their swelling (46:4); and the nations that rage and the kingdoms that are moved upon the earth. God has not only stilled the infernal foes, so that Israel need not again fear an earthquake like the one in 740; he has so tamed the waters that there is a river whose streams make glad his city. In 1 Kgs 1 both Adonijah and Solomon process to the sacred springs outside Jerusalem for their consecration, and Ps 110:7 speaks of the Jewish ruler as drinking of the brook by the way before slaughtering his enemies. It is likely that here also we should think of a procession to the holy spring that is being celebrated; though a river with streams sounds more like the rich waters of the Jordan at Dan than the trickles of Gihon and En-rogel at Jerusalem.

---

[13] Reading וּבַת־צֹר with *BHS* as a vocative. The likelihood that the occasion is the marriage of Ahab to Jezebel has been canvassed since F. Hitzig (*Die Psalmen I–II* [Leipzig and Heidelberg: Winter, 1863-65]). Kraus criticizes this on the ground that many kings of Israel and Judah may have married Tyrian princesses, but this is exaggerated with respect to Judah, and the ivory palace is also suggestive of Ahab. Gunkel derived the psalm from (northern) Israel: see my *Korah*, 121–137.

[14] Psalm 46 is taken as a "cultic" psalm by later 20th century commentators —Mowinckel, *The Psalms in Israel's Worship* (Oxford: Blackwell, 1967), 174, 181, Weiser, Kraus, J. Eaton (Torch Bible; London: SCM Press, 1967), A. Anderson (*The Book of Psalms, I–II* (New Century Bible; London: Oliphants, 1972) — but without closer definition. The suggestions here are my own; cf. *Korah*, 137–49.

The second half of the psalm turns to the earthly enemies: "Come, behold the works of the LORD, who hath made desolations in the earth. ... He breaketh the bow and cutteth the spear in sunder, He burneth the chariots in the fire" (46:10). Who then are to come, and what are they to behold? There is no reason for reducing the language to "Imagine": it is the peoples who are to come, and it is a bonfire of captured enemy munitions that they are to behold. Isaiah speaks of the people's joy as like joy in harvest, as men rejoice when they divide the spoil; "for every boot of the booted warrior, and the garments rolled in blood shall be for burning, for fuel of fire" (Isa 9:6), and again of the great Tophet when a feast is hallowed (Isa 30:29-33). There were bonfires after victories, and a more impressive festal fire would symbolize in edifying fashion the power of the LORD of hosts, the God of Jacob.

Psalm 47 involves a further procession. Representatives of foreign countries are in attendance: "O clap your hands, all ye peoples; Shout unto God with the voice of triumph" (47:2). In fact, with their presence and (implied) tribute, they have virtually become part of Greater Israel: "The princes of the peoples are gathered together [as] the people of the God of Abraham"(47:10).[15] They are there because of Israel's hegemony, because "[Yahweh] subdueth the peoples under us, and the nations under our feet" (47:4). They are participants in the solemn movement in which the cultic focus of the divine presence has been carried up to the Temple: "God has gone up" (עָלָה, 47:6); he has "taken his seat (יָשַׁב) upon his holy throne," he has taken up his reign over the nations (מָלַךְ, 47:9).[16] The procession is punctuated with the

---

[15] So Delitzsch, A. Kirkpatrick (*The Book of Psalms I–III* (The Cambridge Bible for Schools and Colleges; Cambridge: Cambridge University Press, 1891-1901). 1 Kings 22 gives an instance where the client king Jehoshaphat of Judah is included in the king of Israel's council, and his army (עַם) becomes part of the army of Israel.

[16] Gunkel saw Psalm 47 as an eschatological hymn, picturing the ultimate enthronement of Yahweh. Later critics saw more ritual behind it, in view of the parallels with the procession (and enthronement) of 2 Samuel 6 and 2 Kings 11. In his *Psalmenstudien II: Das Thronbesteigungs-fest Jahwäs und der Ursprung der Eschatologie* (Kristiania, Norway: J. Dybwad, 1922 [repr. Amsterdam: P. Schippers, 1966]) 1921–24; and *The Psalms in Israel's Worship*, 106–92, S. Mowinckel — followed by Weiser and Eaton — argues for a ceremony of Yahweh's enthronement (יָשַׁב). Kraus, Anderson and others allow a procession and perhaps an act of homage, but deny any enthronement, since Yahweh was already en-

united cultic shout, the תרועה, with blasts on the trumpet, and with clapping and singing to music (47:6-8). No doubt it began near the city gate, as in 2 Samuel 6, and involved the whole population dancing and cheering. If the celebration was held at Dan, God would be represented by the ephod; when at Jerusalem, by the ark.

Psalm 48 requires yet another procession, this time a circumambulation of the city walls. Psalms 45–49 are all psalms concerned with Israel's victory in war, and 46 and 48 have especially in mind the *Völkersturm*, the attack of the nations on God's city, which he repels (46:7; 48:5-9); Psalm 46 particularly exalts the divine river, 48 the divine mountain.[17] There is a liturgy in the temple area, in which the promise of the city's inviolability is repeated: "As we have heard, so have we seen...We have compared (דמינו) thy lovingkindness In the midst of thy temple" (48:9-10).[18] Then the people are bidden to set off and march around the sacred city: "go round about her, Tell the towers thereof. Mark ye well her bulwarks, Traverse her palaces, That ye may tell it to the generations following" (48:13-14). This is God's city, and it is inexpugnable in perpetuity.

The principal problem with 48, as I have hinted, is its original site. The present text leaves no doubts: "the joy of the whole earth is mount Zion. ... Let mount Zion be glad, And the daughters of Judah rejoice. ... Walk about Zion" (48:3, 12-13).[19] But the earlier verses suggested something different. There the stress seems rather to be on the mountain, which is said to be "fair in height" (יפה נוף), "the boundaries of the north" (ירכתי צפון). Mt. Zion is in fact unimpressive in height, a mere 2,500 feet above sea level, lower than the neighbouring Mount of Olives, and far from the country's northern frontier. By contrast, Dan is on a spur of Mt. Hermon, four times as high at

---

throned on the Ark. But an original northern setting would imply the ephod rather than the ark as Yahweh's symbol, and the ephod was a robe; see *Korah*, 151–59.

[17] Older commentators, followed by Louis Jacquet (*Les Psaumes et le coeur de l'homme I–III* [Gembloux: Duculot, 1975-78]) and others, saw the invasion as a recent real event. Gunkel and Kraus think of a poet's vision, to which the community's march is the response; Mowinckel, Weiser, Eaton and Anderson envisage a regular part of the Jerusalem autumn festival. See my *Korah*, 159–70.

[18] Gunkel properly interprets the verb in its primary meaning, *compare*; Israel has set God's covenanted promise (חסד) alongside historical event, and found it true.

[19] By the sixth century BCE the psalm was familiar as applying to Jerusalem (Lam 2:15).

10,000 feet, and standing precisely on Israel's northern boundary.[20] It is when the kings see the divine city on this enormous pile that they panic and flee (48:6). The thought must arise that an original Dan psalm has been transferred to Jerusalem after 732 BCE.[21]

Psalm 49 is the most controversial psalm of the sequence: I have disputed the standard "wisdom psalm" theory at length elsewhere, and will only resume the argument in outline here.[22] The speaker warns foreign nations ("Hear this, all ye peoples...all ye inhabitants of the world," 49:2) not to trust in their strength (חילם) and their wealth to attack Israel (49:7). He has no reason to fear them "when the iniquity of them that would supplant me compasseth me round about" (49:6). Israel will take no prisoners, so no amount of money will suffice to ransom them: "None can by any means redeem his brother, Nor give to God a ransom for him" (49:8). They think that they will live on for ever and not see corruption; but "they shall see it: wise men die and fools together" (49:10-11). They plan for permanent houses in Israel, and call whole areas by their names; but man shall not pass a night in his war-finery there (אדם ביקר בל־ילין), but shall die like the animals (49:12-13).[23]

Such is the way of fools, and their followers support their boasts

---

[20] The phrase ירכתי צפון occurs four further times in the Bible: in three of these (Ezek 38:6, 15; 39:2) it means "the uttermost parts of the north," i.e. modern Turkey, whence the hosts of Gomer and Togarmah are to come; in Isa 14:13 it is the mythological mountain of the gods.

[21] Kraus notes these points, and attributes them to an older Canaanite mythology underlying the psalm.

[22] *Korah*, 181–95. The psalm has a most unfortunate history of exegesis. For much of the period scholars were looking for hints of a belief in life after death, and Psalm 49 was the best hope—although the evidence was slight, and the key phrases in 49:16 are used elsewhere of life on earth (Hos 13:14; Ps 18:16). This (majority) view was accordingly refused by Kirkpatrick, Gunkel and Mowinckel. But then what is the "wisdom" communicated? That the wealthy will die in the end — a rather banal conclusion following a pretentious introduction. But both theories are disreputable in that they rest on an alarming number of changes to the text: NEB, for instance, confesses to 15 emendations, mostly of consonants, besides transposing a line and adopting four other readings not in the MT — these are referred to as "probable readings."

[23] Warriors of the time went to battle wearing their "precious things" (יקר): Gideon was able to take 1,700 shekels of gold from the slain Midianites (Judges 8), and the women of Ps 68:13 cover their arms with bangles from the spoil of the enemy.

(49:14). "They are appointed as a flock for Sheol; Death shall be their shepherd: And the upright" — the Israelites — "shall have dominion over them in the morning; And their form shall be for Sheol to consume, that there be no habitation for it." Defeat and extermination will be the fate of the invaders: "But God will redeem my soul from the hand of Sheol, For he shall receive me" (49:15-16). There is no suggestion of life after death, just a straight contrast between the destruction of the aggressor and the preservation of Israel's representative, the speaker. As often is the case in these psalms there is a mixture of singular and plural for the speaker; perhaps we should think of a court poet or cantor, מנצח, speaking on behalf of king and community.

The psalm ends with a warning to the people not to be afraid when neighbouring leaders grow in power and wealth: they do not live for ever. The man with finery but without sense (אדם ביקר ולא יבין) will die like the animals (49:17-21).

Psalm 49 is the only psalm in the sequence that does not suggest a ritual, and perhaps there was none. What is striking is the similarity and the difference between it and its immediate predecessors. The social setting for all the sequence seems to be the same: it is a national festival, probably Tabernacles, at which whole days are dedicated to prescribed rituals. The royal party, and the people at large, have come on pilgrimage to the nation's cultic centre (42). Their arrival is followed by a sacrifice the following morning (43). Since these two rites must stand at the beginning of the festal sequence, and 42–43 stand at the beginning of the Korah series, it is likely that the remaining rites follow the order of the Korah psalter. There will then have been a day of national humiliation (44) before the Feast, as later Yom Kippur preceded Sukkot. The Feast itself was an occasion for rejoicing, and opened with the annual reconsecration of the king (45). The second day was marked by a procession to the spring of the sacred river, and a bonfire of enemy arms (46). On the third day the symbol of the divine presence was carried in triumph from the city gate up to the Temple, amid the shouting, singing, clapping, and cheering of the people and their (tributary) allies (47). On the fourth day there was a march round the city walls, the guarantee of God's city from attack (48). On the fifth day (we may suppose), an oracle was produced after much "meditation" (49:4-5), warning off any invaders, and reassuring the people of their safety (49).

Thus far, the social setting seems stable: the occasion was the autumn festival, the theme was God's guarantee of protection for his people. But within this united framework we find two dissonances. The first is in the confidence of the psalmist. Psalms 45–48 are optimistic psalms: Israel's king will massacre his enemies, and his sons will be kings over foreign lands; God is our refuge and strength, when he thunders the earth melts, he makes wars to cease; he is terrible, a great king over all the earth, now resuming his reign; invaders panic and flee when they see his holy mountain — he is our God for ever and ever. This is very different from the tone of Psalms 42–44 and 49. There the psalmist goes mourning; his soul is cast down and disquieted as an ungodly nation continually jibes, "Where is thy God?" The army has turned its back on the enemy and has been as sheep for slaughter; its towns are deserted, a place for jackals, covered with the shadow of death. There is no confidence in Psalm 49 either, for all its bold front. "Wherefore should I fear in the days of evil?," asks the psalmist, "Be not thou afraid when one is made rich" (49:6, 17). The situation presupposed is that a neighbouring country has grown rich and powerful, and that there is ample reason for fear. The days are evil.

The festal setting then suggests an explanation for this. The Korah psalms were not used just once, and then kept in a file. They were repeated annually. The optimistic psalms will come from an earlier period, perhaps the days of Ahab or Jeroboam II, when Israel was a power in the land. But with the rise of Assyria, and especially after the disastrous invasion of 732 (2 Kgs 15:29), a change of tone was called for. One could not pretend that all was well; the thing was to move the heart of God with mourning and prostrations before the festival began (Psalms 42–44), and then to reassure the fearful as it progressed (Psalm 49).

Such a picture of historical adaptation would also account for the dissonance we have noted between signs that the Korah psalms came from Dan and evidence that they were in use in Jerusalem. In the end all surviving psalms survived because they were in use at Jerusalem. The Korah collection would have been written for use at Dan if they belonged to the high days of the ninth and eighth centuries. When the Assyrians finally took over the whole of (northern) Israel in 722, its priesthood will have fled south, taking with it its legal code, its historical traditions and its psalmody. The Jerusalem priesthood might have been pleased to welcome these psalms, and to use them with suitable amendments. There should, of course, be no direct mention of any northern shrine, and any mention of a sacred mountain could be clarified by specifying mount Zion. As a later psalmist was to put it, the dew of Hermon came upon the mountain of Zion (133:3).

## THE DAVIDIC COLLECTION

Form critics are faced by an enigma. They think that many of Psalms 51–72 are individual laments, confessions, and thanksgivings from the post-exilic period; but the community which collected these pieces for some reason attributed them to David. All twenty- two have David's name in the heading, with the exception of 66, 67, 71 (which follows on from 70), and 72, which is "for Solomon." Furthermore, an editor has added, "The Prayers of David the son of Jesse are ended." These elements are in the Septuagint, and are likely to go back at least to the third century.

As it is no longer seriously considered that the collection goes back to David,[24] it is normal to belittle the David tradition. David was traditionally a psalmist, the inaugurator of the Temple music; in time his name was associated with many psalms, eventually with them all. But this does not explain the limitation of David's name to two main collections, 3–41 and 51–72, while none of the Korah or Asaph psalms is ascribed to David, and only a scattered few in Book IV or the Psalms of Ascents. Nor does the wording give a casual impression. It is easy to think that a copyist missed out a few "for David" notes, or added one in when he thought the text reminiscent of David. But in our case the editor is sufficiently confident that he has marked off the end of the sequence as the end of a David series.

It is this feature that is in fact so suggestive. Psalms 51–72 consist of a considerable series of psalms "for David," followed by a single psalm "for Solomon," with the note, "The Prayers of David the son of Jesse are ended." Now the Former Prophets include quite a long series of narratives about David, closing in 1 Kings 1 with his abdication in favour of his son Solomon. The editor's concluding note suggests that this parallel was familiar to him. Furthermore, Psalm 72 reads like an echo of the Solomon legends in 1 Kings "Give the king thy judgements, O God: and thy righteousness unto the king's son" (72:1)

---

[24] In my *The Prayers of David (Psalms 51–72)* (Sheffield: Sheffield Academic Press, 1990), I argued that Psalms 51–72 were written by a court poet for David and his son Solomon. For the purposes of the present article it would be sufficient if a later editor collected and arranged these psalms, some of them being in fact from David's time.

sounds like a prayer for king Solomon, son of king David. Abdication
in favour of one's son was rare. The psalm specifies three blessings
for which God is petitioned, each of which is exemplified in Solomon.
First he should judge the people with righteousness and the poor with
judgement, saving the children of the needy (72:1-6); Solomon was
famous for his wisdom in judgement, and in particular for his verdict
over the two women and the disputed child (1 Kings 3). Secondly,
there should be abundance of peace in his days, and corn in plenty
growing on the hillsides (72:9, 16-17); and this came to pass in Solomon's reign, when every Israelite sat under his vine and his fig-tree
(1 Kings 4). Finally, the king will receive tribute from foreign poten-
tates: "The kings of Tarshish and of the isles shall bring presents: the
kings of Sheba and Seba shall bring gifts ... to him shall be given of
the gold of Sheba" (72:8-15). We have an apparent echo of this in the
gifts brought to Solomon by the Queen of Sheba in 1 Kings 10. The
psalm ends with a thanksgiving, "Blessed be the LORD God, the God
of Israel, Who only doeth wondrous things ...": David's last words in
1 Kings 1 are "Blessed be the LORD the God of Israel who hath given
one to sit on my throne this day, mine eyes even seeing it" (1 Kgs
1:48).

So much can hardly be coincidence. The suggestion must be that
the editor saw these David psalms as a response to the Davidic history
in Samuel-Kings, with Psalm 72 answering to the narrative of
1 Kings 1.[25] But if this were so, where would his sequence begin?
Two possibilities may occur to us. The series might go back all the
way to David's first appearance in 1 Samuel 16; or it could start with
the beginning of the "Succession Narrative." The latter is not merely
the creation of modern scholarship, but forms a continuous narrative
beginning with David's affair with Bathsheba (2 Samuel 11), and
continues, steadily fulfilling Nathan's prophecy, till 1 Kings 1. Now
there can be no two opinions about the view taken by the editor, for he
heads Psalm 51, "A Psalm of David: when Nathan the prophet came

---

[25] The indications are that the dependence is in fact the other way: the rather
general petitions of Psalm 72 have been turned into colourful legends—the two
harlots, the Queen of Sheba—of 1 Kings 3-10. These parallels are usually played
down by commentators, who regard 72 as a psalm written for the accession, or the
reconsecration, of any king. Kraus thinks it is relatively early; Dahood and (tentatively) J. Rogerson and J. Mackay (*Psalms I–III* [Cambridge Bible Commentary
on the *NEB*; Cambridge: Cambridge University Press, 1977]) ascribe it to
Solomon.

unto him, after he had gone in to Bathsheba."

Here again the text of the psalm fits the supposed occasion re-markably well. It is sometimes objected that there is no reference to David's adultery with Bathsheba; but what draws God's judgement in the story is not the adultery but the murder: "thou hast smitten Uriah the Hittite with the sword. ... Now therefore the sword shall never de-part from thine house" (2 Sam 12:9-10). The central prayer of the psalm is at 51:16, "Deliver me from blood-guiltiness (דמים), O God." The speaker has committed murder and needs to escape from the "bloods" on his hands.[26]

A curious feature of Psalm 51 is the status of the speaker. In Israel-ite law the punishment for murder was death (Exod 21:12, etc.), but in this case there is no mention of the possibility of execution. What has been done is sufficiently serious that it cannot be absolved with a sac-rifice: "thou delightest not in sacrifice that I should give it" (51:18). On the other hand, the speaker can look forward to happier times to come, when the walls of Jerusalem are built, and he can offer bullocks on the altar (51:20-21).[27] Both features suggest that the speaker is supposed to be the king. Only kings can excuse themselves the death penalty, and only kings build walls round Jerusalem. The editor has found a psalm that fits the theme of 2 Samuel 12 strikingly well,[28] and this makes us the more curious whether the response-hypothesis can be made plausible all the way.

Such an endeavour would require more space than is available here, and in any case I have offered such a detailed exegesis in my *The Prayers of David*. It must be conceded that some psalms are worded generally, and might be thought suitable for more than one of the situations in the Succession Narrative. But there is one long psalm, 68, which includes a considerable amount of specific detail, and I will limit my comments on the David sequence to 68 as providing some-

---

[26] See my *Prayers*, 53–56, for other interpretations. The most popular is that of B. Duhm (*Die Psalmen* [HKAT 14; 2nd ed., Tübingen: Mohr Siebeck, 1922]) who supposes that the speaker is ill, and prays to be delivered from bloods = death; so also Weiser, Kraus, Anderson. But the equivalence looks forced, and does not ac-count for the enormous sense of guilt which pervades the psalm; the speaker sees himself as conceived in sin (vv. 5–7).

[27] It is common to excise the last two verses of 51, as with so many other in-convenient parts of the text; there is no evidence to support such speculations.

[28] For a detailed comparison of Psalm 51 with the situation described in 2 Samuel 11–12, see my *Prayers*, 51–69.

thing of a test case for the theory.

Psalm 68 is the celebration of a victory in battle. It describes a procession with the ark ("Let God arise...," 68:2) going up to the Temple ("They have seen thy goings, O God, Even the goings of my God, my King, into the sanctuary," 68:25) at Jerusalem (68:30). A choir ("singers") lead; musicians ("minstrels") bring up the rear; the women play their timbrels alongside (68:26). The people line the route in their "congregations," blessing God (68:27).

The vanquished enemy are a coalition. Those mentioned first are "the rebellious" (סוררים), who will be sent to "dwell in a parched land" (68:7), to farm the desert; the widows and orphans of loyalist soldiers who have died will be looked after and given homes (68:5). The rebels are referred to again in 68:19, where their leaders are executed so as to purify the land: "Yea, the rebellious also, that the LORD God might dwell." Feeling is strong against these rebels: they are spoken of as human sacrifices (מתנות באדם),[29] and have their hairy scalps beaten in for the victors to dip their feet in the blood (68:22-24). But the rebels have been supported by allies, whether mercenaries or opportunists, and it is these whose flight is reported by the triumphant loyalist women: "Kings of armies flee, they flee!" (68:13). These kings are tribal chieftains from the southern frontier area. The psalmist closes with a warning to "the wild beast of the reeds, the multitude of the bulls, with the calves of the peoples." In time, princes will come from Egypt and Cush bringing their tribute to Jerusalem (68:31-32). The might of Egypt ("the wild beast of the reeds," "bulls") is felt to be behind the incursion, but the kings will be from the "calves of the peoples," the lesser tribes of the Sinai area.

Can we learn anything more about the rebels? The victory procession leaves some surprising gaps. Those mentioned are "little Benjamin their ruler, the princes of Judah their council, the princes of Zebulun, the princes of Naphtali" (68:29). The core of Israel was the Joseph complex, the tribes of Ephraim and Manasseh (Machir) who are the first to be mentioned in the Song of Deborah (Judg 5:14):[30] it is

---

[29] This seems the best meaning for the context, with *bet essentiae*, "consisting of." Delitzsch, and many others, translate "among men," which seems plethoric.

[30] The links with Judges 5 have suggested to many critics (Gunkel, for example) that behind 68 is an echo of Israel's *Heilsgeschichte*: But this is often problematic. God goes before his people as he did out of Egypt, and the earth trembles as at Sinai; but then he sends plentiful rain as does not happen in Exodus: Gunkel

singular that they are not mentioned here.[31] The main credit goes to the princes of Zebulun and Naphtali in the north; but even there a note of restraint is felt. The mountain of Bashan is a mighty mountain, but it is not to look with jealousy at God's mountain, Zion. The suggestion seems to be that the northern tribesmen prefer to worship at the mountain of Bashan, Mt. Hermon, at the shrine at Dan — but that would be a mistake.

We also learn two things about the campaign. First, the battle was fought at Zalmon in a snowstorm: "When the Almighty scattered kings therein, it snowed in Zalmon" (68:15). Zalmon is in a heavily wooded area near Shechem on the Ephraim-Manasseh border; Abimelech had his men cut down branches from the trees on Mt. Zalmon so as to burn the Shechem acropolis (Judg 9:48). Secondly, the psalm is partly addressed to a human being who has been for some reason in Bashan, that is, northern Transjordan: "The LORD said, I will bring again from Bashan, I will bring again from the deep places of the sea, That thou mayest dip thy foot in blood ..." (68:23-4). The repeated אשיב shows that "the deep places of the sea" are on the earth's surface, as Bashan is. If one were coming back from Bashan to Jerusalem, it might be convenient to cross the Jordan at the ford at Gilgal used by Joshua (Joshua 3–4) near the Dead Sea, well below sea level.

So there is a good deal of detail. Is there any historical event in our tradition that would fit with it? Well, first, it seems to be an early psalm. If "their ruler" (רדם) means the king, all the kings after David were thought of as Judahites. Saul was from Benjamin, and so was David's family. His father Jesse came from Ephrath (1 Sam 17:12), where Rachel died giving birth to Benjamin (Gen 35:16), and her sepulchre was in the territory of Benjamin (1 Sam 10:2). David later settled in Bethlehem, and it became politic in time to think of him as a Judahite — hence the fiction that Ephrath and Bethlehem were two

---

sees the "rain" as manna and quails. Mowinckel in *Der achtundsechzigste Psalm* (Oslo: Dybwad, 1953) combined the Exodus theme with that of creation: the context was a New Year procession with real rain. But both Gunkel and Mowinckel have imaginary battles in the future: the concrete details like Zalmon, the snow, and Bashan, disappear with emendations and questionable symbolism. See my *Prayers*, 191–216, esp. 214–16.

[31] Cf. also 60:8, "I will divide Shechem and mete out the valley of Succoth." Also from the second David collection, this verse suggests a civil war in which Shechem was on the enemy side.

names for the same place (Gen 35:19; Mic 5:2, etc.). So if the king is from Benjamin, he must be Saul or David. We know of no rebellion in which the central tribes rose against Saul; but we do know of a major rising in which "Israel" rebelled against David, under Absalom. This would agree with the element of competition implied between Jerusalem and Dan, soon to become critical with Jeroboam.

2 Samuel 15–19 describe Absalom's revolt. Absalom goes south to Hebron "to sacrifice to the LORD," in fact to raise the rebellion (2 Sam 15:7-12). The two hundred men who accompany him are said to have gone in their innocence, knowing nothing; so the likelihood is that Absalom had hired tribesmen from the Negev to support him, just as David had hired Philistines. But the revolt catches on: the hearts of the men of Israel were after Absalom (15:13), and when the battle is fought, it is said to be against Israel (18:6). In chapter 19, a contrast is drawn between Israel and the men of Judah, so the revolt was supported mainly by northern tribes, of which Ephraim and Manasseh are likely to have been the core. David's commanders, and so his "council," were Joab, Abishai, and Ittai, of whom the former two were Judahites (1 Chron 2:16).

The revolt was at first successful, and David took flight for Mahanaim in Manasseh beyond the Jordan (Bashan). The battle was fought "in the forest of Ephraim" (18:6), that is, on the West Bank, very likely in the wooded area around Mt. Zalmon. David was brought back after the victory, and crossed the Jordan at Gilgal, just north of the Dead Sea, before being escorted up to Jerusalem (19:15). So it looks as if the details provided by Psalm 68 correspond closely with those of 2 Samuel 15–19. (a) King David, "their ruler" was from Benjamin. (b) Joab and Abishai, "their council," were from Judah. (c) It was a civil war, against "rebels," whose leaders were ceremonially executed. These rebels were spoken of as "Israel," and included the central tribes; David was supported by Zebulun and Naphtali, the latter a "handmaid tribe" from the northern frontier of the country. (d) The revolt was raised at Hebron in the south, probably with the assistance of foreign tribesmen, "kings of armies" from "calves of the peoples" near Egypt, "the wild beast of the reeds." (e) David fled to Mahanaim in Bashan, from where he was brought back to Jerusalem. (f) The battle took place in the forest of Ephraim, in the region where Mt. Zalmon stands with its woods. (g) David came back via the crossing at Gilgal, at "the deep places of the sea." We may also note that Psalm 68 stands near the end of the David series, 51–72, in the same way that the battle in 2 Samuel 18 stands near the end of the Succession Narrative, leading on to 1 Kings 1.

## A COMBINED FESTAL SETTING

How then has Book II come to combine the Korah sequence (Psalms 42–49) with the David sequence (Psalms 51–72), with the intrusion of the single Asaph psalm 50 in between? We lack direct evidence, and have to rely on inference. The Korah psalms were the psalmody used for the autumn festival at Dan in the days of the divided monarchy. It provided for a series of rituals before and during the Feast: the pilgrimage, the first sacrifice, the preliminary day of affliction; and then five days of processions and (mostly) triumphalism. No doubt there had been similar rites and psalms in Jerusalem, but under the divided monarchy Israel worshipped at Dan and Bethel, and Jerusalem was small beer in comparison. When the Assyrians took the northern rump over in 722, the Korah priests fled to Jerusalem, and brought their splendid psalms with them.

The Jerusalem priests might have been quite pleased to welcome the newcomers, especially as a counterweight to King Manasseh — provided their priestly rights and incomes were safeguarded. So the Korah psalms were incorporated into the Jerusalem liturgy for Sukkot, with the addition of one or two mentions of Zion and Judah. There was however one tradition the Judahites were not prepared to give up. This was the story of how the line of Solomon came to sit on the throne of David; and this was celebrated with a collection of psalms, some of them at least ancient psalms, which had been assembled as responses to the Succession Narrative. In this way we should have an explanation for the combination. The first five days of Sukkot were now celebrated with the rituals and psalms of the nation, brought down from Dan; the last two days were given over to a recital of King David's passion and triumph, and his commitment of the throne to Solomon his son.

With the catastrophe of 587 came a break. Other psalms, less triumphalist, like the Asaph psalms, may have been put in use. When the exiles began to return, there were no more kings, so the force of the Succession Narrative was lost. It was remembered that the David psalms were responses to individual episodes in David's life, but the notion of a sequence was forgotten. Editors sometimes included "historical" notes in the headings. Such guesses were not always wrong. They were right over Psalms 51 and 72; but otherwise there was a tendency to read complaints of persecution as echoes of the well-known persecution of David by Saul. A further development was the extension of Sukkot to an eight-day festival (Lev 23:36). This would then require an additional psalm; but one would not wish to destroy the fine climax of 72. It seemed suitable therefore to transfer Psalm 50 to bridge the gap between the two collections; 50 was similar to 51 in subject, and in particular stressed the right attitude as well as the action of festal sacrifice.

The term "social setting" has been popular since the work of Gunkel, and the reader may have been disappointed not to read of poor but faithful Israelites oppressed by greedy landlords, suffering from manifold diseases, in prison, under debt, and such trials. My own conclusions on the social setting of Book II are perhaps less colourful, but are not less interesting: for the liturgies in use at Israel's festivals reveal the central concerns of the people's life: peace, justice, plenty, and if war, victory. Like form-critical commentators I have to make inferences from inadequate evidence; but, unlike them, I have based myself on the oldest interpretive traditions: that is, the order in which the psalms have been placed in the Psalter, and the Headings that introduce them.

## SELECT BIBLIOGRAPHY

Anderson, A. A. *The Book of Psalms, I–II* (New Century Bible; London: Oliphants, 1972).

Dahood, M. *Psalms I–III* (AB 16, 17, 17A; New York: Doubleday, 1965-70).

Delitzsch, F. *Biblical Commentary on the Psalms* (4th ed., Lodon: Hodder & Stougton, 1887-88).

Duhm, B. *Die Psalmen* (HKAT 14; 2nd ed., Tübingen: Mohr Siebeck, 1922).

Eaton, J. H. *Psalms* (Torch Bible; London: SCM Press, 1967).

Goulder, M. D. *The Psalms of the Sons of Korah* (JSOTSup 29; Sheffield: JSOT Press, 1982).

—. *The Prayers of David (Psalms 51–72)* (Sheffield: Sheffield Academic Press, 1990).

Gunkel, H. *Die Psalmen* (Gottinger HKAT, 4th ed.; Göttingen: Vandenhoeck & Ruprecht, 1929).

Hitzig, F. *Die Psalmen I–II* (Leipzig and Heidelberg: Winter, 1863-65).

Jacquet, L. *Les Psaumes et le coeur de l'homme I–III* (Gembloux, France: Duculot, 1975-78).

Kirkpatrick, A. F. *The Book of Psalms I–III* (The Cambridge Bible for Schools and Colleges; Cambridge: Cambridge University Press, 1891-1901).

Kraus, H.-J. *Psalmen I–II* (BKAT; Neukirchen-Vluyn: Neukirchener, 1978).

Mowinckel, S. *Psalmenstudien II: Das Thronbesteigungs-fest Jahwäs und der Ursprung der Eschatologie* (Kristiania, Norway: J. Dybwad, 1922 [repr. Amsterdam: P. Schippers, 1966]).

—. *Der achtundsechzigste Psalm* (Oslo: Dybwad, 1953).

—. *The Psalms in Israel's Worship I–II* (Oxford: Blackwell, 1967).

Rogerson, J. W. and J. W. McKay, *Psalms I–III* (Cambridge Bible Commentary on the *NEB*; Cambridge: Cambridge University Press, 1977).

Schmidt, H. *Die Psalmen* (HAT; Tübingen: Mohr Siebeck, 1934).

Weiser, A. *The Psalms* (5th ed., ATD; London: SCM Press, 1962).

# ZUR GESCHICHTE DES VIERTEN DAVIDPSALTERS
## (PSS 138–145)

### KLAUS D. SEYBOLD

Der sogenannte vierte Davidpsalter,[1] dem man die Psalmen 138–145 zuschreibt, wird durch zwei Faktoren konstituiert: einmal durch die allen Texten vorangestellte Zueignungsformel לדוד in den Überschriften, zum andern durch die abgrenzende Gruppierung der Textfolge, welche durch die Einzelpsalmen 135; 136 und 137 auf der einen und die Hymnusgruppe 146–150 auf der andern Seite einen Rahmen markiert. Ist nun die Setzung der Überschriften in den hebräischen und griechischen Hauptzeugen, d.i. in der LXX, in den Q-Handschriften und im MT — bei kleineren Variationen im Einzelnen[2] — hinsichtlich der Zueignung im großen Ganzen einheitlich überliefert, gibt es bei der Textfolge erhebliche Unterschiede. Die von MT und LXX festgelegte Reihenfolge 138–145 wird von den Q-Handschriften nicht bezeugt[3], wie ja überhaupt wahrscheinlich nur die Handschrift MasPs[b] die Psalmenfolge im MT-Psalter unterstützt; vielmehr bietet vor allem die in diesem Textbereich besonders gut erhaltene Handschrift 11QPs[a] eine völlig anderes Bild: Die Reihenfolge ab Psalm 135 ist:

–135–136+Catena–145+Postscript–154–Plea for Deliverance–139–137–
138–Sirach 51–Apostrophe to Zion–93–141–133–144–155–142–143–149
–150–Hymn to the Creator–2.Sam 23–David's Compositions–140–
134–151A–151B // Ende der Psalterhandschrift (vgl. LXX).

Von einer Gruppierung 138–145(150) findet sich in dem 11Q[a]-Psalter scheinbar keine Spur. Doch sieht man näher zu, fällt ins Auge, dass diese etwa 25 Schlusstexte ja samt und sonders als David-Psalmen ausgewiesen

---

[1] Es gibt zu dieser Gruppe wenig spezielle Literatur, vgl. M. Millard, *Die Komposition des Psalters. Ein formgeschichtlicher Ansatz* (FAT 6; Tübingen: Mohr Siebeck, 1994) 45.144ff.

[2] Vgl. J. A. Sanders, *The Psalms Scroll of Qumran Cave 11 [11QPs[a]]* (DJD 4; Oxford: Clarendon Press, 1965); P. W. Flint, *The Dead Sea Psalms Scrolls and the Book of Psalms* (STDJ 17; Leiden: Brill, 1997) (dort weitere Literatur). Die griechische Überlieferung hat z.T. biographische Erweiterungen bei den Psalmen 138 (MT 139), 142 (MT 143), 143 (MT 144). 11QPs[a] liest bei Psalm 145 תפלה statt תהלה sowie eine Unterschrift: זאת לזכרון.

[3] Von der Gruppe der Psalmen 138–145 sind außerhalb von 11QPs[a] nur Ps 141,10 (11QPs[b]), Ps 144,1-2 (11QPs[b]) und Ps 143,2-4.6-8 (4QPs[p]) bezeugt.

sind, sei es durch explizite Angaben und Verweise im Textkorpus oder durch den in David's Compositions vorweggenommenen Kolophon, der offenbar sämtliche Texte des 11Q-Psalters David zuschreiben will. Explizite David-Verfasserschaft machen neben den durch Überschriften ausge wiesenen Psalmen (in 11QPs[a]: 133; 138; 140; 143; 145)[4] geltend: die letzten Worte 2.Samuel 23; Sirach 51; Psalm 151A(B). Bei den Texten Psalm 154; Plea und Psalm 155, die ohne Überschrift sind, kann man eine Übertragung der Zuschreibung aus dem Kontext annehmen, da sie ebenfalls individuelle Gebete sind. Was übrig bleibt, sind hymnische Zionpsalmen, die gegen Ende der Reihe da und dort eingestreut worden zu sein scheinen. So wird man sagen können, dass der 11Q-Psalter zwar im letzten Teil von der masoretischen Reihenfolge der Texte abweicht, dass er aber den Textbestand des vierten Davidpsalters des MT überliefert, wenngleich durch andere David-Texte oder ihresgleichen erweitert und mit Zionpsalmen vermischt. Da ein Gruppierungsprinzip wie beim MT Psalter: 135–137 Ziontexte, 138–145 Davidpsalmen, 146–150 Hymnen nicht erkennbar ist, ist anzunehmen, dass ein solches für 11QPs[a] (noch) nicht bestand oder aus allgemeinen Erwägungen zur generellen David-Verfasserschaft nicht (mehr) relevant war. Trotz dieses etwas komplizierten Sachverhalts der Überlieferung wird man schließen dürfen, dass die in dem letzten Teil der beiden Psalter überlieferten David-Texte insofern als etwas Besonderes angesehen wurden, als sie nicht in die offenbar bereits vorhandenen David-Psalter integriert oder dort addiert wurden, vielmehr nach den großen Komplexen des Psalm 119 und des Wallfahrt-Psalters platziert wurden und insofern insgesamt den Eindruck eines Nachtrags vermitteln. Die Barrieren der genannten Komplexe deuten darauf hin, dass die Sammler und Editoren der Psalmdichtung diese Texte von bereits vorgegebenen anderen Gruppierungen distanzieren wollten.

Beide Psalter haben ihr Material unterschiedlich arrangiert. Dabei wird man nicht davon ausgehen können, dass eine Abhängigkeit in der einen oder andern Richtung besteht. Weder ist der MT-Psalter als Weiterführung und Bearbeitung des 11Q-Psalters anzusehen, in der Weise, dass er die David-Texte selektioniert und als Gruppe für sich konzentriert hätte. Noch ist zu sehen, dass der 11Q-Psalter aus dem MT-Psalter hervorgegangen wäre, dadurch dass er eine vorhandene Gruppierung aufgelöst und mit neuen Texten durchsetzt hätte. Anzunehmen ist vielmehr, dass beide Versionen unterschiedlich vorgegangen sind, wobei ihr editorisches Ziel ein

---

[4] Nicht alle Anfänge sind in 11QPs[a] erhalten. So nicht bei 139; 141; 142. Die Psalmen 93 und 137 sind nach LXX Davidpsalmen.

ähnliches gewesen ist, nämlich die Hervorhebung der David-Verfasserschaft, auch und besonders im letzten Teil einer wahrscheinlich bereits soweit herangewachsenen Sammlung. Die editorische Arbeit an diesem Schlussteil lässt sich wohl in beiden Versionen dadurch charakterisieren, indem man feststellt:

Es war die Aufgabe, Restbestände von Individualtexten sowie hymnische Ziontexte dem bestehenden Psalter beizufügen, ohne sie dort einbringen zu können oder zu wollen, wo bereits solche Teilsammlungen bestanden. Man löste diese so, dass die eine Version Texte auswählte und säuberlich gruppierte (138–145 Davidtexte, 146–150 Hymnen), die andere den Bestand zum Teil durch bereits sanktionierte oder „kanonisierte" Texte (aus 2.Sam), aber auch durch „apokryphe" Texte ergänzte und den ganzen entstehenden Psalter zum David-Psalter erklärte.

In beiden Fällen spielten die hymnischen Zion-Texte und die David-Texte eine je besondere Rolle. Sie gehörten zum vorliegenden Restbestand. Woher kamen diese Texte?

Um dieser Frage im Blick auf die David-Texte weiter nachzugehen, muss zuerst die in den Überschriften dokumentierte Einschätzung der Texte erörtert werden.

## DIE ANGABEN DER ÜBERSCHRIFTEN

Da die Versionen und Editionen in der Bezeugung der Überschriften weithin übereinstimmen, ist zu schließen, dass sie diese bereits in ihrem Material vorfanden. Es ist nicht sehr wahrscheinlich, dass die Bearbeiter bei einigermaßen unterschiedlichem Vorgehen diese fast gleichlautend oder gar gemeinsam gesetzt hätten. Sonst hätten sie doch bei ihrer Tendenz zur Davidisierung die Überschriften —im Sinne der biographischen Erweiterungen der griechischen Fassung — bearbeitet und einander angeglichen oder in irgendeiner Weise, etwa in der Reihenfolge der einzelnen Angaben, anders gestaltet. Die Überschriften müssen ihnen bereits vorgelegen haben, und zwar als zum Textkorpus gehörige Teile, an denen sie willentlich nichts mehr ändern konnten. Somit stellt sich die Frage, wer sie verfasst hat.

Weil wir andererseits als unwahrscheinlich ausschließen, dass die Psalmenüberschriften mit der Abfassung der Psalmen — als von den Verfassern selbst gesetzt — entstanden sind, kommen nur rezeptionelle bzw. redaktionelle Maßnahmen zwischen Abfassung der Einzeltexte und der in den Handschriften bezeugten Psalterversionen und –editionen in Frage. Diese aber halten an der Fiktion fest oder suggerieren die Vorstellung, alle diese Texte seien davidisch, d.h. entweder von David oder für David verfasst, woran der 11Q-Psalter ganz explizit festhält, gefolgt von der LXX, während der MT-Psalter in diesem Punkt sich offener verhält.

Die Probleme der Psalmenüberschriften sind bekanntlich bisher nicht befriedigend gelöst, und man bewegt sich dabei auf wenig gesichertem Boden. Auch ist das Ziel dieser Studie nicht, diese Probleme zu diskutieren. Sie möchte nur die schlichte Frage stellen, weshalb die Psalmen 138–145 überschriftlich „davidisiert" wurden und was das für ihre Einschätzung zu bedeuten hat.

Zunächst der Bestand: Die Überschriften im vierten David-Psalter unterscheiden sich nicht grundsätzlich von denen der andern David-Psalter. Das grundlegende Element ist die Formel לדוד, die mehrheitlich unmittelbar vor dem beginnenden Textkorpus steht. Sie ist häufig verbunden mit einem „Gattungsbegriff", wie מזמור (4-mal), משכיל, תהלה oder תפלה (je 1-mal).[5] Dabei spielt die Reihenfolge offenbar syntaktisch keine Rolle, wie man an der unerklärbaren Umkehrung bei Psalm 139 und Psalm 140 sieht. Dieser Kernbestand ist zwei Mal durch Zusätze erweitert worden: durch die Voranstellung des wohl musikalischen Terminus למנצח (Psalmen 139; 140) und durch die an den Davidnamen angehängte biographische Notiz (Psalm 142), was in der LXX (dort auch bei Psalmen MT 139; 143; 144) vermehrt geschieht. Beide Zusätze scheinen erst sekundär oder tertiär zur Überschrift hinzugekommen zu sein: der Terminus zum Zwecke einer tertiären musikalischen Verwendbarkeit (neben מזמור), die Notiz im Zuge der konsequenten historischen Biographisierung und Verortung im Leben Davids nach der Tradition, wobei die Annahme der Verfasserschaft durch David vorausgesetzt ist.

Bei diesen letzten Zusätzen liegt die Motivation offen. Der Hinweis auf die „Höhle" als Ort der Entstehung von Psalm 142 ergibt sich aus der Assoziation mit dem „Kerker", in dem sich der Psalmist nach eigenem Zeugnis befindet (V. 8). Der Hinweis „für den Chorleiter" jedoch, falls er denn so zu verstehen ist, ist zwar klar, entzieht sich aber der begründeten Einsicht. Weshalb sollen gerade Psalm 139 und Psalm 140 musikalisch besonders gut verwertbar sein? Die Frage ist auch, wie die Setzung der anderen, älteren Teile der Überschrift motiviert ist. Nachvollziehbar ist wohl relativ einfach die Charakterisierung durch die „Gattungsbegriffe": Gesang, Lehrgedicht, Lobpreis, Gebet. Als Gesänge, zur Leier vorgetragen, können die Ich-Psalmen 139; 140; 141; 143 verstanden werden, wie auch Psalm 145 als Lobpreis oder als Gebet. Was an Psalm 142 lehrhaft sein soll, vor allem gegenüber den theologischen und weisheitlichen Texten Psalm 139

---

[5] 11QPs^a bei Psalm 145 תפלה statt תהלה.

oder Psalm 145, denen dieser Titel viel eher zuzuerkennen wäre, bleibt rätselhaft. Vielleicht ist es doch die „Lehre" aus der Höhle des Kerkers, die von den Tradenten besonders hervorgehoben werden sollte. Doch wird ja auch die Bezeichnung „Lehrgedicht" am Ende durch den Begriff „Gebet" ergänzt und korrigiert.

Drei Punkte sind festzuhalten:

1. Die Angaben der Überschriften gruppieren sich um den Kernbegriff der David-Formel, die auch — wie etwas bei Psalm 138 und Psalm 144 — isoliert stehen kann.

2. Sie sind z.T. abhängig von nachträglicher Einschätzung und formaler Einordnung nach dem Psalminhalt oder auch von einer tertiären musikalischen Verwendung.

3. Die David-Formel ist aus den Texten nicht abzuleiten, jedenfalls nicht im Sinne einer Verfasserschaft. Im Gegenteil: Die Erwähnung Davids Ps 144,10 in der dritten Person spricht zumindest bei diesem Text gegen eine Abfassung durch David. Dasselbe gilt von den in den Texten selbst erkennbaren Situationen, die — und das gilt selbst und gerade für die Kerkerszene von Psalm 142 — sich nur schwer mit der aus der Tradition bekannten Biographie David vereinbaren lassen.

Was hat die Formel zu bedeuten?

## DIE ZUEIGNUNGSFORMEL

Die Möglichkeiten der Deutung der Formel sind bekannt und müssen nicht noch einmal aufgelistet werden. Das Problem liegt darin, dass die Bedeutung der Formel sich offenbar im Laufe der Überlieferung verändert, und zwar extrem verändert hat. Ist durch die biographischen Zusätze zumindest die Vorstellung einer davidischen Verfasserschaft als gegeben anzusehen, die außer durch die LXX durch die 11QPs$^a$-Texte David's Compositions und die Letzten Worte explizit gesichert wird, kann diese Deutung offensichtlich nicht die ursprüngliche Meinung der Formulierung gewesen sein. Denn einmal ist ein ל-auctoris im Hebräischen nicht nachzuweisen; vielmehr ist die präpositionale Verbindung als allgmeiner Ausdruck der Zugehörigkeit (*ascriptio*)[6] zu verstehen, was insbesondere die Fälle mit isolierter Formel (Psalmen 138; 144) und damit die wahrscheinliche Grundform der Überschrift betrifft. Eine Verfasserschaft durch David ist so zunächst nicht intendiert, vielmehr eigentlich ausgeschlossen. Zum andern widerlegt die Nennung Davids in dritter Person die Annahme,

---

[6] Vgl. E. Jenni, *Die hebräischen Präpositionen*, Bd.3: *Die Präposition Lamed*, (Stuttgart: Kohlhammer, 2000) *passim*.

das sprechende Ich sei mit David selbst gleichzusetzen (Psalmen 18; 144). Schließlich spricht die Nennung des Tempels und seines Umfelds eigentlich deutlich gegen die davidische Zeit, und dass die geschilderte reale Situation einer Gefangenschaft im Tempelverließ nicht mit der judäischen Höhle vergleichbar ist, müsste auch denen aufgefallen sein, die solche Texte auf dem Hintergrund der Zeugnisse aus den Vorderen Propheten herauszulesen versuchten. Somit wäre für die Erstsetzung der Formel eine ursprünglich andere Bedeutung anzunehmen.

Welche Bedeutung das war, kann m.E. nur aus der Analogie vergleichbarer Zuschreibungen und aus dem gleichgearteten Versuch geschlossen werden, bestimmte Texte bekannten Figuren zuzuordnen, um ihnen dadurch ein stärkeres Gewicht und eine höhere Weihe zu verleihen oder ihnen gar die Würde besonders heiliger Schriften zuzuerkennen. Kurzum, diese Formeln gehören in die Phase der Wertung und Würdigung vorhandener Texte und somit in die bewegte Geschichte der Kanonisierung aktueller Texte. Viel ist über diese Prozesse nicht bekannt, aber schon der Psalter bezeugt mit seinen Zuweisungen an Mose, Salomo, Asaph, sowie die Qorachiten, diese Tendenz, die außerhalb des Psalters im Anschluss an die Mose-Tora des Deuteronomiums und der Priesterschrift, der Weisheitsliteratur usw. literaturgeschichtlich außerordentlich wirksam geworden war.

Dieselbe Tendenz verfolgten ja auch die Tradenten, die versuchten, noch vorhandenes Psalmenmaterial in der bereits kanonischen Tora oder den sich zum Prophetenkanon hin entwickelnden Großarchiven der biblischen Schriften unterzubringen. Es ist nur auf die sog. Mose-Psalmen in Exodus 15 oder Deut 32, auf den Hanna-Psalm, Hiskia-Psalm, Jona-Psalm, Habakuk-Psalm, Nahum-Psalm u.a. zu verweisen, die letzteren Texte nach Art und Herkunft den David-Psalmen unmittelbar vergleichbar, um zu erkennen, wie stark der Drang gewesen sein muss, möglichst viel noch dem werdenden Kanon einzuverleiben.

Offenbar war die Kapazität bald einmal erschöpft und es wurde die Idee entwickelt, die vielen Texte aus den Archiven zu sammeln, zu ordnen und zum Gebrauch aufzubereiten. Auf diese oder ähnliche Weise kam es wohl zur Entstehung von Psaltersammlungen.

Damit aber entstand zugleich das Bedürfnis, die große Menge der Einzeltexte—und am Anfang standen die Einzeltexte—überschaubar zu ordnen, zu sortieren und für den Gebrauch auszuzeichnen. Sie wurden jeweils mit einer Zuschreibung als Etikette, als einer Art Siegel oder Stempel, versehen. Die Formel „für/zu NN" funktioniert ja nur, wenn eine Auswahl von unterschiedlichen Möglichkeiten besteht. Es scheint, als ob die Formel לדוד eben eine bestimmte Gruppe von Texten siegeln und dadurch

kenntlich machen sollte. Neben den Gruppen der Asaph-Texte, der
Qorachiten-Texte, der Mose- und Salomo-Texte bezeichnet sie die größte
Psalmengruppe eben der David-Psalmen. So gesehen ist der Schluss un-
ausweichlich, dass die Formel ursprünglich „nur" als Namensetikett
fungierte, das eine Menge gleichartiger Texte signieren sollte. Die
Gleichartigkeit besteht wohl darin, dass die Texte 1. aus dem Umkreis des
Jerusalemer Tempels stammen (im Unterschied zu der Asaph- und
Qorachiten-Gruppe); dass sie 2. in ihrer Mehrheit als Individualpsalmen
verfasst oder verwendet worden sind; dass sie 3. offenbar nach der Verwendung im Toda-Ritual als Votivtexte abgelegt und archiviert worden
sind; dass sie 4. bis zuletzt, im Unterschied zu allen andern Gruppen, noch
aufgestockt und vermehrt werden konnten (wie man an der Abfolge der
David-Psalter bis hin zu den apokryphen Psalmtexten von 11QPs[a] sehen
kann). Teil und Resultat dieses Prozesses scheint der vierte David-Psalter
zu sein.

## ZUR VERWENDUNG DER TEXTE

Was ergibt sich im Blick auf die Verwendbarkeit der Texte? Es ist ja das
Problem aller Individualtexte vor allem der David-Psalter, dass sie als Vo-
tivtexte persönlich verfasst und biographisch verwurzelt sind, dass eine
Wiederverwendung im Sinne ihrer primären Absicht jedoch kaum möglich
ist. Wo gibt es hasserfüllte Zusammenstöße wie bei Psalm 139, wo Feind-
seligkeiten wie bei Psalm 140, oder Verleumdungen und Anklagen wie bei
Psalm 141 — ein zweites Mal? Wo gibt es mit den Kerkergebeten dieser
Gruppe vergleichbare Situationen? Es ist dasselbe Problem wie bei den
Königspsalmen. Eine Wiederaufnahme und Aneignung solcher Ich-Gebete
ist eigentlich unmöglich. Bei dem Königspsalm 2 lösen die Tradenten das
Problem dadurch, dass sie den Vorbildcharakter des königlichen Handelns
und Sprechens hervorheben: „Wohl allen, die ihm (so) vertrauen!" (2,12)
und diese Lösung scheint auch für die Behandlung der Votivtexte Vorbild
zu sein: Die Texte konnten nicht als solche re–zitiert und nach-gebetet, aber
sie konnten gelesen, meditiert und musiziert werden. Und es scheint, als ob
mit der Davidisierung eine Historisierung intendiert war, welche aus den
aktuellen Gebeten lehrhaft-erbauliche Meditationstexte aus vergangener
„klassischer" Zeit machte. In dieser Absicht treffen sich die Etikettierung
der Jerusalem-Psalmen mit dem David-Siegel wie die Autorisierung als
„heilige Schriften" der David-Zeit und auch die Biographisierung als
„David's Compositions", die sich einer unmittelbaren Aneignung und Verwendung als aktuelle Gebete entziehen. Die Psalmenauslegung in Qumran
wie die neutestamentliche Psalmenverwendung haben — wie man weiß

— dieser Intention entsprochen. Psalmtexte, auch aus dem Bereich des vierten David-Psalters, werden als göttliche Verheißung und heilige Schrift interpretiert.

Auch die in der vierten Höhle von Qumran gefundenen und unter den Sigla 4Q380 und 4Q381 edierten Psalmsammlungen verwenden die Überschriften in analoger Weise. Die beiden gänzlich erhaltenen lauten:

4Q381 24.4  תהלה לאיש האל[הי]ם

4Q381 33.8, die restlichen  תפלה למנשה מלך יהודה בכלו אתו מלך אשור

380.1 ii.8  תהלה לעבדיה

4Q380 4.2  תהלה ל[

Gattungsbezeichnungen mit der Zuschreibungsformel, dann eine biblische Figur, Gottesmann, Manasse, Obadja, z.T. mit biographischen Angaben: Im Endeffekt bezeichnen sie Verfasserschaft. Ob das ursprünglich so war, ist ebenfalls fraglich. Die Angaben fehlen bei andern Texten, die offensichtlich einmal selbständig waren.[7] Die Zuschreibung zeigt deutlich die Intention, diese Texte als „biblisch" zu erweisen und ihnen „kanonische" Würde zu verleihen.

Was ergibt sich aus der Gruppierung der Texte in der MT Reihenfolge? Vielleicht dieses: Der erste Psalm der Gruppe, Psalm 138, steht als „Dankpsalm" in einem gewissen Abstand zu der aktuellen Bedrängnis, blickt zurück auf eine Heilserfahrung im narrativen Stil („Am Tag, da ich rief, da erhörtest du mich", V. 3) und denkt an die Zukunft in der Befürchtung der Wiederholung ähnlicher Ereignisse („Wenn ich [wieder] mitten in Not kommen sollte, halte du mich am Leben...", V. 7). Dagegen sind die Psalmen 139–143 im Gebetsgestus (vgl. 143,6) Bitten und Appelle, die unmittelbar aus aktueller Not heraus gesprochen zu sein scheinen, jedenfalls nach der Selbstdarstellung der Redenden. Das gilt möglicherweise auch von Psalm 144A (V. 1-11), sofern seine Sprechsituation nach V. (7)11 ebenfalls die Bitte in Not zu sein scheint. Anders scheint es bei Psalm 144B (V. 12-15) zu sein (s.u. Exkurs). Psalm 145, der letzte in der MT Reihe, ist nach Form und Inhalt als Lobpreis- und Dankgebet in der reflektierender Distanz zu aktuellen Ereignissen verfasst, welche für allgemeine Feststellungen und theologische Lehrsätze Raum gibt. Er bildet jetzt — auch wenn er nach Psalm 144B als ein Nachtrag anzusehen ware — mit Psalm 138 zusammen einen Rahmen um die Gruppe. Dieser Rahmen aber leitet zugleich zum Verständnis der Texte an, insofern als er

---

[7] Vgl. E. M. Schuller, *Non-Canonical Psalms from Qumran. A Pseudepigraphic Collection* (Atlanta: Scholars Press, 1986) bes. 25ff.

auch die Reihe der Klage- und Bittgebete mit Blick auf die gewendete Not
zu lesen lehrt. Von den mittleren Psalmen sind gewiss 139 und 143 die
Texte mit der kunstvollsten Gestaltung und der größten Tiefenschärfe,
während die mittlere Gruppe Psalmen 140–142 je ihr besonderes Anliegen
scharf profilieren, aber — soweit ich sehe — in ihrer Folge keine konstitutive Struktur erkennen lassen. Der innere Zusammenhang der Gruppe liegt
also nicht in der MT Reihenfolge als solcher, eine Annahme, der ja schon
11QPs<sup>a</sup> mit unterschiedlicher Anordnung nicht günstig wäre. Was aber
verbindet diese Texte untereinander?

*Exkurs:*

Bevor dieser Frage weiter nachzugehen ist, muss noch ein kurzer Vorhalt
in Form eines Exkurses gemacht werden. Psalm 144B (V. 12-15) ist ein
Rätsel und entzieht sich m.E. bisher einer befriedigenden Erklärung. Anzunehmen ist, dass der Text 1. ursprünglich nicht zu Psalm 144A gehört
hat. Der Psalm 144A, eine Collage aus Psalm 18; Psalm 8 u.a. (also vor
allem aus dem ersten Davidpsalter), ist nach V. 11 ein Bittgebet. Es ist
schwer einzusehen, was am Ende eines solchen Texts, selbst als Kon-
glomerat von Zitaten, ein Makarismus auf das Jhwh-Volk soll, ohne
nachweisbare Beziehung zu dem voranstehenden Text. Anzunehmen ist
deshalb 2., dass der Text ein selbständiges Stück eigenen Aussagesinns
und mit besonderer Funktion gewesen ist. Dass diese in einer ver-
gleichenden Absage an die Lebensformen von anderen Völkern besteht,
Völkern, deren Gott Jhwh nicht ist und denen es darum „gerade so" (ככה)
nicht ergeht (V. 15), legt sich mit Hinsicht auf die verwendeten Vergleiche
nahe. Diese scheinen aus einer neuen, vielleicht der modernen hellenis-
tischen Gesellschaft zu stammen. Es ist folglich 3. anzunehmen, dass dieser spät entstandene Text eine Affinität zu Psalm 1 hat, dem offenbar eine
ähnlich abgrenzende Funktion eignet. Das führt schließlich dazu
4. anzunehmen, dass diesem aus genormten Sätzen bestehenden Text bei
der Psalterentstehung zusammen mit Psalm 1 einmal eine rahmende
Funktion zugedacht war, die dann aber durch immer neue Zusätze: Psalm
145; Psalmen 146ff. verdeckt wurde. Von daher gesehen, wäre Psalm 145,
jetzt Abschluss der Gruppe, nachträglich an diese Stelle gebracht worden.
Wie dem auch gewesen sein mag, offenbar überlagern sich an dieser Stelle
zwei dispositionelle Konzepte: das einer David-Gruppe und das einer
Psalter-Rahmung (Psalmen 1–144). Merkwürdigerweise wäre das letztere
als das ältere anzusehen, das durch die David-Reihe (und die Psalmen
145–150) zurückgedrängt wurde. Der Blick auf 11QPs<sup>a</sup> lehrt, dass dieser
Vorgang sich bis hin zur Verdrängung von Psalm 144 aus jeder sichtbaren
strategischen Position zugunsten eines David-Psalters fortgesetzt hat
— Vorgänge, die im Spätstadium der Psalterredaktion stattfanden.

## ZUR HERKUNFT DER TEXTE

Woher stammen die Texte?

Die Annahme, dass die mit לדוד ausgezeichneten Texte aus dem Umkreis des Jerusalemer Tempels kommen, wird durch die internen Angaben der Psalmgruppe 138–145 weithin bestätigt. Dabei ist es kaum unterscheidbar oder feststellbar, ob die Gebete bei ihrem aktuellen ursprünglichen mündlichen Vortrag innerhalb des Tempelbereichs oder im weiteren Umfeld des Heiligtums mit Blick auf den heiligen Ort gesprochen wurden, ob sie in Vorbereitung einer Rezitation vorher oder erst nachträglich aus dem Gedächtnis niedergeschrieben wurden. Man muss sich mit der Einsicht begnügen, dass die Gebete zum einen von individuellen Menschen aus persönlichen Gründen für eine bestimmte einmalige Gelegenheit verfasst wurden. Die in den Anliegen der Gebete — mit Ausnahme des weisheitlich gelehrten Psalms 145 und des collagierten Psalms 144A — angedeuteten sozialen Verhältnisse und die gewählten Formulierungen sind m.E. zu persönlich geprägt, um dabei an Gebetsformulare oder liturgische Vorlagen zu denken. Selbst für Psalm 144A ist das aber keineswegs sicher, obwohl die von ihm benützten psalmischen Ausdrucksformen auf ein künstliches Konstrukt weisen. Doch nicht jeder Beter findet für seine persönlichsten Anliegen auch eigene originelle Worte. Psalm 144A hat sich an Vorlagen gehalten. Seine Situation aber ist wahrscheinlich genauso einmalig gewesen wie die der andern Klagegebete. Psalm 145 ist ebenfalls ein Ich-Psalm, der zwar nichts Persönliches verlauten lässt, der aber zum Ausdruck bringt, dass er sich in hymnischem Lobpreis betätigen will (V. 1f.), offenbar, weil er auch einen persönlichen Anlass dazu hat.

So ist zum zweiten für diese im großen Ganzen biographisch bedingten Gebetstexte anzunehmen, dass sie mit Blickrichtung auf den Ort verfasst worden sind, wo man die Gottheit vornehmlich anzureden, anzuflehen, zu lobpreisen, zu besingen pflegte, wo man die Erhörung der Gebete und Zuwendung der Hilfe am ehesten erwarten konnte. Und da sie — wieder mit möglicher Ausnahme von Psalm 144A, der von Gefangenschaft in fremder Hand spricht, — andere Standorte nicht nennen oder erkennen lassen, wird man schließen dürfen, dass sie in irgendeiner Beziehung zum Jerusalemer (doch wohl: zweiten) Tempel entstanden sind.

Dies wird durch Einzelaussagen bestätigt, auch wenn man diese nur auf den jeweiligen Psalm beziehen darf. So kündigt der Psalmist von Psalm 138 an, dass er in Richtung auf das Tempelheiligtum (אֶל הֵיכַל קָדְשֶׁךָ) anbeten werde (V. 2). Zwar ist nicht sicher, ob sich dies auf den Vortrag des vorliegenden Psalms oder auf ein zukünftiges Gebet bezieht. Doch steht damit dieser Psalm in jedem Fall in einer Beziehung zum Tempel. Psalm 139 ist als Reinigungseid[8] derart eng mit einem entsprechenden Verfahren verflochten, dass man sich einen andern Ort als den Ort der Realpräsenz der Gottheit nicht vorstellen kann. Psalm 140 spricht am Ende seines Hilferufs davon, dass die „Aufrichtigen bei (את eig. „mit") deinem (scil. Jhwhs) Angesicht wohnen werden" (V. 14), was vielleicht für den Psalmisten jetzt noch nicht gilt, aber doch in Erwartung eines solchen Aufenthalts, d.h. im Blick auf das Heiligtum, gesagt ist. Der schwierige Text, das Gebet Psalm 141,[9] soll nach dem noch gut lesbaren Eingangsteil „als Räucherwerk gelten vor deinem Angesicht, meine Handerhebung als Abendopfer" (V. 2), was doch wohl nur bedeuten kann, dass der Verfasser, auch wenn er an den kultischen Ritualen selbst nicht teilnehmen kann (oder diese missachtet?), mit seinen Worten den kultischen Ort der nahen Gottheit sucht. Die gleiche Nähe sucht laut rufend Psalm 142, um „meine Klage vor ihm auszugießen" (אשפך לפניו שחי), was sich doch wohl auf eben diesen Psalm bezieht (vgl. V. 6ff.). Dass sich beim Lobpreis dann „die Gerechten um ihn scharen werden" (V. 8), wäre indes erst auf eine neue gottesdienstliche Gelegenheit zu beziehen, die noch aussteht. Auch Psalm 143 spricht von der größtmöglichen Nähe zu dem, der Gebete erhört und — wie das auch für Psalm 138 gilt — zu beantworten pflegt (V. 7ff., vgl. Ps 138,2.4). In jedem Fall breitet er die Hände zum Gebet mit diesem Psalm[10] (oder dem in V. 7ff. folgenden Gebetsstück), was doch wohl nicht ohne Bezug zum Tempelheiligtum denkbar ist. Von Psalm 144A war bereits die Rede. Er könnte aus der Distanz gesprochen sein, aus fremder Umgebung, aber auch er in der Erwartung, mit einem neuen Lied auf zehnsaitiger Harfe (V. 9) im Lobpreis danken und damit das angefangene Gebet zu Ende bringen zu können. Das bezieht sich auf das Dankritual als der Fortsetzung des Klagegebets, auf das hin alle diese Gebetsklagen ausgerichtet sind. Psalm 144B liegt außerhalb des Gesichtsfelds, es sei denn, er wäre als ein Beitrag zur Dankfeier aufzufassen, worauf aber nichts hinweist. Dagegen stellt sich der alphabetische Psalm 145 selbst zu Beginn als ein solches Dankgebet dar. Es liegt nicht

---

[8] Nach E. Würthweins immer noch gültigem Nachweis: „Erwägungen zu Psalm 139", *VT* 7 (1957) 165–82 (= *Wort und Existenz. Studien zum Alten Testament* [Göttingen: Vandenhoeck & Ruprecht, 1970] 179–96).

[9] Vgl. meinen Versuch einer Deutung: „Psalm 141. Ein neuer Anlauf", in: *Biblische Welten. Festschrift für Martin Metzger,* hg. von W. Zwickel (OBO 23; Fribourg: Universitätsverlag; Göttingen: Vandenhoeck & Ruprecht, 1993) 199–214 (= *Studien zur Psalmenauslegung* [Stuttgart: Kohlhammer, 1998] 173–88).

[10] פרשתי *Perfectum coincidentiae.*

fern, in ihm einen solchen Beitrag zu sehen, der eine allerdings nicht mehr wahrnehmbare Klage abschließt. In jedem Fall aber passt er mit seiner Reich-Gottes-Theologie (V. 1.11ff.) nirgends besser hin als an das Jerusalemer Heiligtum.

Fazit: Die Gebetsklagen 140–144A gehören mitsamt dem Beicht- und Bekenntnispsalm 139 und wie die Dankgebete 138 und 145 in den Umkreis des Jerusalemer Tempels. Sie sind durch das liturgische Klage-Dank-Schema im weitesten Sinne auf den Ort der göttlichen Präsenz bezogen und somit kultisch orientiert, auch wenn ihr realer Ort außerhalb des sakralen Bereichs anzusetzen wäre.

Zu diesem Befund passt die Annahme, dass es sich bei diesen Psalmen um Asyl- und — was fast auf das Gleiche hinausläuft — um Gefangenschaftsgebete handelt.

### GEFANGENSCHAFTSPSALMEN

Dass diese und andere Feindpsalmen im Jerusalemer Tempelasyl[11] entstanden sind, ist eine sehr wahrscheinliche Annahme. Sie entspricht dem sozialen Beziehungsgefüge, das im Hintergrund der Gebete sichtbar wird und kurz gesagt darin besteht, dass die Psalmisten sich zwar an Leib und Leben bedroht fühlen, dass sie aber dennoch sich nicht unmittelbar gegen direkte persönliche Attacken der Feinde wehren müssen, diese vielmehr zunächst — darüber spricht Psalm 140 am deutlichsten — offensichtlich hinter sich wissen und von einer gewissen Distanz zu den Verfolgern profitieren können. Die von ihnen gewählten Formulierungen für diesen Zwischenhalt sind wohl aus der Asylpraxis genommen und gehören in den Zusammenhang der Zulassung zum Tempelbereich. Dies gilt zuerst für die sechs Psalmen 138–143; für die Psalmen 144AB und 145 ist Anderes anzunehmen.

Doch mit der Kennzeichnung Asyl wäre die Situation dieser Psalmisten nur unzureichend beschrieben. Asyl bedeutet in diesem Zusammenhang zugleich Haft und Gefängnis, bis es denn zu einer Lösung des jeweiligen Falles kommt. So wäre auch von Untersuchungshaft zu reden, wie ja das altisraelitische Rechtswesen nur Untersuchungsgefängnisse, aber keine Freiheitsstrafen und keine Gefängnisse für verurteilte Sträflinge kennt.

---

[11] Vgl. L. Delekat, *Asylie und Schutzorakel am Zionheiligtum. Eine Untersuchung zu den privaten Feindpsalmen* (Leiden: Brill, 1967); W. Beyerlin, *Die Rettung der Bedrängten in den Feindpsalmen der Einzelnen auf institutionelle Zusammenhänge untersucht* (FRLANT 99; Göttingen: Vandenhoeck & Ruprecht, 1970).

Die deutlichste Beschreibung eines solchen „Sitzes im Leben" findet sich in Ps 107,10-16:

> Die in Dunkel und Finsternis saßen,
>> gebunden in Haft[12] und Eisen,
> Weil sie den Worten Gottes getrotzt
>> und den Ratschluss des Höchsten verachtet;
> Deren Herz er durch Mühsal gebeugt,
>> die strauchelten, ohne dass jemand half;
> Die dann schrien zu Jhwh in ihrer Not ...

So sind auch die wenigen eindeutigen Angaben der Psalmen zu dem konkreten Aufenthaltsort der Beter zu verstehen. Ps 142,8 spricht vom Kerker (הוציאה ממסגר נפשי „Führe mich doch aus dem Kerker!"[13]) und Ps 143,3 von der Versetzung an „finstere Stellen" (מחשכים),[14] was wohl auf Ähnliches hinausläuft.[15] Obwohl man über konkretere Daten hinsichtlich der Unterbringung von Flüchtlingen und Asylanten im Umkreis des Tempelkomplexes — denn wo sonst sollten solche Verließe sein—der fraglichen Zeit nicht verfügt, gibt doch der Baruch-Bericht aus dem Jeremiabuch eine Vorstellung wie das in der vorexilischen Zeit gehandhabt wurde. Viel anders werden die Flüchtlinge, Verfolgten und Angeklagten auch nicht behandelt worden sein.[16] Dass die Situation der betreffenden inhaftierten Psalmisten deplorabel war, lassen ja auch die knappen Hinweise auf ihr miserables Befinden (Pss 142,4; 143,3f.7) durchblicken. Allgemeine Erwägungen zur Versorgungslage von Gefangenen unter Anklage (vgl. 1.Kön

---

[12] עני könnte wie an andern späten Stellen die spezielle Bedeutung „Gefangenschaft", „Haft" angenommen haben, was schon früher von D. W. Thomas, in: *JTS* 16 (1965) 444–45, vermutet wurde (vgl. *HAL* 810), falls nicht eine Nominalbildung (abgeleitet vom Verbum ענה II „beugen, niederdrücken" u.Ä.) mit dupliziertem *Nun* mit dieser Bedeutung angenommen werden kann (vgl. Ps 105,18). In jedem Fall bezieht sich das Nomen in besonderen Kontexten wie Ps 107,10.41; Hi 36,8; Thr 3,1 u.a. auf das konkrete Elend des „Gebeugtseins" im Sinne des in den Stock Geschlossenen. Ps 140,13 spricht von דין עני, dem Prozess des „Elenden" bzw. Häftlings — in diesem Zusammenhang.

[13] מסגר I „Gefängnis", „Verließ" (Jes 24,22 // בור; Jes 42,7).

[14] Zwar ist der Passus in 143,3 möglicherweise ganz oder teilweise ein Zitat (oder eine Glosse) aus Thr 3,6, trifft aber als solches und im Vergleich der Insaßen mit den „für immer Toten" (מתי עולם) ziemlich genau den Sachverhalt (vgl. Jes 42,16; Pss 88,7; Ps 74,20?).

[15] Die Rede vom Führen „auf ebener Erde" (Ps 143,10) könnte — bei aller Metaphorik — auch mit Vorstellungen von unterirdischen Verließen zu tun haben.

[16] Für die frühchristliche Zeit wäre Act heranzuziehen (Kap. 4f.; 7; 12; 22f.).

22,27 par. 2.Chr 18,26) und auch zu der wohl durchaus üblichen Folterpraxis runden das Bild, wenngleich die Texte über diese ihre Umstände nicht sehr viel sagen.

Ihnen drohte ja weit Schlimmeres. Sie standen unter Anklage. Die Verfolger, die von ihnen so genannten „Bedränger und Feinde", blieben präsent, und ihr Schicksal hing von Entscheiden ab, die über Leben oder Tod befanden,[17] und d.h. doch wohl von Entscheiden in wie immer gearteten Prozessen oder gerichtlichen oder gerichtsähnlichen Verfahren.

Das führt zu der Frage weiter, wessen denn diese Psalmisten beschuldigt wurden. Was war es, das so schwer wog, dass diese Menschen alle um ihr Leben fürchten mussten. Zwei der Texte machen dazu konkretere Angaben. Einmal der Psalmist von Psalm 139, dem offenbar vorgeworfen wurde, auf einem „Weg des Götzen(dienstes)" (דרך עצב)[18] gewandt zu sein. Was das im Klartext heißt, deutet er in der Schlussstrophe seines Gebets (V. 19-22) an. Er wird in seinen Augen fälschlich beschuldigt, mit den „Jhwh-Hassern" und „Rebellen" heimlich gemeinsame Sache gemacht zu haben, wovon er sich öffentlich und dezidiert in dem Reinigungsverfahren distanzieren muss: „Mit vollkommenem Hass hasse ich sie; zu Feinden sind sie mir geworden" (V. 22). Letztere Formulierung konzediert offenbar, dass das nicht immer so war, und dass die Verfolger, als „Frevler" und „Blutmenschen" bezeichnet, möglicherweise doch einen Grund oder Vorwand für ihre Anklage gehabt haben könnten.

Ein Sakraldelikt ist auch hinter den nicht mehr deutlich lesbaren Vorwürfen zu vermuten, die in Psalm 141 angedeutet sind. Dort ging es offenbar um Teilnahme an Mahlfeiern und um das Essen von verbotenen Speisen, die zu Anzeigen führten, zu falschen, wie der Psalmist meint, weshalb er erwartet, dass die „Frevler" sich in ihrem eigenen Netz verfangen. Weil es wieder um Leben oder Tod geht, muss die Anzeige sehr ernst genommen werden. Darum ist anzunehmen, dass ein schweres religiöses Delikt zur Debatte steht.

So deutlich werden die andern Psalmisten der Gruppe nicht. Aber immerhin lässt Psalm 138 — wenn man den Ausdruck: „vor den Göttern" (נגד אלהים) unmittelbar neben der Anrufung Jhwhs so verstehen will

---

[17] Dass es um Leben oder Tod ging zeigen Stellen aus allen Texten der Gruppe: Pss 138,7; 139,19; 140,11-12; 141,8; 142,6; 143,3.12; 144,11 und zusammenfassend Ps 145,20.

[18] Mit Würthwein, vgl. meinen Beitrag: Feindbild und Menschenwürde. Das Zeugnis der Psalmen, in: E. Herms (Hg.), *Menschenbild und Menschenwürde* (Gütersloh: Gütersloher Verlagshaus, 2000) 307–19.

(V. 1) — vermuten, dass es bei der ihm von seinen Feinden zur Last ge-
legten Sache um etwas Religiöses gehandelt hat, das seine Existenz bedroht
hat das er aber nun durch Jhwhs Eintreten (יגמר בעדי) hinter sich gebracht
zu haben glaubt (V. 8) und öffentlich bezeugen will (V. 1).

Die Anklagen gegen den temperamentvollen Psalmisten von Psalm 140
sind nicht klar formuliert, nur die Bosheit und Falschheit und Gefähr-
lichkeit („wie die Schlangen") wird betont und die Hoffnung, wieder zu den
Gerechten und Aufrichtigen gezählt zu werden (V. 14), wenn denn durch
Jhwhs Intervention das „Armengericht" den „Prozess des Elenden" (V. 13)
zum guten Ende geführt hat.

Das sieht der Psalmist von 142 in seinem Verließ nicht anders, ohne zu
sagen, welche „Falle" man denn ihm gestellt hat. Er muss zugeben, dass er
hineingeraten ist und nun auf die Anerkennung seines tadellosen Vorlebens
(V. 4) und seiner Arglosigkeit setzt, die zu dem „Unfall" geführt hat.

Psalm 143 gibt auch keine konkreten Anhaltspunkte. Es ist aber an-
zunehmen, dass der Psalmist in ähnlicher Lage ist wie der Psalmist von
Psalm 142: Er ist in der betreffenden Sache sich seiner Unschuld sehr si-
cher und beruft sich darauf, ein „Knecht (עבד) Jhwhs" zu sein; er hofft auf
Gerechtigkeit und Gnade, die den Fall zu seinen Gunsten und gegen seine
Feinde und Verfolger entscheiden werden (V. 11f.). Es geht auch hier um
Leben und Tod.

Der Psalmist von Psalm 144A befindet sich zwar in der Gewalt von
„Fremden", damit in Gefangenschaft; doch ist nicht sicher, ob dies mit dem
Tempelgefängnis zu tun hat. Man müsste dann ausländisches Aufsichts-
personal annehmen, was nicht sehr naheliegt.[19]

Und was hinter den allgemeinen Aussagen des alphabetischen
Dankpsalms 145 steht, wer die „Gefallenen und Gebeugten" (die Gefangenen?) sind, denen geholfen wurde, und ob sich das Dankgebet für die
Versorgung mit Nahrung in V. 14-16 auf eine selbsterlebte Situation im
Gefängnis bezieht, bleibt offen. Doch ist nicht zu übersehen, dass die Aussagen dieses Texts gleichfalls im Horizont der Gefangenschaftstexte bleiben.

GERICHTLICHE VERFAHREN?

Es gibt also Anzeichen, dass es sich bei diesen Fällen um Anzeigen
wegen angeblicher religiöser Delikte handelt, die offenbar für die Betref-

---

[19] Anders noch in meiner Studie: „Formen der Textrezeption in Psalm 144",
in: *Schriftauslegung in der Schrift, FS Odil Hannes Steck* (BZAW 300; Berlin: de
Gruyter, 2000) 281–90.

fenden lebensbedrohend waren — ob sie nun ins Heiligtumsasyl geflohen sind, wie das von Ps 11,1 bekannt ist, oder zwangsweise dorthin verbracht wurden und zur Aburteilung vorläufig in den Kerker geworfen wurden. Auch die Gruppe der ehemaligen „Gefangenen", die nach Ps 107,10-16 liturgisch auftreten soll, wird von dem eventuell sekundären V. 11 beschuldigt, gegen göttliche Worte und Gebote verstoßen zu haben. Sie waren also aus religiösen Gründen in Haft genommen worden — man erinnert sich an Mt 5,25 —, um auf eine Entscheidung über ihr Leben zu warten, das von einer höheren Instanz getroffen werden sollte.

Soweit ich sehe, gibt es nicht viele Informationen über eine Gerichtsbarkeit am zweiten Tempel, die für solche Sakraldelikte zuständig wäre. Man ist auf einige sporadische Daten und vor allem auf allgemeine Erwägungen angewiesen. Wir versuchen, diese zusammenzustellen, um daraus ein ungefähres Bild zu gewinnen.

1. Eine solche Instanz müsste aus Experten, d.i. aus Priestern bestehen. Dafür gibt die Tempelvision Hesekiels einen Hinweis. Die zadokitischen Priester sollen (auch) in Zukunft nach Hes 44,24 u.a. „bei Streitsachen (על ריב) zu Gericht sitzen, um zu schlichten (יעמדו לשפט) nach meinen (scil. Jhwhs) Rechtssatzungen (במשפטי)", was für ein Tempelgericht spricht. Dafür ist die Chronikstelle 2.Chr 19,8 ein weiterer Beleg. Dem König Josaphat wird zugeschrieben, dass er „auch in Jerusalem eine Anzahl Leviten und Priester und Familienhäupter für das Gericht Jhwhs und für die Rechtshändel der Bewohner Jerusalems" bestellte. Vorsteher sollte der Hohepriester sein und als Beamte sollten Leviten fungieren (V. 11). Das Datum ist gewiss anachronistisch, die Sache selbst aber an sich plausibel und für die Zeit der Chronik vermutlich Realität.

2. Der Stelle Hiob 31,26-28 ist zu entnehmen, dass fremdreligiöse Handlungen wie die Anbetung von Sonnenlicht und Mond als ein „Vergehen für das sakrale Strafgericht" (עון פלילי) geahndet wurde, denn — so die Begründung — Gott im Himmel ist dadurch geleugnet worden.[20]

3. Mittel für die Urteilsfindung waren vor allem Befragungen und Verhöre, sicher auch unter Folter, und Zeugenaussagen, sowie Eidesleistungen, vor allem im Sinne des Reinigungseids (vgl. Hiob 31; Psalm 7), in manchen Fällen möglicherweise auch ein Gottesurteil (Ordal).

4. Die Urteile sollten nach 2.Chr 19,6 „im Namen Jhwhs" gefällt werden.

---

[20] פלילי ist in jedem Fall in diesem Kontext ein juristisch-forensicher Begriff (vgl. HAL 881–82). Nach Hi 31,11 par. 31,28 wird ein solches sakrales Vergehen זמה genannt, ein Terminus der in Ps 26,10 und ähnlich auch in Ps 139,20 und 140,9 begegnet.

Nach dem, was über solche Entscheidungen auszumachen ist, ergehen sie prinzipiell alternativ: bei erwiesener Falschanklage traf es die Ankläger. Bei sakralen Delikten wie z.B. Gotteslästerung oder -fluch (Lev 24,10-16)[21] oder Sabbatschändung (Num 15,32-36) schrieb die Tora anhand von Präzedenzfällen die Todesstrafe vor — in den genannten Fällen in Form der Steinigung. Die Beschuldigten wurden bis zur Entscheidung in Gewahrsam genommen (במשמר) (Lev 24,12; Num 15,34).

5. Die Urteile wurden wahrscheinlich sofort vollzogen — und zwar von den Beteiligten selbst. Eine Partei wurde schuldig, die andere frei gesprochen. Todesstrafe oder Freilassung waren die extremen Möglichkeiten, die vielleicht nicht immer zur Anwendung kamen. An anderer Stelle habe ich vermutet, dass an der bekannten Stelle Hab 2,4 ein solches Urteil überliefert oder wiedergegeben ist,[22] sofern es richtig ist, dass es sich dort ebenfalls um einen Klage- und Feindpsalm handelt.[23] „Siehe das Urteil(?)![24] Nicht aufrichtig ist seine Seele in ihm (scil. dem Schuldigen). Der Gerechte aber soll aufgrund seiner Redlichkeit am Leben bleiben."[25]

Es fällt nicht schwer, die Psalmgebete 138–145 in diese Skizze einzuzeichnen. Dabei ist wohl nicht anzunehmen, dass diese Texte — eventuell mit Ausnahme von Psalm 139 — selbst Teil des Verfahrens waren und etwa als schriftliche Deklarationen abverlangt und dann als entlastende Beweisstücke gewertet wurden, obwohl es nicht unmöglich ist, dass so von Fall zu Fall verfahren wurde. Die schriftliche Aufzeichnung könnte dafür sprechen. Eher schon wird man sie für echte Gebete und Hilferufe im Sinne von Ps 107,13 ansehen, die allerdings das gerichtliche Milieu wider-

---

[21] R. R. Hutton, „The Case of the Blasphemer Revisited (Lev. XXIV 10-23)", *VT* 49 (1999) 532–41: „He blasphemed the divine name by using it illegitimately" (540).

[22] „Habakuk 2,4b und sein Kontext", in: *Zur Aktualität des Alten Testaments. FS Georg Sauer*, hg. von S. Kreuzer und K. Lüthi (Frankfurt: Peter Lang, 1992) 99–107 (= *Studien zur Psalmenauslegung* [Stuttgart: Kohlhammer, 1998] 189–98).

[23] Trotz der beachtenswerten Arbeit von B. Huwyler, „Habakuk und seine Psalmen", in: *Prophetie und Psalmen, FS Klaus* Seybold (AOAT 280; Münster: Ugarit-Verlag, 2001) 231–59, glaube ich immer noch, dass es sich um einen Psalm handelt, der mit der Prophetie Habakuks nichts zu tun hat und nur mehr oder weniger zufällig dort steht.

[24] Vgl. Anm. 20. Dazu auch vom Verf., *Nahum-Habakuk-Zephanja, Zürcher Bibelkommentare 24,2* (Zürich: Theologischer Verlag 1991) 66–67: Konjektur, statt עפלה zu lesen: פעלה „Lohn", „Strafe" oder פלילה „Urteil".

[25] יחיה qal.

spiegeln, in dem sich die Psalmisten befanden. Es gibt in jedem Text einige Hinweise, welche zur konkreten Anschauung der Situation beitragen.

- Psalm 142, im Kerker ausgerufen, beklagt im Blick auf seinen Fall das Fehlen eines מכיר, eines Zeugen,[26] der Auskunft über die hinterhältigen Anschläge seiner Verfolger geben könnte. So ist er auf den angewiesen, der seinen „Pfad" kennt.

- Psalm 140 konzentriert sich vor allem darauf, die Verfolger als „böse Menschen", als Terroristen (V. 2), als schlangenzüngige Verleumder und Giftmischer (V. 3f.) zu charakterisieren, um sie damit als falsche Ankläger hinzustellen, auf die ihre Verleumdungen wie glühende Kohlen regnen sollen, so dass man sie in „Erdlöchern"[27] verscharren muss. Weil denn Verleumder („Männer der Zunge") und Gewalttäter im Lande nichts zu suchen haben, sollen sie vielmehr ihrerseits mit Gitter und Hürden[28] gejagt oder verjagt werden (V. 13f.). Denn — er ist sich sicher — Jhwh führt „die Sache des Elenden, das Gericht der Armen" und ist den Aufrichtigen und Gerechten verpflichtet (V. 14).

- Psalm 141 bietet nur einige unzusammenhängende Reflexe. Die Erwähnung von Gerechten und Frommen könnte besagen, dass die Anklage auf Beteiligung an Mahlfeiern bei „Übeltätern" von ihnen ausging. Jedenfalls schlugen sie den Beschuldigten (V. 5).[29] Richter werden erwähnt, die zuhören und die Rede beurteilen sollen (V. 6). Er erwartet die Hinrichtung der Frevler, die sich in ihren Stellnetzen verfangen haben — er selbst aber wird davonkommen (עבר, V. 9f.).[30]

- Psalm 143 setzt auf die „Wahrheitsliebe" und „Gerechtigkeit" seines Herrn, als dessen Knecht er sich zwei Mal bekennt, dass er ihn in diesem Fall vor gewalttätigen Feinden schützt (V. 1.3). Er wünscht keinen

---

[26] Nach H. J. Boecker, *Redeformen des Rechtslebens im Alten Testament* (WMANT 14; Neukirchen-Vluyn: Neukirchener, 1964 [2 Aufl. 1970]), ein juristischer Terminus (39), vgl. 2.Sam 3,37; Dan 11,39, aber auch Dt 16,19 mit Par.

[27] Zum *Hapax legomenon*, vgl. Sir 12,16.

[28] Mit R. J. Tournay, *Seeing and Hearing God with the Psalms. The Prophetic Liturgy of the Second Temple in Jerusalem* (JSOTSup 118; Sheffield: Sheffield Academic Press, 1991) 194.

[29] הלם „schlagen, prügeln" (vgl. Prv 23,35) könnte auch im Sinne von „foltern" gemeint sein.

[30] Es könnte sein, dass die fast unverständlichen Aussagen in V. 6a.7a, die von „Gestürztwerden", „Felsen", „Mühlstein (?)", „von den Richtern" sprechen in Parallele zum „Zerstreuen von Gebeinen (?) vor der Scheol" zumindest eine Anspielung auf eine Hinrichtung durch Steinigung enthalten. Vgl. dazu den o. Anm. 9 genannten Beitrag.

Prozess, der ihn und sein Leben im Ganzen beurteilt: „Denn vor dir ist kein Lebender gerecht" (V. 2). Er bittet um eine Lösung: Gnade vor Recht (V. 2.8.11f.), die allerdings zur Folge hat, dass der Wahrheit und Gerechtigkeit Genüge getan wird, und die Feinde und Verfolger „vernichtet" und „zugrunde gerichtet" werden, während er selbst am Leben bleibt (חיה *pi.*) (V. 11f.).

- Psalm 144 deutet in V. 8.11 Negatives und Lügnerisches an, lässt aber nicht erkennen, ob er an eine gerichtliche Lösung denkt.

- Psalm 145 nennt nur das Resultat, nach dem solche Ketzerprozesse enden sollten: Verschonung „derer, die Jhwh lieben", und Vernichtung der „Gottlosen" (V. 20).

- Psalm 139 ist viel stärker in den Prozessablauf verwickelt, indem der Beter den ihm offenbar vorgelegten Beichtspiegel für den Reinigungseid (V. 2-18) seinem Gebet zugrunde legt, um an ihm entlang zu gehen und seine Unschuld gegenüber der Anklage zu beweisen. Nach V. 20 lautet die Anklage offenbar auf „Schandtat" (למזמה), dem juristischen Terminus für religiöse Delikte (Jer 11,15). Das im Psalm zugrundegelegte Dokument ist von theologisch großer Bedeutung, weil eine Theologie der Schöpfung und der *praesentia Dei* impliziert. Die vielen eigenen Worte des Psalmisten in V. 19ff. bleiben dahinter zurück: Sie sprechen von seinem „vollkommenen Hass" (תכלית) gegenüber den „Jhwh-Hassern" und „Jhwh-Widersachern" und wünschen den ihn mit falschen Anklagen verfolgenden „Blutmännern" den Tod (V. 19-22).

- Zuletzt Psalm 138, der auf einen erfolgreichen Prozess zurückblicken kann. Auch da ging es um Leben und Tod. Als entscheidend sieht er eine „Äußerung" (אמרה bzw. אמרי פה) seines Gottes an, die wunderbarerweise ergangen ist und die von vielen gehört worden ist. Sehr wahrscheinlich handelt es sich dabei um einen Urteilsspruch, der ja nachweislich im Namen Jhwhs ergeht und den der Beter als persönliche Offenbarung für sich selbst ansah („Du antwortetest mir", V. 3). Rätselhaft bleibt die Erwähnung „aller Könige der Erde (oder des Landes)" als Ohrenzeugen dieses Gotteswortes, die zudem aufgefordert werden, zu lobpreisen und „die Wege Jhwhs" zu besingen (V. 4f.). Das macht wenig Sinn, so dass die Vermutung einer Textentstellung naheliegt. Vielleicht ist nicht מלך, sondern מלאך zu lesen und auf alle „Priester des Landes" bzw. Landpriester zu beziehen, die nach Mal 2,7; Qoh 5,5; Hi 33,23 und Ps 35,5f. in der Spätzeit so genannt wurden: Priester die auf dem Lande verstreut wohnten und von denen es nach Hi 33,23 Tausende gab. Die Richtigkeit dieser Korrektur vorausgesetzt, wäre dem zu entnehmen, dass den Landpriestern, die gelegentlich am Jerusalemer Heiligtum Dienst taten, die besondere Aufgabe oblag, im Tempelgericht ergangene Gerichtsurteile in ihrem Wohnbereich im „Land" zu vertreten und durchzusetzen. Dass die Anerkennung eines Freispruchs im Land ein Problem sein konnte, lassen auch andere Psalmen durchblicken. Psalm 138 hofft auf weitere Bewahrung des Lebens (חיה *pi'el*) bei künftigen Notfällen (V. 7f.).

## WER WAREN DIE VERFASSER?

Wer waren die Verfasser dieser Texte? Wir gehen davon aus, dass es bestimmte individuelle Personen waren, die in ihrem Fall für sich selbst sprachen. Dass sie ghostwriter hatten, Liturgen oder Schreiber, die wussten, wie man solche Gebete formulierte, ist in ihrer Situation unwahrscheinlich. Dass man Formulare für Gebete bereit hielt für solche Fälle, ist nicht auszuschließen, aber doch wohl wegen der Vielfalt der Möglichkeiten nicht naheliegend. Auch wenn Psalm 139 Teile eines Beichtspiegel oder Ähnliches verwendet, ist nicht gesagt, dass das vorliegende Gebet mit V. 19ff. eine Vorlage hatte. Bei Psalm 144A sieht man, was ein um eigene Formulierungen verlegener Psalmist macht: Er greift auf das ihm offenbar zugängliche Repertoire von Psalmenmaterial — etwas wie der erste Davidpsalter[31] — zurück. Was dabei herauskommt, ist aber so wenig professionell wie die Schlussverse von Psalm 139.

Man muss es schon auch einfachen Menschen im alten Israel zutrauen, dass sie solche Gebete formulieren konnten. Ohnehin ist ja nur eine ganz kleine Auswahl davon erhalten. Sie stehen in einer ziemlich stabilen Gebetstradition. Das wird deutlich sichtbar, wenn man zunächst auf die Struktur- und Stilmuster achtet, die sie verwenden. Nur wenige Hinweise zum Formenrepertoire:

(1) Alle Texte verwenden den Parallelismus gleich bemessener Teile als Verstruktur. Wenn nicht versintern, dann extern, wie in der bemerkenswerten Reihenbildungen von Ps 143,7-10 und Psalm 144B.

(2) Alle Texte, mit Ausnahme des alphabetischen Psalms 145, bilden Strophen,[32] die in der Regel etwa gleich groß gewesen zu sein scheinen.

(3) Besondere Formmuster finden sich in Psalm 145: alphabetische Akrostichie;[33] in Psalm 141: verdeckte oder verwischte Akrostichie (V. 2-4a.6: א; V. 4b-5: בא oder ב; V. 7-8: ה);[34] Litaneistil in Ps 144,12-15(B);

---

[31] Pss 8; 18; 39, vgl. o. Anm. 19.

[32] In Psalm 140 unterstrichen durch die סלה-Gliederung.

[33] Die MT fehlende נ-Zeile ist in der LXX und 11QPsᵃ belegt.

[34] Vgl. vom Verf., „Akrostichie im Psalter", in: *Alttestamentliche Forschung*

ausgemalte Metaphorik in Psalm 140;[35] vor allem aber eine kunstvoll strukturierte Gesamtanlage in Psalm 143 mit abgemessenem Stufenaufstieg (V. 1-6), einer Plattform parallel gelegter Balkenzeilen (V. 7-10) und einem gestuften Abstieg (V. 11f.).[36] In der Überzeugung, dass Gebetssprache das Beste zu bieten habe, das verfügbar ist, sind auch diese späten Texte verfasst. Dabei sind Stilunterschiede, ja unterschiedliche Stilebenen, etwa zwischen den Psalmen 143 und 144A, oder den Psalmen 138[37] und 142, oder der Psalms in Psalmen 139 (V. 1-18 // V. 19-24) und 144AB durchaus zu erkennen.

Zum andern schöpfen diese Psalmisten aus der theologisch-liturgischen Tradition und aus den in der Entstehung begriffenen heiligen Schriften.[38] Auch hier nur wenige augenfällige Beispiele: Psalm 139 stützt sich auf einen Beichtspiegel, der eine über Genesis 1 und Psalm 8 hinausgehende, individuell bezogene Theologie der Schöpfung und der göttlichen Gegenwart bietet. Psalm 144 zitiert aus dem ersten Davidpsalter u.a. Psalm 18 und Psalm 8. Psalm 145 zitiert die sog. Gnadenformel aus Ex 34,6. Berührungen ergeben sich zwischen Ps 143,3 und Thr 3,6; Ps 142,4 und Ps 143,4 etc. Auch die nicht wenigen Bekenntnisaussagen: „Jhwh steht für mich ein" (138,8); „Du bist mein Gott" (140,7; 143,10); „auf dich verlasse ich mich" (141,8; 143,8); „Du bist meine Zuflucht" (142,6); „ich bin dein Knecht" (143,12); „mein Gott und König" (145,1) u.a. sind in der Glaubenstradition verwurzelt und werden zitierend aktualisiert.

Die Beobachtung, dass die irgend eines sakralen Vergehens beschuldigten Psalmisten in ihren Gebeten offensichtlich traditionelle Rechtgläubigkeit an den Tag legen, mag mit ihrer Verteidigung zu tun haben und ist aus der konkreten Situation verständlich. Auf der andern Seite mutet es doch seltsam an, dass gerade bekennende Rechtgläubige — die Aufrichtigkeit der Bekenntnisse unterstellt — in solche, möglicherweise von „Gerechten" und „Frommen" ausgehenden Anklagen und gerichtlichen Auseinandersetzungen geraten sind. Freilich wissen wir wenig über den Glaubensalltag

---

*in der Schweiz. Festheft zum Kongress IOSOT XVII, 2001, ThZ 57 (2001) 172–83.*

[35] Schlangenbilder in V. 4.6.10.12(?).

[36] Genauere Messdaten einer vorläufigen metrischen Strukturanalyse: V. 1-6: 3+2+3 // 4+4 // 3+3+3(2) // 3+3//3+3+3// 3+1+3. V. 7-10: 5 (3+2)// 6 // 5 // 6 // 5 // 5 // 5. V. 11f.: 4+4 // 3+3 // 2(3).

[37] Bei Psalm 138 mag eine gewisse Stilnachlässigkeit zu Entstellungen und Missverständnissen geführt haben (V. 1.4) (wie bei Psalm 141?).

[38] Die in Ps 143,5 erwähnte Meditation spricht von einem Traditionsbezug ähnlicher Art.

und über religiöse und soziale Konflikte in jener späten Zeit (das über die Zeugnisse der Psalmen hinausgeht). Doch wird man die Vermutung äußern können, dass diese Texte und ihre realen Hintergründe eine gewisse religiöse Spannung oder Erhitzung und eine gewisse Nervosität erahnen lassen, die möglicherweise mit dem zunehmenden Einfluss des Hellenismus auf das Glaubensleben der Gemeinden um Jerusalem zusammenhängt. Vielleicht könnte Psalm 144B darüber etwas Aufklärung bieten, würde er sich nicht einem befriedigenden Verständnis bisher verweigern.

## LITERATUR IN AUSWAHL

Auffret, P. „O Dieu, connais mon coeur: Études structurelle du Psaume CXXXIX", *VT* 47 (1997) 1–22.

Beyerlin, W. *Die Rettung der Bedrängten in den Feindpsalmen der Einzelnen auf institutionelle Zusammenhänge untersucht* (FRLANT 99; Göttingen: Vandenhoeck & Ruprecht, 1970).

Boecker, H. J. *Redeformen des Rechtslebens im Alten Testament* (WMANT 14; Neukirchen-Vluyn: Neukirchener, 1964 [2. Aufl. 1970]).

Brown, W. P. „Psalm 139", *Int* 50 (1996) 280–84.

Delekat, L. *Asylie und Schutzorakel am Zionheiligtum. Eine Untersuchung zu den privaten Feindpsalmen* (Leiden: Brill, 1967).

Flint, P. W. *The Dead Sea Psalms Scrolls and the Book of Psalms* (STDJ 17; Leiden: Brill, 1997).

Hutton, R. R. „The Case of the Blasphemer Revisited (Lev. XXIV 10–23)", *VT* 49 (1999) 532–41.

Huwyler, B. „Habakuk und seine Psalmen", in: *Prophetie und Psalmen. Festschrift für Klaus Seybold,* hg. von B. Huwyler u.a. (AOAT 280; Münster: Ugarit-Verlag, 2001) 231–59.

Kratz, R. G. „Die Gnade des täglichen Brots. Späte Psalmen auf dem Weg zum Vaterunser", *ZThK* 89 (1992) 1–40.

Mazor, Y. „When Aesthetics Is Harnessed to Psychological Charakterization—,Ars Poetica' in Psalm 139", *ZAW* 109 (1997) 260–71.

Millard, M. *Die Komposition des Psalters. Ein formgeschichtlicher Ansatz* (FAT 6, Tübingen: Mohr Siebeck, 1994).

Sanders, J. A. *The Psalms Scroll of Qumran 11 [11QPsᵃ]* (DJD 4, Oxford: Clarendon Press, 1965).

Seybold, K. „Psalm 141. Ein neuer Anlauf", in: *Biblische Welten. Festschrift für Martin Metzger,* hg. von W. Zwickel (OBO 123, Fribourg, Universitätsverlag; Göttingen: Vandenhoeck & Ruprecht, 1993, 199–214 [= *Studien zur Psalmenauslegung* (Stuttgart: Kohlhammer, 1998) 173–88]).

—. „Habakuk 2,4b und sein Kontext", in: *Zur Aktualität des Alten Testaments. Festschrift für Georg Sauer,* hg. von S. Kreuzer und K. Lüthi (Frankfurt: Peter

Lang, 1992, 99–107 [= *Studien zur Psalmenauslegung* (Suttgart: Kohlhammer, 1998) 189–98]).

—. „Feindbild und Menschenwürde. Das Zeugnis der Psalmen", in: *Menschenbild
und Menschenwürde*, hg. von E. Herms (Gütersloh: Gütersloher Verlagshaus
2000, 307–19).

—. „Formen der Textrezeption in Psalm 144", in: *Schriftauslegung in der Schrift.
Festschrift für Odil Hannes Steck*, hg. von R.G. Kratz u.a. (BZAW 300; Berlin: de Gruyter, 2000) 281–90.

—. „Akrostichie im Psalter", in: *Alttestamentliche Forschung in der schweiz.
Festheft zum Kongress IOSOT* XVII, *ThZ* 57 (2001) 172–83.

Tournay, R. J. *Seeing and Hearing God with the Psalms. The Prophetic Liturgy of
the Second Temple in Jerusalem* (JSOTSup 118, Sheffield: Sheffield Academic Press, 1991).

Würthwein, E. „Erwägungen zu Psalm 139", *VT* 7 (1957) 165–82 (= *Wort und
Existenz. Studien zum Alten Testament* [Göttingen: Vandenhoeck & Ruprecht,
1970)] 179–96).

Zenger, E. „Dass alles Fleisch den Namen seiner Heiligung segne" (Ps 145,21).
Die Komposition Ps 145–150 als Anstoß zu einer christlich-jüdischen Psal-
menhermeneutik, *BZ* 41 (1997) 1–27.

# KING, MESSIAH, AND THE REIGN OF GOD: REVISITING THE ROYAL PSALMS AND THE SHAPE OF THE PSALTER

## GERALD H. WILSON

It is well over twenty years since my early work that suggested certain royal psalms have been employed editorially in the shaping of the Psalter.[1] That initial statement in *The Editing of the Hebrew Psalter* (1981/1985) was followed by an expanded discussion in "The Use of the Royal Psalms at the 'Seams' of the Psalter" (1986),[2] reiterated in a broader context in "The Shape of the Book of Psalms" (1992),[3] and further developed in "Shaping the Psalter: A Consideration of Editorial Linkage in the Book of Psalms" (1993).[4] Let me begin by offering a brief restatement of the thesis offered in these works. I will then proceed to a discussion of some of the issues that have been raised in the intervening years, and offer some new insights along the way.

## REVIEW OF THE THESIS

The basic idea advanced in my early work is that certain royal psalms (in particular Psalms 2, 72, and 89) have been intentionally placed at the seams of the first three books (Psalms 2–89) in order to shape the understanding of those segments of the Psalter as an Exilic response to the loss of the Davidic monarchy. This response offers agonized pleas for deliverance and intends to foster hope for the restoration of the Davidic kingdom and the fortunes of Judah. The first of these psalms (Psalm 2) refers to the establishment of the Davidic covenant and cautions the would-be rebel nations of the world to

---

[1] Gerald H. Wilson, *The Editing of the Hebrew Psalter* (Ph. D. diss., Yale University, 1981). Subsequently published as *The Editing of the Hebrew Psalter* (SBLDS 76; Chico, CA: Scholars Press, 1985). See particularly pp. 207–14.

[2] Gerald H. Wilson, "The Use of Royal Psalms at the 'Seams' of the Hebrew Psalter," *JSOT* 35 (1986) 85–94.

[3] Gerald H. Wilson, "The Shape of the Book of Psalms," *Interpretation* 46 (1992) 129–42.

[4] Gerald H. Wilson, "Shaping the Psalter: A Consideration of Editorial Linkage in the Book of Psalms," in J. C. McCann (ed.), *The Shape and Shaping of the Psalter* (JSOTSup 159; Sheffield: JSOT Press, 1993) 72–82.

submit themselves to the power of Yahweh's king enthroned in Zion. At the conclusion of the second book (which has been combined with the first into a collection of "Prayers of David"),[5] the Solomonic Psalm 72 invokes the continuation of divine blessing on subsequent generations of Davidic monarchs who, it is hoped, will live "as long as the sun" and will rule "from sea to sea, and ... to the ends of the earth."

At the conclusion of the third book, however, Psalm 89 hurls an almost frantic accusation at Yahweh for his failure to live up to his covenant promises by preserving the Davidic kings and kingdom. The first three books thus end with a stinging rebuke of God's incomprehensible rejection of David, and a demand that he rouse himself to faithfulness to restore his promises (89:46-51).

It is further posited that the last two books (Psalms 90–150) were added at a later point as part of the final redaction of the Psalter, a movement that reflects the concerns of the sages, and intends to offer a response to the questions and hopes raised in the earlier books. The intent is to redirect the hopes of the reader away from an earthly Davidic kingdom to the kingship of Yahweh. This final shaping of the Psalter is accomplished in part by: (a) placing wisdom psalms (or at least psalms influenced by the wisdom tradition) in primary positions that bind the earlier collection together with the later one; and (b) by providing the whole Psalter with an extended conclusion. This is particularly evident in the placement of Psalm 1 as an introduction to the whole Psalter, the use of Psalms 90 and 107 to introduce the last two books, the placement of Psalm 145 to conclude the body of the Psalter proper, and to precipitate the concluding *hallel* (Psalms 146–150).[6] In addition, the shift of focus to the Kingship of Yahweh rather than humans is accomplished by foregrounding the *Yahweh Malak* psalms (Psalms 93, 95–99) that form the core of the first answering book (Book Four, Psalms 90–106), and indeed of the whole Psalter in its final form.

The result is a Psalter that recalls the foundational pre-monarchical

---

[5] This is the effect of the only true postscript in the whole Psalter (72:20): "The prayers of David, son of Jesse, are ended." The fact that this postscript *follows* the doxology that concludes the second book of the Psalter (42–72) suggests the first two books have been combined into a collection of "Davidic" prayers.

[6] See the discussion of this final redaction in Gerald H. Wilson, "Shaping the Psalter," 72–82.

faith of Israel (Psalms 90, 105–106),[7] and directs the faithful to trust in Yahweh as king rather than in fragile and failing human princes (Psalms 145–146).

## ISSUES AND ANSWERS

Although there remain many additional details that could be cited, I think this statement offers a fair representation of the original thesis associated with the use of royal psalms in shaping the canonical Psalter. Now let us turn to consider some of the significant issues that have been raised in light of this thesis in the intervening years.

### 1. Two Segments of the Psalter

The recognition of two segments of the Psalter distinguished by methods of arrangement and representing two significantly different periods of redaction has been generally accepted among commentators. Confirmation of these two divisions was initially drawn from the Qumran Psalms manuscripts, where evidence displays almost complete consistency of arrangement for the first three books of the Psalter; while the last two books demonstrate continuing variety of arrangement into the first century CE.[8]

Despite this general recognition and confirmation, many critics fail to take this feature of the Psalter into due consideration in understanding its final form. Many prefer instead to think in terms of a single final redaction of disparate psalms collections, and in so doing confuse elements of these two distinctive editorial movements, so that their interpretation suffers as a result. This is particularly noticeable in regards to two related issues: the date assigned to the final redaction, and the function of Psalm 1 as introduction to the whole Psalter.

### 2. Date of the Final Redaction

Nowhere has there been more resistance to this thesis than at the point of the date that must be assigned to this final shaping of the Psalter. Following the hints of the two distinctive segments of the canonical Psalter, and correlating this with evidence of variation in the Qumran psalms manuscripts, it is difficult to escape the conclusion

---

[7] The appearance of Mosaic and Exodus themes in the fourth book has been noted by others, including Marvin Tate, *Psalms 51–100* (WBC 20; Waco, TX: Word, 1990) 452–53; 458.

[8] See the work of Peter W. Flint, *The Dead Sea Psalms Scrolls and the Book of Psalms* (STDJ 17; Leiden: Brill, 1997) 237–40.

that the final books of the Psalter were still in a state of flux as late as the first century BCE to the first century CE. Whether this is a case of two competing arrangement strategies (represented by canonical Psalms 90–150 and the parallel Qumran arrangement 11QPsª) as suggested by Flint, or of continuing general fluctuation in the arrangement of these psalms as proposed early on by Sanders, the result seems to remain that the canonical Psalter arrangement did not win the day until after the middle of the first century CE.

Critics of this late date for the canonical Psalter often point to an assumed Septuagint translation of the Psalter in or by the second century BCE. However, none have been willing (or able) to offer solid evidence of this translation that takes into consideration the two segments outlined above, and unequivocally confirms the existence of the canonical arrangement of all 150 psalms at that early date. That there was a Psalter in the second century BCE is not the question, but what were its contents! While it is generally agreed that the Torah was translated into Greek in Alexandria, Egypt in the second century BCE,[9] this does not confirm the translation of the Psalter by that time, or especially of the *whole Psalter* given the existence of the two segments and their chronological relationship.[10] More recently, Septuagint scholars of the caliber of Eugene Ulrich have begun to accept the evidence that the Hebrew Psalter (and therefore the LXX Psalter translation) was not closed in its canonical form until the first century CE.[11]

## 3. The Function of Psalm 1 as Introduction

By and large, the placement and function of Psalm 1 as an introduction to the whole Psalter proposed by Childs and others has won general acceptance. As far as the thesis regarding the royal psalms at the "seams" of the Psalter is concerned, the primary issue arises from

---

[9] This is the import granted by most scholars to the legendary account of the Septuagint translation of the Old Testament in the *Letter of Aristeas*.

[10] Even if there *were* a translation of the Psalter in the second century BCE, what is to say that it was not a translation of the first *three books* rather than all five? Arguments for the early closure of the Psalter have generally failed even to discuss this aspect of the issue.

[11] See the comments of Eugene Ulrich, "The Dead Sea Scrolls and Their Implications for an Edition of the Septuagint Psalter," in Anneli Aejmelaeus and Udo Quast (eds.), *Der Septuaginta-Psalter un seine Tochterübersetzungen* (Göttingen: Vandenhoeck & Ruprecht, 2000) 323–36.

those who seek to link together Psalms 1 and 2 to form a combined introduction. Early on the rabbis pointed to the use of the wisdom term אַשְׁרֵי at the beginning of Psalm 1 and at the ending of Psalm 2, as evidence these two psalms were intended to be read together. John T. Willis has effectively undermined any attempt to read these two compositions as an *original* unity,[12] but others, often following the lead of Gerald T. Sheppard,[13] seek to explain these psalms as a *redactional* unity intended to shape the understanding of the *final* form of the Psalter. Sheppard does not recognize the significant placement of other royal psalms at the seams of the first three books. As a result he is unaware of the relationship that exists between Psalm 2 and Psalms 72 and 89. Neither is he aware of the disconnection that occurs by his attempt to bind Psalm 2 so closely to Psalm 1. While it may well be true that an attempt has been made to connect these Psalms at some point, the failure to recognize the connection of Psalm 2 with 72 and 89, leads Sheppard to place too great an emphasis on David as "the one who qualifies under the injunction of Psalm 1 to interpret the Torah as a guide to righteousness."[14] The continued association of Psalm 2 with 72 and 89 mitigates the status of David significantly and opens the way, as we shall shortly see, for a new understanding of the anointed servant of Yahweh that focuses the reader instead on the kingship and kingdom of Yahweh.

Others, including Christoph Rösel,[15] recognize the importance of Psalm 2 as a significant editorial feature of the first three books of the Psalter (Psalms 2–89). Any understanding of the final form of the Psalter would have to take into consideration the function of Psalm 2 in this earlier collection and then understand the effect of any later attempt to bind Psalm 2 (and the collection of which it is a part) to Psalm 1 and the final redaction of the whole Psalter (including Psalms 90–150). Rösel's work strongly suggests that Psalm 2 was already part of a consistent "messianic redaction" of Psalms 2–89 *before* Psalm 1 and the last two books were added to complete the Psalter. If

---

[12] John T. Willis, "Psalm 1—An Entity," *ZAW* 9 (1979) 381–401.

[13] Gerald T. Sheppard, *Wisdom as a Hermeneutical Construct: A Study in the Sapientializing of the Old Testament* (BZAW 151; Berlin: de Gruyter, 1980) 136–44.

[14] Sheppard, *Wisdom as a Hermeneutical Construct*, 142.

[15] Christoph Rösel, *Die Messianische Redaktion des Psalters: Studien zu Entstehung und Theologie der Sammlung Psalm 2–89* (Stuttgart: Calwer, 1999).

this is the case, one needs to ask what effect the addition of Psalm 1 and the last two books was intended to have on this previous messianic psalter. I will return to this question at the end of the discussion of issues.

*4. The Presence of Highly Davidic Psalms in Books Four and Five*

In response to the suggestion that the second segment of the Psalter (Psalms 90–150) responds to the first (Psalms 2–89) by directing the reader *away* from trust in human kings and *toward* the kingship of Yahweh, some critics have countered by drawing attention to the presence of highly Davidic psalms in the last two books, and point in particular to Psalm 132 with its clear references to the Davidic covenant and to an eternal throne for the Davidic descendants (132:1-5; 11-12).[16] The presence of such psalms, it is claimed, flies in the face of any attempt to shift attention away from hopes attached to the Davidic kings.[17] Just a few comments are necessary in this context.

First, only three psalms within the last two books mention David outside the psalm-headings (122:5; 132:10, 11, 17; and 144:10). Of these, two occur within the collection of Ascent Psalms that extend consecutively from Psalms 120 to 134. The appearance of these two psalms (122 and 132) in the fifth book may owe more to their prior inclusion in the Ascent collection than any specific editorial purpose. Even so, Psalm 122 does not offer a very significant challenge to the thesis since its reference is a rather vague, historical one to the "thrones for judgment ... the thrones of the house of David" that reflects the context of a pilgrim's anticipation upon entering the city of Jerusalem.

Psalm 132, however, is a tougher case all together as Bernhard Anderson indicates in his critique of the thesis regarding the royal psalms:

> This is an attractive, even tempting hypothesis. It breaks down, however, on the text of the book of Psalms itself. The Achilles' heel is Psalm 132, which comes after the psalms of God's enthronement. Here we find a re-

---

[16] In reality there are only six psalms in the canonical Psalter that mention David in the body of the psalm. Three of these psalms are found in the first three books (18:50; 78:70; 89:3, 20, 35, 49), while another three appear in the last two books (122:5; 132:10, 11, 17; 144:10).

[17] See in particular the comments of Bernhard W. Anderson in *Out of the Depths. The Psalms Speak for Us Today* (Philadelphia: Westminster John Knox, 2000) 208–209.

statement of the tenets of Davidic theology: the election of the Davidic king to a role in God's cosmic administration, and the choice of the temple of Zion as God's "dwelling place."[18]

Although Psalm 132 may also have come to its position by virtue of its association with the Ascent collection, its strong references to the Davidic covenant require further comment. Despite these references, however, it is remarkable that the psalm concludes in its present form with a description of the eternal enthronement, *not of the Davidic king*, but of Yahweh himself. Hard on the heels of the recollection of Yahweh's "oath to David" that "One of your descendants I will place on your throne — if your sons keep my covenant and the statutes I teach them, then their sons will sit on your throne for ever and ever" (132:11-12), Yahweh's declaration of *self-enthronement* has the effect of undermining the Davidic hopes and replacing them with his own kingship. "For Yahweh has chosen Zion, he has desired it for his dwelling: 'This is my resting place for ever and ever; here I will sit enthroned, for I have desired it'" (132:13-14). The use of the same phrase ("for ever and ever") just employed in reference to the quite *conditional* enthronement of the Davidic descendants has the effect (especially in light of the exilic proof of the *failure* of the Davidic descendants to "keep [God's] covenant")[19] of shifting any hopes attached to the Davidic monarchs on to the rulership of God himself. Yahweh himself is the one who fulfills the role of the monarch by providing abundantly, satisfying the poor with food, and clothing "[Zion's] priests with salvation" (132:15-16).

The psalm does conclude with an anticipated exaltation of "David" in eschatological tones as God promises to "make a horn grow for David and set up a lamp for my anointed one" (132:17). But the words stop just short of an unambiguous declaration of David's kingship. Anointing is of course employed to mark out and sanctify priests as well as kings, and the "crown" (נֵזֶר) mentioned in verse 18 is most often mentioned elsewhere as a sign of special dedication for priests

---

[18] Anderson, *Out of the Depths*, 209.

[19] It seems a bit disingenuous to believe that the readers of this psalm could not have seen the relationship of the condition expressed here to the judgment expressed in the Exile. The condition here is essentially unlike that relayed in 2 Sam 7:14-16 where the Davidic descendant's "wrongdoing" encounters punishment, *not* revocation of the covenant promises. Here continued rule is directly linked to keeping the covenant, a condition the monarchs patently failed to fulfill.

or even adherents to the Nazirite vow,[20] although it does in a few instances refer to the headgear of kings.[21] Coupled with the treatment of David in Psalm 144 (see below), Psalm 132 offers a less than unambiguous affirmation of David, and ultimately leaves the re-establishment of the broken covenant of kingship a question for future resolution.

As for Psalm 144, the reference to David is found within a strong context of human frailty and dependence on Yahweh. God is the one who "gives victory to kings, who delivers his servant David from the deadly sword" (144:10). It is deliverance that the David of Psalm 144 seeks from God, and the voice of the poet exhorts trust in Yahweh as the source of hope and blessing (144:18).[22] Psalm 144 further stands within a broader context of human frailty and acknowledgement of the kingship of Yahweh that marks the end of the whole Psalter. Psalm 145 (a Davidic psalm) opens with the declaration "I will exalt you, my God the King (הַמֶּלֶךְ); I will praise your name for ever and ever" (145:1), and goes on to praise the worthy character and majesty of God and his glorious eternal kingdom (145:11-13). Psalm 146 (along with the remainder of the concluding *Hallel* precipitated by the vow in 145:21) counsels the reader to eschew trust in human princes (the term מֶלֶךְ ["king"] is not even used!) in favor of the sure help provided by God (146:3-5).[23]

In addition to these three psalms where David is explicitly mentioned within the body of each psalm, Bernhard Anderson notes the strong presence of Psalm 110 and its allusions to a ruling presence and

---

[20] See Exod 29:6; 39:30; Lev 8:9; 21:12; Num 6:2, 3, 4, 5, 7, 8, 9, 12, 13, 18, 19, 21; and Jer 7:29.

[21] 2 Sam 1:10; 2 Kgs 11:12; Ps 89:39.

[22] I find it particularly interesting that Psalm 144 ends with parallel lines *both* initiated by the wisdom term אַשְׁרֵי ("blessed"), with which Psalm 2 — at the other end of the Psalter — also concludes. In the competing editorial framing of the Psalter, Psalm 144 stands removed from the end of the Psalter by *one psalm* (Psalm 145) as Psalm 2 stands removed from the beginning of the Psalter by *one psalm* (Psalm 1). For a discussion of these competing editorial frames, see Wilson, "Shaping the Psalter," 72–82.

[23] The appearance in Ps 146:5 of the wisdom term אַשְׁרֵי ("blessed"), commending trust in Yahweh, links back to Ps 144:15 and serves to bind these three psalms (144, 145, 146) into a unit spanning the conclusion of the Psalter. This whole unit links back to the similar combination of Psalms 1 and 2 at the beginning of the Psalter while affirming the basic two-stage development of the canonical collection.

power emanating from Zion. This psalm is picked up often in the New Testament and employed to define the messianic role of Jesus.[24] As Anderson states:

> Psalm 110 which exalts the Davidic "messiah" to a position at the right hand of God's celestial throne, [is also] found in the latter part of the book of Psalms. The truth is that Israelite interpreters, even in the face of harsh realities of history, never surrendered the hope for a coming monarch of the Davidic line who would rule as God's viceregent ...[25]

Let us look more closely at Psalm 110 and see if Anderson's objections hold up. First, the common rendering of the exhortation "rule" in 110:2b is a translation of the Hebrew verb רדה, which more commonly means "exercise authority" or even "supervise the labor of others," rather than kingly rule. The obvious effect of employing this particular verb here (and not the alternatives משל or מלך) is to link this psalm back to the original creation role of humanity (Gen 1:26, 28) more than to kingly rule. The activity normally envisioned by רדה is not exclusively kingly, but can be exercised by decidedly subordinate characters supervising work for the sake of a superior.[26] The use of רדה here opens a window of possible ambiguity that could stand in tension with the overtly kingly context established in the psalms' opening lines. The exploitation of this possibility comes only a bit later in the psalm's development.

The claim in 110:4a that "Yahweh has sworn and will not change his mind ..." recalls the similar passage in Ps 89:33-36, which is itself an allusion to the original text of the Davidic covenant in 2 Sam 7:11-16. On the surface this claim in 110:4a reinforces the kingly context established in verses 1-2, drawing the reader mentally back to the initial proclamation of Yahweh's special relationship with David and his descendants and the promise of an eternal throne. This allusion makes the unexpected completion of God's proclamation — "You are a priest forever, according to the order of Melchizedek" (110:4b) — even more startling. Contrary to all expectation, the one who is commissioned here is *priest* and not *king*! Thus the ambiguity permitted by the choice of the term רדה ("exercise authority") becomes an essential preparation for the sudden reversal accomplished

---

[24] See Matt 22:41-46 = Mark 12:35-37 = Luke 20:41-44; 16:19; Acts 2:34-36; 1 Cor 15:25; Col 3:1; Heb 1:13; 7:17-22.

[25] Anderson, *Out of the Depths*, 209.

[26] See Lev 25:43, 46, 53; 1 Kgs 5:16; 9:23; Jer 5:31; and 2 Chron 8:10.

in 110:4b as an enduring priesthood replaces an eternal (human) kingship!

Some have objected that the name Melchizedek (Heb. מַלְכִּי־צֶדֶק) contains its own reference to kingship. While it is true that the translation of this name is "My king (is) righteous," the reference to kingship here adds weight to the argument I am offering, since the significance of such names is consistently to make claims about *God* and *not* the name-bearer. Thus, this name means in reality "My [heavenly] king (is) righteous." Compare the name borne by Abimelek, the son of Gideon, in Judges 9. In the preceding chapter, Gideon had refused an offer of kingship with the theologically pregnant statement: "I will not rule over you, and my son will not rule over you; the LORD will rule over you" (Judg 8:22-23). The name Gideon subsequently gives his son — אֲבִימֶלֶךְ — makes the same theological claim: "My [heavenly] father is king." So, in Psalm 110, the Davidic descendant is proclaimed "a priest after the order of Melkizedek," an individual whose name proclaimed eternally the righteous kingship of Yahweh!

In light of this unexpected reversal, the tension between the "Lord" (אֲדֹנִי) in verse 1 and the "Lord" (אֲדֹנָי) who dominates the latter part of the psalm receives further clarification. It is אֲדֹנָי ("my Lord," the normal oral replacement for the divine name Yahweh) and not אֲדֹנִי (an obvious reference to the human monarch) who toward the end of this psalm is the active figure "shattering kings" (v. 5); "judging nations" (6a); "heaping up the dead" (6b); and "crushing the rulers of the earth" (6c). Thus, once again in this Davidic psalm, it is ultimately Yahweh who assumes the role of conquering monarch while the Davidic scion is affirmed as "priest forever."

## 5. The Assumption of a Messianic Reading of the Royal Psalms

I find it rather mystifying that the proposal regarding a shift from human kingship to the kingship of Yahweh should have been taken by some critics as undermining a supposed messianic reading of the royal psalms. That has never been my intention, and indeed it has always been my opinion that the developments noted only enhance our understanding of how the royal psalms achieved messianic status. The question in my estimation has never been *whether* the royal psalms came to be read messianically — that has always seemed rather transparently obvious to me. However, the real question remains once the obvious is accepted: *Just what kind of messianic figure comes into view when these psalms are read in concert and within the final shaping of the Psalter as a whole?* Let me offer now a couple of insights that affect how the reader of the Psalter might answer this question.

(1) First, no matter how unexpected it may seem, the role of David is *down-played* in the final form of the Hebrew Psalter. In strong contrast to the highly Davidic character of the first three books (Psalms 2–89) where almost 64 percent of these 88 psalms are attributed to David in their heading, only 17 of the 61 psalms in the last two books (Psalms 90–150) — or about 28 percent — are declared Davidic! Indeed, it is notable that in the 17 psalms of the fourth book (Psalms 90–106) where the kingship of Yahweh is emphasized in the introduction of the *Yahweh Malak* psalms, only 2 psalm-headings include attributions to David — a little less than 12 percent! The result is that as one reads through the final form of the Psalter from beginning to end, the figure of David, while still important, is unmistakably diminished in frequency (and thus prominence) as one moves into the latter two books.

This change is particularly noticeable when the contents of the canonical Hebrew Psalter are compared with the competing visions of David presented in the two alternate psalm collections available to the community of faith toward the end of the first century CE. In the LXX version of the Psalter several canonical psalms that are unattributed in the Hebrew Psalter are supplied with Davidic headings, and the Davidic Psalm 151 is appended at the end of the collection (although clearly labeled as "outside" the official number of psalms). The overall effect is to reinforce the Davidic character of the Greek Psalter by increasing David's frequency and prominence. This is even more true of the Qumran Psalms Scroll (11QPs[a]) where David is further exalted by the inclusion of other Davidic compositions unknown to the canonical Psalter, the addition of Davidic psalm-headings where they do not exist in the canonical collection, and the inclusion of an honorific prose piece describing David's Compositions and his prophetic inspiration.[27] So, by a reduction of emphasis on David in the last 61 psalms, and by its less Davidic character overall — in comparison to other possible arrangements of the Psalter — the canonical Hebrew Psalter commits itself in its final form to a more moderate interpreta-

---

[27] I have compared the alternative shaping of the canonical Hebrew Psalter and 11QPs[a] in "11QPs[a] and the Canonical Psalter: Comparison of Editorial Technique and Shaping," *CBQ* 59 (1997) 448–64.

tion of the role and significance of David.

(2) Another insight involves a study of the distribution of the terms מֶלֶךְ "king" and מָלַךְ "be king; rule" in the 150 psalms of the canonical Psalter.[28] There is a significant difference in the way these terms relating to kingship are employed in relation to the two segments of the Psalter previously discussed. In the first segment (Psalms 2–89) these terms are used in four ways: (1) as a reference in the most general sense to "kings" or "kingship (e.g. Ps 33:16); (2) when describing foreign kings of the non-Israelite world (e.g. Pss 2:2, 10; 45:9; 76:12); (3) in specific allusions to the human kings of Israel/Judah (e.g. Pss 2:6; 21:1, 7; 45:11; 89:18); and (4) to describe the divine kingship of Yahweh (Pss 5:2; 10:16; 24:7, 8, 9, 10; 29:10; 44:4; 47:2, 6, 7; 48:2?; 68:24; 74:12; 84:3). When, however, we survey the later segment of the Psalter (Psalms 90–150), we note a remarkable change in the way these terms are used. While מֶלֶךְ "king" and מָלַךְ "be king; rule" are still employed as before to describe kings in the general sense (e.g. Pss 140:10; 144:10), the kings of the foreign nations (Pss 102:15; 105:14, 20, 30; 110:5; 119:46; etc.), and the kingship of Yahweh (95:1; 98:6; 99:4; 145:1; 149:2), these terms are *never employed* in specific references to the kings of Israel and Judah in the last two books of the Psalter! The effect of this change is to change the way the Davidic monarchs are experienced in this section while highlighting the new emphasis on the kingship of Yahweh established early in the fourth book through the introduction of the *Yhwh Malak* ("Yahweh reigns/has become king") psalms.[29] The change in the use of these terms deflects attention away from *human* kingship in Israel to the enduring kingship and kingdom of Yahweh.

This somewhat subtle shift in the use of these terms receives some confirmation from the contrasting treatment of two other important terms that are employed in the earlier segment of the Psalter to describe the kings of Israel/Judah in general and David in particular. These terms — "servant" (עֶבֶד) and "anointed one" (מָשִׁיחַ) — continue

---

[28] These terms occur 73 times in the text of the Psalter, 46 times in the first three books (63%), and 27 times in the last two books (37%). Even when adjusted for the number of psalms in each section, the appearances of these terms is reduced in the latter books of the Psalter (Books 1–3: 46 appearances in 89 psalms = 52%; Books 4–5: 27 appearances in 61 psalms = 43%).

[29] The *Yhwh malak* psalms include the collected Psalms 93, 95, 96, 97, 98, 99, and the two separated Psalms 47 and 146.

to appear in association with the kings of Israel/Judah in the second Psalter segment as well.[30] One effect of the distribution of all these terms is to refocus attention on the roles of the anticipated Davidic kings as "anointed servants" while distancing them from the kind of "kingly rulership" normally associated with the term מֶלֶךְ.

Indeed, the understanding of the Davidic messiah reflected in this view of the Psalter shaping is consistent with the kind of role described for humans in Genesis 1–2. As I have attempted to show elsewhere, to "exercise dominion" (רדה) and "subdue the earth" (כבשׁ) mean to bring the earth and its inhabitants under *God's* rule. Humans are "servants" who are expected to exercise protective care over God's creation.[31] So at the very beginning of the canon we find the same tension between authority (Gen 1:26-28) and servanthood (Genesis 2) that is embodied in the Psalter's understanding of the Davidic kings toward the end of its canonical development.[32] Both texts understand this tension, in my opinion, by placing human authority within the context of servanthood to God's kingship and kingdom.

This change in the way the Davidic kings were treated in the Psalter implies a shift in the way the royal psalms and other references to the Davidic kings were interpreted. While it is clear that the anointed servants of Israel continue to play a prominent role in the future plans of Yahweh for his people, that role is increasingly distanced from the kind of "rulership" normally associated with מֶלֶךְ. Yahweh is the eternal king (מֶלֶךְ) who rules over his people. In Psalm 110, the Davidic descendant is associated with an eternal priesthood "according to the order of Melchizedek (110:4).[33] Even with the decidedly militant

---

[30] After appearing seven times in six psalms in the first three books (2:2; 18:51; 20:7; 28:8; 84:10; 89:39, 52), the term מָשִׁיחַ occurs only three times in two psalms in the last two books (105:15; 132:10, 17) — a slight reduction in emphasis. The term "servant" (עֶבֶד) also occurs in reference to kings seven times in four psalms in the earlier segment (18:1; 36:1; 78:70; 89:4, 21, 40, 51) and only two times in two psalms (132:10; 144:10) in the latter.

[31] Gerald H. Wilson, "Restoring the Image: Perspectives on a Biblical View of Creation," *Quaker Religious Thought* 24 (1990) 11–21.

[32] Deut 17:14-20 exhibits the same tension. Israel may have a king, but only one who will not exercise the normal modes of kingly power: military, political, or financial.

[33] An association that survives elsewhere in the "two messiahs" — one priestly and one kingly — anticipated in the Qumran documents. Cf. the *Manual of Discipline*, also known as the *Rule of the Congregation* (1QSᵃ) 9:11.

picture of David in Psalm 132 and the reference there to the promise
of an enduring throne for David and his descendants based on the Davidic covenant (cf. Ps 132:10-12), it becomes increasingly clear that it
is *Yhwh who sits enthroned in Zion for ever and ever* as king (132:13-
14). It would have been incredibly difficult for the diaspora community with its long identification with the Davidic monarchy to disasso-
ciate David and his descendants from kingship *entirely*. Nevertheless,
the role of the Davidic מֶלֶךְ recedes in the final form of the Psalter,
while David's role as the eschatological Messiah (מָשִׁיחַ) and Servant
(עֶבֶד) who ushers in the kingdom and reign of Yahweh moves to the
foreground.[34]

It is apparent from the witness of the New Testament Gospels that it
was possible in first century (CE) Palestine to derive at least two views
of Messiah from the same Old Testament canon. While the mainline
Jewish community and the early followers of Jesus shared a body of
scripture, each came ultimately to a radically different understanding
of Messiah that influenced (and was influenced by!) how they understood Jesus' life and teaching. This should not be taken to imply that
each group was employing a distinctively different canon; only that
they had different ways of understanding the one they shared. As an
illustration of the point, the Psalter allows a militant messianic view of
the Davidic kingship (particularly in Psalms 2–89). And yet, as I have
attempted to show, the same collection of psalms offers a subtle alternative emphasizing servanthood subordinated to the rulership of
Yahweh.

The shape of the canonical Psalter would ultimately affect the way
the royal psalms and earlier references to Davidic kingship were interpreted. In light of the distancing that takes place in the later books,
these references would have been increasingly understood *eschatologically* as hopeful anticipation of the Davidic descendant who

---

[34] The attempt to describe a consistent and thorough going "eschatological
programme" that enfuses the whole psalter is the goal of David C. Mitchell in *The
Message of the Psalter: An Eschatological Programme in the Book of Psalms*
(JSOTSup 252; Sheffield: Sheffield Academic Press, 1997). His work is ultimately unpersuasive since it (like earlier attempts to reconstruct an enthronement
festival) is based largely on tenuous connections between particular psalms and a
supposed eschatological program discovered in Zechariah 9–14. While Mitchell's
attempt at least takes the Psalter arrangement seriously, it ultimately fails by
seeking to say too much — or at least more than the psalms themselves clearly
say.

would — as God's anointed servant — establish God's direct rule over all humanity in the Kingdom of God.[35] Of course this shift later provides the grounds for Jesus' own peculiar understanding of his role as the suffering, dying kind of messiah who inaugurates an eternal kingdom of God that is "not of this world" but of the spirit.[36]

## SELECT BIBLIOGRAPHY

Anderson, B. W. *Out of the Depths. The Psalms Speak for us Today* (Philadelphia: Westminster John Knox, 2000).

Brueggemann, W. "Bounded by Obedience and Praise: The Psalms as Canon," *JSOT* 50 (1991) 63–92.

Childs, B. S. *Introduction to the Old Testament as Scripture* (Philadelphia: Fortress, 1979) 513–14.

Flint, P. W. *The Dead Sea Psalms Scrolls and the Book of Psalms* (STDJ 17; Leiden: Brill, 1997) 237–40.

McCann, J. C., ed. *The Shape and Shaping of the Psalter* (JSOTSup 159; Sheffield: JSOT Press, 1993).

Mitchell, D. C. *The Message of the Psalter: An Eschatological Programme in the Book of Psalms* (JSOTSup 252; Sheffield: Sheffield Academic Press, 1997).

Rössel, C. *Die messianische Redaktion des Psalters: Studien zu Enstehung und Theologie der Sammlung Psalm 2–89* (Stuttgart: Calwer, 1999).

Sheppard, G. T. *Wisdom as a Hermeneutical Construct: A Study in the Sapientializing of the Old Testament* (BZAW 151; Berlin: de Gruyter, 1980).

Willis, John T. "Psalm 1—An Entity," *ZAW* 9 (1979) 381–401.

Wilson, Gerald H. *The Editing of the Hebrew Psalter* (SBLDS 76; Chico, CA: Scholars Press, 1985).

—. "Restoring the Image: Perspectives on a Biblical View of Creation," *Quaker Religious Thought* 24 (1990) 11–21.

—. "The Shape of the Book of Psalms," *Interpretation* 46 (1992) 129–42.

—. "11QPsᵃ and the Canonical Psalter: Comparison of Editorial Technique and

---

[35] This may even offer a partial solution for the apparent confusion between king and Yhwh in such passages as Ps 45:2-7, where the king appears in verse 5 to be called "God".

[36] Whether the continued use of the terms "anointed one" (מָשִׁיחַ) and "servant" (עֶבֶד) in the last two books of the Psalter has any relationship to the "suffering servant" songs in Isaiah is not clear. But it is interesting that these two concepts are brought together by the heavenly voice at Jesus' baptism and transfiguration when it quotes portions of Ps 2:7 ("son" = מָשִׁיחַ) and the servant song of Isa 42:1-4 ("in whom I delight" = עֶבֶד). Cf. Jesus' reply to Pilate: "My kingdom is not of this world…" (John 18:36).

Shaping," *CBQ* 59 (1997) 448–64.

—. "The Use of Royal Psalms at the 'Seams' of the Hebrew Psalter," *JSOT* 35 (1986) 85–94. Also available in D. J. A. Clines (ed.), *The Poetical Books. A Sheffield Reader* (Sheffield Academic Press, 1997) 73–83.

—. "A First Century C.E. Date For the Closing of the Hebrew Psalter?," *Jewish Biblical Quarterly* 28 (2000) 102–110.

# THEOPHANIEN DES KÖNIGSGOTTES JHWH: TRANSFORMATIONEN VON PSALM 29 IN DEN TEILKOMPOSITIONEN PS 28–30 UND PS 93–100

ERICH ZENGER

## PSALM 29 ALS FESTHYMNUS DER VOREXILISCHEN TEMPELLITURGIE

Zwar sind die Datierung von Psalmen und die historische Konkretisierung ihrer Verwendungssituationen ein schwieriges und wohl kaum konsensfähiges Feld der Psalmenforschung. Gleichwohl scheint mir, daß zumindest für zwei Gruppen von Psalmen die Wahrscheinlichkeit recht groß ist, sie bzw. ihre Primärfassungen in die vorexilische Zeit zu datieren und für sie Verwendung in der offiziellen Religion bzw. Tempelliturgie anzunehmen. Es handelt sich zum einen um Königspsalmen, die bei unterschiedlichen Anlässen der Amtsführung des Jerusalemer Königs Verwendung fanden. Zu dieser ersten Gruppe gehören die Primärfassungen von Ps 2; 18; 20; 21; 45; 72; 89; 110.[1] Und es handelt sich zum anderen um Psalmen, die JHWH als den im Jerusalemer Tempel residierenden und von dort aus das Chaos bekämpfenden Königsgott feiern. Zu dieser zweiten Gruppe gehören die Primärfassungen von Ps 29; 46–48; 76; 93.[2] Für

---

[1] Zur Gruppe der „Königspsalmen" ist immer noch grundlegend: H. Gunkel & J. Begrich, *Einleitung in die Psalmen. Die Gattungen der religiösen Lyrik Israels* (3. Aufl., HK-Ergänzungsband zur II. Abteilung; Göttingen: Vandenhoeck & Ruprecht, 1975) 140–71; vgl. auch E. Zenger, „Königpsalmen," *NBL* 2 (1995) 510–513. Einen informativen und detaillierten Überblick zum religionsgeschichtlichen Kontext der Königspsalmen Ps 2 18 72 89 110 bieten die Beiträge von M. Arneth, F.-L. Hossfeld, K. Koch, B. Janowski, E. Otto, H. U. Steymans und E. Zenger in: E. Otto & E. Zenger (Hrsg.), *„Mein Sohn bist du," (Ps 2,7). Studien zu den Königspsalmen* (SBS 192; Stuttgart: Katholisches Bibelwerk, 2002). Eine forschungsgeschichtliche Skizze findet sich bei K.-P. Adam, *Der königliche Held. Die Entsprechung von kämpfendem Gott und kämpfendem König in Psalm 18* (WMANT 91; Neukirchen-Vluyn: Neukirchener, 2001) 1–16.

[2] Vgl. dazu—außer den Psalmenkommentaren—besonders: „Die Wasser der Gottesstadt. Zu einem Motiv der Zionstradition und seinen kosmologischen Implikationen," in: B. Ego & B. Janowski (Hrsg.), *Das biblische Weltbild und seine altorientalischen Kontexte* (FAT 32; Tübingen: Mohr Siebeck, 2001) 361–89; „Die heilige Wohnung des Höchsten. Kosmologische Implikationen der

beide Gruppen ist jeweils charakteristisch, daß sie untereinander mo-
tivlich verwandt sind und individuelle Ausprägungen eines über-
greifenden Symbolsystems darstellen.[3] Darüber hinaus ist beiden
Gruppen gemeinsam, daß *alle* diese Psalmen, im einzelnen gewiß unterschiedlich stark, kanaanäische, ägyptische und assyrische Vorstellungen und Bilder aufnehmen.

Daß dies vor allem für Ps 29 gilt, ist in der Forschung unbestritten.
Die Diskussion, die hier nicht detailliert referiert werden soll, geht dabei bekanntlich vor allem um die Frage, ob dem Psalm 29 ein ka-
naanäischer Hymnus zugrundeliegt, der sogar rekonstruiert werden
könne, oder ob hier „nur" Vorstellungen der El- und Baal-
Überlieferung aufgenommen wurden, ohne daß vorgegebene „Texte"
postuliert werden. Autoren, die eine kanaanäische „Textvorlage" annehmen, rechnen mit einer mehrstufigen Wachstumsgeschichte, wobei
man entweder einen „Baal-Psalm" oder einen „El-Psalm" als Grundform annimmt, die dann im einzelnen unterschiedlich bestimmt werden.[4] Ich selbst verzichte auf den Versuch, kanaanäische Textvorla-

---

Jerusalemer Tempeltheologie," in: O. Keel & E. Zenger (Hrsg.), *Gottesstadt und
Gottesgarten. Zu Geschichte und Theologie des Jerusalemer Tempels* (QD 197;
Freiburg: Herder, 2002) 24–68; H. Spieckermann, „Stadtgott und Gottesstadt.
Beobachtungen im Alten Orient und im Alten Testament," *Bib* 73 (1992) 1–31.

[3] Vgl. dazu die den Ansatz von C. Geertz aufnehmenden Überlegungen von
B. Janowski, „Das biblische Weltbild," 15–21; sowie G. Theißen, *Die Religion
der ersten Christen. Eine Theorie des Urchristentums* (Gütersloh: Gütersloher
Verlagshaus, 2000) 20–36.

[4] Die Sekundärliteratur zu Ps 29 ist beinahe unüberschaubar geworden. Einen
Forschungsüberblick bis 1987 bietet O. Loretz, *Ugarit-Texte und Thronbesteigungspsalmen. Die Metamorphose des Regenspenders Baal-Jahwe (Ps
24,7-10; 29; 47; 93; 95–100 sowie Ps 77,17-20; 114)* (UBL 7; Münster: Ugarit-
Verlag, 1988) 76–95 und 232–48 (Bibliographie). An wichtigen Studien danach
sind zu nennen: J. F. Diehl, A. Diesel, A. & A. Wagner, „Von der Grammatik
zum Kerygma. Neue grammatische Erkenntnisse und ihre Bedeutung für das Verständnis der Form und des Gehalts von Psalm XXIX," *VT* 49 (1999) 462–86;
J. Jeremias, *Das Königtum Gottes in den Psalmen. Israels Begegnung mit dem
kanaanäischen Mythos in den JHWH-König-Psalmen* (FRLANT 141; Göttingen:
Vandenhoeck & Ruprecht, 1987) 29–45; M. Klingbeil, *Yahweh Fighting from
Heaven. God as Warrior and as God of Heaven in the Hebrew Psalter and Ancient Near Eastern Iconography* (OBO 169; Fribourg & Göttingen: Vandenhoeck
& Ruprecht, 1999) 84–99; K. Seybold, „Psalm 29. Redaktion und Rezeption," in:
ders., *Studien zur Psalmenauslegung* (Stuttgart: Kohlhammer, 1998) 85–111;
H. Spieckermann, *Heilsgegenwart. Eine Theologie der Psalmen* (FRLANT 148;

gen zu rekonstruieren, gehe aber davon aus, daß der nun gegebene Psalm 29 eine kunstvolle Kombination von El- und Baal-Theologumena darstellt, die JHWH als den in seinem Palast machtvoll als König wirkenden Gott feiert. „Sitz im Leben" dieses JHWH-König-Hymnus war das vermutlich im Herbst bzw. zur Jahreswende am Jerusalemer Tempel gefeierte JHWH-König-Fest. Dieses Verständnis des Psalms soll kurz begründet und erläutert werden.

Auf der Grundlage von Beobachtungen zur Syntax und zur Kolometrie[5] legt sich folgender Aufbau des Psalms nahe:

V 1-2:     Aufforderung zur Huldigung vor dem auf seinem Thron sitzenden König JHWH

V 3-9:     Hymnische Darstellung der Macht des Königs JHWH

V 3-4:     JHWHs Macht über die Chaos-Wasser

V 5-9b:    JHWHs Macht über Götterberge und Wüste

V 9c:      Huldigungsruf im Königspalast

V 10-11:   Proklamation / Akklamation und Definition der Königsherrschaft JHWHs

Grundlegend für das Verständnis des Psalms ist die sich aus diesem Aufbau ergebende Erkenntnis, daß der Psalm nicht beschreibt, wie JHWH *König wird*, sondern wie er sein von Urzeit an gegebenes (V 10 ingressiv-durativ) *Königtum ausübt*[6] und wie dieses erfahren wird. Das wird sogleich im ersten Teil des Psalms V 1-2 unterstrichen, der voraussetzt, daß JHWH bereits als König auf seinem Thron sitzt und von den „Göttersöhnen" als König anerkannt und gefeiert wird. Die für altorientalisches Denken charakteristische Vorstellung, daß die Adoranten mit ihren „Gaben" die Machtfülle des Gott-Königs steigern, indem sie ihm zurückgeben, was ihm zu eigen ist und von ihm ausstrahlt, darf nicht so mißverstanden werden, als sei JHWH noch nicht ein König voller „Kraft" (עז) und „Herrlichkeit"

---

Göttingen: Vandenhoeck & Ruprecht, 1989) 165–79.

[5] Vgl. dazu ausführlicher: E. Zenger, „Psalm 29 als hymnische Konstituierung einer Gegenwelt," in: K. Kiesow & Th. Meurer (Hrsg.), *Textarbeit. Studien zu Texten und ihrer Rezeption aus dem Alten Testament und der Umwelt Israels. FS P. Weimar* (AOAT 294; Münster: Manfried Dietrich & Oswald Loretz, 2002) 569–83.

[6] Das Bikolon V 10 bietet mit seinem Inversionspaar *x-qatal // wajjiqtol-x* des Verbums ישׁב einen synthetischen Parallelismus, der in V 10a einen einmaligen perfektischen Vorgang bezeichnet und in V 10a den daraus resultierenden, andauernden Zustand festhält: „JHWH hat ureinst seinen Thron bestiegen und thront seitdem ..."

(כבוד). Im Gegenteil: Daß die „Göttersöhne" ihm gerade diese im
weiteren Verlauf des Psalms von ihm ausgehenden göttlichen Wirkweisen gleich zu Anfang des Psalms huldigend zusprechen, bestätigt,
daß der Psalm JHWHs von Anfang an gegebenes König-Sein feiert.
Dies zeigt sich auch in V 3-4. Die vier adverbiellen Nominalsätze
V 3a.3c.4a.4b, die paarweise zusammengehören, sind Zustandsaussagen und bilden insofern eine thematische Einheit, als V 4 die adverbiellen Angaben von V 3 explizit: JHWHs Stimme ist nicht einfach
„*über* den Wassern" im Sinne einer bloßen Ortsangabe, sondern sie
erweist *in Bezug* auf diese (Chaos-)Wasser *immerfort* ihre Macht und
Pracht. Dieser Zustand ist, wie das zwischen V 3a und V 3c betont
positionierte Kolon V 3b unterstreicht, eine Folge eines uranfäng-
lichen Machterweises JHWHs als des Gottes der Herrlichkeit. In syntaktischer Hinsicht ist V 3b ein zusammengesetzter Nominalsatz bzw.
ein Pendenssatz[7] wie 10a und drückt, mit Betonung des am Anfang
stehenden Subjekts, einen perfektischen Sachverhalt aus, dessen re-
sultierender Zustand in V 10b mit Inversion *wajjiqtol* und in V 3ac
mit Nominalsätzen festgehalten wird: „Der Gott der Herrlichkeit hat
einmal und zwar ein für allemal so gedonnert", daß seine Stimme nun
machtvoll über den Wassern walten kann.

Die Szenerie des Psalms ist m.E. falsch beschrieben, wenn z.B. B.
Lang sagt:

> In den eröffnenden Zeilen stellt sich der Dichter in den Kreis der
> himmlischen Wesen, d.h. der Engel oder, polytheistisch gesprochen, der
> Götter. Er macht sich zu ihrem Chorführer und ermahnt sie, Gott zu prei-
> sen. Offenbar haben sie sich im himmlischen Tempel versammelt, wo sie
> *der Ankunft des großen Gottes Jahwe* harren (Hervorhebung: E.Z.) ... In
> dem Augenblick, in dem Jahwe seinen Palast betritt, wird er von den Göt-
> tern mit dem Zuruf „Ehre" begrüßt. Er nimmt auf seinem Thron Platz, und
> unter seinen Füßen mag es eine Darstellung der aufrührerischen Wasser
> geben, welche die Erdscheibe umringen.[8]

Diese Interpretation widerspricht nicht nur der Syntax des Psalms,
insbesondere der von V 10, sondern eben auch der in V 1-2 entwor-
fenen Szenerie, die den ganzen Psalm durchlaufend bestimmt, wie die
Vernetzung der drei Teile des Psalms anzeigt.

---

[7] Zur Diskussion über das Konzept des zusammengesetzten Nominalsatzes und
das Plädoyer für das Konzept des Pendens-Satzes vgl. W. Groß, *Doppelt besetztes
Vorfeld. Syntaktische, pragmatische und über-setzungstechnische Studien zum althebräischen Verbalsatz* (BZAW 305; Berlin: de Gruyter, 2001) 31–60.

[8] B. Lang, *Jahwe, der biblische Gott. Ein Porträt* (München: Beck, 2002) 183.

Teil 1 (V 1-2) und Teil 2 (V 3-9) sind durch das Konzept der „Herrlichkeit" (כבוד) miteinander verbunden, die ein Proprium der Königsmacht JHWHs ist und die von ihm bei der Ausübung seiner Königsherrschaft „ausstrahlt" (V 2b: הדרה V 4b: הדר).[9] Gerade die כבוד-Perspektive widerspricht der interpretativen Engführung von V 3-9 als bloßer Schilderung eines Gewitters. Gewiß sind hier Motive des kämpferischen Wettergottes Baal aufgenommen, aber sie sind der Hauptaussage vom fortwährenden[10] königlichen Herrlichkeiterweis des auf seinem Thron sitzenden und von ihm aus machtvoll regierenden JHWH untergeordnet.[11] Die Zusammenbindung von Teil 1 und Teil 2 wird nicht zuletzt durch V 9c bewirkt, weil hier ausdrücklich auf die in V 1-2 konstituierte Szenerie zurückverwiesen wird. V 9c hebt sich in kolometrischer Hinsicht als Monokolon von V 9ab ab, ist aber durch das waw in ובהיכלו sowie durch die auf JHWH bezogenen Suffixe an das Vorangehende eng angeschlossen. In syntaktischer Hinsicht liegt ein partizipialer Nominalsatz vor, „wobei das Partizip des Satzes dazu dient, die ununterbrochene Dauer des Vorgangs und die Gleichzeitigkeit mit den Machterweisen der Stimme JHWHs auszudrücken. Verdeutlichend müßte man übersetzen: ‚Aber in seinem Palast ruft (währenddessen) ein jeder (anhaltend): ‚Glorie!'"[12] bzw. „O Herrlichkeit!". Dieses Monokolon hat eine mehrfache strukturelle Funktion:

- Es schließt zusammenfassend das in V 3-9 hymnisch beschriebene Wirken der Stimme JHWHs ab und deutet es als Manifestation der „Herrlichkeit" JHWHs.
- Durch den Stichwortbezug „Herrlichkeit" schlägt es einen

---

[9] Die Angabe בהדרת־קדש kann entweder auf die בני אלים oder auf יהוה bezogen werden. Da es in V 1-2 durchgehend um Eigenschaften / Wirkweisen JHWHs geht, die im Lobpreis anerkannt werden, legt sich der Bezug auf JHWH nahe, zumal die „Herrlichkeit" von V 1-2 als „Ausstrahlung" der göttlichen „Heiligkeit" verstanden werden kann.

[10] Vgl. die Beobachtungen zur Syntax von Ps 29 in meinem Beitrag: „Psalm 29" (2002).

[11] Daß die Topoi der (rettenden) Theophanie des Wettergottes nicht einfach „naturreligiös" aufgelöst werden dürfen, läßt sich beispielsweise an Ps 18,8-16 gut erkennen; vgl. dazu nun M. Köckert, „Die Theophanie des Wettergottes Jahwe in Psalm 18," in: Th. Richter, D. Prechtel & J. Klinger (Hrsg.), Kulturgeschichten. FS V. Haas (Saarbrücken: Saarbrücker Druckerei und Verlag, 2001) 209–26.

[12] J. Jeremias, Königtum Gottes (1987) 34.

Bogen zurück nach V 3b, also an den Anfang des Abschnitts über die Stimme JHWHs V 3-9.

- Es „nimmt das Thema der Huldigung vor dem Weltenkönig in V 1f auf, aber nicht in Gestalt der Aufforderung, sondern der Beschreibung."[13]

- Es bewirkt eine Zäsur *vor* V 10, so daß die häufig behauptete progressive Linearität von V 3 nach V 10, wonach der in V 3-9 beschriebene Machterweis der Stimme JHWHs bzw. JHWHs selbst dazu führt, daß JHWH gemäß V 10 die Königsherrschaft antreten kann, schon aus syntaktischen Gründen auszuschließen ist.

Teil 3 (V 10-11) ist zunächst durch das Motiv von dem auf seinem Thron sitzenden JHWH eng mit V 9c und damit mit Teil 2 (V 3-9) verknüpft, denn der Thron JHWHs befindet sich zweifelsohne in dem in V 9c genannten Palast. Noch stärker freilich ist die Verbindung, die V 10a nach V 3, dem Anfang von Teil 2, herstellt. Dies gilt vor allem dann, wenn man der von F. Hartenstein vorgeschlagenen Deutung von V 10a folgt, der unter Verweis auf E. Jenni die Präposition ל und V 10a als „Partikel der Beziehung mit *direktionaler* Bedeutung durch Kombination mit einem Substantiv der Orientierung"[14] vorschlägt:

> Für die zwischen *Thronen* (x) und *Flut* (y) durch ל hergestellte Relation würde dann von vornherein eine *räumliche* Beziehung naheliegen, und dies scheint wahrscheinlich, da Thron und Wasserfluten im Sinnhorizont der Jerusalemer Kulttradition auf der *vertikalen Achse* in Opposition zueinander stehen. Die crux interpretum מבול würde dann kaum im Sinne eines „himmlischen Ozeans" zu verstehen sein … sondern als Bezeichnung für den Bereich der *Wasser(tiefen)*, der in der kosmischen Vertikalen den Gegenpol zur „Höhe" des Throns bildet: JHWH hat ureinst seinen Thron bestiegen und thront seitdem „in Richtung auf" die unten befindliche Flut …, d.h. „angesichts" der (Ur)flut, über die er so ständig Kontrolle ausübt.[15]

Wenn diese Interpretation richtig ist, wird zugleich von V 10a ein Bogen geschlagen an den Anfang von Teil 2, wo die „gewaltigen Wasser" ja nicht das Mittelmeer sind, wie verschiedentlich unterstellt

---

[13] J. Jeremias, *Königtum Gottes* (1987) 34.

[14] Vgl. E. Jenni, *Die hebräischen Präpositionen. Band 1: Die Präposition Beth* (Stuttgart: Kohlhammer, 1992) 22.

[15] F. Hartenstein, *Die Unzugänglichkeit Gottes im Heiligtum. Jesaja 6 und der Wohnort JHWHs in der Jerusalemer Kulttradition* (WMANT 75; Neukirchen-Vluyn: Neukirchener, 1997) 59 Anm. 117.

wird,[16] sondern die Chaoswasser, über bzw. gegen[17] die JHWH seine kämpferische Macht ausübt. Schließlich sind auch Teil 1 und Teil 3 nicht nur durch das Thema-Wort „Kraft" (עֹז) miteinander verknüpft, sondern auch durch die Szenerie vom thronenden König JHWH.

Wo aber steht der Palast, von dem aus JHWH das Chaos bekämpft und seinem Volk Kraft und Frieden wirkt? Für die Beantwortung dieser Frage scheinen mir drei kurze Überlegungen hilfreich:

- Im Psalm ist weder vom Himmel noch vom Gottesberg als Ort der Königs-Residenz die Rede. Als entscheidende Bezugspunkte des Throns sind in V 3 „die gewaltigen Wasser" und in V 10 „die Urflut" genannt, die beide räumlich „unter" dem Königspalast verortet werden, wobei diese Relation eher qualitativ gemeint ist.

- Daß der Palast als Ort des Thrones JHWHs in V 9c das auf JHWH bezogene Suffix verwendet, macht deutlich, daß primär der mythische Wohnort JHWHs im Blick ist, „die Sphäre seines Thrones (V. 10), in der alle Göttersöhne (V. 1) dem Weltenherrscher huldigen (V. 1f.9c). Das schließt den *Tempel* als den Ort, an dem der Gottesthron zugänglich wird, nicht aus, sondern ein (vgl. das bewußt inclusive ‚alles' in V. 9c, das für beide Ebenen offen ist)."[18] Wie in den Haupttexten der vorexilischen Zionstheologie, die noch nicht zwischen dem im Himmel thronenden und dem im Jerusalemer Tempel gegenwärtig werdenden Gott unterscheiden, sondern den im Tempel stehenden Gottesthron mythisch bis in den Himmel aufragen lassen,[19] so

---

[16] Vgl. zuletzt wieder M. Klingbeil, *Yahweh Fighting* (1999) 86 Anm. 189, der gleichwohl feststellt: "though a certain polyvalence can be observed."

[17] Zur Bedeutung der Präposition עַל in V 3 als „gegen" vgl. *HALAT* 781.

[18] F. Hartenstein, *Die Unzugänglichkeit Gottes* (1997) 61.

[19] Vgl. Jes 6,1-5; Ps 46,2-8; 47; 48,2-9; 93,1-4. Zu den Implikationen der vorexilischen Tempeltheologie vgl. besonders B. Ego, „Von der Jerusalemer Tempeltheolgie zur rabbinischen Kosmologie. Zur Konzeption der himmlischen Wohnstatt Gottes," in: *Mitteilungen und Beiträge 12/13. Forschungsstelle Judentum* (Leipzig: Thomas, 1997) 36–52; dies., „Die Wasser der Gottesstadt. Zu einem Motiv der Zionstradition und seinen kosmologischen Implikationen," in: B. Ego & B. Janowski (Hrsg.), *Das biblische Weltbild und seine altorientalischen Kontexte* (FAT 32; Tübingen: Mohr Siebeck, 2001) 361–89; B. Janowski, „Die heilige Wohnung des Höchsten. Kosmologische Implikationen der Jerusalemer Tempeltheologie," in: O. Keel & E. Zenger (Hrsg.), *Gottesstadt und Gottesgarten. Zu Geschichte und Theologie des Jerusalemer Tempels* (QD 191; Freiburg:

konzentriert auch Ps 29 seine JHWH-König-Theologie auf den Gottesthron als mythische Chiffre seiner universalen Königsmacht.

• Die geographischen Angaben des Abschnitts V 5-9 verweisen nicht auf ein Gewitter, das sich in Nordsyrien zwischen Libanon und Antilibanon entlädt, sondern die Angaben entwerfen m.E. ein horizontales Weltbild, in dessen Mitte der Jerusalemer Tempel liegt. Ansatzpunkt dieser Deutung ist die von J. Jeremias beobachtete Ringkomposition von V 5-9.[20] Diese wird zunächst auf der Geschehensebene erkennbar: Sturm (V 5), Erdbeben (V 6), Feuer (V 7), Erdbeben (V 8), Sturm (V 9); im Zentrum steht die partizipial geschilderte Macht der Stimme JHWHs, die (wie ein Steinmetz) aus hartem Gestein Feuerfunken und Feuerflammen herausschlägt. Ob hier nicht auf die mit dem Zionsheiligtum verbundene „Feuerpräsenz" JHWHs[21] angespielt werden soll? Für diese Vermutung spricht m.E. die Geographie von V 5-9, die mit dem Libanon im Norden beginnt und mit der Wüste von Kadesch (Barnea) im Süden schließt — und als Mitte eben den Gottesthron in Jerusalem positioniert.

Psalm 29 setzt ein (mythisches) Weltbild voraus, dessen Zentrum sowohl in vertikaler als auch in horizontaler Perspektive der Gottesthron JHWHs ist, der die Mitte seiner Königsresidenz darstellt. Von hier aus bekämpft er die Chaoswasser (V 3-4.10), von hier aus übt er seine machtvolle Weltherrschaft aus (V 5-9) und von hier aus erweist er sich als segnender und rettender König seines Volkes (V 11). Der Psalm spiegelt demnach kein Ritual, mit dessen Rezitation der Wettergott im Herbst eingeladen wurde, die Regenzeit zu beginnen, sondern er ist die hymnische Konstituierung eines „Weltbilds", das JHWH als den königlichen Triumphator über alle Formen des Chaos feiert und so JHWHs die Welt erfüllende und dominierende Herrlichkeit kultisch vergegenwärtigt. Dazu überträgt der Psalm einerseits Eigenschaften bzw. Wirkweisen des kämpfenden Wettergottes Baal und des inmitten seines himmlischen Hofstaates residierenden Götterkönigs El auf JHWH und betont andererseits gleichwohl eine spezifische JHWH-Perspektive, die vor allem im dritten Teil des Psalms zum Ausdruck kommt: Hier wird dezidiert in V 10 durch die

---

Herder, 2001) 24–68.

[20] Vgl. J. Jeremias, *Königtum Gottes* (1987) 33.

[21] Vgl. Jes 4,5; 31,9; Ps 21,10.

zweimalige Setzung des JHWH-Namens unterstrichen, daß es JHWH ist und eben nicht El und / oder Baal, der all dies wirkt, was traditionell El und Baal zugeschrieben wird. Und in V.11 wird noch pointierter die Abgrenzung gegenüber der El- und der Baal-Theologie vollzogen, wenn „das Volk JHWHs" als Empfänger der Gaben JHWHs (עֹז und שָׁלוֹם) präsentiert wird.

Das Nomen עֹז in V 11a nimmt עֹז aus V 1 auf und konstatiert, daß der König JHWH seinem Volk Anteil an seiner eigenen Machtfülle gibt. Wie H.-P.Müller gezeigt hat,[22] gehört die Vorstellung von JHWHs עֹז ursprünglich in den Kontext vom kriegerischen Eingreifen Gottes zum Wohl seines Volkes (V.11b: שָׁלוֹם). Dies gilt umso mehr, wenn V 5-9 JHWHs königliche Macht in der Bildwelt des *kriegerischen* Gewittergottes präsentiert:

Inhaltlich sind sowohl der Hymnus auf Jhwhs Stimme als auch die verbalen und nominalen Jhwh Prädikationen, die den Hymnus immer wieder unterbrechen, durch Motive gekennzeichnet, die auch auf den Krieg passen, als stände Jhwh im Kampf mit natürlichen Instanzen wie den Zedern des Libanon (5), der Wüste Qadeš (8) oder allgemein Bäumen und Wäldern (9a).[23]

Spätestens in V 11 wird das mythische Muster, mit dem der Psalm beginnt, aufgesprengt: Die „Königs-Herrlichkeit" JHWHs erweist sich inmitten seines Volkes, das an seinem „Palast" versammelt ist und ihm „O Herrlichkeit!" zuruft (V 9c).

In der hymnischen Aussage, daß JHWH sich von seinem „Palast" / „Tempel" aus im Kampf gegen das Chaos als rettende עֹז für seine Verehrer erweist, berührt sich Ps 29 mit den vorexilischen Primärfassungen von Ps 46 und Ps 93. In Ps 46,2 faßt das Bekenntnis zu JHWH, der sich als עֹז und מַחְסֶה seiner Verehrer erwiesen hat, den Psalm zusammen, der JHWHs Machterweis wie in Ps 29 ebenfalls in seiner Macht über die Chaoswasser *und* im Ertönen seiner Stimme darstellt. Ps 93 beginnt in V 1 mit dem Bild von JHWH, der sich mit עֹז umgürtet, um so als Kämpfer von seinem Thron aus die Chaosströme zu bändigen. Beide Psalmen dürften wie Ps 29 im Jerusalemer Tempelkult ihre ursprüngliche hymnische Verwendung gehabt haben — als Elemente der offiziellen, nationalen Religion.

---

[22] Vgl. „‚Jhwh gebe seinem Volke Kraft.' Zum Hintergrund der alttestamentlichen Geschichtsreligion," *ZThK* 98 (2001) 265–81.

[23] H.-P.Müller, „Jhwh gebe" (2001) 268.

TRANSFORMATION DER JHWH-KÖNIG-THEOPHANIE IN DEN BEREICH
DER FAMILIALEN RELIGION BZW. DER PRIVATEN FRÖMMIGKEIT:
PSALM 29 ALS TEIL DER KOMPOSITION PS 28–30

Im vorliegenden Psalmenbuch steht Ps 29 als hermeneutische Mitte
zwischen dem Bittgebet Ps 28 und dem Dankpsalm Ps 30. Diese beiden Psalmen sind thematisch und kompositionell aufeinander bezogen
und von der Redaktion gezielt vor bzw. hinter Ps 29 gesetzt worden.
Dadurch erhält die in Ps 29 gefeierte Theophanie JHWHs eine Konkretisierung und umgekehrt konstituiert die Verbindung mit Ps 29 für
die beiden Psalmen 28 und 30 einen neuen Sinnraum.

*Psalm 28*

Die Primärfassung von Psalm 28,[24] nämlich Ps 28,1-7, ist ein indi-
viduelles Klage — bzw. Bittgebet in tödlicher Bedrohung, wobei —
wie üblich — die im Psalm sich aussprechende Not multiperspektiv
ist: V 1 evoziert mit dem Verweis auf die, die hinabsteigen in die
Grube, vielleicht tödliche Krankheit, während V 3 auf soziale Bedrängnis bzw. auf Rechtsnot anzuspielen scheint. Der Psalm könnte
seinen „Sitz im Leben" im Bereich der familialen Religion gehabt haben, sei es bei einem privaten Besuch am Jerusalemer Tempel (vgl.
V 2!), sei es irgendwo „im Lande", aber mit Blick auf den Tempel. Ps
28,1-7 zeigt die typische dreiteilige Struktur des Klagepsalms:

- V 1-2 ist Anrufung Gottes mit Notschilderung in der Form der
  Klage; die Anrufung richtet sich an den im Debir des Tempels
  auf seinem Thron residierenden JHWH (V 2b), wobei das Flehen um einen Gnadenerweis (V 2a) ebenfalls zur Königsmeta-
  phorik paßt.
- V 3-5 sind als Bitten gegen die Übermacht der Akteure des
  Bösen zugleich Bitten um ein Ende der Not. Im Hintergrund der
  Bitten steht der sog. Tun-Ergehen-Zusammenhang bzw. der Ap-
  pell an JHWH, nach dem Prinzip der konnektiven Gerechtigkeit
  dem Treiben der Frevler ein Ende zu setzen und die Gerechtigkeitsordnung wiederherzustellen.
- V 6-7 ist eine Doxologie mit Prolepse der erhofften Rettung und
  mit der Ankündigung eines Dankpsalms für die Hilfe, die zwar
  noch aussteht, deren der Beter aber gewiß ist.

Mit V 6-7 kommt zunächst einmal der in V 2 begonnene

---

[24] Vgl. F.-L. Hossfeld & E. Zenger, *Die Psalmen I. Psalm 1–50* (NEchBAT;
Würzburg: Echter, 1993) 176–80.

Gebetsprozeß an sein Ende, wie der Rückbezug von V 6 nach V 2 und das als Fazit formulierte Bekenntnis V 7a erkennen läßt. Dieses Bekenntnis evoziert mit עז und מגן Kriegsmetaphorik — und verweist zugleich auf den Nachbarpsalm Ps 29. Sowohl der in V 2b gegebene Tempelbezug als auch die Vorstellung von JHWH als der gegen die kriegerischen Feinde schützenden Kraft in V 7a könnten der Anlaß gewesen sein, Ps 28 vor Ps 29 zu stellen.

V 8-9 ist eine Erweiterung der Primärfassung V 1-7. Nun wechselt der Psalm von der individuellen auf die kollektive Ebene („das Volk und JHWHs Gesalbter"). Von einer aktuellen Bedrohung ist nicht mehr die Rede, weder in dem Bekenntnis V 8, das die Aussage von V 7 über JHWH als „Kraft" und als „Schild" des Beters aufgreift und generalisiert, noch in der abschließenden Bitte V 9, die sich einerseits am Nachbarpsalm 29,11 inspiriert und zugleich mit der gegenüber V 2-7 neuen Hirtenmetaphorik das in Ps 29 folgende Königsbild anders akzentuiert.

*Psalm 30*

Psalm 30[25] ist ein individueller Dankpsalm für Rettung aus tödlicher Bedrohung bzw. aus Todesnot. Streng genommen realisiert nur V 2-6 das dreiteilige gattungstypische Muster eines Dankpsalms: V 2 ist Selbstaufforderung zum Gotteslob / Dank in direkter JHWH-Anrede, mit zweifacher Begründung (Rettung des Beters: V 2a, sowie Entmachtung der Feinde des Beters: V 2b); V 3-4 ist Rettunserzählung, abermals mit direkter JHWH-Anrede gestaltet (Rückblick: Not — Hilfeschrei — Rettung aus dem Machtbereich des Totenreichs); V 5-6 ist Aufforderung an die Dankliturgieteilnehmer bzw. die Frommen, sich dem Gotteslob anzuschließen (Wechsel der Sprechrichtung: Rede über JHWH in der 3. Person), das in V 6 mit einem liedhaften „Lehrsatz" zitiert wird.[26] Dieser als Lied zu Musikbe

---

[25] Vgl. Hossfeld & Zenger, *Psalm 1–50* (1993) 186–90; H.-P. Müller, „Formgeschichtliche und sprachliche Beobachtungen zu Psalm 30," *ZAH* 12 (1999) 192–20; sowie B. Janowski, „Dankbarkeit. Ein anthropologischer Grundbefriff im Spiegel der Toda-Psalmen," in: E. Zenger (Hrsg.), *Ritual und Poesie. Formen und Orte religiöser Dichtung im Alten Orient, im Judentum und im Christentum* (HBS 36; Freiburg: Herder, 2003) 91–136.

[26] Dieses „Festlied" ist mit Kontrastmotiven kunstvoll gestaltet. Kontrast 1: Gottes Zorn dauert nur einen kurzen Augenblick, aber seine rettende Güte umfängt das ganze Leben. Kontrast 2: Auf den Abend, mit dem die Nacht als Zeit der Bedrohung, des Schmerzes und der Angst beginnt, folgt der Morgen, der

gleitung gesungene „Lehrsatz" bildet einen guten Abschluß des in V 2
begonnenen Dankpsalms, der als solcher seinen „Sitz im Leben" bei
einer familialen Todafeier im örtlichen Heiligtum bzw. im Tempel
haben konnte.

Mit V 7 setzt der Beter abermals zu einem Rückblick an. Der
Neueinsatz ist zum einen mit betontem ואני markiert, zum anderen
wird er im Wechsel der Sprechrichtung sichtbar. Der Beter wendet
sich nun wieder, wie in V 2-4, an JHWH selbst. Dieser Rückblick
greift nun weiter zurück als der Rückblick von V 2-4, nämlich in die
Zeit vor der tödlichen Bedrohung. V 7-8a charakterisiert diese Zeit
einerseits als eine Zeit des Glücks und der Kraft, die JHWH in seinem
Wohlgefallen (vgl. das gleiche Stichwort רצון in V 6a) dem Beter
geschenkt hatte.[27] Andererseits betrachtete der Beter dieses Glück in
seiner Sorglosigkeit als eine „ewige" Selbstverständlichkeit (V 7b),
bis urplötzlich das Unglück über ihn hereinbrach und ihn so in seinem
Lebensnerv traf, daß er zutiefst erschrocken und schreckensstarr war
(V 8b: הייתי נבהל). In V 9-11 berichtet der Beter von seiner Reaktion
auf diese Erfahrung seiner Gottverlassenheit. Er referiert den Wortlaut
des Hilfeschreis, den er in dieser Situation an seinen Gott gerichtet
hatte. Das Zitat beginnt nicht erst in V 10, wie meist angenommen
wird, sondern in V 9. Die im Rückblick V 7-12 die Vergangenheit
bezeichnende Verbalform ist durchgängig die Suffixkonjugation. Davon weichen die beiden Präfixkonjugationen in V 9 ab, sie können
also nicht auf der gleichen Zeitebene liegen. Sie müssen vielmehr
präsentisch übersetzt werden — genau so wie in Ps 28,1, wo Ps 30,9a
wortgleich steht. Da auch V 9b die in Ps 28,2 gebrauchte Nominal-
verbindung קול תחנוני als Verbalform אתחנן verwendet, liegt in Ps
30,9 entweder eine verbreitete gattungstypische Eröffnung eines
Klage- bzw. Bittgebetes vor — oder, was mir wahrscheinlicher ist
(s.u.), hier wird der Bittpsalm Ps 28 gezielt aufgenommen – und in
Ps 30 als „erhört" präsentiert. Die in V 9-11 zitierte Bitte an JHWH
argumentiert ohnedies ähnlich wie Ps 28,1-2 mit dem Motiv des dro-
henden Todes. Daß das Zitat der Bitte bereits in V 9 beginnt, legt sich
schließlich auch von der Beobachtung her nahe, daß V 9b und V 11a
durch die Verwendung von חנן („ich flehe um Gnade" → „sei mir
gnädig!") eine *inclusio* bilden und daß der Gebetseröffnung V 9a „Zu
dir, JHWH, rufe ich" der Imperativ in V 11a „Höre, JHWH!" korre-

---

Licht und Leben zurückkehren läßt und so Jubel auslöst.

[27] Die eigenartige Formulierung ist offensichtlich tempeltheologisch inspiriert.

spondiert. V 12 beschreibt dann die Rettung durch JHWH mit zwei Metaphern einer grundlegenden Umkehrung der Situation des Beters (V 10a: Totenklage wegen des Hineinfallens in den Machtbereich des Todes — Reigentanz als festliche Feier eines Sieges über den Tod; V 10b: Kleidertausch Bußgewand — Festgewand). V 13a betont die Absicht des Rettungshandelns JHWHs. Behält man den überlieferten Text bei,[28] ergibt sich eine Vorstellung, die eine Variation von Ps 29,9c darstellt: In Ps 29,9c wird die fortwährende Theophanie JHWHs mit dem Huldigungsruf „O Herrlichkeit" beantwortet, den „alle die Seinen", d.h. der Thronrat der Göttersöhne und die am Tempel versammelte Gemeinde, rufen. Nach Ps 30,11a soll das Rettungshandeln am einzelnen Beter ebenfalls mit dem Theophanie-Huldigungsruf „O Herrlichkeit!" gefeiert werden. V 11a betont sogar, daß dieser Ruf nie verstummen soll. Wer gemäß Ps 30,11a den Herrlichkeitsruf singt und spielt, läßt der Psalm unbestimmt. Er denkt zunächst — wie V 11b nahelegt — gewiß an den Beter selbst, aber impliziert darüber hinaus alle die, die den Psalm 30 rezitieren. Vor allem, wenn sie dies im Kontext der redaktionell geschaffenen Abfolge Ps 28–30 tun.

Daß Ps 28–30 als theologisch relevante Psalmenkomposition intendiert ist, wird dadurch angezeigt, daß Ps 30,7-13 eine Erweiterung des vorgegebenen kleinen Dankpsalms 30,2-6 ist, die gezielt die drei Psalmen 28–30 zusammenbindet:

(1) Ps 30,7-13 ist eine nachträgliche Fortschreibung von Ps 30,2-6. Während V 2-6 das Rettungshandeln Gottes und damit den äußeren Vorgang der Rettung in den Blick nimmt, steht in V 7-13 das Ich des Beters im Zentrum; in V 7-13 wird die Rettung als innere Verwandlung des Beters dargestellt. Auch die Not wird in beiden Psalmteilen unterschiedlich charakterisiert. Von der feindlichen Bedrängnis, die in V 2b beklagt wird, ist in V 7-13 nichts zu erkennen. Die Not, aus der JHWH den Beter gemäß V 7-13 rettet, ist hier seine eigene Selbstgewißheit und Gottesblindheit. Da V 2-6 als eigenständiger Dankpsalm „funktioniert", spricht vieles dafür, daß V 7-13 eine jüngere Ergänzung ist, die V 2-6 theologisch vertiefen will. V 7-13 kann man insbesondere als Ausgestaltung der im „Lehrsatz" V 6 ge-

---

[28] Meist wird der Text geändert: Viele lesen im Anschluß an G כְּבוֹדִי, was dann als „mein Herz" oder „meine (bedrängte, aber nun wiederhergestellte) Ehre" oder „mein Ehrenlied" / „mein Lobgesang" gedeutet wird; andere lesen כְּבֵדִי „meine Leber" / „mein Inneres".

bündelten Lebensdeutung begreifen. Die Perspektive „ein Leben — in seinem Wohlgefallen" (V 6a) wird durch das Stichwort „in deinem Wohlgefallen" (V 8a) aufgenommen, während
die Spannung „Weinen" — „Jubel" (V 6b) in V 12 mit den
Paaren „Totenklage" — „Reigentanz" bzw. „Bußgewand" —
„Freudenfestkleid" entfaltet wird.

(2) Mehrere Formulierungen und Vorstellungen in V 7-13 lassen
sich besser verstehen, wenn sie als Rückbezüge nach Ps 28 gelesen werden. Die eigenartige Formulierung Ps 30,8a „JHWH, in
deinem Wohlgefallen hattest du Kraft / Festigkeit als Berg für
mich hingestellt", ist als Rückbezug auf Ps 28,1b („JHWH, du
mein Fels") und Ps 28,7a („JHWH ist meine Kraft / Festigkeit")
und auf Ps 29,11 („JHWH gibt Kraft / Festigkeit seinem Volk")
eine Applikation der tempeltheologischen Aussagen von Ps 28
und Ps 29, zumal dann in Ps 30,8b das Hereinbrechen der Not
abermals mit einer tempeltheologischen Metapher („du hast dein
Angesicht verborgen") beschrieben wird. Daß V 9-11 am plau-
sibelsten als wörtliches Zitat der an JHWH gerichteten Bitte
verstanden wird, haben wir bereits oben angemerkt. Nimmt man
Ps 28–30 als Komposition, ergibt sich dann noch weiter: Ps
30,9-11 ist dann als Kurzfassung des Bittgebets Ps 28,1-7 gemeint. Das wird auch durch 30,11a bestätigt, wo das Rettungs-
geschehen ausdrücklich mit der Wurzel עזר „Hilfe / helfen"
zusammengefaßt wird, genau wie in Ps 28,7c. Der Schlußsatz
Ps 30,13b לעולם אודך nimmt Ps 28,7d אהודנו auf und unterstreicht nochmal den Geschehensbogen, der Ps 28 und Ps 30
zusammenbindet: Ps 28 ist ein Bittgebet in tödlicher Bedrohung,
das gattungstypisch mit der im Dankversprechen 28,6-7 vorweggenommenen (aber de facto noch ausstehenden) Rettung
endet.[29] Ps 30 ist dann der Dankpsalm nach der erfolgten Rettung; daß Ps 30,7-13 den Akzent so stark auf die innere Verwandlung des Beters legt, kündigt sich bereits in Ps 28,7 an, wo
das „Herz" des Beters als der Ort der erhofften Rettung präsentiert wird.

(3) Zwischen den Bittpsalm 28 und den Dankpsalm 30 hat die

---

[29] Zur proleptischen / antizipierenden Funktion des sog. Dankgelübdes im
Klagepsalm vgl. nun die gründliche Diskussion bei B. Janowski, „Das verborgene
Angesicht Gottes. Psalm 13 als Muster eines Klagelieds des einzelnen," *JBTh* 16
(2001) 25–53.

Redaktion gezielt den Theophaniepsalm 29 gesetzt. Ps 28 bot sich wegen mehrerer Motive für die Zusammenstellung mit Ps 29 an: Er beschwört JHWH an seinem Anfang gleich zweimal, JHWH möge sein Schweigen brechen (28,1); wenn Ps 29 dann so massiv das Wirken „der Stimme" JHWHs feiert, wird deutlich, daß JHWH gar nicht schweigen kann. Ps 28,2b erhebt der Beter seine Hände zu dem in seinem Heiligtum gegenwärtigen und von dort aus wirkenden JHWH; genau dies ist die in Ps 29 hymnisch gefeierte Realität. In der Rettungsprolepse 28,7 wird die von JHWH erhoffte Wirkmächtigkeit mit „meine Kraft / Festigkeit" (עזי) charakterisiert; in Ps 29,1 und 29,11 ist עז die Gestalt des כבוד JHWHs, die er seinem Volk mitteilt.[30] Wenn dann Ps 30 der dem Bittpsalm Ps 28 korrespondierende Dankpsalm ist, dann soll der dazwischen gesetzte Ps 29 offenkundig das Geschehen beschreiben, durch das die Bitte von Ps 28 erfüllt wurde / wird, so daß dann der Dankpsalm 30 gesungen werden kann — eben als paradigmatische Konkretisierung der Erfahrung der כבוד JHWHs und als „Mitsingen" jenes Theophanie-Huldigungsrufes, von dem Ps 29,9c redet.

Durch die Zusammenbindung von Ps 29 mit dem Psalmenpaar 28 und 30 wird demnach der „mythische" Theophaniepsalm 29 auf die Ebene der individuellen Begegnung mit dem rettenden Gott „herabgeholt". Und umgekehrt werden die punktuellen Situationen von Bitte und Dank, die den ursprünglichen „Sitz im Leben" der Psalmen 28 und 30 bildeten, durch ihre Anbindung an Ps 29 so „generalisiert", daß die Komposition Ps 28–30 nun als poetische Inszenierung der *condition humaine* gelesen werden kann. Das aber heißt: Hier wird paradigmatisch der Prozeß der Transformation des Rituals zur Poesie sichtbar. [31]

---

[30] Die weiteren Bezüge zwischen Ps 28,8-9 und Ps 29,11 gehen auf eine nochmals jüngere Hand zurück.

[31] Eine nochmals andere Transformation erfährt Ps 30 durch den in der Überschrift hergestellten Bezug zur „Weihe" des (Tempel-)Hauses. Diese Notiz verdankt sich weniger wahrscheinlich der Korrelation des Psalms mit der „Wiedereinweihung" des Tempels durch die Makkabäer 164 v.Chr. bzw. mit dem sich von da herleitenden Chanukka-Fest, sondern hier wird auf die in 1 Chr 21 erzählte Geschichte über den Bau des Tempels durch David angespielt.

### DIE AUFNAHME VON PS 29 DURCH DIE REDAKTOREN DER
### FRÜHNACHEXILISCHEN „TEMPELKANTATE" PS 93* 95* 96* 98 100

Die JHWH-König-Psalmen 93–100 sind in der Forschung als eigene Psalmengruppe anerkannt.[32] Ihre Eigenständigkeit als Gruppe innerhalb des Psalmenbuchs wird durch folgende Eigenheiten und Gemeinsamkeiten nahegelegt:

- die durchgehende Königsmotivik (in unterschiedlichen Ausprägungen: der auf seinem Thron sitzende und von ihm aus amtierende Weltenkönig, der den Kosmos gründet und erhält; der Tempel als seine Königsresidenz, in deren Höfen er Israel und die Völker zur Huldigung bzw. zu Belehrung empfängt; der König als Richter und als Hirte);

- der hymnische Stil (mit Ausnahme von Ps 94) in der gattungstypischen Struktur: Lobaufruf mit anschließender Begründung;

- Verwendung der Formel יהוה מלך (Ps 93 96 97 99), der Prädikation מלך גדול (Ps 95), המלך יהוה (Ps 98);

- die interne stilistisch-semantische Verknüpfung der Psalmen; diese macht auch deutlich, daß die Psalmen 94 und 100 trotz des Fehlens expliziter Königstitulaturen konstitutive Teile dieser Gruppe sind (s.u.);

- mit Ausnahme von Ps 98 und Ps 100 sind alle Psalmen titellos; der kurze Titel מזמור über Ps 98 markiert eine kleine Zäsur hinter Ps 97; die Überschrift מזמור לתודה über Ps 100, die sich an Ps 100,4 inspiriert, markiert den Schluß der Gruppe. Die Psalmen der Gruppe 93–100 lassen sich als Explikation des im Anfangspsalm Ps 93 proklamierten kosmischen Königtums JHWHs begreifen.

---

[32] Ich nehme im Folgenden meine Beobachtungen in N. Lohfink & E. Zenger, *Der Gott Israels und die Völker. Untersuchungen zum Jesajabuch und zu den Psalmen* (SBS 154; Stuttgart: Katholisches Bibelwerk, 1994) 151–78 sowie die Überlegungen aus dem Beitrag F.-L. Hossfeld & E. Zenger, *Psalmenauslegung* (2000) auf und führe sie präzisierend weiter. Eine kritische Auseinandersetzung mit meiner Position bietet H. Leene, „The Coming of YHWH as King. The Contemporary Chracter of Psalms 96 and 98," in: J. W. Dyk et al. (Hrsg.), *Unless Some One Guide Me ... FS K. A. Deurloo* (Amsterdamse Cahiers Sup 2; Maastricht: Shaker, 2001) 211–28. Zu Ps 93–100 als Psalmengruppe vgl. nun auch J. Schnocks, *Vergänglichkeit und Gottesherrschaft. Studien zu Psalm 90 und dem vierten Psalmenbuch* (BBB 140; Berlin: Philo) 2002) 196–211, dessen entstehungsgeschichtliche bzw. redaktionsgeschichtliche Hypothesen mich freilich nicht überzeugt haben.

## Psalm 93

Die Primärfassung von Psalm 93,[33] die dem Ps 29 und den Primärfassungen von Ps 46–48 nahesteht, ist eine Kurzfassung der vorexilischen Tempeltheologie. Ps 93,1-4 ist ein Hymnus auf den Weltkönig JHWH, der in Ausübung seines vor Anfang der Welt bereits
gegebenen Königtums das Chaos, das die Welt immer wieder bedroht,
bändigt und so der Welt Festigkeit und Leben gibt. Diese „Königsthe-
ologie" wird in den beiden Teilen V 1-2 und V 3-4 kontrastiv entfaltet. V 1-2 beginnt mit dem Themasatz יהוה־מלך, der mit Blick auf V 2
so paraphrasiert werden kann: „JHWH ist am Ur-Anfang König geworden und übt seither (V 2: מאז מעולם) dieses Königtum machtvoll
aus." Den Aspekt der Macht der Königsherrschaft JHWHs unterstreicht V 1 mit der Motivik von der Königsinvestitur: JHWH trägt
weder einen Prunkornat noch den herrscherlichen Lichtmantel, sondern eine Kleidung, die Kampfbereitschaft und Kampfkraft ausdrückt.
Mythische Metapher der Königsherrschaft ist der Königsthron, der
gewissermaßen als Zentrum des ganzen Kosmos diesem die Festigkeit
gibt. Dieser Thron steht nicht im Himmel, sondern er steht im Jerusalemer Tempel als der Königsresidenz JHWHs, aber er ragt zugleich
auf „in die Höhe" (V 4) des Kosmos (vgl. ähnlich Ps 29 und Jes 6,1-
3). Weil JHWH „von Anfang an", d.h. vor der Weltzeit, König ist, hat
er bei der Weltschöpfung das als tosende Wasser vorgestellte Ur-
Chaos gebändigt (V 3ab) und er bändigt dieses weiterhin (V 3c).

Die Wasserfluten sind mythische Metapher für die die Welt auf
vielfältige Weise und permanent bedrohende Realität, aber sie prallen
an der überlegenen Mächtigkeit des Weltkönigs JHWH ab. Die spät-
nachexilische Redaktion, die die Gesamtkomposition Ps 93–100 als
Abschluß eines Psalters Ps 2–100* geschaffen hat, hat dieses
Königtumskonzept durch Hinzufügung von V 5 weiter präzisiert: Die
chaosbekämpfende Mächtigkeit JHWHs wird durch die im Tempel
stattfindende Liturgie und durch die von dort ausgehende Tora vermittelt. Die nach Ps 93 folgenden Psalmen 94–100 entfalten dann unterschiedliche Aspekte dieser in Ps 93 proklamierten Königsherrschaft
JHWHs.

---

[33] Vgl. F.-L. Hossfeld & E. Zenger, *Psalmen 51–100* (2.Aufl., HThKAT;
Freiburg: Herder, 2001) 643–49.

*Psalm 94*

Psalm 94[34] ist eine Appellation an JHWH, sein königliches Amt als Richter endlich auszuüben, und zwar einerseits als Strafgericht an den „Stolzen" und Frevlern, die über sein Richteramt spotten (vgl. Ps 94,7), und andererseits als Rettung der personae miserae, die doch in besonderer Weise unter königlichem Rechtsschutz stehen müßten. So beschwört Ps 94 mit Theophaniebildern, JHWH möge sich endlich und konkret als der königliche Gott der Gerechtigkeit offenbaren.

*Psalm 95*

Psalm 95[35] besteht aus zwei Teilen: Der erste Teil (V 1-7c) ist eine doppelte Selbstaufforderung Israels zur Huldigung vor seinem König JHWH im Jerusalemer Tempel als JHWHs königlicher Residenz. Die Aufforderung wird zum einen mit der Singularität dieses Königtums begründet, das ein Königtum „über alle Götter" ist (V 3) und den ganzen Kosmos umfaßt (V 4: in der Vertikalen; V 5 in der Horizontalen); zum anderen hat dieser „Großkönig" eine einzigartige Beziehung zu seinem Volk Israel — als sein Gott, sein Schöpfer und sein guter Hirte. So folgt als zweiter Teil die „Rede" des göttlichen Königs an sein Volk (V 7d-11), die Israel zum Hören auf die Stimme JHWHs auffordert und diese Aufforderung mit dem Verweis auf die Folgen des Ungehorsams der Exodusgeneration untermauert.

*Psalm 96*

Psalm 96[36] weitet den Kreis derer, die zum Königsjubel vor und für JHWH aufgerufen werden, auf die ganze Erde aus, wie bereits der Anfang von Ps 96 (V 1), der eine Art Zusammmenfassung des Psalms bietet, erkennen läßt. Er realisiert dreimal die Struktur „Hymnische Aufforderung — Inhaltliche Begründung / Erläuterung" und zeigt so eine sich in drei Stufen steigernde Ausweitung der Adressaten an: V 1-6 ist Aufforderung an Israel, V 7-10 ist Aufforderung an die Sippen der Völker, V 11-13 ist Aufforderung an den Kosmos. Diese Adressaten werden aufgerufen, ein „neues Lied" zu singen, das ein „neues" bevorstehendes Eingreifen des Weltkönigs JHWH zum Inhalt hat. Dieses „neue" Handeln JHWHs wird die gestörte Weltordnung wiederherstellen und die Vollendungsgestalt der Erde als des universalen Königreichs JHWHs herbeiführen, so daß der ganze Kosmos

---

[34] Vgl. Hossfeld & Zenger, *Psalmen 51–100* (2001) 650–58.

[35] Vgl. Hossfeld & Zenger, *Psalmen 51–100* (2001) 658–65.

[36] Vgl. Hossfeld & Zenger, *Psalmen 51–100* (2001) 665–72.

in einen großen Jubel ausbrechen wird. Ps 96 greift Ps 29 auf und gibt diesem Psalm, wie wir weiter unten zeigen werden, eine neue Bedeutungsdimension.

*Psalm 97*

Psalm 97[37] „malt" das in Ps 96 angekündigte Kommen des Weltkönigs JHWH zur definitiven Durchsetzung seiner Weltordnung. Der erste Teil des Psalms (V 1-6) zeichnet zunächst das Bild von dem im Wolkendunkel verborgenen gegenwärtigen Weltkönig, der sich auf seinen (himmlischen) Thron gesetzt hat, um sein Richteramt auszuüben (V 2). Dieses Amt wir nun in Ps 97 dynamisiert: Der auf seinem „Gerechtigkeitsthron" sitzende JHWH kommt auf die Erde und wird als königlicher Weltenrichter „sichtbar" und „erfahrbar" (V 3-5). Höhepunkt des Geschehens ist, daß die Himmel als Herolde *und* als kosmische Zeugen dieses Kommen JHWHs in „seine" Welt ankündigen.

Der zweite Teil des Psalms (V 7-9) und der dritte Teil (V 10-12) beschreibt die Auswirkungen und die Folgen der Theophanie JHWHs: Wenn vor dem Forum aller Völker offenbar wird, daß JHWH der Gott-König der ganzen Erde ist, werden alle die, die andere Götter oder deren Götterbilder verehren, enttäuscht und beschämt zugleich sein, denn sie feiern Götter, die nur „Gott-Nichtse" bzw. „Göttlein" (אלילים) sind. Ja, diese „Götter" erkennen dies nun selbst und unterwerfen sich JHWH, wie mit abermaligem Rückgriff auf Ps 29 (s.u.) betont wird. Für die Gerechten aber bedeutet diese Theophanie, daß sie nun im Kraftfeld des Lichtes JHWHs leben und aus der Macht der Frevler befreit werden.

*Psalm 98*

Mit Psalm 98[38] kann dann der „Schlußabschnitt" der JHWH-König-Psalmen-Komposition beginnen.[39] Dieser Psalm konstatiert, daß das in Ps 96 angekündigte Kommen JHWHs zur weltweiten und endgültigen Durchsetzung seiner Weltordnung bereits begonnen hat — und zwar mit dem „neuen" Exodus Israels aus dem Exil, wie der

---

[37] Vgl. Hossfeld & Zenger, *Psalmen 51–100* (2001) 672–86. Wie bereits oben angemerkt wurde, insinuiert auch die Psalmenüberschrift מזמור eine diesbezügliche Zäsur.

[38] Vgl. Hossfeld & Zenger, *Psalmen 51–100* (2001) 687–91.

[39] Wie bereits oben angemerkt wurde, insinuiert auch die Psalmenüberschrift מזמור eine diesbezügliche Zäsur.

Psalm mit Anspielungen auf Deuterojesaja sagt. Zur Feier dieses „Ereignisses" fordert der Psalm deshalb — analog der Dreiteilung von Ps 96 — in drei sich steigernden Teilen zunächst „das Haus Israel" (V 1-3), sodann alle Völker (V 4-6) und schließlich die ganze Schöpfung (V 7-9) zum großen Königsjubel vor und für JHWH auf.

## Psalm 99

Psalm 99[40] präsentiert den auf dem Berg Zion auf seinem Kerubenthron sitzenden Weltkönig JHWH und beschreibt in drei Teilen (V 1-3.4-5.6-9) die spezifische Art seiner königlichen Amtsführung. Wie in den vorangehenden Psalmen kulminiert diese Präsentation jeweils mit der Aufforderung zur Königshuldigung, die jeweils mit der Gottesprädikation „Heilig ist er!" zusammengefaßt wird. V 1-3 konstatiert die Universalität der Königsherrschaft JHWHs, V 4-5 charakterisiert die Grundpinzipien seiner königlichen Macht und V 6-9 beschreibt mit dem Blick auf die kanonische Ursprungsgeschichte Israels die konkrete Amtsausübung dieses Königs im Spannungsfeld von gerechter Strafe und vergebender Barmherzigkeit.

## Psalm 100

Psalm 100[41] ist Höhepunkt und Abschuß der JHWH-König-Psalmen-Komposition Ps 93–100. Zwar fehlen im Psalm die יהוה מלך -Formel und eine explizite Königstitulatur, doch ist die Sprache bzw. Motivik von Ps 100 so stark königstheologisch geprägt (V 1: Königsjubel; V 2.4: „hineingehen vor sein Angesicht" bzw. „in die Höfe" = Königsaudienz), daß er sich schon von daher als Psalm über JHWHs Königtum ausweist.[42] Daß Ps 100 als Klimax von Ps 93ff gelesen werden will, ist vor allem dar-aus zu folgern, daß er fast vollständig aus Zitaten der vorangehenden JHWH-König-Psalmen besteht. Gattungsmäßig folgt der Psalm dem Schema des imperativischen Hymnus. V 1b-4 ist eine breit entfaltete, konzentrisch gestaltete Aufforderung an die ganze Erde, gemeinsam mit Israel in der Tempelresidenz des Weltkönigs JHWH das definitive Anbrechen der universalen Königsherschaft JHWHs zu feiern. Zugleich werden

---

[40] Vgl. Hossfeld & Zenger, *Psalmen 51–100* (2001) 691–705.

[41] Vgl. Hossfeld & Zenger, *Psalmen 51–100* (2001) 705–710; sowie Ch. Macholz, „Psalm 100—Israels Toda-Feier mit den Völkern," in: B. Huwyler u.a. (Hrsg.), *Prophetie und Psalmen. FS K. Seybold* (AOAT 280; Münster: Manfried Dietrich & Oswald Loretz, 2001) 143–62.

[42] Vgl. Hossfeld & Zenger, *Psalmen 51–100* (2001) 75–100.

die Völker zur (An-)Erkenntnis aufgerufen, daß der Gott Israels — er allein — auch ihr Schöpfer ist und daß sie deshalb zu ihm in einer — freilich schöpfungstheologisch begründeten — Bundesbeziehung stehen (V 3). V 5 ist die mit gattungstypischem כי eingeleitete Begründung bzw. Durchführung des bei der Festversammlung in der Königsresidenz zu singenden Hymnus, der zunächst die Kurzformel der Tempelliturgie (טוב יהוה) bietet und sodann die beiden zentralen Theologumena der spezifischen Königs-herrschaft JHWHs (חסד und אמונה) betont.

Daß mit Ps 100 ein Kompositionsbogen zu Ende kommt, wird auch daran sichtbar, daß der dann folgende Psalm 101 insofern einen Neueinsatz darstellt, als nun das Wirken des irdischen Königs präsentiert wird, von dem in Ps 93–100 nicht einmal im Ansatz die Rede ist. Trotz mancher Bedenken in der neueren Forschung[43] dürfte die traditionelle Deutung von Ps 101 als Königspsalm immer noch am ehesten zutreffen. Zwar erscheint der Sprecher des Psalms einerseits als vorbildlicher „Privatmann",[44] doch übt er andererseits sein richterliches Amt „im Lande" (V 6 und V 8) und in der „Stadt JHWHs" (V 8: Bezeichnung Jerusalems)[45] aus. So dürfte der Psalm eine Art „Königsspiegel" sein, mit dem der König sein innenpolitisches Amtsverständnis darlegt, das stark an das in Ps 94 entworfene „Amtsverständnis" des Weltkönigs JHWH erinnert. Dann aber geht es in Ps 101 um die „Frage der Umsetzung der Königsherrschaft JHWHs im irdischen Königtum",[46] die zuletzt in Ps 89 bzw. im sog. messianischen Psalter Ps 2–89* thematisiert wurde.

Um die Rezeption bzw. Transformation der JHWH-Theophanie von Ps 29 in den JHWH-König-Psalmen Ps 93–100 präziser erfassen zu können, müssen mehrere redaktionsgeschichtliche Überlegungen vorausgeschickt werden:

(1) Die drei Psalmen 94 97 99 sind in der Komposition Ps 93–100 sekundär:

    (a) Die drei Psalmen präsentieren eine andere Konzeption von JHWH als „Richter". Während die Psalmen 96 und 98 JHWH als Richter „der Erde und des Erdkreises" zeichnen, der die

---

[43] Vgl. die kurze Forschungsskizze bei F.-L. Hossfeld, *Das vierte Psalmenbuch* (2002) 180f.

[44] Vgl. „mein Haus": V 2 und V 7.

[45] Vgl. z.B. Ps 48,2.9.

[46] Hossfeld, *Das vierte Psalmenbuch* (2002) 181.

Weltordnung im Zusammenleben Israels und der Völker
wiederherstellt bzw. definitiv durchsetzt, ist JHWH in Ps 94 97
99 ein Richter, der zwischen Gerechten und Frevlern scheidet
und die Frevler bestraft; außerdem werden hier die Maßstäbe
des Gerichts konkretisiert.

(b) Ps 94 hebt sich, wie bereits angemerkt, durch das Fehlen expliziter Königstitulaturen für JHWH, durch das Fehlen der
hymnischen Elemente und durch den in den übrigen Psalmen
der Gruppe 93–100 nicht mehr auftretenden Ich-Stil (vgl. V 16-
22) ab.[47]

(c) Ps 97 verwendet nicht nur mehrere typische altorientalische
Theophanietopoi, die in den Nachbarpsalmen fehlen, die Theophanie wird hier darüber hinaus als ein Kommen JHWHs
präsentiert, das als Vorgang geschildert wird. Diese Motive
klingen in den Nachbarpsalmen nicht mehr an. Der Psalm selbst
dürfte kaum eine ursprüngliche Einheit sein. In V 10-12 ist die
V 1-9 prägende Königs- und Theophanietheologie nicht erkennbar, während umgekehrt das weisheitstheologische Vokabular von V 10-12[48] in V 1-9 fehlt. Außerdem ergibt V 1-9
einen dramaturgisch stimmigen Theophaniepsalm, der mit dem
Zitat V 9 einen wirkungsvollen Abschluß findet; außerdem
bilden V 1 und V 9 eine *inclusio*. So legt sich die Hypothese
nahe, Ps 97,1-9 sei die Primärfassung des Psalms. Da Ps 97,10-
12 eine sprachliche und konzeptionelle Nähe zu Ps 94 aufweist,
ist anzunehmen, daß V 10-12 auf jene Hand zurückgeht, die Ps
94 und Ps 97 in die Komposition Ps 93–100 eingefügt hat.

(d) Ps 99 hat gegenüber den Nachbarpsalmen einerseits dadurch ein
spezifisches Profil, daß er das Königtum JHWHs durch
Anspielungen auf die kanonische Ursprungsgeschichte Israels
(Mose und Samuel) und insbesondere durch die Aufnahme der
„Gnadenformel" bzw: „Namenformel" Ex 34,6f expliziert. Andererseits hat Ps 99 sprachliche und theologische Gemeinsamkeiten mit den Psalmen 94 und 97.[49]

---

[47] V 23 ist überraschend im Wir-Stil formuliert: redaktionell geschaffene
Überleitung nach Ps 95!

[48] Gegensatz „Gerechte"—„Frevler", doppelte Charakterisierung der Getreuen
/ Gerechten durch „das Böse hassen" und „geraden Herzens sein".

[49] Nur diese drei Psalmen haben das Wortpaar „Recht und Gerechtigkeit":
Ps 94,15; 97,2; 99,4; nur 94,1 und 99,8 haben die Vorstellung vom „rächenden"

(2) Die Psalmenabfolge Ps 93* 95* 96* 98 100 ergibt einen stimmigen Bild- bzw. Geschehenszusammenhang:

(a) Ps 93,5 ist eine jüngere Ergänzung von Ps 93,1-4. Während nach V 1-4 JHWH selbst bzw. sein von Urzeit an im Kosmos stehender (mythischer) Königsthron das den Kosmos bedrohende Chaos bändigt, führt V 5 das Gesetz und den Tempel als Instrumente der Königsherrschaft ein. Zugleich wird die V 1-4 prägende kosmische Bildwelt in V 5 nicht mehr weitergeführt. Der Vers hat demgegenüber Gemeinsamkeiten mit Ps 99. Sowohl der „Gesetzesterminus" עדות als auch die Betonung der „Heiligkeit" des Tempels als des Ortes der Gegenwart JHWHs begegnen nur in Ps 93,5 und in Ps 99,7 bzw. 99,3.5.9. Diese Beobachtungen sprechen dafür, daß Ps 93,5 auf jene Redaktion zurückgeht, die Ps 99 in die Komposition Ps 93–100 eingestellt hat.

(b) Auch Ps 95 scheint mir keine ursprüngliche Einheit zu sein. Zwar kann man die beiden Teile des Psalms V 1-7c und V 7d-11 als eine kompositionelle, sinnvolle Einheit lesen, wie auch wir dies oben getan haben.[50] Die beiden Teile sind sogar durch das Motiv von JHWH als dem Eigentümer und Geber des gelobten Landes für Israel kontrastiv verbunden (V 7 und V 11). Die Abfolge der beiden Teile „Aufruf zur Festversammlung" und „Gottesrede im Ich-Stil" hat auch zwei Parallelen in den mit Ps 95 verwandten asafitischen „Festpsalmen" Ps 50 und 81. Dennoch dürfte Ps 95,1-7c der ursprüngliche Psalm[51] und gerade als solcher die ursprüngliche Fortführung von Ps 93,1-4

---

Gott; falls die Theophaniebilder von Ps 97 auch auf die Sinaitraditionen anspielen, läge auch darin eine Verwandtschaft zwischen Ps 97 und Ps 99 vor.

[50] Einen Überblick über die Auslegungsgeschichte von Ps 95 bietet W. S. Prinsloo, „Psalm 95. If Only You Will Listen To His Voice!," in: M. D. Carroll, D. Clines & Ph. R. Davies (Hrsg.), *The Bible in Human Society. FS J. Rogerson* (JSOTSup 200; Sheffield: Sheffield Academic Press, 1995) 395–410. Die Einheitlichkeit von Ps 95 wird erneut verteidigt von F.-L. Hossfeld in: Hossfeld & Zenger, *Psalmen 51–100* (2001) 660–62; vgl. auch J. S. Fodor, *Psalm 95 und die verwandten Psalmen 81 und 50. Eine exegetische Studie* (Theos 32; Hamburg: Verlag Dr. Kovac, 1999).

[51] Zur Literarkritik von Ps 95 vgl. auch Th. Seidl, „Scheltwort der Befreiungsrede. Eine Deutung der deuteronomistischen Paränese für Israel in Ps 95,7c-11," in: H. Keul & H.-J. Sander (Hrsg.), *Das Volk Gottes. Ein Ort der Befreiung E. Klinger* (Würzburg: Echter, 1998) 107–120.

gewesen sein. Anders als Ps 50 und Ps 81 ruft Ps 95 ja nicht zu
einem Opferfest auf, sondern zur Huldigung vor JHWH als dem
König des Kosmos und dem Gott Israels. Das ist einerseits eine
konsequente Reaktion auf die in Ps 93,1-4 vollzogene hymnische Proklamation des Weltkönigtums JHWHs und andererseits ist es die Präzisierung, daß dieser Weltkönig eine besondere Beziehung zu seinem Volk Israel hat. Die in V 7c-11 folgende direkte Gottesrede gibt dieser Beziehung dann zwar mit
dem Kontrastverweis auf die ungehorsame Exodusgeneration,
die JHWH gerade nicht als „guter Hirte" in das Land der Ruhe
gebracht hatte, eine dialektische Dramatik zwischen Gelingen
und Scheitern. Aber diese Dramatik liegt eher auf der Ebene der
Psalmen 94 97 99 als auf der Linie Ps 93* 95* 96* 98 100.[52]

(c) In Ps 96 gibt es zwei Passagen, die in literar- und redaktions-
kritischer Hinsicht relevant sind. Das gilt zunächst für V 5. Auffällig ist zunächst, daß V 5 im Anschluß an V 4 abermals eine
mit yk eingeleitete Begründung bringt und außerdem in V 5a
einen Subjektwechsel im Kontext V 4-6 bietet (V 5a „die Götter
der Völker" gegenüber JHWH in V 4.5b-6). V 5b unterbricht
außerdem mit seinem Verbalsatz die Kette der Nominalsätze
V 4-6. Vor allem sprengt sein Inhalt den Rahmen des Kontex-
tes: In V 4 und V 6 wird JHWH gepriesen als der den Göttern
überlegene Weltkönig, in V 5 werden diese Götter dagegen zu
„Gott-Nichtsen" bzw. „Göttlein" (אלילים) erklärt, die im
Gegensatz zu JHWH keinerlei Schöpfermächtigkeit haben. V 5
liegt damit sowohl semantisch als auch theologisch auf der
Aussage-Ebene von Ps 97,7. Redaktionsgeschichtlich heißt
dies: 96,5 geht auf jene Redaktion zurück, die Ps 97 in die
Komposition Ps 93–100 eingebracht hat. Des weiteren ist in li-
terarkritischer Hinsicht Ps 96,10c auffällig. Dieses Kolon
schließt V 7-10, den zweiten Teil von Ps 96, ab. Dieser Teil
fordert die Sippen der Völker (משפחות עמים) auf, im Jerusa-
lemer Tempel JHWH als dem Weltkönig zu huldigen, ihm
Tributgaben darzubringen — und dann wieder zu ihren
„Nationen" (גוים) zurückzukehren und dort zu verkünden, daß
JHWH, der Großkönig vom Zion, dem Kosmos Festigkeit und
Ordnung gegeben hat und gibt. Dieser Inhalt der ihnen

---

[52] Die „Festpsalmen" 50 81 könnten dabei durchaus die „Vorlage" zur Erweiterung gewesen sein: vgl. vor allem Ps 50,7; 81,8-9.12-14.

aufgetragenen Botschaft wird in V 10ab durch wörtliches Zitat aus Ps 93,1 wiedergegeben. Dagegen findet sich die in V 10c formulierte Botschaft über das stattfindende Völkergericht nicht in Ps 93. Sachlich greift V 10c der Klimax des gesamten Psalms in V 13 voraus. Da V 10c auch in kolometrischer Hinsicht auffällig ist,[53] ist es naheliegend V 10c als spätere Ergänzung zu beurteilen. Für ihre redaktionsgeschichtliche Einordnung bieten sich zwei Möglichkeiten an: Entweder handelt es sich um eine Glosse, die durch Ps 98,9d angeregt ist, oder das Kolon geht auf eine Hand zurück, die einen makrostrukturellen Bezug nach Ps 9,9 herstellen wollte, wo die engste sprachliche Parallele zu Ps 96,10c vorliegt; da Ps 9 ein junger Psalm ist, der erst nachträglich zusammen mit Ps 10 in seinen jetzigen Kontext eingefügt wurde, erscheint mir die zweite Alternative als wahrscheinlicher.

| Ps 100 | Ps 95 96 98 | Ps 93 |
|---|---|---|
| 1b | 98,4a | 1b |
| 2a | | 1c |
| 2b | 95,6ab; 96,8b | 1d |
| 3a | 95,7a | 3a |
| 3b | 95,6b | 3b |
| 3c | 95,7bc | 3c |
| 4a | 95,2a | 4a |
| 4b | 96,8b | 4b |
| 4c | 96,2a | 4c |
| 5a | | 5a |
| 5b | 98,3a | 5b |
| 5c | 98,3a; 56,13b | 5c |

(d) Daß die ursprüngliche JHWH-König-Psalmen-Komposition nur Ps 93* 95* 96* 98 100 umfaßt, legt sich auch von Ps 100 her nahe. Ps 100 besteht ja fast ausschließlich aus Zitaten der vorangehenden JHWH-König-Psalmen.[54] Keines dieser Zitate stammt aber aus Ps 94 97 99 und darüber hinaus bezieht sich Ps

---

[53] Entweder bestimmt man V 10 als Trikolon, dann paßt V 10c inhaltlich nicht zu V 10ab, oder man bestimmt V 10c als Monokolon, dann ist dies angesichts der ansonsten konsequenten Bikola-Technik in Ps 96 singulär.

[54] Vgl. den detaillierten Nachweis bei J. Jeremias, „Ps 100 als Auslegung von Ps 93–100," *Skrif en Kerk* 19 (1998) 605–15.

100 auch nicht auf Ps 93,5; 95,7c-11; 96,10. Die entsprechenden Zitate und Anspielungen in Ps 100 lassen sich
tabellarisch folgendermaßen zusammenfassen:

Während es zwischen Ps 100 und Ps 95* 96* 98 semantische
Bezüge gibt, liegen die Bezüge zwischen Ps 100 und Ps 93 „nur" auf
formaler Ebene, insofern Ps 100 durchgehend Trikola verwendet. Eine
vergleichbare Trikola-Struktur weist nur noch Ps 93 auf. Allerdings
gibt es hier einen wichtigen Unterschied, der zugleich entstehungsgeschichtlich relevant ist. Während die drei Trikola Ps 93,1bcd.
3abc.4abc die „klassische" Form bieten, stellen die Trikola in Ps 100
(und ebenso das in Ps 93 sekundäre Trikolon Ps 93,5abc) nur eine
Nachahmung dieser klassischen Form dar.[55] Diese Beobachtung zur
Trikolatechnik bedeutet entstehungsgeschichtlich, daß Ps 100 jünger
ist als Ps 93,1-4 und diese poetische Technik offensichtlich nachahmt,
um seine kompositionelle Korrespondenz als Schlußpsalm zu Ps 93,1-
4 als Anfangspsalm der Komposition Ps 93* 95* 96* 98 100 zu unter-
streichen.

(3) Die Komposition Ps 93* 95* 96* 98 100 ist als eine frühnach-
exilische Kantate für die Tempelliturgie, wahrscheinlich für das im
Herbst gefeierte JHWH-König-Fest, entstanden und kann insgesamt
als eine Transformation der JHWH-König-Theologie von Ps 93 und
von Ps 29 verstanden werden.

Ansatzpunkt für diese These sind die beiden Psalmen 96 und 98.
Schon vielfach wurde betont, daß die beiden Psalmen „so eng miteinander verwandt [sind], daß sie nur zusammen ausgelegt werden
können".[56] Beide Psalmen haben, wie oben bereits skizziert, die
gleiche dreiteilige Aufforderungs-Struktur mit dem jeweils sich
ausweitenden Adressatenkreis (Israel: 96,2-6*; 98,1-5; Völker: 96,7-
10*; 98,4-6; Kosmos: 96,11-13; 98,7-9; 96,1 ist eine Art zusammen-

---

[55] So im Anschluß an J. Jeremias, *Psalm 100* (1998). In der „klassischen"
Form bilden die ersten beiden Zeilen durch wörtliche Wiederholung einen
repetierenden Parallelismus und die dritte Zeile steigert dann zur „klimaktischen"
Hauptaussage (z.B. Ps 93,1bcd: „Mit Hoheit *ist er bekleidet. Bekleidet ist* JHWH.
Mit Macht hat er sich umgürtet"). Demgegenüber hat bei den „modernen" Trikola
von Ps 100 die erste Zeile die Hauptaussage und die typischen Wort-
wiederholungen fehlen (z.B. Ps 100, 1b.2ab: „Jauchzet JHWH [im Königsjubel]
zu, du ganze Erde! Dienet JHWH mit Freude! Geht hinein vor sein Angesicht mit
Jubel!").

[56] J. Jeremias, *Königtum Gottes* (1987) 131.

fassende Vorwegnahme des ganzen Psalms!) Beide Psalmen sind vor allem in ihrem Anfang und im Schlußteil weitgehend wörtlich identisch. Allerdings dürfen auch die Unterschiede zwischen beiden Psalmen nicht übersehen werden. Ich nenne hier nur jene Differenzen, die interpretatorisch besonders relevant sind:

(a) In ihrem ersten Teil unterscheiden sich die beiden Psalmen nicht nur darin, daß Ps 98 nur eine einzige imperativische Aufforderung hat (98,1a), an die sich eine lange mit כי eingeleitete Begründung / Explikation anschließt (98,1b-3), während Ps 96 fünf Imperative bietet (96,1-3) und erst dann die mit כי eingeführte Begründung / Explikation folgen läßt. Besonders auffallend (und mit Konsequenzen für das Gesamtverständnis der Psalmen) ist, daß Ps 96,4.6 nur in Nominalsätzen formulierte zeitstufenneutrale bzw. zeitlos gültige Wesens- bzw. Zustandsaussagen über JHWH bringt, während Ps 98,1b-3 eine Kette von Verbalsätzen mit Suffixkonjugation bietet, die ein bereits geschehenes bzw. abgeschlossenes Handeln JHWHs (98,1b-2) und eine damit zusammenhängende Aktion der gesamten Erde (98,3) berichten. Das in Ps 98,1b-3 berichtete Handeln JHWHs nimmt sprachlich Verheißungen Deuterojesajas über das Ende des babylonischen Exils als Machterweis JHWHs als des Retters seines Volkes Israel vor dem Forum der Völkerwelt auf und konstatiert die Erfüllung dieser Verheißungen als Anlaß für Israel, für und über JHWH ein „neues Lied" zu singen. Demgegenüber ist der Inhalt des „neuen Liedes", das Israel nach 96,2-6* singen soll, JHWHs כבוד, seine Überlegenheit über alle Götter und seine machtvolle Präsenz in seinem Heiligtum. Der in Ps 96 wichtige Begriff כבוד fehlt in Ps 98, während umgekehrt die in Ps 98,1b-4 aufgenommenen Zitate bzw. Anspielungen aus Deuterojesaja in Ps 96 nicht begegnen.[57]

(b) Ps 96 zitiert bzw. transformiert mehrere andere Psalmen. Diese Zitate bzw. Anspielungen geben Ps 96 sein typisches Profil; diese Zitate fehlen demgegenüber in Ps 98. So wird Ps 48,2 in 96,4a und Ps 47,3 in 96,4b aufgenommen; Ps 47 und Ps 48 sind Zionspsalmen bzw. Psalmen über den auf dem Zion thronenden und wirkenden König JHWH. Der Anfang von Ps 93 wird als Text der Botschaft zitiert, die die Vertreter der Völker, die an der großen Audienz in der Tempelresidenz JHWHs teilnehmen

---

[57] Lediglich 96,2b gebraucht das Nomen ישועה wie Ps 98,2a = Jes 52,10d.

werden, ihren Nationen überbringen sollen (96,10ab = 93,1aef).
Vor allem bildet Ps 29 die strukturelle und semantische Matrix
für die beiden ersten Teile von Ps 96. Die stärkste Präsenz von
Ps 29 ist im Mittelteil von Ps 96 erkennbar. Ps 96,7-8a.9b zitiert
wörtlich Ps 29,1-2, also den ersten Teil des Theophaniepsalms
29, der die Göttersöhne zur Huldigung vor dem auf seinem
Thron sitzenden Götterkönig als Anerkenntnis der von ihm ausgehenden Macht auffordert. Diese mythische Szene wird in Ps
96 auf zweifache Weise historisiert. Zum einen werden die
Göttersöhne durch die (עמים משפחות) (96,4a) ersetzt. Und zum
anderen wird die Szene nun klar in die Höfe des Jerusalemer
Tempels verlegt (96,8b) und der Vorgang wird zugleich insofern
religions- bzw. weltpolitisch akzentuiert, als diese Vertreter der
Völker Gaben mitbringen sollen, mit denen sie sich als
„Vasallen" des Weltkönigs JHWH ausweisen (96,8b). Wenn
96,9b dann „die ganze Erde" auffordert, vor JHWHs Angesicht
zu „beben" (חיל), liegt eine Zusammenfassung von Ps 29,5-9
vor. Ps 96,3a faßt die Botschaft, die Israel den Nationen überbringen soll, mit dem entscheidenden Themawort von Ps 29
כבוד zusammen. Im übrigen läßt Ps 96 gleich an seinem Anfang
erkennen, daß er Ps 29 aufgreifen, nachahmen und aktualisieren
will. Ps 96,1-2a ahmt die Trikolonstruktur von Ps 29,1-2a = Ps
96,7-8a nach, was nicht nur an der dreimaligen Wiederholung
des gleichen Imperativs zu Beginn der einzelnen Kola erkennbar
ist, sondern auch daran, daß das dritte Kolon auf den Lobpreis
des Namens JHWHs hinausläuft. Aber Ps 96,1-2a erreicht nicht
mehr die kunstvolle Poesie des „klassischen" Trikolon (s.o.),
sondern verwendet die „moderne" Form, der wir auch schon
oben bei der Charakterisierung von Ps 100 begegnet sind. Die
drei Kola bilden keine Klimax auf das dritte Kolon hin, sondern
sind ein mehr oder weniger gleichgeordnetes Nebeneinander,
wobei vielleicht das erste Kolon mit der Ankündigung des
„neuen Liedes" sogar das Toppgewicht hat. Die „Vorlage" Ps 29
wirkt bei der Gestaltung von Ps 96 auch in V 10 insofern weiter,
als nun wie in Ps 29,10 die explizite Proklamation des kosmischen Königtums JHWHs folgt. Allerdings greift dafür Ps 96
nun auf Ps 33 zurück und macht mit dem Kurzzitat des ersten
Teils von Ps 93 deutlich, daß es sich um die Ausübung eben
jenes vorzeitlich gegebenen Königtums handelt, das dem
Erdkreis Festigkeit gibt. In Ps 29 wird die Ausübung des

Königtums JHWHs dann in V 11 mit den Gaben von עז und
שלום an JHWHs Volk expliziert (s.o.). Auch Ps 96 läßt eine Explikation folgen — nämlich in seinem 3. Teil V 11-13, der die
Klimax des Psalms ist. Dieser Teil, der einerseits weitgehend
dem dritten Teil von Ps 98 (V 7-9) wörtlich entspricht, greift
deuterojesanische Texte auf, die den Kosmos zum Jubel au-
frufen bzw. dessen Jubel darstellen, weil JHWH sich als Krieg-
sheld aufmacht, um sein Volk aus der Knechtschaft zu befreien
(vgl. Jes 42,10-13), weil JHWH seinem Volk die Trostbotschaft
verkünden ließ, daß das Exil zu Ende ist (vgl. Jes 49,13), und
wenn Berge und Hügel sowie die Bäume des Feldes sehen, daß
die Verbannten heimkehren (vgl. Jes 55,12). Mit der Aufnahme
dieser Texte weckt der Psalm also ganz bestimmte Erwartungen,
die er dann in V 13 auch erfüllt — und zugleich weiter steigert,
weil er das konkrete Ereignis, das er als Ausübung des Weltkönigtums JHWHs nennt, recht unbestimmt als „Kommen"
JHWHs benennt und die Zielsetzung dieses Kommens so formuliert, daß mit dem Kommen JHWHs ein Geschehen, das dem
Ziele dient, zwar begonnen hat, aber die Vollendung dieses Ziels
steht noch aus. Das entscheidende Ereignis, das den kosmischen
Jubel auslösen soll, nennt V 13ab gleich zweimal:

> (Es freue sich der Himmel und es juble die Erde ...)
> vor JHWH , denn er ist gekommen,
>  denn er ist gekommen, um zu richten die Erde:
> Er richtet (wird richten) den Erdkreis in Gerechtigkeit
>  und die Völker in seiner Verläßlichkeit / Treue (96,13).

Daß hier כי בא zweimal steht, während Ps 98,9 den ki-Satz nur
einmal hat, muß nicht zu einer literarkritischen Operation
führen. Die Wiederholung bedeutet hier vielmehr eine Akzen-
tuierung, so wie ja auch das Verbum שפט in V 13b und V 13c
zweimal gesetzt wird, um die Klimax zu betonen. Zum rechten
Verständnis von V 13 sind drei Beobachtungen wichtig:

- Die Suffixkonjugation בא in V 13ab bezeichnet einen individuellen Sachverhalt der Vergangenheit, muß also wie
  oben übersetzt werden: „er ist gekommen".[58] Die Aussage

---

[58] So auch J. Jeremias, *Königtum Gottes* (1987) 130:
Ist Jahwes Kommen ... prägnant zu deuten, ist schlechterdings nicht einzusehen, warum all mir zugänglichen Kommentare (mit der bemerkenswerten Ausnahme von Kissane) das hebräische Perfekt (anders als etwa

bezieht sich also auf ein einmaliges, bestimmtes Ereignis, das auf der Weltbühne stattgefundenn hat und deshalb vom Kosmos bejubelt werden kann bzw. soll.

- Da Ps 98 auf der Textebene, um die es uns hier zunächst geht, die unmittelbare Fortsetzung von Ps 96,13 ist, wird dort im ersten Teil V 1-4 mit der (gegenüber Ps 96,2-6 auffallenden: s.o.) Kette der Suffixkonjugationen das mit dem „Kommen" JHWHs in 96,13 gemeinte Ereignis konkretisiert: Es ist die „dem Haus Israel" (98,3) aus Güte und aus Verläßlichkeit[59] von JHWH erwirkte Rettung aus dem Exil – „vor dem Angesicht der Völker".

- Mit dieser Rettung des Hauses Israel hat nun aber jenes Geschehen begonnen, das Ps 96,13 (und analog Ps 98,9) mit dem Verbum שפט bezeichnet. Dieses Verbum ist nicht nur der „Schlüsselbegriff der beiden Psalmen 96 und 98", an dessen „Verständnis … schlechterdings alles [hängt]",[60] das Verbum faßt m.E. sogar die Leitidee der gesamten Komposition Ps 93* 95* 96* 98 100 zusammen. Wie auch Ps 82 zeigt, wo שפט ebenfalls Schlüsselbegriff ist, hat das Verbum ein breites Bedeutungsspektrum, das u.a. die Tätigkeiten „einen Prozeß führen bzw. leiten, ein Urteil sprechen und vollziehen, jemandem zu seinem Recht verhelfen, die Rechtsordnung autoritativ durchsetzen, regieren" umfaßt. J. Jeremias bringt die in Ps 96 und 98 gemeinte Bedeutung so auf den Punkt: „שפט bezeichnet kein regelmäßiges, sondern ein ordnungsstiftendes Eingreifen Jahwes, das dann notwendig wird, wenn die Ordnung der Welt gefährdet oder gar teilweise zerstört ist".[61] Da nach der in Ps 96 und 98 vorausgesetzten Theologie Deutero-

---

in Dtn 33,2) im Gefolge der LXX präsentisch wiedergeben (›... denn er kommt, ja kommt‹). In dem oft mit Recht als Sachparallele zitierten Vers Jes 40,10 steht nicht zufällig das Imperfekt יבוא! Allenfalls könnte man in Ps 96,13 ב א als Partizip auffassen, müßte dann freilich genauer übersetzen: ›... denn er ist dabei, die Erde zu richten ...‹ Wahrscheinlicher ist mir vom Kontext her — der ganze Psalm läuft auf V.13 zu — der perfektive Aspekt.

[59] חסד steht in der Komposition 93* 95* 96* 98 100 nur in 98,3 und 100,5; אמונה steht in 96,13d; 98,3 – und ist das letzte Wort der Komposition Ps 93–100!

[60] Jeremias, *Königtum Gottes* (1987) 128.

[61] Jeremias, *Königtum Gottes* (1987) 129.

jesajas das Ende des Exils durch den Perserkönig Kyrus vom Weltkönig JHWH, der sich seines „Gesalbten" Kyrus zur Durchsetzung *seiner* Königsherrschaft zum Wohl Israels bediente, ein „weltpolitisches" Ereignis war, wird verständlich, daß die Komposition 93–100* auf der Basis der „alten" JHWH-KönigTheologie von Ps 93,1-4 und von Ps 29 zu der Sicht gelangen konnte, mit der von JHWH inspirierten Religionspolitik der Perser habe die definitive Durchsetzung einer friedlichen Weltordnung begonnen — die ihr Fundament darin hätte, daß alle Völker JHWH als ihren Großkönig anerkennen.

(c) Da nach Ps 96,13 und Ps 98,9 der in Gang gesetzte Prozeß der Wiederherstellung der Ordnung des friedlichen Zusammenlebens der Völker mit dem Ende des Exils und der Wiedererrichtung des Tempels als der Königsresidenz JHWHs in dieser Welt zwar schon begonnen hat, aber eben noch nicht vollendet ist, lassen die Schöpfer der Komposition Ps 93–100* auf Ps 96 98 nun Ps 100 folgen, der die Vision der feierlichen Aussöhnung „der ganzen Erde" vor dem Weltkönig JHWH mit der Übernahme der entsprechenden Verpflichtungen (100,2a: עבדו את־יהוה) entwirft.

(d) Die skizzierte Abfolge der Psalmen 93* 95* 96* 98 100 läßt sich als eine „Kantate" begreifen, die ihren Sitz im Leben am Zweiten Tempel hatte und das Weltkönigtum JHWHs mit der Vision verband, daß er die Macht seines כבוד als Chaosbekämpfer und als Beschützer seines Volkes Israel als großer „Aussöhner" verwirklichen werde[62] — wie dies analog in der wohl zeitgleich entstandenen Vision Mi 4,1-5 gezeichnet wird.[63] Auf dieser Ebene wäre die Komposition Ps 93* 95*

---

[62] Dieses Gesamtkonzept spricht m.E. auch gegen die *a priori* durchaus vorstellbare Annahme, Ps 96 und 98 seien nicht Rezipienten von Jes 40–55, sondern Spendertexte, wie dies H. Leene, „Psalm 98 and Deutero-Isaiah: Linguistic Analogies and Literary Affinity," in: R. F. Poswick (Hrsg.), *Actes du quatrième Colloque International Bible et Informatique, Amsterdam, 15-18 août 1994* (Paris: Champion, 1995) 313–40, vorschlägt.

[63] Ich gehe davon aus, daß Mi 4,1-5 frühnachexilisch ist und daß Jes 2,1-5 ein aus Mi 4 nach Jes 2 transponierter bzw. transformierter Text ist: vgl. dazu vor allem Schwienhorst-Schönberger, L. „Zion—Ort der Tora. Überlegung zu Mi 4,1-3," in: F. Hahn u.a. (Hrsg.), *Zion—Ort der Begegnung. FS. L. Klein* (BBB 90; Bodenheim: Philo, 1993) 107–125.

96* 98 100 der Text einer Tempelliturgie bzw. ein Ritual, das
JHWH hymnisch feiert und ihn beschwört, diese im Ritual
gefeierte Königsherrschaft endlich Wirklichkeit werden zu
lassen.

## DIE KOMPOSITION PS 93–100 ALS ABSCHLUSS EINES PSALTERS PS 2–100*: VOM RITUAL ZUR POESIE

Wenigstens skizzenhaft soll eine weitere Transformation des „alten" Psalms 29 beschrieben werden, die mit jenem Prozeß verbunden
war, der die Tempelkantate Ps 93* 95* 96* 98 100 durch die Einfügung der Psalmen 94 97 99 sowie durch die Ergänzungen Ps 93,5;
95,7d-11; 96,5 bearbeitete und diese neue JHWH-König-Psalmen-
Komposition an den Schluß eines „theokratischen Psalters" Ps 2–100*
setzte, der als Fortschreibung bzw. Uminterpretation des „messianischen Psalters" Ps 2–89[64] konzipiert war — nicht für die Rezitation in der Liturgie, sondern als theologisches „Lesebuch".

(1) Durch die Einfügung von Ps 94 97 99 verändert sich das
„Gerichtshandeln" JHWHs und insbesondere die Rolle der Völker
bzw. das Verhältnis JHWHs zu den Völkern. Die Neuakzentuierung
wird sofort am Anfang von Ps 94 deutlich, wo JHWH zwar den Titel
שפט הארץ erhält, aber im Kontext von der zweifach vorangestellten
Gottesprädikation אל נקמות.

(2) Der gezielt zwischen die Abfolge Ps 96 und 98 (s.o.) gesetzte
Psalm 97 gibt dem in Ps 96 und 98 konstatierten „Kommen" JHWHs
als dem rettenden Eingreifen JHWHs zugunsten Israels die drama-
tische Perspektive einer Vernichtungstheophanie. Dabei greift Ps 97
wie Ps 96 seinerseits den „alten" JHWH-König-Psalm 29 und die
JHWH-König-Psalmen bzw. Zionspsalmen 46 47 48 auf, gibt diesen
Bezügen aber nun eine andere Tendenz. Die in Ps 97,7c mit Anspielung auf Ps 29,1-2 geschilderte Proskynese der Götter der Völker vor
dem im Feuer gekommenen JHWH ist eine massive Ironisierung: Die
„Götter" werfen sich „huldigend" nieder vor jenem JHWH, der eben
ihre Diener vernichtet hat, weil die Diener von „Götzenbildern" und

---

[64] Zum Konzept und zur zeitgeschichtlichen Situierung des „messianischen
Psalters" vgl. E. Zenger, „‚Es sollen sich niederwerfen vor ihm alle Könige,' (Ps
72,11). Redaktionsgeschichtliche Beobachtungen zu Psalm 72 und zum Pro-
gramm des messianischen Psalters Ps 2–89," in: E. Otto & E. Zenger (Hrsg.),
„Mein Sohn bist du" (Ps 2,7). Studien zu den Königspsalmen (SBS 192; Stuttgart:
Katholisches Bibelwerk, 2002) 66–93.

„Gott-Nichtsen" sind. Von Ps 29 her erhalten darüber hinaus mehrere Einzelzüge in Ps 97 ihre besondere Pointe: die Theophaniebilder in Ps 97,1-9 kann man als Transformation des Mittelteils von Ps 29 (d.h. Ps 29,3-9) lesen. Daß die Völker in Ps 97,6 den vernichtenden kabod JHWHs schauen und nicht, wie Ps 98,3cd sagt, die Rettung Israels, erhält ebenfalls von Ps 29,2.3.9 her ein besonderes Gewicht. Schließlich läßt sich Ps 97,10-12 als „Exegese" und Applikation von Ps 29,11 begreifen. Die in Ps 97 dominierende Götterpolemik bzw. Entdivinisierung der „Götter" hat diese Redaktion nachräglich auch in Ps 96 durch V 5 eingetragen.

(3) Sowohl durch Ps 97, aber insbesondere durch Ps 99 wird die Botschaft vom Weltkönigtum JHWHs im Unterschied zur vorgegebenen „Tempelkantate" stärker futurisiert bzw. „eschatologisiert", aber zugleich auch stärker mit der kanonischen Ursprungsgeschichte Israels verwoben.

(4) Diese Rückbindung der Theologie von der Königsherrschaft JHWHs an die kanonische Geschichte Israels hängt auch mit der neuen Funktion zusammen, die Ps 93–100 als Fortschreibung des „messianischen" Psalters Ps 2–89 erhalten hat. Der gerade in dessen Schlußpsalm 89 beklagten Ohnmacht bzw. „Treulosigkeit" JHWHs setzt die Komposition die Botschaft von der Macht des Weltkönigs JHWH und von seiner „Verläßlichkeit" entgegen. Diese wird, wie die als Verbindungsstück eingefügte Teilkomposition Ps 90–92 entfaltet, nicht mehr nur, wie dies die Tempelkantate Ps 93* 95* 96* 98 100 tat, in der offiziellen Tempelliturgie „gegenwärtig" gesetzt, sondern auch fern vom Tempel, durch die individuelle ethische Realisierung der Gerechtigkeitsordnung JHWHs oder eben durch die poetische Inszenierung im Rezitieren des Psalters Ps 2–100 bzw. besonders seines programmatischen Abschlusses Ps 93–100.

## VERWENDETE LITERATUR

Adam, K.-P. *Der königliche Held. Die Entsprechung von kämpfendem Gott und kämpfendem König in Psalm 18* (WMANT 91; Neukirchen-Vluyn: Neukirchener, 2001).

Diehl, J. F., A. Diesel, A. & A. Wagner. „Von der Grammatik zum Kerygma. Neue grammatische Erkenntnisse und ihre Bedeutung für das Verständnis der Form und des Gehalts von Psalm XXIX," *VT* 49 (1999) 462–86.

Ego, B. „Von der Jerusalemer Tempeltheolgie zur rabbinischen Kosmologie. Zur Konzeption der himmlischen Wohnstatt Gottes," in: *Mitteilungen und Beiträge 12/13 Forschungsstelle Judentum* (Leipzig: Thomas, 1997) 36–52.

—. „Die Wasser der Gottesstadt. Zu einem Motiv der Zionstradition und seinen kosmologischen Implikationen," in: B. Ego & B. Janowski (Hrsg.), *Das biblische Weltbild und seine altorientalischen Kontexte* (FAT 32; Tübingen: Mohr Siebeck, 2001) 361–89.

Fodor, J. S. *Psalm 95 und die verwandten Psalmen 81 und 50. Eine exegetische Studie* (Theos 32; Hamburg: Verlag Dr. Kovac, 1999).

Gross, W. *Doppelt besetztes Vorfeld. Syntaktische, pragmatische und übersetzungstechnische Studien zum althebräischen Verbalsatz* (BZAW 305; Berlin: de Gruyter, 2001).

Hartenstein, F. *Die Unzugänglichkeit Gottes im Heiligtum. Jesaja 6 und der Wohnort JHWHs in der Jerusalemer Kulttradition* (WMANT 75; Neukirchen-Vluyn: Neukirchener, 1997).

Hossfeld, F.-L. & E. Zenger. *Die Psalmen I. Psalm 1–50* (NEchBAT; Würzburg: Echter, 1993).

—. *Die Psalmen II. Psalmen 51–100* (2.Aufl., HThKAT; Freiburg: Herder, 2001).

—. „Psalmenauslegung im Psalter, " in: R. G. Kratz u.a. (Hrsg.), *Schriftauslegung in der Schrift. FS O. H. Steck* (BZAW 300; Berlin & New York: de Gruyter, 2000) 237–57.

—. „Ps 89 und das vierte Psalmenbuch (Ps 90–106)," in: E. Otto & E. Zenger (Hrsg.), *„Mein Sohn bist du" (Ps 2,7). Studien zu den Königspsalmen* (SBS 192; Stuttgart: Katholisches Bibelwerk, 2002) 173–83.

Janowski, B. „Das biblische Weltbild. Eine methodologische Skizze," in: B. Ego & B. Janowski (Hrsg.), *Das biblische Weltbild und seine altorientalischen Kontexte* (FAT 32; Tübingen: Mohr Siebeck, 2001) 3–26.

—. „Das verborgene Angesicht Gottes. Psalm 13 als Muster eines Klagelieds des einzelnen," *JBTh* 16 (2001) 25–53.

—. „Die heilige Wohnung des Höchsten. Kosmologische Implikationen der Jerusalemer Tempeltheologie," in: O. Keel & E. Zenger (Hrsg.), *Gottesstadt und Gottesgarten. Zu Geschichte und Theologie des Jerusalemer Tempels* (QD 191; Freiburg: Herder, 2001) 24–68.

—. „Dankbarkeit. Ein anthropologischer Grundbefriff im Spiegel der Toda-Psalmen," in: E. Zenger (Hrsg.), *Rituel und Poesie. Formen und Orte religiöser Dichtung im Alten Orient, im Judentum und im Christentum* (HBS 36; Freiburg: Herder, 2003) 91–136.

Jenni, E. *Die hebräischen Präpositionen. Band 1: Die Präposition Beth* (Stuttgart: Kohlhammer, 1992).

Jeremias, J. *Das Königtum Gottes in den Psalmen. Israels Begegnung mit dem kanaanäischen Mythos in den JHWH-König-Psalmen* (FRLANT 141; Göttingen: Vandenhoeck & Ruprecht, 1987).

—. „Ps 100 als Auslegung von Ps 93–100," *Skrif en Kerk* 19 (1998) 605–15.

Klingbeil, M. *Yahweh Fighting from Heaven. God as Warrior and as God of Heaven in the Hebrew Psalter and Ancient Near Eastern Iconography* (OBO

169; Fribourg & Göttingen: Vandenhoeck & Ruprecht, 1999).

Köckert, M. „Die Theophanie des Wettergottes Jahwe in Psalm 18," in: Th. Richter, D. Prechtel & J. Klinger (Hrsg.), *Kulturgeschichten. FS V. Haas* (Saarbrücken: Saarbrücker Druckerei und Verlag, 2001) 209–26.

Lang, B. *Jahwe, der biblische Gott. Ein Porträt* (München: Beck, 2002).

Leene, H. „Psalm 98 and Deutero-Isaiah: Linguistic Analogies and Literary Affinity," in: R. F. Poswick (Hrsg.), *Actes du quatrième Colloque International Bible et Informatique, Amsterdam, 15-18 août 1994* (Paris: Champion, 1995) 313–40.

—. „The Coming of YHWH as King. The Contemporary Chracter of Psalms 96 and 98," in: J. W. Dyk et al. (Hrsg.), *Unless Some One Guide Me ... FS K. A. Deurloo* (Amsterdamse Cahiers Sup 2; Maastricht: Shaker, 2001) 211–28.

Lohfink, N. & E. Zenger. *Der Gott Israels und die Völker. Untersuchungen zum Jesajabuch und zu den Psalmen* (SBS 154; Stuttgart: Katholisches Bibelwerk, 1994).

Loretz, O. *Ugarit-Texte und Thronbesteigungspsalmen. Die Metamorphose des Regenspenders Baal-Jahwe (Ps 24,7-10; 29; 47; 93; 95–100 sowie Ps 77,17-20; 114)* (UBL 7; Münster: Ugarit-Verlag, 1988).

Macholz, Ch. „Psalm 100—Israels Toda-Feier mit den Völkern," in: B. Huwyler u.a. (Hrsg.), *Prophetie und Psalmen. FS K. Seybold* (AOAT 280; Münster: Manfried Dietrich & Oswald Loretz, 2001) 143–62.

Müller, H.-P. „,Jhwh gebe seinem Volke Kraft.' Zum Hintergrund der alttestamentlichen Geschichtsreligion," *ZThK* 98 (2001) 265–81.

—. „Formgeschichtliche und sprachliche Beobachtungen zu Psalm 30," *ZAH* 12 (1999) 192–201.

Otto, E. & Zenger, E. (Hrsg.). *„Mein Sohn bist du," (Ps 2,7). Studien zu den Königspsalmen* (SBS 192; Stuttgart: Katholisches Bibelwerk, 2002).

Prinsloo, W. S. „Psalm 95. If Only You Will Listen To His Voice!," in: M. D. Carroll, D. Clines & Ph. R. Davies (Hrsg.), *The Bible in Human Society. FS J. Rogerson* (JSOTSup 200; Sheffield: Sheffield Academic Press, 1995) 395–410.

Schnocks, J. *Vergänglichkeit und Gottesherrschaft. Studien zu Psalm 90 und dem vierten Psalmenbuch* (BBB 140; Berlin: Philo) 2002.

Schwienhorst-Schönberger, L. „Zion—Ort der Tora. Überlegung zu Mi 4,1-3," in: F. Hahn u.a. (Hrsg.), *Zion—Ort der Begegnung. FS. L. Klein* (BBB 90; Bodenheim: Philo, 1993) 107–125.

Seidl, Th. „Scheltwort der Befreiungsrede. Eine Deutung der deuteronomistischen Paränese für Israel in Ps 95,7c-11," in: H. Keul & H.-J. Sander (Hrsg.), *Das Volk Gottes. Ein Ort der Befreiung E. Klinger* (Würzburg: Echter, 1998) 107–120.

Seybold, K. „Psalm 29. Redaktion und Rezeption," in: ders., *Studien zur Psalmenauslegung* (Stuttgart: Kohlhammer, 1998) 85–111.

Spieckermann, H. *Heilsgegenwart. Eine Theologie der Psalmen* (FRLANT 148; Göttingen: Vandenhoeck & Ruprecht, 1989).

—. „Stadtgott und Gottesstadt. Beobachtungen im Alten Orient und im Alten Testament," *Bib* 73 (1992) 1–31.

Theißen, G. *Die Religion der ersten Christen. Eine Theorie des Urchristentums* (Gütersloh: Gütersloher Verlagshaus, 2000).

Zenger, E. „Königpsalmen," *NBL* 2 (1995) 510–13.

—. „‚Es sollen sich niederwerfen vor ihm alle Könige,‘ (Ps 72,11). Redaktionsgeschichtliche Beobachtungen zu Psalm 72 und zum Programm des messianischen Psalters Ps 2–89," in: E. Otto & E. Zenger (Hrsg.), *„Mein Sohn bist du" (Ps 2,7). Studien zu den Königspsalmen* (SBS 192; Stuttgart: Katholisches Bibelwerk, 2002) 66–93.

—. „Psalm 29 als hymnische Konstituierung einer Gegenwelt," in: K. Kiesow & Th. Meurer (Hrsg.), *Textarbeit. Studien zu Texten und ihrer Rezeption aus dem Alten Testament und der Umwelt Israels. FS P. Weimar* (AOAT 294; Münster: Manfried Dietrich & Oswald Loretz, 2002) 569–83.

PART FOUR


TEXTUAL HISTORY AND RECEPTION
IN JUDAISM AND CHRISTIANITY

# SEPTUAGINTAL EXEGESIS AND THE SUPERSCRIPTIONS
# OF THE GREEK PSALTER

## ALBERT PIETERSMA

Some years ago I had occasion to write a review of Joachim Schaper's, *Eschatology in the Greek Psalter*.[1] In that review I took exception to Schaper's view on a number of, what I perceived to be, fundamental issues in Septuagintal exegesis. In this essay I would like to continue that discussion, not so much *contra* Schaper as in the larger context of Septuagintal hermeneutics.

In the broadest of terms one tends to find the field divided between "minimalists," on the one hand, and "maximalists," on the other. In his book Schaper takes particular aim at the so-called Finnish School of Septuagint studies, because of its propensity — so Schaper — for "not seeing the woods for the trees." He takes issue with what he regards as its essentially mechanistic view on the Greek translator's role which (to Schaper) entails that a translator is not "in any way ... influenced by his religious and cultural environment," but instead is a "mere medium."[2] I do not myself think that Schaper's assessment of the Finnish School is accurate or fair, but for my present purposes it will do as a characterization of a "minimalist" approach to exegesis in the Septuagint. Schaper's own approach, by comparison, might then be characterized as one that "does not see the trees for the woods." That is to say, the Greek translator is effectively elevated to the status of an author and his work becomes the same kind of replacement for the original as, for example, an English translation of a novel by Kazantzakis. So Schaper writes in the introduction to his book:

> We shall attempt to look at the Septuagint Psalms not merely from a phi-
> lological point of view, but also from the perspective of the history of
> ideas. Tracing the development of early Jewish eschatology ... and trying
> to assign to the Greek Psalter its proper place in this development will

---

[1] Joachim Schaper, *Eschatology in the Greek Psalter* (WUNT 2.Reihe 76; Tübingen: Mohr Siebeck, 1995). For my review, see *Bibliotheca Orientalis* 54 (1997) 185–90.

[2] Schaper, *Eschatology*, 21.

give us a fresh view of the importance and the formative power of Septuagint texts in early Judaism.[3]

For my immediate purposes, Schaper's view will do as a characterization of a "maximalist" approach to exegeting the Septuagint,
which entails taking the Greek Psalter as a free-standing entity with its
own message, or rather a (more or less) systematically revised message from that of its Hebrew parent. Essentially the same view has
more recently been advocated by Martin Rösel regarding the book of
Genesis.[4] Both Ronald S. Hendel[5] and William P. Brown[6] have raised
strong objection to Rösel's view.

As I see it, the lines between so-called maximalist and minimalist
approaches are increasingly being drawn more sharply, even though
each side maintains that it recognizes the legitimacy in the other's position. So, for example, in the Rösel versus Hendel & Brown debate,
Rösel recognizes that some of the differences between MT and LXX
are textual rather than interpretational. Similarly both Brown and especially Hendel are quite prepared to grant that the LXX is our earliest
commentary on the Hebrew Bible. The crucial question is, When does
the translated text give evidence for one or the other? Rösel is, of
course, correct in emphasizing that each book must in principle be approached differently, since each translator may be expected to have
had his own *modus operandi*. Although a meticulous investigation of
the translational character of each book or translation unit may then
give somewhat different results for different units, that scarcely
means, that we should not try to develop a comprehensive explanatory
framework within which variation can be accounted for and linguistic
oddities (as well as beauty) can be accommodated, both among books
and within books. Such an investigation, however, must clearly deal
with textual variants and translational variants at the same time, without confusing them. Hence, methodologically Schaper and Rösel
should join forces, so to speak, with "the Finnish School" and Brown
and Hendel. In short, the (translated) Septuagint needs to be placed

---

[3] Schaper, *Eschatology*, 6.

[4] M. Rösel, "The Text-Critical Value of Septuagint-Genesis," *BIOSCS* 31
(1998) 62–70.

[5] R. S. Hendel, "On the Text-Critical Value of Septuagint Genesis: A Reply to
Rösel," *BIOSCS* 32 (1999) 31–34.

[6] W. P. Brown, "Reassessing the Text-Critical Value of the Septuagint-Genesis
1: A Response to Martin Rösel," *BIOSCS* 32 (1999) 35–39.

within the emerging discipline of Translation Studies, and more particularly within Descriptive Translation Studies as a branch of that discipline.

## THE CONSTITUTIVE CHARACTER OF THE TRANSLATED TEXT

On the subject of Descriptive Translation Studies (hereafter DTS) I am heavily indebted to the work of Gideon Toury, one of the leading scholars in the field.[7] Within the DTS branch of Translation Studies, according to Toury, three approaches can be used to address three distinct but interdependent aspects of any translation. This is of importance, since the position a translation is intended to occupy within the recipient culture, or sub-culture, has a direct bearing on both the textual-linguistic make-up of that translation as well as on the strategies by which a target text is derived from its original. Secondly, he notes the process-oriented approach, which focuses on the process through which a translation is derived from its parent text, and thirdly, the product-oriented approach which seeks to delineate its textual-linguistic make-up along with the relationships which hold target text and source text together. Great emphasis is placed by Toury on the interdependence of all three aspects, that is to say, function determines product and process but it is equally true that each determines the other in a bi-directional manner. It may be useful to reproduce here Toury's graphic representation (slightly expanded) but to remember that the arrows in it can be made to point in either direction.

The (prospective) systemic position & function
of a translation
(function)

determines

↓

its appropriate surface realization
(= textual-linguistic make-up)
(product)

governs

↓

the strategies whereby a target text (or parts thereof)
is derived from its original, and hence the
relationships which hold them together
(process)

---

[7] G. Toury, *Descriptive Translation Studies and Beyond* (Amsterdam and Philadelphia: Benjamins, 1995)

Since the Septuagint (for the most part) is a translation, Toury's study would seem to be directly applicable to the study of the Septuagint. It is not my purpose here to deal with this issue in any detail but simply to note a few of the major implications. If Toury's delineation of descriptive translational studies is correct, it follows that the three interdependent aspects he delineates, namely, the position or function of the Septuagint in the Alexandrian Jewish community, the process by which it was derived from its source text, and the relationships it bears to its Hebrew (and Aramaic) source text, comprise its constitutive character. Differently put one might say that function, product and process are embedded in the text as a verbal-object of the target culture that produced it. This thought was already adumbrated, apart from Toury's delineation, in Cameron Boyd-Taylor's article of 1999, where he wrote,

> When a translated text is considered with respect to the historical enterprise which gave rise to it, its originating Sitz im Leben, it becomes readily apparent that the verbal character of the document will to some extent reflect the socio-linguistic practices proper to the larger cultural undertaking of which it was a part. We might call this aspect of the text its constitutive character.[8]

In a sentence, it can be stated that the constitutive character of the Septuagint is its interlinearity, that is, its character as a translated text with a pronounced vertical dimension that ties it closely to its original. It is therefore the constitutive character of the text that places constraints on how that text can be interpreted responsibly. Thus what is being advocated here is a theoretically principled approach to the entire text with clear-cut methodological implications and parameters.

Toury further argues that by definition a translation is target-oriented, that is to say, any and every translation answers a felt need within the host or target culture or sub-culture, and is cloaked in the language of that culture. Thus from this perspective even so-called source-oriented translating is fundamentally catered to the target culture and hence at heart target-oriented (for example, the Greek of the Septuagint remains Greek no matter how Hebraized it might be perceived to be). He writes,

---

[8] C. Boyd-Taylor, "A Place in the Sun: The Interpretative Significance of LXX-Psalm 18:5c," *BIOSCS* 31 (1998) 73. This entire article is an excellent piece of exegesis along the lines suggested in this essay. For constitutive character see further NETS xiii–xiv.

in an almost tautological way it could be said that, in the final analysis, a translation is a fact of whatever sector [of the target culture] it is found to be a fact of, i.e., that (sub)system which proves to be best equipped to account for it: function, product and underlying process.[9]

Again let me bring the Septuagint into the picture. For the Septuagint I take this to mean that the most secure way of placing it within Hellenistic Greek culture, within Alexandrian Jewish Greek culture (as a sub-system thereof), within a certain sector of Alexandrian Jewish Greek culture (e.g. worship, law or education), is through an analysis of the text itself by means of the three interdependent approaches Toury has delineated: function, product and process. So, for example, if we find that the translated text in numerous ways is tied to its original and might be said to have a pronounced vertical dimension, which involves a good deal of negative transfer from the source text, that is, violations of the linguistic code of the target language, that should tell us something about its original function. If, on the other hand, we uncover few instances of negative transfer, hence few if any violations of the linguistic code of the target language but instead perhaps a measure of literary beauty, that too should reveal something of its original position within the Jewish community. In other words a text written in vulgar Greek and in translationese points presumably in a different direction from a text that is written with literary beauty and rhetorical flourish. But more importantly for my present purpose, such things have a direct bearing on the question of interpretation and exposition within it. The constitutive character of a translated text dictates its own hermeneutics.

## SOME NECESSARY DISTINCTIONS

As it happens the title chosen by the editors of the current volume provides me with a suitable point to continue. It reads *The Book of Psalms: Composition and Reception*. I read that to mean that the composition of the psalms (or the book of psalms) and their reception history are, though related, nonetheless distinct issues. Thus the composing of a piece of literature is one thing but its history of interpretation is quite another. It may be, of course, that what the composer deliberately encoded in his composition and what a later interpreter decoded from that work turns out to be substantially the same thing (as far as we can tell), but that conclusion must needs be *quod est demon-*

---

[9] *Descriptive Translation Studies*, 29.

*strandum.* In other words, it cannot be presupposed but must instead be demonstrated to exist. Hence the burden of proof is on the person that believes that the two are effectively one and the same. In exactly the same way, the translating of the psalms into Greek is one thing but the reception history of the translated psalms quite another. It is this distinction, as I see it, that informs James Barr's argumentation in his book *The Semantics of Biblical Language*[10] and which he more explicitly states in his response to David Hill's criticism of his work. Barr there writes,

> He [Hill] does not make the obvious and necessary distinction between two sets of mental processes, those of the translators themselves, whose decisions about meaning were reached from the Hebrew text, and those of later readers, most of whom did not know the original ...[11]

Or to cite the general introduction to the recently published NETS translation of Psalms,

> ... just as the [textual] form of the original text differed [in principle] from its later textual descendants, so what the original translator thought his text to mean differed [in principle] from what later interpreters thought the text to mean.[12]

My central interest here is in the original translation, in distinction from later interpretations with which the text may have become endowed. Thus the operative thought here is that *one and the same text* should be assumed to have been understood differently by its originator (author, translator, or redactor) and its subsequent interpreters or exegetes. This should at once be obvious when one reminds oneself that all such activity occurs within certain cultural environments and are designed to meet certain cultural needs.[13] The NETS Introduction suggests the distinction between the Septuagint's constitutive character, on the one hand, and its reception history, on the other.

As I see it, Toury, too, makes a comparable distinction when he writes,

> ... this principle [namely, that function determines textual-linguistic make-up] does not lose any of its validity when the position occupied by a

---

[10] J. Barr, *The Semantics of Biblical Language* (Oxford: Oxford University Press, 1961; repr. London: SCM, 1983).

[11] J. Barr, "Common Sense and Biblical Language," *Biblica* 49 (1968) 379.

[12] A. Pietersma and B. Wright (eds.), *A New English Translation of the Septuagint: The Psalms* (New York and Oxford: Oxford University Press, 2000) x.

[13] Toury, *Descriptive Translation Studies*, 12.

translation in the target culture, or its ensuing functions, happen to differ from the ones it was initially 'designed' to have; e.g., when the translation of a literary work, intended to serve as a literary text too and translated in a way which should have suited that purpose, is nevertheless rejected by the target literary system, or relegated to a position which it was not designed to occupy. In fact, one task of descriptive studies in translation may well be to confront the position which is *actually* assumed by a translation with the one it was *intended* to have....[14]

Or again,

> ... significant is the possibility that translations which retain their status as facts of the target culture may nevertheless change their position in it over time. Of course, such changes can have no bearing on either the intended, or even the final position of a translation.[15]

Applied to the Septuagint, I take this to mean that its original and intended function, embedded in its linguistic make-up and in its relationships to its parent text, could have differed quite radically from the role subsequently assigned to it. More concretely let us suppose for a moment that the Septuagint did begin its existence as a study-aid for the Hebrew (thus a crib), as has been suggested elsewhere,[16] certainly as early as Aristeas its position was that of an independent text, a free standing entity, holy scripture. Likewise for the writers of the New Testament it was itself holy writ. But assuming for the sake of argument that such a development indeed took place, would one then have to conclude as well that its constitutive character had undergone a change commensurate with its change in position or status? To me that issue is scarcely subject to debate.

It was the failure to draw a distinction between the constitutive character of the Septuagint, on the one hand, and its reception history, on the other, that in my judgment vitiated much of Joachim Schaper's book on the Greek Psalter.

I proceed to make a second distinction which is fundamental to my overall argument, and that is the distinction between the original text of the Greek translation and subsequent and therefore secondary changes introduced into that Greek text. The point I wish to make is this: if one intends to focus on the original Greek text, that is, its constitutive character, in order to determine its exegetical dimension vis-

---

[14] Toury, *Descriptive Translation Studies*, 14.

[15] Toury, *Descriptive Translation Studies*, 30.

[16] E.g. *A New English Translation (NETS Psalms)*, ix.

à-vis the Hebrew parent text, whatever can be shown to be secondary to the pristine text ceases to be grist for the mill. Differently put, secondary developments in the Septuagint belong *ipso facto* to its history of textual transmission and its history of interpretation, that is, its reception history, and consequently are not part of its constitutive character. Yet again, secondary elements may tell us a great deal about how the Septuagint text was understood at some point in its long transmission history, within a certain cultural setting; they can tell us nothing about the understanding of the translator himself. As a result, the first thing a modern interpreter of the Septuagint must do is to determine what is primary and what is secondary, whether through private research or through reliance on a critical edition. Needless to say, the labels "primary" and "secondary" are not indicative of ontological status; rather they simply mark logical and chronological precedence and subsequence. Here then, the operative thought is that a given text may be added to or subtracted from, with the result that a new text, a (slightly) different entity, may be created in the process. My interest lies with the first text.

Finally under the present sub-heading, I must briefly return to Rösel, since in a recent article he has gone even farther than he did in the piece I noted earlier. Whereas in the earlier article in *BIOSCS* he already suggested, as Hendel rightly noted, that since the parent text of Septuagint Genesis and our present Hebrew text were substantially the same, where they differ must then be interpretational (rather than textual), in his article on the superscriptions of the Septuagint Psalter[17] he boldly asserts that variants in the Septuagint without external attestation should only be taken to be *textual* variants if (a) they cannot be explained as intra-textual harmonization, (b) as being linguistically motivated, or (c) as exegetically motivated. In so doing, says Rösel, "soll der Eigenwert der griechichen Übersetzung gegen oftmals naive Textkritik stärker pointiert werden." What troubles me about Rösel's assertion is not so much that it prohibits facile recourse to difference in parent text (though it seems overly restrictive), but that it seems to suggest that whatever *can be* regarded as exegetical *should be* so regarded. To be sure, Rösel's point (b) ("linguistically motivated deviation") might provide an important escape hatch; yet I read him to say that all differences between the Hebrew text and the Greek text

---

[17] M. Rösel, "Die Psalmüberschriften des Septuaginta-Psalter," in E. Zenger (ed.), *Der Septuaginta-Psalter* (Freiburg: Herder, 2001) 125–48, esp. 125.

are interpretive in nature — until proven otherwise. If that is indeed Rösel's stance, I fear that the cart is being put before the horse, and that all carts and all horses are of the same colour. Rather than working from a text's constitutive character, beginning with what Toury calls process and product, that is, its textual-linguistic make-up and the relationships of the translated text to its source, we are effectively advised to work from the outside in. This cannot be justified, it seems to me, unless one maintain that textual-linguistic make-up and relationship to the source, in other words, the vertical dimension of the translated text, have no relevance for exposition. Furthermore, it can scarcely be maintained that all interpretation is exposition or exegesis — but more on this below. In fact I would formulate the precisely opposite postulate that would run as follows: No difference between the Hebrew and the Greek texts shall be deemed exegetical, until proven so. An excellent set of eleven postulates on Septuagint exegesis has recently been developed (with graphic representation) by Frank Austermann.[18] His delineations also serve very well to place the Greek Psalter in descriptive translation studies, and thus to establish a general framework within which it should be studied. Unfortunately, Austermann's argumentation seems to have been summarily dismissed by Rösel.[19]

## TRANSLATION AS INTERPRETATION

That translation is, and can only be, interpretation rather than being simply a reproduction (of the parent text) I do not consider to be controversial.[20] If that is correct, the issue on which I want to focus cannot be *whether* interpretation occurred when the Hebrew psalms were translated into Greek but *what level of interpretation* was achieved in any given instance. And that in turn leads to a further question: Is it meaningful to count each and every level of such interpretation as exegesis or exposition? Even an elementary definition of the term in

---

[18] F. Austermann, "Thesen zur Septuaginta-Exegese am Beispiel der Untersuchung des Septuaginta-Psalters," in A. Aejmelaeus and U. Quast (eds.), *Der Septuaginta-Psalter und seine Tochterübersetzungen.* (Göttingen: Vandenhoeck & Ruprecht, 2000) 380–86. For a more discursive discussion, see Boyd-Taylor "A Place in the Sun," 71–77.

[19] M. Rösel, " Psalmüberschriften," 126–27.

[20] See, for example, Hans-Georg Gadamer, *Truth and Method* (New York: Crossroad, 1986) 345–66.

*Webster's New Twentieth Century Dictionary* (1956) suggests other-wise. According to WNTCD exegesis is: "the exposition, critical analysis, or interpretation of a word, literary passage, etc., especially of the Bible." It would thus be fair to say, it seems to me, that exege-sis, in any meaningful sense, presupposes as a minimum (a) deliber-ateness, (b) methodicalness, and (c) a goodly degree of target orient-edness. Unless all three of these are present it makes little sense, I would submit, even to begin to speak of exegesis or exposition. In what follows I will therefore argue that exegesis, since by nature it is contextual, can be said to begin only at a certain level of interpreta-tion.[21] Let me make it perfectly clear, however, that I am not denying that exposition and exegesis exist in the Septuagint. Instead my inter-est lies in ways of identifying such exposition responsibly and scien-tifically.

Though no translator can realistically choose not to interpret, he can decide whether to make his translation more source-oriented or more target-oriented. As Toury has noted, the seventies of the past century were marked by "extreme source-orientedness" and in his words the "preoccupation was mainly with the source text and with the pro-claimed protection of its 'legitimate rights'."[22] This source-orientedness is then contrasted with target-orientedness, without any suggestion that the two are mutually exclusive. In fact I have noted earlier that, for Toury, at a deeper level target-orientedness includes source-orientedness, since by definition a translation is aimed at the target culture. The terms themselves are very helpful since they tell us much about a translator's *modus operandi* and by extension at what level of interpretation one should understand him. Sebastian Brock,[23] in applying these concepts directly to Greek biblical translation from Hebrew, speaks of the difference between, on the one hand, transla-tions that bring the reader to the text and, on the other hand, transla-tions that bring the text to the reader. No doubt the most extreme ex-ample of source-orientedness within the biblical corpus is Aquila, but from Aquila one can draw concentric circles to the rest. Thus the op-erative thought here is that the degree of source- or target-orientedness

---

[21] Similarly, Webster's defines hermeneutics as "the science of interpretation, or of finding the meaning of an author's words and phrases and explaining it to others; exegesis: particularly applied to the interpretation of the Scriptures."

[22] *Descriptive Translation Studies*, 24.

[23] S. Brock, "The Phenomenon of the Septuagint," *OTS* 17 (1972) 17.

of a translation stands in direct proportion to its level of intelligibility, or lack thereof. Whereas Aquila is difficult if not impossible to understand without the help of the Hebrew, for Job it is not infrequently advisable to ignore the Hebrew.

LEVELS OF INTERPRETATION

But if it is correct, as I have suggested, that not all interpretation can be called exegesis or exposition, it will be necessary to differentiate. Accordingly, in what follows I will delineate what I have called "levels of interpretation" and illustrate each, as much as possible, with examples from the superscriptions of the Greek Psalter. My reason is simply that in an earlier article[24] on them I have already raised the question of their interpretive function, and because the superscriptions furnish me with reasonably good examples for most of what I want to illustrate. All levels or categories are, I believe, applicable to any part of the (translated) Septuagint.[25] Furthermore, as I noted earlier, Martin Rösel has written an article on the superscriptions. Since his approach to Septuagint exegesis is different from my own, I can productively interact with what he has written. As will become clear, my basic disagreement with Rösel does not lie so much in the interpretation of individual words and phrases as it does in the contextualizing that he proposes. Since exposition and exegesis are by their very nature a matter of contextualization, my interest in his article should be obvious. As an aside, I might yet note that I tend to read the superscriptions rather atomistically as a series of notes added over a long period of time.

*Level 0: "Interpretation" by Transcription*

The numbering here is deliberate since items of language transfer which I place here are not interpretational in any meaningful sense of the term, since this category is comprised not of just any transcriptions from the source language but of transcriptions that had no prior linguistic status in the target language. Thus what I have in mind here are not items like ἀλληλουιά, which in all probability had a history of

---

[24] A. Pietersma, "Exegesis and Liturgy in the Superscriptions of the Greek Psalter," in B. A. Taylor (ed.), *X Congress of the International Organization for Septuagint and Cognate Studies, Oslo, 1998* (SBLSCS 51; Atlanta: Society of Biblical Literature, 2001) 99–138.

[25] It should also be noted that to begin the levels of interpretation effectively at the word-level appropriately reflects G's segmentation of his source text.

usage in Alexandrian Jewish Greek and — if that is so — had been integrated into the living language before the translation process began, but items that were transcribed *de novo* as products of the translation process. In fact, one can place here all indeclinable, transcribed names (or any Hebrew lexemes treated as names), instances of which are furnished aplenty in the superscriptions of the Psalter. From the superscriptions which are undeniably original I include the following: Abessalom (3), Abimelech (33, 51), Aithan (88), Asaph (49, 72–82), Bersabee (50), Chousi (7), Dauid (3 *et passim*), Doek (51), Haiman (87), Idithoun (38, 61), Iemeni (7), Kore (41, 43–46, 83, 84, 86, 87), Nathan (50), Saoul (17, 51, 53, 56, 58), Soba (59). Since such transcriptions into Greek had no prior history of usage, they lacked reference in Greek. As an aside it may be of interest to note that, whereas they typically had semantic transparency in the source language, this disappeared in the process of translation. Since such items lacked reference in Greek and therefore cannot meaningfully be called interpretive, I have assigned them to Level 0.

In translation literature, apart from names, one thinks immediately of Theodotion who had a penchant for throwing the Hebrew text at his reader without translating it. Yet the phenomenon is well attested also in the Septuagint, particularly in Greek Jeremiah. Such transcriptions are, however, in short supply in the Psalter, since its translator insisted on rendering his source text into Greek, whether or not he understood it. Perhaps the best example from the superscriptions is עַל־מָחֲלַת in 53(52) and עַל־מָחֲלַת לְעַנּוֹת in 88(87), which is generally taken to refer to a tune or chanting pattern to be used with these psalms,[26] and rendered accordingly by the NRSV as "according to Mahalath" and "according to Mahalath Leannoth" respectively. The Greek translator in Psalms 52 and 87 does a bit of transcribing *and* translating. Thus in Psalm 52 he comes up with ὑπὲρ μαελεθ, and in Psalm 87 with ὑπὲρ μαελεθ τοῦ ἀποκριθῆναι, deriving עַנּוֹת from the verb עָנָה ("to answer"). Since in Gen 28:9 Maeleth is a daughter of Ishmael, it is not impossible that the Psalms translator intended a reference to that person, although the press the lady gets in Genesis 28 is not conducive to being mentioned in Psalms superscripts, nor is such a connection made by the Church Fathers,[27] who instead interpreted μαελεθ as

---

[26] M. E. Tate, *Word Biblical Commentary: Psalms 51–100* (WBC 20; Dallas: Word, 1990.)

[27] So, for example, Athanasius, *Expositiones in Psalmos* 27.248, Didymus the

χορός ("dance") or χορεία ("dancing"), gleaned from Aquila, Symmachus and Theodotion, who in turn derived it from Hebrew חול ("whirl/dance/writhe"). Of course, even if the Fathers had connected μαελεθ with Genesis 28, one would simply note it as a fact of reception history rather than of the original text. In Psalms 52 and 87, as elsewhere in the superscriptions, our translator shows no knowledge of cultic or liturgical directives. What later interpreters did with such items might be of interest, but irrelevant to the question posed here. The constitutive character of the text in Psalms 52 and 87 is clearly one of pronounced source-orientedness.

Also to be placed at Level 0 are all textual items that can readily be explained as being due to mechanical error such as misreading of Hebrew letters, haplography, dittography, and parablepsis. If that is correct, none of these can be regarded as expositional in any way.

Quite clearly, this category of "interpretation" is characterized by the highest possible degree of source-orientedness, and consequently demonstrates most vividly the vertical dimension of the translated text, that is, its highly restrictive relationship to its source.

*Level 1: Interpretation at the Word Level*

What happens here is that a lexeme of the source text (Hebrew) is replaced by a lexeme of the target text (Greek), though not necessarily integrated syntactically and therefore supplied with unmarked inflection (nominative). The difference between Levels 0 and 1 is that whereas transcriptions are without reference in the target language, items at Level 1 have an established reference. Differently put, they have meaning but as isolated words cannot be said to convey information. Thus some interpretation does indeed take place, but clearly at a very elementary and restricted level. As an eloquent example one may cite, from the so-called Kaige recension, ἐγώ εἰμι as a representation of אנכי (the long form of the 1st sing. pronoun) even when it occurs with a finite verb. From the superscriptions one may choose the less obvious ψαλμός as a rendering of מזמור. Since both apparently referred to instrumental rather than vocal music, it may well be that the difference between them was minimal, though a close correspondence of this type would have to be labeled accidental to rather than essential for this category of interpretation. Furthermore, if Hebrew זמר can refer to the playing on wind instruments and on string in-

---

Blind, *Fragmenta in Psalmos* 868, Eusebius, *Commentaria in Psalmos* 23.453, and Gregory of Nyssa, *In inscriptiones Psalmorum* 5.74.

struments together with the words, while Greek ψάλλω refers solely to string instruments, one might note that in the transfer from source to target a restriction of meaning has occurred.

That ψαλμός, since it has an established reference in Greek and as such can readily be used in syntactic constituents in explanatory contexts, is of course true, but a separate issue. In the superscriptions it is invariably made to represent מזמור, and is even used in the phrase ἐν ψαλμοῖς in Ps 4:1, where it is scarcely intelligible. What the textual-linguistic evidence suggests is a mental process that substituted ψαλμός for מזמור but not one that deliberately relabeled the piece of literature in question from a מזמור to a ψαλμός. Moreover, to the extent that it did refer to the psalm as a whole, one would in any case have to credit the source text rather than the translator. For the molding of the Greek term to fit its new use, one has to look to reception history. Though in time ψαλμός took on the meaning that "psalm" has in English and other modern languages, there is ample evidence to show that it did not yet have that meaning in Septuagintal times.[28] The point here is that in reference to the entire piece in whose superscript it appears, it is slightly odd, since the piece in question is a descriptive piece of literature rather than a musical performance on strings, and its isolate use will become even clearer presently.

Other terms in the superscriptions that fall into the same category are ᾠδή for שׁיר (Psalms 44[45], 64[65], 75[76], 95[96], 119[120], 121[122]–133[134]) (see further below), ὕμνος for נגינה (Psalms 6, 53[54], 66[67], 75[76]), στηλογραφία for מכתם (Psalms 15[16], 55[56], 56[57], 57[58], 58[59], 59[60]), αἴνεσις[29] for תהלה (32[33], 144[145], 146[147]), προσευχή for תפלה (Psalms 16[17], 101[102], 141[142]), though some of these can also be cited under my next category since they are pushed by the translator to the phrase level, without explicit warrant in the Hebrew. So, for example, the term στηλογραφία is preposed with εἰς (except in Psalm 15) to form some kind of purpose (or general reference) phrase, without explicit warrant

---

[28] See, for example, Amos 5:23. It is further of interest that the Church Fathers still contrast ψαλμός and ᾠδή as instrumental vs. vocal (e.g. Origen on Psalm 29).

[29] Rösel glosses this as "Loblied" but this can only be justified if what the Hebrew term is thought to mean ("song of praise") is superimposed on the Greek. The Greek αἴνεσις as an active verbal noun means nothing more than "praise" or "praising." Contrast, on the other hand, αἶνος in the superscriptions to Psalms 90, 92, 94.

in the Hebrew. Here I simply want to emphasize that interpretation on the word level does indeed take place but that unless such words are *newly* integrated into the context of the translated text at least at the phrase level, they can be said to have meaning but cannot fairly be said to be expositional. That some of these terms happen to make sense in reference to the entire psalm is a bonus, but not to be confused with what took place at the constitutive stage. Again, the Greek term is present as a reflex of its Hebrew counterpart and not because the translator decided that the psalm as a whole could best be so described.

Other items that belong at this level are so-called etymological renderings, that is, Greek words arrived at not because of contextual considerations within the Greek but because an unfamiliar item in the source text is linked to a familiar item and then translated into the target text, whether or not it fits the context. Jan Joosten in his article on exegesis in Greek Hosea has placed such items under the descriptive heading "Giving the Words Their Due."[30] An instance from the superscriptions is τοῦ ἀποκριθῆναι in Psalm 87(88) for לענות, although this is slightly beyond the present level. The Greek translator (hereafter G), not knowing what it means, derives it from ענה ("to answer"). As such it would have to be read as a *qal* construct infinitive with the prefixed preposition ל, indicating purpose. Thus, as is G's practice in such cases, the preposition is glossed by the Greek article in the genitive. Though the Greek infinitive happens to be passive in form, given the nature of the verb, that need not mean that it was intended to be passive in function (so *NETS*). Thus G is responsible for two items of interpretation: a) one Hebrew lexeme (לענות) is rendered into Greek; and b) a second Hebrew (מחלת) is construed as the subject of the infinitive. Since Psalm 87(88) happens to be a prayer (see ἡ προσευχή μου in v. 3) it is not impossible that v. 3 played a role in the latter process. One strongly suspects, however, that his move was purely on the word/phrase level. That his resultant text created potential for future interpretation is doubtlessly true, though the Church Fathers evidently did not make use of that potential.

Further, what should be placed on this level of interpretation is what

---

[30] J. Joosten, "Exegesis in the Septuagint Version Hosea," in J. C. de Moor (ed.), *Intertextuality in Ugarit and Israel* (OTS 40; Leiden: Brill, 1998) 62–85, esp. 72–73. Joosten's article as a whole is very useful for its grouping of phenomena and for its strictly text-based approach.

*NETS* has labeled (semantic) stereotypes, that is, Greek words woodenly paired in the process of translation with Hebrew words often as a closed equation. Since words in different languages seldom, if ever, have the same semantic range, one-to-one representation can cause problems in certain contexts. Because the superscriptions offer minimal context, no good example can be gleaned from them. One might, however, cite the חפץ– θελ- equation in Psalms. Since √חפץ includes the semantic component of "pleasure/delight" but √θελ- does not, the latter does not always smoothly fit its context (cf., for example, Ps 1:2).

Finally, what should be placed here are translated and partially translated names. From the superscriptions one can cite Ζιφαῖοι for זיפים (Psalm 53[54]), Μεσοποταμία for ארם נהרים and Συρία for ארם (59[60]), Ἰσραηλίτης for אזרחי (87[88], 88[89]), and Μωυσῆς for משה (89[90]).

Though on this level of interpretation the source text does not play as restrictive a role as on the preceding one, it remains true that it seriously interferes with the target text, even though the target language is being used. Thus the vertical dimension remains the dominant one. Characteristic at this level of interpretation is that words either have no context or stand in tension with their context. An initial way of testing whether a given item belongs to this category is to determine with what consistency it is made to represent its Hebrew counter part, and to what extent the context is simply reproduced from the source text.

A fascinating exception, although not in the superscriptions, would seem to be διάψαλμα, always used as a rendering for the Hebrew סלה but possibly coined by the translator of Psalms from the same root as ψαλμός, and functionally adjusted accordingly. Since, like Greek διαύλιον, familiar from drama as a musical interlude on the flute (αὐλός), διάψαλμα evidently indicated a musical interlude on a stringed instrument, it is never made to stand at the close of a psalm (see Psalms 3, 23[24], 45[46]).

*Level 2: Interpretation at the Phrase Level*

As the minimum unit of information it is perhaps understandable that at this level the greatest potential for maximalist interpretation comes to the fore. This is so, no doubt, because a phrase out of context or in minimal context gives inherently ambiguous information. Thus here again contextualization is the central issue. In other words, based on the linguistic make-up of the translated text how much new contextualization can legitimately be attributed to the translator? Is the context simply transferred from the source text, or is the context the creation of the translator, as a result of which the target text can be said to have a context different from that of the source? Since the superscriptions of the Psalter are especially rich in phrases, my discussion here will be disproportionately long, though still only illustrative.

*Level 2.1:*

From the superscriptions I take two related examples, namely, ψαλμὸς ᾠδῆς (Psalms 29, 47, 66, 86, 91) and ᾠδὴ ψαλμοῦ (Psalms 65, 82, 87, 107). Needless to say, they occur when the corresponding Hebrew terms, מזמור and שיר stand together. The mental process reflected by the reality of the translated text seems akin to our own, especially when reading unpointed Hebrew. When two Hebrew nouns stand together one might infer a bound construction such as "X of Y," especially if there is no context to correct one's mistake.[31] Though the words themselves have meaning, what were the phrases ψαλμὸς ᾠδῆς and ᾠδὴ ψαλμοῦ intended to convey as units of information? Seemingly about as much as "a performance on strings of a song" and "a song of a performance on strings" would convey in English. Of course, one can massage such phrases into meaning "an accompaniment of a song on strings" or "a song with accompaniment on strings." But if that is what the translator wanted to convey, surely he could have done so by using or forming a word such as ψαλμῳδία "a singing to a harp."[32] Such well-intentioned attempts at making sense of the translator's text, however, miss the nature of the text itself. What happens is that two syntactically unrelated Hebrew words are forged into a phrase, evidently without much reflection on what the combined pair might mean. Thus for context one is forced to invoke the vertical relationship of the translated text to the parent text, since the translator's *modus operandi* wreaks havoc with the horizontal dimension of the Greek. In other words, the best way to account for the Greek text we have is interlinearity, and in this instance of a rather restrictive variety. Thus, beyond the word level, the only interpretation we have here is that two lexemes of the source text are made into

---

[31] See further Psalm 75(74), where the two do not stand together but yet are treated as a bound construction.

[32] For ψαλτῳδέω and ψαλτῳδός see, for example, 2 Chron 5:13 and 1 Chron 6:33, respectively.

a phrase in the target text, irrespective of coherent sense. What context there is beyond this level is simply carried over from the source.

Perhaps not surprisingly, though Patristic commentators on the Psalms understand what the two Greek words mean separately and maintain that allegorically ψαλμός has to do with physical activity while ᾠδή stands for mental activity, the best they can do for their combination is to say that it means the two combined.[33] To illustrate I cite Origen on Psalm 29:

> Ὀργάνῳ δὲ καὶ φωνῇ ὁ ψαλμὸς ἀποτελεῖται διὸ ψαλμὸς ᾠδῆς ἐπιγέγραπται, δηλωτικὸς ὢν τοῦ δεῖν ἡμᾶς καὶ ὀργάνῳ διὰ τῶν σωματικῶν κινήσεων ὑμνεῖν τὸν θεόν, καὶ φωνῇ νοητῇ, διὰ τοῦ τὸν νοῦν ἀνακεῖσθαι τῷ δημιουργῷ.[34]

> The psalm is performed with instrument and voice. Therefore it is titled ψαλμὸς ᾠδῆς, making it very clear that we must sing hymns to God with an instrument, through bodily movements, and with a mental voice, through devoting our mind to the creator.

In my discussion of Level 1, I have already called attention to other phrases that belong to this category, though not all of these are as semantically problematic as those just discussed. Since, however, potential exegesis at the phrase level looms larger in the superscriptions than at any other level, it may be useful to discuss the more important instances in some detail. Rösel, too, concentrates his attempts at extensive contextualization at the phrase level.

A similar phrase to those just discussed is αἶνος ᾠδῆς in Psalms 90, 92, and 94 without counterpart in the MT. Though it is possible that this phrase was original in only one of the three psalms and from there spread to the other two, its structure makes it unlikely that it was secondary everywhere. Semantically it is even more incongruous than either ψαλμὸς ᾠδῆς or ᾠδὴ ψαλμοῦ. Since both terms refer to vocal music and both indicate songs of praise, it is difficult to understand what the two combined might be intended to convey. If, however, one retroverts the Greek phrase into Hebrew on the pattern of either of the other phrases the text becomes transparent. Thus in all likelihood, the phrase αἶνος ᾠδῆς translates שיר תהלה, analogous to מזמור שיר and שיר מזמור.

---

[33] See, for example, Athanasius, *Expos. in Psalmos* 27, 576; Basil, *Hom. super Psalmos* 29, 305; Didymus the Blind, *Comm. in Psalmos* 129; Eusebius, *Comm. in Psalmos* 23, 680.

[34] *Fragmenta in Psalmos* on Ps 74:1.

*Level 2.2:*

The use of ὑπὲρ τῆς κληρονομούσης for אֶל־הַנְּחִילוֹת in Psalm 5. I begin here with the observable facts: (a) that G did not understand the Hebrew word as a musical term; (b) that he derived הַנְּחִילוֹת from נחל√ ("inherit"); (c) that the ' infix made the word into a verbal (*hip'il*) rather than the noun נַחְלָה; (d) that the Hebrew article as well as the וֹת-ending suggest a nominalized participle; (e) that as a participle of נחל√ it would have to be an active participle; (f) that the feminine in-flection of the source text produced a feminine inflection in the target text; (g) that the standard gloss in Psalms for נחל√ ("inherit") is κληρονομ⁻ (22x, with 1 exception). Thus apart from his mistaken identification, which can scarcely count as exposition, the only real expositional move he makes is to construe the Hebrew word as a sin-gular rather than as a plural, a move very similar to the move we saw him make above in Psalm 87(88). That interpretation took place is ob-vious: a Hebrew word is replaced with a Greek word and, more par-ticularly, an unknown Hebrew word is replaced with a known Greek word. But given the questionable though understandable derivation, what G did in the title of Psalm 5 was virtually entirely predictable and, therefore, can scarcely count as deliberate exposition. Again, the larger context must be attributed to the source text, rather than to G.

It is true, of course, that the translator by doing what he did created potential for future exegesis; hence in reception history this potential might well be realized. Rösel, however, would have us believe that already at the constitutive stage much more was deliberately encoded in the translated text. So he writes:

> die Wiedergabe [verweist] nun auf ein weibliches Individuum. Damit lässt sich der Psalm als Lied einer Frau verstehen, die in ihrer Not zu Gott ruft und auf seine Hilfe am Morgen hofft (v. 4).[35]

Rösel is, of course, correct that the Greek text as it now stands has the *potential* for such an interpretation, but that scarcely proves that the Greek translator himself had this in mind, and that, furthermore, he deliberately reinterpreted the entire psalm in feminist terms. While it is true that the psalm is a prayer, I see nothing in the Greek text that even remotely makes reference to a female inheritor. Thus the observable facts as well as the textual linguistic make-up of the trans-lation as a whole testify to something far more mundane: G mistak-

---

[35] M. Rösel, "Psalmenüberschriften," 131–32.

enly but by rather strict rules translated his source, and inadvertently created a text radically at variance with the Hebrew at the phrase level. Finally, if the feminine inflection in Psalm 5 indicates a woman, why not do the same with τῆς ὀγδόης ("the eighth") in Psalms 6 and 11, seeing that it was derived from the source text in the same manner?

*Level 2.3:*

The use of ὑπὲρ τῶν ληνῶν for עַל־הַגִּתִּית in Psalms 8, 80(81), 83(84). Here the observable facts are: (a) that again G fails to understand the Hebrew musical term; (b) that he derives it from גַת ("wine-press"); (c) that he construes the י as a ו and thus ends up with the plural; (d) that he isomorphically renders the entire phrase into Greek. To be sure, interpretation perforce takes place, albeit based on ignorance. But can we speak of exegesis or exposition? Moreover, can we infer a cognitive process that denied that the psalms in question were "Gittith" but had to do with wine-presses instead? Rösel, however, wonders whether, since in prophetic literature ληνός can connote a display of God's power, it might not connote the same in the psalms at hand, since these are thought to be amenable to such an interpretation. Thus ληνός, according to Rösel, should not be understood in its usual sense, even though that is what it normally carries both outside and inside the Septuagint, but should be understood metaphorically. Once again, that G had created a text with some potential, and that later interpreters might understand the Greek metaphorically, cannot be denied. But as I see it, that is not relevant to the present discussion. G proceeds literally, according to his analysis, and the larger context of the phrase is carried over from the source.

*Level 2.4:*

The use of μὴ διαφθείρῃς for אַל־תַּשְׁחֵת in Psalms 57(58), 58(59), 74(75). Rösel makes no attempt at contextualizing this obscure phrase, a decision with which I fully agree. The phrase is nonetheless of interest, not for what G did with it but for what reception history was able to do with it. Origen, for example, in comment on Ps 58:1, refers his readers to David's order to Abishai not to destroy Saul — the same phrase occurs in the Greek — in 1 Rgns 26:9, when the two of them enter Saul's camp and carry off the spear and water jug. And why not, since Psalm 58 is a David psalm and the superscription also refers to Saul's guarding David's house to kill him? But that is reception history not the constitutive character of the translated text.

Or in Austermann's terms, Origen is writing an Auslegungstext, not making an Übersetzung,[36] and, furthermore, one of a formal-correspondence variety. What G does with the phrase in all three psalms is predictable both on the verbal and nominal levels (verb 8x; noun 5x) and there is nothing in the psalms per se that lends support. But as a caveat against Origen's contextualizing of Psalm 58, it should be noted that neither of the other two have conducive detail in the su-perscriptions, and 74 is not even a David psalm. Yet G derived the phrase in question from his source text in exactly the same manner as he did in 58.

*Level 2.5:*

The use of ὑπὲρ τῆς ἀντιλήμψεως τῆς ἑωθινῆς for עַל־אַיֶּלֶת הַשַּׁחַר in Psalm 21(22). Again I begin with the observable facts: (a) that the translator is familiar with Hebrew אַיָּלָה ("doe") as is clear from Psalms 18(17):34, 29(28):9; (b) that he did not know what to do with a doe in the phrase at issue; (c) that he connects אַיָּלָה with אֱיָלוּת ("strength/help"); (d) that אֱיָלוּת occurs in 21:20 where he renders it by ἀντίλημψις; (e) that he then makes use of ἀντίλημψις in the super-scription; (f) that he introduces articles without formal warrant in the Hebrew. There can be no doubt, therefore, that exposition at the phrasal level occurs in the process of translation. And given the fact that he is unfamiliar with musical or liturgical terminology (including first lines of songs) in the superscriptions, given his dislike for tran-scriptions and, finally, given the fact that "concerning the doe of the morning" would make little if any sense even at the phrasal level, he did rather well. But the question that presents itself again is whether his concern for making sense at the phrasal level means that he delib-erately re-labels the psalm as a whole. I can find no reason for such a conclusion. Even the Church Fathers are surprisingly silent on this phrase. The only comment on it that I have been able to find is by Di-dymus the Blind who says that it refers to a spiritual day that is being ushered in by "the sun of righteousness".[37]

*Level 2.6:*

The use of εἰς ἀνάμνησιν for לְהַזְכִּיר in Psalms 37(38), 69(70). The observable facts of the case are: (a) that though the Hebrew √זכר is most often in Psalms translated by the simplex Greek root μνη- (12x),

---

[36] F. Austermann, "Thesen zur Septuaginta-Exegese," 383 (Thesis 6).

[37] Didymus, *Comm. in Psalmos*, 23.

in the superscriptions to these two psalms as well as in 108(109):14 G uses the compound form; (b) that the exceptions cannot be explained by the Hebrew stem (*hip'il*), since not all *hip'il*s are so translated; (c) that no verbal noun of the simplex form is attested. In light of (c) it may well be that G's option is determined linguistically rather than semantically.

M. Rösel sees significance in two things:[38] (a) that the phrase can be used in a cultic context and (b) that the Hebrew infinitive is translated by εἰς + a verbal noun, rather than by an infinitive. Even if we grant Rösel the cultic use of the Greek phrase, we would still have to conclude that no deliberate interpretation took place in the translation process, since the source text would already have had that sense. Rösel's second point, it seems to me, is purely linguistic. That is to say, according to G's standard practice for infinitives with preposed ל, להזכיר would have produced τοῦ ἀναμνησθῆναι. But had he followed standard practice here, "Δαυιδ" would have had to function as its subject. Hence the resultant text would be "A Psalm. Pertaining to Dauid in order that he might commemorate." If one then further regards περὶ σαββάτου in Psalm 37 as original text (which I do not), one would end up with David's being told that he should remember about the sabbath. A similar problem would arise in Psalm 69 if our translator had rigidly stuck to his standard equivalent, and in doing so had perforce created a subject of the infinitive. Thus if the translator was intent on safeguarding what the Hebrew text is thought to mean, to use the purpose infinitive was not a realistic option for him. Thus G is not going beyond the Hebrew at all, except for the fact that הזכיר *may* mean "memorial offering" (so *NRSV*), while ἀνάμνησις simply means "remembering/recalling/commemorating." Thus even if one were to apply the Greek phrase to the psalm as a whole no exposition or exegesis would have taken place beyond what the source text already gives us.

Linguistically, precisely the same phenomenon occurs in Psalm 59(60) where εἰς διδαχήν (εἰς + verbal noun) is used to translate ללמד (an infinitive), and all three (Psalms 37, 59, 69) may be contrasted with τοῦ ἀποκριθῆναι in 87, as discussed in 4.c.1.

---

[38] M. Rösel, "Psalmenüberschriften," 133. The two references Rösel cites in support (3 Rgns 17:18 and Amos 6:10) demonstrate my point.

*Level 2.7:*

The use of ὑπὲρ τοῦ ἀγαπητοῦ for ידידת in Psalm 44(45). The facts of the case are: (a) that G once again fails to understand the import of the Hebrew (cf. *NRSV*, "A love song"); (b) that he (correctly as it seems) derived the word from the Hebrew adjective ידיד ("beloved"); (c) that G ignores the final ת; (d) that he renders ידיד in the same way he renders it all four other times in Psalms (60[59]:7, 64[63]:2, 108[107]:7, 127[126]:2) by ἀγαπητός. Rösel[39] is right in noting that both ὑπέρ and the article are unwarranted by the Hebrew. Hence some interpretation takes place at the phrasal level. Whereas the Hebrew according to G's analysis would mean "a song of a beloved" the Greek would mean "on behalf of the beloved" (ὑπέρ is common in dedicatory statements). But then Rösel links "beloved" here with "beloved" in 67(68):13 where it in fact is used twice for Hebrew ידדון. So what happens is that the latter is equated with ידיד, since he evidently does not know what to do with ידדון. Given the fact that ידיד is consistently glossed with ἀγαπητός, the linguistic connection G forges in 68(67):13 based on ignorance of his source text is understandable, and expositional on the word or phrase level. Furthermore, that same linguistic connection is made with *all other* occurences of ידיד. But can one then also argue, as Rösel does, that since in his judgment τοῦ ἀγαπητοῦ (= ידדון) in 67(68):13 refers to God,[40] it does as well in Psalm 44 on the grounds that there, too, the singular occurs? But since singular and plural occur (for this word) in lockstep with the source text, how can this be deemed expositional in any meaningful way?[41] There can be little doubt that such intra-textual exegetical connections would be made in reception history, but is it already encoded at the constitutive stage? When one approaches the text from within and bases oneself on its linguistic make-up, all such instances appear as purely linguistically based, and expositional purely on the phrasal level. G etymologizes what he doesn't understand and refuses to transcribe and in so doing creates a text that differs more radically from the Hebrew than would have been the case if he had understood the Hebrew. The rest was up to reception history.

---

[39] "Psalmenüberschriften," 133.

[40] This interpretation itself is based on creative contextualizing.

[41] Rösel further states that the reference in 67:13 is "eindeutig eschatologisch" (p. 134 n. 53).

*Level 2.8:*

The use of ὑπὲρ τῶν ἀλλοιωθησομένων for עַל־שֹׁשַׁנִּים in Psalms 44(45), 59(60), 68(69), 79(80). The observable facts of the case are: (a) that G did not understand his source text and derives the Hebrew from √שׁנה ("change"); (b) that he analyzes the form as a non-feminine plural participle of that verb; (c) that the left-over initial שׁ, like the מ in preceding לַמְנַצֵּח, he represents by the Greek article; (d) that in so doing he maintains an isomorphic relationship to the source text; (e) that in Psalms 34(33):1 and 77(76):11 G translates √שׁנה with ἀλλοι- ("change"), which is in fact the standard equation in the Septuagint; (f) that since √שׁנה occurs most often in Daniel, ἀλλοιόω most often occurs there; (g) that most often throughout the Septuagint ἀλλοιόω has a non-eschatological sense. Rösel, however, goes two steps beyond this.

First, to him, the phrase, together with preceding εἰς τὸ τέλος, is "gewiss eschatologisch."[42] Second, the phrase makes the psalms in question into eschatological psalms. That at the phrasal level G engages in exposition is clear from the fact that, although the Greek-Hebrew equation as such is predictable, the use of the future passive participle is not. Thus time-subsequent and passive transformation is being signaled ("those that will be changed"). But even if one were to grant that the word here has a sense it normally does not have, there is no other indication that it was meant to function beyond the phrasal level, except that one of the four psalms in question (44[45]) can be interpreted eschatologically. But what about the other three? The Greek-Hebrew equation, even though it cannot be predicted on the basis of Psalms alone, nevertheless turns out to be predictable in light of the Septuagint as a whole.

That the phrase in question would all the more be read eschatologically beyond its own boundaries in Christian reception history, since, in its superscription, Psalm 44 also features ὑπὲρ τοῦ ἀγαπητοῦ, was inevitable. It thus comes as no surprise that Athanasius, for example, says that "the beloved" is David's son, Christ, and the phrase in question refers to the ἀλλοίωσις brought about by Christ's advent. Cyril, on the other hand, has our phrase refer to Jews and Greeks who, according to Paul, in Christ became one beloved people (cf. Rom 9:25).

---

[42] "Psalmenüberschriften," 134. Didymus the Blind, for example, does the same thing (*Commentarii in Psalmos 40–44*, 336) and, furthermore, brings in Ps 76:11.

I close the present discussion with two phrases which Rösel accords special treatment because of their allegedly even clearer eschatological import, namely, συνέσεως/εἰς σύνεσιν and εἰς τὸ τέλος.

*Level 2.9:*

The observable facts on συνέσεως/εἰς σύνεσιν for מַשְׂכִּיל are as follows: (a) that G did not understand מַשְׂכִּיל as a certain type of song; (b) that he derived the term from the verb √שׂכל ("be prudent"); (c) that in Psalms he translated √שׂכל with συνίημι + cognates some 22 times; (d) that συνίημι + cognates is used to translate √בין ("understand") some 27 times; (e) that in most superscriptions he translates מַשְׂכִּיל with a genitive (Psalms 32[31], 52[51], 53[52], 54[53], 55[54], 74[73], 78[77], 88[87], 89[88], 142[141]); (f) that in three superscriptions he renders it by εἰς σύνεσιν (Psalms 42[41], 44[43], 45[44]).

To be sure, this summary points up some interesting facts. For example, G vividly demonstrates his lack of familiarity with מַשְׂכִּיל as a type of song in Ps 47(46):8 where he translates זמרו מַשְׂכִּיל ("play a Maskil") as ψάλατε συνετῶς ("make music [on strings] with understanding"). Similarly, it is interesting that in all cases he pushes σύνεσις from the word level to the phrase level, either by inflection or by preposing a preposition, though perhaps it deserves noting that verbal nouns in the superscriptions are regularly made to function at the phrasal level whether or not there is explicit warrant in the Hebrew, the only two exceptions being στηλογραφία in Psalm 15 and αἴνεσις in Psalm 144. Thus the reason for turning σύνεσις into a phrase may be chiefly linguistic. Whatever the precise reason, exposition at the phrasal level has occurred. Beyond that, if perchance G opted for εἰς σύνεσιν (as a purpose expression) because of the adjacent phrase τοῖς υἱοῖς Κορε, on the assumption that G thought that the latter could do with a bit of understanding (cf. Num 16), we can even say that an expositional move extended to the propositional level. Rösel,[43] however, wants to push it well beyond that point, since for him it re-labels the entire psalm whenever σύνεσις occurs in the superscription as a gloss for מַשְׂכִּיל. That seems highly questionable, since its occurrence is once again predictable on the basis of the source text, and similarly, on the few occasions that a member of the συνίημι group occurs within the psalm itself (Pss 31:8. 9, 52:3, 77:72), it is again predictable on the basis G's standard equations.

---

[43] "Psalmenüberschriften," 136–37.

That being the case, how can it be argued that the translator is engaged in deliberate interpretation, that is, exposition? All that can be
said is that, since the Hebrew √שׂכל and Greek σύνεσις + cognates do
not have an identical semantic range, interpretation may be taking
place in the translational process. Rösel, however, takes yet another
step, since he writes:

> Das fragliche Nomen ist nun mitsamt dem zugehörigen Verbum συνίημι
> in der Jesaja-LXX wie in der Dan-LXX eindeutig im Sinne eines escha-
> tologisch-apokalyptischen Verstehens der Wege Gottes konnotiert; man
> erinnere sich nur an die berühmte Übersetzung von Jes 7,9 mit "glaubt ihr
> nicht, so versteht ihr nicht."[44]

He then proceeds to certain passages in the Psalter where σύνεσις or a
cognate thereof might carry the same sense, for example: Psalms
15(16):7; 48(49):13, 21; 146(147):5 and 110(111):10. Thus Rösel's
argument here is effectively that, since σύνεσις elsewhere in the LXX
*can* have an eschatological-apocalyptic sense, it should be given that
meaning whenever a given text can bear it. But that ignores two fundamental facts: that συνίημι + cognates, both without and within the
LXX, rarely carries that meaning, and furthermore, that in three of the
four passages he cites in the Psalter the Greek word is predictable.
That leaves Ps 15(16):7 where συνετίζω ("to make to understand")
translates Hebrew יעץ ("to give counsel"). Since in this case συνετίζω
is a non-default rendering for יעץ (= βουλεύομαι 4x, ἐπιστηρίζω 1x),
it of course attracts exegetical interest; but scarcely gives it an eschatological-apocalyptic meaning. That σύνεσις anywhere has such a
meaning is *quod est demonstrandum*. Similarly, what G does has more
than an indirect and non-deliberate effect on the psalms in question is
equally *quod est demonstrandum*.

*Level 2.10:*

Perhaps the most lavish interpretation Rösel reserves for εἰς τὸ
τέλος, a phrase that occurs in the superscriptions more often than any
other (*ca.* 55), with the exception of τῷ Δαυιδ (*ca.* 73). The observable facts are: (a) that εἰς τὸ τέλος and למנצח form a closed Greek-
Hebrew equation; (b) that G was unfamiliar with the meaning "leader"
(*NRSV*) or "director" (BDB); (c) that G arrived at his translation via
his equation of εἰς τέλος with לנצח. As in the case of σύνεσις, Rösel
would have us believe that εἰς τὸ τέλος should be understood

---

[44] "Psalmenüberschriften," 136.

eschatologically. He briefly entertains others possibilities, but then writes:

> Sinnvoller ist die Übersetzung mit "Ende", die man wohl auf die Endzeit beziehen muss; die entsprechenden Lieder zielen demnach auf die Endzeit. Diese Überlegung wird durch die auffällige Verwendung des Artikels unterstützt, die m. E. eindeutig auf ein bestimmtes Ende zielt.[45]

If such a claim could be substantiated it would mean that our Greek translator in the act of translating has made some 55 psalms into psalms about the end time. But the argument that leads to such a conclusion seems fatally flawed. I begin with Hebrew נצח for which τέλος regularly serves as a gloss. According to the lexica it would seem safe to say that the root has essentially three components of meaning: "(pre-)eminence, successfulness, perpetuity." It is thus little wonder that לנצח is commonly glossed in English as "forever," that is to say, "in perpetuity." Though τέλος can have a great many meanings and clearly has considerable semantic overlap with נצח, the component not covered very well, if at all, by τέλος is that of perpetuity, that is, the temporal dimension.

This becomes at once clear when one investigates how נצח is translated in the Septuagint. Outside of the Psalter the root occurs some 35 times: five times one finds εἰς τέλος ("completely," Hab 1:4; Job 4:20, 14:20, 20:7, 23:7), five times εἰς νῖκος ("victoriously," 2 Sam 2:26; Jer 3:5; Amos 1:11, 8:7; Lam 5:20) + τοῦ νικῆσαι ("to win victory," Hab 3:19), and ἡ νίκη ("victory," 1 Chron 29:11).[46] Seemingly related to the concept of "victory" are ἰσχύω ("to be powerful/prevail") in Isa 25:8, κατισχύω ("to prevail over") in Jer 15:18, and ἐνισχύω ("to prevail in") in 1 Chron 15:21. And again trading on the notion of pre-eminence are glosses like ἐργοδιώκτης ("taskmaster") in 1 Chron 23:4 and 2 Chron 2:17, as well as ἐπισκοπέω ("to oversee") in 2 Chron 34:12. Thus there is plenty that reflects the components of "(pre-)eminence" and "successfulness." Interestingly, however, when the component of "perpetuity" comes into play נצח is glossed by temporal phrases: εἰς τὸν αἰῶνα (Isa 28:28; Jer 27[50]:39), εἰς τὸν αἰῶνα χρόνον (Isa 13:20, 33:20), χρόνον πολύν (Isa 34:10), διὰ παντός (Isa 57:16) and ἔτι (Job 34:36).

Thus one can conclude with reasonable assurance that outside of the Psalter τέλος does not seem to have a temporal dimension. Yet that is

---

[45] Psalmenüberschriften," 138.

[46] Aquila and Quinta use εἰς νῖκος for לנצח.

precisely what Rösel claims for the Psalter in his lead-up to "die Endzeit."[47] To prove his point he makes reference to three passages in the Psalms where εἰς τέλος appears as a parallel to εἰς τὸν αἰῶνα (Pss 9:19, 76:8f[?], 102:9). The inference is, therefore, that "parallel" means "identical." That seems to me problematic. One can in fact argue that in Psalms, too, τέλος is *not* perceived to have a strictly temporal dimension, since in Ps 49(48):20 where the Hebrew has עד־נצח and where the meaning is patently temporal, G switches to ἕως αἰῶνος. Since this is a non-default rendering of נצח it can be taken to have some exegetical significance.

Rösel's proposal to read εἰς τὸ τέλος eschatologically raises a by now familiar problem. In non-philosophical Classical and Hellenistic literature τέλος as a nominal means nothing more often than "conclusion" (natural or logical) and as an adverbial it means nothing more frequently than "in conclusion" or "completely/finally," with no more of an eschatological overtone than the English glosses I have used. Polybius, for example, regularly uses εἰς τέλος. Similarly, within the Septuagint (some 94 occurrences according to Hatch-Redpath, not counting the Psalter) τέλος rarely has an eschatological sense. In light of all that, with what justification can the claim be made that the phrase εἰς τὸ τέλος has an eschatological sense and is thus an exegetical contribution of the translator? Is it because of the article, which Rösel sees as supporting such a claim? But the article is there simply to maintain isomorphism with the source text, and perhaps more importantly to allow G to reproduce a contrast in his source text: εἰς τέλος = לנצח and εἰς τὸ τέλος = למנצח while deriving both from the same root.

The fact that the Fathers of the Church, who read the entire Septuagint as a *praeparatio euangelica* would read εἰς τὸ τέλος, and in fact τέλος generally from an eschatological perspective. is of course true. So, for example, Asterius the Sophist in commenting on Ps 9:1 exclaims:

> What is τὸ τέλος? The beginning of the proclamation of the Gospel, which is the τέλος of the Law and the Prophets (τί τὸ τέλος; ἡ ἀρχὴ τοῦ εὐαγγελικοῦ κηρύγματος, ὅ ἐστι τέλος τοῦ νόμου καὶ τῶν προφητῶν).

In similar vein 1 Pet 4:7 writes that "the end of all things is near" (πάντων δὲ τὸ τέλος ἤγγικεν). But to superimpose such a meaning onto the Septuagint runs afoul of what I consider to be a basic and vi-

---

[47] Psalmenüberschriften," 138.

tal distinction between the chronologically oldest and logically prior Septuagint, on the one hand, and its reception history on the other. What the original text meant has to be determined on the basis of its constitutive character.

## Level 3: Interpretation at the Sentence Level

In earlier comment on εἰς σύνεσιν in Psalms 41, 43, and 44 I have already suggested that the structure of the phrase may have been determined by the preceding phrase τοῖς υἱοῖς Κορε. If that is the case we can speak of contextualization from the phrasal to the propositional and, therefore, to the clausal or sentence level.

As an example of intra-clausal exegetical activity one might cite Psalm 3: ὁπότε ἀπεδίδρασκεν ἀπὸ προσώπου Αβεσσαλωμ τοῦ υἱοῦ αὐτοῦ for בברחו מפני אבשלום בנו. Though the grammatical information is transferred almost isomorphically to the Greek, it is of interest that in the case of the Hebrew infinitival construction G opts for ὁπότε plus an imperfect verb. Since both the conjunction and the imperfect indicative verb are uncommon and therefore marked items in the Psalter as well as the Septuagint corpus, one can infer a certain deliberateness on the part of the translator. So here he portrays David's flight from his son as a withdrawal in progress, something the Hebrew does not show explicitly. But since the information conveyed by this clause was already in the parent text, G cannot be said to have contextualized the sentence at the paragraph level, that is, the entire psalm or even a part thereof. What exposition he did, he did purely within the sentence.

As I have suggested elsewhere,[48] there can be no doubt that all such "historical" superscriptions played an important exegetical role in the transmission history of the Book of Psalms, both before and after they were translated into Greek. But if our interest lies in the specific contributions of the Greek translator to this history of exegesis, it must be ascertained whether or not such items — be they word, phrase, or sentence — were introduced as part of the translational process. To the extent that such items are also attested by the Masoretic Text, one can safely assume that they were inherited by G from his source text. That being the case, he can be given expositional credit only for what exposition he is shown to have accomplished at the sentence level.

For a final possible example one might turn to Psalm 55(56), ὑπὲρ

---

[48] A. Pietersma, "Exegesis and Liturgy," 99–138.

τοῦ λαοῦ τοῦ ἀπὸ τῶν ἁγίων μεμακρυμμένου for רחקים על־יונת אלם.
At the phrasal level G does not know what to do with a "dove" (יונה)
any more than he knows what to do with a "doe" in Psalm 21(22). As
a result, here as in 21(22) he comes up with something that makes
sense at least within the phrase.[49] Though it is likely that G did not
stray very far from the consonantal text, one wonders whether the
sense he gave the phrase is related to the last clause in the superscription which states that David was in a foreign land, away from Israel's
shrine. If that is so we have here another instance of clausal and
phrasal contextualization. Since as in the previous example the items
as such were already in the parent text, G cannot be credited with exposition beyond the sentence level.

*Level 4: Interpretation at the Paragraph Level*

At this level of interpretation significant exposition of the source
text clearly takes place, and like all other levels of interpretation it too
can be found in the translated corpus. In connection with the superscriptions, one naturally thinks of the superscriptions in the Greek
which are lacking in the Masoretic text. But as I have already noted, if
our interest lies in the contribution of the translator, that is, in the constitutive character of the translated text, not only do we have to remove from consideration items G inherited from his source text, but
also items that belong to the reception history of the Greek text. In an
earlier article I have dealt extensively with this issue. Here a single
example must suffice.

While in the MT the superscription of Psalm 27(26) is a simple
לדוד, the Greek text adds πρὸ τοῦ χρισθῆναι ("before he [David] was
anointed"). What happened here in the reception history of the Book
of Psalms is reasonably clear. From being simply a "David psalm," it
became a psalm associated with a particular period in David's life,
namely, before he was anointed king over Judah (2 Sam 2:4) and over
Israel (2 Sam 5:3). The impetus for the addition arose from the Greek
text of verse 5:

ὅτι ἔκρυψέν με ἐν σκηνῇ ἐν ἡμέρᾳ κακῶν μου·
ἐσκέπασέν με ἐν ἀποκρύφῳ τῆς σκηνῆς αὐτοῦ,
ἐν πέτρᾳ ὕψωσέν με·

---

[49] For a discussion of G's possible misreadings of the consonantal text see
Martin Flashar, "Exegetische Studien zum Septuagintapsalter," *ZAW* 32(1912)
244.

For he hid me in the tabernacle in the day of my troubles;
he sheltered me in a secret spot of his tabernacle;
he set me high on a rock. (*NETS*)

This verse was thought to refer to David's stopover at the tabernacle at Nob (1 Samuel 21), an event which unmistakably predated his becoming king. Though theoretically the extra clause could have been part of G's source text, this becomes unlikely once one realizes that the terms for "tabernacle" in this verse are סכה and אהל, but not משכן. While linkage with the tabernacle would not be impossible within Hebrew transmission history, the Greek text makes it all but inevitable, since in Greek σκηνή is the standard term for the old desert shrine. The crucial question becomes, however, whether it was the translator who added the exegetical note based on information supplied in v. 5, or whether it was the reception history of the Greek text that was responsible. Even though there is evidence to suggest that G reserved σκηνή for the tabernacle (hence the *NETS* translation), I consider it more likely that the piece of exegesis belongs to the history of interpretation of the Greek Psalter (hence the square brackets in *NETS*). Be that as it may, for my present purpose suffice it to say that if the clause is attributable to G, we have clear evidence that G at times engaged in exposition at the paragraph level, that is, the psalm as a whole. If, on the other hand, the clause stems from reception history, it ought not be cited as evidence for exegesis in the Septuagint itself.[50]

## CONCLUSION

I have sought to argue that though genuine exegesis and exposition can be found in the Septuagint, including in the Greek Psalter, it needs to be identified on the basis of its textual-linguistic make-up. If its textual-linguistic make-up argues for a translation characterized more by formal correspondence than by dynamic equivalency, one's approach to hermeneutics in the Septuagint should be governed by these findings. As I see it, that means at a minimum that exegesis needs to demonstrated, not presupposed. From that perceptive I would suggest that one work from the least intelligible phenomena to the more intelligible; that one proceed from the word level to higher levels of constituent structure; that one pay more attention to the translator's deviations from his Hebrew-Greek defaults than to his defaults and stan-

---

[50] For another instance of exegesis beyond the sentence level, see Boyd-Taylor "A Place in the Sun," 77–105.

dard equations or, to put it differently, that greater weight be given to what is unpredictable than to what is predictable; that one assign greater context to segments of the Greek text than to the corresponding segments of the Hebrew text only as a last resort.

To read the translated text in the light of its constitutive character is one thing, but to read it in the light of a culturally reassigned function and position is quite another.

## SELECT BIBLIOGRAPHY

Austermann, F. "Von der Tora im hebräischen Psalm 119 zum Nomos im griechischen Psalm 118," in E. Zenger (ed.), *Der Septuaginta-Psalter* (Freiburg: Herder, 2001) 331–47.

—. "Thesen zur Septuaginta-Exegese am Beispiel der Untersuchung des Septuaginta-Psalters," in A. Aejmelaeus and U. Quast (eds.), *Der Septuaginta-Psalter und seine Tochterübersetzungen.* (Göttingen: Vandenhoeck & Ruprecht, 2000) 380–86.

Barr, J. *The Semantics of Biblical Language.* Oxford 1961 (SCM edition 1983).

—. "Common Sense and Biblical Language," *Biblica* 49 (1968) 337–87.

Boyd-Taylor, C. "A Place in the Sun: The Interpretative Significance of LXX-Psalm 18:5c," *BIOSCS* 31(1998) 71–105.

Brock, S. "The Phenomenon of the Septuagint," *OTS* 17 (1972) 17.

Brown, W. P. "Reassessing the Text-Critical Value of the Septuagint-Genesis 1: A Response to Martin Rösel," *BIOSCS* 32 (1999) 35–39.

Flashar, M. "Exegetische Studien zum Septuagintapsalter," *ZAW* 32 (1912) 81–116, 161–89, 241–68.

Hendel, R. S. "On the Text-Critical Value of Septuagint Genesis: A Reply to Rösel," *BIOSCS* 32 (1999) 31–34.

Joosten, J. "Exegesis in the Septuagint Version Hosea," in J. C. De Moor (ed.), *Intertextuality in Ugarit and Israel* (OTS 40; Leiden: Brill, 1998) 62–85.

Kooij, A. van der. "Zur Frage der Exegese im LXX-Psalter. Ein Beitrag zur Verhältnissbestimmung zwischen Original und Übersetzung," in A. Aejmelaeus and U. Quast (eds.), *Der Septuaginta-Psalter und seine Tochterübersetzungen.* (Göttingen: Vandenhoeck & Ruprecht, 2000) 366–79.

Pietersma, A. Review of Schaper, *Bibliotheca Orientalis* 54 (1997) 185–90.

—. *The Psalms*, in A. Pietersma and B. Wright (eds.), *A New English Translation of the Septuagint* (New York and Oxford: Oxford University Press, 2000).

—. "Exegesis and Liturgy in the Superscriptions of the Greek Psalter," in B. A. Taylor (ed.), *X Congress of the International Organization for Septuagint and Cognate Studies, Oslo, 1998.* (SBLSCS 51; Atlanta: Society of Biblical Literature, 2001) 99–138.

—. "The Present State of the Critical Text of the Greek Psalter," in A. Aejmelaeus and U. Quast (eds.), *Der Septuaginta-Psalter und seine Tochterübersetzungen.* (Göttingen: Vandenhoeck & Ruprecht, 2000) 12–32.

Rösel, M. "Die Psalmüberschriften des Septuaginta-Psalter," in E. Zenger (ed.), *Der Septuaginta-Psalter* (Freiburg: Herder, 2001) 125–48.

—. "The Text-Critical Value of Septuagint-Genesis," *BIOSCS* 31 (1998) 62–70.

Schaper, J. *Eschatology in the Greek Psalter* (Wissenschaftliche Untersuchungen zum Neuen Testament. 2.Reihe 76; Tübingen: Mohr Siebeck, 1995).

Thesaurus Linguae Graecae (TLG). CD ROM# e. 1999.

Toury, G. *Descriptive Translation Studies and Beyond* (Amsterdam and Philadelphia: Benjamins, 1995).

# A JEWISH READING OF PSALMS: SOME OBSERVATIONS ON THE METHOD OF THE ARAMAIC TARGUM

## INTRODUCTION

In light of the size of the book of Psalms and its multidimensional significance within Jewish tradition, it is perhaps surprising, at first glance, that the Aramaic version of Psalms has been relatively neglected when compared with the Aramaic versions of other biblical books.[1] The fact that it has not been the object of a great deal of scholarly scrutiny may be attributed to any one of a variety of factors: its unwieldy size, its presumed "late" date, its non-employment in Jewish liturgy, or some combination of those phenomena as well as others.[2]

---

[1] We shall speak of the "targum" in the singular, whether it is the product of one hand or of many. If the targum of Psalms, for example, is not the product of a single hand, it still possesses a commonality of aim and method that allows us to think of it as the product of a single school or tradition of translation and interpretation.

[2] The most important and thorough treatment of Targum Psalms remains W. Bacher, "Das Targum zu den Psalmen," *MGWJ* 21 (1872) 408–16, 463–73; the chapter on this targum by P. Churgin in תרגום כתובים [*Targum of the Hagiographa*] (New York: Horeb, 1945) 17–62 is also noteworthy. Among the other fairly sparse studies of this Aramaic version are: Y. Komlosh, "קווים אופייניים בתרגום תהלים" ["Characteristic Features in the Targum of Psalms"], in J. M. Grintz and J. Liver (eds.), *Studies in the Bible Presented to M. H. Segal (Sefer Segal)* (Jerusalem: Israel Society for Biblical Research, 1964) 265–70; L. Diez Merino, "Haggadic Elements in the Targum of Psalms," *Proceedings of the Eighth World Congress of Jewish Studies. Division A* (Jerusalem: World Union of Jewish Studies, 1982) 131–37; and J. Shunary, "Avoidance of Anthropomorphism in the Targum of Psalms," *Textus* 5 (1966) 134–44.

The commentary by A. T. Wein, ייט טוב (Rehovot, 1985) consists of a translation of the standard text of the targum into Hebrew with fairly sparse notes, mostly linking targumic comments with rabbinic literature. An important recent article is E. M. Cook, "The Psalms Targum: Introduction to a New Translation, with Sample Texts," in P. V. Flesher (ed.), *Targum and Scripture: Studies in Aramaic Translation and Interpretation in Memory of Ernest G. Clarke* (Studies in the Aramaic Interpretation of Scripture 2; Leiden: Brill, 2002) 185–201; this is an introduction to his translation of the targum found on the website of the *Newsletter for Targumic*

## The Text

One of the serious deficiencies in the study of this Aramaic version in the past has been the absence of a critical edition; for the first two "books" of Psalms (1–72), we now have the 1988 work of Emanuel White, "A Critical Edition of the Targum of Psalms: A Computer Generated Text of Books I and II."[3] On p. v, White lists the sixteen MSS and the *editio princeps* (Venice, dated 1524-25) which he employed, and describes them in greater detail on pp. 36–60. Several years earlier, Luis Diez Merino had published the MS *Vill-Amil n. 5 de Alfonso de Zamora*[4] (not included by White in his edition because it is "virtually identical to the Salamanca MS"). The present essay relies for Books 1 and 2 of Psalms (1–72) primarily on White's collations of those manuscripts, supplemented by my own collations (both before and after receiving a copy of his thesis), and for the rest of Psalms on my own incomplete examinations of the manuscripts.[5]

## Provenance

The rabbinic tradition of the Babylonian Talmud knows of no "official" or "authorized" translation of the Hagiographa into Aramaic, in the way in which it acknowledges "Onqelos" to the Pentateuch and "Jonathan" to the Prophets.[6] Although there is an *en passant* tannaitic

---

*and Cognate Studies*, http://www.targum.org.

[3] Unpublished Ph.D. thesis, McGill University, 1988. Dr. White was kind enough to furnish me with a copy of his thesis a number of years ago after I had begun my own intensive studies on this Aramaic version. References in this essay to "White, 'Critical Edition'" are to this thesis.

[4] *Targum de Salmos: Edición del Ms. Vill-Amil n. 5 de Alfonso de Zamora* (Biblia Poliglota Complutense–Tradición Sefardi de la Biblica Aramaea IV,1; Madrid: Consejo Superior de Investiaciones Cientificas/Instituto "Francisco Suarez," 1982). The fullest list of the MSS of the targum of Psalms has been compiled, I believe, by Willem Smelik, who was kind enough to furnish me with a copy in fall 2001: "Extant Manuscripts of the Targum of Psalms: An Eclectic List" (September, 2001) <http://www.ucl.ac.uk/hebrew-jewish/staff/willem.htm>.

[5] In the course of my research on this version, dating back to the early 1980s, I have done a "selective" collation of virtually all the manuscripts, including a complete collation of a Genoa MS that was apparently not available to White. My colleague at Yeshiva College, Dr. Richard T. White, produced several years ago on my behalf a computer-generated concordance to this targum based on Lagarde's printed text (in *Hagiographa Chaldaice*) which has been invaluable for my work.

[6] Cf. b*Megilla* 3a, according to which Jonathan ben Uzziel wanted to proceed from his translation of the Prophets to a translation of the Hagiographa, but was

reference to an Aramaic translation of Job at b*Shabbat* 115a, and a
tannaitic allusion to the *targum* of the book of Esther and the "Hallel"
(Psalms 113–118) at b*Megilla* 21b, the former very possibly speaks of
a work of non-rabbinic provenance, while the latter two deal with
translation in liturgical contexts.[7] Unlike the targum of Esther, the targum of Psalms was furthermore apparently unknown to the geonim in
Babylonia later on. R. Hai Gaon writes (speaking of an Aramaic version of Esther),

> Whence do you have the translation [of the Hagiographa] which you do?
> And who said it? For Jonathan ben Uzziel never revealed the *targum* of the
> Hagiographa at all. The one which you have in your possession can only be
> the translation of common folk (תרגום של הדיוטות). Furthermore, we have
> here in Babylonia several versions of targum Esther, differing from each
> other; one has many additions and midrashim in it, while another does not.[8]

Despite this absence of recognition in authoritative Babylonian
sources, an Aramaic version of the Hagiographa — except for the
books of Daniel and Ezra-Nehemiah, each of which contains material
written in Aramaic — has found a place in the standard Rabbinic Bible
(*miqra'ot gedolot*).

Regarding the translation of Psalms into Aramaic, in particular, although no "official" Aramaic version is acknowledged by the Talmud,
there is at least one verse cited in the Babylonian Talmud at *Ta'anit* 5a
with the same text as appears in the "standard" targum. There Ps
122:3 (ירושלם הבנויה כעיר שחברה לה יחדו) is rendered as ירושלם
דמתבניא ברקיע היך קרתא דאתחברא לה בארעא ("Jerusalem which is
built in heaven is like the city which is joined to it on earth").[9]

---

precluded by a heavenly voice "because it contains the end-time of the Messiah."

[7] The reference to the targum of Job in Shabbat, especially in light of the decision by Rabban Gamliel the elder that it be cemented into a row of bricks, has become a *locus classicus* for Qumran scholars ever since the discovery and publication of the Aramaic version of Job from Qumran (11QtgJob).

[8] B. M. Lewin, *Otzar ha-Gaonim (Thesaurus of the Gaonic Responsa and
Commentaries: Megilla)* (Jerusalem: Hebrew University Press Association, 1932)
5.5.

[9] The targum of Psalms was certainly not widely known to the early medieval
Jewish exegetes (*rishonim*); for the data, see White, "Critical Edition," 14–17. R.
Nathan b. Yehiel of Rome (1035-1105), in his classic dictionary of rabbinic Hebrew and Aramaic, cites the Aramaic version of Psalms more than 80 times according to the *Index ad Citata Biblica, Targumica, Talmudica atque Midrashica*
in A. Kohut's edition of the *Aruch Completum* (Vienna: Fanto, 1892; repr. New

We thus possess no hard information on the circles from which the Aramaic version of Psalms, emerged, and we likewise have no reliable facts regarding its date of composition.[10] From a linguistic perspective, it appears to be composed in that late amalgam of Palestinian and Babylonian Aramaic which characterizes texts such as the pseudo-Jonathan version of the Pentateuch and most of the other Hagiographa targumim (with the well-known exception of Proverbs whose dialect seems most closely related to Syriac).[11]

*Function and Significance*

Because we have no evidence that the book of Psalms was ever recited liturgically accompanied by an Aramaic translation, we have no reason to assume that the Aramaic version was composed for synagogue or other liturgical performance.[12] It is therefore quite reasonable to surmise that the goal of the translation was in some sense pri-

---

York: Pardes, 1955) 8.26–27. White, "Critical Edition," 17 n. 65, points out that over 50 of those references are to Psalms 1–72.

[10] White, "Critical Edition," 19, expresses a widely accepted, and very likely, position that "Tar[gum ]Ps[alms] is a relatively late Targum." Cook, "Psalms Targum," 186, feels that the evidence White adduces does not warrant his inference of a late date: "The weak influence of the targum may have other explanations. It is possible that the targum, like many ancient compositions, is the accumulation of several generations' work." On that point, there should not be much dispute. The targum to Ps 108:11 (מי ילכני עיר מבצר מי נחני עד אדום) has often been cited as pointing toward a pre-476 CE date because of the targum's joint references to Rome and Constantinople, since almost all MSS read there מן אוביל יתי עד כרכא דרומי רשיעא מן דברני עד קושטינא דאדום ("who will bring me to the fortified city *of wicked Rome* and who will lead me to *Constantinople* of Edom"). Since Rome, capital of the Western Roman Empire, fell in 476, it is not likely to have been alluded to after that point. But this verse can only point toward its own date, not that of the targum as a whole. Cf. the brief discussion in White, "Critical Edition," 19–20.

[11] For a brief, but pointed, discussion of the language of the Psalms targum, cf. Cook, "Psalms Targum," 186–89, as well as the discussion in White, "Critical Edition," 17–19.

[12] White, "Critical Edition," 5, calls this "first and foremost a literary composition," but it is nonetheless appropriate to ask for what purpose or under what circumstances such a literary composition would come into being. This uncertainty regarding circumstances of translation is not unique to the targum of Psalms, but exists regarding all the other books of the Hagiographa which were also not employed liturgically (other than the *Megillot*) but for which translations into Aramaic exist.

marily pedagogical, even though we cannot point to its being employed in formal educational contexts either.

The text-critical value of the targum of Psalms is very limited for several reasons. First, its fairly late date and its connection to rabbinic tradition together reduce the likelihood of its preserving any substantive variants. Second, and perhaps more significant, the flexible approach of the Psalms targum — like that of most of the other Aramaic versions — to the translation of the Hebrew text in difficult passages, makes it very hazardous to retrovert with any confidence to an underlying Hebrew *Vorlage*. This is not to deny that the targum may on rare occasions be based on a text which diverges from the MT, but the student of the translation must always be wary of the possibility that the midrashic interpretive translation technique of the Aramaic version can lead it to create in translation what may look like the product of variant Hebrew texts.[13]

Furthermore, it is not primarily as an exemplar of very early biblical translation that the targum of Psalms is likely to attract our interest. It is probably relatively late both among the Aramaic versions, since all the translations to the Hagiographa clearly post-date those to the Pentateuch and Prophets, and among other ancient translations of the Psalms, since it certainly postdates at the very least the Septuagint, Peshitta and Vulgate. We should rather value this version as a repository of Jewish interpretive traditions, some of them early, on a biblical book whose influence was widespread among Jews and Christians alike. Whereas a work such as *Midrash Tehillim*,[14] for example, could comment on the biblical text selectively, picking and choosing which verses to omit from its commentary and which were to be the subject of multiple comments, the targum of Psalms, like other translations,

---

[13] Thus at 76:5, almost all the witnesses to the targum render the MT (= LXX, Peshitta) reading נאור by דחיל ("feared"), as if the text read נורא (which is certainly smoother contextually). The printed text reads נהיר דחיל, a double translation reflecting both נורא and נאור. On the other hand, the morphological deviation in the translation of הביט וראה at 142:5 by אסתכלית וחמית is very unlikely to indicate that the Vorlage of the targum read הבטתי וראיתי.

[14] *The Midrash of Psalms* — also known from its opening words as *Shoḥer Tov*, based on its opening citation of Prov 11:27 — is a composite text of uncertain date, although it certainly does not belong anywhere in the earliest strata of rabbinic midrash. For brief discussion and bibliography, see H. L. Strack and G. Stemberger, *Introduction to the Talmud and Midrash* (Minneapolis: Fortress, 1996) 322–23.

had to deal with each and every sentence of the poetic Hebrew text and to present a version of it to its audience. The ways in which the targumim do this is often quite different from the approaches of the Septuagint, Peshitta and Vulgate; it is therefore valuable to observe the methodology of a translator or school of translators operating on a biblical text that is not always easily translatable, and to attempt to classify the targumic translation techniques that are indeed often quite different from those of the other ancient versions.

In an essay of this length, there is unfortunately not sufficient room to present a full description of all aspects of the methodology employed by the targum of Psalms in its rendition of the Hebrew text, especially the most fundamental level, that of translation technique. I have chosen instead to offer the reader samples of three aspects of this targum: (1) its exegetical methodology, that is, the way the targum operates on the biblical text; (2) one feature of its interpretive process, the introduction of historical "data" into unhistorical text; and (3) the targum's theology: the system of values and beliefs which it brings to the biblical text.[15]

## EXEGETICAL DEVICES

In order to gain fuller insight into the approach of any translation of a biblical text, we must be aware of the technical devices which it employs. The translator of Psalms into Aramaic utilized a variety of exegetical and interpretive strategies, both in order to clarify more expansively the meaning of texts whose meaning is fundamentally clear but which are densely formulated in the Hebrew original, as well as to "elucidate" passages in the text which do not lend themselves to translation because of more intractable features. In this essay, we shall present two of those techniques: the introduction of similes into the translation, and the specification of speakers in passages where they are not present in the biblical original.

### Similes

The poetic biblical text of Psalms is replete with various forms of figurative language, including similes and metaphors, which convey its messages; the targum, however, resorts particularly to the simile

---

[15] Also for reasons of space, I shall make no attempt to describe the relationship of the targum of Psalms to the interpretation of Psalms found in rabbinic literature, other than a few comments which are not to be taken as systematic.

even in cases where the Hebrew text has a metaphor, and similes are employed frequently even where the Hebrew text has neither simile nor metaphor. We shall examine the targum's utilization of similes, beginning with the simplest cases where it transforms the biblical metaphor into a simile through the addition of a word such as היך ("like") between the terms of the metaphor. From there we shall proceed to cases where there is in the Hebrew text only one term of the comparison, the metaphorical one, without specification of the object of its description, and the targum transforms the Hebrew into a full-fledged simile. Finally, we shall examine cases where there is no comparison at all implied in the biblical text, and the targum invents the whole simile, occasionally counter to the simple sense of the original. In these latter cases, where the targum employs similes unexpectedly, we shall be able to observe how the simile is one of the implements in the targum's exegetical toolkit, as well as the textual and theological motivations for its use.

In most of the cases where the targum adds היך or a similar term to the translation of the biblical text, it shifts a metaphor in the original to a simile. A few examples should suffice:

Ps 5:10 קבר פתוח גרונם

Tg היך שיול פתיח גרונהון

Ps 141:2 תכון תפלתי קטרת לפניך משאת כפי מנחת ערב

Tg תתכוין צלותי היך קטרת בוסמין קדמך זקפות ידי בצלו היך דורון בסים דמתקרב ברמש

Ps 22:13 פצו עלי פיהם אריה טרף ושאג

Tg ¹⁶פתחו עלי פומהון היך כאריא

Sometimes, the appearance of a simile in the targum, while formally equivalent to these examples, is motivated by more than mere formality. It may be intended to overcome theological difficulties, such as:

Ps 82:6 אנא אמרתי אלהים אתם

Tg אנא אמרית כמלאכיא אתון חשיבין

The addressees of the psalm are neither divine nor angels for the targum, and the simile solves the problem.

At times, a bit more than the comparative particle is added to create the simile; a verb, noun or adjective may be supplied as well in order to limit the sphere of comparison. Thus Ps 119:105 נר לרגלי דבריך

---

¹⁶ Others of this simple sort can be found at 48:3, 57:5, 66:11 (*targum aḥer*), 73:22, 83:10, 105:39, 41, and 124:6. At times some of the textual witnesses of the targum have a simile, while other MSS translate the metaphor.

becomes in the Tg היך שרגא דמנהרא לרגלי דבירך, while Ps 45:2 ממלל לשני היך קולמוס ספרא רגילא results in Tg לשני עט סופר מהיר. These similes, despite the fact that they introduce more than just a particle, often express what is probably the simple sense of the text: In Ps 59:8 חרבות בשפתותם is a metaphor for slander, so we might expect the targum's מילי דשנינן היך סייפא בספוותהון; and in Ps 80:9 Israel is the vine described in גפן ממצתים תסיע, so the targum's בית ישראל דמתילין לגופנא ממצרים אטילתא is unexceptional. Slightly more complicated is Ps 51:9 תחטאני באזוב ואטהר where the targum expands תדי עלי היך כהנא דמדי באזובא על מסאבא. The Hebrew text is understood as if it were כבאזוב, and the targum then expands with a description of how the hyssop is employed in the purification process. The fundamental sense of the simile, however, remains that of the biblical text.

At other times, the employment of the simile can actually clarify texts which might support two different readings. For example, Ps 104:4 עשה מלאכיו רוחות can be rendered as both "He makes his messengers winds" and "He makes winds his messengers." The targum, by translating דעבד אזגדוי סרהובין היך רוחא, indicates that it chooses the former ("swift as the wind"). Similarly, לך דמיה תהלה (Ps 65:2) can be rendered "Silence is praise for thee," but the targum chooses קדמך מתחשבא היך שתיקותא תושבחתא ("Praise is considered as silence for thee)."

Quite frequently, biblical metaphors which have a single term are transformed by the targum into two-term similes. The imagery of water overwhelming a victim is not uncommon in Psalms; whether the psalmist fears actual drowning or is employing it as a metaphor for being overwhelmed by a "sea of troubles" is not relevant for our purpose. Choosing two out of many such examples, we find:

Ps 69:2 באו מים עד נפש becomes
Tg מטו משירית חיבין עד די אעיקון לי היך מיא דמטו עד נפשא;
Ps 144:7 והצילני ממים רבים becomes
ושיזיב יתי מאוכלוסין דמתילין למיין סגיאין.[17]

---

[17] The text of Psalm 69 attracts a number of these similes in the targum, and these are also to be found at 124:5 and 32:6. Closely related are passages where the "pit" and "slime" of the Hebrew text are seen by the targum as a metaphor for exile in Pss 69:3, 15 and 88:7. These metaphorical renderings are not, however, ubiquitous in TgPs; cf. Ps 40:13 ויעלני מבור שאון מטיט היון, which is translated literally.

In the targum the water becomes a simile for the "encampment of the wicked who oppress me like water which has reached my soul" or "crowds who are like water".

Some of the most interesting uses of this device in the targum's translation of Psalms, however, occur in passages where it produces similes which are probably quite remote from the simple sense of the Hebrew text. From a formal standpoint, the methodology of the targum does not differ between cases where the simile unpacks a metaphor which is implicit in the Hebrew and when the targum creates one afresh. Twice (Pss 90:14, 101:8) the Hebrew word for morning is understood metaphorically as the "world to come." Thus Ps 101:8 לעלמא דאתי דמתיל לנהור becomes לבקרים אצמית כל רשעי ארץ צפרא אמגר כל רשיעי ארעא. The targum's eschatological interests are likely to have generated these readings.[18]

Finally, in the course of dealing with an intractable verse (Ps 68:14), a *targum aḥer* that is found in a few MSS introduces no fewer than *four* similes. The text reads אם תשכבון בין שפתים כנפי יונה נחפה בכסף ואברותיה בירקרק חרוץ.[19] The targum writes: "<u>You wicked kings</u> if you sleep <u>in theaters</u> *which are compared to* garbage heaps, <u>behold the congregation of the children of Israel</u> *who are compared to* the wings of a dove, <u>relaxing themselves</u> (?) <u>in the verses of the Torah</u> *which are compared to* silver and <u>its students</u> *who are compared* to the body of a dove in pure gold."[20] The device of introducing similes is taken to the limit in this verse, and the result bears no resemblance to the original either in form or in meaning, but it enables the targum to contrast Israel and the nations, and to highlight one of its pet themes, the study of Torah.

---

[18] At times the targum can accomplish the same goal without the simile; thus at 90:15 בקר is rendered עלמא דאתי in a non-simile translation.

[19] Note the similarity of two contemporary translations, one calling this "the most difficult of the psalms to interpret" and the other writing, "the coherence of this psalm and the meaning of many of its passages are uncertain." *NRSV*: "[The women at home divide the spoils] though they stay among the sheepfolds — the wings of a dove covered with silver, its pinions with green gold." *NJPS*: "[housewives are sharing in the spoils;] even for those of you who lie among the sheepfolds there are wings of a dove sheathed in silver, its pinions in fine gold."

[20] The "regular" targum has only one simile, but shares more than that with the *targum aḥer*: "If you wicked kings lie among the garbage heaps, the congregation of Israel <u>which is like</u> a dove is shaded by clouds of glory, dividing up the plunder of the Egyptians, pure silver and treasure houses filled with pure gold."

## Specification of Speakers

One of the most characteristic features of the targum of Psalms is "specification," a technique by which elements are introduced into the translation, thereby making the Aramaic version more specific and more narrowly focused than the Hebrew original. These elements which modify the text may be adjectives, adverbs, prepositional phrases or whole clauses, and are employed in a variety of contexts to a variety of effects. Sometimes the specification merely clarifies the meaning which inheres to the Hebrew text, but at others is part of the way in which the targum rewrites the text either to solve intractable language or to convey a theological message.

The psalms cannot be described, as a rule, as dialogue or conversation, although it is certainly likely that in the actual recitation of psalms in a variety of cultic contexts different voices may have spoken different parts. One of the technical devices which the targum of Psalms employs is the introduction into the Aramaic text of markers which identify the speakers of passages where no such indicator is present in the biblical text.[21] As we examine this technique, we shall find that not all of its occurrences are of the same nature. Some of the time the insertion of the speaker is obvious and fairly trivial, while in other instances the creation of dialogue is a response to a real or perceived exegetical or theological difficulty.

It is important to realize that the insertion of speakers at the beginning of a sentence in the targum of Psalms is a sub-category of a feature which I call "introductory narrative plus." In order to make its translation flow more smoothly, the targum at times supplements its translation with a freely composed (i.e. not text-based) subordinate temporal or circumstantial clause (usually) at the beginning of a verse.

---

[21] This device is not unique to the targum of Psalms among the Aramaic versions; it is the subject of R. P. Gordon, "Dialogue and Disputation in the Targum to the Prophets," *JSS* 39 (1994) 7–17. Earlier students of the targum of Psalms noted its presence as well, but this has not been analyzed in a systematic fashion. In general, the most elaborate and extended examples of dialogue have been studied, without giving any sense of the employment of this device by the targum on a smaller, and thus broader, scale. There has been a tendency to attribute the introduction of speakers into the text to a desire by the targum to dramatize, and — although vividness is certainly a result of the assignment of speakers to the text — I should argue that in most cases the interpolation of speakers by the targum is related to the exigencies of the biblical text or the targumist's worldview, and not merely to an attempt to make the text "come alive."

These often midrashic additions contextualize the translation of the verse in some way in order to clarify its meaning. Here I shall use the terms "dialogue" and "insertion of speakers" fairly synonymously for instances where the targum places quotation marks around a verse or part of a verse, and introduces references to one or more interlocutors who are not present in the biblical text. First I shall examine cases where a single speaker is introduced, attempt to classify the reasons for their presence, and then proceed to more complicated examples.

The book of Psalms, unlike narrative, or even prophetic, works of the Bible, does not require indication of speakers in the vast majority of its text. Although the poetic text is terse and occasionally ambiguous, the difficulties presented are not usually solved by the awareness of who the speaker is or where speakers may be said to alternate. In a surprising number of cases, however, real or perceived difficulties in the biblical text can be alleviated in such a fashion. We shall observe instances where the insertion of a speaker by the targum is paralleled in a modern translation. The simplest form of insertion of speaker consists of the targum's inserting words like אמר דוד ("David said") at some point in a psalm. Such examples are to be found at Pss 18:4, 21; 49:16; 60:3; 84:9, and are not necessarily meaning-laden. But most of the examples of this feature in the targum of Psalms can be seen as responses to something present or lacking in the biblical text.

Shifts in person or number in the verbs of the Hebrew text can generate the marking of speakers by the targum. Thus Ps 20:1-5 has no indication of speaker; the words are addressed to an unnamed listener, and God is the subject of the verbs. With verse 6, however, there is a shift to a first person plural cohortative נרננה ("let us rejoice"), and the targum marks it with the insertion of יימרון עמך ("your people shall say"), so that the words are not those of the speaker of the psalm but of others. A similar motivation probably governs the targumist's rendition of Ps 65:5, אשרי תבחר ותקרב ישכן חצריך נשבעה בטוב ביתך קדש היכלך. The awkward sequence of second person and third person singular, followed by first person plural cohortative נשבעה, is resolved, in part, by the targum through the insertion of יימרון צדיקיא ("the righteous will say"), thus furnishing a subject for the first person plural verb.[22]

---

[22] Likewise Ps 48:5-8, which describes the expedition of a group of kings to Jerusalem, is followed in the Hebrew text by כאשר שמענו כן ראינו ("as we have heard, so have we seen"). Despite the reference in the opening line of the psalm

Sometimes the insertion of the speaker alone is not enough to resolve such difficulties in the flow of a psalm. The reading in Ps 76:10,
בקום למשפט אלהים ("when God arises for judgment") is presumably
a temporal clause modifying the previous verse, "From the heavens
you made justice heard; the earth feared and was silent." But the targum does not read the syntax that way, possibly because the previous
several verses all refer to God in the second person, and this one is in
the third. The targum therefore inserts the words יימרון צדיקיא ("the
righteous will say") *and* translates בקום as a finite verb, "God will
arise." These two changes together create a much smoother flow for
the translation. Similarly, Psalm 45 is an address to the royal bride-
groom in the second person, but the targum introduces new speakers
before the words בעידנא ההוא תימרון (45:18), אזכירה שמך בכל דר ודר
("at that time shall you [pl.] say"), while at the same time shifting the
translation of the singular אזכירה to the plural.[23]

In his edition of the Aramaic version of Job from Qumran, Michael
Sokoloff notes:

> A recurring characteristic of the translator is his telescoping of two phrases
> which appear in the H text in *parallelismus membrorum*. The translator
> combined the parallel words or phrases into one unit, thus destroying the
> poetic character of the original, but gaining compactness of style.[24]

The targum of Psalms also ignores the parallelism of the Hebrew poetry, but treats it in a way which may be seen as the opposite of
11QtgJob's. Rather than compressing the "synonymous" terminology
of the biblical parallelism into single phrases or clauses, it frequently
expands each of the balanced clauses in such a way that they are no
longer parallel.[25] The result is the same as that of the Job translation,

---

(48:2) to "the city of our God," which implies a first person plural, the abrupt shift
at line 9 impels the targum to add יימרון כולהון כחדא ("they all shall say together") — or יימרון בני ישראל in some MSS — in order to furnish a speaker for
the first person plural verb.

[23] All this despite the fact that Ps 45:1 begins with a first person remark (presumably the psalmist), so that the presence of a first person in the final verse need
not be seen as anomalous.

[24] M. Sokoloff, *The Targum to Job from Qumran Cave XI* (Ramat-Gan: Bar-
Ilan University, 1974) 8.

[25] The term often applied to this exegetical approach in rabbinic biblical interpretation is "omnisignificance," following the suggestions of J. L.Kugel, *The Idea
of Biblical Poetry* (New Haven, CT: Yale University Press, 1981) 104. Willem
Smelik suggests the term "diversification of parallelism" for phenomena like this.

in that the "poetic character of the original" is destroyed, but the impression produced is very different.

The introduction of different speakers for the two half verses is one way in which the targum can accomplish this. A good example is at Ps 129:8, ולא אמרו העברים ברכת ה׳ עליכם ברכנו אתכם בשם ה׳ ("And the passersby did not say, 'may the blessing of the Lord be upon you; we bless you in the name of the Lord'"). For the targum the second half-verse must say something different from the first, and it therefore renders as ולא אמרו דעברין מתמן בירכתא דה׳ עליכון ולא יתיבון להון בריכנא יתכון בשמא בה׳. For the targum the second half-line is a response, "nor will they respond to them (i.e. the passerby) 'we bless you, etc.'" The two halves have different speakers addressing one another.

This tendency may be further stimulated by the presence of slight differences between the two halves of the verse. Thus in Ps 18:32, כי מי אלוה מבלעדי ה׳ ומי צור זולתי אלהינו ("Who is a god beside the Lord, and who is a rock other than our God"), the presence of a first person plural in the second half-verse but not in the first may be responsible for the targumic expansion. The targum reads ארום על ניסא ופורקנא דתעביד למשיחך ולשיורי עמך דישתארון יודון כל עממיא אומיא ולישניא ויימרון לית אלהא ... ועמך יימרון לית דתקיף אלא אלהנא ("For because of the miracle and redemption which you will perform for your messiah and the remainder of your people who survive, all the peoples, nations and tongues will confess and say, 'there is no god…,' while your people will say, 'there is none as powerful as our god'"). Each half of the sentence has been furnished with a speaker; the confession of the nations to God's power is paralleled by the exultation of Israel in its God.

Cruces in the biblical text could not be treated by the ancient versions after the fashion of modern translations or commentaries, marking a word or a verse as "hopelessly corrupt." The targum employs a variety of techniques to resolve such difficulties, including that of identification of speakers. Thus at Ps 59:8 הנה יביעון בפיהם הרבות בשפתותיהם כי מי שמע, where *BHS* marks the last three words with "perhaps a gloss," the Aramaic version both introduces speakers and adds to the quotation: אמרין נתגבר ארום מן הוא דשמע ויתפרע ("they say, we shall triumph, for who will listen and exact punishment"?). The last three words of the verse are thus a quotation, and the rest of the supplement denies the notion of reward and punishment. The *NJPS* translation here translates very similarly, "[they think], 'who hears?'"

Ps 101:2 also presents to any translator a problem that the targum solves through specification of speakers. The Hebrew text reads אשכילה בדרך תמים מתי תבוא אלי אתהלך בתם לבבי בקרב ביתי. The previous verse was addressed by the psalmist (אזמרה) to God (לך ה'), while this one contains two clauses, each of which has a first person singular verb, with the ambiguous תבא (2nd m.s. or 3rd f.s. with דרך as subject). The targum chooses the former reading of תבא, but as a result has a different problem. If the speaker is the subject of אשכילה, then God is the subject of תבא, and it may not be theologically appropriate for God to be visiting the psalmist (man should go to God, not vice-versa). This exegetico-theological problem is resolved by the targum with אמר אלהא אשכלינך באורח שלים אימתי תיעול לוותי אמר דוד אתלהך בשלימות לבבי בגו בית אולפבי ("God said, 'I shall enlighten you in a wholesome path before me, when you will come to me;' David said, 'I shall walk in wholesomeness of heart within my study-hall'").[26] God is the subject of אשכילה, and David is the subject of תבא, as well as אתהלכה. It is not likely that the targum's reading of תבא is the simple sense of the biblical text, but once the targum has chosen the second person reading, it is virtually forced to resort to the use of dialogue within its version of the Hebrew to create a satisfactory overall rendering.

A *targum aḥer* which is found in about a half dozen MSS at Ps 127:2 invents a remarkable piece of dialogue to solve an exegetical crux. The Hebrew text reads שוא לכם משכימי קום מאחרי שבת אכלי לחם העצבים כן יתן לידידו שנא.[27] One of the favored themes of the targum of Psalms is the contrast between the righteous and the wicked, and here it creates a dialogue between those two groups.[28] "The wicked say to the righteous, 'It is a mistake for you to get up early and pray in the morning, and to sit at length at night to study Torah, eating the

---

[26] It is interesting that there are Hebrew MSS which read אשכילך, which may imply the exegesis of the targum.

[27] *NRSV*: "It is in vain that you rise up early and go late to rest, eating the bread of anxious toil; for he gives sleep to his beloved" (or "for he provides for his beloved during sleep"); *NJPS*: "In vain do you rise early and stay up late, you who toil for the bread you eat; He provides as much for His loved ones while they sleep" (with the final clause marked "meaning of Hebrew uncertain").

[28] On this theme, see my "The Righteous and the Wicked in the Aramaic Version of Psalms," *Journal of the Aramaic Bible* 3 (Michael L. Klein Memorial Volume, 2002) 5–26.

bread of pain.' The righteous respond, 'In truth the Lord gives to his
beloved a full reward doubled.'" Once again, this is not anything close
to a legitimate reading of the Hebrew text, but it is a good example of
the targum's use of dialogue to "interpret" a difficult passage, and to
superimpose upon it many of the ideological values which he holds
dear, such as the contrast between righteous and wicked, the study of
Torah and prayer.

Finally, let us turn our attention to one of the three passages in
Psalms where there is a more substantial division of the text among
speakers and which has been mentioned in ealier analyses of this issue
in the targum.[29] These are not typical of the phenomenon which we
have been discussing to this point, although they are striking and
memorable, and, indeed, represent the logical extension of the techniques which we have seen employed on a much smaller scale.[30]

Psalm 91 is a text unassigned by heading to author or speaker,
plunging directly into its prayer without introduction. Verse 2 asserts
in the first person אמר לה׳ מחסי ומצודתי אלהי אבטח בו ("Let me say
of the Lord, 'He is my refuge and fortress etc.'"), while vv. 3-8, beginning כי הוא יצילך מפח יקוש ("for He will save you from the
fowler's trap"), has a series of second person singular addresses.
Verse 9, once again, has a first person statement, כי אתה ה׳ מחסי
("for you, Lord, are my refuge"), followed by an address to an uni-
dentified addressee in vv. 10-13 and God's concluding words in vv.
14-16 guaranteeing His protection to the individual spoken of in the
first portion of the psalm.

The exegetical challenge of this text is met head-on by the targum.
The speaker of v. 2 is David, and his words in vv. 3-8 are addressed to
his son Solomon. Verse 9 is Solomon's affirmation of his acceptance
of the Lord's protection. Beginning with v. 10, God himself announces (אתיב מרי עלמא) that Solomon will be protected by him. It appears
that the targum ignores the problem of מלאכיו ("his angels") in v. 11,
which should have been "my angels" if God were the speaker, as well
as references to the addressee in the third person in vv. 14-16 which

---

[29] Cf., for example, Churgin, תרגום כתובים, 46.

[30] I have discussed one of the other cases (Ps 137:3-9) in detail in "Translation
Technique in the Targum to Psalms: Two Test Cases. Psalms 2 and 137," *SBL
Seminar Papers 1994* (Atlanta: Scholars Press, 1994) 340–43. Cook, "Psalms Targum," 193–94, has more recently discussed the third passage, Ps 118:23-29, which
has the most extensive indications of change of speaker in all of targum Psalms.

read awkwardly together with the second person language of vv. 10-13 in the targum's version. Nevertheless, it is clear that — granted the targum's willingness to set out speakers in this text, had it thought there was another speaker who was to be introduced — the targum would not have hesitated to insert it into the text. At any rate, the targum sees the solution to the shifting persons and direction of the text in the presence of a variety of speakers, which are not explicitly indicated in the Hebrew, but supplied for the reader's convenience in the Aramaic.

## "HISTORICIZATION" IN THE TARGUM OF PSALMS

The exegetical technique of introducing speakers into a psalm text, which we examined above, is but one of many sorts of specification. In this section, we shall investigate another sort of specification which the targum of Psalms employs, one which it shares with rabbinic midrashic technique: the interpretation of ahistorical passages in Psalms in relation to specific historical events and historical characters.

The book of Psalms is, to a large degree, devoid of historical markers, except in psalm titles[31] and in such texts as Psalms 68, 78, 105, 106, 135, and 136. Historical characters, too, do not play a significant role in very many psalms, and it appears that the reason for this may be to make the text of Psalms non-specific, both temporally and personally. This feature contributes to the timeless popularity of the poetry which describes Everyman's confrontation with his God, his world and his fellow man. The targum of Psalms, however, moves away from this historical generality toward specification. It assigns allusions in the biblical text to specific historical events or figures rather than allowing them to remain vague and unallusive. There is little attention paid, on the whole, to whether or not the historical allusion is compatible with the interpretation of the rest of the text or whether it is completely atomistic.

The historical material within the book of Psalms centers on the Exodus, the desert wanderings and the conquest of Canaan, with a number of titles alluding to events in the life of David. It should not

---

[31] In other ancient versions of Psalms, such as the Septuagint and the Peshitta, the tradition of assigning psalms to specific historical contexts through indicators in the title is expanded. Cf. B. S. Childs, "Psalm Titles and Midrashic Exegesis," *JSS* 16 (1971) 137–50.

surprise us, then, that the bulk of the historical allusions in the targum
centers about the same events as those found in the biblical text. References to individuals, which often consist merely of the specification
by the targum of the individual to whom a given text refers, are a bit
more diverse than those found in the Hebrew. I shall present a representative survey of the way the targum utilizes this midrashic technique.

Psalm titles, which, as we have noted, occasionally contain historical allusions, furnish an opportunity for the targum to introduce further historical data. Thus in two exegetically related passages, Ps 7:1
על דברי כוש בן ימיני is taken by the targum to refer to Saul son of
Kish (קיש) from the tribe of Benjamin,[32] while Ps 110:1 נאם ה׳
לאדני שב לימיני עד אשית איביך הדום לרגליך is seen as a warning to
David to wait for the kingship of Saul the Benjamite to come to an
end, and not attempt to usurp any of the time allotted for his predeces-
sor's rule.[33] There is nothing in the text or targumic exegesis of the
rest of these Psalms that would generate these readings, which are
thus seen to be atomistically connected to the term ימיני in both cases.

Two consecutive non-Davidic psalm titles are expanded by the targum with reference to Moses. Ps 45:1 למנצח על ששנים לבני קרח is
linked to the Sanhedrin of Moses, presumably through the exegesis of
the Hebrew as *sheshonim* = "those who learn [Torah]."[34] Perhaps the
authorship by the sons of Korah, contemporaries of Moses, suggests
this association. More interesting, however, is the interpretation of Ps
46:1 למנצח לבני קרח על עלמות שיר, the key word of which the targum renders through בזמן דאתכסי אבוהון מבהון והיבון אשתיזבו ואמרו
שירתא ("when their father was *concealed* from them"), probably alluding to Korah's being swallowed by the earth while they survived
(Num 26:11). The fact that this psalm deals with something like an
earthquake may furnish an additional "excuse" for the targumic
reading.[35]

---

[32] Cf. *Midrash Tehillim* 7:13, 15-16 (ed. S. Buber; Vilna: Romm, 1881) 69–70
and b*Mo ʿed Qatan* 16b.

[33] There are two expansions to this verse in the targumic tradition; only this
version, and not the other, has an historical one. The two versions alternate in the
MS tradition in the place of base text and *targum aḥer*.

[34] This "exegesis" is also found in the titles of Pss 69:1 and 80:1, but only here
is it associated with Moses.

[35] A further possible allusion to the Korah incident is in the targum of verse 3.

Outside of titles, the simplest form of historical allusion in the targum consists of explicit reference to an event which the biblical text
has alluded to implicitly. In this fashion, Ps 74:2 זכר עדתך קנית קדם
גאלת שבט נחלתך receives the modifier ממצרים after the equivalent of
גאלת in the targum. A *targum aḥer* identifies Ps 78:64
ואלמונתיו לא תבכינה כהניו בחרב נפלו with the slain priests Hophni and
Phineas and their wives.[36]

Modern Psalms scholarship associates passages like Ps 74:13-15
אתה פוררת בעזך ים שברת ראשי תנינים על המים אתה רצצת ראשי לויתן
תתננו למאכל לעם לציים אתה בקעת מעין ונחל אתה הובשת נהרות איתן
with the Near Eastern mythological motifs of the battle of Baal and
Yam, employed in a fashion that indicates the triumph of the one God
over natural forces which in Canaanite cultures were considered divinities. The targum rewrites these verses to describe the splitting of
the Red Sea at the Exodus, with a double literal-metaphorical translation of שברת ראשי תנינים, wherein the תנינים are the Egyptians, and the
"heads of leviathan" become "the heads of Pharaoh's warriors."[37] The
extraction of water and drying up of rivers is related to the rock in the
wilderness which produced water when struck, and the drying up of
Arnon, Jabbok and Jordan during the conquest.[38]

Two of the sorts of historical allusions linked to David involve his
opponents and his son, Solomon. The addressee in Ps 55:14 ואתה אנוש
כערכי אלופי ומידעי, according to the targum is Ahitophel, described
in rabbinic tradition on the basis of this verse as David's partner in
Torah study.[39] But two verses later, the targum names Ahitophel and
Doeg as the specific enemies of David who are the object of the curse
ישימות (ק' ישי מות) עלימו. The same pair, according to the targumic
reading, are the concerns of Ps 140:9-10, with Doeg being identified
as the רשע of v. 9, and Ahitophel, once again characterized as ריש
עמל שפתימו יכסומו (ק' יכסימו) סנהדרי תלמידי, is subjected to the curse.
David, according to the targumic version of Ps 140:11, prays that their
punishment be the fire of Gehenna and absence of eternal life. The

---

[36] Likewise, Ps 66:6 הפך ים ליבשה בנהר יעברו ברגל is associated by the targum with the crossings of the Red Sea and the Jordan, while גוים הורשת ותטעם
receives the specifications "Canaanite" and "Israelite."

[37] Note that at Ezek 29:3 תנים is used symbolically for Egypt.

[38] References to God's power in conjunction with water frequently attract
identification with the events of the Exodus in the targum.

[39] Cf. b*Sanh.* 106b, citing Pss 55:14-15 and 41:10.

presumption is that the audience of the targum was familiar with these characters and their relationship with David in both biblical and rabbinic versions, and that the Aramaic version could allude to them in this fashion without further remark.

We have already seen, in our earlier discussion of the introduction of speakers into the translation of the Hebrew text, how the targum introduces Solomon as an interlocutor in the Aramaic version of Psalm 91. In two passages based on the same midrashic tradition, the targum alludes to Solomon's bringing the Ark into the Temple in a Davidic context. David's request of God, Ps 86:17 עשה עמי אות לטובה ויראו שנאי ויבשו כי אתה ה' עזרתני ונחמתני, is specified "at the time that my son Solomon brings the Ark into the Temple, let the gates open on my behalf." This would be the sign that David has been completely forgiven by God. The same event is identified at Ps 132:10 בעבור דוד עבדך אל תשב פני משיחך, where the time is indicated by "when the Ark enters within the gates," and משיחך is identified with Solomon. It is only on the merits of David, according to the tradition, that the Temple is "willing" to open its doors to the Ark.[40] Again, the audience is presumed to be familiar with that tradition.

There are a number of passages in Psalms where "Joseph" is used to represent a part of the Israelite nation. The targum, it appears, does not recognize such allusions in positive contexts, and interprets the passages as referring to the son of Jacob, with interesting results.[41] Ps 77:16 גאלת בזרוע עמך בני יעקב ויוסף סלה identifies those redeemed as "the children whom Jacob bore and Joseph sustained," employing separate verbal specifications for the two patriarchs. Ps 80:2 נהג כצאן יוסף is rendered "who leads like sheep the coffin of Joseph." This unexpected employment of the simile technique in translation is necessary to avoid calling the Israelites in the desert by the name of Joseph. Finally, Ps 81:6 עדות ביהוסף שמו בצאתו על ארץ מצרים, which follows upon חק לישראל and משפט לאלהי יעקב, is taken to refer to Joseph the individual (and not a group parallel to "Israel" and "Jacob"), and is "translated" as follows: "He set testimony regarding Joseph that he did not come near to the wife of his master; on that day he went forth from prison and ruled over the land of Egypt."

Finally, let us look at a psalm text which, *prima facie*, is the last

---

[40] Cf. *Midrash Tehillim* 24:10 (ed. Buber, p. 208); b*Sanh.* 107b.

[41] In a negative reference to the Northern Kingdom such as Ps 78:67 the targum is willing to allow "Joseph" to refer to a group of Israelites.

place where one would expect historicization to take place, the familiar-to-all Psalm 23. We read (following the MSS rather than the printed text):

> [1]The Lord sustained <u>his people in the desert; they</u> lacked nothing. [2]<u>In a place of dryness</u>, in the pleasantness of greenery he causes me to dwell; he leads me beside restful waters. [3]He restores my soul <u>with manna (and quails)</u>; he leads me in the way of righteousness for the sake of his name.... [5]You set before me a table <u>with manna</u> in the presence of my oppressors; you have fattened <u>with fat birds my body</u> and with <u>anointing</u> oil <u>the head of my priests</u>...

The text, albeit with some awkwardness, has been transformed from an individual psalm of trust to a more narrowly focused reflection on the Israelite experience in the desert (expressed, in all but the first verse, through the words of an individual). It is here perhaps worthwhile to call attention to rabbinic parallels to this targum in *Midrash Tehillim* on Psalm 23.[42] These associate Ps 23:1 with the journeys through the desert, and particularly with the manna; like the targum, the midrash links v. 3 with the manna, but via the words במעגלי צדק which attract no such expansion in the Aramaic. The midrashic comment, "'You arrange before me a table': this is the table of manna and quail" is almost verbatim in the targum. However, although the targum shares certain readings with classic rabbinic material, its presentation is as often unique.

## WELTANSCHAUUNG/THEOLOGY

When we attempt to enter the world of ideas in the targum, the complex of ideals and values which it brings to the translated Hebrew text, and which are not necessarily intrinsic to that text, we must be exceptionally cautious in our methodology.[43] Because the Aramaic

---

[42] *Midrash Tehillim* (ed. Buber), 199–201.

[43] In much of my published and unpublished work on the Aramaic versions of the Bible, I have tried to stress these methodological issues: the published material includes "Torah and Its Study in the Targum of Psalms," in J. Gurock and Y. Elman (eds.), *Ḥazon Naḥum: Studies in Honor of Dr. Norman Lamm on the Occasion of His Seventieth Birthday* (Hoboken, NJ: Yeshiva University Press, 1997) 39–67, esp. 39-41; "The Aramaic Versions of Deuteronomy 32: A Study in Comparative Targumic Theology," in P. V. Flesher (ed.), *Targum and Scripture: Studies in Aramaic Translation and Interpretation in Memory of Ernest G. Clarke* (Studies in the Aramaic Interpretation of Scripture 2; Leiden: Brill, 2002) 29–52; "The Righteous and the Wicked in the Aramaic Version of Psalms," *Journal of the Ara-*

versions of the Hebrew Bible are translations of the Hebrew text before they are anything else, we must be very careful not to impute to
the targum a *Weltanschauung* which is really that of its Hebrew original. In order to make sure that we are investigating the theology of the
targum and not that of the Hebrew text, we should first put aside any
theological statements or concepts which are wholly due to the underlying biblical text. A straightforward translation of the Hebrew text
furnishes us with the least evidence or information about the beliefs of
a targum. It is thus of no significance if, for example, the targum
would employ משיחא where the Hebrew text has משיח; it would tell us
nothing of the targum's conception of messianism. Once we have
done that, we must also discount temporarily features or phenomena
of the targum which are products of the way in which it operates on
the biblical text, that is, its translation technique and exegetical methodology. This is not to say that translation and exegesis may not serve
as theological guideposts, but we have no right to presume that they
do so without further evidence. This sort of prudence is not always
observed in contemporary targumic scholarship.

We therefore have to pay particularly close attention to targumic
use of terminology in non-translation contexts, that is, material in the
Aramaic version which does not stand in one-to-one correspondence
to the biblical text. By doing this, we allow the Aramaic text itself to
determine what in it is theologically significant, and do not run the
risk of imposing the theological framework of the modern scholar on
the targum. Sometimes this "non-translation" language is "triggered"
by the language of the verse and can thus be said to be a natural out-
come of the translation process. But on other occasions, those we describe as "untriggered pluses," the targumic material cannot be seen as
directly connected with the translation of the text and can only be ascribed to the targum's own theological interests. Both of these types
of targumic material give us the greatest insight into the way the Ara-

---

*maic Bible* 3 (2002) 5–26. Cf. also my comments in "The Aramaic Versions and the
Many Faces of the Jewish Biblical Experience," in G.J. Brooke (ed.), *Jewish Ways
of Reading the Bible. Proceedings of the British Association for Jewish Studies Annual Meeting, June 1999* (JSS Sup 11; Oxford: Oxford University Press, 2000)
133–64, esp. 161–64. Over the last 20 years or so, I have given a number of papers
at conferences on theological aspects of the targum of Psalms which I hope to inte-
grate for publication in the near future. The present section of this essay, aside from
the first two paragraphs which are taken almost verbatim from my "The Righteous
and the Wicked," 7–8, is based in part on that hitherto unpublished material.

maic versions present their beliefs and opinions. Once we have sketched the outlines of the theological interests of the translator on the basis of freely produced material, we can return to the translation and exegetical material to see how they support and fill in that picture.

*Prayer in the Targum of Psalms*

In order to illustrate the ways in which the targum conveys its theological message over and above its translation, I have selected the related themes of prayer and sacrifice. There is no doubt that the language of the Hebrew text of Psalms contains many terms for prayerful communication between man and God — the verbs שוע, התפלל, התחנן, קרא, and the nouns from these roots — to name but a few. It is due in part to this phenomenon that the book of Psalms has become the Jewish book of prayer, par excellence, through the ages. The theme of prayer is taken further by the Aramaic translation in ways that indicate its significance, beyond the biblical, in the targumic world-view. Among the Aramaic targumim, prayer is not a theme unique to the targum of Psalms, but its importance in the Hebrew text of Psalms allows us to view issues of translation and theology simultaneously on a number of levels in the Aramaic version.[44]

On the strictly lexical plane, many of the terms for communication between man and God are rendered צלי \ צלותא by the targum. I believe that this is not due to the paucity of Aramaic vocabulary, but to a conscious effort by the translation to emphasize this theme. Furthermore, on the exegetical/idiomatic plane, a number of terms in the Hebrew text generate צלי \ צלותא in the targum, even though the Hebrew does not, strictly speaking, demand such a rendering. In some cases these are standard targumic exegeses, but in others they are not. Finally, the significance of prayer can be documented by the number of texts which do not refer to prayer in the Hebrew, whether idiomatically or by standard association, but for which the targum has supplied a plus (whether triggered or not) pertaining to prayer.

In conjunction with references to prayer, it will be interesting to ex-

---

[44] It is difficult, at times, to gauge the prominence of themes in this targum. Prayer does not appear to be as pervasive in non-translation pluses as others such as Torah and "righteous and wicked," which I have already discussed in my published work. It is interesting thay neither of two the recent attempts to list "theological" concepts in the targum of Psalms — by Diez Merino, in the introduction to his edition of the Zamora MS, and by Wein in ייַ הטוב — includes prayer as a significant concept in the targum of Psalms.

amine targumic allusions to sacrifice, particularly when they are in contexts where prayer is also mentioned. The replacement of sacrifice by prayer became a commonplace theme in Judaism after the destruction of the Temple, and it may prove instructive to discover whether the targum's interpretation reflects this dichotomy. Is there a "pro-prayer/anti-sacrifice" tendency in the targum? We present our analysis, moving from translation technique to exegesis to free supplementation, even though in gathering the data we have followed the methodology described above.

Most of the approximately 135 occurrences of צלי \ צלותא in the targum of Psalms are translations of Hebrew words for prayer: among nouns, תפלה, תחנון, קול, רנה, שיח; and among verbs, התחנן, חלה, צעק, שוע, קרא, התפלל. There is no doubt that the targum could have employed Aramaic קרא for Hebrew קרא, but it appears to disdain the poetic variation of the original and to employ the single term "prayer" for all of these roots. As a result, the targum loses the color and texture of the original, and, at the same time, "prayer" becomes the object and focus of the audience's attention. Closely linked to the employment of צלי to translate all of these roots is the targum's constant קבל צלותא ("hear the prayer") for the biblical verb ענה ("answer"), when God is the subject of the verb. It keeps the idea of prayer in the foreground.

Idioms which the targum employs in translation that add the word "prayer" to the literal translation of the Hebrew are typical of the way in which the Aramaic versions on the whole operate. Thus נשא ("raise"), פרש ("stretch out"), and שטח ("spread") + יד ("hand") all become "lift/spread out one's hands in prayer" in the targum. While it is natural to expand such literal biblical phrases with "prayer," since the posture described is one of entreaty, the metaphorical נשא נפש (literally, "lift one's soul") also becomes "lift one's soul in prayer" in the targum. The supplement sounds natural to our ears, but must be distinguished from "lift one's hands in prayer" by the fact that the latter is physical and not metaphorical. In fact, out of all the Hebrew Bible it is only in Psalms that נשא יד (28:2; 134:2) and נשא נפש (25:1; 86:4; 143:8) are rendered as "prayer" in the targumim.[45] This may certainly give us insight into the priorities of our translator. It is but a short step,

---

[45] For example, נשא נפש: Deut 24:15; Jer 22:27; 44:14; Hos 4:8 all could have been translated in that fashion, but none of them is. Similarly, Lam 1:17 פרשה ציון בידיה could easily have attracted "prayer," but it does not.

then, for the targumic exegete to take the word בפרש without יי at Ps 68:15 and render it "when she spread <u>her hands in prayer</u> at the sea," or ידיו without פרש or נשא at 68:32 and translate "<u>to spread</u> their hands in prayer." The standard Hebrew idioms are stimulated by the single words, and the supplementary reference to prayer follows naturally.

The appearance of "prayer" as an unexpected translation for Hebrew words is also a sign of the significance of the theme in this targum. So if Ps 2:11 גילו ברעדה has the targum צלו ברתיתא ("pray in fear"), it may be that the targumist feels that any of the usual renditions of גיל (i.e. דוץ, בוע, רנן) were at odds with רעדה, and abandoned the literal translation (here alone in all the targumim) for terminology more suitably parallel with עבדו in the first half of the sentence. Similarly, Ps 120:7 אני שלום וכי <u>אדבר</u> המה למלחמה is rendered אצלי. Since the Hebrew term דבר is almost never translated this way, this somewhat eccentric rendering is likely due to the translator's interest in prayer.

From the foregoing discussion, it should be clear that "prayer" appears in the targum of Psalms more frequently than we might have expected. But in order to claim real theological or ideological significance for this language, we must look at untriggered pluses and supplements to the text where the targum is most free to delineate what is important in its world-views. We shall observe that prayer makes frequent appearances in these pluses in unexpected contexts. The prayers of the patriarchs are recalled at Ps 46:5 לפנות בקר ("<u>for the sake of Abraham who prayed for it</u> at morning time"); Ps 132:6 שדה יער ("the <u>Lebanon</u> forests <u>where the patriarchs of old prayed</u>"); and Ps 99:6 ("and Samuel prayed for them to the Lord <u>like the patriarchs of old who prayed</u>").

Somewhat surprisingly, it is not only the righteous who pray in the targum; the רשע addressed by God at Ps 50:16 is described by the targum as "the wicked one <u>who has not repented, but prays in rebellion</u>." Those who "lie to God with their tongues" (Ps 78:36) do so, according to most MSS "at the time that they pray." Neither of these allusions to prayer is expected in the slightest. Presumably in order to heighten the depravity of the wicked, they are said to pray rebelliously or falsely.[46]

Difficult verses are "explicated" by the targum by the introduction of references to prayer. Ps 72:5 <u>ייראוך עם שמש ולפני ירח דור דורים</u>

---

[46] Similarly, the idiom פרש יד at Ps 44:21 becomes for the targum פרש יד בצלו in an idolatrous context.

is not translated in strict parallelism by the targum, but the second half is rendered "<u>let</u> generation after generation <u>pray for you</u> before <u>the light</u> of the moon." The insertion of prayer in parallelism with "fear" is not unreasonable, but it is certainly not demanded by the text. A more difficult text, Ps 4:5 רגזו ואל תחטאו אמרו בלבבכם על משכבכם ודמו סלה is expanded by the targum to read "So tremble <u>from him</u> and do not sin, recite <u>your entreaty with your mouths and your request</u> in your hearts <u>pray</u> on your beds and <u>remember the day of death</u> forever."[47] The three synonyms for prayer inserted into the verse clearly indicate the importance of prayer for the targumist.

*Sacrifice in the Targum of Psalms*

It should be clear that there is no anti-sacrificial bias in the targum because sacrifice is introduced freely in a variety of untriggered pluses. Thus the targum of Ps 43:4 reads "I shall approach the altar of God <u>to offer sacrifices</u>"; Ps 68:30 "From thy Temple over Jerusalem" becomes in the targum "From thy Temple <u>you shall receive sacrifices; your Shekhina dwells</u> over Jerusalem"; the pious who rejoice (Ps 132:4) do so <u>over sacrifices</u>; "the watchers for the morning" (Ps 130:6) is taken by the targum to be the equivalent of "those who watch <u>to offer</u> the morning <u>sacrifice</u>." If the targum had wanted to de-emphasize sacrifice, even these few pluses should not have been introduced.

In the translation of Psalms, the targum behaves unexceptionally vis-à-vis terms meaning "offering" or "sacrifice," rendering them literally, on the whole. There is, however, a group of passages in Psalm 50 which appear to contain vacillating judgments on the value and importance of sacrifice. Overtly positive attitudes are evinced by 50:5 "who make my covenant over sacrifice"; 50:14 "sacrifice a thankoffering to God and pay your vows to the Most High"; and 50:23 "he who sacrifices a thankoffering honors me." On the other hand, 50:8-9 "I rebuke you not for your sacrifices, and your burntofferings which are ever before me. I shall not take from your house a bull, nor from your paddocks he-goats," seems to indicate a less receptive attitude to sacrifice, as does 50:13: "Shall I eat the flesh of bulls or drink the blood of he-goats?" Note that the last verse stands before 50:14 which, we saw above, seems to present a more positive attitude.

---

[47] There is a good deal of orthographical variety among the MSS, but almost all have expansions that resemble the one I have translated.

All of the "positive" verses are modified by the targum, using the exegetical technique of introducing similes, ‏די גזרו קיימי וקיימו אורייתי‎ ‏ואתעסקו בצלותא דאמתילא לקורבנא‎ ("those who made my covenant and fulfilled my Torah and engaged in prayer which is compared to sacrifice" [on Ps 50:5]). Sacrifice was not the activity engaged in, but prayer which is compared to sacrifice. The two verses dealing positively with the thankoffering (14 and 23) are both turned by the targum into similes with a slightly different context. Ps 50:14 becomes ‏כבשו יצרא בישא ויתחשב קדם ה' כנכסת קודשא‎ ("suppress the evil inclination and it will be considered before the Lord as holy sacrifice").[48] The metaphorical translation of ‏זבח‎ appears to be ‏כבשו‎, and the suppression of the evil impulse is compared to animal sacrifice. The targum of 50:23 ‏זבח תודה יכבדנני‎ likewise compares the sacrifice of the evil impulse to the thankoffering ‏דדבח יצרא בישא היך קורבן‎ ‏יתחשב ליה ומוקיר לי‎ ("one who slaughters the evil inclination like a sacrifice it will be considered for him and he honors me").[49]

On the other hand, the passages which seem not overtly positive are also rewritten by the targum. Verses 8-9 and 13 become

> I did not rebuke you for the sacrifices which you did not offer to me in exile, for your burntofferings which your ancestors offered are ever before me. From the day that the home of my Shekhina was destroyed, I have not accepted a bull from your hand or rams from your flock.... From the day my Temple was destroyed, I have not received the flesh of sacrifice of fattened oxen, and the blood of rams the priests did not sprinkle before me.[50]

Although we have seen the targum substituting prayer and moral behavior for sacrifice in the other passages, in these verses it did not allow possibly negative words about sacrifice to remain unchanged. The emphasis of the targum is on the absence of sacrifice during the exile, after the Temple was destroyed. Sacrifice is a positive phenomenon,

---

[48] A minority MS tradition goes even further in the "non-sacrificial" reading, appending to the verse "which you vowed at Sinai to observe the commandments." In this translation, ‏נדריך‎ also does not refer to vows of sacrifice.

[49] The same exegesis is reflected at Ps 4:6 ‏זבחו זבחי צדק‎, when it is translated ‏כבשו יצריכון ויתחשב לכון כנכסת קודשא‎. Incidentally, we see here the intersection of targumic technique and targumic theology, as several verses with parallel language are interpreted employing the simile technique in order to highlight a theologoumenon that is dear to the translator.

[50] My version of 9 and 13 follows the MSS; the printed texts do not have the material supplementary to the translation of the Hebrew.

and the sacrifices of the patriarchs stand in for their descendants' lack of offerings.[51]

## CONCLUDING REMARKS

It should already be clear, from this rather limited survey of a few ways in which the Aramaic targum handles the biblical book of Psalms, that the goal of the translator was much more than to transform the words of the Hebrew text into Aramaic unadorned. First, the full meaning of that text had to be clarified, and we have demonstrated two of the devices that were used to achieve that end: similes and specification of speakers. Of course, both of those devices function at the same time to enhance the ideological messages of the targum as well.

In the historicization of the text we see, to some degree, simply a product of the attempt to endow the biblical verses with more narrowly focused meaning — but the process goes beyond the mere technique of introducing similes or dialogue into a text. This approach to the biblical Psalms allows them to function, in their Aramaic version, as another vehicle to transmit information about the Jewish past, while at the same time endowing nameless, faceless, timeless poetic texts with life through historical identifications. When the psalms are overlaid with biblical and midrashic history, they become more than isolated pieces of poetry in the hands of the targumist; they become vehicles through which he can link his readers to their national and religious history.

When the targum takes the theme of prayer which already inheres to the book of Psalms in so many ways, expands its presence both through translational and exegetical devices, and then further superimposes it freely onto passages where it cannot be seen in the original text at all, the concept of prayer is one to which it wishes to give prominence. More than the introduction of historical identifications into the psalms, the overlay of theological concepts on the translation is intended to convey to the audience the values that are important in the targum's eyes. As opposed to a theologoumenon such as "the world to come," for example — which had to be superimposed *de*

---

[51] Ps 50:12 "If I were hungry I would not tell you," is rendered by the targum "If the time of the morning daily sacrifice arrives, I would not tell you." This perhaps indicates the same line of reasoning that if man cannot offer up the requisite sacrifices due to circumstances beyond his control, God waives his due.

*novo* on a biblical text in which it did not appear already — in the case of the theme of prayer, the targum had a ready-made framework in its presence already in the biblical book. All it had to do was employ its various techniques of interpretation and expansion of the Hebrew text in order to send its message.

## BIBLIOGRAPHY

Bacher, W. "Das Targum zu den Psalmen," *MGWJ* 21 (1872) 408–16, 463–73

Bernstein, M. J. "Translation Technique in the Targum to Psalms: Two Test Cases. Psalms 2 and 137," *SBL Seminar Papers 1994* (Atlanta: Scholars Press, 1994) 326–45.

—. "Torah and Its Study in the Targum of Psalms," in J. Gurock and Y. Elman (eds.), *Ḥazon Naḥum: Studies in Honor of Dr. Norman Lamm on the Occasion of His Seventieth Birthday* (Hoboken, NJ: Yeshiva University Press, 1997) 39–67.

—. "The Righteous and the Wicked in the Aramaic Version of Psalms," *Journal of the Aramaic Bible* 3 (Michael L. Klein Memorial Volume, 2002) 5–26.

Churgin, P. תרגום כתובים [*Targum of the Hagiographa*] (New York: Horeb, 1945) 17–62.

Cook, E. M. "The Psalms Targum: Introduction to a New Translation, with Sample Texts," in P. V. Flesher (ed.), *Targum and Scripture: Studies in Aramaic Translation and Interpretation in Memory of Ernest G. Clarke* (Studies in the Aramaic Interpretation of Scripture 2; Leiden: Brill, 2002) 185–201.

Diez Merino, Luis (ed.). *Targum de Salmos: Edición del Ms. Vill-Amil n. 5 de Alfonso de Zamora* (Biblia Poliglota Complutense–Tradición Sefardi de la Biblica Aramaea IV,1; Madrid: Consejo Superior de Investiaciones Cientificas/ Instituto "Francisco Suarez," 1982).

—. "Haggadic Elements in the Targum of Psalms," *Proceedings of the Eighth World Congress of Jewish Studies. Division A* (Jerusalem: World Union of Jewish Studies, 1982) 131–37.

Edwards, T.M. "The Old, the New and the Rewritten: The Interpretation of the Biblical Psalms in the Targum of Psalms, in Relationship to other Exegetical Traditions, both Jewish and Christian" (D.Phil. thesis, University of Oxford, 2003).

Gordon, R. P. "Dialogue and Disputation in the Targum to the Prophets," *JSS* 39 (1994) 7–17.

Komlosh, Y. "קווים אופייניים בתרגום תהלים" ["Characteristic Features in the Targum of Psalms"], in J. M. Grintz and J. Liver (eds.), *Studies in the Bible Presented to M. H. Segal (Sefer Segal)* (Jerusalem: Israel Society for Biblical Research, 1964) 265–70.

Shunary, J. "Avoidance of Anthropomorphism in the Targum of Psalms," *Textus* 5 (1966) 134–44.

Smelik, W. F. "Extant Manuscripts of the Targum of Psalms: An Eclectic List" (September, 2001) <http://www.ucl.ac.uk/hebrew-jewish/staff/willem.htm>.

Wein, A. T. ין הטוב [*Yein ha-Tov*, A Hebrew Commentary on Targum Psalms] (Rehovot, 1985).

White, Emanuel. "A Critical Edition of the Targum of Psalms: A Computer Generated Text of Books I and II" (unpublished Ph.D. thesis, McGill University, 1988).

# THE PLACE OF THE SYRIAC VERSIONS
# IN THE TEXTUAL HISTORY OF THE PSALTER

ROBERT J. V. HIEBERT

## INTRODUCTION

The Classical Syriac[1] versions of the Bible are of considerable text critical significance, as a perusal of editions like *Biblia Hebraica Stuttgartensia* (*BHS*), *Septuaginta: Vetus Testamentum Graecum* (Göttingen), and *The Greek New Testament* (United Bible Societies) makes clear. When it comes to the Old Testament, the fact that Syriac was the first Semitic language into which the whole of the original Hebrew/Aramaic canon was translated[2] further demonstrates that the importance of this segment of the larger textual history must not be underestimated. In this essay, highlights of that history are surveyed and comparisons of Hebrew, Greek, and Syriac versions are carried out in order that the kinds of textual relationships that exist among them may be explicated.

## ORIGINS OF THE SYRIAC BIBLE

Textual scholars have debated when the process of translating the Hebrew Scriptures into Syriac began. Some have associated it with developments in the mid-first century CE in the kingdom of Adiabene in Mesopotamia east of the Tigris River. The Jewish historian Josephus and midrashic sources describe members of the royal house at that time reading the Torah and converting to Judaism.[3] Such accounts, it

---

[1] This dialect is sometimes called Eastern Aramaic. It is to be distinguished from Christian Palestinian Aramaic or Palestinian Syriac, a Western Aramaic dialect, into which the Old Testament was translated from the Septuagint. Only parts of this translation are extant (S. P. Brock, "Syriac Versions," *ABD* 6.794–99, esp. 794; A. Vööbus, "Syriac Versions," *IDBSup*, 848–54, esp. 849–50). The focus in this essay is on Classical Syriac versions of the Bible.

[2] M. P. Weitzman, *The Syriac Version of the Old Testament: An Introduction* (University of Cambridge Oriental Publications 56; Cambridge: Cambridge University Press, 1999) 2.

[3] Josephus (*Ant.* 20.17–53, 71, 75) reports on the conversion of Queen Helena

has been suggested, would presuppose the existence of those Scriptures in the vernacular of the region. It has also been argued that the *Vorlage* for such a version would not have been the original Hebrew text, but a Western Aramaic, Palestinian Targum. Furthermore, this Targum would have been the basis either for a *Vetus Syra* (an old Syriac version or an assortment of such versions which, in turn, would have been revised to produce the principal version of the Syriac Old Testament, the Peshitta)[4] or for the Peshitta itself. Others have asserted that the initial impetus for the production of the Syriac Bible is to be found in the circumstances surrounding the origins of Christianity in Mesopotamia — either in Adiabene or in Osrhoene, one of whose principal cities, Edessa, was by the second century a centre from which this faith spread generally eastward.[5]

---

and her son Izates. Significantly, Josephus also describes Izates reading the law of Moses and, subsequently, of being circumcised. In *Genesis Rabbah* 46:10, it is said that Izates and his brother Monobazus were both motivated to become circumcised upon reading God's command to that effect issued to Abraham in Gen 17:11.

[4] The term *Peshitta*, apparently meaning "simple," is first attested in the writings of Moses bar Kēphā (c. 813–903) to designate this version in distinction from the very literal and stylistically more cumbersome Syrohexapla (M. P. Weitzman, "The Interpretative Character of the Syriac Old Testament," in M. Sæbø [ed.], *Hebrew Bible / Old Testament: The History of Its* Interpretation, Vol. 1/1: *From the Beginnings to the Middle Ages (Until 1300): Antiquity* [Göttingen: Vandenhoeck & Ruprecht, 1996] 587–611, esp. 588; Weitzman, *Syriac Version*, 2–3), about which more will be said below.

[5] Labubna bar Sennak, *The Doctrine of Addai the Apostle* (ed. and trans. George Phillips; London: Trubner & Co., 1876); I. Guidi (ed. and trans.), *Chronicon Edessenum. Chronicon anonymum de ultimis regibus Persarum* (2 vols. in 1; part 1 of *Chronica Minora*; CSCO, Scriptores Syri, series 3, tome 4; Paris: E Typographeo Reipublicae, 1903); Eusebius, *Hist. Eccl.* 1.13; J. Perles, *Meletemata Peschitthoniana* (Breslau: Typis Grassii, Barthii et Socii [W. Friedrich], 1859) 7–8; A. Baumstark, "Pešiṭta und palästinensisches Targum," *Biblische Zeitschrift* 19 (1931) 257–70; P. Kahle, *Masoreten des Westens* (2 vols., Stuttgart: W. Kohlhammer, 1927–30) 2:3*-4*; idem, *The Cairo Geniza* (2d ed., Oxford: Blackwell, 1959) 265–83; A. Vööbus, *Peschitta und Targumim des Pentateuchs. Neues Licht zur Frage der Herkunft der Peschitta aus dem altpalästinischen Targum* (Papers of the Estonian Theological Society in Exile 9; Stockholm: ETSE, 1958); L. G. Running, "An Investigation of the Syriac Version of Isaiah," *AUSS* 3 (1965) 138–57; *AUSS* 4 (1966) 37–64, 135–48; Y. Maori, *Peshitta Version of the Pentateuch and Early Jewish Exegesis* (Hebrew; Jerusalem: Magnes, 1995); Vööbus, "Syriac Versions," 848–49; D. Bundy, "Christianity in Syria," *ABD* 1.970–79;

However, the scholarly consensus that seems to have emerged with regard to the origins of the Syriac Scriptures is that the textual evidence is best accounted for with the assumption that the first version of the Old Testament was the Peshitta and its *Vorlage* was the original Hebrew. The argument for a *Vetus Syra* that antedated the Peshitta is based upon the textual divergences observed in biblical quotations in Syriac patristic sources and in Arabic translations from the Syriac. Yet these can more easily be accounted for as free quotations, paraphrases, and other such ad hoc textual adjustments on the part of the church fathers and translators. The theory of a Palestinian Targum base for the Peshitta is also suspect, inasmuch as the parallels between the two seem to be readily attributable both to a common exegetical tradition and to coincidental agreements produced independently by those who translated the same Hebrew original into dialects of essentially the same language (i.e. Aramaic and Syriac). Furthermore, the Peshitta often diverges from the Targums in its rendering of the Hebrew and, in fact, includes the books of Daniel, Ezra, and Nehemiah for which there are no Targums. The theories about Adiabenian origins of the Syriac Bible are problematic as well. In the first place, the aforementioned traditions concerning the reading of the Torah do not constitute evidence that the version employed would have been in the dialect encountered in the Peshitta, since a related though distinctive one was spoken in that region. The Syriac of the Peshitta, on the other hand, was spoken in Osrhoene, as is demonstrated by inscriptional evidence at Edessa. An Edessene context is also suggested by the substitution for place names in the original biblical text of local toponyms such as Harran (1 Chron 19:6, אֲרַם מַעֲכָה [MT]), Mabbūg (2 Chron 35:20, כַּרְכְּמִישׁ [MT]), and Nisibis (1 Chronicles 18–19: צוֹבָה [MT]). It should also be noted that neither Josephus nor the creators of the Midrash mention a translation. One could conclude, therefore, that they are referring to the Hebrew text. Although that suggestion might be regarded by some as logistically improbable, given the kinds of contacts attested between Adiabenians and Jews of both that region

---

Weitzman, "Interpretative Character," 587–88, 610; idem, *Syriac Version*, 1–2, 86–88, 125–26, 247–53, 258–62; L. van Rompay, "The Christian Syriac Tradition of Interpretation," in M. Sæbø (ed.), *Hebrew Bible / Old Testament: The History of Its* Interpretation, Vol. 1/1: *From the Beginnings to the Middle Ages (Until 1300): Antiquity* (Göttingen: Vandenhoeck & Ruprecht, 1996) 612–41, esp. 612–14.

and Palestine the possibility of the Hebrew Bible being read either by royal personages themselves or by some courtier who could translate it for them should not be ruled out.[6] In short, one cannot assume that the traditions about the Adiabenians support, or even imply, the existence of a Syriac version of the Scriptures in the first century CE.

The preceding considerations point to the likelihood of an Osrhoenian / Edessene provenance for the Peshitta. As for the time of its execution, there is enough diversity of translation technique among the books to render it unlikely that any single date is applicable (and thus that any single translator was responsible) for the entire corpus. On the other hand, certain ubiquitous translation equivalences and intertextual connections make it probable that this is to be regarded as a single undertaking. Several lines of historical, literary, lexical, and grammatical evidence point to the second half of the second century and perhaps the first part of the third century CE as the period during which the Peshitta was translated.[7]

There is also evidence to suggest that the community which produced the Peshitta was Jewish, though that too has been a matter of debate. In the first place, the use of the Hebrew Bible as the basis of translation — rather than the Septuagint, which assumed pride of place in the early church — would be expected in a Jewish context. This is not to say that there are no markers of Septuagint influence on the Peshitta, but its role was clearly subordinate to that of the Hebrew. Secondly, there are numerous parallels between the Peshitta and the Targums and rabbinic sources that are indicative of a common Jewish exegetical tradition. Thirdly, in Chronicles the translator exhibits a sense of identification with the Jews in some freely rendered sections of what was apparently for him a rather damaged Hebrew *Vorlage*. The same sort of phenomenon is manifest at times in some other books. The kind of Judaism that shines through in the Peshitta is, however, a distinctive one that betrays a particular theological out-

---

[6] Weitzman, *Syriac Version*, 1–2, 12–13, 48–49, 87–88, 126, 149, 247; idem, "Interpretative Character," 602–3, 610; P. V. M. Flesher (ed.), *Targum and Peshitta* (vol. 2 of *Targum Studies*; South Florida Studies in the History of Judaism 165; Atlanta: Scholars Press, 1998); Z. Garber has an online review of the preceding volume in *Review of Biblical Literature*, accessed 6 December 2001 (http://www.bookreviews.org); van Rompay, "Christian Syriac Tradition," 614; Brock, "Syriac Versions," 794–99.

[7] Weitzman, *Syriac Version*, 2, 164–205, 248–58; Brock, "Syriac Versions," 794.

look. It eschews cultic sacrifice and other forms of ritual, is non-rabbinic, and places a premium on faith, prayer, and charitable deeds. Yet as the rabbinic brand of Judaism became predominant and the Peshitta came to be adopted as the Holy Writ of the eastern churches (possibly in conjunction with the conversion to Christianity of these non-rabbinic Jews who brought their Syriac Bible with them), it — like the Septuagint — ceased to find a welcome within mainstream Judaism. Instead, it was preserved and transmitted by the Syriac-speaking church(es) from the eastern Mediterranean to Mesopotamia and beyond.[8]

In describing the nature of the translation in the Peshitta, M. P. Weitzman characterizes it, on the whole, as "idiomatic, though faithful," with the translators conveying "not the words but the content" in a "combination of fidelity with intelligibility."[9] To that end they selected equivalences with a view to communicating precisely a perceived nuance in the Hebrew (even though that might result in semantic differentiation), filled out Hebrew ellipses with contextually acceptable insertions, resolved Hebrew metaphors, improved the logic of texts, made adjustments to enhance contemporaneity, condensed perceived Hebrew redundancies, and the like.[10]

As indicated above, most textual scholars acknowledge that there is evidence for some influence by the Septuagint on the Peshitta. The degree of such influence varies from book to book, ranging from considerable to little or none. Some of that influence appears to have been exerted on the translators and some of it on revisers/copyists of the Syriac text. However much of a connection between the Septuagint and the Peshitta one is prepared to admit, it is clear that an increasing conviction among early Syriac biblical scholars as to the accuracy and authoritativeness of the Septuagint led, over the course of approximately four centuries following the translation of the Peshitta, to the creation of Syriac translations that were ever more closely aligned with the Greek.[11]

---

[8] Weitzman, *Syriac Version*, 1, 13, 86–125, 149–60, 206–207, 208–27, 244–45, 258–62; idem, "Interpretative Character," 587; van Rompay, "Christian Syriac Tradition," 614.

[9] *Syriac Version*, 61–62.

[10] Weitzman, "Interpretative Character," 590–92.

[11] J. F. Berg, *The Influence of the Septuagint upon the Pešiṭta Psalter* (New York: no publ.; Leipzig: W. Drugulin, 1895); W. E. Barnes, "On the Influence of

SUBSEQUENT SYRIAC TRANSLATIONS/REVISIONS

A number of Syriac translations of the Greek Scriptures are mentioned in Syriac sources. One such version was attributed by ʿAbdīšōʿ bar Bᵉrīkā (d. 1318) to Mar ʾĀbā who taught at the School of Nisibis in the first half of the sixth century and who, according to ʿAbdīšōʿ, translated the Old Testament. However, there is currently no textual evidence for this version, so the claim cannot now be verified.[12] A sixth century translation for which there is both literary and textual evidence is the one completed in 508 under the auspices of Philoxenus, the Monophysite bishop of Mabbūg, by his chorepiscopus (i.e. rural bishop) Polycarp.[13] In that same century, Moses of Aghel

the Septuagint on the Peshitta," *JTS* 2 (1901) 186–97; J. Gwynn, *Remnants of the Later Syriac Versions of the Bible in Two Parts* (London: Williams & Norgate, 1909) 1.xxxi; L. Haefeli, *Die Peschitta des Alten Testamentes, mit Rücksicht auf ihre textkritische Bearbeitung und ihre Herausgabe* (ATA 11/1; Münster: Verlag der Aschendorffschen Verlagsbuchhandlung, 1927); A. Vogel, "Studien zum Pešiṭṭa-Psalter: Besonders im Hinblick auf sein Verhältnis zu Septuaginta," *Biblica* 32 (1951) 32–56, 198–231, 336–63, 481–502; M. P. Weitzman, "The Origin of the Peshitta Psalter," in J. A. Emerton and S. C. Reif (eds.), *Interpreting the Hebrew Bible: Essays in Honour of E. I. J. Rosenthal* (Cambridge: Cambridge University Press, 1982) 277–98, esp. 284 and n. 39); Weitzman, "Interpretative Character," 594–95; idem, *Syriac Version*, 62, 68–86, 181; and van Rompay, "Christian Syriac Tradition," 615. J. Lund is reluctant to admit any direct influence of the Septuagint on the Peshitta (*The Influence of the Septuagint on the Peshitta: A Re-evaluation of Criteria in Light of Comparative Study of the Versions in Genesis and Psalms* [Jerusalem: Hebrew University, 1988]; idem, "Grecisms in the Peshitta Psalms," in P. B. Dirksen and A. van der Kooij [eds.], *The Peshitta as a Translation* [Monographs of the Peshitta Institute, Leiden 8; Leiden: Brill, 1995] 85–102).

[12] J. S. Assemanus, *Bibliotheca Orientalis Clementino-Vaticana* (3 vols., Rome: Typis sacrae congregationis de propaganda fide, 1719–28) 3/1:75; S. P. Brock, *A Brief Outline of Syriac Literature* (Mōrān ʾEthʾō 9; Baker Hill, Kottayam, India: St. Ephrem Ecumenical Research Institute, 1997) 44, 80; J. Gwynn, "Thomas (8) Edessenus," *DCB* 986–87; A. Vööbus, *History of the School of Nisibis* (CSCO 266, Subsidia 26; Louvain: Secrétariat du Corpus SCO, 1965) 167–68; idem, *The Hexapla and the Syro-Hexapla* (Papers of the Estonian Theological Society in Exile 22; Stockholm: ETSE, 1971) 48.

[13] E. Venables, "Philoxenus (4) (Xenaias)," *DCB* 4.391–93; J. Gwynn, "Polycarpus (5)," *DCB* 4.431–34; A. de Halleux, *Philoxène de Mabbog: sa vie, ses écrits, sa théologie* (Louvain: Imprimerie orientaliste, 1963) 122–25; R. G. Jenkins, "Some Quotations from Isaiah in the Philoxenian Version," *Abr-Nahrain* 20 (1981–82) 20–36 (esp. 24); Brock, *Brief Outline*, 39; and idem, "Syriac

referred, in a letter, to the Psalms as well as the New Testament in the Philoxenian version,[14] while in the thirteenth century, Eli of Qartamin asserted that this translation included the Old and New Testaments.[15] Philoxenus himself stated that he had authorized the translation of the Greek Scriptures into Syriac due to the inadequacy of earlier versions vis-à-vis the Greek,[16] and though he did not specify the scope of that translation, it evidently included most or all of the New Testament.[17] While the authenticity of the claims about the Old Testament has been called into question,[18] there is in the great Milan manuscript of the Syrohexapla published by Antonio Ceriani a scholion containing a

---

Versions," 795, 797–98.

[14] ܢܘܢܝܢ ... ܟܬܒܘܝܢ ܟܬܒܘܩܣܡ "the version of the New (Testament) ... and of David" (*Letter to Paphnutius*, in I. Guidi, "Mosè di Aghel e Simeone Abbate," *Rendiconti della R. Accademia dei Lincei* 4/2 [1886] 397–416, 545–57, esp. 404).

[15] Eli of Qartamin, *Mēmrā sur S. Mār Philoxène de Mabbog* (ed. and trans. A. de Halleux; CSCO 234, Scriptores Syri 101; Louvain: Secrétariat du Corpus SCO, 1963) 5; cf. "Victory of Mar Akhsnaya, who is Philoxenus, bishop of the town of Mabbūg" (A. Mingana, "New Documents on Philoxenus of Hierapolis, and on the Philoxenian Version of the Bible," *The Expositor* 8/19 [1920] 149–60, esp. 150–53).

[16] Philoxène de Mabbog: *Commentaire du prologue johannique (Ms. Br. Mus. Add. 14,534)* (ed. and trans. A de Halleux; CSCO 380, Scriptores Syri 165; Louvain: Secrétariat du Corpus SCO, 1977) 53; S. P. Brock, in E. J. Epp and G. D. Fee (eds.), *New Testament Textual Criticism—Its Significance for Exegesis: Essays in Honour of Bruce M. Metzger* (Oxford: Clarendon Press, 1981) 325–43, esp. 328.

[17] The most compelling evidence for this is Thomas of Harkel's testimony that his own Syriac version of the New Testament is a revision of the Philoxenian. That testimony is contained in manuscript colophons:

Gospels: J. White (ed.), *Sacrorum Evangeliorum versio syriaca Philoxeniana* (Oxford: Clarendon Press, 1778) 561–62. Note that White mistakenly calls the Harklean version "Philoxenian."

Acts and Catholic Epistles: J. White (ed.), *Actuum Apostolorum et Epistolarum tam Catholicarum quam Paulinarum, versio syriaca Philoxeniana* (2 vols., Oxford: Clarendon Press, 1799–1803) 1.274–75.

Corpus Paulinum: W. Wright and S. A. Cook, *A Catalogue of the Syriac Manuscripts Preserved in the Library of the University of Cambridge* (2 vols., Cambridge: University Press, 1901) 1.11.

Apocalypse: A. Vööbus, *The Apocalypse in the Harklean Version* (CSCO 400, Subsidia 56; Louvain: Secrétariat du CorpusSCO, 1978) 35*, 52–62.

[18] See, for example, J. Lebon, "La version philoxénienne de la Bible," *Revue d'histoire ecclésiastique* 12 (1911; repr. 1967) 413–36, esp. 435.

variant reading to the Syrohexapla of Isaiah $9:6(5)^{b}$-$7(6)^{a\alpha}$ attributed to Philoxenus,[19] a reading that is solidly supported in non-hexaplaric witnesses (particularly *L* manuscripts) of the text type associated with Lucian of Antioch.[20] This is the same text type exhibited in a fragmentary Isaiah manuscript[21] (for which chapter 9 is unfortunately no longer extant) designated Syl for "syrolukianisch" by Joseph Ziegler, the editor of this volume in the Göttingen *Septuaginta* edition. Comparisons between Syl and Philoxenus' quotations of Isaiah reveal that he employed a version which agrees in distinctive fashion with Syl against the Peshitta. Thus the case for a Philoxenian version of at least Isaiah in the Old Testament corpus, though admittedly based on circumstantial evidence, seems nonetheless to be reasonably well established.[22] The possibilities with regard to a Philoxenian Psalter will be considered presently.

A little more than a century after the Philoxenian Bible had been completed, a translation project characterized by extreme fidelity to the Greek was undertaken. Paul of Tella supervised the production of the Syrohexapla[23] which was based for the most part on Origen's

---

[19] Folio 176r, Milan, Ambr. Libr., C. 313. Inf., published in a facsimile edition as *Codex Syro-Hexaplaris Ambrosianus photolithographice editus* (Monumenta sacra et profana 7; Milan: Typis et impensis Bibliothecae Ambrosianae, 1874).

[20] J. Ziegler (ed.), *Isaias* (vol. 14 of *Septuaginta: Vetus Testamentum Graecum*; Göttingen: Vandenhoeck & Ruprecht, 1967).

[21] Ms Br. Mus. Add. 17,106, published by A. Ceriani in *Esaiae fragmenta syriaca versionis anonymae et recensionis Jacobi Edesseni* (Monumenta sacra et profana 5/1; Milan: Typis et impensis Bibliothecae Ambrosianae, 1868) 1–40.

[22] L. Delekat, "Die syrolukianische Übersetzung des Buches Jesaja und das Postulat einer alttestamentlichen Vetus Syra," *ZAW* N.F. 28 (1957) 21–54, esp. 23–24; R. G. Jenkins, "Some Quotations from Isaiah in the Philoxenian Version," 20–36; idem, *The Old Testament Quotations of Philoxenus of Mabbug* (CSCO 514, Subsidia 84; Louvain: E. Peeters, 1989) 3–4, 83–129, 178–86, 204; Brock, *Brief Outline*, 90; idem, "Syriac Versions," 795, 797; R. J. V. Hiebert, *The "Syrohexaplaric" Psalter* (SBLSCS 27; Atlanta: Scholars Press, 1989) 250–51, 299–301 nn. 24, 27; idem, "The 'Syrohexaplaric' Psalter: Its Text and Textual History," in A. Aejmelaeus and U. Quast (eds.), *Der Septuaginta-Psalter und seine Tochterübersetzungen* (Abhandlungen der Akademie der Wissenschaften in Göttingen; MSU 24; Göttingen: Vandenhoeck & Ruprecht, 2000) 123–46. esp. 133–35.

[23] Manuscript and literary sources that associate Paul with the Syrohexapla include a Catena Patrum in Ms Br. Mus. Add. 12,168, fol. 161b (W. Wright, *Catalogue of Syriac Manuscripts in the British Museum* [3 vols., London: British Mu-

(hexaplaric) recension of the Old Greek version of the Jewish Scriptures, and Thomas of Harkel produced what he referred to as a revision of the Philoxenian New Testament.[24] Political and ecclesiastical events in the second decade of the seventh century converged to bring these two Mesopotamian Monophysite clerics, fleeing hostile Persian forces, to the Antonian monastery at the Enaton, a relay post nine miles from Alexandria, Egypt. There they worked for several years on their stylistically similar translations. Mention is made in manuscript colophons to a Thomas who assisted Paul in the translation of 4 Kingdoms and to a Paul who rendered the *Pericope de Adultera* in John 7:53–8:11. Though of course these might be other men with the same names as the renowned clerics, it is possible that the references are to the clerics themselves and that these notices are indicative of the sort of collaboration that characterized this enterprise.[25]

Manuscript colophons provide other interesting and noteworthy evidence as to the complex textual history that lies behind the Syrohexapla. Some speak of the Hexapla as the Greek *Vorlage*, others the Tetrapla, and one of the Heptapla — all designations for various configurations of Origen's multi-version Old Testament. For the books of Genesis and Joshua, both the Tetrapla and the Hexapla are mentioned. For both Exodus and Numbers, it is reported that part of the textual history involves a Hebrew text that had been collated to the Samaritan version. These and other collation/correction sequences that are

---

seum, 1870–72] 2.906–907); the 4 Kingdoms colophon in Ms Par. syr. 27, fol. 90a (P. de Lagarde, *Bibliothecae Syriacae...quae ad philologiam sacram pertinent* [Göttingen: Prostant in aedibus Dieterichianis Luederi Horstmann, 1892] 256; H. Middeldorpf (ed.), *Codex Syriaco-Hexaplaris* [Berlin: Enslin, 1835] 66); Moses bar Kēphā's commentary on the Hexaemeron (cited by J. P. P. Martin, *Introduction à la critique textuelle du Nouveau Testament* [5 vols., Paris: Maisonneuve frères et C. Leclerc, 1884–85] 1.101, from Ms Par. syr. 241); Barhebraeus' *prooemium* to his *Auṣar Rāzē*, i.e. *Horreum Mysteriorum*, (M. Sprengling and W. C. Graham [eds.], *Barhebraeus' Scholia on the Old Testament* [The University of Chicago Oriental Institute Publications 13; Chicago: University of Chicago Press, 1931] 4–5).

[24] See note 17 above.

[25] J. Gwynn, "Paulus (48) Tellensis," *DCB* 4.266–71; idem, "Thomas (17) Harklensis," *DCB* 4.1014–21; R. J. V. Hiebert, "Syriac Biblical Textual History and the Greek Psalter," in R. J. V. Hiebert, C. E. Cox, and P. J. Gentry (eds.), *The Old Greek Psalter: Studies in Honour of Albert Pietersma* (JSOTSup 332; Sheffield: Sheffield Academic Press, 2001) 178–204, esp. 179–80); idem, *The "Syrohexaplaric" Psalter*, 253–54, 256, 311 nn. 74, 75.

described reflect an ongoing desire to reconstruct a more pristine text, a desire that continued to manifest itself as much in the work of Syriac textual scholars as it had in their Greek predecessors.[26]

Paul of Tella's *Vorlage* was, as mentioned above, normally Origen's hexaplaric recension of the Old Greek, but he apparently did not restrict himself to that textual tradition. It will be remembered that, like Thomas of Harkel, Paul is known to have made use of a version that he identified in a colophon to Isaiah 9 as Philoxenian. I have argued elsewhere that there is good reason to suspect that Paul's Syriac translation base for the Psalter — which, uncharacteristically, features a non-hexaplaric text type associated by Alfred Rahlfs, the editor of Psalms in the Göttingen *Septuaginta* edition, with the Lucianic recension[27] — was the Philoxenian Psalter mentioned by Moses of Aghel. Distinctive translation patterns, not to mention the anomalous text type, make that a possibility worth considering, even though no textual evidence for a Philoxenian Psalter in its original state has yet been discovered. My collation and analysis of the available manuscripts of this so-called Syrohexaplaric Psalter, designated SyrPss, have shown that there are in fact three Syriac textual traditions represented. The majority group, SyrPs, consists of eight of the eleven manuscript sources[28] that were collated ($a$-$g$, $h_1$). SyrPs$^a$ is contained in the first part of manuscripts $h$ and $j$ up to Psalm 27:6, and SyrPs$^b$ in those

---

[26] Hiebert, "Syriac Biblical Textual History," 182–84.

[27] A. Rahlfs (ed.), *Septuaginta: Vetus Testamentum Graecum*, Vol. 10: *Psalmi cum Odis* (Göttingen: Vandenhoeck & Ruprecht, 1931) 60–70.

[28] $a$ = Milan, Ambr. Libr., C. 313. Inf., folios 6b–38b (Ceriani's A): eighth/ninth century.

$b$ = Br. Mus., Add. 14,434, folios 1–79 (Ceriani's B): eighth century.

$c$ = Br. Mus., Add. 14,434, folios 80–128 (Ceriani's C): eighth century.

$d$ = Br. Mus., Add. 17,257, folios 84–94 (Ceriani's E): thirteenth century.

$e$ = Cambridge, Univ. Libr., Orient. 929, folios 1a–184a: fourteenth century.

$f$ = Baghdad, Libr. of the Chald. Patr., 211, folios 8b–152a (Mosul Cod. 4): twelfth century.

$g$ = Vat. Libr., Borg. sir. 113, folios 1–135 (copy of f): nineteenth century.

$h$ = Baghdad, Libr. of the Chald. Patr., 1112, folios 1a–127b (Diarbakir Cod. 2): twelfth century.

$h_1$ = Baghdad, Libr. of the Chald. Patr., 1112, folios 128a–129a (Diarbakir Cod. 2): fifteenth century.

$j$ = Paris, Nat. Libr., Syr. 9, folios 165b–228a (Ceriani's D): thirteenth century.

$k$ = Moscow, Publičnaja Biblioteka S.S.S.R. im. V. I. Lenina, Gr. 432, 4 folios (Norov 74): eighth century.

same witnesses from Ps 27:7 onward as well as in the extant fragments of manuscript *k* (parts of Psalms 70, 73, 77, and 79). I have
demonstrated that the Greek *Vorlage* of SyrPs, SyrPs$^a$, and SyrPs$^b$ is
usually the same, and that most divergences among them can be classified as either inner-Syriac adjustments or distinctive renderings of
identical Greek texts by different translators. Stylistically, whereas all
three are characterized by rigid, quantitative conformity to the Greek,
SyrPs$^a$ is the most servile of the group, with SyrPs$^b$ standing closer to
SyrPs in this regard.

In the absence of any sources that attribute specifically SyrPss to
Paul of Tella, I have developed the hypothesis that he was responsible
for the revision of the Philoxenian Psalter toward the Greek that resulted in SyrPs (five of whose manuscripts feature the kind of apparatus of non-Septuagintal readings in their margins that appear in
other books of the Syrohexapla), and that Thomas of Harkel produced
an independent revision/translation along the same lines that is preserved in SyrPs$^a$ (one of whose manuscripts [*h*] has been identified as
Harklean). SyrPs$^b$, for its part, may have been produced by some unknown individual who lightly reworked SyrPs in accordance with
some techniques employed in the creation of SyrPs$^a$.[29]

The next major development in Syriac biblical textual history following the appearance of the so-called Enaton Bible was the making
of a revision of at least parts of the Old Testament by Jacob of Edessa
in c. 705. Jacob's work — which is extant with some gaps in the Pentateuch, 1 and 2 Samuel, and the beginning of 1 Kings, Isaiah, Ezekiel, Daniel and Susannah, and in fragments and citations of some
other books including Psalms — entailed the blending of readings
from the Peshitta and the Syrohexapla. It therefore represented a move
in the direction of more normal Syriac idiom in comparison to the
translation technique of Paul of Tella and Thomas of Harkel.[30]

---

[29] Hiebert, *"Syrohexaplaric" Psalter*, chapter 5; idem, "Text and Textual
History," 125–45; idem, "Syriac Biblical Textual History," 185–94, 198–204.

[30] C. J. Ball, "Jacobus (24) Edessenus," *DCB* 3:332–35; W. Baars, *New Syro-
Hexaplaric Texts* (Leiden: Brill, 1968) 149; idem, "Ein neugefundenes Bruch-
stück aus der syrischen Bibelrevision des Jakob von Edessa," *VT* 18 (1968)
548–54; A. Rücker (ed.), *Die syrische Jakobosanaphora nach der Rezension des
Ja'qôb(h) von Edessa* (Liturgiegeschichtliche Quellen 4; ed. P. K. Mohlberg and
A. Rücker; Münster: Verlag der Aschendorffschen Verlagsbuchhandlung, 1923);
Vööbus, "Syriac Versions," 850; Brock, *Brief Outline*, 57–59, 90; idem, "Syriac
Versions," 795; Weitzman, *Syriac Version*, 62; L. van Rompay, "Development of

TRANSMITTING TEXTUAL TRADITIONS

Jacob of Edessa's revision appears to have been the last of the prominent Syriac versions of the Old Testament to be produced. The Peshitta, of course, remained the most popular among Syriac-speaking Christians, though the versions of Paul of Tella and Jacob of Edessa continued to be reproduced by copyists, cited by scholars and commentators, and even employed in some lectionaries. Syriac exegetes noted the distinctions between readings in the Peshitta and those attested elsewhere. Divergent readings were identified by a number of terms. "The Hebrew" (ܥܒܪܝܐ) was sometimes used to signify the Hebrew language or a specific Hebrew word, but it seems also to have been employed in a more generic sense to designate material derived ultimately from targumic, midrashic and Hebrew sources. "The Greek" (ܝܘܢܝܐ) or "the seventy" (ܫܒܥܝܢ) appeared in contexts where the Peshitta and the Septuagint are substantially different to mark materials that commentators had drawn from Greek sources, including the Septuagint, or the Syrohexapla.[31]

Noteworthy exegetes who made use of various textual traditions include Moses bar Kēphā, Išoʿdad of Merv, Dionysius bar Ṣalibi, and Barhebraeus. The most remarkable of the works produced by these Syriac luminaries is ʾAuṣar Rāzē ("Storehouse of Mysteries") by the polymath Barhebraeus (1226–86). This systematic collection of notes or comments on the Old and New Testaments contains readings from an impressive array of Bible translations (including Syriac, Greek, Armenian, and "Egyptian"), as well as remarks on matters of textual criticism, exegesis, lexicography, phonology, and chronology.[32]

---

Biblical Interpretation in the Syrian Churches of the Middle Ages," in M. Sæbø (ed.), *Hebrew Bible / Old Testament: The History of Its Interpretation*, Vol. 1/2: *From the Beginnings to the Middle Ages (Until 1300): The Middle Ages* (Göttingen: Vandenhoeck & Ruprecht, 2000) 559–77, esp. 561.

[31] Vööbus, "Syriac Versions," 850; Weitzman, *Syriac Version*, 62, 139–42; idem, "Interpretative Character," 611; Baars, *New Syro-Hexaplaric Texts*, 2, 17–20, 41–149; Vööbus, *The Hexapla and the Syro-Hexapla*, 54–60; Hiebert, "Syriac Biblical Textual History," 181–82; L. van Rompay, "Christian Syriac Tradition," 615–16; idem, "Development of Biblical Interpretation," in M. Sæbø (ed.), *Hebrew Bible / Old Testament.* 1/2: *The Middle Ages* (see note above) 559–77, esp. 570.

[32] Van Rompay, "Development of Biblical Interpretation," 562–63, 569–70, 573–75; Brock, *Brief Outline*, 75–80.

## CASE STUDIES FROM THE PSALTER

The preceding synopsis of Syriac textual history serves as an introduction to the following exercise in textual analysis designed to demonstrate the kinds of relationships and parallels that exist among the
versions. Psalm 24(23) in its entirety and brief excerpts from other
Psalms have been selected for this investigation. Psalm 24(23) is a
good choice because it is extant in a number of fragmentary Syriac
translations that I wish in include in this profile.

The psalm is divided below into units of text that allow for ready
comparison of parallel lines of each of the relevant versions. MT (the
Masoretic Text), P (the Peshitta), and LXX (the Septuagint/Old
Greek) readings are taken from the standard editions that are well
known to biblical scholars.[33] SyrPss is the edition of the so-called
Syro-hexaplaric Psalter — with its three manuscript groups, SyrPs,
SyrPs$^a$, and SyrPs$^b$ — that I have published.[34] A$^1$ is the siglum for the
Syriac translation of *Expositio in Psalmos* by Athanasius, Patriarch of
Alexandria (c. 296–373).[35] Portions of this translation, including the
complete text of Psalm 24(23), are preserved in Ms British Museum,
Add. 14568.[36] A$^2$ is the considerably abbreviated Syriac version of
Athanasius' *Expositio* in Ms British Museum, Add. 12168,[37] in which
only parts of the psalm are quoted. B is the designation for

---

[33] MT = K. Elliger and W. Rudolph (eds.), *Biblia Hebraica Stuttgartensia*
(Stuttgart: Deutsche Bibelgesellschaft, 1983); P = The Peshitta Institute (ed.), *The
Old Testament in Syriac according to the Peshitta Version*. Vol. 2/3: *The Book of
Psalms* (Leiden: Brill, 1980); LXX = Rahlfs (ed.), *Psalmi cum Odis*. See the ap-
pendix at the conclusion of this essay for the apparatus of Rahlfs' edition of the
LXX, an electronic version of which I am indebted to Albert Pietersma for mak-
ing available to me. I have supplemented this apparatus with collations from ad-
ditional sources mentioned in the appendix.

[34] *The "Syrohexaplaric" Psalter*, chapters 1 and 2. SyrPs$^b$ is not, however,
extant for this Psalm.

[35] F. L. Cross and E. A. Livingstone (eds.), "Athanasius, St. (c. 296–373),"
*ODCC*, 101–102.

[36] R. W. Thomson (ed.), *Athanasiana Syriaca*. Part 4: *Expositio in Psalmos*
(CSCO 386, Scriptores Syri 167; Louvain: Secrétariat du CorpusSCO, 1977)
117–88. Thomson remarks that its text is "similar to—but not identical with—the
composite Greek text published in Migne, *PG* 27.60–545" (R. W. Thomson
(trans.), *Athanasiana Syriaca*. Part 4: *Expositio in Psalmos* [CSCO 387, Scriptores Syri 168; Louvain: Secrétariat du Corpus SCO, 1977] i).

[37] Thomson (ed.), *Expositio in Psalmos* (CSCO 386) 1–116.

Barhebraeus' citations from the Peshitta associated with his notes on the Psalms, while B<sup>y</sup> signifies his excerpts from "the Greek" (*yawnāyā* = ܝܘܢܝܐ). Barhebraeus does not quote the full text of either version, and in a few cases below only part of a line is attested. B<sup>g</sup> is employed when the reading of manuscript g of the edition published by Paul de Lagarde varies from the readings of other manuscripts. It should be noted that because de Lagarde has reproduced the Syriac text in Aramaic script and has not employed *s<sup>e</sup>yāmē* dots to mark the plural, plural emphatic forms are sometimes indistinguishable from singular ones.[38]

The lines of MT, P, B (where extant), LXX, and SyrPs(s) readings in the layout below are always arranged in the same sequence. SyrPss is the designation used when the SyrPs and SyrPs<sup>a</sup> textual traditions are in agreement; when they do not agree, they are cited separately. The lines that follow the preceding ones contain the extant readings of the other translations, typically ordered in a sequence from most to least like SyrPs(s). Relevant variants to the lemmas of the versions are recorded in parentheses beside the cited texts.

1. PSALM 24(23)

*Verse 1*

| | |
|---|---|
| MT | לְדָוִד מִזְמוֹר |
| LXX | ψαλμὸς τῷ Δαυιδ· τῆς μιᾶς σαββάτων |
| SyrPss | ܫܘܒܚܐ ܠܕܘܝܕ ܘ(ܫܘܒܚܐ ] ܫܘܒܚܐ ܕܐܚܕ ܒܫܒܐ ܠܕܘܝܕ ܘܫܘܒܚܐ *fg*) |
| A² | ܕܐܚܕ ܒܫܒܐ ܠܕܘܝܕ ܘ ܫܘܒܚܐ |
| B<sup>y</sup> | מזמורא לדויד דחד בשבא |
| A¹ | ܕܐܚܕ ܒܫܒܐ ܘܕܕܘܝܕ ܫܘܒܚܐ |

P lacks a Psalm title.[39] All other witnesses reverse the word order of לְדָוִד מִזְמוֹר in MT, but only A¹ employs the sign of the genitive ܕ as the counterpart to לְ = τῷ. All except MT agree with LXX in attesting τῆς μιᾶς σαββάτων, a phrase that is under the obelus in Ga but lacking in S 2110 O (teste Tht) L<sup>pau</sup>. It is impossible to know whether the Syriac counterpart to σαββάτων was marked in B<sup>y</sup> as a plural *à la*

---

[38] P. de Lagarde, ed., כתבא דמזמורא מן כתבא דאוצר ארזא, *Praetermissorum libri duo* (Göttingen: Sumptibus editoris in officina academica Dieterichiana, 1879).

[39] P. Weitzman suggests that the omission of these titles is attributable to the freedom that P translators felt to make modifications vis-à-vis their *Vorlage* ("Interpretative Character," 591).

SyrPss-*fg* or was written without *s*^e^*yāmē* as in manuscripts *fg* and in A² and A¹. Note also that manuscripts *fg* use ܟܠ rather than ܕ to introduce the Greek genitive construction.

| | |
|---|---|
| MT | לַיהוָה הָאָרֶץ וּמְלוֹאָהּ |
| P | ܘܕܡܪܝܐ ܗܝ ܐܪܥܐ ܒܡܠܐܗ̇ |
| B | דמריא הי ארעא במלאה |
| LXX | Τοῦ κυρίου ἡ γῆ καὶ τὸ πλήρωμα αὐτῆς |
| SyrPs | ܘܕܡܪܝܐ ܗܝ ܐܪܥܐ ܘܡܘܠܝܐ ܕܝܠܗ̇ |
| A² | ܘܕܡܪܝܐ ܗܝ ܐܪܥܐ ܘܡܘܠܝܐ ܕܝܠܗ̇ |
| SyrPs^a^ | ܘܕܡܪܝܐ ܐܪܥܐ ܘܡܘܠܝܐ ܕܝܠܗ̇ |
| B^y^ | דמריא ארעא ומוליא דילה |
| A¹ | ܘܕܡܪܝܐ ܗܝ ܐܪܥܐ ܘܡܠܐܗ̇ |

All Syriac witnesses reflect an initial genitive construction as is found in LXX, rather than a dative construction like the one in MT. SyrPs^a^ and B^y^ lack the pronoun functioning as a copula and thus conform even more closely to LXX than do SyrPs and A² which have the pronoun. Only P = B have a preposition prefixed to the last word of this excerpt; all other versions have a conjunction. The readings of SyrPs and A² are identical, as are those of SyrPs^a^ and B^y^, while A¹ accords with P = B, except for the conjunction rather than the preposition prefixed to the concluding lexeme.

| | |
|---|---|
| MT | תֵּבֵל וְיֹשְׁבֵי בָהּ |
| P | ܬܒܝܠ ܘܟܠܗܘܢ ܒܥܡܘܪܝܗ̇ |
| B | תביל |
| LXX | ἡ οἰκουμένη καὶ πάντες οἱ κατοικοῦντες ἐν αὐτῇ |
| SyrPs | ܡܬܥܡܪܢܝܬܐ ܘܟܠܗܘܢ ܐܝܠܝܢ ܕܥܡܪܝܢ ܒܗ̇ |
| SyrPs^a^ | ܡܬܥܡܪܢܝܬܐ ܘܟܠܗܘܢ ܗܢܘܢ ܕܥܡܪܝܢ ܒܗ̇ |
| B^y^ | מתעמרניתא |
| A¹ | ܬܒܝܠ ܘܟܠ ܕܥܡܪܝܢ ܒܗ̇ |

MT, P, B, and A¹ attest cognates for the first word (תֵּבֵל, ܬܒܝܠ), while SyrPs, SyrPs^a^, and B^y^ have ܡܬܥܡܪܢܝܬܐ. All extant versions except MT specify "all" of the world's inhabitants, with the equivalent for πάντες under the obelus in Ga. As is usual for SyrPs^a^, ܗܢܘܢ is the counterpart to the article of the Greek plural articulated participle, rather than ܐܝܠܝܢ of SyrPs.[40] A¹ and P have no such equivalent. MT, LXX, SyrPs, SyrPs^a^, and A¹ each have a participial construction designating the world's inhabitants, while P has a simple substantive.

[40] Hiebert, *"Syrohexaplaric" Psalter*, 257, 313 n. 80.

*Verse 2*

| | |
|---|---|
| MT | כִּי־הוּא עַל־יַמִּים יְסָדָהּ |
| P | ܡܛܠ ܕܗܘ̣ ܒܝܡܐ ܣܡ ܫܬܐ̈ܣܝܗ̇ |
| LXX | αὐτὸς ἐπὶ θαλασσῶν ἐθεμελίωσεν αὐτὴν |
| SyrPs | ܗܘ̣ ܥܠ ܝ̈ܡܡܐ ܫܬܣܗ̇ |
| SyrPs[a] | ܗܘ̣ ܥܠ ܝ̈ܡܡܐ ܫܬܐܣܗ̇ |
| A[1] | ܗܘ ܥܠ ܝ̈ܡܡܐ ܣܡ ܫܬܐ̈ܣܝܗ̇ |
| A[2] | ܗܘ̣ ܫܬܐ̈ܣܝܗ̇ |

Of the witnesses represented above, only MT and P make this a causal clause. Ga has *quia* under the asterisk. MT, SyrPs, SyrPs[a], and A[1] use the *ʿl* preposition (עַל, ܥܠ) with which LXX's ἐπί is consistent, while P is distinct from the other Syriac traditions in its employment of ܒ (the same applies in the next excerpt). MT, LXX, SyrPs, SyrPs[a], and A[1] attest the plural "seas," whereas P alone has the singular "sea." SyrPs and SyrPs[a] differ orthographically in spelling the last word. However, A[1] follows P which translates יְסָדָהּ with the phrase ܣܡ ܫܬܐ̈ܣܝܗ̇. The reading of A[2] conveys an idea that differs dramatically from what is stated in all the other witnesses, and appears to be more of an interpretative gloss than a citation of any particular version.

| | |
|---|---|
| MT | וְעַל־נְהָרוֹת יְכוֹנְנֶהָ |
| P | ܘܒܢܗܪ̈ܘܬܐ ܐܬܩܢܗ̇ |
| B | ובנהרותא אתקנה |
| LXX | καὶ ἐπὶ ποταμῶν ἡτοίμασεν αὐτήν |
| SyrPs | ܘܥܠ ܢܗܪ̈ܘܬܐ ܐܬܩܢܗ̇ |
| A[1] | ܘܥܠ ܢܗܪ̈ܘܬܐ ܐܬܩܢܗ̇ |
| SyrPs[a] | ܘܥܠ ܢܗܪ̈ܘܬܐ ܛܝܒܗ̇ |
| B[y] | טיבה |
| A[2] | ܘܒܢܗܪ̈ܘܬܐ ܬܘܒ ܛܝܒܬܗ̇ |

Regarding the preposition, see the preceding paragraph. The wording of P and B is identical, and SyrPs and A[1] are likewise in agreement with one another. SyrPs[a] and B[y] attest ܛܝܒܗ̇ instead of ܐܬܩܢܗ̇ which is found in P = B, SyrPs, and A[1].[41] Again, as in the preceding paragraph, the reading of A[2] seems to be more of a free paraphrase (seemingly influenced in part by P = B) than a precise quotation.

---

[41] At Psalm 23(22):5, the counterpart to ἑτοιμάζω is also the *Poʿel* of ܛܘܒ in SyrPs[a] and the *ʾAphel* of ܬܩܢ in SyrPs (as well as A[2] and B[y]). P = B has ܣܕܪܬ, while A[1] is not extant.

*Verse 3*

| | |
|---|---|
| MT | מִי־יַעֲלֶה בְהַר־יְהוָה |
| P | ܡܢܘ ܢܣܩ ܠܛܘܪܗ ܕܡܪܝܐ |
| B | מנו נסק לטורה דמריא |
| LXX | τίς ἀναβήσεται εἰς τὸ ὄρος τοῦ κυρίου |
| SyrPs | ܡܢܘ ܢܣܩ ܠܛܘܪܗ ܕܡܪܝܐ |
| A$^2$ | ܡܢܘ ܢܣܩ ܠܛܘܪܗ ܕܡܪܝܐ |
| SyrPs$^a$ | ܡܢܘ ܢܣܩ ܠܛܘܪܐ ܕܡܪܝܐ |
| A$^1$ | ܡܢܘ ܢܣܩ ܠܛܘܪܗ ܕܡܪܝܘ |

P = B, SyrPs, and A$^2$ have identical readings. None of the versions reproduce the בְּ preposition of MT. The Syriac ones have ܠ, to which εἰς of LXX is equivalent. SyrPs$^a$, as usual,[42] avoids the use of the proleptic suffix before ܕ in a genitival construction, while all other Syriac versions include it. The form ܡܪܝܘ in A$^1$ is anomalous (see the regular spelling ܡܪܝܐ in verses 1, 5, 8, and 10 of this manuscript).

| | |
|---|---|
| MT | וּמִי־יָקוּם בִּמְקוֹם קָדְשׁוֹ |
| P | ܘܡܢܘ ܢܩܘܡ ܒܛܘܪܗ ܩܕܝܫܐ |
| LXX | καὶ τίς στήσεται ἐν τόπῳ ἁγίῳ αὐτοῦ |
| SyrPss | ܘܡܢܘ ܢܩܘܡ ܒܕܘܟܬܐ ܩܕܝܫܬܐ ܕܝܠܗ |
| A$^2$ | ܘܡܢܘ ܢܩܘܡ ܒܕܘܟܬܐ ܩܕܝܫܬܐ ܕܝܠܗ |
| A$^1$ | ܐܘ ܡܢܘ ܢܩܘܡ ܒܐܬܪܗ ܩܕܝܫܐ |

SyrPss and A$^2$ are in agreement regarding the wording of this clause. Only A$^1$ begins with something other than the ܘ conjunction—namely, the disjunctive particle ܐܘ which agrees with η, the reading attested by LXX witnesses Bo U' 2110 R'' Ga *L*Thtp 55 et Cyp.p, rather than with Rahlfs' lemma καί. Only P's ܒܛܘܪܗ reiterates the reference to "mountain" in the preceding clause. All other witnesses follow MT (בִּמְקוֹם) in choosing a term for place: ἐν τόπῳ (LXX); ܒܕܘܟܬܐ (SyrPss and A$^2$); ܒܐܬܪܗ (A$^1$).

*Verse 4*

| | |
|---|---|
| MT | נְקִי כַפַּיִם וּבַר־לֵבָב |
| P | ܐܢܐ ܕܕܟܝ̈ܢ ܐ̈ܝܕܘܗܝ ܘܓܒܐ ܒܠܒܗ (ܕܕܟܝ̈ܢ] ܕܟܝ̈ܢ 12t1) |
| B | אינא דדכין אידוהי וגבא בלבה |
| LXX | ἀθῷος χερσὶν καὶ καθαρὸς τῇ καρδίᾳ |
| SyrPs | ܕܕܟܝ ܒܐ̈ܝܕܘܗܝ ܘܕܟܐ ܒܠܒܗ |

42 Hiebert, *"Syrohexaplaric" Psalter*, 15, 17–18.

A[1] ܐܝܢܐ ܕܙܟܝ ܒܐܝ̈ܕܘܗܝ ܘܕܟܐ ܒܠܒܗ
B[y] אינא דזכי באידוהי ודכא בלבה
SyrPs[a] ܙܟܝܐ ܒܐܝ̈ܕܝܐ ܘܕܟܝܐ ܒܠܒܐ
A[2] ܐܝܢܐ ܕܐܝܬܘܗܝ ܕܟܝܐ ܒܡܫܠܡܘܬܐ ܘܒܬܐܘܪܝܐ

In P=B, A[1] and B[y] (whose wording is identical), and A[2], this excerpt begins with the relative pronoun construction ܐܝܢܐ ܕ. SyrPs has the simple relative pronoun ܕ which more closely approximates LXX and MT than the preceding reading does, but SyrPs[a] is closest of all to the Greek and Hebrew with its rendering that lacks a pronominal construction altogether. P=B, SyrPs, A[1], and B[y] all exhibit suffixes in the words ܐܝ̈ܕܘܗܝ /ܒܐܝ̈ܕܘܗܝ and ܒܠܒܗ. Although ܒܐܝ̈ܕܘܗܝ in SyrPs, A[1], and B[y] is somewhat closer to LXX's dative construction than ܐܝ̈ܕܘܗܝ in P=B is, the text of SyrPs[a] without pronominal suffixes, etc., matches that of LXX. The reading of A[2], on the other hand, is an interpretative comment rather than a direct quotation from any particular translation.

MT אֲשֶׁר לֹא־נָשָׂא לַשָּׁוְא נַפְשִׁי
P ܘܠܐ ܝܡܐ ܒܢܦܫܗ ܒܕܓܠܘܬܐ
B ולא ימא בנפשה בדגלותא
LXX ὃς οὐκ ἔλαβεν ἐπὶ ματαίῳ τὴν ψυχὴν αὐτοῦ
SyrPs ܗܘ ܕܠܐ ܢܣܒ ܥܠ ܣܪܝܩܘܬܐ ܢܦܫܐ ܕܝܠܗ
B[y] הו דלא נסב על סריקותא נפשה
A[1] ܗܘ ܕܠܐ ܢܣܒ ܠܣܪܝܩܘܬܐ ܢܦܫܗ
SyrPs[a] ܗܘ ܕܠܐ ܫܩܠ ܥܠ ܣܪܝܩܘܬܐ ܢܦܫܐ ܕܝܠܗ
A[2] ܘܠܐ ܐܬܟܠܠ ܠܬܟܬܘܫܬܐ ܥܒܕ̈ܬܐ

Only P=B do not make this a relative clause, apparently interpreting the idea of MT under the influence of the following clause which also talks about making an oath. The counterpart to ἔλαβεν is ܢܣܒ in SyrPs, B[y], and A[1], but it is ܫܩܠ in SyrPs[a].[43] The preposition ܥܠ in SyrPs, B[y], and SyrPs[a] reflects ἐπί of LXX, while ܠ of A[1] parallels the cognate counterpart in MT. The third person possessive pronoun associated with ܢܦܫܐ/ψυχήν in P=B, LXX, SyrPs, B[y], A[1], and SyrPs[a] — in contrast to the first person of MT (and of LXX Codex Alexandrinus) — is presumably correct. SyrPs and SyrPs[a] opt for the independent possessive pronoun (rather than the suffixed form of B[y],

[43] These are the same respective equivalents for SyrPs and SyrPs[a] at Psalm 15(14):3 and 18(17):17(16)—except note ܘܫܩܘܠܝܢ *h*, ܘܫܩܠܝܢ *j* (= P and B). At 15(14):3, P=B have ܡܣܒܒܠ. A[2] has a reading for only 18(17):17(16) where it attests ܢܣܒ. In A[1], neither passage is extant.

A[1], and P = B) in order to match the Greek quantitatively. The reading of A[2] appears once again to be an interpretative paraphrase.

MT וְלֹא נִשְׁבַּע לְמִרְמָה
P ܘܠܐ ܝܡܐ ܒܢܟܠܐ
LXX καὶ οὐκ ὤμοσεν ἐπὶ δόλῳ τῷ πλησίον αὐτοῦ
SyrPss ܘܠܐ ܝܡܐ ܥܠ ܢܟܠܐ ܠܩܪܝܒܐ ܕܝܠܗ
A[1] ܘܠܐ ܐܝܡܐ ܒܢܟܠܐ ܠܩܪܝܒܗ

The difference between ܝܡܐ in P and SyrPss and ܐܝܡܐ in A[1] is simply orthographic. P and A[1] agree on ܒܢܟܠܐ over against ܥܠ ܢܟܠܐ in SyrPss, a reading that is closer to LXX. SyrPss and A[1] follow LXX in rendering τῷ πλησίον αὐτοῦ, a phrase that has no counterpart in MT or in P. However, SyrPss has the independent possessive pronoun, whereas A[1] employs the pronominal suffix.

*Verse 5*

MT יִשָּׂא בְרָכָה מֵאֵת יְהוָה
P ܗܢܐ ܢܩܒܠ ܒܘܪܟܬܐ ܡܢ ܡܪܝܐ
LXX οὗτος λήμψεται εὐλογίαν παρὰ κυρίου
SyrPs ܗܢܐ ܢܶܣܰܒ ܒܘܪܟܬܐ ܡܢ ܡܪܝܐ
A[1] ܗܢܐ ܢܣܒ ܒܘܪ̈ܟܬܐ ܡܢ ܡܪܝܐ
SyrPs[a] ܗܢܐ ܢܶܣܰܒ ܒܘܪܟܬܐ ܡܢ ܠܘܬ ܡܪܝܐ

The Syriac versions all begin with the demonstrative pronoun ܗܢܐ, which is equivalent to οὗτος of LXX but has no explicit equivalent in MT. In contrast to ܢܩܒܠ in P, the verb in SyrPs, A[1], and SyrPs[a] is ܢܶܣܰܒ. It will be remembered that, in SyrPs and A[1] of the preceding verse, this latter root also serves as the counterpart to a form of λαμβάνω, though ܩܰܒܶܠ is the equivalent there in SyrPs[a]. In the present verse, only A[1] uses a plural form ܒܘܪ̈ܟܬܐ to describe the favourable prospects of the qualified worshipper. In both this and the following clause, P, SyrPs, and A[1] opt for the preposition ܡܢ, whereas SyrPs[a] employs the construction ܡܢ ܠܘܬ, its usual counterpart to παρά + genitive in the LXX.[44]

MT וּצְדָקָה מֵאֱלֹהֵי יִשְׁעוֹ
P ܘܙܕܝܩܘܬܐ ܡܢ ܐܠܗܐ ܦܪܘܩܢ
LXX καὶ ἐλεημοσύνην παρὰ θεοῦ σωτῆρος αὐτοῦ
SyrPs ܘܙܕܩܬܐ ܡܢ ܐܠܗܐ ܦܪܘܩܗ (ܘܙܕܩܬܐ] ܘܙܕܝܩܘܬܐ c = P)
A[1] ܘܡܪܚܡܢܘܬܐ ܡܢ ܐܠܗܐ ܦܪܘܩܗ

[44] Hiebert, "Syriac Biblical Textual History," 202.

SyrPs[a] ܘܡܪܚܡܢܘܬܐ ܡܢ ܠܘܬ ܐܠܗܐ ܦܪܘܩܐ ܕܝܠܗ

The terms ܙܕܝܩܘܬܐ "righteousness, alms, beneficence" in P and SyrPs manuscript *c* and ܙܕܩܬܐ "alms" in other SyrPs manuscripts are cognate counterparts of צְדָקָה "righteousness, vindication" in MT,[45] whereas ܡܪܚܡܢܘܬܐ of A[1] and SyrPs[a] seems in its primary sense of "mercy" (if not the secondary one of "beneficence, alms") to be semantically closer to ἐλεημοσύνη of LXX.[46] As for ܡܢ (P, SyrPs, A[1]) and ܡܢ ܠܘܬ (SyrPs[a]), see the preceding paragraph. Only P associates the first common plural possessive pronoun (in the form of a suffix) with the last noun; the other versions have a third person possessive. Of the Syriac versions, SyrPs[a], as is typical, opts for the independent possessive pronoun rather than the pronominal suffix attested in the others.[47]

*Verse 6*

| | |
|---|---|
| MT | זֶה דּוֹר דֹּרְשָׁו |
| P | ܗܢܘ ܕܪܐ ܕܒܥܐ |
| LXX | αὕτη ἡ γενεὰ ζητούντων αὐτόν |
| SyrPs | ܗܢܐ ܕܪܐ ܕܒܥܝܢ ܠܡܪܝܐ |
| A[1] | ܗܢܐ ܕܪܐ ܕܐܝܠܝܢ ܕܒܥܝܢ ܠܗ |
| SyrPs[a] | ܗܢܐ ܕܪܐ ܕܒ̈ܥܝܢ ܠܡܪܝܐ |

P exhibits the contracted demonstrative form ܗܢܘ (ܗܢܐ plus ܗ̣ܘ) while SyrPs, A[1], and SyrPs[a] show the simple demonstrative pronoun ܗܢܐ . P concludes this line with the singular ܕܒܥܐ whereas the remaining Syriac versions have plural forms that correspond to LXX and MT *q$^{e}$rê* דֹּרְשָׁיו (*k$^{e}$tîb* is דֹּרְשׁוֹ). P is the only version that has no object of the verb/participle; MT, LXX, and A[1] show a pronoun object, while SyrPs and SyrPs[a] read ܠܡܪܝܐ which agrees with LXX witnesses Bo U'-1093 R´Aug *L´* 55.

| | |
|---|---|
| MT | מְבַקְשֵׁי פָנֶיךָ יַעֲקֹב סֶלָה |
| P | ܘܡܫܡܫܝܢ. ܠܦܪ̈ܨܘܦܐ ܕܐܦܝܟ ܐܠܗܗ ܕܝܥܩܘܒ |
| LXX | ζητούντων τὸ πρόσωπον τοῦ θεοῦ Ιακωβ διάψαλμα |

---

45 J. Payne Smith (ed.), "ܙܕܝܩ, ܙܕܝܩܘܬܐ" and "ܙܕܩܬܐ, ܙܕ̈ܩܬܐ," *A Compendious Syriac Dictionary*, 110, 111; F. Brown, S. R. Driver, and C. A. Briggs (eds.), "צדק," BDB, 841.

46 Payne Smith, "ܡܪܚܡܢܘܬܐ," *A Compendious Syriac Dictionary* (Oxford: Clarendon Press, 1994 [1st edition, 1903]]) 301; H. G. Liddell, R. Scott, and H. S. Jones, "ἐλεημοσύνη," LSJ, 531.

47 Hiebert, *"Syrohexaplaric" Psalter*, 15–17, 257.

SyrPs ܘܒܥܝܢ ܠܦܪ̈ܨܘܦܐ ܕܐܠܗܗ ܕܝܥܩܘܒ. ܕܦܣܠܡܘܢ (ܕܦܣܠܡܘܢ] ܕܐܦܣܐܠܡܐܘܢ *e*; ܕܦܣܠܡܐ *fg*)[48]
A[1] ܘܒܥܝܢ ܠܦܪ̈ܨܘܦܐ ܕܐܠܗܗ ܕܝܥܩܘܒ
SyrPs[a] ܘܒܥܝܢ ܦܪ̈ܨܘܦܐ ܕܐܠܗܐ ܕܝܥܩܘܒ. ܕܐܦܣܠܡܐ (ܕܐܦܣܠܡܐ *h* ] ܕܐܦܠܡܠܡܐ [sic] *j*)

Only P has a singular verbal form (consistent in number with the verb that precedes it) to which the conjunction is prefixed (ܘܡܒܥܐ), though clause division between the previous and present lines in P differs from that in the other versions. Of the Syriac translations, SyrPs[a] alone does not prefix the ܠ preposition to ܦܪ̈ܨܘܦܐ. P seems to have a doublet on the Hebrew term פנים[49] to which is affixed the second person singular pronominal suffix (yielding פָּנֶיךָ), attached to the second of the Syriac words for face in P (ܐ̇ܦܝܟ). Only MT and P make this clause vocative: in MT, Jacob is addressed directly, whereas in P, it is the God of Jacob.[50] The other versions make the phrase, "the face of the God of Jacob," the direct object of the participle. P and A[1] do not have counterparts to סֶלָה / διάψαλμα, whereas the other Syriac witnesses exhibit various transliterated forms of the Greek term.

*Verse 7*

MT שְׂאוּ שְׁעָרִים רָאשֵׁיכֶם
P ܐܪܝܡܘ ܬܪ̈ܥܐ ܪ̈ܫܝܟܘܢ
B ארימו תרעא רשיכון
LXX ἄρατε πύλας, οἱ ἄρχοντες ὑμῶν
SyrPss ܐܪܝܡܘ ܬܪ̈ܥܐ ܪ̈ܫܢܐ ܕܠܟܘܢ
A[1] ܐܪܝܡܘ ܬܪ̈ܥܐ ܪ̈ܫܟܘܢ

This entire verse may be compared with verse 9. The readings of P, B, and A[1], which mirror MT, are the same except for the orthographic difference between P and the other two in the last word. SyrPss follows LXX in construing the term for gates as the direct object of the verb rather than as a vocative, and in interpreting the heads as human rulers who are addressed vocatively rather than as gate lintels which

[48] Note that manuscripts *fg* do not contain continuous texts of SyrPs as they do of the Peshitta, but interlinear glosses of SyrPs readings where these versions differ. Hence, throughout this paper no *e silentio* conclusions about the existence of *fg* readings, other than ones explicitly recorded, may be drawn.

[49] Vogel, "Studien zum Pešiṭta-Psalter," 492.

[50] According to the *BHS* apparatus, this is also the case in two Hebrew manuscripts.

constitute the direct object of the verb.

MT      וְהִנָּשְׂאוּ פִּתְחֵי עוֹלָם

P       ܐܬܬܪܝܡܘ ܬܖܥܐ ܕܡܢ ܥܠܡ

B       אתתרימו תרעא דמן עלם

LXX     καὶ ἐπάρθητε, πύλαι αἰώνιοι

SyrPss  ܘܐܬܬܪܝܡܘ ܬܖܥܐ ܕܠܥܠܡ

A¹      ܘܐܬܬܪܝܡܘ ܬܖܥܐ ܕܡܢ ܥܠܡ

Only P = B do not begin the clause with a conjunction. Apart from
that, the wording in A¹ is the same. So ܕܡܢ ܥܠܡ, the counterpart in
these witnesses to עוֹלָם, differs from ܕܠܥܠܡ in SyrPss. Only MT
has a word for doors in this clause that differs from the word in the
preceding clause.

MT      וְיָבוֹא מֶלֶךְ הַכָּבוֹד

P       ܢܥܘܠ ܡܠܟܐ ( ܢܥܘܠ ] pr. *dalath* 8a1* 8t1ᵗˣᵗ 9a1 9t2.3
        10t1.2.5 12a1 12t2.5.7 →)

B       נעול מלכא דאיקרא

LXX     καὶ εἰσελεύσεται ὁ βασιλεὺς τῆς δόξης

SyrPss  ܘܢܥܘܠ ܡܠܟܐ ܕܬܫܒܘܚܬܐ

A¹      ܘܢܥܘܠ ܡܠܟܐ ܕܬܫܒܘܚܬܐ

P = B alone do not begin this line with a conjunction. Only in P (= B?)
is there a plural word for glory, a different term than the one encountered in the other Syriac witnesses (see the next clause). SyrPss and
A¹ have identical wording which is in accord with the readings of
LXX and MT.

*Verse 8*

MT      מִי זֶה מֶלֶךְ הַכָּבוֹד

P       ܡܢܘ ܗܢܐ ܡܠܟܐ ܕܐܝܩܪܐ

B       מנו הנא מלכא דאיקרא

LXX     τίς ἐστιν οὗτος ὁ βασιλεὺς τῆς δόξης

SyrPss  ܡܢܘ ܐܝܬܘܗܝ, ܗܢܐ ܡܠܟܐ ܕܬܫܒܘܚܬܐ

A²      ܡܢܘ ܐܝܬܘܗܝ, ܗܢܐ ܡܠܟܐ ܕܬܫܒܘܚܬܐ

A¹      ܡܢ ܐܝܬܘܗܝ, ܗܢܐ ܡܠܟܐ ܕܬܫܒܘܚܬܐ

The interrogative and demonstrative pronouns in MT are rendered in
P = B by a contraction of the interrogative pronoun of common gender
(ܡܢ) plus the personal pronoun as a copula (ܗܘ), and a demonstrative pronoun, respectively. LXX and the other Syriac versions insert the copula verb or equivalent between the interrogative and the
demonstrative. In SyrPss and A² (whose wording is identical), the

interrogative is the contracted form described above, while in A[1], it is the simple pronoun of common gender, which is in fact quantitatively closest to מִי of MT and τίς of LXX. With regard to the word for glory in P and B, see the preceding paragraph.

| | |
|---|---|
| MT | יְהוָה עִזּוּז וְגִבּוֹר |
| P | ܡܪܝܐ ܥܫܝܢܐ ܘܓܢܒܪܐ |
| B | מריא עשינא וגנברא |
| LXX | κύριος κραταιὸς καὶ δυνατός |
| SyrPs | ܡܪܝܐ ܐܚܝܕܐ ܘܥܫܝܢܐ (ܐܚܝܕܐ] ܚܝܕܐ *f*, ܚܝܕܐ *g*) |
| A[2] | ܡܪܝܐ ܐܚܝܕܐ ܘܥܫܝܢܐ |
| SyrPs[a] | ܡܪܝܐ ܥܫܝܢܐ ܘܚܝܠܬܢܐ |
| A[1] | ܡܪܝܐ ܥܫܝܢܐ ܘܓܢܒܪܐ |

The readings of P=B and A[1] are identical, as are those of SyrPs[-fg] and A[2]. SyrPs[-fg] and A[2] attest ܐܚܝܕܐ as the first adjective (compare the counterparts in manuscripts *f* and *g*); P = B, SyrPs[a], and A[1] agree on ܥܫܝܢܐ. MT, P=B, and A[1] are cognately equivalent as far as the second adjective is concerned, while the second adjective in SyrPs and A[2] is ܥܫܝܢܐ and in SyrPs[a] it is ܚܝܠܬܢܐ.[51]

| | |
|---|---|
| MT | יְהוָה גִּבּוֹר מִלְחָמָה |
| P | ܡܪܝܐ ܓܢܒܪܐ ܘܡܩܪܒܬܢܐ |
| LXX | κύριος δυνατὸς ἐν πολέμῳ |
| SyrPs | ܡܪܝܐ ܥܫܝܢܐ ܒܩܪܒܐ |
| A[2] | ܡܪܝܐ ܥܫܝܢܐ ܒܩܪܒܐ |
| SyrPs[a] | ܡܪܝܐ ܚܝܠܬܢܐ ܒܩܪܒܐ |
| A[1] | ܡܪܝܐ ܓܢܒܪܐ ܒܩܪܒܐ |

SyrPs and A[2] have identical readings. All witnesses employ the same lexeme for the second word as they do for the last word in the preceding clause. MT's מִלְחָמָה is interpreted creatively as a conjunction plus adjective in P. For their part, LXX and the other Syriac witnesses interpret the Hebrew quite appropriately as a prepositional phrase.

*Verse 9*

MT שְׂאוּ שְׁעָרִים רָאשֵׁיכֶם

[51] SyrPs and SyrPs[a] have the same respective equivalents at Psalm 18(17):18(17), 20(19), and in the clause that follows the present one in 24(23):8. The textual evidence for these three passages in other witnesses is: P (1. ܥܫܝܢܐ; 2. no reading; 3. ܓܢܒܪܐ ); B (1. no reading; 2. no reading; 3. no reading); A[1] (1. no reading; 2. no reading; 3. ܓܢܒܪܐ ); A[2] (1. no reading; 2. no reading; 3. ܥܫܝܢܐ).

P ܐܪܝܡܘ ܬܪ̈ܥܐ ܪ̈ܝܫܝܟܘܢ
B רשיכון ארימו תרעא (רשיכון ] רישיכון Bg)
LXX ἄρατε πύλας, οἱ ἄρχοντες ὑμῶν
SyrPss ܐܪܝܡܘ ܬܪ̈ܥܐ ܪ̈ܝܫܢܐ ܕܝܠܟܘܢ (ܪ̈ܝܫܢܐ] ܪ̈ܫܢܐ c)
By ארימו תרעא רשנא דילכון (רשנא ] רישנא Bg)
A1 ܐܪܝܡܘ ܬܪ̈ܥܐ ܪ̈ܫܝܟܘܢ

The readings of P, B, and A1 are the same except for orthographic differences involving the last word. The same can be said for SyrPss and By regarding the second last word. On the syntactical and semantic distinctions among the versions, see the discussion on verse 7 above.

MT וְשְׂאוּ פִּתְחֵי עוֹלָם
P ܐܬܬܪܝܡܘ ܬܪ̈ܥܐ ܕܡܢ ܥܠܡ
LXX καὶ ἐπάρθητε, πύλαι αἰώνιοι
SyrPss ܘܐܬܬܪܝܡܘ ܬܪ̈ܥܐ ܕܠܥܠܡ (ܕܠܥܠܡ] ܕܡܢ ܥܠܡ e)
A1 ܘܐܬܬܪܝܡܘ ܬܪ̈ܥܐ ܕܡܢ ܥܠܡ

Only P does not begin the clause with a conjunction. Apart from that, the wording in A1 and SyrPss manuscript *e* agrees with that of P. So ܕܡܢ ܥܠܡ, their counterpart to עוֹלָם, differs from ܕܠܥܠܡ in SyrPss$^{-e}$. Only MT does not have a passive verb form (contrast verse 7). As in verse 7, only MT has a word for doors in this clause that differs from the word in the preceding clause.

MT וְיָבֹא מֶלֶךְ הַכָּבוֹד
P ܕܢܥܘܠ (ܕܢܥܘܠ] om. *dalath* 6t1 8a1c 8t1 10t4.6 12t1.3.4[*vid.*] →) ܡܠܟܐ ܕܐܝܩܪ̈ܐ
B נעול מלכא דאיקרא
LXX καὶ εἰσελεύσεται ὁ βασιλεὺς τῆς δόξης
SyrPss ܘܢܥܘܠ ܡܠܟܐ ܕܫܘܒܚܬܐ
A1 ܘܢܥܘܠ ܡܠܟܐ ܕܫܘܒܚܬܐ

SyrPss and A1 have identical readings, mirroring LXX and MT. The P lemma alone begins the clause with a purpose conjunction (ܕ) rather than a copulative conjunction (ܘ); B has neither. The verb in MT is spelled defectively (contrast verse 7). As in verse 7, only P (= B?) has a plural word for glory, and it is different from the one in the other Syriac witnesses.

*Verse 10*

MT מִי הוּא זֶה מֶלֶךְ הַכָּבוֹד
P ܡܢܘ ܗܢܐ ܡܠܟܐ ܕܐܝܩܪ̈ܐ (ܕܐܝܩܪ̈ܐ] ܕܫܘܒܚܬܐ 12t2.5)
LXX τίς ἐστιν οὗτος ὁ βασιλεὺς τῆς δόξης

SyrPss ܡܢܘ ܐܝܬܘܗܝ ܗܢܐ ܡܠܟܐ ܕܬܫܒܘܚܬܐ
A[1] ܡܰܢ ܐܝܬܘܗܝ ܗܢܐ ܡܠܟܐ ܕܬܫܒܘܚܬܐ

MT's reading מִי הוּא זֶה contrasts with מִי זֶה in verse 8, whereas the other versions have the same wording as in verse 8. The counterpart in P to this Hebrew phrase and its Greek translation in the present verse is now a quantitative equivalent. The rendering in A[1] which includes the interrogative pronoun of the common gender (ܡܰܢ) and the copula can also be understood this way. The same could be true of SyrPss which includes the contraction of interrogative pronoun (ܡܰܢ) plus personal pronoun (ܗܘ) and the copula, though having both the personal pronoun and the copula is, strictly speaking, redundant.

MT יְהוָה צְבָאוֹת
P ܡܪܝܐ ܚܝܠܬܢܐ
B מריא חילתנא
LXX κύριος τῶν δυνάμεων
SyrPss ܡܪܝܐ ܕܚܝ̈ܠܘܬܐ
A[1] ܡܪܝܐ ܕܚܝ̈ܠܘܬܐ
A[2] ܡܪܝܐ ܕܚܝ̈ܠܘܬܐ

P = B render צְבָאוֹת with a singular attributive adjective, whereas the other versions have genitive plural nouns meaning "hosts/forces," which are more precise equivalents of the Hebrew.

MT הוּא מֶלֶךְ הַכָּבוֹד סֶלָה
P ܗܘܝܘ ܡܠܟܐ ܡܫܒܚܐ ܠܥܠܡ (ܗܘܝܘ ] pr. *waw* 9a1 9t3 10t1 12t7; ܠܥܠܡ] pr. *dalath* 12t7)
LXX αὐτός ἐστιν ὁ βασιλεὺς τῆς δόξης
SyrPss ܗܘ ܐܝܬܘܗܝ ܡܠܟܐ ܕܬܫܒܘܚܬܐ
A[1] ܗܘ ܐܝܬܘܗܝ ܡܠܟܐ ܕܬܫܒܘܚܬܐ

SyrPss and A[1] have identical readings that mirror LXX, including the combination of pronoun plus copula at the beginning of the line that serves as an appropriate translation of MT. P's ܗܘܝܘ — a contraction of two third masculine singular personal pronouns, the semantic range of the resulting term being "that is to say, *id est*, the same, that very"[52] — might be interpreted either as introducing an appositional clause or as the subject plus copula of a verbless clause. Only the latter sense, of course, conveys the meaning of MT. P's ܡܫܒܚܐ functions as an attributive adjective, as opposed to ܕܬܫܒܘܚܬܐ in the other Syriac

[52] Payne Smith, "ܗܘ, " and "ܗܘܝܘ," *A Compendious Syriac Dictionary*, 101, 102.

witnesses which reflects the genitive noun constructions in MT and LXX. P alone translates סֶלָה, rendering it as ܠܥܠܡ, "for ever." This equivalence accords with the one that appears regularly in the Targums (לעלמין), though that may be the result of polygenesis or of P and the Targums drawing from a common tradition, rather than evidence for the former's textual dependence upon the latter.[53]

The preceding analysis of Psalm 24(23) has not provided an opportunity to profile the version of Jacob of Edessa since it is not extant in this section of the Psalter. However, there are excerpts of other parts of his recension of Psalms, which I designate below as J$^{E}$, in a published liturgical text.[54] It is instructive to compare that text with those of the versions examined above.

2. PSALM 4:7(6)

| | |
|---|---|
| MT | אוֹר פָּנֶיךָ יְהוָה |
| P | ܢܘܗܪܐ ܕܦܪܨܘܦܗ (ܢܘܗܪܐ] pr. *beth* 9t2) |
| B | נוהרא דפרצופה |
| LXX | τὸ φῶς τοῦ προσώπου σου, κύριε |
| SyrPs | ܢܘܗܪܐ ܕܦܪܨܘܦܗ ܕܡܪܝܐ (ܕܦܪܨܘܦܗ] ܕܦܪܨܘܦܐ ܕܝܠܗ *fg*; ܕܦܪܨܘܦܗ ܕܡܪܝܐ] ܕܦܪܨܘܦܟ ܡܪܝܐ *a*$^{c}$) |
| A$^{2}$ | ܢܘܗܪܐ ... ܕܦܪܨܘܦܗ ܕܡܪܝܐ |
| B$^{y}$ | נוהרא דפרצופך מריא |
| SyrPs$^{a}$ | ܢܘܗܪܐ ܕܦܪܨܘܦܐ ܕܝܠܟ ܡܪܝܐ |
| J$^{E}$ | ܢܘܗܪܐ ܕܦܪܨܘܦܐ ܕܝܠܟ |

MT, LXX, the corrector of SyrPs manuscript *a*, B$^{y}$, SyrPs$^{a}$, and J$^{E}$ all attest a second person possessive pronoun in conjunction with the word for face. Furthermore, in all of these same witnesses except J$^{E}$ (from which version only the three words of this verse recorded above are cited in the liturgical text), the term for the deity follows in the vocative case. J$^{E}$, like SyrPs$^{a}$, employs the independent possessive pronoun rather than the pronominal suffix of *a*$^{c}$ and B$^{y}$.

3. PSALM 9:9(8)

| | |
|---|---|
| MT | תֵּבֵל בְּצֶדֶק |
| P | ܬܒܝܠ ܒܟܐܢܘܬܐ (ܬܒܝܠ] pr. *lamadh* 9t3 12a1 12t2.5 →) |
| B | תביל בקושתא |

[53] Weitzman, *Syriac Version*, 121.

[54] Rücker (ed.), *Die syrische Jakobosanaphora*, 18 line 2 (Ps. 9:9[8]), 26 lines 5-7 (Ps. 25[24]:7), 42 line 6 (Ps. 4:7[6]).

LXX τὴν οἰκουμένην ἐν δικαιοσύνῃ
SyrPs ܠܡܥܡܪܬܐ ܒܙܕܝܩܘܬܐ
B[y] לעמרתא בזדיקותא
SyrPs[a] ܠܡܬܥܡܪܢܝܬܐ ܒܙܕܝܩܘܬܐ (*h** transposes ܠܡܬܥܡܪܢܝܬܐ and the preceding word ܗܘ)
J[E] ܠܬܐܒܝܠ ܒܙܕܝܩܘܬܐ (ܠܬܐܒܝܠ] ܠܬܒܝܠ M R)

In this excerpt, J[E] exhibits a reading that constitutes a blend of elements from P=B (ܬܒܝܠ; cf. MT) and SyrPs=B[y] and SyrPs[a] (ܒܙܕܝܩܘܬܐ).

4. PSALM 25(24):7

MT חַטֹּאות נְעוּרַי וּפְשָׁעַי אַל־תִּזְכֹּר
P ܘܣܟܠܘܬܐ ܕܛܠܝܘܬܝ ܠܐ ܬܕܟܪ ܠܝ (ܬܕܟܪ] ܬܬܕܟܪ 6t1[c] 8a1 10t4.5* 12a1 12t2.3.7 →: ܬܬܟܪ 10t5[c] →: *l.n.* 12t4)
B וסכלותא דטליותי לא תתדכר לי
LXX ἁμαρτίας νεότητός μου καὶ ἀγνοίας μου μὴ μνησθῇς
SyrPs ܚܛܝܬܐ ܕܛܠܝܘܬܝ ܘܠܐ ܝܕܥܬܐ ܕܝܠܝ ܠܐ ܬܬܕܟܪ (ܬܬܕܟܪ] ܬܕܟܪ *cfg*)
J[E] ܚܛ̈ܗܐ ܕܛܠܝܘܬܝ ܘܠܐ ܝܕܥ̈ܬܐ ܕܝܠܝ ܠܐ ܬܬܕܟܪ (ܬܬܕܟܪ] + ܠܝ ܡܪܝܐ KO)
SyrPs[a] ܚܛܝܬܐ ܕܛܠܝܘܬܐ ܕܝܠܝ ܘܕܠܐ ܝܕܥܬܐ ܕܝܠܝ ܠܐ ܬܬܕܟܪ
A[1] ...]ܕܠܐ ܝܕܥܬܝ ܠܐ ܬܬܕܟܪ
A[2] ܘܚܛ̈ܗܐ ܘܠܐ ܝܕܥܬܐ ܕܛܠܝܘܬܐ ܠܐ ܢܬܕܟܪ ܠܗ

Among the Syriac versions of this clause, the reading in J[E] is closest to the SyrPs lemma which, in turn, aligns itself in distinctive fashion with LXX against MT, P, and B. However, instead of ܚܛܝܬܐ and ܠܐ ܝܕܥܬܐ, J[E] has the respective cognates ܚܛ̈ܗܐ (whose plurality accords with the forms in all other extant witnesses above except SyrPs and SyrPs[a])[55] and ܠܐ ܝܕܥ̈ܬܐ. A[2]'s free paraphrase also includes ܚܛ̈ܗܐ, but in comparison to SyrPs, J[E], and SyrPs[a], it reverses the order of the counterparts to νεότητος and ἀγνοίας. In addition, A[2] agrees with SyrPs (against J[E]) on the term ܠܐ ܝܕܥܬܐ.

MT כְּחַסְדְּךָ זְכָר־לִי־אַתָּה
P ܐܠܐ ܐܝܟ ܣܘܓܐܐ ܕܪ̈ܚܡܝܟ ܐܬܕܟܪܢܝ (om. 9a1)
LXX κατὰ τὸ ἔλεός σου μνήσθητί μου σὺ
SyrPs ܐܝܟ ܪ̈ܚܡܝܟ ܐܬܕܟܪܢܝ ܐܢܬ
SyrPs[a] ܐܝܟ ܪ̈ܚܡܐ ܕܝܠܟ ܐܬܕܟܪܢܝ ܐܢܬ

---

55 In the apparatus of *Psalmi cum Odis*, Rahlfs asserts (correctly) that the LXX term is accusative plural (rather than genitive singular).

A[1]    ܐܝܟ ܝܡܬܘܢܝ ܐܝܕܪܒܝܘ

J[E]    ܐܠܐ ܐܝܟ ܗܩܠܐܐ ܕܝܡܬܘܢܝ ܐܝܕܪܒܝܘ ܐܬܐ (ܐܬܐ > K)

J[E] reproduces P exactly, except that the second person masculine singular personal pronoun is added (save in K) in accordance with MT, LXX, SyrPs, and SyrPs[a].

## CONCLUSION

The preceding textual analysis, though limited in scope, provides clear documentation concerning the textual relationships that exist among the profiled versions. The series of statements below, formulated on the basis of these data, summarize those relationships and generally corroborate what previous studies about the textual character of these witnesses have concluded (see sections 2, 3, and 4 above).

(1) (= B) is a quite faithful, but not slavish, translation of the MT which also exhibits some parallels with the LXX against MT.

(2) LXX is a rather literal translation of MT, though there are necessary concessions to Greek syntax and idiom as well as a few variant readings.

(3) SyrPs and SyrPs[a] are independent, literal translations of the LXX. However, SyrPs[a] not infrequently reflects the Greek even more precisely than SyrPs does.

(4) B[y] is naturally in the SyrPss tradition. Yet when SyrPs and SyrPs[a] diverge, B[y] seems as likely to side with one as with the other.

(5) A[1] exhibits a significant degree of comparability to SyrPss. Agreements with P, usually in combination with either SyrPs and SyrPs[a] or just with SyrPs, are also not uncommon. On a number of occasions, A[1] reflects the LXX but with wording that differs, to one degree or another, from other Syriac witnesses.

(6) A[2] is characterized by agreements with SyrPss or with SyrPs when it diverges from SyrPs[a]. In addition, there are several contexts in which the reading is a free paraphrase rather than a precise quotation of a particular version.

(7) J[E] shows evidence of dependence on P and SyrPss, SyrPs, or SyrPs[a].

## SELECT BIBLIOGRAPHY

Baars, W. "Ein neugefundenes Bruchstück aus der syrischen Bibelrevision des Jakob von Edessa," *VT* 18 (1968) 548–54.

—. *New Syro-Hexaplaric Texts* (Leiden: Brill, 1968).

Barnes, W. E. "On the Influence of the Septuagint on the Peshitta," *JTS* 2 (1901) 186–97.

Baumstark, A. "Pešiṭta und palästinensisches Targum," *Biblische Zeitschrift* 19 (1931) 257–70.

Berg, J. F. *The Influence of the Septuagint upon the Pešiṭta Psalter* (New York: no publ.; Leipzig: W. Drugulin, 1895).

Brock, S. P. "The Resolution of the Philoxenian/Harclean Problem," in E. J. Epp and G. D. Fee (eds.), *New Testament Textual Criticism—Its Significance for Exegesis: Essays in Honour of Bruce M. Metzger* (Oxford: Clarendon Press, 1981) 325–43.

—. "Syriac Versions," *ABD* 6.794–99.

—. *A Brief Outline of Syriac Literature* (Mōrān ʾEthʾō 9; Baker Hill, Kottayam, India: St. Ephrem Ecumenical Research Institute, 1997).

Bundy, D. "Christianity in Syria," *ABD* 1.970–79.

Delekat, L. "Die syrolukianische Übersetzung des Buches Jesaja und das Postulat einer alttestamentlichen Vetus Syra," *ZAW* N.F. 28 (1957) 21–54.

Eli of Qartamin, *Mēmrā sur S. Mār Philoxène de Mabbog* (ed. and trans. A. de Halleux; CSCO 234, Scriptores Syri 101; Louvain: Secrétariat du Corpus SCO, 1963).

Flesher, P. V. M. (ed.). *Targum and Peshitta* (vol. 2 of *Targum Studies*; South Florida Studies in the History of Judaism 165; Atlanta: Scholars Press, 1998),

Gwynn, J. *Remnants of the Later Syriac Versions of the Bible in Two Parts* (London: Williams and Norgate, 1909).

Haefeli, L. *Die Peschitta des Alten Testamentes, mit Rücksicht auf ihre textkritische Bearbeitung und ihre Herausgabe* (ATA 11/1; Münster: Verlag der Aschendorffschen Verlagsbuchhandlung, 1927).

Halleux, A. de. *Philoxène de Mabbog: sa vie, ses écrits, sa théologie* (Louvain: Imprimerie orientaliste, 1963).

Hiebert, R. J. V. *The "Syrohexaplaric" Psalter* (SBLSCS 27; Atlanta: Scholars Press, 1989).

—. "The 'Syrohexaplaric' Psalter: Its Text and Textual History," in A. Aejmelaeus and U. Quast (eds.), *Der Septuaginta-Psalter und seine Tochterübersetzungen* (Abhandlungen der Akademie der Wissenschaften in Göttingen; MSU 24; Göttingen: Vandenhoeck & Ruprecht, 2000) 123–46.

—. "Syriac Biblical Textual History and the Greek Psalter," in R. J. V. Hiebert, C. E. Cox, and P. J. Gentry (eds.), *The Old Greek Psalter: Studies in Honour of Albert Pietersma* (JSOTSup 332; Sheffield: Sheffield Academic Press, 2001) 178–204.

Jenkins, R. G. "Some Quotations from Isaiah in the Philoxenian Version," *Abr-Nahrain* 20 (1981–82) 20–36.

—. *The Old Testament Quotations of Philoxenus of Mabbug* (CSCO 514, Subsidia 84; Louvain: E. Peeters, 1989).

Kahle, P. *Masoreten des Westens* (2 vols.; Stuttgart: W. Kohlhammer, 1927–30).

—. *The Cairo Geniza* (2d ed., Oxford: Blackwell, 1959).

Lagarde, P. de (ed.). כתבא דמזמורא מן כתבא דאוצר ארזא, *Praetermissorum libri duo* (Göttingen: Sumptibus editoris in officina academica Dieterichiana, 1879).

Lund, J. *The Influence of the Septuagint on the Peshitta: A Re-evaluation of Criteria in Light of Comparative Study of the Versions in Genesis and Psalms* (Jerusalem: Hebrew University, 1988).

—. "Grecisms in the Peshitta Psalms," in P. B. Dirksen and A. van der Kooij (eds.), *The Peshitta as a Translation* (Monographs of the Peshitta Institute, Leiden 8; Leiden: Brill, 1995) 85–102.

Maori, Y. *Peshitta Version of the Pentateuch and Early Jewish Exegesis* (Hebrew; Jerusalem: Magnes, 1995).

Peshiṭta Institute (ed.). *The Old Testament in Syriac according to the Peshiṭta Version.* Vol. 2/3: *The Book of Psalms* (Leiden: Brill, 1980).

Philoxène de Mabbog. *Commentaire du prologue johannique (Ms. Br. Mus. Add. 14,534)* (ed. and trans. A de Halleux; CSCO 380, Scriptores Syri 165; Louvain: Secrétariat du Corpus SCO, 1977).

Rahlfs, A. (ed.). *Septuaginta: Vetus Testamentum Graecum*, Vol. 10: *Psalmi cum Odis* (Göttingen: Vandenhoeck & Ruprecht, 1931).

Rompay, L. van. "The Christian Syriac Tradition of Interpretation," in M. Sæbø (ed.), *Hebrew Bible / Old Testament: The History of Its Interpretation*, Vol. 1/1: *From the Beginnings to the Middle Ages (Until 1300): Antiquity* (Göttingen: Vandenhoeck & Ruprecht, 1996) 612–41.

—. "Development of Biblical Interpretation in the Syrian Churches of the Middle Ages," in M. Sæbø (ed.), *Hebrew Bible / Old Testament: The History of Its Interpretation*, Vol. 1/2: *From the Beginnings to the Middle Ages (Until 1300): The Middle Ages* (Göttingen: Vandenhoeck & Ruprecht, 2000) 559–77.

Rücker, A. (ed.). *Die syrische Jakobosanaphora nach der Rezension des Jaʿqôb(h) von Edessa* (Liturgiegeschichtliche Quellen 4; ed. P. K. Mohlberg and A. Rücker; Münster: Verlag der Aschendorffschen Verlagsbuchhandlung, 1923).

Running, L. G. "An Investigation of the Syriac Version of Isaiah," *AUSS* 3 (1965) 138–57; *AUSS* 4 (1966) 37–64, 135–48.

Thomson, R. W. (ed.). *Athanasiana Syriaca.* Part 4: *Expositio in Psalmos* (CSCO 386, Scriptores Syri 167; Louvain: Secrétariat du Corpus SCO, 1977).

—. (trans.). *Athanasiana Syriaca.* Part 4: *Expositio in Psalmos* (CSCO 387, Scriptores Syri 168; Louvain: Secrétariat du CorpusSCO, 1977).

Vogel, A. "Studien zum Pešiṭta-Psalter: Besonders im Hinblick auf sein Verhältnis zu Septuaginta," *Biblica* 32 (1951) 32–56, 198–231, 336–63, 481–502.

Vööbus, A. *Peschitta und Targumim des Pentateuchs. Neues Licht zur Frage der*

*Herkunft der Peschitta aus dem altpalästinischen Targum* (Papers of the Estonian Theological Society in Exile 9; Stockholm: ETSE, 1958).

Vööbus, A. *History of the School of Nisibis* (CSCO 266, Subsidia 26; Louvain: Secrétariat du Corpus SCO, 1965).

—. *The Hexapla and the Syro-Hexapla* (Papers of the Estonian Theological Society in Exile 22; Stockholm: ETSE, 1971).

—. A. "Syriac Versions," *IDBSup*, 848–54.

Weitzman, M. P. "The Origin of the Peshitta Psalter," in J. A. Emerton and S. C. Reif (eds.), *Interpreting the Hebrew Bible: Essays in Honour of E. I. J. Rosenthal* (Cambridge: Cambridge University Press, 1982) 277–98.

—. "The Interpretative Character of the Syriac Old Testament," in M. Sæbø (ed.), *Hebrew Bible / Old Testament: The History of Its* Interpretation, Vol. 1/1: *From the Beginnings to the Middle Ages (Until 1300): Antiquity* (Göttingen: Vandenhoeck & Ruprecht, 1996) 587–611.

—. *The Syriac Version of the Old Testament: An Introduction* (University of Cambridge Oriental Publications 56; Cambridge: University Press, 1999).

## APPENDIX

Excerpts from the Apparatus of Rahlfs' *Psalmi cum Odis*[56]

### Psalm 23 (𝔐 24)

1 τω Δαυιδ ] ܒ̄ܕܕ A¹ | της μιας (των) σαββατων ] ÷ Ga, > S 2110 O(teste Tht) L^pau = 𝔐 | της μιας ] της > L^pau, τη μια U, εις μιαν L^pau 55 | σαββατων ] pr. των U L^b R^c, σαββατου L^d(sil)He A, ܟ̈ܒ̄ܐ *fg* A¹ A² B^y | παντες ] ÷ Ga | εν αυτη > U

2 init. ] pr. ⁕ *quia* Ga

3 του > L^pau: cf. 2 12 | και B' Tht^pSyrPss A² A' et Cyp.^p ] η Bo U' 2110 R'' Ga LTht^p A¹ 55 et Cyp.^p: cf. 14 1 17 32 | αγιω ] αγιασματος U' 2110: item α' θ' | στησεται ] στηθησεται 2110

4 χερσιν SyrPs^a ] ,ܡܢܐ̈ܪܟ SyrPs A¹ B^y | τη καρδια SyrPs^a ] ܡܒܠܒ SyrPs A¹ B^y | αυτου 1° ] μου A = K^ere⁻ | και ουκ ] ουδε U, ουδ 2110 | τω πλησιον αυτου (ex 14 4?) ] αυτου > S A'(non 1219)

5 ευλογιαν SyrPss ] ܟܒ̈ܪܝܢܒ A¹ | ελεημοσυνην ] ελεος U' 2110 | θεου ] *domino* La^G

6 αυτον B' La^G Ga A¹ A et Cyp. = 𝔐 ] τον κυριον Bo U'-1093 R'Aug L'SyrPss 55 | το > U | του θεου > La^G = 𝔐 | διαψαλμα > A¹

7 υμων ] ημων 2110 R L^pau 55: item in 9 | υμων cum πυλας connectunt Bo Sa

---

[56] These excerpts have been supplemented with collations from SyrPs, SyrPs^a, A¹, A², J^E, B^y, and the important Greek witness, Papyrus Bodmer XXIV = 2110 (R. Kasser and M. Testuz [eds.], *Papyrus Bodmer XXIV: Psaumes XVII–CXVIII* [Cologny-Genève: Bibliotheca Bodmeriana, 1967]).

Ga (*uestras*), cum αρχοντες La (*uestri*: sic, ut uid., etiam Tert. et Cyp.): item in 9

8 κραταιος ܟܢܝܐ *ace* A², ܟܘܬܢ SyrPsᵃ A¹ ] ܟܢܝܝ *f*, ܟܢܢܝܝ *g* | κραταιος ... δυνατος ] tr. U' | fin. ] + διαψαλμα USaᴸ

10 ουτος > *L*ᵖᵃᵘ | των > U | ο βασιλευς ult. (sic etiam Tert. et Cyp.) ] pr. ουτος B'(non Bo) 55: ex 10 ₁; ουτος ο βασ. της δοξης ult. est stichus singularis in B solo

## Psalm 9 (1–21 = 𝔐 Psalm 9; 22–39 = 𝔐 Psalm 10)

9 την οικουμενην ] + *totam* Bo | δικαιοσυνη ... ευθυτητι ] ευθ. ... δικ. R = *aequitate ... iustitia* La Ga, sed sic La Ga uarietatis causa uertisse uidentur, ne pro „δικαιοσυνη, κρινει“ dicerent „*iustitia, iudicabit*“ cf. 5

## Psalm 24 (𝔐 25)

7 αμαρτιας est acc. plur. = 𝔐: sic recte Bo Sa 2110 La Ga A²(ܟܡܠܢ̈) Jᴱ(idem) (sed gen. sing. SyrPss [ܟܕܠܝ]) | μου 1° > Laᴿ | αγνοιας R *L*'Bᶜ A″ ] est acc. plur. in B*(uid.)' U 2110 τας praemittentibus et in Sa Ga SyrPs(ܟܕܠܝܢ ܟܠ ) A²(idem) Jᴱ(ܟܕܠܢ̈ ܟܠ ) = 𝔐, est gen. sing. in Bo La SyrPsᵃ(ܟܕܠܢ ܟܠܢ ) A¹(item) | μου 2° > B' | κατα ] pr. ܟܠܟ Jᴱ(= P) | ελεος ] πληθος του ελεους U' Jᴱ(= P): cf. **1054₅**; ελεους [sic] 2110 | συ U' 2110 *L*'SyrPss Jᴱ(praeter K) 1219' = 𝔐 ] hab. Ga sub ÷ (pro ※?); *deus* Aug; > B″ R″ A¹ A: exciditne post μου?

## Psalm 4

7 του προσωπου σου κυριε *a*ᶜ SyrPsᵃ Bʸ Jᴱ(sine κυριε) ] ܟܢܝܢܢ ܡܓܢܝܓܢ *a*b A²; ܡܠܢ ܟܓܢܝܓܢ pro του προσωπου σου *fg*

# THE PSALMS IN EARLY SYRIAC TRADITION

HARRY F. VAN ROOY

The Psalms played a major part in the life of many communities in Jewish and Christian traditions. For example, more than 200 of the nearly 900 manuscripts found at Qumran may be classified as biblical scrolls. Thirty-six manuscripts from Qumran and three from other locations contain (parts of) the Psalter, the most of any biblical book.[1] With regard to the Greek version of the Psalter, more translations have been made into Greek than for every other book of the Old Testament, and more than ten times the number of Septuagint manuscripts are available for the Psalter than for any other book.[2]

In the same way the Psalter played an enormous role in the history of the Syriac-speaking churches. The majority of the manuscripts containing the Psalms in the Peshitta are Psalters, that is Hymnbooks or books for ecclesiastical services.[3] Of the forty-two manuscripts used for the critical edition of the Peshitta, only four are complete Bibles (7a1, 8a1, 9a1 and 12a1).[4] The remainder are all Psalters, representing different branches of Syriac Christianity.[5] The place of the Syriac versions in the textual history of the Psalter is the subject of a separate contribution in this volume. The present contribution will deal with the translation of the Psalter in Syriac, the headings of the Psalms, commentaries on the Psalms and a small collection of Syriac Apocryphal Psalms.

---

[1] See P. W. Flint, "Variant Readings of the Dead Sea Psalms Scrolls, against the Massoretic Text and the Septuagint Psalter," in A. Aejmelaeus & U. Quast (eds.), *Der Septuaginta-Psalter und seine Tochterübersetzungen* (MSU XXIV; Göttingen: Vandenhoeck & Ruprecht, 2000) 339.

[2] A. Pietersma, "The Present State of the Critical Text of the Greek Psalter," in Aejmelaeus & Quast (eds.), *Der Septuaginta-Psalter*, 25.

[3] W. E. Barnes, *The Peshitta Psalter According to the West Syrian Text* (Cambridge: Cambridge University Press, 1904) xxxv.

[4] For manuscripts used in the critical edition of the Peshitta, the notation of that edition is used, see Peshitta Institute, *List of Old Testament Peshitta Manuscripts* (Leiden: Brill, 1961).

[5] See D. M. Walter, *The Old Testament in Syriac*. Part II/3: *The Book of Psalms* (Leiden: Brill, 1980).

THE PSALMS IN SYRIAC TRANSLATION

The version of the Psalms contained in the Peshitta must be regarded as the most important and the oldest of the extant Syriac versions of the Psalter. The translations of the different books of the Peshitta are related to a Hebrew original[6] (or rather a number of originals for the different books of the Old Testament that were translated into Syriac). This Hebrew original was fairly close to the Masoretic text, although not identical in all respects.[7] Questions for debate are where, by whom, and for whom this translation was made. There is no consensus regarding these issues, with the result that one may still say that the origins of the Peshitta are obscure.[8]

A detailed view on these questions is to be found in M. Weitzman's substantial introduction to the Syriac Old Testament.[9] He discusses these issues in his chapter 5,[10] and situates the origin of the Peshitta in Edessa at about 150 CE. According to Weitzman, the translators were Jews, but Jews who can be described as non-rabbinic and anti-ritual.[11] This community gradually converted to Christianity and took their translation with them, which accounts for why a translation made by Jews was not transmitted by Jews, but by the church.[12] The transition happened over a period of time, explaining why the books that were translated last, perhaps at about 200 CE (Ezra-Chronicles), were not part of the original Syriac canon. They did not form part of the corpus of translated books the original converts brought with them. Although the Peshitta originated in Jewish circles, it was not accepted by the Jews, just as was the case eventually with the Septuagint.[13] Alison Salvesen agrees to some extent with this view, but is somewhat more

---

[6] See A. Vogel, "Studien zum Pešiṭta-Psalter," *Biblica* 32 (1951) 32.

[7] M. P. Weitzman, *The Syriac Version of the Old Testament* (University of Cambridge Oriental Publications 56; Cambridge: Cambridge University Press, 1999) 15.

[8] A. Salvesen, " Jacob of Edessa and the text of Scripture," in L. V. Rutgers, P. van der Horst, H. W. Havelaar, H. W. & L. Teuvels (eds.), *The Use of Sacred Books in the Ancient World* (Contributions to Biblical Exegesis and Theology 22; Leuven: Peeters, 1998) 235–45, esp 235.

[9] Weitzman, *Syriac Version.*

[10] Weitzman, *Syriac Version,* 206–62.

[11] Weitzman, *Syriac Version,* 258.

[12] Weitzman, *Syriac Version,* 259.

[13] Weitzman, *Syriac Version,* 261.

cautious, stating that the Pentateuch was translated first, probably by Jews. The other books, she adds, were translated later on, either by Jews (non-rabbinical, thus also Weitzman) or by Christian Jews.[14]

A question frequently asked is to what extent did the Septuagint influence the translation of the Psalms from the Hebrew. A frequently expressed view is that in the Peshitta the influence of the Septuagint is especially clear for the Psalter. This position is discussed in detail by A. Vogel, the original editor of the Psalms in the critical edition of the Peshitta published at Leiden.[15] He finds some evidence of influence from the Septuagint on the Peshitta's transmission, but not on the original translation.[16] However, J. Lund demonstrates convincingly that even this view exaggerates the influence of the Greek Bible, and that one cannot accept a major influence of the Septuagint on the Peshitta Psalter.[17]

Whatever the origin of the Peshitta, it is evident that the transmission of this translation was in the hands of the church.[18] This church was, especially at its inception, in many respects dependent on the Greek-speaking churches and Greek Fathers, such as Athanasius of Alexandria and Theodore of Mopsuestia. This will be discussed when looking at Psalms commentaries.

The Peshitta was, however, not the only translation of the Psalter in Syriac. Especially well-known is the translation called the Syro-Hexapla, attributed to Paul of Tella, who made his translation in the years 616–17 CE, from the Septuagint.[19] Unlike the remainder of the Syro-Hexapla, the Syro-Hexaplaric Psalter is not inherently a hexaplaric text, which was already indicated by A. Rahlfs, who regarded the Syro-Hexaplaric Psalter as part of his Lucianic witnesses to the Greek Psalter.[20] R. Hiebert has indicated that the different

---

[14] Salvesen, " Jacob of Edessa," 236.

[15] Vogel, "Pešiṭta-Psalter," 32–56, 198–231, 336–63, 481–502.

[16] Vogel, "Pešiṭta-Psalter," 501.

[17] J. Lund, "Grecism in the Peshitta Psalms," in P. B. Dirksen and A. van der Kooij (eds.), *The Peshitta as a Translation. Papers Read at the II Peshitta Symposium Held at Leiden 19–21 August 1993* (Leiden: Brill, 1995) 85–102, esp. 102.

[18] See R. A. Taylor, "The Syriac Old Testament in Recent Research," *Journal for the Aramaic Bible* 2/1 (2000) 119–39, esp. 134.

[19] See R. J. V. Hiebert, *The "Syrohexaplaric" Psalter* (SBLSCS 27; Atlanta: Scholars Press, 1989) 1.

[20] A. Rahlfs, *Psalmi cum Odis* (3rd ed., Vetus Testamentum Graecum X; Göttingen: Vandenhoeck & Ruprecht, 1979) 66–67.

manuscripts of the Syro-Hexapla contain three different traditions. The basic tradition he regards as a recension of the Philoxenian Psalter, probably done by Paul of Tella.[21] The second tradition is possibly a different recension of the Philoxenian Psalter, perhaps by Thomas of Harkel, while a third tradition is possibly a revision of the first tradition in the light of the second.[22]

Hiebert has made a good case for the existence of a Philoxenian Psalter.[23] In a paper read at the Peshitta Symposium at Leiden in 2001, a study was made of the text of the Psalms in the longer Syriac version of the commentary of Athanasius on the Psalms.[24] The text of the Psalms in this longer version of the commentary presents a mixed form, with a text in between the Peshitta and the Syro-Hexapla having probably been used as a base-text. In agreement with the thesis of Hiebert, this text can probably be identified as the Psalter of Philoxenus. It may even be the case that the text of the Psalms in this longer version of the commentary is Philoxenian, but this would be difficult to prove.

In this regard, Barbara Aland has published an important study with regard to the Philoxenian-Harklean translation tradition.[25] She refers to an earlier study that was done by S. Brock on the Syriac Euthalian

---

[21] See Hiebert, *"Syrohexaplaric" Psalter*, 252–57.

[22] Hiebert, *"Syrohexaplaric" Psalter*, 257–60.

[23] Hiebert, *"Syrohexaplaric" Psalter*, 248–51.

[24] H. F. van Rooy, "The Peshitta and Biblical Quotations in the Longer Syriac Version of the Commentary of Athanasius on the Psalms (B. M. Additional Manuscript 14568) with Special Attention to Psalm 23 (24) and 102 (103)," paper read at the III Peshitta Symposium, Leiden 2001. There are two Syriac versions of this commentary of Athanasius, the longer (fragmentary) version dating from the late Sixth Century, and a shorter version, dating from the Eight or Ninth Century. The text and a translation of the two commentaries were published by R. W. Thomson:

Text: *Athanasiana Syriaca Part IV. Expositio in Psalmos. 1. Abbreviated version. 2. Longer version* (CSCO 386, Scriptores Syri Tomus 167; Louvain: Peeters, 1977).

Translation: *Athanasiana Syriaca Part IV. Expositio in Psalmos. 1. Abbreviated version. 2. Longer version* (CSCO 387, Scriptores Syri Tomus 168; Louvain: Peeters, 1977).

[25] B. Aland, "Die philoxenianisch-harklensische Übersetzungstradition. Ergebnisse eine Untersuchung der neutestamentliche Zitate in der syrischen Literatur," *Museon* 94 (1981) 321–83.

material,[26] comparing the Old Testament quotations in the Euthalian introduction to the Pauline epistle in the Greek, Peshitta, three Syriac manuscripts containing the Euthalian material, and the Harklean translation. In two of the manuscripts the quotations agree with the Harklean translation, but in the third it is Philoxenian.[27] Brock's conclusion is that the Philoxenian New Testament stands mid-way between the Peshitta and the Harklean translation; the Philoxenian translation is a revision of the Peshitta.[28] Aland agrees with Brock's conclusions about the Euthalian material.[29] She defines what is meant by mid-way between the Peshitta and the Harklean translation, namely that the Philoxenian is with regard to literalness of the translation mid-way between the relatively free translation of the Peshitta and the Harklean with its tendency to follow the Greek closely.

A. Juckel[30] holds that the Philoxenian version falls between the Peshitta and the revision of Thomas of Harkel. It retained much of the vocabulary and syntax of the Peshitta, but it also anticipated some of the lexicographical and syntactical features of the Harklean revision. Aland links the use of the Philoxenian translation to a specific Syriac genre, namely Monophysite translations of Greek commentaries.[31] In these commentaries the New Testament text is often quoted in a form agreeing with the mid-way character of the Philoxenian translation. This is not found in Nestorian commentaries, or in original Syriac commentaries; she thinks that the translators used the Philoxenian as a base text for their translation.[32] Aland prefers to speak of a Philoxenian-Harklean tradition of translation.[33]

---

[26] See S. P. Brock, "The Syriac Euthalian material and the Philoxenian version of the New Testament," *ZNW* 70 (1979) 120–30.

[27] Brock, "Euthalian material," 120–21.

[28] Brock, "Euthalian material," 127.

[29] Aland, "philoxenianisch-harklensische Übersetzungstradition," 322.

[30] A. Juckel, "Introduction to the Harklean Text," in G. A. Kiraz, *Comparative Edition of the Syriac Gospels* (New Testament Tools and Studies Volume 25/1; Leiden: Brill, 1996) xxxiii, n. 9.

[31] L. van Rompay, "The Christian Syrian Tradition of Interpretation," in M. Saebø, *Hebrew Bible / Old Testament. The History of its Interpretation I.1: From the Beginning to the Middle Ages* (Göttingen: Vandenhoeck & Ruprecht, 1996) 618, refers to the translation of works of Cyril of Alexandria and Athanasius in the Fifth Century, leading to a distinctive West Syrian branch of exegesis.

[32] Aland, "philoxenianisch-harklensische Übersetzungstradition," 324.

[33] Aland, "philoxenianisch-harklensische Übersetzungstradition," 334.

Her thesis of the text of translated commentaries being close to the Philoxenian, whereas commentaries written in Syriac tend to follow the Peshitta, also holds true for commentaries on the Psalms. Whereas the translated longer commentary of Athanasius has a text related to the Philoxenian, the commentary of Daniel of Salach follows the Peshitta in the first two Psalms.[34] This supports the theory that the longer version of Athanasius' Psalms commentary in Syriac contains the Philoxenian Psalter, or at least a text very close to it.

## THE HEADINGS OF THE PSALMS IN THE SYRIAC TRADITION

With regard to the headings of the Psalms in Syriac tradition, one must distinguish between the headings in the Peshitta and those in the Syro-Hexapla. The headings in the Syro-Hexapla are related to the Septuagint. Rahlfs accordingly dealt with the headings from the Ambrosian Syro-Hexapla in his critical edition of the Septuagint Psalter,[35] not using all the manuscripts of the Syro-Hexapla that were published later by Hiebert. A complete study of all the headings in the Syro-Hexapla still remains to be done. In one study that was carried out on the headings in the first book of the Psalms, a number of important conclusions were drawn:[36]

- The distinction made by Hiebert between three traditions in the manuscripts of the Syro-Hexapla is valid for the headings as well.
- Manuscript f as listed by Hiebert (12t3 in the Leiden notation) frequently goes its own way.[37]
- The headings in the Syro-Hexapla frequently agree with Rahlfs' Lower Egyptian group and with the group of A. Whereas the body of the Syro-Hexaplaric Psalms may be regarded as

---

[34] The first two homilies were published by G. Diettrich, *Eine jakobitische Einleitung in den Psalter in Verbindung mit zwei Homilien aus den grossen Psalmkommentar des Daniel von Salah.* (BZAW 5; Giessen: Ricker'sche Verlagsbuchhandlung, 1901).

[35] See Rahlfs, *Psalmi*, 18–19.

[36] H. F. van Rooy, "The Psalm Headings in Book One of the Syro-Hexapla Psalms," in B. A. Taylor (ed.) *X Congress of the International Organization for Septuagint and Cognate Studies. Oslo 1988* (SBLSCS 51; Atlanta: Society of Biblical Literature, 2001) 373–92, esp. 391–92.

[37] The headings of this manuscript were dealt with at a paper read at the meeting of the International Organization for Septuagint and Cognate Studies in Boston, 1999: H. F. van Rooy, "The Syro-Hexaplaric Headings of the Psalms in Manuscript 12t3." [forthcoming]

Lucianic, this may not be valid for the headings.

With regard to the headings in the Peshitta, a totally different picture emaerges. The headings of the Hebrew Psalter were not retained in the Peshitta. The Psalms in the different manuscripts or editions of the Peshitta either have no headings at all, or headings different from that in the Masoretic text. In his study of the headings of the Psalms in the East Syrian Church, W. Bloemendaal[38] distinguishes four groups:

- Headings of the East Syrian tradition.
- Headings of the West Syrian tradition, as in Codex Ambrosianus.
- Headings in the edition of Sionita, Lee and the Polyglotts.
- Manuscripts with a mixture of headings.

Bloemendaal published a critical edition of the headings of the East Syrian tradition, although he was unable to use some of the most important manuscripts. No such edition of the West Syrian tradition has been undertaken yet.[39] It has been proven without doubt that the headings of the East Syrian tradition should be linked to the commentary on the Psalms by Theodore of Mopsuestia.[40] The exact situation with regard to the headings of the Western tradition is still unclear, although a link to the commentary on the psalms by Daniel of Salach is evident in some instances.[41] In any case, these headings are important for the study of the interpretation of the Psalms in the different traditions. The East Syrian headings are not all exactly the same in all the manuscripts, but the tradition as a whole is fairly consistent. They reflect the interpretation of the Psalms by Theodore of Mopsuestia, regarded as the exegete par excellence in the Nestorian tradition. As an example, one may consider the headings of the four Psalms that were regarded as Messianic by Theodore:

- Psalm 2: "He prophesies about the things that were done by the Jews during the Passion of our Lord and reminds us of his human nature as well."

---

[38] W. Bloemendaal, *The Headings of the Psalms in the East Syrian Church* (Leiden: Brill, 1960) 2–3.

[39] In a paper read at the Peshitta Symposium in Leiden during August 2001, D. G. K. Taylor reported work being done at present: "The Psalm Headings in the West Syrian Tradition."

[40] Bloemendaal, *Headings*, 12.

[41] S. P. Brock, *Catalogue of Syriac Fragments (New Finds) in the Library of the Monastery of Saint Catherine, Mount Sinai* (Athens: Mount Sinai Foundation, 1995) xxi.

• Psalm 8: "He prophesies about the Messiah our Lord and he makes known to us concerning the division of the natures."
• Psalm 45: "He prophesies about the Messiah our Lord and about the establishment of the faithful church."
• Psalm 110: "About the rule of our Saviour the Messiah."

These headings may be compared to the Theodore's commentary on these Psalms, where the interpretation of each Psalm is prefaced by an introduction, summarising his exegesis. Frequently the first sentence of that introduction is important for the history of the East Syrian headings. In the case of Psalm 2, the first sentence is as follows[42]: "In the second Psalm the blessed David narrates, while prophesying, all that were done by the Jews at the time of the Passion of our Lord." A little later in the introduction Theodore makes reference to the two natures of Christ: "He indicates both the right to rule and the power to govern which above all, sustained by God, the Man received after the resurrection."[43]

Psalm 8 begins as follows in the commentary: "In this Psalm the blessed David, filled with a prophesying spirit, predicted concerning the incarnation of the Lord and he said those things about Christ that were later fulfilled in essence, by which truly all the depravity of the Jewish contradictions was refuted."[44] These examples are sufficient to demonstrate that the East Syrian headings followed the messianic interpretation of Theodore in these Psalms.

The consistency of the East Syrian headings does not appear in the headings in the West Syrian tradition, however. This is clear, for example, in the following headings for Psalm 7 in three different manuscripts. Codex Ambrosianus (7a1) has the following heading: "Spoken by David when he was fleeing from Absalom his son." The heading in 9t3 is related to this heading, but not identical: "Spoken by David when Absalom send a mighty army against him to pursue him." The heading in 9t2 connects this Psalm to David's flight before Absalom as well, but inserts a reference to Cush: "Spoken by David about Cush the Ethiopian (the Benjaminite), when he fled before Absalom his son." The last heading is clearly related to the heading of

---

[42] Translated from the edition of Theodore's commentary by R. Devreesse, *Le Commentaire de Theodore de Mopsueste sur les Psaumes 1–80* (Studi e Testi 93, 1939) 7.

[43] Devreesse, *Commentaire*, 8.

[44] Devreesse, *Commentaire*, 42.

Psalm 7 in the Masoretic Text, which mentions a Benjaminite Cush.

There are instances where manuscripts contain headings that are totally unrelated, as in the case of Psalm 142. Codex Ambrosianus (7a1) has the following heading: "Spoken by David when David was speaking to the Edomites who came to him on account of King Hadarezer."[45] Quite a few East Syrian headings link a number of Psalms to the Maccabees. Manuscript 9t2 has a heading for Psalm 142 with a reference to the Maccabees: "Spoken by David concerning the prayer of the Maccabees in the time of their distress." Manuscript 9t3 links the Psalm to an attempt of Saul to kill David: "Spoken by David when Saul sent to kill him."

A manuscript with very interesting headings is 12t4,[46] which has at least four headings preceding each Psalm, and frequently has five. Three of the headings are ascribed to early Church Fathers (Eusebius, Athanasius, and Theodore of Mopsuestia). The fourth (the first mentioned in every instance) is called "Hebrew." This heading is frequently followed by an alternative, ascribed to another manuscript or other manuscripts. As an example, the headings to Psalm 63 are quoted:

- Hebrew: "A Psalm of David when he was in the desert of Judah."
- Another manuscript: "A Psalm of David when he was in the desert of Edom."
- Eusebius: "A thanksgiving of the one made perfect by God."
- Athanasius: "Of those Psalms that are a thanksgiving. And when you, while you are persecuted, go to the desert, do not fear as if you are alone there, because God is already there for you. Sing then while you precede him."
- Theodore: "He prophesies about the virtuous amongst the people in Babel."

The so-called Hebrew headings are frequently related to the headings of the Psalms in the Syro-Hexapla, but are not identical to them. In this instance the Hebrew heading is that found in one of the manuscripts used by Hiebert in his edition of the Syro-Hexaplaric Psalter, while the heading ascribed to another manuscript is the same as in all the other manuscripts used by Hiebert.[47] The heading

---

[45] See 2 Samuel 8.

[46] See H. F. van Rooy, *Studies on the Syriac Apocryphal Psalms* (JSSSup 7; Oxford: Oxford University Press, 1999) 11–25.

[47] Hiebert, *"Syrohexaplaric" Psalter*, 84.

ascribed to Eusebius is a translation of the short heading of this Psalm
in a list of short headings in the Greek edition of his commentary.[48]
The heading ascribed to Athanasius is not related to his commentary
on the Psalms, but rather to his letter to Marcellinus.[49] The heading of
Athanasius in manuscript 12t4 consists of two parts; the first part
classifies the Psalm as a thanksgiving and the second links the Psalm
to a departure of the desert. The first part corresponds to Athanasius'
classification of this Psalm[50], and the second part to his note about the
use of this Psalm.[51] The heading ascribed to Theodore of Mopsuestia
is the well-known heading to this Psalm in the East Syrian tradition.[52]
These different headings demonstrate the variety of influences on
Biblical interpretation in Syriac traditions. Manuscript 12t4 is an
eastern manuscript, but contains headings of Fathers who had more of
an influence on Biblical interpretation in western circles.

COMMENTARIES ON THE PSALMS
AND PSALMS IN COMMENTARIES

The development of the interpretation of the Old Testament and
commentaries used and produced in Syriac was discussed by L. Van
Rompay in an important contribution,[53] as well as in a paper read at
the Third Peshitta conference in Leiden during 2001.[54] For the
Eastern tradition, the work of Theodore of Mopsuestia was especially
important. His commentaries, including the one on the Psalms, were
translated into Syriac and played a decisive role in determining the
orientation in Eastern Syriac circles.[55] In agreement with Theodore,
allegorical interpretation was rejected in favour of a more historical
interpretation. Theodore's influence can clearly be seen, as indicated
above, in the headings of the Psalms in East Syrian tradition, and his
Commentary on the Psalms was translated into Syriac quite early

---

[48] Eusebius, *Commentaria in Psalmos* (P.G. 23) 67–72.

[49] Athanasius, *Epistula ad Marcellinum* (P.G. 27) 11–46.

[50] Athanasius, *Epistula ad Marcellinum* (P.G. 27) 25–28.

[51] Athanasius, *Epistula ad Marcellinum* (P.G. 27) 27, 33.

[52] See Bloemendaal, *Headings*, 58.

[53] Van Rompay, "The Christian Syriac Tradition," 612–41.

[54] L. van Rompay, "Between the School and the Monk's cell. The Syriac Old
Testament Commentary Tradition," paper read at the III Peshitta Symposium,
Leiden, 2001.

[55] Van Rompay, "The Christian Syriac Tradition," 634.

on.[56] The interpretation of Theodore had a profound influence on the Psalms interpretation in the East Syrian tradition, as may be seen in the Psalms commentary of Ishodad of Merv.[57]

For the West Syrian tradition the (as yet) unpublished Psalms commentary of Daniel of Salach is very important.[58] He did not follow the school of Theodore, but also did not follow the Alexandrian allegorical approach. Daniel commences with a historical interpretation, and then moves into a more allegorical direction. In this he linked up with Ephrem and Greek authors such as Chrysostom, Athanasius, Cyril of Alexandria and the Cappadocians. In both the Eastern and Western traditions the historical setting played a signifi-cant role,[59] as seen in the Eastern and Western headings to the Psalms.

Reference was already made to the two Syriac translations of the Psalms commentary of Athanasius. The longer version is extant in fragmentary form, and is contained in a manuscript dating from 597 CE.[60] The original translation of this commentary may be quite a few years older, making it possible that Daniel of Salach could have used this Syriac translation. The influence and importance of the work of Athanasius[61] must have contributed to the creation of the shorter version, a few centuries later, just as the importance of Theodore's work resulted in abridged versions of his commentary, such as the commentary of Dencha and the anonymous commentary contained in manuscript Sachau 215.

David Lane has conducted an interesting study on the use of the Psalms in Syriac authors,[62] examining ways in which the Psalms were

---

[56] Text: L. van Rompay, *Théodore de Mopsueste. Fragments syriaques du Commentaire des Psaumes (Psaume 118 et Psaumes 138–148)* (CSCO 435, Scriptores Syri Tomus 189; Louvain: Peeters, 1982).

Translation: L. van Rompay, *Théodore de Mopsueste. Fragments syriaques du Commentaire des Psaumes (Psaume 118 et Psaumes 138–148)* (CSCO 436, Scriptores Syri Tomus 190; Louvain: Peeters, 1982).

[57] This was the conclusion of C. Leonhard, who made a comparison of the Syriac fragments of Theodore's commentary and the corresponding sections of the commentary of Ishodad. (*Ishodad of Merv's Exegesis of the Psalms 119 and 139–147* [CSCO 585, Subsidia 107; Louvain: Peeters, 2001]).

[58] Van Rompay, "The Christian Syriac Tradition," 639.

[59] Van Rompay, "The Christian Syriac Tradition," 640.

[60] See Thomson, *Athanasiana Syriaca*, (text) IX.

[61] See Bloemendaal, *Headings*, 16.

[62] D. J. Lane, "'Come here ... and let us sit and read ...': the use of Psalms in

used by five authors, viz., Narsai from the Fifth Century, Jacob of
Serugh from the Fifth and Sixth Century, John of Dalyatha and Joseph
Chazzaya from the Eight Century, and Ishodad of Merv from the
Ninth Century. Lane concluded that the Psalms played an important
role in Syriac ascetical and liturgical life.[63]

These five authors may be seen as representatives of two
contrasting approaches, namely expository and exegetical, between
which the differences are significant. The expository approach makes
conceptual points, for which quotations from Psalms may provide
examples, allusions, or illustrations. This may be seen in the work of
Jacob of Serugh, John of Dalyatha, and Joseph Chazzaya. On the
other hand, exegetical authors, such as Narsai and Ishodad, take a
theme or (rather) a biblical text and explain difficulties, with an
explanation or illustration from other biblical passages, science,
philosophy, or history.[64]

APOCRYPHAL PSALMS

In a discussion of the Psalms in the early Syriac Church, the
collection of five Syriac Apocryphal Psalms warrants a few remarks.
The existence of these five Psalms has been known to the scholarly
world since the Eighteenth Century, when they were mentioned in a
catalogue of manuscripts in the Vatican Library.[65] W. Wright first
published them in 1887,[66] with critical editions following in 1930 and
1972.[67] Psalm 151 was already well known from the Septuagint, but
the others were unknown until the discovery of 11QPs$^a$.[68] This scroll
from Qumran contains Psalm 151, in two sections, quite different

---

Five Syriac Authors," in A. Rapaport-Albert and G. Greenberg (eds.), *Biblical
Hebrew, Biblical texts. Essays in Memory of Michael P. Weitzman* (JSOTSup
333; The Hebrew Bible and Its Versions 2; London: Sheffield, 2001) 412–30.

[63] Lane, "Come here," 415.

[64] Lane, "Come here," 416.

[65] S. E. & J. E. Assemanus, *Bibliothecae Apostolicae Vaticanae Codicum
Manuscriptorum Catalogus Partis Primae. Tomus Tertius* (Rome, 1756) 385–86.

[66] W. Wright, "Some Apocryphal Psalms in Syriac," *Proceedings of the
Society of Biblical Archaeology 9* (1887) 257–66.

[67] M. Noth, "Die fünf syrisch überlieferten apokryphen Psalmen," *ZAW* 48
(1930) 1–23, and W. Baars, *The Old Testament in Syriac*. Part IV/6: *Apocryphal
Psalms* (Leiden: Brill, 1972).

[68] J. A. Sanders, *The Psalms Scroll of Qumran Cave 11 (11QPs$^a$)* (DJD 4;
Oxford: Clarendon Press, 1965).

from the version known from the Greek, as well as the Syriac Psalms 154 and 155.

As one would expect, Psalm 151 occurs in manuscripts of the Syro-Hexapla; but it is found, however, in a number of Peshitta manuscripts as well.[69] The oldest known version of this Psalm in Syriac occurs at the end of the longer version of Athanasius' Commentary on the Psalms, referred to above. The version in this commentary is older than that contained in the Syro-Hexapla, but almost identical to it; thus the version in the Syro-Hexapla must depend on an older version of this Psalm.[70] In the case of Psalm 154 and 155, the Syriac versions must be translations of Hebrew texts quite similar to the texts found at Qumran, but not identical to them.[71]

These five Syriac Apocryphal Psalms occur in only one Peshitta Psalms manuscript, namely 12t4, the same one that contained the different sets of headings, as was discussed above. In addition to this manuscript, these Psalms occur in a manuscript of the prophets and in a number of manuscripts of a work of Elias of al-Anbar. Although these texts are very interesting and important, they are no more than a footnote with respect to the use of the Psalms in the early Syriac church.

## CONCLUSION

The origin of the Syriac translations of the Psalms will remain an area of fruitful research for some time to come. The possibility of a Jewish origin seems plausible, but several questions remain unanswered. The influence of Theodore of Mopsuestia was probably responsible for the interesting history of the headings of the Psalms. The Masoretic headings were not retained and the headings developed in different Syriac traditions. The translation of commentaries from the Greek influenced the exegesis of the Psalms in the early Syriac church, with again a very special value attached to the work of Theodore. It is clear that the Psalms played an important role in the early Syriac church, with the history of five Apocryphal Psalms as a short footnote to this role.

---

[69] Baars, *Apocryphal Psalms*, viii.

[70] See Van Rooy, *Apocryphal Psalms*, 109.

[71] See Van Rooy, *Apocryphal Psalms*, 146–47 and 160–61.

SELECT BIBLIOGRAPHY

Aejmelaeus, A. and U. Quast (eds.). *Der Septuaginta-Psalter und seine Tochter-übersetzungen* (MSU XXIV; Göttingen: Vandenhoeck & Ruprecht, 2000).

Barnes, W. E. *The Peshitta Psalter According to the West Syrian Text* (Cambridge: Cambridge University Press, 1904).

Bloemendaal, W. *The Headings of the Psalms in the East Syrian Church* (Leiden: Brill, 1960).

Devreesse, R. *Le Commentaire de Theodore de Mopsueste sur les Psaumes 1–80* (Studi e Testi 93, 1939).

Hiebert, R. J. V. *The "Syrohexaplaric" Psalter* (SBLSCS 27; Atlanta: Scholars Press, 1989).

Leonhard, C. *Ishodad of Merv's Exegesis of the Psalms 119 and 139–147* (CSCO 585, Subsidia 107; Louvain: Peeters, 2001).

Lund, J. "Grecism in the Peshitta Psalms," in P. B. Dirksen, and A. van der Kooij (eds.), *The Peshitta as a Translation. Papers Read at the II Peshitta Symposium held at Leiden 19–21 August 1993* (Leiden: Brill, 1995) 85–102.

Rapaport-Albert, A and G. Greenberg (eds.). *Biblical Hebrew, Biblical Texts. Essays in Memory of Michael P. Weitzman* (JSOTSup 333; The Hebrew Bible and Its Versions 2; London: Sheffield, 2001).

Taylor, R. A. "The Syriac Old Testament in recent research," *Journal for the Aramaic Bible* 2/1 (2001) 119–39.

Van Rompay, L. "The Christian Syriac Tradition of Interpretation," in M. Saebø (ed.) *Hebrew Bible / Old Testament. The History of its Interpretation I.1: From the Beginning to the Middle Ages* (Göttingen: Vandenhoeck & Ruprecht, 1996) 612–41.

Van Rooy, H. F. "The Psalm Headings in Book One of the Syro-Hexapla Psalms," in B. A. Taylor (ed.), X *Congress of the International Organization for Septuagint and Cognate Studies, Oslo 1988* (SBLSCS 51; Atlanta: Society of Biblical Literature, 2001) 373–92.

Van Rooy, H. F. *Studies on the Syriac Apocryphal Psalms* (JSSSup 7; Oxford: Oxford University Press, 1999).

Vogel, A. "Studien zum Pešiṭta-Psalter," *Biblica* 32 (1951) 32–56, 198–231, 336–63, 481–502.

Walter, D. M. *Old Testament in Syriac*. Part II/3: *The Book of Psalms* (Leiden: Brill, 1980).

Weitzman, M. P. *The Syriac Version of the Old Testament* (University of Cambridge Oriental Publications 56; Cambridge: Cambridge University Press, 1999).

# PRAISE AND PROPHECY IN THE PSALTER
# AND IN THE NEW TESTAMENT

CRAIG A. EVANS

## INTRODUCTION

Quotations of and allusions to the Psalter abound in the New Testament. According to the Index of Quotations in the United Bible Societies Greek New Testament there are more than four hundred quotations and allusions.[1] Of these some 130 are quotations, 70 of which are introduced with formulas. It is not hard to see why the Psalter was so important to early Christians.[2] The Royal Psalms readily lent themselves to emerging christology, while the Lament Psalms clarified aspects of Jesus' Passion and the suffering and persecution many of his followers experienced. Psalms of praise contributed to the early church's liturgy and thankfulness to God for what had been accomplished in his Son the Messiah Jesus.

The Psalter was understood in early Christian circles as prophetic, much as it was at Qumran, whose scholars produced commentaries (or *pesharim*) on several Prophets and Psalms. Indeed, the Risen Christ in Luke 24 instructs his disciples concerning all that is written in "the Law and the Prophets and Psalms." Luke's grammar here suggests that "Psalms" are closely linked with "the Prophets."[3]

---

[1] As compiled in K. Aland, M. Black, C. M. Martini, B. M. Metzger, and A. Wikgren (eds.), *The Greek New Testament* (2nd ed., Stuttgart: Deutsche Bibelgesellschaft, 1968) 906–909.

[2] The most frequently used Psalms are 2, 22, 33, 34, 35, 39, 50, 69, 78, 89, 102, 105, 106, 107, 110, 116, 118, 119, 135, 145, and 147; cf. H. M. Shires, *Finding the Old Testament in the New* (Philadelphia: Westminster, 1974) 131–35.

[3] The Greek reads: δεῖ πληρωθῆναι πάντα τὰ γεγραμμένα ἐν τῷ νόμῳ Μωϋσέως καὶ τοῖς προφήταις καὶ ψαλμοῖς περὶ ἐμοῦ ("everything written about me in the law of Moses and the Prophets and Psalms must be fulfilled"). The RSV translates " ... the Prophets and the Psalms ...," which is misleading. There is no definite article preceding "Psalms." We do not have here an instance of the tripartite canon (i.e. the Law, the Prophets, and the Writings), but only the first two divisions—the Law and the Prophets, the latter of which was understood to include the Psalms. This is probably how the reference in 4QMMT should be

It is not surprising that the Psalter was regarded as inspired and as prophetic. Its association with David was doubtless a major reason for its authoritative reception in early Judaism and Christianity. The tradition of an inspired David reaches back to ancient Scripture. We are told that when David was anointed the Spirit of the Lord came upon him mightily (cf. 1 Sam 16:13). David and others were said to "prophesy" with musical instruments (cf. 1 Chron 25:1). Probably the most important scriptural tradition refers to inspired utterance (cf. 2 Sam 23:1-2):

> 1 Now these are the last words of David: The oracle of David, the son of Jesse, the oracle of the man who was raised on high, the anointed of the God of Jacob, the sweet psalmist of Israel: 2 "The Spirit of the LORD speaks by me, his word is upon my tongue."

The tradition of an inspired, even prophetic David grows in the intertestamental period. According to 11QPs[a] 27:11: "All these he (David) spoke through prophecy which was given him from before the Most High."[4] Similarly says Josephus: "the Deity abandoned Saul and passed over to David, who, when the divine spirit had removed to him, began to prophesy" (*Ant.* 6.8.2 §166). Further evidence of David's inspiration is seen in healing powers attributed to some of his Psalms that were "for making music over the stricken" (11QPs[a] 27:10; cf. 1 Sam 16:16-23; 18:10; 19:9; Ps 91:5-6; *Tg.* Ps 91:5-6).

The tradition of a prophetic David is presupposed in the New Testament as well. According to Acts 1:16, "the Holy Spirit spoke beforehand by the mouth of David" (προεῖπεν τὸ πνεῦμα τὸ ἅγιον διὰ στόματος Δαυίδ); Acts 2:30-31, "Being therefore a prophet [προφήτης οὖν ὑπάρχων] ... he foresaw and spoke of the resurrection of the Christ"; and Acts 4:25, "who by the mouth of our father David, thy servant, didst say by the Holy Spirit [τοῦ πατρὸς ἡμῶν διὰ

---

understood: "We have also written to you that you should examine the book of Moses and the books of the Prophets and David [ובדויד הנביאים ובספרי]" (4Q397 frgs. 14–21 line 10).

[4] For Hebrew text and translation, see J. A. Sanders, *The Psalms Scroll of Qumrân Cave 11* (DJD 4; Oxford: Clarendon Press, 1965) 92. Recent years have seen an increase in interest in David in the Dead Sea Scrolls. For further discussion, see E. Jucci, "Davide a Qumran," *RSB* 7 (1995) 157–73; C. A. Evans, "David in the Dead Sea Scrolls," in S. E. Porter and C. A. Evans (eds.), *The Scrolls and the Scriptures: Qumran Fifty Years After* (RILP 3; JSPSup 26; Sheffield: Sheffield Academic Press, 1997) 183–97; J. C. R. de Roo, "David's Deeds in the Dead Sea Scrolls," *DSD* 6 (1999) 44–65.

πνεύματος ἁγίου στόματος Δαυὶδ]" (Ps 2:2 is then quoted).[5] This exalted view of David is not unique to the author of Luke-Acts. According to Heb 4:7, "again he (God) sets a certain day, 'Today,' saying through David so long afterward, in the words already quoted, 'Today, when you hear his voice, do not harden your hearts'" (quoting Ps 95:7-8). God speaks through David.

It comes as no surprise, then, that the Psalter, as much as did the Prophets, played a vital role in the development of New Testament theology, beginning with Jesus himself, and continuing in the New Testament writings. The major contributions of the Psalter in the thought of Jesus and of major New Testament writers will be treated in the sections that follow.

## JESUS AND THE PSALMS

Jesus' message and self-understanding are to a great extent informed by four books: (1) Isaiah, (2) Daniel, (3) Zechariah, and (4) the Psalter. Jesus of course quotes or alludes to passages from the Law of Moses,[6] but his understanding of mission derives principally from

---

[5] Luke's introduction of an utterance of David with the words διὰ στόματος Δαυὶδ parallels the evangelist's introduction of utterances of the prophets, e.g. Luke 1:70 "as he spoke by the mouth of his holy prophets [διὰ στόματος τῶν ἁγίων ... προφητῶν] from of old"; Acts 3:18 "But what God foretold by the mouth of all the prophets [διὰ στόματος πάντων τῶν προφητῶν], that his Christ should suffer, he thus fulfilled"; Acts 3:21 "... all that God spoke by the mouth of his holy prophets [διὰ στόματος τῶν ἁγίων...προφητῶν] from of old." Luke's introductory formula is scriptural, e.g. Deut 8:3 "man lives by everything that proceeds out of the mouth of God [διὰ στόματος θεοῦ]" (cf. Matt 4:4); 2 Chron 35:22 "Josiah ... did not listen to the words of Neco from the mouth of God [διὰ στόματος θεοῦ]"; 2 Chron 36:21 "to fulfill the word of the LORD by the mouth of Jeremiah [διὰ στόματος Ιερεμίου]"; 2 Chron 36:22 "that the word of the LORD by the mouth of Jeremiah [διὰ στόματος Ιερεμίου] might be accomplished."

[6] For examples, cf. Exod 20:12 and 21:17 in Mark 7:10; Gen 1:27 and 2:24 in Mark 10:6-8; Exod 20:12-16 in Mark 10:19; Exod 3:6 in Mark 12:26; Deut 6:4-5 and Lev 19:18 in Mark 12:29-31. On the Law in Jesus' teaching, see K. Berger, *Die Gesetzesauslegung Jesu: Ihr historischer Hintergrund im Judentum und im Alten Testament.* Teil I: *Markus und Parallelen* (WMANT 40; Neukirchen-Vluyn: Neukirchener Verlag, 1972); R. Banks, *Jesus and the Law in the Synoptic Tradition* (SNTSMS 28; Cambridge: Cambridge University Press, 1975); H. Hübner, *Das Gesetz in der synoptischen Tradition* (Göttingen: Vandenhoeck & Ruprecht, 2nd ed., 1986); F. Vouga, *Jésus et la loi selon la tradition synoptique* (Le monde de la Bible 563; Paris: Labor et Fides, 1988); W. R. G. Loader, *Jesus'*

books that he and his contemporaries regarded as prophetic.

Another important feature that must be taken into account is that Jesus' interaction with these scriptures is often refracted through an Aramaic prism. At many points Jesus' appeal to Isaiah, Zechariah, and the Psalter reflects Aramaic interpretive tradition.[7] Daniel, of course, is partly in Aramaic and has no Targum.[8] In some of the examples that will be considered below we shall see that Psalms Targum can shed light.

The Psalter becomes especially important for Jesus when he enters the city of Jerusalem. This is hardly surprising, given the role played by the Psalter in pilgrimages to Jerusalem and the temple (e.g. 24:3; 100:4; 116:18-19; 118:19; 122:1-5), for worship in Jerusalem (e.g. 66:13, 15; 68:18; 102:21; 147:12), prayer for Jerusalem (e.g. 122:6; 128:5; 137:5-7), and so forth. Moreover, it is in Jerusalem that God dwells (e.g. 24:7-9; 135:21). Jesus himself refers to Jerusalem as the "city of the great King" (cf. Matt 5:35; quoting Ps 48:2). It is only to be expected that the proclaimer of the kingdom of God wished to visit the city of God. Indeed, the theme of the kingship of God in the Psalms almost certainly contributed to Jesus' understanding of the kingdom that he proclaimed.[9]

---

*Attitude towards the Law: A Study of the Gospels* (WUNT 2.97; Tübingen: Mohr Siebeck, 1997).

[7] For examples of Isaiah, see Mark 1:15 and *Tg.* Isa 40:9 and 52:7; Mark 4:11-12 and *Tg.* Isa 6:9-10; Mark 9:43-48 and *Tg.* Isa 66:24; Mark 12:1-9 and *Tg.* Isa 5:1-7; Matt 26:52 and *Tg.* Isa 50:11. For examples of Zechariah, see Mark 11:16 and *Tg.* Zech 14:20-21; and Mark 14:27 and *Tg.* Zech 13:7. Examples from the Aramaic Psalter will be considered below. For studies of the importance of Isaiah for Jesus, emphasizing the Targum, see B. D. Chilton, *A Galilean Rabbi and His Bible: Jesus' Use of the Interpreted Scripture of His Time* (GNS 8; Wilmington, DE: Glazier, 1984); C. A. Evans, "Introduction: An Aramaic Approach Thirty Years Later," in M. Black, *An Aramaic Approach to the Gospels and Acts* (3rd ed., Oxford: Clarendon Press, 1967; repr. Peabody, MA: Hendrickson, 1998) v–xxv.

[8] For examples of Aramaic Daniel, see Matt 11:25-26 and Dan 2:21-23; Mark 2:10 and Dan 7:13-14; Mark 14:58 and Dan 2:44-45; and Mark 14:62 and Dan 7:13. For studies of the importance of Daniel for Jesus, see D. Wenham, "The Kingdom of God and Daniel," *ExpTim* 98 (1987) 132–34; C. A. Evans, "Daniel in the New Testament: Visions of God's Kingdom," in J. J. Collins and P. W. Flint (eds.), *The Book of Daniel: Composition and Reception* (VTSup 83.2; FIOTL 2.2; Leiden: Brill, 2001) 490–527.

[9] See B. D. Chilton, "The Kingdom of God in Recent Discussion," in B. D.

Two Psalms appear to be especially important for Jesus in his teaching and activities in Jerusalem.[10] They appear in four passages in Mark, though they will be treated in only three sections. Another cluster of quotations and allusions to the Psalms appears in the Passion itself, in the words of the Last Supper and in the crucifixion of Jesus. These quotations and allusions are mostly from the Lament Psalms. Some of them are uttered by Jesus, others are editorial, deriving from the early community or from the evangelists

---

Chilton and C. A. Evans (eds.), *Studying the Historical Jesus: Evaluations of the State of Current Research* (NTTS 19; Leiden: Brill, 1994) 255–80, esp. 273–74. The Psalms that portray God as king or as enthroned and that are also associated with Jerusalem or Zion include 29, 47, 48, 114, 145.

[10] The Psalter plays an important role in the temptation of Jesus and also in his ministry of exorcism. In Q's expanded tripartite form of the temptation tradition, the Devil urges Jesus to cast himself from the pinnacle of the temple, trusting in God's care, "for it is written, 'He will give his angels charge of you,'" etc. (Matt 4:6 = Luke 4:10-11). The Devil has quoted Ps 91:11-12. That this Psalm is appropriate for such a context is clear enough in the Hebrew, which in vv. 5 and 6 speaks of "terror of the night," "pestilence that stalks in darkness," and "destruction that wastes at noonday." But its appropriateness for the temptation context becomes even clearer when the Targum is taken into account. In the Aramaic vv. 5-6 read: "Be not afraid of the terror of demons who walk at night, of the arrow of the angel of death that he looses during the day; of the death that walks in darkness, of the band of demons that attacks at noon." The verses that the Devil quoted to Jesus are prefaced in the Hebrew with the word of assurance, "no evil shall befall you, no scourge come near your tent" (Ps 91:10); but in the Aramaic this verse reads, "No harm shall happen to you; and no plague or demon shall come near to your tents." The explicit references to demons in Psalm 91 suggests that the Targum reflects an interpretive orientation that reaches back to the time of Jesus.

Jesus' assurance to his disciples, in reference to their power of Satan and his evil allies, lends further support to the probability that the Aramaic Psalter contains in places early tradition. According to Luke 10:19, Jesus assures his disciples, "Behold, I have given you authority to tread upon serpents and scorpions, and over all the power of the enemy; and nothing shall hurt you." Most commentators rightly recognize the allusion to Ps 91:13 "You will tread on the lion and the adder, the young lion and the serpent you will trample under foot." It is assumed that the adder approximates the scorpion (because of their venomous bite), which in turn is a symbol of an evil spirit. The Aramaic version of Psalm 91 encourages this assumption, while the contextualization of this Psalm at Qumran confirms the antiquity of the demonic interpretation and application. See 11QapocrPs, which contains four exorcism Psalms, of which the first three are apocryphal and the fourth is Psalm 91!

themselves. These will be treated in a fourth section.

## 1. The Triumphal Entry

When Jesus enters the city of Jerusalem, mounted on a colt, evidently in keeping with the prophecy of Zech 9:9 (cf. Mark 11:7-8), the accompanying crowd cries out (cf. Mark 11:9-10):

ὡσαννά· εὐλογημένος ὁ ἐρχόμενος ἐν ὀνόματι κυρίου· εὐλογημένη ἡ ἐρχομένη βασιλεία τοῦ πατρὸς ἡμῶν Δαυίδ· ὡσαννὰ ἐν τοῖς ὑψίστοις.

Hosanna! Blessed is he who comes in the name of the Lord! Blessed is the kingdom of our father David that is coming! Hosanna in the highest!

The cry of the crowd is an unmistakable allusion to Ps 118:25-26:

25 Save us, we beseech thee, O LORD! O LORD, we beseech thee, give us success!

26 Blessed be he who enters in the name of the LORD! We bless you from the house of the LORD.

Mark's "Hosanna" (ὡσαννά) transliterates the Hebrew הוֹשִׁיעָה נָּא ("save now!"). The evangelist does not make use of the LXX's translation σῶσον δή (117:25-26):

25 אָנָּא יְהוָה הוֹשִׁיעָה נָּא אָנָּא יְהוָה הַצְלִיחָה נָּא

26 בָּרוּךְ הַבָּא בְּשֵׁם יְהוָה בֵּרַכְנוּכֶם מִבֵּית יְהוָה

25 ὦ κύριε σῶσον δή ὦ κύριε εὐόδωσον δή

26 εὐλογημένος ὁ ἐρχόμενος ἐν ὀνόματι κυρίου εὐλογήκαμεν ὑμᾶς ἐξ οἴκου κυρίου

Mark's citation of Ps 118:25-26 is mostly a paraphrase. "Hosanna" is taken from v. 25. "Blessed is he who comes in the name of the LORD!" is taken from v. 26 and agrees verbatim with the LXX (which translates literally the Hebrew).[11] But Mark's "Blessed is the kingdom of our father David that is coming," although it loosely reflects the second clause in v. 26, agrees with neither the LXX nor with the Hebrew. Both the Hebrew and the LXX have two parallel lines that "bless" the approaching pilgrim, but nowhere in Psalm 118 do we find mention of David or of his kingdom.

It is only in the Aramaic version of Psalm 118 that we find David. The Psalm is rewritten to reflect the story of David, how as a youth he

---

[11] J. A. Fitzmyer, "Aramaic Evidence Affecting the Interpretation of *Hosanna* in the New Testament," in G. F. Hawthorne and O. Betz (eds.), *Tradition and Interpretation in the New Testament* (E. E. Ellis Festschrift; Grand Rapids: Eerdmans, 1987) 110–18. Fitzmyer rightly questions attempts to find messianic meaning in the word "Hosanna." It is a greeting, not a call for messianic action.

was initially rejected by the "builders" (i.e. the religious leaders) but then was later recognized as Israel's rightful king. In v. 22 he is said to be "worthy to be appointed king and ruler," while in v. 26 it is the young David who speaks the second line: "'They will bless you from the sanctuary of the LORD,' said David."

The shout of the crowd in Mark's form of the entrance narrative seems to reflect the interpretive orientation of the Psalms Targum.[12] If so, then we have two scriptural components in the entrance narrative that point to the presence of an underlying royal messianism on the part of Jesus and his following. The second appearance of Psalm 118 in Jesus' teaching will add further support to this conclusion.

## 2. The Parable of the Vineyard

Mark's parable of the Vineyard, or Wicked Vineyard Tenants (i.e. Mark 12:1-9) concludes with a quotation of Ps 118:22-23:

οὐδὲ τὴν γραφὴν ταύτην ἀνέγνωτε· λίθον ὃν ἀπεδοκίμασαν οἱ οἰκοδομοῦντες, οὗτος ἐγενήθη εἰς κεφαλὴν γωνίας· παρὰ κυρίου ἐγένετο αὕτη καὶ ἔστιν θαυμαστὴ ἐν ὀφθαλμοῖς ἡμῶν;

Have you not read this scripture: "The very stone which the builders rejected has become the head of the corner; this was the Lord's doing, and it is marvelous in our eyes"?

The quotation follows the LXX exactly, which in turn represents a very literal translation of the Hebrew.

Psalm 118 was the last of the six so-called Egyptian Hallel Psalms (i.e. Psalms 113–118). These Psalms were associated with three of Israel's major feasts. Although Psalm 118 was probably more at home with the Feast of Tabernacles, it was linked to the fourth cup of wine consumed during the Passover Seder. Parts of the Psalm were sung publicly and antiphonally (cf. *Midr. Pss.* 118.22 [on Ps 118:25-29]). Thus, allusion to Psalm 118 as Jesus entered the city, from the east, approaching the temple mount, one week before Passover was appropriate. Entering the temple precincts (cf. Mark 11:11) coheres with Ps 118:19 "Open to me the gates of righteousness, that I may enter through them and give thanks to the LORD."

Jesus appends Ps 118:22-23 to the conclusion of his parable of the Vineyard, a parable that tells us of the murder of the son of the

---

[12] Psalm 118 is understood in a messianic sense in late rabbinic tradition; cf. *y. Meg.* 2.1; *b. Pesaḥ.* 117b; *Midr. Ps.* 118:22 (on Ps 118:24-29). The interpretive orientation of the Psalms Targum is probably older, at least in places.

vineyard owner. Because the parable is based on Isaiah's juridical
song of the Vineyard (Isa 5:1-7), which in the Targum was applied
against the temple establishment (an interpretive orientation that
evidently predated the time of Jesus, as seen in 4Q500), the ruling
priests are said to have understood that Jesus had told the parable
"against them" (Mark 12:12). But why append the passage from
Psalm 118?

Prior to its christological interpretation in the early church (cf. Acts
4:11; 1 Pet 2:4, 7) Ps 118:22 was probably understood as in reference
to the nation of Israel.[13] The "stone" probably alluded to the stone that
God laid in Zion (cf. Isa 28:16).[14] In later Jewish interpretation, as
seen in the Targum and in rabbinic midrash (cf. *Midr. Pss.* 118.21 [on
Ps 118:23] "'This is the Lord's doing' alludes to king David"), the
stone was understood to refer to David (and the Messiah as well),
while the "builders" referred to those who opposed him, whether of
priestly vocation or otherwise.[15] We shall return to this point shortly.

---

[13] For example, see W. O. E. Oesterley, *The Psalms: Translated with Text-
Critical and Exegetical Notes* (2 vols., London: SPCK; New York: Macmillan,
1939) 2:484; idem, *A Fresh Approach to the Psalms* (London: Ivor Nicholson and
Watson, 1937) 204. According to Oesterley and others, the "stone" is Israel and
the "builders" are Israel's enemies.

[14] C. A. Briggs and E. G. Briggs, *A Critical and Exegetical Commentary on
the Book of Psalms* (ICC; 2 vols., Edinburgh: T. & T. Clark, 1906–7) 2.407.

[15] For discussion of Psalm 118 in early Jewish interpretation, see M. Berder,
*"La pierre rejetée par les bâtisseurs": Psaume 118,22-23 et son emploi dans les
traditions juives et dans le Nouveau Testament* (EBib 31; Paris: Gabalda, 1996).
Ps 118:22-23 is quoted and alluded to in *T. Solomon* 22–23. Although underlying
this work may well be Jewish material reaching back to the first century, it is a
Christian composition. The function of Ps 118:22-23 in this writing probably tells
us nothing of its pre-Christian Jewish understanding. However, Ps 118:20, 22, 27
may be alluded to and commented upon in the fragmentary 4Q173 (= 4QpPs[b])
frg. 5 lines 1–6. See J. M. Allegro, *Qumrân Cave 4.1 (4Q158–4Q186)* (DJD 5;
Oxford: Clarendon Press, 1968) 52–53; Berder, *"La pierre rejetée par les
bâtisseurs"*, 183–85. We have reference to "house of stumbling" (line 2, which
could involve a combination of Ps 118:22 and Isa 8:14), "horns of the altar" (line
3; cf. Ps 118:27), and "the gate of God, the righteous" (line 4; cf. Ps 118:20).
Fragment 5, however, probably does not belong to 4Q173; cf. J. Strugnell, "Notes
en marge du volume V des 'Discoveries in the Judaean Desert of Jordan," *RevQ* 7
(1969–71) 163–276, esp. 219–20; M. P. Horgan, *Pesharim: Qumran Interpretations of Biblical Books* (CBQMS 8; Washington: Catholic Biblical
Association, 1979) 226–27, 266. This small fragment is tantalizing, but what

In the Hebrew Ps 118:22 reads as follows:[16]

אֶבֶן מָאֲסוּ הַבּוֹנִים הָיְתָה לְרֹאשׁ פִּנָּה

The stone that the builders rejected has become the head of the corner.

But in the Targum the verse reads (with italics denoting departures from the Hebrew):

טליא שביקו ארדיכליא הות ביני בניא דישי וזכה לאתמנאה למליך ושולטן:

*The boy* that the builders *abandoned was among the sons of Jesse and he is worthy to be appointed king and ruler.*

Based on a wordplay between "stone" (*eben*) and "son" (*ben*),[17] the Aramaic verse speaks of a rejected boy. We thus have remarkable coherence between the parable proper, which speaks of a son rejected and murdered, and the concluding quotation of Ps 118:22, which according to the Aramaic and rabbinic interpretation speaks of David who also was rejected initially. The fact that the two passages that are involved — Isa 5:1-7, on which the parable is based, and Ps 118:22, with which the parable concludes — become intelligible when the Aramaic is taken into account argues for great antiquity of the tradition, probably its derivation from Jesus himself, rather than derivation from the later, largely Greek-speaking church.[18]

---

point was being made cannot be determined. Finally, Ps 118:2 may be alluded in 2Q23 frg. 1 line 6 "you will be pushed away from the corner stone [מאבן פנת]." The fragmentary context is judgmental. See M. Baillet, J. T. Milik, and R. de Vaux, *Les 'Petites Grottes' de Qumrân* (DJD 3; Oxford: Clarendon Press, 1962) 82–84; Berder, *"La pierre rejetée par les bâtisseurs,"* 185–88.

[16] Ps 118:22 is not preserved at Qumran.

[17] John the Baptist's "from these stones God is able to raise up children to Abraham" (cf. Matt 3:9 = Luke 3:8) probably also presupposes a wordplay between stone and son. See also Josephus, *J.W.* 5.6.3 §272. On the wordplay, see M. Black, "The Christological Use of the Old Testament in the New Testament," *NTS* 18 (1971–72) 1–14, esp. 11–14. The wordplay was suggested some three and a half centuries ago by John Lightfoot, *Horae Hebraicae et Talmudicae* (4 vols., Oxford: Oxford University Press, 1859 [Latin orig. 1658–74]) 2.435.

[18] This point is well made in G. J. Brooke, "4Q500 1 and the Use of Scripture in the Parable of the Vineyard," *DSD* 2 (1995) 268–94. It has been fashionable to claim that the parable of the Vineyard is a piece of Christian allegory that sums of the story of salvation; cf. E. Schweizer, *The Good News according to Mark* (Atlanta: John Knox, 1970) 239. It is asserted the parable lacks Semitic elements and so must derive from a Hellenistic setting; cf. U. Mell, *Die "anderen" Winzer: Eine exegetische Studie zur Vollmacht Jesu Christi nach Markus 11,27–12,34* (WUNT 77; Tübingen: Mohr Siebeck, 1995) 97–117; J. S. Kloppenborg Verbin,

In all probability the "builders" of Ps 118:22 would have been readily identified with the ruling priests who oppose Jesus. This is so not only because in the Aramaic they are understood this way, but also because religious leaders despised by Qumran are called builders (cf. CD 4:19; 8:12, 18), Paul calls himself a "master builder" who "laid a foundation" (cf. 1 Cor 3:10), and in later rabbinic literature the rabbis are themselves sometimes called builders (cf. *b. Ber.* 64a; *b. Shab.* 114a; *Exod. Rab.* 23.10 [on Exod 15:11]; *Song Rab.* 1:5 §3). The metaphor is thus widespread and was used either in a positive sense (as in Paul and the later rabbis) or in a negative sense (as in the *Damascus Document*). In *Tg.* Ps 118:22 the builders initially oppose the young son of Jesse, but they quickly come to accept him (and this is consistent with the Midrash on the Psalms, cited above).

It seems then that the use of Psalm 118 that so significantly shaped early christology has its origins in the teaching and actions of Jesus himself. To be sure, the early church expanded this interpretation, linking Ps 118:22 to other stone passages (such as Isa 28:16 and Isa 8:14), but the train of thought itself seems to have got under way in the Aramaic context of Jesus' ministry.[19]

### 3. The Question of David's "Son"

Psalm 110, royal in outlook and probably dating from Israel's monarchic period,[20] is another Psalm that plays an important role in

---

"Egyptian Viticultural Practices and the Citation of Isa. 5:1–7 in Mark 12:1–9," *NovT* 44 (2002) 134–59. But this is not correct; there are Semitic features throughout the parable and a general lack of agreement with the LXX version of Isa 5:1-7; cf. C. A. Evans, *Mark 8:27–16:20* (WBC 34B; Nashville: Nelson, 2001) 224–30; idem, "How Septuagintal is Isa. 5:1–7 in Mark 12:1–9?" *NovT* 45 (2003) 105–10.

[19] Psalm 118 apparently continued to exert its influence in the family of Jesus, for Ps 118:19-20 ("Open to me the gates of righteousness . . . This is the gate of the Lord; the righteous/just shall enter through it") may well lie behind the sobriquet "the Just" given to James the brother of Jesus. Moreover, Ps 118:25-26 is alluded to in tradition about the ministry of James in Jerusalem and in the temple precincts (cf. Eusebius, *Hist. Eccl.* 2.23.12–14). For discussion of the place of Psalm 118 in the family of Jesus, see C. A. Evans, "Jesus and James: Martyrs of the Temple," in B. D. Chilton and C. A. Evans (eds.), *James the Just and Christian Origins* (NovTSup 98; Leiden: Brill, 1999) 233–49.

[20] Briggs and Briggs, *The Book of Psalms*, 2:374–75; Oesterley, *The Psalms*, 2:463; A. Weiser, *The Psalms* (OTL; Philadelphia: Westminster, 1962) 693–94; J. Bowker, "Psalm CX," *VT* 17 (1967) 31–41; G. Gerleman, "Psalm CX," *VT* 31

the development of early christology. It is the most quoted and alluded to Old Testament passage in the New Testament and early Christian literature.[21] Indeed, the theology of the book of Hebrews turns on this Psalm. In the Gospels it appears twice on the lips of Jesus; once in dispute with teachers in the temple precincts, where Jesus raises the question about David's son, and again in the hearing before Caiaphas and the Jewish council. Our focus is principally on the first passage, though some comment will be made on the second.

---

(1981) 1–19; L. C. Allen, *Psalms 101–150* (WBC 21; Dallas: Word, 1983) 83–85. The hypothesis of the Maccabean origin of Psalm 110 has been recently resurrected by H. Donner, "Der verläßliche Prophet: Betrachtungen zu 1 Makk 14,41f. und Ps 110," in R. Liwah and S. Wagner (eds.), *Prophetie und geschichtliche Wirklichkeit im Alten Testament* (S. Herrmann Festschrift; Stuttgart: Kohlhammer, 1991) 89–98; repr. in Donner, *Aufsätze zum Alten Testament aus vier Jahrzehnten* (BZAW 224; Berlin: de Gruyter, 1994) 213–23. The linkage between kingship and priesthood in Ps 110:4 is suggestive, to be sure, but there are many problems with this line of interpretation. See their summary in Briggs and Briggs (above).

[21] There are five quotations of Ps 110:1 in the New Testament: Mark 12:36 = Matt 22:44 = Luke 20:42-43; Acts 2:34-35; Heb 1:13 (and there are two quotations in the Apostolic Fathers: *1 Clem.* 36:5; *Barn.* 12:10), and nineteen allusions in the New Testament: Mark 14:62 = Matt 26:64 = Luke 22:69; Mark 16:19; Acts 2:33; 5:31; 7:55, 56; Rom 8:34; 1 Cor 15:25; Eph 1:20; 2:6; Col 3:1; Heb 1:3; 8:1; 10:12-13; 12:2; 1 Pet 3:22; Rev 3:21. There are also several quotations of and allusions to other parts of Psalm 110 in the New Testament. For this summary I am indebted to D. E. Aune, "Christian Prophecy and the Messianic Status of Jesus," in J. H. Charlesworth (ed.), *The Messiah: Developments in Earliest Judaism and Christianity* (Minneapolis: Fortress, 1992) 404 n. 4. For major treatments of the history of interpretation of Psalm 110, see D. M. Hay, *Glory at the Right Hand: Psalm 110 in Early Christianity* (SBLMS 18; Nashville: Abingdon, 1973); J. Dupont, "'Assisa à la droite de Dieu': L'interpretation du Ps 110,1 dans le Nouveau Testament," in E. Dhanis (ed.), *Resurrexit: Actes du Symposium international sur la resurrection de Jésus (Rome, 1970)* (Rome: Libreria Editrice Vaticana, 1974) 340–422; M. Gourgues, *A la droite de Dieu: Résurrection de Jésus et actualisation du Psaume 110,1 dans le Nouveau Testament* (EBib; Paris: Gabalda, 1978); W. R. G. Loader, "Christ at the Right Hand—Ps. CX in the New Testament," *NTS* 24 (1978) 199–217; M. Hengel, "'Setze dich zu meiner Rechten!' Die Inthronisation Christi zur Rechten Gottes und Psalm 110,1," in M. Philonenko (ed.), *Le Trône de Dieu* (WUNT 69; Tübingen: Mohr Siebeck, 1993) 108–94; English Transl.: "'Sit at My Right Hand!' The Enthronement of Christ at the Right Hand of God and Psalm 110:1," in Hengel, *Studies in Early Christology* (Edinburgh: T. & T. Clark, 1995) 119–225.

Placed in the context of the temple precincts, Jesus asks the crowd (cf. Mark 12:35-37):[22]

πῶς λέγουσιν οἱ γραμματεῖς ὅτι ὁ χριστὸς υἱὸς Δαυίδ ἐστιν; αὐτὸς Δαυὶδ εἶπεν ἐν τῷ πνεύματι τῷ ἁγίῳ· εἶπεν κύριος τῷ κυρίῳ μου· κάθου ἐκ δεξιῶν μου, ἕως ἂν θῶ τοὺς ἐχθρούς σου ὑποκάτω τῶν ποδῶν σου. αὐτὸς Δαυὶδ λέγει αὐτὸν κύριον, καὶ πόθεν αὐτοῦ ἐστιν υἱός;

How can the scribes say that the Christ is the son of David? David himself, inspired by the Holy Spirit, declared, "The Lord said to my Lord, Sit at my right hand, till I put thy enemies under thy feet." David himself calls him Lord; so how is he his son?

Jesus has quoted Ps 110:1, which in the Hebrew reads:[23]

לְדָוִד מִזְמוֹר נְאֻם יְהוָה לַאדֹנִי שֵׁב לִימִינִי עַד־אָשִׁית אֹיְבֶיךָ הֲדֹם לְרַגְלֶיךָ

A Psalm to David: An oracle of the LORD[24] to my lord: "Sit at my right hand, until I make your enemies a footstool for your feet."

According to the LXX (i.e. 109:1) the passage reads:

τῷ Δαυιδ ψαλμός εἶπεν ὁ κύριος τῷ κυρίῳ μου κάθου ἐκ δεξιῶν μου ἕως ἂν θῶ τοὺς ἐχθρούς σου ὑποπόδιον τῶν ποδῶν σου

A Psalm to David: The LORD said to my lord: "Sit at my right hand, until I make your enemies a footstool for your feet."

The superscription "Psalm to David" (לְדָוִד מִזְמוֹר/τῷ Δαυιδ ψαλμός) is ambiguous, meaning either that David composed the Psalm (i.e. a "Psalm of David," as in the RSV), or that the Psalm "pertains to David."[25] The former understanding supports the view that it is David himself who speaks the words of the Psalm, and that is what Jesus assumes when he says, "David himself ... declared," while the latter understanding supports the view that the Psalm, even if spoken by someone else, at least relates to the famous king. Either interpretation

---

[22] The appearance of the Pharisees in Matt 22:41 is Matthean redaction (cf. Mark 12:12 = Matt 21:45; Mark 12:28 = Matt 22:34). According to Mark, Pharisees appear only at 12:13, in the company of the "Herodians," to trap Jesus in the question about paying tax to Caesar. The Markan evangelist places the teaching in the temple precincts and refers to a "great crowd" (12:37b). There is nothing about the teaching in itself that requires a setting in either Jerusalem or the temple precincts themselves.

[23] Psalm 110 is not preserved at Qumran.

[24] The RSV renders נְאֻם יְהוָה "the LORD says." But the text is literally "oracle of the LORD"; cf. Oesterley, *The Psalms*, 2:462.

[25] As is rendered in A. Pietersma, *The Psalms: A New English Translation of the Septuagint (NETS)* (Oxford: Oxford University Press, 2000) 112.

accommodates messianic interpretation. When Jesus says, "inspired by the Holy Spirit," he shares the widely-held assumption of David's prophetic gift (as noted above).

Interpretation of Psalm 110 in early Judaism is diverse. There are hints of messianic interpretation, but it is not dominant.[26] The point that Jesus makes, however, is only incidental to the interpretation of this Psalm. Jesus simply questions the scribal habit of referring to the Messiah as the "son of David."

The point Jesus makes hinges on a textual observation and on a cultural given in the Middle East. The textual observation is that David calls his descendant his "Lord."[27] The cultural given is that fathers do not address their sons or descendants in this way. Therefore, when we consider what David says in Ps 110:1, what justifies the scribal habit of referring to the Messiah as the "son of David," which implies that he is in some sense subordinate or inferior to David?[28]

---

[26] Hay, *Glory at the Right Hand*, 19–33; Hengel, "'Sit at My Right Hand!'," 175–214.

[27] The linguistic issues concerning "Lord" in Greek, Hebrew, and Aramaic have been sorted out by J. A. Fitzmyer, "The Contribution of Qumran Aramic to the Study of the New Testament," *NTS* 20 (1973–74) 382–407; repr. in his *A Wandering Aramean: Collected Essays* (SBLMS 25; Missoula, MT: Scholars Press, 1979) 85–113, esp. 90; idem, "Der semitische Hintergrund des neutesta-mentlichen Kyriostitels," in G. Strecker (ed.), *Jesus Christus in Historie und Theologie* (H. Conzelmann Festschrift; Tübingen: Mohr Siebeck, 1975) 267–98; rev. English Transl: "The Semitic Background of the New Testament *Kyrios*-Title," in Fitzmyer, *A Wandering Aramean*, 115–42, esp. 141 n.71. Fitzmyer shows that the Aramaic מר ("lord") was sometimes used to translate the Hebrew יהוה and אדני, as well as the Greek κύριος. Accordingly, there are no compelling grounds for contending that the function of Ps 110:1 in Mark 12:35-37 works only in Greek (which Jesus presumably would not have quoted) and therefore cannot derive from Jesus. Jesus could have said in Aramaic, אמר מרא למראי, "the Lord said to my lord ...," which renders the Hebrew literally and then subsequently in turn is rendered in Greek the way we find it in the Synoptic Gospels. See also the discussion in Hengel, "'Sit at My Right Hand!'," 155–56 and 156 n. 81.

[28] In raising this question, Jesus is not implying that Israel's Messiah is not in fact a descendant of David. R. Bultmann (*The History of the Synoptic Tradition* [Oxford: Blackwell, 1972] 136–37) completely misunderstands the thrust of Mark 12:35-37. Had this been the point of his teaching, then we must wonder why Davidic descent of the Messiah (and of Jesus himself, according to the genealogies of Matthew and Luke) is assumed and apparently uncontested in

Why is Jesus not happy with the messianic epithet "son of David," an epithet that becomes commonplace in Jewish literature?[29] The most probable explanation is that he believed the Messiah to be God's Son, not David's son. There is sufficient scriptural warrant for this view (e.g. Ps 2:2, 7; 2 Sam 7:14; 1 Chron 22:10).[30] Moreover, in all probability Jesus understood himself as the "son of man" figure of Dan 7:13-14, who received from the Ancient of Days kingdom and authority.

Our suspicion is confirmed by the conflated quotation of Ps 110:1 and Dan 7:13 in Jesus' reply made to the Jewish high priest in Mark 14:61-62:

> But he was silent and made no answer. Again the high priest asked him, "Are you the Christ, the Son of the Blessed?" And Jesus said, "I am; and you will see the Son of man seated at the right hand of Power, and coming with the clouds of heaven."

The Messiah is no mere "son of David," a junior David, as it were. The Messiah is the Son of God, seated at the right hand of God, and invested in heavenly power and authority.[31]

It should come as no surprise that Ps 110:1 made such a vital contribution to early christology. It was not simply one proof text

---

early Christian literature (e.g. Rom 1:3-4; 2 Tim 2:8).

[29] For examples, see *Pss. Sol.* 17:21; *T. Sol.* 1:7; *b. Sukkah* 52a; *b. Meg.* 17b; *b. Sanh.* 38a; *b. Yoma* 10a; *Exod. Rab.* 25. 12 (on Exod 16:29); *Num. Rab.* 14.1 (on Num 7:48).

[30] The tradition of the divine voice at the baptism of Jesus and at the Mount of Transfiguration (cf. Mark 1:11; 9:7), whatever its origin, attests the antiquity of the contribution that these Old Testament passages (esp. Ps 2:7) made to the emerging story of Jesus.

[31] Jesus is not the only one to link Ps 110:1 and Dan 7:13, but he may have been the first. For examples of texts that either allude to or seem to presuppose these passages, see *1 Enoch* 51:3; 55:4; 61:8; 62:2-3; *Midr. Ps.* 2.9 (on Ps 2:7); *Hekhalot Rabbati* §125–126. For arguments in support of the authenticity of the dominical tradition preserved in Mark 12:35-37 and 14:61-62, see Evans, *Mark 8:27–16:20*, 270–76, 448–52. It has been plausibly suggested that Ps 8:4-7 ("What is man that thou art mindful of him, and the son of man that thou dost care for him? Yet thou hast made him little less than God, and dost crown him with glory and honor. Thou hast given him dominion over the works of thy hands; thou hast put all things under his feet ...") and Ps 80:17 ("But let thy hand be upon the man of thy right hand, the son of man whom thou hast made strong for thyself!") facilitated the linkage of Ps 110:1 (enthronement, right hand) and Dan 7:13 (son of man). On this point, see Hengel, "'Sit at My Right Hand!'," 163–72.

among many that Jesus' followers found and applied in creative ways
to the story of Jesus; it was a text that their Lord and Master himself
had claimed, in order to identify his role and his relationship to God.

## 4. The Lament Psalms in the Passion

The extent of the influence that Old Testament Scripture had upon
the Passion Narrative has been a topic of ongoing study.[32] Of special
interest is the contribution made by the Lament Psalms. The allusions
to and echoes of several Lament Psalms in the crucifixion and death
scene of Jesus may be tabulated as follows:[33]

| Psalm | Topic | Gospel |
|---|---|---|
| 6:3 | troubled soul | Jn 12:27(?) |
| 22:1 | Why have you forsaken me? | Mk 15:34; Mt 27:46 |
| 22:6 | reviling | Mk 15:32 |
| 22:7a | all who see me mock me | Lk 23:35a |
| 22:7b | mockery, wagging head | Mk 15:29; Mt 27:39 |
| 22:8 | Save yourself! | Mk 15:30-31; Mt 27:43 |
| 22:14a | like water poured out | Jn 19:34b |
| 22:15 | thirst | Jn 19:28 |
| 22:16b | pierced | Jn 19:34a |
| 22:18 | division of garments | Mk 15:24; Mt 27:35; Lk 23:34b; Jn 19:24 |
| 27:2 | evildoers assail me | Jn 18:6(?) |
| 27:12 | false witnesses testify | Mk 14:57-58(?) |
| 31:5 | into your hand . . . | Lk 23:46 |
| 31:13 | they counsel together . . . | Mt 26:3-4a |
| 35:4 | turned back and confounded | Jn 18:6(?) |
| 35:11 | against me . . . slandered | Mk 14:57-58(?) |
| 35:19 | they hate me without cause | Jn 15:25 |
| 37:32 | he seeks to put him to death | Mk 14:55 |
| 38:11 | looking on at a distance | Mk 15:40a; Mt 27:55a; Lk 23:49 |
| 38:13-15 | in his mouth are no rebukes | Mk 14:61; 15:4-5 |
| 41:9a | one eating with me | Mk 14:18 |
| 41:9b | lifted his heel against me | Jn 13:18 |
| 42:5, 6; 43:5 | my soul is very sorrowful | Mk 14:34; Mt 26:38; Jn 12:2 |

---

[32] For example, see D. J. Moo, *The Old Testament in the Gospel Passion
Narratives* (Sheffield: Almond Press, 1983) 264–83.

[33] Based on Shires, *Finding the Old Testament in the New*, 202–206; Moo, *The
Old Testament in the Gospel Passion Narratives*, 285–86; J. Marcus, *The Way of
the Lord: Christological Exegesis of the Old Testament in the Gospel of Mark*
(Louisville: Westminster/John Knox, 1992) 175. Marcus (p. 172) prefers to speak
of these Psalms as the "Psalms of the Righteous Sufferer."

| 69:4  | they hate me without cause | Jn 15:25 |
| 69:9  | zeal for your house ...    | Jn 2:17 |
| 69:21 | gave him vinegar to drink  | Mk 15:36; Mt 27:34, 48; Lk 23:36; Jn 19:29-30 |
| 140:8 | do not deliver me to a sinner | Mk 14:41 |

A few of these words, phrases, and allusions are on the lips of Jesus himself. The cry of abandonment (Mark 15:34; Matt 27:46), which quotes Ps 22:1 in Aramaic, is almost certainly an authentic utterance. It is hard to see why the early Christian community would place this saying on the lips of Jesus (note its omission in Luke and nonappearance in John). Less certain is Jesus' allusion to Ps 41:9 (Mark 14:18; John 13:18), though reference to the righteous one who complains of betrayal at the hands of a friend is plausible had Jesus become aware of Judas' defection. It is also plausible that Jesus would have alluded to phraseology in Pss 42:5, 6; 43:5 ("Why are you grieved [περίλυπος], O Soul?") on the occasion of the garden prayer, "My soul is very grieved [περίλυπος], even to death" (Mark 14:34), and perhaps also to the phraseology of Ps 140:8 (cf. LXX 139:9 "Do not hand me over, O Lord, to a sinner") as the arresting party approached, "the Son of man is betrayed into the hands of sinners."

Most of the allusions to the Lament Psalms reflect the work of the early community, as it searched for a theological context, in which the suffering of Jesus might be placed. Nevertheless, it is probable that the interpretation of Jesus' passion in the language of the Lament Psalms began with Jesus himself. Later tradents, including the evangelists themselves, enriched the Gospel story with additional allusions.[34]

Appeal to the Lament Psalms was not motivated out of a general desire to find scriptural antecedents, even rationale, for the dreadful experience that overtook Jesus. Rather, appeal was made to these Psalms because they were viewed as prophetic, as on par with the Prophets themselves (see discussion above). The suffering of Jesus was part of the eschatological suffering through which the righteous must pass (cf. Dan 7:13-27, where the "saints," which presumably

---

[34] Marcus (*Way of the Lord*, 175–76) is correct when he says that "allusions to Psalms of the Righteous Sufferer were part of the common narrative that was used by both Mark and John." The Johannine tradition is probably literarily independent of Mark and the Synoptic tradition, while Matthew and Luke made use of Mark and possibly some parallel tradition.

includes the "son of man," struggle and suffer before finally winning the kingdom of God).[35]

We find a similar phenomenon in the Dead Sea Scrolls. The parallels may be tabulated in the same way:

| Psalm | Topic | Dead Sea Scroll |
|---|---|---|
| 5:2-3a | Listen to my cry | 4Q174 3:14 |
| 6:1-4 | O Lord, how long? | 4Q177 12+13 i.7-8 |
| 11:1-2 | I have taken refuge | 4Q177 5+6.7-8 |
| 12:1 | superscription | 4Q177 5+6.11-12 |
| 12:6 | purified in a furnace | 4Q177 10.1 |
| 13:1-2 | How long shall my enemy? | 4Q177 10.8-9 |
| 13:4 | lest the enemy say . . . | 4Q177 10.11-12 |
| 17:1 | listen to my complaint | 4Q177 1.4 |
| 17:2 | from you flows judgment | 4Q177 1.6 |
| 26:12 | I will bless your name | 1QH 10:29-30 |
| 37:7 | wait on the Lord | 4Q171 1–10 i.17-19 |
| 40:2 | up from the pit, from the bog | 4Q160 3–5.2-3 |
| 42:5 | my soul is cast down | 1QH 16:32 [olim 8:32] |
| 51:17 | strengthen the repentant | 4Q436 1 i.1 |
| 86:16 | be gracious to me | 4Q381 15.2 |
| 86:17 | show me a good omen | 4Q381 15.2-3 |

Only one parallel to Psalm 37 is given in the tabulation above. However, the whole of the text in which it is found is a *pesher* on Psalm 37 (i.e. 4Q171 or 4QpPs37). Like the other *pesharim*, 4Q171 is eschatological. But in keeping with the perspective of the Lament Psalms, 4Q171 focuses on the suffering through which the righteous must pass before the end of the wicked final comes:

> "Very soon there will be no wicked man; look where he was, he's not there" (Ps 37:10). This refers to all of the wicked at the end of the forty years. When they are completed, there will no longer be any wicked person on the earth. (4Q171 1–10 ii.5-8)[36]

Most of the other examples tabulated above function the same way. The author (in some instances probably the founding teacher) appeals

---

[35] Marcus (*Way of the Lord*, 177) rightly observes that the orientation of the Lament Psalms was originally focused on vindication in this world, while their use in the New Testament and in other sources (chiefly apocalyptic) shifts the emphasis to the Eschaton.

[36] Translation is based on M. O. Wise, M. G. Abegg Jr., and E. M. Cook, *The Dead Sea Scrolls: A New Translation* (San Francisco: Harper San Francisco, 1996) 221.

to these laments for comfort and assurance in the face of treachery and
deadly opposition, all of which, it is believed, must take place before
eschatological vindication. Appeal is also made to Ps 41:9, just as it is
in Mark 14:18:

> But I myself have become [...], strife and contentions for my fellows,
> jealousy and anger to those who have entered into my covenant, a
> grumbling and a complaining to all who are my comrades. Ev[en those
> who sha]re my bread have lifted up their heel against me (Ps 41:9), and all
> those who have committed themselves to my counsel speak perversely
> against me with unjust lips. The men of my [coun]cil rebel and grumble
> round about. And concerning the mystery which you hid in me, they go
> about as slanderers to the children of destruction. (1QH 13:22-25 [*olim*
> 5:22-25])[37]

It is fascinating to observe that the use Ps 41:9 matches quite closely
its use in Mark. The author of the *Hodayot* complains that his closest
followers, his comrades, those who have committed themselves to his
counsel, men of his council, and the like, speak against him. This fits
Judas' betrayal, who not only led the ruling priests to the place where
Jesus retired for prayer, but, we should assume, also gave evidence
against Jesus as well.

It seems clear that for Jesus and his following, for the men of the
Renewed Covenant (a.k.a. Essenes), and for other individuals and
groups with eschatological orientation, the Lament Psalms were
mined much as were the Prophets and were applied to the bitter
experiences of these individuals and groups. Given this combination
of suffering and eschatological hope, it is not too surprising that
certain groups found relevant and reassuring the Psalter's agonized
"How long?" (e.g. 6:3; 13:1-2; 35:17; etc.).

### THE EARLY CHURCH AND THE PSALMS

The christological and prophetic use of the Psalms originated in
Jesus and was extended and developed further in the early Christian
community. Some of the Psalms to which Jesus made reference were
subjected to further exegetical and theological rumination, while other
Psalms, to which he had made no reference (so far as is known) were

---

[37] Translation based on Wise, Abegg, and Cook, *The Dead Sea Scrolls*, 98.
Marcus (*Way of the Lord*, 178) discusses this text. 1QH then alludes to Ps 22:15
("my strength is dried up like a potsherd, and my tongue cleaves to my jaws"): "I
have put on the garment of mourning, and my tongue clings to the roof of my
mouth" (13:31 [*olim* 5:31]). Marcus's comments (pp. 177–86) are very helpful.

discovered and mined for further clarification of this point or that.

*1. Replacing a Traitor*

Appeal to Pss 69:25 and 109:8 is part of early Christian use of Psalm 69. In the Johannine community, it is remembered—in reflection upon the significance of Jesus' action in the temple precincts (John 2:13-22; cf. Mark 11:15-19; Matt 21:12-13; Luke 19:45-48)—that Jesus' zeal fulfilled Ps 69:9, "Zeal for thy house will consume me" (John 2:17), while hatred of Jesus fulfilled Ps 69:4, "They hated me without cause" (John 15:25). It is possible too that the offer of vinegar to the dying Jesus (Mark 15:36; Matt 27:34, 48; Luke 23:36; John 19:29-30) alluded to Ps 69:21, "They gave me poison for food, and for my thirst they gave me vinegar to drink." The probability of an allusion here is supported by the explicit use of Ps 69:25 in Acts 1:20,

> For it is written in the book of Psalms, "Let his habitation become
> desolate, and let there be no one to live in it" [γενηθήτω ἡ ἔπαυλις αὐτοῦ
> ἔρημος καὶ μὴ ἔστω ὁ κατοικῶν ἐν αὐτῇ]; and "His office let another
> take" [τὴν ἐπισκοπὴν αὐτοῦ λαβέτω ἕτερος].[38]

Thus, it seems that Psalm 69 was as well known in Synoptic circles as it was in the Johannine circle.

Usage of Psalm 69 illustrates the sense of corporate solidarity between the righteous founder of the community (i.e. Jesus) and his following. What happens to the founder also happens to his followers. The following examples return to the christological use of the Psalms.

*2. Not abandoning the Holy One*

In his Pentecost discourse (Acts 2:14-36) Peter appeals to Ps 16:8-11 as prophecy of the resurrection of Jesus.[39] The discourse is complex, countering first the charge that the disciples are drunk, next

---

[38] The quotation of Ps 69:25 has been supplemented with words from Ps 109:8, "May his days be few; may another seize his goods!" See the discussion in C. K. Barrett, *A Critical and Exegetical Commentary on the Acts of the Apostles* (2 vols., ICC; Edinburgh: T. & T. Clark, 1994–98) 1:100; J. A. Fitzmyer, *The Acts of the Apostles* (AB 31; New York: Doubleday, 1998) 225–26. Fitzmyer wonders if Psalm 109 might not be alluded in Mark 15:29 = Matt 27:39 (cf. Ps 109:2-3).

Appearance of the word ἐπισκοπή ("office" or "office of bishop"; cf. 1 Tim 3:1; 1 Pet 2:12) made the use of Ps 109:8 ( = LXX 108:8) irresistible.

[39] Much of what will be said of the Pentecost discourse applies to Paul's discourse at Pisidian Antioch in Acts 13:13-52, where Ps 16:10 is quoted (at Acts 13:35) and a host of other prophecies and Psalms are quoted also.

explaining that the Spirit has come as foretold by the prophet Joel, then explaining that all of this has been occasioned by the ministry, death, and resurrection of Jesus. According to the Lukan Peter (i.e. Acts 2:24-28):

24 ὃν ὁ θεὸς ἀνέστησεν λύσας τὰς ὠδῖνας τοῦ θανάτου, καθότι οὐκ ἦν δυνατὸν κρατεῖσθαι αὐτὸν ὑπ᾽ αὐτοῦ.

25 Δαυὶδ γὰρ λέγει εἰς αὐτόν· προορώμην τὸν κύριον ἐνώπιόν μου διὰ παντός, ὅτι ἐκ δεξιῶν μού ἐστιν ἵνα μὴ σαλευθῶ.

26 διὰ τοῦτο ηὐφράνθη ἡ καρδία μου καὶ ἠγαλλιάσατο ἡ γλῶσσά μου, ἔτι δὲ καὶ ἡ σάρξ μου κατασκηνώσει ἐπ᾽ ἐλπίδι,

27 ὅτι οὐκ ἐγκαταλείψεις τὴν ψυχήν μου εἰς ᾅδην οὐδὲ δώσεις τὸν ὅσιόν σου ἰδεῖν διαφθοράν.

28 ἐγνώρισάς μοι ὁδοὺς ζωῆς, πληρώσεις με εὐφροσύνης μετὰ τοῦ προσώπου σου.

24 But God raised him up, having loosed the pangs of death, because it was not possible for him to be held by it.

25 For David says concerning him, "I saw the Lord always before me, for he is at my right hand that I may not be shaken;

26 therefore my heart was glad, and my tongue rejoiced; moreover my flesh will dwell in hope.

27 For thou wilt not abandon my soul to Hades, nor let thy Holy One see corruption.

28 Thou hast made known to me the ways of life; thou wilt make me full of gladness with thy presence."

The quotation of Ps 16:8-11 follows the LXX (i.e. 15:8-11) exactly, though the last part of v. 11 is omitted (τερπνότητες ἐν τῇ δεξιᾷ σου εἰς τέλος ["delights are in your right hand to the end"]), and offers a fairly literal translation of the Hebrew text:[40]

8 שִׁוִּיתִי יְהוָה לְנֶגְדִּי תָמִיד כִּי מִימִינִי בַּל־אֶמּוֹט

9 לָכֵן שָׂמַח לִבִּי וַיָּגֶל כְּבוֹדִי אַף־בְּשָׂרִי יִשְׁכֹּן לָבֶטַח

10 כִּי לֹא־תַעֲזֹב נַפְשִׁי לִשְׁאוֹל לֹא־תִתֵּן חֲסִידְךָ לִרְאוֹת שָׁחַת

11 תּוֹדִיעֵנִי אֹרַח חַיִּים שֹׂבַע שְׂמָחוֹת אֶת־פָּנֶיךָ נְעִמוֹת בִּימִינְךָ נֶצַח

8 I keep the LORD always before me; because he is at my right hand, I shall not be moved.

9 Therefore my heart is glad, and my soul rejoices; my body also dwells secure.

10 For thou dost not give me up to Sheol, or let thy godly one see the Pit.

11 Thou dost show me the path of life; in thy presence there is fullness of joy, in thy right hand are pleasures for evermore.

---

[40] At Qumran (i.e. 4QPsᶜ) only fragments of vv. 8-10 of our passage are extant. There are no significant variants.

There are a few minor differences: the LXX's ἐπ' ἐλπίδι ("in hope") renders the Hebrew's לָבֶטַח ("in security"), and διαφθοράν ("corruption," "decay") renders שַׁחַת ("pit," "grave"), though in this instance there is some semantic overlap (cf. BDB).

Psalm 16 is yet another Lament Psalm, which may explain in part its appearance in the early church's scriptural arsenal. Originally the Psalm probably did not envision resurrection or any form of postmortem survival.[41] However, what the Psalmist hoped for — that God would in some way remain with him, even in death — is a step on the trajectory that will lead to articulation of the resurrection hope.[42]

In the intertestamental period hope in the resurrection is clearly expressed in texts such as Dan 12:2 ("And many of those who sleep in the dust of the earth shall awake, some to everlasting life, and some to shame and everlasting contempt") and Isa 26:19 ("Thy dead shall live [יִחְיוּ מֵתֶיךָ], their bodies shall rise. O dwellers in the dust, awake and sing for joy!"). The latter text is probably alluded to in the much talked about 4Q521: "For he shall heal the wounded; he shall make alive the dead [ומתים יחיה]" (2+4 ii 12). In light of these expressions, all of which were in late antiquity associated in various ways with eschatology, it is not surprising that Ps 16:10 came to be added to the list of Scriptures understood to promise resurrection.

Far from being abandoned in Hades,[43] Jesus the righteous finds himself at the Lord's right hand (Ps 16:8; Acts 2:25). Reference to the *right hand* provides the link to the allusion to Ps 110:1 in Acts 2:33 and to its formal quotation in Acts 2:34. Here lies the principal point of the Pentecost discourse: the enthronement of Jesus as the Lord's Messiah, seated at the right hand of God. We are accordingly taken right back to Jesus' conviction, expressed explicitly before the Jewish council in Mark 14:61-62 but also implied in other contexts, that he is the "one like a son of man" who in the vision of Daniel 7 received

---

[41] Oesterley, *The Psalms*, 1:157: "There is no reference to life hereafter."

[42] Briggs and Briggs, *The Book of Psalms*, 1:121. See also T. K. Cheyne, *The Book of Psalms* (2 vols., London: Kegan Paul, Trench, Trübner, 1904) 1:50; Weiser, *The Psalms*, 176–78.

[43] The confident expression, "For you will not abandon [LXX 21:2: ἐγκατέλιπές με] my soul to Sheol," may explain why the Lukan evangelist omitted the quotation of Ps 22:1 in his Markan source: "My God, my God, why have no abandoned me [ἐγκατέλιπές με]?" (cf. Mark 15:34); rightly suggested by Barrett, *Acts*, 1:145.

authority and kingdom. Invested with this authority, attested by the resurrection, which Jesus fulfilled — not David — Jesus now sits at God's right hand.

### 3. Ascending and Descending with a Shout

After the risen Jesus promises his disciples that they will receive power when the Holy Spirit comes upon them, "he was lifted up, and a cloud took him out of their sight" (Acts 1:9). While looking on, two men appear and say to them:

ἄνδρες Γαλιλαῖοι, τί ἑστήκατε [ἐμ]βλέποντες εἰς τὸν οὐρανόν; οὗτος ὁ Ἰησοῦς ὁ ἀναλημφθεὶς ἀφ᾽ ὑμῶν εἰς τὸν οὐρανὸν οὕτως ἐλεύσεται ὃν τρόπον ἐθεάσασθε αὐτὸν πορευόμενον εἰς τὸν οὐρανόν.

"Men of Galilee, why do you stand looking into heaven? This Jesus, who was taken up from you into heaven, will come in the same way as you saw him go into heaven" (Acts 1:11).

A form of this tradition probably lies behind Paul's word of assurance to the Christians of Thessalonica, some of whom are grieving the recent passing of friends and relatives:

15 Τοῦτο γὰρ ὑμῖν λέγομεν ἐν λόγῳ κυρίου, ὅτι ἡμεῖς οἱ ζῶντες οἱ περιλειπόμενοι εἰς τὴν παρουσίαν τοῦ κυρίου οὐ μὴ φθάσωμεν τοὺς κοιμηθέντας· 16 ὅ τι αὐτὸς ὁ᾽ κύριος ἐν κελεύσματι, ἐν φωνῇ ἀρχαγγέλου καὶ ἐν σάλπιγγι θεοῦ, καταβήσεται ἀπ᾽ οὐρανοῦ καὶ οἱ νεκροὶ ἐν Χριστῷ ἀναστήσονται πρῶτον, 17 ἔπειτα ἡμεῖς οἱ ζῶντες οἱ περιλειπόμενοι ἅμα σὺν αὐτοῖς ἁρπαγησόμεθα ἐν νεφέλαις εἰ᾽ς ἀπάντησιν τοῦ κυρίου εἰς ἀέρα·

15 For this we declare to you by the word of the Lord, that we who are alive, who are left until the coming of the Lord, shall not precede those who have fallen asleep. 16 For the Lord himself will descend from heaven with a cry of command, with the archangel's call, and with the sound of the trumpet of God. And the dead in Christ will rise first; 17 then we who are alive, who are left, shall be caught up together with them in the clouds to meet the Lord in the air. (1 Thess 4:15-17a)

Over twenty-five years ago C. F. D. Moule tentatively suggested that LXX Ps 46:6 may be echoed in 1 Thess 4:16.[44] Comparison of the relevant texts suggests that he is probably correct:

---

[44] C. F. D. Moule, *The Origin of Christology* (Cambridge: Cambridge University Press, 1977) 42.

| Ps 47:6 | LXX Ps 46:6 | 1 Thess 4:16 |
|---|---|---|
| עָלָה אֱלֹהִים בִּתְרוּעָה<br>יְהֹוָה בְּקוֹל שׁוֹפָר | ἀνέβη ὁ θεὸς ἐν<br>ἀλαλαγμῷ κύριος ἐν<br>φωνῇ σάλπιγγος | αὐτὸς ὁ κύριος ἐν<br>κελεύσματι, ἐν φωνῇ<br>ἀρχαγγέλου καὶ ἐν<br>σάλπιγγι θεοῦ, κατα-<br>βήσεται ἀπ' οὐρανοῦ |

Seven of the nine words of LXX Ps 46:6 are found in 1 Thess 4:16. The principal parallels are as follows: (1) The main verb is -βαίνω, with ἀναβαίνω in the LXX and καταβαίνω in 1 Thessalonians. (2) The subject of Ps 46:6 and 1 Thess 4:16 is θεός/κύριος. (3) Whereas in the LXX God ascends ἐν ἀλαλαγμῷ ("with a joyous shout"; that this shout is indeed joyful is confirmed by the parallel line in v. 2: ἀλαλάξατε τῷ θεῷ ἐν φωνῇ ἀγαλλιάσεως ["shout to God with a voice of rejoicing"]), in Paul the Lord descends ἐν κελεύσματι ("with a command"). This difference may well be due to the shift from the original liturgical setting of Psalm 47 to the apocalyptic scenario envisioned by Paul. (4) Whereas the LXX reads ἐν φωνῇ σάλπιγγος ("with the sound of a trumpet"), the saying in 1 Thessalonians reads ἐν φωνῇ ἀρχαγγέλου ("with the sound [or voice] of the archangel") and ἐν σάλπιγγι θεοῦ ("with the trumpet of God"). (5) Although the LXX does not explicitly say that God ascended *into heaven*, which would correspond with Paul's explicit statement that the Lord will descend ἀπ' οὐρανοῦ ("from heaven"), the text could, and in fact was, so interpreted. The only truly unparalleled component is the appearance of ἀρχαγγέλου ("archangel"). Its appearance in a context such as this, of course, is not difficult to explain. Angels and archangels play prominent roles in the Jewish and Christian literatures of late antiquity, especially in apocalyptic (cf. Dan 10:13, 21; 12:1; 4 Ezra 4:36; Mark 13:27; Jude 9; Rev 7:1; 8:2; 12:7 *passim*). Moreover, the appearance of an angel in this "word of the Lord" is an important link with Matt 24:31, which says that angels will be sent out with a loud trumpet call.[45]

---

[45] The *Psalms Targum* renders Ps 47:5 literally, excepting possibly the verb at the beginning of the verse: "Let the LORD be exalted with a shout." Like the MT, the Targum has עלי (or עלה), which means "ascend." But in the Targum the verb is presented as an *ithpaʿel* (יתעלי) and so probably should be rendered "Let him be exalted" (as also in v. 10; on this, see Jastrow). Such a change in nuance is in keeping with the Targum's reluctance to describe the Deity in anthropomorphic terms (i.e. as ascending or climbing, the way a human does).

One obvious point that could tell against LXX Ps 46:6 as the biblical text echoed in 1 Thess 4:16 is that whereas the latter speaks of *descent*, the former speaks of *ascent*. Perhaps this explains why few commentators,[46] despite such a high percentage of verbal and conceptual agreement, have considered this verse from the Greek Psalter. Early Jewish and Christian exegesis, however, lends support to the suggestion that the eschatological scenario to which Paul refers is indeed indebted to Ps 47:6 (Eng. 47:5; LXX 46:6).

In Jewish exegesis the sound of the trumpet (usually the shofar, as we have in Ps 47:6) often figures in eschatology. Commenting on Exod 19:19 ("as the sound of the trumpet grew louder and louder") a Tanna cites Ps 47:6, along with Isa 27:13 ("and in that day a great trumpet will be blown, and those who were lost in the land of Assyria ... will come and worship the Lord") and Zech 9:14 ("then the Lord will appear ... the Lord God will sound the trumpet"), and says: "In the sacred writings wherever the horn is mentioned it augurs well for Israel, as when it says: 'God has gone up with a shout'" (*Mekilta* on Exod 19:19 [*Bahodesh* §4]).[47] There are other examples of eschatological interpretation of Ps 47:6,[48] including one in reference to the Messiah: "As for the king, the Messiah .... What is written in Scripture? 'God has gone up with a shout ...'."[49]

In patristic exegesis Ps 47:6 (LXX Ps 46:6) is linked several times with the ascension of the risen Jesus.[50] For our purposes the most

---

[46] An exception is F. F. Bruce, *1 & 2 Thessalonians* (WBC 45; Waco: Word Books, 1982) 101.

[47] Translation based on J. Z. Lauterbach, *Mekilta De-Rabbi Ishmael* (3 vols., Philadelphia: Jewish Publication Society, 1933) 2:222–23.

[48] See *Lev. Rab.* 29.3 (on Lev 23:24); *Midr. Ps.* 47.2 (on Ps 47:9); *Pesiq. R.* 40.5; *Pesiq. Rab Kah.* 1.4.

[49] Translation based on J. J. Slotki, "Numbers," in H. Freedman and M. Simons (eds.), *Midrash Rabbah* (10 vols.; London and New York: Soncino, 1983) 6.655. For more Jewish parallels, most from even later periods, see J. Klausner, *From Jesus to Paul* (New York: Macmillan, 1943) 537–47.

[50] For examples, see Justin Martyr, *Dialogue with Trypho* §37 and §38; John Chrysostom, *Pater, si possibile est* §2; idem, *Expositiones in Psalmos* on LXX Ps 46:6; idem, *De Prophetiarum Obscuritate* (Homily 2.2–3); idem, *In Ascensionem* (Sermon 2); idem, *In Psalmum 50*; Eusebius, *Demonstratio Evangelica* (*GCS* 23.2); idem, *Commentaria in Psalmos* (*PG* 23.224); Epiphanius, *Testimonia ex Divinis et Sacris Scripturis* 86.1; Athanasius, *Epistula ad Marcellinum de Interpretatione Psalmorum* (*PG* 27.17); idem, *Expositiones in Psalmos* on LXX

important exegesis comes from Origen, or at least from an early Greek Father whose selected comments on the Psalms came to be identified with the famous exegete and theologian:

> "God went up with a shout, etc." Even as the Lord will come "with the voice of an angel, and with the trumpet of God he will descend from heaven," so "God went up with a shout." But the Lord "with the sound of a trumpet" (went up) meaning possibly with the shout of all the nations clapping their hands, shouting to God with the sound of rejoicing. To these ones I expect God to ascend. But if some one should praise him with the sound of a trumpet, even the one who ascends will himself ascend with the sound of a trumpet.[51]

Not only has Origen interpreted LXX Ps 46:6 in terms of the ascension of the risen Jesus, as several Greek and Latin Fathers did, he explicitly relates the verse from the Psalm to 1 Thess 4:16 "Even as the Lord ... 'will descend [καταβήσεται] from heaven,' so 'God went up [ἀνέβη] with a shout.'" Apparently what draws the two passages together is their common language, especially ἀναβαίνειν/καταβαίνειν. It seems that patristic exegesis supports Moule's suggestion that Paul alludes to Ps 47:6 (or LXX Ps 46:6) when he has assured the grieving faithful of Thessalonica that Jesus "will descend from heaven with a cry of command."[52] Once again a Psalm has contributed to an important piece of early Christian theology in a significant way.[53]

---

Ps 46:6 (*PG* 27.217); Cyril of Jerusalem, *De Christi Resurrectione* (*Catechesis* 14.24).

[51] *Selecta in Psalmos* on LXX Ps 46:6 (*PG* 12.1437). There is some doubt about the authorship of the *Selecta*.

[52] It is interesting to note that the Fathers typically cite and apply verses to Christ that had been cited and similarly applied in the New Testament. For example, Chrysostom (*Pater, si possibile est* §2) speaks "with reference to the resurrection" and then cites Ps 16(15):10 (cf. Acts 2:31; 13:35), speaks "with reference to the ascension" and then cites Ps 47:5(46:6), and then speaks "with reference to the seating at the right hand" and then cites Ps 110(109):1 (cf. Acts 2:34; *passim*). From this we may infer that Chrysostom assumed that his christological interpretation of Psalm 47, like those of Psalms 16 and 110, was apostolic. Similarly, in *Expositiones in Psalmos* he cites Hos 13:14 (cf. 1 Cor 15:55), Ps 47(46):6, and Ps 68:18(67:19) (cf. Eph 4:8-10). Should we assume that he regarded his citation of Psalm 47 as different, in that it lacked the authority that the New Testament had invested in the other two citations? In all of these examples, Chrysostom cites the Old Testament passages without reference to the New Testament passages that had cited them.

[53] I explore this example more fully in C. A. Evans, "Ascending and

## 4. Giving Gifts to Humanity

In the patristic exegesis already cited reference is sometimes made to Ps 68:19 and Eph 4:8.[54] We have here another interesting use of one of the Psalms, to clarify points of christology and, in the case of Ephesians 4, ecclesiology. In Hebrew Ps 68:19 (Eng. v. 18) reads:

סָעֲלִיתָ לַמָּרוֹם שָׁבִיתָ שֶּׁבִי
לָקַחְתָּ מַתָּנוֹת בָּאָדָם וְאַף סוֹרְרִים
לִשְׁכֹּן יָהּ אֱלֹהִים:

Thou didst ascend the high mount, leading captives in thy train, and receiving gifts among men, even among the rebellious, that the LORD God may dwell there.

It is rendered in the LXX (i.e. 67:19) as follows:

ἀνέβης εἰς ὕψος ἠχμαλώτευσας αἰχμαλωσίαν ἔλαβες δόματα ἐν ἀνθρώπῳ καὶ γὰρ ἀπειθοῦντες τοῦ κατασκηνῶσαι κύριος ὁ θεὸς εὐλογητός.

You ascended on high, you led captivity captive, you received gifts among people; for indeed they were disobedient when they tented there; may the Lord God be blessed.[55]

We have a fascinating exegesis of this passage in Eph 4:8-10:

8 διὸ λέγει· ἀναβὰς εἰς ὕψος ἠχμαλώτευσεν αἰχμαλωσίαν, ἔδωκεν δόματα τοῖς ἀνθρώποις. 9 τὸ δὲ ἀνέβη τί ἐστιν, εἰ μὴ ὅτι καὶ κατέβη εἰς τὰ κατώτερα [μέρη] τῆς γῆς; 10 ὁ καταβὰς αὐτός ἐστιν καὶ ὁ ἀναβὰς ὑπεράνω πάντων τῶν οὐρανῶν, ἵνα πληρώσῃ τὰ πάντα.

8 Therefore it is said, "When he ascended on high he led a host of captives, and he gave gifts to men." 9 (In saying, "He ascended," what does it mean but that he had also descended into the lower parts of the earth? 10 He who descended is he who also ascended far above all the heavens, that he might fill all things.)

---

Descending with a Shout: Psalm 47.6 and 1 Thessalonians 4.16," in C. A. Evans and J. A. Sanders (eds.), *Paul and the Scriptures of Israel* (JSNTSup 83; SSEJC 1; Sheffield: Sheffield Academic Press, 1993) 238–53.

[54] As in John Chrysostom, *Expositiones in Psalmos* on LXX Ps 46:6 (*PG* 56.213); Eusebius, *Demonstratio Evangelica* (*GCS* 23.2).

[55] Pietersma (*The Psalms*, 64) renders the middle part of the verse differently: "indeed they being disobedient in tenting there." Admittedly, the Greek is obscure and cryptic, and either does not translate the second half of the verse literally or is based on a different Hebrew text. As it stands, the reference is to what happened at Sinai (see the preceding verse). The disobedience had to do with idolatry *while encamped* at the foot of Sinai, not simply for *being there*, as Pietersma's translation seems to suggest.

The author's "he gave gifts to men" (ἔδωκεν δόματα τοῖς ἀνθρώποις) agrees with neither the Hebrew (לָקַחְתָּ מַתָּנוֹת בָּאָדָם) nor the LXX (ἔλαβες δόματα ἐν ἀνθρώπῳ), both of which literally read "you received gifts among man." But this reading will not work for the author of Ephesians, who wishes to make the point that the risen Jesus, who ascended to heaven, gave gifts to the church (cf. Eph 4:7 "But grace was given to each of us according to the measure of Christ's gift"). These gifts are said to be apostles, prophets, evangelists, pastors, and teachers (cf. v. 11).

Although at one time it was thought that the author of Ephesians intentionally misquoted Ps 68:19, we now recognize that he has followed an interpretive tradition akin to the Aramaic version:

סליקתא לרקיע משה נבייא שביתא שבייתא
אלפתא פיתגמי אוריתא יהבתא להון מתנן לבני נשא
וברם סרבניא די מתגיירין תייבין בשרת
עליהון שכינת יקרא דיהוה אלהים:

> You ascended to the firmament, O prophet Moses; you captured captives,
> you learned the words of Torah, you gave them as gifts to the sons of man,
> and even the stubborn who are converted turn in repentance,
> [and] the glorious presence of the LORD God abides upon them.

The Aramaic version not only accommodates the point the author of Ephesians is trying to make,[56] its reference to conversion and repentance is completely in step with the nature of the gifts mentioned in Eph 4:11 (i.e. "apostles," "evangelists"). Indeed, even the reference to "Prophet Moses" coheres with the gift of "prophets."

The author of Ephesians makes two principal points from his quotation of Ps 68:19. The first is to provide scriptural testimony for the claim that the risen Jesus has provided gifts to his Church. But the second point is to exalt Christ as the one who has "ascended far above all the heavens" (v. 10), which resembles Paul's exegesis in Romans 10, where appeal is made to Deut 30:12-14 and where again we hear of ascending and descending. As here in Eph 4:18 and its exegesis of Ps 68:19, so in Romans 10 Christ is linked with the Law. What is intriguing in the exegesis of Romans is that again it is the Aramaic (this time *Targum Neofiti*) that clarifies the apostolic exegesis.[57]

---

[56] See M. McNamara, *The New Testament and the Palestinian Targum to the Pentateuch* (AnBib 27A; 2nd ed., Rome: Pontifical Biblical Institute, 1978) 78–81.

[57] See McNamara, *The New Testament and the Palestinian Targum*, 70–78.

## CONCLUSION

The prophetic authority accorded the Psalter in early Judaism and Christianity is on par with that accorded the Prophets themselves. The examples that have been reviewed in this study document the great importance that the Psalter had in aiding the early Church in its efforts to understand and clarify the ministry, death, resurrection, and ascension of Jesus. That the Psalter functioned in this way is in itself intriguing, for it testifies to a convergence of worship and prophecy that characterized the charismatic nature of the early Christian community.

Israel's Psalter, understood as prophetic and charismatic, left a mark on the early Church that in some ways was more profound than that left by any other part of Scripture. Isaiah clarified the content of the Gospel (namely, the rule of God)[58] and Daniel clarified the identity and role of God's vice-regent (namely, the "son of man"),[59] but it is the Psalter that explicates the life and ministry of the new community, which are enabled by the gifts of him who ascended to heaven and sits at the right hand of God.

## SELECT BIBLIOGRAPHY

Berder, M. *"La pierre rejetée par les bâtisseurs": Psaume 118,22-23 et son emploi dans les traditions juives et dans le Nouveau Testament* (EBib 31; Paris: Gabalda, 1996).

Chilton, B. D. "The Kingdom of God in Recent Discussion," in B. D. Chilton and C. A. Evans (eds.), *Studying the Historical Jesus: Evaluations of the State of Current Research* (NTTS 19; Leiden: Brill, 1994) 255–80.

Dupont, J. "'Assisa à la droite de Dieu': L'interpretation du Ps 110,1 dans le Nouveau Testament," in E. Dhanis (ed.), *Resurrexit: Actes du Symposium international sur la resurrection de Jésus* (Rome, 1970) (Rome: Libreria Editrice Vaticana, 1974) 340–422.

Evans, C. A. "David in the Dead Sea Scrolls," in S. E. Porter and C. A. Evans (eds.), *The Scrolls and the Scriptures: Qumran Fifty Years After* (RILP 3; JSPSup 26; Sheffield: Sheffield Academic Press, 1997) 183–97.

---

[58] C. A. Evans, "From Gospel to Gospel: The Function of Isaiah in the New Testament," in C. C. Broyles and C. A. Evans (eds.), *Writing and Reading the Scroll of Isaiah: Studies of an Interpretive Tradition* (VTSup 70.2; FIOTL 1.2; Leiden: Brill, 1997) 651–91.

[59] Evans, "Daniel in the New Testament: Visions of God's Kingdom," in Collins and Flint (eds.), *The Book of Daniel*, 2:490–527.

Gourgues, M. *A la droite de Dieu: Résurrection de Jésus et actualisation du Psaume 110,1 dans le Nouveau Testament* (EBib; Paris: Gabalda, 1978).

Hay, D. M. *Glory at the Right Hand: Psalm 110 in Early Christianity* (SBLMS 18; Nashville: Abingdon, 1973).

Loader, W. R. G. "Christ at the Right Hand—Ps. CX in the New Testament," *NTS* 24 (1978) 199–217;

Hengel, M. "'Setze dich zu meiner Rechten!' Die Inthronisation Christi zur Rechten Gottes und Psalm 110,1," in M. Philonenko (ed.), *Le Trône de Dieu* (WUNT 69; Tübingen: Mohr Siebeck, 1993) 108–94; English Trans.: "'Sit at My Right Hand!' The Enthronement of Christ at the Right Hand of God and Psalm 110:1," in Hengel, *Studies in Early Christology* (Edinburgh: T. & T. Clark, 1995) 119–225.

Marcus, J. *The Way of the Lord: Christological Exegesis of the Old Testament in the Gospel of Mark* (Louisville: Westminster/John Knox, 1992).

Moo, D. J. *The Old Testament in the Gospel Passion Narratives* (Sheffield: Almond Press, 1983).

Roo, J. C. R. de. "David's Deeds in the Dead Sea Scrolls," *DSD* 6 (1999) 44–65.

Shires, H. M. *Finding the Old Testament in the New* (Philadelphia: Westminster, 1974).

PART FIVE


THEOLOGY OF THE PSALTER

# THE PSALMS IN THEOLOGICAL USE: ON
# INCOMMENSURABILITY AND MUTUALITY

WALTER BRUEGGEMANN

The Psalms have "theological use" both through their *liturgical* repetition and through their *didactic* authority as a way of shaping, schooling, and nurturing the singing, learning community of faith in a peculiar way. The work of the Psalter is to trope Israel's imagination with reference to a God who is odd and incomparable. That the Psalter is an enterprise of trope means that it is distinctly "unfamiliar" in its claims and offers not a common-sense characterization of Israelite life in the world, but a strenuous, alternative presentation that intends always to subvert and delegitimate Israel's ordinary, common-sense entry into the world.[1]

## THE INCOMPARABILITY OF GOD IN THE PSALTER

Specifically, the God to whom Israel's life is endlessly referred in the Psalter is offered as "incomparable," both in power (the accent of the hymns) and in solidarity (as stressed in the complaints).[2] That unarguable quality of YHWH that in turn bespeaks Israel's incomparable character is YHWH's *relatedness to Israel* as a defining mark of YHWH. That relatedness ("You shall be my people") that recharac-

---

[1] See Patrick D. Miller, "The Theological Significance of Biblical Poetry," *Language, Theology, and the Bible: Essays in Honour of James Barr* ed. Samuel F. Balentine and John Barton (Oxford: Clarendon Press, 1994) 213–30 [repr. in Patrick D. Miller (ed.), *Israelite Religion and Biblical Theology* (JSOTSup; Sheffield: Sheffield Academic Press, 2000) 233–49].

On the defining "unfamiliarity" of the text, attention may usefully be given to both Karl Barth, "The Strange New World within the Bible," *The Word of God and the Word of Man* (New York: Harper, 1957) 28–50; and Martin Buber, "The Man of Today and the Bible," *On the Bible: Eighteen Studies* (New York: Schocken, 1982) 1–13. See more generally, Wesley A. Kort, *Take, Read: Scripture, Textuality, and Cultural Practice* (University Park, PA: Pennsylvania State University Press, 1996).

[2] For a review of the data, see C. J. Labuschagne, *The Incomparability of Yahweh in the Old Testament* (Leiden: Brill, 1966). See also my summary, Brueggemann, *Theology of the Old Testament: Testimony, Dispute, Advocacy* (Minneapolis: Fortress, 1997) 139–44.

terizes both parties has been famously articulated by John Calvin at the beginning of his *Institutes*:

> Nearly all the wisdom we possess, that is to say, true and sound wisdom, consists of two parts: the knowledge of God and of ourselves. But, while joined by many bonds, which one precedes and brings forth the other is not easy to discern. In the first place, no one can look upon himself without immediately turning his thought to the contemplation of God, in whom he "lives and moves" [Acts 17:28]. For, quite clearly, the mighty gifts with which we are endowed are hardly from ourselves, indeed, our very being is nothing but subsistence in the one God...Accordingly, the knowledge of ourselves not only arouses us to seek God, but also, as it were, leads us by the hand to find him...We must infer that man is never sufficiently touched and affected by the awareness of this lowly state until he has compared himself with God's majesty...Yet, however the knowledge of God and of ourselves may be mutually connected, the order of right teaching requires that we discuss the former first, then proceed afterward to treat the latter.[3]

While Calvin observes that finally we could begin either way and work toward the other, it is a matter of great import for Calvin that the beginning point is with God. Moreover, we notice that Calvin speaks of "man," whereas our focus here more modestly is "Israel," though, as I have suggested, in the Old Testament Israel functions paradigmatically for humanity with God.[4]

The precise nature of the interrelatedness that is definitional for both parties, however, is not obvious. I am, moreover, unconvinced that Calvin's articulation, sweeping as it is, in the end does full justice to the oddness of the relationship in the Psalter. We may advance with some precision beyond Calvin to Serene Jones, herself a distinguished Calvin scholar, who considers the interplay between the work of Luce Irigaray and Karl Barth. She concludes:

> The interplay does, however, illuminate a direction in which contemporary theology is called to move if it takes seriously the challenges raised by both French feminists and postliberal Barthians. It is a direction that, if followed, promises adventure and risk, and most importantly, conflict. Its signposts are not clear and its ending is not predetermined. What is clear, however, is that the God confessed by each is, contrary to traditional metaphysics, a God who is not One but multiple, active, and relational. And if this God is truly to meet humanity in a relationship of *mutuality*, then this God must

---

[3] John Calvin, *Institutes of the Christian Religion* (The Library of Christian Classics 20; Philadelphia: Westminster, 1960) Book One 1.1–3, 35–39.

[4] Brueggemann, *Theology of the Old Testament*, 450–91.

also be respected as *incommensurable* other, as a sign as well as an actual event of true alterity.[5]

Jones articulates an enormous challenge for theological interpretation. Her juxtaposition of *incommensurability* and *mutuality* seems to me exactly correct and a fortuitous phrasing. I shall take that double characterization as my point of focus. Put broadly, I shall want to insist that this God-in-relation offered in the Psalter is an anticipation of the I-Thou interactionism so famously given by Martin Buber (and Franz Rosenzweig) and later echoed in fresh ways by Emmanuel Levinas.[6]

Most broadly construed, we may suggest that Israel's life with YHWH, as troped in the Psalter, is definitively covenantal, so long as we keep the notion of covenant theological and do not let it drift off into the critical problems of the pancovenantalism that came to be derived from the work of George Mendenhall and Klaus Baltzer. That covenantal characterization of YHWH with Israel, moreover, in the imaginative work of Martin Buber and Abraham Heschel, came to be a decisive and I believe effective response to and refutation of Cartesian autonomy.

It is important to recognize that Buber's work, deeply grounded in Hebrew scripture, was not simply an act of Jewish piety or scholarship, but it was a broad and deep response to the philosophical assumptions of modernity, an exercise of quintessential Jewishness

---

[5] Serene Jones, "This God Which is Not One: Irigaray and Barth on the Divine," in C. W. Maggie Kim et. al. (eds.), *Transfigurations: Theology and the French Feminists* (Minneapolis: Fortress, 1993) 141. (Italics mine)

[6] Hans Urs von Balthasar, *Theo-Drama: Theological Dramatic Theory I; Prolegomena* (San Francisco: Ignatius, 1988) 626, has stunningly noted the convergence on this interactionist theme in 1918 in a way that featured Martin Buber, Ferdinand Ebner, Gabriel Marcel, and Franz Rosenzweig:

> It is not insignificant that, in 1918, the year Simmel died, and in the following year, one of the strangest phenomena of "acausal contemporeneity" in the history of the intellect took place. This was the simultaneous emergence of the "dialogue principle in thinkers who could not be farther apart."

Of these the best known is Martin Buber. Derivatively from Buber, the most important advances, in my judgment, are those undertaken by Emmanuel Levinas, *Totality and Infinity: An Essay on Exteriority* (Pittsburgh: Duquesne University Press, 1969). Levinas's own work, of course, has continued to develop since that early and programmatic statement.

against the mistaken categories of modernity.[7] I shall argue, consequently, that Israel's Psalmic trope of its life with YHWH is not only a gift of *Israel's own peculiar identity* in the world, but the Psalter is as well an invitation issued to a *larger public concerning reality that is at bottom an enigmatic relatedness*. My comments then are situated not with particular reference to Luce Irigaray and Karl Barth, as Jones has done, but to the specific issues of the postmodern crisis of interpretation.

### THE RELATIONAL GOD OF THE PSALTER

I shall in turn consider this subversive alternative offer of *reality as relationship* in three rubrics: *genre analysis, institutional thematization,* and finally *the canonical whole.* In each of these I will consider the way in which the God of Israel is known to be *incommensurate* and *mutual.*

First then I consider how the *genre analysis* of Hermann Gunkel, Claus Westermann, and Erhard Gerstenberger may serve us in discerning the God of Israel as enigmatically incommensurate and mutual. I will work with the largest genre categories without refinement, because my purpose is not to advance genre analysis, but to see how that analysis is directly useful for theological interpretation.

The genres that give voice to YHWH's incommensurability are *hymns* and *songs of thanksgiving.* (While I believe there is merit in Westermann's coalescence of these two genre for some purposes, I am persuaded by Harvey Guthrie's accent on the different intentions and milieus that they reflect).[8] By *incommensurability,* I mean that God is for God's self, concerned for God's own life and honor, whereby Israel is aware of the huge, decisive differential between itself and the God whom it praises.

The incommensurability of YHWH is rooted in the acknowledgement that YHWH does "wonders, works, and awesome deeds" that are beyond understanding and without parallel, on which the life of

---

[7] On the development of Jewish postmodern interpretation from Buber and Rosenzweig, see Steven Kepnes, Peter Ochs, and Robert Gibbs (eds.), *Reasoning After Revelation: Dialogues in Postmodern Jewish Philosophy* (Boulder, CO: Westview, 1998). I thank my colleague Mark Douglas for this reference.

[8] Harvey H. Guthrie, Jr., *Theology as Thanksgiving: From Israel's Psalms to the Church's Eucharist* (New York: Seabury, 1981) esp. 2–30.

the world and the life of Israel depend.

Victory songs and declarative hymns name the particularities of such wonders that assert that YHWH is utterly beyond any interpretive categories of Israel and beyond any rivals or competitors. But of course it is the descriptive Psalms that begin to summarize, stylize, and give inventory to YHWH's wondrous works that are characteristic and defining of YHWH:

> One generation shall laud your works to another,
>     and shall declare your mighty acts.
> On the glorious splendor of your majesty,
>     and on your wondrous works, I will mediate.
> The might of your awesome deeds shall be proclaimed,
>     and I will declare your greatness.
> They shall celebrate the fame of your abundant goods news,
>     and shall sing aloud of your righteousness (Ps 145:4-7).

These verses are noteworthy for the rich vocabulary of splendor and majesty that set YHWH well beyond the scope of Israel's own life: "mighty acts, majesty, wondrous works, awesome deeds, greatness, fame, goodness, righteousness." Particularly the terms *niphleʾôth* and *noreʾôth* bespeak the claims of YHWH beyond human characterization or definition.

It is, moreover, characteristic that Israel's doxology concerns both of what we have come to call "history and creation," because both arenas, insofar as they may be distinguished, are simply venues out of which YHWH's stunning incommensurability is noticed and voiced.[9] Out of its own sense of its own life, Israel affirms YHWH to be the one who transforms social life in the interest of the denied and disadvantaged:

> ... who executes justice for the oppressed;
> who gives food to the hungry.
> The LORD sets the prisoners free;
> the LORD opens the eyes of the blind.
> The LORD lifts up those who are bowed down;

---

[9] Many scholars have subsequently written on the interface of "creation" and "history" and have noticed the one-sidedness of an accent on "history" in the mid-fifties in Old Testament studies. Among the earliest and most important of such discernments was Claus Westermann, "Creation and History in the Old Testament," in Vilmos Vajta (ed.), *The Gospel and Human Destiny* (Minneapolis: Augsburg, 1971) 11–38.

The LORD loves the righteous.
The LORD watches over strangers;
he upholds the orphan and the widow.
But the way of the wicked he brings to ruin (Ps 146:7-9).
Praise the LORD!
How good it is to sing praises to our God;
for he is gracious, and a song of praise is fitting.
The LORD builds up Jerusalem;
he gathers the outcasts of Israel.
he heals the brokenhearted,
and binds up their wounds (Ps 147:1-3).

This amazing capacity of YHWH applies of course to Israel and concretely to Jerusalem. Doxologically, however, it cannot be contained in Israel and becomes generic toward all such needy in every circumstance of powerlessness.

The same hymns of incommensurability make no distinction between history and creation, so that in the same Psalms, accent on the wonder, order, and food-producing reliability of creation is voiced:

Happy are those whose help is the God of Jacob,
whose hope is in the LORD their God,
who made heaven and earth,
the sea, and all that is in them (Ps 146:5-6).
He determines the number of the stars,
he gives to all of them their names...
He gives to the animals their food,
and to the young ravens when they cry (Ps 147:4, 9).

The data that are offered doxologically are beyond analysis and take Israel's breath away:

Great is our LORD, and abounding in power,
his understanding is beyond measure [without number]   (Ps 147:5).

Perhaps the most complete, stylized voicing of God beyond Israelite categories is Psalm 136 that moves easily from the wonders of creation to the wonders of Israel's own life (Ps 136:4-9, 10-15). Israel makes no attempt to penetrate that mystery. If it had done so, we would have carefully nuanced theology. But theology is of little use with a God beyond, and therefore instead of the discipline of theology there is simply the grateful helplessness of doxology.

The matter of incommensurability occurs in a somewhat different form in Israel's songs of thanksgiving, as Guthrie has seen. It is more concrete, more immediate, more direct. Nonetheless, Israel

knows in these songs as well that the action of YHWH evokes gratitude that is inescapably inadequate to the reality of YHWH. YHWH's
decisive action or gift is not seen or explained. Israel only knows
what was "before" and what is "after," and credits the move from
before to after as the move beyond human capacity. A classic example is Psalm 107 in which Israel offers four cases. Each of them proceeds in the same way:

- a statement of trouble: dislocation, prison, sickness, storm at sea.
- a plea to YHWH: "they cried to the Lord."
- an affirmation: "he delivered them from their distress."
- a response in two parts, generic thanks for YHWH's "wonders"
  and a specific naming the deed of rescue and rehabilitation.

The shift from hymn to thanksgiving perhaps entails a shifted emphasis from the *power* of YHWH to the *fidelity* of YHWH, but in all
cases it is the convergence of *power and fidelity* that evokes Israel's
doxology beyond all explanatory efforts.

YHWH is affirmed to be, in terms of both power and fidelity, beyond anything Israel can picture and beyond anything Israel has ever
seen in any other agent. This staggering awareness produces Israel's
formulae of incomparability and that evokes responses appropriate to
that incommensurability:

- Israel's primal response is one of *awe, wonder*, and *amazement.*
  The very act of praise in which Israel moves completely outside
  itself does not seek to understand, explain, or control, but only to
  yield in gladness, for praise is essentially a glad, unrestrained,
  total yielding.
- Israel's primal response is *gratitude* for the unfathomable wonder of the great God who attends to Israel and, derivatively, to
  all the little ones who might not be noticed:

  > Who is like the Lord our God,
  > who is seated on high ...
  > He raises the poor from the dust,
  > and lifts the needy from the ash heap,
  > to make them sit with princes,
  > with the princes of his people (Ps 113:5-7).

For that reason *praise* is characteristically linked to *thanks*, the basis
for Westermann's proposed convergence:

> I will give to the Lord the thanks due his righteousness, and sing praise to
> the name of the Lord, the Most High (Ps 7:18).

Indeed, it is most plausible to suggest that *hymns of awe* and *thank-songs of gratitude* together as "thanks and praise" are Israel's full recognition of *how unlike Israel YHWH is*, how unlike YHWH is to anyone or anything, none like YHWH in splendid power, none like YHWH in awesome fidelity. Israel's primal response is *obedience*, to be among those

> who fear him...who love him (Ps 145:19-20)
> who receive his statutes and ordinances (Ps 147:19)
> who are faithful, who are close to him (Ps 148:14).

Indeed the entire Torah framing of the Psalter understands that a response of obedience is appropriate, for the wonders establish sovereignty that is as gracious as it is uncompromising.[10]

Now I have taken this long to review what is no doubt an obvious point in order to prepare for my next point. Thus far I simply observe that the genres of hymn and song of thanksgiving assert, affirm, and accept YHWH's *incommensurate* sovereignty that evokes glad obedience and *incomparable* generosity that evokes glad gratitude. These are the genre of amazed obedience and glad gratitude.

## THE URGENCY OF LAMENT IN THE PSALTER

It is, however, the genre of *lament/complaint* that preoccupies much of Israel's troping energy. It is, moreover, lament/complaint that warrants careful attention if we are to focus on "theological use," for lament and complaint do not — in their radicality, daring, and honesty — easily fit into conventional theology, certainly not conventional Calvinism. As a consequence, conventional theology must most often disregard this genre of theological utterance or at least tone it down and make it liturgically innocuous, even if it is pastorally indispensable.

Lament/complaint is perhaps the trade-mark of Psalmic piety, even though it violates standard popular notions of biblical piety. We may, for our purposes, accept the conventional hypothesis that the lament/complaint is an address to God that characterizes the trouble for God

---

[10] I have lined out a grid of *obedience and praise* as a way of seeing the wholeness of the Psalter; see Brueggemann, "Bounded by Obedience and Praise: The Psalms as Canon," in Patrick D. Miller (ed.), *The Psalms and the Life of Faith* (Minneapolis: Fortress, 1995) 189–213.

(*Klage*), that petitions God for redress (*Bitte*), that evokes from God
an intervening response perhaps signaled by a salvation oracle, and
that culminates in praise, thanks, and an assurance of being heard
(*Lobe*).[11] We may give different nuance to the odd transaction
whereby YHWH responds to petition in actions and utterances of rehabilitation, whether we focus upon *God's responsiveness* or we rely
upon the insistences and *shrillness of Israel* that evokes or requires
or forces or coerces YHWH's response. How the transaction is understood varies according to the theological inclination of the interpreter and a judgment about how realistically interactive the exchange is.[12]

However that may be, what I want to consider is the daring ma-
neuver of Israel in its speech of insistent imperative address to
YHWH, speaking in a tone of urgency that lives very close to com-

---

[11] See especially Erhard Gerstenberger, *Die bittende Mensch: Bittritual und
Klagelied des Einzelnen im alten Testament* (Habilitationsschrift, Heidelberg, 1970),
"Der Klagende Mensch: Anmerkungen zu den Klagegattungen in Israel," in Hans
Walter Wolff (ed.), *Probleme biblischer Theologie: Gerhard von Rad zum 70. Ge-
bürtstag* (München: Kaiser, 1971) 64–72. See also Patrick D. Miller, *They Cried to
the Lord: The Form and Theology of Biblical Prayer* (Minneapolis: Fortress Press,
1994) 55–134, idem., "Prayer and Divine Action," in Tod Linafelt and Timothy K.
Beal (eds.), *God in the Fray: A Tribute to Walter Brueggemann* (Minneapolis: Fortress, 1998) 211–32. See also my several articles in *Psalms and the Life of Faith*.

[12] Harold Fisch, "Psalms: the Limits of Subjectivity," in *Poetry with a Purpose:
Biblical Poetics and Interpretation* (Bloomington, IN: Indiana University Press,
1990) 108–109, sharply insists that the prayers of the Psalter are real interactions
not subjective imaginations:

> Can we therefore conclude that the Hebrew term "meditation" suggests
> something like romantic self-consciousness—a self-consciousness that ex-
> presses itself especially in monologue? The answer is that the Psalms are
> not monologues but insistently and at all times dialogue-poems, poems of
> the self but of the self in the mutuality of relationship with the other...To
> speak of relationality pure and simple, is, however, misleading. The Psalms
> are not exercises in existential philosophy; we are not speaking of an en-
> counter for the sake of merely discovering the existence of the other and of
> the self in relation to the other. The "Thou" *answers* the plea of the "I" and
> that answer signals a change in the opening situation. The Psalms are in this
> sense dynamic, they involve action, purpose.... In nearly every Psalm
> something does happen. The encounter between the "I" and the "Thou" is
> the signal for a change not merely in the inner realm of consciousness but in
> the realm of outer events.

mand. I have suggested that in this moment of utterance, there is a *provisional role reversal* whereby, for the moment, needy Israel (or a needy Israelite) who has no other visible resource with which to cope with trouble, dares to assume the upper hand and the initiating voice and action in the relationship in order to "compel" YHWH to act.[13] To be sure, this imperative of urging that has the strong tone of command is spoken in a faith context (perhaps a liturgical context) of long practice of praise and thanks that count on and affirm YHWH's incommensurability.

This remarkable act of petition, however, violates that habit of *incommensurability*, breaks through the habitual practices of awe, gratitude, and obedience, and calls YHWH to accountability, either because YHWH has been negligent and has permitted "enemies" to do bad things, or has been actively unreliable in perpetrating bad things.[14] For purposes of such speech, a distinction between *negligence* and *active unreliability* is not very important, for they express only shades of difference in a failure of fidelity to which YHWH is pledged and upon which Israel counts heavily. In this daring moment of utterance — so daring that worshiping communities tend to avoid them — the habit of incommensurability is shattered or overcome, and Israel dares to engage in a season of *mutuality* with YHWH in which YHWH is not more than a partner met on level ground for dispute.[15]

---

[13] See Walter Brueggemann, "Prerequisites for Genuine Obedience," *Calvin Theological Journal* 36 (2001) 34–41.

[14] On "neglect," see Fredrik Lindström, *Suffering and Sin: Interpretations of Illness in the Individual Complaint Psalms* (Stockholm: Almqvist & Wiksell, 1994); on perpetration, see David R. Blumenthal, *Facing the Abusing God: A Theology of Protest* (Louisville, KY: Westminster/John Knox, 1993).

[15] To be sure, laments and complaints continue to be capable of cadences of incomparability. Israel does not abandon its characteristic rhetoric:

All my bones shall say,
"O LORD, who is like you?
You deliver the weak from those too strong for them,
the weak and needy from those who despoil them (Ps 35:10).
There is none like you among the gods, O LORD,
nor are there any works like yours." (Ps 86:8).

Such usage, however, performs a rhetorical, strategic function very different from the same formulae in hymns and songs of thanksgiving. In complaints and laments,

I use the term "mutuality" to mean that the two parties are, for the occasion of speaking, on level ground; for the occasion YHWH's accustomed place of privilege is inoperative. Speaking Israel is, on such occasions of utterance, not intimidated, not deferential, not deterred by awe, not restrained by gratitude, not disciplined by obedience. Rather speaking Israel now assumes rights, privileges, and entitlements based upon prior agreement, prior covenant promises, prior commitments that YHWH has made to Israel. In situations of need, distress, and desperation, Israel asserts its claim upon YHWH who is for an instant treated as a fellow bargainer and fellow suppliant, who has obligations and who is now called upon to honor those obligations not out of inclination but out of duty.

This daring act of utterance perhaps has its quintessential embodiment in the readiness of Job to go to court with YHWH (Job 31:35-37). Partly Job understands that he is approaching the bench to be judged by YHWH; but partly Job treats YHWH as a fellow petitioner who is also in the dock over issues of justice. That is, Job is partly ready to recognize YHWH's incommensurability, but partly he conducts himself on a basis with God as fellow suppliant also at risk in the process. The utterance of Job is a characteristically daring and remarkable achievement to offer rhetoric so that God's *incommensurability* is for the moment overcome and God is reduced to a *mutuality* in dispute.[16]

- The lament/complaint is not ordinary speech. It is indeed, in terms of Paul Ricoeur, a "limit expression" that is used and seen to be legitimate only in the most dire circumstance when the habits of incommensurability are no longer adequate or credible.[17] It is a strategy whereby Israel honors its own pain and refuses to cover over its own pain for the sake of YHWH's reputa-

---

such utterance is not only ground for petition; it is also a summons that implies some impatience and indignation toward YHWH, challenging YHWH to be YHWH's true, faithful self which is not presently the case. Thus in these uses, the formulae of incomparability are utilized in an act of assertive mutuality.

[16] It is for this reason that liberation theologians such as Gustavo Gutierrez, *On Job: God-Talk and the Suffering of the Innocent* (Maryknoll: Orbis, 1987) are deeply interested in the book of Job. As Job provisionally undermines YHWH's incommensurability, so such speech models subversion of earthly monopolies of power.

[17] Paul Ricoeur, "Biblical Hermeneutics," *Semeia* 4 (1975) 107–45.

tion. This "genre of mutuality" attests that Israel understood its own bodily, social suffering as a theological datum to which the Worker of Wonders must come to terms.

- The speech is incredibly daring and requires enormous theological *hutzpah* to speak against long-standing habits of incommensurability which, in the case of Job, are represented by his friends. I mean specifically theological, not social *hutzpah*, because I believe the matter is the same theologically, even if, with Gerstenberger and Miller, the genre has a setting in local, intimate, relative private enactment. It is therefore not at all surprising that the capacity to sustain such daring speech is provisional and limited; it characteristically reverts to more acceptable speech of incommensurability, so that complaints regularly culminate in new affirmation of incomparability. That such speech is provisional and is not normally sustained to the end of the Psalm, however, is no argument against its daring upheaval of conventional relationships.

- As Fredrik Lindström has pointed out, with such speech of mutuality that treats YHWH as a partner in disputation who is equally at risk, Israel does not characteristically give in to admission of guilt whereby the failure of the lesser party overcomes any charges against the greater party.[18] This is the point at which Israel's daring practice of lament/complaint most sharply parts company with conventional theology, most particularly Augustinian -Lutheran theology that tends to reduce pain to guilt and cannot entertain the full legitimate voice of pain that on occasion dares to assert it is the other partner, YHWH, who now stands charged, if not with abuse, at least with neglect.[19]

Thus it is my suggestion that genre analysis of hymn, song of thanksgiving, lament/complaint offers a model for theological interaction that is normally one of glad *incommensurability* but in emergencies is one of stark *mutuality*. Genre analysis as such has shown us a great deal, but it is the *interplay* of these genres that here concerns me,

---

[18] Lindström, *Suffering and Sin*, 7–11 and *passim*.

[19] See the shrewd comments of Johann Baptist Metz, *A Passion for God: The Mystical-Political Dimension of Christianity* (New York: Paulist, 1998) 62–71 on the Augustinian tradition.

that is, the interplay of incommensurability and mutuality. In Christian extrapolation, moreover, I suggest it is this theological interplay that leads to the interaction of Friday and Sunday and the strange, haunting enigmatic formulation, "truly divine, truly human." Given that Christian extrapolation, moreover, it is stunning that even such a Christian theologian as Jürgen Moltmann has been principally instructed by Abraham Heschel who, as a Jew, had already seen what has become in Christian theology, patripassionism.[20] It is Israel's utterance of lament/complaint that creates a field for YHWH's pathos, brought by such generative imperative from the splendor of incommensurability to the risk of mutuality.

### THE PSALTER IN THE COMMUNITY

Having established my primary point about "theological use," I want to consider what I have called "institutional thematization." By this term I mean simply that we are able to see that certain Psalms reflect certain institutional interests and practices, and operate through those interests and practices. While it is the case that the hymn and lament/complaint may be situated variously in the *Grosskult* or the *Kleinkult*, we may take them as generally undifferentiated in their usage.[21] We are in a different situation when we consider Torah Psalms, wisdom psalms and royal psalms. Strictly speaking these tend not to be form critical categories, but appeal much more to theme and substance. (I shall not consider here the ways in which these Psalms provide clues to the canonical shape of the Psalter, although that enterprise is worth pursuing.)[22] Here I simply observe that these Psalms offer a particular staging of the interplay of incommensurability and mutuality that I have exposited.

---

[20] See Jürgen Moltmann, *The Crucified God: The Cross of Christ as the Foundation and Criticism of Christian Theology* (San Francisco: Harper & Row, 1974) 270–74; and Abraham Heschel, *The Prophets* (San Francisco: Harper & Row, 1962).

[21] The categories are from Rainer Albertz, *Persönliche Frömmigkeit und offizielle Religio: Religionsinterner Pluralismus in Israel und Babylon* (Calwer Theologische Monographien 9; Stuttgart: Calwer, 1978), and have been decisive for Erhard Gerstenberger as well.

[22] See J. Clinton McCann (ed.), *The Shape and Shaping of the Psalter* (JSOTSup 159; Sheffield: Sheffield Academic Press, 1993).

*The Torah psalms* of course exhibit a high affirmation of incommensurability. This is a relationship between lord and vassal, between king and people.[23] It is YHWH who commands and Israel who obeys, without question or reservation. As Psalm 1 makes clear, as long as the structure of this relation is honored and practiced, everything works well; there is abundance and prosperity and life. This is the premise of the theology of Deuteronomy, which pervades the Psalter at important points.[24] The incommensurability that defines the relationship is accepted in these Psalms as a matter of course.

In the rhetoric of Israel, it is clear that the sovereign God who gives Torah requires and expects full obedience. On occasion, in rather grand style, the Holy One of Israel is astonished and affronted that questions should be raised about how the Torah-giving God has ordered creation:

> Will you question me about my children,
> or command me concerning the work of my hands (Isa 45:11)?
> Who is this that darkens counsel by words without knowledge?...
> Shall a faultfinder contend with the Almighty?
> Anyone who argues with God must respond...
> Will you even put me in the wrong?
> Will you condemn me that you may be justified? (Job 38:2; 40:2, 8).

These texts are perhaps exilic, or from some such circumstance where the old, unquestioned incommensurability has begun to unravel.

The jeopardy of the Torah structure of faith, which was decisively important for Israel, is mostly voiced not in grand, majestic challenge as in Job or II Isaiah, but in what must have been the more common practice of complaint. That is, the claims and guarantees of Torah, offered in Torah psalms and entrance liturgies, are not available among those who protest and wonder and wait:

> If you try my heart, if you visit me by night,
> if you test me, you will find no wickedness in me;
> my mouth does not transgress (Ps 17:3).

---

[23] See James L. Mays, "The Place of the Torah Psalms in the Psalter," *The Lord Reigns: A Theological Handbook to the Psalms* (Louisville, KY: Westminster/John Knox, 1994).

[24] See Patrick D. Miller, "Deuteronomy and Psalms: Evoking a Biblical Conversation," *JBL* 118 (1999) 3–18.

> I cry to God Most High,
> to God who fulfills his purpose for me (Ps 57:3).

This is the rhetoric of unrequited fidelity that counts on the Torah relation, that trusts it and holds YHWH to it, but sees no evidence of it. In such Psalms, with some deference, YHWH is drawn into the trouble and is addressed in urgent imperative. Even the Torah-giving God is drawn down into dispute about fidelity in a way that assumes some mutuality and refuses, for the occasion, the conventions of incomparability. It is the courage of Israel, together with the discerned unresponsiveness of YHWH, that events such daring mutuality. It is the complaints that draw the God of Torah-incomparability into mutuality.

In the *Royal psalms* the daring assumption is that YHWH is the true King enthroned among the gods who appoints and anoints a human regent to maintain fruitful order. It is in the interest of the community gathered around royal claims to keep YHWH exalted and to "exalt by association" the human, Davidic king. That is, the court language of incomparability is important to the royal claim (see 2 Sam 7:22). In this regard, I will cite three of the best known royal Psalms, all of them apparently placed as canonical markers. First, in Psalm 2,

> He who sits above the heavens laughs,
> The Lord has them in derision (v. 4).

While the human anointee is on the earth, he enjoys the guarantees of the incommensurate God. In Psalm 72, the commands of righteousness and justice to the king that echo Torah themes and the high claims for creation surely present a God high above earthly traffic. Moreover, the exalted language of the court draws the king into the orbit of the creator, for it is the human king who will have "dominion" from sea to sea (Ps 72:8). And in Psalm 89, the high, "once for all" claim of covenant serves as a guarantee for the throne that is exempt from historical vagaries (vv. 35-37). Indeed, the royal ideology seeks to place the David monarchy beyond approach by any actual circumstance, that is, incommensurate along with the incommensurate God. That mood will hold only as long as things work well.

The royal Psalms accent the incomparability of YHWH, both to enhance YHWH among the gods but also to enhance, derivatively, the Davidic king who has access to the incomparable God. (See the prayer of David that trades on this incomparability, 2 Sam 7:18-29.)

This high claim for YHWH, however, is abruptly interrupted in Ps 89:39-52, presumably written in exile when the royal incomparability is no longer sustainable. In these verses, royal rhetoric is revised in the utterance of a characteristic complaint. As we have seen under the rubric of Torah psalms, the complaint has the effect of voicing mutuality whereby the lesser party dares to make claims in a striking act of parity. In verses 39-46 we are offered a series of "you statements" accusing YHWH of spurning covenant. The "you statements" are remarkably direct and terse, no longer with the royal deference of court style. Finally in verse 50, YHWH is questioned about *ḥesed* and *'amûnah*, the ingredients of covenant loyalty precisely celebrated in verses 25, 29, 34. Now the rhetoric shows how the lower one can make claims against a stronger party, thereby refusing the old comfort and assurance of incomparability.

*The wisdom psalms* are likely not cultic but instructional. If we take Psalm 37 as a characteristic wisdom Psalm — an instruction that could easily be lodged in the book of Proverbs — YHWH is affirmed as the good, reliable guarantor of created order, who does not intervene but who stands at a distance, but as a sure guarantor.[25] Psalm 37 is a disciplined presentation of a well-ordered world in which the righteous and obedient end up possessing the land.[26] The assurances of such wisdom reflection are in close parallel to those of the Torah psalms. Both Torah and wisdom statements see the world working under YHWH's rule in order to assure order and to reward righteousness.

We do not find in the Psalms a clear departure from sapiential incomparability; but we may notice an impulse in that direction. Gerstenberger suggests that Psalm 39 is a "meditative prayer" with sapiential overtones.[27] The Psalm reflects upon mortality and asserts complete reliance upon YHWH. And yet, because of the reality of

---

[25] See Lennart Bostrom, *The God of the Sages: The Portrayal of God in the Book of Proverbs* (CBOT 29; Stockholm: Almqvist & Wiksell, 1990).

[26] See Walter Brueggemann, "Psalm 37: Conflict of Interpretation," in Heather A. McKay and David J. A. Clines (eds.), *Of Prophets' Visions and the Wisdom of Sages: Essays in Honour of R. Norman Whybray on His Seventieth Birthday* (JSOTSup 162; Sheffield: Sheffield Academic Press, 1993) 229–56.

[27] Erhard Gerstenberger, *Psalms Part I with an Introduction to Cultic Poetry* (FOTL 14; Grand Rapids: Eerdmans, 1988) 165–68.

fractured well-being, the Psalmist makes accusation against YHWH, refusing to accept a more settled serenity:

> *You* have made my days a few handbreadths,
> and my lifetime is as nothing in your sight ...
> Remove *your* stroke from me;
> I am worn down by the blows of *your* hand.
> *You* chastise mortals in punishment for sin,
> consuming like a moth what is dear to them;
> surely everyone is a mere breath (Ps 39:6, 11-12).

The guarantees of reliable moral coherence given in conventional wisdom are here found not to be adequate. A more nearly mutual impulse creeps in, as the Psalmist dares to protest. Of course this model that moves to a new tone gains full form in Job that Wester-mann has seen as a series of Psalm-like utterances.[28]

All three "institutional thematizations" that I have considered — *Torah, royal, sapiential* — seek to assure an order authorized and guaranteed by an incomparable God. In each case, however,

complaint questions *Torah* assurances,

complaint wonders about *hesed* to the *king*;

complaint appeals to *wise order* not now visible.

The order has not held in particular circumstance as the dominant, long-held claims of incomparability had proposed. In each case, the guarantee for order (and well-being) from the incomparable God is found to be less than sufficient.

In each case Israel must adopt a new position and speak in a new tone, thereby departing from *incomparability* toward a new, daring *parity*, a parity made both possible and necessary by unbearable circumstance. This does not mean, of course, that the traditional theological claims of Torah, royal ideology, or wisdom are invalidated; Israel, however, must now face the reality of disorder where characteristic institutional thematizations on behalf of YHWH are not fully credible. The rhetoric of Israel — and consequently also the character of YHWH — are open enough in the Psalter to allow YHWH to be available in very different modes, modes in which YHWH is addressed strongly, compellingly from "below" by those who find courage to break the silence of deference, guilt, and

---

[28] Claus Westermann, *The Structure of the Book of Job: A Form-Critical Analysis* (Philadelphia; Fortress, 1981).

pain.[29] Israel breaks the silence through an act of courage, to fend off despair by utterance that speaks truth to power. It is this truth-to-power praxis that deconstructs incomparability in the direction of mutuality. In the process, traditional institutional claims laden with power and authority are placed in jeopardy.

## THE PSALTER IN THE CANON

Finally, I add only a note about the dialectic of incommensurability and mutuality as concerns the canonical structure of the Psalter. In my article "Bounded by Obedience and Praise," I have suggested that the final form of the text moves from something of a calculated Torah obedience in Psalm 1 with its quid-pro-quo to self-abandoning doxology in the concluding Psalm 150, by way of the vigor and abrasiveness of complaint and lament.[30] There is no doubt that Psalm 1 vigorously works its Torah insistence and postulates an incommensurability between Torah-giver and Torah-keepers upon which everything for the future depends. There is no doubt, in equal fashion, that Psalm 150 presents an exuberant incommensurability between the one who praises and the one praised, in which the speaking community is at a distance from the one praised, a distance marked by gladness, awe, gratitude, and an absence of self-regard.

This defining movement from one kind of incommensurability (obedience) to another kind of incommensurability (praise) is, I suggest, marked by the crucial canonical placement and function of Psalm 73.[31] It is clear that the *good* "to be near God" in Ps 73:28 is very different form the *good* that God does to the "upright" (Ps 73:1). The move from "good" as *benefit* to "good" as *communion* is a primary theological transformation accomplished through the Psalter. I should insist that this move from a *prudential* good to a

---

[29] On speech from below that beaks the silence of deference, guilt and pain, see Elaine Scarry, *The Body in Pain: The Making and Unmaking of the World* (New York: Oxford University Press, 1985); and Judith Lewis Herman, *Trauma and Recovery: The Aftermath of Violence—from Domestic Abuse to Political Terror* (New York: Basic Books, 1992).

[30] See note 9 above.

[31] See Walter Brueggemann, "Bounded by Obedience and Praise," and Walter Brueggemann and Patrick D. Miller, "Psalm 73 as a Canonical marker," *JSOT* 72 (1996) 45–56.

*relational* good is accomplished (and can be accomplished) only through an active, abrasive disruption of incommensurability that features a daring, claiming, asserting mutuality in which the lesser party freely and in risky ways assumes provisional parity, if not leverage, over the greater party. It is *this intense articulation of mutuality that recharacterizes, reshapes, and redescribes incommensurability.* It is this intense feature of mutuality that is decisive for the Psalter, that is so problematic in conventional pious and theological usage of the Psalter, and that peculiarly marks the community of faith and the God who is the source of and reference of its life. The staggering disclosure is that this move made in the process of undenied rights, unsilenced pain, and unintimidated truth-telling is that this season of mutuality is not characteristically an affront to the Holy One; it is received by, embraced, and responded to in commensurate way by the One who is first and last incommensurate. Thus the practice of *disruption*, reflected in the shape of the Palter, is seen to be a sketch of the oddness of this God who makes a different life possible, a life of incommensurability disrupted and then reconstrued.

## CONCLUSION

The God of the Psalter is first and last an incommensurate sovereign who creates, redeems, and consummates.[32] This is, nonetheless, a God whose incommensurability is interrupted, perforce, by the unsilenceable insistence of Israel's pain and indignity. In the end this is an incommensurability interrupted by YHWH's own willingness to be interrupted because this is a God unlike any other. It is this interrupted incommensurability, marked by daring, risk-taking mutuality, that most characterizes this God and that makes this literature so powerful liturgically, so inescapable pastorally, and so haunting theologically.

The recognition of this dynamic — that I have briefly explicated in terms of *genres*, *themes*, and *canonical shape* — invites a major theological rethink, as Serene Jones has indicated. First, it invites a

---

[32] See Patrick D. Miller, "The Sovereignty of God," in Donald G. Miller (ed.), *The Hermeneutical Quest: Essays in Honor of James Luther Mays on His Sixty-Fifth Birthday* (Allison Park, PA: Pickwick, 1986) 129–44. See also my exposition, Brueggemann, *Theology of the Old Testament* , 267–313.

rethink of "traditional metaphysics" (for example an appeal to Calvin's opening of the *Institutes*) in order to allow for a mutuality that
is not obvious in the diction of incommensurability. Second, it opens
a way, as is occasionally recognized pastorally and liturgically if not
theologically, for a theology of the cross.[33] For that reason the utilization of the Psalms in the Passion Narrative of Jesus are not incidental but rather a defining articulation of the *mutuality of Friday*
that makes possible the *incommensurate, inexplicable triumph of
Easter.*

My concern in the end, however, looks through these theological
issues and beyond them to the crisis of humanness now to be faced in
our culture. I suggest that it is precisely an uncriticized incommensurability — reflected through Cartesian autonomy and certitude
— that is fundamentally at work in the brutalizing military and economic power among us. The god(s) of incommensurability invite
state and corporate power that is always on the make, consumer ideology of the incommensurate self who needs and owes nothing and
can receive nothing. That way lies death for self, community, and the
earth.

The decisive break with such *uncriticized incommensurability*
— an incommensurability of course wildly extrapolated in undisci-
plined and frantic ways — is made in the Psalter in the *interruption
of mutuality* that reshapes, recharacterizes, and redescribes incommensurability. It is mutuality that permits the lesser, denied, silenced
ones to dare make noises about their worth and their future, noises
that oddly enough are heeded. It is *the voice of mutuality* that began
the Exodus event:

> The Israelites groaned under their slavery, and cried out. Out of the slavery
> their cry for help rose up to God. God heard their groaning, and God re-
> membered his covenant with Abraham, Isaac, and Jacob. God looked upon
> the Israelites, and God took notice of them (Exod 2:23-25).

It is *the voice of mutuality* that secured sight for the blind Bartimeus:

> When he heard it was Jesus of Nazareth, he began to shout out and say,
> "Jesus, Son of David, have mercy on me!" Many sternly ordered him to be
> quiet, but he cried out even more loudly, "Son of David, have mercy on

---

[33] The more public implications of a theology of the cross have been well seen
by Douglas John Hall, *Lighten Our Darkness: Toward an Indigenous Theology of
the Cross* (Philadelphia: Westminster, 1976).

me!" Jesus stood still and said, "Call him here." (Mark 10:47-49).

It is *the voice of mutuality* that marks the God of the Psalter, in the end as incommensurable, but incommensurability that is shrilly interrupted and redefined.

The kind of mutuality that issues in transformative interaction that puts both parties at some risk is a huge relearning in much Christian theology. It was the burden of Martin Buber in the face of Cartesian absoluteness and autonomy. It is the more recent offer of Emmanuel Levinas who seeks a way outside totality. It is the oddity that causes Kathleen Norris, following Sebastian Moore, to observe that, "God behaves in the psalms in ways he is not allowed to behave in systematic theology."[34] In the end the capacity of YHWH to be *assertive* or *interrupted* and Israel's capacity to be *receiving* or *interrupting* is the fullness of communion. It is only then, and not before, that the Psalmist can say:

Whom have I in heaven but you?
And there is nothing on earth that I desire other than you (Ps 73:25).

## SELECT BIBLIOGRAPHY

Blumenthal, D. R. *Facing the Abusing God: A Theology of Protest* (Louisville, KY: Westminster/John Knox, 1993).

Brueggemann, W. "Bounded by Obedience and Praise: The Psalms as Canon," in P. D. Miller (ed.), *The Psalms and the Life of Faith* (Minneapolis: Fortress, 1995) 189–213.

—. *Theology of the Old Testament: Testimony, Dispute, Advocacy* (Minneapolis: Fortress, 1997).

Fisch, H. *Poetry with a Purpose: Biblical Poetics and Interpretation* (Bloomington, IN: Indiana University Press, 1990).

Gerstenberger, E. *Psalms Part I with an Introduction to Cultic Poetry* (FOTL 14; Grand Rapids: Eerdmans, 1988) 165–68.

Guthrie, H. H., Jr. *Theology as Thanksgiving: From Israel's Psalms to the Church's Eucharist* (New York: Seabury, 1981) esp. 2–30.

Labuschagne, C. J. *The Incomparability of Yahweh in the Old Testament* (Leiden: Brill, 1966)

Lindström, F. *Suffering and Sin: Interpretations of Illness in the Individual Complaint Psalms* (Stockholm: Almqvist & Wiksell, 1994.

Mays, J. L. "The Place of the Torah Psalms in the Psalter," in *The Lord Reigns: A*

---

[34] Kathleen Norris, *The Cloister Walk* (New York: Riverhead Books, 1996) 91.

*Theological Handbook to the Psalms* (Louisville, KY: Westminster/John Knox, 1994).

McCann, J. Clinton (ed.). *The Shape and Shaping of the Psalter* (JSOTSup 159; Sheffield: Sheffield Academic Press, 1993).

Miller, P. D. *They Cried to the Lord: The Form and Theology of Biblical Prayer* (Minneapolis: Fortress Press, 1994) 55–134.

—. "Prayer and Divine Action," in T. Linafelt and T. K. Beal (eds.), *God in the Fray: A Tribute to Walter Brueggemann* (Minneapolis: Fortress, 1998) 211–32

—. "The Theological Significance of Biblical Poetry," *Language, Theology, and the Bible: Essays in Honour of James Barr* ed. Samuel F. Balentine and John Barton (Oxford: Clarendon Press, 1994) 213–30 [repr. in P. D. Miller (ed.), *Israelite Religion and Biblical Theology* (JSOTSup Press; Sheffield: Sheffield Academic Press, 2000) 233–49].

Moltmann, J. *The Crucified God: The Cross of Christ as the Foundation and Criticism of Christian Theology* (San Francisco: Harper & Row, 1974) 270–74.

Ricoeur, P. "Biblical Hermeneutics," *Semeia* 4 (1975) 107–45.

Westermann, C. "Creation and History in the Old Testament," in V. Vajta (ed.,), *The Gospel and Human Destiny* (Minneapolis: Augsburg, 1971) 11–38.

# THEOLOGIES IN THE BOOK OF PSALMS

ERHARD S. GERSTENBERGER

## POINTS OF DEPARTURE

How can Biblical Theology, the very goal of our work, be approached? In this purview focusing on the Psalter as a prime example for theological reasoning in liturgical contexts I am departing from several assumptions.

One simply says, that God-talk or theology can hardly be uniform, universal, and valid through the ages. Rather, God-talk, for deeply divine and human reasons, for the very heart of faith must be contextual, temporary, unfinished and in a certain concordance with changing customs, cultures, social conditions.[1] Our theological discourse must not be taken as eternal truth. We think and talk as transitory beings, firmly tied to the textures of our socialization and cultural identities.

Secondly, since there are great varieties of cultural and social patterns — in coexistence as well as in conflict with each other — we certainly have to count on quite different modes of talking about God, with different experiences and conceptualizations of the Divine. Living side by side, nowadays, with many other godfearing or godignoring people, intensely feeling the challenges of our pluralistic societies, we have the unique opportunity to test our own theological affirmations and learn of their richness and deficiencies, and their precious, human relativity — that is, affinity — to our own cultural settings.

What rarely has been recognized, however, is that pluralism (to a certain degree this always has been the case) has invaded even the stronghold of individual being. Each of us lives at the same time in very different social contexts. We are on the one hand members of small, intimate groups of family and friends, and on the other of various economic, political and religious associations. In both kinds

---

[1] Cf. Erhard S. Gerstenberger, *Theologien im Alten Testament* (Stuttgart: Kohlhammer, 2001); English transl., *Theologies in the Old Testament* (London: T. & T. Clark; Minneapolis: Augsburg Fortress); idem, and Ulrich Schoenborn (eds.), *Hermeneutik–sozialgeschichtlich* (exuz 1, Münster: LIT-Verlag, 1999).

of social conglomeration we play our roles according to different tunes. Personal experience may tell us that theological concepts and argumentations are distinctly different in either context. God is perceived on the one hand in terms of personal relations, in I–Thou terms, and on the other as an ordering power with increasingly superpersonal authority. God, the companion who exercises solidarity with his (or her) people, cannot easily be reconciled with that divine being who speaks through thunderstorms, smites the enemies, and administers justice to all mankind.

The Psalter is a uniquely opportune work to test out the manifold and multilayered theological discourse I have tried to suggest above. Most biblical "books" do have some cohesion, plot, or structure. The "book of Psalms," however, seems to be a much more loosely-knit compilation of liturgical texts, used for different kinds of interactions, rites, ceremonies, gatherings.[2] In any case, the broad confluence of texts from greatly different sources in the Psalter provides a very coourful picture of human conditions and longings. This makes the biblical Psalms an unmatched treasure of diverse theological concepts.

## LIFE-SETTINGS

The early masters of formcritical analysis, Hermann Gunkel and Sigmund Mowinckel,[3] emphasized social and communicative settings in establishing their genre-classifications of the psalms. They traced complaints, hymns, royal songs, and wisdom poems back to determined groups of people interacting with each other and with their God, at different "recurring" opportunities. Although large differences exist among form-critics, in detailed evaluations the basic human associations producing and using those principal genres emerge clearly enough in socio-historical and formcritical research.[4] We may identify four main types of human association, not precluding

---

[2] Naturally, not all experts will agree at this point. Many defend a well-thought out organization of the material at hand. But there is a good deal of consensus as to the various fountain-heads of individual psalms and genres.

[3] Their classical studies are: Hermann Gunkel and Joachim Begrich, *An Introduction to the Psalms* (Macon, GA: Mercer University Press, 1998); Sigmund Mowinckel, *The Psalms in Israel's Worship* (2 vols., Nashville: Abingdon, 1962).

[4] Overviews of research offer, e.g. Martin J. Buss, *Form-Criticism*; Henning Graf Reventlow, *Gebet*; Hans-Peter Müller, "Formgeschichte/Formenkritik I," *TRE* 11.271 – 285.

sub-divisions and overlappings, with each of these basic social conditions producing its proper psalm types.

(1) The first type is the small intimate family cluster, the age-old economic and religious nucleus of humankind, resorted to cultic means, whenever one member fell seriously ill or was threatened by demonic powers. Petitionary rituals were held, often on the precincts of the patient's home, as may be learnt from hundreds of Akkadian (Assyrian-Babylonian) incantations. A ritual expert would lead the ceremony and let the endangered person recite the decisive prayer of complaint, confession, and petition.[5] This pattern of ceremonial healing is common in most tribal societies to this very day. Even modern religions maintain some of those archaic proceedings; for example, prayer-services for the sick, last unctions, exorcisms, and secularized remnants may be discovered even in today's medical and psychotherapeutic practices. Exuberant thanksgivings after graces attained and fortunes restored were the counterpart of complaint and petition, also being celebrated among intimate circles of family and neighbours. Oferings to God, opulant meals, testimony of the saved one and merriment were characteristic elements of this "private" festivity.

(2) A second layer of religious or cultic action without doubt was the regional aggregation of families in village or township with their own local sanctuary. The Old Testament quite often refers to the *bamah*, the open-air shrine, of a neighbourhood, whose existence archaeology has amply confirmed in many Israelite sites. People were united by common interests principally according to the seasonal calendar, with respect to personal *rites de passage*, and in spontaneous cases of common grief and joy. Early victory songs may pertain to this category, led by inspired women (cf. Exod 15:21). The noisy crowd would join in shouting refrains, as cheerleaders intoned the lines: "Yahweh is good," "His loyalty endures forever" (Ps 136:1-26). Appealing to and hailing the God of weather and fertility, protection and victory was the main end of such cults of local and regional dimension. Countless religious activities survive even today in burroughs, clubs, rural centers, *et cet-*

---

[5] Cf. Erhard S. Gerstenberger, *Der bittende Mensch* (WMANT 51; Neukirchen-Vluyn: Neukirchener, 1980).

*era*, destined to support the communitarian life of people not related by blood but tied together by vital interests on a smaller scale, on a person-to-person basis.

(3) Gradually, with growth and diversification of society, cultic activity passes into the larger ambit of tribal and national concerns. Anonymity grows with the sheer number of persons involved in cultic interactions or assemblies. Rules of communication — as well as common interests — change considerably, and with such changes theological concepts also fall into different patterns, gaining a new profile. To complicate matters, state cults in the Ancient Near East are dynasty-centered, managed by professionals, and, as a rule, do discourage popular responsibility. With the establishment of divine or semidivine monarchies (a switch that causes much concern in Judges 9 and 1 Samuel 7–12), state cults become restricted to officially-appointed royal priesthoods. Since the hymnic material of the Davidic court (if anything from that source has survived at all) was used and remodelled by the exilic / post-exilic community (cf. Psalms 18; 20; 21; 45; 72; 132; 144) also in terms of messianic expectations (cf. Pss 2; 110), we cannot be sure how much authentic material of the pre-exilic state-cult has been preserved. In any case, the "highest" level of Old-Israelite social organization falls into line with bureaucratic and autocratic forms of government, which reduced the anonymous mass of citizens to a subservient state, while permitting freely, as it were, all kinds of family, local and regional cults on their respective social levels and with their specific theological interests. In addition, Ancient Near Eastern monarchies always purported to truly serve — in the name of highest deities — the needs of the weakest elements of society (cf. Psalm 72 and Hammurapi's prologue to his law-edicts).

(4) After Israel's final defeat of 587 BC and the loss of monarchic structures, a complete reorganization of the people of Yahweh was inevitable. National ambitions could only survive underground. Local communities, apparently, soon rallied around old family- and tribal-traditions. In retrospect, monarchy, temple, and prophecy all became unifying factors for a new Israel, which identified herself with *tora*, sabbath, circumcision, temple, and the holy land as the people elected by Yahweh, creator of heaven and earth and supreme king over all nations.

This new, unheard of community of faith,[6] without state government, was the decisive social group shaping the sacred traditions and handing them down to the Jewish, Christian, and even Muslim communities. Exclusive adoration of Yahweh — much later erroneously designated as "monotheism"— is the hallmark of this religious body of local congregations. In many ways the Book of Psalms carries the stamp of this latest period in Old Testament history.[7] As far as contemporary songs and prayers are concerned, we should consider the so-called "wisdom" poems as products of that early Jewish community. The main spiritual need of the congregation was for divine guidance in a pluriform religious environment and under foreign domination. *Tora*-psalms such as 1, 19, and 119 occupy important positions in the Psalter. Reflections about life, death and the ups and downs of faith (cf. Psalms 9/10; 23; 37; 39; 49; 73; 90; 139) in the midst of internal strife about true righteousness and fidelity are typical for the latest layer in Old Testament psalmody. Theological wrestling with historical developments leading to a loss of national and religious independence (cf. Psalms 44; 89; 106; 137) are sure signs of the communities' state of mind in those crucial 6th/5th centuries BCE. Of course, the community of faith was not a homogeneous social block. Different liturgical needs of varying groups persisted, such as attendance to the sick, ostracism of pilgrims on their way to distant Jerusalem, members of congregation stricken by poverty, or priestly groups particularly attached to a Zionist theology. These groups maintained specific songs and liturgies, as still extant in the Psalter.

In summary, the different genres of psalms reflect specific social and cultic groupings, consisting always of real flesh and blood people, in Israel's long history of faith. The trajectory of psalmodic expressions runs from small-group, domestic services to regional as-

---

[6] Possibly, the followers of Zoroaster in ancient Persia, had earlier formed communities of faith transcending family ties. See Mary Boyce, *History of Zoroastrianism* (2 vols., Leiden: Brill 1980, 1982).

[7] While working on a form-critical commentary (*Psalms* [2 vols., FOTL 14 and 15; Grand Rapids: Eerdmans, 1988 and 2001]), I became more and more convinced that much reworking of older Psalms is evident in the canonical text: e.g. in meditative, homiletical, and late hymnic genres.

semblies and royal state rituals back to parochial community worship related to our Christian Sunday-morning gatherings. Moreover, to remind us of our presuppositions, these modes of religious expression were and are tied to determined social bodies which do not simply form a historical chain or sequence, but may exist contemporaneously, side by side, at any given time. Many of the theological problems and blessings connected with the Book of Psalms have their origin in this fundamental, at least four-part social setup experienced by the early Jewish fathers and mothers: In sociological terms we are dealing with psalm theology coming out of (a) family and clan milieux; (b) regional neighbourhoods; (c) royal state cults; and (d) the newly-founded religious comunity of faith, representing a quite new kind of communal organiztion somewhere between FAMILY- and state-structures and conceptions.[8]

The exilic-postexilic community of faith thus left us with its powerful heritage of spiritual and theological patterns of contemporary social mouldings, together with its own complexities and confusions. We should now enquire after the specific religious experiences and conceptualizations of the Divine, that is, for the contextual theologies on each level of social organization. For practical purposes I am drawing together stages (a) and (b), since they are close to each other in featuring organic face-to-face relationships between members.

PERSONAL GOD, FAMILY, AND NEIGHBORHOOD RELIGION

For millennia, before taking the step towards sedentary life and organized communities of a larger scope, humankind existed in isolated bands structured according to kinship lines. Even the Israelites, latecomers in the Near Eastern theatre, visualized a prehistoric stage occupied by patriarchal and sometimes perhaps matriarchal families with their specific customs and beliefs. Modern research from Albrecht Alt to Karel van der Toorn and Leo G. Perdue, etc., acknowledges this particular religious setting which does bring forth a distinct mode of theological conceptualization. It is interesting to note that researchers in modern small-group sociology tend to confirm the existence of a specific kind of religious faith within primary social clusters. This means that the original structuring of faith has not been lost over the ages. And the Psalms, having one of their an-

---

[8] Cf. Erhard S. Gerstenberger, "Conflicting Theologies in the Old Testament," *Horizons in Biblical Theology* 22 (2000) 120–34.

cient roots in family environment, can give us a vivid impression of how family-religion has come about and is still in operation.

The principal deity of the family, primarily aligned to the male or female (in my opinion, more to the latter! House-cults of old were probably administered by chief women)[9] leader of the small unit, was more or less considered a member of the group, even if a prominent or supreme one. Affinities with ancestor worship probably existed.[10] The "God of my father" (although not attested, we should expect also "of my mother"!) becomes the deity of every member of the group, a helper and saviour in daily troubles from birth to grave. God — committed to a particular group — was (and still is!) a defender of his or her client's interest (cf. Jacob's conditional vow to serve the deity he finds at Bethel, Gen 28:20-21). From this very intimate relationship between God and small group arise dimension and atmosphere of family faith down to our own days:

> It was you who took me from the womb;
>> you kept me safe on my mother's breast.
> On you I was cast from my birth,
>> and since my mother bore me you have been my God.
>> (Ps 22:9-10 *NRSV* [MT v. 10-11])

> O God, from my youth you have taught me,
>> and I still proclaim your wondrous deeds.
> So even to old age and gray hairs,
>> O God, do not forsake me,
> until I proclaim your might
>> to all the generations to come. (Ps 71:17-18a, *NRSV*)

Personal faith is embedded in family-relationships, the most horrible experience being abandonment by close kinsfolk and becoming the object of naked aggression on their part (cf. Pss 27:10; 41:5-9 [MT

---

[9] Cf. Erhard S. Gerstenberger, *Yahweh the Patriarch* (Minneapolis: Fortress, 1996) 55–66.

[10] Cf. Josef Tropper, *Nekromantie* (AOAT 223; Kevelaer: Butzon & Becker; Neukirchen: Neukirchener, 1989); Oswald Loretz, "Die Teraphim als 'Ahnen-Götter-Figur(in)en'," *UF* 24 (1993) 133–78; idem, "Nekromantie und Totenevoka-tion in Mesopotamien, Ugarit und Israel." in B. Janowski, K. Koch & G. Wilhelm (eds.), *Religionsgeschichtliche Beziehungen zwischen Kleinasien, Nord-syrien und dem Alten Testament. Internationales Symposion Hamburg 17.–21. März 1990* (OBO 129; Fribourg: Universitätsverlag; Göttingen: Vandenhoeck & Ruprecht, 1993) 285–315.

vv. 6-10]; 88:8, 18 [MT 9:19]).[11]

God is experienced totally in personal categories, not as an abstract power. The I-Thou relationship, so influential and precious in our whole religious heritage, has grown out of ancient family faith. Some of the highest values of Jewish-Christian theology — childlike trust in God, personalized hope for divine solidarity and help, courage to argue with the divine protector, expectation that he or she may heal aberrations, broken relationships, illnesses, social disruptions — all these familiar features of personal faith do have their beginnings with family religion. Faith is grounded in belongingness, and belongingness generates the deepest kind of trust. Therefore, formulas of "kinship" and expressions of confidence abound in individual psalms of complaint or thanksgiving.[12] "You are [he is] my God (helper, shield, shepherd, castle; rock, refuge, etc.)" is a very concise statement of this basic relationship of trust (for example, Ps 22:10[MT v. 11]; 31:14[MT v. 15]; 63:1[MT v. 2]; 118:28; 140:6 [MT v. 7]; 7:10[MT v. 11]; 54:4[MT v. 6]; 71:3, etc.). Some psalms may be classified as "songs of confidence," because trust is their dominant mood (cf. Psalms 4; 11; 16; 23; 27; 56; 62; 131).

The vocabulary in the Psalter expressing confidence in and nearness to God is large, and the form-element, as already indicated, propels prayer to the personal, familiar God. Interestingly, these individual petitions and thanksgivings do not need the notions of exodus, covenant, torah, king, or Zion. They are more directly related to the deity, being independent of secondary institutions. God belongs to their social group. God is dwelling in the midst of the faithful. We may again refer to domestic cults in Israel, clearly attested in Gen 31:34; Exod 21:6; Judg 17:1-5; 1 Sam 19:13, 16. The "household idols" actually were personal, familial deities represented by figurines. Perhaps they were identical with those clay models found by the hundreds in Israelite homes of monarchic times, for the most

---

[11] For all psalm-expositions in this essay cf. also "Introduction to Cultic Poetry" and interpretations of individual texts by Erhard S. Gerstenberger, *Psalms* (FOTL 14 and 15).

[12] The motif or form-element expressing confidence in God is an essential item in individual complaints; see Erhard S. Gerstenberger, *Psalms* (FOTL 14 and 15), glossaries under "Affirmation of Confidence"; Patrick D. Miller, *They Cried to the Lord: The Form and Theology of Biblical Prayer* (Minneapolis: Fortress, 1994) 127–30.

part of nude female deities.[13] We need not, in my opinion, shun away from this testimony to "alien" Gods in Israel. On the contrary: If the above line of argumentation is at all sustainable, we find household religion an incredible enrichment of theological experience within the Bible.[14] Encountering the divine on the lowest social level, experiencing inclusively the female side of the deity, is basic for faith and theological insight. We should be grateful for the width and depth of biblical tradition. The Yahweh-alone theology is to be understood inclusively, not exclusively: God offers contacts and revelations on all levels of human social organization, in each and every cultural sphere, for all kinds of people.

The point just made is underlined by another piece of evidence. A host of personal names in the Hebrew Scriptures testifies most clearly to the prevalence of well-defined family-outlooks on life, kinship, blessing, salvation from evils, etc.,[15] to the exclusion of national religious concerns. In personal names,

> individual relationships to God are put on the same foundation as in individual complaints and salvation oracles: they do imply an archaic, creational state of affairs.[16]

God assists the mother to give birth (cf. *Jiftah*, "[God] opened [the womb]"; *Elnatan*, "God gave [a child]"; *Amminadab*, "my uncle [= God] promotes [birth?]," sustains and saves the child,[17] and indeed is

---

[13] Cf. Urs Winter, *Frau und Göttin* (OBO 53, Fribourg: Universitätsverlag; Göttingen: Vandenhoeck & Ruprecht, 1983); Silvia Schroer, *In Israel gab es Bilder* (OBO 74; Fribourg: Universitätsverlag; Göttingen: Vandenhoeck & Ruprecht, 1987).

[14] Like many other exegetes Karel van der Toorn, *Family Religion in Babylonia, Syria and Israel* (Leiden: Brill, 1996) 181–82, 218–25, 373–79, judges that state religion eventually supersedes family faith. In my opinion, family experiences of God never have ceded to any superior influences, but maintained their autonomy into our own times.

[15] Cf. Rainer Albertz, *Persönliche Frömmigkeit und offizielle Religion* (Stuttgart: Calwer, 1978) 49–77. Albertz points out that: (a) personal names in the Old Testament are all but lacking references to "national" creeds in Yahweh's salvific deeds; and (b) these names rather refer to familial experiences of divine benevolence, sustenance and help in regard to birth, illness, threats, dangers, upkeep, blessing, etc.

[16] Albertz, *Persönliche Frömmigkeit*, 59.

[17] Albertz lists 58 names attributing to the personal deity all sorts of care, protection, help, salvation, vindication etc. (*Persönliche Frömmigkeit*, 61–65).

his or her "Father" (*Abihu*, "my father is he").

> A trustful relationship of individuals to their gods antedates their existence;
> it is anchored in being created by the deity. Trust is not initiated by a hu-
> man decision .... Personal ties to God are in a way unalienable, just like
> the relationship between parents and children normally is not liable ever to
> be cancelled.[18]

We may conclude, therefore, that familial faith has been thoroughly
routed, as far as the psalmic literature of Israel and her neighbours is
concerned, in the ambit of small-group structures and outlooks. The
psalmists, at this level, are taking over the role the deity's children:
"I have calmed and quieted my soul, like a child quieted at its
mother's breast" (Ps 131:2).

From this infant's perspective there is a thread to expressions of
confidence even in the majestic deity portrayed in many psalms:
"hide me under the shadows of thy wings" (Ps 17:8; cf. similar expressions in Pss 36:8; 57:2; 63:8; 91:4), if "wings"[19] really is referring to the guardians of the ark and not — as in the famous Jesus
saying — the protection of a roosting hen (Mt 23,37). Language of
confidence has also been drawn from the imagery of war and protection, that is, from the realm of larger social social structures (God
is "my king," "my shield," "my castle," etc.). For millennia families
lived within widespread organizations and experienced the pressures
and opportunities of such more ample and anonymous contexts. They
were certainly familiarized with the language and metaphors of a
wider society. But apparently the real roots of personal trust are age-
old experiences: to be sheltered within the intimate kinship group
and the neighborhood in village and small townships, which partially
function on kinship ties. In distinction to mere family bounds, ancient neighborhoods as a rule operated according to common interests in agricultural and seasonal tasks, defence against hostile outsid-
ers, and internal peace-keeping. Anthropological insights help us to
differentiate between family and village life. The latter have to build
on custom and law that already exists, while families live on the solidarity of "natural" kinsfolk. In consequence, faith and theology in a
village community, although partly prolonging family-attitudes towards the larger group, reach out for a God who is less tied to mi-
cro-groups but rather deals with seasonal and political affairs. This

---

[18] Albertz, *Persönliche Frömmigkeit*, 75.

[19] Cf. W. Dommershausen, *kanap*, *ThWAT* 4.243–46.

local deity was venerated in early Israel at open-air sanctuaries. The challenge originating from community religion clearly was for all participants to overcome self-centered family interests.[20]

From this perspective it seems fully clear, then, that the material and spiritual interests articulated in expressions of confidence and belongingness are those of the familial group. This means that faith and theology revolve around basic needs of life, health, survival of the individual, and his or her immediate surroundings. Accordingly, God is provider of food, housing, and group-harmony (Psalm 133), midwife of the newly born (Ps 22:10), protector against fire and water, disease and bad luck (Ps 91:2-6), healer of all illnesses (Psalm 38), and protector against demonic onslaught (Psalm 91). Naturally, the personal and familial God takes sides in group conflicts in favour of his adherents. Thus, some of the frequent references to "enemies and evildoers" in the Book of Psalms certainly pertain to the inner circle of familial piety, especially in those prayers which show strictly personal, individual traits of suffering, persecution and defence (e.g. Psalms 22; 38; 55), as well as of revenge (Ps 109). On the other hand, the God of the rural community has to take care of weather and soil, herds and plantations, inter-familial relations and customs, evil-minded neighbors, and seasonal feasts (cf. Psalms 8, 12, 65, 118, etc.).

One of the most spectacular features of familial theology has always been noted with a certain surprise by those modern Christian theologians who believe the Almighty must be a sovereign of sorts, ruling all the world and therefore not suffering any obstacles to his or her rule. Family religion of old, however, did not visualize God in terms of national or world dominion, nor does a modern family faith do so. That means that familial deities — belonging to the small group and facing competition from other small-group divinities — were accessible for argument and rebuke. Individual complaints in the Bible and in the Ancient Near East (much like in tribal societies around the world) have been vehicles of serious censure and violent complaints against God, which is only possible on the basis of that intimate familial relationship. Wherever we meet similar characteristics in communal laments (cf. "city-laments," or "communal complaints" as in Lamentations and Psalms 44 and 89) we need to

---

[20] For more on village and small-town religion, see in Erhard S. Gerstenberger, *Theologien im Alten Testament*, chap. 5.

identify the life-settings and consider the possibility that familial forms have been used in a congregational or national service. Originally, direct and aggressive language against God from his own followers most likely arose in the religious family tradition of the kinship-God.

My contention, all in all, is simply this: Kinship theology, both at home in familial groups and to some extent in village communities — realized primarily in house-cults (mostly under direction of women?) and familial pilgrimages to regional shrines as that of Elkanah, Hanna, and Peninna (1 Samuel 1) — is primeval and the primary theology of all mankind. The faith of the small kinship group forms the basis for all subsequent theological systems, and still is most essential for human existence. It persists into our own time as a distinct type of religious faith. After all, where else than in small groups face-to-face with co-religionists could we exercise our faiths and become human beings? The hallmarks of family religion are intimacy, inter-personal-relations, limitations to individual lives and necessities, and struggle for wholesome solidarity, both human and divine. Correspondingly, the features of God in kinship theologies should lack tyrannical, arbitrary, majestic traits, since his or her face is human:

> Yahweh is merciful and gracious,
>     slow to anger and abounding in steadfast love.[21]
> He will not always accuse,
>     nor will he keep his anger forever.
> He does not deal with us according to our sins,
>     nor repay us according to our iniquities.
> For as heavens are high above the earth
>     so great is his steadfast love toward those who fear him;
> as far as the east is from the west,
>     so far he removes our transgressions from us.
> As a father has compassion for his children,
>     so Yahweh has compassion for those who fear him. (Ps 103:8-13)

Psalm 103 is in my opinion a "communal hymn" that shows typical concerns of a congregation in a tradition-minded and universalistic setting. Nevertheless, the individual member of the group is voicing his or her eulogies to Yahweh, probably in common worship. And

---

[21] The concept of *hesed* ("steadfast love,"better: "solidarity") is central to the family and kinship ethos. Cf. Eckart Otto, *Theologische Ethik des Alten Testaments* (Stuttgart: Kohlhammer, 1994) 64–67, 81–94.

the portrayal of the fatherly deity taking care of all believers has certainly been derived from family experiences and traditions.

## FAITH IN SOCIETY AT LARGE

All other kinds of social organizations apart from family and kinship-groups emerged fairly late in cultural or civil development.[22] We may distinguish several of such "secondary" or "tertiary" societal arrangements in antiquity and modernity: the tribe, state, ethnic entity, political and trade associations, professional societies, religious and gender alliances, etc. In the present context, however, we are interested only in one common feature: larger associations very soon tend to become anonymous entities in which the individual does function differently from his or her own family environment. In other words, larger and anonymous groupings develop their own set of rules, no longer based on kinship values (no matter how insistently the participants clamour for "brotherhood" and "sisterhood"), but now governed by more "objective," impersonal norms and perspectives. In fact, emergent "law," with its offshoots in village customs, is one prominent indicator of a society's growing anonymity. "Bureaucracy" and "loss of solidarity" are others. As far as "law" is concerned, strict impartiality must prevail in the name of justice, while family solidarity, in contrast, is built on individual and group needs. (To "consider the person" is against the law! Compare Exod 23:3; Deut 1:17; 16:19, but this is necessary within the family ethos).

The Psalter also reflects the secondary level of socialization, consisting, as it were, not only of prayers of the small-group type. A good number of texts have their origin in ceremonies or rituals oriented towards military and political organizations of Israel and/or Judah. In modern research these are often named "collective" or "national" psalms, serving distinct opportunities in the life of the nation. Conspicuous are situations of complaint (cf. Psalms 44; 89), thanksgiving (cf. Psalm 124), victory (cf. Psalm 68), hymnic praise (cf. Psalms 105; 136; 148), public education (cf. Psalm 78), and national mourning and penitence (cf. Psalm 106; Nehemiah 9). All these texts were no doubt adapted, used, and reused among the exilic and postexilic communities, thus serving the ends of a group of worshippers that was markedly different from either family or state or-

---

[22] Cf. Darcy Ribeiro, *O processo civilisatório* (5th ed., Petrópolis, Brazil: Editora Vozes, 1979).

ganization.[23] But sociologically speaking, these texts also preserve sufficient traces of that anonymous larger body of people that outgrew the limits of kinship structures.

Would anyone doubt that in larger associations, with their different ways of life, a different type of faith and theology needs to emerge? In other words, the concepts of God (by necessity?) have to be different, when they emerge from so disparate a social setting as anonymous organizations. The main characteristics of theological models are:

- God assumes hierarchical leadership, which is mirrored in monarchic structures.
- The city, state, or ethnic group, with its peculiar organization and interests, also becomes the matrix of theological thinking.
- The state economy and contemporary ideas about property, commerce, and political associations play a significant role.

One prominent realm — attributed by some scholars along the lines of J. Wellhausen as the decisive influence on Old Testament theological thought — is the "military camp," where war-rituals were celebrated and where Yahweh was envisioned as the Lord of battle. The image of God was one of a terrifying hero, wielding superhuman powers in favour of his followers and against their enemies:

> Then the earth reeled and rocked;
>> the foundation of the mountains trembled
>> and quaked, because he was angry.
> Smoke went up from his nostrils,
>> and devouring fire from his mouth;
>> glowing coals flamed forth from him.
> He bowed the heavens, and came down;
>> thick darkness was under his feet.
> He rode on the cherub, and flew;
>> he came swiftly upon the wings of the wind.
> He made darkness his covering around him,
>> his canopy thick clouds dark with water.
> Out of the brightness before him
>> there broke through his clouds,
>> hailstones and coals of fire.

---

[23] See the following section, THE ONLY GOD OF THE EXCLUSIVE CONGREGATION.

Yahweh also thundered in the heavens,
  and the Most High uttered his voice.
And he sent out his arrows, and scattered them;
  he flashed forth lightnings, and routed them.
Then the channels of the sea were seen,
  and the foundations of the world were laid bare
at your rebuke, O Yahweh,
  at the blast of the breath of your nostrils.
  (*NRSV* Ps 18:7-15; MT vv. 8-16)

The "theophany report" occurs frequently in the Hebrew Scriptures (cf. Pss 68:7-10[MT vv. 8-11]; 77:16-19[MT vv. 17-20]; 97:2-5; Hab 3:3-15, etc.).[24] The inherent concept of God here has nothing to do with mercy and care, or the individual's well-being and daily concerns. It is instead oriented towards the crises of a threatened larger entity, a political body of sorts, which has to fight back in order to survive. Unconditional confrontation — war until the enemy's annihilation — is the order of the day. God is consequently pictured as warrior,[25] with his anger (more literally, his "nostrils") raging, and nature reeling with anxiety. God's armament is superior, and nobody can resist his fierce onslaught.[26] Thus he intervenes in favour of Israel, saving his clients from extreme dangers. Should this frightening picture of Yahweh really be fundamental to Israel's faith? We must at least admit that a deity like the warrior-god did play an important role in certain contexts of biblical times.

There are other models of God that belong to different situations in the life of Yahweh's people. Suffice it to point out a few of the resulting portrayals of the deity.

- Any larger association of people wants its own God to be first in power and authority. Psalm 29 challenges other deities by using elements of Canaanite myth to acknowledge the supremacy to Israel's God: "Ascribe to Yahweh, O heavenly beings, ascribe to Yahweh glory and strength ..." (v. 1).
- Psalm 104, apparently following Egyptian hymnic tradition,

---

[24] Cf. Jörg Jeremias, *Theophanie* (WMANT 10, 2nd ed., Neukirchen-Vluyn: Neukirchener, 1977).

[25] Cf. Patrick D. Miller, Jr., *The Divine Warrior in Early Israel* (HSM 5, Cambridge, MA: Harvard University Press, 1973).

[26] The Pentateuch and the Prophets quite frequently touch on Yahweh's battles for his people, cf., for example, Exodus 14–15; 17:8-16; Deuteronomy 20; Judges 4–5. A terrible description of the blood-splashed warrior-god appears in Isa 63:1-6.

lauds the heavenly constructor of the world in a theological
effort to show his creative capacities: "O Yahweh, my God,
you are very great, you are clothed with honour and majesty
...!" (v. 1; cf. the mythical narration of the chaos battle in
vv. 2-9).

- The sustenance of the world-order in which Israel has been
  living is guaranteed by the divine judge over all law-
  enforcing powers that exist: "God has taken his place in the
  divine council; in the midst of the gods he holds judgement
  ..." (Ps 82:1).
- The supreme authority of Yahweh over nature, kingdoms and
  powers is majestically expressed in Psalms 95–99, which belong to the Yahweh-Kingship type. These Psalms also demonstrate the adamant will of the people "called by his name"
  to be recognized, probably in marked contrast to their actual
  state of destitution, as a valid part of humankind and possibly
  as the leading one.

On the side of human macro-organizations the most important issues are these: (1) How can we establish and maintain a solid identity
over against other political, ethnic, and religious entities? (2) In what
ways may internal administration of justice be guaranteed?

Leaving aside for the time being traces of tribal religion centering
on the war-god Yahweh, we now briefly turn to Israel's statehood.
The Book of Psalms, although composed pretty much in exilic and
postexilic times, retains some valuable information on the theological
workings of monarchy (e.g. in Psalms 45; 89; 110) and on ancient
Zionism (cf. Psalms 46; 48; 76; 132). These memories — be  they
authentic or modified by exilic and eschatological concerns — demonstrate to what degree hierarchic theological thinking superseded
older kinship and tribal outlooks and values. The will and help of
God is now channeled by way of dynasty and national symbols of in-
vincibility. Yahweh — who  had come into the early tradition as a
fierce warrior-god fighting for his tribal clients — becomes, in a
way, a state official who is cultically manipulated by the royal government in Samaria or Jerusalem (cf., for example, 2 Kings 22). As
such, he is the Lord of internal order and potentially of dominion
over less powerful neighbours. Needless to say, kinship religion and
local cults that cannot be identified with official state ideology persisted side by side with royal Yahwism, perhaps borrowing here and
there concepts and names from the "superior" cult.

Theologically speaking, the Psalms represent a full measure of state-supporting theology around Davidic kingship and Zion-mythology, but do not provide many hints of the prophetic critique so well known from the second part of the canon. Psalms 18; 20; 21; 72 and 144, for example, paint the picture of a victorious monarch, while only a few (later?) exhortations alert to the dangers of human pride, stubbornness and abuse of power (cf. Psalms 78; 95:7-11; 106; 144:3-4; 147:10). The individual supplicant is subsumed under society at large, for society's very well-being is at stake. The state God does not live in solidarity with small groups; his or her face is not the parent-type image, but he or she governs or runs — with equity and justice — a large company of human beings. In spite of all criticism within the Bible itself (e.g. by prophets) we have to admit that theology in the context of larger and anonymous societies is legitimate and necessary to a certain degree. General principles must take a certain precedence over individual needs. Royal Judaean theology, with its hierarchical state-order, is an attempt to do justice to that particular social context. But to build all theological reflection on a macro-organism such as this, together with its governing deity, would be disastrous. Sadly enough, it was not long before Christian theologies indulged in such error.

### THE ONLY GOD OF THE EXCLUSIVE CONGREGATION

We have already pointed out[27] the changes that came about during the 6th and 5th centuries within the exilic Judaean communities. A new type of organization, sociologically speaking to be located between kinship group and macro-society, emerged among the deportees in Babylonia and afterwards with the returnees to Judaea. A decapitated nation turned into a community of faith, existing, as it were, as a separate entity within the pluralistic empires of Babylonian and Persian provenance.[28]

From a sociological perspective, the newly emerging Jewish faith, which was dissected into several creative centers, lacked political unity, hierarchical (monarchic) order. It had, therefore, to build a new identity by utilizing traditions of family, tribal past, priestly extract, etc. In contrast to many displaced peoples and emigrants of

---

[27] See LIFE-SETTINGS above.

[28] For a more detailed analysis and synthesis, cf. Erhard S. Gerstenberger, *Theologien*, 166–216 (chap. 8).

various epochs, the emerging Jewish community succeeded in organizing itself in congregations that rallied around religious symbols such as Torah, Sabbath, and circumcision. The only and exclusive deity became Yahweh, who had proven sufficiently independent of state authorities to remain the God of the religious community. The new structures of life and faith of the Judaean groups in Palestine, Babylonia, Egypt, and possibly other countries were characterized by several focal points:

- Identification via confessing Yahweh as the exclusive personal and communal God.
- Experience of pluralistic and globalizing societies.
- Submission under foreign rule with concomitant economic exploitation.
- Internal strife in order to assert exclusivist positions.
- Most important, communal life was at one and the same time oriented towards the believing individual and his autonomous decision to adhere to Yahweh alone, and towards the needs and wellbeing of the local communities — in more modern terms, towards the parochial entity, and towards the world-wide Jewish community as symbolized in Temple and Torah.

These focal points of spiritual life became the generative matrixes of theological thinking.

The Psalter, more than most other Hebrew writings, is a treasury of early Jewish theologies. Since the Psalms focus on the exemplaric needs of congregations and their theological solutions, but always with the members as persons in view, several features may be highlighted:

- The importance of individual prayers within the context of congregational worship (cf. the great number of individual psalms in the Psalter).
- The astonishingly strong motivation to draw conclusions from prior salvation history (cf. the so-called history-psalms such as 78; 105; 106; 136).
- The endeavour to concentrate on the Mosaic Torah as the backbone of Jewish identity.
- Numerous examples of psalmic homilies or teachings.[29]

---

[29] For the latter item, cf. Erhard S. Gerstenberger, "Höre, mein Volk, lass mich reden!" (Ps 50,7), *BK* 56 (2001) 21–25.

The image of Yahweh that emerges is of a supreme God, creator and maintainer of the world order, yet also an exclusive, zealous Overlord of his religious community, and the consoler, teacher and provider of each individual adherent.

Yahweh is teacher, wise man, counsellor. He himself gives vital instruction to the younger generation, through his precepts (which are probably written: each block of eight acrostic verses features up to ten synonyms for *torah*). Psalm 119 addresses throughout this Instructor-God of the Torah-community:

> Blessed are you, O Yahweh;
>> teach me your statutes.
> With my lips I declare
>> all the ordinances of your mouth. (vv. 12-13)
> I rise before dawn and cry for help;
>> I put my hope in your words.
> My eyes are awake before each watch of the night,
>> that I may meditate on your promise (vv. 147-48)
> Yet you are near, O Yahweh,
>> and all your commandments are true.
> Long ago I learned from your decrees,
>> that you have established them forever. (vv. 151-52)

The vocabulary of "teaching," "making understand," and "open the eyes" is prominent in the entire, extensive text. Torah implies salvation, grace and shalom ("all-round wellbeing, bliss," cf. Psalm 1), and Torah is synchronized with the cosmic order:

> The heavens are telling the glory of God;
>> and the firmament proclaims his handiwork ...
> In the heavens he has set a tent for the sun,
>> which comes out like a bridegroom from his wedding canopy ...
> The law [*torah*] of Yahweh is perfect,
>> reviving the soul;
> Yahweh's decrees are sure,
>> making wise the simple... (Ps 19:1, 4c, 5a, 7)

In consonance with the universalistic world views of Babylonian and Persian cultures, and in sheer defence against spiritual subjugation by the ruling powers Judaeans claimed the absolute sovereignty of Yahweh over all the earth (Ps 24:1), without forgetting the response of individual persons (Ps 24:2-4). Thus in their temple rituals they elevated their God to the top position:

> Lift up your heads, O gates!
>> and be lifted up, O ancient doors!
>> that the King of glory may come in.

Who is the King of glory?
  Yahweh, strong and mighty,
  Yahweh, mighty in battle.
Lift up your heads, O gates!
  And be lifted up, O ancient doors!
  that the King of glory may come in.
Who is this King of glory?
  Yahweh of hosts,
  he is the King of glory. (Ps 24:7-10)

The ancient war traditions of the Yahweh tribes come to the fore in order to give expression to the new, universal theology. Yahweh-Kingship hymns and eschatological songs in the Psalter sometimes underscore more aggressively the quest for Yahweh's world dominion (cf. Psalms 47; 93; 95–99; and Psalms 2; 110, etc.). Reminiscences of past statehood-structures linger in the minds of postexilic Judaeans; they are worked over and partially condensed in feverish expectations of a new reign of David or of the final kingdom of God.

To my mind, this plurality of divine functions in the emerging Jewish community points to a segmentation of theology in different discourses, subject to social groupings within the whole entity of the faithful all over the world — a situation that is also familiar in our churches today. We may consider this a kind of fragmentation of reality, and consequently a breaking up of the Divine. Which do we really prefer: the illusion of wholeness and uniformity, or the stark reality of disquieting, piecemeal theological insight and practice of faith? Ancient communities called upon the personal God with respect to individual and familial necessities. The God of state-order and general ethos played a role in legal administration and in the preaching of equity among the congregation. Yahweh, the God of heaven and earth, was finally the supreme guarantee in all questions of one's larger identity and all instances of conflict with the universalizing ideologies of the time. Naturally, the borderlines between different groups and discourses also allowed for a good amount of fluctuation in terms of language, metaphors, and contents.

From this perspective, the Book of Psalms neither diachronically nor synchronically represents a uniform theology. To the contrary, it exhibits multilayered conceptions of God. We may also suggest possible differences between laypersons' models of God and learned reflections, between wealthy congregants and poor ones, perhaps even between male and female adherents, to the all-embracing Yahweh-faith.[30]

## CONCLUSIONS FOR OUR WORLD

Recognizing layers of theological thinking and conceptualizations within the Psalter does not mean abandoning the basic idea of one world and one all-inclusive God. But it does presuppose the hiddenness of this concept. In our limited theological discourse we are dealing only with contextual models of God; affirmations about an ultimate and exclusivistic Oneness are left to God him/her/itself, but with hope for and belief in a firm foundation of this world and a final convergence of all the centrifugal forces of life.

On the other hand, our own lives according to day-to-day experience are partitioned and dissociated into several levels of existence. The witness of the Psalter, it seems to me, is thus of utmost importance to us. Its depth and theological diversity stimulates an ecumenical chorus of singers and supplicants, mediators and confessors.[31] Just as the early Jewish community in its prayers and songs treasured texts for various groups and occasions — admitting distinctly different models of God side by side (Pentateuch, prophetic canon and wisdom literature still contribute more to these variations) — we also are allowed (better: commissioned) to preach differently in various social contexts. My own experience as a pastor tells me this: The Christian message becomes flesh in particular ways with small groups (for example, in personal counselling and family celebrations), with communal worship and interfaith dialogue, or with national and international discourse on the burning issues of humankind. God today is at one and the same time — and these models are not reconcilable, nor to be smoothed over theologically — the personal partner, the guarantor of justice and equity, and the hidden principle and critical yardstick of evolution, science and the world economy.

The quest for unity remains alive in our thinking, because we can hardly exist without a vision of coherence and belongingness. After all, we feel like one determined person with respect to defined

---

[30] Cf. Erhard S. Gerstenberger, "Weibliche Spiritualität in Psalmen und Hauskult," in Walter Dietrich and Martin A. Klopfenstein (eds.), *Ein Gott allein?* (Fribourg: University Press 1994) 349–63.

[31] Cf., for example, Erhard S. Gerstenberger, "Singing a New Song: On Old Testament and Latin American Psalmody," *Word & World* 5 (1985) 155–67.

groups and entities. Our identity seeks to be one and the same in different walks of life. If this is correct, we should remind ourselves that this desired unity does not reside in our own existence. It is not given into our hands, but we are pilgrims on the way toward such a peaceful state of affairs (cf. Psalm 39). We must not claim that unity in order to coerce others to receive it from our hands and be subdued to our whims. The unity of God, the world and human-kind — unity of our own individual existence — is a goal, a gift, and a future glory:

> O Yahweh, you have searched me and known me.
> You know when I sit down and when I rise up;
>> you discern my thoughts from far away.
> You search out my path and my lying down,
>> and are acquainted with all my ways.
> Even before a word is on my tongue,
>> O Yahweh, you know it completely.
> You hem me in, behind and before,
>> and lay your hand upon me.
> Such knowledge is too wonderful for me;
>> it is so high that I cannot attain it. (Ps 139:1-4)

## SELECT BIBLIOGRAPHY

Albertz, R. *Persönliche Frömmigkeit und offizielle Religion* (Stuttgart: Calwer, 1978).

Blenkinsopp, J. *Sage, Priest, Prophet* (Louisville: Westminster John Knox, 1995).

Brueggemann, W. *The Psalms and the Life of Faith* (Minneapolis: Fortress, 1995).

—. *Theology of the Old Testament* (Minneapolis: Fortress, 1997).

Buss, M. J. *Biblical Form-Criticism* (JSOTSup 274; Sheffield: Sheffield Academic Press, 1999).

Gerstenberger, E. S. *Der bittende Mensch* (WMANT 51; Neukirchen-Vluyn: Neukirchener, 1980).

—. *Psalms* (2 vols., FOTL 14 and 15; Grand Rapids: Eerdmans, 1988 and 2001).

Gunkel, H. and J. Begrich. *An Introduction to the Psalms* (Macon, GA: Mercer University Press, 1998).

Hossfeld, F.-L. & E. Zenger. *Psalmen 51–100* (2nd ed., HThKAT; Freiburg: Herder, 2001).

Miller, P. D. *They Cried to the Lord: The Form and Theology of Biblical Prayer* (Minneapolis: Fortress, 1994).

Mowinckel, S. *The Psalms in Israel's Worship* (2 vols., Nashville: Abingdon, 1962).

Perdue, L. G. (ed.). *Families in Ancient Israel* (Louisville, KY: Westminster John Knox, 1997).

Reventlow, H. G. *Gebet im Alten Testament* (Stuttgart: Kohlhammer, 1986).

Seybold, K. and E. Zenger (eds.). *Neue Wege der Psalmenexegese* (2nd ed., HBS 1; Freiburg: Herder, 1995).

Toorn, K. van der. *Family Religion in Babylonia, Syria and Israel* (Leiden: Brill, 1996).

# INDICES

1. SCRIPTURE INDEX

2. APOCRYPHA AND PSEUDEPIGRAPHA

3. DEAD SEA SCROLLS

4. OTHER ANCIENT WRITINGS

5. MODERN AUTHORS

# INDICES

1. Scripture Index...........................................................................627
2. Apocrypha and Pseudepigrapha ...................................................661
3. Dead Sea Scrolls.........................................................................662
4. Other Ancient Writings...............................................................664
5. Index of Modern Authors............................................................669

## 1. SCRIPTURE INDEX

### 1. HEBREW BIBLE/OLD TESTAMENT

#### Genesis

| | |
|---|---|
| Genesis (Book) | 313, 331, 444n.4, 444n.5, 444n.6, 450, 474, 475, 510n.11, 513, 534 |
| Genesis 1–2 | 403 |
| Genesis 1 | 102n.27, 388, 474 |
| 1:26-28 | 403 |
| 1:26 | 399 |
| 1:27 | 553n.6 |
| 1:28 | 399 |
| Genesis 2 | 403 |
| 2:24 | 553n.6 |
| 5:24 | 284 |
| 6:11 | 176 |
| 14:18-20 | 62 |
| 17:11 | 506n.3 |
| 19:19 | 228n.11 |
| 20:13 | 228n.11 |
| 24:12 | 228 |
| 24:27 | 228 |
| 24:42 | 228 |
| 24:48 | 228 |
| Genesis 28 | 454, 455 |
| 28:9 | 454 |
| 28:20-21 | 609 |
| 31:34 | 610 |
| 35:16 | 363 |
| 35:19 | 364 |
| 39:4 | 213n.28 |
| 40:4 | 213n.28 |
| Genesis 41 | 209 |
| 41:39 | 209n.12, 209n.13 |
| 41:46 | 209 |

#### Exodus

| | |
|---|---|
| Exodus (Book) | 78, 238, 290, 291, 334n.63, 362n.30, 513 |
| Exodus 1–18 | 184n.5, 301n.47 |
| Exodus 1–15 | 301 |
| Exodus 1–14 | 293, 302, 307 |
| 2:23-25 | 600 |
| 3:6 | 553n.6 |
| 4:22 | 48 |
| Exodus 14–15 | 300n.37, 303, 617n.26 |
| Exodus 15 | 291, 293, 293n.19, 296, 298, 300, 300n.37, 300n.41, 301, 301n.47, 306, 373 |
| 15:1 | 130n.64, 131, 298 |
| 15:1-21 | 288 |
| 15:1-18 | 98 |
| 15:11 | 560 |
| 15:21 | 130n.64, 298, 605 |
| 16:29 | 564n.29 |
| 17:8-16 | 617n.26 |
| 19:3ff. | 45 |
| 19:19 | 574 |
| 20:5-6 | 229 |
| 20:7 | 250 |
| 20:12-16 | 553n.6 |
| 20:12 | 553n.6 |
| 20:16 | 250 |
| 21:12 | 361 |
| 21:16 | 610 |
| 21:17 | 553n.6 |
| 23:3 | 615 |
| 23:14-17 | 109 |
| 23:15 | 350 |

| | |
|---|---|
| 23:26 | 193 |
| 24:13 | 213n.28 |
| 25:8 | 80 |
| 25:20 | 260 |
| 28:35 | 213n.28 |
| 29:6 | 398n.20 |
| 29:45-46 | 80 |
| 33:11 | 213n.28 |
| 34:6 | 388 |
| 34:6-7 | 292 |
| 34:6-7 | 428 |
| 34:18-24 | 109 |
| 34:20 | 350 |
| 37:9 | 260 |
| 39:30 | 398n.20 |

**Leviticus**

| | |
|---|---|
| Leviticus 1–16 | 188n.19 |
| 1:5 | 262 |
| 1:8-9 | 257n.11 |
| 1:12 | 257n.11 |
| 8:9 | 398n.20 |
| 15:13 | 193 |
| 15:28 | 193 |
| Leviticus 16 | 109 |
| 19:18 | 553n.6 |
| 21:12 | 398n.20 |
| 23:4-44 | 109 |
| 23:16 | 193 |
| 23:24 | 574n.48 |
| 23:36 | 366 |
| 24:10-16 | 384, 384n.21 |
| 24:12 | 384 |
| 25:43 | 399n.26 |
| 25:46 | 399n.26 |
| 25:53 | 399n.26 |

**Numbers**

| | |
|---|---|
| Numbers (Book) | 78, 513 |
| 1:50 | 213n.28 |
| 1:52 | 39 |
| 2:2 | 39 |
| 6:2 | 398n.20 |
| 6:3 | 398n.20 |
| 6:4 | 398n.20 |
| 6:5 | 398n.20 |
| 6:7 | 398n.20 |
| 6:8 | 398n.20 |
| 6:9 | 398n.20 |
| 6:12 | 398n.20 |
| 6:13 | 398n.20 |
| 6:18 | 398n.20 |

| | |
|---|---|
| 6:19 | 398n.20 |
| 6:21 | 398n.20 |
| 7:48 | 564n.29 |
| 10:35 | 55, 108n.68, 252 |
| 11:28 | 213n.28 |
| 14:44-45 | 108n.68 |
| 15:32-36 | 384 |
| 15:34 | 384 |
| 16 | 467 |
| 21:17 | 298 |
| 23-24 | 293 |
| 26:11 | 492 |

**Deuteronomy**

| | |
|---|---|
| Deuteronomy (Bk.) | 48n.91, 78, 80n.29, 204, 215n.32, 216n.35, 238n.53, 290, 290n.12, 293, 302, 594, 594n.24 |
| Deuteronomy 1–11 | 80n.29 |
| 1:17 | 615 |
| 2:7 | 204 |
| 2:35 | 188 |
| 5:11 | 250 |
| 5:20 | 250 |
| 6:4-5 | 553n.6 |
| 6:6b | 213n.29 |
| 6:7a | 213n.29 |
| 6:8 | 213n.29 |
| 7:9 | 229n.18 |
| 7:12 | 229n.18 |
| 8:3 | 553n.5 |
| 8:9 | 168 |
| 9:27 | 228n.14 |
| 14:29 | 204 |
| 16:1-17 | 109 |
| 16:19 | 385n.26, 615 |
| 17:8-13 | 254n.6 |
| 17:12 | 213n.28 |
| 17:14-20 | 403n.32 |
| Deuteronomy 20 | 617n.26 |
| 24:15 | 498n.45 |
| 24:19 | 204 |
| 26:13-14 | 250 |
| 26:15 | 80 |
| 26:19 | 48 |
| 28:1 | 48 |
| 28:9 | 73 |
| 28:12 | 204 |
| 30:12-14 | 577 |
| Deuteronomy 31 | 307 |
| Deut 31–32 | 300 |
| 31:9-11 | 351n.10 |

| | |
|---|---|
| 31:19 | 298 |
| 31:21 | 298 |
| 31:22 | 298 |
| 31:30 | 298 |
| Deuteronomy 32 | 291, 293n.19, 296, 301, 302, 305, 305n.67, 373, 495n.43 |
| 32:1-43 | 88n.5, 96, 288 |
| 32:4 | 204 |
| 32:30 | 199 |
| 32:44-45 | 298 |
| Deuteronomy 33 | 298, 302 |
| 33:2 | 436n.58 |

**Joshua**

| | |
|---|---|
| Joshua (Book) | 513 |
| 1:8 | 188 |
| 1:12 | 188 |
| 2:12 | 228n.11 |
| 2:14 | 228n.11 |
| Joshua 3–4 | 363 |
| Joshua 6 | 187 |
| 6:3 | 187 |
| 6:4-13 | 252 |
| 6:4 | 187 |
| 6:7 | 187 |
| 6:11 | 187n.13 |
| 6:14 | 187 |
| 6:15 | 187 |
| 10:1 | 188 |
| 23:10 | 199 |

**Judges**

| | |
|---|---|
| 1:8 | 188 |
| 1:12 | 188 |
| Judges 4–5 | 292n.17, 293, 300n.37, 303, 617n.26 |
| Judges 4 | 290, 300 |
| Judges 5 | 288, 290, 290n.9, 291, 293n.19, 296, 298, 300, 301, 302, 362n.30 |
| 5:1 | 298 |
| 5:3 | 298 |
| 5:12 | 68 |
| 5:14 | 362 |
| Judges 8 | 356n.23 |
| 8:22-23 | 400 |
| Judges 9 | 48, 400, 606 |
| 9:7-15 | 43 |
| 9:48 | 363 |
| 12:6 | 203 |
| 16:1-17 | 288 |
| 17:1-5 | 610 |

**Ruth**

| | |
|---|---|
| 2:20 | 228n.11 |

**1 & 2 Samuel**

| | |
|---|---|
| 1 & 2 Samuel | 21, 27, 27n.41, 29, 50, 54, 290, 293, 295, 296n.27, 301, 302, 305n.67, 314, 360, 515 |

**1 Samuel**

| | |
|---|---|
| 1 Samuel (Book) | 58, 186n.10, 473 |
| 1 Samuel 1–2 | 290n.10 |
| 1 Samuel 1 | 291n.13, 614 |
| 1 Samuel 2 | 291, 301, 303, 305 |
| 2:1 | 298 |
| 2:1-20 | 288 |
| 2:11 | 213n.28 |
| 1 Samuel 4–6 | 78, 80 |
| 4:4-6 | 108n.68 |
| 4:4 | 252 |
| 1 Samuel 7–12 | 606 |
| 1 Samuel 8 | 48, 291n.13 |
| 10:2 | 363 |
| 15:6 | 228n.11 |
| 1 Samuel 16 | 360 |
| 16:13 | 552 |
| 16:14-23 | 54 |
| 16:16-23 | 552 |
| 17:12 | 363 |
| 18:6-9 | 293 |
| 18:10 | 54, 552 |
| 1 Samuel 19–24 | 58 |
| 19:4 | 59 |
| 19:9 | 54, 552 |
| 19:11 | 59 |
| 19:13 | 610 |
| 19:16 | 610 |
| 20:8 | 229 |
| 20:14 | 228n.11 |
| 20:15 | 228n.11 |
| 1 Samuel 21 | 315, 473 |
| 21:5 | 473 |
| 21:11-16 | 57, 59 |
| 21:12 | 293 |
| 21:13 | 57 |
| 21:14 | 59 |
| 1 Samuel 22–30 | 315 |
| 1 Samuel 22 | 58 |
| 22:1 | 57, 59 |
| 22:9 | 58 |
| 23:2 | 57 |
| 23:4 | 57 |
| 23:11 | 57 |

23:12 57
23:14-28 58
23:17 203
23:27 57
1 Samuel 24 59
24:5 59
24:15 186n.10
1 Samuel 26 315
29:5 293

**2 Samuel**

2 Samuel (Book) 2, 21n.39, 27, 30, 186n.10, 231n.30, 291, 370
1:10 398n.21
1:17-27 288
1:17 54, 298
1:19-27 291n.15
2:4 472
2:26 469
3:8 228n.11
3:33-34 288, 293
3:33 298
3:37 385n.26
5:3 472
2 Samuel 6 55, 100, 354n.16, 355
6:2 249, 252
6:12 249
6:15 249
2 Samuel 7 20, 21, 26, 27, 27n.41, 28, 28n.44, 30, 31, 49n.94, 78, 100
7:1-17 21n.39
7:1 28n.44
7:6 28n.44, 79
7:8 22
7:9-11a 28n.44
7:9 22, 31
7:9a 28n.44
7:9b 28n.44(2x)
7:10 23, 28n.44
7:10b 23
7:11-16 399
7:11 23, 31
7:11a 28n.44
7:11b 27n.41, 27n.42, 28n.44(3x), 29
7:12 24, 28n.44
7:13 24
7:13b 28n.44
7:14-16 397n.19
7:14 23, 564
7:14b 28n.44
7:15 25, 26, 230n.25
7:16 25, 27n.41
7:18-29 595
7:22 595
2 Samuel 8 58, 111, 545n.45
8:1-14 59
8:1-13 113n.86
8:2 54
8:6 110
2 Samuel 9 229
9:8 186n.10
10 58
11 360
2 Samuel 11–12 58, 361n.28
11:11 108n.68
2 Sam 12 58, 315, 361
12:9-10 361
12:13 58
12:18 73n.15
12:22 202n.29
2 Samuel 15–19 364
2 Samuel 15–17 54, 59
2 Samuel 15 315
15:7-12 364
15:12 55
15:13 364
15:23 59
15:25 59
15:28 59
15:29 108n.68
15:32 55
16:2 59
16:8 55
16:17 231
2 Samuel 17 55, 56
2 Samuel 18 365
18:6 364
18:21-32 55
2 Samuel 19 364
19:15 364
19:22 60
2 Samuel 21–24 294
2 Samuel 22 16, 19, 43, 60, 288, 288n.1, 291, 291n.15, 295, 296, 301, 302, 305
22:1-51 291n.15
22:1 298
2 Samuel 23 302, 368, 369
23:1-7 291n.15
23:1-2 552
23:1 53, 60
23:5 32n.50

| | |
|---|---|
| 24:13 | 194 |

**Kings**

| | |
|---|---|
| Kings | 313, 360 |

**1 Kings**

| | |
|---|---|
| 1 Kings (Book) | 2, 359, 515 |
| 1 Kings 1 | 353, 359, 360, 365 |
| 1:11 | 106n.63, 107n.63 |
| 1:18 | 106n.63, 107n.63 |
| 1:48 | 360 |
| 1 Kings 2 | 291n.13 |
| 2:1-4 | 61 |
| 2:3 | 61 |
| 2:11 | 111 |
| 2:14 | 61 |
| 1 Kings 3–10 | 360n.25 |
| 1 Kings 3 | 360 |
| 3:1 | 110 |
| 3:8 | 193n.10 |
| 1 Kings 4 | 360 |
| 5:1-8 | 113n.86 |
| 5:1 | 111 |
| 5:11 | 14 |
| 5:16 | 399n.26 |
| 6:23-28 | 108n.69 |
| 1 Kings 8 | 78, 100 |
| 8:2 | 349 |
| 8:5 | 193n.10 |
| 8:6-7 | 108n.69 |
| 8:7 | 260 |
| 8:11 | 213n.28 |
| 8:22 | 262n.17 |
| 8:23 | 229n.18 |
| 8:31-32 | 254n.6 |
| 8:42 | 38 |
| 8:65 | 110 |
| 9:23 | 399n.26 |
| 1 Kings 10 | 360 |
| 10:23-25 | 113n.86 |
| 11:36 | 62 |
| 11:42 | 111 |
| 14:11 | 185 |
| 16:4 | 185 |
| 1 Kings 17–18 | 166 |
| 17:18 (LXX, 3 Rgns) | 464n.38 |
| 18:33 | 257n.11 |
| 20:31 | 228n.11 |
| 21:24 | 185 |
| 1 Kings 22 | 354n.15 |
| 22:27 | 380, 381 |

**2 Kings**

| | |
|---|---|
| 4 Kingdoms (LXX) | 513, 513n.23 |
| 2 Kings 6–7 | 162 |
| 6:15 | 187 |
| 8:12 | 69 |
| 8:13 | 186n.10 |
| 2 Kings 11 | 354n.16 |
| 11:12 | 398n.21 |
| 12:10 | 262n.17 |
| 14:7 | 69 |
| 15:29 | 358 |
| 2 Kings 17 | 81n.31 |
| 2 Kings 20 | 290 |
| 21:23 | 222n.55 |
| 2 Kings 22 | 618 |
| 23:15 | 40 |

**Chronicles**

| | |
|---|---|
| Chronicles | 20n.36, 21, 52, 262n.17, 302, 508 |

**1 Chronicles**

| | |
|---|---|
| 2:16 | 364 |
| 6:16 | 54 |
| 6:17 | 213n.28 |
| 6:33 | 459n.32 |
| 15:16 | 298 |
| 15:19 | 298 |
| 15:21 | 469 |
| 15:27 | 298 |
| 1 Chonickes 16 | 100, 290n.11, 293, 296, 298, 302, 305 |
| 16:4-7 | 54 |
| 16:8-36 | 288, 288n.1 |
| 16:9 | 298 |
| 16:41 | 302n.50 |
| 1 Chonickes 17 | 21, 26 |
| 17:7-8 | 22 |
| 17:9 | 23 |
| 17:9b | 23 |
| 17:10 | 23 |
| 17:11-13 | 24 |
| 17:13 | 23, 231 |
| 17:14 | 25 |
| 17:16 | 231 |
| 18-19 | 507 |
| 19:6 | 507 |
| 1 Chonickes 21 | 421n.31 |
| 22:10 | 564 |
| 23:4 | 469 |
| 23:5 | 54 |
| 25:1 | 552 |
| 28:2 | 108n.70 |
| 28:18 | 260 |
| 29:11 | 469 |

**2 Chronicles**

| | |
|---|---|
| 2 Chronicles | 262n.17, 302 |
| 2:6 | 16n.25 |
| 2:17 | 469 |
| 5:6 | 193n.10 |
| 5:13 | 302n.50, 459n.32 |
| 6:14 | 229n.18 |
| 6:16-29 | 16n.25 |
| 7:3 | 302n.50 |
| 7:6 | 302n.50 |
| 8:10 | 399n.26 |
| 16:9 | 214n.32 |
| 18:26 | 381 |
| 19:6 | 383 |
| 19:8 | 383 |
| 19:11 | 383 |
| 22:3-4 | 210n.15, 210n.16 |
| 24:8 | 262n.17 |
| 24:22 | 228n.11 |
| 25:2 | 214n.32, 215n.32 |
| 25:11-12 | 69n.10 |
| 2 Chronicles 29 | 77n.24 |
| 29:26-27 | 54 |
| 33:24 | 222n.55 |
| 34:12 | 469 |
| 35:20 | 507 |
| 35:22 | 553n.5 |
| 36:21 | 553n.5 |
| 36:22 | 553n.5 |

**Ezra**

| | |
|---|---|
| Ezra | 302, 478, 507 |
| 3:11 | 302n.50 |
| 4:36 | 573 |

**Nehemiah**

| | |
|---|---|
| Nehemiah | 478, 507 |
| 1:5 | 229n.18 |
| Nehemiah 9 | 615 |
| 9:32 | 229n.18 |
| 12:36 | 54 |

**Esther** 478

**Job**

| | |
|---|---|
| Job (Book) | 88n.5, 96, 296n.27, 453, 478n.7, 487, 487n.24, 591n.16, 592, 594, 597, 597n.28 |
| Job 4–14 | 122n.28, 137 |
| 4:6 | 242n.71 |
| 4:20 | 469 |
| 5:13 | 188 |
| 5:15 | 187n.15 |

| | |
|---|---|
| 5:16 | 242n.71 |
| 6:8 | 242n.71 |
| 6:19 | 242n.71 |
| 7:6 | 242n.71 |
| 7:7-8 | 199 |
| 7:16 | 196 |
| 8:13 | 242n.71 |
| 10:22 | 148n.18 |
| 11:18 | 242n.71 |
| 11:20 | 242n.71 |
| 14:2 | 199 |
| 14:7 | 242n.71 |
| 14:20 | 469 |
| 17:15 | 242n.71 |
| 19:10 | 242n.71 |
| 20:7 | 469 |
| 20:8 | 200, 200n.24 |
| 23:7 | 469 |
| 24:13-17 | 187 |
| 27:8 | 242n.71 |
| Job 31 | 383 |
| 31:26-28 | 383 |
| 31:35-37 | 591 |
| 34:36 | 469 |
| 38:2 | 594 |
| 40:2 | 594 |
| 40:8 | 594 |

**Psalms/Psalter**

| | |
|---|---|
| Psalms/Psalter | 1, 2, 3, 4, 5, 6, 9, 10n.4, 11n.8, 11n.9, 12, 12n.10, 12n.12, 14n.16, 14n.20, 15n.21, 15n.22, 16n.27, 17n.27, 20n.35, 20n.39, 21, 27n.42, 38, 39, 39n.67, 42n.79, 42n.80, 43n.81, 44n.84, 47n.88, 50, 51, 52, 53, 53n.1, 54, 55n.3, 55n.4, 55n.5, 56, 56n.6, 56n.7, 57n.9, 57n.10, 58, 58n.12, 60, 60n.17, 61, 62, 63, 64, 65, 66, 69n.10, 70, 72, 72n.14, 75, 76, 76n.21, 77n.23, 79n.28, 81n.33, 81n.34, 84, 87, 87n.3, 89, 91, 96, 97, 97n.1, 98, 99, 99n.4, 99n.5, 99n.6, 100n.7, 100n.8, 101n.21, 101n.28, 102n.28, 103n.32, 103n.33, 103n.34, 103n.35, 103n.36, |

**Psalms** (contd.)    103n.37, 103n.38,
103n.39, 103n.40,
103n.42, 103n.45, 105,
105n.57, 106n.57, 109,
110n.74, 112, 112n.80,
113, 114, 114n.88,
116n.2, 117, 117n.8,
118n.11, 118n.12,
119n.16, 120, 120n.18,
120n.21, 121n.24,
122n.28, 123n.33,
123n.35, 123n.35,
124n.36, 125n.42,
130n.67, 137, 138, 139,
139n.2, 140, 141, 142,
142n.7, 142n.8, 142n.9,
142n.10, 143, 143n.11,
143n.12, 143n.13, 144,
144n.14, 148n.18,
149n.19, 149n.20, 150,
150n.21, 150n.22, 151,
151n.24, 152, 153,
158n.9, 158n.11,
159n.14, 160n.20,
161n.22, 162n.25,
163n.29, 164n.31,
164n.32, 164n.33,
167n.42, 171n.56,
177n.64, 178n.65, 180,
181, 184, 184n.1,
185n.6, 185n.7, 185n.8,
186n.12, 189, 190n.2,
191n.4, 191n.5,
193n.11,199n.21,
201n.26, 202n.28,
202n.30, 205, 206n.2,
207n.7, 223, 224,
225n.1, 233n.36,
234n.40, 235n.43,
235n.44, 235n.46,
236n.49, 236n.50,
238n.52, 239n.55,
239n.56, 243n.73,
243n.74, 243n.75,
245n.78, 246, 247,
248n.1, 253, 257, 260,
262n.18, 263n.20, 264,
266n.22, 271n.27,
271n.28, 277n.33, 287,
288, 289, 289n.6,
292n.16, 297n.32, 298,
299, 299n.37, 303,
304n.61, 305, 305n.63,
305n.65, 305n.67,
305n.68, 306n.69,
306n.71, 307n.73, 308,

**Psalms** (contd.)    311, 311n.1, 311n.2,
312, 313, 314, 314n.5,
315, 315n.7, 316,
316n.9, 316n.10, 317,
317n.13, 318, 319,
319n.16, 319n.18, 320,
320n.20, 320n.21, 321,
321n.23, 322, 322n.26,
323, 323n.29, 324, 325,
325n.35, 325n.38, 326,
327, 327n.43, 328,
329n.46, 329n.50, 330,
330n.51, 331, 332, 333,
333n.61, 333n.62, 334,
334n.63, 335, 335n.65,
335n.66, 335n.67, 336,
336n.68, 337, 338, 340,
340n.1, 340n.2, 341,
342, 343, 344n.3, 345,
346, 346n.5, 347, 348,
349, 350n.7, 351n.9,
351n.10, 353n.14,
354n.15, 354n.16,
355n.17, 360n.25,
361n.26, 366, 367,
368n.2, 375n.7,
384n.23, 385n.28, 389,
391, 391n.1, 391n.3,
391n.4, 392, 392n.6,
393, 393n.8, 394,
394n.10, 394n.11,
395n.15, 396n.16,
396n.17, 398n.22,
398n.23, 401, 401n.27,
402, 402n.28, 403, 404,
404n.34, 405, 405n.36,
406, 407, 407n.1, 410,
416n.24, 426n.41, 440,
441, 442, 443, 443n.1,
447, 448, 448n.12, 449,
449n.16, 450, 450n.17,
451, 451n.18, 453,
453n.24, 454, 458, 459,
460, 461, 463, 463n.37,
466, 467, 468, 470, 471,
473, 474, 475, 476, 477,
478, 479, 480, 481, 483,
486, 489n.28, 490, 491,
491n.31, 494, 497, 498,
502, 503, 505, 510n.11,
511, 512n.22, 513n.25,
514, 517n.33, 518, 533,
534, 537, 537n.1,
537n.5, 538, 539, 540,
540n.24, 542, 542n.37,
543, 543n.38, 546,

**Psalms** (contd.)    546n.48, 547, 547n.62,
548, 548n.68, 549, 550,
551, 551n.3, 552,
552n.4, 553, 554, 555,
555n.9, 555n.10,
558n.13, 558n.14,
560n.20, 562n.24,
562n.25, 568, 569,
571n.41, 571n.42,
574n.50, 575, 575n.51,
575n.52, 576n.54,
576n.55, 578, 581, 582,
583, 584, 585, 588,
588n.10, 589n.12, 593,
593n.22, 594, 594n.23,
594n.24, 596, 596n.27,
597, 598, 599, 600, 601,
602, 603, 604, 604n.2,
607, 607n.7, 608, 610,
610n.11, 610n.12, 613,
618, 620, 622, 623,
623n.30, 624, 625

Psalms 1–144      376
Psalms 1–80       550
Psalms 1–75       103n.36
Psalms 1–72       121n.24, 138, 477,
479n.9
Psalms 1–59       64, 101n.14, 101n.15,
101n.16, 108n.65,
108n.67, 117n.8, 138,
139n.3, 152, 225n.1,
254n.6, 255n.7,
261n.15, 266n.23,
270n.24, 275n.30, 287
Psalms 1–50       13n.14, 16n.27, 17n.27,
18n.31, 33n.57, 41n.75,
50, 117n.8, 120n.20,
123n.34, 137, 238n.54,
264n.21, 270n.25,
271n.26, 287, 319n.18,
337, 416n.24, 417n.25,
440
**Book I**
Pss 1–41 (Book I)   1, 3, 57
Psalms 1–2         52, 341, 342, 343, 395
376
Psalm 1            14n.16, 60, 63, 139,
142, 323, 325n.35, 340,
342, 343, 345, 347, 392,
393, 393n.8, 395,
395n.12, 396, 398n.22,
398n.23, 405, 607, 621
1:1                219n.48, 342, 344
1:1-2              341, 346
1:1-3              60n.15

1:2                60, 342, 343, 345, 458
1:3                343
1:6                60n.16, 342, 343
Psalms 2–100       438, 439
Psalms 2–89        51, 391, 395, 395n.15,
396, 401, 402, 404, 405,
427, 438, 438n.64, 442,
439
Psalm 2            9, 10, 11, 14, 14n.16,
15, 16, 16n.27, 18, 45,
46, 49n.94, 60, 61, 63,
100, 108, 139, 139n.1,
142, 317, 318, 320,
320n.21, 342, 343,
344n.3, 374, 391, 395,
398n.22, 398n.23, 407,
490n.30, 503, 543, 544,
551n.2, 595, 606, 622
2:1-3              188
2:1                342
2:2                60, 188, 402, 403n.30,
553, 564
2:4                188, 595
2:6-11             10
2:6                60, 123n.34, 402
2:7                15, 32n.50, 51, 52, 63,
405n.36, 407n.1,
438n.64, 440, 441, 564,
564n.30, 564n.31
2:7ff.             10n.4
2:8                188
2:9                46
2:10               402
2:11               343, 499
2:12               61, 341, 342, 343, 345,
347, 374
2:12d              344n.3
Psalms 3–41        314, 314n.5, 342, 359
Psalms 3–17        140, 140n.4
Psalms 3–9         56
Psalms 3–7         56
Psalm 3            55, 56, 58, 63, 116n.2,
135n.75, 144, 144n.14,
315, 343, 347, 458, 471
3:1[0]             53
3:2[1]             55
3:3[2]             55
3:3                347
3:5[4]             55
3:6[5]             55, 56
3:7                243n.72
3:8                233n.36
3:8[7]             55

| | | | |
|---|---|---|---|
| 3:9 | 347 | 6:8 | 287 |
| Psalm 4 | 536, 610 | Psalm 7 | 55, 56, 58, 116n.2, 118, |
| Psalms 4–6 | 56 | | 142, 144n.14, 254n.6, |
| 4:1 | 456 | | 383, 544, 545 |
| 4:5 | 244n.76, 500 | Psalms 7–14 | 142 |
| 4:6 | 501n.49 | 7:1 | 243n.72, 492 |
| 4:7[6] | 530, 530n.54 | 7:2 | 233n.36 |
| 4:9[8] | 56 | 7:2-3 | 186 |
| Psalm 5 | 253, 254, 254n.6, 255, | 7:3-5 | 254n.6 |
| | 258, 259, 261, 264, 266, | 7:9 | 265 |
| | 270, 273, 274, 275, 278, | 7:10 | 243n.72 |
| | 284, 285, 286, 461, 462 | 7:10[11] | 610 |
| 5:2-4 | 255, 257, 257n.12, 259, | 7:12 | 186 |
| | 273 | 7:18 | 587 |
| 5:2-3a | 567 | Psalm 8 | 56, 97, 140n.4, 142, |
| 5:2 | 402 | | 376, 388, 462, 544, 613 |
| 5:3 | 259 | 8:4-7 | 564n.31 |
| 5:3a | 268 | 8:5 | 240n.60 |
| 5:4a | 268 | 8:11 | 376 |
| 5:4[3] | 56 | 8:15 | 376 |
| 5:5-8 | 255 | Psalms 9–10 | 66n.1, 607 |
| 5:5-7 | 217n.40, 255, 257, | Psalm 9 | 56, 139n.3, 142, 431, |
| | 257n.12, 258, 259, 260, | | 536 |
| | 274 | 9:1[0] | 56 |
| 5:5 | 256, 257, 258, 281, 282 | 9:1 | 470 |
| 5:6 | 255, 256, 257, 258, 264, | 9:9[8] | 530, 530n.54 |
| | 273, 281, 282 | 9:19 | 470 |
| 5:7 | 227n.5, 254, 257, | Psalm 10 | 139n.3, 142, 342, 431, |
| | 257n.13, 258, 264, 272, | | 536 |
| | 277, 281, 282 | 10:1-11 | 343 |
| 5:8-9 | 257, 257n.12 | 10:9 | 186 |
| 5:8 | 123n.34, 255, 256, 257, | 10:16 | 402 |
| | 258, 259, 260, 264 | Psalm 11 | 142, 462, 610 |
| 5:9-10 | 259 | 11–14 | 136 |
| 5:9 | 255, 256, 260, 264, 283, | 11:1-2 | 567 |
| | 284 | 11:1 | 383 |
| 5:10 | 254, 260, 272, 277, 482 | Psalm 12 | 142, 613 |
| 5:10a | 254 | 12:1 | 243n.72, 567 |
| 5:10b | 254 | 12:3-4 | 254 |
| 5:10-13 | 257 | 12:6 | 567 |
| 5:10-11 | 255, 257n.12, 260 | Psalm 13 | 3, 116, 117n.8, 118, |
| 5:11 | 69, 255, 256, 260, 264, | | 119n.15, 120, 120n.22, |
| | 272, 273, 282 | | 121, 121n.24, 122, |
| 5:12-13 | 257n.12, 260 | | 123n.34, 124, 124n.40, |
| 5:12 | 256, 261, 272, 283, 285 | | 129n.60, 131, 132, 133, |
| 5:13 | 258, 260 | | 135, 136, 137, 138, 142, |
| Psalm 6 | 118, 199, 332, 456, 462 | | 420n.29, 440 |
| 6:1-4 | 567 | 13:1-4 | 121 |
| 6:3 | 565, 567 | 13:1-2 | 567, 568 |
| 6:4 | 227n.5, 243n.72 | 13:2-5 | 124 |
| 6:5 | 208n.8, 233n.36 | 13:2ab | 124, 125 |
| 6:5[4] | 237 | 13:2a | 121, 124, 124n.37, 126, |
| 6:7[6] | 56 | | 133 |

| | | | |
|---|---|---|---|
| 13:2b | 121, 125, 128 | | 259n.14, 263, 265, 268, 272, 273, 278, 282 |
| 13:3ab | 124, 125, 125n.43 | | |
| 13:3a | 121, 121n.27, 123n.33, 123n.34 | 15:3 | 249, 268, 272, 278, 282 |
| | | 15[LXX14]:3 | 522n.43 |
| 13:3b | 121, 121n.27, 123n.33, 123n.34, 124n.37, 129, 134 | 15:4 | 249, 250, 260, 265, 272, 279 |
| | | 15:4a | 250 |
| 13:3c | 121, 121n.27, 124, 125, 125n.44 | 15:5 | 263, 265, 266, 268, 277, 278 |
| 13:4 | 122, 122n.28, 567 | 15:5a | 250 |
| 13:4ab | 122n.28, 125, 126, 133 | 15:8-11 (LXX) | 570 |
| 13:4a | 121, 125 | 15:8 | 260 |
| 13:4b | 122, 125, 125n.43, 128, 133 | 15:9 | 260 |
| | | 15:11 | 260 |
| 13:4c, 5ab | 122n.28, 125, 126, 130 | Psalm 16 | 571, 575n.52, 610 |
| 13:4c | 122, 122n.28, 125, 126 | Psalm 16 [LXX 15] | 456 |
| 13:4-6 | 122 | 16:6 | 243n.72 |
| 13:5 | 122, 122n.28, 126, 227n.5, 244n.76 | Psalm 16[LXX15]:7 | 468 |
| | | 16:8 | 571 |
| 13:5a | 122, 123, 123n.34, 125, 125n.44 | 16:8a | 218 |
| | | 16[LXX15]:8-11 | 569, 570 |
| 13:5ab | 122, 122n.28, 125, 126 | 16:8-10 | 570n.40 |
| 13:5b | 117n.8, 122, 123, 123n.34, 125, 126, 127, 128, 130, 134 | 16:10 | 569n.39, 571 |
| | | 16[LXX15]:10 | 575n.52 |
| | | 16:11 | 570 |
| 13:6 | 47, 117n.8, 120n.20, 122n.28, 124, 126, 132n.71, 134, 134n.73, 135 | Psalm 17 | 238, 254n.6 |
| | | 17:1 | 238, 567 |
| | | 17:2 | 238, 567 |
| 13:6ab | 127n.50 | 17:3 | 243n.72, 594 |
| 13:6a | 122, 123, 123n.34, 127, 127n.54, 128, 129, 130, 134 | 17:6 | 238 |
| | | 17:7-8 | 261 |
| | | 17:7 | 239, 243n.72 |
| 13:6b | 122, 123n.33, 126, 129, 130, 130n.67, 131, 134 | 17:8 | 238, 612 |
| | | 17:13 | 238 |
| 13:6c-d | 130 | 17:14a | 238 |
| 13:6c | 122, 126, 129, 130, 130n.64, 131, 131n.70 | Psalm 18 | 11, 15, 16, 16n.27, 19, 43, 45, 46, 47, 56, 57, 60, 61, 64, 140, 141, 142, 144, 144n.14, 288n.1, 373, 376, 388, 407, 407n.1, 411n.11, 439, 441, 606, 619 |
| Psalm 14 | 142 | | |
| Psalm 15 | 2, 97, 140n.4, 248, 248n.2, 249, 250, 251, 253, 257, 258, 259, 260, 263, 264, 264n.21, 265, 266, 268, 270, 272, 273, 274, 277, 280, 285, 286, 287, 456, 467 | | |
| | | Psalms 18–24 | 140 |
| | | Psalms 18–21 | 140 |
| | | 18:1[0] | 53, 56 |
| 15:1 | 251, 256, 257, 258, 262n.16, 263, 265, 268, 276, 278 | 18:1 | 46, 403n.30 |
| | | 18:1-3 | 140 |
| | | 18:2 | 15n.24, 243n.72 |
| 15:1-5 | 270 | 18:3 | 47, 243n.72 |
| 15:2-5 | 253, 273 | 18:4 | 486 |
| 15:2-4 | 278 | 18:5c (LXX) | 446n.8 |
| 15:2-3 | 260, 268, 270 | 18:7-15[8-16] | 617 |
| 15:2 | 249, 257, 257n.13, 258, | 18:7 | 46, 271 |

| | | | |
|---|---|---|---|
| 18:8-16 | 411n.11 | 20:9 | 36, 142, 243n.72 |
| 18:10-12 | 271 | 20:10 | 37, 39, 39n.69, 42 |
| 18:16 | 356n.22 | Psalm 21 | 10, 11, 15, 16n.27, |
| 18:17 [LXX 17:16] | 522n.43 | | 41n.76, 61, 140, 142, |
| 18:18 [LXX 17:17] | 527n.51 | | 143, 407, 606, 619 |
| 18:21[20] | 61 | 21:1 | 142, 402 |
| 18:21 | 86 | 21:2 | 47 |
| 18:22[21] | 61 | 21:2 (LXX) | 571n.43 |
| 18:25[24] | 61 | 21:5 | 15, 142 |
| 18:27 | 243n.72 | 21:6 | 47 |
| 18:28 | 47 | 21:7 | 140, 142, 402 |
| 18:28[27] | 61 | 21:8 | 128n.55 |
| 18:31 | 15n.24 | 21:9-14 | 46 |
| 18:31[30] | 61 | 21:10 | 414n.21 |
| 18:32 | 488 | 21:20 | 463 |
| 18:33-51[32-50] | 57 | 21:21 | 243n.72 |
| 18[LXX17]:34 | 463 | Psalm 22 | 3, 116n.2, 118n.10, |
| 18:44[43] | 57 | | 135n.75, 138, 139, |
| 18:46 | 15n.24 | | 139n.1, 140, 141, 142, |
| 18:50 | 227n.5, 396n.16 | | 143, 144, 145, 145n.15, |
| 18:51[50] | 60 | | 146, 147, 148, 149, 151, |
| 18:51 | 47, 403n.30 | | 152, 347, 551n.2, 613 |
| Psalm 19 | 140, 305n.65, 607 | Psalm 22 [LXX 21] | 463, 472 |
| 19:1 | 140, 621 | 22:1-5 | 143 |
| 19:4c | 621 | 22:1-2 | 143, 144, 145, 146, 147, |
| 19:5a | 621 | | 149 |
| 19:7 | 621 | 22:1 | 141, 142, 143, 565, 566, |
| Psalms 20–21 | 142 | | 571n.43 |
| Psalm 20 | 5, 9, 10, 11, 15, 16, 19, | 22:2 | 141, 142, 143 |
| | 20, 35, 41, 41n.76, | 22:3-5 | 144, 146, 147, 149 |
| | 42n.80, 44, 61, 90, 91, | 22:3 | 145 |
| | 92, 140, 142, 143, 407, | 22:4-5 | 142 |
| | 606, 619 | 22:4 | 244n.76 |
| Psalm 20 [LXX 19] | 527n.51 | 22:5 | 244n.76 |
| 20:1-5 | 486 | 22:6-8 | 144, 145, 146, 147, 149 |
| 20:1 | 35, 142 | 22:6 | 141, 144, 151, 565 |
| 20:2 | 35 | 22:7 | 12, 151 |
| 20:3 | 36, 46 | 22:7a | 565 |
| 20:4-5 | 44 | 22:7b | 565 |
| 20:4 | 35, 36, 38, 41, 42 | 22:8 | 565 |
| 20:5-6 | 142 | 22:9-10 | 144, 146, 147, 149, 151 |
| 20:5 | 36, 38 | 22:9 | 144, 145 |
| 20:6 | 36, 38, 42, 42n.78, 47, | 22:9-10[10-11] | 609 |
| | 140, 142, 243n.72, 486 | 22:10 | 144, 244n.76, 613 |
| 20:6b | 39 | 22:10[11] | 610 |
| 20:7-10 | 47 | 22:11 | 144, 145, 146, 147, 148, |
| 20:7[6] | 61 | | 149 |
| 20:7 | 15, 36, 39, 40, 41, | 22:12 | 141 |
| | 41n.75, 42, 42n.80, 44, | 22:12-18 | 144, 146, 147, 149 |
| | 403n.30 | 22:13-14 | 186 |
| 20:8-9 | 42n.80 | 22:13 | 482 |
| 20:8 | 36, 39, 41 | 22:14-16 | 141 |

| | |
|---|---|
| 22:14a | 565 |
| 22:15-17 | 142 |
| 22:15 | 148, 565, 568n.37 |
| 22:16 | 144, 148, 151 |
| 22:16b | 565 |
| 22:18 | 565 |
| 22:19-21 | 144, 146, 147, 149 |
| 22:19 | 148 |
| 22:20 | 144 |
| 22:21 | 144, 147, 149 |
| 22:22-31 | 144, 146, 147, 149 |
| 22:22 | 186, 233n.36 |
| 22:23 | 12 |
| 22:26 | 12 |
| 22:27 | 144 |
| 22:28 | 144 |
| 22:31 | 149 |
| Psalm 23 | 3, 139, 140, 141, 142, 143, 146, 147, 148, 149, 151, 161n.22, 249n.3, 455, 460n.33, 495, 607, 610 |
| 23:1-2 | 141 |
| 23:1 | 495 |
| 23:3 | 284, 495 |
| 23:4 | 141, 148, 151 |
| 23:5 | 148 |
| 23[22]:5 | 520n.41 |
| 23:6 | 141, 149 |
| Psalm 24 | 2, 3, 97, 100, 108, 139, 140, 141, 142, 143, 147, 149, 150, 150n.22, 151, 248, 249, 250, 251, 252, 253, 257, 258, 259, 260, 263, 264, 264n.21, 265, 268, 269, 270, 270, 272, 273, 277, 280, 285, 286, 331, 458, 535, 540n.24 |
| Psalm 24 [LXX 23] | 150n.22, 517, 518, 530 |
| 24:1-2 | 150 |
| 24:1 | 151, 621 |
| 24[LXX23]:1 | 518, 521 |
| 24:2-4 | 621 |
| 24[LXX23]:2 | 520 |
| 24:3-6 | 150, 248, 252 |
| 24:3-5 | 270 |
| 24:3 | 150, 257, 258, 263, 265, 273, 282, 554 |
| 24[LXX23]:3 | 521 |
| 24:4-6 | 347 |
| 24:4 | 150, 151, 258, 263, 265, 268, 272, 277, 278, 280 |
| 24[LXX23]:4 | 521 |
| 24:5 | 150, 251, 258, 260, 272 |
| 24[LXX23]:5 | 521, 523 |
| 24:6 | 251, 270, 281 |
| 24[LXX23]:6 | 524 |
| 24:7-10 | 150, 252, 259, 263, 283, 284, 408n.4, 441, 622 |
| 24:7-9 | 141, 554 |
| 24:7 | 252, 402 |
| 24[LXX23]:7 | 525, 528 |
| 24:8-9 | 270 |
| 24:8 | 402 |
| 24[LXX23]:8 | 521, 527n.51, 529 |
| 24:8a | 252 |
| 24:8b | 252 |
| 24:9-10 | 151 |
| 24:9 | 252, 402 |
| 24[LXX23]:9 | 525, 527 |
| 24:10 | 402 |
| 24[LXX23]:10 | 521, 528 |
| 24:10a | 252 |
| 24:10b | 252 |
| Psalms 25–28 | 141n.6, 147n.16 |
| Psalm 25 | 88, 92, 141, 142 |
| Psalm 25 [LXX 24] | 536 |
| 25:1 | 251, 498 |
| 25:3 | 185n.8 |
| 25[LXX24]:7 | 530, 531 |
| 25:11 | 240n.59, 241, 241n.63 |
| Psalm 26 | 253, 254, 254n.6, 261, 264, 265, 266, 267, 269, 270, 273, 275, 284, 285, 287 |
| 26:1-4 | 267 |
| 26:1-3 | 265 |
| 26:1-2 | 265 |
| 26:1 | 128n.55, 128n.56, 244n.76, 259n.14, 263, 264, 265, 266, 278, 282, 286 |
| 26:2 | 263, 265 |
| 26:3 | 263, 265 |
| 26:4-8 | 265 |
| 26:4-5 | 219n.48, 261 |
| 26:4 | 263 |
| 26:4a | 261 |
| 26:5 | 262, 263, 264, 265, 267 |
| 26:5b | 261 |
| 26:6-7 | 267 |
| 26:6 | 262, 262n.17, 263, 265, 280 |
| 26:7 | 262, 283 |
| 26:8-9 | 267 |

| | | | |
|---|---|---|---|
| 26:8 | 261, 262, 263, 264, 265, 268, 283, 284 | 28:7d | 420 |
| | | 28:8-9 | 269, 417, 421n.30 |
| 26:9 | 261, 264, 265, 267, 268, 273 | 28:8 | 47, 48n.93, 266, 269, 278, 403n.30, 417 |
| 26:9-11 | 265 | 28:9 | 243n.72, 267, 269, 417 |
| 26:9-10 | 265 | Psalm 29 | 2, 4, 97, 142, 153, 154, |
| 26:10 | 261, 263, 383n.20 | | 157n.7, 158n.8, 158n.9, |
| 26:11 | 123n.34, 259n.14, 263, 265, 266 | | 159n.12, 161n.22, 165, 165n.34, 166, 170, |
| 26:11b | 261 | | 170n.53, 171n.54, |
| 26:12 | 261, 262, 263, 265, 266, 285, 567 | | 171n.55, 172, 172n.58, 173, 174, 175, 176, 177, |
| Psalm 27 | 460n.33, 610 | | 178, 178n.66, 179, |
| Psalm 27 [LXX 26] | 472 | | 179n.68, 180, 180n.68, |
| 27:2 | 565 | | 180n.69, 181, 407, 408, |
| 27:3 | 128n.56, 244n.76 | | 408n.4, 409, 409n.5, |
| 27:4-6 | 249 | | 411n.10, 414, 415, 416, |
| 27[LXX26]:5 | 472 | | 417, 420, 421, 422, 425, |
| 27:6 | 514 | | 427, 432, 434, 437, 438, |
| 27:7 | 515 | | 439, 441, 442, 456n.28, |
| 27:10 | 609 | | 459, 460, 460n.33, 617 |
| 27:11 | 284 | 29:1-2 | 158, 160, 160n.20, 162, |
| 27:12 | 565 | | 163, 164n.29, 164n.32, |
| Psalm 28 | 2, 12, 253, 254, 254n.6, | | 179, 180n.68, 410, 411, |
| | 261, 266, 269, 270, 273, | | 411n.9, 413, 434, 438 |
| | 275, 278, 284, 285, 286, | 29:1-2a | 160, 160n.20 |
| | 416, 417, 418, 420, 421 | 29:1 | 113, 154, 156, 157, 158, |
| Psalms 28–30 | 407, 416, 419, 420, 421 | | 160, 161, 161n.21, 163, |
| 28:1-7 | 416, 417, 420 | | 164, 179, 409, 413, 415, |
| 28:1-4 | 267, 269, 270 | | 421, 617 |
| 28:1-2 | 416, 418 | 29:2-4 | 167n.40 |
| 28:1 | 416, 418, 421 | 29:2 | 154, 156, 158, 163, 164, |
| 28:1b | 420 | | 164n.31, 176, 178, 439 |
| 28:2-7 | 417 | 29:2b | 160, 160n.20, 411 |
| 28:2 | 267, 268, 269, 416, 417, | 29:3-4, 10 | 414 |
| | 418, 498 | 29:3-9 | 158, 162, 171, 409, 411, |
| 28:2a | 268, 416, 417 | | 412, 439 |
| 28:2b | 416, 417, 421 | 29:3-4 | 409, 410 |
| 28:3-5 | 266, 416 | 29:3 | 154, 156, 158n.11, 159, |
| 28:3 | 257n.13, 266, 267, 268, | | 160, 161, 163n.29, 164, |
| | 270, 273, 281, 416 | | 164n.29, 165, 176, 179, |
| 28:3a | 268 | | 410, 412, 413, 439 |
| 28:3b | 268 | 29:3a | 410 |
| 28:4 | 267, 268, 269 | 29:3ac | 410 |
| 28:4b | 268 | 29:3b | 410, 412 |
| 28:5-8 | 267 | 29:3c | 410 |
| 28:5 | 253, 266, 267, 269 | 29:4-5a | 161 |
| 28:6 | 267, 269, 417 | 29:4 | 154, 156, 158n.11, 159, |
| 28:6-7 | 269, 416, 420 | | 164, 164n.31, 410 |
| 28:7 | 244n.76, 266, 267, 269, | 29:4a | 410 |
| | 285, 417, 420, 421 | 29:4b | 410, 411 |
| 28:7a | 278, 420 | 29:5-9 | 179, 414, 415, 434 |
| 28:7c | 420 | 29:5-9b | 409 |
| | | 29:5 | 154, 156, 157, 159,176, |

| | |
|---|---|
| | 414, 415 |
| 29:5-6 | 176, 178 |
| 29:6 | 154, 156, 157, 161, 177, 178n.65, 414 |
| 29:7 | 154, 156, 157, 167, 167n.41, 168, 176, 180, 414 |
| 29:8-9 | 176 |
| 29:8 | 154, 156, 157, 169, 178, 414, 415 |
| 29[LXX28]:9 | 463 |
| 29:9 | 155, 156, 157, 158n.11, 162, 163, 163n.29, 164, 167n.42, 176, 414, 439 |
| 29:9a | 415 |
| 29:9ab | 411 |
| 29:9c | 163, 163n.29, 409, 411, 412, 413, 415, 419, 421 |
| 29:10-13 | 179, 180 |
| 29:10-11 | 158, 163, 163n.29, 164n.32, 171, 409, 412 |
| 29:10 | 155, 156, 157, 158, 165, 166, 170, 171, 176, 178n.67, 179n.68, 402, 409, 409n.6, 410, 412, 413, 414, 434 |
| 29:10a | 409n.6, 410, 412 |
| 29:10b | 410 |
| 29:11 | 155, 156, 157, 158, 158n.11, 164n.29, 164n.31, 171, 176, 177, 178n.67, 179, 414, 415, 417, 420, 421, 421n.30, 435, 439 |
| 29:11a | 415 |
| 29:11b | 415 |
| 29:12 | 155 |
| 29:13 | 155 |
| Psalm 30 | 30, 416, 417, 417n.25, 418, 419, 420, 421, 421n.31, 441 |
| 30:2-6 | 417, 419 |
| 30:2-4 | 418 |
| 30:2 | 417, 418 |
| 30:2a | 417 |
| 30:2b | 417, 419 |
| 30:3-4 | 417 |
| 30:5-6 | 417 |
| 30:6 | 417, 419 |
| 30:6a | 418, 420 |
| 30:6b | 420 |
| 30:7-13 | 419, 420 |
| 30:7-12 | 418 |

| | |
|---|---|
| 30:7-8a | 418 |
| 30:7 | 123n.34, 418 |
| 30:7b | 418 |
| 30:8a | 420 |
| 30:8b | 418, 420 |
| 30:9-11 | 418, 420 |
| 30:9 | 35, 418 |
| 30:9ab | 418 |
| 30:9a | 418 |
| 30:9b | 418 |
| 30:10 | 418 |
| 30:10a | 419 |
| 30:10b | 419 |
| 30:11a | 418, 419, 420 |
| 30:11b | 419 |
| 30:12 | 419, 420 |
| 30:13a | 419 |
| 30:13b | 420 |
| Psalm 31 | 116n.2, 141n.6, 142, 347 |
| 31:2 | 243n.72 |
| 31:4 | 284 |
| 31:5 | 565 |
| 31:6 | 244n.76 |
| 31:7 | 123n.34, 127n.52, 128n.56 |
| 31:8 | 467 |
| 31:9 | 467 |
| 31:10 | 240n.59 |
| 31:13 | 565 |
| 31:14 | 244n.76 |
| 31:14[15] | 610 |
| 31:15 | 123n.34, 127n.52, 128n.56 |
| 31:16 | 243n.72 |
| 31:17 | 233n.36 |
| 31:17[16] | 237 |
| 31:23 | 123n.34 |
| Psalms 32–34 | 342 |
| Psalm 32 | 139n.3, 332, 344 |
| Psalm 32 [LXX 31] | 467 |
| 32:1-2 | 344, 345, 346 |
| 32:1 | 341 |
| 32:2 | 341 |
| 32:5 | 240n.59, 245n.83 |
| 32:6 | 483n.17 |
| 32:8 | 284 |
| 32:8a | 208 |
| 32:10 | 244n.76, 344, 345 |
| 32:11 | 344 |
| Psalm 33 | 88, 97, 139n.3, 305n.65, 342, 344, 434, 551n.2 |

| | | | |
|---|---|---|---|
| Psalm 33 [LXX 32] | 456 | 36:8-10 | 273 |
| 33:1 | 344 | 36:8 | 261, 271, 272, 283, 612 |
| 33:5 | 227n.3, 345 | 36:9-10 | 270, 277 |
| 33:12 | 341, 344, 345, 346 | 36:9 | 261, 274 |
| 33:16 | 402 | 36:10 | 271 |
| 33:18-19a | 244 | 36:11-12 | 274 |
| 33:18 | 242n.70, 345 | 36:11 | 272 |
| 33:21 | 244n.76, 344 | 36:12 | 270, 271, 273, 274, 281 |
| 33:22 | 227n.5, 242n.70, 244, 345 | 36:13 | 270, 273, 274, 277, 282 |
| Psalm 34 | 58, 59, 88, 92, 144n.14, 344, 551n.2 | Psalm 37 | 88, 161n.22, 464, 464, 567, 596, 596n.26, 607 |
| 34[LXX33]:1 | 466 | 37:7 | 567 |
| 34:1[0] | 57 | 37:10 | 567 |
| 34:4[3] | 59 | 37:11 | 347 |
| 34:5[4] | 57, 59 | 37:32 | 565 |
| 34:6 | 243n.72 | 37:40 | 243n.72 |
| 34:8[7] | 57 | Psalms 38–40 | 141n.6 |
| 34:9 | 341, 344, 345 | Psalm 38 | 199, 332, 613 |
| 34:12[11] | 59 | 38 [LXX 37] | 463 |
| 34:18 | 243n.72 | 38:4 | 240n.59 |
| 34:20 | 344 | 38:11 | 565 |
| Psalms 35–36 | 141n.6 | 38:13-15 | 565 |
| Psalm 35 | 116n.2, 551n.2 | 38:16 | 35, 242 |
| 35:3 | 117n.6 | 38:18 | 240n.59 |
| 35:4-8 | 69 | Psalm 39 | 191, 192, 195, 196, 199, 202, 551n.2, 596, 607, 624 |
| 35:4 | 565 | | |
| 35:5-6 | 386 | 39:2-4a | 192 |
| 35:8 | 188 | 39:2-3 | 196 |
| 35:9 | 47 | 39:5-7 | 196 |
| 35:10 | 590n.15 | 39:5 | 191n.7, 192, 193, 194, 195, 196, 200, 202, 205 |
| 35:11 | 565 | 39:5a | 193 |
| 35:17 | 567 | 39:5c | 194 |
| 35:19 | 565 | 39:6-7 | 193, 194, 196 |
| 35:24 | 265 | 39:6 | 597 |
| Psalm 36 | 253, 254, 254n.6, 261, 266, 270, 273, 275, 284, 285, 286 | 39:6b | 196 |
| | | 39:7-8a[8-9a] | 243 |
| 36:1 | 46, 271, 403n.30 | 39:8 | 196 |
| 36:2-5 | 253, 270, 271, 273, 278, 279 | 39:8[7] | 242 |
| | | 39:9 | 196 |
| 36:2 | 270, 272, 274 | 39:8-12 | 193 |
| 36:2a | 271n.26 | 39:10-14 | 196 |
| 36:3 | 254, 272 | 39:10-11 | 196 |
| 36:4 | 221n.54, 258, 272, 277, 281 | 39:11 | 240n.59 |
| | | 39:11-12 | 597 |
| 36:5 | 227n.4, 272, 273, 274, 277, 281 | 39:12c | 193 |
| | | 39:13-14 | 193 |
| 36:6-10 | 270, 271, 274 | Psalm 40 | 66n.1 |
| 36:6-7 | 271 | 40:2 | 567 |
| 36:6 | 243n.72 | 40:5 | 341, 344, 345, 346 |
| 36:7 | 227n.4 | 40:9 | 227n.5 |

| | | | |
|---|---|---|---|
| 40:10 | 227n.4 | | 471, 607, 613, 615 |
| 40:11 | 345 | Psalm 44 [LXX 43] | 467 |
| 40:12 | 240n.59 | 44:2-9 | 197 |
| 40:13 | 483n.17 | 44:2 | 204, 351, 351n.10 |
| Psalms 40–44 | 466n.42 | 44:3-4 | 352 |
| Psalms 40–41 | 341, 342 | 44:3 | 243n.72 |
| Psalm 41 | 342, 344, 344n.4, 345, | 44:4 | 74, 402 |
| | 347, 348, 471 | 44:5 | 259 |
| 41:2 | 341, 342, 344, 346 | 44:7 | 243n.72 |
| 41:4 | 345 | 44:9 | 351, 351n.10, 352 |
| 41:5-9[6-10] | 609, 610 | 44:10-20 | 351, 352 |
| 41:9 | 218, 566, 567 | 44:10 | 72 |
| 41:9a | 565 | 44:11 | 72 |
| 41:9b | 565 | 44:13 | 72 |
| 41:10 | 345, 347, 493n.39 | 44:14-15 | 72 |
| 41:12 | 345 | 44:16 | 351 |
| Psalm 42 | 349, 349n.2, 351, 357 | 44:17 | 72 |
| Psalm 42 [LXX 41] | 467 | 44:18 | 73n.15 |
| Psalms 42–44 | 358 | 44:18-22 | 72, 73 |
| Psalms 42–43 | 66n.1, 184n.4, 351n.8, | 44:18-19 | 73 |
| | 351n.9, 352n.12, 357, | 44:18[17] | 72 |
| | 365 | 44:19 | 352 |
| Psalms 42–49 | 2, 349, 365 | 44:20 | 72 |
| **Book  II** | | 44:21 | 72, 73, 499n.46 |
| Pss 42–72 (Book II) | 1, 2, 3, 58, 392n.5 | 44:22 | 72, 73 |
| 42:2-3 | 350 | 44:24-27 | 72 |
| 42:3 | 208n.8 | 44:24 | 351 |
| 42:4 | 350 | 44:26 | 227n.4 |
| 42:4d | 184n.4 | 44:27 | 352 |
| 42:5 | 242n.70, 350, 565, 566, | Psalm 45 | 15, 112, 352, 357, 407, |
| | 567 | | 487, 544, 606, 618 |
| 42:6 | 184n.4, 565, 566 | 45 [LXX 44] | 456, 465, 466, 467 |
| 42:7 | 349, 350, 350n.6 | 45 [LXX 46] | 458 |
| 42:8 | 227n.3, 350 | 45:1 | 487n.23, 492 |
| 42:9 | 350n.6, 351 | 45:2-7 | 405n.35 |
| 42[LXX41]:9 | 227n.8 | 45:2 | 483 |
| 42:10 | 184n.4, 349 | 45:5 | 405n.35 |
| 42:11 | 242n.70, 350 | Psalms 45–49 | 355 |
| 42:11d | 184n.4 | Psalms 45–48 | 358 |
| 42:12 | 184n.4 | 45:7 | 46, 47, 352 |
| Psalm 43 | 349n.2, 351, 357, 471 | 45:9 | 352, 402 |
| 43:1 | 350 | 45:11 | 353, 402 |
| 43:2 | 184n.4, 349 | 45:13 | 44, 353 |
| 43:3-4 | 351 | 45:16 | 353 |
| 43:3 | 284, 351 | 45:18 | 487 |
| 43:4 | 500 | Psalm 46 | 70, 97, 353, 353n.14, |
| 43:5 | 184n.4, 242n.70, 565, | | 355, 357, 415, 438, 618 |
| | 566 | Psalms 46–48 | 407 |
| Psalms 44–49 | 349n.2 | 46:1 | 492 |
| Psalm 44 | 65, 66n.1, 71, 73, 76, | 46:2 | 415 |
| | 351, 351n.9, 352, | 46:2-8 | 413n.19 |
| | 352n.12, 357, 465, 466, | 46:2 (LXX) | 573 |

| | | | |
|---|---|---|---|
| 46:3 | 492n.35 | 49:10-11 | 356 |
| 46:4 | 353 | 49:12-13 | 356 |
| 46:5 | 271, 499 | 49:12 | 240n.60 |
| 46:6 | 574, 575n.50 | 49[LXX48]:13 | 468 |
| 46:6 (LXX) | 572, 573, 574, 574n.50, | 49:14 | 357 |
| | 575, 575n.51, 576n.54 | 49:15-16 | 357 |
| 46:7 | 186, 355 | 49:15 | 243n.72 |
| 46:10 | 354 | 49:16 | 284, 356n.22, 484 |
| Psalm 47 | 97, 101, 112, 114, | 49:17-21 | 357 |
| | 114n.88, 354, 354n.16, | 49:17 | 358 |
| | 357, 402n.29, 408n.4, | 49[LXX48]:20 | 470 |
| | 413n.19, 433, 438, 441, | 49[LXX48]:21 | 468 |
| | 459, 555n.9, 573, | Psalm 50 | 70, 97, 327, 349, 365, |
| | 575n.52, 622 | | 366, 429n.50, 430, |
| 47:2 | 100, 354, 402 | | 430n.52, 440, 500, |
| 47:3 | 433 | | 551n.2, 574n.50 |
| 47:4 | 354 | 50:5 | 500, 501 |
| 47:5 | 573n.45 | 50:7 | 430n.52, 620n.29 |
| 47:5[LXX46:6] | 575n.52 | 50:8-9 | 500, 501 |
| 47:6-8 | 355 | 50:9 | 501n.50 |
| 47:6 | 354, 402, 573, 575, | 50:12 | 502n.51 |
| | 576n.53 | 50:13 | 500, 501, 501n.50 |
| 47[LXX46]:6 | 575n.52 | 50:14 | 500, 501 |
| 47:7 | 100, 113, 402 | 50:16-21 | 279 |
| 47:8 | 100, 101 | 50:16 | 499 |
| 47[LXX46]:8 | 467 | 50:23 | 243n.72, 500, 501 |
| 47:9 | 354, 574n.48 | Psalms 51–100 | 13n.14, 14n.17, 16n.25, |
| 47:9[8] | 107n.63 | | 17n.27, 18n.31, 27n.42, |
| 47:10 | 354, 573n.45 | | 29n.45, 29n.46, 30n.47, |
| Psalm 48 | 70, 97, 150n.22, 331, | | 50, 58n.13, 64, |
| | 355, 433, 438, 555n.9, | | 106n.63, 185n.6, 189, |
| | 618 | | 191n.6, 279n.34, 287, |
| 48:2-9 | 413n.19 | | 360, 361, 361n.28, 365, |
| 48:2 | 402, 427n.45, 433, | | 366, 393n.7, 424n.34, |
| | 487n.22, 554 | | 424n.35, 424n.36, |
| 48:3 | 38, 349, 355, 482n.16 | | 425n.37, 425n.38, |
| 48:5-9 | 355 | | 426n.40, 426n.41, |
| 48:5-8 | 486n.22 | | 426n.42, 429n.50, 440, |
| 48:6 | 356 | | 454n.26, 624 |
| 48:9 | 427n.45 | Psalms 51–72 | 2, 314, 314n.5, 315n.7, |
| 48:9-10 | 355 | | 319, 337, 349, 359, |
| 48:12-13 | 349, 355 | | 359n.24, 364, 365, 366 |
| 48:13-14 | 355 | Psalms 51–64 | 58 |
| 48:13 | 187 | Psalm 51 | 58, 66n.1, 144n.14, 145, |
| Psalms 49–51 | 171n.55 | | 315, 327, 332, 360, 361, |
| Psalm 49 | 191, 356, 356n.22, 357, | | 361n.28, 365, 366 |
| | 358, 607 | 51:1 | 227n.3 |
| 49:2 | 356 | 51:1-2 | 145 |
| 49:4-5 | 357 | 51:2 | 240n.59 |
| 49:5 | 240n.59 | 51:2[0] | 58 |
| 49:6 | 356, 358 | 51:5 | 240n.59 |
| 49:7 | 240n.60, 356 | 51:5-7 | 361n.26 |
| 49:8 | 356 | 51:6 | 245n.83 |

| | | | |
|---|---|---|---|
| 51:6[4] | 58 | 56:1-2a | 145 |
| 51:9 | 240n.59, 245n.83, 483 | 56:1[0] | 59 |
| 51:16 | 361 | 56:4 | 128n.56, 243n.72 |
| 51:16[14] | 58 | 56:8-9 | 212 |
| 51:17 | 567 | 56:13b | 431 |
| 51:18 | 361 | 56:14 | 212 |
| 51:19[17] | 58 | 56:14[13] | 59 |
| 51:20-21 | 361, 361n.27 | Psalm 57 | 58, 59, 118, 144n.14, 224 |
| Psalm 52 | 58, 144n.14, 253, 254, 254n.6, 261, 266, 270, 275, 278, 284, 285, 286, 315, 454, 455 | Psalm 57 [LXX 56] | 456 |
| | | 57:1[0] | 59 |
| Psalm 52 [LXX 51] | 467 | 57:1 | 224 |
| 52:1 | 275 | 57:2 | 224, 261, 612 |
| 52:2 | 275 | 57:2[1] | 59 |
| 52:2[0] | 58 | 57:3 | 224, 227n.5, 595 |
| 52:3 | 187n.15, 278, 279, 281, 467 | 57:4 | 224 |
| | | 57:5 | 187n.15, 224, 482n.16 |
| 52:3-7 | 253, 276, 279 | 57:6 | 224 |
| 52:3-6 | 275, 276, 278, 279, 280 | 57:7 | 224 |
| 52:4 | 275, 276, 277, 278, 281 | 57:8 | 224 |
| 52:5 | 277, 281 | 57:9 | 224 |
| 52:6 | 258, 276, 277, 281 | 57:10 | 224 |
| 52:7 | 262n.16, 273, 275, 276, 277, 277n.33, 278, 279, 280, 282 | 57:11 | 224 |
| | | Psalm 58 | 90, 91, 92, 92n.11, 462, 463 |
| 52:7[5] | 58 | Psalm 58 [LXX 57] | 456, 462 |
| 52:8-9 | 276, 276n.32, 277, 280 | 58:1 | 462 |
| 52:9 | 275n.31, 276, 278, 282, 285 | 58:4 | 92n.11 |
| | | 58:11 | 92n.11 |
| 52:10-11 | 277 | Psalm 59 | 5, 58, 59, 144n.14, 184, 184n.2, 184n.3, 185, 185n.6, 187, 188, 189, 464 |
| 52:10 | 127n.52, 128n.56, 276, 277, 278, 279, 280 | | |
| 52:11 | 280 | Psalm 59 [LXX 58] | 456, 462 |
| Psalm 53 [LXX 52] | 467 | 59:1[0] | 59 |
| 53:6[7] | 243 | 59:2 | 184n.3, 243n.72 |
| Psalm 54 | 58, 144n.14, 326 | 59:3 | 233n.36 |
| Psalm 54 [LXX 53] | 456, 458, 467 | 59:4 | 184n.3, 187n.14, 188 |
| 54:1 | 243n.72 | 59:4[3] | 59 |
| 54:2[0] | 58 | 59:5 | 184n.3, 187, 188 |
| 54:3 | 233n.36 | 59:6 | 185, 185n.6, 188 |
| 54:4[6] | 610 | 59:7 | 184, 187, 188, 189 |
| Psalm 55 | 613 | 59:8 | 187, 188, 483, 488 |
| Psalm 55 [LXX 54] | 467 | 59:9 | 185n.6, 188 |
| Psalm 55 [LXX 56] | 456, 471 | 59:10-11 | 184 |
| 55:14-15 | 493n.39 | 59:10 | 184n.3 |
| 55:14 | 493 | 59:12 | 184n.3 |
| 55:16 | 243n.72 | 59:12[11] | 59 |
| 55:22 | 187n.15 | 59:13 | 188 |
| 55:24 | 127n.52, 128n.56 | 59:14 | 184n.2, 188, 189 |
| Psalm 56 | 58, 59, 116n.2, 144, 144n.14, 212, 610 | 59:15 | 184, 185, 187, 188, 189 |
| | | 59:16 | 184n.2, 184n.3, 189 |

| | | | |
|---|---|---|---|
| 59:17-18 | 184n.3 | 68:7 | 362 |
| 59:18 | 184 | 68:13 | 356n.23, 362 |
| Psalms 60–150 | 61n.18, 64, 74n.16, | 68[LXX67]:13 | 465, 465n.41 |
| | 74n.17, 101n.17, | 68:14 | 484 |
| | 101n.18, 201n.26, | 68:15 | 363, 499 |
| | 206n.1, 211n.21, 222 | 68:16-17 | 349 |
| Psalm 60 | 58, 59, 66n.1, 76, | 68:18 | 554 |
| | 144n.14, 560n.20 | 68:18[LXX67:19] | 575n.52 |
| Psalm 60 [LXX 59] | 456, 458, 464, 466 | 68:19 | 113n.86, 362, 576, 577 |
| 60:5 | 243n.72 | 68:19[18] | 576 |
| 60[LXX59]:7 | 465 | 68:22-24 | 362 |
| 60:3 | 486 | 68:23-24 | 363 |
| 60:8-10[6-8] | 59 | 68:24 | 402 |
| 60:8 | 363n.31 | 68:25 | 259, 362 |
| 61:3 | 284 | 68:26 | 362 |
| 61:5 | 249, 249n.3, 261 | 68:27 | 271, 362 |
| 61:7 | 17, 249n.3 | 68:29 | 362 |
| 61:8[7] | 237 | 68:30 | 113n.86, 362, 500 |
| Psalm 62 | 610 | 68:31-32 | 362 |
| 62:1 | 243n.72 | 68:32 | 499 |
| 62:2[1] | 243 | 68:34-36 | 271 |
| 62:7 | 243n.72 | Psalm 69 | 65, 66n.1, 74, 464, |
| Psalm 63 | 58, 59, 144n.14, 315 | | 483n.17, 551n.2, 569 |
| 63:1[0] | 53 | Psalm 69 [LXX 68] | 466 |
| 63:1[2] | 610 | 69:1 | 243n.72, 492n.34 |
| 63:3-6 | 271 | 69:2 | 233n.36, 483 |
| 63:3[2] | 59 | 69:3 | 242n.70, 483n.17 |
| 63:8 | 261, 612 | 69:4 | 566, 569 |
| 63:12 | 17 | 69:9 | 566, 569 |
| 63:12[11] | 59 | 69:10-12 | 74 |
| Psalm 64 | 118 | 69:10 | 74 |
| 64[LXX63]:2 | 465 | 69:13 | 243n.72 |
| 64:4-5 | 187n.15 | 69:14[13]b | 237 |
| 64:10 | 204 | 69:15 | 483n.17 |
| Psalm 65 | 459, 613 | 69:17[16]a | 237 |
| Psalm 65 [LXX 64] | 456 | 69:21 | 566, 569 |
| 65:2 | 483 | 69:23-28 | 69 |
| 65:3 | 240n.59, 245n.83 | 69:23 | 70 |
| 65:5 | 249, 341, 346, 486 | 69:25 | 569, 569n.38 |
| Psalm 66 | 66n.1, 349n.3, 359, 459 | 69:27 | 74 |
| Psalm 66A | 97 | 69:29 | 243n.72 |
| 66:6 | 493n.36 | 69:31-32 | 74 |
| 66:11 | 482n.16 | 69:34 | 74 |
| 66:13 | 554 | 69:35 | 243n.72 |
| 66:15 | 554 | 69:36 | 75 |
| Psalm 67 | 349n.3, 359 | 69:36-37 | 74 |
| Psalm 67 [LXX 66] | 456 | Psalm 70 | 116n.2, 359, 515 |
| Psalm 68 | 349, 361, 362, 362n.30, | 70 [LXX 69] | 463 |
| | 364, 491, 615 | 70:4 | 243n.72 |
| 68:2 | 362 | Psalms 71–72 | 314 |
| 68:5 | 362 | Psalm 71 | 14, 118, 349n.3, 359 |
| 68:7-10[8-11] | 617 | 71:2 | 233n.36, 243n.72 |

| | | | |
|---|---|---|---|
| 71:3 | 243n.72, 610 | 73:23 | 127n.52 |
| 71:9 | 314 | 73:24 | 283, 284 |
| 71:14 | 127n.52, 242n.70 | 73:25 | 601 |
| 71:17-18a | 609 | 73:27 | 282 |
| Psalm 72 | 10, 11, 14, 16, 17, | 73:28 | 272, 283, 284, 285, 598 |
| | 17n.27, 18, 45, 61, 64, | Psalm 74 | 66, 66n.1, 76, 76n.21, |
| | 100, 314, 317, 318, 320, | | 199, 463 |
| | 344n.4, 349, 359, 360, | Psalm 74 [LXX 73] | 467 |
| | 360.25, 365, 366, 391, | 74:1 | 460n.34 |
| | 392, 395, 407, 442, 595, | 74:2 | 493 |
| | 606, 619 | 74:9 | 194, 194n.12 |
| 72:1-7 | 46 | 74:10 | 208n.8 |
| 72:1-6 | 360 | 74:12-17 | 197 |
| 72:1-3 | 61 | 74:12 | 243n.72, 259, 402 |
| 72:1 | 359 | 74:13-15 | 493 |
| 72:4 | 47, 243n.72 | 74:20 | 380n.14 |
| 72:5 | 499 | Psalm 75 | 97 |
| 72:8-15 | 360 | Psalm 75 [LXX 74] | 459n.31, 462 |
| 72:8 | 595 | 75:8-10 | 43n.81 |
| 72:9 | 360 | 75:10 | 38n.63 |
| 72:11 | 438n.64, 442 | Psalm 76 | 70, 97, 402, 618 |
| 72:12-14 | 61 | 76 [LXX 75] | 456 |
| 72:13 | 47, 243n.72 | 76:5 | 480n.13 |
| 72:16-17 | 360 | 76:8-9 | 470 |
| 72:16 | 61 | 76:9 | 243n.72 |
| 72:18-19 | 14 | 76:10 | 487 |
| 72:18 | 14 | 76:11 | 466n.42 |
| 72:19a | 14 | 76:12 | 402 |
| 72:19b | 14 | Psalm 77 | 66n.1, 135n.74, 138, |
| 72:20 | 314, 316n.9, 392n.5 | | 199, 515 |
| Psalms 73–150 | 79n.28, 85 | 77[LXX76]:11 | 466 |
| Psalms 73–83 | 17 | 77:12-21 | 197 |
| Psalm 73 | 280, 283, 284, 515, 607 | 77:13 | 204 |
| **Book III** | | 77:16-19[17-20] | 617 |
| Pss 73–89 (Book III) | 1, 3, 62 | 77:16 | 494 |
| 73:1 | 280, 598 | 77:16-20 | 298 |
| 73:2 | 282 | 77:17-20 | 408n.4, 441 |
| 73:3 | 280, 281, 284 | 77:72 | 467 |
| 73:3-12 | 283 | Psalm 78 | 65, 77n.22, 78, 78n.25, |
| 73:6 | 281 | | 80, 80n.30, 81n.31, |
| 73:8-9 | 281 | | 81n.33, 82n.37, 83, 85, |
| 73:11 | 280 | | 86, 100, 491, 551n.2, |
| 73:12 | 282 | | 615, 619, 620 |
| 73:13-14 | 280 | Psalm 78 [LXX 77] | 467 |
| 73:13 | 263n.20, 280 | 78:2-4 | 82 |
| 73:15 | 281 | 78:9 | 82 |
| 73:16-17 | 280 | 78:11 | 82 |
| 73:17 | 280, 283, 284 | 78:36 | 499 |
| 73:18-20 | 284 | 78:38 | 245n.83 |
| 73:18 | 282 | 78:54-56 | 82 |
| 73:20 | 282 | 78:56-64 | 76, 77, 83 |
| 73:22 | 482n.16 | 78:57 | 185n.8 |

| | | | |
|---|---|---|---|
| 78:58-60 | 80 | Psalm 84 | 70, 97, 100 |
| 78:59-70 | 75, 78 | Psalm 84 [LXX 83] | 462 |
| 78:59-67 | 78 | Psalms 84–89 | 349n.1 |
| 78:59-63 | 77n.22 | Psalms 84–88 | 14 |
| 78:59-60 | 83 | 84:3 | 402 |
| 78:59 | 78 | 84:4 | 259 |
| 78:60 | 77, 78, 79 | 84:5 | 341, 346 |
| 78:61-66 | 80 | 84:6 | 341 |
| 78:61 | 78, 80 | 84:9-10 | 259 |
| 78:62 | 78 | 84:9 | 486 |
| 78:63 | 78 | 84:10 | 17, 46, 403n.30 |
| 78:64 | 78, 80, 493 | 84:12 | 259n.14 |
| 78:65 | 78 | 84:13 | 341, 346 |
| 78:66 | 78, 80, 82n.36 | Psalm 85 | 66, 199, 239 |
| 78:67-68 | 80 | 85:2 | 245n.83 |
| 78:67 | 77, 78, 80, 494n.41 | 85:5 | 204 |
| 78:68 | 77, 79 | 85:8[7] | 239 |
| 78:69 | 79, 80, 81n.32 | Psalm 86 | 235, 459 |
| 78:70-71 | 46 | 86:1 | 235 |
| 78:70 | 79, 396n.16, 403n.30 | 86:2 | 46, 236, 243n.72 |
| Psalm 79 | 66, 66n.1, 76, 76n.21, 77n.24, 81n.33, 515 | 86:4 | 46, 251, 498 |
| | | 86:5 | 241, 241n.63 |
| 79:2 | 46 | 86:7 | 236 |
| 79:6-7 | 78n.24 | 86:8 | 590n.15 |
| 79:8 | 245n.83 | 86:13 | 236 |
| 79:10 | 69, 350n.4 | 86:14 | 236 |
| 79:13 | 95 | 86:16 | 46, 243n.72, 567 |
| 79:20 | 46 | 86:17 | 494, 567 |
| Psalm 80 | 66n.1, 76 | Psalm 87 | 70, 97, 100, 454, 455, 459, 464 |
| Psalm 80 [LXX 79] | 466 | | |
| 80:1 | 492n.34 | 87:3 | 457 |
| 80:2 | 494 | 87:7 | 271 |
| 80:3 | 243n.72 | Psalm 88 | 16n.25, 199 |
| 80:5 | 208n.8 | Psalm 88 [LXX 87] | 85, 457, 458, 461, 467 |
| 80:7 | 243n.72 | 88:7 | 380n.14, 483n.17 |
| 80:9-12 | 197 | 88:8 | 610 |
| 80:9 | 483 | 88:18 | 610 |
| 80:17 | 564n.31 | Psalm 89 | 10, 11, 14, 16, 17, 18, 19, 20, 20n.35, 21, 21n.39, 26, 27, 27n.41, 28n.43, 29, 30, 48n.93, 50, 52, 62, 63, 66, 66n.1, 100, 168n.46, 183n.5, 271, 317, 318, 320, 344n.4, 391, 392, 395, 407, 427, 439, 440, 551n.2, 595, 607, 613, 615, 618 |
| 80:19 | 243n.72 | | |
| Psalm 81 | 97, 150n.22, 331, 429n.50, 430, 440 | | |
| 81 [LXX 80] | 462 | | |
| 81:6 | 494 | | |
| 81:8-9 | 430n.52 | | |
| 81:12-14 | 430n.52 | | |
| Psalm 82 | 97, 150n.22, 331, 459 | | |
| 82:1 | 618 | | |
| 82:6 | 482 | 89 [LXX 88] | 458, 467 |
| Psalm 83 | 66n.1, 76 | 89:1-2 | 29 |
| 83:3 | 185 | 89:1 | 16n.25 |
| 83:10-13 | 197 | 89:2-38 | 20n.38, 197 |
| 83:10 | 482n.16 | 89:2-4 | 26 |

| | | | |
|---|---|---|---|
| 89:3-6 | 26 | 89:35-37 | 595 |
| 89:3 | 396n.16 | 89:35 | 19n.34, 25, 396n.16 |
| 89:4 | 46, 403n.30 | 89:35[34] | 62 |
| 89:4-5 | 10, 15, 14n.29, 21, 26, 29, 31, 52 | 89:36 | 19n.34, 25, 27n.42, 29 |
| | | 89:37-38[36-37] | 62 |
| 89:4[3] | 62 | 89:37 | 25 |
| 89:5-7 | 29 | 89:38 | 25 |
| 89:6 | 26 | 89:39-52 | 14, 317, 596 |
| 89:8-11a | 28 | 89:39-46 | 596 |
| 89:10bβ | 27 | 89:39-40[38-39] | 62 |
| 89:11 | 27 | 89:39 | 48n.93, 398n.21, 403n.30 |
| 89:12aαβ | 27 | | |
| 89:13 | 168n.46 | 89:40 | 19, 19n.34, 26, 46, 403n.30 |
| 89:13a | 27 | 89:46-51 | 392 |
| 89:15-16 | 271 | 89:47-52[46-51] | 62 |
| 89:15 | 27, 32n.50, 271 | 89:49 | 396n.16 |
| 89:16 | 29, 341, 346 | 89:50[49] | 63 |
| 89:18-19 | 29 | 89:50 | 19n.34, 26, 596 |
| 89:18 | 46, 402 | 89:51-52 | 49 |
| 89:20-38 | 9, 10, 15, 17n.29, 19, 21n.39, 52 | 89:51 | 46, 403n.30 |
| | | 89:52[51] | 63 |
| 89:20ff. | 10n.4 | 89:52 | 48n.93, 403n.30 |
| 89:20 | 22, 38, 46, 396n.16 | 89:53 | 14 |
| 89:21 | 22, 403n.30 | **Book IV** | |
| 89:21[20] | 63 | Psalms 90–150 | 392, 394, 395, 396, 401, 402 |
| 89:22 | 22 | | |
| 89:23-26 | 28 | Pss 90–106 (Bk IV) | 1, 3, 392, 401, 440 |
| 89:23-24 | 46 | Psalms 90–92 | 439 |
| 89:23 | 22, 23 | Psalm 90 | 3, 66n.1, 190, 190n.1, 191, 191n.5, 192, 196, 197, 198n.19, 198n.20, 199, 200, 200n.22, 200n.23, 205, 317, 318, 319, 320, 391, 392, 393, 422n.32, 456n.29, 460, 607 |
| 89:24 | 22 | | |
| 89:25 | 23, 26, 29, 596 | | |
| 89:26 | 22, 23 | | |
| 89:27-28 | 15 | | |
| 89:27 | 23, 24, 29, 32n.50, 47 | | |
| 89:28 | 24, 47, 230n.25 | | |
| 89:28[27] | 62 | | |
| 89:29-38 | 26n.40 | Psalm 90 [LXX 89] | 458 |
| 89:29-30 | 19, 26 | 90:1-12 | 191 |
| 89:29 | 19n.34, 24, 26, 29, 32n.50, 596 | 90:1-6 | 199 |
| | | 90:1-5 | 202 |
| 89:29[28] | 62 | 90:1-2 | 198 |
| 89:30 | 24, 26 | 90:1-2b | 197 |
| 89:30[29] | 62 | 90:1 | 198, 198n.19, 204 |
| 89:31-34 | 26 | 90:1b-12 | 204 |
| 89:31 | 20, 25 | 90:1b-6 | 191, 198, 199 |
| 89:32 | 25 | 90:1b-2 | 197, 200 |
| 89:33-36 | 399 | 90:1b | 197 |
| 89:33 | 25, 230n.25 | 90:3-10 | 198 |
| 89:34 | 25, 596 | 90:3-6 | 197, 199, 200 |
| 89:34-35 | 19, 26 | 90:3-5 | 199 |
| 89:34a | 26 | 90:3 | 198, 205 |
| 89:35-36 | 32n.50 | 90:3a | 198 |

| | | | |
|---|---|---|---|
| 90:4-8 | 240n.60 | 91:14-16 | 490 |
| 90:4-6 | 199 | Psalm 92 | 150n.22, 331, 456n.29, 460 |
| 90:5-6 | 205 | | |
| 90:5 | 205 | 92:13-15 | 276 |
| 90:6 | 198 | Psalm 93 | 97, 101, 111, 112, |
| 90:7-12 | 199, 200 | | 150n.22, 331, 368, |
| 90:7-10 | 191, 191n.5, 197, 198, | | 369n.4, 392, 402n.29, |
| | 199, 201n.27, 202 | | 407, 408n.4, 415, 422, |
| 90:7 | 199, 202 | | 423, 429, 430, 431, 432, |
| 90:7a | 199 | | 433, 434, 436, 436n.59, |
| 90:8 | 218, 240n.59 | | 437, 438, 439, 441, 622 |
| 90:9-10 | 198 | Psalms 93ff. | 426 |
| 90:9 | 199, 202, 204 | 93:1-4 | 430, 413n.19, 423, 429, |
| 90:9b | 199 | | 432, 437 |
| 90:10-12 | 201n.26 | 93:1-2 | 423 |
| 90:10 | 200n.23 | 93:1 | 101, 415, 423, 431 |
| 90:10c | 200 | 93:1aef | 434 |
| 90:10d | 200 | 93:1bcd | 432, 432n.55 |
| 90:11-13 | 202 | 93:1b | 431 |
| 90:11-12 | 190, 191,191n.7, 200, | 93:1c | 431 |
| | 202, 203 | 93:1d | 431 |
| 90:11 | 199, 201, 202 | 93:2 | 423 |
| 90:11a | 202 | 93:3-4 | 423 |
| 90:12 | 191n.4, 191n.7, 192, | 93:3abc | 432 |
| | 201, 201n.25, 201n.26, | 93:3a | 431 |
| | 202, 203, 205 | 93:3b | 431 |
| 90:12b | 204 | 93:3c | 431 |
| 90:13 | 46, 198, 208n.8 | 93:4 | 423 |
| 90:13a | 204 | 93:4abc | 432 |
| 90:13b | 204 | 93:4a | 431 |
| 90:14 | 198, 204, 484 | 93:4b | 431 |
| 90:13-17 | 197, 204 | 93:4c | 431 |
| 90:13-16 | 198 | 93:5 | 204, 429, 429, 432, 438 |
| 90:14-15 | 198 | 93:5abc | 432 |
| 90:15 | 198, 204, 484n.18 | 93:5a | 431 |
| 90:16 | 46, 198, 204 | 93:5b | 431 |
| 90:16b | 204 | 93:5c | 431 |
| 90:17 | 198 | 93:7c-11 | 430 |
| 90:17a | 204 | 93:10 | 431n.53 |
| Psalm 91 | 459, 490, 494, 555n.10, | 93:10c | 431n.53 |
| | 613 | Psalms 93-100 | 95n.14, 95n.15, 96, |
| 91:2 | 490 | | 106n.59, 112n.78, |
| 91:2-6 | 613 | | 112n.79, 114, 422, |
| 91:3-8 | 490 | | 422n.32, 426, 427, 428, |
| 91:4 | 260, 612 | | 429, 430, 431n.53, |
| 91:5-6 | 552, 555n.10 | | 436n.59, 437, 438, 439, |
| 91:9 | 490 | | 440 |
| 91:10-13 | 490, 491 | Psalms 93-99 | 18 |
| 91:10 | 490, 555n.10 | Psalm 94 | 66n.1, 88, 112, 150n.22, |
| 91:11-12 | 555n.10 | | 331, 407, 422, 424, 427, |
| 91:11 | 490 | | 428, 430, 431, 438, |
| 91:13 | 555n.10 | | 456n.29, 460 |
| | | 94:1 | 428n.49 |

| | | | |
|---|---|---|---|
| 94:3 | 208n.8 | 96:3a | 434 |
| 94:7 | 424 | 96:4-6 | 430 |
| 94:8 | 208n.8 | 96:4, 5b-6 | 430 |
| 94:12 | 341, 346 | 96:4, 6 | 433 |
| 94:15 | 428n.49 | 96:4 | 182, 430 |
| 94:16-22 | 428 | 96:4a | 433, 434 |
| 94:23 | 428n.47 | 96:5 | 182, 430, 438, 439 |
| Psalm 95 | 97, 112, 402n.29, 422, | 96:5a | 430 |
| | 424, 428n.47, 429n.50, | 96:5b | 430 |
| | 429n.51, 431, 432, 436, | 96:6 | 179, 182, 430 |
| | 436n.59, 437, 438, 439, | 96:7-10 | 180n.68, 424, 430, 432 |
| | 440, 441 | 96:7-9 | 179 |
| Psalms 95–100 | 408n.4, 441 | 98:7-8a | 434 |
| Psalms 95–99 | 392, 618, 622 | 96:7 | 182 |
| 95:1-7c | 424, 429 | 96:9-13 | 182 |
| 95:1 | 402 | 96:9b | 434 |
| 95:2a | 431 | 98:9b | 434 |
| 95:7c-11 | 432 | 96:8 | 182 |
| 95:7d-11 | 429 | 96:8b | 431, 434 |
| 95:3 | 424 | 96:9 | 183 |
| 95:4 | 424 | 96:10 | 101, 183, 432 |
| 95:5 | 424 | 96:10ab | 431, 434 |
| 95:6ab | 431 | 96:10c | 430, 431 |
| 95:6b | 431 | 96:11-13 | 424, 432, 435 |
| 95:7-11 | 619 | 96:11-12 | 113 |
| 95:7-8 | 553 | 96:11 | 183 |
| 95:7 | 429 | 96:13 | 431, 435, 436, 436n.58, |
| 95:7a | 431 | | 437 |
| 95:7bc | 431 | 96:13ab | 435 |
| 95:7c-11 | 429n.51, 441 | 96:13b | 435 |
| 95:7d-11 | 424, 438 | 96:13c | 435 |
| 95:11 | 429 | 96:13d | 436n.59 |
| Psalm 96 | 4, 97, 112, 178n.66, | Psalm 97 | 97, 112, 402n.29, 422, |
| | 179, 179n.68, 180, | | 425, 427, 428, 429n.49. |
| | 180n.68, 180n.69, 182- | | 430, 431, 438, 439 |
| | 83, 402n.29, 422, | 97:1-9 | 428, 439 |
| | 422n.32, 424, 425, 427, | 97:1-6 | 425 |
| | 429, 430, 431, 432, 433, | 97:1 | 101, 428 |
| | 434, 435, 436, 436n.59, | 97:2-5 | 617 |
| | 437, 437n.62, 438, 439, | 97:2 | 425, 428n.49 |
| | 441 | 97:3-5 | 425 |
| Psalm 96 [LXX 95] | 456 | 97:6 | 439 |
| 96:1-13a | 288n.1 | 97:7-9 | 425 |
| 96:1-8 | 182 | 97:7 | 113, 430 |
| 96:1-6 | 179, 424 | 97:7c | 438 |
| 96:1-3 | 433 | 97:8 | 428 |
| 96:1-2a | 434 | 97:10-12 | 425, 428, 439 |
| 96:1 | 182, 183n.4, 424, 432 | Psalm 98 | 97, 112, 178n.66, |
| 96:2-6 | 432, 433, 436 | | 402n.29, 422, 422n.32, |
| 96:2 | 182 | | 425, 427, 429, 431, 432, |
| 96:2a | 431 | | 433, 436, 436n.59, 437, |
| 96:2b | 433n.57 | | 437n.62, 438, 439, 441 |
| 96:3 | 182 | | |

| | | | |
|---|---|---|---|
| 98:1-5 | 432 | 100:4a | 431 |
| 98:1-4 | 436 | 100:4b | 431 |
| 98:1 | 243n.72 | 100:4c | 431 |
| 98:1a | 433 | 100:5 | 427, 436n.59 |
| 98:1b-4 | 433 | 100:5a | 431 |
| 98:1b-3 | 433 | 100:5b | 431 |
| 98:1b-2 | 433 | 100:5c | 431 |
| 98:2-3 | 234 | Psalms 101–150 | 234n.40, 561n.20 |
| 98:3 | 243n.72, 436, 436n.59, 433 | Psalm 101 | 5, 12, 61, 61n.18, 64, 206, 206n.3, 207, 207n.6, 208, 210, 211n.22, 212n.22, 213n.27, 214, 216, 217, 217n.40, 218n.41, 218n.43, 219n.47, 220, 221, 222, 222n.55, 327, 427 |
| 98:3a | 431 | | |
| 98:3cd | 439 | | |
| 98:4-6 | 432 | | |
| 98:4a | 431 | | |
| 98:6 | 402 | | |
| 98:7-9 | 432, 435 | | |
| 98:9 | 435, 436, 437 | | |
| 98:9d | 431 | 101:1 | 207n.7 |
| Psalm 99 | 97, 101, 111, 112, 402n.29, 422, 427, 428, 429, 429n.49, 431, 438, 439 | 101:1b | 211n.22 |
| | | 101:2a-5a | 207n.7 |
| | | 101:2 | 207, 208, 212, 213n.26, 214, 216, 221, 222, 427n.44, 489 |
| 99:1-3 | 426 | | |
| 99:1 | 101 | 101:2a | 208, 210, 211, 211n.22, 212, 214n.30, 217 |
| 99:3 | 429 | | |
| 99:4-5 | 426 | 101:2aβ | 211 |
| 99:4 | 402, 428n.49 | 101:2b-3a | 220 |
| 99:5 | 108n.70, 429 | 101:2b | 207, 212, 213, 214, 214n.30, 216, 221, 213, 213n.26 |
| 99:6-9 | 426 | | |
| 99:6 | 499 | 101:2bα | 213, 213n.26 |
| 99:7 | 429 | 101:2bβ | 213 |
| 99:8 | 428n.49 | 101:3-7 | 207, 217n.40 |
| 99:9 | 429 | 101:3-5 | 207 |
| Psalm 100 | 90, 94, 97, 112, 327, 422, 426, 426n.41, 427, 429, 431, 431n.53, 432, 432n.55, 434, 436, 436n.59, 437, 438, 439, 441 | 101:3 | 207 |
| | | 101:3a | 217n.40, 218, 221 |
| | | 101:3b | 217n.40, 218, 221 |
| | | 101:4a | 214n.30, 218 |
| | | 101:4aβ | 221 |
| | | 101:4b | 217n.40, 219 |
| 100:1 | 426 | 101:5a | 217 |
| 100:1b | 431 | 101:5b | 214n.30 |
| 100:2a | 431 | 101:5bβ | 220 |
| 100:2b | 431 | 101:6-7 | 207, 213n.27 |
| 100:1b, 2ab | 432 | 101:6 | 427 |
| 100:1b-4 | 426 | 101:6a | 214n.30, 220, 220n.50 |
| 100:2 | 426 | 101:6b-8a | 207n.7 |
| 100:2a | 437 | 101:6b | 217, 219, 220 |
| 100:3 | 427 | 101:6bα | 213, 213n.26 |
| 100:3a | 431 | 101:7 | 207, 427n.44 |
| 100:3b | 431 | 101:7a | 213, 217, 219, 220 |
| 100:3c | 431 | 101:7ab | 220 |
| 100:4 | 422, 426, 554 | 101:7b | 217, 217n.40, 218 |

| | | | | |
|---|---|---|---|---|
| 101:8 | 207, 427, 484 | | 107:11 | 383 |
| 101:8a | 217n.40 | | 107:13 | 243n.72, 384 |
| 101:8b | 212n.25, 214n.30, 217, | | 107:14-15 | 237 |
| | 217n.40 | | 107:15 | 236 |
| Psalm 102 | 66, 66n.1, 332, 551n.2 | | 107:19 | 237, 243n.72 |
| Ps 102 [LXX 101] | 456 | | 107:21 | 236 |
| 102:3-11 | 199 | | 107:31 | 236 |
| 102:9 | 470 | | 107:33-39 | 236n.50 |
| 102:15 | 402 | | 107:41 | 380n.12 |
| 102:21 | 554 | | Psalms 108–109 | 14 |
| Psalm 103 | 66n.1, 90, 614 | | Psalm 108 | 142 |
| Ps 103 [LXX 102] | 540n.24 | | 108:6 | 243n.72 |
| 103:3 | 241n.63, 245n.83 | | 108:7-8 | 15 |
| 103:8-13 | 614 | | 108[LXX107]:7 | 465 |
| 103:15-16 | 199 | | 108:8 (LXX) | 569n.38 |
| Psalm 104 | 102n.27, 617 | | 108:11 | 479n.10 |
| 104:1 | 618 | | Psalm 109 | 14, 14n.19, 142, |
| 104:2-9 | 618 | | | 569n.38, 613 |
| 104:4 | 483 | | 109:1 | 562 |
| Psalm 105 | 14n.19, 66, 90, 93, 491, | | 109:2-3 | 569n.38 |
| | 551n.2, 615, 620 | | 109:8 | 569, 569n.38 |
| Psalms 105–106 | 393 | | 109[LXX108]:14 | 464 |
| 105:1-15 | 288n.1 | | 109:21 | 237 |
| 105:14 | 402 | | 109:26 | 233n.36, 237, 243n.72 |
| 105:15 | 48n.93, 403n.30 | | 109:31 | 243n.72 |
| 105:18 | 380n.12 | | Psalm 110 | 10, 10n.4, 11, 14, 15, |
| 105:20 | 402 | | | 16, 16n.26, 17n.27, 18, |
| 105:30 | 402 | | | 45, 46, 62, 334n.63, |
| 105:39 | 482n.16 | | | 398, 399, 400, 403, 407, |
| 105:41 | 482n.16 | | | 544, 551n.2, 560, |
| Psalm 106 | 66, 66n.1, 83, 83n.39, | | | 561n.20, 561n.21, |
| | 234, 491, 551n.2, 607, | | | 562n.23, 563, 575n.52, |
| | 615, 619, 620 | | | 578, 579, 606, 618, 622 |
| 106:1 | 234, 288n.1 | | 110[LXX109]:1 | 575n.52 |
| 106:3 | 341, 346 | | 110:1-2 | 399 |
| 106:4 | 235 | | 110:1 | 400, 492, 561n.21, 562, |
| 106:8 | 243n.72 | | | 563, 563n.27, 564, |
| 106:10 | 243n.72 | | | 564n.31, 571, 579 |
| 106:47-48 | 288n.1 | | 110:2b | 399 |
| 106:47 | 243n.72 | | 110:4 | 62, 403, 561n.20 |
| Psalms 107–145 | 334n.63, 339 | | 110:4a | 399 |
| Psalm 107 | 142, 236, 392, 459, | | 110:4b | 399, 400 |
| | 551n.2, 587 | | 110:5-6 | 62 |
| **Book  V** | | | 110:5 | 400, 402 |
| Pss 107–150 (Bk V) | 112, 329n.46, 337 | | 110:6a | 400 |
| 107:2 | 236 | | 110:6b | 400 |
| 107:4-9 | 236n.50 | | 110:6c | 400 |
| 107:4-7 | 237 | | 110:7 | 353 |
| 107:2-3 | 236n.50 | | Psalms 111–112 | 305n.65 |
| 107:8 | 236 | | Psalm 111 | 88, 92, 159n.15 |
| 107:10-16 | 380, 383 | | 111:3 | 204 |
| 107:10 | 380n.12 | | 111:7-8 | 316 |
| | | | 111[LXX110]:10 | 468 |

| | |
|---|---|
| Psalm 112 | 88, 92 |
| 112:1 | 341, 346 |
| Psalms 113–118 | 330, 334n.63, 478, 557 |
| 113:5-7 | 587 |
| Psalm 114 | 97, 157n.7, 180, 331, 331n.53, 408n.4, 441, 555n.9 |
| Psalms 115–116 | 331 |
| Psalm 115 | 14n.19 |
| 115:1 | 331n.53 |
| 115:2 | 350n.4 |
| 115:9-10 | 244 |
| Psalm 116 | 212, 551n.2 |
| 116:6 | 243n.72 |
| 116:7 | 131n.69 |
| 116:9 | 212, 331n.53 |
| 116:16 | 46 |
| 116:18-19 | 554 |
| Psalm 117 | 305n.65 |
| 117:25-26 | 556 |
| 117:25 | 556 |
| 117:26 | 556 |
| Psalm 118 | 14n.19, 97, 233, 234, 474, 547n.56, 551n.2, 556, 557, 557n.12, 558, 558n.15, 560, 560n.19, 613 |
| 118:1 | 234 |
| 118:2 | 559n.15 |
| 118:14 | 235 |
| 118:15a | 235 |
| 118:19-20 | 560n.19 |
| 118:19 | 554, 557 |
| 118:20 | 558n.15, 559 |
| 118:21 | 235 |
| 118:22-23 | 557, 558n.15, 578 |
| 118:22 | 558, 558n.15, 559, 559n.16, 560 |
| 118:23-29 | 490n.30 |
| 118:23 | 558 |
| 118:24-29 | 557n.12 |
| 118:25-29 | 557 |
| 118:25-26 | 556, 560n.19 |
| 118:25 | 243n.72 |
| 118:26 | 12, 556, 557 |
| 118:27 | 558n.15 |
| 118:28 | 610 |
| 118:29 | 234 |
| Psalm 119 | 87, 88, 88n.4, 91n,7, 96, 208n.9, 234n.40, 305n.65, 334n.63, 369, 474, 547n.57, 550, 551n.2, 607, 621 |
| 119:1-2 | 346 |
| 119:1 | 341 |
| 119:2 | 341 |
| 119:12-13 | 621 |
| 119:17 | 46, 243n.72 |
| 119:41 | 234 |
| 119:43 | 242n.70 |
| 119:46 | 402 |
| 119:49 | 242n.70 |
| 119:64 | 234n.40 |
| 119:74 | 242n.70 |
| 119:77 | 234n.40 |
| 119:81-88 | 208n.9 |
| 119:81 | 242n.70 |
| 119:82 | 208n.8 |
| 119:84 | 208n.8 |
| 119:94 | 243n.72 |
| 119:105 | 482 |
| 119:114 | 242n.70 |
| 119:146 | 243n.72 |
| 119:147-48 | 621 |
| 119:147 | 242n.70 |
| 119:151-52 | 621 |
| Psalms 120–136 | 334n.63 |
| Psalms 120–134 | 15, 328, 329n.45, 329n.48, 337, 338, 396 |
| Psalm 120 | 329n.49 |
| Ps 120 [LXX 119] | 456 |
| 120:7 | 499 |
| 122–34[LXX121–33] | 456 |
| Psalm 122 | 70, 100, 329n.49, 396 |
| 122:1-5 | 554 |
| 122:1 | 60 |
| 122:3 | 478 |
| 122:5 | 60, 396, 396n.16 |
| 122:6 | 554 |
| Psalm 123 | 66n.1 |
| Psalm 124 | 615 |
| 124:5 | 483n.17 |
| 124:6 | 482n.16 |
| 125:1 | 128n.55 |
| Psalm 126 | 66 |
| 127:1 | 204 |
| 127:2 | 489 |
| 127[LXX126]:2 | 465 |
| 127:5 | 341 |
| 128:1 | 341, 346 |
| 128:5 | 554 |
| Psalm 129 | 460n.33 |
| 129:8 | 488 |
| Psalm 130 | 239, 240n.57, 241, 243n.74, 244, 245n.79, |

|  |  |  |  |
|---|---|---|---|
|  | 247, 305n.65, 332 |  | 86, 368, 369n.4, |
| 130:[1] | 239 |  | 490n.30, 503, 607 |
| 130:2 | 240, 241 | 137:1-9 | 67 |
| 130:3 | 240, 245 | 137:1-2 | 67 |
| 130:4 | 240, 241, 245 | 137:1 | 66, 67 |
| 130:5 | 241, 242 | 137:2 | 67, 68 |
| 130:6 | 241, 245n.81, 500 | 137:3-9 | 490n.30 |
| 130:7 | 244, 245 | 137:3-4 | 67, 68, 70 |
| 130:8 | 245 | 137:3 | 67, 68n.6, 70 |
| Psalm 131 | 610 | 137:4 | 67, 68 |
| 131:2 | 612 | 137:5-7 | 554 |
| 131:3 | 242n.70 | 137:5-6 | 68 |
| Psalm 132 | 10, 11, 15, 15n.22, 16, | 137:5 | 66, 67 |
|  | 17n.27, 50, 61, 63, 64, | 137:6 | 67 |
|  | 97, 100, 100n.10, 396, | 137:7-9 | 69, 69n.10 |
|  | 397, 398, 404, 606, 618 | 137:7 | 67 |
| 132:1-5 | 61, 63, 396 | 137:8 | 67, 341 |
| 132:4 | 500 | 137:9 | 67, 70, 341 |
| 132:6 | 499 | Psalms 138–148 | 547n.56 |
| 132:7 | 108n.70 | Psalms 138–145 | 2, 15, 368, 368n.3, 377, |
| 132:8 | 108n.68 |  | 369, 370, 371, 384 |
| 132:9-10 | 47 | Psalms 138–143 | 379 |
| 132:9 | 15, 46 | Psalm 138 | 368, 369, 372, 375, 378, |
| 132:10 | 46, 48n.93, 62, 63, 396, |  | 379, 381, 386, 388n.37 |
|  | 396n.16, 403n.30, 494 | 138:1 | 382, 388n.37 |
| 132:10-12 | 404 | 138:2 | 377, 378 |
| 132:11-18 | 10, 15 | 138:3 | 375, 386 |
| 132:11-12 | 32, 62, 396, 397 | 138:4-5 | 386 |
| 132:11 | 62, 396, 396n.16 | 138:4 | 378, 388n.37 |
| 132:13-14 | 397, 404 | 138:7-8 | 387 |
| 132:15-16 | 397 | 138:7ff. | 378 |
| 132:16 | 15, 47 | 138:7 | 243n.72, 375, 381n.17 |
| 132:17 | 48n.93, 62, 63, 396, | 138:8 | 382, 388 |
|  | 396n.16, 397, 403n.30 | Psalm 139 | 368, 369n.4, 371, 374, |
| 132:18 | 397 |  | 376, 378, 378n.8, 379, |
| Psalm 133 | 15, 368, 369, 613 |  | 381, 384, 386, 388, 389, |
| 133:2-3 | 15 |  | 390, 607 |
| 133:3 | 359 | Ps 139 [LXX 138] | 368n.2, 387 |
| Psalm 134 | 15, 368 | 139:1-18 | 388 |
| 134:2 | 498 | 139:1-4 | 624 |
| Psalm 135 | 305n.65, 368, 491, | Psalms 139–143 | 375 |
|  | 551n.2 | Psalms 139–147 | 547n.57, 550 |
| Psalms 135–137 | 369 | 139:2-18 | 386 |
| 135:21 | 554 | 139:9 (LXX) | 566 |
| Psalm 136 | 66n.1, 491, 586, 615, | 139:19-24 | 388 |
|  | 620 | 139:19-22 | 381, 386 |
| Psalm 136 + Catena | 368 | 139:19ff. | 386 |
| 136:1-26 | 605 | 139:19 | 381n.17 |
| 136:4-9 | 586 | 139:20 | 250, 383n.20 |
| 136:10-15 | 586 | 139:22 | 381 |
| Psalm 137 | 65, 66, 66n.1, 68n.7, | 139:24 | 284 |
|  | 68n.8, 69n.9, 69n.10, | Psalm 140 | 368, 369, 371, 374, 379, |
|  | 69n.11, 70, 71, 84, 85, |  |  |

|  |  |  |  |
|---|---|---|---|
|  | 385, 388 | 143:6-8 | 368n.3 |
| Psalms 140–144A | 379 | 143:6 | 375 |
| Psalms 140–142 | 376 | 143:7-10 | 387, 388, 388n.36 |
| 140:2 | 385 | 143:7 | 380 |
| 140:3-4 | 385 | 143:8 | 251, 386, 388, 498 |
| 140:4 | 388n.35 | 143:10 | 380n.15, 388 |
| 140:6 | 388n.35 | 143:11-12 | 382, 386, 388, 388n.36 |
| 140:6[7] | 610 | 143:12 | 381n.17, 388 |
| 140:7 | 388 | Psalm 144 | 11, 15, 16, 18, 45, 46, |
| 140:8 | 566 |  | 47, 305n.65, 334n.63, |
| 140:9-10 | 493 |  | 368, 371, 372, 373, 376, |
| 140:9 | 383n.20, 493 |  | 382n.19, 386, 388, 390, |
| 140:10 | 388n.35, 402 |  | 398, 398n.22, 398n.23, |
| 140:11-12 | 381n.17 |  | 467, 606, 619 |
| 140:11 | 493 | Ps 144 [LXX 143] | 368n.2 |
| 140:12 | 388n.12 | Psalm 144AB | 379, 388 |
| 140:13-14 | 385 | Psalm 144A | 376, 377, 378, 382, 387, |
| 140:13 | 380n.12, 382 |  | 388 |
| 140:14 | 378, 382, 385 | Psalm 144B | 375, 376, 378, 387, 388 |
| Psalm 141 | 15, 15n.21, 368, 369n.4, | 144A:1-11 | 375 |
|  | 371, 374, 378n.9, 381, | 144:1-2 | 368n.3 |
|  | 385, 387, 388, 389 | 144:1 | 60 |
| 141:2 | 378, 482 | 144:3-4 | 619 |
| 141:5 | 385 | 144:7 | 483 |
| 141:6 | 385 | 144A:(7)11 | 375 |
| 141:6a | 385n.30 | 144:8 | 386 |
| 141:7a | 385n.30 | 144:9-10 | 63 |
| 141:8 | 381n.17, 388 | 144A:9 | 378 |
| 141:9-10 | 385 | 144:10-15 | 47 |
| 141:10 | 368n.3 | 144:10 | 46, 60, 372, 396, |
| Psalm 142 | 144n.14, 315, 368, |  | 396n.16, 398, 402, |
|  | 369n.4, 371, 372, 382, |  | 403n.30 |
|  | 385, 388, 545 | 144:11 | 381n.17, 386 |
| Ps 142 [LXX 141] | 456, 467 | 144A:(7)11 | 375 |
| 142:4 | 380, 382, 388 | 144:12ff. | 46 |
| 142:5 | 480n.13 | 144B:12-15 | 375, 376, 387 |
| 142:6ff. | 378 | 144:15 | 346, 398n.23 |
| 142:6 | 381n.17, 388 | 144:15a | 341 |
| 142:8 | 131n.69, 368, 371, 378, | 144:15b | 341 |
|  | 380 | 144:18 | 398 |
| Psalm 143 | 15n.21, 332, 369, 371, | Psalm 145 | 18, 88, 90, 368. 368n.2, |
|  | 376, 378, 382, 385, 388 |  | 369, 371, 371n.5, 372, |
| Ps 143 [LXX 142] | 368n.2 |  | 375, 376, 377, 378, 379, |
| 143:1-6 | 388, 388n.36 |  | 382, 386, 387, 388, 392, |
| 143:1 | 385 |  | 398, 398n.22, 398n.23, |
| 143:2-4 | 368n.3 |  | 551n.2, 555n.9 |
| 143:2 | 240n.59, 245, 38 | Ps 145 + Postscript | 368 |
| 143:3-4 | 380 | Ps 145 [LXX 144] | 456 |
| 143:3 | 380, 380n.14, 381n.17, | 144:18 | 398 |
|  | 385, 388 | Psalms 145–146 | 393 |
| 143:4 | 388 | Psalms 145–150 | 376, 390 |
| 143:5 | 204, 388n.38 | 145:1-2 | 377 |
|  |  | 145:1 | 379, 388, 398, 402 |

| | | | |
|---|---|---|---|
| 145:2-4a, 4b-5 | 387 | 4:14 | 219n.48 |
| 145:2-4a | 387 | 4:19 | 187 |
| 145:4-7 | 585 | Proverbs 5 | 88 |
| 145:4b-5 | 387 | 5:22 | 188 |
| 145:6 | 387 | 6:2 | 188n.20 |
| 145:7-8 | 387 | 6:16-19 | 218n.41 |
| 145:11ff. | 379 | 7:5 | 255 |
| 145:11-13 | 398 | 8:1-11 | 88 |
| 145:14-16 | 382 | 8:12-21 | 88 |
| 145:19-20 | 588 | 8:22-31 | 88 |
| 145:19 | 243n.72 | 8:32-36 | 88 |
| 145:20 | 381n.17, 386 | 9:1-18 | 88 |
| 145:21 | 398, 390 | 10:28 | 242, 242n.71 |
| Psalms 146–150 | 330n.52, 346, 368, 369, 370, 392 | 11:7 | 242, 242n.71 |
| | | 11:23 | 242n.71 |
| Psalms 146ff. | 376 | 11:27 | 480n.14 |
| Psalm 146 | 18, 305n.65, 346, 398, 398n.23, 402n.29 | 16:12 | 210n.16 |
| | | 19:18 | 242n.71 |
| 146:3-5 | 398 | 23:1 | 220 |
| 146:3 | 346 | 23:5 | 200 |
| 146:5-6 | 586 | 23:18 | 242n.71 |
| 146:5 | 341, 346, 398n.23 | 23:35 | 385n.29 |
| 146:7-9 | 586 | 24:1 | 219n.48 |
| 146:10 | 346 | 24:14 | 242n.71 |
| Psalm 147 | 178n.66, 551n.2 | 24:22 | 202n.29 |
| Ps 147 [LXX 146] | 456 | 25:4-5 | 210n.16 |
| 147:1-3 | 586 | 25:5 | 219n.49 |
| 147:4 | 586 | 26:12 | 242n.71 |
| 147:5 | 586 | 28:23 | 255 |
| 147[LXX146]:5 | 468 | 29:12 | 210n.16 |
| 147:9 | 586 | 29:20 | 242n.71 |
| 147:10 | 619 | Proverbs 31 | 88, 88n.5, 89n.6, 96 |
| 147:11 | 242n.70, 244 | | |
| 147:12 | 554 | **Ecclesiastes (Qohelet)** | |
| 147:19 | 588 | Ecclesiastes (Book) | 200n.23 |
| Psalm 148 | 66n.1, 615 | 1:3 | 200n.23 |
| 148:14 | 588 | 2:3 | 193 |
| Psalm 149 | 97, 368 | 3:21 | 202n.29 |
| 149:2 | 402 | 5:5 | 386 |
| Psalm 150 | 327, 368, 598 | 5:17 | 193 |
| **Apocryphal Psalms** | | 6:12 | 193, 202n.29 |
| Psalm 151 | 53, 369, 401, 548, 549 | 9:14 | 187 |
| Psalm 151AB | 369 | 7:28 | 199 |
| Psalm 154 | 549 | | |
| Psalm 155 | 549 | **Song of Songs (Canticles)** | |
| | | Song of Songs (Bk) | 299 |
| **Proverbs** | | 3:2 | 187 |
| Proverbs (Book) | 88, 340, 596n.25 | 3:3 | 187 |
| Proverbs 1–9 | 88 | 5:7 | 187 |
| Proverbs 2 | 88, 88n.5, 89n.6, 96, 159n.13, 183n.5 | **Isaiah** | |
| 2:16 | 255 | Isaiah (Book) | 15n.24, 49n.93, 101, 112, 117, 118n.11, 180, |

|  |  |
|---|---|
|  | 225, 226, 290, 308, 346n.5, 405n.36, 422n.32, 433, 437, 437n.62, 441, 468, 506n.5, 510n.13, 512, 512n.20, 512n.22, 515, 533, 534, 553, 554, 554n.7, 578, 578n.58 |
| 1:13 | 220n.52 |
| Isaiah 2 | 180, 437n.63 |
| 2:1-5 | 437n.63 |
| 4:5 | 414n.21 |
| 5:1-7 | 558, 559, 560n.18 |
| 5:2 | 168 |
| 5:12 | 267 |
| Isaiah 6 | 412n.15, 440 |
| 6:1 | 108n.70 |
| 6:1-5 | 413n.19 |
| 7:9 | 468 |
| 8:14 | 558n.15, 560 |
| Isaiah 9 | 512, 514 |
| 9:6 | 354 |
| Isaiah 9:6[5]–7[6] | 512 |
| 11:1-9 | 18 |
| 13:16 | 69 |
| 13:20 | 469 |
| 14:13 | 356n.20 |
| 17:12 | 186 |
| 22:16-19 | 279 |
| 22:16 | 168 |
| 23:16 | 187 |
| 24:22 | 380n.13 |
| 25:8 | 469 |
| 25:9 | 242 |
| 26:8 | 244 |
| 26:19 | 571 |
| 27:13 | 574 |
| 28:16 | 558, 560 |
| 28:28 | 469 |
| 29:1 | 209n.10 |
| 30:17 | 199 |
| 30:29-33 | 354 |
| 31:9 | 414n.21 |
| 33:14b-16 | 248 |
| 33:20 | 469 |
| 34:10 | 469 |
| Isaiah 38 | 290, 292, 294, 296 |
| 38:9-20 | 10, 288 |
| 38:9 | 298 |
| 40:7-8 | 199 |
| 40:10 | 436n.58 |
| Isaiah 40–55 | 230n.26, 247, 346, |

|  |  |
|---|---|
|  | 346n.5, 437n.62 |
| 41:1-5 | 15n.24 |
| 41:8-13 | 117n.6 |
| 41:8 | 228n.14 |
| 41:10 | 117 |
| 41:13 | 117 |
| 41:14-16 | 117n.6 |
| 41:14 | 117 |
| 42:1-4 | 405n.36 |
| 42:7 | 380n.13 |
| 42:10-13 | 435 |
| 42:16 | 380n.14 |
| 43:1-3 | 117n.6 |
| 43:1 | 117 |
| 43:5 | 117, 117n.6 |
| 44:2-5 | 117n.6 |
| 45:1-3 | 15n.24 |
| 45:11 | 594 |
| 48:17-19 | 117n.6 |
| 49:7 | 117n.6 |
| 49:13 | 435 |
| 49:14-15 | 117n.6 |
| 51:7-8 | 117n.6 |
| 52:10d | 433n.57 |
| 52:3 | 72 |
| 53:3 | 193 |
| 54:4-8 | 117n.6 |
| 54:7 | 230 |
| 54:8 | 230, 230n.25 |
| 55:3-5 | 48n.93 |
| 55:3 | 48n.93 |
| 55:4 | 49n.93 |
| 55:12 | 435 |
| 57:16 | 469 |
| 61:2-3 | 74 |
| 61:3 | 75 |
| 63:1-6 | 617n.26 |
| 63:7-14 | 197 |

**Jeremiah**

| Jeremiah (Book) | 32n.50, 81, 81n.31, 81n.34, 83, 380 |
|---|---|
| 1:10 | 267 |
| 3:5 | 469 |
| 3:6-8 | 185 |
| 3:11 | 185 |
| 3:12 | 230n.25 |
| Jeremiah 4–5 | 380n.16 |
| 5:26 | 188, 256n.10 |
| 5:31 | 399n.26 |
| Jeremiah 7 | 78, 79n.28, 81, 81n.34, 85, 380n.16 |

| | | | |
|---|---|---|---|
| 7:12-14 | 79 | 33:23 | 386 |
| 7:12 | 79, 80 | 36:8 | 380n.12 |
| 7:29 | 83, 398n.20 | 38:6 | 356n.20 |
| 10:25 | 78n.24 | 38:15 | 356n.20 |
| 11:15 | 386 | 39:2 | 356n.20 |
| Jeremiah 12 | 380n.16 | 44:24 | 383 |
| 15:18 | 469 | 44:26 | 193 |
| Jeremiah 22–23 | 380n.16 | | |
| 22:27 | 498n.45 | **Daniel** | |
| 24:6 | 267 | Daniel (Book) | 292, 294, 468, 478, 507, |
| 25:10-11 | 200 | | 515, 553, 554, 554n.8, |
| 25:11-12 | 194 | | 578, 578n.59 |
| 26:6 | 78 | Daniel 1 | 209 |
| 26:9 | 78 | 1:18 | 209 |
| 29:10 | 194, 200 | 1:19 | 209 |
| 30:10 | 117n.6 | Daniel 2 | 290, 292, 296 |
| 30:11 | 117n.6 | 2:20-23 | 288 |
| Jeremiah 31 | 204n.33 | 2:21-23 | 554n.8 |
| 31:28 | 267 | 2:44-45 | 554n.8 |
| 31:31-34 | 18 | Daniel 3 | 288, 290 |
| 42:10 | 267 | Daniel 7 | 571 |
| 44:14 | 498n.45 | 7:13-27 | 566 |
| 45:4 | 267 | 7:13-14 | 554n.8, 564 |
| 46:27 | 117n.6 | 7:13 | 554n.8, 564, 564n.31 |
| 46:28 | 117n.6 | 9:4 | 229n.18 |
| 48:13 | 39 | 10:13 | 573 |
| 49:7-22 | 69n.10, 85 | 10:21 | 573 |
| 50[LXX 27]:39 | 469 | 11:39 | 385n.26 |
| 51:14 | 251 | 12:1 | 573 |
| | | 12:2 | 571 |
| **Lamentations** | | 12:4 | 573 |
| Lamentations (Book) 77, 77n.22, 77n.23, 78 | | | |
| Lamentations 1–4 | 88 | **Hosea** | |
| 1:21-22 | 69 | Hosea (Book) | 178, 180, 457, 457n.30, |
| 2:1 | 108n.70 | | 474 |
| 2:15 | 355 | 2:19 | 230n.25 |
| 3:1 | 380n.12 | 4:8 | 498n.45 |
| 3:6 | 380n.14, 388 | 5:7 | 185n.8 |
| 3:57 | 117n.6 | 6:2 | 195n.18 |
| 3:64-66 | 69 | 9:11 | 200 |
| 4:21-22 | 69 | 13:7 | 256n.10 |
| Lamentations 5 | 76, 88 | 13:14 | 356n.22, 575n.52 |
| 5:20 | 469 | 14:1 | 69 |
| | | | |
| **Ezekiel** | | **Joel** | |
| Ezekiel (Book) | 373, 515 | Joel 1–2 | 352n.11 |
| 3:27 | 193, 194 | 2:14 | 202n.29 |
| Ezekiel 18 | 204n.33 | | |
| 28:14 | 260 | **Amos** | |
| 28:16 | 260 | 1:11 | 469 |
| 29:3 | 493n.37 | 4:13 | 288 |
| 31:11 | 383n.20 | 5:8 | 288 |
| 31:28 | 383n.20 | 5:23 | 456n.28 |
| | | 6:5 | 54 |

| | |
|---|---|
| 6:8 | 251 |
| 6:10 | 464n.38 |
| 6:13 | 70 |
| 7:13 | 44 |
| 8:7 | 469 |
| 9:5-6 | 288 |

**Obadiah**

| | |
|---|---|
| Obadiah (Book) | 69n.10, 85, 375 |

**Jonah**

| | |
|---|---|
| Jonah (Book) | 290, 292, 296n.28, 373 |
| 1:9 | 292 |
| 2 | 290n.11, 294, 296, 305 |
| 2:2 | 298 |
| 2:3-10 | 288 |
| 3:9 | 202n.29 |
| 4:2 | 292 |

**Micah**

| | |
|---|---|
| Micah 4 | 437n.63 |
| 4:1-3 | 437n.63, 441 |
| 4:1-5 | 437, 437n.63 |
| 5:2 | 364 |
| 6:8 | 228 |

**Nahum**

| | |
|---|---|
| Nahum (Book) | 373, 384n.24 |
| 3:10 | 69 |

**Habakkuk**

| | |
|---|---|
| Habakkuk (Book) | 308, 373, 384n.23, 384n.24, 389 |
| 1:4 | 469 |
| 2:4 | 384 |
| 2:4b | 384n.22, 389 |
| 2:18-19 | 279 |
| Habakkuk 3 | 288, 293n.18, 298, 298n.36, 308 |
| 3:1 | 298 |
| 3:3-15 | 617 |
| 3:3 | 298 |
| 3:9 | 298 |
| 3:15 | 298 |
| 3:19 | 298, 469 |

**Zephaniah**

| | |
|---|---|
| Zephaniah (Book) | 384n.24 |
| 2:4 | 70 |

**Haggai** 48

**Zechariah**

| | |
|---|---|
| Zechariah (Book) | 48, 553, 554, 554n.7 |
| 7:3-5 | 75 |
| 7:3 | 74 |

| | |
|---|---|
| Zechariah 9–14 | 404n.34 |
| 9:9 | 556 |
| 9:14 | 574 |
| 14:16 | 98 |

**Malachi**

| | |
|---|---|
| 2:7 | 386 |
| 2:11 | 185n.8 |

**2. NEW TESTAMENT**

**Matthew**

| | |
|---|---|
| Matthew (Book) | 563n.28, 566n.34 |
| 3:9 | 559n.17 |
| 4:4 | 553n.5 |
| 4:6 | 555n.10 |
| 5:5 | 347 |
| 5:8 | 347 |
| 5:25 | 383 |
| 5:35 | 554 |
| 11:25-26 | 554n.8 |
| 21:12-13 | 569 |
| 21:45 | 562n.22 |
| 22:34-39 | 347 |
| 22:34 | 562n.22 |
| 22:41-46 | 399 |
| 22:41 | 562n.22 |
| 22:44 | 561n.21 |
| 23 | 612 |
| Matthew 24:31 | 573 |
| 26:3-4a | 565 |
| 26:38 | 565 |
| 26:52 | 554n.7 |
| 26:64 | 561n.21 |
| 27:34 | 566, 569 |
| 27:35 | 565 |
| 27:39 | 565, 569n.38 |
| 27:43 | 565 |
| 27:46 | 565, 566 |
| 27:48 | 566, 569 |
| 27:55a | 565 |
| 37 | 612 |

**Mark**

| | |
|---|---|
| Mark (Book) | 559n.18, 565n.33, 566n.34, 579 |
| 1:11 | 564n.30 |
| 1:15 | 554n.7 |
| 2:10 | 554n.8 |
| 4:11-12 | 554n.7 |
| 7:10 | 553n.6 |
| Mark 8:27–16:20 | 560n.18, 564n.31 |
| 9:7 | 564n.30 |

| | | | |
|---|---|---|---|
| 9:43-48 | 54n.7 | 16:19 | 399n.24 |
| 10:6-8 | 553n.6 | 19:45-48 | 569 |
| 10:19 | 553n.6 | 20:41-44 | 399n.24 |
| 10:47-49 | 601 | 20:42-43 | 561n.21 |
| 11:7-8 | 556 | 20:42 | 53 |
| 11:9-10 | 556 | 22:53 | 187 |
| 11:11 | 557 | 22:69 | 561n.21 |
| 11:15-19 | 569 | 23:34b | 565 |
| 11:16 | 554n.7 | 23:35a | 565 |
| Mark 11:27–12:34 | 559n.18 | 23:36 | 566, 569 |
| 12:1-9 | 554n.7, 557, 560n.18 | 23:46 | 565 |
| 12:12 | 558, 562n.22 | 23:49 | 565 |
| 12:13 | 562n.22 | Luke 24 | 551 |
| 12:26 | 553n.6 | | |
| 12:28 | 562n.22 | **John** | |
| 12:29-31 | 553n.6 | John (Book) | 566, 566n.34 |
| 12:35-37 | 399n.24, 562, 563n.27, 563n.28, 564n.31 | 2:13-22 | 569 |
| | | 2:17 | 566, 569 |
| 12:36 | 53, 561n.21 | John 7:53–8:11 | 513 |
| 12:37b | 562n.22 | 12:2 | 565 |
| 13:27 | 573 | 12:27 | 565 |
| 14:18 | 565, 566, 568 | 13:18 | 565, 566 |
| 14:27 | 554n.7 | 13:30 | 187 |
| 14:34 | 565, 566 | 15:25 | 565, 566, 569 |
| 14:41 | 566 | 18:6 | 565 |
| 14:55 | 565 | 18:36 | 405n.36 |
| 14:57-58 | 565 | 19:24 | 565 |
| 14:58 | 554n.8 | 19:28 | 565 |
| 14:61-62 | 564, 564n.31, 571 | 19:29-30 | 566, 569 |
| 14:61 | 565 | 19:34a | 565 |
| 14:62 | 554n.8, 561n.21 | 19:34b | 565 |
| 15:4-5 | 565 | | |
| 15:24 | 565 | **Acts** | |
| 15:29 | 565, 569n.38 | Acts (Book) | 511n.17, 569n. 38, 571n.43 |
| 15:30-31 | 565 | | |
| 15:32 | 565 | 1:9 | 572 |
| 15:34 | 565, 566, 571n.43 | 1:11 | 572 |
| 15:36 | 566, 569 | 1:16 | 53, 552 |
| 15:40a | 565 | 1:20 | 569 |
| 16:19 | 561n.21 | 2:14-36 | 569 |
| | | 2:24-28 | 570 |
| **Luke** | | 2:24 | 570 |
| Luke (Book) | 290, 563n.28, 566, 566n.34 | 2:25 | 53, 570, 571 |
| | | 2:26 | 270 |
| Luke 1 | 303 | 2:27 | 270 |
| Luke 1–2 | 303 | 2:28 | 270 |
| 1:46-55 | 288 | 2:30-31 | 11n.7, 552 |
| 1:67-79 | 288 | 2:31 | 575n.52 |
| 1:70 | 553n.5 | 2:33 | 561n.21, 571 |
| 3:8 | 559n.17 | 2:34-36 | 399n.24 |
| 4:10-11 | 555n.10 | 2:34-35 | 561n.21 |
| 10:19 | 555n.10 | 2:34 | 571, 575n.52 |
| | | 3:18 | 553n.5 |

3:21            553n.5
4:11            558
4:25            53, 552
5:31            561n.21
7:55            561n.21
7:56            561n.21
13:13-52        569n.39
13:33           14n.16
13:35           569n.39, 575n.52
17:28           582

**Romans**
Romans (Book)   577
1:3-4           564n.28
4:6             53
8:34            561n.21
9:25            466
Romans 10       577
11:9            53

**1 Corinthians**
3:10            560
15:25           399n.24, 561n.21
15:55           575n.52

**Ephesians**
Ephesians (Book)  577
1:20            561n.21
2:6             561n.21
Ephesians 4     576
4:7             577
4:8-10          575n.52, 576
4:8             576
4:10            577
4:11            577
4:18            577

**Colossians**
3:1             399n.24, 561n.21

**1 Thessalonians**
1 Thessalonians (Bk) 573

4:15-17a        572
4:16            572, 573, 574, 575,
                576n.53

**1 Timothy**
3:1             569n.38

**2 Timothy**
2:8             564n.28

**1 Peter**
2:4             558
2:7             558
2:12            569n.38
3:22            561n.21
4:7             470

**2 Peter**
3:8             190

**Hebrews**
Hebrews (Book)  561
1:3             561n.21
1:13            399n.24, 561n.21
4:7             553
7:17-22         399n.24
8:1             561n.21
10:12-13        561n.21
12:2            561n.21

**Jude**
9               573

**Revelation (Apocalypse)**
1:16            187n.15
3:21            561n.21
7:1             573
8:2             573
12:7            573
19:15           187n.15

## 2. APOCRYPHA AND PSEUDEPIGRAPHA *(IN ALPHABETICAL ORDER)*

**Additions to Daniel**
Additions to Daniel  294, 296
1               298
3               292
Susannah        515

**Baruch**          380

**Ben Sira (See Sirach)**

*1 Enoch*
51:3            564n.31
55:4            564n.31
61:8            564n.31
62:2-3          564n.31

**Judith**
Judith (Book)   290, 296, 296n.28, 298,
                303

| | |
|---|---|
| 15:13 | 298 |

**Letter of Aristeas**

| | |
|---|---|
| Letter of Aristeas | 394n.9,  449 |

**1 Maccabees**

| | |
|---|---|
| 1 Maccabees (Book) | 302,  302n.51 |
| 4:24 | 302n.50 |
| 14:41-42 | 561n.20 |

**2 Maccabees**

| | |
|---|---|
| 2:13 | 53 |

**Psalms**

| | |
|---|---|
| Ps 136 + Catena | 368 |
| Ps 145 + Postscript | 368 |
| Ps 151 | 53, 401, 548, 549 |
| Ps 151AB | 369 |
| Ps 154 | 369,  549 |

| | |
|---|---|
| Ps 155 | 369,  549 |

**Psalms  of  Solomon**

| | |
|---|---|
| 17:21 | 564n.29 |

**Sirach  (Ben  Sira)**

| | |
|---|---|
| Sirach (Book) | 88n.5, 96, 369 |
| 12:16 | 385n.27 |
| 51 | 368 |

**Testament  of  Solomon**

| | |
|---|---|
| 1:7 | 564n.29 |

**Tobit**

| | |
|---|---|
| Tobit (Book) | 290, 292, 296 |
| 13 | 88 |

# 3. DEAD SEA SCROLLS INDEX

With very few exceptions this Index uses the sigla and names for the Scrolls as found in Appendix III by E. Tov: "A List of the Texts from the Judaean Desert," in P. W. Flint and J. C. VanderKam (eds.), *The Dead Sea Scrolls After Fifty Years: A Comprehensive Assessment* (2 vols., Leiden: Brill, 1998-99) 2.669–717. As indicated in the Terms, Sigla and Abbreviations of the present volume, the following sigla are generally used:

| | |
|---|---|
| 2:4–5 | The second extant column of the manuscript, lines 4–5 |
| 10.4–5 | Fragment 10, lines 4–5 |
| 10 ii.4–5 | Fragment 10, column 2, lines 4–5 |

**1. CAIRO GENIZEH**

**Damascus  Document**

| | |
|---|---|
| CD | 560 |
| 4:19 | 560 |
| 8:12 | 560 |
| 8:18 | 560 |

**2. QUMRAN**

**1QHª**

| | |
|---|---|
| (Hodayot) | 568,  568n.37 |
| 10:29-30 | 567 |
| 3[olim 5]:22-25 | 568 |
| 16[olim 8]:32 | 567 |
| 13[olim 5]:31 | 568n.37 |

**1QSª (Rule  of  the  Congregation)**

| | |
|---|---|
| 9:11 | 403n.33 |

**2Q23 (apocrProph)**

| | |
|---|---|
| frg. 1.6 | 559n.15 |

**4Q160  (VisSam)**

| | |
|---|---|
| 3–5.2-3 | 567 |

**4Q171**

| | |
|---|---|
| (4QpPsª) | 567 |
| 1–10 i.17-19 | 567 |
| 1–10 ii.5-8 | 567 |

**4Q174  (Florilegium)**

| | |
|---|---|
| (4QMidrEschª?) | 49n.94 |
| 3:14 | 567 |

**4Q177  (Catena  A)**

| | |
|---|---|
| (4QMidrEschatᵇ?) | |
| 12+13 i.7-8 | 567 |
| 5+6.7-8 | 567 |
| 5+6.11-12 | 567 |
| 10.1 | 567 |
| 10.8-9 | 567 |
| 10.11-12 | 567 |
| 1.4 | 567 |

1.6                         567

**4Q85**
(4QPs^c)                    570n.40

**4Q87**
(4QPs^e)                    14

**4Q88**
(4QPs^f)                    142

**4Q97** (*olim* **4Q237**)
(4QPs^p)                    368n.3

**4Q98g** (*olim* **4Q236**)
(4QPs^x)                    20, 21, 27n.42, 28n.43,
                           31
line 1                      22
line 2                      22
line 3                      22
line 4                      22
lines 5–6                   23
line 5                      22
line 6                      22
line 7                      23

**4Q158–186**
(*Misc. Texts*)             558n.15

**4Q173**
(4QpPs^b)                   558n.15

**4Q380**
(*Non-Can. Pss A*)          375
4.2                         375

**4Q381**
(*Non-Can. Pss B*)          375
15.2-3                      567
15.2                        567
24.4                        375
33.8                        375
380.1 ii.8                  375

**4Q394–399** (*MMT*)
(*Halakhic Letter*)         551n.3
4Q397
frgs. 14–21.10              552n.3

**4Q436**
(*Barkhi Nafshi^c*)
1 i.1                       567

**4Q500**
(*papBened*)                558
1                           559n.18

**4Q521**
(*Messianic Apoc.*)         571
2+4 ii.12                   571

**11Q11**
(*apocrPs*)                 555n.10

**11Q5–6**
(11QPs^a+b)                 14n.19, 15

**11Q5**
(11QPs^a)                   15, 20, 54, 368, 368n.2,
                           368n.3, 369,  369n.4,
                           371n.5, 372, 374, 376,
                           387n.33, 389, 401,
                           401n.27, 405, 548,
                           548n.68
24:3-17                     10
27                          53
27:10                       552
27:11                       11n.7, 552
136 + Catena                368
145 + Postscript            368
151AB                       368, 369
154                         369
155                         369
Apostrophe to Zion          368
David's Comp                368
Hymn to Creator             368
Plea for Deliverance        368

**11Q6**
(11QPs^b)                   368n.3

**11Q10**
(*11QtgJob*)                478n.7, 487

**3. OTHER SITES FROM THE
JUDEAN DESERT**

**Naḥal Ḥever**
5/6Ḥev1b (5/6ḤevPs)
(*olim* 5/6Ḥev 40, XḤev/Se 4) 142

**Masada**
MasPs^b                     368

## 4. OTHER ANCIENT WRITINGS

Here the following groups are indexed: 1. Ancient Near East. 2. Classical Greek and Roman Literature. 3. Hellenistic Jewish Literature. 4. Targumic Literature. 5. Rabbinic Literature and Authorities. 6. Christian *Apocrypha* and Other Early Writings. 7. Church Fathers (Western and Eastern). 8. Other

**1. ANCIENT NEAR EAST**

*Ahiqar*                301

*Akkadian Enthonement Text*
CoS 1.472-474          44n.85

*Amarna Letters*
Amarna Letters        186, 186n.9, 186n.11,
                      189
EA 60:7               186
EA 61:3               186n.10
EA 67                 186
EA 67:15-18           186
EA 147:13-14          167n.42
EA 201:15             186n.10
EA 202:13             186n.10
EA 247:15             186n.10

*Amherst Papyrus 63*
Amherst Pap. 63       5, 13, 33n.51, 33n.56,
                      34n.60, 35, 51, 52
II–V                  51
VI:12-18              41
IX (X):1-13, 13-17    42
IX:17-20, 20-23       42
XI/XII                35
XI                    32, 35
XI:11-19              35
XII                   35 (2x)
XII:1-3               37
XII:11-19             32, 51
XII:11                35
XII:12                35
XII:13                36
XII:14                36
XII:15, 17            35
XII:15                36
XII:16                36
XII:17                36
XII:18                37
XII/XIII              35, 42, 42n.78, 42n.81,
                      43n.81
XII/XIII:1-3          35
XIII                  35, 37
XIII:1                37
XIII:2                37

XIII:3                37
XIII:4                37
XIII:5                37
XV (XIV):13-17        40
XVI:1-6               40, 43
RIA 3.170             13n.15
RIA 165a              44n.86
TUAT 2.775            13n.15

*Amon Papyrus*
(Leiden I 350)        13n.15
ÄHG Nr.132–42         13n.15
TUAT 2.868–71         13n.15

*Aqhat Epic*
Aqhat Epic            203
KTU 1.4.7.19          175n.59
KTU 1.17.2.43         203
KTU 1.17.6.29         203n.31

*Atrahasis Epic*
I:34                  203n.32
I:36                  203n.32
I:279                 203
III:6                 199n.20

*Baal Epic*
2.iv.2-32             252n.4

*Babylonian Text (King)*
VS 24.92              211n.19(2x), 222

*Gilgamesh Epic*
X.vi                  198n.20

*Ludlul bel nemeqi* 195

*Lachish Letters*
2.4                   186n.10
5.4                   186n.10
6.3                   186n.10

*Maqlu*
I:144                 210n.17

*Neo-Assyrian Grants*
Royal Grants          214, 214n.31, 215n.33,
                      215n.34, 216n.36, 222,
                      223
I:144                 210n.17

*Ras Shamra*

| | |
|---|---|
| RS 24.252:1 | 195, 195n.17 |
| RS 24.252:1 | 165n.35, 166 |
| RS 2.[003]+ | 166 |
| RS 2.[014]+ | |
| ii.6, 20, 24, 30 | 168 |
| RS 2.002:65 | 169 |
| RS 2.002 | 169, 170n.53 |
| RS 24.258:23-24 | 169 |
| RS 94. 2391:16' | 170n.51 |
| RS 2.[008] + | |
| iv | 176 |
| vi.15 | 175n.60 |
| vii.14-52 | 172, 173-75 |
| vii.17-19 | 176 |
| vii.19 | 175n.60, 176 |
| vii.24-25 | 175n.60 |
| vii.25-28 | 175n.60 |
| vii.27-28 | 175n.59, 176 |
| vii.29-30 | 176 |
| vii.31-49 | 174 |
| vii.32 | 175n.60 |
| vii.34-35 | 176 |
| vii.35-36 | 176 |
| vii.35-37 | 176 |
| vii.41 | 176 |
| vii.42-43 | 176 |
| vii.50-52 | 175, 176 |
| vii.51-52 | 176 |

## 2. CLASSICAL GREEK AND ROMAN LITERATURE

**Cicero**

| | |
|---|---|
| *Consolatio* | 192 |

**Polybius** 470

**Seneca**

| | |
|---|---|
| *Ad Marciam* | 192 |

**Sulpicius Rufus** 192

## 3. HELLENISTIC JEWISH LITERATURE

**Josephus**

| | |
|---|---|
| Josephus | 505, 506n.3, 507 |
| *Antiquities* | |
| 6.8.2 §166 | 552 |
| 20.17-53, 71, 75 | 505n.3 |
| *Jewish War* | |
| 5.6.3 §272 | 559n.17 |

**Philo** 306

**Pseudo-Philo** 306

## 4. TARGUMIC LITERATURE

*Targum aḥer* 484n.20, 492n.33, 493

*Tg. Onqelos* 477

*Tg. Pseudo Jonathan* 477

*Tg. Numbers*

| | |
|---|---|
| 26:11 | 492 |

*Tg. Deuteronomy*

| | |
|---|---|
| 24:15 | 498n.45 |
| 32 | 495n.43 |

*Tg. Isaiah*

| | |
|---|---|
| Tg. Isaiah | 554 |
| 5:1-7 | 554n.7 |
| 6:9-10 | 554n.7 |
| 40:9 | 554n.7 |
| 50:11 | 554n.7 |
| 52:7 | 554n.7 |
| 66:24 | 554n.7 |

*Tg. Jeremiah*

| | |
|---|---|
| 22:27 | 498n.45 |
| 44:14 | 498n.45 |

*Tg. Ezekiel*

| | |
|---|---|
| 29:3 | 493n.37 |

*Tg. Hosea*

| | |
|---|---|
| 4:8 | 498n.45 |

*Tg. Zechariah*

| | |
|---|---|
| Tg. Zechariah | 554 |
| 13:7 | 554n.7 |
| 14:20-21 | 554n.7 |

*Tg. Psalms*

| | |
|---|---|
| Tg. Psalms | 489n.28, 490, 490n.30, 495n.43, 498, 503, 504, 557, 557n.12, 573n.45 |
| 2:11 | 499 |
| 4:5 | 500 |
| 4:6 | 501n.49 |
| 5:10 | 482 |
| 7:1 | 492 |
| 18:4 | 486 |
| 18:21 | 486 |
| 18:32 | 488 |
| 20:1-5 | 486 |

| | | | |
|---|---|---|---|
| 20:6 | 486 | 72:5 | 499 |
| 22:13 | 482 | 73:22 | 482n.16 |
| Psalm 23 | 495 | 74:2 | 493 |
| 25:1 | 498 | 74:13-15 | 493 |
| 28:2 | 498 | 76:5 | 480n.13 |
| 32:6 | 483n.17 | 76:10 | 487 |
| 40:13 | 483n.17 | 77:16 | 494 |
| 41:10 | 493n.39 | Psalm 78 | 491 |
| 43:4 | 500 | 78:36 | 499 |
| 44:21 | 499n.46 | 78:64 | 493 (aḥer) |
| Psalm 45 | 487 | 78:67 | 494n.41 |
| 45:1 | 487n.23, 492 | 80:1 | 492n.34 |
| 45:2 | 483 | 80:2 | 494 |
| 45:18 | 487 | 80:9 | 483 |
| 46:1 | 492 | 81:6 | 494 |
| 46:3 | 492n.35 | 82:6 | 482 |
| 46:5 | 499 | 83:10 | 482n.16 |
| 47:5 | 573n.45 | 84:9 | 486 |
| 47:10 | 573n.45 | 86:4 | 498 |
| 48:2 | 487n.22 | 86:17 | 494 |
| 48:3 | 482n.16 | 88:7 | 483n.17 |
| 48:5-8 | 486n.22 | 90:14 | 484 |
| 49:16 | 486 | 90:15 | 484n.18 |
| Psalm 50 | 500 | Psalm 91 | 490, 494 |
| 50:5 | 500, 501 | 91:2 | 490 |
| 50:8-9 | 500, 501 | 91:3-8 | 490 |
| 50:9 | 501n.50 | 91:5-6 | 552, 552n.10 |
| 50:12 | 502n.51 | 91:9 | 490 |
| 50:13 | 500, 501, 501n.50 | 91:10-13 | 491 |
| 50:14 | 500, 501 | 91:10 | 490 |
| 50:16 | 499 | 91:11 | 490 |
| 50:23 | 500, 501 | 91:14-16 | 490 |
| 51:9 | 483 | 99:6 | 499 |
| 55:14-15 | 493n.39 | 101:2 | 489 |
| 55:14 | 493 | 101:8 | 484 |
| 57:5 | 482n.16 | 104:4 | 483 |
| 59:8 | 483, 488 | Psalm 105 | 491 |
| 60:3 | 486 | 105:39 | 482n.16 |
| 65:2 | 483 | 105:41 | 482n.16 |
| 65:5 | 486 | Psalm 106 | 491 |
| 66:6 | 493n.36 | 108:11 | 479n.10 |
| 66:11 | 482n.16 (aḥer) | 110:1 | 492 |
| Psalm 68 | 491 | 118:22 | 560 |
| 68:14 | 484 (aḥer) | 118:23-29 | 490n.30 |
| 68:15 | 499 | 119:105 | 482, 483 |
| 68:30 | 500 | 120:7 | 499 |
| 68:32 | 499 | 122:3 | 478 |
| Psalm 69 | 483n.17 | 124:5 | 483n.17 |
| 69:1 | 492n.34 | 124:6 | 482n.16 |
| 69:2 | 483 | 127:2 | 489 (aḥer) |
| 69:3 | 483n.17 | 129:8 | 488 |
| 69:15 | 483n.17 | 130:6 | 500 |

| | |
|---|---|
| 132:4 | 500 |
| 132:6 | 499 |
| 132:10 | 494 |
| 134:2 | 498 |
| Psalm 135 | 491 |
| Psalm 136 | 491 |
| Psalm 137 | 490n.30, 503 |
| 137:3-9 | 490n.30 |
| 140:9 | 493 |
| 140:9-10 | 493 |
| 140:11 | 493 |
| 141:2 | 482 |
| 142:5 | 480n.13 |
| 143:8 | 498 |
| 144:7 | 483 |

**Tg. Job** 478n.7, 487, 487n.24

**Tg. Lamentations**
| | |
|---|---|
| 1:17 | 498n.45 |

**Tg. Esther** 478

## 5. RABBINIC LITERATURE AND AUTHORITIES

**Mishnah**
*m. Pesaḥim*
| | |
|---|---|
| 5.7 | 330n.52 |
| 9.3 | 330n.52 |
| 10.5 | 330n.52 |
| *m. Tamid* | 150 |
| 7.4 | 150n.22, 331n.55, 331n.57 |

**Jerusalem Talmud**
*y. Megillah*
| | |
|---|---|
| 2.1 | 557n.12 |

**Babylonian Talmud**
(in alphabetical order)
*b. Baba Batra*
| | |
|---|---|
| 14b | 53 |

*b. Berakhot*
| | |
|---|---|
| 56a | 330n.52 |
| 64a | 560 |

*b. Megillah*
| | |
|---|---|
| 3a | 477n.6 |
| 17b | 564n.29 |
| 21b | 478 |

*b. Moʾed Qaṭan*
| | |
|---|---|
| 16b | 492n.32 |

*b. Pesaḥim*
| | |
|---|---|
| 117a | 53 |
| 117b | 557n.12 |
| 118a | 330n.52, 331 |

*b. Sanhedrin* 493n,39, 494n.40
| | |
|---|---|
| 38a | 564n.29 |

*b. Shabbat*
| | |
|---|---|
| 114a | 560 |
| 115a | 478 |

*b. Soṭa*
| | |
|---|---|
| 48b | 11n.7 |

*b. Roš Haššanah*
| | |
|---|---|
| 31a | 331n.56 |

*b. Sukkah*
| | |
|---|---|
| 52a | 564n.29 |

*b. Yoma*
| | |
|---|---|
| 10a | 564n.29 |

**Midrashim**
| | |
|---|---|
| Mekilta | 574, 574n.47 |
| Exod 19:19 (Bahodesh §4) | 574 |

*Megillat Taʿanit*
| | |
|---|---|
| 5a | 478 |
| *Midrash Rabbah* | 574n.49 |

*Genesis Rabbah*
| | |
|---|---|
| Gen 46:10 | 506n.3 |

*Exodus Rabbah*
| | |
|---|---|
| Exod 23.10 | 560 |
| Exod 25.12 | 564n.29 |

*Leviticus Rabbah*
| | |
|---|---|
| Lev 29.3 | 574n.48 |
| *Numbers Rabbah* | 564n.29 |

*Songs Rabbah*
| | |
|---|---|
| Songs 1:5 §3 | 560 |

*Midrash Tehillim (Psalms)*
| | |
|---|---|
| Midrash Tehillim | 147, 315, 316, 329, 331, 480, 495n.42 |
| Ps 1:2 | 53 |
| Ps 2:9 | 564n.31 |
| Ps 3:2 | 315n.8, 316 |
| Ps 7:13 | 492n.32 |
| Ps 7:15-16 | 492n.32 |
| Ps 18:1 | 321n.23 |
| Ps 24:10 | 494n.40 |
| Ps 47:2 | 574n.48 |
| Ps 120:1 | 329n.47 |
| Ps 118:21 | 558 |
| Ps 118:22 | 557, 557n.12 |

**Other Jewish Writings**
*Pesiqta Rabbati*
| | |
|---|---|
| 40.5 | 574n.48 |

*Pesiqta de Rab Kahana*
| | |
|---|---|
| 1.4 | 574n.48 |

*Hekhalot Rabbati*
| | |
|---|---|
| §125-126 | 564n.31 |

Aquila (Bible)          452, 453, 469n.46
Rabbi Hai Gaon          478
Ibn Ezra                329n.47
David Qimḥi             316n.9, 316n.12,
                        329n.47
*Quinta* (Bible)        469n.46
ben Uzziel, J.          477n.6, 478

## 6. CHRISTIAN *APOCRYPHA* AND OTHER EARLY WRITINGS

*Epistle of Barnabas*   561n.21
*Quinta* (Bible)        469n.46

## 7. CHURCH FATHERS (WESTERN AND EASTERN)

### Athanasius

Athanasius              327n.42, 335n.66,
                        454n.27, 460n.33, 466,
                        517, 517n.35, 517n.36,
                        539, 540n.24, 541n.31,
                        542, 545, 546, 547,
                        547n.60, 549, 574n.50
*Letter to Marcellinus*
*PG* 27                 335, 335n.66, 546n.49,
                        546n.50, 546n.51
*PG* 27.17              574n.50
*Expositiones in Psalmos*
*Expositiones*          517, 517n.36,
                        517n.37, 534
*PG* 27.217             574-75n.50

### Clement of Alexandria

*1 Clement* 36:5        561n.21

### Cyril of Jerusalem

*De Christi Resurrectione*
Catechesis 14.24        575n.50

### John Chrysostom

John Chrysostom         547, 547n.50, 575n.52
*Expositiones in Psalmos*
(on LXX Ps 46:6)        574n.50, 575n.52
*PG* 56.213             576n.54

*De Prophetiarum Obscuritate*
Homily 2.2-3            574n.50
*In Ascensionem*
Sermon 2               574n.50
*In Psalmum*
50                      574n.50
*Pater, si possibile est*
§2                      574n.50, 575n.52

### Epiphanius

Epiphanius              574n.50
*Testimonia ex Divinis et Historia Ecclesiastica*
1.13                    506n.5
2.23.12-14              560n.19
*Testimonia ex Divinis et Sacris Scripturis*
86.1                    574n.50

### Eusebius

Eusebius                545, 546
*Commentaria in Psalmos*
*Comm. in Psalmos*      460n.33
*PG* 23                 546n.48
*PG* 23.224             574n.50
*PG* 23.453             455n.27
*Demonstratio Evangelica*
*GCS* 23.2              574n.50, 576n.54

### Justin Martyr

*Dialogue with Trypho*
§37                     574n.50
§38                     574n.50

### Origen

Origen                  456n.28, 460, 462, 463,
                        512, 575
*Fragmenta in Psalmos*
on Ps74:1               460n.34
*Selecta in Psalmos*    575n.51

## 8. OTHER

**Zoroaster**           607n.6

# INDEX 5

## MODERN AUTHORS

A.P.-Thomas, D. R., 97n.1
Aalen, S., 103, 103n.48
Abegg, M. G. Jr., 567n.36, 568n.37
Abou-Assaf, A., 216n.37
Abramsky, S., 77n.22, 84
Ackroyd, P. R., 66n.1
Adam, K.-P., 407n.1, 439
Aejmelaeus, A., 233n.36, 236n.48, 246,
  394n.11, 451n.18, 474, 512n.22, 533,
  537n.1, 537n.2, 550
Ahlstrom, G. W., 50, 183n.5
Aland, B., 540, 540n.25, 541, 541n.29,
  541n.32, 541n.33
Aland, K., 551n.1
Albertz, R., 593n.21, 611n.15, 611n.16,
  611n.17, 612n.18, 624
Allegro, J. M., 558n.15
Allen, L. C., 561n.20
Alt, A., 608
Anderson, A, A., 112, 234n.40, 235n.47,
  239n.55, 245n.78, 353n.14, 354n.16,
  355n.17, 361n.26, 366, 399, 399n.25
Anderson, B. W., 396, 396n.17, 397n.18,
  398, 405
Anderson, G. A., 70, 71, 71n.13
Angenendt, A., 52
Arneth, M., 10n.5, 17n.29, 44n.85, 50,
  407n.1
Arnold, B. T., 340n.1, 348
Assemanus, J. E., 548n.65
Assemanus, J. S., 510n.12
Assemanus, S. E., 548n.65
Assman, J., 13n.15, 50, 304n.62
Auffret, P., 157n.8, 158n.11, 163n.29, 180,
  389
Aune, D. E., 561n.21
Austermann, F., 451, 451n.18, 463,
  463n.36, 474
Auwers, J.-M., 15n.22, 50, 333n.61, 336
Ayguan, M., 330, 330n.51

Baars, W., 515n.30, 516n.31, 532, 548n.67,
  549n.69
Bar-Efrat, S., 67n.3, 84

Bacher, W., 476n.2, 503
Bailey, R. C., 291n.13
Baillet, M., 559n.15
Baker, D. W., 340n.1, 348
Bal, M., 292n.17
Balentine, S. F., 581n.1, 602
Ball, C. J., 515n.30
Balthasar, H. U. von, 583n.6
Baltzer, K., 583
Banks, R., 553n.6
Barnes, W. E., 103, 103n.39, 245n.78,
  509n.11, 533, 537n.3, 550
Baron, H., 86
Barr, J., 448, 448n.10, 448n.11, 474,
  581n.1, 602
Barré, M. L., 5, 186n.9, 186n.11, 190n.1,
  195, 212n.24
Barrett, C. K., 569n.38, 571n.43
Barrick, W. B., 183n.5
Barth, K., 581n.1, 582, 584
Barton, J., 581n.1, 602
Baudissin, W. W. G. von, 225n.1
Bauer, J. B., 230, 230n.24
Baumgartner, W., 230n.22
Baumstark, A., 506n.5, 533
Bayer, B., 68n.5, 85
Beal, T. K., 589n.11, 602
Beaucamp, E., 79n.28, 85
Begrich, J., 11n.9, 50, 99n.4, 116, 116n.3,
  117, 117n.4, 117n.5, 117n.6, 117n.7,
  118, 137, 171n.54, 180, 225, 225n.1,
  235n.44, 245n.78, 407n.1, 604n.3, 624
Bellinger, W. H. Jr., 143n.13, 149n.20,
  238n.52
Bentzen, A., 12n.11, 50, 102, 102n.23
Berder, M., 558n.15, 559n.15, 578
Berg, J. F., 509n.11, 533
Berger, K., 553n.6
Berlin, A., 5
Bernstein, M. J., 4, 503
Betz, O., 556n.11
Beyerlin, W., 51, 52, 121n.22, 137,
  233n.36, 236n.50, 246, 254n.6,
  261n.15, 266n.23, 287, 379n.11, 389

Black, M., 551n.1, 554n.7, 559n.17
Blaiklock, E. M., 236n.49
Blenkinsopp, J., 624
Bloemendaal, W., 543, 543n.38, 543n.40, 546n.52, 547n.61, 550
Blumenthal, D, R., 590n.14, 601
Boadt, L., 77n.24
Boecker, H. J., 385n.26, 389
Bohl, F. M. Th., 102, 102n.21
Booij, T., 205
Bordreuil, P., 165n.35
Borger, R., 194n.13, 211n.20
Bostrom, L., 596n.25
Botterweck, J., 185n.6, 186n.11
Bouzard, C, Jr., 76n.21, 78n.24
Bowker, J., 560n.20
Boyce, M., 607n.6
Boyd-Taylor, C., 446, 446n.8, 451n.18, 473n.50, 474
Bradshaw, P., 335n.67, 337
Bratcher, R. G., 234n.39
Braude, W. G., 147n.17, 152, 315n.8, 329n.47, 337
Brenner, A., 292n.17
Brettler, M. Z., 106, 106n.61, 112, 112n.77, 112n.81, 112n.82, 112n.83, 112n.84, 113, 113n.85, 114
Brichto, H. C., 188n.19
Briggs, C. A., 185n.8, 189, 245n.78, 524n.45, 558n.14, 560n.20, 571n.42
Briggs, E. G., 185n.8, 189, 245n.78, 558n.14, 560n.20, 571n.42
Brock, S. P., 452, 452n.23, 474, 505n.1, 508n.7, 510n.12, 510n.13, 511n.16, 512n.22, 515n.30, 516n.32, 533, 540, 541, 541n.26, 541n.27, 541n.28, 543n.41
Brooke, G. J., 49n.94, 51, 496n.43, 559n.18
Brown, F., 524n.45
Brown, W. P., 389, 444, 444n.6, 474
Broyles, C. C., 2, 7, 271n.27, 271n.28, 287, 578n.58
Bruce, F, F., 574n.46
Brueggemann, W., 6, 107, 107n.64, 114, 150, 151n.24, 152, 291n.13, 322, 322n.26, 323, 323n.27, 323n.29, 325n.35, 325n.36, 332n.58, 337, 405, 581n.2, 582n.4, 588n.10, 589n.11, 590n.13, 596n.26, 598n.31, 599n.32, 601, 602, 624

Brunell, A., 7
Buber, M., 492n.32, 494n.40, 495n.42, 581n.1, 583, 583n.6, 584n.7, 601
Buber, S., 492n.32, 494n.40, 495n.42
Bultmann, D. R., 563n.28
Bultmann, R., 242n.68, 246
Bundy, D., 506n.5, 533
Burkert, W., 305n.62, 308
Buss, M. J., 604n.4, 624
Buttenwieser, M., 103, 103n.45

Cales, J., 102, 103n.32
Campbell, P., 238n.53
Cancik-Kirschbaum, E., 211n.19, 222
Carroll, M. D., 429n.50, 441
Cartledge, T. W., 225n.1
Cassian, J., 327n.42
Ceriani, A., 511, 512n.21
Charlesworth, J. H., 561n.21
Cheyne, T. K., 161n.22, 571n.42
Childs, B. S., 55n.3, 55n.4, 57n.11, 64, 312n.3, 337, 336, 336n.69, 394, 405, 491n.31
Chilton, B. D., 554n.7, 554n.9, 555n.9, 560n.19, 578
Churgin, P., 476n.2, 490n.29, 503
Clark, G. R., 228n.13, 232n.33, 233n.35, 246
Clarke, E. G., 476n.2, 495n.43, 503
Classen, W. T., 236n.48, 246
Clifford, R. J., 3, 82n.37, 85, 199n.20, 205
Clines, D. J. A., 184n.3, 189, 406, 429n.50, 441, 596n.26
Cloete, W. T. W., 297n.32
Coats, G. W., 186n.10
Cogan, M., 67n.3, 70n.12, 85, 88n.5, 290n.10
Cohen, M. E., 105n.55
Collins, J. J., 7, 554n.8, 578n.59
Combs, A. E., 105n.57
Conzelmann, H., 563n.27
Cook, E. M., 476n.2, 479n.10, 479n.11, 490n.30, 503, 567n.36, 568n.37
Cook, S. A., 233n.35, 511n.17
Cook, S. L., 296n.27
Cox, C. E., 513n.25, 533
Craigie, P., 117n.8, 123n.35, 137, 158n.9, 264n.21, 270, 270n.25, 271n.26, 287
Craigie, P. C., 238n.53, 238n.54
Creach, J. F. D., 344n.3, 346n.5, 348

Crenshaw, J. L., 202n.29
Croatto, J. S., 186n.11
Cross, F. L., 517n.35
Cross, F. M., 112, 166n.37, 177n.63, 180
Crow, L. D., 329n.48, 337
Crusemann, F., 205
Culley, R., 69n.10, 303n.55
Cunchillos, J.-L., 158n.9, 159n.12,
  160n.18, 164, 165n.34, 170n.53, 180,
  180n.69
Curtis, A. H. W., 51

Dahood, M., 161n.22, 185n.6, 185n.7, 189,
  234n.40, 236n.50, 245n.78, 266n.22,
  360n.25, 171n.56, 287, 366
Dalglish, E. R., 40n.70
Davies, P. R., 429n.50, 441
Davisdon, R., 150n.23, 191n.4
Davis, E. F., 145, 145n.15, 146, 152
Day, J., 49n.94, 50
Day, L., 296n.28
de Groot, J., 103, 103n.42
de Lagarde, P., 518, 518n.38, 534
de Langhe, R., 102n.21
de Moor, J. C., 289, 289n.5, 290n.12,
  297n.32, 298n.35, 308, 457n.30, 474
de Roo, J. C. R., 552n.4, 579
de Vaux, R., 559n.15
deClaissé-Walford, N. L., 3, 142n.7,
  143n.13, 152, 319n.16, 337
Deissler, A., 234n.40, 235n.47
Delekat, L., 379n.11, 389, 512n.22, 533
Delitzsch, F., 193n.11, 245n.78, 351n.9,
  354n.15, 362n.29, 366
del Olmo Lete, G., 170n.52
Deurloo, K. A., 422n.32, 441
Deusen, N. van, 335n.67, 338
Devreesse, R., 544n.42, 544n.43, 544n.44,
  550
Dhanis, E., 561n.21, 578
Di Lella, A. A., 88n.5, 96
Diehl, J. F., 408n.4, 439
Diesel, A., 408n.4, 439
Dietrich, M., 167n.39
Dietrich, W. D, 27n.41, 50, 623n.30
Diettrich, G., 542n.34
Diez Merino, L., 476n.2, 477, 497n.44, 503
Dillard, R. B., 262n.17
Dirksen, P. B., 510n.11, 534, 539n.17, 550
Dobbs-Allsopp, F. W., 66n.1, 75, 76,

76n.21, 78n.24, 85
Dommershausen, W., 612n.19
Donin, R. R., 331n.53, 331n. 54, 337
Donnor, H., 16n.26, 561n.20
Douglas, M., 584n.7
Driver, S. R., 524n.45
Dudley, M. R., 335n.67, 337
Duhm, B., 12n.10, 15n.22, 16, 20n.39, 50,
  158n.11, 240n.58, 361n.26, 366
Dumortier, J. B., 20n.38
Dupont, J., 561n.21, 578
Durand, J.-M., 168n.44
Dyk, J., 292n.16, 422n.32, 441

Eaton, J. H., 185n.6, 189, 236n.49,
  353n.14, 354n.16, 355n.17, 366
Ebner, F., 583n.6
Edwards, T. M., 503
Eerdmans, B. D., 103, 103n.40
Ego, B., 19n.33, 50, 407n.2, 413n.19, 439,
  440
Ehlers, K., 118n.10, 137
Ehrlich, A. B., 202, 202n.30
Eichler, B. L., 67n.3, 85, 290n.10
Eichrodt, W., 226n.2
Eissfeldt, O., 103, 103n.41
Elliger, K., 517n.33
Ellis, E. E., 556n.11
Elman, Y., 495n.43, 503
Emerton, J. A., 85, 510n.11, 535
Emmendorfer, M., 19n.34, 50
Empson, W., 4
Engelken, K., 40n.73
Engell, I., 102, 102n.24
Epp, E. J., 511n.16, 533
Erbele-Kuster, D., 119, 119n.16, 120n.17,
  120n.18, 120n.19, 137
Erlandsson, S., 185n.8
Eslinger, L., 289, 289n.8
Etzelmuller, G., 118n.10, 119, 119n.13,
  137
Evans, C. A., 4, 7, 49n.94, 552n.4, 554n.7,
  554n.8, 555n.9, 560n.18, 560n.19,
  564n.31, 575n.53, 576n.53, 578,
  578n.58, 578n.59

Fabry, H.-J., 15n.21, 15n.23, 50, 186n.11
Fee, G. D., 511n.16, 533
Feininger, B., 108, 109n.71
Fisch, H., 589n.12, 601

Fitzgerald, A., 77n.24
Fitzmyer, J. A., 556n.11, 563n.27, 569n.38
Flashar, M., 472n.49, 474
Flesher, P. V., 476n.2, 495n.43, 503, 508n.6, 533
Fleury, M., 168n.44
Flint, P. W., 7, 15n.21, 50, 142n.8, 142n.9, 152, 368n.2, 389, 393n.8, 394, 405, 537n.1, 554n.8, 578n.59
Fodor, J. S., 429n.50, 440
Follis, E., 68n.8
Fokkelmann, J. P., 122n.28, 137
Fordor, J. S., J. P., 429n.51
Forster, C., 191, 191n.5, 200n.23, 205
Foster, B. R., 195n.17
Freedman, D. N., 4, 87n.2, 87n.3, 88n.4, 88n.5, 89, 89n.6, 91n.7, 96, 112, 177n.62, 177n.63, 180
Freedman, H., 574n.49
Fuchs, O., 118n.10, 137, 138
Füglister, N., 85

Gadamer, H-G., 451n.20
Galán, J. M., 186n.11, 189
Garber, Z., 508n.6
Gattungen, R. von, 11
Geertz, C., 408n.3
Gelston, A., 105n.57
Gentry, P. J., 513n.25, 533
Geoghegan, J. C., 87n.3, 96
Gerhards, A., 335n.67, 337
Gerleman, G., 560n.20
Gerstenberger, E. S., 6, 77, 109, 110n.74, 111, 118n.9, 137, 246, 306n.71, 311n.1, 336n.68, 337, 584, 589n.11, 592, 593n.21, 596n.27, 601, 603n.1, 605n.5, 608n.8, 609n.9, 610n.11, 610n.12, 613n.20, 619n.28, 620n.29, 623n.30, 623n.31, 624
Gevirtz, S., 159n.15
Gibbs, R., 584n.7
Gibson, J. C. L., 167n.39, 252n.4, 287
Gillingham, S. E., 289, 289n.6, 297n.32, 305, 305n.68, 306, 306n.69, 307, 308, 320n.21, 337
Ginsberg, H. L., 153, 157n.7, 165n.34, 169, 170n.53, 178n.66, 179n.68, 180
Girard, M., 158n.9, 159n.14, 160n.20, 162n.25, 163n.29, 164n.31, 164n.32, 164n.33, 167n.40, 167n.42, 180
Gleßmer, U., 20n.35

Glueck, N., 228, 228n.11, 228n.12, 228n.15, 228n.16, 228n.17, 229, 234, 234n.41
Gordon, R. P., 485n.21, 503
Gosling, F. A., 82n.35
Goulder, M., 2, 315n.7, 329n.46, 337, 366
Gourgues, M., 561n.21, 579
Graham, W. C., 513n.23
Gray, 166n.38, 169n.50
Greenberg, G., 548n.62, 550
Greenberg, M., 42n.80, 67n.3, 85, 88n.5, 96, 290n.10
Greenstein, E. L., 76, 77, 77n.22, 80n.30, 83n.38, 85, 160, 160n.19, 160n.20, 167n.41, 167n.43, 180
Greinacher, N., 205
Grimal, N.-C., 300n.38
Grintz, J. M., 476n.2, 503
Groot, J. de, 103, 103n.42
Groß, W., 127, 127n.50, 128n.57, 129n.63, 137, 410n.7, 440
Groves, J. W., 300n.41
Grundmann, W., 245n.82
Gruber, M. I., 242n.69, 246
Guidi, I., 506n.5, 511n.14
Guillaume, A., 68
Gunkel, H., 9, 9n.1, 10, 10n.2, 11, 11n.9, 12, 13, 20n.39, 50, 97, 99, 99n.4, 104, 109, 116n.3, 120n.21, 137, 191, 202n.28, 225n.1, 235n.44, 235n.47, 245n.78, 311, 350n.7, 353n.13, 354n.16, 355n.17, 355n.18, 356n.22, 362n.30, 363n.30, 366, 407n.1, 584, 604, 604n.3, 624
Gunneweg, A. H. J.,, 32n.50
Gurock, J., 495n.43, 503
Guthrie, H. H., Jr., 584, 584n.8, 586, 601
Gutierrez, G., 591n.16
Gwynn, J., 510n.11, 510n.12, 510n.13, 513n.25, 533

Haag, E., 78n.25, 85
Haas, V., 411n.11, 441
Haefeli, L., 510n.11, 533
Hahn, F., 437n.63, 441
Hake, J. A. vor der, 102n.21
Hakham, A., 73n.15
Hall, D. J., 600n.33
Halleux, A. de, 510n.13, 511n.15, 511n.16, 533, 534
Hallo, W. W., 31n.48, 33n.52, 50, 166n.36

Halpern, 82n.37, 85
Hanson, P. D., 177n.63
Harrelson, W. A., 205
Harrison, R. K., 244n.77
Hartberger, B., 85
Hartenstein, F., 19n.33, 50, 412, 412n.15, 413n.18, 440
Hauge, M. R., 118n.12, 137
Hausmann, J., 40n.74, 51
Havelaar, H. W., 538n.8
Hawthorne, G. F., 556n.11
Hay, D. M., 561n.21, 563n.26, 579
Healey, J. F., 51
Heim, K. M., 48n.93, 50
Hendel, R. S., 444, 444n.5, 450, 474
Hengel, M., 561n.21, 563n.27, 564n.31, 579
Herion, G. A., 32n.50
Herkenne, H., 102, 103n.33
Herman, J. L., 598n.29
Herms, E., 381n.18, 390
Heschel, A., 583, 593, 593n.20
Hiebert, R. J. V., 4, 512n.22, 513n.25, 514n.26, 515n.29, 516n.31, 519n.40, 521n.42, 523n.44, 524n.47, 533, 539, 539n.19, 540, 540n.21, 540n.22, 540n.23, 542, 545, 545n.47, 550
Hill, D., 448
Hinrichs, J. C., 215n.33
Hitzig, F., 353n.13, 366
Hoglund, K. G., 225n.1
Holladay, W. L., 139n.3, 152, 185n.7, 189
Holliday, W. L., 242n.67
Hooke, S. H., 102n.25
Hoppe, L. J., 77n.24, 78n.24, 81n.33
Horgan, M. P., 558n.15
Horst, P. van der, 538n.8
Hossfeld, F. -L., 13, 13n.14, 14n.17, 16n.25, 16n.27, 17n.27, 18, 18n.31, 27n.42, 29n.45, 29n.46, 30n.47, 33n.57, 41n.75, 50, 58n.13, 60n.14, 64, 120n.18, 120n.20, 122n.28, 123n.33, 123n.35, 125n.42, 130n.67, 137, 191n.6, 311n.2, 314n.5, 319, 319n.18, 319n.19, 320, 337, 338, 407n.1, 416n.24, 417n.25, 422n.32, 423n.33, 424n.34, 424n.35, 424n.36, 425n.37, 425n.38, 426n.40, 426n.41, 426n.42, 427n.43, 427n.46, 429n.50, 440, 624
House, P. R., 298n.36, 308

Howard, D. M. Jr., 95n.14, 95n.15, 96, 106n.59, 106n.63, 112, 112n.78, 112n.79, 114, 143, 143n.12, 340n.1, 348
Hubbard, A. M., 139n.1
Hübner, H., 553n.6
Humbert, P., 102, 102n.27
Hunt, J. I., 243n.74, 247
Hurvitz, A., 112, 112n.80
Hutton, R. R., 384n.21, 389
Huwyler, B., 384n.23, 389, 426n.41, 441

Irigaray, L., 582, 584
Irsigler, H., 120, 120n.22, 126n.48, 127n.54, 129n.60, 129n.62, 130n.66, 130n.67, 131n.68, 133, 137
Iwry, S., 177n.62

Jacquet, L., 355n.17, 366
Janowski, B., 19n.33, 39n.68, 50, 51, 119, 119n.15, 120n.20, 121, 121n.23, 122n.29, 128n.55, 129n.60, 130n.67, 133, 135, 137, 407n.1, 407n.2, 408n.3, 413n.19, 417n.25, 420n.29, 440, 609n.10
Jastrow, M., 573n.45
Jenkins, R. G., 510n.13, 512n.22, 533
Jenni, E., 122n.30, 122n.31, 137, 232n.33, 372n.6, 412, 412n.14, 440
Jeremias, J., 408n.4, 411n.12, 412n.13, 414n.20, 431n.54, 432n.55, 432n.56, 435n.58, 436, 436n.60, 436n.61, 440, 617n.24
Johnson, A. R., 102, 102n.25
Jones, H. S., 524n.46
Jones, S., 582, 583, 583n.5, 599
Joosten, J., 457, 457n.30, 474
Jucci, E., 552n.4
Juckel, A., 541, 541n.30

Kahle, P., 506n.5, 534
Kassar, R., 535n.56
Kataja, L., 214n.31, 215n.33, 215n.34, 222
Keck, L.E., 139n.2
Keel, O., 123n.34, 137, 239n.56, 247, 253n.5, 262, 287, 408n.2, 413n.19, 440
Keet, C. C., 329n.46, 338
Keil, C. F., 193n.11
Kellenberger, E., 128n.59, 138
Kellermann, U., 69n.11

Kempf, W., 48n.91
Kenik, H. A., 210n.14, 222
Kepnes, S., 584n.7
Keul, H., 429n.51, 441
Kiesow, K., 409n.5, 442
Kilian, R., 118n.10, 137
Kim, J., 297n.32
Kiraz, G. A., 541n.30
Kirkpatrick, A., 354n.15, 356n.22, 366
Kirkpatrick, A. F., 236n.50, 245n.78
Kitchen, K. A., 106n.57
Kissane, E. J., 102, 103n.34, 236n.50, 245n.78
Klausner, J., 574n.49
Kleer, S. M., 55n.4, 57n.11, 60n.14, 64
Klein, L., 437n.63, 441
Klein, M. L., 489n.28, 503
Klein, R. W., 66n.1
Kleinig, J., 289, 289n.7, 304, 304n.60, 308
Klingbeil, M., 408n.4, 413n.16, 440
Klinger, E., 429n.51, 441
Klinger, J., 411n.11, 441
Kloos,, C., 153n.2, 153n.3, 158n.9, 158n.10, 162n.24, 163n.27, 171n.54, 180
Klopfenstein, M. A., 623n.30
Knibb, M., 84n.40, 85
Knight, D. A., 113n.87, 114, 188n.18, 189
Knight, J. C., 243n.74, 247
Koch, K., 2, 4, 10n.3, 10n.4, 13n.13, 14n.20, 15n.24, 16n.27, 17n.27, 17n.28, 38n.65, 38n.66, 40n.73, 40n.74, 47n.89, 48n.90, 48n.92, 49n.93, 51, 214n.32, 407n.1, 609n.10
Köchert, M., 51
Köckert, M., 411n.11, 441
Köehler, L., 105n.57, 227, 230, 230n.22
Kohut, A., 478n.9
Komolosh, Y., 476n.2, 503
Kooij, A. van der, 474, 510n.11, 534, 539n.17, 550
Korpel, M. C. A., 175n.60, 181
Kort, A., 177n.62
Kort, W. A., 581n.1
Kottsieper, I., 33n.51, 33n.56, 34n.59, 38n.64, 41n.75, 41n.76, 51
Kratz, R. G., 389, 390, 440
Kraus, H. J., 21n.39, 27n.42, 51, 61n.18, 64, 73, 74, 74n.16, 74n.17, 100, 100n.9, 100n.11, 100n.12, 101,

101n.13, 101n.14, 101n.15, 101n.16, 101n.17, 101n.18, 103, 104, 104n.49, 106n.57, 107, 108, 108n.65, 108n.67, 109, 111, 117n.8, 124, 124n.36, 138, 139n.3, 152, 201n.26, 206n.1, 211n.21, 222, 225n.1, 243n.73, 243n.75, 254, 254n.6, 255, 255n.7, 261n.15, 266, 266n.23, 270, 270n.24, 275, 275n.30, 287, 350n.4, 350n.6, 351n.10, 353n.13, 353n.14, 354n.16, 355n.17, 356n.21, 360n.25, 361n.26, 367
Kreuzer, S., 384n.22, 389
Krüger, T., 190, 191, 191n.5, 198n.19, 200, 205
Kruse, H., 100n.10
Kselman, J., 5, 190n.1, 206n.3, 207, 207n.6, 213n.27, 217n.40, 218n.41, 218n.43, 219n.47, 222
Küchler, F., 116n.3, 225n.1
Kugel, J., 297, 297n.31, 487n.25
Kugler, R. A., 7
Kuiper, M. (editor), 7
Kuyper, L. J., 229, 229n.21

Labuschagne, C. J., 290n.12, 581n.2, 601
Lafont, B., 168n.44
Lagarde, P. de, 518, 518n.38, 534
Lambert, W. G., 195n.16
Lamm, N., 495n.43, 503
Lane, D. J., 547, 547n.62, 548, 548n.63, 548n.64
Lang, B., 410, 410n.8, 441
Langhe, R. de, 102n.21
Lauterbach, J. Z., 574n.47
Lebon, J., 511n.18
Lee, A. C. C., 82n.36, 85
Lee, S.-H., 3
Leene, H., 422n.32, 437n.62, 441
Lemaire, A., 7
Lenowitz, H., 68n.8
Leonhard, C., 547n.57, 550
Leslie, E. A., 102, 102n.28
Lettmann, B. R., 52
Levenson, J. D., 82n.37, 85
Levinas, E., 583, 583n.6, 601
Lewin, B. M., 478n.8
Lichtheim, M., 300n.38
Liddell, H. G., 524n.46
Limburg, J., 143n.13
Linafelt, T., 589n.11, 602

Lindström, F., 118, 118n.12, 124n.40, 126n.46, 126n.47, 128n.59, 129n.61, 132, 134, 138, 590n.14, 592. 592n.18, 601

Lipinski, E., 20n.38, 102n.21, 106n.57

Lipshitz, O., 86

Littledale, R. F., 330n.51, 338

Liver, J., 476n.2, 503

Livingstone, A., 105n.55, 210n.18, 222, 517n.35

Liwah, R., 561n.20

Lloyd, J. B., 167n.39

Loader, W. R. G., 553n.6, 561n.21, 579

Loewenstamm, S. E., 81n.32, 85

Lofthouse, W. F., 230, 230n.23, 231, 232n.31, 247

Lohfink, N., 48n.91, 422n.32, 441

Long, B. O., 69n.10, 303n.55

Loretz, O., 33n.56, 37n.62, 39n.69, 42n.80, 43, 43n.83, 48n.93, 51, 158n.8, 160, 161n.22, 165n.34, 167n.39, 170n.53, 171, 172, 179n.68, 180, 408n.4, 441, 609n.10

Lund, J., 510n.11, 534, 539, 539n.17, 550

Luria, S. B. Z., 77n.22, 84

Luthi, K., 384n.22, 389

Macholz, C., 426n.41, 441

Mackay, J., 360n.25

Maori, Y., 506n.5, 534

Marcel, G., 583n.6

Marcus, J., 565n.33, 566n.34, 567n.35, 568n.37, 579

Marfoe, L., 169n.48

Margulis, B., 158n.9

Markschies, C., 119, 119n.14, 127n.53, 129n.60, 133, 138

Martin, J. P. P., 513n.23

Martini, C. M., 551n.1

Martinze, F. G., 290n.12

Masing, U., 247

Mathys, H.-P., 288, 288n.3, 289, 290n.9, 290n.10, 290n.11, 291n.15, 292n.16, 293n.19, 294, 294n.20, 295, 301, 302n.48, 303, 304, 304n.58, 304n.59, 305, 305n.63, 305n.64, 305n.66, 306, 308

Matouš, L., 209n.10

Mayer, W. R., 211n.19

Mays, J. L., 53n.1, 57n.9, 64, 190, 201, 234, 234n.42, 240, 240n.61, 247, 340,

340n.2, 348, 594n.23, 599n.32, 601

Mazor, Y., 389

McBride, S. D., 177n.63

McCambley, C., 316n.10, 337

McCann, J. C. Jr., 3, 60n.17, 139, 139n.2, 142, 142n.7, 142n.10, 143, 143n.11, 143n.13, 148n.18, 149, 149n.19, 149n.20, 152, 317n.13, 319, 319n.16, 319n.17, 320, 325n.38, 338, 391n.4, 405, 593n.22, 602

McCarter, P. K. Jr., 186n.10, 231n.30

McKay, H. A., 596n.26

McKay, J. W., 367

McKeating, H., 241n.62, 245n.80, 247

McKenzie, S. L., 81n.34

McKinnon, J. W., 335n.67, 338

McNamara, M., 577n.56, 577n.57

Meer, W. van der, 297n.32

Meij, H. van der (editor), 7

Mell, U., 559n.18

Melugin, R. F., 230n.26, 247

Mendenhall, G., 32n.50, 583

Merrill, A. L., 205

Metz, J. B., 592n.19

Metzger, B. M., 511n.16, 533, 551n.1

Metzger, M., 378n.9, 389

Meurer, Th., 409n.5, 442

Meyer, H., 327n.43, 327n.44, 338

Miano, D., 4

Michel, D., 105n.57, 106, 106n.58, 106n.63, 107, 108, 114

Middeldorpf, H., 513n.23

Milgrom, J., 188, 188n.19

Milik, J. T., 559n.15

Millard, M., 55n.5, 56n.6, 56n.7, 58n.12, 64, 311n.2, 334n.63, 338, 368n.1, 389

Miller, D. G., 599n.32

Miller, P. D., 7, 60n.17, 64, 113, 113n.87, 114, 118n.10, 137, 142n.7, 152, 177n.63, 247, 248n.2, 287, 581n.1, 588n.10, 589n.11, 592, 594n.24, 598n.31, 599n.32, 601, 602, 610n.12, 617n.25, 624

Mitchell, D. C., 404n.34, 405

Mittmann, S., 157n.8, 158n.11, 159n.17, 160, 160n.17, 181

Mohlberg, P. K., 515n.30

Moltmann, J., 593, 593n.20, 602

Montgomery, J. A., 232n.34

Moo, D. J., 565n.33, 565n.32, 579

Moor, J. C. de, 289, 289n.5, 290n.12, 297n.32, 298n.35, 308, 457n.30, 474
Moore, S., 601
Moran, W. L., 186n.9, 186n.11, 189
Morschauser, S., 177n.62
Morse, J., 296n.27
Mosca, P. G., 262n.17, 287
Motyer, J. A., 49n.93
Moule, C. F. D., 572, 572n.44, 575
Mowinckel, S., 2, 12, 12n.12, 47n.88, 51, 97, 97n.1, 98, 98n.2, 99, 100, 101, 102, 103, 104, 105, 105n.54, 106, 106n.63, 107, 107n.63, 108, 109, 113, 114, 185n.6, 189, 206n.2, 222, 225n.1, 266n.22, 287, 304, 304n.61, 311, 353n.14, 354n.16, 355n.17, 356n.22, 363n.30, 367, 604, 604n.3, 625
Mrozek, A., 78n.27
Muffs, Y., 215n.33, 216, 216n.35
Muilenburg, J., 225n.1
Muller, A. R., 118n.10, 120n.16, 138
Müller, H.-P., 198, 198n.20, 205, 415, 415n.23, 417n.25, 441, 604n.4
Murphy, R. E., 225n.1
Myers, J. M., 214n.32

Nasuti, H. P., 1, 338
Naumann, T., 27n.41, 50
Neale, J. M., 330n.51, 338
Neuhaus, G. O., 302n.51
Neumann, P. H. A., 99n.2
Niehr, H., 40n.73
Nims, F., 33n.51, 51
Noll, K., 289, 289n.7, 289n.8, 291n.15, 295, 295n.25, 295n.26, 308
Norris, K., 601, 601n.34
Noth, M., 304n.61, 548n.67
Notscher, F., 103, 103n.35

O'Connor, M., 209n.10, 245n.78
Ochs, P., 584n.7
Oesterley, W. O. E., 235n.47, 538n.13, 560n.20, 571n.41
Ogden, G. S., 69n.10, 85
Ollenburger, B. C., 106n.62
Olmo Lete, G. del, 170n.52
Olyan, S., 69n.10, 303n.55
Oppenheim, A. L., 188n.17, 189
Otto, E., 17n.29, 51, 52, 407n.1, 438n.64, 440, 441, 442, 614n.21

Overholt, T. W., 205

Pap, L. I., 103, 103n.46
Pardee, D., 4, 5, 153n.3, 158n.10, 159n.13, 163n.28, 165n.35, 169n.49, 169n.50, 176n.61, 183n.5
Patton, C. L., 296n.27
Pederson, J., 102, 102n.22
Perdue, L. G., 608, 625
Perles, J., 506n.5
Perowne, J. J. S., 72, 72n.14
Petty, R. J., 243n.74, 245n.79, 247
Pfeiffer, R. H., 103, 103n.43
Phillips, G., 506n.5
Philonenko, M., 561n.21, 579
Pietersma, A., 4, 448n.12, 453n.24, 471n.48, 474, 513n.25, 517n.33, 533, 537n.2, 562n.25, 576n.55
Pietsch, M., 21n.39
Ploger, O., 302n.53
Plumer, W. S., 234n.40
Podechard, E., 103, 103n.36
Poethig, E. B., 292n.17
Porter, S. E., 552n.4, 578
Postgate, J. N., 215n.33, 215n.34, 216n.36, 222
Poswick, R. F., 437n.62, 441
Prechtel, D., 411n.11, 441
Preuß, H. D., 40n.74, 51
Prinsloo, W. S., 429n.50, 441
Propp, W. H. C., 184n.5, 301n.47
Prosser, M., 175n.59

Quast, U., 394n.11, 451n.18, 474, 475, 512n.22, 533, 537n.1, 537n.2, 550
Quell, G., 245n.82

Raabe, P. R., 5, 184, 184n.1, 184n.2, 186n.12, 189
Rad, G. von, 102, 102n.29, 205, 589n.11
Rahlfs, A., 514, 514n.27, 517n.33, 521, 531n.55, 534, 535, 539, 539n.20, 542, 542n.35
Rains, R. R., 332n.60, 338
Rapaport-Albert, A., 548n.62, 550
Ravasi, G., 185n.6, 189, 206n.1
Reif, S. C., 510n.11, 535
Reinelt, H., 78n.25, 86
Rendsburg, G., 68n.7, 69n.9, 178n.65
Rendsburg, S., 68n.7, 69n.9

Rendtorff, R., 311n.2, 337, 338
Reventlow, H. G., 604n.4, 625
Reyburn, W. D., 234n.39
Ribeiro, D., 615n.22
Richter, T., 411n.11, 441
Ricoeur, P., 591, 591n.17, 602
Ridderbos, J., 105n.57
Ringgren, H., 235n.45
Rom-Shiloni, D., 66n.1, 84n.40, 85
Roberts, J. J. M., 2, 114, 194, 194n.12
Roberts, R., 7
Robinson, H. W., 227n.10, 229, 229n.19, 229n.20
Roeder, G., 13n.15, 51
Rogerson, J., 360n.25, 367, 429n.50, 441
Röllig, W., 40n.70
Römer, T. C., 81n.34
Rompay, L. van, 507n.5, 508n.6, 509n.8, 510n.11, 515n.30, 516n.31, 516n.32, 534, 540n.24, 541n.31, 546, 546n.53, 546n.54, 546n.55, 547n.56, 547n.58, 547n.59, 550
Roo, J. C. R. de, 552n.4, 579
Rooy, H. F. van, 4, 542n.36, 542n.37, 545n.46, 549n.70, 549n.71, 550
Rösel, C, 18, 18n.30, 51, 95, 395, 395n.15, 405
Rösel, M., 33, 33n.54, 34. 34n.59, 35n.61, 38n.63, 38n.65, 43n.81, 44n.84, 51, 444, 444n.4, 444n.6, 450, 450n.17, 451, 451n.19, 453, 456n.29, 460, 461, 461n.35, 462, 464, 464n.38, 465, 465n.41, 466, 467, 468, 470, 474, 475
Rosenthal, E. I. J., 510n.11, 535
Rosenzweig, F., 583, 583n.6, 584n.7
Rost, L., 27n.41, 32n.50, 51, 103, 103n.44
Rowley, H. H., 238n.53, 304n.61
Rücker, A., 515n.30, 530n.54, 534
Rudolph, W., 517n.33
Running, L. G., 506n.5, 534
Rutgers, L. V., 538n.8

Sabourin, L., 245n.78
Sæbø, M., 506n.4, 507n.5, 516n.30, 516n.31, 534, 535, 550
Sakenfeld, K. D., 230, 231, 231n.27, 231n.28, 231n.29, 231n.30, 247
Salvesen, A., 538, 538n.8, 539n.14
Sander, H.-J., 429n.51, 441
Sanders, J. A., 368n.2, 389, 394, 548n.68, 552n.4, 576n.53

Sanmartîn, J., 170n.52
Sarna, N., 150n.21, 152
Sauer, G., 384n.22
Savran, G., 67n.3, 69n.11, 85
Sawyer, J. F., 47n.87
Scarry, E., 598n.29
Schaefer, K., 207n.7
Schaper, J., 443, 443n.1, 443n.2, 444n.3, 449, 475
Schearing, L. S., 81n.34
Schiffman, L. H., 49n.94, 52
Schmidt, H., 98, 98n.2, 99, 104, 114, 247, 367
Schmidt, L., 233n.36, 235n.47, 247
Schmidt, W. H., 205, 239, 240, 240n.57
Schneemelcher, W., 303n.53
Schniedewind, W. M., 21n.39
Schnocks, J., 190, 205, 422n.32, 441
Schoenborn, U., 603n.1
Schoors, A., 245n.78
Schreiner, J., 86, 205
Schroeder, C. O., 118, 118n.11, 138
Schroer, S., 611n.13
Schuller, E. M., 375n.7
Schulz, A., 103, 103n.37
Schwartz, B. J., 81n.32
Schweizer, E., 559n.18
Schwienhorst-Schönberger, L., 437n.63, 441
Scott, J. M., 84n.40, 85, 86
Scott, R., 524n.46
Scourfield, J. H. D., 192n.9
Segal, M. H., 476n.2, 503
Seidl, T., 429n.51, 441
Sekine, M., 32n.50
Sellin, E., 103, 103n.44
Sennak, L. B., 506n.5
Seybold, K., 2, 4, 14n.20, 16n.27, 17n.27, 39n.67, 39n.69, 42n.79, 51, 52, 117n.8, 120n.22, 121n.22, 137, 138, 190, 191, 201n.26, 311n.1, 329n.48, 337, 338, 384n.23, 384n.24, 387n.34, 389, 408n.4, 426n.41, 441, 625
Sheppard, G., 60n.17, 64, 294, 294n.21, 305, 338, 395, 395n.13, 395n.14, 405
Shires, H. M., 551n.2, 579
Shunary, J., 476n.2, 503
Simons, M., 574n.49
Sinclair, L. A., 243n.74, 247
Skehan, P. W., 88n.5, 96

Slomovic, E., 55n.3, 64
Slotki, J. J., 574n.49
Smelik, K. A. D., 292n.16
Smelik, W. F., 477n.4, 487n.25, 504
Smith, G., 195n.14
Smith, G. A., 233n.35
Smith, J. P., 227n.6, 524n.45, 524n.46, 529n.52
Smith, M. S., 77n.24, 301n.47
Smith, R. P., 227, 227n.6, 227n.7
Smith, W. R., 227n.10
Snaith, N. H., 103, 103n.47, 227n.9, 232n.32
Soden, W. von, 31n.48, 205, 215n.33
Sokoloff, M., 487, 487n.24
Soll, W., 208n.9
Spencer, J. R., 183n.5
Spieckermann, H., 408n.2, 408n.4, 442
Sprengling, M., 513n.23
Stamm, J. J., 101, 101n.19, 102, 102n.20, 102n.29, 102n.30, 102n.31, 104, 104n.50, 115
Staehlin, G., 245n.82
Steck, O. H., 109, 109n.72, 123n.34, 124, 124n.41, 125n.45, 138, 382n.19, 390, 440
Steiner, R. C., 33, 33n.51, 33n.55, 38n.65, 51, 52, 127n.49, 138
Stemberger, G., 480n.14
Stern, P. D., 78n.25, 81n.31, 86
Steymans, H. U., 10, 17n.29, 19n.34, 21n.39, 26n.40, 30n.47, 31n.48, 31n.49, 52, 407n.1
Stoebe, H. J., 128n.59, 138, 232, 232n.33, 247
Strecker, G., 563n.27
Stolz, F., 305n.62, 308
Strack, H. L., 480n.14
Streck, M., 215n.33
Strugnell, J., 558n.15
Sylva, D., 235, 235n.43, 235n.46, 247

Tadmor, H., 188n.18, 189
Taft, R., 335n.67, 338
Tallqvist, K. L., 210n.17
Talshir, Z., 67n.3, 76n.22, 85, 86
Tate, M. E., 106n.63, 107n.63, 185n.6, 189, 279n.34, 287, 393n.7, 454n.26
Taylor, B. A., 453n.24, 474, 542n.36, 550
Taylor, D. G. K., 543n.39

Taylor, R. A., 539n.18, 550
Testuz, M., 535n.56
Teuvels, H. W., 538n.8
Teuvels, L., 538n.8
Theißen, G., 408n.3, 442
Thomas, D. W., 61, 304n.61, 380n.12
Thomson, R. W., 517n.36, 517n.37, 534, 540n.24, 547n.60
Tigay, J. H., 67n.3, 80n.29, 85, 290n.10
Tita, H., 130n.65, 138
Toorn, K. van der, 608, 611n.14, 625
Torrance, T. F., 232, 232n.34, 247
Tournay, R. J., 103, 103n.38, 177n.64, 181, 385n.28, 390
Toury, G., 445, 445n.7, 446, 447, 448, 448n.13, 449n.14, 449n.15, 451, 452, 475
Tov, E., 290n.10
Tropper, J., 167n.39, 184n.2, 189, 609n.10
Trudinger, P., 331n.58, 332n.58
Tsevat, M., 205
Tucker, W. D., 344n.4, 348
Tucker, G. M., 113n.87, 114, 188n.18, 189

Ulrich, E., 20n.36, 52, 394, 394n.11
Ulrichson, J.H., 105n.57, 106, 106n.57, 106n.60, 115
Ungnad, A., 209n.10

VanderKam, J. C., 49n.94, 51, 52
Vajta, V., 602
van der Horst, P., 538n.8
van der Kooij, A., 474, 510n.11, 534, 539n.17, 550
van der Meer, W., 297n.32
van der Meij, H. (editor), 7
van der Toorn, K., 608, 611n.14, 625
van Deusen, N., 335n.67, 338
van Rompay, L., 507n.5, 508n.6, 509n.8, 510n.11, 515n.30, 516n.31, 516n.32, 534, 540n.24, 541n.31, 546, 546n.53, 546n.54, 546n.55, 547n.56, 547n.58, 547n.59, 550
van Rooy, H. F., 4, 542n.36, 542n.37, 545n.46, 549n.70, 549n.71, 550
van Veldhuisen, A., 102n.21
Vaux, R. de, 559n.15
Veijola, T., 20n.39, 21n.39, 52
Veldhuisen, A. van, 102n.21
Venables, E., 510n.13

Verbin, J. S. K., 559n.18

Vermeylen, J., 291n.13

Viviers, H., 328n.45, 338

Vleeming, S. P., 33n.51, 52

Vogel, A., 510n.11, 525n.49, 534, 538n.6, 539, 539n.15, 539n.16

Vogt, E., 264n.21, 287

von Rad, G., 102, 102n.29, 205, 589n.11

von Soden, W., 205, 215n.33

Vööbus, A., 505n.1, 506n.5, 510n.12, 511n.17, 515n.30, 516n.31, 534

vor der Hake, J. A., 102n.21

Vorgrimler, H., 52

Vouga, F., 553n.6


Wagner, A. & A., 408n.4, 439

Wagner, S., 561n.20

Wahl, H.-M., 201, 204, 205

Walford, deClaisse, N. L., 319n.16

Walkte, B. K., 208n.10, 209n.10, 245n.78

Walsh, P. G., 329n.50, 337

Walter, D. M., 537n.5, 550

Waschke, E. J., 21n.39

Waschke, G., 241n.66

Watson, W. G. E., 87n.1, 88n.5, 96, 167n.39, 217n.40, 242n.69, 289, 289n.5, 297n.32, 298n.35, 308

Watts, J. W., 5, 288n.2, 290n.9, 290n.10, 290n.11, 290n.12, 291n.13, 291n.14, 291n.15, 292n.16, 292n.17, 293n.18, 293n.19, 294n.20, 295n.24, 296n.29, 297n.34, 298n.35, 298n.36, 299n.36, 299n.37, 300n.38, 300n.39, 300n.41, 301n.46, 301n.47, 302n.50, 302n.51, 302n.52, 303n.53, 303n.54, 303n.56, 307n.72, 308, 308n.74, 308n.75

Weber, B., 3, 86, 121n.24, 135n.74, 138

Wei, T. F., 110n.76

Weimar, P., 409n.5, 442

Wein, A. T., 476n.2, 497n.44, 504

Weinfeld, M., 80n.29, 187n.16, 189, 215n.32, 216, 216n.35

Weiser, A., 99, 99n.5, 99n.6, 100, 100n.7, 100n.8, 105, 235n.47, 236n.50, 243n.75, 245n.78, 351n.10, 353n.14, 354n.16, 355n.17, 356n.26, 361n.26, 367, 560n.20

Weitzman, M. P., 505n.2, 506n.4, 507n.4, 508n.6, 508n.7, 509, 509n.8, 509n.10, 510n.11, 515n.30, 516n.31, 518n.39, 530n.53, 535, 538, 538n.7, 538n.9,

538n.10, 538n.11, 538n.12, 538n.13, 539, 548n.62, 550

Weitzman, S., 288, 288n.4, 289, 290n.9, 290n.10, 290n.11, 290n.12, 291n.14, 291n.15, 292n.16, 293n.19, 294, 294n.20, 294n.22, 294n.23, 295, 296, 296n.30, 297, 297n.33, 299n.37, 300, 300n.40, 300n.41, 301, 301n.42, 301n.43, 301n.44, 301n.45, 302, 302n.49, 303, 303n.55, 303n.57, 306, 306n.70, 306n.71, 307n.73, 308

Wellhausen, J., 9, 616

Welton, P., 104, 105, 105n.56, 106n.58, 109, 109n.73, 115

Wenham, D., 554n.8

Werline, R. A., 84n.40, 86

Wesselius, J. W., 33, 33n.51, 34, 43n.81, 52

Westermann, C., 117n.8, 120n.21, 127n.53, 138, 206n.2, 222, 225n.1, 232n.33, 241n.66, 245n.78, 584, 585n.9, 587, 597, 597n.28, 602

White, E., 477, 477n.3, 478n.9, 479n.9, 479n.10, 479n.11, 479n.12, 504

White, J., 511n.17

White, R. T., 477n.5

Whiting, R., 214n.31, 215n.33, 215n.34, 222

Whitley, C., 205

Whitley, C. F., 233n.38, 247

Whybray, R. N., 312 n.3, 338, 596n.26

Widengren, G., 102, 102n.26

Wikgren, A., 551n.1

Wilhelm, G., 51, 609n.10

Williamson, H. G. M., 262n.17

Willis, J. T., 395, 395n.12, 405

Wilson, G. H., 3, 13n.13, 14n.16, 14n.18, 18n.32, 52, 140n.3, 317, 318, 318n.14, 319, 320, 321n.20, 322, 322n.25, 325n.35, 338, 391n.1, 391n.2, 391n.3, 391n.4, 392n.6, 398n.22, 403n.31, 405

Wilson, R. R., 81n.34

Winckler, H., 195n.15

Winter, U., 611n.13

Wischnowsky, M., 84n.40, 86

Wise, M. O., 567n.36, 568n.37

Wolff, H. W., 205, 589n.11

Wolter, H., 48n.91

Wright, B., 448n.12, 474

Wright, W., 511n.17, 512n.23, 548, 548n.66

Würthwein, E., 378n.8, 381n.18, 390

Wyatt, N., 167n.39

Yon, M., 165n.34
Younger, K. L., 166n.36

Zakovitch, Y., 68n.7, 69n.10, 86, 303n.55
Zauzich, Z., 34n.60
Zenger, E., 2, 4, 9, 13, 13n.14, 14n.16,
    14n.17, 16n.25, 16n.27, 17n.27,
    17n.29, 18, 18n.31, 27n.42, 29n.45,
    29n.46, 30n.47, 33n.57, 40n.75, 42,
    42n.80, 50, 51, 52, 58n.13, 60n.14,
    64, 117n.8, 120n.20, 121n.22,
    122n.29, 123n.33, 123n.34, 123n.35,
    125n.42, 130n.67, 137, 138, 191,
    191n.6, 200n.23, 311n.1, 311n.2, 314n.5,
    319, 319n.18, 320, 320n.21, 334n.63,
    335n.67, 337, 338, 339, 390, 407n.1,
    408n.3, 409n.5, 413n.19, 416n.24,
    417n.25, 422n.32, 423n.33, 424n.34,
    424n.35, 424n.36, 425n.37, 425n.38,
    426n.40, 426n.41, 426n.42, 429n.50,
    438n.64, 440, 441, 442, 450n.17, 474,
    475, 624, 625

Ziegler, J., 512, 512n.20
Zimmerli, W., 244n.77
Zmijewski, J., 78n.25, 85, 86
Zobel, H.-J., 38n.63, 40n.74, 51, 227n.9,
    233n.36
Zwickel, W., 378n.9, 389

# SUPPLEMENTS TO VETUS TESTAMENTUM

2. POPE, M.H. *El in the Ugaritic texts.* 1955. ISBN 90 04 04000 5
3. *Wisdom in Israel and in the Ancient Near East.* Presented to Harold Henry Rowley by the Editorial Board of Vetus Testamentum in celebration of his 65th birthday, 24 March 1955. Edited by M. NOTH and D. WINTON THOMAS. 2nd reprint of the first (1955) ed. 1969. ISBN 90 04 02326 7
4. *Volume du Congrès* [international pour l'étude de l'Ancien Testament]. *Strasbourg 1956.* 1957. ISBN 90 04 02327 5
8. BERNHARDT, K.-H. *Das Problem der alt-orientalischen Königsideologie im Alten Testament.* Unter besonderer Berücksichtigung der Geschichte der Psalmenexegese dargestellt und kritisch gewürdigt. 1961. ISBN 90 04 02331 3
9. *Congress Volume, Bonn 1962.* 1963. ISBN 90 04 02332 1
11. DONNER, H. *Israel unter den Völkern.* Die Stellung der klassischen Propheten des 8. Jahrhunderts v. Chr. zur Aussenpolitik der Könige von Israel und Juda. 1964. ISBN 90 04 02334 8
12. REIDER, J. *An Index to Aquila.* Completed and revised by N. Turner. 1966. ISBN 90 04 02335 6
13. ROTH, W.M.W. *Numerical sayings in the Old Testament.* A form-critical study. 1965. ISBN 90 04 02336 4
14. ORLINSKY, H.M. *Studies on the second part of the Book of Isaiah.* — The so-called 'Servant of the Lord' and 'Suffering Servant' in Second Isaiah. — SNAITH, N.H. Isaiah 40-66. A study of the teaching of the Second Isaiah and its consequences. Repr. with additions and corrections. 1977. ISBN 90 04 05437 5
15. *Volume du Congrès* [International pour l'étude de l'Ancien Testament]. *Genève 1965.* 1966. ISBN 90 04 02337 2
17. *Congress Volume, Rome 1968.* 1969. ISBN 90 04 02339 9
19. THOMPSON, R.J. *Moses and the Law in a century of criticism since Graf.* 1970. ISBN 90 04 02341 0
20. REDFORD, D.B. *A Study of the Biblical Story of Joseph.* 1970. ISBN 90 04 02342 9
21. AHLSTRÖM, G.W. *Joel and the Temple Cult of Jerusalem.* 1971. ISBN 90 04 02620 7
22. *Congress Volume, Uppsala 1971.* 1972. ISBN 90 04 03521 4
23. *Studies in the Religion of Ancient Israel.* 1972. ISBN 90 04 03525 7
24. SCHOORS, A. *I am God your Saviour.* A form-critical study of the main genres in Is. xl-lv. 1973. ISBN 90 04 03792 2
25. ALLEN, L.C. *The Greek Chronicles.* The relation of the Septuagint I and II Chronicles to the Massoretic text. Part 1. The translator's craft. 1974. ISBN 90 04 03913 9
26. *Studies on prophecy.* A collection of twelve papers. 1974. ISBN 90 04 03877 9
27. ALLEN, L.C. *The Greek Chronicles.* Part 2. Textual criticism. 1974. ISBN 90 04 03933 3
28. *Congress Volume, Edinburgh 1974.* 1975. ISBN 90 04 04321 7
29. *Congress Volume, Göttingen 1977.* 1978. ISBN 90 04 05835 4
30. EMERTON, J.A. (ed.). *Studies in the historical books of the Old Testament.* 1979. ISBN 90 04 06017 0
31. MEREDINO, R.P. *Der Erste und der Letzte.* Eine Untersuchung von Jes 40-48. 1981. ISBN 90 04 06199 1
32. EMERTON, J.A. (ed.). *Congress Volume, Vienna 1980.* 1981. ISBN 90 04 06514 8
33. KOENIG, J. *L'herméneutique analogique du Judaïsme antique d'après les témoins textuels d'Isaïe.* 1982. ISBN 90 04 06762 0

34. BARSTAD, H.M. *The religious polemics of Amos.* Studies in the preachings of Amos ii 7B-8, iv 1-13, v 1-27, vi 4-7, viii 14. 1984. ISBN 90 04 07017 6
35. KRAŠOVEC, J. *Antithetic structure in Biblical Hebrew poetry.* 1984. ISBN 90 04 07244 6
36. EMERTON, J.A. (ed.). *Congress Volume, Salamanca 1983.* 1985. ISBN 90 04 07281 0
37. LEMCHE, N.P. *Early Israel.* Anthropological and historical studies on the Israelite society before the monarchy. 1985. ISBN 90 04 07853 3
38. NIELSEN, K. *Incense in Ancient Israel.* 1986. ISBN 90 04 07702 2
39. PARDEE, D. *Ugaritic and Hebrew poetic parallelism.* A trial cut. 1988. ISBN 90 04 08368 5
40. EMERTON, J.A. (ed.). *Congress Volume, Jerusalem 1986.* 1988. ISBN 90 04 08499 1
41. EMERTON, J.A. (ed.). *Studies in the Pentateuch.* 1990. ISBN 90 04 09195 5
42. McKENZIE, S.L. *The trouble with Kings.* The composition of the Book of Kings in the Deuteronomistic History. 1991. ISBN 90 04 09402 4
43. EMERTON, J.A. (ed.). *Congress Volume, Leuven 1989.* 1991. ISBN 90 04 09398 2
44. HAAK, R.D. *Habakkuk.* 1992. ISBN 90 04 09506 3
45. BEYERLIN, W. *Im Licht der Traditionen.* Psalm LXVII und CXV. Ein Entwicklungszusammenhang. 1992. ISBN 90 04 09635 3
46. MEIER, S.A. *Speaking of Speaking.* Marking direct discourse in the Hebrew Bible. 1992. ISBN 90 04 09602 7
47. KESSLER, R. *Staat und Gesellschaft im vorexilischen Juda.* Vom 8. Jahrhundert bis zum Exil. 1992. ISBN 90 04 09646 9
48. AUFFRET, P. *Voyez de vos yeux.* Étude structurelle de vingt psaumes, dont le psaume 119. 1993. ISBN 90 04 09707 4
49. GARCÍA MARTÍNEZ, F., A. HILHORST and C.J. LABUSCHAGNE (eds.). *The Scriptures and the Scrolls.* Studies in honour of A.S. van der Woude on the occasion of his 65th birthday. 1992. ISBN 90 04 09746 5
50. LEMAIRE, A. and B. OTZEN (eds.). *History and Traditions of Early Israel.* Studies presented to Eduard Nielsen, May 8th, 1993. 1993. ISBN 90 04 09851 8
51. GORDON, R.P. *Studies in the Targum to the Twelve Prophets.* From Nahum to Malachi. 1994. ISBN 90 04 09987 5
52. HUGENBERGER, G.P. *Marriage as a Covenant.* A Study of Biblical Law and Ethics Governing Marriage Developed from the Perspective of Malachi. 1994. ISBN 90 04 09977 8
53. GARCÍA MARTÍNEZ, F., A. HILHORST, J.T.A.G.M. VAN RUITEN, A.S. VAN DER WOUDE. *Studies in Deuteronomy.* In Honour of C.J. Labuschagne on the Occasion of His 65th Birthday. 1994. ISBN 90 04 10052 0
54. FERNÁNDEZ MARCOS, N. *Septuagint and Old Latin in the Book of Kings.* 1994. ISBN 90 04 10043 1
55. SMITH, M.S. *The Ugaritic Baal Cycle. Volume 1.* Introduction with text, translation and commentary of KTU 1.1-1.2. 1994. ISBN 90 04 09995 6
56. DUGUID, I.M. *Ezekiel and the Leaders of Israel.* 1994. ISBN 90 04 10074 1
57. MARX, A. *Les offrandes végétales dans l'Ancien Testament.* Du tribut d'hommage au repas eschatologique. 1994. ISBN 90 04 10136 5
58. SCHÄFER-LICHTENBERGER, C. *Josua und Salomo.* Eine Studie zu Autorität und Legitimität des Nachfolgers im Alten Testament. 1995. ISBN 90 04 10064 4
59. LASSERRE, G. *Synopse des lois du Pentateuque.* 1994. ISBN 90 04 10202 7
60. DOGNIEZ, C. *Bibliography of the Septuagint – Bibliographie de la Septante (1970-1993).* Avec une préface de PIERRE-MAURICE BOGAERT. 1995. ISBN 90 04 10192 6
61. EMERTON, J.A. (ed.). *Congress Volume, Paris 1992.* 1995. ISBN 90 04 10259 0

62. SMITH, P.A. *Rhetoric and Redaction in Trito-Isaiah*. The Structure, Growth and Authorship of Isaiah 56-66. 1995. ISBN 90 04 10306 6

63. O'CONNELL, R.H. *The Rhetoric of the Book of Judges*. 1996. ISBN 90 04 10104 7

64. HARLAND, P.J. *The Value of Human Life*. A Study of the Story of the Flood (Genesis 6-9). 1996. ISBN 90 04 10534 4

65. ROLAND PAGE JR., H. *The Myth of Cosmic Rebellion*. A Study of its Reflexes in Ugaritic and Biblical Literature. 1996. ISBN 90 04 10563 8

66. EMERTON, J.A. (ed.). *Congress Volume, Cambridge 1995*. 1997.
ISBN 90 04 106871

67. JOOSTEN, J. *People and Land in the Holiness Code*. An Exegetical Study of the Ideational Framework of the Law in Leviticus 17–26. 1996.
ISBN 90 04 10557 3

68. BEENTJES, P.C. *The Book of Ben Sira in Hebrew*. A Text Edition of all Extant Hebrew Manuscripts and a Synopsis of all Parallel Hebrew Ben Sira Texts. 1997. ISBN 90 04 10767 3

69. COOK, J. *The Septuagint of Proverbs – Jewish and/or Hellenistic Proverbs?* Concerning the Hellenistic Colouring of LXX Proverbs. 1997. ISBN 90 04 10879 3

70,1 BROYLES, G. and C. EVANS (eds.). *Writing and Reading the Scroll of Isaiah*. Studies of an Interpretive Tradition, I. 1997. ISBN 90 04 10936 6 (*Vol.* I);
ISBN 90 04 11027 5 (*Set*)

70,2 BROYLES, G. and C. EVANS (eds.). *Writing and Reading the Scroll of Isaiah*. Studies of an Interpretive Tradition, II. 1997. ISBN 90 04 11026 7 (*Vol.* II);
ISBN 90 04 11027 5 (*Set*)

71. KOOIJ, A. VAN DER. *The Oracle of Tyre*. The Septuagint of Isaiah 23 as Version and Vision. 1998. ISBN 90 04 11152 2

72. TOV, E. *The Greek and Hebrew Bible*. Collected Essays on the Septuagint. 1999.
ISBN 90 04 11309 6

73. GARCÍA MARTÍNEZ, F. and NOORT, E. (eds.). *Perspectives in the Study of the Old Testament and Early Judaism*. A Symposium in honour of Adam S. van der Woude on the occasion of his 70th birthday. 1998. ISBN 90 04 11322 3

74. KASSIS, R.A. *The Book of Proverbs and Arabic Proverbial Works*. 1999.
ISBN 90 04 11305 3

75. RÖSEL, H.N. *Von Josua bis Jojachin*. Untersuchungen zu den deuteronomistischen Geschichtsbüchern des Alten Testaments. 1999. ISBN 90 04 11355 5

76. RENZ, Th. *The Rhetorical Function of the Book of Ezekiel*. 1999.
ISBN 90 04 11362 2

77. HARLAND, P.J. and HAYWARD, C.T.R. (eds.). *New Heaven and New Earth Prophecy and the Millenium*. Essays in Honour of Anthony Gelston. 1999.
ISBN 90 04 10841 6

78. KRAŠOVEC, J. *Reward, Punishment, and Forgiveness*. The Thinking and Beliefs of Ancient Israel in the Light of Greek and Modern Views. 1999.
ISBN 90 04 11443 2.

79. KOSSMANN, R. *Die Esthernovelle – Vom Erzählten zur Erzählung*. Studien zur Traditions- und Redaktionsgeschichte des Estherbuches. 2000. ISBN 90 04 11556 0.

80. LEMAIRE, A. and M. SÆBØ (eds.). *Congress Volume, Oslo 1998*. 2000.
ISBN 90 04 11598 6.

81. GALIL, G. and M. WEINFELD (eds.). *Studies in Historical Geography and Biblical Historiography*. Presented to Zecharia Kallai. 2000. ISBN 90 04 11608 7

82. COLLINS, N.L. *The library in Alexandria and the Bible in Greek*. 2001.
ISBN 90 04 11866 7

83,1 COLLINS, J.J. and P.W. FLINT (eds.). *The Book of Daniel*. Composition and Reception, I. 2001. ISBN 90 04 11675 3 (*Vol.* I);
ISBN 90 04 12202 8 (*Set*)

83,2 COLLINS, J.J. and P.W. FLINT (eds.). *The Book of Daniel*. Composition and Reception, II. 2001. ISBN 90 04 12200 1 (*Vol.* II); ISBN 90 04 12202 8 (*Set*).

84. COHEN, C.H.R. *Contextual Priority in Biblical Hebrew Philology*. An Application of the Held Method for Comparative Semitic Philology. 2001. ISBN 90 04 11670 2 (In preparation).

85. WAGENAAR, J.A. *Judgement and Salvation*. The Composition and Redaction of Micah 2-5. 2001. ISBN 90 04 11936 1

86. McLAUGHLIN, J.L. *The Marzēaḥ in sthe Prophetic Literature*. References and Allusions in Light of the Extra-Biblical Evidence. 2001. ISBN 90 04 12006 8

87. WONG, K.L. *The Idea of Retribution in the Book of Ezekiel* 2001. ISBN 90 04 12256 7

88. BARRICK, W. Boyd *The King and the Cemeteries*. Toward a New Understanding of Josiah's Reform. 2002. ISBN 90 04 12171 4

89. FRANKEL, D. *The Murmuring Stories of the Priestly School*. A Retrieval of Ancient Sacerdotal Lore. 2002. ISBN 90 04 12368 7

90. FRYDRYCH, T. *Living under the Sun*. Examination of Proverbs and Qoheleth. 2002. ISBN 90 04 12315 6

91. KESSEL, J. *The Book of Haggai*. Prophecy and Society in Early Persian Yehud. 2002. ISBN 90 04 12368 7

92. LEMAIRE, A. (ed.). *Congress Volume, Basel 2001*. 2002. ISBN 90 04 12680 5

93. RENDTORFF, R. and R.A. KUGLER (eds.). *The Book of Leviticus*. Composition and Reception. 2003. ISBN 90 04 12634 1

94. PAUL, S.M., R.A. KRAFT, L.H. SCHIFFMAN and W.W. FIELDS (eds.). *Emanuel*. Studies in Hebrew Bible, Septuagint, and Dead Sea Scrolls in Honor of Emanuel Tov. 2003. ISBN 90 04 13007 1

95. VOS, J.C. DE. *Das Los Judas*. Über Entstehung und Ziele der Landbeschreibung in Josua 15. ISBN 90 04 12953 7

96. LEHNART, B. *Prophet und König im Nordreich Israel*. Studien zur sogenannten vorklassischen Prophetie im Nordreich Israel anhand der Samuel-, Elija- und Elischa-Überlieferungen. 2003. ISBN 90 04 13237 6

97. LO, A. *Job 28 as Rhetoric*. An Analysis of Job 28 in the Context of Job 22-31. 2003. ISBN 90 04 13320 8

98. TRUDINGER, P.L. *The Psalms of the Tamid Service*. A Liturgical Text from the Second Temple. 2004. ISBN 90 04 12968 5

99. FLINT, P.W. and P.D. MILLER, JR. (eds.) with the assistance of A. Brunell. *The Book of Psalms*. Composition and Reception. 2004. ISBN 90 04 13842 8

100. WEINFELD, M. *The Place of the Law in the Religion of Ancient Israel*. 2004. ISBN 90 04 13749 1

101. FLINT, P.W., J.C. VANDERKAM and E. TOV. (eds.) *Studies in the Hebrew Bible, Qumran, and the Septuagint*. Essays Presented to Eugene Ulrich on the Occasion of his Sixty-Fifth Birthday. 2004. ISBN 90 04 13738 6

102. MEER, M.N. VAN DER. *Formation and Reformulation*. The Redaction of the Book of Joshua in the Light of the Oldest Textual Witnesses. 2004. ISBN 90 04 13125 6

103. BERMAN, J.A. *Narrative Analogy in the Hebrew Bible*. Battle Stories and Their Equivalent Non-battle Narratives. 2004. ISBN 90 04 13119 1

104. VAN KEULEN, P.S.F. *Two Versions of the Solomon Narrative*. An Inquiry into the Relationship between MT 1Kgs. 2-11 and LXX 3 Reg. 2-11. 2004. ISBN 90 04 13895 1